Complete Computer Concepts and Microcomputer Applications:
WordPerfect 5.1
Lotus 1-2-3 Release 2.2
dBASE IV Version 1.1

GARY B. SHELLY
THOMAS J. CASHMAN
GLORIA A. WAGGONER
WILLIAM C. WAGGONER

  SHELLY CASHMAN SERIES

boyd & fraser publishing company

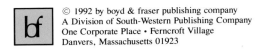

© 1992 by boyd & fraser publishing company
A Division of South-Western Publishing Company
One Corporate Place • Ferncroft Village
Danvers, Massachusetts 01923

1 2 3 4 5 6 7 8 9 10 BC 6 5 4 3 2

Developed by Susan Solomon Communications
Manufactured in the United States of America

ISBN 0-87835-529-4 (Perfect Bound)
ISBN 0-87835-531-6 (Spiral Bound)

PHOTO CREDITS

CHAPTER 1 *Opening Page*, ©Robert Holmgren; *Figure 1-1*, Texas Instruments; *Figure 1-2*, (pc) International Business Machines Corp.; (printer) Panasonic Communications and Systems Co.; *Figure 1-3*, International Business Machines Corp.; *Figure 1-4*, International Business Machines Corp.; *Figure 1-7*, (pc) Dell Computer Corp. (palmtop) Hewlett-Packard Co.; (laptop) International Business Machines Corp.; (supercomputer) Paul Shambroom, courtesy of Cray Research, Inc.; *Figure 1-9*, Curtis Fukuda; *Figure 1-15*, Hewlett-Packard Co.; *Figure 1-16*, International Business Machines Corp.; *Figure 1-17*, International Business Machines Corp.; *Figure 1-18*, UNISYS Corp.; *Figure 1-19*, Lockheed Corp.; *Figure 1-20*, NCR Corp.; *Figure 1-21*, UNISYS Corp.; *Figure 1-22*, Hewlett-Packard Co.; *Figure 1-23*, Intertec Diversified Systems; *Figure 1-24*, International Business Machines Corp.; *Figure 1-25*, (1) Compaq Computer Corp. All rights reserved.; (2) International Business Machines Corp.; (3) UNISYS Corp.; (4) Compaq Computer Corp. All rights reserved.; (5) International Business Machines Corp.; (6) Zenith Data Systems; (7) International Business Machines Corp.; (8) International Business Machines Corp.; (9) Hewlett-Packard Co. **TIMELINE** *Page 1 (1937–52)*, (top left three photos of Atanosoff, Berry, ABC) Iowa State University, News Service, Photo Dept.; (top right) Princeton University; (bottom three photos) UNISYS Corp. *Page 2 (1952–60)*, (top three photos of Dr. Hopper, COBOL, FORTRAN) U.S. Department of the Navy; (top-IBM 650) International Business Machines Corp.; (bottom-core memory) M.I.T.; (bottom two photos of transistors) International Business Machines Corp.; *Page 3 (1964–69)*, (top left-IBM 360) International Business Machines Corp.; (top right-DEC) Digital Equipment Corp.; (bottom left-Kemeny) Dartmouth College News Service; (bottom right-Hoff) Intel Corp.; (bottom right-4004) Intel Corp.; *Page 4 (1970–80)*, (top two photos on the left-LSI) International Business Machines Corp.; (top right-MITS) The Computer Museum; (bottom-Wozniak) Apple Computer, Inc.; (bottom-first Apple) Apple Computer, Inc.; (bottom right-VisiCalc) ©Ira Wyman; *Page 5 (1981–84)*, (top left-Gates) Microsoft Corp.; (top right-IBM) International Business Machines Corp.; (bottom left-Lotus) Lotus Development Corp.; (bottom left-Kapor) Lotus Development Corp.; (bottom right-Apple) Apple Computer, Inc.; *Page 6 (1987–90)*, (top left-Compaq) Compaq Computer Corp. All rights reserved.; (top right-Intel) Intel Corp.; (bottom right-NeXT) NeXT Computer, Inc.; (bottom right-Windows) Microsoft Corp. **CHAPTER 2** *Opening Page*, Stan Musilek Photography; *Figure 2-1*, (far left) Curtis Fukuda; 2-1, (icons) Microsoft Corp.; 2-1, (mouse) Apple Computer, Inc.; *Figure 2-2*, (left) Curtis Fukuda; (right) Hewlett-Packard Co.; *Figure 2-3*, Reference Software Intl.; *Figure 2-14*, Dubl-Click Software, Inc.; *Figure 2-15*, Lotus Development Corp.; *Figure 2-23*, Hewlett-Packard Co.; *Figure 2-25*, Curtis Fukuda; *Figure 2-35*, International Business Machines Corp.; *Figure 2-36*, Business & Professional Software, Inc. Image created with BPS's 35mm Express Software; *Figure 2-37*, Compaq Computer Corp. All rights reserved.; *Figure 2-38*, Prodigy; *Figure 2-39*, Microsoft Corp.; *Figure 2-40*, Borland International ©1991; *Figure 2-41*, Symantic Corp.; *Figure 2-42*, The Aldridge Co.; *Figure 2-43*, Curtis Fukuda; 2-44, (bottom left) Curtis Fukuda; 2-44, (bottom right) Wink Data Products **CHAPTER 3** *Opening Page*, Hank Morgan/Rainbow; *Figure 3-6*, International Business Machines Corp.; *Figure 3-7*, (left) Applied Data Signs; 3-7, (right) Hewlett-Packard Co.; *Figure 3-8*, Compaq Computer Corp. All rights reserved.; *Figure 3-9*, International Business Machines Corp.; *Figure 3-10*, (top) Microsoft Corporation; (bottom) Curtis Fukuda; *Figure 3-11*, Logitech, Inc.; *Figure 3-12*, Hewlett-Packard Co.; *Figure 3-13*, Kensington Microware; *Figure 3-14*, International Business Machines Corp.; *Figure 3-15*, Design Technology; *Figure 3-16*, Summagraphics Corp.; *Figure 3-17*, CalComp Digitizer Products Group; *Figure 3-18*, Compaq Computer Corp. All rights reserved.; *Figure 3-19*, GRID Systems Corp.; *Figure 3-20*, Texas Instruments; *Figure 3-21*, Hewlett-Packard Co.; *Figure 3-22*, Logitech, Inc.; *Figure 3-23*, Wang Laboratories, Inc.; *Figure 3-24*, (both) Spectra-Physics Scanning Systems, Inc.; *Figure 3-25*, (close-up) Soricon Corp.; (less close) International Business Machines Corp.; *Figure 3-28*, Caere Corp.; *Figure 3-29*, Scantron Corp.; *Figure 3-30*, NCR Corp.; *Figure 3-31*, International Business Machines Corp.; *Figure 3-32*, Symbol Technologies, Inc.; *Figure 3-33*, Photo courtesy of Intermec Corp.; *Figure 3-34*, International Business Machines Corp.; *Figure 3-41*, Microsoft Corp.; *Figure 3-47*, Acme Visible Records **CHAPTER 4** *Opening Page*, Chuck O'Rear/West Light; *Figure 4-19*, Intel Corp.; *Figure 4-20*, International Business Machines Corp.; *Figure 4-21*, Intel Corp.; *Figure 4-22*, International Business Machines Corp.; *Figure 4-23*, International Business Machines Corp.; *Making a Chip*: (1) Intel Corp.; (2) Intel Corp.; (3) AT&T; (4) Siltec Corp.; (5) Siltec Corp.; (6) Micron Technology, Inc.; (7) Intel Corp.; (8) Micron Technology, Inc.; (9) Intel Corp.; (10) National Semiconductor Corp.; (11) International Business Machines Corp.; (12) AT&T Bell Laboratories; (13) 3M Corp. **CHAPTER 5** *Opening Page*, ©Robert Holmgren; *Figure 5-1*, Hewlett-Packard Co.; *Figure 5-7*, Britannica Software Inc.; *Figure 5-8*, Owens-Corning Fiberglas Corp.; *Figure 5-11*, Panasonic Communications and Systems Co.; *Figure 5-12*, (both) Printronix, Inc.; *Figure 5-13*, Dataproducts Corp.; *Figure 5-18*, (left) Storage Technology Corp.; (right) Atchison, Topeka and Santa Fe Railway Co.; *Figure 5-19*, Epson America, Inc.; *Figure 5-20*, Dataproducts Corp.; *Figure 5-22*, McDonnell Douglas Automation Co.; *Figure 5-23*, Dataproducts Corp.; *Figure 5-25*, International Business Machines Corp.; *Figure 5-26*, NEC Technologies, Inc.; *Figure 5-28*, Hewlett-Packard Co.; *Figure 5-29*, Xerox Corp.; *Figure 5-31*, Radius, Inc.; *Figure 5-33*, (left) Ramtek Corp.; (right) Evans & Southerland; *Figure 5-35*, International Business Machines Corp.; *Figure 5-36*, Toshiba America Information Systems, Inc.; *Figure 5-39*, Proxima Corp.; *Figure 5-40*, Electrohome Ltd.; *Figure 5-41*, Hewlett-Packard Co.; *Figure 5-42*, (both) CalComp Digitizer Products Group. **CHAPTER 6** *Opening Page*, Stan Musilek Photography; *Figure 6-2*, Greg Hadel; *Figure 6-3*, Jerry Spagnoli; *Figure 6-10*, Seagate Technology, Inc.; *Figure 6-11*, Amdahl Corp.; *Figure 6-12*, International Business Machines Corp.; *Figure 6-13*, Microscience International Corp.; *Figure 6-14*, ©Robert Holmgren; *Figure 6-18*, Control Data Corp.; *Figure 6-19*, Plus Development Corp.; *Figure 6-20*, Plus Development Corp.; *Figure 6-21*, Jerry Spagnoli; *Figure 6-22*, Hewlett-Packard Co.; *Figure 6-24*, International Business Machines Corp.; *Figure 6-25*, Hewlett-Packard Co.; *Figure 6-26*, Everex Systems, Inc.; *Figure 6-30*, Plasmon Data Systems, Inc.; *Figure 6-32*, 3M Corp.; *Figure 6-33*, EMC Corp.; *Figure 6-34*, Storage Technology Corp.; *Figure 6-35*, Applied Systems Institute, Inc.; *Figure 6-36*, Canon **CHAPTER 7** *Opening Page*, Charles Thatcher/Tony Stone; *Figure 7-20*, UNISYS Corp.; *Figure 7-21*, (left) Borland International, Inc.; (right) Ashton-Tate Corp. **CHAPTER 8** *Opening Page*, A. Tennenbaum/Sygma; *Figure 8-2*, Inmac; *Figure 8-3*, Inmac; *Figure 8-4*, Siecor Corporation of America; *Figure 8-6*, Hewlett-Packard Co.; *Figure 8-7*, NASA; *Figure 8-8*, Photonics Corp.; *Figure 8-9*, Motorola Mobile Data Division; *Figure 8-18*, (left) Hayes Microcomputer Products, Inc.; (right) Hayes Microcomputer Products, Inc. ©1991 Hayes Microcomputer Products, Inc.; *Figure 8-19*, Hayes Microcomputer Products, Inc. ©1991 Hayes Microcomputer Products, Inc.; *Figure 8-20*, Panasonic Industrial Co.; *Figure 8-22*, International Business Machines Corp.; *Figure 8-23*, (left) Hayes Microcomputer Products, Inc. ©1991 Hayes Microcomputer Products, Inc.; (right) Hayes Microcomputer Products, Inc. ©1991 Hayes Microcomputer Products, Inc.; *Figure 8-24*, Digital Communications Associates, Inc.; *Figure 8-27*, EDS Corp. **CHAPTER 9** *Opening Page*, Steve Smith/West Light; *Figure 9-9*, UIS, Inc.; *Figure 9-11*, Apple Computer, Inc.; *Figure 9-12*, International Business Machines Corp.; *Figure 9-13*, Microsoft Corp. **CHAPTER 10** *Opening Page*, New York Stock Exchange; *Figure 10-4*, International Business Machines Corp.; *Figure 10-5*, Zenith Data Systems; *Figure 10-6*, (both) COMSHARE Incorporated; *Figure 10-7*, Frito-Lay, Inc.; *Figure 10-8*, Neuron Data; *Figure 10-10*, Ford Motor Co. **CHAPTER 11** *Opening Page*, Hewlett-Packard Co.; *Figure 11-14*, PC Magazine, Sept. 26, 1989 Copyright ©1989, Ziff Communications Co.; *Figure 11-15*, International Business Machines Corp.; *Figure 11-16*, Curtis Fukuda; *Figure 11-22*, Hewlett-Packard Co.; *Figure 11-23*, Intersolv, Inc.; *Figure 11-24*, International Business Machines Corp.; *Figure 11-25*, Curtis Fukuda **CHAPTER 12** *Opening Page*, ©Robert Holmgren; *Figure 12-27*, (both) Oracle Corp.; *Figure 12-28*, Oracle Corp. **CHAPTER 13** *Opening Page*, Lannie Duka/Tony Stone; *Figure 13-1*, Tandy Corp.; *Figure 13-2*, Hewlett-Packard Co.; *Figure 13-4*, Egghead Software; *Figure 13-5*, Tandy Corp.; *Figure 13-6*, International Business Machines Corp.; *Figure 13-12*, The Interface Group; *Figure 13-13*, Jerry Spagnoli **CHAPTER 14** *Opening Page*, R. Ian Lloyd Singapore/West Light; *Figure 14-1(a)*, Compaq Computer Corp. All rights reserved.; 14-1(b), Microsoft Corp.; 14-1(c), Macromind, Inc.; 14-1(d), International Business Machines Corp.; 14-1(e), Hewlett-Packard Co.; *Figure 14-2*, NEC Technologies, Inc.; *Figure 14-3*, Compression Labs, Inc.; *Figure 14-4*, (both) Computervision, A Prime Company; *Figure 14-5*, NASA; *Figure 14-6*, Ford Motor Co.; *Figure 14-8*, Prodigy; *Figure 14-9*, ComputorEdge Magazine; *Figure 14-10*, (both) Broderbund Software; *Figure 14-11*, Electronic Arts; *Figure 14-12*, Quicksoft, Inc.; *Figure 14-13*, (Eyedentify) Eyedentify, Inc.; (Identix) Identix, Inc.

◆ CONTENTS

◆ CHAPTER 1   An Overview of Computer Concepts   1.1

◆ CHAPTER 2   Microcomputer Applications: User Tools   2.1

CHAPTER 7   File and Database Management

 CHAPTER 8   Communications   8.1

 CHAPTER 9   Operating Systems and Systems Software   9.1

CHAPTER 10   Management Information Systems   10.1

CHAPTER 11   The Information System Life Cycle   11.1

CHAPTER 12   Program Development   12.1

CHAPTER 13   Career Opportunities in Information Processing   13.1

INTRODUCTION TO DOS

WORD PROCESSING USING WORDPERFECT 5.1

PROJECT 6   Macros, Windows, Sorting, and the Thesaurus   WP182

 SPREADSHEETS USING LOTUS 1-2-3 RELEASE 2.2

 PROJECT 1   Building a Worksheet   L2

PROJECT 2   Formatting and Printing a Worksheet   L44

 PROJECT 3   Enhancing Your Worksheet   L92

PROJECT 4   Building Worksheets with Functions and Macros   L153

◆ **PROJECT 5   Graphing with 1-2-3 and Allways   L192**

◆ **PROJECT 6   Sorting and Querying a Worksheet Database   L228**

◆ **APPENDIX—Command Structure Charts for Release 2.2   L257**

DATABASE MANAGEMENT USING dBASE IV VERSION 1.1

 PROJECT 1   Creating a Database   dB3

PROJECT 2   **Displaying Records in a Database**   **dB43**

 PROJECT 3   **Sorting and Report Preparation**   **dB74**

 PROJECT 4   **More on Adding, Changing, and Deleting**   **dB113**

 PROJECT 5   **Additional Topics**   **dB138**

 PROJECT 6   **Generating Applications**   **dB181**

◆ PREFACE

Congratulations! You are about to use a Shelly Cashman Series textbook. In doing so, you join millions of other students and instructors who have discovered why this is the best-selling computer education series of all time.

The Shelly Cashman Series offers superior materials from which to learn about computers. The series includes books on computer concepts, microcomputer applications, and introductory programming. No matter what you cover in your class, the Shelly Cashman Series provides the appropriate texts.

Traditionally bound series texts are shown in the table below. If you do not find the exact combination that fits your needs, boyd & fraser's unique Custom Editions Program allows you to choose from a number of options and create a text perfectly suited to your course. This exciting new program is explained in detail on page xiv of this preface.

Traditionally Bound Texts in the Shelly Cashman Series

Computer Concepts	*Essential Computer Concepts* *Complete Computer Concepts*
Computer Concepts Study Guide	*Workbook and Study Guide with Computer Lab Software Projects to accompany Complete Computer Concepts*
Computer Concepts and Microcomputer Applications	*Essential Computer Concepts with Microcomputer Applications: WordPerfect 5.0/5.1, Lotus 1-2-3 Release 2.2, and dBASE III PLUS* *Complete Computer Concepts and Microcomputer Applications: WordPerfect 5.1, Lotus 1-2-3 Release 2.2, and dBASE III PLUS* (also available in spiral bound edition) *Complete Computer Concepts and Microcomputer Applications: WordPerfect 5.1, Lotus 1-2-3 Release 2.2, and dBASE IV Version 1.1* (also available in spiral bound edition)
Computer Concepts and Programming	*Complete Computer Concepts and Microsoft BASIC* *Complete Computer Concepts and QuickBASIC*
Microcomputer Applications	*Learning to Use Microcomputer Applications: WordPerfect 5.1, Lotus 1-2-3 Release 2.2, and dBASE III PLUS* (also available in spiral bound edition) *Learning to Use Microcomputer Applications: WordPerfect 5.1, Lotus 1-2-3 Release 2.2, and dBASE IV Version 1.1* (also available in spiral bound edition)
Word Processing	*Learning to Use Microcomputer Applications: WordPerfect 5.1* *Learning to Use WordPerfect 4.2* (WordPerfect 4.2 Educational Version Software available) *Learning to Use Microsoft Word 5.0* *Learning to Use WordStar 6.0* (with WordStar 6.0 Academic Edition Software)
Spreadsheets	*Learning to Use Microcomputer Applications: Lotus 1-2-3 Release 2.3* *Learning to Use Microcomputer Applications: Lotus 1-2-3 Release 2.2* *Learning to Use Lotus 1-2-3 Release 2.01* *Learning to Use Microcomputer Applications: Quattro Pro* *Learning to Use Microcomputer Applications: Quattro with 1-2-3 Menus* (with Quattro Educational Version Software)
Database	*Learning to Use dBASE III PLUS* (dBASE III PLUS Educational Version Software available) *Learning to Use Microcomputer Applications: dBASE IV Version 1.1* *Learning to Use Microcomputer Applications: Paradox 3.5* (with Paradox Educational Version Software)
Programming	*Programming in Microsoft BASIC* *Programming in QuickBASIC*

CONTENT

◆ Shelly Cashman Series texts assume no previous experience with computers and are written with continuity, simplicity, and practicality in mind.

Computer Concepts

The Shelly Cashman Series computer concepts textbooks offer up-to-date coverage to fit every need. *Essential Computer Concepts* is a brief concepts text that covers the topics most commonly found in short courses on computer concepts. *Complete Computer Concepts* offers a more comprehensive treatment of computer concepts.

All Shelly Cashman Series computer concepts textbooks are lavishly illustrated with hundreds of photographs and carefully developed illustrations—features that have become a hallmark of the Shelly Cashman Series. The impact of microcomputers and the user's point of view are consistently addressed throughout these texts. In addition they include coverage of important topics to help students understand today's rapidly changing technology:

- A chapter on Management Information Systems that presents information as an asset to organizations, discusses how computer-based systems effectively manage information, and addresses recent trends in decision support and expert systems.
- An innovative approach to the phases of the Information System Life Cycle.
- Up-to-date coverage of local area networks, pen-based and notebook computers, graphic user interfaces, multi-media, object-oriented programming, page printers, and desktop publishing.

Each concepts chapter concludes with:

- A Chapter Summary to help students recall and comprehend key concepts.
- Key Terms to reinforce terminology introduced in the chapter.
- Review Questions to test students' mastery of the chapter content.
- Controversial Issues to stimulate classroom discussion and critical thinking.
- Research Projects to provide opportunity for in-depth investigation of chapter content.

Microcomputer Applications

The Shelly Cashman Series microcomputer applications textbooks include projects on DOS, word processing, spread-sheets, and database management. In each project students learn by way of a unique and time-tested problem-solving approach, in which problems are presented and then *thoroughly* solved in a step-by-step manner. Numerous, carefully labeled screens and keystroke sequences illustrate the exact order of operations. Using this approach, students are visually guided as they perform the various commands and quickly come up to speed.

The DOS materials are divided into two projects. Project 1 covers the essential commands on file management and Project 2 presents directory and subdirectory file management concepts.

Each word processing application contains six projects. After an introduction to the keyboard, students are guided through the word processing cycle—starting the software, creating a document, entering text, saving, viewing, printing, and exiting to DOS. To reinforce their understanding of the cycle, students restart the software, retrieve the document they created, revise the document, save the changes, print the document, and exit to DOS again. In subsequent projects students learn to use the speller and thesaurus; to format, move, search, and replace text; to merge documents, create footnotes, and to use windows. They learn these skills by creating memos, letters, reports, and resumes.

Each spreadsheet application contains six projects. In Project 1 students learn spreadsheet terminology and basic spreadsheet characteristics and apply this know-how to create a company's first quarter sales report. In Project 2 students continue to use this sales report, learning such skills as adding summary totals, formatting, changing column widths, replication, debugging, and printing. In Project 3 students create a more complex quarterly report using what-if analysis and other skills such as inserting and deleting rows and columns, changing default settings, and copying absolute cell addresses. Projects 4, 5, and 6 cover functions and macros, graphing, and database functions, respectively.

Each database application contains six projects. In Project 1 students design and create a database of employee records, which they use as an example throughout the remaining five projects. Project 2 teaches students how to display records in a database in a variety of ways and also how to use statistical functions. Sorting and report generation are taught in Project 3. Project 4 introduces the processes of adding, changing, and deleting records. Students change the structure of the employee database, and create and use indexes and views in Project 5. Finally, in Project 6 students create custom forms for data entry and learn how to generate applications.

In all of the microcomputer applications, two beneficial learning and review tools are included at the end of each project—the Project Summary, which lists the key concepts covered in the project, and the Keystroke Summary, which is an exact listing of each keystroke used to solve the project's problem.

Following the last project in each application, an easy-to-use Quick Reference is included for each project. The Quick Reference is divided into three parts—the activity, the procedure for accomplishing the activity, and a description of what actually occurs when the keys are pressed.

Finally, each project concludes with a wealth of Student Assignments. These include: true/false and multiple-choice questions; exercises that require students to write and/or explain various commands; a series of realistic problems for students to analyze and solve by applying what they have learned in the project; and minicases for the database projects.

Programming

The Shelly Cashman Series includes QuickBASIC and Microsoft BASIC programming textbooks. They are divided into six projects that provide students with knowledge that is central to a real programming environment. They present the essentials of the language as well as structured and top-down programming techniques. In each project a problem is presented and then *thoroughly* solved step by step with a program.

In Project 1 students learn the program development cycle, the basic characteristics of the programming language, and the operating environment. Project 2 presents computations, summary tools, report editing, and report printing. In Project 3 students learn about decision making. Topics include implementing If-Then-Else and Case structures, and the use of logical operators. Unlike the first three projects, which use the READ and DATA statements to integrate data into a program, Project 4 shows students how to use the INPUT statement to accomplish this task. Also included is coverage of how to use For loops to implement counter-controlled loops, and how to design top-down programs. Project 5 introduces students to creating and processing a sequential data file. In Project 6 students learn how to write programs that can look up information in tables; they are then acquainted with the most often used built-in functions and, if applicable, special variables, of the language. Finally, an appendix on debugging techniques introduces students to debugging features that are built into the language.

Each programming project includes one or more sets of Try It Yourself Exercises, paper-and-pencil practice exercises to help master the concepts presented. Each project concludes with challenging and field-tested Student Assignments. All programming assignments include a problem statement, sample input data, and sample output results. Also included is a Reference Card that lists all statements, functions, and features of the language.

SHELLY CASHMAN SERIES CUSTOM EDITIONS

◆ The Shelly Cashman Series provides a new textbook option so flexible that you can easily put together a unique, customized computer textbook reflecting the exact content and software requirements of your course. Because all of the Shelly Cashman Series materials use a consistent pedagogy, you can easily "mix and match" them while maintaining a clear, cohesive text. It has all been designed to work together in any combination.

When you order your custom edition, you will receive individually packaged text materials that you selected for your course needs. The customized materials arrive in a sealed box together with a durable spine binding and two covers ready for your students to assemble in seconds.

Features of the custom bound editions include:

- Text that reflects the content of your course.
- Shelly Cashman Series quality, including the same full-color materials and proven Shelly Cashman Series pedagogy found in the traditionally bound books.
- Flexibility so you can also include your own handouts and worksheets.
- Affordably priced so your students receive the Custom Edition at a cost similar to the traditionally bound books.
- Guaranteed quick order processing where your materials are sent to your bookstore within forty-eight hours of receipt of your order.
- Applications materials are continually updated to reflect the latest software versions.

The materials available in the Shelly Cashman Series Custom Edition program are listed below.

Materials Available for Shelly Cashman Series Custom Editions

Concepts	*Introduction to Computers* *Essential Computer Concepts* *Complete Computer Concepts*
Operating Systems	*Introduction to DOS* (all versions using commands) *Introduction to DOS 5.0* (using menus)
Word Processing	*Word Processing Using WordPerfect 5.1* *Word Processing Using WordPerfect 4.2* *Word Processing Using Microsoft Word 5.0* *Word Processing Using WordStar 6.0*
Spreadsheets	*Spreadsheets Using Lotus 1-2-3 Release 2.3* *Spreadsheets Using Lotus 1-2-3 Release 2.2* *Spreadsheets Using Lotus 1-2-3 Release 2.01* *Spreadsheets Using Quattro Pro* *Spreadsheets Using Quattro with 1-2-3 Menus*
Database	*Database Management Using dBASE IV Version 1.1* *Database Management Using dBASE III PLUS* *Database Management Using Paradox 3.5*
Programming	*Programming in Microsoft BASIC* *Programming in QuickBASIC*

SUPPLEMENTS

 Ten available supplements complement the various textbooks in the Shelly Cashman Series.

Workbook and Study Guide with Computer Lab Software Projects

This highly popular supplement contains completely new activities to enhance the concepts chapters and to simulate computer applications that are not usually available to beginning students. Included for each chapter are:

- Chapter Objectives that help students measure their mastery of the chapter content.
- A Chapter Outline that guides students through the organization of the chapter.
- A Chapter Summary that helps students recall and comprehend key concepts.
- Key Terms with definitions that reinforce terminology introduced in the chapter.
- Six projects which range from self-testing on paper and communications skills activities to on-line computerized testing with self-scoring. Answers are included for all projects and exercises.

The Computer Lab Software Projects simulate the following applications in an interactive environment:

- Home banking
- Airline reservations
- On-line information services
- Electronic mail
- Desktop publishing
- Presentation graphics

Instructor's Manual to accompany the Workbook and Study Guide with Computer Lab Software Projects

The Instructor's Manual to accompany the workbook includes answers and solutions for the entire workbook, and the software for the on-line, self-testing projects as well as for the Computer Lab Software Projects.

Educational Versions of Applications Software

Free educational versions of WordPerfect 4.2, WordStar 6.0, Quattro 1.01, Paradox 2.04, and dBASE III PLUS are available to adopting institutions. This software is available for IBM or IBM compatible systems.

Instructor's Guide Including Answer Manual and Test Bank

The Instructor's Guide and Answer Manual includes Lesson Plans for each chapter or project. The Lesson Plans begin with behavorial objectives and an overview of each chapter or project to help instructors quickly review the purpose and key concepts. Detailed outlines of each chapter and/or project follow. These outlines are annotated with the page number of the text on which the outlined material is covered; notes, teaching tips, and additional activities that the instructor might use to embellish the lesson; and a key for using the Transparency Masters and/or Color Transparencies. Complete answers and solutions for all Exercises, Discussion Questions, Projects, Controversial Issues, Student Assignments, Try It Yourself Exercises, and Minicases are also included.

This manual also contains three types of test questions with answers and is a hard copy version of MicroSWAT III (see below). The three types of questions are—true/false, multiple choice, and fill-in. Each chapter or project has approximately 50 true/false, 25 multiple choice, and 35 fill ins.

MicroSWAT III

MicroSWAT III, a microcomputer-based test-generating system, is available free to adopters. It includes all of the questions from the Test Bank in an easy-to-use, menu-driven package that allows testing flexibility and customization of testing documents. For example, with MicroSWAT III a user can enter his or her own questions and can generate review sheets and answer keys. MicroSWAT III will run on any IBM or IBM compatible system with two diskette drives or a hard disk.

Transparency Masters

Transparency Masters are available for *every* illustration in all of the Shelly Cashman Series textbooks. The transparency masters are conveniently bound in a perforated volume; they have been photographically enlarged for clearer projection.

Color Transparencies

One hundred high-quality, full-color acetates contain key illustrations found in *Complete Computer Concepts*. Each transparency is accompanied by an interleaved lecture note.

Instructor's Data Disks

The Instructor's Data Disks contain the files used in the DOS projects; the letters and memos, and the final versions of documents used to teach the word processing projects; the project worksheets and Student Assignment worksheet solutions for the spreadsheet projects; the databases that students will create and use in the database Minicases; the data for the employee database example, and program solutions to all of the programming assignments.

HyperGraphics®

This software-based, instructor-led classroom presentation system is available to assist adopters in delivering top-notch lectures. It allows instructors to present much of the text's content using graphics, color, animation, and instructor-led interactivity. It requires an LCD projection panel, a microcomputer, and an overhead projector.

ACKNOWLEDGMENTS

◆ The Shelly Cashman Series would not be the success it is without the contributions of many outstanding publishing professionals, who demand quality in everything they do: Jeanne Huntington, typographer; Ken Russo, Anne Craig, Mike Bodnar, John Craig and Julia Schenden, illustrators; Janet Bollow, book design and cover design; Sarah Bendersky, photo researcher; Virginia Harvey, manuscript editor; Pat Stephan, manufacturing coordinator; Greg Hadel and Tim Davis, cover photography; Becky Herrington, director of production and art coordinator; Susan Solomon, director of development; and Thomas K. Walker, publisher and vice president of boyd & fraser publishing company. We hope you will find using this text an enriching and rewarding experience.

Gary B. Shelly
Thomas J. Cashman

An Overview of Computer Concepts

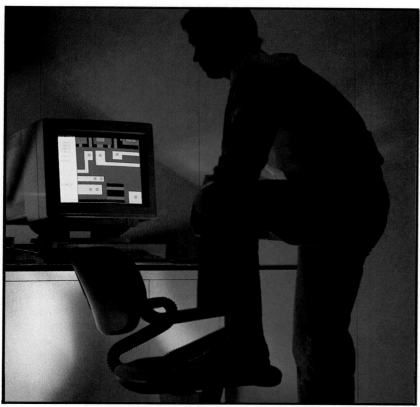

OBJECTIVES

◆ Explain what a computer is and how it processes data to produce information

◆ Identify the four operations of the information processing cycle: input, process, output, and storage

◆ Explain how the operations of the information processing cycle are performed by computer hardware and software

◆ Identify the major categories of computers

◆ Describe the six elements of an information system: equipment, software, data, personnel, users, and procedures

◆ Explain the responsibilities of information system personnel

◆ Explain the use of computers in our world

◆ Describe the evolution of the computer industry

Every day computers play a key role in how we work and how we live. Today, even the smallest organizations usually have computers to help them operate more efficiently. Computers also affect our lives in many unseen ways. When we buy groceries at the supermarket, use an automatic teller machine, or make a long-distance phone call, we are also using computers.

As they have for a number or years, personal computers continue to make an increasing impact on our lives. Both at home and at work, these small desktop systems help us do our work faster, more accurately, and in some cases, in ways that previously would not have been possible.

Today, many people believe that knowing how to use a computer, especially a personal computer, is a basic skill necessary to succeed in business or to function effectively in society. Given the increasing use and availability of computer systems, such knowledge will continue to be an essential skill. The purpose of this book is to give you this knowledge so that you will understand how computers are used today and so that you can adapt to how computers will be used in the future.

In this first chapter we will give you an overview of computer concepts. You will begin to learn what a computer is, how it processes data into information, and what elements are necessary for a successful information system. While you are reading, remember that this chapter is an overview and that many of the terms and concepts that are introduced will be discussed in more detail in later chapters.

WHAT IS A COMPUTER?

The most obvious question related to understanding computers and their impact on our lives is, "What is a computer?". A **computer** is an electronic device, operating under the control of instructions stored in its own memory unit, that can accept data (input), process data arithmetically and logically, produce output from the processing, and store the results for future use. While broader definitions of a computer exist, this definition includes a wide range of devices with various capabilities. For example, the tiny microcomputer chip shown in Figure 1-1 can be called a computer. Generally the term is used to describe a collection of devices that function together to process data. An example of the devices that make up a computer is shown in Figure 1-2.

FIGURE 1-1
Small enough to fit in the palm of a baby's hand, this microcomputer chip contains the electronic circuits that perform the operations of a computer.

WHAT DOES A COMPUTER DO?

Whether small or large, computers can perform four general operations. These operations comprise the **information processing cycle** and are: input, process, output, and storage. Collectively, these operations describe the procedures that a computer performs to process data into information and store it for future use.

All computer processing requires data. **Data** refers to the raw facts, including numbers and words, given to a computer during the input operation. In the processing phase, the computer manipulates the data to create information. **Information** refers to data that has been processed into a form that has meaning and is useful. The production of information by processing data on a computer is called **information processing**, or sometimes **data processing (DP)**. During the output operation, the information that has been created is put into some form, such as a printed report, that people can use. The information can also be stored electronically for future use.

screen

printer

processor
unit

keyboard

FIGURE 1-2
Devices that comprise a
microcomputer.

The people who either use the computer directly or use the information it provides
are called **computer users**, **end users**, or sometimes just simply **users**. Figure 1-3
shows a computer user and demonstrates how the four operations of the information
processing cycle can occur on a personal computer. ①The computer user inputs data
by pressing the keys on the keyboard. ②The data is then processed by the unit called
the processor. ③The output, or results, from the processing are displayed on the
screen or printed on the printer, providing information to the user. ④Finally, the output may be stored on a disk for future reference.

WHY IS A COMPUTER SO POWERFUL?

The input, process, output, and storage operations that a
computer performs may seem very basic and simple. However,
the computer's power derives from its capability to perform
these operations very quickly, accurately, and reliably. In a
computer, operations occur through the use of electronic
circuits contained on small chips as shown on the next
page in Figure 1-4. When data flows along these circuits it travels at close to the speed of light.
This allows processing to be accomplished
in billionths of a second. The electronic
circuits in modern computers are
very reliable and seldom fail. Storage capability is another reason
why computers are so powerful.
They can store enormous amounts
of data and keep that data readily
available for processing. This
capability combined with the factors of speed, accuracy, and reliability are why a computer is
considered to be such a powerful
tool for information processing.

FIGURE 1-3
The use of this personal computer illustrates the four operations of the information
processing cycle: input, process, output, and storage.

input

process

storage

output

FIGURE 1-4
Inside a computer are chips and other electronic components that process data in billionths of a second.

HOW DOES A COMPUTER KNOW WHAT TO DO?

For a computer to perform the operations in the information processing cycle, it must be given a detailed set of instructions that tell it exactly what to do. These instructions are called a **computer program**, **program instructions**, or **software**.

Before the information processing cycle for a specific job begins, the computer program corresponding to that job is stored in the computer. Once the program is stored, the computer can begin to process data by executing the program's first instruction. The computer executes one program instruction after another until the job is complete.

THE INFORMATION PROCESSING CYCLE

Your understanding of the information processing cycle introduced in this chapter is fundamental to understanding computers and how they process data into information. To review, the information processing cycle consists of four operations. They are: input, process, output, storage.

The first three of these operations, **input**, **process**, and **output**, describe the procedures that a computer performs to process data into information. The fourth operation, **storage**, describes a computer's electronic storage capability. As you learn more about computers, you will see that these four operations apply to both the computer equipment and the computer software. The equipment, or devices, of a computer are classified according to the operations that they perform. Computer software is made up of instructions that describe how the operations are to be performed.

WHAT ARE THE COMPONENTS OF A COMPUTER?

Data is processed by specific equipment that is often called computer **hardware** (Figure 1-5). This equipment consists of: input devices, a processor unit, output devices, and auxiliary storage units.

FIGURE 1-5
A computer is composed of input devices through which data is entered into the computer; the processor that processes data stored in main memory; output devices on which the results of the processing are made available; and auxiliary storage units that store data for future processing.

Input Devices

Input devices are used to enter data into a computer. A common input device is the **keyboard**, shown in Figure 1-6⟨a⟩. As the data is entered, or keyed, it is stored in the computer and displayed on a screen.

FIGURE 1-6
The components of a computer perform the four operations of the information processing cycle.

Processor Unit

Figure 1-6⟨b⟩ shows the **processor unit** of a computer, which contains the electronic circuits that actually cause the processing of data to occur. The processor unit is divided into two parts, the central processing unit and main memory. The **central processing unit (CPU)** contains a **control unit** that executes the program instructions and an **arithmetic/logic unit (ALU)** that performs math and logic operations. **Arithmetic operations** include numeric calculations such as addition, subtraction, multiplication, and division. Comparisons of data to see if one value is greater than, equal to, or less than another are called **logical operations**.

 Main memory, also called **primary storage**, is a part of the processor unit. Main memory electronically stores data and program instructions when they are being processed.

Output Devices

Output from a computer can be presented in many forms. The two most commonly used **output devices** are the **printer** and the computer **screen** shown in Figure 1-6⟨c⟩. Other frequently used names for the screen are the **monitor**, or the **CRT**, which stands for **cathode ray tube**.

Auxiliary Storage Units

Auxiliary storage units, shown in Figure 1-6⟨d⟩, store instructions and data when they are not being used by the processor unit. A common auxiliary storage device on personal computers is a diskette drive, which stores data as magnetic spots on a small plastic disk called a **diskette**. Another auxiliary storage device is called a hard disk drive. **Hard disk** drives contain nonremovable metal disks and provide larger storage capacities than diskettes.

As you can see, each component shown in Figure 1-6 plays an important role in information processing. Collectively, this equipment is called a **computer system**, or simply a computer. The term computer is also used to refer to the processing unit where the actual processing of data occurs. The input devices, output devices, and auxiliary storage units that surround the processing unit are sometimes referred to as **peripheral devices**.

CATEGORIES OF COMPUTERS

Figure 1-7 shows the following four major categories of computers: microcomputers, minicomputers, mainframe computers, and supercomputers.

Computers are generally classified according to their size, speed, processing capabilities, and price. However, rapid changes in technology make firm definitions of these categories difficult. This year's speed, performance, and price classification of a mainframe might fit next year's classification of a minicomputer. Even though they are not firmly defined, the categories are frequently used and should be generally understood.

FIGURE 1-7

ⓐ Microcomputers are small desktop-sized computers. These machines have become so widely used that they are sometimes called desktop appliances. ⓑ Minicomputers can perform many of the functions of a mainframe computer, but on a smaller scale. ⓒ Mainframe computers are large, powerful machines that can handle many users concurrently and process large volumes of data. ⓓ Supercomputers are the most powerful and expensive computers.

Microcomputers, shown in Figure 1-7⟨a⟩, also called **personal computers** or **micros**, are the small desktop-sized systems that have become so widely used in recent years. These machines are generally priced under $10,000. This category also includes hand-held, notebook, laptop, portable, and supermicrocomputers.

Minicomputers, shown in Figure 1-7⟨b⟩, are more powerful than microcomputers and can support a number of users performing different tasks. Originally developed to perform specific tasks such as engineering calculations, their use grew rapidly as their performance and capabilities increased. These systems can cost from approximately $15,000 up to several hundred thousand dollars. The most powerful minis are called superminicomputers.

Mainframe computers, shown in Figure 1-7⟨c⟩, are large systems that can handle hundreds of users, store large amounts of data, and process transactions at a very high rate. Mainframes usually require a specialized environment including separate air conditioning, cooling, and electrical power. Raised flooring is often built to accommodate the many cables connecting the system components underneath. The price range for mainframes is from several hundred thousand dollars to several million dollars.

Supercomputers, shown in Figure 1-7⟨d⟩, are the most powerful category of computers and, accordingly, the most expensive. The capability of these systems to process hundreds of millions of instructions per second is used for such applications as weather forecasting, engineering design and testing, space exploration, and other jobs requiring long, complex calculations. These machines cost several million dollars.

Computers of all categories, especially microcomputers, are sometimes wired together to form networks that allow users to share data and computing resources.

COMPUTER SOFTWARE

As we mentioned previously, a computer is directed by a series of instructions called a computer program (Figure 1-8), which specifies the sequence of operations the computer will perform. To do this, the program must be stored in the main memory of the computer. Computer programs are commonly referred to as **computer software**. Many instructions can be used to direct a computer to perform a specific task. For example, some instructions allow data to be entered from a keyboard and stored in main memory; some instructions allow data in main memory to be used in calculations such as adding a series of numbers to obtain a total; some instructions compare two values stored in main memory and direct the computer to perform alternative operations based on the results of the comparison; and some instructions direct the computer to print a report, display information on the screen, draw a color graph on a screen, or store data on a disk.

FIGURE 1-8
A computer program contains instructions that specify the sequence of operations to be performed. This program is written in a language called BASIC. It allows the user to generate a telephone directory of names, area codes, and telephone numbers.

COMPUTER PROGRAM LISTING

```
100 REM TELLIST          SEPTEMBER 22          SHELLY CASHMAN
110                                                         REM
120 REM THIS PROGRAM DISPLAYS THE NAME, TELEPHONE AREA CODE
130 REM AND PHONE NUMBER OF INDIVIDUALS.
140                                                         REM
150 REM VARIABLE NAMES:
160 REM    A.....AREA CODE
170 REM    T$....TELEPHONE NUMBER
180 REM    N$....NAME
190                                                         REM
200 REM ••••• DATA TO BE PROCESSED •••••
210                                                         REM
220 DATA 714, "749-2138", "SAM HORN"
230 DATA 213, "663-1271", "SUE NUNN"
240 DATA 212, "999-1193", "BOB PELE"
250 DATA 312, "979-4418", "ANN SITZ"
260 DATA 999, "999-9999", "END OF FILE"
270                                                         REM
280 REM ••••• PROCESSING •••••                              REM
290                                                         REM
300 READ A, T&, N$                                          REM
310                                                         REM
320 WHILE N$ <> "END OF FILE"
330    PRINT N$, A, T$
340    READ A, T$, N$
350 WEND
360                                                         REM
370 PRINT " "
380 PRINT "END OF TELEPHONE LISTING"
390 END
```

Most computer programs are written by people with specialized training. They determine the instructions necessary to process the data and place the instructions in the correct sequence so that the desired results will occur. Complex programs may require hundreds or even thousands of program instructions.

Computer software is the key to productive use of computers. With the correct software, a computer can become a valuable tool. Software can be categorized into two types: system software and application software.

System Software and Application Software

System software consists of programs that are related to controlling the actual operations of the computer equipment. An important part of the system software is a set of programs called the operating system. The instructions in the **operating system** tell the computer how to perform functions such as how to load, store, and execute an application program and how to transfer data between the input/output devices and main memory. For a computer to operate, an operating system must be stored in the main memory of the computer. Each time a computer is started, or turned on, the operating system is loaded into the computer and stored in the computer's main memory. Many different operating systems are available for computers. An operating system commonly used on many microcomputers is called DOS. The letters stand for Disk Operating System.

Application software consists of programs that tell a computer how to produce information. When you think of the different ways that people use computers in their careers or in their personal lives, you are thinking of examples of application software. Business, scientific, and educational programs are all examples of application software.

Application Software Packages

Most end users do not write their own programs. In large corporations, the information processing department develops programs for unique company applications. Programs required for common business and personal applications can be purchased from software vendors or stores that sell computer products (Figure 1-9). We often refer to purchased programs as **application software packages**, or simply **software packages**.

FIGURE 1-9
Many programs commonly required for business and personal applications can be purchased from computer stores.

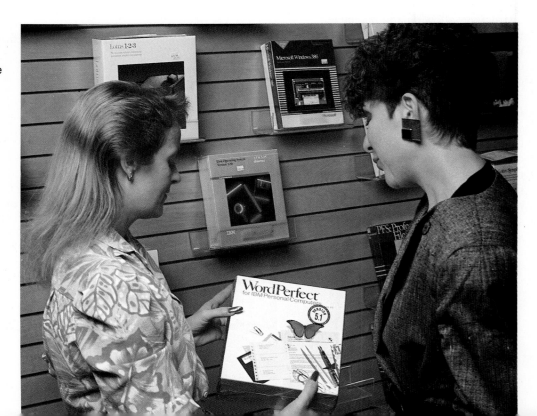

Microcomputer Applications Software Packages

Personal computer users often use applications software packages. Some of the most commonly used packages, shown in Figure 1-10, are: word processing software, electronic spreadsheet software, computer graphics software, and database software.

word processing

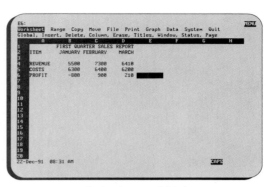

electronic spreadsheet

FIGURE 1-10
Commonly used microcomputer applications software packages.

Word processing is used to write letters, memos, and other documents. As the user keys in words and letters, they display on the screen. The user can easily add, delete, and change any text entered until the document is exactly what he or she wants. The user can then save the document on auxiliary storage and can also print it on a printer.

Electronic spreadsheet software is frequently used by people who work with numbers. The user enters the data and the formulas to be used on the data; then the program applies the formulas to the data and calculates the results. A powerful feature of electronic spreadsheet software is the capability to ask what-if questions by changing the data and quickly recalculating the new results. For example, the user could direct the software to recalculate the total sales based on a percentage increase in the second quarter sales.

computer graphics

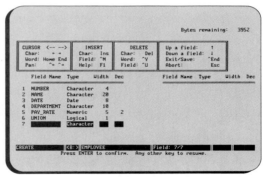

database

Computer graphics software provides the capability to transform a series of numeric values into graphic form for easier analysis and interpretation. In this example, the sales values from an electronic spreadsheet have been transformed into a pie chart. Using graphics software, these graphs can be produced in seconds instead of the hours that were required for a graphic artist to hand draw each graph.

Database software allows the user to enter, retrieve, and update data in an organized and efficient manner. This screen shows how a database is created by defining the information that can be stored in each database record. After the database is defined, the user can add, delete, change, display, print, or reorganize the database records.

Word processing software is used to create and print documents that would otherwise be prepared on a typewriter. A key advantage of word processing software is its capability to make changes easily in documents, such as correcting spelling, changing margins, and adding, deleting, or relocating entire paragraphs. These changes would be difficult and time consuming to make on a typewriter. With a word processor, documents can be printed quickly and accurately and easily stored on a disk for future use.

Electronic spreadsheet software allows the user to add, subtract, and perform user-defined calculations on rows and columns of numbers. These numbers can be changed and the **spreadsheet** quickly recalculates the new results. Electronic spreadsheet software eliminates the tedious recalculations required with manual methods.

Graphics software converts numbers and text into graphic output that visually conveys the relationships of the data. Some graphics software allows the use of color to further enhance the visual presentation. Line, bar, and pie charts are the most frequent forms of graphics output. Spreadsheet information is frequently converted into a graphic form. In fact, graphics capabilities are included in most spreadsheet packages.

Database software allows the user to enter, retrieve, and update data in an organized and efficient manner. These software packages have flexible inquiry and reporting capabilities that allow users to access the data in different ways and create custom reports.

FIGURE 1-11
After the diskette is inserted in the disk drive, the spreadsheet program is copied into main memory. In this example we use English statements for ease of understanding.

A TYPICAL BUSINESS APPLICATION

Electronic spreadsheets are one of the most widely used software applications. In the following example, a user develops a budget spreadsheet for the first quarter of a year. After loading the operating system and spreadsheet program, the user enters the revenues and the costs for the first three months of the year. The spreadsheet program then calculates the total revenues and total costs, the profit for each month (determined by subtracting costs from revenues), and the profit percentage (obtained by dividing the profit by the revenues). In addition, the spreadsheet program calculates the total profit and the total profit percentage.

The diagrams shown in Figures 1-11 and 1-12, and on page 1.12 in Figure 1-13 show the steps that occur to obtain the spreadsheet output. A more complete description of these steps follows.

MAIN MEMORY
Accept input data
Perform calculations
Display spreadsheet on CRT
Display spreadsheet on printer
Save spreadsheet on disk

ELECTRONIC SPREADSHEET PROGRAM

ELECTRONIC SPREADSHEET PROGRAM

Load the Operating System

When the user turns on the power to the computer, a copy of the operating system is transferred from the hard disk into the main memory of the computer. When this process is complete, the computer is ready to load the application software.

Loading the Application Software

For processing to occur, the application software must also be stored in the main memory of the computer. In this example, the application software is a spreadsheet program that is stored on a diskette. The process of getting the program into the main memory is called loading the program.

In Figure 1-11 the diskette on which the program is stored is inserted into the disk drive. The user then issues a command that instructs the operating system to load a copy of the program from the diskette into main memory. After loading the program, the operating system instructs the computer to begin executing the program.

Input: Enter the Data

The next step is to input the data (Figure 1-12). The user does this by using a keyboard. As the user enters the data on the keyboard ⟨1⟩, the data displays on the screen ⟨2⟩, and it is stored in main memory ⟨3⟩.

The data in this example consists of the words indicating the contents of each of the columns and rows on the screen and the numbers on which the calculations are to be performed.

FIGURE 1-12
In this example, the user enters on the keyboard a report heading, column and row headings, the revenues for January, February, and March, and the costs for the three months ⟨1⟩, the data displays on the screen ⟨2⟩, and it is stored in main memory ⟨3⟩.

Process: Perform the Calculations

FIGURE 1-13

After the data has been entered, the program specifies the following processing steps: ① Perform calculations. ② Display the entire spreadsheet, with the calculation results, on the screen. ③ Print the spreadsheet. ④ Store the spreadsheet data and results on auxiliary storage.

As Figure 1-13 shows, the user has entered the data ①, and the program will direct the processor to perform the required calculations ②. In this example, the program calculates the profit for each month, the total revenue, costs, and profit for the quarter, the profit percent for each month, and the total profit percent.

The preceding operations illustrate the calculating capability of computers. Whenever any calculations are performed on data, the data must be stored in main memory. The results of the calculations are also stored in main memory. If you desire, the program can issue instructions to store the results on an auxiliary storage device such as a hard disk or diskette.

Output: Display the Results

After completing the calculations, the program specifies that the spreadsheet, with the results of the calculations, display on the screen. The program also specifies that the results are printed on the printer ③. When this instruction is executed, the spreadsheet is printed on paper so the results of the processing can be used by someone other than the computer user.

Storage: Save the Results

The spreadsheet is also stored on a disk, in this example a hard disk, so that at a later time it can be retrieved and used again ◇4◇.

WHAT ARE THE ELEMENTS OF AN INFORMATION SYSTEM?

◆ Obtaining useful and timely information from computer processing requires more than just the equipment and software we have described so far. Other elements required for successful information processing include accurate data, trained information systems personnel, knowledgeable users, and documented procedures. Together these elements are referred to as an **information system** (Figure 1-14).

FIGURE 1-14
An information system requires computer equipment; software, which runs the equipment; data, which the computer manipulates; people, including both computer personnel who manage the equipment and users who use the information that the equipment produces; and finally procedures, which help the entire system run efficiently.

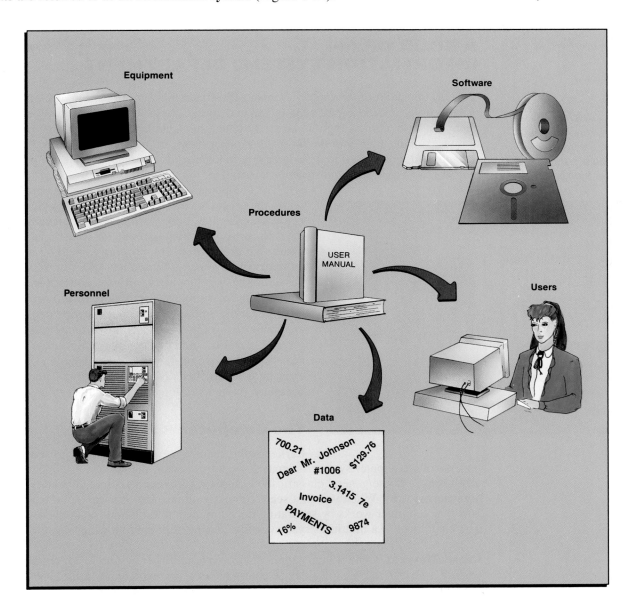

For an information system to provide accurate, timely, and useful information, each element in the system must be strong and all of the elements must work together. The equipment must be reliable and capable of handling the expected work load. The software must have been carefully developed and tested, and the data entered to be processed must be accurate. If the data is incorrect, the resulting information produced from it will be incorrect. Properly trained data processing personnel are required to run most medium and large computer systems. Users are sometimes overlooked as an important element of an information system, but with expanding computer use, users are taking increasing responsibility for the successful operation of information systems. This includes responsibility for the accuracy of both the input and output. In addition, users are taking a more active role in the development of computer applications. They work closely with information systems department personnel in the development of computer applications that relate to their areas of expertise. Finally, all information processing applications should have documented procedures covering not only the computer operations but any other related procedures as well.

A TOUR OF AN INFORMATION SYSTEMS DEPARTMENT

To this point in the chapter, we have illustrated most of the concepts you have learned using microcomputer equipment and applications. To show you how the concepts you have learned apply to larger systems, this section will take you on a narrative and visual tour of an information systems department. In this section we also discuss how computers are used in a business environment and the responsibilities of personnel that work in an information systems department.

FIGURE 1-15
A terminal contains a keyboard and a screen. The screen displays the data entered via the keyboard.

The computers used in a business are generally under the control of a separate department within the company called the **information systems department**, the **data processing department**, or sometimes just the **computer department**. In our tour we will be visiting an information systems department of a company that has a multiuser computer. **Multiuser computers** concurrently process requests from more than one user. For example, if the employees in the accounting department are connected to the computer, one or more accounts receivable clerks could be entering cash receipts at the same time that one or more accounts payable clerks are entering invoices. Let's begin our tour by visiting the computer room and seeing the computer equipment.

The Computer Room

Earlier in the chapter, we identified the hardware components of a computer system as input devices, processor, output devices, and auxiliary storage. These general classifications apply to all computers including a multiuser computer system. When you first see a computer of any size, it is easier to understand how that computer works by separating the equipment into the four component areas. The equipment of a multiuser system can be separated in the following way.

Input Devices The primary input device on a multiuser system is a **terminal** (Figure 1-15). A terminal is a device consisting of a keyboard and a screen, which is connected through a communication line, or cable, to a computer. Sometimes personal computers are used as terminals. While there may be a few terminals in the computer room, most of the terminals are located on the desktops of employees throughout the organization.

FIGURE 1-16
This mainframe computer processes data for hundreds of users. Such a computer is usually placed in a room designed specifically for the machine. Special air conditioning, humidity control, electrical wiring, and flooring are required for many of these installations.

Processor   One of the main pieces of equipment in the computer room is the processor unit (Figure 1-16). The processor unit of a multiuser computer allocates computer resources to the programs that are being processed. Modern computer processors are so fast that they can usually handle numerous users and still provide very quick response time.

Output Devices   The most commonly used output devices for a multiuser computer are a printer (Figure 1-17) and a terminal (Figure 1-18). When large volumes of printed output must be produced, high-speed printers are used. Some terminals can display both text material and graphics in either monochrome or color.

Auxiliary Storage   The two major types of auxiliary storage for a multiuser computer are magnetic disk and magnetic tape.
   Magnetic disk is the most widely used auxiliary storage on multiuser computers. When using magnetic disk, data is recorded on an oxide coated metal platter (the disk) as a series of magnetic spots. Disk drives can store data on either removable disks or hard disks, sometimes called fixed disks. **Removable disks** refer to disk packs that can be taken out of the disk drive. In Figure 1-19, the containers for the removable disk packs can be seen sitting on the disk drives. Most hard disks contain platters that are enclosed in sealed units to prevent contamination of the disk surface.

FIGURE 1-18
A terminal is both an input and an output device. Here, the user is viewing a color graphics display.

FIGURE 1-17
High-speed printers are necessary to print the large volume of reports generated by a multiuser computer system.

FIGURE 1-19
Removable disk packs are mounted on the disk drives. The multiple disk drives shown here are common in large computer installations.

FIGURE 1-20
This magnetic tape drive uses reels of one-half-inch tape. Tape is often used to backup the data stored on disk drives.

FIGURE 1-21
The console allows the computer operator to monitor the processing.

Magnetic tape (Figure 1-20) stores data as magnetic spots on one-quarter- to one-half-inch tape on cartridges or reels. On systems with disk drives, tape is most often used to store data that does not have to be accessed frequently. Another common use of tape is for backup storage. The contents of the disk drives are regularly copied to tape to provide protection against data loss.

Computer Operators The **computer operator** works in the computer room and is responsible for a number of different tasks. When the computer is running, the operator's console displays messages that indicate the status of the system (Figure 1-21). For example, a message may indicate that a special form, such as a check, must be placed in a printer. The operator responds to these messages to keep the computer running. In many instances, more than one operator is required to run a large computer.

The Data Library

The information systems department keeps its software and data on either disks or tapes. When a disk pack or tape is not in use, it is stored in a **data library** (Figure 1-22). The data library is usually located close to the computer room and is usually staffed by a **data librarian**. The disk packs and tapes in the library must be catalogued so that when they are required, they can be located quickly and taken to the computer room for use.

FIGURE 1-22
The data library stores disk packs and tapes when they are not in use.

Depending on the amount of disk storage available and how frequently it is used, some software applications and data are always available for processing. An example would be order processing software that enters orders into the computer while the sales clerk is on the phone with the customer. Because a phone call can come in at any time, this software application and the data associated with it must always be available for processing.

Offices of Information Systems Personnel

To implement applications on a computer, the information systems department usually employs people who have specialized training in computers and information processing. These employees may include computer operators who work in the computer room and run the equipment; data entry personnel who prepare and enter data into the computer; systems analysts who design the software applications; programmers who write specialized programs; a database administrator who controls and manages data; and managers who oversee the use of the computer.

Data Entry Personnel   **Data entry personnel** (Figure 1-23) are responsible for entering large volumes of data into the computer system. Data is usually entered on terminals from **source documents**, which are original documents such as sales invoices. The accuracy of the data is important because it will affect the usefulness of the resulting information.

FIGURE 1-23
Data entry personnel specialize in entering large amounts of data from source documents.

Systems Analysts   **Systems analysts** review current or proposed applications within a company to determine if the applications should be implemented using a computer. The systems analyst would consider applications for computer implementation if, among other things, productivity can be increased or more timely information can be generated to aid in the management of the company. If an application is to be *computerized*, the systems analyst studies the application to identify what data is used, how the data is processed, and other aspects of the application that are pertinent to the new system. The systems analyst then designs the new system by defining the data required for the computer application, developing the manner in which the data will be processed in the new system, and specifying the associated activities and procedures necessary to implement the application using the computer. Systems analysts work closely with both the people who will be using and benefiting from the new system and the programmers in the information systems department who will be writing the computer programs (Figure 1-24).

FIGURE 1-24
Programmers, systems analysts, and users all work closely in developing new computer applications.

Computer Programmers   **Computer programmers** design, write, test, and implement specialized programs that process data on a computer. The design specifications from the systems analyst tell the programmer what processing needs to be accomplished. The programmer develops the specific programs of computer instructions that process the data and create the required information. The systems analyst specifies *what* is to be done; the programmer decides *how* to do it.

Database Administrator   An important function within the information systems department is the management of data. In many companies, this task is the responsibility of the **database administrator**. Among other things, the database administrator must develop procedures to ensure that correct data is entered into the system, that confidential company data is not lost or stolen, that access to company data is restricted to those who need the data, and that data is available when it is needed. Data administration is very important. In a business, billions of pieces of data are processed on the computer, and the loss or misappropriation of that data could be extremely detrimental.

Information Systems Department Management   Management within an information systems department varies depending on the size and complexity of the department. Most information systems departments have an operations manager, a systems manager, a programming manager, and a manager of the entire department. The **systems manager** oversees the activities in the systems analysis and design area of the department. The **programming manager** is in charge of all programmers within the department. Each of the managers we previously mentioned may also have project

HOW COMPUTERS ARE USED TODAY

managers within their own areas. The **operations manager** oversees the operational aspects of the department such as the scheduling, maintenance, and operation of the equipment. The information systems department manager is in charge of the entire department and may have the title **vice president of information systems**, or **chief information officer (CIO)**.

Summary of the Tour of an Information Systems Department

During the tour of the information systems department we have seen the computer room, data library, and the offices of information systems personnel. You should know more about an information systems department and how a multiuser computer is used in a business.

HOW COMPUTERS ARE USED TODAY

In addition to business, the use of computer technology is widespread in our world. Figure 1-25 shows a variety of computers and their applications. New uses for computers and improvements to existing technology are continually being developed. How do computers affect your life? How will you use computers in the future?

FIGURE 1-25
Here we see computers being used in a wide variety of applications and professions. New applications are being developed every day.

SUMMARY OF AN INTRODUCTION TO COMPUTERS

◆ In this chapter we presented a broad introduction to concepts and terminology that are related to computers. You now have a basic understanding of what a computer is, how it processes data into information, and what elements are necessary for a successful information system. You have also seen some examples of different types of computers and how they are used. The photo essay at the end of the chapter is a time line that shows the evolution of modern computers.

CHAPTER SUMMARY

1. A **computer** is an electronic device, operating under the control of instructions stored in its own memory unit, that can accept data (input), process data arithmetically and logically, produce output from the processing, and store the results for future use.
2. A computer can perform **input**, **process**, **output**, and **storage** operations. These operations are called the **information processing cycle**.
3. **Data** refers to the raw facts, including numbers and words, that are processed on a computer.
4. **Information** is data that has been processed into a meaningful and useful form.
5. The production of information by processing data on a computer is called **information processing**, or **data processing (DP)**.
6. **Computer users** are the people who either directly use the computer or utilize the information it provides.
7. A computer is a powerful tool because it is reliable and can process data quickly and accurately.
8. A **computer program** is a detailed set of instructions that tells the computer exactly what to do.
9. Computer processing can produce many different forms of information from a single set of data.
10. Processing data on a computer is performed by computer equipment including input devices, the processor unit, output devices, and auxiliary storage units. Computer equipment is often referred to as **hardware**.
11. **Input devices** are used to enter data into a computer.
12. The **processor unit** contains the electronic circuits that cause processing to take place.
13. The processor unit contains the central processing unit (CPU) and main memory.
14. The **central processing unit (CPU)** contains the **control unit** and the **arithmetic and logic unit (ALU)**.
15. **Arithmetic operations** are numeric calculations such as addition, subtraction, multiplication, and division that take place in the processor.
16. **Logical operations** are comparisons of data in the processor to see if one value is greater than, equal to, or less than another value.
17. **Main memory** electronically stores data and program instructions.
18. **Output devices** are used to print or display data and information.
19. **Auxiliary storage units** are used to store program instructions and data when they are not being used in the main memory of the computer.
20. The four major categories of computers are microcomputers, minicomputers, mainframes, and supercomputers.
21. Types of **microcomputers** include hand-held, notebook, laptop, portable, desktop, and supermicrocomputers.
22. **Minicomputers** address the needs of users who want more processing power than a microcomputer but do not need the power of a mainframe. Minicomputers can support a number of users performing different tasks.
23. **Mainframe** computers are large systems that can handle hundreds of users, store large amounts of data, and process transactions at a very high rate.
24. **Supercomputers**, the most powerful and expensive category of computers, can process hundreds of millions of instructions per second and perform long, complex calculations.
25. **Computer software** is another name for computer programs.
26. A computer program must first be loaded into main memory before it can be executed.
27. **System software** consists of programs that are related to controlling the actual operations of the computer equipment.

28. An important part of the system software is a set of programs called the **operating system**, which tells the computer how to perform its various functions.
29. **Application software** consists of programs that tell a computer how to produce information.
30. Programs purchased from computer stores or software vendors are called **application software packages**.
31. Commonly used personal computer software packages are word processing, electronic spreadsheet, graphics, and database software.
32. **Word processing software** is used to create and print documents.
33. **Electronic spreadsheet software** performs calculations on rows and columns of numeric data based on formulas entered by the user.
34. **Graphics software** provides the capability to transform numbers and text into a graphic format.
35. **Database software** allows the user to enter, retrieve, and update data efficiently.
36. The elements of an information system are equipment, software, data, personnel, users, and procedures.
37. **Multiuser computers** can concurrently process requests from more than one user.
38. A **terminal**, consisting of a keyboard and screen, is the most commonly used input device for a large computer.
39. Modern computer processors are so fast that they can usually handle numerous users and still provide very quick response time.
40. The most commonly used output devices for large computers are terminals and high-speed printers.
41. Auxiliary storage devices used on a large computer include magnetic disk and magnetic tape.
42. **Computer operators** run the computer equipment and monitor processing operations.
43. A **data library** stores disk packs and tapes when they are not in use.
44. **Source documents** are original documents, such as sales invoices, from which data can be entered.
45. **Data entry personnel** prepare and enter data into the computer.
46. **Systems analysts** review and design computer applications. Systems analysts work closely with users and programmers.
47. **Computer programmers** design, write, test, and implement programs, that process data on a computer.
48. A **database administrator** is responsible for managing an organization's computerized data.
49. Management within an information systems department includes a **systems manager**, **programming manager**, **operations manager**, and a department manager, who is sometimes called the **vice president of information systems**, or **chief information officer (CIO)**.
50. The use of computer technology is widespread in our world.

KEY TERMS

ALU (Arithmetic/Logic Unit) *1.5*
Application software *1.8*
Application software package *1.8*
Arithmetic/Logic Unit (ALU) *1.5*
Arithmetic operation *1.5*
Auxiliary storage unit *1.5*
Cathode ray tube (CRT) *1.5*
Central processing unit (CPU) *1.5*
Chief information officer (CIO) *1.19*
Computer *1.2*
Computer department *1.14*
Computer operator *1.16*
Computer program *1.4*
Computer programmer *1.18*
Computer software *1.7*
Computer system *1.6*
Computer users *1.3*
Control unit *1.5*

CPU (central processing unit) *1.5*
CRT (cathode ray tube) *1.5*
Data *1.2*
Data entry personnel *1.17*
Data librarian *1.16*
Data library *1.16*
Data processing (DP) *1.2*
Data processing department *1.14*
Database administrator *1.18*
Database software *1.10*
Diskette *1.6*
Electronic spreadsheet software *1.10*
End users *1.3*
Graphics software *1.10*
Hard disk *1.6*
Hardware *1.4*
Information *1.2*

Information processing *1.2*
Information processing cycle *1.2*
Information system *1.13*
Information systems department *1.14*
Input *1.4*
Input device *1.5*
Keyboard *1.5*
Logical operation *1.5*
Magnetic disk *1.15*
Magnetic tape *1.16*
Main memory *1.5*
Mainframe *1.7*
Micro *1.7*
Microcomputer *1.7*
Minicomputer *1.7*
Monitor *1.5*
Multiuser computer *1.14*

Operating system *1.8*
Operations manager *1.18*
Output *1.4*
Output device *1.5*
Peripheral device *1.6*
Personal computer *1.7*
Primary storage *1.5*
Printer *1.5*
Process *1.4*

Processor unit *1.5*
Program instruction *1.4*
Programming manager *1.18*
Removable disk *1.15*
Screen *1.5*
Software *1.4*
Software package *1.8*
Source document *1.17*
Spreadsheet *1.10*

Storage *1.4*
Supercomputer *1.7*
Systems analyst *1.17*
Systems manager *1.18*
System software *1.8*
Users *1.3*
Vice president of information
  systems *1.19*
Word processing software *1.10*

REVIEW QUESTIONS

1. What is the definition of a computer?
2. Define the term computer user.
3. What is the difference between data and information? How is information derived from data?
4. What is the information processing cycle?
5. Describe the four hardware units found on a microcomputer.
6. What is the difference between main memory and auxiliary storage? Why are both necessary?
7. Identify some of the differences among microcomputers, minicomputers, mainframe computers, and super-computers.
8. What is computer software? How does a computer use software?
9. What is system software? List two functions that the operating system performs.
10. Identify four application software packages often used with personal computers.
11. What are the six elements of an information system?
12. What is the user's role in an information system?
13. Who are some of the personnel who work in an information systems department?
14. What is the role of a systems analyst? How does that position differ from the job of a computer programmer?
15. Describe the key developments in the evolution of the modern computer during the 1960s.

CONTROVERSIAL ISSUES

1. At what grade level should computers be introduced to students? Should all high school or college graduates have a minimum computer skill level? If yes, what should the minimum skill level include?
2. Do computers make mistakes, or is it the humans that program and operate the computers who make the mistakes? Discuss what you think caused recent *computer errors* that you experienced or read about.

RESEARCH PROJECTS

1. Write or call a manufacturer of a minicomputer or mainframe, such as IBM, Bull, DEC, or HP, and ask for a brochure describing one of its popular models. Prepare a report for your class based on what you learned.
2. Prepare a report for your class describing the use of computers at your school. You may focus on a single department or prepare a general report about computer use throughout the school.
3. Prepare a detailed report on an individual who made a contribution to the history of computing.

The Evolution of the Computer Industry

The electronic computer industry began about fifty years ago. This time line summarizes the major events in the evolution of the computer industry.

Dr. John V. Atanasoff and his assistant Clifford Berry designed and began to build the first electronic digital computer during the winter of 1937–38. Their machine, the Atanasoff-Berry-Computer, or ABC, provided the foundation for the next advances in electronic digital computers.

Dr. John von Neumann is credited with writing a brilliant report in 1945 describing several new hardware concepts and the use of stored programs. His breakthrough laid the foundation for the digital computers that have since been built.

1937   1945   1951   1952

During the years 1943 to 1946, Dr. John W. Mauchly and J. Presper Eckert, Jr. completed the ENIAC (Electronic Numerical Integrator and Computer), the first large-scale electronic digital computer. The ENIAC weighed thirty tons, contained 18,000 vacuum tubes, and occupied a thirty-by-fifty-foot space.

In 1951–52, after much discussion, IBM decided to add computers to their line of business equipment products. This led IBM to become a dominant force in the computer industry.

J. Presper Eckert, Jr., standing left, explains the operations of the UNIVAC 1, to newsman Walter Cronkite, right. This machine was the first commercially available electronic digital computer.

UNIVAC on Election Night

8:30 PM

IT'S AWFULLY EARLY, BUT I'LL GO OUT ON A LIMB.
UNIVAC PREDICTS—with 3,398,745 votes in—

	STEVENSON	EISENHOWER
STATES	5	43
ELECTORAL	93	438
POPULAR	18,986,436	32,915,049

THE CHANCES ARE NOW 00 to 1 IN FAVOR OF THE ELECTION OF EISENHOWER.

Public awareness of computers increased when in 1951 the UNIVAC I, after analyzing only 5% of the tallied vote, correctly predicted that Dwight D. Eisenhower would win the presidential election.

In 1952, Dr. Grace Hopper, a mathematician and commodore in the U.S. Navy, wrote a paper describing how to program a computer with symbolic notation instead of the detailed machine language that had been used.

The IBM model 650 was one of the first widely used computer systems. Originally IBM planned to produce only 50 machines, but the system was so successful that eventually they manufactured over 1,000.

Dr. Hopper was instrumental in developing high-level languages such as COBOL, a business applications language introduced in 1960. COBOL uses English-like phrases and can be run on most computers, making it one of the most widely used languages in the world.

FORTRAN (FORmula TRANslator) was introduced in 1957 proving that efficient, easy-to-use programming languages could be developed. FORTRAN is still in use.

1952   1953   1957   1958   1959   1960

By 1959 over 200 programming languages had been created.

Core memory, developed in the early 1950s, provided much larger storage capacities and greater reliability than vacuum tube memory.

In 1958, computers built with transistors marked the beginning of the second generation of computer hardware. Previous computers built with vacuum tubes were first-generation machines.

Third-generation computers, with their controlling circuitry stored on chips, were introduced in 1964. The IBM System/360 computers were the first third-generation machines.

From 1958 to 1964, it is estimated, the number of computers in the U.S. grew from 2,500 to 18,000.

Digital Equipment Corporation (DEC) introduced the first mini-computer in 1965.

1964   **1965**   **1968**   **1969**

In 1965, Dr. John Kemeny of Dartmouth led the development of the BASIC programming language. BASIC is the language most commonly used on microcomputers. More people program in BASIC than any other language.

The software industry emerged in the 1960s. In 1968, Computer Science Corporation became the first software company to be listed on the New York Stock Exchange.

In 1969, under pressure from the industry, IBM announced that some of its software would be priced separately from the computer hardware. This "unbundling" allowed software firms to emerge in the industry.

In 1969, Dr. Ted Hoff of Intel Corporation developed a microprocessor, or microprogrammable computer chip, the Intel 4004.

1974

The MITS, Inc. Altair computer, sold in kits for less than $400, was the first commercially successful microcomputer.

The fourth-generation computers built with chips that used LSI (large-scale integration) arrived in 1970. The chips used in 1965 contained as many as 1,000 circuits. By 1970, the LSI chip contained as many as 15,000.

1970   1975   1976   1979   1980

In 1976, Steve Wozniak and Steve Jobs built the first Apple computer.

The VisiCalc spreadsheet program written by Bob Frankston and Dan Bricklin was introduced in 1979. This product was originally written to run on Apple II computers. Together, VisiCalc and Apple II computers rapidly became successful. Most people consider VisiCalc to be the singlemost important reason why microcomputers gained acceptance in the business world.

In 1980, IBM offered Microsoft Corporation's founder Bill Gates the opportunity to develop the operating system for the soon-to-be-announced IBM personal computer. With the development of MS-DOS, Microsoft achieved tremendous growth and success.

The IBM PC was introduced in 1981, signaling IBM's entrance into the micro-computer marketplace. The IBM PC quickly garnered the largest share of the personal computer market and became the personal computer of choice in business.

It is estimated that 313,000 microcomputers were sold in 1981. In 1982, the number jumped to 3,275,000.

1981   **1982**   **1983**   **1984**

The Lotus 1-2-3 integrated software package, developed by Mitch Kapor, was introduced in 1983. It combined spread-sheet, graphics, and database programs in one package.

Apple introduced the Macintosh computer, which incorporated a unique graphics interface making it easy to learn.

The Intel 80486 became the world's first 1,000,000-transistor microprocessor. It crammed 1.2 million transistors on a sliver of silicon that measured .4" × .6" and executed instructions at 15 MIPS (million instructions per second)—four times as fast as its predecessor, the 80386.

Several microcomputers using the powerful Intel 80386 microprocessor were introduced in 1987. These machines could handle processing performed previously only by large systems.

In early 1990, estimates indicated that over 54 million computers were in use in the United States.

1987　　**1988**　　**1989**　　**1990**

In October of 1988, former Apple founder Steve Jobs announced his long-awaited NeXT computer. Innovative features included the capability to record and process sound and the use of erasable optical disk storage.

Microsoft released Windows 3.0, a substantially enhanced version of its Windows graphics user interface first introduced in 1985. The software allows users to run multiple applications on a personal computer and more easily move data from one application to another. The package became an instant success selling hundreds of thousands of copies.

The computer industry will continue to evolve as improved technology and innovation lead to a variety of new computer applications.

Microcomputer Applications: User Tools

OBJECTIVES

◆ Identify the most widely used general microcomputer software applications

◆ Describe how each of the applications can help users

◆ Explain the key features of each of the major microcomputer applications

◆ Explain integrated software and its advantages

◆ List and describe six guidelines for purchasing software application packages

◆ List and describe learning aids and support tools that help users to use microcomputer applications

Today, understanding the applications commonly used on micro-computers is considered a part of being computer literate. In fact, a knowledge of these applications is now considered by many educators and employers to be more important than a knowledge of programming. Because of this, we introduce microcomputer applications, focusing on the most widely used applications early in this book. Learning about each application will help you understand how people use microcomputers in our modern world.

AN INTRODUCTION TO GENERAL MICROCOMPUTER APPLICATIONS

The applications discussed in this chapter are usually called **general microcomputer applications**. This software is called *general* because it is useful to a broad range of users. Word processing is a good example of a general application. Regardless of the type of business a company does, word processing can be used as a tool to help employees generate documents.

An important advantage of general applications is that you do not need any special technical skills or ability to use them. These programs are designed to be **user friendly**, in other words, easy to use. You do not need detailed computer instructions. Instead, you use the software through simple commands. **Commands** are instructions that tell the software what you want to do. For example, when you are finished using an application and you want to save your work, you issue an instruction called a SAVE command. In some applications you must type the command, in other applications the command is entered through a user interface.

User interfaces (Figure 2-1) are methods and techniques that make using an application simpler. They include function keys, screen prompts, menus, icons, and a device called a mouse. To help you understand how to use the software, we include an introduction to these features in this chapter. We present a more thorough discussion in Chapter 3.

FIGURE 2-1
User interfaces.

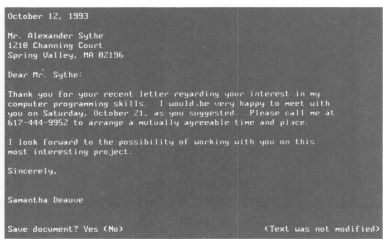

▲ Screen prompts — such as the question in the lower left of this screen — indicate that the software is waiting for the user to respond.

▲ Function keys — programmed to execute commonly used instructions.

Menus — such as this "pull-down" menu — offer a list of possible processing selections. ▶

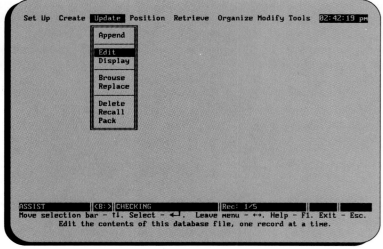

The **function keys** that are included on computer keyboards are a type of user interface. Pressing a function key in an applications program is a shortcut that takes the place of entering a command. The software defines exactly what the function key causes to happen. If you used a function key to save your work as we discussed in the previous example, pressing one key instead of several could issue the entire command.

Screen **prompts** are the messages that the program displays to help you while you are using an application. **Menus**, a special kind of screen prompt, are used in applications to provide a list of processing options. You make a selection from the menu by pressing the number or letter key that corresponds with the option you desire. Some applications use a menu called a **pull-down menu**. In this menu style the selections are displayed across the top of the screen. As you use the arrow keys to move from one selection to the next, the options associated with that selection appear to be *pulled down* from the top of the screen like a window shade. **Icons** refer to pictures instead of words that are displayed on the screen to show you various program options. A user interface that extensively uses icons to graphically represent files and processing options is called a **graphic user interface (GUI)**.

A **mouse** is a small input device that is used to move the cursor and input commands. The **cursor** is a symbol, such as an underline character or an arrow, that indicates where you are working on the screen. Many applications require you to move the cursor around on the screen. You do this by using the arrow keys on the keyboard or by moving the mouse. For example, a mouse could be used to move the cursor so that it is pointing to a selection you want to make on a menu. You can then press a button on the mouse to select that menu option.

These are some of the user interfaces that help to make application packages user friendly. User interfaces help minimize the technical computer knowledge you need when you are using general applications packages.

▲ Icons — symbols that represent program options.

Mouse — used to control the movement of the cursor on the screen. By pressing a button on the mouse, menu selections and other processing options can be chosen. ▶

Many kinds of general applications are available. Some of the most widely used software includes:

- Word processing
- Desktop publishing
- Electronic spreadsheet
- Database
- Graphics
- Data communications

Although we will discuss these applications as they are used on microcomputers, they are actually available on computers of all sizes. The concepts you will learn about each application package on microcomputers will also apply if you are working on a larger system.

WORD PROCESSING SOFTWARE: A DOCUMENT PRODUCTIVITY TOOL

The most widely used general application is word processing. If you need to create **documents**, such as letters or memos, you can increase your productivity by learning to use this software tool. Some of the popular packages used today include WordPerfect, Microsoft Word, and WordStar. This section discusses using a word processor to create a document.

Word processing software is used to prepare documents electronically (Figure 2-2). It allows you to enter text on the computer keyboard in the same manner as you create documents on a typewriter. As you enter the characters, they are displayed on the screen and stored in the computer's main memory. Because the document is in an electronic format, you can easily **edit** it by making changes and corrections to the text. You can correct errors and add, move, or delete characters, words, sentences, paragraphs, and large blocks of text. When the document is complete, you enter a command and have the computer send the document to the printer. The document's format is also under your control. You can specify the margins, define the page length, and select the print style. The document can be printed as many times as you like. Each copy is an original and looks the same as the other copies. The computer's storage capability allows you to store your documents so they can be used again. It is an efficient way to file documents because many documents can fit on one disk. If you wish, previously stored documents can be combined to make new documents, and you do not have to reenter the text as you would on a typewriter.

FIGURE 2-2
Word processing using a computer is faster, more accurate, and less tedious than using a typewriter.

The value of word processing is that it reduces the time required to prepare and produce written documents. Any editing you want to do in the document is easy because the software allows you to make changes quickly and efficiently. In addition, you can eliminate the tedious task of typing a final draft.

Most word processing packages include additional support features such as a spelling checker and a thesaurus. In addition, software may be purchased for grammar checking that is designed to work with word processors.

Spelling Checker

Spelling checker software allows you to check individual words or the entire document for correct spelling. To check a document for misspelled words, you enter a command that instructs the software to check the spelling. The words in the text will then be checked against an electronic dictionary stored on a disk that is part of the spelling checker software. If an exact match is not found, the word is highlighted. A menu is then superimposed on the screen, giving you a list of similar words that may be the correct spelling. You can select one of the words displayed on the menu, edit the highlighted word, leave the word unchanged, or add the word to the dictionary.

Some spelling checker dictionaries contain over 120,000 words. Many users customize their software dictionaries by adding company, street, city, and personal names so that the software can check the correct spelling of those words.

While spelling checkers can catch misspelled words and words that are repeated such as the the, they cannot identify words that are used incorrectly. A thesaurus and grammar checker will help you to choose proper words and use them in a correct manner.

Thesaurus

Thesaurus software allows you to look up synonyms for words in a document while you are using your word processor. Using a thesaurus is similar to using a spelling checker. When you want to look up a synonym for a word, you place the cursor on the word that you want to check, enter a command through the keyboard, and the thesaurus software displays a menu of possible synonyms. If you find a word you want to use, you select the desired word from the list and the software automatically incorporates it in the document by replacing the previous word.

Grammar Checker

Grammar checker software is used to check for grammar, writing style, and sentence structure errors (Figure 2-3). This software can check documents for excessive use of a word or phrase, identify sentences that are too long, and find words that are used out of context such as four example.

Whereas many word processors include a spelling checker and a thesaurus, grammar checkers are usually purchased separately. A popular grammar checker that is compatible with many word processing packages is Grammatik.

FIGURE 2-3
This grammar checker software is named Grammatik. It can proofread a document for mistakes in grammar, usage, punctuation, and spelling. The document being proofread is shown in the top portion of the screen. The possible problem identified by the software is displayed in the lower portion of the screen.

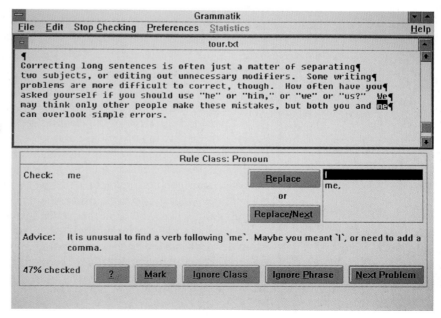

A Word Processing Example

Figures 2-4 through 2-11 illustrate the following word processing example. Let's say that Julia Broderick, Vice President of Sales of a company, wants to send a memo announcing a meeting of all sales personnel. She remembers that last month she sent a similar memo to just the sales managers. Thus, the first thing she does is load last month's memo into main memory so it will appear on the screen (Figure 2-4). This memo might be stored on a hard disk or on a diskette.

FIGURE 2-4
Last month's memo that will be changed for this month's meeting.

```
DATE:      June 21

FROM:      Julia Broderick, Vice President of Sales

TO:        All Sales Managers

SUBJECT:   Sales Meeting

A sales  meeting will  be held at  the Corporate  Training Center
from 8:00 AM to 12:00 noon, on Thursday, June 30.

This month's presentation will be on our new product line.

Please let  me know as  soon as possible  if you have  a schedule
conflict.
```

Word processing changes are usually one of three types: inserting text, deleting text, or moving text. When you **insert**, you add characters and words to the existing text in your document. When you **delete**, text is removed from your document. Often it makes sense to do your insertions and deletions at the same time; as you edit your document, you delete the existing word or phrase and insert the new one. Figure 2-5 shows the document with the text to be deleted. Figure 2-6 shows the document after she enters the new text.

FIGURE 2-5
The shaded areas indicate text to be deleted.

```
DATE:      June 21

FROM:      Julia Broderick, Vice President of Sales

TO:        All Sales Managers

SUBJECT:   Sales Meeting

A sales  meeting will  be held at  the Corporate  Training Center
from 8:00 AM to 12:00 noon, on Thursday, June 30.

This month's presentation will be on our new product line.

Please let  me know as  soon as possible  if you have  a schedule
conflict.
```

■ = Items to be deleted

FIGURE 2-6
The shading on the computer screen shows the new text inserted into last month's memo.

```
DATE:      July 19

FROM:      Julia Broderick, Vice President of Sales

TO:        All Sales Personel

SUBJECT:   Sales Meeting

A sales  meeting  will  be held at  the Corporate  Training Center
from 8:00 AM to 12:00 noon, on Friday, July 29.

John Smith, our  new vice  president of  marketing, will  make a
presentation.

Please let  me know as  soon as possible  if you have  a schedule
conflict.
```

■ = Inserted information

The Move command allows you to either cut (remove) or copy a sentence, paragraph, or block of text. In our example, Julia decides she wants to **move** the existing third paragraph in front of the existing second paragraph (Figure 2-7). First, she highlights, or marks, the text to be moved. Next, she indicates that she wants to *cut* and not *copy* the marked text. With a **cut**, you are removing text from an area. With a **copy**, the word processor makes a copy of the marked text but leaves the marked text where it was. After you perform either the cut or the copy, the word processor needs to know where you want to place, or **paste**, the text. This is usually done by moving the cursor to the point where you want the moved text to begin. You then give a command to execute the move and the text is inserted. Figure 2-8 shows the cut text *pasted* into a position that now makes it the second paragraph. This capability to easily move text from one location to another is often referred to as *cut and paste*.

```
DATE:      July 19
FROM:      Julia Broderick, Vice President of Sales
TO:        All Sales Personel
SUBJECT:   Sales Meeting
A sales  meeting will  be held at  the Corporate  Training Center
from 8:00 AM to 12:00 noon, on Friday, July 29.
John  Smith, our  new vice  president  of  marketing, will  make a
presentation.
Please let  me know as  soon as possible  if you have  a schedule
conflict.
```

▬▬ = Block to be moved to second paragraph

FIGURE 2-7

The shading shows the text to be moved from the third to the second paragraph.

```
DATE:      July 19
FROM:      Julia Broderick, Vice President of Sales
TO:        All Sales Personel
SUBJECT:   Sales Meeting
A sales  meeting will  be held at  the Corporate  Training Center
from 8:00 AM to 12:00 noon, on Friday, July 29.
Please let  me know as  soon as possible  if you have  a schedule
conflict.
John  Smith, our  new vice  president  of  marketing, will  make a
presentation.
```

▬▬ = Block that was moved

FIGURE 2-8

Memo after the third paragraph was moved to the second paragraph.

After the text changes are made, Julia runs a spelling checker. The spelling checker matches each word in the document against its spelling dictionary and discovers an unrecognized word: personel. Figure 2-9 shows how a spelling checker might present two alternatives for the correct spelling of the word. Julia merely has to enter the letter B and the word processor changes personel to personnel (Figure 2-10).

Before printing the memo, Julia reviews its format. She decides that the length of the lines in the document are too wide and she increases the margins. Figure 2-11 shows the document with the wider, 1 1/2-inch margins.

Now that the text and format are correct, Julia saves the document before printing it in case a system or power failure occurs during printing. Once she saves it, she can print the document as often as necessary. With the document saved, it is readily available to be retrieved by the word processor at any time.

FIGURE 2-9

Spelling checker highlighting unrecognized word and showing two possible spellings.

```
DATE:      July 19
FROM:      Julia Broderick, Vice President of Sales
TO:        All Sales Personel
SUBJECT:   Sales Meeting
A sales  meeting will  be held at  the Corporate  Training Center
-------------------------------------------------------------------
A. personal          B. personnel




Not Found:
1 Skip Once; 2 Skip; 3 Add; 4 Edit; 5 Look Up; 6 Ignore Numbers : 0
```

▬▬ = Unrecognized word

FIGURE 2-10

Correct spelling of personnel inserted into text by spelling checker.

```
DATE:      July 19
FROM:      Julia Broderick, Vice President of Sales
TO:        All Sales Personnel
SUBJECT:   Sales Meeting
A sales  meeting will  be held at  the Corporate  Training Center
from 8:00 AM to 12:00 noon, on Friday, July 29.
Please let  me know as  soon as possible  if you have  a schedule
conflict.
John  Smith, our  new vice  president  of  marketing, will  make a
presentation.
```

▬▬ = Correctly spelled word

```
DATE:      July 19
FROM:      Julia Broderick, Vice President of Sales
TO:        All Sales Personnel
SUBJECT:   Sales Meeting
A sales  meeting will be held at  the Corporate  Training
Center from 8:00 AM to 12:00 noon, on Friday, July 29.
Please let  me know as  soon as possible  if you have  a
schedule conflict.
John  Smith, our  new vice  president  of  marketing, will
make a presentation.
```

FIGURE 2-11

Memo after margins are changed.

Word processing software is a productivity tool that allows you to create, edit, format, print, and store documents. Each of the many word processing packages available may have slightly different capabilities, but most have the features summarized in Figure 2-12.

FIGURE 2-12
Common features of word processing software.

WORD PROCESSING FEATURES	
INSERTION AND MOVING Insert character Insert word Insert line Move sentences Move paragraphs Move blocks Merge text **DELETE FEATURES** Delete character Delete word Delete sentence Delete paragraph Delete entire text **SCREEN CONTROL** Scroll up and down by line Scroll by page Word wrap Uppercase and lowercase display Underline display Screen display according to defined format Bold display Superscript display Subscript display	**SEARCH AND REPLACE** Search and replace word Search and replace character strings **PRINTING** Set top and bottom margins Set left and right margins Set tab stops Print columns Single, double, triple space control Variable space control within text Right, left, full justification Center lines Subscripts Superscripts Underline Boldface Condense print Enlarge print Special type fonts Proportional spacing Headers Footers Page numbering Print any page from file

While our discussion of word processing has focused on the creation of documents that contain only text, you should know that some word processing packages now incorporate desktop publishing features that allow graphics to be included with the text. As you will see in the next discussion, the areas of word processing and desktop publishing are closely related.

DESKTOP PUBLISHING SOFTWARE: A DOCUMENT PRESENTATION TOOL

◆ **Desktop publishing (DTP) software** allows users to design and produce professional looking documents that contain both text and graphics (Figure 2-13). Two popular desktop publishing packages are Ventura Publisher and PageMaker. This software produces documents, such as newsletters, marketing literature, technical manuals, and annual reports, that contain art as well as text. Documents of this type were previously created by slower, more expensive traditional publishing methods such as typesetting. With desktop publishing, users can now create professional looking documents on their own computers and produce work that previously could only be done by graphic artists. By using desktop publishing, both the cost and time of producing quality documents is significantly decreased.

As we previously mentioned, some word processing packages now have desktop publishing capabilities. Packages such as WordPerfect and Microsoft Word contain enough features to satisfy the needs of many users. However, most desktop publishing packages still exceed the capabilities of word processing software. On the other hand, the word processing features of many desktop publishing packages are not as complete as those offered by word processing packages. Therefore, text is usually created with a word processor and then transferred into the desktop publishing package.

The graphic art used in the documents created with desktop publishing usually comes from one of three sources:

1. Art can be selected from clip art collections. **Clip art** refers to collections of art that are stored on disks and are designed for use with popular desktop publishing packages (Figure 2-14).
2. Art can be created on the computer with software packages that are specifically designed to create graphics, or through software such as spreadsheet packages that can create pie, line, and bar charts.
3. An input device called a scanner can be connected to the computer and used to electronically capture copies of pictures, photographs, and drawings and store them on a disk for use with desktop publishing software.

An important feature of desktop publishing is page composition. This means that a user is able to design on the screen an exact image of what a printed page will look like. This capability is called WYSIWYG. **WYSIWYG** is an acronym for What You See Is What You Get. Some of the page composition or layout features that are available include the use of columns for text, the choice of different type sizes and font (type) styles, and the capability to place, edit, enlarge, and reduce the size of charts, pictures, and illustrations in the document. Also, numerous special effects such as borders and backgrounds can be used to enhance the appearance of a document.

As new versions of word processing and desktop publishing software are introduced, the capabilities of both applications will increase and the differences between the two applications will decrease.

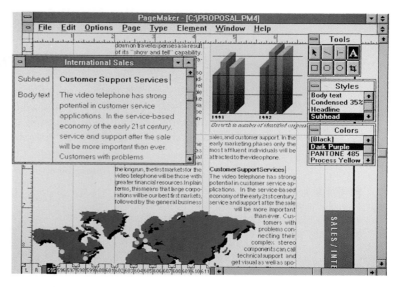

FIGURE 2-13
High-quality printed documents can be produced with desktop publishing software.

FIGURE 2-14
Clip art consists of previously created figures, shapes, and symbols that can be added to documents.

ELECTRONIC SPREADSHEET SOFTWARE: A NUMBER PRODUCTIVITY TOOL

◆ **Electronic spreadsheet software** allows you to organize numeric data in a worksheet or table format called an **electronic spreadsheet** or **spreadsheet**. Manual methods, those done by hand, have long been used to organize numeric data in this manner (Figure 2-15). You will see that the data in an electronic spreadsheet is organized in the same manner as it is in a manual spreadsheet. Within a spreadsheet, data is organized horizontally in **rows** and vertically in **columns**.

FIGURE 2-15

The electronic spreadsheet on the right still uses the row-and-column format of the manual spreadsheet on the left.

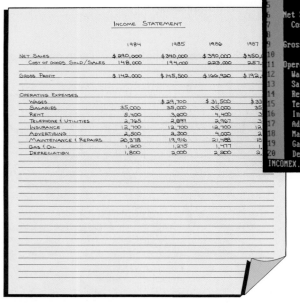

The intersection where a row and column meet is called a **cell** (Figure 2-16). Cells are named by their location in the spreadsheet. In Figure 2-16, the cursor is on cell C2, the intersection of column C and row 2.

Cells may contain three types of data: labels (text), values (numbers), and formulas. The text, or **labels**, as they are called, identify the data and document the worksheet. Good spreadsheets contain descriptive titles. The rest of the cells in a spreadsheet may appear to contain numbers, or **values**. However, some of the cells actually contain formulas. The **formulas** perform calculations on the data in the spreadsheet and display the resulting value in the cell containing the formula.

FIGURE 2-16

In a spreadsheet, rows refer to the horizontal lines of data and columns refer to the vertical lines of data. Rows are identified by numbers and columns are identified by letters. The intersection of a row and column is called a cell. The highlighted cell is the cursor. You can move the cursor by pressing the arrow keys on the keyboard.

To illustrate this powerful tool, we will show you how to develop the spreadsheet that we used as an example in Chapter 1. Recall that the completed spreadsheet contains revenues, costs, profit, and profit percentage for three months and the totals for the three months. By looking at Figure 2-17, you can see that the first step in creating the spreadsheet is to enter the labels or titles. These should be short but descriptive, to help you organize the layout of the data in your spreadsheet.

The next step is to enter the data or numbers in the body of the spreadsheet (Figure 2-18). The final step is to enter the formulas that calculate the totals. (Some users enter the formulas before they enter the data.)

In a manual spreadsheet, you would have to calculate each of the totals by hand or with your calculator. In an electronic spreadsheet, you simply enter a formula into the cell where the total is to appear. The total is calculated and displayed automatically (Figure 2-19).

Once a formula is entered into a cell, it can be copied to any other cell that requires a similar formula. As the formula is copied, the formula calculations are performed automatically (Figure 2-20). After entering the remaining formulas, the spreadsheet is complete (shown on the next page in Figure 2-21). You can now give the commands to print the spreadsheet and to store it on a disk.

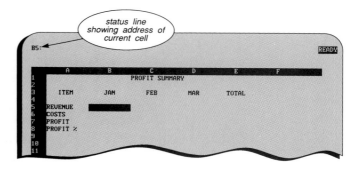

FIGURE 2-17
Labels such as JAN, FEB, REVENUE, and COSTS are entered in the spreadsheet to identify columns and rows of data. The status line shows the address and contents of the current cell. The address of a cell is the intersection of the column letter and row number. Here, the current cell is B5 (column B, row 5). Nothing has been entered for this cell, so the status line shows only the cell address.

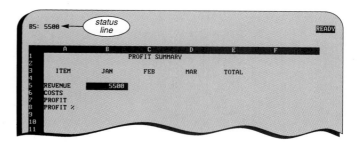

FIGURE 2-18
The value 5500 is entered and stored in cell B5. The status line now displays both the cell address and the cell value.

FIGURE 2-19
The remaining values are entered in cells C5, D5, B6, C6, and D6. A formula is entered in cell E5. The formula specifies that cell E5 is to be the sum of the values in cells B5, C5, and D5. Cell E5 displays the numeric sum. The status line at the top of the screen, however, shows the formula that calculates the value in that cell.

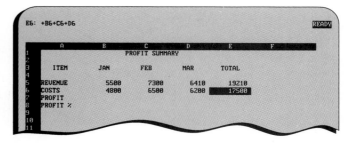

FIGURE 2-20
The formula required for cell E6 is similar to the one for cell E5; it totals the amounts in the three previous columns. When we copy the formula from E5 into E6, the software automatically changes the cell references from B5, C5, and D5 to B6, C6, and D6.

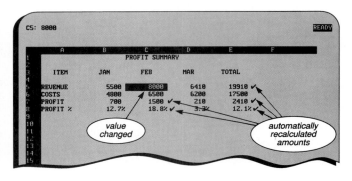

FIGURE 2-21

This screen shows the completed spreadsheet. The value in cell E8 is derived from the formula on the status line, which specifies that the value in cell E7 is to be divided by the value in cell E5 (the slash character indicates division). Since the value in E7 is the total profit and the value in E5 is the total revenue, the result of the division operation is the profit percentage.

FIGURE 2-22

This screen shows the capability of a spreadsheet to recalculate totals when data is changed. This capability gives the user the ability to quickly see the total impact of changing one or more numbers in a spreadsheet. Using the spreadsheet shown in FIGURE 2-21, one number was changed; the REVENUE amount for February. This one change results in five numbers automatically recalculating in the spreadsheet (the recalculated numbers are shown with a check mark). In a manual spreadsheet, each of these five numbers would have to be recalculated separately.

FIGURE 2-23

The what-if testing capability of electronic spreadsheets is a powerful feature used to aid managers in making decisions.

One of the most powerful features of the electronic spreadsheet occurs when the data in a spreadsheet changes. To appreciate the capabilities of spreadsheet software, let's discuss how a change is handled in a manual system. When a value in a manual spreadsheet changes, you must erase it and write a new value into the cell. You must also erase all cells that contain calculations referring to the value that changed and then you must recalculate these cells and enter the new result. For example, the row totals and column totals would be updated to reflect changes to any values within their areas. In large manual spreadsheets, accurately posting changes and updating the values affected can be time consuming and new errors can be introduced. But posting changes on an electronic spreadsheet is easy. You change data in a cell by simply typing in the new value. All other values that are affected are updated automatically. Figure 2-22 shows that if you changed the value in cell C5, the column and row totals that use the value in C5 will automatically change. All other values and totals in the spreadsheet remain unchanged. On a computer, the updating happens very quickly. As row and column totals are recalculated, the changes are said to *ripple* through the spreadsheet.

An electronic spreadsheet's capability to recalculate when data is changed makes it a valuable tool for decision making. This capability allows people to perform what-if testing by changing the numbers in a spreadsheet (Figure 2-23). The resulting values that are calculated by the spreadsheet software provide valuable decision support information based on the alternatives tested.

An electronic spreadsheet is a productivity tool that organizes and performs calculations on numeric data. Spreadsheets are one of the most popular software applications. They have been adapted to a wide range of business and non-business applications. Some of the popular packages used today are Lotus 1-2-3, Excel, and Quattro. Most spreadsheet software has the features shown in Figure 2-24.

DATABASE SOFTWARE: A DATA MANAGEMENT TOOL

◆ A **database** refers to a collection of data that is stored in files. **Database software** allows you to create a database and to retrieve, manipulate, and update the data that you store in it. In a manual system (Figure 2-25), data might be recorded on paper and stored in a filing cabinet. In a database on the computer, the data will be stored in an electronic format on an auxiliary storage device such as a disk.

SPREADSHEET FEATURES

WORKSHEET	MOVE
Global format	Move from cells
Insert column	Move to cells
Insert row	
Delete column	**FILE**
Delete row	Save
Set up titles	Retrieve
Set up windows	Erase
	List
RANGE	
Format range of data	**PRINT**
Erase cells	Set up margins
	Define header
COPY	Define footer
Copy from cells	Specify range to print
Copy to cells	Define page length
	Condense print

FIGURE 2-24
Common features of spreadsheet software.

FIGURE 2-25
An electronic database is similar to a manual system; related data items are stored in files.

When you use a database, you need to be familiar with the terms file, record, and field. Just as in a manual system, the word **file** is a collection of related data that is organized in records. Each **record** contains a collection of related facts called **fields**. For example, a file might consist of records containing information about a checking account. All the data that relates to one check would be considered a record. Each fact, such as the check number or amount, is called a field.

The screens in Figures 2-26 through 2-32 present the development of a database containing personal checking account information using the popular database program dBASE III PLUS. To begin creating the database, you would select the Create menu by moving the cursor until Create was highlighted, as shown in Figure 2-26.

FIGURE 2-26
A menu used to create a file in the popular database program dBASE III PLUS.

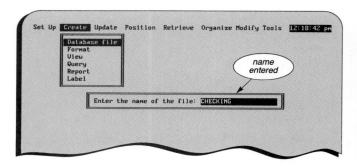

FIGURE 2-27
Screen used to enter the name of the file.

FIGURE 2-28
CREATE FILE screen showing definition of fields for records in the CHECKING file.

FIGURE 2-29
Data entry screen with the word Utility partially entered.

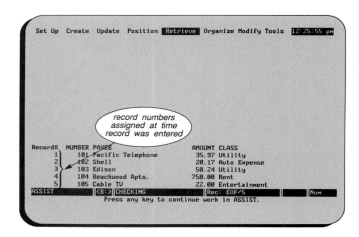

FIGURE 2-30
Display of all records sorted by record number.

Using the pull-down menu displayed under Create, you would select the "Database file" option. After identifying the disk drive to use, the screen would look like Figure 2-27. A prompt asks you to enter a file name, the name under which the file being created will be stored on disk. In this example, you would enter the name "CHECKING".

You are then asked to enter descriptions for each field (Figure 2-28). A field description consists of a field name, the type of data to be stored in the field (C for character, N for numeric data), and the number of characters in the field. In a numeric field, if you want to put digits to the right of the decimal point, you must specify the number of digits to the right. Thus, for the amount field, the designation 6.2 means that the field is six characters wide with two digits to the right of the decimal point. Because the decimal point takes one of the positions, the largest number that can be displayed in this field is 999.99.

Once you have defined the fields in the records, you enter data into the records (Figure 2-29). The software prompts you to enter data for each record. As you type the data into each field it is stored. Thus, after the field name NUMBER, you enter the check number. You complete each field in the same manner, and continue to enter data until all data is entered for the checking account file.

After the file has data stored in it, you can use the file to produce information. For example, suppose you want to display the checks in order by check number. You can use the "Organize" and "Retrieve" options on the menu to enter commands that sort all records by NUMBER and display the sorted list on the screen. Figure 2-30 shows a display of the sorted list. Suppose you also want to display your utility expenses.

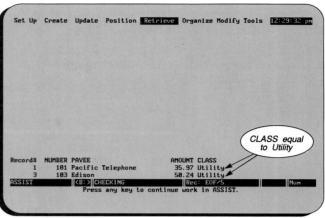

FIGURE 2-31
The software is directed to display only records with a
CLASS equal to Utility.

FIGURE 2-32
Display of only the Utility CLASS records.

In Figure 2-31, you direct the system to display only
those records where the class is equal to Utility. As a
result, only those records for which the classification is
Utility are retrieved and displayed (Figure 2-32).

As shown in our checkbook example, database software assists users in creating files and storing, manipulat-
ing, and retrieving data. Popular software packages that
perform these functions include dBASE III PLUS,
dBASE IV, R:Base, and Paradox. Figure 2-33 lists some
of the common features of these packages.

Recall that when you use a microcomputer database
software application, you do not need to have any special
technical knowledge. Database software is a general
application tool that is designed to help you easily and
efficiently manage data electronically.

FIGURE 2-33
Common features of database software.

GRAPHICS SOFTWARE: A DATA PRESENTATION TOOL

◆ Information presented in the form of a graph or a chart is commonly referred to
as **graphics**. Studies have shown that information presented as graphics can be understood much faster than information presented in writing. Three common forms of
graphics are **pie charts**, **bar charts**, and **line charts** (on the next page in Figure 2-34).

Today, many software packages can create graphics, including most spreadsheet
packages. The graphics capabilities of these packages can be grouped into two categories: analytical graphics and presentation graphics.

Bar charts display blocks, or bars, to show relationships among data clearly.

Pie charts, so called because they look like pies cut into pieces, are particularly effective for showing the relationship of parts to a whole.

FIGURE 2-34

Line charts are effective for showing a trend as indicated by a rising or falling line.

FIGURE 2-35
Color can enhance the presentation of graphic information.

Analytical graphics is widely used by management personnel when they analyze information and when they communicate information to others within their organization (Figure 2-35). For example, a production manager who is planning a meeting with the president of the company may use color graphics to show him the expenses of the producton department. This graphic display would have more impact and lead to better understanding than would a printed column of numbers.

To create analytical graphics on your computer, you must follow the directions that apply to your graphics software package. Most packages will prompt you to enter the data the graph will represent, and then ask you to select the type of graph you would like. After entering the data, you can select several different graphic forms to see which one will best convey your message. When you decide on a graph, you can print it and also store it for future reference.

As its name implies, **presentation graphics** goes beyond analytical graphics by offering the user a wide choice of presentation effects. These include three-dimensional displays, background patterns, multiple text fonts, and image libraries that contain illustrations of factories, people, coins, dollar signs, and other symbols that can be incorporated into the graphic (Figure 2-36). Figure 2-37 shows an example of presentation graphics projected.

Using graphics software as a presentation tool allows you to efficiently create professional quality graphics that can help you communicate information more effectively. Persuasion and Harvard Graphics are two popular presentation graphics packages.

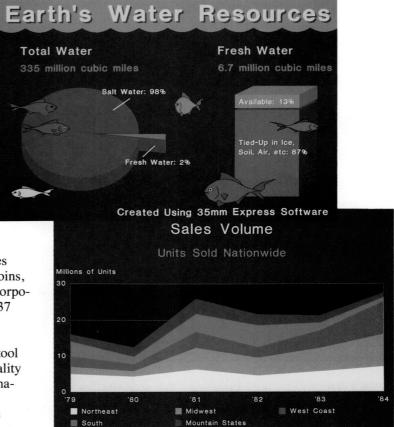

FIGURE 2-36
Examples of presentation graphics.

FIGURE 2-37
Presentation graphics can be an effective way to communicate information to a large group. Presenters can use devices such as the computer projection device shown. When this device is connected to a microcomputer, it can project everything on the microcomputer screen onto a large screen.

DATA COMMUNICATIONS SOFTWARE: A CONNECTIVITY TOOL

◆ **Data communications software** is used to transmit data from one computer to another. It gives users access to databases such as stock prices and airline schedules, and services such as home banking and shopping (Figure 2-38).

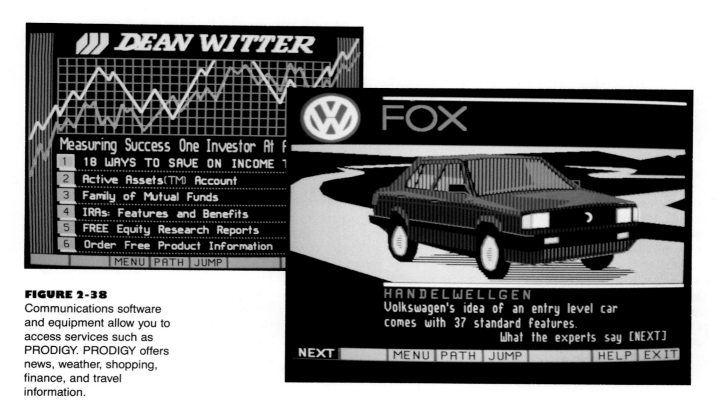

FIGURE 2-38
Communications software and equipment allow you to access services such as PRODIGY. PRODIGY offers news, weather, shopping, finance, and travel information.

For two computers to communicate, they each must have data communications software, data communications equipment, and be connected to a telephone line. To establish a communications link, you would use the data communications software to dial the phone number of the computer you want to call. Once the connection is established, you would enter commands and answer responses to control the transmission of data between the computers. Popular communication software packages include CROSSTALK Communicator and PROCOMM PLUS.

INTEGRATED SOFTWARE: A COMBINATION PRODUCTIVITY TOOL

◆ Software packages such as databases and electronic spreadsheets are generally used independently of each other. But what if you wanted to place information from a database into a spreadsheet? The data in the database would have to be reentered in the spreadsheet. This would be time consuming and errors could be introduced as you reentered the data. The inability of separate programs to communicate with one another and use a common set of data has been overcome through the use of integrated software.

Integrated software refers to packages that combine applications such as word processing, electronic spreadsheet, database, graphics, and data communications into a single, easy-to-use set of programs. The applications that are included in integrated packages are designed to have a consistent command structure; that is, the user can use the same set of common commands such as SAVE or LOAD in all the applications in the package. Besides these consistent commands, a key feature of integrated packages is their capability to pass data quickly and easily from one application to another. For example, revenue and cost information from a database on daily sales could be quickly loaded into a spreadsheet. The spreadsheet could be used to calculate gross profits. Once the calculations are completed, all or a portion of the spreadsheet data can be passed to the graphics program to create pie, bar, line, or other graphs. Finally, the graphic (or the spreadsheet) can be transferred to word processing to create a printed report. A possible disadvantage of an integrated package is that individual integrated programs may not have all the features that are available in nonintegrated packages. Two popular integrated software packages are Microsoft Works and Lotus Works.

Integrated programs frequently use windows. A **window** is a rectangular portion of the screen that is used to display information. They are called *windows* because of their capability to *see* into another part of a program. Many people consider windows to be like multiple sheets of paper on top of a desk. In the same way that each piece of paper on the desk contains different information, each window on the screen contains different information. And just as papers can be moved from the bottom of a pile to the top of the desk when they are needed, windows can be created on a screen and used to show information when it is needed. Windows are used to display a variety of information including: help information about the commands of the program you are using; text from different documents in a word processor and; different parts of a large spreadsheet. With some integrated packages, windows can be used to display data from separate applications such as a spreadsheet and a word processing document. Many programs today use windows and can display multiple windows on the screen at the same time (Figure 2-39). These programs allow you to easily move between applications by moving from one window to another.

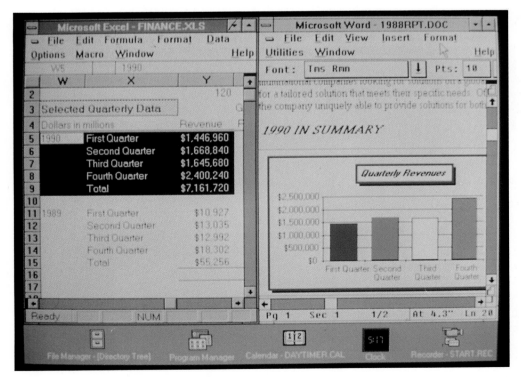

FIGURE 2-39
This screen shows two windows. The window on the left shows a spreadsheet, whereas the window on the right displays a word processing document. The user can work on information displayed in either application.

OTHER POPULAR MICROCOMPUTER APPLICATIONS

The applications we have discussed so far are the most widely used microcomputer applications. Three other application areas that are becoming increasingly popular are software for personal information management, project management, and utilities.

Personal Information Management

Personal information management (PIM) software helps users keep track of the miscellaneous bits of personal information that each of us deals with every day. This information can take many forms: notes to ourselves or from others, phone messages, notes about a current or future project, appointments, and so on. Programs that keep track of this type of information, such as electronic calendars, have been around for some time. In recent years, however, such programs have been combined, or integrated, so that one package can keep track of all of a user's personal information.

Because of the many types of information that these programs can manage, it is difficult to precisely define personal information software. However, the category can be applied to programs that offer any of the following capabilities: appointment calendars, outliners, electronic notepads, data managers, and text retrieval. Some personal information software packages also include communications software capabilities such as phone dialers and electronic mail. Appointment calendars allow you to schedule activities for a particular day and time (Figure 2-40). Most of them will warn you if two activities are scheduled for the same time. Outliners allow you to *rough out* an idea by constructing and reorganizing an outline of important points and subpoints. Electronic notepads allow the user to record comments and assign them to one or more categories that can be used to retrieve the comments. Data managers are simple file management systems that allow the input, update, and retrieval of related records such as name and address lists or phone numbers. Text retrieval provides the capability to search files for specific words or phrases such as Sales Meeting. Two popular personal information management packages are Lotus Agenda and GrandView.

FIGURE 2-40
Personal information management software packages include calendars that help the user schedule and keep track of appointments.

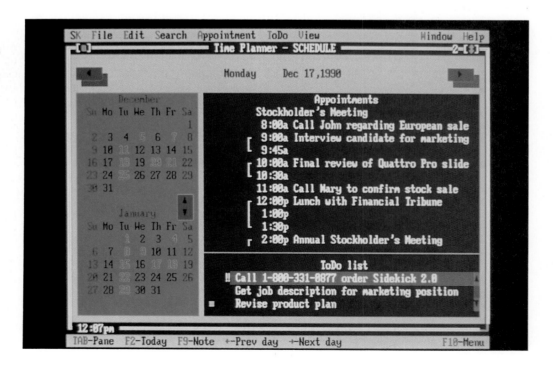

Project Management

Project management software allows users to plan, schedule, track, and analyze the events, resources, and costs of a project (Figure 2-41). For example, a construction company might use this type of software to manage the building of an apartment complex or a campaign manager might use it to coordinate the many activities of a politician running for office. The value of project management software is that it provides a method for managers to control and manage the variables of a project to help ensure that the project will be completed on time and within budget. Popular project management packages include Timeline and Microsoft Project.

FIGURE 2-41
This output was prepared using project management software. It shows the individual tasks that make up the project and the elapsed time that each task is scheduled to take.

Utilities

As its name implies, **utility software** includes a variety of programs to help you manage and maintain the data on your computer system. One of the more valuable utility features is the ability to recover *deleted* files. This is made possible by the fact that when a file is deleted, the data is still on the disk. The process of deletion only modifies the disk directory to indicate that the area of the disk that contains the file information is now available for new data. The disk directory is a special file on a disk that is used to keep track of which files are stored on the disk and where each file is located. If the data has not been overwritten, the utility software can rebuild the disk directory to allow access to the previously deleted file. Another common utility software feature is a defragmenter. When a file is written to the disk it sometimes has to be stored in separate areas because no one area is large enough to hold it all. In such cases, the file is said to be *fragmented*. The **defragmenter** analyzes and reorganizes the disk so that related file information is stored in one continuous area. Other common utility software features include visual directory listings (Figure 2-42), file management capabilities, and disk defect analysis. Popular utility software packages include the Norton Utilities (Advanced Edition), PC Tools Deluxe, and Mace Utilities.

FIGURE 2-42
This visual directory listing, sometimes called a directory tree, makes it easier to see the relationship of the files that are on a disk.

GUIDELINES FOR PURCHASING
MICROCOMPUTER APPLICATIONS SOFTWARE

◆ To ensure that applications software will meet your needs, you should follow these six steps when you purchase the software (Figure 2-43).

FIGURE 2-43
Shop carefully for software, evaluating the available packages and suppliers. Many people spend more on software than they do on their computer equipment.

1. **Read software product reviews.** A good place to start shopping for microcomputer applications software is in computer magazines such as *PC Magazine* and *MACWORLD*. These magazines regularly review applications packages and publish articles and charts to help you choose the package best suited to your needs.

2. **Verify that the software performs the task you desire**. In some cases, software that is supposed to perform particular functions either does not perform the functions or performs them in a manner that will be unacceptable to you. The best method of verifying that the software performs satisfactorily is to try it out prior to purchase. Many computer stores and software vendors will allow you to try software to see if it meets your needs before you purchase it. Some software developers even have special demonstration versions that allow you to try package features on a limited-use basis.

3. **Verify that the software will run on your computer**. The best way to verify this is to run the software on a computer that is the same as yours. Such factors as the number of disk drives, whether the software can run on a computer without a hard disk, main memory requirements, and graphics capabilities or requirements must be evaluated before you buy. For example, it would be unwise to purchase a package that is incompatible with your printer or one with graphics capabilities that your computer cannot handle.

4. **Make sure that the software is adequately documented**. The written material that accompanies the software is known as documentation. Even the best software may be unusable if the documentation does not clearly and completely describe what the software does, how it does it, how to recover from processing errors, and how to back up data.

5. **Purchase software from a reputable software developer or software publisher**. Regardless of the care taken, software sometimes contains errors. A reputable software developer or publisher will correct those errors or replace your software.

6. **Obtain the best value, but keep in mind that value might not mean the lowest price**. Different stores or distributors will sell the same software package for different prices. Be sure to compare prices, but also ask about product support. Sometimes a store will offer training on products that you buy from them; other vendors, such as mail order houses, provide no support or training but offer discount prices. Also, some vendors offer telephone service so that you can call to ask questions about the software.

If you keep these factors in mind when buying application software packages, you are likely to be pleased with the software you buy.

LEARNING AIDS AND SUPPORT TOOLS FOR APPLICATION USERS

◆ Learning to use an application software package involves time and practice. In addition to taking a class to learn how to use a software application, several learning aids and support tools are available to help you including: tutorials, online help, trade books, and keyboard templates (Figure 2-44).

FIGURE 2-44
Four ways to learn application software packages are shown here.

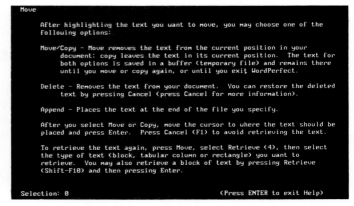

Software tutorials help you learn an application while using the actual software on your computer.

Online help gives you assistance without your having to leave the application.

Trade books are available for the popular software applications.

Keyboard templates give you quick reference to software commands.

    Tutorials are step-by-step instructions using real examples that show you how to use an application. Some tutorials are written manuals, but more and more, tutorials are in the software form, allowing you to use your computer to learn about a package.
    Online help refers to additional instructions that are available within the application. In most packages, a function key or special combination of keys are reserved for the help feature. When you are using an application and have a question, pressing the designated *help* key will temporarily overlay your work on the screen with information on how to use the package. When you are finished using the help feature, pressing another key allows you to return to your work.

The documentation that accompanies software packages is frequently organized as reference material. This makes it very useful once you know how to use a package, but difficult to use when you are first learning it. For this reason, many **trade books** are available to help users learn to use the features of microcomputer application packages. These books can usually be found where software is sold and are frequently carried in regular bookstores.

     Keyboard templates are plastic sheets that fit around a portion of your keyboard. The keyboard commands to select the various features of the application programs are printed on the template. Having a guide to the commands readily available is helpful for both beginners and experienced users.

SUMMARY OF MICROCOMPUTER APPLICATIONS

◆   By reading this chapter, you have learned about several of the commonly used microcomputer applications. You have also learned some guidelines for purchasing microcomputer software and seen some of the learning aids and support tools that are available for applications software. Knowledge about these topics increases your computer literacy and helps you to understand how microcomputers are being used.

CHAPTER SUMMARY

1. Understanding the software applications commonly used on microcomputers is considered a part of being computer literate.
2. Software that is useful to a broad range of users is sometimes referred to as **general microcomputer applications** software.
3. **User interfaces** are methods and techniques including **function keys**, screen **prompts**, **menus**, **icons**, and a device called a **mouse** that make using an application simpler.
4. A **graphic user interface (GUI)** makes extensive use of icons to graphically represent files and processing options.
5. The most widely used microcomputer software applications are word processing, desktop publishing, electronic spreadsheet, database, graphics, and data communications.
6. **Word processing software** is used to prepare documents electronically. With word processing software you **insert**, **delete**, and **move** text.
7. The MOVE command allows you to **cut**, **copy**, and **paste** text.
8. Additional support for a word processing application can include a spelling checker, thesaurus, and grammar checker.
9. **Spelling checker software** allows you to check individual words or an entire document for correct spelling.
10. **Thesaurus software** allows you to look up synonyms for words in a document while you are using your word processor.
11. **Grammar checker software** is usually purchased separately from a word processing package and is used to identify possible grammar, writing style, and sentence structure errors.
12. Word processing software is a document productivity tool that allows you to create, edit, format, print, and store documents.
13. **Desktop publishing software** allows you to design and produce professional looking documents that contain both text and graphics.
14. **WYSIWYG** is an acronym for What You See Is What You Get and describes the capability of a desktop publishing package to display on the screen an exact image of what the printed page will look like.
15. **Electronic spreadsheet software** allows you to organize numeric data in a worksheet or table format.
16. A **spreadsheet** is composed of **rows** and **columns**. Each intersection of a row and column is a **cell**.
17. A spreadsheet cell can contain one of the following: a **label**, a **value**, or a **formula**.

18. The what-if capability of electronic spreadsheet software is a powerful feature that is widely used by management personnel for decision support information.
19. A **database** refers to a collection of data that is stored in files. **Database software** allows you to create a database and to retrieve, manipulate, and update data that you store in it.
20. Just as in a manual system, the word **file** is a collection of related data that is organized in records. Each **record** contains a collection of related facts called **fields**.
21. Information presented in the form of a graph or a chart is commonly referred to as **graphics**. Three popular graphics used to present information include **pie charts**, **bar charts**, and **line charts**.
22. **Analytical graphics** is widely used by management personnel when analyzing information and when communicating information to others within their organization.
23. **Presentation graphics** allows you to create professional quality graphics that can be used to communicate information more effectively.
24. **Data communications software** allows you to transmit data from one computer to another.
25. **Integrated software** packages combine several applications in one package and allow data to be shared between the applications.
26. **Personal information management (PIM) software** packages include capabilities such as appointment calendars, outliners, electronic notepads, data managers, and text retrieval.
27. **Project management software** allows users to plan, schedule, track, and analyze the events, resources, and costs of a project.
28. **Utility software** includes a variety of programs to help you manage and maintain the data on your computer system.
29. When you purchase software, you should follow these six steps: (1) Read software product reviews. (2) Verify that the software performs the task desired. (3) Verify that the software runs on your computer. (4) Make sure the software documentation is adequate. (5) Purchase software from a reputable developer or publisher. (6) Obtain the best value.
30. Aids such as tutorials, online help, trade books, and keyboard templates are useful in learning and using microcomputer applications.

KEY TERMS

Analytical graphics *2.16*
Bar chart *2.15*
Cell *2.10*
Clip art *2.9*
Column *2.10*
Command *2.2*
Copy *2.6*
Cursor *2.3*
Cut *2.6*
Database *2.13*
Database software *2.13*
Data communications software *2.18*
Defragmenter *2.21*
Delete *2.6*
Desktop publishing (DTP) software *2.8*
Document *2.4*
Edit *2.4*
Electronic spreadsheet *2.10*
Electronic spreadsheet software *2.10*
Field *2.13*

File *2.13*
Formula *2.10*
Function keys *2.3*
General microcomputer applications *2.2*
Grammar checker software *2.5*
Graphic user interface (GUI) *2.3*
Graphics *2.4*
Icon *2.3*
Insert *2.6*
Integrated software *2.19*
Keyboard template *2.24*
Label *2.10*
Line chart *2.15*
Menu *2.3*
Mouse *2.3*
Move *2.6*
Online help *2.23*
Paste *2.6*
Personal information management (PIM) software *2.20*
Pie chart *2.15*

Presentation graphics *2.17*
Project management software *2.21*
Prompt *2.3*
Pull-down menu *2.3*
Record *2.13*
Row *2.10*
Spelling checker software *2.5*
Spreadsheet *2.10*
Thesaurus software *2.5*
Trade books *2.24*
Tutorials *2.23*
User friendly *2.2*
User interfaces *2.2*
Utility software *2.21*
Values *2.10*
Window *2.19*
Word processing software *2.4*
WYSIWYG (What You See Is What You Get) *2.9*

REVIEW QUESTIONS

1. What is a user interface? List five examples.
2. What is general microcomputer applications software?
3. List six of the most widely used microcomputer application packages and describe how each application helps users.
4. What is a grammar checker? Give three examples of how a grammar checker works.
5. Describe three sources for art that is used in desktop publishing.
6. What are the three types of data that can be entered into a spreadsheet cell? Explain the purpose of each type of data.
7. Write a definition of the terms database and database software.
8. List the three most commonly used computer graphics. Draw an example of each.
9. Describe the advantage of using integrated software. What is a possible disadvantage? What are windows and how are they used in integrated software packages?
10. Describe how you would make a communications link between your microcomputer and another computer.
11. What is project management software and how is it used?
12. Explain why data files that have been deleted can sometimes be recovered by using a utility software application.
13. List the six steps that should be performed when purchasing software.
14. List and describe four learning aids that can help you use general microcomputer application packages.

CONTROVERSIAL ISSUES

1. As the owner of a small business you are trying to decide whether to purchase a word processor, a desktop publishing software package, or both. Some people have advised you that a word processor is all you need. Other people say you will be disappointed unless you have a desktop publishing package. Discuss the advantages and disadvantages of each option.
2. Some organizations insist that their employees use an integrated package so that data can be easily transferred between users. Other organizations let their users make individual decisions on which package they want to use for a particular application. Discuss the advantages and disadvantages of both policies.

RESEARCH PROJECTS

1. Interview a person who uses a desktop publishing package on a regular basis. Write a report on the types of documents he or she prepares. Include the person's comments on the different desktop publishing features.
2. Find someone who has developed an electronic spreadsheet. Ask him or her to review with you the formulas that he or she used in the spreadsheet.
3. Assume that you have decided to use a database package to keep track of all the members of a ski club. Define the fields that would make up your database record.

Input to the Computer

3

I N P U T

CHAPTER

OBJECTIVES

◆ Review the four operations of the information processing cycle: input, process, output, and storage

◆ Define the four types of input and how the computer uses each type

◆ Define data and explain the terms used to describe data: field, record, file, database

◆ Describe the standard features of keyboards, and explain how to use the cursor control and function keys

◆ Explain the three types of terminals and how they are used

◆ Describe several input devices other than the keyboard and terminal

◆ Explain user interfaces and list the features that a good user interface should have

◆ Discuss how data entry differs in interactive and batch processing

◆ List and explain the systems and procedures associated with data entry

◆ Explain the term ergonomics and describe some of the important features of good equipment design

The information processing cycle is basic to all computers, large or small. It is important that you understand this cycle, for much of your success in understanding computers and what they do depends on having an understanding or *feeling* for the movement of data as it flows through the information processing cycle and becomes information. In this chapter we discuss the information processing cycle focusing on input operations. We examine the nature of data and how it is organized, describe some of the devices used for input, and explain the ways that both hardware and software are designed to make input operations easier for the user. We also discuss data entry methods and the design, arrangement, and usage of equipment.

OVERVIEW OF THE
INFORMATION PROCESSING CYCLE

◆ As we saw in Chapter 1, the information processing cycle consists of four operations: input, processing, output, and storage (Figure 3-1). Regardless of the size and type of computer, these operations process data into a meaningful form called information.

INPUT

keyboard

PROCESS

screen

OUTPUT

processor unit

diskette drive

AUXILIARY STORAGE

hard disk drive

printer

FIGURE 3-1
A computer consists of input devices, the processor unit, output devices, and auxiliary storage units. This equipment, or hardware, is used to perform the operations of the information processing cycle.

The operations in the information processing cycle are carried out through the combined use of computer equipment, also called computer hardware, and computer software. The computer software, or programs, contain instructions that direct the computer equipment to perform the tasks necessary to process data into information. In the information processing cycle, the input operation must take place before any data can be processed and any information produced and stored.

WHAT IS INPUT?

◆ **Input** refers to the process of entering programs, commands, user responses, and data into main memory. Input can also refer to the media (e.g., disks, tapes, documents) that contain these input types. These four types of input are used by a computer in the following ways:

- **Programs** are instructions that direct the computer to perform the necessary operations to process data into information. The program that is loaded and stored in main memory determines the processing that the computer will perform. When a program is first created it is input by using a keyboard. Once the program has been entered and stored on auxiliary storage, it can be transferred to main memory by a command.
- **Commands** are key words and phrases that the user inputs to direct the computer to perform certain activities. For example, if you wanted to use a payroll program, you might issue a command such as LOAD "PAYROLL" to load the program named

PAYROLL into main memory from auxiliary storage. To begin the execution of the program you would enter another command such as RUN (Figure 3-2).

- **User responses** refer to the data that a user inputs to respond to a question or message from the software. Usually these messages appear on a screen and the user responds through a keyboard. One of the most common responses is to answer "Yes" or "No" to a question. Based on the answer, the computer program will perform specific actions. For example, typing the letter Y in response to the message "Do you want to save this file?" will result in the file being saved (written) to the auxiliary storage device.
- **Data** refers to the raw facts, including numbers and words, that a computer receives during the input operation and processes to produce information. Data must be entered and stored in main memory for processing to occur. For example, data entered from sales orders can be processed by a computer program to produce sales reports useful to management. Data is the most common type of input.

Because data is such an important part of the input operation it is important for you to understand what data is and how it is organized.

HOW IS DATA ORGANIZED?

Data is comprised of **characters**. These characters are classified as **alphabetic** (A–Z), **numeric** (0–9), or **special** (all characters other than A–Z and 0–9 such as ()*&%#@,). The raw facts that we refer to as data are made up of a combination of these three kinds of characters. In the monthly sales application example shown in Figure 3-3, the date 01/31 is made up of the numeric characters 0 1 3 and the special character /. In the payroll example (Figure 3-4), the Social Security number contains numeric characters and the special character -. The name Haynes contains only alphabetic characters.

FIGURE 3-2
In this example, the computer user first entered a command to load the program called "PAYROLL" and then issued the command RUN, which will execute the program.

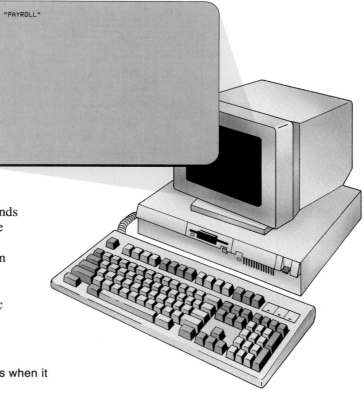

```
LOAD  "PAYROLL"
RUN
```

FIGURE 3-3
By itself, the month-ending date, 01/31, is not as useful as when it is related to the monthly sales amount.

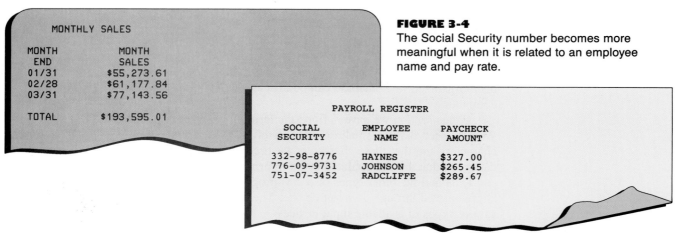

```
      MONTHLY SALES

   MONTH          MONTH
   END            SALES
   01/31          $55,273.61
   02/28          $61,177.84
   03/31          $77,143.56

   TOTAL          $193,595.01
```

FIGURE 3-4
The Social Security number becomes more meaningful when it is related to an employee name and pay rate.

```
            PAYROLL REGISTER

   SOCIAL          EMPLOYEE        PAYCHECK
   SECURITY        NAME            AMOUNT

   332-98-8776     HAYNES          $327.00
   776-09-9731     JOHNSON         $265.45
   751-07-3452     RADCLIFFE       $289.67
```

Each fact or unique piece of data is referred to as a **data item**, **data field**, or simply a **field**. Fields are classified by the characters that they contain. For example, a field that contains only alphabetic characters, such as the name field which contains Haynes, is called an **alphabetic field**. A field that contains numeric characters is called a **numeric field**. Numeric fields may also contain some special characters that are commonly used with numbers such as a decimal point (.) and the plus (+) and minus (–) signs. Even with the plus sign (+) and decimal point (.), the number + 500.00 is still called a numeric field. Fields that contain a combination of character types, such as the date 01/31 (numeric and special characters), are called **alphanumeric fields**. Although the word *alphanumeric* implies only alphabetic and numeric characters, it also includes fields that contain special characters. The term alphanumeric is used to describe all fields that do not fall into the alphabetic or numeric classifications.

A field is normally most meaningful when it is combined with related fields. To illustrate, the month and day 01/31 by itself is not as useful as when it is related to monthly sales (Figure 3-3). Also, the Social Security number 332-98-8776 is more useful when it is related to the name HAYNES and to the paycheck amount $327.00 (Figure 3-4). Because related fields are more meaningful if they are together, fields are organized into groups called records.

A **record** is a collection of related fields. Each record normally corresponds to a specific unit of information. For example, a record that could be used to produce the payroll report in Figure 3-4 is illustrated in Figure 3-5. The fields in the record are the Social Security number, employee name, and paycheck amount. This example shows that the data in each record is used to produce a line on the payroll report. The first record contains all the data concerning the employee named HAYNES. The second record contains all the data concerning the employee named JOHNSTON. Each subsequent record also contains all the data for a given employee. Thus, you can see how related data items are grouped together to form a record.

FIGURE 3-5
The records of this payroll file are stored one after another on magnetic tape. The file contains the Social Security number, name, and paycheck amount for all employees.

A collection of related records is called a **file**. The payroll file in Figure 3-5, for example, contains all the records required to produce the payroll register report. Files on a computer are usually stored on magnetic tape or magnetic disk.

Data is frequently organized in a **database**. As we discussed in Chapter 2, a database provides an efficient way to establish a relationship between data items and implies that a relationship has been established between multiple files. Data that has been organized in a database can be efficiently manipulated and retrieved by a computer.

In this section we have defined the terms used to describe how data is organized. We have seen that the smallest elements of data are alphabetic, numeric, and special characters and that these characters are used to build the fields, records, files, and databases that are manipulated by an information system to create information.

Data and the other types of input, programs, commands and user responses, will all be entered through an input device. The next section of this chapter discusses the various types of available input devices.

THE KEYBOARD

The **keyboard** is the most commonly used input device. Users input data to a computer by pressing the keys on the keyboard. Keyboards are connected to other devices that have screens, such as a personal computer or a terminal. As the user enters data through the keyboard, the data appears on the screen.

The keyboards used for computer input are very similar to the keyboards used on the familiar office machine, the typewriter. They contain numbers, letters of the alphabet, and some special characters (Figure 3-6). In addition, many computer keyboards are equipped with a **numeric keypad** on the right-hand side of the keyboard. These numeric keys are arranged in an adding machine or calculator format and aid the user with numeric data entry.

Keyboards also contain keys that can be used to position the cursor on the screen. A **cursor** is a symbol, such as an underline character or an arrow, that indicates where on the screen the next character entered will appear. The keys that move the cursor are called **arrow keys** or **cursor control keys**. Cursor control keys have an up arrow, a down arrow, a left arrow, and a right arrow. When you press any of these keys, the cursor moves one space in the same direction as the arrow. In addition, many keyboards contain other cursor control keys such as the Home key, which when you press it can send the cursor to a beginning position such as the upper left position of the screen or document.

Some computer keyboards also contain keys that can alter or edit the text displayed on the screen. For example, the Insert and Delete keys allow characters to be inserted into or deleted from data that appears on the screen.

Function keys are keys that can be programmed to accomplish certain tasks that will assist the user. For example, a function key might be programmed for use as a help key when a terminal is used for word processing. Whenever the key is pressed, messages will appear that give helpful information about how to use the word processing software. Function keys can also save keystrokes. Sometimes several keystrokes

FIGURE 3-6
The IBM PS/2 Model 30 keyboard contains a numeric keypad, cursor control keys, and function keys. The keys on the numeric keypad are arranged in the same order as the keys on an adding machine or a calculator. This arrangement allows people who are skilled in entering numbers to input numeric data at a much faster rate than if the number keys were positioned across the top of the keyboard as they are on a typewriter. The four cursor control keys are identified by up ↑, down ↓, left ←, and right → arrows. When the user presses one of these keys, the cursor moves one position in the direction indicated by the arrow. Function keys are used for specific commands that are either programmed by the user or determined by the application software. Function keys can be in different places, but on most keyboards they are either on the left side or along the top.

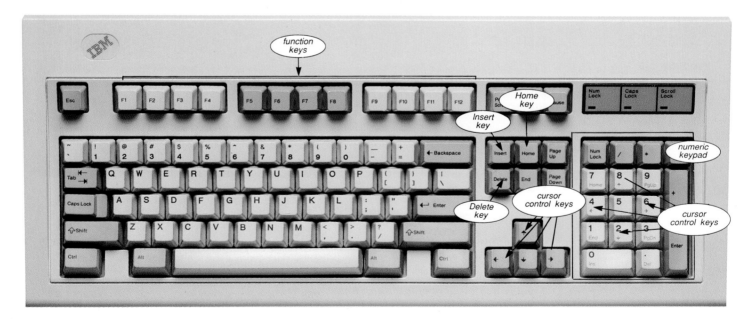

are required to accomplish a certain task, for example, printing a document. Some application software packages are written so that the user can either enter the individual keystrokes or press a function key and obtain the same result.

The disadvantage of using a keyboard as an input device is that training is required to use it efficiently. Users who do not know how to type are at a disadvantage because of the time they spend looking for the appropriate keys. While other input devices are appropriate in some situations, users should be encouraged to develop their keyboard skills.

TERMINALS

Terminals, sometimes called **display terminals** or **video display terminals (VDTs)**, consist of a keyboard and a screen. They fall into three basic categories: dumb terminals, intelligent terminals (sometimes called programmable terminals) and special-purpose terminals. We explain the features of each type in the following sections. Figure 3-7 shows a dumb and an intelligent terminal.

FIGURE 3-7
A dumb terminal (left) and a group of intelligent terminals (right). From appearance alone, it is often difficult to tell in which category a terminal belongs. Intelligent terminals have built-in processing capabilities.

Dumb Terminals

A **dumb terminal** consists of a keyboard and a display screen that can be used to enter and transmit data to or receive and display data from a computer to which it is connected. A dumb terminal has no independent processing capability or auxiliary storage and cannot function as a stand-alone device.

Intelligent Terminals

Intelligent terminals have built-in processing capabilities and often contain not only the keyboard and screen, but also disk drives and printers. Because of their built-in capabilities, these terminals can perform limited processing tasks when they are not communicating directly with the central computer. Intelligent terminals are also known as **programmable terminals** or **smart terminals** because they can be programmed by the user to perform many basic tasks, including arithmetic and logic operations. Personal computers are frequently used as intelligent terminals (Figure 3-8).

FIGURE 3-8
This WYSE pc 286 personal computer can function as both a stand-alone computer or as a terminal when it is connected to another computer system.

FIGURE 3-9
This point-of-sale terminal has been specifically designed for use in a restaurant. The operator can press separate keys to enter the prices of certain menu items.

As the amount of processing power that is incorporated into intelligent terminals increases, more processing can occur at the site of the terminal. This means that the large minicomputer or mainframe at the central site can perform the main processing and serve multiple users faster, rather than having to use its resources to perform tasks that can be performed by the intelligent terminal.

Special-Purpose Terminals

Terminals are found in virtually every environment that generates data for processing on a computer. While many are general terminals like those we previously described, others are designed to perform specific jobs and contain features uniquely designed for use in a particular industry.

The terminal shown in Figure 3-9 is called a point-of-sale terminal. **Point-of-sale (POS) terminals** allow data to be entered at the time and place where the transaction with a customer occurs, such as in fast-food restaurants or hotels, for example. Point-of-sale terminals serve as input to either minicomputers located at the place of business or larger computers located elsewhere. The data entered is used to maintain sales records, update inventory, make automatic calculations such as sales tax, verify credit, and perform other activities associated with the sales transactions and critical to running the business. Point-of-sale terminals are designed to be easy to operate, requiring little technical knowledge. As shown in Figure 3-9, the keys are labeled to assist the user.

OTHER INPUT DEVICES

◆ Besides keyboards and terminals, there is an increasing variety of other input devices. This section describes some of the devices used for general-purpose applications.

FIGURE 3-10

The mouse can be moved to control the cursor on the screen. You press the button on the top of the mouse to make selections or perform functions, depending on the software you are using. The ball on the underside of the mouse moves as you push the mouse around on a hard, flat surface. The movement of the ball causes the cursor to move correspondingly on the screen.

Mouse

The mouse is a unique device used with personal computers and some computer terminals. A **mouse** is a small, lightweight device that easily fits in the palm of your hand. You move it across a flat surface such as a desktop (Figure 3-10) to control the movement of the cursor on a screen.

The mouse is attached to the computer by a cable. On the bottom of the device is a small ball. As the mouse moves across the flat surface, the computer electronically senses the movement of the ball. The movement of the cursor on the screen corresponds to the movement of the mouse (Figure 3-11). When you move the mouse left on the surface of the table or desk, the cursor moves left on the screen. When you move the mouse right, the cursor moves right, and so on.

On top of the mouse are one or more buttons. By using the mouse to move the cursor on the screen and pressing the buttons on the mouse, you can perform many actions such as making menu selections, editing a word processing document, and moving data from one point on the screen to another.

The primary advantage of a mouse is that it is easy to use. Proponents of the mouse say that with a little practice, a person can use a mouse to point to locations on the screen just as easily as using a finger.

There are two major disadvantages of the mouse. The first is that it requires empty desk space where it can be moved about (Figure 3-12). The second disadvantage is that the user must remove a hand from the keyboard and place it on the mouse whenever the cursor is to be moved or a command is to be given. Some keyboard experts have noted that taking hands from the keyboard slows the speed of data entry considerably.

FIGURE 3-11

Here, a mouse is being moved from one side to another. This action will result in the cursor moving from one side of the screen to the other. The buttons on top of the mouse can be used instead of keys on the keyboard.

FIGURE 3-12

Notice that some amount of clear desk space is required for moving the mouse.

Thus, some people have said the mouse is not an effective tool in those environments where keying must be performed rapidly, such as in word processing applications. Others, however, say that using a mouse is far superior to using the cursor control keys on a keyboard.

Trackball

A **trackball** is a graphic pointing device like a mouse only with the ball on the top of the device instead of the bottom (Figure 3-13). To move the cursor with a trackball, all you have to do is rotate the ball in the desired direction. With a mouse, you have to move the entire device. To accommodate movement with both the fingers and palms of a hand, the ball on top of a trackball is larger than the ball on the bottom of a mouse. The main advantage of a trackball over a mouse is that it doesn't require the clear desk space.

Touch Screens

Touch screens allow users to touch areas of the screen to enter data. They let the user interact with a computer by the touch of a finger rather than typing on a keyboard or moving a mouse. The user enters data by touching words or numbers or locations identified on the screen (Figure 3-14).

Several electronic techniques change a touch on the screen into electronic impulses that can be interpreted by the computer software. One of the most common techniques uses beams of infrared light that are projected across the surface of the screen. A finger or other object touching the screen interrupts the beams, generating an electronic signal. This signal identifies the location on the screen where the touch occurred. The software interprets the signal and performs the required function.

Touch screens are not used to enter large amounts of data. They are used, however, for applications where the user must issue a command to the software to perform a particular task or must choose from a list of options to be performed.

There are both advantages and disadvantages to touch screens. A significant advantage is that they are very *natural* to use; that is, people are used to pointing to things. With touch screens, users can point to indicate the processing they want performed by the computer. In addition, touch screens are usually easy for the user to learn. As quickly as pointing a finger, the user's request is processed. This is considerably faster than repeatedly pressing arrow keys to move the cursor from one location on the screen to another.

FIGURE 3-13
The trackball is similar to the mouse but does not require the same amount of clear desk space. The user rotates the ball to move the cursor and then presses one of the keys shown at the top of this trackball device.

FIGURE 3-14
Touch screens allow the user to make choices and execute commands by actually touching areas of the screen. Touch screens require special software that determines where the user touched the screen and what action should be taken.

There are some disadvantages to touch screens. First, the resolution of the touching area is not precise. Thus, while a user can point to a box or a fairly large area on the screen and the electronics can determine the location of the touch, it is difficult to point to a single character in a word processing application, for example, and indicate that the character should be deleted. In cases such as these, a keyboard is easier to use. A second disadvantage is that after a period of reaching for the screen, the user's arm might become tired.

Graphic Input Devices

Graphic input devices are used to translate graphic input data, such as photos or drawings, into a form that can be processed on a computer. Three devices that are often used for graphic input are light pens, digitizers, and graphics tablets. A **light pen** is used by touching it on the display screen to create or modify graphics (Figure 3-15). An electronic grid on the screen senses the light generated at the tip of the light pen when it is touched to the screen. A **digitizer** converts points, lines, and curves from a sketch, drawing, or photograph to digital impulses and transmits them to a computer (Figures 3-16 and 3-17). The user indicates the data to be input by pressing one or more buttons on the hand-held digitizer device. A **graphics tablet** works in a manner similar to a digitizer, but it also contains unique characters and commands that can be automatically generated by the person using the tablet (Figure 3-18).

Pen Input Devices

Pen input devices allow the user to input hand-printed letters and numbers to record information. These devices work with a type of hand-held computer sometimes called *scratchpad computers*. These systems consist of a flat screen and the pen device (Figure 3-19). As the characters are printed, special circuitry records the movement of the pen on the screen.

FIGURE 3-15
Placing the light pen at a point on the screen activates a sensing device within the pen. The activated pen transmits the location of the light to the computer, where the program can perform the desired tasks.

FIGURE 3-16
The device in the engineer's hand reads and translates the coordinates on the drawing into data that can be stored in the computer and later used to reproduce the drawing on a screen or a printer.

FIGURE 3-17
Digitizers are used to create original drawings or to trace and reproduce existing drawings quickly and accurately.

FIGURE 3-18
The color template on the graphics tablet allows the user to select processing options by placing a hand-held device over the appropriate location on the tablet and pressing a button.

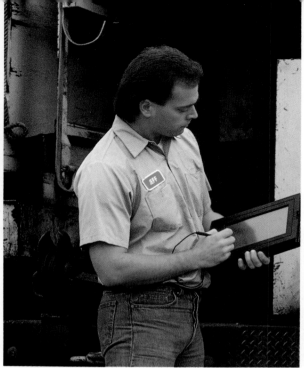

The computer translates the pen strokes into characters. The characters are then processed as text or as a user response to a message displayed on the screen. The advantage of pen input systems is that many workers who may have a difficult time using a keyboard can use the more familiar pen to enter data.

FIGURE 3-19
Pen input systems allow the user to use an electronic pen to enter data or select processing options without using a keyboard. This method is easy to learn by individuals who have worked with a pencil and paper.

Voice Input

One of the more exciting recent developments is the use of voice input, sometimes referred to as voice or speech recognition. As the name implies, **voice input** allows the user to enter data and issue commands to the computer with spoken words (Figure 3-20).

Most systems require the user to *train* the system to recognize their voice by first speaking the words that will be used a number of times. As the words are spoken, they are digitized by the system; that is, they are broken down into digital components that the computer can recognize. After each word has been spoken several times, the system develops a digital pattern for the word that can be stored on auxiliary storage. When the user later speaks a word to the system to request a particular action, the system compares the word to words that were previously entered and that it is trained to *understand*. When it finds a match, the software performs the activity associated with

FIGURE 3-20
Voice input systems allow the user to enter data without using the keyboard. The microphone headset is attached to the personal computer. Special software and hardware are used to interpret the voice commands.

the word. For example, in voice-controlled word processing systems, spoken words can control such functions as single- and double-spacing, choosing type styles, and centering text. The major advantage of voice input is that the user does not have to key, move, or touch anything to enter data into the computer. Many experts believe that voice input will be used extensively in the years to come.

INPUT DEVICES DESIGNED FOR SPECIFIC PURPOSES

Some input devices are designed to perform specific tasks. Examples are scanners, MICR readers, and data collection devices.

Scanners

Scanners include a variety of devices that *read* printed codes, characters, or images and convert them into a form that can be processed by the computer. This section describes several different types of scanning devices.

Page Scanners A **page scanner** is an input device that can electronically capture an entire page of text or images such as photographs or art work (Figure 3-21). The scanner converts the text or image on the original document into digital information that can be stored on a disk and processed by the computer. The digitized information can be printed or displayed separately or merged into another document such as a newsletter. Hand-held devices that can scan a portion of a page are also available (Figure 3-22) as well as color scanners.

Image Processing Much of the data input to a computer is taken from source documents. Usually, you input only a portion of the data on the source document, but sometimes you might find it necessary to store the entire source document, such as legal document with a signature or a drawing. In these situations, organizations often implement image processing systems. **Image processing systems** use software and special equipment, including scanners, to input and store an actual image of the source document. These systems are like electronic filing cabinets that allow users to rapidly access and review exact reproductions of the original documents (Figure 3-23).

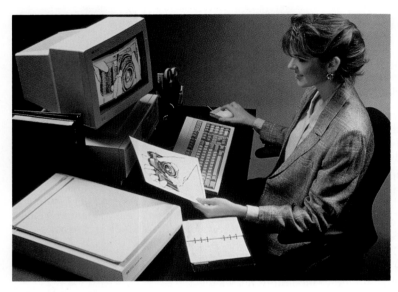

FIGURE 3-21
This scanner can input text, graphics, or photographs for use in word processing or desktop publishing applications.

FIGURE 3-22
A hand-held scanner can enter text or graphics less than a page wide. Software allows you to join separately scanned items to make up a complete page.

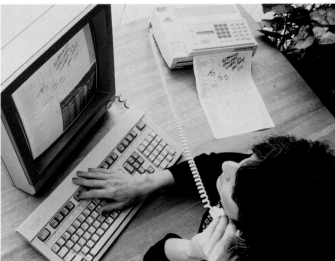

FIGURE 3-23
Image processing systems record and store an exact copy of a document. These systems are often used by insurance companies that may need to refer to any of hundreds of thousands of documents.

FIGURE 3-24
Most modern grocery stores use optical scanning devices such as the one shown here. A laser beam, emitted from the opening on the counter, reads the bar code on the product package. Most retail products have the Universal Product Code (UPC) imprinted somewhere on the label or package (located at the bottom of the can in the photo below). The UPC code uniquely identifies both the manufacturer and the product. The scanning device is connected to a computer system that uses the UPC code to look up the price of the product and add the price into the total sale. A keyboard above the scanner is used to code the numbers for items such as fruit, which do not have UPC labels.

Laser Scanners   A scanning device often used by modern grocery stores at checkout counters is a **laser scanner**, also called a **bar code reader** (Figure 3-24). These devices use a laser beam to scan and read the special bar code printed on the products.

Optical Character Readers   Optical character recognition (OCR) devices are scanners that read type-written, computer-printed, and in some cases hand-printed characters from ordinary documents. OCR devices range from large machines that can automatically read thousands of documents per minute to hand-held wands (Figure 3-25).

FIGURE 3-25
This hand-held optical character recognition device is being used to read a typed document one line at a time. Other OCR devices can scan an entire page at one time.

FIGURE 3-26
The full OCR-A standard character set. Characters such as B and 8, S and 5, and 0 and the letter O are designed so the reading device can easily distinguish between them.

FIGURE 3-27
These hand-printed characters can be read by some types of OCR devices. The two small dots in each square identify where certain portions of each numeric digit must be placed.

An OCR device scans the shape of a character on a document, compares it with a predefined shape stored in memory, and converts the character into the corresponding computer code. The standard OCR typeface, called OCR-A, is illustrated in Figure 3-26. The characters can be read easily by both humans and machines. OCR-B is a set of standard characters widely used in Europe and Japan.

Some optical character readers can read hand-printed characters. Building a machine capable of reading and interpreting hand-printed characters is a challenging task even in this era of high technology. The characters must be carefully printed according to a strict set of rules regarding their shapes. The example in Figure 3-27 illustrates the shape of hand-printed characters that can be read with an OCR device.

The most widespread application of OCR devices is for reading turn-around documents prepared by computer printers. A **turn-around document** is designed to be returned to the organization in which it was originally issued. When the document is returned (*turned around*), the data on it is read by an OCR device. For example, many utility bills, department store bills, insurance premium statements, and so on request that the consumer return the statement with a payment (Figure 3-28). The statement is printed with characters that can be read by OCR devices. When the customer returns it, the machine reads it to give proper credit for the payment received. Some OCR devices, such as the one shown at the bottom of this page in Figure 3-28, are small enough to fit on top of a desk.

Optical Mark Readers   An **optical mark reader (OMR)** is a scanning device that can read carefully placed pencil marks on specially designed documents. The pencil marks on the form usually indicate responses to questions and can be read and interpreted by a computer program. Optical mark readers are frequently used to score tests (shown on the next page in Figure 3-29).

FIGURE 3-28
Here, utility company payment receipts are being read by an OCR device. These receipts are examples of turn-around documents because they were designed to be returned to the utility with the customer's payment.

FIGURE 3-29
The pencil marks made on this test answer sheet can be read by an optical mark reader. The reader can mark the incorrect answers, report the number of correct answers, and report the average score of all tests.

MICR Readers

MICR readers, used almost exclusively in the banking industry for processing checks, are a type of input device. **MICR (magnetic ink character recognition)** is a type of machine-readable data. In the 1950s, the industry chose MICR as the method to be used to encode and read the billions of checks written each year.

When MICR is used, special characters encoded on checks identify such items as the bank number and the account number. When a check is processed, the amount is added to the previously encoded data. The MICR characters (Figure 3-30) use a special ink that can be magnetized during processing. MICR readers interpret the electronic signals generated from the magnetized characters so checks can be sorted and processed to prepare bank statements for customers. MICR devices can process over 1,000 checks per minute (Figure 3-31). MICR also is used in utility companies, credit card companies, and other industries that must process large volumes of data.

FIGURE 3-30
The characters at the bottom of the check are being read by the magnetic ink character recognition (MICR) device. Banks in the United States and in many foreign countries use these codes for checks.

FIGURE 3-31
This MICR reader-sorter can process over a thousand documents per minute. After the documents are read, they are sorted into the vertical bins on the right side of the machine. This device can be connected directly to a computer to allow the documents to be input as they are read.

Data Collection Devices

Many **data collection devices** are designed and used for obtaining data at the site where the transaction or event being reported takes place. For example, in Figure 3-32, a man is taking inventory in a warehouse. Rather than write down the number and type of items and then enter this data, he uses a portable data collection device to record the inventory count in the device's memory. After he takes the inventory, he can transmit the data to a computer for processing.

Sometimes data collection equipment is needed in environments where heat, humidity, and cleanliness are difficult or impossible to control (Figure 3-33). In addition, these devices are often used by people whose primary task is not entering the data. Entering the data is only a small portion of their job duties. Data collection devices used in this manner must be designed and built for use in uncontrolled environments and they must be easy to operate.

Using data collection devices can provide important advantages over alternative methods of input. Because the data is entered as it is collected, clerical costs and transcription errors are reduced or eliminated. If the data collection devices can be connected directly to the computer, the data is immediately available for processing.

Data collection devices range from portable devices that can be carried throughout a store or factory to sophisticated terminal systems with multiple input stations that feed directly into a central computer (Figure 3-34). These devices will continue to improve and find increased use in data entry applications.

FIGURE 3-32
This portable data collection device is being used to take an inventory in a warehouse. The data is stored in memory and can later be transferred to a computer system for processing.

FIGURE 3-33
This data collection terminal has been designed to accommodate the user. Data collection devices should be simple and quick to operate, so that entering the data does not interfere with the main job of the person using the terminal.

FIGURE 3-34
A data collection device located in a production area. Data collected at this station is transferred to the main computer that keeps track of total production.

Figure 3-35 summarizes the most commonly used input devices. Although each device has advantages and disadvantages, each is appropriate for specific applications.

DEVICE	DESCRIPTION
Keyboard	Most commonly used input device. Special keys may include numeric keypad, cursor control keys, and function keys.
Terminal	Can be dumb, intelligent, or special-purpose.
Mouse or Trackball	Input devices used to move the cursor on a screen and select options.
Touch screens	User interacts with the computer by touching the screen.
Graphic input	Light pens, digitizers, and graphics tablets translate graphic data into a form that can be processed by a computer.
Pen	Allows input or hand-printed characters.
Voice input	User enters data and issues commands with spoken words.
MICR reader	Used primarily in banking to read the magnetic ink characters printed on checks.
Scanner	A variety of devices that read printed codes, characters, or images.
Data collection	Used to input data where it is generated.

FIGURE 3-35
This table summarizes some of the more common input devices.

With the widespread use of terminals, personal computers, and other input devices, input operations are performed by many types of users whose computer knowledge and experience varies greatly. Some users have a limited knowledge of computers and others have many years of experience. In addition, some users interact with computers daily, while others use them only occasionally. Information systems need to provide all users with a means of interacting with the computer efficiently. This is accomplished through user interfaces.

USER INTERFACES

A **user interface** is the combination of hardware and software that allows a user to communicate with a computer system. Through a user interface, users are able to input values that (1) respond to messages presented by the computer, (2) control the computer, and (3) request information from the computer. Thus, a user interface provides the means for communication between an information system and the user.

Both the hardware and software working together form a user interface. A terminal is an example of hardware that is frequently part of a user interface. The screen on the terminal displays messages to the user. The devices used for responding to the messages and controlling the computer include the keyboard, the mouse, and other types of input devices. The software associated with an interface are the programs. These programs determine the messages that are given to the user, the manner in which the user can respond, and the actions that will take place based on the user's responses.

In the following sections we discuss two of the most commonly found user interface techniques—prompts and menus—and describe how these interface techniques have improved communication between the user and the computer.

FIGURE 3-36
Prompts aid the user in entering data. They can tell the user what data to enter as well as the required format (as shown for the date entry). Prompts were one of the first types of interfaces designed to assist the user in utilizing the computer.

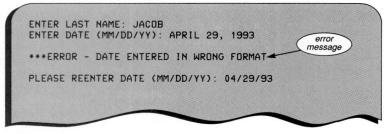

FIGURE 3-37
The software used for this screen checks the date entered and gives an error message if the date is entered in the wrong format.

FIGURE 3-38
A menu consists of a title, the selections that can be made, and a prompt for the user to make an entry.

Prompts

A **prompt** is a message to the user that appears on the screen and provides helpful information or instructions regarding an entry to be made or action to be taken. The example in Figure 3-36 illustrates the use of prompts.

On the first line, the prompt "ENTER LAST NAME:" appears on the screen. This message tells the user to enter his or her last name. After the user enters the last name, a second prompt displays. This prompt, "ENTER DATE (MM/DD/YY):", indicates not only what the user is to enter but also exactly how the user should enter it. MM/DD/YY means to enter the date as a two-digit month number followed by a slash (/), a two-digit day number followed by a slash, and a two-digit year number. Thus, the entry 04/05/93 is valid, but 4/5/93 is not.

To help ensure that the user inputs valid data, the software should use **data editing**, the capability to check the data for proper format and acceptable values. When data is entered incorrectly, a message should appear to identify the error so the user can enter the correct data. The example in Figure 3-37 illustrates what might occur if a user does not enter data in the correct format. An error message appears and requests the user to reenter the date.

Menus

A **menu** is a screen display that provides a list of processing options for the user and allows the user to make a selection. A menu generally consists of three parts: a title, the selections, and a prompt (Figure 3-38). The title identifies the menu and orients the user to the choices that can be made. The selections consist of the words that describe each selection. The prompt asks the user to choose one of the selections.

The user can choose a menu selection in several ways. Figure 3-39 illustrates four common techniques, each of which is described as follows.

1. **Sequential Number**. Numbers are used to identify each of the selections. The user enters the number that corresponds to his or her selection and then presses the Enter key.
2. **Alphabetic Selection**. Letters of the alphabet identify the various processing options. The user enters the letter or letters that correspond to the selection and then presses the Enter key.
3. **Cursor Positioning**. The user presses the arrow or cursor control keys to position the cursor adjacent to the desired selection and then presses the Enter key.

4. **Reverse Video**. **Reverse video**, also called **inverse video**, means that the normal screen display, such as amber characters on a black background, is reversed to black characters on an amber background to highlight and draw attention to a certain character, word, or section on the screen. The directions instruct the user to move the reverse video from one selection to another by pressing the Spacebar (or arrow keys). Pressing the Spacebar once moves the reverse video from word processing to graphics; pressing it again highlights the database selection. When the desired selection is highlighted the user presses the Enter key to make that selection.

FIGURE 3-39

This example illustrates four different types of menus and menu selection methods.

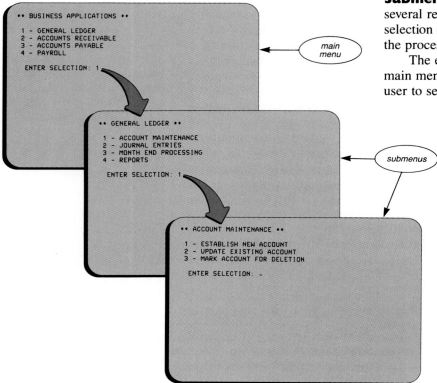

Submenus Some applications require the use of several related menus. When a user chooses a selection on a menu, a **submenu** further defines the processing options that are available.

The example in Figure 3-40 illustrates the main menu from Figure 3-38, which allows the user to select GENERAL LEDGER, ACCOUNTS RECEIVABLE, ACCOUNTS PAYABLE, or PAYROLL. Also shown are two submenus. When the GENERAL LEDGER function is selected, a submenu appears. This submenu contains more detailed functions. Depending on the submenu selection, additional menus could be displayed. For example, if the user selected option 1, ACCOUNT MAINTENANCE, a third menu would appear that displays selections relative to establishing a new account, updating an existing account, or marking an existing account for deletion.

FIGURE 3-40
A submenu is used when additional selections can be made within an application. In this example, the first submenu shows additional General Ledger selections. The second submenu shows General Ledger Account Maintenance options.

Menus: Advantages and Disadvantages Menus are a type of user interface that is used with all sizes and types of computers. There are both advantages and disadvantages to menus. Some of the advantages are:

- The user does not have to remember special commands. He or she merely chooses a selection from a list of possible operations that appear on the menu.
- The user can become productive with minimum training. Instead of having to learn a lot of technical computer information, he or she needs only to learn the application and the results of choosing a particular selection from the menu.
- The user is guided through the application because the selections that are available appear on the menus.

The disadvantage most often associated with menus, according to some experienced users, is that they can be slow and restrictive. For example, the menus illustrated in Figure 3-40 are good for the novice or infrequent computer user because they take him or her step by step through the possible operations that can be performed. The experienced user, however, knows which operations to perform. Therefore, he or she may prefer to enter a few quick commands and immediately begin work instead of having to view and respond to two or more menus. Some menus allow users to go directly to a processing option by entering a code such as the first one or two letters of the processing option name. For example, the user could enter AM to go directly to the Account Maintenance menu.

GRAPHIC USER INTERFACE

◆ A **graphic user interface (GUI)** uses on-screen pictures, called **icons** to represent data or processing options (Figure 3-41). Rather than typing a command to open a file or start a program, with a GUI, the user uses a mouse to select one of the graphic images on the screen. Although they were first developed in the early 1970s by Xerox, GUIs did not become popular until the mid 1980s when Apple introduced the Macintosh computer. Today, many software products offer a GUI. The advantages of a GUI include ease of use, a shorter learning time, and quicker execution of commands.

FIGURE 3-41
A graphic user interface (GUI) uses pictures (called icons) to represent data or functions that the user can select. The user selects an icon by using a mouse or similar device to place the cursor on top of the picture and then pressing a button.

FEATURES OF A USER INTERFACE

◆ The following list identifies some features that should be included in a good user interface.

1. Meaningful responses to the user—System responses are the messages a computer displays and the actions the computer takes when a user enters data into the computer. In a well-designed system, the user receives a response for every action he or she takes. Without a response, the user does not know if the computer accepted the input. A system response from the computer avoids user confusion.
2. Good screen design—The design of the messages and pictures that appear on the screen can have a significant impact on the usability of the system. The most important rule is to keep the screen uncluttered and simple. Each message and each action that a user must take should be clear and easily understood. All messages, menus, and prompts within a system should follow a consistent format. This reduces the time needed for users to learn how to use a system and increases ease of use for experienced users.
3. Simple user responses—In general, the simpler the response required from the user, the better the user interface. If the user does not have to enter a large number of characters, data entry will be faster and fewer errors will occur.

4. Error recovery procedures—Errors are inevitable, thus users should be able to easily recover from them. Whenever the user makes an error, three user interface activities should take place: (1) the user should be alerted that an error has been made; (2) the error should be identified as specifically as possible; and (3) the user should be told how to recover from the error.

5. Control and security—Many multiuser computer systems require users to *sign on* to the computer by entering identification such as a name or account number followed by a password. A **password** is a value, such as a word or number, which identifies the user. The computer will only allow a user to sign on if he or she enters the correct password. These procedures help to ensure that only authorized users obtain access to the computer.

Computer professionals should keep these features in mind when they are designing and developing user interfaces. Users should also consider them when they are evaluating software or hardware for purchase.

The question that must be asked when designing or deciding on a user interface is, *Who will be using it and what is their level of computer experience?* A good user interface must be appropriate for the people who are going to use it.

DATA ENTRY

◆ Of the four types of input—program, commands, user responses, and data—the most common type of input is data. Sometimes data is entered by professional data entry operators who are specially trained in data entry procedures and techniques. However, it is becoming more common for data to be entered at its source by users working where the data is generated. The next section explains data entry techniques.

DATA ENTRY FOR INTERACTIVE AND BATCH PROCESSING

◆ Two methods of processing data on a computer are interactive processing and batch processing. **Interactive processing** means that data is processed immediately as it is entered. In **batch processing**, data is collected and, at some later time, all the data that has been gathered is processed as a group or *batch*. As you will see in the following sections, the methods used to enter data for interactive and batch processing differ.

Data Entry for Interactive Processing

Data entered in the interactive processing mode generates immediate output. In most interactive data entry, the person entering the data is communicating directly with the computer that will process the data. Therefore, data entry for interactive processing is said to be **online data entry**, meaning that the device from which the data is being entered is connected directly to the computer.

The output generated from interactive data entry processing is not always produced at the location where the data was entered. In Figure 3-42, for example, the data is entered from a terminal located in the order entry department. The data entered concerns a purchase by a customer. After the data is entered, a picking slip is printed in the warehouse. The worker in the warehouse then retrieves the item purchased (in this case, a lawn mower) and packages it for shipping. The terminal operator in the order entry department never sees the output generated, yet this is interactive processing because the data entered is processed immediately.

FIGURE 3-42
In this example of data entry for interactive processing, the data is entered by a terminal operator in the order entry department. The output generated, a picking slip, is printed in the warehouse. In addition, a record of the order is stored on disk.

The person entering the order in the order entry department may enter hundreds of such orders each day. When large amounts of data are entered by a terminal operator whose only job is to enter the data, the data entry function is called **production data entry**.

Data Entry for Batch Processing

FIGURE 3-43

In online batch data entry, data is input directly to the computer and stored on disk or tape. At a later time, the stored data will be processed as a group by the computer.

When data is entered for processing in the batch processing mode, it is stored on a storage medium (usually tape or disk) for processing at a later time. Data for batch processing can be entered in either an online or offline manner. As we noted previously, online data entry means that the device from which the data is being entered is connected directly to the computer that will process it (Figure 3-43).

data is accumulated in a batch and processed as a group

Offline data entry means that the device from which the data is being entered is not connected to the computer that will process it (Figure 3-44). Instead, the data is entered using a dedicated computer or other device devoted to the data entry function. This computer or special device accepts the input data and stores it on disk or tape. At a later time, the disk or tape can be transported to the site where the data will be entered for processing in a batch mode to produce information.

When offline data entry is used, source documents are accumulated prior to entering the data. Then the data on these documents is entered into the computer system. For example, in a payroll application, time cards for hourly employees would be the source documents from which data entry operators would enter the hours each employee worked.

To ensure that data is entered and processed accurately, controls are established within applications. Controls are the methods and procedures that ensure the accuracy and reliability of data and processing techniques. In a credit card payment application, for example, payments are usually divided into batches for processing. The payments for each batch are added manually and recorded prior to data entry. When the payment batches are processed on the computer, the total amount of the payments calculated by the computer for each batch is compared to the total determined from the manual addition performed prior to data entry. If the totals are the same, the data was input to the computer accurately. If the totals are not the same, then either the data was entered incorrectly or the manually determined batch total was calculated incorrectly. This technique of balancing to a predetermined total is called a **batch control**.

Summary of Interactive and Batch Data Entry

Entering data to produce information can take place online or offline. Online data entry is always used for interactive processing and often for batch processing as well. Offline data entry is used for batch processing. When using offline data entry, source documents from which the data is obtained must be gathered prior to the data being entered. Regardless of the processing method, producing information often requires a large amount of data entry.

OFFLINE DATA ENTRY

source
documents

INPUT DATA

to computer

FIGURE 3-44
In offline data entry, the data is input to a computer other than the one that will eventually process it. Often computers used for offline data entry are dedicated to data input functions and perform little if any processing. The data entered is later transferred to another computer for processing.

DATA ENTRY PROCEDURES

The procedures developed for the data entry function are important because accurate data must be entered into a computer to ensure data integrity. In addition, since users are interacting directly with the computer during the data entry function, procedures and documentation must be quite clear. The following questions must be answered in order to implement a data entry application successfully:

■ *Who originates the data?* Data entered for processing on a computer is generated from many sources. It is important to identify which people and operations will generate the data so that appropriate procedures can be written to specify what data is to be gathered, how it is to be gathered, and who is to gather it.

■ *Where will the data be entered?* Data is generally entered either from the centralized data entry section of the information systems department or from various locations throughout an organization. The hardware, software, and personnel needs vary depending upon which of these two methods is used. In a **centralized data entry** operation, the data is keyed by trained operators from source documents. When data is entered in the centralized data entry section, it is usually processed in a batch processing mode.

Entering data from various locations in an organization is called **distributed data entry**. Quite often the data entry takes place at the site where the data is generated, for example, sales orders being entered by the sales department. Often, data entered using distributed data entry is processed in an interactive processing mode.

■ *How soon will the data be entered?* The amount of time that can elapse between when the event being reported takes place and when the data about that event must be entered should be specified. In some applications, an event can occur but the data need not be entered until hours or even days later. For example, in the payroll application, the time cards are retrieved by a clerk on Monday at 4:00 p.m. These time cards record the workers' time for the previous week. Data entry personnel might not enter this data until Tuesday. Therefore, more than a week might elapse between when the event occurred and when the data about the event was entered. In most cases when entry time is not a critical factor, the data is recorded on source documents and given to data entry personnel to enter at either a centralized or distributed location. In other applications, however, the data must be entered as the event or transaction is occurring and at the location where it is occurring. This process is sometimes called **source data collection**. For example, when a retail sale is made using a point-of-sale terminal, the data must be entered at the moment the sale is made so that the sale can be completed with the customer. Therefore, the documentation for the data entry system should specify the timing requirements for entering data.

■ *How will the data be entered?* Based on many of the factors discussed in the first three questions, the procedures must specify how the data will be entered, identifying devices and methods. For example, data will be entered from source documents using terminals in an online, centralized environment.

■ *How much data will be entered?* The amount of data entered for a given time period and location must be estimated. Any particularly high or low volumes may require special procedures.

■ *How will data errors be identified and corrected?* The documentation must specify the editing for the entered data and the steps to take if the data is not valid. Although different applications will have specific criteria for validating input data, several tests can be performed on input data before the data is processed in a computer. Some of these tests are:

   ■ Tests for numeric or alphabetic data—For example, in the United States a ZIP code must always be numeric. Therefore, the program performing the editing can check the values in the ZIP code field. If they are not numeric, the data is incorrect (Figure 3-45).

FIGURE 3-45
In this example, a nonnumeric ZIP code is entered and an error message displays. When a numeric ZIP code is entered, the data is accepted and no error message displays. An additional test could be performed to match the entry against a file of valid ZIP codes.

- Tests for data reasonableness—A reasonableness check ensures that the data entered is within normal or accepted boundaries. For example, suppose no employee within a company is authorized to work more than 80 hours per week. If the value entered in the hours worked field is greater than 80, the value in the field would be indicated as a probable error.
- Tests for data consistency—In some cases, data entered cannot, by itself, be found to be invalid. If, however, the data is examined in the context of other data entered for the same record or group of fields, discrepancies might be found. For example, in an airline reservation system, passengers often purchase round-trip tickets (Figure 3-46). If the terminal operator enters the date on which the passenger is leaving, the editing program can only check whether the date entered is valid. Similarly, when the return date is entered, the program can again make sure it is a valid date. The return date can also be compared to the departure date. If the return date is earlier than the departure date, it is likely that an error has been made when entering one of the dates.
- Tests for transcription and transposition errors—There is always a possibility that an operator will make an error when entering data. A **transcription error** occurs when an error is made in copying the values from a source document. For example, if the operator keys the customer number 7165 when the proper number is 7765, the operator has made a transcription error. A **transposition error** happens when the operator switches two numbers. Such an error has occurred when the number 7765 is entered as 7756.
- *How will data be controlled?* The controls and security that will be applied to the data must be defined. This includes what the controls and security measures are, how they are to be implemented, and what action is to be taken if the security of the data is compromised in any way.
- *How many people are needed?* Specifying personnel requirements includes defining who will gather the data, who will enter it, and how many people will be required. Personnel must be educated about gathering and entering the data. They must be trained in using the equipment and software, ensuring reliable data entry, entering the data according to specified procedures, and interpreting any output received from the computer during interactive processing.

FIGURE 3-46
On this airline reservation screen, the user entered a return date earlier than the departure date and the system displayed an error message.

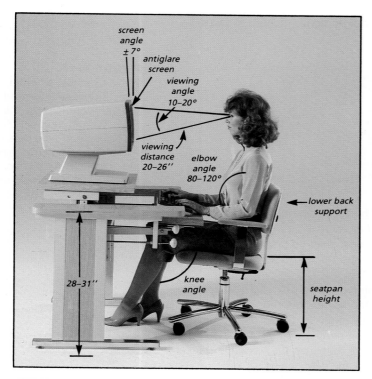

FIGURE 3-47
Here, we see some of the ergonomic factors that should be considered when using a terminal for an extended period of time.

ERGONOMICS

Because of the increased use of computers, many people now spend part or all of their day in front of a computer terminal. In order to make this work environment more comfortable, many equipment manufacturers and users have turned to ergonomics. **Ergonomics** is the study of the design and arrangement of equipment so that people will interact with the equipment in a healthy, comfortable, and efficient manner. As related to computer equipment, ergonomics is concerned with such factors as the physical design of the keyboard, screens, related hardware, computer furniture, and the manner in which people interact with this equipment.

The first computer terminals contained the keyboard and screen as a single unit. The screen frequently displayed white characters on a black background. Early studies found significant user dissatisfaction with these terminals. One study reported that many of the people who used them complained of health problems, including eye fatigue, blurred vision, itching and burning eyes, and back problems. As a result of these and other studies, a number of design recommendations have been made, including the following:

1. Computer keyboards should be detached from the screen so that they can be positioned on a desk for the convenience and comfort of the user.
2. The screen should be movable, and the angle at which the user views the contents of the screen should be adjustable.
3. The screen should be high quality to eliminate any flickering of the image and characters on the screen. The characters displayed on the screen should appear as solid as possible and the images on the screen should be in sharp focus over the entire screen area.
4. The screen should have brightness and contrast adjustments.
5. The screen should have an antiglare coating. Screen glare has been a common complaint of many terminal users, and it is known that glare can be harmful to eyes. A flat screen, now used on some terminals, can also reduce glare.
6. Terminals with screens that display amber or green characters on a black background are preferable to those that display black characters on a white background or white characters on a black background.
7. The screen and keyboard should be positioned at an appropriate height for the user.
8. Users should sit directly in front of the screen and keyboard and use an adjustable chair that has a lower-back support.

Figure 3-47 illustrates some of these recommendations. The keyboard is detachable, the screen is adjustable and has an antiglare coating. The illustration also shows the use of a chair with a lower-back support. Notice the position of the user's body in relation to the terminal.

As more workers use terminals and personal computers, the importance of ergonomically designed equipment increases. Manufacturers are now aware of the importance of ergonomic design and, as a result, are designing and building terminals and personal computers that incorporate ergonomic design for the health and comfort of users.

SUMMARY OF INPUT TO THE COMPUTER

In this chapter we presented an overview of the information processing cycle and discussed how data is organized. We also discussed the four types of input, a variety of input devices, user interfaces, data entry, and ergonomics. After reading this chapter you should have a better overall understanding of computer input.

C H A P T E R   S U M M A R Y

1. In the **information processing cycle** (input, processing, output, and storage), the input operation must take place before any data can be processed and any information produced and stored.
2. **Input** refers to the process of entering programs, commands, user responses, and data into main memory.
3. **Data** refers to the raw facts and consists of the numbers and words that a computer receives and processes to produce information.
4. Data is composed of **characters**. These include **alphabetic** (A–Z), **numeric** (0–9), and **special** characters, such as ()*&%#@,.
5. Individual facts are referred to as **data items**, **data fields**, or **fields**.
6. Fields may be classified as **numeric**, **alphabetic**, or **alphanumeric**.
7. A **record** is a collection of related fields.
8. A collection of related records is called a **file**.
9. Files on a computer are usually stored on magnetic tape or magnetic disk.
10. A **database** provides an efficient way to establish a relationship between data items and implies that a relationship has been established between multiple files.
11. A **cursor** is a symbol, such as an underline character or an arrow, that indicates where on the screen the next character entered will appear.
12. The **keyboard** is the most commonly used input device. Special keys may include the **numeric keypads**, **cursor control keys**, and **function keys**.
13. Terminals may be classified as **dumb terminals**, **intelligent terminals**, and **special-purpose terminals**.
14. A **mouse** is a small input device used to control the movement of the cursor and to select options displayed on the screen.
15. A **trackball** is a graphic pointing device like a mouse only with the ball on the top of the device instead of on the bottom.
16. **Touch screens** allow the user to interact with a computer by merely touching the screen.
17. **Light pens**, **digitizers**, and **graphics tablets** are **graphic input devices** used to translate graphic input data into a form that can be processed by the computer.
18. **Pen input devices** allow the user to input hand-printed letters and numbers to record information.
19. **Voice input** allows the user to enter data and issue commands to a computer with spoken words.
20. **Scanners** are devices that read printed codes, characters, or images and convert them into a form that can be processed by the computer.
21. A **page scanner** is an input device that can electronically capture an entire page of text or images such as photos and art work.
22. **Image processing systems** use software and special equipment, including scanners, to input and store an actual image of a source document.
23. A scanning device called a **laser scanner**, or a **bar code reader**, uses a laser beam to scan and read the special bar code printed on products.

24. **Optical character recognition (OCR)** devices are scanners that read typewritten, computer-printed, and in some cases hand-printed characters from ordinary documents.
25. An **Optical mark reader (OMR)** is a scanning device that can read carefully placed pencil marks on a specially designed form.
26. **Magnetic ink character recognition (MICR)** is a type of machine-readable data. **MICR readers**, used almost exclusively in the banking industry, are a type of input device used to process checks.
27. **Data collection devices** are designed and used for obtaining data at the site where the transaction or event being reported takes place.
28. A **user interface** is the combination of hardware and software that allows a user to communicate with a computer system.
29. A **prompt** is a message to the user that is displayed on the screen and provides information or instructions regarding some entry to be made or action to be taken.
30. **Data editing** is used to check input data for proper format and acceptable values. It helps to ensure that valid data is entered by the user.
31. A **menu** is a screen display that provides a list of processing options for the user and allows the user to make a selection. There are several types of menu-selection techniques including sequential number, alphabetic selection, cursor positioning, and reverse video.
32. **Submenus** are used to further define the processing options that are available.
33. A **graphic user interface (GUI)** uses on-screen pictures, called **icons** to represent data or processing options.
34. Features that relate to good interfaces include: system responses, screen design, user responses, error recovery, and control and security.
35. A **password** is a value, such as a word or number, which identifies the user.
36. **Interactive processing** means that data is processed immediately as it is entered.
37. In **batch processing**, data is collected and, at some later time, all the data that has been gathered is processed as a group or *batch*.
38. Data entry for interactive processing is said to be **online data entry**, meaning that the device from which the data is being entered is connected directly to the computer.
39. Data for batch processing can be entered in either an online or offline manner. **Offline data entry** means that the device from which the data is being entered is not connected to the computer that will process it.
40. Controls are the methods and procedures that ensure the accuracy and reliability of data and processing techniques. For example, balancing to a predetermined total is called a **batch control**.
41. Data entry procedures are important because accurate data must be entered into a computer to ensure data integrity.
42. **Centralized data entry** is performed by trained operators from source documents.
43. **Distributed data entry** often takes place at the site where the data is generated and is input to the computer by a variety of users.
44. **Source data collection** refers to data that is entered as the event or transaction is occurring and at the location where it is occurring.
45. Several tests can be performed on the input prior to processing. Some of these are numeric and alphabetic testing, tests for reasonableness and consistency, and transcription and transposition tests.
46. **Transcription errors** refer to operator errors made at the time of input, such as entering 7165 instead of 7665.
47. **Transposition errors** refer to operator errors where two characters are switched, such as entering 7756 instead of 7765.
48. **Ergonomics** is the study of the design and arrangement of equipment so that people will interact with the equipment in a healthy, comfortable, and efficient manner.

KEY TERMS

Alphabetic character *3.3*
Alphabetic field *3.4*
Alphanumeric field *3.4*
Arrow keys *3.5*
Bar code reader *3.13*
Batch control *3.25*
Batch processing *3.22*
Centralized data entry *3.26*
Character *3.3*
Command *3.2*
Cursor *3.5*
Cursor control keys *3.5*
Data *3.3*
Database *3.4*
Data collection device *3.16*
Data editing *3.18*
Data field *3.4*
Data item *3.4*
Digitizer *3.10*
Display terminal *3.6*
Distributed data entry *3.26*
Dumb terminal *3.6*
Ergonomics *3.28*
Field *3.4*
File *3.4*

Function keys *3.5*
Graphic input device *3.10*
Graphic user interface (GUI) *3.21*
Graphics tablet *3.10*
Icon *3.21*
Image processing system *3.12*
Input *3.2*
Intelligent terminal *3.6*
Interactive processing *3.22*
Inverse video *3.19*
Keyboard *3.5*
Laser scanner *3.13*
Light pen *3.10*
Magnetic ink character recognition
   (MICR) *3.15*
Menu *3.18*
MICR reader *3.15*
Mouse *3.8*
Numeric character *3.3*
Numeric field *3.4*
Numeric keypad *3.5*
Offline data entry *3.24*
Online data entry *3.22*
Optical character recognition
   (OCR) *3.13*

Optical mark reader (OMR) *3.14*
Page scanner *3.12*
Password *3.22*
Pen input device *3.10*
Point-of-sale (POS) terminal *3.7*
Production data entry *3.23*
Programmable terminal *3.7*
Program *3.2*
Prompt *3.18*
Record *3.4*
Reverse video *3.19*
Scanners *3.12*
Smart terminal *3.7*
Source data collection *3.26*
Special character *3.3*
Submenu *3.20*
Touch screen *3.9*
Trackball *3.9*
Transcription error *3.27*
Transposition error *3.27*
Turn-around document *3.14*
User interface *3.17*
User response *3.3*
Video display terminal (VDT) *3.6*
Voice input *3.13*

REVIEW QUESTIONS

1. List the four operations of the information processing cycle. What types and sizes of computers use the information processing cycle?
2. What is input? What are the four types of input used by a computer?
3. What is data? What terms are used to describe how data is organized for processing?
4. Describe the different types of keys on a keyboard and how they are used.
5. Name three types of terminals. Describe how they are different.
6. How is a mouse used? Describe the advantages and disadvantages of using a mouse. How is a trackball different from a mouse?
7. How does a touch screen work? What are the advantages and disadvantages of a touch screen?
8. Describe three different types of graphic input devices.
9. Describe several applications that use scanners.
10. What types of applications use data collection devices? How do they differ from other input devices?
11. What is the purpose of a user interface?
12. Describe several commonly used user interface techniques.
13. How is a graphic user interface (GUI) different from other interface techniques?
14. Name several features that a good user interface should have.
15. What are the differences between data entry for interactive and batch processing?
16. What are some of the questions that should be answered in order to implement a data entry application?
17. What is ergonomics? Describe several ergonomic features that a terminal or personal computer workplace should have.

CONTROVERSIAL ISSUES

1. Some people believe that the keyboard and the mouse are difficult to learn and use. They believe that voice and pen input systems will someday be the most widely used input devices. Discuss the advantages and disadvantages of each type of device.
2. Some local governments have passed laws regulating the work environment of people who work with terminals. The laws address such issues as proper lighting, furniture, and the amount of time that workers can spend in front of a screen. Other organizations have passed voluntary guidelines. Do you believe that such issues should be regulated?

RESEARCH PROJECTS

1. At school or a local computer store, use a program that allows the use of both function keys and a mouse. Perform several operations using only the function keys or only the mouse. Report on which method you liked best and why.
2. Visit a retail or grocery store in your area that uses laser scanners to check out the merchandise. Ask the clerks what they like and dislike about the system they use. Report back to your class. (You may need to obtain the store manager's approval.)
3. Find a document that is used for input to the computer. Examples might be school registration forms, job applications, or membership applications. Does it appear to be well designed to help both the person completing the document as well as the person who inputs the data to the computer?
4. Visit a fast food franchise that uses point-of-sale terminals. Write a report on how orders are taken, reported to the cooks, and eventually cleared from the system.

The Processor Unit

OBJECTIVES

◆ Identify the components of the processor unit and describe their use

◆ Define a bit and describe how a series of bits in a byte is used to represent characters

◆ Discuss how the ASCII and EBCDIC codes represent characters

◆ Describe why the binary and hexadecimal numbering systems are used with computer systems

◆ List and describe the four steps in a machine cycle

◆ Discuss the three primary factors that affect the speed of the processor unit

◆ Describe the characteristics of RAM and ROM memory, and list several other types of memory

◆ Describe the process of manufacturing integrated circuits

The information processing cycle consists of input, processing, output, and storage operations. When an input operation is completed and both a program and data are stored in main memory, processing operations can begin. During these operations, the processor unit executes, or performs, the program instructions and processes the data into information.

In this chapter we examine the components of the processor unit, describe how main memory stores programs and data, and discuss the sequence of operations that occurs when instructions are executed on a computer.

THE PROCESSOR UNIT

FIGURE 4-1
The processor unit of a computer contains two components: the central processing unit (CPU) and main memory. The CPU includes the control unit and the arithmetic/logic unit.

WHAT IS THE PROCESSOR UNIT?

◆ The term computer is usually used to describe the collection of devices that perform the information processing cycle. This term is also used more specifically to describe the processor unit, because this is where the *computing* actually occurs. It is in the processor unit that the computer programs are executed and the data is manipulated. The main components of the processor unit are the central processing unit, or CPU, and the main memory (Figure 4-1).

The Central Processing Unit

The central processing unit (CPU) contains the control unit and the arithmetic/logic unit. These two components work together using the program and data stored in main memory to perform the processing operations.

The control unit can be thought of as the *brain* of the computer. Just as the human brain controls the body, the control unit *controls* the computer. The **control unit** operates by repeating the following four operations: fetching, decoding, executing, and storing. **Fetching** means obtaining the next program instruction from main memory. **Decoding** is translating the program instruction into the commands that the computer can process. **Executing** refers to the actual processing of the computer commands, and **storing** takes place when the result of the instruction is written to main memory.

The second component of the CPU is the **arithmetic/logic unit (ALU)**. This unit contains the electronic circuitry necessary to perform arithmetic and logical operations on data. **Arithmetic operations** include addition, subtraction, multiplication, and division. Often, the result of one arithmetic calculation is used in a subsequent operation. An example would be a payroll calculation where the gross pay (hours worked times pay rate) is used to calculate the payroll taxes (tax rate times gross pay). **Logical operations** consist of comparing one data item to another to determine if the first data item is *greater than*, *equal to*, or *less than* the other. Based on the result of the comparison, different processing may occur. For example, two part numbers in different records can be compared. If they are equal, the part quantity in one record can be added to the quantity in the other record. If they are not equal, the quantities would not be added.

Both the control unit and the ALU contain **registers**, temporary storage locations for specific types of data. Separate registers exist for the current program instruction, the address of the next instruction, and the values of data being processed.

Main Memory

In addition to the CPU, **main memory**, or **primary storage**, is also contained in the processor unit of the computer. Main memory (Figure 4-2) stores three items: the *operating system* that directs and coordinates the computer equipment; the *application programs* containing the instructions that will direct the work to be done; and the *data* currently being processed by the application programs. Data is stored in areas of main memory referred to as input and output areas and working storage.

The input and output areas receive and send data to the input and output devices. *Working storage* is used to store any other data that is needed for processing.

Within main memory, each storage location is called a **byte**. Just as a house on a street has a unique address that indicates its location on the street, each byte in the main memory of a computer has an address that indicates its location in memory (Figure 4-3). The number that indicates the location of a byte in memory is called a **memory address**. Whenever the computer references a byte, it does so by using the memory address, or location, of that byte.

The size of main memory is normally measured in kilobytes. A **kilobyte** (abbreviated as **K** or **KB**) is equal to 1,024 bytes. Often, memory is referred to as if a kilobyte contained only 1,000 bytes. The difference between the actual and the approximate size of memory is usually unimportant and if the exact size of memory is needed, it can be calculated by using the value 1,024. For example, 640K is approximately 640,000 bytes (640 × 1,000). The exact size of 640K is 655,360 bytes (640 × 1,024). When memory exceeds 1,000K or one million bytes, it is referred to in **megabytes**, abbreviated **MB**.

MEMORY USAGE

FIGURE 4-2
Main memory is used to store several types of data and programs. The amount of memory space in use changes as program instructions are executed and data is input and output.

FIGURE 4-3
Just as each house on a street has its own address, each byte in main memory is identified by a unique address.

HOW PROGRAMS AND DATA ARE REPRESENTED IN MEMORY

◆ Program instructions and data are made up of a combination of the three types of characters: alphabetic (A through Z), numeric (0 through 9) and special (all other characters such as *,?/&). To understand how program instructions and data are stored in main memory, it is helpful to think of them as being stored character by character. Generally speaking, when we think of characters being stored in main memory, we think of one character being stored in one memory location, or byte. Thus, the name TOM would take three memory locations, or bytes, because there are three letters in that name. The address 125 Elm St. would take eleven memory locations, or bytes, because it contains eleven characters (including the spaces and .) (Figure 4-4).

FIGURE 4-4
Each character (alphabetic, numeric, or special) requires one memory location (byte) for storage.

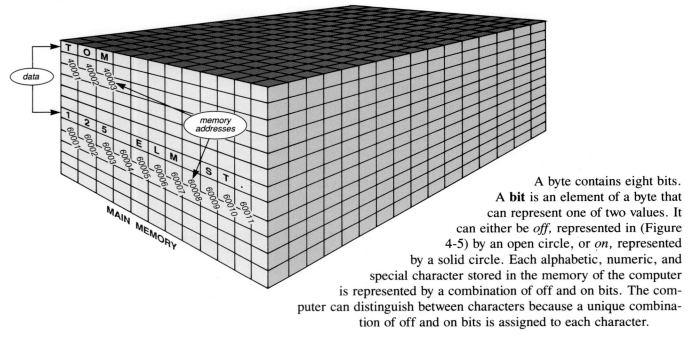

A byte contains eight bits. A **bit** is an element of a byte that can represent one of two values. It can either be *off,* represented in (Figure 4-5) by an open circle, or *on,* represented by a solid circle. Each alphabetic, numeric, and special character stored in the memory of the computer is represented by a combination of off and on bits. The computer can distinguish between characters because a unique combination of off and on bits is assigned to each character.

0 1 0 0 0 0 0 1
8-bit byte

FIGURE 4-5
A graphic representation of an eight-bit byte with two bits on and six bits off. The on bits (solid circles) are represented by the binary number 1 and the off bits (open circles) are represented by the binary 0. (This combination of bits represents the letter A in ASCII code.)

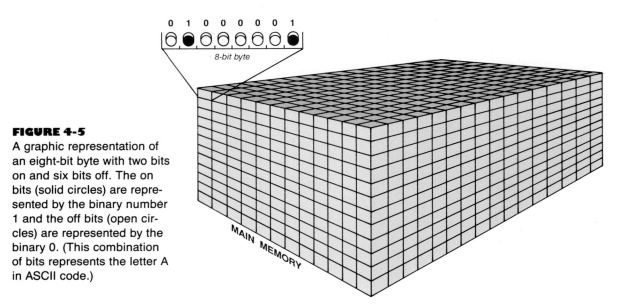

A mathematical way of representing the off and on conditions of a bit is to use 0 to represent off and 1 to represent on. The **binary** number system (base 2) represents quantities by using only two symbols, 0 and 1. For this reason, binary is used to represent the electronic status of the bits inside the processor unit. The term bit was derived from the a combination of words *b*inary dig*it*.

Two popular codes that use combinations of zeros and ones to represent characters in memory and on auxiliary storage are the ASCII and EBCDIC codes. Figure 4-6 summarizes these codes. Notice how the combination of bits, represented in binary, is unique for each character.

SYMBOL	ASCII	EBCDIC	SYMBOL	ASCII	EBCDIC	SYMBOL	ASCII	EBCDIC
(space)	0100000	01000000	?	0111111	01101111	^	1011110	
!	0100001	01011010	@	1000000	01111100	_	1011111	
"	0100010	01111111	A	1000001	11000001	a	1100001	10000001
#	0100011	01111011	B	1000010	11000010	b	1100010	10000010
$	0100100	01011011	C	1000011	11000011	c	1100011	10000011
%	0100101	01101100	D	1000100	11000100	d	1100100	10000100
&	0100110	01010000	E	1000101	11000101	e	1100101	10000101
'	0100111	01111101	F	1000110	11000110	f	1100110	10000110
(	0101000	01001101	G	1000111	11000111	g	1100111	10000111
)	0101001	01011101	H	1001000	11001000	h	1101000	10001000
*	0101010	01011100	I	1001001	11001001	i	1101001	10001001
+	0101011	01001110	J	1001010	11010001	j	1101010	10010001
,	0101100	01101011	K	1001011	11010010	k	1101011	10010010
−	0101101	01100000	L	1001100	11010011	l	1101100	10010011
.	0101110	01001011	M	1001101	11010100	m	1101101	10010100
/	0101111	01100001	N	1001110	11010101	n	1101110	10010101
0	0110000	11110000	O	1001111	11010110	o	1101111	10010110
1	0110001	11110001	P	1010000	11010111	p	1110000	10010111
2	0110010	11110010	Q	1010001	11011000	q	1110001	10011000
3	0110011	11110011	R	1010010	11011001	r	1110010	10011001
4	0110100	11110100	S	1010011	11100010	s	1110011	10100010
5	0110101	11110101	T	1010100	11100011	t	1110100	10100011
6	0110110	11110110	U	1010101	11100100	u	1110101	10100100
7	0110111	11110111	V	1010110	11100101	v	1110110	10100101
8	0111000	11111000	W	1010111	11100110	w	1110111	10100110
9	0111001	11111001	X	1011000	11100111	x	1111000	10100111
:	0111010	01111010	Y	1011001	11101000	y	1111001	10101000
;	0111011	01011110	Z	1011010	11101001	z	1111010	10101001
<	0111100	01001100	[	1011011	01001010	{	1111011	
=	0111101	01111110	\	1011100		}	1111101	
>	0111110	01101110	]	1011101	01011010			

FIGURE 4-6
This chart shows alphabetic, numeric, and special characters as they are represented in the ASCII and EBCDIC codes. Each character is represented in binary using a unique ordering of zeros and ones.

The ASCII Code

FIGURE 4-7
Pressing the letter A key on
the keyboard sends an electronic signal to the computer
①. Computer circuts convert
the signal into a particular
combination of bits that are
on and off. The combination
of bits shown here represents
the letter A ②. The character
is displayed on the screen ③.

The **American Standard Code for Information Interchange**, called **ASCII** (pronounced ask-ee), is the most widely used coding system to represent data. Figure 4-7
illustrates the letter A stored in an eight-bit byte in main memory using the ASCII
code. When you type the letter A on the keyboard, the electronic circuitry of the computer interprets the character and stores it in main memory as a series of off and on
bits. When the character A appears on the screen or is printed, the ASCII code is converted back into the alphabetic symbol A.

As you can see by looking at Figure 4-6, the ASCII code uses only the rightmost
seven bits of the eight bits in a byte to represent characters. These seven bits provide
128 orderings of zeros and ones, enough to represent all the standard characters including numeric, uppercase and lowercase alphabetic, and special. An extended version of
the ASCII code has been developed that allows certain foreign alphabetic letters and
additional special characters to be stored. This extended version makes use of the
eighth bit.

The EBCDIC Code

The ASCII code is widely used on personal computers and many minicomputers.
Another common coding scheme used primarily on mainframes is called the **Extended
Binary Coded Decimal Interchange Code**, or **EBCDIC** (pronounced eb-see-dick).

Binary Representation of Numbers

When the ASCII or EBCDIC code is used, each character that is represented is stored in one byte of memory. There are other binary formats, however, that the computer sometimes uses to represent numeric data. For example, a computer may store, or *pack* two numeric characters in one byte of memory. These binary formats are used by the computer to increase storage and processing efficiency.

PARITY

◆ Regardless of whether ASCII, EBCDIC, or other binary methods are used to represent characters in main memory, it is important that the characters be stored accurately. For each byte of memory, most computers have at least one extra bit, called a **parity bit**, that is used by the computer for error checking. A parity bit can detect if one of the bits in a byte has been inadvertently changed. Such an error could occur because of voltage fluctuations, static electricity, or a memory chip failure.

parity — T — 3 bits on parity off
parity — O — 5 bits on parity off
parity — M — 4 bits on parity on

Computers are either odd or even parity machines. In computers with **odd parity**, the total number of *on* bits in the byte (including the parity bit) must be an odd number (Figure 4-8). In computers with **even parity**, the total number of on bits must be an even number. Parity is checked by the computer each time a memory location is used. When data is moved from one location to another in main memory, the parity bits of both the sending and receiving locations are compared to see if they are the same. If the system detects a difference or if the wrong number of bits is on (e.g., an even number in a system with odd parity), an error message displays. Some computers use multiple parity bits that enable them to detect and correct a single-bit error and detect multiple-bit errors.

NUMBER SYSTEMS

◆ This section describes the number systems that are used with computers. Whereas thorough knowledge of this subject is required for technical computer personnel, a general understanding of number systems and how they relate to computers is all most users need.

As you have seen, the binary (base 2) number system is used to represent the electronic status of the bits in main memory. It is also used for other purposes such as addressing the memory locations. Another number system that is commonly used with computers is **hexadecimal** (base 16). Figure 4-9 shows how the decimal values 0 through 15 are represented in binary and hexadecimal.

FIGURE 4-8
In a computer with odd parity, the parity bit is turned on or off in order to make the total number of on bits (including the parity bit) an odd number. Here, the letters T and O have an odd number of bits and the parity bit is left off. However, the number of bits for the letter M is even, so in order to achieve odd parity, the parity bit is turned on. Turning on the parity bit makes the total number of bits in the byte an odd number (five).

FIGURE 4-9
The chart shows the binary and hexadecimal representation of decimal numbers 0 through 15. Notice how letters represent the numbers 10 through 15.

DECIMAL	BINARY	HEXADECIMAL
0	0000	0
1	0001	1
2	0010	2
3	0011	3
4	0100	4
5	0101	5
6	0110	6
7	0111	7
8	1000	8
9	1001	9
10	1010	A
11	1011	B
12	1100	C
13	1101	D
14	1110	E
15	1111	F

The mathematical principles that apply to the binary and hexadecimal number systems are the same as those that apply to the decimal number system. To help you better understand these principles, we will start with the familiar decimal system, then progress to the binary and hexadecimal number systems.

The Decimal Number System

The decimal number system is a base 10 number system (*deci* means ten). The *base* of a number system indicates how many symbols are used in it. Decimal uses 10 symbols, 0 through 9. Each of the symbols in the number system has a value associated with it. For example, you know that 3 represents a quantity of three and 5 represents a quantity of five. The decimal number system is also a *positional* number system. This means that in a number such as 143, each position in the number has a value associated with it. When you look at the decimal number 143, you know that the 3 is in the ones, or units, position and represents three ones or (3 × 1); the 4 is in the tens position and represents four tens or (4 × 10); and the 1 is in the hundreds position and represents one hundred or (1 × 100). The number 143 is the sum of the values in each position of the number (100 + 40 + 3 = 143). The chart in Figure 4-10 shows how the positional values (hundreds, tens, and units) for a number system can be calculated. Starting on the right and working to the left, we raise the base of the number system, in this case 10, to consecutive powers (10^2, 10^1, 10^0). These calculations are a mathematical way of determining the place values in a number system.

FIGURE 4-10
This chart shows the positional values in the decimal number 143.

power of 10	10^2	10^1	10^0
positional value	100	10	1
number	1	4	3

$(1 \times 10^2) + (4 \times 10^1) + (3 \times 10^0) =$
$(1 \times 100) + (4 \times 10) + (3 \times 1) =$
$100 + 40 + 3 = 143$

When you use number systems other than decimal, the same principles apply. The base of the number system indicates the number of symbols that are used, and each position in a number system has a value associated with it. The positional value can be calculated by raising the base of the number system to consecutive powers beginning with zero.

The Binary Number System

As we have discussed, binary is a base 2 number system (*bi* means two), and the symbols that are used are 0 and 1. Just as each position in a decimal number has a place value associated with it, so does each position in a binary number. In binary, the place values are successive powers of two (2^3, 2^2, 2^1, 2^0) or (8 4 2 1). To construct a binary number, you place ones in the positions where the corresponding values add up to the quantity you want to represent; you place zeros in the other positions. For example, the binary place values are 8, 4, 2, and 1, and the binary number 1001 has ones in the positions for the values 8 and 1 and zeros in the positions for 4 and 2. Therefore, the quantity represented by binary 1001 is 9 (8 + 0 + 0 + 1) (Figure 4-11).

power of 2	2^3	2^2	2^1	2^0
positional value	8	4	2	1
binary	1	0	0	1

$$(1 \times 2^3) + (0 \times 2^2) + (0 \times 2^1) + (1 \times 2^0) =$$
$$(1 \times 8) + (0 \times 4) + (0 \times 2) + (1 \times 1) =$$
$$8 + 0 + 0 + 1 = 9$$

FIGURE 4-11
This chart shows how to convert the binary number 1001 to the decimal number 9. Each place in the binary number represents a successive power of 2.

The Hexadecimal Number System

Many computers use a base 16 number system called hexadecimal. The hexadecimal number system uses 16 symbols to represent values. These include the symbols 0 through 9 and A through F (Figure 4-9). The mathematical principles we previously discussed also apply to hexadecimal (Figure 4-12).

power of 16	16^1	16^0
positional value	16	1
hexadecimal	A	5

$$(10 \times 16^1) + (5 \times 16^0) =$$
$$(10 \times 16) + (5 \times 1) =$$
$$160 + 5 = 165$$

FIGURE 4-12
This chart shows how the hexadecimal number A5 is converted into the decimal number 165. Notice that the value 10 is substituted for the A during calculations.

The primary reason why the hexadecimal number system is used with computers is because it can represent binary values in a more compact form and because the conversion between the binary and the hexadecimal number systems is very efficient. An eight-digit binary number can be represented by a two-digit hexadecimal number. For example, in the EBCDIC code, the decimal number 5 is represented as 11110101. This value can be represented in hexadecimal as F5.

One way to convert a binary number to a hexadecimal number is to divide the binary number (from right to left) into groups of four digits; calculate the value of each group; and then change any two-digit values (10 through 15) into the symbols A through F that are used in hexadecimal (Figure 4-13).

positional value	8421	8421
binary	1111	0101
decimal	15	5
hexadecimal	F	5

FIGURE 4-13
This chart shows how the EBCDIC code 11110101 for the value 5 is converted into the hexadecimal value F5. Each group of four binary digits is converted to a hexadecimal symbol.

Summary of Number Systems

As we mentioned at the beginning of the section on number systems, binary and hexadecimal are used primarily by technical computer personnel. A general user does not need a complete understanding of numbering systems. The concepts that you should remember about number systems are that binary is used to represent the electronic status of the bits in main memory and auxiliary storage. Hexadecimal is used to represent binary in a more compact form.

HOW THE PROCESSOR UNIT EXECUTES PROGRAMS AND MANIPULATES DATA

◆ The program instructions that users write are usually in a form similar to English. Before these instructions can be executed, they must be translated by the computer into a form called machine language instructions. A **machine language instruction** is one that the electronic circuits in the CPU can interpret and convert into one or more of the commands in the computer's instruction set. The **instruction set** contains commands, such as ADD or MOVE, that the computer's circuits can directly perform. To help you understand how the processor unit works, let's look at an example of a machine language instruction.

Machine Language Instructions

A machine language instruction is usually composed of three parts: an operation code; values that indicate the number of characters to be processed by the instruction; and the addresses in main memory of the data to be used in the execution of the instruction (Figure 4-14).

FIGURE 4-14
A machine language instruction consists of an operation code, the lengths of the field to be processed, and the main memory addresses of the field.

The **operation code** is a unique value that is typically stored in the first byte in the instruction. This unique value indicates which operation is to be performed. For example, the letter A stored as the operation code might mean *addition*. The letter M might mean *move*.

The number of characters to be processed is included in the machine language instruction so the CPU will manipulate the proper number of bytes. For example, if a four-digit field were to be added to another four-digit field, the number of characters specified in the instruction for each field would be four. The main memory addresses of the fields involved in the operation are also specified in the instruction. This specification of the main memory address enables the CPU to locate where in main memory the data to be processed is stored. The steps involved in executing a computer instruction are illustrated in Figure 4-15. The instruction A44 7000 9000 indicates that the four-digit fields that begin in locations 7000 and 9000 are to be added together. When this instruction is executed, the following steps occur:

1. The instruction is fetched from main memory and placed in an instruction register. An **instruction register** is an area of memory within the control unit of the CPU that can store a single instruction at a time.

2. The control unit decodes the instruction, and then fetches the data specified by the two addresses in the instruction from main memory.

3. The arithmetic/logic unit executes the instruction by adding the two numbers.

4. The control unit then stores the result of the processing by moving the sum to main memory. This basic sequence of fetch the instruction, decode the instruction, execute the instruction, and store the results, is the way most computers process instructions.

FIGURE 4-15
The four steps involved in executing a program instruction.

The Machine Cycle

These four steps—fetch, decode, execute, and store—are called the **machine cycle**. As shown in Figure 4-16, the machine cycle is made up of the instruction cycle and the execution cycle. The **instruction cycle** refers to the fetching of the next program instruction and the decoding of that instruction. The **execution cycle** includes the execution of the instruction and the storage of the processing results. One machine cycle is completed when the computer is again ready to fetch the next program instruction.

PROCESSOR SPEEDS

◆   Although the machine cycle may appear to be cumbersome and time consuming, computers can perform millions of machine cycles in one second. In fact, the processing speed of computers is often measured in **MIPS**—million instructions per second. A computer with a rating of 1 MIPS can process one million instructions per second. The most powerful personal computers today are rated at between 10 and 15 MIPS. Larger computers can process 75 to 100 MIPS and supercomputers are capable of over 200 MIPS. The speed at which a computer can execute the machine cycle is influenced by three factors: the system clock, the buses, and the word size (Figure 4-17).

FIGURE 4-16
The machine cycle consists of four steps: fetching the next instruction, decoding the instruction, executing the instruction, and storing the result. Fetching and decoding are part of the instruction, or I, cycle. Executing and storing are part of the execution, or E, cycle.

FACTOR	AFFECT ON SPEED
System clock	The system clock generates electronic pulses used to synchronize processing. Faster clock speed results in more operations in a given amount of time.
Bus width	Bus width determines how much data can be transferred at any one time. A 32-bit bus can transfer twice as much data at one time as a 16-bit bus.
Word size	Word size is the number of bits that can be manipulated at any one time. A computer with a 32-bit word size can manipulate twice as much data at one time as a system with a 16-bit word size.

FIGURE 4-17
Factors affecting computer speed.

System Clock

The control unit utilizes the **system clock** to synchronize, or control the timing of, all computer operations. The system clock generates electronic pulses at a fixed rate, measured in **megahertz**. One megahertz equals one million pulses per second. The speed of the system clock varies among computers. Some personal computers can operate at speeds in excess of 30 megahertz.

Buses

As we explained, computers store and process data as a series of electronic bits. These bits are transferred internally within the circuitry of the computer along paths capable of transmitting electrical impulses. The bits must be transferred from input devices to memory, from memory to the CPU, from the CPU to memory, and from memory to output devices. Any path along which bits are transmitted is called a **bus**. Buses can transfer multiples of eight bits at a time. An eight-bit bus has eight lines and can transmit eight bits at a time. On a 16-bit bus, bits can be moved from place to place 16 bits at a time, and on a 32-bit bus, bits are moved 32 bits at a time. Separate buses are used for memory addresses, control signals, and data (Figure 4-18).

PROCESSOR UNIT

CPU

INPUT DEVICES

BUSES

OUTPUT DEVICES

MAIN MEMORY

FIGURE 4-18
Data is transmitted between computer components via electrical pathways called buses. Separate buses exist for memory addresses, control signals, and data. Input and output devices are connected to the buses by electrical cables.

The larger the number of bits that are handled by a bus, the faster the computer can transfer data. For example, assume a number in memory occupies four eight-bit bytes. With an eight-bit bus, four steps would be required to transfer the data from memory to the CPU because on the eight-bit bus, the data in each eight-bit byte would be transferred in an individual step. A 16-bit bus has 16 lines in the bus, so only two transfers would be necessary to move the data in four bytes. And on a 32-bit bus, the entire four bytes could be transferred at one time. The fewer number of transfer steps required, the faster the transfer of data occurs.

Word Size

Another factor that affects the speed of a computer is the word size. The **word size** is the number of bits that the CPU can *process* at one time, as opposed to the bus size, which is the number of bits the computer can *transmit* at one time. Like a bus, the word size of a machine is measured in bits. Processors can have 8-bit, 16-bit, 32-bit, or 64-bit word sizes. A processor with an eight-bit word size can manipulate eight bits at a time. If two four-digit numbers are to be added in the ALU of an eight-bit processor, it will take four operations because a separate operation will be required to add each of the four digits. With a 16-bit processor, the addition will take two operations; with a 32-bit processor, only one operation would be required to add the numbers together. Sometimes the word size of a computer is given in bytes instead of bits. For example, a word size of 16 bits may be expressed as a word size of two bytes because there are eight bits in a byte. The larger the word size of the processor, the faster the capability of the computer to process data.

In summary, the speed of a computer is influenced by the system clock, the size of the buses, and the word size. When you purchase a computer, the speed requirements you want should be based on your intended use of the computer. Sixteen-bit computers are widely used today for applications such as word processing, electronic spreadsheets, or database. Thirty-two-bit computers are considered powerful and are useful for applications that require complex and time-consuming calculations such as graphics. The more powerful personal computers, many minicomputers, and most mainframes are 32-bit computers. Most supercomputers are 64-bit computers.

ARCHITECTURE OF PROCESSOR UNITS

◆ The processor unit of a computer can be designed and built in many different ways. For example, the processor for a personal computer may be housed on a single printed circuit board while a larger machine may require a number of circuit boards for the CPU, main memory, and the related electronic circuitry.

Microprocessors

The smallest processor, called a **microprocessor** (Figure 4-19), is a single integrated circuit that contains the CPU and sometimes memory. An **integrated circuit**, also called an **IC**, **chip**, or **microchip**, is a complete electronic circuit that has been etched on a small chip of nonconducting material such as silicon. Microcomputers are built using microprocessors for their CPU.

Figure 4-20 shows the location of the microprocessor chip in the main circuit board, called a **motherboard**, of a personal computer. Some of the microprocessors commonly used in personal computers today are listed on the next page in Figure 4-21.

FIGURE 4-19
The Intel 80486 microprocessor has a word size and bus width of 32 bits and can operate at between 25 and 33 megahertz.

FIGURE 4-20
The main circuit board (motherboard) of an IBM PS/2 personal computer. The microprocessor is shown in the lower left corner.

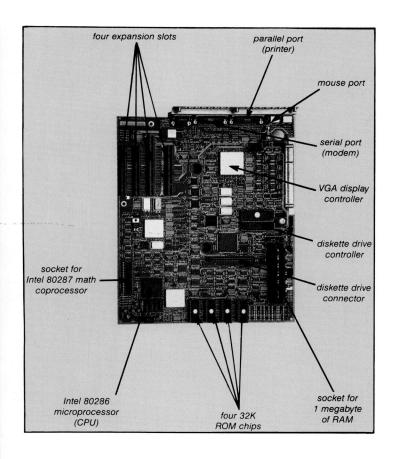

MICROPROCESSOR	MANUFACTURER	WORD SIZE (BITS)	I/O BUS WIDTH (BITS)	CLOCK SPEED (MHz)	MICROCOMPUTERS USING THIS CHIP
6502	MOS Technology	8	8	4	Apple IIe Atari 800
8088	Intel	16	8	8	IBM PC and XT HP 150 Compaq Portable
8086	Intel	16	16	8	Compaq Deskpro Many IBM compatibles
80286	Intel	16	16	8–12	IBM PC/AT Compaq Deskpro 286
68000	Motorola	32	16	12–20	Apple Macintosh SE Commodore Amiga
68020	Motorola	32	32	12–33	Apple Macintosh II
80386	Intel	32	32	16–33	Compaq Deskpro 386 IBM PS/2
68030	Motorola	32	32	16–40	Apple Macintosh SE/30 Apple Macintosh IIfx
68040	Motorola	32	32	25–33	Engineering Workstations
80486	Intel	32	32	25–33	IBM PS/2 Model 70 Compaq Systempro

FIGURE 4-21
A comparison of some of the more widely used microprocessor chips.

Coprocessors

One way computers can increase their productivity is through the use of a **coprocessor**, a special microprocessor chip or circuit board designed to perform a specific task. For example, math coprocessors are commonly added to computers to greatly speed up the processing of numeric calculations. Other types of coprocessors extend the capability of a computer by increasing the amount of software that will run on the computer.

Parallel Processing

Most computers contain one central processing unit (CPU) that processes a single instruction at a time. When one instruction is finished, the CPU begins execution of the next instruction, and so on until the program is completed. This method is known as **serial processing**. **Parallel processing** involves the use of multiple CPUs, each with their own memory. Parallel processors divide up a problem so that multiple CPUs can work on their assigned portion of the problem simultaneously. As you might expect, parallel processors require special software that can recognize how to divide up problems and bring the results back together again. Parallel processors are often used in supercomputers.

RISC Technology

As computers have evolved, more and more commands have been added to hardware instruction sets. In recent years, however, computer designers have reevaluated the need for so many instructions and have developed systems based on RISC technology.

RISC, which stands for reduced instruction set computing (or computers), involves reducing the instructions to only those that are most frequently used. Without the burden of the occasionally used instructions, the most frequently used instructions operate faster and overall processing capability, or throughput, of the system is increased (Figure 4-22).

In summary, you can see that computers have many different types of processor architecture. Regardless of the architecture used, the important concept to remember is that the processor units on all computers perform essentially the same functions.

TYPES OF MEMORY

◆ Recall that electronic components are used to store data in computer memory. The actual materials and devices used for memory have changed throughout the years. The first device used for storing data was the vacuum tube. After the vacuum tube, core memory was used. **Core memory** consisted of small, ring-shaped pieces of material that could be magnetized, or polarized, in one of two directions. The polarity indicated whether the core was on or off. Today, semiconductor memory is used in virtually all computers (Figure 4-23). **Semiconductor memory** is an integrated circuit containing thousands of transistors. A **transistor** is an electronic component that can be either on or off and represents a bit in memory.

When core memory was used as main memory, the time required to access data stored in the memory was measured in microseconds. A **microsecond** is one millionth of a second. Access to data stored in semiconductor memory is measured in nanoseconds. A **nanosecond** is one billionth of a second. In addition, the cost of semiconductor memory is just a fraction of the cost for core memory. Figure 4-24 shows how the storage capacity of semiconductor memory has increased over recent years, while the cost of semiconductor memory has decreased. The trend is expected to continue.

FIGURE 4-22
This IBM computer uses reduced instruction set computer (RISC) technology to obtain performance of over 27 million instructions per second. This level of processing power is best used in applications that require numerous calculations such as computer-aided design (CAD).

FIGURE 4-23
This semiconductor memory chip can store one million bits of information. Memory chips that can store up to 64 million bits are also available.

FIGURE 4-24
The declining cost and increased storage capacity of semiconductor storage are shown here.

Chip manufacturers say that by the end of the century it will be possible to store over a billion components on a chip. As you can see, semiconductor memory is compact, fast, and inexpensive. Several different types of semiconductor memory chips are used in computers. They are RAM, ROM, PROM, EPROM, and EEPROM chips.

RAM Memory

Random access memory, or **RAM**, is the name given to the integrated circuits, or chips, that are used for main memory. This is the type of memory we have discussed so far in this chapter. Data and programs are transferred into and out of RAM, and data stored in RAM is manipulated by computer program instructions.

There are two types of RAM memory chips: dynamic RAM and static RAM. **Dynamic RAM (DRAM)** chips are smaller and simpler in design than static RAM chips. With dynamic RAM, the current, or charge, on the chip is periodically regenerated by special regenerator circuits, which allow the chip to retain the stored data. **Static RAM** chips are larger and more complicated than dynamic RAM and do not require the current to be periodically regenerated. The main memory of most computers uses dynamic RAM chips.

Figure 4-25 illustrates the processing that could occur as a series of area codes are entered into RAM (computer memory) from a terminal. The first area code, 212, is entered from the keyboard and stored at memory locations 66000, 66001, and 66002. Once in memory, this field can be processed as it is required.

FIGURE 4-25
The instruction in the program specifies that the telephone area code is to be read into adjacent memory locations beginning with location 66000. After the data is placed in the locations, it can be processed by the program. When the same instruction is executed the second time, the value 714 entered by the terminal operator is stored on locations 66000, 66001, and 66002, where it can be processed by the same instructions that processed area code 212.

MEMORY—
AFTER READING
FIRST ENTRY

MEMORY—
AFTER READING
SECOND ENTRY

ENTER AREA CODE: 212
AREA CODE 212 HAS BEEN PROCESSED

ENTER AREA CODE: 714

Read area code from terminal and store beginning at location 66000 } COMPUTER PROGRAM

Read area code from terminal and store beginning at location 66000 } COMPUTER PROGRAM

When the instruction to read (input) data into memory from the keyboard is executed again, the second area code entered from the keyboard, area code 714, would replace the previous value (212) at locations 66000, 66001, and 66002 in memory. Area code 714 could then be processed by the same instructions that processed area code 212.

Some computers improve their processing efficiency by using a limited amount of high-speed RAM memory between the CPU and main memory (Figure 4-26). High-speed memory used in this manner is called **cache memory** (pronounced cash). When the processor needs the next program instruction or data, it first checks the cache memory. If the required instruction or data is present in cache, the processor will execute faster than if the instruction or data had to be retrieved from the slower main memory. Cache memory is used to store the most frequently used instructions and data.

RAM memory is said to be **volatile** because the programs and data stored in RAM are erased when the power to the computer is turned off. As long as the power remains on, the programs and data stored in RAM will remain intact until they are replaced by other programs and data. Programs and data that are needed for future use must be transferred from RAM to auxiliary storage before the power is turned off.

ROM Memory

ROM stands for **read only memory**. With ROM, data is permanently recorded in the memory when it is manufactured. ROM memory retains its contents even when the power is turned off. The data or programs that are stored in ROM can be read and used, but cannot be altered, hence the name *read only*. ROM is used to store items such as the instruction set of the computer. In addition, many of the special-purpose computers used in automobiles, appliances, and so on use small amounts of ROM to store instructions that will be executed repeatedly. Instructions that are stored in ROM memory are called **firmware** or **microcode**.

Other Types of Memory

PROM means **programmable read only memory**. PROM acts the same as ROM when it is part of the computer; that is, it can only be read, and its contents cannot be altered. With PROM, however, the data or programs are not stored in the memory when they are manufactured. Instead, PROM can be loaded with specially selected data or programs prior to installing it in a computer. A variation of PROM is **EPROM** (pronounced ee-prom), which means **erasable programmable read only memory**. In addition to being used in the same way as PROM, EPROM allows the user to erase the data stored in the memory and to store new data or programs in the memory. EPROM is erased through the use of special ultraviolet light devices that destroy the bit settings within the memory.

EEPROM (pronounced double-ee-prom), or **electronically erasable programmable read only memory**, allows the stored data or programs to be erased electronically. The advantage of EEPROM is that it does not have to be removed from the computer to be changed.

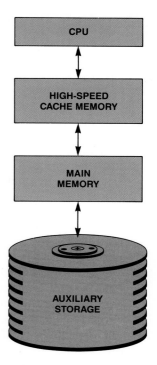

FIGURE 4-26
Some computers use an area of high-speed RAM memory, called cache memory, between the CPU and main memory. If the required data or instruction is found in cache, a program will run faster than if the information has to be retrieved from main memory or auxiliary storage.

SUMMARY

◆ In this chapter we examined various aspects of the processor unit including its components, how programs and data are stored, and how the processor executes program instructions to process data into information. Although a detailed understanding of this material is not a prerequisite for computer literacy, understanding these principles will increase your overall comprehension of how processing occurs on a computer.

CHAPTER SUMMARY

1. The central processing unit and the main memory are contained in the processor unit.
2. The central processing unit, or CPU, contains the **control unit** and the **arithmetic/logic unit (ALU)**. The control unit directs and coordinates all the activities on the computer. The arithmetic/logic unit performs arithmetic and logic operations.
3. **Arithmetic operations** consist of adding, subtracting, multiplying, and dividing.
4. **Logical operations** consist of comparing one data item to another to determine if the first data item is greater than, equal to, or less than the other.
5. **Registers** are temporary storage locations in the CPU that store specific data such as the address of the next instruction.
6. The **main memory**, also called **primary storage**, stores the operating system, application programs, and data.
7. Each storage location in main memory is called a **byte** and is identified by a **memory address**.
8. The size of main memory is normally expressed in terms of **kilobytes (KB)**. Each kilobyte is equal to 1,024 bytes.
9. A byte consists of eight **bits**. A bit can represent one of two values—off and on.
10. When a letter is entered into main memory from a keyboard, the electronic circuitry interprets the character and stores the character in memory as a series of off and on bits. The computer can distinguish between characters because a unique combination of off and on bits are assigned to each character.
11. One of the most widely used codes to represent characters is the **American Standard Code for Information Interchange**, called the **ASCII code**.
12. A code used for mainframes is the **Extended Binary Coded Decimal Interchange Code (EBCDIC)**.
13. Computers use **parity bits** for error checking.
14. The **binary** (base 2) number system is used by the computer for purposes such as representing memory addresses and the electronic status of the bits in main memory. **Hexadecimal** (base 16) is used to represent binary in a more compact form.
15. A **machine language instruction** can be decoded and executed by the CPU.
16. A machine language instruction is usually composed of an **operation code**; values indicating the number of characters to be processed; and main memory addresses of the data to be processed.
17. Steps in the **machine cycle** consist of: fetch the next instruction; decode the instruction; execute the instruction; and store the results.
18. The speed of a computer is influenced by the system clock, the bus size, and the word size.
19. The **system clock** is used by the control unit to synchronize all computer operations.
20. A **bus** is any line that transmits bits between memory and the input/output devices, and between memory and the CPU.
21. The number of bits that the CPU can process at one time is called the **word size**.
22. Computers can be 8-bit, 16-bit, 32-bit, or 64-bit machines.
23. **Microprocessors** are used for the CPU in microcomputers.
24. **Coprocessors** can be used to enhance and expand the capabilities of a computer.
25. Parallel processors divide up a problem so that multiple CPUs can work on their assigned portion of the problem simultaneously.
26. **RISC** technology involves reducing a computer's instruction set to only those instructions that are the most frequently used.
27. **Core memory** consisted of small, ring-shaped pieces of material that could be magnetized, or polarized, in one of two directions.
28. **Semiconductor memory** is now used in most computers. It consists of transistors etched into a semiconductor material such as silicon.
29. A **microsecond** is a millionth of a second. A **nanosecond** is a billionth of a second. Access to data stored in semiconductor memory is measured in nanoseconds.
30. **RAM**, which stands for **random access memory**, is used for main memory.

31. Some computers improve their processing efficiency by using a limited amount of high-speed memory, called **cache memory**, between the CPU and main memory.
32. RAM memory is said to be **volatile** because the programs and data stored in RAM are erased when the power to the computer is turned off.
33. **ROM** stands for **read only memory**. Data or programs are stored in ROM when the memory is manufactured, and they cannot be altered.
34. **PROM** means **programmable read only memory**. PROM acts the same as ROM except data can be stored into the PROM memory prior to being installed in the computer.
35. **EPROM**, or **erasable programmable read only memory**, can be erased through the use of special ultraviolet devices.
36. **EEPROM**, or **electronically erasable programmable read only memory**, can be electronically erased without being removed from the computer.

KEY TERMS

American Standard Code for Information Interchange (ASCII) *4.6*
Arithmetic/logic unit (ALU) *4.2*
Arithmetic operations *4.2*
ASCII code *4.6*
Binary *4.5*
Bit *4.4*
Bus *4.12*
Byte *4.3*
Cache memory *4.17*
Chip *4.13*
Control unit *4.2*
Coprocessor *4.14*
Core memory *4.15*
Decoding *4.2*
Dynamic RAM (DRAM) *4.16*
EBCDIC *4.6*
EEPROM *4.17*
Electronically erasable programmable read only memory (EEPROM) *4.17*
EPROM *4.17*
Erasable programmable read only memory (EPROM) *4.17*
Even parity *4.7*
Executing *4.2*
Execution cycle *4.11*

Extended Binary Coded Decimal Interchange Code (EBCDIC) *4.6*
Fetching *4.2*
Firmware *4.17*
Hexadecimal *4.7*
IC *4.13*
Instruction cycle *4.11*
Instruction register *4.10*
Instruction set *4.10*
Integrated circuit (IC) *4.13*
K *4.3*
KB *4.3*
Kilobyte (K or KB) *4.3*
Logical operations *4.2*
Machine cycle *4.11*
Machine language instruction *4.10*
Main memory *4.2*
MB *4.3*
Megabyte (MB) *4.3*
Megahertz *4.11*
Memory address *4.3*
Microchip *4.13*
Microcode *4.17*
Microprocessor *4.13*
Microsecond *4.15*
MIPS *4.11*

Motherboard *4.13*
Nanosecond *4.15*
Odd parity *4.7*
Operation code *4.10*
Parallel processing *4.14*
Parity bit *4.7*
Primary storage *4.2*
Programmable read only memory (PROM) *4.17*
PROM *4.17*
RAM *4.16*
Random access memory (RAM) *4.16*
Read only memory (ROM) *4.17*
Registers *4.2*
RISC (reduced instruction set computing) *4.15*
ROM *4.17*
Semiconductor memory *4.15*
Serial processing *4.14*
Static RAM *4.16*
Storing *4.2*
System clock *4.11*
Transistor *4.15*
Volatile *4.17*
Word size *4.12*

REVIEW QUESTIONS

1. Identify the components of the processor unit and describe the functions of each.
2. What are the three items that are stored in main memory? Draw a diagram of main memory and label each of the areas.
3. Define the terms bit and byte. Illustrate how the number 12 is represented in binary, hexadecimal, ASCII, and EBCDIC.
4. What do the letters KB and MB stand for when referring to main memory? What quantity does each represent?
5. Describe how a group of characters entered into the computer as a field are stored in main memory. Draw a diagram to illustrate how the letters in your last name would be stored using the ASCII code. Begin at main memory address 55231.
6. What is parity and how is it used?
7. Why are the binary and hexadecimal number systems used with computers?
8. List and describe the four steps of the machine cycle.
9. What are the three factors that influence the speed of a processor?
10. What is parallel processing and how is it used?
11. Define RAM memory. How is cache memory used by the computer?
12. Describe the process of manufacturing integrated circuits.

CONTROVERSIAL ISSUES

1. Some people feel that industry standards should be set to eliminate the problems caused by incompatibility. For example, unless special enhancements are made, software that is written for an IBM personal computer system will not run on an Apple Macintosh computer. Others feel that standards would restrict competition and product development. Write a paper to discuss your opinions on this topic.
2. The importation of computer goods from foreign manufacturers has affected the computer industry in this country. In addition, the lower cost of producing electronic components outside the United States has caused many U.S. companies to become involved in offshore manufacturing. Discuss whether restrictions should be placed on integrated circuits and other computer goods that are imported or manufactured offshore.

RESEARCH PROJECTS

1. The semiconductor industry continues to develop and introduce new microprocessor and memory chips. Prepare a report on the latest microprocessor and memory chips that are available. Include information on speed and storage capabilities.
2. Research the history of main memory and prepare a report. Include information on the way the data was stored, the speed of the memory, any limitations of the method, the amount of memory that could be used, and the cost of the memory.

◆ A chip is made by building layers of electronic pathways and connections by using conducting and nonconducting materials on a surface of silicon. The combination of these materials into specific patterns forms microscopic electronic components such as transistors, diodes, and capacitors that make up the integrated chip circuit. The application of the materials to the silicon is done through a series of technically sophisticated chemical and photographic processes. Some of the manufacturing steps are shown in the following photographs.

A chip begins with a design developed by an engineer using a computer-aided circuit design program. Some circuits take only a month or two to design, whereas others may take a year or more. The computer-aided design system allows the engineer to rearrange the design of the circuit pathways and then see them displayed on the screen ◁1▷. Most chips have at least four to six layers, but some have up to fifteen. A separate design is required for each layer of the chip circuit. To better review the design, greatly enlarged printouts are prepared ◁2▷. After the design is finalized, a glass photo mask is prepared for each layer ◁3▷. To provide for mass production of the chips, the design is reduced to the actual size of the circuit, approximately 1/4-inch square, and duplicated over one hundred times on the surface of the photo mask. In a process similar to printing a picture from a negative, the photo mask will be used to project the circuit design onto the material used to make the chips.

Although other materials can be used, the most common raw material used to make chips is silicon crystals that have been refined from quartz rocks ◇4◇. The silicon crystals are melted and *grown* into a cylinder, called an ingot, two to three feet long and eight inches in diameter ◇5◇. After being smoothed, the silicon ingot is sliced into wafers four to eight inches in diameter and 4/1000 of one inch thick. Much of the chip manufacturing process is performed in special laboratories called clean rooms. Because even the smallest particle of dust can ruin a chip, rooms are kept 1,000 times cleaner than a hospital operating room. People who work in these facilities must wear special protective clothing called bunny suits ◇6◇. After the wafer has been polished and sterilized, it is placed in a diffusion oven where the first layer of material is added to the wafer surface ◇7◇. These layers of materials will be etched away to form the circuits.

Before etching, a soft gelatin-like emulsion called photoresist is added to the wafer. During lithography ⟨8⟩, the photoresist is covered by a photo mask and exposed to ultraviolet light. The exposed photoresist becomes hard and the covered photoresist remains soft. The soft photoresist and some of the sur-face materials are etched away with chemicals or hot gases leaving what will become the circuit pathways. In some facilities, the etching process is done by a robot ⟨9⟩.

The process of adding material and photoresist to the wafer, exposing it to ultraviolet light, and etching away the unexposed surface, is repeated using a different photo mask for each layer of the circuit. After the circuits are tested on the wafer, they are cut into pieces called die by the use of a diamond saw ⟨10⟩ or a laser.

The individual chip die ◇11◇, approximately 1/4-inch square, are packaged in a hard plastic case ◇12◇. This case contains pins that connect the chip to a socket on a circuit board ◇13◇.

Output from the Computer

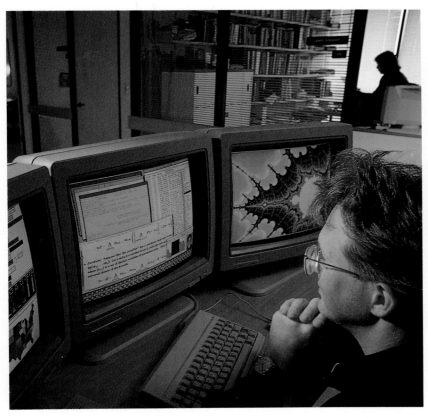

OBJECTIVES

◆ Define the term output

◆ List the common types of reports that are used for output

◆ Describe multimedia

◆ Describe the features and classification of printers

◆ Identify and explain impact printers

◆ Identify and explain nonimpact printers

◆ Describe the types of screens available and list common screen features

◆ List and describe other types of output devices used with computers

Output is the way the computer communicates with the user; there-fore, it is important to know the many forms output can take. In this chapter we discuss the types of output and the devices computers use to produce output.

FIGURE 5-1
Here, you see the same output in hard-copy and soft-copy form. An advantage of hard copy is that the user can write comments on it and route it to other users.

WHAT IS OUTPUT?

◆ **Output** is data that has been processed into a useful form called information that can be used by a person or a machine. Output that is used by a machine, such as a disk or tape file, is usually an intermediate result that eventually will be processed into output that can be used by people.

TYPES OF OUTPUT

◆ The type of output generated from the computer depends on the needs of the user and the hardware and software that are used. Two common types of output are reports and graphics. These types of output can be printed on a printer or displayed on a screen. Output that is printed is called **hard copy** and output that is displayed on a screen is called **soft copy** (Figure 5-1). An exciting method of displaying information, called multimedia, combines several types of output on a single screen.

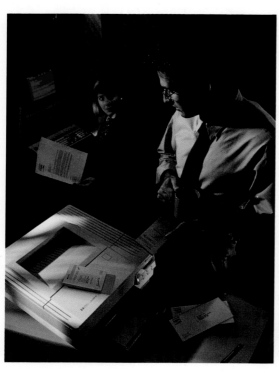

Reports

A **report** is information presented in an organized form. Most people think of reports as items printed on paper or displayed on a screen. For example, word processing documents can be considered reports. Information printed on forms such as invoices or payroll checks can also be considered types of reports. One way to classify reports is by who uses them. An **internal report** is used by individuals in the performance of their jobs. For example, a daily sales report that is distributed to sales personnel is an internal report because it is used only by personnel within the organization. An **external report** is used outside the organization. Sales invoices that are printed and mailed to customers are external reports.

Reports can also be classified by the way they present information. The four types of common reports are: narrative reports, detail reports, summary reports, and exception reports.

Narrative reports may contain some graphic or numeric information, but are primarily text-based reports. These reports, usually prepared with word processing software, include the various types of correspondence commonly used in business such as memos, letters, and sales proposals (Figure 5-2). Detail, summary, and exception reports are primarily used to organize and present numeric-based information.

FIGURE 5-2 ▼
A word processing document is an example of a narrative report.

```
Date:       March 10

To:         Gloria Gilbert

From:       Charlene Kim

Subject:    Electronics Trade Show

The recent Electronics Trade Show was a great success!

At the show, we booked orders of over $2 million.  Most of the
orders were for our new computer product line that was introduced
in January.

In addition to the actual orders, we obtained the names of over
two hundred businesses that are interested in our products.  We
have already added these names to the prospect database and will
be following up with literature and direct phone calls in the
next two weeks.  These names will also be passed along to our
dealers where appropriate.

Based on these successful results, I strongly recommend that we
attend the Computer Products Show next September.  I will obtain
the necessary information and forward it to you as soon as I
receive it.
```

In a **detail report**, each line on the report usually corresponds to one input record that has been read and processed. Detail reports contain a great deal of information and can be quite lengthy. They are usually required by individuals who need access to the day-to-day information that reflects the operating status of the organization. For example, people in the warehouse of a hardware distributor should have access to the location and number of units on hand for each product. The Detail Inventory Report in Figure 5-3 contains a line for each warehouse location for each part number. Separate inventory records exist for each line on the report.

As the name implies, a **summary report** summarizes data. It contains totals for certain values found in the input records. The report shown in Figure 5-4 contains a summary of the total quantity on hand for each part. The information on the summary report consists of totals for each part from the information contained in the detail report in Figure 5-3. Detail reports frequently contain more information than most managers have time to review. With a summary report, however, a manager can quickly review information in summarized form.

An **exception report** contains information that is outside of *normal* user-specified values or conditions, called the exception criteria. Records meeting this criteria are an *exception* to the majority of the data. For example, if an organization wants to know when to reorder inventory items to avoid running out of stock, it would design an exception report. The report would tell which inventory items fell below the reorder points and therefore need to be ordered. An example of such a report is shown in Figure 5-5.

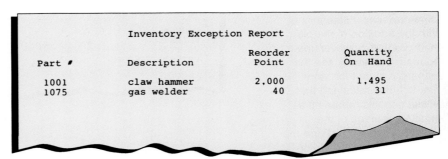

```
                    Detail Inventory Report
                       By Part Number

                                                    Quantity
    Part #          Description        Location      On   Hand
    1001            claw hammer           W1         1,000
    1001            claw hammer           W2           420
    1001            claw hammer           W3            75
    1049            pipe wrench           W2           725
    1075            gas welder            W1            13
    1075            gas welder            W2             7
    1075            gas welder            W4            11
```

FIGURE 5-3
The data for this detail report was obtained from each input record that was read and processed. A line was printed for each record.

```
                   Summary Inventory Report
                       By Part Number
                                       Quantity
    Part #          Description        On   Hand
    1001            claw hammer         1,495
    1049            pipe wrench           725
    1075            gas welder            31
```

FIGURE 5-4
This summary report contains the total on-hand quantity for each part. The report can be prepared using the same data that prepared the report in Figure 5-3.

```
                  Inventory Exception Report

                                    Reorder      Quantity
    Part #          Description       Point       On   Hand
    1001            claw hammer       2,000        1,495
    1075            gas welder           40           31
```

FIGURE 5-5
This exception report lists inventory items with an on-hand quantity below their reorder points. These parts could have been selected from thousands of inventory records. Only these items met the user's exception criteria.

Exception reports help users focus on situations that may require immediate decisions or specific actions. The advantage of exception reports is that they save time and money. In a large department store, for example, there may be over 100,000 inventory items. A detail report containing all inventory items could be longer than 2,000 pages. To search through the report to determine the items whose on-hand quantity was less than the reorder point would be a difficult and time-consuming task. The exception report, however, could select these items, which might number 100 to 200, and place them on a two- to four-page report that could be reviewed in just a few minutes.

Reports are also sometimes classified by how often they are produced. **Periodic reports**, also called **scheduled reports**, are produced on a regular basis such as daily, weekly, or monthly. **On-demand reports** are created for information that is not required on a scheduled basis, but only when it is requested.

Graphics

Another common type of output is computer graphics. In business, **computer graphics** are often used to assist in analyzing data. Computer graphics display information in the form of charts, graphs, or pictures so that the information can be understood easily and quickly (Figure 5-6). Facts contained in a lengthy report and data relationships that are difficult to understand in words can often be summarized in a single chart or graph.

In the past, graphics were not widely used in business because each time data was revised, a graphic artist would have to redraw the chart or graph. Today, relatively inexpensive graphics software makes it possible to redraw a chart, graph, or picture within seconds rather than the hours or days that were previously required. Many application software packages, such as spreadsheets, include graphics capabilities. Analytical and presentation graphics software, discussed in Chapter 2, offer powerful tools for the business user who must present data in a meaningful manner or for the manager who must review, analyze, and make decisions based on data relationships.

FIGURE 5-6
This report lists sales of magazines by school category. With the addition of the pie chart graphic, however, the manager can easily see that colleges account for more than half the sales and that private schools represent a small percentage of the sales. Both the report and the graphic use the same information, but the graphic helps the manager to understand the information more quickly.

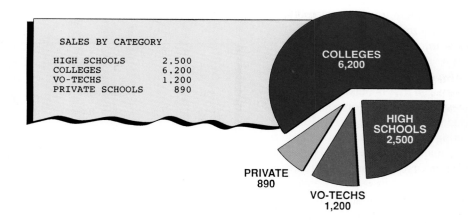

Multimedia

Multimedia is the mixing of text, graphics, video (pictures) and audio (sound) output on a screen. An example would be a multimedia encyclopedia where in addition to the standard text, an animated image with sound is displayed (Figure 5-7).

FIGURE 5-7
Compton's Multimedia Encyclopedia includes 15,000 illustrations, 45 animated sequences, and 60 minutes of sound.

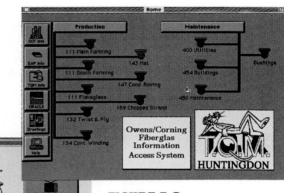

A powerful aspect of multimedia presentations is that the viewer can decide how to proceed. For example, if a technician is viewing a multimedia presentation on machine repair, he or she can select only the repair procedures with which he or she is unfamiliar. With multimedia, the presentation can also include sounds that can help the technician identify a specific problem (Figure 5-8).

One of the technical issues that multimedia developers are working on is the tremendous amount of storage required by full-motion video. One minute of full-motion video requires over two billion bytes of storage. Because of this requirement, most multimedia presentations use animation instead of TV-quality video. The key to more widespread use of full motion is **video compression**, making the large amounts of data take up less storage space. One compression technique currently being developed is **digital video interactive (DVI)**. This technique can reduce storage requirements by a factor of 100 or more.

A variety of devices produce the output created in the information processing cycle. The following sections describe the devices most commonly used.

FIGURE 5-8
Owens/Corning Fiberglas has a multimedia equipment maintenance system that provides general and specific information on pieces of equipment. The multimedia presentation includes sounds that can be used to identify a specific repair problem.

PRINTERS

Printing requirements vary greatly among computer users. For example, the user of a personal computer generally uses a printer capable of printing 100 to 200 lines per minute. Users of mainframe computers, such as large utility companies that send printed bills to hundreds of thousands of customers each month, need printers that are capable of printing thousands of lines per minute. These different needs have resulted in the development of printers with varying capabilities. Due to the many choices available and because printed output is so widely used, users must be familiar with printer features and printer technology when choosing a printer.

Printer Features

To decide which printer to choose for a particular application, it is important to know the different features that a printer might have. The main feature choices include speed, paper types and sizes, print quality, and typefaces. Other features include the capability to print color, printer size, and the type of printer interface.

Speed Printers can be rated as low speed, medium speed, high speed, and very high speed. Low-speed printers print one character at a time and are sometimes called character printers. The rate of printing for low-speed printers is expressed in **characters per second (cps)**. Low-speed printers can print from 50 to 400 characters per second. Medium-speed and high-speed printers are called **line printers** because they can print multiple characters on a line at the same time. The rate of printing for these machines is expressed in the number of **lines per minute (lpm)** that can be printed. Medium-speed printers can print from 300 to 600 lines per minute. Printers that can print from 600 to 3,000 lines per minute are classified as high-speed printers. Very high-speed printers can print in excess of 3,000 lines per minute; some, more than 20,000 lines per minute. Some printers produce an entire page at one time. The speed of these printers is rated in **pages per minute (ppm)**.

Paper Types and Sizes Most printers use either continuous-form or single-sheet paper. Some printers can use both. The pages of **continuous-form paper** are connected together for a continuous flow through the printer. The advantage of continuous-form paper is that it doesn't need to be changed frequently; thousands of pages come connected together. A disadvantage of continuous-form paper is that sometimes the individual pages of the report have to be separated. The advantage of using single-sheet printers is that different types of paper, such as letterhead, can be changed quickly.

Continuous-form paper usually has a page size of 8 1/2 by 11 inches or 11 by 14 inches. Single-sheet paper is usually either standard letter size (8 1/2 by 11 inches) or legal size (8 1/2 by 14 inches). Numerous variations on these sizes are available.

FIGURE 5-9
Many printers can now print different typefaces. Here, examples of the Avant Garde, Helvetica, and Times Roman typefaces are shown in regular, italics, and bold type.

Print Quality When users require high-quality printed output, such as for business or legal correspondence, a printer that provides letter-quality output is chosen. The term **letter quality (LQ)** means that the printed character is a fully formed, solid character like those made by a typewriter. Printers that cannot make fully formed characters, but still offer good print quality are said to provide **near letter quality (NLQ)**. **Draft-quality** printers provide output that a business would use for internal purposes and not for correspondence.

REGULAR	ITALIC	BOLD
Avant Garde	*Avant Garde*	**Avant Garde**
Helvetica	*Helvetica*	**Helvetica**
Times Roman	*Times Roman*	**Times Roman**

Typefaces A **typeface** is a set of letters, numbers, and special characters that have a similar design. Commonly used typefaces include Avant Garde, Helvetica, and Times Roman. Each typeface can be printed in a variety of styles and sizes. An example of a different style is *italics* where the characters are slanted or **bold** where the characters are darker (Figure 5-9). Character size is measured in points. A **point** is 1/72 of an inch. Common point sizes for text used in the body of a document are 10 or 12 points. A complete set of characters in the same typeface, style, and size is called a **font**. One feature you should consider when evaluating a printer is the number of fonts it can print. Some printers can print only a limited number of fonts, whereas others are capable of printing numerous fonts.

Other Printer Features   Other features that you should consider when you evaluate a printer include color output, the amount of desk space the printer requires (referred to as the *footprint*) and the printer interface, which is the way the printer electronically communicates with the computer to which it is attached. With a **serial interface**, data is sent to the printer a single bit at a time. With a **parallel interface**, an entire byte (eight bits) is sent at the same time. Printers with a parallel interface must be located close to the computer, generally within fifty feet. Serial interface printers can be located up to 1,000 feet away from the computer and can even be used at remote locations where the printed information is transmitted over a communication link such as a phone line.

How Are Printers Classified?

Printers can be classified by how they transfer characters from the printer to the paper, either by impact or nonimpact.

Impact printers transfer the image onto paper by some type of printing mechanism striking the paper, ribbon, and character together. One technique is front striking in which the printing mechanism that forms the character strikes a ribbon against the paper from the front to form an image. This is similar to the method used on typewriters. The second technique utilizes a hammer striking device. The ribbon and paper are struck against the character from the back by a hammer to form the image on the paper (Figure 5-10).

Nonimpact printing means that printing occurs without having a mechanism striking against a sheet of paper. For example, ink is sprayed against the paper or heat is used to fuse a fine black powder into the shape of a character.

Impact and nonimpact methods of printing each have advantages and disadvantages. Impact printing can be noisy because the paper is struck when printing occurs. But because the paper is struck, specially treated multipart paper can be used to create multiple copies of a report at one time, such as an invoice, that is routed to different people. Nonimpact printers are quiet and produce high-quality output. However, they do not strike the paper and can therefore only create one printed copy at a time. If additional copies are needed, they must each be printed separately.

IMPACT PRINTERS

The increased use of computers has resulted in the development of a variety of impact printers that vary significantly in speed, quality, and price. Some of these printers, such as dot matrix, daisy wheel, and small page printers, are commonly used on microcomputers or small minicomputers. As the demand for printing information from a computer increases, the use of higher speed printers is required. In industry, minicomputers and mainframes are frequently used to process and print large volumes of data. The two types of impact printers often used to print large volumes of data are chain printers and band printers. The following sections describe the various types of impact printers.

Dot Matrix Printers

Dot matrix printers are used extensively because they are versatile and relatively inexpensive. The Panasonic printer shown in Figure 5-11 is a well-known dot matrix printer that is used with personal computers. Figure 5-12 shows a popular Printronix dot matrix printer that is frequently used with minicomputers. A **dot matrix printer** is an impact printer. Its print head consists of a series of small tubes containing pins that, when pressed against a ribbon and paper, print small dots. The pins are activated by electromagnets that are arranged in a radial pattern. The combination of small dots printed closely together forms the character (Figure 5-13).

◄ FIGURE 5-12
This dot matrix line printer can print up to 800 lines per minute and is used in many business applications. Print heads at each print position allow this device to print an entire line at one time.

FIGURE 5-13 ▼
The print head assembly for a dot matrix printer consists of a series of pins that are fired at the paper by electromagnets. When activated, the pins strike the ribbon that strikes the paper, creating a dot on the paper.

To print a character using a dot matrix printer, the character stored in main memory is sent to the printer's electronic circuitry. The printer circuitry activates the pins in the print head that correspond to the pattern of the character to be printed. The selected pins strike the ribbon and paper and print the character. Most dot matrix printers used with personal computers have a single print head that moves across the page. Dot matrix printers used with larger computers usually have fixed print mechanisms at each print position and can print an entire line at one time.

Dot matrix printers can contain a varying number of pins, depending on the manufacturer and the printer model. Print heads consisting of 9, 18 (two vertical rows of 9), and 24 pins (two vertical rows of 12) are most common. Figure 5-14 illustrates the formation of the letter E using a nine-pin dot matrix printer.

The print quality of dot matrix printers can be improved by overlapping the printed dots. Nine-pin print heads accomplish the overlapping by printing the line twice. The character is slightly offset during the second printing. This results in the appearance of solid characters (Figure 5-15).

Eighteen-pin and 24-pin printers can accomplish the overlapping on a single pass because their multiple rows of pins are slightly offset (Figure 5-16).

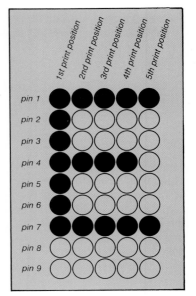

FIGURE 5-14
The letter E is formed with seven vertical and five horizontal dots. As the nine-pin print head moves from left to right, it fires one or more pins into the ribbon, which makes a dot on the paper. At print position 1, it fires pins 1 through 7. At print positions 2 through 4, it fires pins 1, 4, and 7. At print position 5, it fires pins 1 and 7. Pins 8 and 9 are used for lowercase characters such as p, q, y, g, and j that extend below the line.

FIGURE 5-15
The letter E in this example is formed by overlapping, or printing the character twice. When it is printed the second time, the character is printed slightly offset so that much of the space between the dots is filled in. This gives the character a better appearance and makes it easer to read.

FIGURE 5-16
The two rows of pins on this 24-pin print head are slightly offset (one is higher than the other) so that they will overlap and produce a more solid looking character or a smoother line.

```
CONDENSED PRINT - NORMAL CHARACTERS
CONDENSED PRINT - EMPHASIZED CHARACTERS


STANDARD PRINT - NORMAL CHARACTERS
STANDARD PRINT - EMPHASIZED CHARACTERS


ENLARGED PRINT — NORMAL CHARACTERS
ENLARGED PRINT — EMPHASIZED CHARACTERS
```

FIGURE 5-17
Three type sizes are shown in this example—condensed, standard, and enlarged. All three are printed using normal and emphasized (also called bold) print density.

Many dot matrix printers can also print characters in a variety of sizes and densities. Typical sizes include condensed print, standard print, and enlarged print. In addition, each of these print sizes can be printed with increased density or darkness, called bold, or emphasized, print. Figure 5-17 illustrates condensed, condensed bold, standard, standard bold, enlarged, and enlarged bold print.

Dot matrix printers are designed to print in a **bidirectional** manner. That is, the print head, the device that contains the mechanism for transferring the character to the paper, can print as it moves from left to right, and from right to left. The printer does this by storing the next line to be printed in its memory and then printing the line forward or backward as needed. Bidirectional printing greatly increases the speed of the printer.

The feed mechanism determines how the paper moves through the printer. Two types of feed mechanisms found on dot matrix printers are tractor feed and friction

FIGURE 5-18
Each sheet of continuous-form paper is connected with the next. A feed mechanism pulls the paper through the printer using the holes on each side of the form. Perforations between each page allow a printed report to be folded to be separated into individual pages.

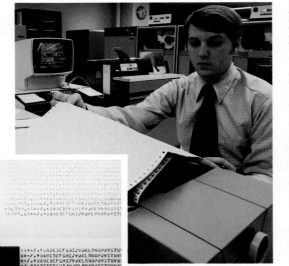

feed. **Tractor feed mechanisms** transport continuous-form paper through the printer by using sprockets, small protruding prongs of plastic or metal, which fit into holes on each side of the paper (Figure 5-18). Where it is necessary to feed single sheets of paper into the printer, **friction feed mechanisms** are used. As the name implies, paper is moved through friction feed printers by pressure on the paper and the carriage, as it is on a typewriter. As the carriage rotates, the paper moves through the printer.

Dot matrix printers are built with a standard, medium, or wide carriage. A standard carriage printer can accommodate paper up to 8 1/2 inches wide. A medium carriage can accommodate paper up to 11 inches wide, and a wide carriage printer can accommodate paper up to 14 inches wide. Using a normal character size, most printers can print from 80 characters per line on a standard carriage to 132 characters per line on a wide carriage.

Some dot matrix printers can print in multiple colors using ribbons that contain the colors red, yellow, and blue in addition to the standard black. Color output is obtained by repeated printing and repositioning of the paper, print head, and ribbon.

Such printers can be useful in printing graphs and charts, but other types of color printers offer a higher quality of color output.

Most dot matrix printers have a graphics mode that enables them to print pictures and graphs (Figure 5-19). In graphics mode, the individual print head pins can be activated separately or in combination to form unique shapes or continuous lines. The flexibility of the dot matrix printer has resulted in widespread use of this type of printer by all types of computer users.

FIGURE 5-19
Some dot matrix printers can produce color output using multicolor ribbons.

Daisy Wheel Printers

The **daisy wheel printer** is an impact printer. The daisy wheel type element resembles the structure of a flower, with many long, thin petals (Figure 5-20). Each *petal* has a raised character at the tip. When printing occurs, the type element (daisy wheel) rotates so that the character to be printed is in the printing position. A hammer extends, striking the selected character against the ribbon and paper, printing the character. Because of the time required to rotate the daisy wheel, the daisy wheel printer is normally slower than a dot matrix printer; however, the print quality is higher because fully formed characters are printed. Printing speeds vary from 20 to 80 characters per second.

An additional feature of the daisy wheel printer is that the daisy wheel can be easily replaced. Daisy wheels come in a variety of sizes and fonts. Therefore, whenever the user wants to change fonts, he or she can remove one daisy wheel and put another wheel on the printer.

The disadvantage of a daisy wheel printer is that it is capable of printing only the characters that are on the wheel. It cannot, therefore, print graphic output. Although daisy wheel printers are still used, they are being replaced by other letter-quality printers.

FIGURE 5-20
The daisy wheel print element consists of a number of arms, each with a character at the end. When the printer is running, the wheel spins until the desired character is lined up with the hammer. The hammer then strikes against the ribbon and paper, printing the character.

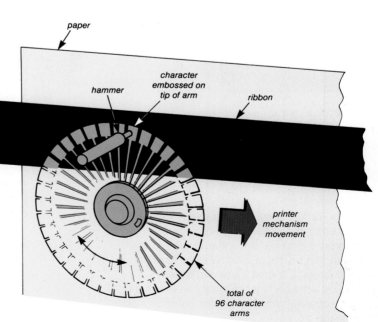

paper

character embossed on tip of arm

hammer

ribbon

printer mechanism movement

total of 96 character arms

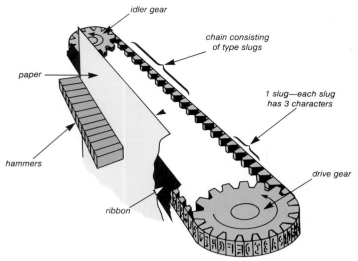

FIGURE 5-21 ▲
The chain printer contains a complete set of characters on several sections of a chain that rotates at a high, constant rate of speed. Print hammers are located at each horizontal print position. The paper and ribbon are placed between the hammers and the chain. As the chain rotates, the hammers fire when the proper characters are in front of their print positions.

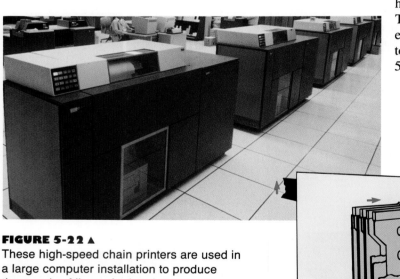

FIGURE 5-22 ▲
These high-speed chain printers are used in a large computer installation to produce thousands of lines of printed output per minute.

FIGURE 5-23 ▶
A band printer uses a metal band that contains solid characters. Print hammers at each print location strike the paper and the ribbon, forcing them into the band to print the character. A print band and a four-position print hammer mechanism that have been removed from the printer are shown on the right.

Chain Printers

The **chain printer** is a widely used high-speed printer. It contains numbers, letters of the alphabet, and selected special characters on a rotating chain (Figure 5-21). The chain consists of a series of type slugs that contain the character set. The character set on the type slugs is repeated two or more times on the chain mechanism. The chain rotates at a very high speed. Each possible print position has a hammer that can strike against the back of the paper, forcing the paper and ribbon against the character on the chain. As the chain rotates, the hammer strikes when the character to be printed is in the proper position.

The chain printer has proven to be very reliable. It produces good print quality up to 3,000 lines per minute. The printers in the large computer installation in Figure 5-22 are chain printers.

Band Printers

Band printers, similar to chain printers, use a horizontal, rotating band containing characters. The characters are struck by hammers located at each print position behind the paper and ribbon to create a line of print on the paper (Figure 5-23).

Interchangeable type bands can be used on band printers. The different type bands contain many different fonts, or print styles. A band printer can produce up to six carbon copies, has good print quality, high reliability, and depending on the manufacturer and model of the printer, can print in the range of 300 to 2,000 lines per minute.

NONIMPACT PRINTERS

Just as there are a variety of impact printers, there are also a variety of nonimpact printers. Ink jet, thermal, and small page printers are frequently used on microcomputers and small minicomputers. Medium- and high-speed page printers are used on minicomputers, mainframes, and supercomputers. The following sections discuss the various types of nonimpact printers.

Ink Jet Printers

A popular type of nonimpact printer is an **ink jet printer**. To form a character, an ink jet printer uses a nozzle that shoots electronically charged droplets of ink onto the page. The droplets pass between electrically charged deflection plates that guide the droplets to the correct position on the paper (Figure 5-24). Ink jet printers produce high-quality print and graphics and are quiet because the paper is not struck as it is by dot matrix or daisy wheel printers. Disadvantages are that ink jet printers cannot use multipart paper, and the ink sometimes smears on soft, porous paper. Ink jet printers that produce color output are also available (Figure 5-25).

◄ FIGURE 5-24
Ink jet printers spray thousands of tiny ink drops toward the paper. The drops are directed to form characters or images by electrically charged deflection plates.

FIGURE 5-25 ▼
An IBM color ink jet printer.

Thermal Printers

Thermal printers use heat to produce fully formed characters and graphic images on special chemically treated paper. Disadvantages of thermal printers are their use of special paper and their relatively slow printing speed. A category of thermal printers called **thermal transfer printers** are used for color printing (Figure 5-26).

Page Printers

The **page printer** is a nonimpact printer that operates similar to a copying machine. The page printer converts data from the computer into light that is directed to a positively charged revolving drum. Each position on the drum touched by the light becomes negatively charged and attracts the toner (powdered ink). The toner is transferred onto the paper and then fused to the paper by heat and pressure. Several methods are used to direct light to the photosensitive drum and create the text or image that will be transferred to the paper. **Laser printers** use a laser beam aimed at the drum by a spinning mirror (Figure 5-27). Other page printers use light emitting diode (LED) arrays or liquid crystal shutters (LCS). With these methods, the light can expose thousands of individual points on the drum. All page printers produce high-quality text and graphics suitable for business correspondence.

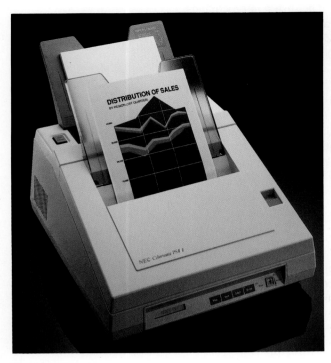

FIGURE 5-26
This thermal transfer printer can produce high-quality color output.

FIGURE 5-27
Laser printers use a process similar to a copying machine. Data from the computer, such as the word SALES ①, is converted into a laser beam ② that is directed by a mirror ③ to a photosensitive drum ④. The sensitized drum attracts toner particles ⑤ that are transferred to the paper ⑥. The toner is fused to the paper with heat and pressure ⑦.

A wide range of page printers are available. Page printers commonly used with personal computers are capable of printing from 4 to 16 pages a minute (Figure 5-28).

Various page printers used with larger computers can print from 20 to 100 pages a minute. **High-speed page printers** can produce printed output at the rate of several hundred pages per minute. As shown in Figure 5-29, these high-speed printers usually consist of a dedicated computer and tape drive to maximize the printing speed.

CONSIDERATIONS IN CHOOSING A PRINTER

◆ In addition to understanding the features and capabilities of the various types of printers that are available, you must consider several other factors before choosing a printer. These include factors such as how much output will be produced and who will use the output. Considering these and the other factors stated in Figure 5-30 will help you to choose a printer that will meet your needs.

FIGURE 5-28
The output shown here was produced by a laser printer. Notice that the output contains a mixture of different sizes and styles of print.

FIGURE 5-29
This laser printer can operate at speeds up to 120 pages per minute. On the left is a tape drive that is used as an input device.

QUESTION	EXPLANATION
How much output will be produced?	Desktop printers are not designed for continuous use. High volume (more than several hundred pages a day) requires a heavy-duty printer.
Who will use the output?	Most organizations want external reports to be prepared on a high-quality printer.
Where will the output be produced?	If the output will be produced at the user's desk, a sound enclosure may be required to reduce the noise of some printers to an acceptable level.
Are multiple copies required?	Some printers cannot use multipart paper.

FIGURE 5-30 Factors that affect the choice of a printer.

SCREENS

The **screen**, also called the **monitor**, **CRT (cathode ray tube)**, or **VDT (video display terminal)**, is another important output device. Screens are used on both personal computers and terminals to display many different types of output. For example, when a user queries a database, the resulting information is frequently displayed on a screen. A screen can also be used to display electronic spreadsheets, electronic mail, and graphs.

Screen Features

Some of the features that should be considered when selecting a screen include size, resolution, and color. A discussion of these and other features follows.

Size The most widely used screens are equivalent in size to a 12- to 16-inch television screen. Although there is no standard number of displayed characters, screens are usually designed to display 80 characters on a line with a maximum of 25 lines displayed at one time. The twenty-fifth line is often reserved for messages or system status reports, not for data. By reducing the character size, some terminals can display up to 132 characters on a single horizontal line. Screens designed for use with desktop publishing or engineering applications come in even larger sizes that can display one or sometimes two 8 1/2 by 11 inch pages of data. One company even makes a screen that can be tilted 90 degrees to display either a long or wide page (Figure 5-31).

FIGURE 5-31
Radius manufactures a screen that can be tilted 90 degrees to display the equivalent of one long or two wide pages.

Resolution The **resolution**, or clarity, of the image on the screen depends on the number of individual dots that are displayed on the screen. Each dot that can be illuminated is called a **picture element**, or **pixel** (Figure 5-32). The greater the number of pixels, the better the screen resolution. The resolution of a screen is important, especially when the screen will be used to display graphics or other nontext information.

Screens used for graphics are called **dot-addressable displays**, or sometimes **bit-mapped displays**. On these monitors, the number of addressable locations on the screen corresponds to the number of pixels, or dots, that can be illuminated. The number of pixels on a screen is determined through a combination of the software in the computer, the graphics capability of the computer, and the screen itself.

◄ **FIGURE 5-32**
The word pixel shown here is made up of pixels as they would be displayed on a dot-addressable or bit-mapped screen. Each pixel is a small spot of light that appears on the screen at the point where it is activated by an electron beam.

Devices are currently available that offer very high-resolution graphics. The resolution of these devices is high enough to provide an image that is almost equivalent to the quality of a photograph (Figure 5-33). High-resolution graphics require a great deal of storage and are more difficult electronically to maintain as a steady image on the screen. In the past few years, however, picture resolutions have greatly improved. In addition, costs have been reduced so that high-resolution graphics are now widely used.

Several graphics standards have been developed, including CGA (Color Graphics Adapter), EGA (Enhanced Graphics Adapter), VGA (Video Graphics Array), super VGA, and 1024. As shown in Figure 5-34, each standard provides for a different number of pixels and colors. Some manufacturers offer even higher resolution screens.

FIGURE 5-33 ▲
Very high-resolution graphics can depict features such as shading, reflections, and highlights as shown in the top photo. Very high-resolution graphics can also be used for simulation exercises; in this case, a flying situation as shown in the bottom photo. Through the use of the computer, this simulation could be changed quickly to show the plane taking off and landing.

FIGURE 5-34
A summary of the graphics resolution standards for display screens.

STANDARD	CGA	HERCULES	EGA	VGA	SUPER VGA	1024
Year	1981	1982	1984	1986	1988	1989
Resolution (W × H)	640 × 200	720 × 348	640 × 350	640 × 480	800 × 600	1024 × 768
Available Colors	16	None	64	262,144	256	262,144
Maximum Displayed Colors	4	None	16	256	16	256

Color Some screens can display information in color. The range of colors available depends on what software and hardware is being used. Microcomputers are available with screens that can simultaneously display 256 colors.

Cursor A **cursor** is a symbol such as an underline character or an arrow that indicates where you are working on the screen. Most cursors blink when they are on the screen so the user can quickly find their location.

Scrolling **Scrolling** is a method of moving lines displayed on the screen up or down one line at a time. For example, as a new line is added to the bottom of the screen, an existing one, from the top of the screen, is removed. The line removed from the screen remains in the computer's memory even though it no longer appears. When the screen is scrolled in the opposite direction (in this example, down), the line from the top that was removed reappears on the screen and the line at the bottom is removed. In addition to scrolling one line at a time, most screens allow users to scroll forward or backward one full screen at a time. This feature is useful in applications such as word processing when a user wants to move quickly through sections of a long document.

Other Screen Features Screen features also include several options that emphasize characters: reverse video, underlining, bold, and blinking. **Reverse video**, also called **inverse video**, refers to reversing the normal display on the screen. For example, it is possible to display a dark background with light characters or a light background with dark characters. Thus, if the normal screen had amber characters on a black background, reverse video shows black characters on an amber background. This feature permits single characters, whole words or lines, and even the entire screen to be reversed. The **underlining** feature allows characters, words, lines, or paragraphs to be underlined. Another feature used for emphasis is bold. **Bold** means that characters are displayed at a greater brightness level than the surrounding text. The **blinking** feature makes characters or words on a screen blink, thus drawing attention to them.

Types of Screens

Several types of screens are used with computers. The most common types are monochrome screens, color screens, plasma screens, and LCD screens. Plasma and LCD screens, which do not use the conventional cathode ray tube technology, are sometimes called **flat panel display screens** because of their relatively flat screens.

Monochrome screens designed for use with personal computers or as computer terminals usually display a single color such as white, green, or amber characters on a black background (Figure 5-35) or black characters on a white background.

FIGURE 5-35
Many users prefer amber or green characters rather than white characters.

FIGURE 5-36
Toshiba manufactures laptop computers that use liquid crystal display (LCD) screens, such as the model T1000 on the left, and plasma technology, such as the T5200 on the right.

The use of **color screens** is increasing. Although they are more expensive than monochrome, they are desireable because much of today's software uses color. Color enables users to more easily read and understand the information on the screen. When color software is used with a monochrome monitor, the output displays as shades of a single color such as shades of grey.

With the development of truly portable computers, that could be conveniently carried by hand or in a briefcase, came a need for an output display that was equally as portable. **Liquid crystal displays (LCD)** and **plasma screens** are flat screens that are used as output displays for a number of laptop computers (Figure 5-36).

How Images Are Displayed on a CRT Screen

Most screens used with personal computers and terminals use cathode ray tube (CRT) technology. When these screens produce an image, the following four steps occur (Figure 5-37):

1. The image to be displayed on the screen is sent electronically from the CPU to the cathode ray tube.
2. An electron gun generates an electron beam of varying intensity, depending on the electronic data received from the CPU.
3. The yoke, which generates an electromagnetic field, moves the electron beam horizontally and vertically on the phosphor-coated screen.
4. The electron beam causes the desired phosphors to emit light. The higher the intensity of the beam, the brighter the phosphor glows. It is the phosphor-emitted light that produces an image on the screen.

FIGURE 5-37
The process of forming an image on a screen begins when the information to be displayed is sent to the CRT ①. Then the electron gun ② generates an electron beam. The yoke ③ directs the beam to a specific spot on the screen ④, where the phosphors struck by the electron beam begin to glow and form an image on the screen.

electron gun

yoke

electron beam

phosphor-coated screen

On most screens, the phosphors that emit the light causing the image on the screen do not stay lit very long. They must be refreshed by having the electron beam light them again. If the screen is not scanned enough times per second, the phosphors will begin to lose their light. When this occurs, it appears that the image on the screen is flickering. To eliminate flicker, the entire screen is refreshed 30 times per second.

The brightness of the image on the screen depends on the intensity of the electron beam striking the phosphor, which in turn depends on the voltage applied to the beam. As the beam scans each phosphor dot, the intensity is varied precisely to turn each dot on or off.

How Color Is Produced   Color is produced on a screen in several ways. Remember that on a monochrome screen, a single electron beam strikes the phosphor-coated screen, causing the chosen phosphor dot to light. If the characters are green on a black background, the phosphors emit a green light when they are activated. Similarly, if the characters are amber on black, the phosphors emit an amber light.

To show color on a screen, each pixel must have three phosphor dots. These dots are red, blue, and green (Figure 5-38). The electron beam must turn on the desired color phosphors within the pixel to generate an image. In the simplest configuration, eight colors can be generated—no color (black), red only, blue only, green only, red and blue (magenta), red and green (yellow), blue and green (blue-green), and red, blue, and green together (white). By varying the intensity of the electron beam striking the phosphors, many more colors can be generated.

Two types of color screens are composite video monitors and RGB monitors. Both monitors produce color images, and both monitors can be used for color graphics. A **composite video monitor** uses a single electron signal to turn on the color phosphors within the pixel. An **RGB monitor** uses three signals, one for each color, red, green, and blue, to turn on the required phosphors. The difference is that the RGB monitor produces a much clearer display with much better color and character resolution.

How Flat Panel Displays Work   A plasma screen is one type of flat panel display. It consists of a grid of conductors sealed between two flat plates of glass. The space between the glass is filled with neon/argon gas. When the gas at an intersection in the grid is electronically activated, it creates an image. Each intersection of the grid of wires in a plasma screen is addressable. Therefore, this type of screen can display characters in a variety of typefaces and graphics such as line drawings, charts, or even pictures.

In an LCD display, a liquid crystal material is deposited between two sheets of polarizing material. When an electrical current passes between crossing wires, the liquid crystals are aligned so that light cannot shine through, producing an image on the screen.

FIGURE 5-38
On color monitors, each pixel contains three phosphor dots: one red, one green, and one blue. These dots can be turned on individually or in combinations to display a wide range of colors.

OTHER OUTPUT DEVICES

Although printers and display devices provide the majority of computer output, other devices are available for particular uses and applications. These include data projectors, plotters, computer output microfilm devices, and voice output devices.

Data Projectors

A variety of devices are available to take the image that appears on a computer screen and project it so that it can be clearly seen by a room full of people. Smaller, lower cost units, called **projection panels**, use liquid crystal display (LCD) technology and are designed to be placed on top of an overhead projector (Figure 5-39).

Larger, more expensive units use technology similar to large screen projection TV sets; separate red, green and blue beams of light are focused onto the screen (Figure 5-40). The projection panels are easily portable and depending on the overhead projector with which they are used, can be located at different distances from the projection screen. The three-beam projectors must be focused and aligned for a specific distance and thus once installed, are usually not moved.

Plotters

A **plotter** is an output device used to produce high-quality line drawings such as building plans, charts, or circuit diagrams. These drawings can be quite large; some plotters are designed to handle paper up to 40 inches by 48 inches, much larger than would fit in a standard printer. Plotters can be classified by the way they create the drawing. The two types are pen plotters and electrostatic plotters.

As the name implies, **pen plotters** create images on a sheet of paper by moving one or more pens over the surface of the paper or by moving the paper under the tip of the pens.

Two different kinds of pen plotters are flatbed plotters and drum plotters. When a **flatbed plotter** is used to plot, or draw, the pen or pens are instructed by the software to move to the down position so the pen contacts the flat surface of the paper. Further instructions then direct the movement of the pens to create the image. Most flatbed plotters have one or more pens of varying colors or widths. The plotter shown in Figure 5-41 is a flatbed plotter that can create color drawings. Another kind of flatbed plotter holds the pen stationary and moves the paper under the pen.

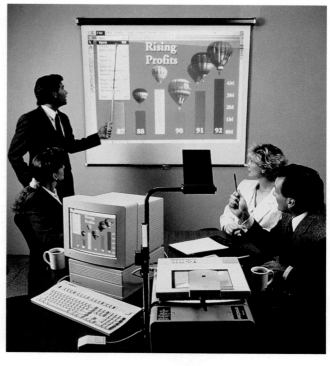

FIGURE 5-39
Projection panels are used together with overhead projectors to display computer screen images to a room full of people.

FIGURE 5-40
This data projector uses three separate red, green, and blue beams to project data onto a screen.

FIGURE 5-41
A color flatbed plotter.

A **drum plotter** uses a rotating drum, or cylinder, over which drawing pens are mounted. The pens can move to the left and right as the drum rotates, creating an image (Figure 5-42). An advantage of the drum plotter is that the length of the plot is virtually unlimited, since roll paper can be used. The width of the plot is limited by the width of the drum.

With an **electrostatic plotter**, the paper moves under a row of wires (called styli) that can be turned on to create an electrostatic charge on the paper. The paper then passes through a developer and the drawing emerges where the charged wires touched the paper. The electrostatic printer image is composed of a series of very small dots, resulting in relatively high-quality output. In addition, the speed of electrostatic plotting is faster than with pen plotters.

Computer Output Microfilm

Computer output microfilm (COM) is an output technique that records output from a computer as microscopic images on roll or sheet film. The images stored on COM are the same as the images that would be printed on paper. The COM recording process reduces characters 24, 42, or 48 times smaller than would be produced on a printer. The information is then recorded on sheet film called **microfiche** or on 16mm, 35mm, or 105mm roll film.

FIGURE 5-42
This drum plotter utilizes eight pens of different colors to create diagrams. As the paper moves forward and back, the pens move left and right and, under software control, draw where instructed.

The data to be recorded by the device can come directly from the computer (online) or from a magnetic tape that was previously produced by the computer (offline) (Figure 5-43). After the COM film is processed, the user can view it.

Microfilm has several advantages over printed reports or other storage media for certain applications. Some of these advantages are:

1. Data can be recorded on the film up to 30,000 lines per minute—faster than all but very high-speed printers.
2. Costs for recording the data are lower. The cost of printing a three-part, 1,000-page report is approximately $28, whereas the cost of producing the same report on microfilm is approximately $3.
3. Less space is required to store microfilm than printed materials. Microfilm that weighs one ounce can store the equivalent of 10 pounds of paper.
4. Microfilm provides a less expensive way to store data. For example, the cost per million characters (megabyte) on a disk is approximately $10, whereas the cost per megabyte on microfilm is approximately 65 cents.

To access data stored on microfilm, a variety of readers are available. They utilize indexing techniques to provide a quick reference to the data. Some microfilm readers can perform automatic data lookup, called **computer-assisted retrieval (CAR)**, under the control of an attached computer. With the powerful indexing software and hardware now available for microfilm, a user can usually locate any piece of data in a 200 million character database in less than 10 seconds, at a far lower cost per inquiry than using an online inquiry system consisting of a computer system that stores the data on a hard disk.

Voice Output

Another important means of generating output from a computer is voice output. **Voice output** consists of spoken words that are conveyed to the user from the computer. Thus, instead of reading words on a printed report or monitor, the user hears the words over earphones, the telephone, or other devices from which sound can be generated.

The data that produces voice output is usually created in one of two ways. First, a person can talk into a device that will encode the words in a digital pattern. For example, the words *The number is* can be spoken into a microphone, and the computer software can assign a digital pattern to the words. The digital data is then stored on a disk. At a later time, the data can be retrieved from the disk and translated back from digital data into voice, so that the person listening will actually hear the words.

A second type of voice generation that holds great promise is called a **voice synthesizer**. It can transform words stored in main memory into speech. The words are analyzed by a program that examines the letters stored in memory and generates sounds for the letter combinations. The software can apply rules of intonation and stress to make it sound as though a person were speaking. The speech is then projected over speakers attached to the computer.

You may have heard voice output used by the telephone company for giving number information. Automobile and vending machine manufacturers are also incorporating voice output into their products. The potential for this type of output is great and it will undoubtedly be used in many products and services in the future.

FIGURE 5-43
The computer output microfilm (COM) process is illustrated here. The computer generates printed images on an output tape that is transferred to the tape drive attached to the COM machine ◇1◇. The COM machine reads the tape and produces reduced images of the printed output on the film ◇2◇—in this example, microfiche sheet film. Then the film can be viewed using special microfilm reader devices ◇3◇.

SUMMARY OF OUTPUT FROM THE COMPUTER

FIGURE 5-44
Some of the more common output devices are summarized in this table.

The output step of the information processing cycle uses a variety of devices to provide users with information. The equipment we discussed in this chapter, including printers, screens, and other output devices are summarized in Figure 5-44.

OUTPUT DEVICE	DESCRIPTION
Printers—Impact	
Dot matrix	Prints text and graphics using small dots.
Daisy wheel	Prints letter-quality documents—no graphics.
Chain	High-speed printer to 3,000 lines per minute—designed to print text.
Band	High-speed printer to 2,000 lines per minute—designed to print text.
Printers—Nonimpact	
Ink jet	Sprays ink onto page to form text and graphic output—prints quietly.
Thermal	Uses heat to produce fully formed characters.
Page	Produces high-quality text and graphics.
Screens	
Monochrome	Displays white, green, or amber images on a black background.
Color	Uses multiple colors to enhance displayed information.
Plasma	A flat screen that produces bright, clear images with no flicker.
LCD	A flat screen used on many laptop computers.
Data Projector	Projects computer screen images to a room full of people.
Plotters	Produces hard-copy graphic output.
COM	Records reduced-size information on sheet film called microfiche or on roll film.
Voice	Conveys information to the user from the computer in the form of speech.

CHAPTER SUMMARY

1. **Output** is data that has been processed into a useful form called information that can be used by a person or a machine.
2. Output that is printed is called **hard copy** and output that is displayed on a screen is called **soft copy**.
3. A **report** is information presented in an organized form.
4. An **internal report** is used within an organization by people performing their jobs.
5. An **external report** is used outside the organization.
6. The major consideration for internal reports is that they are clear and easy to use. For external reports, the quality of the printed output may be important.
7. **Narrative reports** may contain some graphic or numeric information, but are primarily text-based reports.
8. In a **detail report**, each line on the report usually corresponds to one input record.
9. A **summary report** contains summarized data, consisting of totals from detailed input data.
10. An **exception report** contains information that will help users to focus on situations that may require immediate decisions or specific actions.
11. **Periodic reports**, also called **scheduled reports**, are produced on a regular basis such as daily, weekly, or monthly.
12. **On-demand reports** are created for information that is not required on a scheduled basis, but only when it is requested.
13. **Computer graphics** are used to present information so it can be quickly and easily understood.
14. **Multimedia** combines text, graphics, video, and audio output on a screen.

15. The key to use of full-motion video in multimedia is **video compression**, making large amounts of data take up less storage space. **Digital video interactive (DVI)** is one compression technique currently being developed.
16. Computer printer features include speed, paper types and sizes, print quality, typefaces, color capability, size, and interface.
17. The printing rate for low-speed printers is rated in **characters per second (cps)**. The printing rate for medium- and high-speed printers is rated in either **lines per minute (lpm)** or **pages per minute (ppm)**.
18. The pages of **continuous-form paper** are connected for continuous flow through the printer.
19. Print quality is rated as **letter quality (LQ)**, **near letter quality (NLQ)**, or **draft quality**.
20. A **typeface** is a set of letters, numbers, and special characters that have a similar design.
21. Character sizes are measured in points. A **point** is 1/72 of an inch.
22. A complete set of characters in the same typeface, style, and size is called a **font**.
23. Computer printers fall into two broad categories: impact printers and nonimpact printers.
24. **Impact printing** devices transfer the image onto paper by some type of printing mechanism striking the paper, ribbon, and character together.
25. A **nonimpact printer** creates an image without having characters strike against a sheet of paper.
26. Although impact printing is noisy, multiple copies can be made at the same time.
27. Nonimpact printers are quiet and produce high-quality output.
28. **Dot matrix printers** can print text and graphics and are used with more personal computers than any other type of printer.
29. Dot matrix printers have small pins that are contained in a print head. The pins strike the paper and ribbon to print a character.
30. The quality of a dot matrix printer is partly dependent on the number of pins used to form the character.
31. Most dot matrix printers can print condensed print, standard print, and enlarged print.
32. Most dot matrix printers print **bidirectionally**, meaning the print head can print while moving in either direction.
33. **Tractor feed mechanisms** transport continuous-form paper by using sprockets inserted into holes on the sides of the paper.
34. **Friction feed mechanisms** move paper through a printer by pressure between the paper and the carriage.
35. Some dot matrix printers can print in color.
36. **Daisy wheel printers** can print high-quality text, but they cannot print graphics.
37. **Chain printers** use a rotating chain to print up to 3,000 lines per minute.
38. **Band printers** can use interchangeable bands with different fonts.
39. An **ink jet printer** uses a nozzle to spray liquid ink drops onto the page. Some ink jet printers print in color.
40. **Thermal printers** use heat to produce fully formed characters, usually on chemically treated paper.
41. **Page printers** use a process similar to a copying machine to produce high-quality text and graphic output.
42. **High-speed page printers** use a dedicated computer and tape drive and can print several hundred pages per minute.
43. **Screens**, also referred to as **monitors**, **CRTs**, or **VDTs** are used to display data.
44. Most screens are 12 to 16 inches and display 80 characters per line with 25 lines on the screen at one time.
45. The **resolution**, or clarity, of a screen is determined by the number of **pixels** that can be illuminated.
46. The **cursor** is a symbol such as an underline character or an arrow that indicates where you are working on the screen.
47. **Scrolling** refers to the movement of screen data up or down one line or one screen at a time.
48. **Reverse video**, also called **inverse video**, **underlining**, **bold**, and **blinking** are screen features that can be used to emphasize displayed characters.
49. Types of screens include **monochrome screens**, **color screens**, **plasma screens**, and **LCD screens**.
50. **Monochrome screens** usually display green, white, or amber images on a black background or black images on a white background.
51. **Color screens** are being used more because color enables the user to more easily read and understand the information displayed on the screen.
52. **Plasma screens** and **liquid crystal display (LCD) screens** are flat screens often used with portable computers.
53. Most screens utilize cathode ray tube (CRT) technology.
54. To display color on a color monitor, three separate dots (red, blue, and green) are turned on by an electron beam.
55. Two types of color monitors are: **composite video monitors** and **RGB monitors**.
56. **Data projectors** can be used to project a screen image so that it can be seen by a room full of people.
57. A **plotter** is an output device that can create line drawings, diagrams, and similar types of output.

58. **Computer output microfilm (COM)** is an output technique that records output from a computer as microscopic images on roll or sheet film.
59. COM offers the advantages of faster recording speed, lower costs of recording the data, less space required for storing the data, and lower costs for storing the data.
60. Some microfilm readers can perform automatic data lookup, called **computer-assisted retrieval (CAR)**.
61. **Voice output** consists of spoken words that are conveyed to the computer user from the computer.
62. A **voice synthesizer** can transform words stored in main memory into human speech.

KEY TERMS

Band printer *5.12*
Bidirectional *5.10*
Bit-mapped display *5.16*
Blinking *5.18*
Bold *5.18*
Chain printer *5.12*
Characters per second (cps) *5.6*
Color screen *5.19*
Composite video monitor *5.20*
Computer-assisted retrieval (CAR) *5.23*
Computer graphics *5.4*
Computer output microfilm (COM) *5.22*
Continuous-form paper *5.6*
CRT (cathode ray tube) *5.16*
Cursor *5.18*
Daisy wheel printer *5.11*
Detail report *5.3*
Digital video interactive (DVI) *5.5*
Dot-addressable display *5.16*
Dot matrix printer *5.8*
Draft quality *5.6*
Drum plotter *5.22*
Electrostatic plotter *5.22*
Exception report *5.3*
External report *5.2*

Flatbed plotter *5.21*
Flat panel display screen *5.18*
Font *5.6*
Friction feed mechanism *5.10*
Hard copy *5.2*
High-speed page printer *5.15*
Impact printer *5.7*
Ink jet printer *5.13*
Internal report *5.2*
Inverse video *5.18*
Laser printer *5.14*
Letter quality (LQ) *5.6*
Line printer *5.6*
Lines per minute (lpm) *5.6*
Liquid crystal display (LCD) *5.19*
Microfiche *5.22*
Monitor *5.16*
Monochrome screen *5.18*
Multimedia *5.4*
Narrative report *5.2*
Near letter quality (NLQ) *5.6*
Nonimpact printing *5.7*
On-demand report *5.4*
Output *5.2*
Page printer *5.14*
Pages per minute (ppm) *5.6*
Parallel interface *5.7*

Pen plotter *5.21*
Periodic report *5.4*
Picture element *5.16*
Pixel *5.16*
Plasma screen *5.19*
Plotter *5.21*
Projection panel *5.21*
Report *5.2*
Resolution *5.16*
Reverse video *5.18*
RGB monitor *5.20*
Scheduled report *5.4*
Screen *5.16*
Scrolling *5.18*
Serial interface *5.7*
Soft copy *5.2*
Summary report *5.3*
Thermal printer *5.14*
Thermal transfer printer *5.14*
Tractor feed mechanism *5.10*
Typeface *5.6*
Underlining *5.18*
VDT (video display terminal) *5.16*
Video compression *5.5*
Voice output *5.23*
Voice synthesizer *5.23*

REVIEW QUESTIONS

1. Name and describe four types of commonly used reports.
2. What is multimedia? Give an example of multimedia.
3. Define the terms typeface, point, and font.
4. Identify the two major classifications of printers and discuss the advantages and disadvantages of each.
5. How does a dot matrix printer produce an image? What techniques are used on dot matrix printers to improve the print quality?
6. What are the two types of impact printers often used to print large volumes of data?
7. How does an ink jet printer produce images?
8. Explain how a page printer works.
9. List four graphics standards that have been developed for screens.
10. List the steps involved in displaying an image on a CRT screen.
11. Identify two types of flat panel display screens that are commonly used with portable computers.
12. What is a projection panel and how is it used?
13. List several advantages of microfilm over printed reports.
14. Describe the two ways of creating voice output.

CONTROVERSIAL ISSUES

1. When computers were first used in business, some people predicted the paperless office; a place where most documents would only exist electronically in the computer database. While some people think this will still happen, others believe that the widespread use of computers, word processing and spreadsheet software, and low-cost printers has actually resulted in an increase in the amount of paperwork. Do you think computers increase or decrease the amount of paper required?
2. Some people believe that multimedia will revolutionize the way information is presented and the way people learn. Others believe multimedia will have only a limited number of successful applications. For which new applications do you think multimedia can be used?

RESEARCH PROJECTS

1. Make a list of the places where you have heard synthesized voice output. Discuss these with others in your class.
2. Visit a computer store and obtain information on the lowest and highest priced printers. Make a presentation explaining the differences between the two printers.

Auxiliary Storage

OBJECTIVES

◆ Define auxiliary storage

◆ Identify the primary devices used for auxiliary storage

◆ Explain how data is stored on diskettes and hard disks

◆ Describe how data stored on magnetic disks can be protected

◆ Explain how magnetic tape storage is used with computers

◆ Describe three other forms of auxiliary storage: optical disks, solid-state devices, and mass storage devices

◆ Describe how special-purpose storage devices such as smart cards are used

Storage is the fourth and final operation in the information processing cycle. In this chapter we explain storage operations and the various types of auxiliary storage devices that are used with computers. Combining what you learn about storage with your knowledge of input, processing, and output will allow you to complete your understanding of the information processing cycle.

WHAT IS AUXILIARY STORAGE?

◆ It is important to understand the difference between how a computer uses main memory and how it uses auxiliary storage. As you have seen, main memory temporarily stores programs and data that are being processed. **Auxiliary storage**, also called **secondary storage**, stores programs and data when they are not being processed, just as a filing cabinet is used in an office to store records. Records that are not being used are kept in the filing cabinet until they are needed. In the same way, data and programs that are not being used on a computer are kept in auxiliary storage until they are needed. Auxiliary storage devices that are used with computers include devices such as disk and tape drives (Figure 6-1).

FIGURE 6-1
Auxiliary storage is like a filling cabinet in which data is stored until you need it.

computer

tape drive

disk drive

filing cabinet

Most auxiliary storage devices provide a more permanent form of storage than main memory because they are **nonvolatile**, that is, data and programs stored on auxiliary storage devices are retained when the power is turned off. Main memory is volatile, which means that when power is turned off, whatever is stored in main memory is erased.

Auxiliary storage devices can be used as both input and output devices. When they are used to receive data that has been processed by the computer, they are functioning as output devices. When some of their stored data is transferred to the computer for processing, they are functioning as input devices.

User auxiliary storage needs can vary greatly. Personal computer users might find the amount of data to be stored to be relatively small. For example, the names, addresses, and telephone numbers of several hundred friends or customers of a small business might require only 20,000 bytes of auxiliary storage (200 records × 100 characters per record). Users of large computers, such as banks or insurance companies, however, might need auxiliary storage devices that can store billions of characters. To meet the different needs of users, a variety of storage devices are available. We discuss magnetic disk, magnetic tape, and other auxiliary storage devices in this chapter.

FIGURE 6-2
Here, a user is inserting a diskette into the disk drive of an IBM personal computer.

MAGNETIC DISK STORAGE

Magnetic disk is the most widely used storage medium for all types of computers. **Magnetic disk** offers high storage capacity, reliability, and the capability to directly access stored data. There are several types of magnetic disk including diskettes, hard disks, and removable disk cartridges.

Diskettes

In the early 1970s, IBM introduced the diskette as a new type of auxiliary storage. These diskettes were eight inches in diameter and were thin and flexible, hence the name **floppy disks**, or *floppies*. Today, **diskettes** are used as a principal auxiliary storage medium for personal computers (Figure 6-2). This type of storage is convenient, reliable, and inexpensive.

Diskettes are available in a number of different sizes. The most common sizes today are 5 1/4" and 3 1/2" diameters (Figure 6-3).

A diskette consists of a circular piece of thin mylar plastic (the actual disk), which is coated with an oxide material similar to that used on recording tape. On a 5 1/4" disk, the circular piece of plastic is enclosed in a flexible square protective jacket. The jacket has an opening so that a portion of the disk's surface is exposed for reading and writing (recording) as shown on the next page in Figure 6-4.

FIGURE 6-3
The most commonly used diskette for personal computers are 5 1/4" and 3 1/2".

FIGURE 6-4

A 5 1/4" diskette consists of the disk itself enclosed within a protective jacket, usually made of vinyl material. The liner of the diskette is essentially friction-free so that the disk can turn freely, but the liner does contact the disk and keep it clean. The magnetic surface of the diskette, which is exposed through the window in the jacket, allows data to be read and stored. The large hole (hub) in the diskette is used to mount the diskette in the disk drive. The small hole is used by some disk drives as an indicator for where to store data.

On a 3 1/2" disk, the circular piece of plastic is enclosed in a rigid plastic cover and a piece of metal called the shutter covers the reading and writing area. When the 3 1/2" diskette is inserted into a disk drive, the drive slides the shutter to the side to expose the diskette surface (Figure 6-5).

How Is a Diskette Formatted?   Before a diskette can be used for auxiliary storage, it must be formatted. The **formatting** process prepares the diskette so that it can store data and includes defining the tracks, cylinders, and sectors on the surfaces of a diskette (Figure 6-6). A **track** is a narrow recording band forming a full circle around the diskette.

FIGURE 6-5

In a 3 1/2" diskette, the flexible plastic disk is enclosed between two liners that clean the disk surface of any microscopic debris and help to disperse static electricity. The outside cover is made of a rigid plastic material, and the recording window is covered by a metal shutter that slides to the side when the disk is inserted into the disk drive.

FIGURE 6-6

Each track on a diskette is a narrow, circular band. On a diskette containing 40 tracks, the outside track is called track 0 and the inside track is called track 39. The distance between track 0 and track 39 on a 5 1/4" diskette is less that one inch. The disk surface is divided into sectors. This example shows a diskette with nine sectors.

A **cylinder** is defined as all tracks of the same number. For example, track 0 on side 1 of the diskette and track 0 on side 2 of the diskette would be called cylinder 0. The term **sector** is used to refer to a pie-shaped section of the disk. It is also used to refer to a section of a track. When data is read from a diskette, a minimum of one full sector of a track is read. When data is stored on a diskette, at least one full sector of a track is written. The number of tracks and sectors created on a diskette when it is formatted varies based on the capacity of the diskette, the capabilities of the diskette drive being used, and the specifications in the software that does the formatting. Many 5 1/4" diskettes are formatted with 40 tracks and 9 sectors on the surface of the diskette. The 3 1/2" diskettes are usually formatted with 80 tracks and 9 sectors on each side. Even though it is smaller in size, a 3 1/2" diskette has a larger storage capacity than a 5 1/4" diskette.

Formatting is not usually done by the disk manufacturer because different operating systems define the surface of the diskette differently. In addition to defining the disk surface, the formatting process erases any data that is on the disk, analyzes the disk surface for any defective spots, and establishes a directory that will be used to record information about files stored on the diskette.

What Is the Storage Capacity of a Diskette? Knowing the storage capacity of a diskette gives you an idea of how much data or how many programs you can store on the diskette. The amount of data you can store depends on three factors: (1) the number of sides of the diskette used; (2) the recording density of the bits on a track; and (3) the number of tracks on the diskette.

Early diskettes and drives were designed so that data could be recorded on only one side of the diskette. These drives are called **single-sided drives**. Similarly, diskettes on which data can be recorded on one side only are called **single-sided diskettes**. Today, disk drives are designed to record and read data on both sides of the diskette. Drives that can read and write data on both sides of the diskette are called **double-sided drives** and the diskettes are called **double-sided diskettes**. The use of double-sided drives and diskettes *doubles* the amount of data that can be stored on the diskette.

Another factor in determining the storage capacity of a diskette is the recording density provided by the drive. The **recording density** is the number of bits that can be recorded on one inch of the innermost track on the diskette. This measurement is referred to as **bits per inch (bpi)**. The higher the recording density, the higher the storage capacity of the diskette.

The third factor that influences the amount of data that can be stored on a diskette is the number of tracks onto which data can be recorded. This measurement is referred to as **tracks per inch (tpi)**. As we saw earlier in this chapter, the number of tracks depends on the size of the diskette, the drive being used, and how the diskette was formatted.

The capacity of diskettes varies and increases every two or three years as manufacturers develop new ways of recording data more densely. Commonly used diskettes are referred to as either low density or high density. **Low-density diskettes** can store 360K for a 5 1/4" diskette and 720K for a 3 1/2" diskette. Personal computers using **high-density diskettes** (sometimes abbreviated as HD) can store 1.2 megabytes (million characters) on a 5 1/4" diskette and 1.44 megabytes on a 3 1/2" diskette.

How Is Data Stored on a Diskette? Regardless of the type of diskette or how it is formatted, the method of storing data on a diskette is essentially the same. When a 5 1/4" diskette is inserted in a disk drive, the center hole fits over a hub mechanism that positions the diskette in the unit (Figure 6-7). The circular plastic diskette rotates within its cover at approximately 300 revolutions per minute. Data is stored on tracks of the disk, using the same code, such as ASCII, that is used to store the data in main memory. To do this, a recording mechanism in the drive called the **read/write head** rests on the surface of the rotating diskette, generating electronic impulses (Figure 6-8). The electronic impulses change the magnetic polarity, or alignment, of magnetic spots along a track on the disk. The plus or minus polarity represents the 1 or 0 bits being recorded. To access different tracks on the diskette, the drive moves the read/write head from track to track. When reading data from the disk, the read/write head senses the magnetic spots that are recorded on the disk along the various tracks and transfers the data to main memory. When writing, the read/write head transfers data from main memory and stores it as magnetic spots on the tracks on the recording surface.

FIGURE 6-7
A cutaway drawing of a 5 1/4" disk drive. When you insert a diskette in a drive, the center hole is positioned between the collet and the hub. After you close the door to the disk drive, the disk is engaged and begins rotating within the protective jacket at approximately 300 RPM.

What Is Access Time? Data stored in sectors on a diskette must be retrieved and placed in main memory to be processed. The time required to access and retrieve the data is called the **access time**.

The access time for a diskette drive depends on four factors:

1. **Seek time**, the time it takes to position the read/write head over the proper track.
2. **Rotational delay** (also called **latency**), the time it takes for the sector containing the data to rotate under the read/write head.
3. **Settling time**, the time required for the read/write head to be placed in contact with the disk.
4. **Data transfer rate**, the time required to transfer the data from the disk to main memory.

FIGURE 6-8
The read/write heads move back and forth over the openings on both sides of the protective jacket to read or write data on the disk.

The access time for diskettes varies from about 175 milliseconds (one millisecond equals 1/1000 of one second) to approximately 300 milliseconds. What this means to the user is that, on the average, data stored in a single sector on a diskette can be retrieved in approximately 1/5 to 1/3 of one second.

The Care of Diskettes With reasonable care, diskettes provide an inexpensive and reliable form of storage. In handling diskettes, you should take care to avoid exposing them to heat, magnetic fields, and contaminated environments such as dust, smoke, or salt air. One advantage of the 3 1/2" diskette is that its rigid plastic cover provides more protection for the data stored on the plastic disk inside than the flexible cover on a 5 1/4" diskette. Figure 6-9 shows you ways to properly care for your diskettes. Because the read/write head actually comes in contact with the diskette surface, wear takes place and the diskette will eventually become unreadable. To protect against loss, you should backup or copy data onto other diskettes.

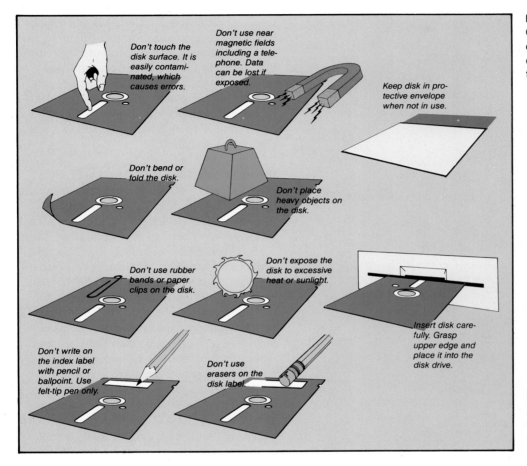

FIGURE 6-9
Guidelines for the proper care of 5 1/4" diskettes. Most of the guidelines also apply to 3 1/2" diskettes.

FIGURE 6-10
A hard disk consists of one or more disk platters. Each side of the platter is coated with an oxide substance that allows data to be magnetically stored.

Hard Disks

Hard disks provide larger and faster auxiliary storage capabilities than diskettes. **Hard disks** consist of one or more rigid metal platters coated with an oxide material that allows data to be magnetically recorded on the surface of the platters (Figure 6-10). These disks are permanently mounted inside the computer and are not removable like diskettes. On hard disks, the metal platters, the read/write heads, and the mechanism for moving the heads across the surface of the disk are enclosed in an airtight, sealed case. This helps to ensure a clean environment for the disk.

FIGURE 6-11
A high-speed, high-capacity fixed disk drive in a stand-alone cabinet.

FIGURE 6-12
A mainframe computer can have dozens of fixed disk storage devices attached to it.

FIGURE 6-13
This hard disk drive shows the access arm and the read/write heads, which are over the surface of the disks. These heads are extremely stable. They can read and write tracks very close together on the surface of the disk.

spindle

disc surface

read/write head

access arm

On minicomputers and mainframes, hard disks are sometimes called **fixed disks** because they cannot be removed like diskettes. They are also referred to as **direct-access storage devices (DASD)**. These hard disks are larger versions of the hard disks used on personal computers and can be either mounted in the same cabinet as the computer or enclosed in their own stand-alone cabinet (Figure 6-11).

While most personal computers are limited to two to four disks drives, minicomputers can support 8 to 16 disk devices, and mainframe computers can support over 100 high-speed disk devices. Figure 6-12 shows a large number of disk units attached to a single mainframe computer.

What Is the Storage Capacity of a Hard Disk? Hard drives contain a spindle on which one or more disk platters are mounted (Figure 6-13). On many drives, each surface of a platter can be used to store data. Thus, if one platter is used in the drive, two surfaces are available for data. If two platters are used, four surfaces are available for data, and so on. Naturally, the more platters, the more data that can be stored on the drive.

The storage capacity of hard drives is measured in megabytes or millions of bytes (characters) of storage. Common sizes for personal computers range from 20MB to 100MB of storage and even larger sizes are available; 20MB of storage is equivalent to approximately 10,000 double-spaced typewritten pages. Some disk devices used on large computers can store billions of bytes of information (Figure 6-14). A billion bytes of information is called a **gigabyte**.

FIGURE 6-14
The IBM 3390 disk drive, shown here being assembled, can store 22.7 billion bytes of data.

How Is Data Stored on a Hard Disk?

Storing data on hard disks is similar to storing data on diskettes. In order to read or write data on the surface of the spinning disk platter, the disk drives are designed with access arms, or actuators. The **access arms**, or **actuators**, contain one or more read/write heads per disk surface. As the disk rotates at a high rate of speed, usually 3600 revolution per minute, the read/write heads move across its surface. These read/write heads *float* on a cushion of air and do not actually touch the surface of the disk. The distance between the head and the surface varies from approximately ten to twenty millionths of an inch. As shown in Figure 6-15, the close tolerance leaves no room for any type of contamination. If some form of contamination is introduced or if the alignment of the read/write heads is altered by something accidentally jarring the computer, the disk head can collide with and damage the disk surface, causing a loss of data. This event is known as a **head crash**. Because of the time needed to repair the disk and to reconstruct the data that was lost, head crashes can be extremely costly to users in terms of both time and money.

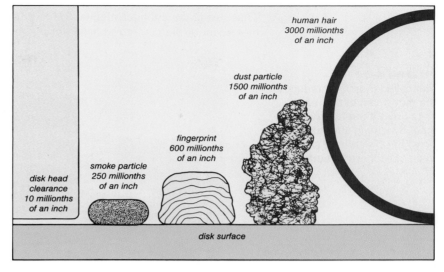

FIGURE 6-15
The clearance between a disk head and the disk surface is about 10 millionths of an inch. With this small difference, contamination such as a smoke particle, fingerprint, dust particle, or human hair could render the drive unusable. Sealed disk drives are designed to minimize contamination.

How Is Data Physically Organized on a Hard Disk?

Depending on the type of disk drive, data is physically organized in one of two ways. One way is the sector method and the other is the cylinder method.

The **sector method** for physically organizing data on disks divides each track on the disk surface into individual storage areas called sectors (Figure 6-16). Each sector can contain a specified number of bytes. Data is referenced by indicating the surface, track, and sector where the data is stored.

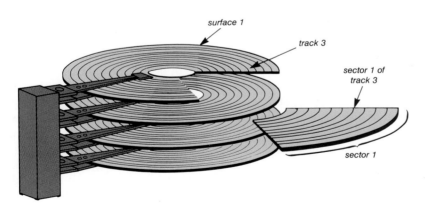

FIGURE 6-16
The sector method of disk addressing divides each track into a number of sectors. To locate data, the surface, track, and sector where the data is stored are specified.

With the **cylinder method**, all tracks of the same number on each recording surface are considered part of the same cylinder (shown on the next page in Figure 6-17). For example, the fifth track on all surfaces would be considered part of cylinder five. All twentieth tracks would be part of cylinder twenty, and so on. When the computer requests data from a disk using the cylinder method, it must specify the cylinder, recording surface, and record number. Because the access arms containing the read/write heads all move together, they are always over the same track on all surfaces. Thus, using the cylinder method to record data *down* the disk surfaces reduces the movement of the read/write head during both reading and writing of data.

FIGURE 6-17
The cylinder method reduces the movement of the read/write head (thereby saving time) by writing information *down* the disk on the same track of successive surfaces.

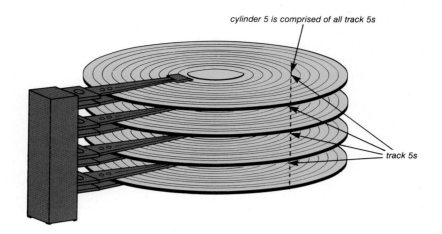

cylinder 5 is comprised of all track 5s

track 5s

Advantages of Using a Hard Disk on a Personal Computer

A hard disk drive on a personal computer provides many advantages for users. Because of its large storage capacity, a hard disk can store many software application programs and data files. When a user wants to run a particular application or access a particular data file on a hard disk, it is always available. The user does not have to find the appropriate diskette and insert it into the drive. In addition, the faster access time of a hard disk reduces the time needed to load programs and access data. The typical access time of a hard disk for a personal computer is between 15 and 80 milliseconds.

Other Types of Hard Disks

We discuss other devices that use hard disk technology in this section. These include removable disks, hard cards, and disk cartridges.

Removable Disks Removable disk units were introduced in the early 1960s and for nearly 20 years were the most prevalent type of disk storage on minicomputers and mainframes. During the 1980s, however, removable disks began to be replaced by hard fixed disks that offered larger storage capacities and higher reliability.

Removable disk devices consist of the drive unit, which is usually in its own cabinet, and the removable recording media, called a **disk pack**. Removable disk packs consist of five to eleven metal platters that are used on both sides for recording data. The recording capacity of these packs varies from 10 to 300 megabytes of data. One advantage of removable disk packs is that the data on a disk drive can be quickly changed by removing one pack and replacing it with another. This can be accomplished in minutes. When removable disk packs are not mounted in a disk drive they are stored in a protective plastic case. When the packs are being used, the plastic case is usually placed on top of the drive unit. Figure 6-18 shows a large installation of removable disk devices with the empty protective disk pack cases on top of the drives.

FIGURE 6-18
A large installation of removable disk drives showing the protective disk pack cases on top of the drive units.

Hard Cards One option for installing a hard disk in a personal computer is a hard card. The **hard card** is a circuit board that has a hard disk built onto it. Hard cards provide an easy way to expand the storage capacity of a personal computer because the board can be installed into an expansion slot of the computer (Figure 6-19).

access arm

read/write head

disc surface

spindle

FIGURE 6-19
A hard card is a hard disk on a circuit board that can be mounted in a computer's expansion slot. Notice that a transparent cover (above) allows you to see the disk platter and access arm.

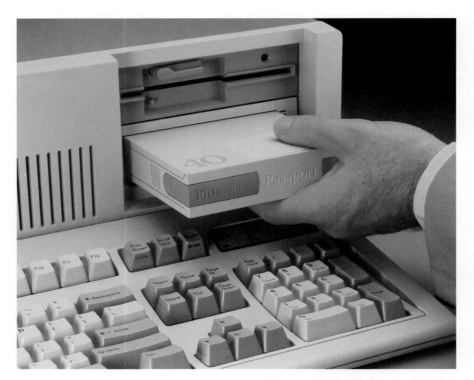

FIGURE 6-20
A removable hard disk cartridge allows a user to remove and transport the entire hard disk from computer to computer or to lock it up in a safe.

Disk Cartridges Another variation of disk storage available for use with personal computers is the removable disk cartridge. **Disk cartridges**, which can be inserted and removed from a computer (Figure 6-20), offer the storage and fast access features of hard disks and the portability of diskettes. Disk cartridges are often used when data security is an issue. At the end of a work session, the disk cartridge can be removed and locked up, leaving no data on the computer.

Protecting Data Stored on a Disk

Regardless of whether you are using diskettes or hard disks, you must protect the data you store on the disk from being lost. Disk storage is reusable, and data that is stored on a disk may be overwritten and replaced with new data. This is a desirable feature allowing users to remove or replace unwanted files. However, it also raises the possibility of accidentally removing or replacing a file that you wanted to keep. To protect programs and data stored on disks, there are several things you can do.

How Is a Diskette Write-Protected? One way to protect the data and programs stored on a 5 1/4" diskette is to use the write-protect notch. This notch is located on the side of the diskette. To prevent writing to a diskette, you cover this notch with a small piece of removable tape. Before writing data onto a diskette, the disk drive checks the notch. If the notch is open, the drive will proceed to write on the diskette. If the notch is covered, the disk drive will not write on the diskette (Figure 6-21). On 3 1/2" diskettes, the situation is reversed. Instead of a write-protect notch, there is a small window in the corner of the diskette. A piece of plastic in the window can be moved to open and close the window. If the write-protect window is closed, the drive can write on the diskette. If the window is open, the drive will not write on the diskette.

Backup Storage Another way to protect programs and data stored on disks is by creating backup storage. Backup storage means creating a copy of important programs and data. To backup diskettes, simply copy the data on one diskette to another diskette. Diskettes are also commonly used to backup the data stored on a hard disk of a personal computer. Because hard disks can store large quantities of data (20MB, 40MB, or even 100MB) many diskettes are required for backup. For example, approximately thirty 3 1/2" diskettes (720,000 characters each) are required to back up a hard disk containing 20 million characters. Data stored on the hard disks of minicomputers and mainframes must also be backed up. Magnetic tape, another form of auxiliary storage, is commonly used to backup data stored on large-capacity hard disks.

FIGURE 6-21
Data cannot be written on the 3½-inch diskette on the upper left because the window in the corner of the diskette is open. A small piece of plastic covers the window of the 3½-inch diskette on the upper right, so data can be written on this diskette. The reverse situation is true for the 5¼-inch diskettes. The write-protect notch of the 5¼-inch diskette on the lower left is covered and, therefore, data cannot be written to the diskette. The notch of the 5¼-inch diskette on the lower right, however, is open. Data can be written to this diskette.

MAGNETIC TAPE

During the 1950s and early 1960s, prior to the introduction of removable disk pack drives, magnetic tape was the primary method of storing large amounts of data. Today, even though tape is no longer used as the primary method of auxiliary storage, it still functions as a cost-effective way to store data that does not have to be accessed immediately. In addition, tape serves as the primary means of backup for most medium and large systems and is often used when data is transferred from one system to another.

Magnetic tape consists of a thin ribbon of plastic. The tape is coated on one side with a material that can be magnetized to record the bit patterns that represent data. The most common types of magnetic tape devices are reel-to-reel and cartridge. Reel-to-reel tape is usually 1/2-inch wide and cartridge tape is 1/4-inch wide (Figure 6-22).

FIGURE 6-22
A computer operator is positioning a reel of magnetic tape on a tape device (top). A standard 10 1/2-inch reel of magnetic tape (left).

FIGURE 6-23
The tape read/write head senses and records the electronic bits that represent data.

FIGURE 6-24
Older style reel-to-reel magnetic tape storage devices are shown behind newer style tape units.

FIGURE 6-25
Newer style tape drives allow the user to slide the tape into a slot at the front of the unit. The drive automatically threads the tape onto an internal take-up reel.

Reel-to-Reel Tape Devices

Reel-to-reel tape devices use two reels: a supply reel to hold the tape that will be read or written on, and the take-up reel to temporarily hold portions of the supply reel tape as it is being processed. At the completion of processing, tape on the take-up reel is wound back onto the supply reel. As the tape moves from one reel to another, it passes over a read/write head (Figure 6-23), an electromagnetic device that can read or write data on the tape.

Older style tape units (Figure 6-24) are vertical cabinets with vacuum columns that hold five or six feet of slack tape to prevent breaking during sudden start or stop operations.

Newer style tape units (Figure 6-25) allow a tape to be inserted through a slot opening similar to the way videotapes are loaded in a videocassette recorder. This front-loading tape drive takes less space and can be cabinet mounted. The drive automatically threads the end of the tape onto an internal take-up reel. Because of their size and cost, reel-to-reel tape drives are used almost exclusively on minicomputer and mainframe systems.

Reels of tape usually come in lengths of 300, 1,200, 2,400 and 3,600 feet and can store up to 200 megabytes of data.

Cartridge Tape Devices

Cartridge tape is frequently used for backup on personal computers. Faster and higher storage capacity cartridge tapes are also increasingly replacing reel-to-reel tape devices on minicomputers and mainframes. Cartridge tape units are designed to be internally mounted or in a separate external cabinet (Figure 6-26).

How Is Data Stored on Magnetic Tape?

Tape is considered a **sequential storage** media because the computer must record and read tape records one after another. Binary codes, such as ASCII and EBCDIC, are used to represent data stored on magnetic tape. Within a code, each character is represented by a unique combination of bits. The bits are stored on tape in the form of magnetic spots (Figure 6-27). The magnetic spots are organized into rows, called channels, that run the length of the tape. A combination of bits in a vertical column (one from each channel) is used to represent a character. An additional bit is used as a parity bit for error checking.

FIGURE 6-26
Cartridge tape drives are an effective way to back up and store data that would otherwise require numerous diskettes.

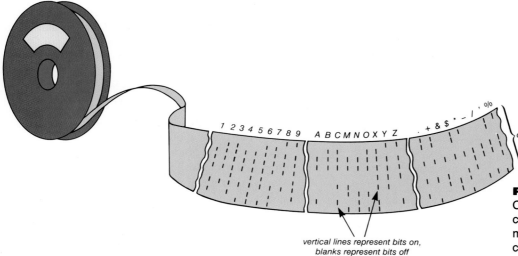

vertical lines represent bits on, blanks represent bits off

FIGURE 6-27
One of the most common coding structures found on magnetic tape is the EBCDIC code, which is stored in nine channels on the tape. Eight channels are used to store the bits representing a character. The ninth channel is for the error-checking parity bit.

Tape density is the number of bits that can be stored on an inch of tape. As on disk drives, tape density is expressed in bits per inch, or bpi. Commonly used tape densities are 800, 1,600, 3,200 and 6,250 bpi. Some of the newer cartridge tape devices can record at densities of over 60,000 bpi. The higher the density, the more data that can be stored on a tape.

Data is recorded on tape in **blocks** which usually consist of two or more records. The individual records are referred to as **logical records**. The group of records making up the block is referred to as a **physical record**. For example, there could be three employee payroll records (three logical records) contained within one block (one physical record) on tape. Each time a tape read or write operation takes place, one physical record is processed. In between each block is a gap of approximately .6 inches called and **interblock gap (IBG)**, or an **interrecord gap (IRG)**. This gap provides room for the tape to slow down and stop after each block has been read. Blocking logical records together has two advantages. First, the space on the tape is used more efficiently than if logical records were written one at a time. Second, because an entire

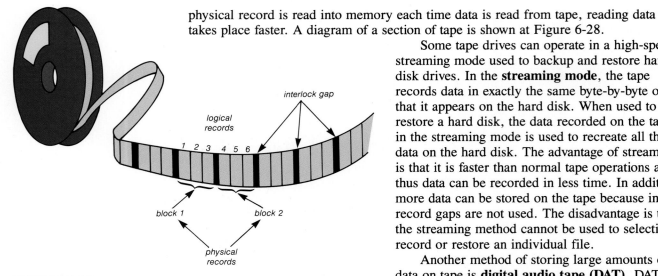

physical record is read into memory each time data is read from tape, reading data takes place faster. A diagram of a section of tape is shown at Figure 6-28.

Some tape drives can operate in a high-speed streaming mode used to backup and restore hard disk drives. In the **streaming mode**, the tape records data in exactly the same byte-by-byte order that it appears on the hard disk. When used to restore a hard disk, the data recorded on the tape in the streaming mode is used to recreate all the data on the hard disk. The advantage of streaming is that it is faster than normal tape operations and thus data can be recorded in less time. In addition, more data can be stored on the tape because inter-record gaps are not used. The disadvantage is that the streaming method cannot be used to selectively record or restore an individual file.

Another method of storing large amounts of data on tape is **digital audio tape (DAT)**. DAT uses **helical scan technology** to write data at much higher densities across the tape at an angle instead of down the length of the tape (Figure 6-29). Using this method, tape densities can be as high as 61,000 bpi.

FIGURE 6-28
Three logical records are stored in each block, or physical record, in this diagram. An entire block of records is brought into main memory each time the tape file is read.

FIGURE 6-29
Using helical scan technology, data is recorded at a higher density across the tape at an angle. Conventional tape drives record data in channels running the length of the tape.

OTHER FORMS OF AUXILIARY STORAGE

The conventional disk and tape devices we just described comprise the majority of auxiliary storage devices and media, but other means for storing data are sometimes used. These include optical disks, solid-state devices, and mass storage devices.

Optical Disks

Enormous quantities of information are stored on **optical disks** by using a laser to burn microscopic holes on the surface of a hard plastic disk (Figure 6-30).

FIGURE 6-30
To record data on an optical disk (left), a laser burns microscopic holes on the surface (right).

A lower power laser reads the disk by reflecting light off the disk surface. The reflected light is converted into a series of bits that the computer can process (Figure 6-31).

FIGURE 6-31
To record data on an optical disk, a high-power laser heats the surface and makes a microscopic pit. To read data, a low-power laser light is reflected from the smooth unpitted areas and is interpreted as a 1 bit. The pitted areas do not reflect the laser beam and are interpreted as 0 bits.

A full-size, 14-inch optical disk can store 6.8 billion bytes of information. Up to 150 of these disks can be installed in automated disk library systems that provide over one trillion bytes (called a **terabyte**) of online storage. The smaller disks, just under five inches in diameter, can store over 800 million characters, or approximately 1100 times the data that can be stored on a standard density 3 1/2" diskette. That's enough space to store approximately 400,000 pages of typed data. The smaller optical disks are called **CDROM**, an acronym for compact disk read-only memory (Figure 6-32). They use the same laser technology that is used for the CDROM disks that have become popular for recorded music.

FIGURE 6-32
An optical compact disk can store hundreds of times the data as on a diskette of similar dimensions.

Most optical disks are prerecorded and cannot be modified by the user. These disks are used for applications such as an auto parts catalog where the information is changed only occasionally, such as once a year, and a new updated optical disk is created. Optical disk devices that provide for one-time recording are called **WORM** devices, an acronym for write once, read many. Erasable optical disk drives are just starting to be used. The most common erasable optical drives use **magneto-optical technology**, in which a magnetic field changes the polarity of a spot on the disk that has been heated by a laser.

FIGURE 6-33
Solid-state storage devices use rows of RAM chips to emulate a conventional rotating disk drive. This solid-state device, with a RAM memory board shown in front, can transfer data 15 to 20 times faster than a rotating disk system.

Because of their tremendous storage capacities, entire catalogs or reference materials can be stored on a single optical disk. Some people predict that optical disks will someday replace data now stored on film such as microfiche.

Solid-State Devices

To the computer, solid-state storage devices act just like disk drives, only faster. As their name suggests, they contain no moving parts, only electronic circuits. **Solid-state storage** devices use the latest in random access memory (RAM) technology to provide high-speed data access and retrieval. Rows of RAM chips (Figure 6-33) provide megabytes of memory that can be accessed much faster than the fastest conventional disk drives. Solid-state storage devices are significantly more expensive than conventional disk drives offering the same storage capacity. Unlike disk or tape systems, solid-state storage devices are volatile; if they lose power their contents are lost. For this reason, these devices are usually attached to emergency power backup systems.

Mass Storage Devices

Mass storage devices provide automated retrieval of data from a library of storage media such as tape or data cartridges. Mass storage is ideal for extremely large databases that require all information to be readily accessible even though any one portion of the database may be infrequently required. Mass storage systems take less room than conventional tape storage and can retrieve and begin accessing records within seconds. Figure 6-34 shows a mass storage system that uses tape cartridges.

FIGURE 6-34
This is the inside of an automated mass storage system that uses tape cartridges. A robot arm with a camera mounted on top can access and load any one of thousands of tape cartridges in an average of 11 seconds. Each cartridge is a 4 × 4-inch square and about one-inch thick and can hold up to 200 megabytes of data. The tapes are stored in a circular cabinet referred to as a silo.

Special-Purpose Storage Devices

Several devices have been developed for special-purpose storage applications. Two of these are smart cards and optical cards.

Smart cards are the same size and thickness of a credit card and contain a thin microprocessor capable of storing recorded information (Figure 6-35). When it is inserted into compatible equipment, the information on the smart card can be read and if necessary, updated. A current user of smart cards is the U.S. Marine Corps, who issues the cards to recruits instead of cash. Each time a recruit uses the card, the transaction amount is subtracted from the previous balance. Other uses of the card include employee time and attendance tracking (instead of time cards) and security applications where detailed information about the card holder is stored in the card.

Optical cards can store up to 800 pages of text or images on a device the size of a credit card (Figure 6-36). Applications include automobile records and the recording of personal and health-care data.

FIGURE 6-35
Smart cards are credit card-sized devices that contain a microprocessor in the left center of the card. The microprocessor can store up to 64,000 bits of information.

FIGURE 6-36
This optical card can store up to 800 pages of information and images. It is about the size of a credit card.

SUMMARY OF AUXILIARY STORAGE

◆ Auxiliary storage is used to store programs and data that are not currently being processed by the computer. In this chapter, we discussed the various types of auxiliary storage used with computers. The chart on the next page in Figure 6-37 provides a summary of the auxiliary storage devices we covered. What you have learned about

FIGURE 6-37
A summary of the various
auxiliary storage devices.

these devices and storage operations in general can now be added to what you have learned about the input, processing, and output operations to complete your understanding of the information processing cycle.

DEVICE	DESCRIPTION
Magnetic Disk	
Diskette	Plastic storage media that is reliable and low in cost.
Hard disk	Fixed metal platter storage media that provides large storage capacity and fast access.
Removable disk	Large disk drives with removable disk packs.
Hard card	Hard disk that is built on a circuit board and installed in an expansion slot of a personal computer.
Disk cartridge	Combines storage and access features of hard disks and portability of diskettes.
Magnetic Tape	
Reel tape	Magnetic tape device using the reel-to-reel method of moving tape.
Tape cartridge	Magnetic tape device using the cartridge method of holding tape.
Other Storage Devices	
Optical storage	Uses lasers to record and read data on a hard plastic disk. Provides high quality and large storage capacity.
Solid-state	Uses RAM chips to provide high-speed data access and retrieval.
Mass storage	Automated retrieval of storage media such as tape or data cartridges.
Special-Purpose Storage Devices	
Smart card	Contains a thin microprocessor capable of storing recorded information.
Optical card	Credit card-sized device that stores text and images.

CHAPTER SUMMARY

1. **Auxiliary storage** is used to store data that is not being processed on the computer.
2. **Magnetic disk** is the most widely used storage medium for all types of computers and offers high storage capacity, reliability, and the capability to directly access stored data.
3. The most common diskette sizes are 5 1/4" and 3 1/2" in diameter.
4. A diskette consists of a plastic disk enclosed within a square protective jacket. A portion of the surface of the disk is exposed so data can be stored on it.
5. The **formatting** process prepares the diskette so that it can store data and includes defining the tracks, cylinders, and sectors on the surfaces of a diskette.
6. Data is stored along the tracks of a diskette. A **track** is a narrow recording band forming a full circle around the diskette.
7. A **cylinder** is defined as all tracks of the same number.
8. The term **sector** is used to refer to a pie-shaped section of the disk. It is also used to refer to a section of a track.
9. When data is read from a diskette, a minimum of one full sector of a track is read. When data is stored on a diskette, at least one full sector of a track is written.
10. The factors affecting disk storage capacity are the number of sides of the disk used; the recording density; and the number of tracks on the disk.
11. The **recording density** is stated as the number of bits that can be recorded on one inch of the innermost track on a disk. The measurement is referred to as **bits per inch (bpi)**.
12. To read or write data on a diskette, it is placed in the disk drive. Within its protective covering the diskette rotates at about 300 revolutions per minute. The **read/write head** rests on the diskette and senses the magnetic spots or generates electronic impulses that represent the bits.

13. The time required to access and retrieve data stored on a diskette is called the **access time**.
14. Access time depends on four factors: (1) **seek time**, the time it takes to position the read/write head on the correct track; (2) **rotational delay time**, or **latency**, the time it takes for the data to rotate under the read/write head; (3) **settling time**, the time required for the head to be placed in contact with the disk; and (4) **data transfer rate**, the amount of data that can be transferred from the disk to main memory.
15. Diskettes should not be exposed to heat or magnetic fields. With proper care, diskettes provide an inexpensive and reliable form of storage.
16. A **hard disk** consists of one or more rigid metal platters coated with an oxide material.
17. On hard disks, the metal platters, read/write heads, and access arm are enclosed in an airtight, sealed case.
18. To read and write data on a hard disk, an **access arm** moves read/write heads in and out. The heads float very close to the surface of the disk, generating or sensing the magnetic spots that represent bits.
19. The **sector method** (identifying the surface, track, and sector number) or the **cylinder method** (identifying the cylinder, recording surface, and record number) can be used to physically organize and address data stored on disk.
20. **Removable disk** devices consist of the drive unit, which is usually in its own cabinet, and the removable recording media, called a **disk pack**.
21. A **hard card** consists of a circuit board that has a hard disk built onto it. The board can be installed into an expansion slot of a personal computer.
22. **Disk cartridges**, which can be inserted and removed from a computer, offer the storage and fast access features of hard disks and the portability of diskettes.
23. The write-protect notch on 5 1/4" diskettes and the window on 3 1/2" diskettes can be used to protect the data stored on a disk from being overwritten.
24. To backup storage means to create a copy of important programs and data on a separate disk or tape.
25. The normal method for diskette backup is to copy the data onto another diskette. For large-capacity hard disks, the data is often copied to magnetic tape.
26. **Magnetic tape** consists of a thin ribbon of plastic. The tape is coated on one side with a material that can be magnetized to record the bit patterns that represent data.
27. The most common types of magnetic tape devices are reel-to-reel and cartridge.
28. Data is recorded on magnetic tape as a series of magnetic spots along a horizontal channel. Each spot represents a bit in a coding scheme.
29. **Tape density** is the number of bits that can be stored on one inch of tape. Common densities are 800, 1,600, 3,200, and 6,520 bytes per inch.
30. Data is recorded on tape in **blocks** which usually consist of two or more records. The individual records are referred to as **logical records**. The group of records making up the block is referred to as a **physical record**.
31. An **interblock gap (IBG)**, also called an **interrecord gap (IRG)**, separates the blocks stored on tape.
32. In the **streaming mode**, a tape records data in exactly the same byte-by-byte order as it appears on the disk.
33. **Digital audio tape (DAT)** uses **helical scan technology** to write data at much higher densities across the tape at an angle instead of down the length of the tape.
34. **Optical disks** use a laser to burn microscopic holes on the surface of a hard plastic disk. Optical disks can store enormous quantities of data.
35. **CDROM** is an acronym for compact disk read-only memory.
36. Optical disks that provide for one-time recording are called **WORM** devices.
37. Most erasable optical disk drives use **magneto-optical technology** that uses a magnetic field to change the polarity of a spot on the disk that has been heated by a laser.
38. RAM chips are used in **solid-state storage** devices to provide fast data access and retrieval. These devices are volatile.
39. Automated retrieval of storage media is provided by **mass storage** devices.
40. **Smart cards** are the same size and thickness of a credit card and contain a thin microprocessor capable of storing recorded information.
41. **Optical cards** can store up to 800 pages of text or images on a device the size of a credit card.

KEY TERMS

Access arm *6.9*
Access time *6.6*
Actuator *6.9*
Auxiliary storage *6.2*
Bits per inch (bpi) *6.5*
Block *6.15*
Cartridge tape *6.14*
CDROM *6.17*
Cylinder *6.5*
Cylinder method *6.9*
Data transfer rate *6.6*
Digital audio tape (DAT) *6.16*
Direct-access storage device
  (DASD) *6.8*
Disk cartridge *6.12*
Diskette *6.3*
Disk pack *6.10*
Double-sided diskette *6.5*
Double-sided drive *6.5*
Fixed disk *6.8*
Floppy disk *6.3*

Formatting *6.4*
Gigabyte *6.8*
Hard card *6.11*
Hard disk *6.7*
Head crash *6.9*
Helical scan technology *6.16*
High-density diskette *6.5*
Interblock gap (IBG) *6.15*
Interrecord gap (IRG) *6.15*
Latency *6.6*
Logical record *6.15*
Low-density diskette *6.5*
Magnetic disk *6.3*
Magnetic tape *6.13*
Magneto-optical technology *6.17*
Mass storage *6.18*
Nonvolatile *6.3*
Optical card *6.19*
Optical disk *6.16*
Physical record *6.15*
Read/write head *6.6*

Recording density *6.5*
Reel-to-reel *6.14*
Removable disk *6.10*
Rotational delay *6.6*
Secondary storage *6.2*
Sector *6.5*
Sector method *6.9*
Seek time *6.6*
Sequential storage *6.14*
Settling time *6.6*
Single-sided diskette *6.5*
Single-sided drive *6.5*
Smart card *6.19*
Solid-state storage *6.18*
Streaming mode *6.16*
Tape density *6.15*
Terabyte *6.17*
Track *6.4*
Tracks per inch (tpi) *6.5*
WORM *6.17*

REVIEW QUESTIONS

1. Write a definition for auxiliary storage. Explain how auxiliary storage differs from main memory.
2. Draw a diagram of a diskette and label the main parts.
3. Explain the terms track, cylinder, and sector.
4. What are the three factors influencing the storage capacity of a diskette? Briefly describe each of them.
5. What is the difference in storage capacity between low-density and high-density diskettes? Give values for both 5 1/4" and 3 1/2" diskettes.
6. What is access time? List the four factors that influence the access time of a disk drive.
7. Describe how data is stored on a hard disk.
8. What are the advantages of using a hard disk drive on a personal computer?
9. Explain how 5 1/4" and 3 1/2" diskettes may be write-protected.
10. Write a definition for magnetic tape. What are the two most common types of magnetic tape devices?
11. What is the streaming mode of tape operation and how is it used?
12. What is a WORM device? How do they differ from magneto-optical technology?

CONTROVERSIAL ISSUES

1. Some people believe that the increasing capacities and decreasing costs of storage devices such as CDROM will eventually result in the replacement of most books, magazines, and other printed matter. What do you think?
2. Many personal computer users and some businesses do not regularly backup the data on their computer systems. Rather than spending time each day to perform backup, they are willing to take the risk that they may have to spend a considerable amount of time recreating their database if their system should experience a disk failure. Discuss the pros and cons of such a policy.

RESEARCH PROJECTS

1. Visit a computer store and obtain information on the different types of hard disk drives that are available for personal computers. Summarize your findings and include data on price, storage capacity, and access speed. Calculate the cost per megabyte of storage for each drive.
2. Pick several different types of businesses. Write a paper on how their information storage requirements differ. Comment on what types of data should be online and available for immediate access.
3. Write a paper on the possible applications of smart card technology.

File and Database Management

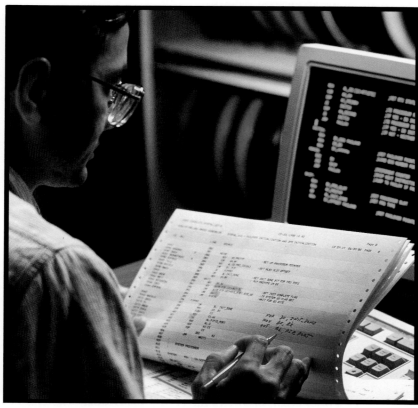

OBJECTIVES

◆ Discuss data management and explain why it is needed

◆ Describe sequential files, indexed files, and direct (or relative) files

◆ Explain the difference between sequential retrieval and random retrieval of records from a file

◆ Describe the data maintenance procedures for updating data including adding, changing, and deleting

◆ Discuss the advantages of a database management system (DBMS)

◆ Describe hierarchical, network, and relational database systems

◆ Explain the use of a query language

◆ Describe the responsibilities of a database administrator

◆ Discuss personal computer database systems

In order to provide maximum benefit to a company, data must be carefully managed, organized, and used. The purpose of this chapter is to explain the need for data management, how files on auxiliary storage are organized and maintained (kept current), and the advantages, organization, and use of databases. Learning this information will help you to better understand how data and information is stored and managed on a computer.

DATA MANAGEMENT

◆ For data to be useful, it must be accurate and timely. **Data management** refers to procedures that are used to keep data accurate and timely and provide for the security and maintenance of data. The purpose of data management is to ensure that data required for an application will be available in the correct form and at the proper time for processing. Both data processing professionals and users share the responsibility for data management.

To illustrate the need for data management, we use an example of a credit bureau (Figure 7-1). A summary of the application follows.

FIGURE 7-1
A credit bureau must carefully manage the data in its database because the data is what the credit bureau sells to its customers. Data management procedures must be in place to make sure the data is accurate and timely and to provide for the proper security and maintenance of the data.

- Data entered into the database of the credit bureau is acquired from numerous sources such as banks and stores. The data includes facts such as income, history of paying debts, bankruptcies, and certain personal information.
- When the data is entered into the computer, it becomes a part of the database. The database is stored on an auxiliary storage device such as a hard disk.
- Customers of the credit bureau can call and request information about an individual. The credit bureau employee uses a terminal to retrieve information from the database and gives the caller a brief credit history of the person in question. The system also generates a record that causes a complete credit history to be printed that night. The credit report will be mailed to the credit bureau customer the following day.

Data Accuracy

For a user, such as a credit bureau customer, to have confidence in the information provided by a computer system, he or she first must be confident that the data used to create the information is accurate. **Data accuracy**, sometimes called **data integrity**, means that the source of the data is reliable and the data is correctly reported and entered. For example, if someone incorrectly reports to the credit bureau that an individual did not pay a bill and this information becomes part of the database, a customer could be denied credit unjustly. Users must be confident that the people and organizations providing data to the credit bureau provide accurate data. In addition, the data they obtain must be entered into the computer correctly. This is called reliable data entry. In the credit bureau example, if a bank reports that the balance on a credit card account is $200.00, but the balance is incorrectly entered as $2,000.00, the information generated would be invalid.

Accurate data must also be timely. Timely data has not lost its usefulness because time has passed. For example, assume that two years ago a salary of $15,000.00 was entered for an individual. Today, that data is not timely because two years have passed and the person may be earning either less or more.

Data Security

Data management also includes managing data security. **Data security** refers to protecting data to keep it from being misused or lost. This is important because misuse or loss of data can have serious consequences. In the credit bureau example, a person's credit rating and history of financial transactions are confidential. People do not want their credit information made available to unauthorized persons. Therefore, the credit bureau must develop systems and procedures that allow only authorized personnel to access the data stored in the database. In addition, if the data in the database should be lost or destroyed, the credit bureau must have a way to recover the correct data. Therefore, data in an information system is periodically copied, or backed up. **Backup** refers to making copies of data files so that if data is lost or destroyed, a timely recovery can be made and processing can continue. Backup copies are normally kept in fireproof safes or in a separate building so that a single disaster, such as a fire, will not destroy both the primary and the backup copy of the data.

Data Maintenance

Data maintenance, another aspect of data management, refers to the procedures used to keep data current. When data is maintained it is called **updating** and includes procedures for **adding** new data, such as creating a record for a new person to include in the credit bureau database; **changing** existing information, such as posting a change of address to an existing record; and **deleting** obsolete information, such as removing inactive records.

Summary of Data Management

Data management includes managing data accuracy, data security, and data maintenance (Figure 7-2). If your attention to data management is inadequate, the information processing system will not perform as intended and the output will have little value.

ACCURACY	SECURITY	MAINTENANCE
Reliable Source Data	Authorized Access	Updating:
Reliable Data Entry	Backup	Adding
Timeliness		Changing
		Deleting

FIGURE 7-2
Data management is concerned with data accuracy, data security, and data maintenance.

The data accumulated by companies is stored in files and databases. In the next section we discuss files and how they are organized and maintained. Then we continue with a discussion of databases.

FIGURE 7-3
This payroll file stored on a diskette contains payroll records. Each payroll record contains a social security field, a name field, and a paycheck amount field.

WHAT IS A FILE?

A *file* is a collection of related records that is usually stored on an auxiliary storage device. A *record* is a collection of related fields and a *field*, also called a *data item* or *data element*, is a fact. Figure 7-3 shows a portion of a payroll file that is stored on a diskette. The file contains a separate record for each employee. Each record contains a social security field, a name field and a paycheck amount field. Files contain data that relates to one topic. For example, a business can have separate files that contain data related to payroll, personnel, inventory, customers, vendors, and so forth. Most companies have hundreds, sometimes thousands of files that store the data pertaining to their business. Files that are stored on auxiliary storage devices can be organized in several different ways, and there are advantages and disadvantages to each of these types of file organization.

TYPES OF FILE ORGANIZATION

Three types of file organization are used on auxiliary storage devices. These are sequential, indexed, and direct or relative, file organization.

Sequential File Organization

Sequential file organization means that records are stored one after the other, normally in ascending or descending order, based on a value in each record called the key. The **key** is a field that contains unique data, such as a Social Security number, part number, or customer number that is used to identify the records in a file (Figure 7-4). Files stored on tape are processed as sequential files. Files on disk may be sequential, indexed, or direct.

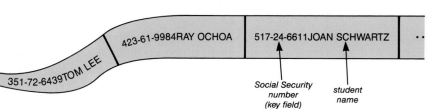

Social Security number (key field)   *student name*

FIGURE 7-4
The student records in this file are stored sequentially in ascending order using the Social Security number as the key field. The records in this file will be retrieved sequentially.

Records stored using sequential file organization are also retrieved sequentially. **Sequential retrieval**, also called **sequential access**, means that the records in a file are retrieved one record after another in the same order that the records are stored. For example, in Figure 7-4, the file contains student records stored in sequence by Social Security number. The data in the file is retrieved one record after another in the same sequence that it is stored in the file.

Sequential retrieval has a major disadvantage — since records must be retrieved one after another in the same sequence as they are stored, the only way to retrieve a record is to read all preceding records first. Therefore, in Figure 7-4, if the record for Joan Schwartz must be retrieved, the records for Tom Lee and Ray Ochoa must be read before retrieving the Joan Schwartz record. Because of this, sequential retrieval is not used when fast access to a particular record is required. However, sequential retrieval is appropriate when records are processed one after another. An example is a weekly payroll application where employee records are processed sequentially.

A common use of sequential files in a computer center is as backup files, where data from a disk is copied onto a tape or another disk so that if the original data becomes unusable, the original file can be restored from the backup file. Sequential files can also be used for batch processing where records are all processed at one time.

Indexed File Organization

A second type of file organization is called **indexed file organization**. Just as in a sequential file, records are stored in an indexed file in an ascending or descending sequence based on the value in the key field of the record.

An indexed file, however, also has an index which itself is a file. An **index** consists of a list containing the values of a key field and the corresponding disk address for each record in a file (Figure 7-5). In the same way that an index for a book points to the page where a particular topic is covered, the index for a file points to the place on a disk where a particular record is located. The index is updated each time a record is added to or deleted from the file. The index is retrieved from the disk and placed in main memory when the file is to be processed.

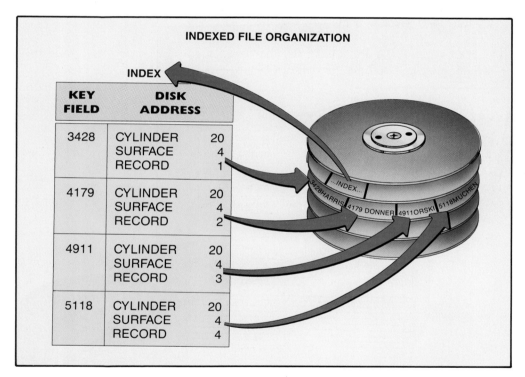

INDEXED FILE ORGANIZATION

FIGURE 7-5
The index in an indexed file contains the record key and the corresponding disk address for each record in the file. Here, the index contains the employee number, which is the key for the employee file and the disk address for the corresponding employee record.

Records can be accessed in an indexed file both sequentially and randomly. As we previously discussed, sequential retrieval means that the records in a file are retrieved one record after another in the same order that the records are stored. **Random retrieval**, also called **random access** or **direct access**, means the system can go directly to a record without having to read the preceding records. For example, with sequential retrieval, to read the fiftieth record in a file, records 1 through 49 would be read first. With random retrieval, the system can go directly to the fiftieth record. To directly access a record in an indexed file, the index is searched until the key of the record to be retrieved is found. The address of the record (also stored in the index) is then used to retrieve the record directly from the file without reading any other records. For example, if the personnel office asked for the name of employee number 5118, the index could be searched until key 5118 was found (Figure 7-6). The corresponding disk address (cylinder 20, surface 4, record 4) would then be used to read the record directly from the disk into main memory. An advantage of indexed files is that usually more than one index can be maintained. Each index can be used to access or report records in a particular order. For example, an employee file might have three separate indexes; one for employee number, a second for employee name, and a third for Social Security number. A disadvantage of indexed files is that searching an index for a record in a large file can take a long time. In addition, maintaining one or more indexes adds to the processing time whenever a record is added or deleted.

FIGURE 7-6
In this example of random retrieval using an indexed file, the user has requested the employee name of employee number 5118 ①. When the employee number is placed in main memory ②, the index for the file would be searched until employee number 5118 is found ③. The corresponding disk address in the index ④ is then used to access the record stored at that address. Here, the record containing the employee name Muchen is retrieved and placed in main memory ⑤. This name is then sent back to the terminal to answer the user's request ⑥.

Direct or Relative File Organization

A **direct file** or **relative file** (sometimes called a random file) uses the key value of a record to determine the location on the disk where the record is or will be stored. For example, a program could establish a file that has nine locations where records can be stored. These locations are sometimes called **buckets**. A bucket can contain multiple records. If the key in the record is a one-digit value (1–9), then the value in the key would specify the relative location within the file where the record was stored. For example, the record with key 3 would be placed in relative location, or bucket, 3, the record with key 6 would be placed in relative location 6, and so on.

Usually, the storage of records in a file is not so simple. For instance, what if the maximum number of records to be stored in a direct file is 100 and the key for the record is a four-digit number? In this case, the key of the record could not be used to specify the relative or actual location of the record because the four-digit key could result in up to 9,999 records. In cases such as these, an arithmetic formula is used to calculate the relative or actual location in the file where the record is stored. The process of using a formula and performing the calculation to determine the location of a record is called **hashing**.

One hashing method is the division/remainder method. With this method, the computer uses a prime number close to but not greater than the number of records to be stored in the file. A **prime number** is a number divisible by only itself and 1. For example, suppose you have 100 records. The number 97 is the closest prime number to 100 without being greater than 100. The key of the record is then divided by 97 and the remainder from the division operation is the relative location where the record is stored. For example, if the record key is 3428, the relative location where the record will be stored in the file is location 33 (Figure 7-7).

Direct files present one problem you do not encounter with sequential or indexed files. In all three file organization methods, the key in the record must be unique so that it can uniquely identify the record. For example, the employee number, when acting as the key in an employee file, must be unique. No two employees can have the same number. When a hashing technique is used to calculate a disk address, however, it is possible that two different keys could identify the same location on disk. For example, employee number 3331 generates the same relative location (33) as employee number 3428. When the locations generated from the different keys are the same, they are called **synonyms**. The occurrence of this event is called a **collision**. A method that is often used to resolve collisions is to place the record that caused the collision in the next available storage location. This location may be in the same bucket (if multiple records are stored in a bucket) or in the next bucket (Figure 7-8).

FIGURE 7-7
When the value 3428 is divided by the prime number 97, the remainder is 33. This remainder is used as the bucket where the record with key 3428 is stored in the direct file.

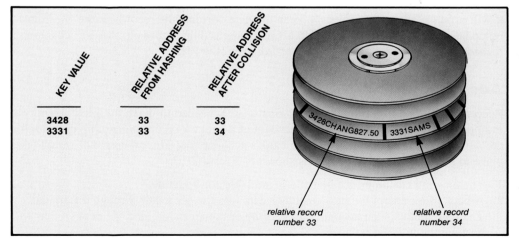

FIGURE 7-8
Sometimes the hashing computation produces synonyms, or records that have the same relative address. In this example, both records have a relative address of 33. When the computer tries to store the second record and finds that location 33 is already full, it stores the second record at the next available location. Here, record 3331 would be stored in location 34.

Once a record is stored in its relative location within a direct file, it can be retrieved either randomly or sequentially. The method normally used with direct files is random retrieval. A record is retrieved from a direct file by performing three steps.

1. The program obtains the key of the record to be retrieved. The value of the key, such as a part number, is entered by the user or is read from another file record such as a sales invoice.

2. The program determines the location of the record to be retrieved by performing the same hashing process as when the record was initially stored. Thus, to retrieve the record with key 3428, the key value would be divided by the prime number 97. The remainder, 33, specifies the location of the bucket where the record is stored.

3. The software directs the computer to bucket 33 to retrieve the record.

Sequential retrieval from a direct file can be accomplished by indicating that the record from the first relative location is to be retrieved, followed by the record from the second relative location, and so on. All the records in the file are retrieved based on their relative location in the file.

Summary of File Organization Concepts

Files are organized as either sequential, indexed, or direct files. Sequential file organization can be used on tape or disk and requires that the records in the file be retrieved sequentially. Indexed files must be stored on disk and the records can be accessed either sequentially or randomly. Direct files are stored on disk and are usually accessed randomly (Figure 7-9).

FIGURE 7-9
The types of storage and the access methods that can be used with each of the three file types.

FILE TYPE	TYPE OF STORAGE	ACCESS METHOD
Sequential	Tape or Disk	Sequential
Indexed	Disk	Random* or Sequential
Direct (Relative)	Disk	Random* or Sequential

* *Primarily accessed as random files*

HOW IS DATA IN FILES MAINTAINED?

Data stored on auxiliary storage must be kept current so that when it is processed it will produce accurate results. To keep the data current, the records in the files must be updated. Updating records within a file means adding records to the file, changing records within the file, and deleting records from the file.

Adding Records

Records are added to a file when additional data is needed to make the file current. For example, if a customer opens a new account at a bank, a record containing the data for the new account must be added to the bank's account file. The process that would take place to add this record to the file is shown in Figure 7-10.

1. The existing customer account file is available for updating.
2. A bank clerk enters the new customer data into the computer through a terminal. The data includes the account number, the customer name, and the deposit that will become the account balance.
3. The update program moves the data entered by the user into the new record area in main memory.
4. The update program writes the new record to the file. The location on the disk where the record is written will be determined by the program that manages the disk. In some cases, a new record will be written between other records in the file. In other cases, such as illustrated in Figure 7-10, the new record will be added to the end of the file.

FIGURE 7-10
In this example of adding records, the file first exists without the new account ◇1◇. The bank clerk enters the account number, customer name, and deposit ◇2◇. This data is used to create a record ◇3◇ that is then added to the file ◇4◇.

Whenever data is stored on auxiliary storage for subsequent use, the capability to add records must be present in order to keep the data current.

Changing Records

Changing data takes place for two primary reasons: (1) to correct data that is known to be incorrect, and (2) to update data when new data becomes available.

As an example of the first type of change, assume in Figure 7-10 that instead of entering HUGH DUNN as the name for the customer, the bank clerk enters HUGH DONE. The error is not noticed and the customer leaves the bank. When the customer receives his statement he notices the error and contacts the bank to request that the spelling of his name be corrected. To do this, the bank clerk would enter HUGH DUNN as a change to the name field in the record. This change replaces data known to be incorrect with data known to be correct.

The bank account example also illustrates the second reason for change—to update data when new data becomes available. This type of change is made when a customer deposits or withdraws money. In Figure 7-11, Jean Martino withdraws $500.00. The following steps occur when the record for Jean Martino must be changed to reflect her withdrawal.

CHANGING RECORDS

** CUSTOMER WITHDRAWAL **

ENTER ACCOUNT NUMBER: 52-4417
ENTER WITHDRAWAL AMOUNT: 500.00

WITHDRAWAL COMPLETE

Obtain account number
Obtain withdrawal amount
Retrieve account record
  subtract withdrawal from balance
Rewrite account record

COMPUTER PROGRAM

|52-4417|
Account Number

|500.00|
Withdrawal

|52-4417JEAN MARTINO2541.71|
Account Record

|52-4417JEAN MARTINO2041.71|
Updated Account Record

FIGURE 7-11
When Jean Martino withdraws $500.00, the bank's records must be changed to reflect her new account balance. In this example, the teller enters Jean Martino's account number and withdrawal amount ①, the account number is used to retrieve Jean's account balance record ②; and the account balance is reduced by the amount of the withdrawal ($500.00) ③. The updated record is then written back to the disk ④.

BEFORE CHANGE

account number
customer name
account balance

52-4417JEAN MARTINO2541.71
77-8972SUSAN BLAKE5411.68
29-4468HUGH DUNN1650.00
45-6641HAL GRUEN 0.00
31-8722NORM DAVIS

AFTER CHANGE

account number
customer name
account balance

52-4417JEAN MARTINO2041.71
77-8972SUSAN BLAKE5411.68
29-4468HUGH DUNN1650.00
45-6641HAL GRUEN 0.00
31-8722NORM DAVIS

1. The bank clerk enters Jean Martino's account number 52-4417 and the amount 500.00.
2. The update program retrieves the record for account number 52-4417 and stores the record in main memory.
3. The program subtracts the withdrawal amount from the account balance in the record. This changes the account balance to reflect the correct balance in the account.
4. After the balance has been changed in memory, the updated record is written back onto the disk. After the change, the account balance has been updated, and the record stored on auxiliary storage contains the new correct account balance.

Changing data stored on auxiliary storage to reflect the correct and current data is an important part of the updating process that is required for data.

Deleting Records

Records are deleted when they are no longer needed as data. Figure 7-12 shows the updating procedures to delete a record for Hal Gruen who has closed his account. The following steps occur to delete the record.

FIGURE 7-12
Here, the account number entered by the teller ①️ is used to retrieve Hal Gruen's account record ②️. The account record is identified as deleted by placing an asterisk in the first position of the record ③️. The record is then written back to the file ④️. The application software is designed to not process records that begin with an asterisk.

1. The teller enters Hal Gruen's account number (45-6641).
2. The update program retrieves the record from the disk using the account number as the key. The record is placed in main memory.

3. The actual processing that occurs to delete a record from a file depends on the type of file organization being used and the processing requirements of the application. Sometimes the record is removed from the file. Other times, as in this example, the record is not removed from the file. Instead, the record is *flagged*, or marked in some manner, so that it will not be processed again. In this example, an asterisk (*) is added at the beginning of the record.
4. After the asterisk is added, the record is written back to the file. The application program is designed to not process records that begin with an asterisk. Even though the record is still physically stored on the disk, it is effectively deleted because it will not he retrieved for processing.

Flagged records are used in applications where data should no longer be processed but must be maintained for some period of time, such as until the end of the year. Periodically, the user can run a utility program that reorganizes the current records and removes the flagged records. Deleting records from auxiliary storage removes records that are no longer needed and makes additional disk space available.

Summary of How Data Is Maintained

Data maintenance is updating or adding, changing, and deleting data stored on auxiliary storage. The maintenance of data is essential for information derived from the processing of that data to be reliable. When updating data, it does not matter if the data is stored as a single file or if it is part of a series of files organized into a database. The concept of adding, changing, and deleting data to keep it current remains the same.

DATABASES: A BETTER WAY TO MANAGE AND ORGANIZE DATA

Most business people realize that next to the skills of their employees, data (and the information it represents) is one of a company's most valuable assets. They recognize that the information accumulated on sales trends, competitors' products and services, employee skills, and production processes is a valuable resource that would be difficult if not impossible to replace.

Unfortunately, in many cases this resource is located in different files in different departments throughout the organization, often known only to the individuals who work with their specific portion of the total information. In these cases, the potential value of the information goes unrealized because it is not known to people in other departments who may need it or it cannot be accessed efficiently. In an attempt to organize their information resources and provide for timely and efficient access, many companies have implemented databases.

WHAT IS A DATABASE?

Previously in this chapter, we've discussed how data elements (characters, fields, and records) can be organized in files. In file-oriented systems, each file is independent and contains all the information necessary to process the records in that file. In a **database**, the data is organized in multiple related files. Because these files are related, users can access data in multiple files at one time. A **database management system (DBMS)** is the software that allows the user to create, maintain, and report the data and file relationships. By contrast, a **file management system** is software that allows the user to create, maintain, and access one file at a time.

WHY USE A DATABASE?

◆ The following example (Figure 7-13) illustrates some of the advantages of a database system as compared to a file-oriented system. Assume that a business periodically mails catalogs to its customers. If the business is using a file-oriented system, it would probably have a file used for the catalog mailing application that contains information about the catalog plus customer information such as customer account number, name, and address. Files that are used in a file-oriented system are independent of one another. Therefore, other applications such as the sales application, that also need to have customer information would each have files that contain the same customer information stored in the catalog mailing file. Thus, in a file-oriented system, the customer data would be duplicated several times in different files. This duplication of data wastes auxiliary storage space. In addition, it makes maintaining the data difficult because when a customer record must be updated, all files containing that data must be individually updated.

In a database system, however, only one of the applications would have a file containing the customer name and address data. That is because in a database system, files are integrated; that is, related files are linked together by the database software either through predefined relationships or through common data fields. In this example, the link could be the customer account number. If the sales file contained the customer account number, name, and address, the catalog mailing file would only need to contain the customer's account number plus the other catalog information. When the catalog application software is executed, the customer's name and address would be obtained from the sales file. The advantage of the database is that because the files are integrated, the customer name and address would only be stored once. This saves auxiliary storage space. It also allows data to be maintained more easily because update information need only be entered once.

As the previous example illustrates, a database system offers a number of advantages over a file-oriented system. These advantages and several others are summarized as follows:

■ **Reduced data redundancy**. Redundant, or duplicate, data is greatly reduced in a database system. Frequently used data elements such as names, addresses, and descriptions are stored in one location. Having such items in one instead of many locations lowers the cost of maintaining the data.

■ **Improved data integrity**. Closely related to reduced data redundancy is the database advantage of improved data integrity. Because data is only stored in one place, it is more likely to be accurate. When it is updated, all applications that use the data will be using the most current version.

FIGURE 7-13

In a file-oriented system, each file contains the customer name and address. In the database system, only the customer file contains the name and address. Other files, such as the catalog file, use the customer number to retrieve the customer name and address when it is needed for processing.

■ **Integrated files**. As we demonstrated by the catalog mailing example in Figure 7-13, a key advantage of a database management system is its capability to *integrate*, or join together, data from more than one file for inquiry or reporting purposes.

■ **Improved data security**. Most database management systems allow the user to establish different levels of security over information in the database. For example, a department manager may have *read only* privileges on certain payroll data: the manager could inquire about the data but not change it. The payroll supervisor would have *full update* privileges: the supervisor could not only inquire about the data but could also make changes. A nonmanagement employee would probably have no access privileges to the payroll data and could neither inquire about nor change the data.

■ **Reduced development time**. Because data is better organized in a database, development of programs that use this data is more efficient and takes less time. The need to create new files is reduced. Instead, new attributes are added to existing files.

Now that we've discussed some of their advantages, let's discuss the ways that databases can be organized.

TYPES OF DATABASE ORGANIZATION

◆ There are three major types of database organization: hierarchical, network, and relational.

Hierarchical Database

In a **hierarchical database** (Figure 7-14), data is organized in a series like a family tree or organization chart (the term hierarchy means an organized series). Like a family tree, the hierarchical database has branches made up of parent and child records. Each **parent record** can have multiple child records. However, each **child record** can have only one parent. The parent record at the top of the database is referred to as the **root record**.

FIGURE 7-14

In this hierarchical database, Johnson, Jefferson, and Longtree are the children of Finance, and Finance is their parent. Finance and Accounting are the children of Business, and Business is their parent. These relationships must be established before the database can be used.

HIERARCHICAL DATABASE

DEPARTMENT — Business

COURSE — Accounting 201 — Finance 301

STUDENT — 2492 Johnson | 2845 Jefferson | 3432 Alvarez | 2492 Johnson | 2845 Jefferson | 3691 Longtree

Hierarchical databases are the oldest form of database organization and reflect the fact that they were developed when the disk and memory capacity of computers was limited and most processing was done in batch mode. Data access is sequential in the sense that an inquiry begins at the root record and proceeds down the branch until the requested data is found. All parent-child relationships are established when the database is created in a separate process that is sometimes called *generating the database*.

After the database is created, access must be made through the established relationships. This points out two disadvantages of hierarchical databases. First, records located in separate branches of the database cannot be accessed easily at the same time. Second, adding new fields to database records or modifying existing fields, such as adding the four-digit ZIP code extension, requires the redefinition of the entire database. Depending on the size of the database, this redefinition process can take a considerable amount of time. The advantage of a hierarchical database is that because the data relationships are predefined, access to and updating of data is very fast.

Network Database

A **network database** (Figure 7-15) is similar to a hierarchical database except that each child record can have more than one parent. In network database terminology, a child record is referred to as a **member** and a parent record is referred to as an **owner**. Unlike the hierarchical database, the network database is able to establish relationships between different branches of the data and thus offers increased access capability for the user. However, like the hierarchical database, these data relationships must be established prior to the use of the database and must be redefined if fields are added or modified.

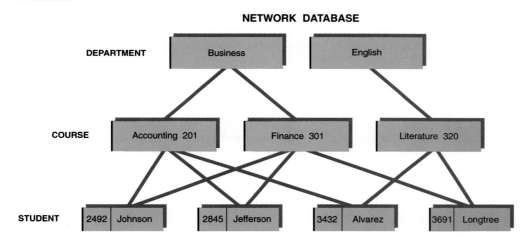

NETWORK DATABASE

FIGURE 7-15
In a network database, lower level (member) records can be related to more than one higher level (owner) record. For example, Longtree's owners are Finance and Literature. Accounting has three members, Johnson, Jefferson, and Alvarez. As in a hierarchical database, these relationships must be established before the database can be used.

Relational Database

The relational database structure is the most recently developed of the three methods and takes advantage of large-capacity, direct-access storage devices that were not available when the hierarchical and network methods were developed. In a **relational database**, data is organized in tables that in database terminology are called **relations**. The tables are further divided into rows (called **tuples**) and fields (called **attributes**). The tables can be thought of as files and the rows as records. The range of values that an attribute can have is called a **domain**. These terms with a Student Master Table are illustrated on the next page in Figure 7-16.

FIGURE 7-16
In a relational database, the terms used to describe files are called tables.

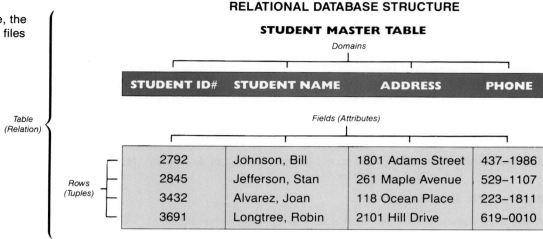

RELATIONAL DATABASE STRUCTURE

STUDENT MASTER TABLE

Domains

STUDENT ID#	STUDENT NAME	ADDRESS	PHONE

Table (Relation)

Fields (Attributes)

Rows (Tuples)

2792	Johnson, Bill	1801 Adams Street	437–1986
2845	Jefferson, Stan	261 Maple Avenue	529–1107
3432	Alvarez, Joan	118 Ocean Place	223–1811
3691	Longtree, Robin	2101 Hill Drive	619–0010

Recall that a key advantage of a database is its capablity to link multiple files together. A relational database accomplishes this by using a common field that exists in each file. For example, in a database for a college, the link between files containing student information could be the student identification number. Hierarchical and network databases can also extract data from multiple files, but in these database structures, the data relationships that will enable the multiple file combination must be defined when the database is created. The advantage of a relational database is that the data relationships do not have to be predefined. The relational database needs only a common field in both data files to make a relationship between them (Figure 7-17). Because it is sometimes difficult to know ahead of time how data will be used, the flexibility provided by a relational database is an important advantage.

FIGURE 7-17
In a relational database, files (called tables) do not require predefined relationships as they do with hierarchal or network databases. Instead, common fields are used to link one table to another. For example, Student ID# could be used to link the Student Master Table in Figure 7-16 above with the Course-Student Table (a). Department ID could be used to link the Department Table (b) with the Course-Master Table (c).

(a) COURSE–STUDENT TABLE

COURSE #	STUDENT ID#
ACC201	2942
ACC201	2845
ACC201	3432
FIN301	2492
FIN301	2845
FIN301	3691
LIT320	3691

(b) DEPARTMENT TABLE

DEPARTMENT ID	DEPARTMENT NAME
BUS	Business
ENG	English

(c) COURSE–MASTER TABLE

COURSE #	COURSE NAME	DEPARTMENT ID	UNITS	MAX ENROLLMENT
ACC201	Advanced Accounting	BUS	4	50
FIN301	Investments	BUS	2	30
LIT320	Modern Literature	ENG	3	20

Another advantage of a relational database is its capability to add new fields. All that need be done is to define the fields in the appropriate table. With hierarchical and network database systems, the entire database has to be *redefined*: existing relationships have to be reestablished to include the new fields. A disadvantage of a relational database is that its more complex software requires more powerful computers to provide acceptable performance.

DATABASE MANAGEMENT SYSTEMS

A number of common database management system features are available, including the following described in Figure 7-18.

FEATURE	DESCRIPTION
Data Dictionary	Defines data files and fields.
Utility Program	Creates files and dictionaries, monitors performance, copies data, and deletes unwanted records.
Security	Controls different levels of access to a database.
Query Language	Allows user to specify report content and format.

FIGURE 7-18
A summary of common database management system features.

- **Data dictionary**. The data dictionary defines each data field that will be contained in the database files. The dictionary is used to record the field name, size, description, type of data (e.g., text, numeric, or date), and relationship to other data elements.
- **Utilities**. Database management system utility programs provide for a number of maintenance tasks including creating files and dictionaries, monitoring performance, copying data, and deleting unwanted records.
- **Security**. Most database management systems allow the user to specify different levels of user access privileges. The privileges can be established for each user for each type of access (retrieve, update, and delete) to each data field. Be aware that without some type of access security, the data in a database is more subject to unauthorized access than in a decentralized system of individual files.
- **Query language**. The query language is one of the most valuable features of a database management system. It allows the user to retrieve information from the database based on the criteria and in the format specified by him or her.

QUERY LANGUAGES: ACCESS TO THE DATABASE

A **query language** is a simple English-like language that allows users to specify what data they want to see on a report or screen display. Although each query language has its own grammar, syntax, and vocabulary, these languages can generally be learned in a short time by persons without a programming background.

A Query Example

Figure 7-19 shows how a user might query a relational database. In this example, we illustrate the relational operations that might be performed when a relational database inquiry is made. These three **relational operations** are select, project, and join. They allow the user to manipulate the data from one or more files to create a unique **view**, or subset, of the total data.

FIGURE 7-19

The three relational operations (select, project, and join) that would be used to produce a response to the query. The query response is referred to as a view.

Query: Display customer name and quantity ordered for all sales orders for Part C-143

SALES ORDERS

SALES ORDER NO.	CUSTOMER NUMBER	PART #	QUANTITY ORDERED
1421	1100	M-200	100
1422	2600	C-143	15
1423	1425	A-101	65
1424	2201	C-143	1000
1425	1087	B-231	4
1426	2890	D-388	140

CUSTOMERS

CUSTOMER NUMBER	NAME	ADDRESS	PHONE
1087	Smith	1820 State	436-8800
1100	Ramirez	231 Elm	619-2200
1425	Gilder	3300 Main	232-0108
2201	Hoffman	675 Oak	457-7030
2600	Redman	1400 College	976-2400
2890	Ingles	117 Adams	629-9021

SELECT: PART C-143

JOIN: BY CUSTOMER NUMBER

PROJECT: CUSTOMER NAME

SALES ORDER	CUSTOMER NUMBER	CUSTOMER NAME	PART #	QUANTITY ORDERED
1422	2600	Redman	C-143	15
1424	2201	Hoffman	C-143	1000

Response to Query (view)

The **select relational operation** selects certain records (rows or tuples) based on user-supplied criteria. In the example, the user queries the database to select records from the sales order file that contain part number C-143. Selection criteria can be applied to more than one field and can include tests to determine if a field is greater than, less than, equal to, or not equal to a value specified by the user. Connectors such as AND and OR can also be used.

The **project relational operation** specifies the fields (attributes) that appear on the query output. In the example, the user wants to see the names of the customers who placed orders for part number C-143.

The **join relational operation** is used to combine two files (relations or tables). In the example, the customer number, a field contained in each file, is used to join the two files. After the query is executed, most query languages allow the user to give the query a unique name and save it for future use.

Structured Query Language

One of the most widely used query languages is **Structured Query Language**, often referred to as **SQL** or *sequel*. Originally developed during the 1970s by IBM, SQL has been incorporated into a number of relational database software packages including ORACLE by Oracle Corporation and INGRES by Relational Technology. IBM actively supports SQL and incorporates it into their two major relational database system products, SQL/DS and DB2. SQL received increased support as the emerging relational database management system query language when, in 1985, the American National

Standards Institute formed a committee to develop industry standards for SQL. The standards were issued in 1987. Today, most database software vendors have incorporated SQL into their products. The standardization of SQL will further accelerate its implementation on a wide range of computer systems from micros to supercomputers. This fact, coupled with the increasing dominance of relational databases, will mean that SQL will be available to many computer users. Figure 7-20 shows an example of the SQL statements that would be used to create the response (view) shown in Figure 7-19.

```
SELECT ORDNO, CUSTNO, CUSTNAME, PARTNO, QTYORD
FROM SALESORDERS, CUSTOMERS
WHERE SALESORDERS.CUSTNO = CUSTOMERS.CUSTNO
ORDER BY ORDNO
```

FIGURE 7-20
These Structured Query Language (SQL) statements will generate the response (view) shown in Figure 7-19. The statements specify that the sales order number (ORDNO), customer number (CUSTNO), part number (PARTNO), and quantity ordered (QTYORD) appear on the report. This information will be taken from the SALESORDERS and CUSTOMERS files. The report information will be taken from records where the customer number (CUSTNO) in the SALESORDERS file matches the customer number in the CUSTOMERS file. Information on the report will be listed in sales order (ORDNO) sequence.

DATABASE ADMINISTRATION

The centralization of an organization's data into a database requires a great deal of cooperation and coordination on the part of the database users. In file-oriented systems, if a user wanted to keep track of some data, he or she would just create another file, often duplicating some data that was already being tracked by someone else. In a database system, the user must first check to see if some or all of the data is already on file and if not, how it can be added to the system. The role of coordinating the use of the database belongs to the database administrator.

The Database Administrator

The **database administrator**, or **DBA**, is the person responsible for managing all database activities (Figure 7-21). In small organizations, this person usually has other responsibilities such as the overall management of the computer resources. In medium and large organizations, the role of the DBA is a full-time job for one or more people. The job of the DBA usually includes the following responsibilities:

- **Database design.** The DBA determines the design of the database and specifies where to add additional data files and records when they are needed.
- **User coordination.** The DBA is responsible for letting users know what data is available in the database and how the users can retrieve it. The DBA also reviews user requests for additions to the database and helps establish priorities for their implementation.
- **Backup and recovery.** The centralization of data in a database makes an organization particularly vulnerable to a computer system failure. The DBA is often responsible for minimizing this risk, making sure that all data is regularly backed up and preparing (and periodically testing) contingency plans for a prolonged equipment or software malfunction.
- **System security.** The DBA is responsible for establishing and monitoring system access privileges to prevent the unauthorized use of an organization's data.

FIGURE 7-21
The database administrator plays a key role in the managing of a company's data. The DBA should possess good technical and management skills.

■ **Performance monitoring**. The performance of the database, usually measured in terms of response time to a user request, can be affected by a number of factors such as file sizes and the types and frequency of inquiries during the day. Most database management systems have utility programs that enable the DBA to monitor these factors and make adjustments to provide for more efficient database use.

In addition to the DBA, the user also has a role in a database management system.

The Responsibility of the User in a Database Management System

One of the user's first responsibilities is to become familiar with the data in the existing database. First-time database users are often amazed at the wealth of information available to help them perform their jobs more effectively.

Another responsibility of the user, in organizations of any size, is to play an active part in the specification of additions to the database. The maintenance of an organization's database is an ongoing task that must be constantly measured against the overall goals of the organization. Therefore, users must participate in designing the database that will be used to help them achieve those goals and measure their progress.

PERSONAL COMPUTER DATABASE SYSTEMS

A variety of software packages are available for personal computers, ranging from simple file management programs to full relational database management systems. Some of the popular database packages designed for personal computer include dBASE III PLUS, dBASE IV, Paradox, Rbase and Foxpro (Figure 7-22).

FIGURE 7-22
Paradox and dBASE IV are two of the more popular database software packages. The screen on the left shows an order entry form that was designed with Paradox. The screen on the right shows a name and address file developed using dBASE IV.

As with large system packages, many personal computer software vendors have developed or modified existing packages to support Structured Query Language (SQL). The advantage of SQL packages for personal computers is that they can directly query mainframe databases that support SQL.

The increased computing power of the newest personal computers now allows modified versions of database management packages originally written for mainframe computers to be run on the personal computers. ORACLE (Oracle Corporation) and INFORMIX-SQL (Informix Software) are two SQL-based packages that have been adapted to personal computers.

With so many software packages available (a recent survey included 43), it's difficult to decide which one to choose. If you have simple needs, a file management package is probably all that you need. If you need the capability of a database, one of the more popular database management systems will offer you increased capability and growth potential. For your complex database requirements, the packages originally developed on mainframes should provide all the database resources you require. If you need to select a database software package for your personal computer, you may want to refer to the sections in Chapter 2 that discuss personal computer databases and how to choose software packages for a personal computer.

SUMMARY OF FILE AND DATABASE MANAGEMENT

◆ Understanding the data management, file, and database concepts that we have presented in this chapter gives you a knowledge of how data is stored and managed on a computer. This information will be useful to you, whether you are a home computer user who wants to store personal data on diskettes or a hard drive, or a computer user accessing the database of the company where you are employed.

CHAPTER SUMMARY

1. **Data management** refers to procedures that are used to keep data accurate and timely and provide for the security and maintenance of data.
2. **Data accuracy**, sometimes called **data integrity**, means that the source of the data is reliable and the data is correctly reported and entered.
3. Accurate data must also be timely meaning that it has not lost its usefulness because time has passed.
4. **Data security** refers to protecting data to keep it from being misused or lost.
5. **Backup** procedures provide for maintaining copies of data so that in the event the data is lost or destroyed it can be recovered.
6. Data maintenance refers to **updating** data. This includes **adding**, **changing**, or **deleting** data in order to keep it current.
7. A **file** is a collection of related records that is usually stored on an auxiliary storage device.
8. The three types of file organization are sequential, indexed, and direct or relative.
9. When **sequential file organization** is used, records are stored one after the other, normally in ascending or descending order, based on a value in each record called the key.
10. The **key** is a field that contains unique data, such as a Social Security number, that is used to identify the records in a file.
11. **Sequential retrieval** means that the records on a tape or disk file are retrieved (accessed) one after another in the same order that the records are stored on the tape or disk.
12. With **indexed file organization**, the records are stored on the disk in an indexed file in ascending or descending sequence based on a key field. An index is used to retrieve records.
13. An **index** is a file that consists of a list containing the key field and the corresponding disk address for each record in a file.
14. **Random retrieval**, or **random access**, means the system can go directly to a record without having to read the preceding records.
15. An advantage of indexed files is that usually more than one index can be maintained. Each index can be used to access the records in a file in a particular order.
16. A **direct file**, or **relative file**, uses the key value of a record to determine the location on the disk where the record is or will be stored.
17. The locations on a disk where records in a direct file can be stored are called **buckets**.
18. **Hashing** means the program managing the disk uses a formula or performs a calculation to determine the location (position) where a record will be placed on a disk.
19. A **collision** occurs when the hashing operation generates the same disk location (called **synonyms**) for records with different key values.

20. In a **database**, the data is organized in multiple related files.
21. A **database management system (DBMS)** is the software that allows the user to create, maintain, and report the data and file relationships.
22. By contrast, a **file management system** allows a user to access only one file at a time.
23. The major advantages of using a database include: **reduced data redundancy** (data is not duplicated in several different files); **improved data integrity** (data accuracy); **integrated files** (joining data from more than one file); **improved data security** (ensuring that the data is accessible only to those with the proper authorization); and **reduced development time** (for program development and data preparation).
24. A **hierarchical database** is organized in a top to bottom series of parent-child relationships. Each **parent record** can have multiple child records. However, each **child record** can have only one parent. The parent record at the top of the hierarchy is called the **root record**.
25. A **network database** is organized similar to a hierarchical database except each child record (called a **member**) may have more than one parent record (called an **owner**).
26. Data relationships in both the hierarchical database and the network database must be established prior to the use of the database.
27. A **relational database** is organized into tables called **relations**. The relations are divided into **tuples** (rows) and **attributes** (fields). Each attribute is given a unique name, called the **domain**.
28. In a relational database, a common field is used to connect multiple files.
29. The advantage of a relational database is that the data relationships do not need to be predefined.
30. The database management system (DBMS) consists of a **data dictionary** that defines each data field to be used in the database; **utilities**, or programs, that provide a number of special functions (such as copying data, creating files, and deleting records); **security levels** that control access to the data; and a **query language** that allows users to specify what data they wish to view.
31. When a user queries a relational database, the three **relational operations** are the select, project, and join.
32. The **select relational operation** selects certain records (rows or tuples) based on user-supplied criteria.
33. The **project relational operation** specifies the fields (attributes) that appear on the query output.
34. The **join relational operation** is used to combine two files.
35. A widely used query language is **Structured Query Language (SQL)**.
36. The **database administrator (DBA)** is the person who coordinates all database activities.
37. The database administrator is responsible for database design, user coordination, backup and recovery, database security, and database performance monitoring.
38. Users should become familiar with the data in their organization's database and should actively participate in the specification of additions to the database that will affect their jobs.
39. A variety of data management systems are available for personal computers, ranging from file management programs to full relational database management systems.

KEY TERMS

REVIEW QUESTIONS

1. List and describe the three areas of data management.
2. Describe sequential file organization. What is a key?
3. What is an indexed file? Describe how the index is used to retrieve records from an indexed file.
4. Write a definition for a direct file.
5. What is hashing? What are buckets?
6. Write a definition for the term database.
7. Describe what a database management system allows a user to do.
8. What are the advantages of a database management system over a file-oriented system?
9. Draw an example of a hierarchical and network database.
10. Describe how data is organized in a relational database.
11. Discuss two advantages and one disadvantage of a relational database.
12. What are the common features of database management systems?
13. How is a database query used?
14. What are the responsibilities of a database administrator?
15. What are the responsibilities of the user in a database management system?

CONTROVERSIAL ISSUES

1. Database management systems allow the user to establish different levels of security that can be used to restrict access and update privileges. Using a student record file as an example, discuss the different access and update privileges that students, teachers, administrators, and outside organizations should have concerning student file records.
2. Commercial attempts to market databases consisting of personal information on citizens have met strong opposition from critics that contend that the dissemination of such information is an invasion of privacy. Discuss how such a database could be used and misused. What limits, if any, should be placed on the creation of databases that contain information on private citizens?

RESEARCH PROJECTS

1. Visit a local computer store and obtain information on a file management system and a database management system. What features does the database management system have that the file management system does not have?
2. Prepare a report on a database management system that supports Structured Query Language (SQL).

Communications

OBJECTIVES

◆ Define the term communications

◆ Describe the basic components of a communications system

◆ Describe the various transmission media used for communications channels

◆ Describe the different types of line configurations

◆ Describe how data is transmitted

◆ Identify and explain the communications equipment used in a communications system

◆ Describe the functions performed by communications software

◆ Explain the two major categories of networks and describe three common network configurations

◆ Describe how bridges and gateways are used to connect networks

Computers are well recognized as important computing devices. They should also be recognized as important communications devices. It is now possible for a computer to communicate with other computers anywhere in the world. This capability, sometimes referred to as *connectivity*, allows users to quickly and directly access data and information that otherwise would have been unavailable or that probably would have taken considerable time to acquire. Banks, retail stores, airlines, hotels, and many other businesses use computers for communications purposes. Personal computer users communicate with other personal computer users. They can also access special databases available on larger machines to quickly and conveniently obtain information such as weather reports, stock market data, airline schedules, news stories, or even theater and movie reviews.

In this chapter we provide an overview of communications with an emphasis on the communication of data and information. We explain some of the terminology, equipment, procedures, and applications that relate to computers and their use as communications devices. Chapter 14 explains more about some of the specialized communications devices that have been developed for transmitting text, graphics, voice, and video over communications channels.

WHAT IS COMMUNICATIONS?

Communications, sometimes called **data communications**, refers to the transmission of data and information over a communications channel such as a standard telephone line, between one computer or terminal and another computer. Other terms such as telecommunications and teleprocessing are also used to describe communications. **Telecommunications** describes any type of long-distance communications including television signals. **Teleprocessing** refers to the use of telephone lines to transmit data. As communications technology continues to advance, the distinction between these terms is blurred. Therefore, most people refer to the process of transmitting data or information of any type as data communications, or simply communications.

A COMMUNICATIONS SYSTEM MODEL

Figure 8-1 shows the basic model for a communications system. This model consists of the following equipment:

FIGURE 8-1
The basic model of a communications system. In addition to the equipment, communications software is also required.

- A computer or a terminal
- Communications equipment that sends (and can usually receive) data
- The communications channel over which the data is sent
- Communications equipment that receives (and can usually send) data
- Another computer

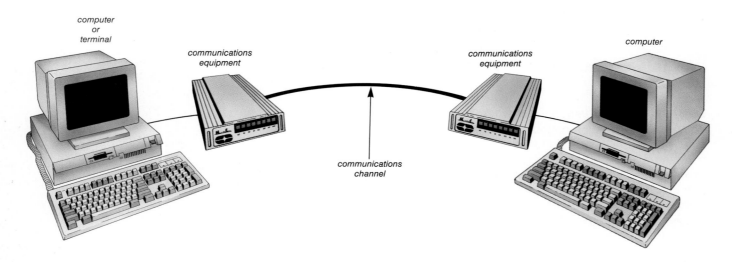

computer or terminal

communications equipment

communications channel

communications equipment

computer

The basic model also includes communications software. If two computers are communicating with each other, compatible communications software is required on each system. If a computer is communicating with a terminal, communications are directed by either a separate program running on the computer or the computer operating system.

COMMUNICATIONS CHANNELS

A **communications channel**, also called a **communications line** or **communications link**, is the path that the data follows as it is transmitted from the sending equipment to the receiving equipment in a communications system. These channels are made up of one or more **transmission media**, including twisted pair wire, coaxial cable, fiber optics, microwave transmission, satellite transmission, and wireless transmission.

Twisted Pair Wire

Twisted pair wire (Figure 8-2) consists of pairs of copper wires that are twisted together. To insulate and identify the wires, each wire is covered with a thin layer of colored plastic. Twisted pair wire is commonly used for telephone lines. It is an inexpensive transmission medium, and it can be easily strung from one location to another. The disadvantage of twisted pair wire is that it can be affected by outside electrical interference generated by machines such as fans or air conditioners. While this interference might be acceptable on a voice call, it can garble the data as it is sent over the line, causing transmission errors to occur.

Coaxial Cable

A **coaxial cable** is a high-quality communications line that is used in offices and laid under the ground and under the ocean. Coaxial cable consists of a copper wire conductor surrounded by a nonconducting insulator that is in turn surrounded by a woven metal outer conductor, and finally a plastic outer coating (Figure 8-3). Because of its more heavily insulated construction, coaxial cable is not susceptible to electrical interference and can transmit data at higher data rates over longer distances than twisted pair telephone wire.

There are two types of coaxial cable, named for the transmission techniques they support: baseband and broadband. **Baseband** coaxial cable carries one signal at a time. The signal, however, can travel very fast — in the area of ten million bits per second for the first 1,000 feet. The speed drops significantly as the length of the cable increases, and special equipment is needed to amplify (boost) the signal if it is transmitted more than approximately one mile.

Broadband coaxial cable can carry multiple signals at one time. It is similar to cable TV where a single cable offers a number of channels to the user. A particular advantage of broadband channels is that data, audio, and video transmission can occur over the same line.

Fiber Optics

Fiber optics is a technology that may eventually replace conventional wire and cable in communications systems. This technology is based on the capability of smooth, hair-thin strands of glass to conduct light with high efficiency (Figure 8-4). The major advantages of fiber optics over wire cables include substantial weight and size savings and increased speed of transmission. Another advantage is that fiber-optic cable is not affected by electrical and magnetic fields. A single fiber-optic cable can carry several hundred thousand voice communications simultaneously. The disadvantages of fiber-optic cable are that it is more expensive than twisted pair or coaxial cable and it is more difficult to install and modify than metal wiring. Fiber optics is frequently being used in new voice and data installations.

FIGURE 8-2 ▲
Twisted pair wire is most commonly used as telephone wire. It is inexpensive but can be affected by electrical interference that can cause errors in data transmission.

FIGURE 8-3 ▼
On coaxial cable, data travels through the copper wire conductor. The outer conductor is made of woven metal mesh that acts as an electrical ground. Coaxial cable can carry up to 100 times as many communication signals as twisted pair wire.

FIGURE 8-4 ▼
The two-strand, fiber-optic cable (bottom) can transmit as much information as the 1,500-pair copper cable (top).

Microwave Transmission

Microwaves are radio waves that can be used to provide high-speed transmission of both voice and data. Data is transmitted through the air from one microwave station to another in a manner similar to the way radio signals are transmitted (Figure 8-5). A disadvantage of microwaves is that they are limited to line-of-sight transmission. This means that microwaves must be transmitted in a straight line and that there can be no obstructions, such as buildings or mountains, between microwave stations. For this reason, microwave stations are characterized by antennas positioned on tops of buildings, towers, or mountains.

Satellite Transmission

Communications satellites receive signals from earth, amplify the signals, and retransmit the signals back to the earth. **Earth stations** (Figure 8-6) are communications facilities that use large, dish-shaped antennas to transmit and receive data from satellites. The transmission *to* the satellite is called an **uplink** and the transmission *from* the satellite to a receiving earth station is called a **downlink**.

Communications satellites are usually placed about 22,300 miles above the earth in a **geosynchronous orbit** (Figure 8-7). This means that the satellite is placed in an orbit where it rotates with the earth, so that the same dish antennas on earth that are used to send and receive signals can remain fixed on the satellite at all times.

FIGURE 8-5 ▲
The round antenna on this tower is used for microwave transmission. Microwave transmission is limited to line-of-sight. Antennas are usually placed 25 to 75 miles apart.

25 to 75 miles *25 to 75 miles*

FIGURE 8-6 ▶
Earth stations use large dish antennas to communicate with satellites.

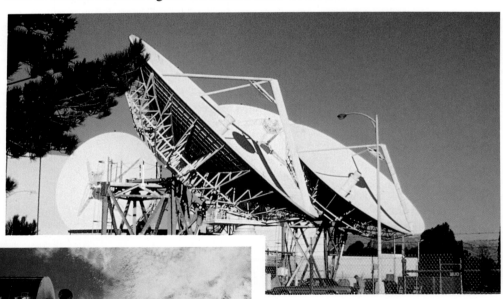

◀ FIGURE 8-7
Communications satellites are placed in geosynchronous orbits approximately 22,300 miles above the earth.

Wireless Transmission

Wireless transmission uses one of three techniques to transmit data: light beams, radio waves, or carrier-connect radio, which uses the existing electrical wiring of a building. These methods are sometimes used by companies to connect devices that are in the same general area such as an office or business park. For example, the unit shown in Figure 8-8 uses light beams to transmit or receive data over a distance up to 70 feet. Local wireless systems offer design flexibility and portability, but provide slower transmission speed than wired connections.

For longer distances, radio-wave wireless systems are becoming more widely used. IBM and Motorola combined their private nationwide radio networks and are selling its use to other companies. The combined network contains over 1,100 radio base stations that can serve over 8,000 cities in 50 states. Potential users include companies with large numbers of service personnel who need access to their company's computer data when they are at a customer site. For example, a repair technician may need to know the nearest location of a particular part. Using a portable radio data terminal (Figure 8-9) the technician could access the company's inventory database and obtain information about the availability of the required part.

A wireless device available to the general public that offers many of the same advantages as private radio networks is a cellular telephone. A **cellular telephone** uses radio waves to communicate with a local antenna assigned to a specific geographic area called a cell. Each cell is shaped like a hexagon (Figure 8-10) so that it will precisely fit with adjacent cells. Cellular phones are often used in automobiles. As a cellular telephone user travels from one cell to another, a computer that monitors the activity in each cell switches the conversation from one radio channel to another. By switching channels in this manner, the same channel can be used by another caller in a nonadjacent cell. Individual cells range from one to ten miles in width and use between 50 and 75 radio channels.

FIGURE 8-8
Wireless communications devices are well suited for open office environments where they can be mounted on office partitions. The units work by bouncing light beams off reflective surfaces such as a ceiling or a wall. Multiple terminals or computers can be connected to each device.

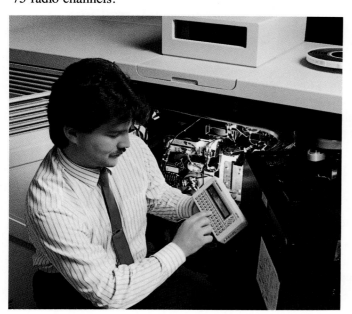

◄ **FIGURE 8-9**
This portable terminal uses radio waves to communicate with a base radio station that is connected to a host computer. Using such a terminal, service technicians can instantly inquire as to the availability of repair parts.

FIGURE 8-10►
Each cell in a cellular phone system is shaped like a hexagon so that it precisely fits with adjacent cells. If a cellular phone user is traveling between cells, such as in a car, a central computer automatically transfers the communication signal from one antenna to another.

An Example of a Communications Channel

When data is transmitted over long distances, several different transmission media are generally used to make a complete communications channel. Figure 8-11 illustrates how some of the various transmission media could be used to transmit data from a personal computer on the west coast of the United States to a large computer on the east coast. An example of the steps that could occur are as follows.

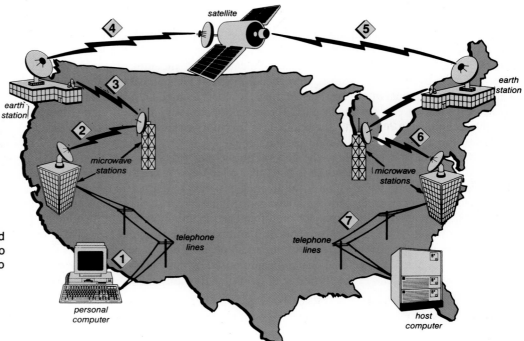

FIGURE 8-11
The use of telephone wires, microwave transmission, and a communications satellite to allow a personal computer to communicate with a large host computer.

⟨1⟩ An entry is made on the personal computer. The data is sent over telephone lines from the computer to a microwave station.

⟨2⟩ The data is then transmitted from one microwave station to another.

⟨3⟩ The data is transmitted from the last microwave station to an earth station.

⟨4⟩ The earth station transmits the data to the communications satellite.

⟨5⟩ The satellite relays the data to another earth station on the other side of the country.

⟨6⟩ The data received at the earth station is transmitted to microwave stations.

⟨7⟩ The data is sent by the telephone lines to the large computer.

This entire transmission process would take less than one second. Not all data transmission is as complex as this example, but such sophisticated communications systems do exist to meet the needs of some users.

LINE CONFIGURATIONS

Two major **line configurations** (types of line connections) commonly used in communications are: point-to-point lines and multidrop, or multipoint, lines.

Point-to-Point Lines

A **point-to-point line** is a direct line between a sending and a receiving device. It may be one of two types: a switched line or a dedicated line (Figure 8-12).

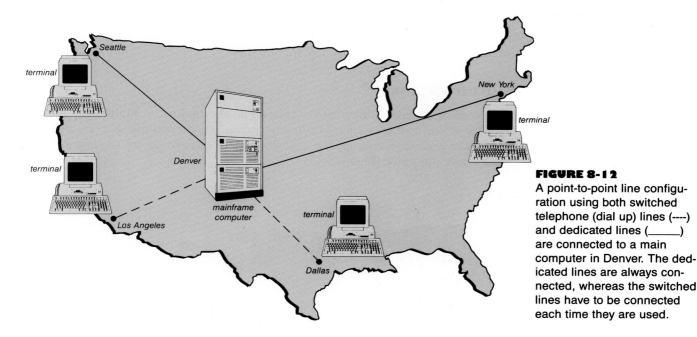

FIGURE 8-12
A point-to-point line configuration using both switched telephone (dial up) lines (----) and dedicated lines (_____) are connected to a main computer in Denver. The dedicated lines are always connected, whereas the switched lines have to be connected each time they are used.

Switched Line   A **switched line** uses a regular telephone line to establish a communications connection. Each time a connection is made, the line to be used for the call is selected by the telephone company switching stations (hence the name switched line). Using a switched line for communicating data is the same process as one person using a telephone to call another person. The communications equipment at the sending end dials the telephone number of the communications equipment at the receiving end. When the communications equipment at the receiving end answers the call, a connection is established and data can be transmitted. The process of establishing the communication connection is sometimes referred to as the **handshake**. When the transmission of data is complete, the communications equipment at either end terminates the call by hanging up and the line is disconnected.

An advantage of using switched lines is that a connection can be made between any two locations that have telephone service and communications equipment. For example, a personal computer could dial one computer to get information about the weather and then hang up and place a second call to another computer to get information about the stock market. A disadvantage of a switched line is that the quality of the line cannot be controlled because the line is chosen at random by the telephone company switching equipment. The cost of a switched line is the same for data communications as for a regular telephone call.

Dedicated Line   A **dedicated line** is a line connection that is always established (unlike the switched line where the line connection is reestablished each time it is used). The communications device at one end is always connected to the device at the other end. A user can create his or her own dedicated line connection by running a wire or cable between two points, such as between two offices or buildings, or the dedicated line can be provided by an outside organization such as a telephone company or some other communications service company. If the dedicated line is provided by an outside organization, it is sometimes called a **leased line**, or a **private line**. The quality and consistency of the connection is better than on a switched line because a dedicated line is always established. Use of dedicated lines provided by outside organizations are usually charged on a flat-fee basis, a fixed amount each month regardless of how much time the line is actually used to transmit data. The cost of dedicated lines varies based on the distance between the two connected points and, sometimes, the speed at which data will be transmitted.

Multidrop Lines

The second major line configuration is called a **multidrop line**, or **multipoint line**. This type of line configuration is commonly used to connect multiple devices, such as terminals or personal computers, on a single line to a main computer, sometimes called a **host computer** (Figure 8-13).

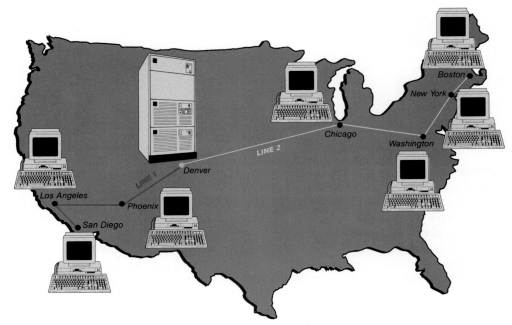

FIGURE 8-13
Two multidrop lines connect several cities with a computer in Denver. Each line is shared by terminals at several locations. Multidrop line configurations are less expensive than individual lines to each remote location.

For example, a ticket agent could use a terminal to enter an inquiry requesting flight information from a database stored on a main computer (Figure 8-14). While the request is being transmitted to the main computer, other terminals on the line are not able to transmit data. The time required for the data to be transmitted to the main computer, however, is short—most likely less than one second. As soon as the inquiry is received by the computer, a second terminal can send an inquiry. With such short delays, it appears to the users that no other terminals are using the line, even though multiple terminals may be sharing the same line.

The number of terminals to be placed on one line is a decision made by the designer of the system based on the anticipated amount of traffic on the line. For example, 100 or more terminals could be contained on a single line, provided each one would send only short messages, such as inquiries, and each terminal would use the communications line only a few hours per day. But if longer messages, such as reports, were required and if the terminals were to be used almost continuously, the number of terminals on one line would have to be smaller.

FIGURE 8-14
On a multidrop line, several terminals share the same line. Only one terminal at a time can transmit data to the host computer.

A leased line is almost always used for multidrop line configurations. The use of multidrop lines can decrease line costs considerably because one line is used by many terminals.

CHARACTERISTICS OF COMMUNICATIONS CHANNELS

The communications channels we have just discussed can be categorized by a number of characteristics including the type of signal, transmission mode, transmission direction, and transmission rate.

Types of Signals: Digital and Analog

Computer equipment is designed to process data as **digital signals**, individual electrical pulses that represent the bits that are grouped together to form characters. Telephone equipment was originally designed to carry only voice transmission, which is comprised of a continuous electrical wave called an **analog signal** (Figure 8-15). Thus, a special piece of equipment called a *modem* is used to convert between the digital signals and analog signals so that telephone lines can carry data. We discuss modems in more detail later in this chapter.

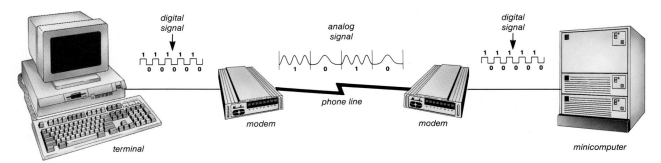

FIGURE 8-15
Individual electrical pulses of the digital signal are converted into analog (electrical wave) signals for transmission over voice telephone lines. The 1s represent ON bits and the 0s represent OFF bits. At the main computer receiving end, another modem converts the analog signals back into digital signals that can be processed by the computer.

To provide better communications services, telephone companies are now offering **digital data service**, communications channels specifically designed to carry digital instead of voice signals. Digital data service is available within and between most major metropolitan areas and provides higher speed and lower error rates than voice lines. Modems are not needed with digital data service; instead, users connect to the communications line through a device called a **data service unit (DSU)**.

Transmission Modes: Asynchronous and Synchronous

In **asynchronous transmission mode** (Figure 8-16), individual characters (made up of bits) are transmitted at irregular intervals, for example, when a user enters data. To distinguish where one character stops and another starts, the asynchronous communication mode uses a start and a stop bit. An additional bit called a *parity bit* is sometimes included at the end of each character. As you learned in our discussion of memory in Chapter 4, parity bits are used for error checking, and they detect if one of the data bits has been changed during transmission. The asynchronous transmission mode is used for lower speed data transmission and is used with most communications equipment designed for personal computers.

FIGURE 8-16
In asynchronous transmission mode, individual characters are transmitted. Each character has start, stop, and error-checking bits. In synchronous transmission mode, multiple characters are sent in a block with start bytes at the beginning of the block and error-checking bits and stop bytes at the end of the block. Synchronous transmission is faster and more accurate.

ASYNCHRONOUS TRANSMISSION MODE

CHARACTER	IDLE	CHARACTER	IDLE	CHARACTER	IDLE	CHARACTER	IDLE

SYNCHRONOUS TRANSMISSION MODE

START BYTES	CHARACTER	CHARACTER	CHARACTER	CHARACTER	ERROR-CHECK BITS	STOP BYTES	IDLE

In the **synchronous transmission mode** (Figure 8-16), large blocks of data are transmitted at regular intervals. Timing signals synchronize the communications equipment at both the sending and receiving ends and eliminate the need for start and stop bits for each character. Error-checking bits and start and end indicators called sync bytes are also transmitted. Synchronous transmission requires more sophisticated and expensive equipment, but it does give much higher speeds and accuracy than asynchronous transmission.

Direction of Transmission: Simplex, Half-Duplex, and Full-Duplex

The direction of data transmission is classified as either simplex, half-duplex, or full-duplex (Figure 8-17). In **simplex** transmission, data flows in one direction only. Simplex is used only when the sending device, such as a temperature sensor, never requires a response from the computer. For example, if a computer is used to control the temperature of a building, numerous sensors are placed throughout it. Each sensor is connected to the computer with a simplex transmission line because the computer only needs to receive data from the temperature sensors and does not need to send data back to the sensors.

FIGURE 8-17
Simplex transmission allows data to flow in one direction only. Half-duplex transmission allows data to flow in both directions but not at the same time. Full-duplex transmission allows data to flow in both directions simultaneously.

In **half-duplex** transmission, data can flow in both directions but in only one direction at a time. An example is a citizens band radio. The user can talk or listen but not do both at the same time. Half-duplex is often used between terminals and a central computer.

In **full-duplex** transmission, data can be sent in both directions at the same time. A normal telephone line is an example of full-duplex transmission. Both parties can talk at the same time. Full-duplex transmission is used for most interactive computer applications and for computer-to-computer data transmission.

Transmission Rate

The transmission rate of a communications channel is determined by its bandwidth and its speed. The **bandwidth** is the range of frequencies that a channel can carry. Since transmitted data can be assigned to different frequencies, the wider the bandwidth, the more frequencies, and the more data that can be transmitted at the same time.

The speed at which data is transmitted is usually expressed as bits per second or as a baud rate. **Bits per second (bps)** is the number of bits that can be transmitted in one second. Using a 10-bit byte to represent a character (7 data bits, 1 start, 1 stop, and 1 parity bit), a 2,400 bps transmission would transmit 240 characters per second. At this rate, a 20-page, single-spaced report would be transmitted in approximately five minutes. The **baud rate** is the number of times per second that the signal being transmitted changes. With each change, one or more bits can be transmitted. At speeds up to 2,400 bps, usually only one bit is transmitted per signal change and, thus, the bits per second and the baud rate are the same. To achieve speeds in excess of 2,400 bps, more than one bit is transmitted with each signal change and, thus, the bps will exceed the baud rate.

FIGURE 8-18
An external modem is connected to a terminal or computer and to a telephone outlet.

COMMUNICATIONS EQUIPMENT

◆ If a terminal or a personal computer is within approximately 1,000 feet of another computer, the two devices can usually be directly connected by a cable. Over 1,000 feet, however, the electrical signal weakens to the point that some type of special communications equipment is required to increase or change the signal to transmit it farther. A variety of communications equipment exists to perform this task, but the equipment that a user is most likely to encounter is a modem, a multiplexor, and a front-end processor.

Modems

FIGURE 8-19
An internal modem is mounted inside a personal computer.

A **modem** converts the digital signals of a terminal or computer to analog signals that are transmitted over a communications channel. It also converts analog signals it receives into digital signals that are used by a terminal or computer. The word modem comes from a combination of the words *mo*dulate, which means to change into a sound or analog signal, and *dem*odulate, which means to convert an analog signal into a digital signal. A modem is needed at both the sending and receiving ends of a communications channel.

An **external modem** (Figure 8-18) is a separate, or stand-alone, device that is attached to the computer or terminal by a cable and to the telephone outlet by a standard telephone cord. An advantage of an external modem is that it can be easily moved from one terminal or computer to another.

An **internal modem** (Figure 8-19) is a circuit board that is installed inside a computer or terminal. Internal modems are generally less expensive than comparable external modems but once installed, they are not as easy to move.

An **acoustic modem**, also called an **acoustic coupler**, is designed to be used with a telephone handset (Figure 8-20). The acoustic coupler converts the digital signals generated by the terminal or personal computer into a series of audible tones, which are picked up by the mouthpiece in the headset in the same manner that a telephone picks up a person's voice. The analog signals are then transmitted over the communications channel. An acoustic coupler provides portability, but is generally less reliable than an internal or external modem because small outside sounds can be picked up by the acoustic coupler and cause transmission errors. Acoustic couplers are no longer common and are primarily used for special applications, such as with portable computers.

Modems can transmit data at rates from 300 to 38,400 bits per second (bps). Most personal computers would use either a 1,200 or 2,400 bps modem. Business or heavier volume users would use faster and more expensive modems.

FIGURE 8-20
The acoustic coupler (lower left) allows a portable computer user to communicate with another computer over telephone lines. The telephone handset is placed in the molded rubber cups on the acoustic coupler.

Multiplexors

A **multiplexor**, sometimes referred to as a MUX, combines more than one input signal into a single stream of data that can be transmitted over a communications channel (Figure 8-21). The multiplexor at the sending end codes each character it receives with an identifier that is used by the multiplexor at the receiving end to separate the combined data stream into its original parts. A multiplexor may be connected to a separate modem or may have a modem built in. By combining the individual data streams into one, a multiplexor increases the efficiency of communications and saves the cost of individual communications channels.

terminal

terminal

terminal

terminal

MUX

modem

phone line

modem

MUX

minicomputer

FIGURE 8-21
At the sending end, a multiplexor (MUX) combines separate data transmissions into a single data stream. At the receiving end, the multiplexor separates the single stream into its original parts.

FIGURE 8-22
This IBM Series 1 minicomputer is often used as a front-end processor to relieve the main computer of communications tasks.

Front-End Processors

A front-end processor (Figure 8-22) is a computer that is dedicated to handling the communications requirements of a larger computer. Relieved of these tasks, the large computer is then dedicated to processing data, while the front-end processor communicates the data. Tasks that the front-end processor would handle include **polling** (checking the connected terminals or computers to see if they have data to send), error checking and correction, and access security to make sure that a connected device or the user of the connected device is authorized to access the computer.

COMMUNICATIONS SOFTWARE

◆ Sometimes communications equipment is preprogrammed to accomplish its designed communications tasks. Other times, the user must load a program before transmitting data. These programs, referred to as **communications software**, can perform a number of tasks including dialing (if a switched telephone line is used), file transfer, terminal emulation, and data encryption (Figure 8-23).

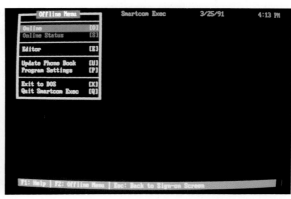

FIGURE 8-23
Communications software performs a variety of tasks that assist the user in operating communications equipment.

Dialing software allows you to store, review, select and dial telephone numbers of computers that can be called (Figure 8-24). The software provides a variety of meaningful messages to assist you in establishing a connection before transmitting data. For example, a person who uses a personal computer at home to communicate with a computer at the office could use dialing software to establish the communications connection. The software would display the office computer's telephone number on the user's personal computer screen. The user would enter the appropriate command for the dialing software, working with a modem, to begin dialing the office computer and to establish a connection. During the 10 or 15 seconds that this process takes, the software would display messages to indicate specifically what was happening, such as "DIALING," "CARRIER DETECT" (which means that the office computer has answered), and "CONNECTED" (to indicate that the communications connection has been established and data transmission can begin).

File transfer software allows you to move one or more files from one system to another. Generally, you have to load the file transfer software on both the sending and receiving computers.

Terminal emulation software allows a personal computer to imitate or appear to be a specific type of terminal, so that the personal computer can connect to another usually larger computer. Most minicomputers and mainframes are designed to work with terminals that have specific characteristics such as speed and parity. Terminal emulation software performs the necessary speed and parity conversion.

FIGURE 8-24
This screen from *Crosstalk Communicator* is a popular communications software package for personal computers. The screen shows the information that is displayed when the software is being used to dial the CompuServe Information Service.

Data encryption protects confidential data during transmission. **Data encryption** is the conversion of data at the sending end into an unrecognizable string of characters or bits and the reconversion of the data at the receiving end. Without knowing how the data was encrypted, someone who intercepted the transmitted data would have a difficult time determining what the data meant.

COMMUNICATIONS PROTOCOLS

Communications software is written to work with one or more protocols. A **protocol** is a set of rules and procedures for exchanging information between computers. Protocols define how the communications link is established, how information is transmitted, and how errors are detected and corrected. Using the same protocol, different types and makes of computers can communicate with each other. Over the years, numerous protocols have been developed. Today, however, there are strong efforts to establish standards that all computer and communications equipment manufacturers will follow. The International Standards Organization (ISO) based in Geneva, Switzerland has defined a set of communications protocols called the **Open Systems Interconnection (OSI) model**. The OSI model has been endorsed by the United Nations.

COMMUNICATIONS NETWORKS

A communications **network** is a collection of terminals, computers, and other equipment that uses communications channels to share data, information, hardware, and software. Networks can be classified as either local area networks or wide area networks.

Local Area Networks (LANs)

A **local area network**, or LAN, is a communications network that is privately owned and that covers a limited geographic area such as an office, a building, or a group of buildings.

The LAN consists of a communications channel that connects either a series of computer terminals together with a minicomputer or, more commonly, a group of personal computers to one another. Very sophisticated LANs can connect a variety of office devices such as word processing equipment, computer terminals, video equipment, and personal computers.

Two common applications of local area networks are hardware resource sharing and information resource sharing. **Hardware resource sharing** allows each personal computer in the network to access and use devices that would be too expensive to provide for each user or would not be justified for each user because of only occasional use. For example, when a number of personal computers are used on the network, each may need to use a laser printer. Using a LAN, a laser printer could be purchased and made a part of the network. Whenever a user of a personal computer on the network needed the laser printer, it could be accessed over the network. Figure 8-25 depicts a simple local area network consisting of four personal computers linked together by a cable. Three of the personal computers (computer 1 in the sales and marketing department, computer 2 in the accounting department, and computer 3 in the personnel department) are available for use at all times. Computer 4 is used as a **server**, sometimes called a **network control unit**, which is dedicated to handling the communications needs of the other computers in the network. The users of this LAN have connected the laser printer to the server. Using the LAN, all computers and the server can use the printer.

LOCAL AREA NETWORK

Information resource sharing allows anyone using a personal computer on the local area network to access data stored on any other computer in the network. In actual practice, hardware resource sharing and information resource sharing are often combined. For example, in Figure 8-25, the daily sales records could be stored on the hard disk associated with the server unit personal computer. Anyone needing access to the sales records could use this information resource. The capability to access and store data on common auxiliary storage is an important feature of many local area networks.

Information resource sharing is usually provided by using either the file-server or client-server method. Using the **file-server** method, the server sends an entire file at a time. The requesting computer then performs the processing. With the **client-server** method, as much processing as possible is done on the server system before data is transmitted. Figure 8-26 illustrates how the two methods would process a request for information stored on the server system for customers with balances over $1,000. With the file-server method, the user transmits a request for the customer file to the server unit ①. The server unit locates the customer file ② and transmits the entire file to the requesting computer ③. The requesting computer selects customers with balances over $1,000 and prepares the report ④. With the client-server method, the user transmits a request for customers with a balance over $1,000 to the server unit ①. The server unit selects the customer records that meet the criteria ② and transmits the selected records to the requesting computer ③. The requesting computer prepares the report ④. The client-server method greatly reduces the amount of data sent over a network but requires a more powerful server system.

FILE-SERVER

① Request for customer file
③ Entire customer file transmitted

SERVER UNIT

② Server locates and transmits entire customer file

④ Requesting computer selects customers with balances over $1,000 and prepares report

CLIENT-SERVER

① Request for balances over $1,000
③ Records of customers with balances over $1,000 transmitted

SERVER UNIT

② Server selects customers with balances over $1,000

④ Requesting computer prepares report

FIGURE 8-26
A request for information about customers with balances over $1,000 would be processed differently by file-server and client-server networks.

Frequently used software is another type of resource that is often shared on a local area network. For example, if all users need access to word processing software, the software can be stored on the hard disk of the server and accessed by all users as needed. This is much more convenient and faster than having the software stored on a diskette and available at each computer. Sharing software is a common practice for both in-house and commercial software. Many software vendors now sell a network version of their software. When a commercial software package is accessed by many users, it is sometimes necessary to obtain a special agreement from the software vendor, called a **site license**. The site license fee is usually based on the number of computers on the network and is less than if individual copies of the software package were purchased for each computer.

Wide Area Networks (WANs)

A **wide area network**, or **WAN**, is geographic in scope (as opposed to local) and uses telephone lines, microwaves, satellites, or a combination of communications channels. Public wide area network companies include so-called **common carriers** such as the telephone companies. Telephone company deregulation has encouraged a number of companies to build their own wide area networks. For example, EDS has built one of the largest private communications network (Figure 8-27) to handle the needs of their computer services business and the needs of their parent company, General Motors.

FIGURE 8-27
The control room for EDSNET, the private communications network of Electronic Data Systems Corporation (EDS). The network was built by EDS over a three-year period and a cost of more than $1 billion. The network provides communications for EDS, its computer services customers, and its parent company, General Motors.

Communications companies, such as MCI, have built WANs to compete with other communications companies. Companies called **value-added carriers** lease channels from the common carriers to provide specialized communications services referred to as **value-added networks**. For example, Tymnet, Inc. and Telenet provide packet-switching services. **Packet-switching** combines individual packets of information from various users and transmits them together over a high-speed channel. The messages are separated and distributed over lower speed channels at the receiving end. Sharing the high-speed channel is more economical than each user having their own high-speed channel. Most common carriers are now offering **Integrated Services Digital Network (ISDN)** services. ISDN is an international standard for the digital transmission of both voice and data using different channels and communications companies. Using ISDN lines, data can be transmitted over one or more separate channels at 64,000 bits per second. Future plans for ISDN include the use of fiber-optic cable that will allow transmission rates up to 2.2 billion bits per second. These higher speeds will allow full-motion video images to be transmitted.

NETWORK CONFIGURATIONS

The configuration, or physical layout, of the equipment in a communications network is called **topology**. Communications networks are usually configured in one or a combination of three patterns. These configurations are star, bus, and ring networks. Although these configurations can be used with wide area networks, we illustrate them with local area networks. Devices connected to a network, such as terminals, printers, or other computers, are referred to as **nodes**.

FIGURE 8-28
A star network contains a single, centralized host computer with which all the terminals or personal computers in the network communicate. Both point-to-point and multidrop lines can be used in a star network.

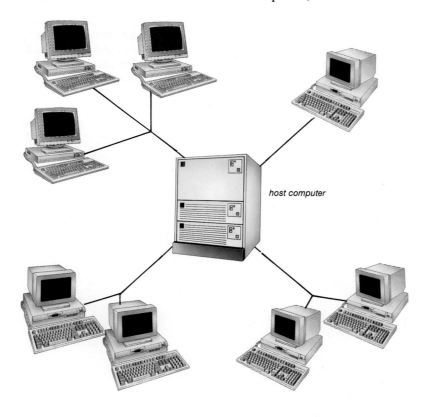

host computer

Star Network

A **star network** (Figure 8-28) contains a central computer and one or more terminals or personal computers connected to it, forming a star. A pure star network consists of only point-to-point lines between the terminals and the computer, but most star networks, such as the one shown in Figure 8-28, include both point-to-point lines and multidrop lines. A star network configuration is often used when the central computer contains all the data required to process the input from the terminals, such as an airline reservation system. For example, if inquiries are being processed in the star network, all the data to answer the inquiry would be contained in the database stored on the central computer.

A star network can be relatively efficient, and close control can be kept over the data processed on the network. Its major disadvantage is that the entire network is dependent on the central computer and the associated hardware and software. If any of these elements fail, the entire network is disabled. Therefore, in most large star networks, backup computer systems are available in case the primary system fails.

Bus Network

When a **bus network** is used, all the devices in the network are connected to and share a single cable. Information is transmitted in either direction from any one personal computer to another. Any message can be directed to a specific device. An advantage of the bus network is that devices can be attached or detached from the network at any point without disturbing the rest of the network. In addition, if one computer on the network fails, this does not affect the other users of the network. Figure 8-25 illustrates a simple bus network.

Ring Network

A **ring network** does not use a centralized host computer. Rather, a circle of computers communicate with one another (Figure 8-29). A ring network can be useful when the processing is not done at a central site, but at local sites. For example, computers could be located in three departments: accounting, personnel, and shipping and receiving. The computers in each of these departments could perform the processing required for each of the departments. On occasion, however, the computer in the shipping and receiving department could communicate with the computer in the accounting department to update certain data stored on the accounting department computer. Data travels around a ring network in one direction only and passes through each node. Thus, one disadvantage of a ring network is that if one node fails, the entire network fails because the data does not get past the failed node. An advantage of a ring network is that less cable is usually needed and therefore network cabling costs are lower.

FIGURE 8-29
In a ring network, all computers are connected in a continuous loop. Data flows around the ring in one direction only.

CONNECTING NETWORKS

Sometimes you might want to connect separate networks. You do this by using gateways and bridges. A **gateway** is a combination of hardware and software that allows users on one network to access the resources on a *different* type of network. For example, a gateway could be used to connect a local area network of personal computers to a mainframe computer network. A **bridge** is a combination of hardware and

FIGURE 8-30
These two personal computer networks are connected to a mainframe computer system with a bridge. A gateway is used to connect the personal computer network with the mainframe. All communications with the mainframe are controlled by a separate computer called a front-end processor. Modems are used to connect the networks to leased and dial telephone lines.

software that is used to connect *similar* networks. For example, if a company had similar but separate local area networks of personal computers in their accounting and marketing departments, the networks could be connected with a bridge. In this example, using a bridge makes more sense than joining all the personal computers together in one large network because the individual departments only occasionally need to access information on the other network.

AN EXAMPLE OF A COMMUNICATIONS NETWORK

The diagram in Figure 8-30 illustrates how two personal computer networks and a mainframe computer can be connected to share information with each other and with outside sources.

The marketing department operates a bus network of four personal computers ①. Frequently used marketing data and programs are stored in the server unit ②. The personal computers in the marketing department share a laser printer ③. A modem ④ is attached to the marketing server unit so that outside sales representatives can use a dial telephone line ⑤ to call the marketing system and obtain product price information.

The administration department operates a bus network of three personal computers ⑥. As with the marketing network, common data and programs are stored on a server unit ⑦ and the administration personal computers share a laser printer ⑧. Because the administration department sometimes needs information from the marketing system, the two similar networks are connected with a LAN bridge ⑨. The bridge allows users on either network to access data or programs on the other network.

Administration department users sometimes need information from the company's mainframe computer system ⟨10⟩. They can access the mainframe through the use of a gateway ⟨11⟩ that allows different types of network systems to be connected. All communications with the mainframe computer are controlled by a front-end processor ⟨12⟩. A dial telephone line ⟨13⟩ connected to a modem ⟨14⟩ allows remote users to call the mainframe and allows mainframe users to call other computers. A leased telephone line ⟨15⟩ and a modem ⟨16⟩ are used for a permanent connection to the computer at the corporate headquarters, several hundred miles away. The leased line can carry the signals of up to four different users. The signals are separated by the use of a multiplexor (MUX) ⟨17⟩. A bridge ⟨18⟩ connects the front-end processor and mainframe system to a microwave antenna ⟨19⟩ on the roof of the building. The microwave antenna sends and receives data from a computer at the manufacturing plant located two miles away. The front-end processor also controls mainframe computer terminals located throughout the company ⟨20⟩.

SUMMARY OF COMMUNICATIONS

Communications will continue to affect how people work and how they use computers. Individuals and organizations are no longer limited to local data resources but instead, with communications capabilities, they can obtain information from anywhere in the world at electronic speed. With communications technology rapidly changing, today's businesses are challenged to find ways to adapt the technology to provide better products and services for their customers and make their operations more efficient. For individuals, the new technology offers increased access to worldwide information and services, and provides new opportunities in business and education.

CHAPTER SUMMARY

1. **Communications**, sometimes called **data communications** refers to the transmission of data or information over a communications channel between one computer or a terminal and another computer.
2. **Telecommunications** describes any type of long-distance communications including television signals.
3. **Teleprocessing** refers to the use of telephone lines to transmit data.
4. The basic components of a communications system are: a personal computer or terminal; communications equipment that sends (and can usually receive) data; the communications channel over which data is sent; communications equipment that receives (and can usually send) data; and a computer. Communications software is also required.
5. A **communications channel**, also called a **communications line** or **communications link** is the link, or path, that the data follows as it is transmitted from the sending equipment to the receiving equipment in a communications system.
6. A communications channel can consist of various **transmission media** including twisted pair wire, coaxial cable, fiber optics, microwave transmission, satellite transmission, and wireless transmission.
7. **Twisted pair wire** is the color-coded copper wires that are twisted together and commonly used as telephone wire.
8. **Coaxial cable** is a high-quality communications line that is used in offices and laid underground and under the ocean. Coaxial cable consists of a copper wire conductor surrounded by a nonconducting insulator that is in turn surrounded by a woven metal mesh outer conductor, and finally a plastic outer coating.
9. Coaxial cable can be either **baseband**, carrying one signal at a time at very high rates of speed, or **broadband**, carrying multiple signals at a time.
10. **Fiber optics** uses technology based on the capability of smooth, hair-thin strands of glass that conduct light waves to rapidly and efficiently transmit data.

11. **Microwaves** are radio waves that can be used to provide high-speed transmissions of voice and data that are sent through the air between microwave stations.
12. **Communications satellites** are man-made space devices that receive, amplify, and retransmit signals from earth.
13. **Earth stations** are communications facilities that contain large, dish-shaped antennas used to transmit data to and receive data from communications satellites.
14. The transmission *to* the satellite is called an **uplink** and the transmission *from* the satellite to a receiving earth station is called a **downlink**.
15. Communications satellites are normally placed about 22,300 miles above the earth in a **geosynchronous orbit**.
16. **Wireless systems** use one of three transmission techniques: light beams, radio waves, or carrier-connect radio.
17. A **cellular telephone** uses radio waves to communicate with a local antenna assigned to a specific geographic area called a cell.
18. **Line configurations** can be either point-to-point lines or multidrop lines.
19. A **point-to-point line** is a direct line between a sending and receiving device. It may be either a **switched line** (a connection established through regular telephone lines) or a **dedicated line** (a line whose connection between devices is always established).
20. If the dedicated line is provided by an outside organization, it is sometimes called a **leased line**, or a **private line**.
21. The process of establishing the communications connection is sometimes referred to as the **handshake**.
22. A **multidrop line**, also known as a **multipoint line**, uses a single line to connect multiple devices to a main computer.
23. A multidrop line, or multipoint line, configuration is commonly used to connect multiple devices, such as terminals or personal computers, on a single line to a main computer sometimes called a **host computer**.
24. Computer equipment processes data as **digital signals**, which are individual electrical pulses representing the bits that are grouped together to form characters.
25. **Analog signals** are continuous electrical waves that are used to transmit data over standard telephone lines.
26. Companies offering **digital data service** provide communications channels specifically designed to carry digital instead of voice signals.
27. Modems are not needed with digital data service; instead, users connect to the communications line through a device called a **data service unit (DSU)**.
28. There are two modes of transmitting data: **asynchronous transmission mode**, which transmits one character at a time at irregular intervals using start and stop bits, and **synchronous transmission mode**, which transmits blocks of data at regular intervals using timing signals to synchronize the sending and receiving equipment.
29. Transmissions may be classified according to the direction in which the data can flow on a line: sending only (**simplex transmission**); sending or receiving but in only one direction at a time (**half-duplex transmission**); and sending and receiving at the same time (**full-duplex transmission**).
30. The transmission rate of a communications channel depends on the **bandwidth** and its speed. The wider the bandwidth, the greater the number of signals that can be carried on the channel at one time and the more data that can be transmitted.
31. **Bits per second (bps)** is the number of bits that can be transmitted in one second.
32. The **baud rate** is the number of times per second that the signal being transmitted changes. With each change, one or more bits can be transmitted.
33. A **modem** converts the digital signals of a terminal or computer to analog signals that are transmitted over a communications channel.
34. There are three basic types of modems: an **external modem**, which is a separate, stand-alone device attached to the computer or terminal by a cable and to the telephone outlet by a standard telephone cable; an **internal modem**, which is a circuit board installed inside a computer or terminal; and an **acoustic modem**, or **acoustic coupler**, which is a device used with a telephone handset.
35. A **multiplexor**, or MUX, combines more than one input signal into a single stream of data that can be transmitted over a communications channel.
36. A **front-end processor** is a computer dedicated to handling the communications requirements of a larger computer.
37. A front-end processor would use **polling** to check the connected terminals or computers to see if they have data to send.
38. **Communications software** consists of programs that perform tasks such as **dialing** (software that stores, selects, and dials telephone numbers); **file transfer**; (moving files from one system to another); **terminal emulation**

(software that allows the personal computer to imitate or appear to be a specific type of terminal, so that the personal computer can connect to specific types of computers); and **data encryption** (software that can code and decode transmitted data for security purposes).

39. A **protocol** is a set of rules and procedures for exchanging information between computers.
40. A **network** is a collection of terminals, computers, and other equipment that use communications channels to share data, information, hardware, and software.
41. A **local area network (LAN)** is a communications network that covers a limited geographic area and is privately owned.
42. Two common uses of local area networks are **hardware resource sharing**, which allows all network users to access a single piece of equipment rather than each user having to be connected to his or her own device, and **information resource sharing**, which allows the network users to access data stored on other computers in the network.
43. A **server**, sometimes called a **network control unit**, is a computer that is dedicated to handling the communications needs of the other computers in a network.
44. Information sharing is usually provided by using either the **file-server** of **client-server** method.
45. When a commercial software package is accessed by many users within the same organization, a special agreement called a **site license** can usually be obtained from the software vendor.
46. A **wide area network (WAN)** is a network that covers a large geographical area.
47. Public wide area network companies include so-called **common carriers** such as the telephone companies.
48. Companies called **value-added carriers** lease channels from the common carriers to provide specialized communications services referred to as **value added networks**.
49. **Packet-switching** combines individual packets of information from various users and transmits them together over a high-speed channel.
50. **Integrated Services Digital Network (ISDN)** services is an international standard for the digital transmission of both voice and data using different channels and communications companies.
51. Network **topology** describes the configuration, or physical layout, of the equipment in a communications network.
52. Devices connected to a network, such as terminals, printers, or other computers, are referred to as **nodes**.
53. A **star network** contains a central computer and one or more terminals or computers connected to it, forming a star.
54. In a **bus network**, all the devices in the network are connected to and share a single cable.
55. A **ring network** has a series of computers connected to each other in a ring.
56. A **gateway** is a combination of hardware and software that allows users on one network to access the resources on a *different* type of network.
57. A **bridge** is a combination of hardware and software that is used to connect *similar* networks.

KEY TERMS

Acoustic coupler *8.13*
Acoustic modem *8.13*
Analog signal *8.10*
Asynchronous transmission
   mode *8.10*
Bandwidth *8.12*
Baseband *8.3*
Baud rate *8.12*
Bits per second (bps) *8.12*
Bridge *8.19*
Broadband *8.3*
Bus network *8.19*
Cellular telephone *8.5*
Client-server *8.16*
Coaxial cable *8.3*

Common carrier *8.17*
Communications channel *8.3*
Communications line *8.3*
Communications link *8.3*
Communications satellite *8.4*
Communications *8.2*
Communications software *8.14*
Data communications *8.2*
Data encryption *8.15*
Data service unit (DSU) *8.10*
Dedicated line *8.7*
Dialing software *8.14*
Digital data service *8.10*
Digital signal *8.10*

Downlink *8.4*
Earth station *8.4*
External modem *8.12*
Fiber optics *8.3*
File transfer software *8.15*
File-server *8.16*
Front-end processor *8.14*
Full-duplex transmission *8.11*
Gateway *8.19*
Geosynchronous orbit *8.4*
Half-duplex transmission *8.11*
Handshake *8.7*
Hardware resource sharing *8.16*
Host computer *8.8*

R E V I E W   Q U E S T I O N S

1. Draw and label the basic components of a communications system.
2. List six kinds of transmission media used for communications channels.
3. Describe the two major types of line configurations. What are the advantages and disadvantages of each?
4. List and describe the three types of data transmission (direction) that are used.
5. Why is a modem used? Describe three types of modems that are available.
6. List and explain four tasks that communications software can perform.
7. What is a communications protocol?
8. Discuss the reasons for using a local area network.
9. Name three topologies, or configurations, that are used with networks. Draw a diagram of each.
10. Explain bridges and gateways and how they are used.

C O N T R O V E R S I A L   I S S U E S

1. Some people believe that better control is maintained if data is stored and processed on a central minicomputer or mainframe. Others believe that personal computer networks that provide decentralized storage and processing are best. Discuss the advantages and disadvantages of both types of systems.
2. Some personal computer users have used communications equipment and software to illegally gain access to private databases. These individuals, known as *hackers*, often claim that their illegal access was only a harmless prank. Do you think this type of computer usage is harmless? Explain your position.

R E S E A R C H   P R O J E C T S

1. Call or visit a communications company and obtain information relating to the types of services they provide for customers who transmit computer data. Prepare a report on this information for your class.
2. Obtain information about modems for personal computers. Prepare a report for your class that discusses the features and cost of both internal and external models.

Operating Systems and Systems Software

9

SYSTEMS SOFTWARE

OBJECTIVES

◆ Describe the three major categories of systems software

◆ Define the term operating system

◆ Describe the various types of operating systems and explain the differences in their capabilities

◆ Describe the functions of an operating system, including allocating system resources, monitoring system activities, and disk and file management

◆ Explain the difference between proprietary and portable operating systems

◆ Name and briefly describe the major operating systems that are being used today

◆ Discuss utilities and language translators

When most people think of software they think of applications software such as word processing, spreadsheet, and database software. For applications software to run on a computer, however, another type of software is needed to interface between the user, the applications software, and the equipment. This software consists of programs that are referred to as the operating system. The operating system is part of what is called systems software.

In this chapter, we discuss operating system features of both large and small computer systems. It is important to understand the features of large computer operating systems because these features are steadily being implemented on small systems such as personal computers.

USER

APPLICATIONS SOFTWARE

SYSTEMS SOFTWARE

Operating System
System Programs

COMPUTER EQUIPMENT

FIGURE 9-1
The operating system
and other systems soft-
ware programs act as an
interface between the
user, the applications
software, and the com-
puter equipment.

WHAT IS SYSTEMS SOFTWARE?

◆ **Systems software** consists of all the programs including the operating system that are related to controlling the operations of the computer equipment. Some of the functions that systems software perform include: starting up the computer; loading, executing, and storing applications programs; storing and retrieving files; and performing a variety of functions such as formatting disks, sorting data files, and translating program instructions into machine language. Systems software can be classified into three major categories; operating systems, utilities, and language translators.

WHAT IS AN OPERATING SYSTEM?

◆ An **operating system (OS)** consists of one or more programs that manage the operations of a computer. These programs function as an interface between the user, the applications programs, and the computer equipment (Figure 9-1).

The operating system is usually stored on a disk. For a computer to operate, the essential and most frequently used instructions in the operating system must be copied from the disk and stored in the main memory of the computer. This *resident* portion of the operating system is called by many different names: the **supervisor**, **monitor**, **executive**, **master program**, **control program**, or **kernel**. The *nonresident* portion of the operating system, which consists of the less frequently used instructions, remains stored on a disk and is available to be loaded into main memory whenever it is needed.

LOADING AN OPERATING SYSTEM

◆ The process of loading an operating system into main memory is called **booting** the system. Figure 9-2 shows the steps that occur when an operating system is loaded on a personal computer. This process is not identical to that used on large computers, but it is similar.

1. A diskette that contains the operating system is placed in the disk drive. If the operating system is already stored on a hard disk, the diskette would not be necessary.
2. When the computer is turned on, a series of instructions stored in ROM called the boot routine issue the commands to load the operating system into main memory. To do this, a copy of the operating system is transferred from the diskette or hard disk into main memory.

3. The instructions that loaded the operating system transfer control of the computer to the operating system. In many cases, the operating system displays a message requesting that the user enter the correct date and time, after which the **operating system prompt** appears. This prompt indicates to the user that the operating system has been loaded and is ready to accept a command such as to begin an application program.

FIGURE 9-2
To load the operating system into a personal computer ①, a copy of the operating system is transferred from the disk ② and stored in main memory (RAM) ③. After the user enters the date and time ④, the system prompt A> appears on the screen.

Once the operating system is loaded into main memory, it usually remains in memory until the computer is turned off. The operating system controls the loading and manages the execution of each application program that is requested by the user. When an application program completes its task or a user finishes using the application program, the operating system displays the system prompt again.

TYPES OF OPERATING SYSTEMS

The types of operating systems include single program, multiprogramming, multiprocessing, and virtual machine operating systems. These operating systems can be classified by two criteria: (1) whether they allow more than one user to use the computer at the same time and (2) whether they allow more than one program to run at the same time (Figure 9-3).

	SINGLE PROGRAM	**MULTIPROGRAMMING**	**MULTIPROCESSING**	**VIRTUAL MACHINE**
NUMBER OF PROGRAMS RUNNING	One	More than one	More than one on each CPU	More than one on each operating system
NUMBER OF USERS	One	One or more than one (Multiuser)	More than one on each CPU	More than one on each operating system

FIGURE 9-3
Operating systems can be classified by whether they allow more than one user and more than one program to be operating at the same time.

Single Program

Single program operating systems allow only a single user to run a single program at one time. This was the first type of operating system developed. Today, many personal computers use this type of operating system. For example, if you are working on a personal computer with a single program operating system you can load only one application, such as a spreadsheet, into main memory. If you want to work on another application, such as word processing, you must exit the spreadsheet application and load the word processing program into memory.

Multiprogramming

Multiprogramming operating systems, also called **multitasking** operating systems, allow more than one program to be run at the same time on one computer. Even though the CPU is only capable of working on one program instruction at a time, its capability to switch back and forth between programs makes it appear that all programs are running at the same time. For example, with a multiprogramming operating system the computer could be performing a complex spreadsheet calculation and at the same time be downloading a file from another computer while the user is writing a memo with the word processing program.

Multiprogramming operating systems on personal computers can usually support a single user running multiple programs. Multiprogramming operating systems on some personal computers and most minicomputers and mainframes can support more than one user running more than one program. This version of a multiprogramming operating system is sometimes called a **multiuser-multiprogramming** operating system. Most of these operating systems also allow more than one user to be running the same program. For example, a wholesale distributor may have dozens of terminal operators entering sales orders using the same order entry program on the same computer.

Multiprocessing

Computers that have more than one CPU are called **multiprocessors**. A **multiprocessing** operating system coordinates the operations of computers with more than one CPU. Because each CPU in a multiprocessor computer can be executing one program instruction, more than one instruction can be executed simultaneously. Besides providing an increase in performance, most multiprocessors offer another advantage. If one CPU fails, work can be shifted to the remaining CPUs. In addition to an extra CPU, some systems, called **fault-tolerant computers**, are built with redundant components such as memory, input and output controllers, and disk drives. If any one of the components fail, the system can continue to operate with the duplicate component. Fault-tolerant systems are used for airline reservation systems, communications networks, bank teller machines, and other applications where it is important to keep the computer operating at all times.

Virtual Machine — on LSD

A **virtual machine** (VM) operating system allows a single computer to run two or more different operating systems. The VM operating system allocates system resources such as memory and processing time to each operating system. To users it appears that they are working on separate systems, hence the term virtual machine. The advantage of this approach is that an organization can run different operating systems (at the same time) that are best suited to different tasks. For example, some operating systems are best for interactive processing and others are best for batch processing. With a VM operating system both types of operating systems can be run concurrently.

FUNCTIONS OF OPERATING SYSTEMS

◆ The operating system performs a number of functions that allow the user and the applications software to interact with the computer. These functions apply to all operating systems but become more complex for operating systems that allow more than one program to run at a time. The functions can be grouped into three types: allocating system resources, monitoring system activities, and disk and file management (Figure 9-4).

ALLOCATING RESOURCES	MONITORING ACTIVITIES	DISK AND FILE MANAGEMENT
CPU management	System performance	Formatting
Memory management	System security	Copying
Input/output management		Deleting

FIGURE 9-4
Operating system functions.

Allocating System Resources

The primary function of the operating system is to allocate, or assign, the resources of the computer system. That is, like a police officer directing traffic, the operating system decides what resource will currently be used and for how long. These resources include the CPU, main memory, and the input and output devices such as disk and tape drives and printers.

CPU Management Because a CPU can only work on one program instruction at a time, a multiprogramming operating system must keep switching the CPU among the different instructions of the programs that are waiting to be performed. A common way of allocating CPU processing is time slicing. A **time slice** is a fixed amount of CPU processing time, usually measured in milliseconds (thousandths of a second). With this technique, each user in turn receives a time slice. Since some instructions take longer to execute than others, some users may have more instructions completed in their time slice than other users. When a user's time slice has expired, the operating system directs the CPU to work on another user's program instructions, and the most recent user moves to the end of the line to await the next time slice (Figure 9-5). Unless the system has a heavy work load, however, users may not even be aware that their program has been temporarily set aside. Before they notice a delay, the operating system has allocated them another time slice and their processing continues.

FIGURE 9-5

With the time slice method of CPU management, each application is allocated one or more fixed amounts of time called slices. Higher priority (more important) applications receive more consecutive slices than lower priority applications. When its processing time has expired, an application goes to the end of the line until all other applications have received at least one time slice. Here, application 2 is the lowest priority and so receives only one time slice. Application 1 is the highest priority and receives three time slices.

APPLICATIONS WAITING TO BE PROCESSED

Processing Priorities:
Application 1 High 3 Time Slices
Application 2 Low 1 Time Slice
Application 3 Medium 2 Time Slices

Because some work has a higher priority or is more important than other work, most operating systems have ways to adjust the amount of time slices a user receives, either automatically or based on user-specified criteria. One technique for modifying the number of time slices is to have different priorities assigned to each user. For each time slice received by the lowest priority, the highest priority would receive several consecutive time slices. For example, it would be logical to assign a higher priority to a program that processes orders and records sales than to an accounting program that could be run at a later time. Another way to allocate time slices is based on the type of work being performed. For example, some operating systems automatically allocate more time slices to interactive processes such as keyboard entry than they do to CPU-only processes such as calculations or batch processing. This gives a higher priority to users entering data than to a report being output to a printer.

Another way of assigning processing priorities is to designate each job as either foreground or background. **Foreground** jobs receive a higher processing priority and therefore more CPU time. Data entry would be an example of a job that would be classified as a foreground job. **Background** jobs receive a lower processing priority and less CPU time. Printing a report or calculating payroll are examples of jobs that could be classified as background jobs. Background jobs usually involve batch processing or require little or no computer operator intervention.

Memory Management During processing, main memory stores such items as the operating system, application program instructions for one or more programs, data waiting to be processed, and work space used for calculations, sorting, and other temporary tasks. It is the operating system's job to allocate, or assign, each of these items to areas of main memory. Data that has just been read into main memory from an input device or is waiting to be sent to an output device is stored in areas of main memory called **buffers**. The operating system assigns the location of the buffers in main memory and manages the data that is stored in them.

Operating systems allocate at least some portion of memory into fixed areas called partitions (Figure 9-6). Some operating systems allocate all memory on this basis while others use partitions only for the operating system instructions and buffers.

Another way of allocating memory is called virtual memory management, or virtual storage. **Virtual memory management** increases the effective (or *virtual*) limits of memory by expanding the amount of main memory to include disk space. Without virtual memory management, an entire program must be loaded into main memory during execution. With virtual memory management, only the portion of the program that is currently being used is required to be in main memory. Virtual memory management is used with multiprogramming operating systems to maximize the number of programs using memory at the same time. The operating system performs virtual memory management by transferring data and instructions to and from memory and the disk by using one or both of the two methods, segmentation and paging.

In **segmentation**, programs are divided into logical portions called **segments**. For example, one segment of a program might edit data and another segment might perform a calculation. Because the segments are based on logical portions of a program, some segments are larger than others. When a particular program instruction is required, the segment containing that instruction is transferred from the disk into main memory.

In **paging**, a fixed number of bytes is transferred from the disk each time data or program instructions are required. This fixed amount of data is called a **page**, or a **frame**. The size of a page, generally from 512 to 4,000 bytes, is determined by the operating system. Because a page is a fixed number of bytes, it may not correspond to a logical division of a program like a segment.

In both segmentation and paging, a time comes when memory is full but another page or segment needs to be read into memory. When this occurs, the operating system makes room for the new data or instructions by writing back to disk one or more of the pages or segments currently in memory. This process is referred to as **swapping** (Figure 9-7). The operating system usually chooses the least recently used page or segment to transfer back to disk.

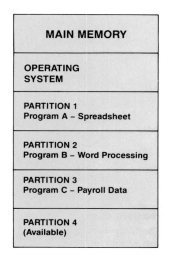

FIGURE 9-6
Some computer systems allocate memory into fixed blocks called partitions. The CPU then keeps track of programs and data by assigning them to a specific partition.

FIGURE 9-7
With virtual memory management, the operating system expands the amount of main memory to include available disk space. Data and program instructions are transferred to and from memory and disk as required. The segmentation technique transfers logical portions of programs that might be different sizes. The paging technique transfers pages of the same size. To make room for the new page or segment, the least recently used page or segment is *swapped*, or written back to the disk.

Input and Output Management   At any given time, more than one input device can be sending data to the computer. At the same time, the CPU could be ready to send data to an output device such as a terminal or printer or a storage device such as a disk. The operating system is responsible for managing these input and output processes.

Some devices, such as a tape drive, are usually allocated to a specific user or application program. This is because tape is a sequential storage medium, and generally it would not make sense to have more than one application writing records to a single tape. Disk drives are usually allocated to all users because the programs and data files that users need are stored on these devices. The operating system keeps track of disk read and write requests, stores these requests in buffers along with the associated data for write requests, and usually processes them sequentially. A printer could be allocated to all users or restricted to a specific user. For example, a printer would be restricted to a specific user if the printer was going to be used with preprinted forms such as payroll checks.

Because the printer is a relatively slow device compared to other computer system devices, the technique of spooling is used to increase printer efficiency and reduce the number of printers required. With **spooling** (Figure 9-8), a report is first written (saved) to the disk before it is printed. Writing to the disk is much faster than writing to the printer. For example, a report that may take one-half hour to print (depending on the speed of the printer) may take only one minute to write to the disk. After the report is written to the disk, the CPU is available to process other programs. The report saved on the disk can be printed at a later time or, on a multiprogramming operating system, a print program can be run (at the same time other programs are running) to process the **print spool** (the reports on the disk waiting to be printed).

FIGURE 9-8
Spooling increases both CPU and printer efficiency by writing reports to the disk before they are printed. After the reports are written to disk, the CPU can begin processing other programs. Writing to the disk is much faster than writing directly to the printer.

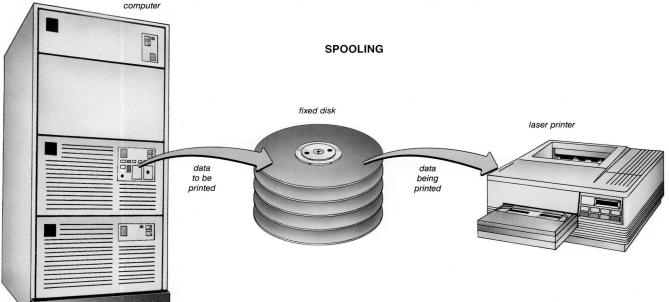

SPOOLING

computer

fixed disk

laser printer

data to be printed

data being printed

Because many input and output devices use different commands and control codes to transmit and receive data, programs called **device drivers** are used by the operating system to control these devices. For example, a different device driver would be required for a high-resolution color monitor than for a standard-resolution monochrome monitor. Output device drivers for monitors and printers are usually supplied by applications software developers along with their specific application such as word processing or spreadsheet. Input device drivers for equipment such as a mouse or scanner are usually supplied by the equipment manufacturer.

Monitoring System Activities

Another function of the operating system is monitoring the system activity. This includes monitoring system performance and system security.

System Performance   System performance can be measured in a number of ways but is usually gauged by the user in terms of response time. **Response time** is the amount of time from the moment a user enters data until the computer responds. Response time can vary based on what the user has entered. If the user is simply entering data into a file, the response time is usually within a second or two. However, if the user has just completed a request for a display of sorted data from several files, the response time could be minutes.

FIGURE 9-9
System performance measurement programs report the amount of time the CPU is actually working and not waiting to process data.

A more precise way of measuring performance is to run a program that is designed to record and report system activity. Among other information, these programs usually report **CPU utilization**, the amount of time that the CPU is working and not idle, waiting for data to process. Figure 9-9 shows a CPU performance measurement report.

Another measure of performance is to compare the CPU utilization with the disk input and output rate, referred to as disk I/O. We previously discussed how a virtual memory management operating system swaps pages or segments from disk to memory as they are needed. Systems with heavy work loads and insufficient memory or CPU power can get into a situation called **thrashing**, where the system is spending more time moving pages to and from the disk than processing the data. System performance reporting can alert the computer operations manager to this problem.

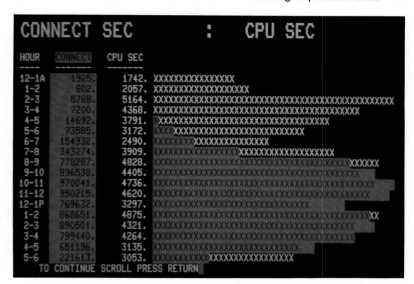

System Security   Most multiuser operating systems provide for a logon code, a user ID, and a password that must all be entered correctly before a user is allowed to use an application program (Figure 9-10). Each is a word or series of characters. A **logon code** usually identifies the application that will be used, such as accounting, sales, or manufacturing. A **user ID** identifies the user, such as Jeffrey Ryan or Mary Gonzales. The **password** is usually confidential; often it is known only to the user and the computer system administrator. The logon code, user ID, and password must match entries in an authorization file. If they don't match, the user is denied access to the system. Both successful and unsuccessful logon attempts are often recorded in a file so that management can review who is using or attempting to use the system. These logs can also be used to allocate data processing expenses based on the percentage of system use by an organization's various departments.

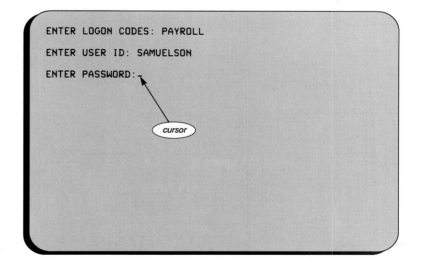

FIGURE 9-10
The logon code, user ID, and password must all be entered correctly before the user is allowed to use the computer. Because the password is confidential, it is usually not displayed on the screen when the user enters it.

Disk and File Management

In addition to allocating system resources and monitoring system activities, most operating systems contain programs that can perform functions related to disk and file management. Some of these functions include formatting disks and diskettes, deleting files from a disk, copying files from one auxiliary storage device to another, and renaming stored files.

POPULAR OPERATING SYSTEMS

The first operating systems were developed by manufacturers for the computers in their product line. When the manufacturers came out with another computer or model, they often produced an improved and different operating system. Since programs are designed to be used with a particular operating system, this meant that users who wanted to switch computers, either from one vendor to another or to a different model from the same vendor, would have to convert their existing programs to run under the new operating system. Today, however, the trend is away from operating systems limited to a specific model and toward operating systems that will run on any model by a particular manufacturer. For example, part of Digital Equipment Corporation's success has been attributed to the fact that their VMS operating system is used on all their computer systems.

Going even further, many computer users are supporting the move away from **proprietary operating systems** (meaning privately owned) and toward **portable operating systems** that will run on many manufacturers' computers. The advantage of portable operating systems is that the user is not tied to a particular manufacturer. Using a portable operating system, a user could change computer systems, yet retain existing software and data files, which usually represent a sizable investment in time and money. For example, say a small business purchased a computer system to handle their immediate needs and to provide for several years of anticipated growth. Five years later, the business has reached the capacity of the computer; no more memory or terminals can be added. In addition, the manufacturer of the five-year-old computer does not make a larger or more powerful model. But because they originally chose a computer that used a portable operating system, the business can purchase a more powerful computer from another manufacturer that offers the same portable operating system and continue to use their existing software and data files.

One of the most popular portable operating systems is UNIX, which we will discuss along with the several personal computer operating systems.

UNIX

The **UNIX** operating system was developed in the early 1970s by scientists at Bell Laboratories. It was specifically designed to provide a way to manage a variety of scientific and specialized computer applications. Because of federal regulations, Bell Labs (a subsidiary of AT&T) was prohibited from actively promoting UNIX in the commercial marketplace. Instead, for a low fee Bell Labs licensed UNIX to numerous colleges and universities where it obtained a wide following. With the deregulation of the telephone companies in the 1980s, AT&T was allowed to enter the computer system marketplace. With AT&T's increased promotion and the trend toward portable operating systems, UNIX has aroused tremendous interest. One of the advantages of UNIX is its extensive library of over 400 instruction modules that can be linked together to perform almost any programming task. Today, most major computer manufacturers offer a multiuser version of the UNIX operating system to run on their computers.

With all its strengths, however, UNIX has not yet obtained success in the commercial business systems marketplace. Some people attribute this to the fact that UNIX has never been considered user friendly. For example, most of the UNIX program modules are identified by obscure names such as MAUS, SHMOP, and BRK. Other critics contend that UNIX lacks the file management capabilities to support the online interactive databases that more and more businesses are implementing. With the support of most major computer manufacturers, however, these problems are being worked on and UNIX has a good chance of becoming one of the major operating systems of the coming years.

MS-DOS

The Microsoft Disk Operating System, or **MS-DOS**, was released by Microsoft Corporation in 1981. MS-DOS was originally developed for IBM for their first personal computer system. IBM calls their equivalent version of the operating system **PC-DOS**. Because so many personal computer manufacturers followed IBM's lead and chose MS-DOS for their computers, MS-DOS quickly became an industry standard. Other personal computer operating systems exist, but by far the majority of personal computer software is written for MS-DOS. This single-user operating system is so widely used that it is often referred to simply as DOS.

Macintosh

The Apple **Macintosh** multiprogramming operating system provides a graphic interface that uses icons (figures) and windows (Figure 9-11). Macintosh users interface with the operating system through the use of features called Finder and Multifinder. Finder allows the user to run single programs and perform utility functions such as organizing and finding files.

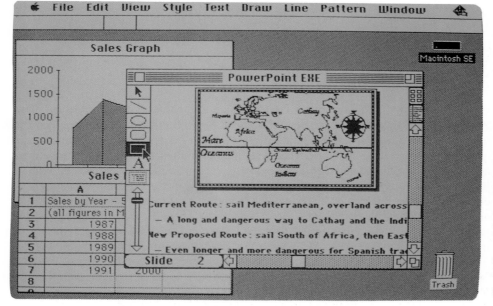

FIGURE 9-11
The Macintosh operating system offers a graphic user interface and the capability to display information in separate windows.

Multifinder allows the user to have certain processes, such as printing a document, run in the background while other processes, such as working on a spreadsheet, are currently being accessed. The Macintosh operating system has set the standard for operating system ease of use and has been the model for most of the new graphic user interfaces developed for non-Macintosh systems.

OS/2

In 1988, IBM released the **OS/2** operating system for its new family of PS/2 personal computers (Figure 9-12). Microsoft Corporation, which developed OS/2 for IBM, also released their equivalent version, called MS-OS/2. OS/2 is designed to take advantage of the increased computing power of the Intel 80286, 80386, and 80486 microprocessors and will run only on systems that use these chips. OS/2 also requires more computing power to operate. For example, OS/2 requires 5MB of hard disk and a minimum of 2MB of main memory just to run the operating system. Additional features offered by OS/2 include the capability to run larger and more complex programs and the capability to do multiprogramming (OS/2 can have up to 12 programs running at the same time).

FIGURE 9-12

IBM's OS/2 operating system takes advantage of the increased processing power of the latest personal computer systems.

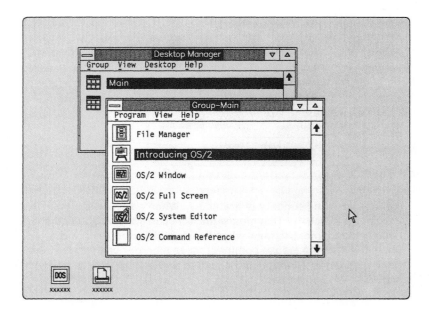

Other Operating Systems

Other popular operating systems exist in addition to the ones we just discussed. The ProDos operating system is used on millions of Apple II computer systems. The PICK operating system is a portable operating system that runs on personal, minicomputers, and mainframes. The PICK operating system incorporates a relational database manager and has had much success in the business data processing marketplace. Minicomputer manufacturers usually provide operating systems that operate only on their equipment. Most minicomputer companies, however, now offer versions of the UNIX and Pick operating systems as well. Most mainframe operating systems are unique to a particular make of computer or are designed to be compatible with one of IBM's operating systems such as DOS/VS, MVS, or VM, IBM's virtual machine operating system.

Although not yet widely used, the MACH operating system has been called a possible replacement for the increasingly popular UNIX operating system and possibly the standard operating system of the future. Considered a streamlined version of UNIX, MACH has the support of several large governmental and educational organizations. Currently being developed by Carnegie Mellon University, MACH has also been chosen by the Open Software Foundation (OSF), a 170 member organization that is trying to establish an industrywide operating system standard.

OPERATING ENVIRONMENTS

◆ Because of the success of the Macintosh operating system, systems software developers have looked for ways to make other operating systems easier to use. One way has been to create an operating environment. An **operating environment**, sometimes called a **windowing environment**, is a graphic interface between the user and the operating system such as DOS, OS/2, or UNIX. Some operating environments, such as Microsoft's Windows (Figure 9-13), are separate software programs that can be added to existing DOS-based systems. Other operating environments, such as IBM's Presentation Manager for OS/2, are included with the operating system. Common features and advantages of an operating environment include use of a mouse, pull-down menus, the capability to have several applications open at the same time, and the capability to easily move data from one application such as a spreadsheet to another application such as a word processing document.

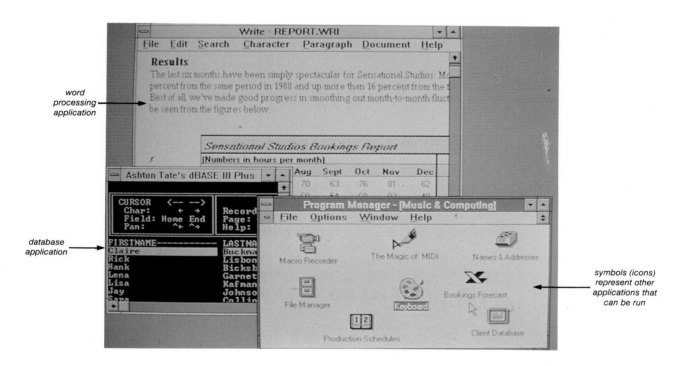

Closely related to operating environments are operating system shell programs. Like an operating environment, a **shell** program acts as an interface between the user and the operating system. Shell programs, however, usually offer a limited number of utility functions such as file maintenance and do not offer applications windowing or graphics.

UTILITIES

◆ In addition to the programs in the operating system, systems software also contains programs called utilities. **Utilities** are programs that provide commonly needed tasks such as file backups, sorting, and editing. Sort utilities place the data stored in files into ascending or descending order based on a value stored in one or more specified fields of each record in a file. For example, a sort utility program could be used

FIGURE 9-13
Microsoft's Windows operating environment provides a graphic user interface for computers that use the DOS operating system. Windows provides the capability to have different applications running in separate windows. The window on the left shows a dBASE III PLUS database application. The window at the top shows a word processing document. The window at the lower right is used to start other application programs represented by the symbols (called icons) shown in the window.

FIGURE 9-14
Utility programs such as PC Tools Deluxe offer a number of functions to help the user perform routine tasks more efficiently. The functions available for maintaining files appear on the screen.

to sort the records in a personnel file in alphabetical order by the employees' last names. An **editor** is a utility program that allows users to make direct changes to programs and data. A programmer can use an editor to change a program instruction that was incorrect or needs to be modified.

Microcomputer operating systems usually contain programs that provide some utility functions such as copying files. In addition, software packages can be purchased to enhance a user's library of systems software. Three popular packages are The Mace Utilities, PC Tools Deluxe, and The Norton Utilities, Advanced Edition. Figure 9-14 shows the file utility functions that are part of PC Tools Deluxe. With larger computer systems, a set of utility programs are usually supplied by the vendor as part of the systems software that is delivered with the computer system.

LANGUAGE TRANSLATORS

Special-purpose systems software programs called **language translators** are used to convert the programming instructions written by programmers into the machine instructions that a computer can understand. Language translators are written for specific programming languages and computer systems. Language translators are explained in more detail in Chapter 12, Program Development.

SUMMARY OF OPERATING SYSTEMS AND SYSTEMS SOFTWARE

Systems software, including the operating system, utilities, and language translators, are essential parts of a computer system and should be understood by users who want to obtain the maximum benefits from their computer. This is especially true for the latest personal computer operating systems that include features such as virtual memory management and multiprogramming. Understanding and being able to use these and other features will give users more control over their computer resources.

CHAPTER SUMMARY

1. **Systems software** consists of all the programs including the operating system that are related to controlling the operations of the computer.
2. An **operating system (OS)** consists of one or more programs that manage the operations of a computer.
3. Operating systems function as an interface between the user, the application programs, and the computer equipment.
4. The essential and most frequently used instructions in an operating system must be stored in main memory for the computer to operate.

5. The *resident* portion of the operating system is called by many different names: the **supervisor, monitor, executive, master program, control program,** or **kernel**.

6. The *nonresident* portion of the operating system, which consists of the less frequently used instructions, remains stored on a disk and is available to be loaded into main memory whenever it is needed.

7. **Booting** the system is the process of loading the operating system into the main memory of a computer.

8. The **operating system prompt** indicates that the operating system has been loaded and is ready to accept a command.

9. **Single program** operating systems allow a single user to run a single program at one time.

10. **Multiprogramming** operating systems, also called **multitasking** operating systems, allow more than one program to be run at the same time.

11. A multiprogramming operating system that allows multiple users is called a **multiuser-multiprogramming** operating system.

12. A **multiprocessor** computer has more than one CPU. **Multiprocessing** operating systems coordinate the operations of these computers.

13. **Fault-tolerant computers** are built with redundant components to allow processing to continue if any single component fails.

14. A **virtual machine (VM)** operating system allows a single computer to run two or more different operating systems.

15. The functions of an operating system include allocating system resources, monitoring system activities, and disk and file management.

16. The system resources that the operating system allocates include the CPU, main memory, and the input/output devices.

17. A **time slice** is a common way for an operating system to allocate CPU processing time.

18. **Foreground** jobs have a higher priority than **background** jobs and thus receive more CPU time.

19. **Buffers** are areas of main memory used to store data that has just been read or is being sent to an output device.

20. **Virtual memory management** increases the effective (or *virtual*) limits of memory by expanding the amount of main memory to include disk space. With virtual memory management, the operating system transfers data and programs between main memory and the disks by segmentation and paging.

21. In **segmentation**, programs are divided into logical portions called **segments**.

22. In **paging**, a fixed number of bytes called a **page**, or **frame**, is transferred from the disk each time data or program instructions are required.

23. The operating system is responsible for managing the input and output processes of the computer.

24. **Spooling** increases printer and computer system efficiency by writing a report to disk before it is printed.

25. The **print spool** refers to reports that have been stored on the disk and are waiting to be printed.

26. **Device drivers** are programs used by the operating system to control different input and output equipment.

27. **Response time** is the amount of time from the moment a user enters data until the computer responds.

28. System performance can be measured by the response time and by comparing the **CPU utilization** with the disk I/O to determine if the system is **thrashing**.

29. Most multiuser operating systems provide for a **logon code**, a **user ID**, and a **password** which all must be entered correctly before a user is allowed to use an application program.

30. Most operating systems contain programs that perform functions that are related to disk and file management.

31. Many computer users are supporting the move away from **proprietary operating systems** and toward **portable operating systems**.

32. Some of the popular operating systems being used today include **UNIX, MS-DOS, PC-DOS, Macintosh,** and **OS/2**.

33. An **operating environment**, sometimes called a **windowing environment**, is a graphic interface between the user and the operating system.

34. A **shell** program acts as an interface between the user and the operating system.

35. **Utilities** are programs that provide commonly needed tasks such as file backups, sorting, and editing.

36. An **editor** is a utility program that allows users to make direct changes to programs and data.

37. **Language translators** are used to convert the programming instructions written by programmers into the machine instructions that a computer can understand.

KEY TERMS

Background *9.6*
Booting *9.2*
Buffer *9.6*
Control program *9.2*
CPU utilization *9.9*
Device driver *9.8*
Editor *9.14*
Executive *9.2*
Fault-tolerant computer *9.5*
Foreground *9.6*
Frame *9.7*
Kernel *9.2*
Language translators *9.14*
Logon code *9.9*
Macintosh *9.11*
Master program *9.2*
Monitor *9.2*

MS-DOS *9.11*
Multiprocessing *9.4*
Multiprocessor *9.4*
Multiprogramming *9.4*
Multitasking *9.4*
Multiuser-multiprogramming *9.4*
Operating environment *9.13*
Operating system (OS) *9.2*
Operating system prompt *9.3*
OS/2 *9.12*
Page *9.7*
Paging *9.7*
Password *9.9*
Portable operating system *9.10*
Print spool *9.8*
Proprietary operating system *9.10*
PC-DOS *9.11*

Response time *9.9*
Segment *9.7*
Segmentation *9.7*
Shell *9.13*
Single program *9.4*
Spooling *9.8*
Supervisor *9.2*
Swapping *9.7*
Systems software *9.2*
Time slice *9.5*
Thrashing *9.9*
UNIX *9.10*
User ID *9.9*
Utilities *9.13*
Virtual machine (VM) *9.5*
Virtual memory management *9.7*
Windowing environment *9.13*

REVIEW QUESTIONS

1. How does systems software differ from applications software?
2. Describe how to boot an operating system on a personal computer.
3. What are the different types of operating systems? How are they different?
4. The functions of an operating system can be grouped into which three types?
5. How does an operating system use time slices to assign different processing priorities to jobs?
6. Describe how an operating system uses the disk drive to perform virtual memory management.
7. How does spooling increase printer and computer system efficiency?
8. Discuss several techniques used to measure computer system performance.
9. Describe three types of authorization that an operating system can use to provide system access security.
10. What are the advantages of a portable operating system.
11. List several tasks that the utility programs can perform.

CONTROVERSIAL ISSUE

1. Many people believe that a graphics user interface will eventually be part of all operating systems. Others prefer a nongraphic, command-line operating system. Discuss the advantages and disadvantages of both.

RESEARCH PROJECTS

1. Prepare a paper comparing the MS-DOS and Unix operating systems.

Management Information Systems

OBJECTIVES

◆ Define the term management information systems

◆ Describe why information is important to an organization

◆ Discuss the different levels in an organization and how the information requirements differ for each level

◆ Explain the qualities that all information should have

◆ Define the term information system and identify the six elements of an information system

◆ Describe the different types of information systems and the trend toward integration

◆ Explain how personal computers are used in management information systems

Management information systems, often abbreviated MIS, is a frequently used computer industry term. It is often used, however, to mean different things. It can describe the total system from which information flows to employees of an organization. This could include manual and automated methods as well as computerized systems. The term MIS can also be used to refer to only those portions of a system that provide information to management. Finally, MIS can refer to the department that manages the computer resources of an organization. For the purposes of this chapter, we use a broad definition of **management information systems (MIS)** to mean any computer-based system that provides timely and accurate information for managing an organization. To better understand how a MIS system provides this information, we first need to discuss why information is important to an organization.

WHY IS INFORMATION IMPORTANT TO AN ORGANIZATION?

◆ More and more organizations are realizing that the information in their databases is an important asset that must be protected. Like more tangible assets such as buildings and equipment, an organization's information assets have both a present and future value and have costs associated with their acquisition, maintenance, and storage. Information is no longer thought of as a by-product of doing business, but rather as a key ingredient in both short- and long-range decision making.

Several factors have contributed to the increased need for timely and accurate information. Among these factors are expanded markets, increased competition, shorter product life cycles, and government regulation.

Expanded markets means that to be successful today, many businesses must sell their products in as many markets as possible. Often this means national as well as international distribution of a product. Companies that produce a product for local or regional use are at a disadvantage against companies that produce larger volumes of products for a wider distribution. When companies expand their markets they must have more information about a larger number of potential selling areas (markets) and the different ways of getting their products to those markets. Automobiles are an example of this trend. The number of automobile producers has decreased, and the surviving companies are moving toward worldwide distribution of their products.

Increased competition means that competing companies are financially stronger and better organized. It is, therefore, more important for organizations to have current information on how competitors are selling their products. Many companies now maintain large databases that include information on competitive product features, prices, and methods of distribution. For consumer product companies, this information often includes sales and percent of the total market. This information is important in measuring the impact of advertising campaigns. For example, many companies will measure the impact of a new advertising campaign in a limited geographic area such as a large metropolitan city, before they use the advertising nationwide.

Shorter product life cycles means that companies have less time to perfect a product. More often than not, the product has to be successful when it is first introduced because companies will have less time to make corrections after a product is introduced. This means that before they introduce products, they must have accurate information about what potential customers want. This has led to the increased use of test marketing. Company managers then use the results of tests to decide on advertising, packaging, and product features. Shorter product life cycles also require companies to begin work earlier on the next generation of products. To do this, managers must have information about existing product features that customers want changed and new features they want added.

Government regulation has also contributed to the need for more information. One good example of this is in human resource management. To comply with equal employment opportunity (EEO) guidelines and laws, organizations must keep detailed records on testing, hiring, and promotion practices. The employee database, once used almost exclusively for payroll purposes, has now been expanded to include valuable information on employee skill and education levels as well as the results of performance reviews. With this information companies can document their compliance with government regulations and guidelines.

HOW DO MANAGERS USE INFORMATION?

◆ All employees in an organization need information to effectively perform their jobs; but the primary users of information are managers. **Managers** of an organization are the men and women responsible for directing the use of resources such as people, money, materials, and information so the organization can operate efficiently and prosper. Managers work toward this goal by performing the four management tasks of planning, organizing, directing, and controlling.

1. *Planning* involves establishing goals and objectives. Upper levels of management also plan by establishing the strategies of the organization that will help meet these goals and objectives. For example, upper management often prepares a three- to five-year plan that includes strategies on how to enter new markets or increase existing market share. Lower levels of management plan by establishing specific policies and procedures to implement the strategies. A lower level management plan might include a specific inventory quantity to be maintained for a part.
2. *Organizing* includes identifying and bringing together the resources necessary to achieve the plans of an organization. Resources include people, money, materials (facilities, equipment, raw materials), and information. Organizing also involves establishing the management structure of an organization such as the departments and reporting relationships. For example, to introduce a new product, a company can assign responsibility to an existing department or form a new group whose sole responsibility is the new product.
3. *Directing* involves instructing and authorizing others to perform the necessary work. To direct effectively, managers must be able to communicate what needs to be done and motivate people to do the work. Directing often takes place at daily or weekly meetings where managers meet with their employees to discuss job priorities.
4. *Controlling* involves measuring performance and, if necessary, taking corrective action. Daily production reports are a control device that give managers the information they need to make any necessary adjustments in production rate or product mix.

Figure 10-1 shows how the four management tasks are usually performed in a sequence that becomes a recurring cycle. Actual performance is measured against a previously established plan as part of the control task; this often results in a revised plan. The revised plan may result in additional organizational and directional activities, and so the cycle repeats itself. The four tasks are related and a change in one task usually affects one or more of the other tasks.

All managers perform these management tasks but their area of focus, such as finance or production, and the information they need to perform the tasks is influenced by their level in the organization.

FIGURE 10-1
The four management tasks performed by management are to plan, organize, direct, and control. These tasks are part of a recurring cycle; actions connected with any one task usually affect one or more of the other tasks.

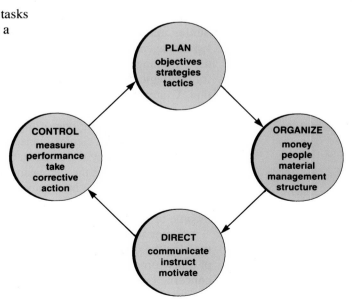

MANAGEMENT LEVELS IN AN ORGANIZATION

◆ Management is usually classified into three levels. The names for these levels can vary; we call them senior management, middle management and operational management. As shown in Figure 10-2, these three levels of management are above a fourth level of the organization consisting of the production, clerical, and nonmanagement staff. Together, these four levels make up the entire organization. The following sections discuss these levels and their different information requirements.

ORGANIZATION MODEL

FIGURE 10-2
The model of an organization's management includes three levels with a fourth level made up of the production, clerical, and other non-management employees. Each level makes different types of decisions and requires different types and amounts of information.

Senior Management — Strategic Decisions

Senior management, also referred to as executive or top management, includes the top management positions in an organization. Senior management is concerned with the long-range direction of the organization. Senior managers are primarily responsible for **strategic decisions** that deal with the overall goals and objectives of an organization. Examples of strategic decisions are whether to add or discontinue a product line or whether to diversify into a new business. The time frame for such decisions is usually long-range starting one or more years in the future and continuing for several years or indefinitely. Senior management decisions often involve factors that cannot be directly controlled by the organization such as the changing trends of society. An example of such a trend is the increasing average age of the population. Senior management decisions often require information from outside the company such as industry statistics, consumer surveys, or broad economic indicators such as the change in personal income or the number of new houses being built.

Senior management is also responsible for monitoring how current operations are meeting the objectives of previously made strategic decisions. For example, are sales of a new product meeting previously forecasted levels? Because senior management is concerned with all areas of an organization, it must rely on summarized information to review all operations in a timely manner. Often information on current operations is presented only if it is significantly above or below what was planned. This helps senior management to focus on only the variations that require its involvement.

Another senior management responsibility is to supervise middle management personnel.

Middle Management — Tactical Decisions

Middle management is responsible for implementing the strategic decisions of senior management. To do this, middle managers make **tactical decisions** that implement specific programs and plans necessary to accomplish the stated objectives. Tactical decisions could include how to best advertise and promote a company's products. Such decisions usually involve a shorter time frame than strategic decisions but often cover an entire year. Although they are interested in external events that may influence their work, middle managers are more concerned with the internal operations of the organization and, therefore, rely on information generated by the organization. Middle management also uses summarized and exception-oriented reports although not to the extent of senior management. Middle management sometimes must review detailed information in order to understand performance variances.

Middle management is also responsible for supervising operational management.

Operational Management — Operational Decisions

Operational management supervises the production, clerical, and nonmanagement staff of an organization. In performing their duties, operational managers make **operational decisions** that usually involve an immediate action such as accepting or rejecting an inventory delivery or approving a purchase order. The decision time frame of operational managers tasks is usually very short, such as a day, a week, or a month. Operational managers directly supervise the production and support of an organization's product or service; thus they need detailed information telling them what was produced. Summary and exception reporting, long an important tool for senior and middle level managers, is increasingly being used by operational managers. There are two reasons for this change. First, upper levels of management are allowing lower levels of management to make more decisions. Second, because of computerized systems, the information necessary to make decisions at lower levels is more easily available.

Nonmanagement Employees — On-the-Job Decisions

Nonmanagement employees, which include production, clerical, and staff personnel, also need frequent information to perform their jobs. The trend toward flexible manufacturing systems has increased the need for information to be available to the production worker. Instead of working at the same task all the time, production workers often work as a group on related tasks. Some manufacturing plants allow a group of workers to move with the product from the beginning of production to the end. Such changes require production workers to understand more about the production process than ever before. Often, this information is made available to the workers through the use of production-floor terminals that can be used to inquire on the next production process or tool required. Some systems tell the workers what job they should work on next.

Today, clerical and nonproduction workers also have more information available to them than in the past. For example, more documentation of administrative systems is being placed on-line for immediate access. As we previously mentioned, this is part of a trend toward giving lower level, nonmanagement employees the information they need to make decisions made formerly by managers.

Although we have classified the organization and its corresponding information requirements into four levels as is usually done, in the real world there is often a crossover from one level to another. For example, management and nonmanagement employees frequently join together in committees where all participants have an equal voice. Organizations have realized that formal or informal distinctions between managers and employees hinder communication and can restrict the flow of useful ideas and information. As we will discuss later in this chapter, recent technology, especially the personal computer, has significantly contributed to the flow of timely information to all levels within an organization.

Now that we have discussed why information is important to an organization and how it is used by the various levels, we explain the characteristics, or qualities, that all information should have.

QUALITIES OF INFORMATION

As we have discussed, the purpose of processing data is to create information. Just as data should have certain characteristics, so too should information. These characteristics are often called the qualities of information (Figure 10-3). Terms used to describe these qualities include: accurate, verifiable, timely, organized, meaningful, useful, and cost effective.

Although it may seem obvious, the first quality of information is that it should be *accurate*. Inaccurate information is often worse than no information at all. Accuracy is also a characteristic of data. Although accurate data does not guarantee accurate information, it is impossible to produce accurate information from erroneous data. The computer jargon term **GIGO** states this point very well; it stands for *Garbage In, Garbage Out*.

Closely related to accuracy is that information be *verifiable*. This means that if necessary, the user can confirm the information. For example, before relying on the amounts in a summary report, an accountant would want to know that the totals could be supported by details of the transactions. The accountant could verify the accuracy of the report totals by testing some or all of the totals by adding up the supporting detail records and comparing the results to the report.

Another quality of information is that it must be *timely*. Although most information loses its value with time, some information, such as trends, becomes more valuable as time passes and more information is obtained. The point to remember is that the timeliness must be appropriate for any decisions that will be made based on the information. Up-to-the-minute information may be required for some decisions such as the inventory level of a key part, while older information may be satisfactory or more appropriate for other decisions such as the number or employees planning vacations next month.

To be most valuable, information should be *organized* to suit users' requirements. For example, a sales manager that assigns territories on a geographic basis would need prospect lists sorted by ZIP code and not by prospect name.

Meaningful information indicates that the information is relevant to the person who receives it. Certain information is only meaningful to specific individuals or groups within an organization. Management should eliminate extraneous and unnecessary information and always consider the audience when it is accumulating or reporting information.

To be *useful*, information should result in an action being taken or specifically being not taken, depending on the situation. Often, this quality can be improved through exception reporting, which focuses only on the information that exceeds certain limits. An example of exception reporting is an inventory report showing items whose balance on hand is less than a predetermined minimum quantity. Rather than looking through an entire inventory report to find such items, the exception report would quickly bring these items to the attention of the managers responsible for maintaining the inventory.

Last, but not least, information must be *cost effective*. That is, the cost to produce the information must be less than the value of the information. This can sometimes be hard to determine. If the value of the information cannot be determined, perhaps the

QUALITIES OF INFORMATION

- ☑ Accurate
- ☑ Verifiable
- ☑ Timely
- ☑ Organized
- ☑ Meaningful
- ☑ Useful
- ☑ Cost Effective

FIGURE 10-3
The qualities of information are characteristics that all information should have, whether or not it is produced by a computer.

information should be produced only as managers require it, instead of on a regular basis. Many organizations periodically review the information they produce in reports to determine if the reports maintain the qualities of information we just described. The cost of producing these reports can therefore still be justified or possibly reduced.

Although we have discused the qualities of information in conjunction with computer systems, these qualities apply to all information regardless of how it is produced. Knowing these qualities will help you evaluate the information you receive and you provide every day, whether or not it is generated by a computer.

The elements of an information system and the general categories of information systems are discussed in the next section.

WHAT IS AN INFORMATION SYSTEM?

◆ An **information system** is a collection of elements that provides accurate, timely, and useful information. As we discussed in Chapter 1, all information systems that are implemented on a computer are comprised of the six elements: equipment, software, accurate data, trained information systems personnel, knowledgeable users, and documented procedures. Each element contributes to a successful information system and conversely, a weakness in any of these elements can cause an information system to fail. People who create, use, or change any type of information system should consider all six elements to ensure success.

Information systems that are implemented on a computer are generally classified into four categories: (1) operational systems; (2) management information systems; (3) decision support systems; and (4) expert systems.

Operational Systems

Operational systems process data generated by the day-to-day transactions of an organization (Figure 10-4). Some examples of operational systems are billing systems, inventory control systems, and order entry systems.

When computers were first used for processing business applications, the information systems developed were primarily operational systems. Usually, the purpose was to computerize an existing manual system. This approach often resulted in faster processing, reduced clerical costs, and improved customer service. Although these operational systems were originally designed to process daily transactions, they were modified over time to provide summaries, trends, and exception data useful to management. Today, operational systems are often a part of management information systems, which we discuss in the next section.

Management Information Systems

In this section we discuss management information systems defined as systems that provide information to management. The concept of management information systems evolved as managers realized that computer processing could be used for more than just day-to-day transaction processing and that the computer's capability to perform rapid calculations and compare data could be used to produce meaningful information

FIGURE 10-4
Operational systems process the day-to-day transactions of an organization.

for management. As we stated at the beginning of the chapter, a management information system (MIS) refers to a computer-based system that generates timely and accurate information for managing an organization. Frequently a management information system is integrated with an operational system. For example, to process a sales order, the operational system would record the sale, update the customer's accounts receivable balance, and make a deduction from the inventory. In the related management information system, reports would be produced that show slow or fast moving items, customers with past due accounts receivable balances, and inventory items that need reordering. In the management information system, the focus is on the information that management needs to do its job (Figure 10-5).

FIGURE 10-5
Management information systems focus on the summary information and exceptions that managers use to perform their jobs.

A special type of management information system is the executive information system. **Executive information systems (EIS)** are management information systems that have been designed for the information needs of senior management. Company-wide management information systems usually address the information needs of all levels of management. Because senior managers may not be familiar (or comfortable) working with computer systems, EIS have features that make them easier for executives to use. The EIS user interface often uses a mouse or a touch screen to help executives that are not familiar with using a keyboard. One leading system uses a remote control device similar to those used to control a television set. Another aspect of the EIS user interface is the graphic presentation of information. EIS rely heavily on graphic presentation of both the processing options (Figure 10-6) and data. Again, this is designed to make the system easier to use.

FIGURE 10-6
Executive information systems (EIS) often use graphics and touch screens to make the systems easier to use by executives who are not familiar with computers.

Because executives focus on strategic issues, EIS often have access to external databases such as the Dow Jones News/Retrieval service. Such external sources of information can provide current information on interest rates, commodity prices, and other leading economic indicators.

Although they offer great promise, many EIS have not been successfully implemented and many executives have stopped using them. A common reason cited in several failed attempts is the mistake of not modifying the system to the specific needs of the individual executives who will use the system. For example, many executives prefer to have information presented in a particular sequence with the option of seeing different levels of supporting detail information such as cost data on a spreadsheet. The desired sequence and level of detail varies for each executive. It appears that EIS must be tailored to the executives' requirements or the executives will continue to manage with information they have obtained through previously established methods.

Decision Support Systems

Frequently, management needs information that is not routinely provided by operational and management information systems. For example, a vice president of finance may want to know the net effect on company profits if interest rates on borrowed money increase and raw material prices decrease. Operational or management information systems do not usually provide this type of information. Decision support systems have been developed to provide this information.

A **decision support system (DSS)** is a system designed to help someone reach a decision by summarizing or comparing data from either or both internal and external sources. Internal sources include data from an organization's database such as sales, manufacturing, or financial data. Data from external sources could include information on interest rates, population trends, new housing construction, or raw material pricing. Frito Lay, for example, collects and reports sales data on its own and competitors products every day (Figure 10-7). The information is part of a DSS that allows Frito Lay to analyze important trends in days or weeks instead of the months that it used to take.

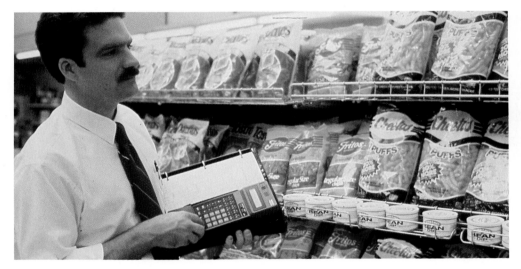

FIGURE 10-7
Frito Lay, a major producer of snack foods, has developed a decision support system that uses sales information collected daily on hand-held terminals by over 10,000 salespeople. The system helps Frito Lay spot sales trends in days or weeks instead of the months it used to take.

Decision support systems often include query languages, statistical analysis capabilities, spreadsheets, and graphics to help the user evaluate the decision data. More advanced decision support systems also include capabilities that allow users to create a model of the variables affecting a decision. With a **model**, users can ask *what-if* questions by changing one or more of the variables and seeing what the projected results would be. A simple model for determining the best product price would include factors for the expected sales volume at each price level. Many people use electronic spreadsheets for simple modeling tasks. DSS are sometimes combined with executive information systems (EIS). Generally speaking, DSS are more analytical and are designed

FIGURE 10-8
Nexpert Object is a powerful expert system that provides a highly visual presentation of its data, rules, and conclusions.

to work on unstructured problems that do not have a predefined number of variables. For example, a problem involving how to finance a company's growth would involve estimates of sales, income, depreciation, interest rates, and other variables that would best be handled by a DSS. EIS are primarily oriented toward collecting and presenting meaningful information from a variety of sources.

Expert Systems

Expert systems combine the knowledge on a given subject of one or more human experts into a computerized system that simulates the human experts' reasoning and decision making processes (Figure 10-8). Thus, the computer also becomes an *expert* on the subject. Expert systems are made up of the combined subject knowledge of the human experts, called the **knowledge base** and the **inference rules** that determine how the knowledge is used to reach decisions. Although they may appear to *think*, the current expert systems actually operate within narrow preprogrammed limits and cannot make decisions based on common sense or on information outside of their knowledge base. An example of how a simple expert system uses rules to identify an animal is shown in Figure 10-9.

FIGURE 10-9
A simulated dialogue between a user and a simple expert system is designed to identify an animal based on observations about the animal provided by the user. Notice how answers to certain questions result in other questions that narrow the possible conclusions. Once a conclusion is reached, the expert system can display or print the rules upon which the conclusion was based.

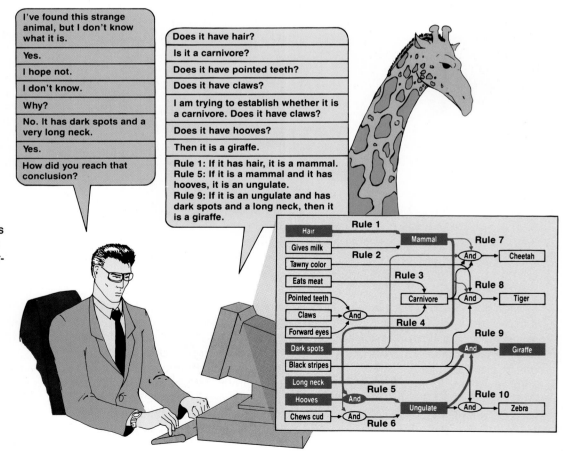

A more practical application of an expert system has been implemented by Ford Motor Company to help their dealers diagnose engine repair problems. Previously, when they encountered an engine problem that they could not solve, dealers would call Dearborn, Michigan to talk with Ford engine expert Gordy Kujawski. Now dealers can access a nationwide computer system that Ford has developed to duplicate the reasoning that Kujawski uses when troubleshooting a problem (Figure 10-10).

Although expert systems can be used at any level in an organization, to date they have been primarily used by nonmanagement employees for job-related decisions. Expert systems have also been successfully applied to problems as diverse as diagnosing illnesses, searching for oil, and making soup. These systems are part of an exciting branch of computer science called **artificial intelligence**, the application of human intelligence to computer systems.

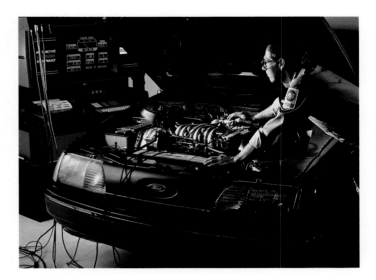

FIGURE 10-10
Ford Motor Company has developed an expert system that incorporates the knowledge of engine repair expert Gordy Kujawski. Instead of calling Kujawski, Ford dealers can now access the expert system when they are trying to diagnose engine problems.

INTEGRATED INFORMATION SYSTEMS

With today's sophisticated software, it can be difficult to classify a system as belonging uniquely to one of the four types of information systems we have discussed. For example, much of today's application software provides both operational and MIS information and some of the more advanced software even includes some decision support capabilities. Although expert systems still operate primarily as separate systems, the trend is clear: combine all of an organization's information needs into a single, integrated information system.

THE ROLE OF PERSONAL COMPUTERS IN MANAGEMENT INFORMATION SYSTEMS

The personal computer is playing an increasingly significant role in modern management information systems. Some professionals have said that the personal computer is the right tool at the right time. As organizations have moved toward decentralizing decision making, personal computers have given managers access to the information they need to make their decisions. Nonmanagement employees also benefit from having information available through networked personal computers on their desk or in the production area. For many MIS applications, personal computers are more cost effective than larger systems. One study estimated that the cost to process a million transactions on a mainframe is fifty times more expensive than on a personal computer. Flexibility is another advantage of personal computers. Individual or networks of personal computers can often be added more quickly than the corresponding amount of equipment that would be needed with minicomputer or mainframe systems. Many professionals believe that the ideal MIS decision involves a network of personal computers attached to a central mainframe, minicomputer, or file server that stores the common information that many users access. This centralized data and decentralized computing arrangement allow users and organizations the most flexibility over controlling their information resources.

SUMMARY OF MANAGEMENT INFORMATION SYSTEMS

Numerous factors have combined to make information an increasingly important asset for most organizations. Organizations manage this asset through the use of management information systems, computer-based systems that provide the information necessary to manage the activities of the organization. Management information systems provide different types of information based on the users' needs, which is often related to the users' levels in the organization.

The trend of management information systems is to combine and integrate operational, MIS, decision support, and expert systems that previously operated independently.

CHAPTER SUMMARY

1. **Management information system (MIS)** refers to any computer-based system that provides timely and accurate information for managing an organization.
2. Information that is stored in a database is no longer thought of as a by-product of doing business, but rather as a key ingredient in both short- and long-range decision making.
3. Factors that have contributed to the increased need for information include: expanded markets; increased competition; shorter product life cycles; and government regulation.
4. **Managers** of an organization are responsible for performing four different types of tasks: planning, organizing, directing, and controlling.
5. Management is usually divided into three levels: senior management, middle management, and operational management. A fourth level of an organization consists of the production, clerical, and nonmanagement staff.
6. **Senior management** makes strategic decisions and is concerned with the long-range direction of the company.
7. **Strategic decisions** deal with the overall goals and objectives of an organization.
8. **Middle management** makes tactical decisions and is responsible for implementing the strategic decisions of senior management.
9. **Tactical decisions** involve specific programs and plans necessary to accomplish the strategic objectives of an organization.
10. **Operational management** makes operational decisions and provides direct supervision over the production, clerical, and nonmanagement staff of an organization.
11. **Operational decisions** usually involve an immediate action such as accepting or rejecting an inventory delivery or approving a purchase order.
12. The terms used to describe the qualities of information include accurate, verifiable, timely, organized, meaningful, useful, and cost effective.
13. **GIGO** is an acronym that stands for *Garbage In, Garbage Out*.
14. An **information system** is a collection of elements that provide accurate, timely, and useful information. These elements include: equipment, software, accurate data, trained information systems personnel, knowledgeable users, and documented procedures.
15. The types of computer information systems include: (1) operational systems; (2) management information systems; (3) decision support systems; and (4) expert systems.
16. **Operational systems** process data generated by the day-to-day transactions of an organization.
17. **Executive information systems (EIS)** are management information systems that have been designed for the information needs of senior management.
18. A **decision support system (DSS)** is a system designed to help someone reach a decision by summarizing or comparing data from either or both internal and external sources.
19. Some decision support systems allow users to create a **model** where they can ask *what-if* questions by changing one or more of the variables and see what the projected results will be.

20. **Expert systems** combine the knowledge on a given subject of one or more human experts into a computerized system that simulates the human experts' reasoning and decision-making processes.
21. Expert systems are made up of the combined subject knowledge of the human experts, called the **knowledge base** and the **inference rules** that determine how the knowledge is used to reach decisions.
22. An exciting branch of computer science is **artificial intelligence**, the application of human intelligence to computer systems.
23. The trend is to combine all of an organization's information needs into a single, integrated information system.
24. The personal computer is playing an increasingly significant role in modern management information systems.

KEY TERMS

Artificial intelligence *10.11*
Decision support system
 (DSS) *10.9*
Executive information system
 (EIS) *10.8*
Expert system *10.10*
GIGO *10.6*

Inference rules *10.10*
Information system *10.7*
Knowledge base *10.10*
Manager *10.2*
Management information system
 (MIS) *10.1*
Middle management *10.5*

Model *10.9*
Operational decision *10.5*
Operational management *10.5*
Operational system *10.7*
Senior management *10.4*
Strategic decision *10.4*
Tactical decision *10.5*

REVIEW QUESTIONS

1. Define the term management information systems. Discuss three ways that the term is used.
2. List five factors that have contributed to the increased need for organizations to have information.
3. Describe the four different types of tasks that managers perform.
4. Identify the three levels of management in an organization, and describe the types of decisions that are made at each level.
5. What are the six qualities that information should have?
6. List the four general types of information systems.
7. What is an EIS? What are some of the user interfaces frequently used with an EIS?
8. Discuss how the personal computer is being used in management information systems.

CONTROVERSIAL ISSUE

1. Some people are concerned that the increased application of expert systems will lead to real life situations of robots gone wild or uncontrollable computers as they are sometimes portrayed in science fiction. Discuss what limits you think should be placed on computerized decision making.

RESEARCH PROJECTS

1. Think of an application for an expert system. Make a list of the inference rules that would be used.
2. Interview a manager at a local company or your school. Ask him or her what information he or she uses to make decisions. Identify the information that is not provided by the computer system being used at the local company or the school. Could it be provided by the system?

The Information System Life Cycle

ANALYSIS/DESIGN

OBJECTIVES

◆ Explain the phases and paths of the information system life cycle

◆ Explain the importance of project management and documentation

◆ Define commercial applications software and describe the difference between horizontal and vertical applications

◆ Discuss each of the steps of acquiring commercial applications software

◆ Discuss the reasons for developing custom software

◆ Describe how various analysis and design tools, such as data flow diagrams, are used

◆ Explain how program development is part of the information system life cycle

◆ Explain several methods that can be used for a conversion to a new system

◆ Discuss the installation and maintenance of an information system

Every day, competition, government regulations, and other such influences cause people to face new challenges as they try to obtain the information they need to perform their jobs. A new product, a new sales commission plan, or a change in tax rates are just three examples of why an organization must change the way it processes information. Sometimes, these challenges can be met by existing methods but other times, meeting the challenge requires an entirely new way of processing data. In these cases, a new or modified information system is needed. As a computer user, either as an individual or within your organization, it is very likely that someday you will participate in acquiring, developing, or modifying a system. Creating an information system can be described by phases known as the information system life cycle. In this chapter, we illustrate each phase of the system life cycle by using a case study about the wholesale auto parts division of the Sutherland Company.

WHAT IS THE INFORMATION SYSTEM LIFE CYCLE?

The **information system life cycle (ISLC)** is an organized approach to obtaining an information system. Regardless of the type or complexity of an information system, the structured process of the information system life cycle should be followed whenever an information system is acquired or developed. The activities of the information system life cycle can be grouped into distinct phases.

The Phases of the Information System Life Cycle

As shown in Figure 11-1, the phases of the information system life cycle are:

- Analysis
- Acquisition or Design
- Customizing or Development
- Implementation
- Maintenance

FIGURE 11-1
The information system life cycle consists of several phases. The phases of the acquistion path are analysis, acquisition, customizing, implementation, and maintenance. The phases of the development path include analysis, design, development, implementation, and maintenance.

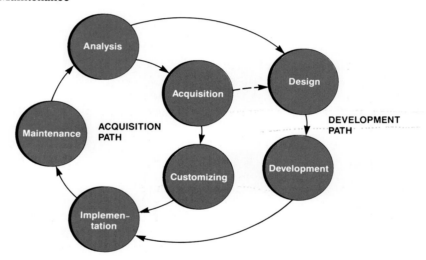

Each of the phases includes important activities that relate to the acquisition or development of an information system.

As Figure 11-1 also shows, there is an acquisition path and a development path in the information system life cycle. After the analysis phase, an organization can either choose to acquire a system by purchasing software or develop one by writing their own software. If an organization does not find a suitable system during the acquisition phase, it will move to the design phase of the development path. All systems have analysis, implementation, and maintenance phases.

Before explaining each of the phases, we will discuss project management and documentation because these two activities are ongoing processes that are performed throughout the cycle. First, we will identify the information system specialists and users who participate in the various phases of the ISLC.

Project Management

Project management involves planning, scheduling, reporting, and controlling the individual activities that make up the information system development life cycle. These activities are usually recorded in a **project plan** on a week-by-week basis that includes an estimate of the time to complete the activity and the start and finish dates. As you might expect, the start of many activities depends on the successful completion of other activities. For example, implementation activities cannot begin until you have completed at least some, if not all, of the development activities. An effective way of showing the relationship of project activities is with a Gantt chart (Figure 11-2). A Gantt chart usually shows time across the top of the chart and a list of activities to be completed down the left side. Marks on the chart indicate when an activity begins and is completed. Lines or bars between the marks indicate progress toward completing the task.

The importance of maintaining a realistic schedule for project management cannot be overstated. Without a realistic schedule, the success of a development project is in jeopardy from the start. If project members do not believe the schedule is realistic, they may not participate to the full extent of their abilities. Project management is a place for realistic, not wishful, thinking.

Project management should be practiced throughout the development process. In most projects, activities need frequent rescheduling. Some activities will take less time than originally planned and others will take longer. To measure the impact of the actual results and revised estimates, they should be recorded regularly and a revised project plan issued. Project management software provides an efficient method of recording results and revising project plans.

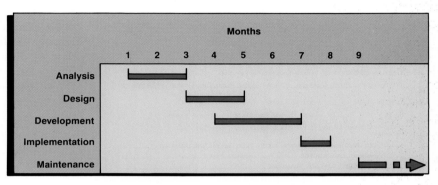

FIGURE 11-2
A Gantt chart is often used in project management to show the time relationships of the project activities.

Documentation

Documentation refers to written materials that are produced as part of the information system development life cycle such as a report describing the overall purpose of the system or layout forms that are used to design reports and screens. Documentation should be identified and agreed on prior to beginning the project. Well-written, thorough documentation makes it easier for users and others to understand why particular decisions are made. Too often, documentation is put off until the completion of a project and is never adequately finished. Documentation should be an ongoing part of the entire development process and should not be thought of as a separate phase. Well-written, thorough documentation can also extend the useful life of a system. Unfortunately, systems are sometimes replaced simply because no one understands how they work.

Who Participates in the Information System Development Life Cycle?

Every person who will be affected by the new system should have the opportunity to participate in its development. The participants fall into two categories: users and information system personnel such as systems analysts and computer programmers. The systems analyst works closely with both the users and the programmers to define the system. The systems analyst's job is challenging, requiring good communication, analytical, and diplomatic skills to keep the development process on track and on schedule. Good communication skills are especially important during analysis, the first phase of the information system life cycle.

ANALYSIS PHASE

Analysis is the separation of a system into its parts to determine how the system works. In addition, the analysis phase of a project also includes the identification of a proposed solution to the problems identified in the current system. A system project can originate in several ways, but a common way is for the manager of a user department, such as accounting or personnel, to contact the information systems department with a request for assistance. The initial request may be oral, but it is eventually written on a standard form that becomes the first item of documentation (Figure 11-3). In most organizations, requests for new system projects exceed the capacity of the information systems department to implement them. Therefore, the manager of the systems department must review each request and make a preliminary determination as to the potential benefit for the company. Requests for large development projects, such as an entirely new system, are often reviewed by committees made up of both user and information systems personnel and representatives of top management. When the managers of both the user and information systems departments determine that a request warrants further review, one or more systems analysts will be assigned to begin a preliminary investigation, the first step in the analysis phase.

FIGURE 11-3
The system development project usually starts with a request from a user. The request should be documented on a form such as this one to provide a record of the action taken.

The Preliminary Investigation

The purpose of the **preliminary investigation** is to determine if a request justifies further detailed investigation and analysis. The most important aspect of the preliminary investigation is **problem definition**, the identification of the true nature of the problem. Often the stated problem and the real problem are not the same. For example, suppose the manager of the accounting department requests a new accounts receivable report that shows recent customer payments. An investigation might reveal that the existing accounts receivable reports would be acceptable if the customer payments were recorded daily instead of once a week. The real problem is that customer payments are being recorded too late to be included in the existing reports. Thus, the preliminary investigation determines the real source of the problem.

The preliminary investigation begins with an interview of the manager who submitted the request. Depending on the request, other users can be interviewed as well. For example, a request might involve data or a process that affects more than one department or clerical workers may have to be interviewed to obtain detail information.

The preliminary investigation is usually quite short when compared to the remainder of the project. At the end of the investigation, the systems analyst presents the findings to both user and information system management and recommends the next action. Sometimes the results of a preliminary investigation indicate an obvious solution that can be implemented at minimal cost. Other times, however, the only thing the preliminary investigation does is confirm that there is a problem that needs further study. In these cases, detailed system analysis is recommended. The user, the information systems management, and the systems analyst work together to decide how to proceed.

Detailed System Analysis

Detailed system analysis involves both a thorough study of the current system and at least one proposed solution to the problems found.

The study of the current system is important for two reasons. First, it helps increase the systems analyst's understanding of the activities that a new system might perform. Second, and perhaps most important, studying the current system builds a relationship between the systems analyst and the user. The systems analyst will have much more credibility with users if he or she understands how the users currently do their job. This may seem an obvious point, but surprisingly, many systems are created or modified without studying the current system or without adequately involving the users.

The basic fact-gathering techniques used during the detailed system analysis are: (1) interviews, (2) questionnaires, (3) reviewing current system documentation, and (4) observing current procedures. During this phase of the system study, the systems analyst must develop a critical, questioning approach to each procedure within the current system to determine what is actually taking place. Often systems analysts find that operations are being performed not because they are efficient or effective, but because they have always been done this way.

Information gathered during this phase includes: (1) the output of the current system, (2) the input to the current system, and (3) the procedures used to produce the output.

An increasingly popular method for documenting this information is called structured analysis. **Structured analysis** is the use of analysis and design tools such as data flow diagrams, data dictionaries, process specifications, structured English, decision tables, and decision trees to document the specifications of an information system.

Data Flow Diagrams   One of the difficulties in analyzing any system is how to document the findings in a way that can be understood by users, programmers, and other systems analysts. Structured analysis addresses this problem by using graphics to represent the flow of data. These graphics are called data flow diagrams.

A **data flow diagram (DFD)** graphically shows the flow of data through a system. The key elements of a DFD (Figure 11-4) are arrows, or vectors, called data flows that represent data; circles (also called bubbles) that represent processes such as verifying an order or creating an invoice; parallel lines that represent data files; and squares, called sources, or sinks, that represent either or both an originator or a receiver of data such as a customer.

FIGURE 11-4
The symbols used to create data flow diagrams.

RFP

Because they are visual, DFDs are particularly useful for reviewing the existing or proposed system with the user (Figure 11-5). One of the features of DFDs is that they are done on a level-by-level basis. The top level would only identify major processes and flows. Lower levels further define the higher levels. For example, in Figure 11-5 the Apply Invoice Payment process in the lower left corner could have its own separate DFD to define subprocesses that take place.

FIGURE 11-5
Data flow diagrams (DFDs) are used to graphically illustrate the flow of information through a system. The customer (box) both originates and receives data (arrows). The circles indicate where actions take place on the data. Files are shown as parallel lines.

CUSTOMER ORDER PROCESSING
DATA FLOW DIAGRAM

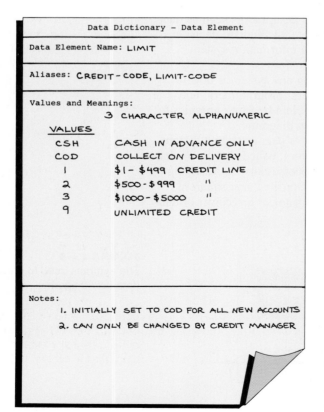

Data Dictionaries   The **data dictionary** describes the elements that make up the data flow. Each element can be thought of as equivalent to a field in a record. The data dictionary also includes information about the attributes of each element such as length, where the element is used (which files and data flows include the element), and any values or ranges the element might have, such as a value of 2 in Figure 11-6 for a credit limit code to indicate a purchase limit of $1,000.00. The data dictionary is created by the systems analyst in the analysis phase and is used in all subsequent phases of the information system life cycle. Although data dictionaries are often first prepared manually, they are usually entered and maintained on a computer system.

FIGURE 11-6
A data dictionary form such as this one is used to document each of the data elements that are included in the data flows. The form records the length, type of data, and possible values for each data element.

Structured English **Process specifications** describe and document what happens to a data flow when it reaches a process circle. For example in Figure 11-5, process specifications describe what goes on in each of the circles. One way of writing process specifications is to use **structured English**, a style of writing and presentation that highlights the alternatives and actions that are part of the process. Figure 11-7 shows an example of a structured English process specification describing a policy for order processing.

```
If the order amount exceeds $1,000,
     If customer has any unpaid invoices over 90 days old,
          Do not issue order confirmation,
          Write message on order reject report.
     Otherwise (account is in good standing),
          Issue order confirmation.
Otherwise (order is $1,000 or less),
     If customer has any unpaid invoices over 90 days old,
          Issue order confirmation,
          Write message on credit follow-up report.
     Otherwise (account is in good standing),
          Issue order confirmation.
```

FIGURE 11-7
Structured English is an organized way of describing what actions are taken on data. This structured English example describes an order processing policy.

Decision Tables and Decision Trees Another way of documenting the system during the analysis phase is with a decision table or decision tree. A **decision table** or a **decision tree** identifies the actions that should be taken under different conditions. Figures 11-8 and 11-9 show a decision table and decision tree for the order processing policy described with structured English in Figure 11-7. Decision tables and trees are an excellent way of showing the desired action when the action depends on multiple conditions.

	Rules			
	1	2	3	4
Conditions				
1. Order > $1,000	Y	Y	N	N
2. Unpaid invoices over 90 days old	Y	N	Y	N
Actions				
1. Issue confirmation	N	Y	Y	Y
2. Reject order	Y	N	N	N
3. Credit follow-up	N	N	Y	N

FIGURE 11-8
Decision tables help a user quickly determine the course of action based on two or more conditions. This decision table is based on the order processing policy described in Figure 11-7. For example, if an order is $1,000 or less and the customer has an unpaid invoice over 90 days old, the policy (Rule 3) is to issue an order confirmation and perform a credit follow-up on the past due invoice.

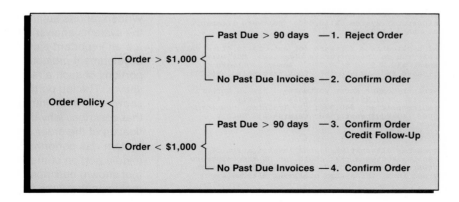

FIGURE 11-9
Like a decision table, a decision tree illustrates the action to be taken based on the given conditions, but presents it graphically. This decision tree is based on the order processing policy described in Figure 11-7.

Making the Decision on How to Proceed

Just as at the completion of the preliminary investigation, at the completion of the analysis phase, the user, systems analyst, and management face another decision on how to proceed. At this point the systems analyst should have completed a study of the current system and, using the same tools and methods, developed one or more proposed solutions to the current system's identified problems. Sometimes, the systems analyst is asked to prepare a feasibility study and a cost/benefit analysis. These two reports are often used together. The **feasibility study** discusses whether the proposed solution is practical and capable of being accomplished. The **cost/benefit analysis** identifies the estimated costs of the proposed solution and the benefits (including potential cost savings) that are expected. If there are strong indications at the beginning of the project that some type of new system will likely be developed, the feasibility study and cost/benefit analysis are sometimes performed as part of the preliminary investigation.

The systems analyst presents the results of his or her work in a written report (Figure 11-10) to both user and information systems management who consider the alternatives and the resources, such as time, people, and money of the organization. The end of the analysis phase is usually when organizations decide either to acquire a commercial software package from an outside source or to develop the software. If a decision is made to proceed, the project enters the acquisition phase if a software package is going to be obtained or the design phase if software is going to be developed. If a suitable software package cannot be found, an organization will start the design phase of the development path.

```
DATE:     April 1, 1992
TO:       Management Review Committee
FROM:     George Lacey, Corporate Systems Manager
SUBJECT:  Detailed Investigation and Analysis of Order Entry System


Introduction

     A detailed system investigation and analysis of the order entry system
was conducted as a result of approval given by the Management Review
Committee on March 1.  The findings of the investigation are presented
below.

Objectives of Detailed Investigation and Analysis

     The study investigated reported problems of the wholesale auto parts
order entry system.  We have received complaints that orders were not being
shipped promptly and that customers were not notified about out-of-stock
parts when they placed their orders.  In addition, invoices are not sent to
customers until twelve to sixteen days after orders are shipped.  The
objective of this study was to determine where the problems existed and to
develop alternative solutions.

Findings of the Detailed Investigation and Analysis

     The following problems appear to exist within the order entry system:
```

```
Possible Solutions:

1.   Acquire a separate minicomputer system and order entry software.
     Estimated costs:  Minicomputer system, $150,000.  Software license,
     $50,000.  Annual maintenance, $20,000.

2.   Investigate commercial applications software for auto parts order entry
     and invoicing that would run on the corporate computer.  Estimated
     costs:  Software license, $50,000 to $100,000.  Annual software
     maintenance, 10% of license fee.  Equipment (four terminals), $6,000.

3.   Internally develop necessary order entry software to run on corporate
     computer.  Estimated costs:  (1) Systems analysis and design, $26,000;
     (2) Programming and implementation, $40,000; (3) Training, new forms,
     and maintenance, $7,000; (4) Equipment (four terminals), $6,000.

Recommended Action

The systems department recommends alternative 2, the investigation of
existing commercial applications software that could run on the corporate
computer.  If suitable software cannot be found, we recommend the design of
a computerized order entry and invoicing system utilizing alternative 3.

George Lacey
```

FIGURE 11-10
Written reports summarizing the systems analyst's work are an important part of the development project. Two portions of such a report are shown. The top portion shows the report introduction that describes why the investigation of the order entry system was performed. The middle portion of the report (not shown) describes the problems that were found during the investigation. The bottom portion shows three possible solutions and the action recommended by the corporate systems manager.

ANALYSIS AT SUTHERLAND

◆ The Sutherland Company is a large corporation with three separate divisions that sell tools, electric motors, and auto parts. Although the tool and electric motor divisions have been computerized for some time, the auto parts division, started just two years ago, has been small enough that it has relied on manual procedures. In the last six months, however, auto parts sales doubled and the manual order entry and invoicing systems are incapable of keeping up with the increased work load.

Mike Charles, the auto parts sales manager, decides to submit a request for system services to the information systems department that provides computer services for all three Sutherland divisions. George Lacey, the head of the Information Systems department assigns Frank Peacock, a senior systems analyst, to investigate Mike's request.

As part of the preliminary investigation, Frank interviews Mike to try to determine the problem. During his interview with Mike and a subsequent tour of the auto parts sales department, Frank discovers that invoices are not being sent to customers until twelve to sixteen days after their parts orders have shipped. In addition, Frank discovers that customers complain about shipments being late and about not being notified when parts they ordered are not available. To quantify the expected increases in sales volume, Frank has Mike prepare the transaction volume summary shown in Figure 11-11. As a result of his preliminary investigation, Frank recommends a detailed system analysis. George Lacey, the corporate systems manager, agrees with Frank's recommendation and assigns systems analyst Mary Ruiz to perform a detailed analysis.

Transaction Volume Summary

	LAST YEAR	CURRENT	1 YEAR	3 YEARS
Number of Customers	175	300	400	600
Orders per Month	525	950	1250	1900
Invoices per Month	600	1100	1375	2100

FIGURE 11-11
A transaction volume summary should be prepared to estimate the projected growth of an application. Systems should be designed to handle the projected volume of transactions, not just the current volume.

Mary reviews Frank's notes and begins to perform a detailed analysis of the auto parts order entry and invoicing systems. As part of her study, Mary interviews several people in the auto parts division and prepares several documents including a data flow diagram (Figure 11-5), a data dictionary definition for the different credit limits assigned to customers (Figure 11-6), and a structured English statement of the order processing policy (Figure 11-7).

After studying the manual procedures for a week, Mary discusses her findings with her supervisor, George Lacey. Based on Mary's work, George writes a report to the management review committee recommending that the order entry and invoicing systems be computerized (Figure 11-10). The report contains three possible solutions; one, obtain a separate minicomputer system; two, obtain a commercial applications software package to run on the corporate computer; and three, internally develop the necessary software for the corporate computer. Before proceeding to develop the necessary software internally, George recommends that Sutherland try to find a suitable commercial software package that would run on Sutherland's central computer. The management review committee meets every month to review requests for additional computer equipment and software. The committee is made up of top management representatives from each division, the finance department, and the information systems department. Based on George's report, the management review committee authorizes the corporate systems department to try and find a commercial package to satisfy the auto parts division's order entry and invoicing requirements.

ACQUISITION PHASE

Once the analysis phase has been completed, the **acquisition** phase begins; it has four steps: (1) summarizing the application requirements, (2) identifying potential software vendors, (3) evaluating software alternatives, and (4) making the purchase. Before we describe these steps, let's discuss commercial applications software.

What is Commercial Applications Software?

Commercial applications software is software that has already been developed and is available for purchase. Prewritten software is available for computers of all sizes. Most users know about the numerous application packages available for microcomputers. In addition, users should be aware that numerous packages are available for larger machines. This section discusses the categories of commercial applications software that are available, how to determine software requirements, and how to acquire the software. This information is important to know because it is very likely that some day you will either acquire applications software for yourself or participate in software selection for your organization.

It's probably safe to say that at least some part of every type of business, government branch, or recreational pastime has been computerized. Figure 11-12 is an excerpt from a category listing from an applications software catalog. Within each category, numerous programs are available to perform different types of tasks. This catalog contains listings for over 20,000 individual software packages. Notice that this list is divided into two parts: nonindustry specific and industry specific. The more commonly used terms are horizontal and vertical applications.

FIGURE 11-12
An excerpt from a category listing in an applications software catalog that contains information on over 20,000 individual software packages.

Horizontal application software is software that can be used by many different types of organizations. Accounting packages are a good example of horizontal applications because they apply to most organizations. If, however, an organization has a unique way of doing business, then it requires a package that has been developed specifically for that job. Software developed for a unique way of doing business, usually within a specific industry, is called **vertical application software**. Examples of specific industries that use vertical software include food service, construction, and real estate. Each of these industries has unique information processing requirements.

The difference between horizontal and vertical application software is important to understand. If you become involved in selecting software, one of the first things you will have to decide is how unique is the task for which you are trying to obtain software. If the task is not unique to your business, you will probably be able to use a horizontal application package. Horizontal application packages tend to be widely available (because they can be used by a greater number of organizations) and less expensive. If your task is unique to your type of organization, you will probably have to search for a vertical software solution. Often an organization's total software requirements are made up of a combination of unique and common requirements.

Now that we understand what commercial applications software is, let's discuss the steps used to acquire it.

Summarizing the Application Requirements

One way organizations summarize their software requirements is in a request for proposal. A **request for proposal**, or **RFP**, is a written list of an organization's software requirements. This list is given to prospective software vendors to help the vendors determine if they have a product that is a possible software solution. Just as the depth of application evaluations varies, so do RFPs. RFPs for simple applications might be only a single page consisting of the key features and a transaction volume summary. Other RFPs for large systems might consist of over a hundred pages that identify both key and secondary desired features. An example of a page from an RFP is shown in Figure 11-13.

FIGURE 11-13
A request for proposal (RFP) documents the key features that a user wants in a software package.

Identifying Potential Software Vendors

After you have an idea of the software features you want, your next step is to locate potential vendors that sell the type of software you are interested in buying. If the software will be implemented on a personal computer, a good place to start looking for software is a local computer store. Most computer stores have a wide selection of applications software and can suggest several packages for you to consider. If you have prepared an RFP, even a simple one, it will help the store representative to narrow the choices. If you require software for a minicomputer or mainframe, you won't find it at the local personal computer store. For this type of software, which can cost tens to hundreds of thousands of dollars, the best place to start is the computer manufacturer.

In addition to having some software themselves, most manufacturers have a list of software companies with which they work—companies that specialize in developing software for the manufacturer's equipment. **Software houses** are businesses that specialize in developing software for sale. **System houses** not only sell software but also sell the equipment. System houses usually take full responsibility for equipment, software, installation, and training. Sometimes, they even provide equipment maintenance, although this is usually left to the equipment manufacturer. The advantage of dealing with a system house is that the user has to deal with only a single company for the entire system.

Another place to find software suppliers, especially for vertical applications, is to look in trade publications, magazines written for specific businesses or industries. Companies and individuals who have written software for these industries often advertise in the trade publications. Some industry trade groups also maintain lists of companies that provide specific software solutions.

For horizontal applications, many computer magazines publish regular reviews of individual packages and often have annual reviews of several packages of the same type. Figure 11-14 shows a software review of an accounting package.

FIGURE 11-14
Many publications regularly evaluate applications software. This review includes a narrative discussion of the package.

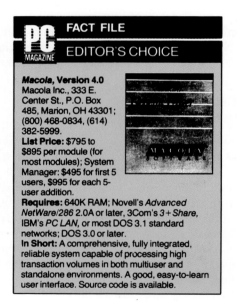

Another way to identify software suppliers is to hire a knowledgeable consultant. Although the fee paid to a consultant increases your software costs, it may be worth it, considering the real cost of making a bad decision. Many consultants specialize in assisting organizations of all sizes to identify and implement software packages. A good place to start looking for a consultant would be to contact professional organizations in your industry. Your accountant may also be able to recommend a possible software solution or a consultant.

Evaluating Software Alternatives

After you have identified several possible software solutions, you have to evaluate them and choose one. First, match each choice against your original requirements list. Be as objective as possible—try not to be influenced by the salesperson or representative demonstrating the software or the appeal of the marketing literature. Match each package against your list or RFP and give each package a score. If some key features are more important than others, take that into consideration. Try to complete this rating either during or immediately after a demonstration of the package while the features are still fresh in your mind (Figure 11-15).

The next step is to talk to existing users of the software. For minicomputer and mainframe software packages, software vendors routinely provide user references. User references are important because if a software package does (or doesn't) work for an organization like yours, it probably will (or won't) work for you. For personal computer packages, if the computer store can't provide references, call the software manufacturer directly.

Finally, try the software yourself. For a small application, this may be as simple as entering a few simple transactions using a demonstration copy of the software at the computer store. For large applications, it may require one or more days of testing at the vendor's office or on your existing computer to be sure that the software meets your needs.

If you are concerned about whether the software can handle a certain transaction volume efficiently, you may want to perform a benchmark test. A **benchmark test** measures the time it takes to process a set number of transactions. For example, a benchmark test might consist of measuring the time it takes a particular software package to produce a sales summary report using 1,000 sales transactions. Comparing the time it takes different packages to perform the same task using the same data and the same equipment is one way of measuring the packages' relative performance.

FIGURE 11-15
You should ask to see a demonstration of any program you are considering purchasing. During or after the demonstration, you should rate how well the package meets your requirements.

Making the Purchase

When you purchase software you usually don't own it. What you are actually purchasing is a **software license** (Figure 11-16), the right to use the software under certain terms and conditions. One of the usual terms and conditions of a software license is that you can use the software on a single computer only. In fact, some software is licensed to a specific computer and the serial number of the system is recorded in the license agreement. Other license restrictions include prohibitions against making the software available to others (for example, renting it or leasing it) and modifying or translating the software into another language. These restrictions are designed to protect the rights of the software developer, who doesn't want someone else to benefit unfairly from the developer's work. For personal computer users, software license terms and conditions usually cannot be modified. But for minicomputer and mainframe users, terms of the license agreements can be modified and, therefore, should be carefully reviewed and considered a part of the overall software selection process. Modifications to the software license are generally easier to obtain before the sale is made than after.

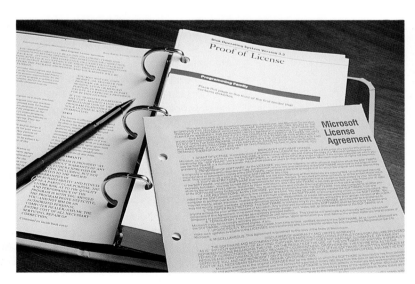

FIGURE 11-16
A software license grants the purchaser the right to use the software but does not include ownership rights.

ACQUISITION AT SUTHERLAND

Based on the directions of the management review committee, a software selection committee is formed with Mike Charles as the chairperson. Mary Ruiz and Frank Peacock from the MIS department are also members as are the order entry and billing supervisors from the auto parts division. Also asked to participate is Bill Comer, computer systems specialist with Sutherland's CPA firm. Mary and Frank take the information developed during the analysis phase and summarize it into a request for proposal (RFP). The RFP is sent to ten software vendors which Bill Comer has identified. Eight of the ten vendors send a response to the RFP within the one month deadline set by Sutherland. Most of the vendors had contacted and visited the auto parts operation to gather information necessary for their responses. Of the eight replies, Sutherland chooses three vendors for further discussions. The committee eliminates five of the vendors because they believe that these systems do not meet the requirements of an auto parts distributor. The software selection committee visits the offices of all three remaining software vendors for a thorough demonstration of their respective packages. In addition, the committee visits a customer of each of the three vendors. The vendor and customer site visits are conducted over a one-month period.

At this point, Sutherland faces a difficult choice. None of the commercial software packages is significantly better than the other and all three have areas that have to be substantially modified to meet Sutherland's way of doing business. The software selection committee summarizes their findings in a report to the management review committee. After discussing the report, the management review committee authorizes the MIS department to begin development of an order entry and invoicing system to run on Sutherland's existing computer system.

COMMERCIAL APPLICATIONS VERSUS CUSTOM SOFTWARE

Each year, the number of applications software packages increases. With all that software available, why would an organization choose to develop its own applications? There could be several reasons. The most common reason is that the organization's software requirements are so unique that it is unable to find a package that will meet its needs. In such a case, the organization would choose to develop the software itself or have it developed specifically for them. Applications software that is developed by the user or at the user's request is called **custom software**. An example of a requirement for custom software might be a government agency that is implementing a new medical assistance service. If the service has new forms and procedures and is different from previous services, it is unlikely that any appropriate software exists. Another reason to develop rather than buy software is that the new software must work with existing custom software. This is an important point to keep in mind; once an organization chooses to use custom software, it will usually choose custom software for future applications as well. This is because it is often difficult to make custom software work with purchased software. The following example illustrates this point.

Let's say a company that has previously developed a custom inventory control software system now wants to computerize their order entry function. Order entry software packages allow the user to sell merchandise from stock and, therefore, must work closely with the inventory files. In fact, many order entry systems are sold together with inventory control systems. If the company wants to retain its existing inventory control application, it would probably have a hard time finding a commercial order entry package that would be able to work with its custom inventory files. This is because the software and the file structures used in the commercial package will not be the same as the existing software. For this reason, the company would probably decide to develop a custom order entry application.

Both custom and commercial software have their advantages and disadvantages. The advantage of custom software is that if it is correctly done, it will match an organization's exact requirements. The disadvantages of custom software are that it is one of a kind, difficult to change, often poorly documented, and usually more expensive than commercial software. In addition, custom software projects are often difficult to manage and complete on time.

The advantage of commercial software is that it's ready to install immediately. After sufficient training, usually provided by the vendor who developed or sold the software, people can begin using the software for productive work. The disadvantage of commercial software is that an organization will probably have to change some of its methods and procedures to adapt to the way the commercial software functions.

A good guideline for evaluating your need for custom or commercial software is to look for a package with an 80% or better fit with your requirements. If there is less than an 80% fit, an organization should either consider custom software or reevaluate its requirements. Figure 11-17 shows the most likely software solutions for different application requirements.

FIGURE 11-17
Software guidelines for different types of applications.

APPLICATION CHARACTERISTICS	APPLICATION EXAMPLE	MOST LIKELY SOFTWARE SOLUTION
Applicable to many different types or organizations	Accounts receivable	Horizontal application package
Specific to a particular type of business or organization	Hotel room reservations	Vertical application package
Unique to a specific organization or business	Space shuttle launch program	Custom software

CUSTOMIZING PHASE

Ideally, acquired commercial applications software will meet 80% or more of an organization's requirements. But what about the other 20% or so? For these requirements, the organization has two choices: change their way of doing business to match the way the software works or modify the way the software works to match their organization. Usually, they will choose a combination of the two alternatives.

Modifying a commercial application package is usually referred to as **customizing**, or **tailoring**. The process of customizing a commercial package involves the following four steps:

1. Identifying potential modifications.
2. Determining the impact of changing current operations to match the software and thus avoiding making a modification.
3. Specifying the amount of work required to make the modifications and the corresponding cost.
4. Choosing which modifications will be made. If possible, the modifications should be made prior to the system being implemented. This avoids users having to relearn how the system works.

Some software vendors do not recommend or support modifications to their packages. Other vendors facilitate modifications by providing copies of the programs or by doing the modifications themselves, usually for a fee. Generally speaking, the larger and more expensive the application package, the more likely that modifications will be required and will be permitted.

CUSTOMIZING AT SUTHERLAND

Because the software selection committee does not choose a commercial applications software package, the customizing phase does not take place at Sutherland.

DESIGN PHASE

The proposed solution developed as part of the analysis phase usually consists of what is called a **logical design**, which means that the design was deliberately developed without regard to a specific computer or programming language and that no attempt was made to identify which procedures should be automated and which procedures should be manual. This approach avoids early assumptions that might limit the possible solutions.

During the **design** phase the logical design will be transformed into a **physical design** that will identify the procedures to be automated, choose the programming language, and specify the equipment needed for the system.

Structured Design Methods

The system design usually follows one of two methods, top-down design or bottom-up design.

Top-Down Design Top-down design, also called **structured design**, focuses on the major functions of the system, such as recording a sale or generating an invoice, and keeps breaking those functions down into smaller and smaller activities, sometimes called modules, that can eventually be programmed. Top-down design is an increasingly popular method because it focuses on the total requirements and helps users and systems analysts reach an early agreement on what the major functions of the new system are.

Bottom-Up Design Bottom-up design focuses on the data, particularly the output of the system. The approach used determines what output is needed and moves *up* to the processes needed to produce the output.

In practice, most systems analysts use a combination of the top-down and bottom-up designs. Some information requirements such as payroll checks, for example, have required data elements that lend themselves to bottom-up design. Other requirements, such as management-oriented exception reports that are based on the needs of a particular user, are better suited to a top-down design. Regardless of the structured design method he or she uses, the systems analyst will eventually need to complete the design activities.

Design Activities

Design activities include individual tasks that a systems analyst performs to design an information system. These include designs for the output, input, database, processes, system controls, and testing.

Output Design   The design of the output is critical to the successful implementation of the system. Output provides information to the users, and information is the basis for the justification of most computerized systems. For example, most users don't know (or necessarily care) how the data will be processed, but they usually do have clear ideas on how they want the information output to look. Often, requests for new or modified systems begin with a user-prepared draft of a report that the current system doesn't produce. During **output design**, the systems analyst and the user document specific screen and report layouts for output to display or report information from the new system. The example in Figure 11-18 illustrates a report layout form.

FIGURE 11-18
The report layout form is used to design printed output. Column titles, data width, and report totals are shown on the layout form.

Input Design   During **input design** the systems analyst and the user identify what information needs to be entered into the system to produce the desired output, and where and how the data will be entered. With interactive systems, the systems analyst and the user must determine the sequence of inputs and computer responses, called a **dialogue**, that the user will encounter when he or she enters data. Figure 11-19 shows a display screen layout form commonly used to document the format of a screen display.

FIGURE 11-19
The display screen layout sheet is similar to the report layout form but is used only for information that will be displayed on a screen. Each row and column corresponds to a row and column on the screen.

Database Design   During **database design** the systems analyst uses the data dictionary information developed during the analysis phase and merges it into new or existing system files. During this phase of the design, the systems analyst works closely with the database administrator to identify existing database elements that can be used to satisfy design requirements.

Efficient file design can be a challenging task, especially with relational database systems that stress minimum data redundancy (duplicate data). The systems analyst must also consider the volume of database activity. For example, large files that will be frequently accessed may need a separate index file to allow inquiries to be processed in an amount of time acceptable to the user.

Process Design   During **process design**, the systems analyst specifies exactly what actions will be taken on the input data to create output information. Decisions on the timing of actions are added to the logical processes he or she identified in the analysis phase. For example, the systems analyst might have found in the analysis phase that an exception report should be produced if inventory balances fall below a certain level. During the process design phase, the frequency of the report will be determined.

One way to document the relationship of different processes is with a **system flowchart** (Figure 11-20). The system flowchart shows the major processes (each of which may require one or more programs), reports (including their distribution), data files, and the types of input devices such as terminals or tape drives, that will provide data to the system.

FIGURE 11-20

The system flowchart documents the equipment used to enter data, such as the terminals for the salespeople and the order department, the processes that will take place, such as the Verify Customer process, the files that will be used, such as the Parts and Customer files, and the reports that will be produced, such as the Shipping Order. Dotted lines indicate additional copies of reports, such as the copy of the Invoice that is sent to the accounts receivable department.

The special symbols used in a system flowchart are shown in Figure 11-21.

During process design the systems analyst, the user, and the other members of the development project sometimes meet to conduct a **structured walk-through**, a step-by-step review of the process design. The purpose of these sessions is to identify any design logic errors and to continue the communication between the systems analyst and the user.

FIGURE 11-21
Symbols used for preparing a system flowchart.

System Controls   An important aspect of the design phase is the establishment of a comprehensive set of system controls. **System controls** ensure that only valid data is accepted and processed. Adequate controls must be established for two reasons: (1) to ensure the accuracy of the processing and the information generated from the system, and (2) to prevent computer-related fraud.

There are four types of controls that must be considered by the systems analyst. These controls are: (1) source document controls, (2) input controls, (3) processing controls, and (4) accounting controls.

1. **Source document controls** include serial numbering of input documents such as invoices and paychecks, document registers in which each input document is recorded and time-stamped as it is received, and batch totaling and balancing to predetermined totals to assure the accuracy of processing.

2. **Input controls** are established to assure the complete and accurate conversion of data from the source documents or other sources to a machine-processable form. Editing data as it enters the system is the most important form of input controls.

3. **Processing controls** refer to procedures that are established to determine the accuracy of information after it has been input to the system. For example, the accuracy of the total accounts receivable could be verified by taking the prior day's total, adding the current day's sales invoices, and subtracting the current day's payments.

4. **Accounting controls** provide assurance that the dollar amounts recorded in the accounting records are correct. One type of accounting control is making sure that detail reports are created to support the summary reports used to make entries in an organization's financial system. For example, many companies record sales by product line based on a summary report showing product line totals. In addition to this summary report, a detail report showing individual product sales should also be prepared and agreed to the summary report.

Testing Design   During the design phase, test specifications are developed. The exact tests to be performed should be specified by someone other than the user or the systems analyst, although both should be consulted. Users and systems analysts have a tendency to test only what has been designed. An impartial third party, who has not been actively involved in the design, is more likely to design a test for, and therefore discover, a procedure or type of data that may have been overlooked in the design. Sometimes organizations avoid test design and test their systems with actual transactions. While such *live* testing is valuable, it might not test all conditions that the system is designed to process. This is especially true of error or exception conditions that do not occur regularly. For example, payroll systems are usually designed to reject input for hours worked over some limit, say 60 hours in a week. If only actual data are used to test the system, this limit may not be tested. Thus, it is important to design testing specifications that will test each system control that is part of the system by using both valid and invalid data.

Design Review

At the end of the design phase, management performs a **design review** and evaluates the work completed so far to determine whether to proceed (Figure 11-22). This is a critical point in any development project and all parties must take equal responsibility for the decision.

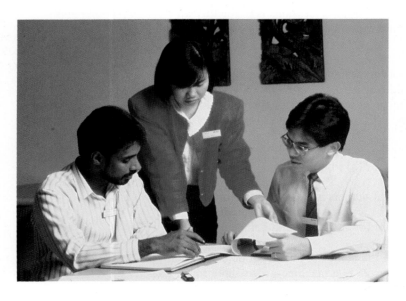

FIGURE 11-22
The design review is a critical point in the development process. Representatives from the user and information systems departments and top management meet to determine if the system should be developed as designed or if additional design work is necessary.

Usually, the design review will result only in requests for clarification of a few items. But sometimes an entire project will be terminated. Although canceling or restarting a project from the beginning is a difficult decision, in the long run it is less costly than implementing the wrong or an inadequate solution. If management decides to proceed, the project enters the development phase.

Before discussing the development phase, we describe prototyping, a development method that can be used in several phases of a system development project, and computer-aided software engineering, an automated approach to system design.

Prototyping

Prototyping is building a working model of the new system. The advantage of prototyping is that it lets the user actually experience the system before it is completed. Some organizations use prototyping during the analysis phase, others use it during the design phase. Still other companies use prototyping to go directly from the preliminary investigation to an implemented system. These companies just keep refining the prototype until the user says that it is acceptable. A disadvantage of such an accelerated approach is that key features of a new system, especially exception conditions, may be overlooked. Another disadvantage is that documentation, an important part of any system development effort, is usually not as well or as thoroughly prepared. Used as a tool to show the user how the system will operate, prototyping can be an important system development tool.

Computer-Aided
Software Engineering (CASE)

Many organizations are now using computer software specifically developed to aid the information system life cycle process. **Computer-aided software engineering (CASE)** refers to
the use of automated computer-based tools to design and manage a software system (Figure 11-23). Sometimes these tools,
such as a data dictionary, exist separately. Other CASE vendors
have combined several tools into an integrated package referred
to as a **CASE workbench**. CASE workbench tools might
include:

- *Analysis and design tools* such as data dictionaries, decision
  tables, or data flow diagram builders
- *Prototyping tools* that can be used to create models of the
  proposed system
- *Code generators* that create actual computer programs
- An *information repository* that cross references and organizes all information about a system
- *Management tools* that assist in the management of a systems project

In addition to the benefits of increased productivity, CASE
tools promote the completion of the design work before development begins. Starting the development work before the
design is completed often results in work that has to be redone.

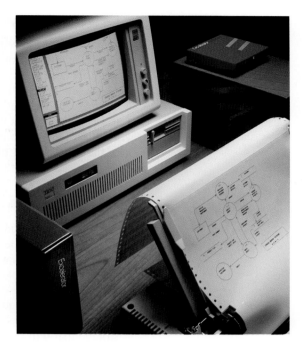

FIGURE 11-23

Computer-aided software engineering (CASE) packages help users design complex systems. Excelera-
tor by Index Technologies allows users to create
and revise data flow diagrams, data dictionary elements, screens, reports, and process
specifications.

DESIGN AT SUTHERLAND

Upon approval by the management review committee, Mary Ruiz begins designing the order entry and invoicing system. After she studies existing manually prepared
documents and talks to users, Mary designs printed reports and screen displays.
According to Mike Charles, one of the most important reports is the daily invoice register. Using a report layout form (Figure 11-18), Mary shows Mike how the report will
look after it is programmed. Using a similar form for screen displays (Figure 11-19),
Mary also shows Mike what the order clerks will see when they enter auto parts
orders. To graphically show how the overall system will work, Mary prepares a system
flowchart (Figure 11-20). The system flowchart shows that auto parts orders will be
entered on terminals in the sales department and will use data in the Parts and Customer files to verify that the orders are valid. Shipping orders and invoices are two of
the reports produced. An important part of Mary's design time involves specifying the
system controls used during processing. These controls include verifying the customer
number before processing the order and checking to see if the ordered part is in stock.
If the ordered part is not in stock, the customer is notified immediately.

After completing her design work, Mary meets with representatives from the user
and information systems departments and top management to review her design. After
Mary explains the design, the committee agrees to develop the system.

DEVELOPMENT PHASE

Once the system design phase has been completed, the project enters the system
development phase. There are two parts to **development**: program development and
equipment acquisition.

Program Development

The process of developing the software, or programs, required for a system is called **program development** and includes the following steps: (1) reviewing the program specifications, (2) designing the program, (3) coding the program, (4) testing the program; and (5) finalizing the program documentation. The primary responsibility for completing these tasks is assumed by computer programmers who work closely with the systems analyst who designed the system. Chapter 12 explains program development in depth. The important concepts to understand now are that this process is a part of the development phase of the information system life cycle and that its purpose is to develop the software required by the system.

Equipment Acquisition

During the development phase, final decisions will be made on what additional equipment, if any, will be required for the new system. A preliminary review of the equipment requirements would have been done during the analysis phase and included in the written report prepared by the systems analyst. Making the equipment acquisition prior to the development phase would be premature because any equipment selected should be based on the requirements specified in the design phase. Equipment selection is affected by factors such as the number of users who will require terminals and the disk storage that will be required for new files and data elements. In some cases, even a new or upgraded CPU is required. If an organization chose to acquire a commercial software package instead of developing software, the equipment acquisition would take place during the acquisition phase.

DEVELOPMENT AT SUTHERLAND

During the development phase, Mary works closely with the two programmers who are assigned to the project. She regularly meets with the programmers to answer questions about the design and to check on the progress of their work. Prior to starting the programming, Mary arranges for the programmers to meet with the auto parts sales employees so that the programmers will have a better understanding of the purpose of the new system.

When the programming is nearly completed, Mary arranges for the terminals to be installed in the sales department.

IMPLEMENTATION PHASE

Implementation is the phase of the system development process when people actually begin using the new system. This is a critical phase of the project that usually requires careful timing and the coordination of all the project participants. Important parts of this phase that will contribute to the success of the new system are training and education, conversion, and post-implementation evaluation.

Training and Education

Someone once said, "If you think education is expensive, you should consider the cost without it." The point is that untrained users can prevent the estimated benefits of a new system from ever being obtained or, worse, contribute to less efficiency and more costs than when the old system was operational. Training consists of showing people exactly how they will use the new system (Figure 11-24). This might include classroom-style lectures, but should definitely include hands-on sessions with the equipment they will be using, such as terminals, and realistic sample data. Education consists of learning new principles or theories that help people to understand and use the system. For example, before implementing a modern manufacturing system, many companies now require their manufacturing personnel to attend classes on material requirements planning (MRP), shop floor control, and other essential manufacturing topics.

FIGURE 11-24
All users should be trained on the system before they have to use it to process actual transactions. Training could include both classroom and hands-on sessions.

Conversion

Conversion refers to the process of changing from the old system to the new system. A number of different methods of conversion can be used including direct, parallel, phased, and pilot.

With **direct conversion**, the user stops using the old system one day and begins using the new system the next. The advantage of this approach is that it is fast and efficient. The disadvantage is that it is risky and can seriously disrupt operations if the new system does not work correctly the first time.

Parallel conversion consists of continuing to process data on the old system while some or all of the data is also processed on the new system. Results from both systems are compared, and if they agree, all data is switched to the new system (Figure 11-25).

Phased conversion is used with larger systems that can be broken down into individual modules that can be implemented separately at different times. An example would be a complete business system that could have the accounts receivable, inventory, and accounts payable modules implemented separately in phases. Phased conversions can be direct, parallel, or a combination of both.

Pilot conversion means that the new system will be used first by only a portion of the organization, often at a separate location such as a plant or office.

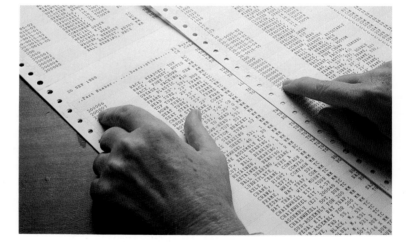

FIGURE 11-25
During parallel conversion, the user compares results from both the old and the new systems to determine if the new systems is operating properly.

Post-Implementation Evaluation

After a system is implemented, it is important to conduct a **post-implementation evaluation** to determine if the system is performing as designed, if operating costs are as anticipated, and if any modifications are necessary to make the system operate more effectively.

IMPLEMENTATION AT SUTHERLAND

Before they begin to use the new system to enter real transactions, the users participate in several training sessions about the equipment and the software. Because this is the first application in the auto parts division to be computerized, Mary begins the training sessions with an overview of how the central computer system processes data.

She conducts a basic data entry class to teach the employees how to use the terminals (Figure 11-24).

Before the system can be used, the Parts and Customer files have to be created from existing manual records. Temporary employees trained in data entry skills are hired for this task. Their work is carefully reviewed each day by Mike Charles and other permanent department employees.

Although he knows it means extra work, Mike decides that a parallel conversion is the safest way to implement the new system. Using this method, Mike verifies the results of the new system with those of the existing manual system. Actual use of the system begins on the first business day of the month so that transaction totals can be balanced to accounting reports.

Because they are thoroughly trained, the order clerks feel comfortable when they begin entering real orders. They encounter a few minor problems, such as orders for special parts not on the Parts file. These problems become less frequent and at the end of the month, after Mike compares the manual and computerized report totals, he decides to discontinue the use of the manual system.

During the post-implementation review, Mike and Mary discover that nine out of ten customer orders are now shipped the same day as the order is received. Before the new system was implemented, less than half the orders were shipped within two days of receipt. Invoices, which once lagged twelve to sixteen days behind shipments, are now mailed on the same day. Perhaps the most positive benefit of the new system is that customer complaints about order processing are practically eliminated.

MAINTENANCE PHASE

◆ **Maintenance** is the process of supporting the system after it is implemented. Maintenance consists of three activities: performance monitoring, change management, and error correction.

Performance Monitoring

Performance monitoring is the ongoing process of comparing response times, file sizes, and other system performance measures against the estimates that were prepared during the analysis, design, and implementation phases. Variances from these estimates may indicate that the system requires additional equipment resources, such as more memory or faster disk drives.

Change Management

Change is an inevitable part of any system; thus, all users of the system should be familiar with methods and procedures that provide for change. Sometimes, changes are required because existing requirements were overlooked. Other times, new information requirements caused by external sources such as government regulations will force change. A key part of change management is documentation. The same documentation standards that were followed during the analysis and design phases should also be used to record changes. In fact, in many organizations, the same document that is used to request new systems (Figure 11-3) is used to request changes to an existing system (Figure 11-26). Thus, the information system development cycle continues as the analysis phase begins on the change request.

Error Correction

Error correction deals with problems that are caused by programming and design errors that are discovered after the system is implemented. Often these errors are minor problems, such as the ZIP code not appearing on a name and address report, that can be quickly fixed by a programmer. Other times, however, the error requires more serious investigation by the systems analyst before a correction can be determined. Design errors that are not found until after a system is implemented are much more expensive to correct than had they been found earlier.

MAINTENANCE AT SUTHERLAND

◆ During the months following the system implementation, users discover a number of minor errors in the system. The programming staff quickly corrects most of these errors, but in one case involving special credit terms for a large customer, Mary Ruiz becomes involved and prepares specifications for the necessary program changes.

Approximately one year after Mike Charles submits his original request for a computerized order entry and invoicing system, he submits another request (Figure 11-26) for a change to the system to provide for a new county sales tax. This type of request does not require a preliminary investigation and is assigned to Mary Ruiz as soon as she is available. Mike submits his request five months before the tax is scheduled to go into effect, which allows ample time for the necessary program changes to be implemented.

REQUEST FOR SYSTEM SERVICES

ISD CONTROL #: 4703

I. To Be Completed By Person Requesting Services
SUBMITTED BY: MIKE CHARLES DEPT: AUTO PARTS SALES DATE: 2/1/93

REQUEST TYPE: ✓ MODIFICATION ☐ NEW SYSTEM
NEED: ✓ ASAP ☐ IMMEDIATE ☐ LONG RANGE
BRIEF STATEMENT OF REQUEST (attach additional material, if necessary)
SALES INVOICE PROGRAM NEEDS TO PROVIDE FOR 1% COUNTY TAX THAT WILL GO INTO EFFECT JULY 1, 1993

✓ ADDITIONAL MATERIAL ATTACHED COUNTY TAX RATE SCHEDULE

II. To Be Completed By Information Systems Department
REQUEST INVESTIGATED BY: _____ DATE: _____
COMMENTS: _____

III. Disposition
  ☐ REQUEST APPROVED FOR IMMEDIATE IMPLEMENTATION
  ☐ ANALYST ASSIGNED: _____
  ☐ REQUEST APPROVED FOR IMPLEMENTATION AS SOON AS POSSIBLE
  ☐ REQUEST REJECTED
COMMENTS: _____

SIGNED: _____ DATE: _____

FIGURE 11-26
The same form used to request a new system (Figure 11-3) is also used to request a modification to an existing system.

SUMMARY OF THE INFORMATION SYSTEM LIFE CYCLE

◆ Although the information system development process may appear to be a straightforward series of steps, in practice it is a challenging activity that calls for the skills and cooperation of all involved. New development tools have made the process more efficient but the success of any project always depends on the commitment of the project participants. The understanding you have gained from this chapter will help you participate in information system development projects and give you an appreciation for the importance of each phase.

CHAPTER SUMMARY

1. The **information system life cycle (ISLC)** is an organized approach to obtaining an information system.
2. Planning, scheduling, reporting, and controlling the individual activities that make up the information system development life cycle is called **project management**. These activities are usually recorded in a **project plan**.
3. **Documentation** refers to written materials that are produced throughout the information system development life cycle.

4. All users and information system personnel who will be affected by the new system should have the opportunity to participate in its development.

5. The **analysis** phase is the separation of a system into its parts in order to determine how the system works. This phase consists of the preliminary investigation, detailed system analysis, and making the decision to proceed.

6. The purpose of the **preliminary investigation** is to determine if a request warrants further detailed investigation. The most important aspect of this investigation is **problem definition**.

7. **Detailed system analysis** involves both a thorough study of the current system and at least one proposed solution to any problems found.

8. **Structured analysis** is the use of analysis and design tools such as **data flow diagrams (DFDs)**, **data dictionaries**, **process specifications**, **structured English**, **decision tables**, and **decision trees** to document the specifications of an information system.

9. A **feasibility study** and **cost/benefit analysis** are often prepared to show whether the proposed solution is practical and to show the estimated costs and benefits that are expected.

10. The **acquisition** phase involves four steps: (1) summarizing application requirements, (2) identifying potential software vendors, (3) evaluating software alternatives, and (4) making the purchase.

11. **Commercial applications software** is software that has already been developed and is available for purchase.

12. Software packages that can be used by many different types of organizations, such as accounting packages, are called **horizontal application software**.

13. Software developed for a unique way of doing business, usually within a specific industry, is called **vertical application software**.

14. A **request for proposal (RFP)** is a written list of an organization's software requirements that is given to prospective software vendors.

15. Identifying potential software vendors for personal computers can usually be done at a local computer store. For larger applications sources include computer manufacturers, **software houses**, **system houses**, trade publications, computer periodicals, and consultants.

16. To evaluate software alternatives, match the features of each possible solution against the original requirements list or RFP.

17. A **benchmark test** involves measuring the time it takes to process a set number of transactions.

18. A **software license** is the right to use software under certain terms and conditions.

19. Application software that is developed by a user or at the user's request is called **custom software**.

20. Modifying a commercial applications package is usually referred to as **customizing** or **tailoring**.

21. During the **design** phase the **logical design** that was created in the analysis phase is transformed into a **physical design**.

22. There are two major structured design methods: **top-down design** (or **structured design**) and **bottom-up design**.

23. **Output design**, **input design**, and **database design** all occur during the design phase.

24. A **dialogue** is the sequence of inputs and computer responses that a user will encounter when he or she enters data on an interactive system.

25. During the **process design**, the systems analyst specifies exactly what actions will be taken on the input data to create output information.

26. One method of documenting the relationship of different processes is with a **system flowchart**.

27. A **structured walk-through**, or a step-by-step review, is sometimes performed on the process design.

28. **System controls** are established to (1) ensure that only valid data is accepted and processed and (2) to prevent computer-related fraud. Types of system controls include **source document controls**, **input controls**, **processing controls**, and **accounting controls**.

29. At the end of the design phase, a **design review** is performed to evaluate the work completed so far.

30. **Prototyping** is building a working model of the new system.

31. **Computer-aided software engineering (CASE)** refers to the use of automated computer based tools to design and manage a software system.

32. A **CASE workbench** provides several CASE tools in an integrated package. These tools might include analysis and design tools, prototyping tools, code generators, information repository, and management tools.

33. The **development** phase consists of program development and equipment acquisition.

34. **Program development** includes: (1) reviewing the program specifications, (2) designing the program, (3) coding the program, (4) testing the program, and (5) finalizing the program documentation.

35. The **implementation** phase is when people actually begin using the new system. This phase includes training and education, conversion, and the **post-implementation evaluation**.

36. The process of changing from the old system to the new system is called a **conversion**. The conversion methods that may be used are **direct**, **parallel**, **phased**, and **pilot**.
37. The **maintenance** phase is the process of supporting the information system after it is implemented. It consists of three activities: **performance monitoring**, change management, and error correction.

KEY TERMS

Accounting controls *11.19*
Analysis *11.4*
Benchmark test *11.13*
Bottom-up design *11.16*
CASE workbench *11.21*
Commercial applications software *11.10*
Computer-aided software engineering (CASE) *11.21*
Conversion *11.23*
Cost/benefit analysis *11.8*
Custom software *11.14*
Customizing *11.15*
Database design *11.18*
Data dictionary *11.6*
Data flow diagram (DFD) *11.5*
Decision table *11.7*
Decision tree *11.7*
Design *11.16*
Design review *11.20*
Detailed system analysis *11.5*
Development *11.21*

Dialogue *11.17*
Direct conversion *11.23*
Documentation *11.3*
Feasibility study *11.8*
Horizontal application software *11.11*
Implementation *11.22*
Information system life cycle (ISLC) *11.2*
Input controls *11.19*
Input design *11.17*
Logical design *11.16*
Maintenance *11.24*
Output design *11.17*
Parallel conversion *11.23*
Performance monitoring *11.24*
Phased conversion *11.23*
Physical design *11.16*
Pilot conversion *11.23*
Post-implementation evaluation *11.23*
Preliminary investigation *11.4*

Problem definition *11.4*
Process design *11.18*
Processing controls *11.19*
Process specification *11.7*
Program development *11.22*
Project management *11.2*
Project plan *11.2*
Prototyping *11.20*
Request for proposal (RFP) *11.11*
Software house *11.12*
Software license *11.13*
Source document controls *11.19*
Structured analysis *11.5*
Structured design *11.16*
Structured English *11.7*
Structured walk-through *11.19*
System controls *11.19*
System flowchart *11.18*
System house *11.12*
Tailoring *11.15*
Top-down design *11.16*
Vertical application software *11.11*

REVIEW QUESTIONS

1. Draw a diagram showing the phases of the information system life cycle.
2. Describe project management and when it should be performed.
3. What is the preliminary investigation? What is the most important aspect of the preliminary investigation?
4. Briefly describe detailed system analysis. What are the fact-finding techniques used during detailed system analysis?
5. What is commercial applications software? Explain the difference between horizontal and vertical applications.
6. Describe the information that an RFP should contain and how the RFP is used.
7. What is custom software and why is it appropriate for some applications?
8. Describe several things that a user can do to evaluate a software package before purchasing it. What is a benchmark test?
9. What is a software license? Describe some of the terms and conditions that are included in a software license.
10. What are the symbols used in data flow diagrams? Why are data flow diagrams useful?
11. Explain the difference between the logical and physical design of an information system.
12. What are the two methods of structured design? Briefly describe each method.
13. What is prototyping?
14. Write a description of the four types of conversion methods.
15. Describe the three major activities of system maintenance.

CONTROVERSIAL ISSUES

1. Some organizations claim that consultants have saved them considerable sums of money when acquiring applications software. Others say that they would have been better off not using a consultant. What role, if any, do you feel a consultant should play in helping an organization to select applications software?
2. "The difficulty in developing and implementing an information processing system is the user," proclaimed a systems analyst. "Users never know what they want. When they are shown what the system will do, they give their approval, but when the system is implemented they are never happy. They always want changes. It's impossible to satisfy them." How do you feel about these comments? Are the systems analyst's comments about users correct?

RESEARCH PROJECTS

1. Use the yellow pages, computer magazines or newspapers, or computer store references to locate a computer consultant. Interview the consultant over the phone or in person and ask him or her how he or she helps a user choose a computer system. Prepare a report for your class.
2. Prepare a data flow diagram of how you registered for class. Document your work by obtaining copies of any forms that you used during the registration process.

Program Development

OBJECTIVES

◆ Define the term computer program

◆ Describe the five steps in program development: review of program specifications, program design, program coding, program testing, and finalizing program documentation

◆ Explain the concepts of structured program design including modules, control structures, and single entry/ single exit

◆ Explain and illustrate the sequence, selection, and iteration control structures used in structured programming

◆ Define the term programming language and discuss the various categories of programming languages

◆ Briefly discuss the programming languages that are commonly used today, including BASIC, COBOL, C, FORTRAN, Pascal, and Ada

◆ Explain and discuss application generators

◆ Explain and discuss object-oriented programming

◆ Explain the factors that should be considered when choosing a programming language

The information system life cycle covers the entire process of taking a plan for processing information through various phases until it becomes a functioning information system. During the development phase of this cycle, computer programs are written. The purpose of these programs is to process data and produce information as specified in the information system design. In this chapter we focus on the steps taken to write a program and the available tools that make the program development process more efficient. Also in this chapter we discuss the different languages used to write programs.

Although you may never write a program yourself, you might someday request information that will require a program to be written or modified; thus, you should understand how a computer program is developed.

WHAT IS A COMPUTER PROGRAM?

A **computer program** is a detailed set of instructions that directs a computer to perform the tasks necessary to process data into information. These instructions, usually written by a computer programmer, can be coded (written) in a variety of programming languages that we discuss later in this chapter. To create programs that are correct (produce accurate information) and maintainable (easy to modify), programmers follow a process called program development.

WHAT IS PROGRAM DEVELOPMENT?

Program development is the process of producing one or more programs to perform specific tasks on a computer. The process of program development has evolved into a series of five steps that most experts agree should take place when any program is developed (Figure 12-1).

FIGURE 12-1
The five steps of program development. Although the process steps are shown sequentially, program development usually requires returning to previous steps to correct errors.

1. *Review of program specifications*. The programmer reviews the specifications created by the systems analyst during the system design phase.
2. *Program design*. The programmer determines and documents the specific actions the computer will take to accomplish the desired tasks.
3. *Coding*. The programmer writes the actual program instructions.
4. *Testing*. The written programs are tested to make sure they perform as intended.
5. *Finalizing documentation*. Throughout the program development process the programmer documents, or writes, explanatory information about the program. In this final step the documentation produced during steps 1 through 4 is brought together and organized.

Although we list these five steps sequentially, the program development process usually requires returning to previous steps to correct errors that are discovered.

FIGURE 12-2
Program development occurs during the Development phase of the information system life cycle.

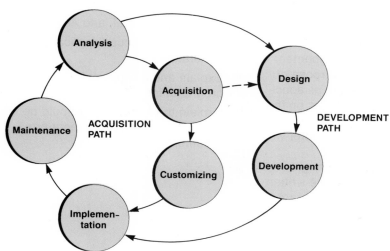

To help you to better understand how the steps in the program development process relate to the overall development of an information system, let's review the phases of the information system life cycle. As you can see in Figure 12-2, program development is a phase on the development path of the information system life cycle. If, after the analysis phase, an organization is unable to acquire commercial software that meets its needs, it moves or it proceeds to the design phase. The development phase, which refers to program development, follows the design phase and includes the five steps shown in Figure 12-1.

STEP 1—REVIEWING THE PROGRAM SPECIFICATIONS

The first step in the program development cycle is a review of the program specifications. **Program specifications** can consist of data flow diagrams, system flowcharts, process specifications that indicate the action to be taken on the data, a data dictionary identifying the data elements that will be used, screen formats, report layouts, and actual documents such as invoices or checks. These documents help the programmer understand the work that needs to be done by the program. Also, the programmer meets once or more with the user and the systems analyst who designed the system to understand the purpose of the program from the user's point of view.

If the programmer believes some aspect of the design should be changed, such as a screen layout, he or she discusses it with the systems analyst and the user. If the change is agreed on, the written design specification is changed. However, the programmer should not change the specified system without the agreement of the systems analyst and the user. If a change is authorized, it should be recorded in the system design. The systems analyst and the user, through the system design, have specified what is to be done. It is the programmer's job to determine *how* to do it.

Large programming jobs are usually assigned to more than one programmer. In these situations, a good system design is essential so that each programmer can be given a logical portion of the system to be programmed.

STEP 2—DESIGNING THE PROGRAM

After the programmer has carefully reviewed the specifications, program design begins. During **program design** a logical solution to the programming task is developed and documented. The logical solution, or **logic**, for a program is a step-by-step solution to a programming problem. Determining the logic for a computer program can be an extremely complex task. To aid in program design and development, a method called structured program design is commonly used.

Structured Program Design

Structured program design is a methodology that emphasizes three main program design concepts: modules, control structures, and single entry/single exit. Use of these concepts helps to create programs that are easy to write, read, understand, check for errors, and modify.

Modules With structured design, programming problems are *decomposed* (separated) into smaller parts called modules. Each **module**, sometimes referred to as a **subroutine** in programming, performs a given task within the program. The major benefit of this technique is that it simplifies program development because each module of a program can be developed individually. When the modules are combined, they form a complete program that accomplishes the desired result.

Structure charts, also called **hierarchy charts**, are often used to decompose and represent the modules of a program. When the program decomposition is completed, the entire structure of a program is illustrated by the hierarchy chart (on the next page in Figure 12-3), which shows the relationship of the modules within the program.

FIGURE 12-3
In this structure chart, the relationship of individual program modules are graphically shown as boxes. The text below each box indicates the processing steps that would be performed.

Control Structures   In structured program design three basic **control structures** are used to form the logic of a program. All logic problems can be solved by a combination of these structures. The three basic control structures are: sequence, selection, and iteration.

1. In the **sequence structure**, one process occurs immediately after another. In Figure 12-4, each rectangular box represents a particular process that is to occur. For example, a process could be a computer instruction to move data from one location in main memory to another location. Each process occurs in the exact sequence specified, one process followed by the next.

2. The second control structure, called the **selection structure**, or **if-then-else structure**, gives programmers a way to represent conditional program logic (Figure 12-5). Conditional program logic can be expressed in the following way: *If* the condition is true, *then* perform the true condition processing, *else* perform the false condition processing. When the if-then-else structure is used, the if portion of the structure tests a given condition. The true portion of the statement is executed if the condition tested is true, and the false portion of the statement is executed if the condition is false. An if-then-else structure might be used to determine if an employee is hourly or salaried and then process the employee accordingly. To do this, an employee code might be tested to determine if an employee is hourly. If the employee is hourly, the true portion of the structure would be executed and hourly pay would be calculated. If the employee is not hourly, the false portion of the structure would be executed and salary pay would be calculated. The selection, or if-then-else, structure is used by programmers to represent conditional logic problems.

SEQUENCE

FIGURE 12-4
Each box in the sequence control structure represents a process that will occur immediately after the preceding process.

FIGURE 12-5
The selection, or if-then-else, control structure is used to direct the program to one process or another based on the test of a condition.

SELECTION

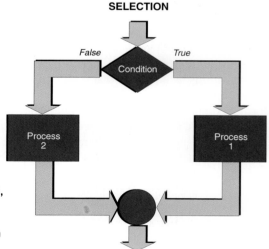

A variation of the selection structure is the case structure. The **case structure** is used when a condition is being tested that can lead to more than two alternatives (Figure 12-6). In a program, a menu is an example of a case structure because it provides multiple processing options.

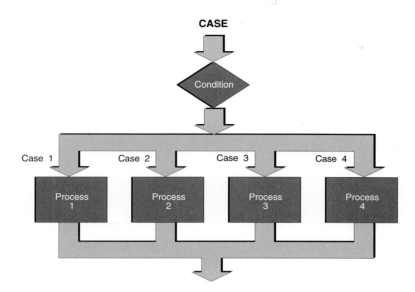

CASE

FIGURE 12-6
A case control structure with four possible processing paths is similar to the if-then-else control structure except that it provides for more than two alternatives.

3. The third control structure, called the **iteration structure**, or **looping structure**, means that one or more processes continue to occur as long as a given condition remains true. There are two forms of this control structure: the **do-while structure** and the **do-until structure** (Figure 12-7). In the do-while structure a condition is tested. If the condition is true, the process is performed. The program then *loops* back and tests the condition again. If the condition is still true, the process is performed again. This looping continues until the condition being tested is false. At that time, the program exits the loop, moves to another section of the program, and performs some other processing. An example of this type of testing would be a check to see if all records have been processed. The do-until control structure is similar to the do-while except that the condition tested is at the end instead of the beginning of the loop. Processing continues *until* the condition is met.

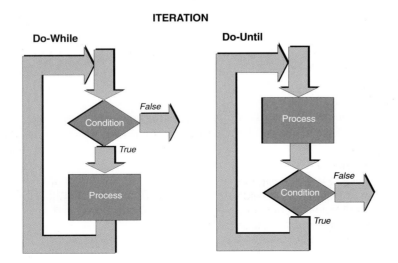

ITERATION

FIGURE 12-7
The iteration control structure has two forms, do-while and do-until. In the do-while structure, the condition is tested before the process. In the do-until structure, the condition is tested after the process.

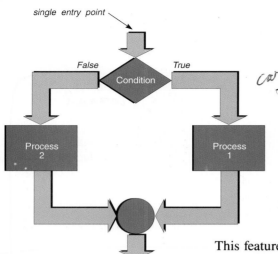

single entry point

False   Condition   True

Process 2

Process 1

single exit point

FIGURE 12-8

Structured programming concepts require that all control structures have a single entry point and a single exit point. This contributes to programs that are easier to understand and maintain.

Programmers combine these three control structures—sequence, selection, and iteration—to create program logic solutions. A structured program design rule that applies to these control structures and how they are combined is the single entry/single exit rule.

Cardinal rule #1

Single Entry/Single Exit   An important concept in structured programming is **single entry/single exit**, meaning that there is only one entry point and one exit point for each of the three control structures. An **entry point** is the point where a control structure is entered. An **exit point** is the point where the control structure is exited. For example, in Figure 12-8, when the if-then-else structure is used, the control structure is entered at the point where the condition is tested. When the condition is tested, one set of instructions will be executed if the condition is true and another set will be executed if the condition is false. Regardless of the result of the test, however, the structure is exited at the single exit point.

This feature substantially improves the logic of a program because, when reading the program, the programmer can be assured that whatever happens within the if-then-else structure, the control structure will always be exited at a common point. Prior to the use of structured programming, many programmers would transfer control to other parts of a program without following the single entry/single exit rule. This practice led to poorly designed programs that were extremely difficult to read, check for errors, and modify. Because the logic path of such programs jumps from one section of the program to another, the programs are sometimes referred to as *spaghetti code*.

Program Design Tools

Programmers use several popular program design tools to develop and document the logical solutions to the problems they are programming. Three commonly used design tools are program flowcharts, pseudocode, and Warnier-Orr diagrams.

Program Flowcharts   Program flowcharts were one of the first program design tools. Figure 12-9 shows a flowchart drawn in the late 1940s by Dr. John von Neumann, a computer scientist and one of the first computer programmers. In a **program flowchart** all the logical steps of a program are represented by a combination of symbols and text.

A set of standards for program flowcharts was published in the early 1960s by the American National Standards Institute (ANSI). These standards, which are still used today, specify symbols, such as rectangles and diamonds, that are used to represent the various operations that can be performed on a computer (Figure 12-10). Program flowcharts were used as the primary means of program design for many years prior to the introduction of structured program design. During these years, programmers designed programs by focusing on the detailed steps required for a program and creating logical solutions for each new combination of conditions as it was encountered. Developing programs in this manner led to programs that were poorly designed.

Today, programmers are taught to apply the structured design concepts when they create program flowcharts (Figure 12-11). When they use basic control structures, program flowcharts are a valuable program design tool.

FIGURE 12-9

An example of an early flowchart developed by computer scientist Dr. John von Neumann in the 1940s to solve a problem involving game theory. This flowchart was drawn prior to the standardization of flowchart symbols and the development of structured design techniques.

FIGURE 12-10 ▶
Standard symbols used to create program flowcharts.

DECISION
The decision function used to document points in the program where a branch to alternate paths is possible based upon variable conditions.

PROCESSING
A group of program instructions which perform a processing function of the program.

TERMINAL
The beginning, end, or a point of interruption in a program.

OFFPAGE CONNECTOR
A connector used instead of the connector symbol to designate entry to or exit from a page.

INPUT/OUTPUT
Any function of an input/output device (making information available for processing, recording processing information, etc.).

PREDEFINED PROCESS
A group of operations not detailed in the particular set of flowcharts.
external

CONNECTOR
An entry from, or an exit to, another part of the program flowchart.

internal

◀ FIGURE 12-11
This flowchart displays the logic required to solve a payroll calculation task using standard flowcharting symbols and the three control structures of structured programming.

```
Open the files
Read a record
PERFORM UNTIL end of file
    Move employee number, name, regular pay, and
        overtime pay to the report area
    IF bonus code is alphabetic or not numeric
        Move error message to report area
    ELSE
        IF first shift
            Calculate total pay = regular pay +
                overtime pay
            Set bonus pay to zero
        ELSE
            If second shift
                Calculate total pay = regular pay +
                    overtime pay + 5.00
                Set bonus pay to 5.00
            ELSE
                If third shift
                    Calculate total pay = regular pay +
                        overtime pay + 10.00
                    Set bonus pay to 10.00
                ELSE
                    Move error message to report area
                ENDIF
            ENDIF
        ENDIF
    ENDIF
    Write a line
    Read a record
ENDPERFORM
Close the files
End the program
```

FIGURE 12-12
This pseudocode is another way of documenting the logic shown in the flowchart in Figure 12-11.

Pseudocode Some experts in program design advocate the use of pseudocode when designing the logic for a program. In **pseudocode**, the logical steps in the solution of a problem are written as English statements and indentations are used to represent the control structures (Figure 12-12). An advantage of pseudocode is that it eliminates the time spent with flowcharting to draw and arrange symbols while attempting to determine the program logic. The major disadvantage is that unlike flowcharting, pseudocode does not provide a graphic representation, which many people find useful and easier to interpret when they examine programming logic.

Warnier-Orr In the **Warnier-Orr technique** (named after Jean Dominique Warnier and Kenneth Orr), the programmer analyzes output to be produced from an application and develops processing modules that are needed to produce the output. The example in Figure 12-13 illustrates a completed Warnier-Orr diagram for the same program as Figures 12-11 and 12-12. Each curly brace ({ }) represents a module in the program. The statements within the braces identify the processing that is to occur within the modules.

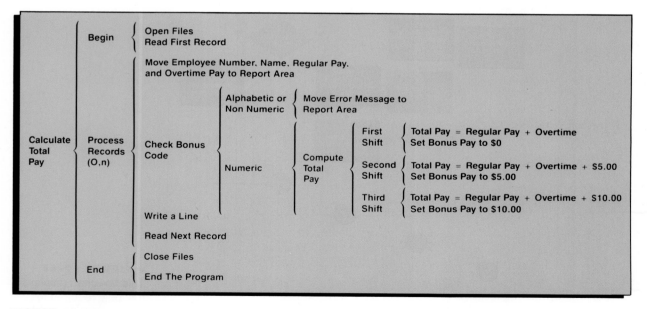

FIGURE 12-13
This Warnier-Orr diagram also illustrates the logic for the payroll calculation problem used for Figures 12-11 and 12-12.

Regardless of the design tool you use, it is important that the program design is efficient and correct. To help ensure this, many organizations use structured walk-throughs.

Structured Walk-Through

After a program has been designed, the programmer schedules a structured walk-through of the program. The programmer, other programmers in the department, and the systems analyst attend. During the walk-through, the programmer who designs the program explains the program logic. The purpose of the design walk-through is to review the logic of the program for errors, and if possible, improve program design. Early detection of errors and approval of program design improvements reduces the overall development time and therefore the cost of the program. It is much better to find errors and make needed changes to the program during the design step than to make them later in the program development process.

Once the program design is complete, the programmer can begin to code the program.

STEP 3—CODING THE PROGRAM

◆ **Coding** the program refers to the process of writing the program instructions that will process the data and produce the output specified in the program design. As we previously mentioned, programs are written in different languages, which each have particular rules on how to instruct the computer to perform specific tasks, such as read a record or multiply two numbers.

If the program design is thorough, logical, and well structured, the coding process is greatly simplified and can sometimes be a one-for-one translation of a design step into a program step. Today, program code, or instructions, are usually entered directly into the computer via a terminal and stored on a disk drive. Using this approach, the programmer can partially enter a program at one time and finish entering it at a later time. Program instructions are added, deleted, and changed until the programmer believes the program design has been fully translated into program instructions and the program is ready for testing.

STEP 4—TESTING THE PROGRAM

◆ Before a program is used to process *real* data and produce information that people rely on, it should be thoroughly tested to make sure it is functioning correctly. A programmer can perform several different types of tests.

Desk checking is the process of reading the program and mentally reviewing its logic. This is a simple process that can be performed by the programmer who wrote the program or by another programmer. This process can be compared to proofreading a letter before you mail it. The disadvantage of this method is that it is difficult to detect other than obvious errors.

Syntax errors are violations of the grammar rules of the language in which the program was written. An example of a syntax error would be the program command READ being misspelled REED. Syntax errors missed by the programmer during desk checking are identified by the computer when it decodes the program instructions.

Logic testing is what most programmers think of when the term testing is used. During **logic testing**, the sequence of program instructions is tested to make sure it provides the correct result. Logic errors may be the result of a programming oversight, such as using the wrong data to perform a calculation, or a design error, such as forgetting to specify that some customers do not have to pay sales tax when they purchase merchandise.

Logic testing is performed with **test data**, data that simulates the type of input that the program will process when it is implemented. To obtain an independent and unbiased test of the program, test data and the review of test results should be the responsibility of someone other than the programmer who wrote the program. The test data should be developed by referring to the system design but it should also try to *break* the program by including data outside the range of data that will be input during normal operations. For example, if the specifications of a payroll program stated that the input for an employee should never exceed 60 hours of work per week, the program should be designed, coded, and tested to properly process transactions in excess of 60 hours. It would do this by displaying an error message or in some other way indicating that an invalid number of hours has been entered. Other similar tests should include alphabetic data when only numeric data is expected, and negative numbers when only positive numbers are normally input.

One of the more colorful terms of the computer industry is **debugging**, which refers to the process of locating and correcting program errors, or **bugs**, found during testing. The term was coined when the failure of one of the first computers was traced to a moth that had become lodged in the electronic components (Figure 12-14).

FIGURE 12-14
In 1945, the cause of the temporary failure of the world's first electromechanical computer, the Mark 1, was traced to a dead moth (shown taped to the log book) caught in the electrical components. The term *bug*, meaning a computer error, has been part of computer jargon ever since.

STEP 5—FINALIZING PROGRAM DOCUMENTATION

Documentation, or the preparation of documents, that explains the program is an essential but sometimes neglected part of the programming process. Documentation should be an ongoing part of developing a program and should only be finalized, meaning organized and brought together, after the program is successfully tested and ready for implementation. Documentation developed during the programming process should include a narrative description of the program, program design documents such as flowcharts or pseudocode, program listings, and test results. Comments in the program itself are also an important part of program documentation (Figure 12-15).

Data entry and computer operations procedures should also be documented prior to implementation. Obtaining adequate documentation may be difficult because some programmers can and do develop programs without it; when they have finished coding the program, they have little incentive to go back and complete the documentation after the fact. In addition to helping programmers develop programs, documentation is valuable because it helps the next programmer who, six months or one year later, is asked to make a change to the program. Proper documentation can substantially reduce the amount of time the new programmer will have to spend learning enough about the program to know how best to make the change.

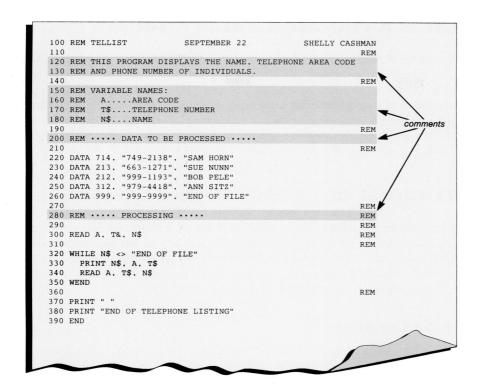

```
100 REM TELLIST          SEPTEMBER 22          SHELLY CASHMAN
110                                                         REM
120 REM THIS PROGRAM DISPLAYS THE NAME. TELEPHONE AREA CODE
130 REM AND PHONE NUMBER OF INDIVIDUALS.
140                                                         REM
150 REM VARIABLE NAMES:
160 REM    A.....AREA CODE
170 REM    T$....TELEPHONE NUMBER
180 REM    N$....NAME
190                                                         REM
200 REM ••••• DATA TO BE PROCESSED •••••
210                                                         REM
220 DATA 714. "749-2138". "SAM HORN"
230 DATA 213. "663-1271". "SUE NUNN"
240 DATA 212. "999-1193". "BOB PELE"
250 DATA 312. "979-4418". "ANN SITZ"
260 DATA 999. "999-9999". "END OF FILE"
270                                                         REM
280 REM ••••• PROCESSING •••••                              REM
290                                                         REM
300 READ A. T&. N$                                          REM
310                                                         REM
320 WHILE N$ <> "END OF FILE"
330    PRINT N$. A. T$
340    READ A. T$. N$
350 WEND
360                                                         REM
370 PRINT " "
380 PRINT "END OF TELEPHONE LISTING"
390 END
```

comments

FIGURE 12-15
Most programming languages allow programmers to place explanatory comments directly in the program. This is an effective way of documenting the program. In this program, comment lines are identified by the letters REM, which is an abbreviation for REMARK.

PROGRAM MAINTENANCE

Program maintenance includes all changes to a program once it is implemented and processing real transactions. Sometimes, maintenance is required to correct errors that were not found during the testing step. Other times, maintenance is required to make changes that are the result of the users' new information requirements. It may surprise you to learn that the majority of all business programming today consists of maintaining existing programs, not writing new programs.

Because so much time is spent on maintenance programming, it should be subject to the same policies and procedures, such as design, testing, and documentation, that are required for new programs. Unfortunately, this is not always the case. Because maintenance tasks are usually shorter than new programming efforts, they often aren't held to the same standards. The result is that over time, programs can become unrecognizable when compared with their original documentation. Maintaining high standards for program maintenance can not only lower overall programming costs, but also lengthen the useful life of a program.

SUMMARY OF PROGRAM DEVELOPMENT

The key to developing quality programs for an information system is to follow the steps of the program development process. Program specifications must be carefully reviewed and understood. Programmers should use structured concepts to design programs that are modular, use the three control structures, and follow the single entry/single exit rule. Programmers should carefully code and test the program and finalize documentation. If each of these steps is followed, programmers will create quality programs that are correct and that can be easily read, understood, and maintained.

WHAT IS A PROGRAMMING LANGUAGE?

As we mentioned at the beginning of this chapter, computer programs can be written in a variety of programming languages. People communicate with one another through language, established patterns of words and sounds. A similar definition can also be applied to a **programming language**, which is a set of written words and symbols that allow the programmer or user to communicate with the computer. As with English, Spanish, Chinese, or other spoken languages, programming languages have rules, called syntax, that govern their use.

CATEGORIES OF PROGRAMMING LANGUAGES

There are hundreds of programming languages, each with its own syntax. Some languages were developed for specific computers and others, because of their success, have been standardized and adapted to a wide range of computers. Programming languages can be classified into one of four categories: machine language, assembly language, high-level languages, and fourth-generation languages.

Machine Language

A **machine language** is the fundamental language of the computer's processor. Programs written in all other categories of languages are eventually converted into machine language before they are executed. Individual machine language instructions exist for each of the commands in the computer's instruction set, the operations such as add, move, or read that are specific to each computer. Because the instruction set is unique for a particular processor, machine languages are different for computers that have different processors. The advantage of writing a program in machine language is that the programmer can control the computer directly and accomplish exactly what needs to be done. Therefore, well-written machine language programs are very efficient. The disadvantages of machine language programs are that they take a long time to write and they are difficult to review if the programmer is trying to find an error. In addition, because they are written using the instruction set of a particular processor, the programs will only run on computers with the same type of processor. Because they are written for specific processors, machine languages are also called **low-level languages**. Figure 12-16 ⓐ shows an example of machine language instructions.

FIGURE 12-16

Program instruction chart for: ⓐ machine language (printed in a hexadecimal form), ⓑ assembly language, and ⓒ a high-level language called C. The machine language and assembly language instructions correspond to the high-level instructions and were generated when the high-level language statements were translated into machine language. As you can see, the high-level language requires fewer program instructions and is easier to read.

ⓐ MACHINE LANGUAGE	ⓑ ASSEMBLY LANGUAGE	ⓒ HIGH-LEVEL LANGUAGE

9b df 46 0c
9b d9 c0
9b db 7e f2
9b d9 46 04
9b d8 c9
9b d9 5e fc
	`        fild WORD PTR [bp+12];qty`
	`fld  ST(0)`
	`        fstp TBYTE PTR [bp-14]`
	`        fld  DWORD PTR [bp+4];price`
	`fmul ST(0),ST(1)`
	`        fstp DWORD PTR [bp-4];gross`
		`gross = qty * price;`

9b d9 c0
9b dc 16 ac 00
9b dd d8
9b dd 7e f0
90 9b
8a 66 f1
9e
9b dd c0
76 19
	`fld  ST(0)`
	`        fcom QWORD PTR $T20002`
	`fstp ST(0)`
	`        fstsw    WORD PTR [bp-16]`
	`        fwait`
	`mov  ah,BYTE PTR [bp-15]`
	`     sahf`
	`ffreeST(0)`
	`     jbe  $I193`
		`if  (qty > ceiling)`

9b d9 46 fc
9b dc 0e b4 00
9b de e9
9b d9 5e 08
90 9b
 	
eb 0d
90
	`        fld  DWORD PTR [bp-4];gross`
	`        fmul QWORD PTR $T20003`
	`fsub`
	`        fstp DWORD PTR [bp+8];net`
	`        fwait`
	
	`        jmp SHORT $I194`
	`        nop`
	`$I193:`
		`net = gross - (gross * discount_rate);`
		
		`else`

8b 46 fc
8b 56 fe
89 46 08
89 56 0a
	`        mov  ax,WORD PTR [bp-4];gross`
	`        mov  dx,WORD PTR [bp-2]`
	`        mov  WORD PTR [bp+8],ax ;net`
	`        mov  WORD PTR [bp+10],dx`
	`        $I194:`
		`net = gross;`

Assembly Language

To make it easier for programmers to remember the specific machine instruction codes, assembly languages were developed. An **assembly language** is similar to a machine language, but uses abbreviations called **mnemonics** or **symbolic operation code** to represent the machine operation code. Another difference is that assembly languages usually allow **symbolic addressing**, which means that a specific computer memory location can be referenced by a name or symbol, such as TOTAL, instead of by its actual address as it would have to be referenced in machine language. Assembly language programs can also include **macroinstructions** that generate more than one machine language instruction. Assembly language programs are converted into machine language instructions by a special program called an **assembler**. Even though assembly languages are easier to use than machine languages, they are still considered a low-level language because they are so closely related to the specific design of the computer. Figure 12-16⟨b⟩ shows an example of assembly language instructions.

High-Level Languages

The evolution of computer languages continued with the development of high-level languages in the late 1950s and 1960s. **High-level languages** more closely resemble what most people would think of as a language in that they contain nouns, verbs, and mathematical, relational, and logical operators that can be grouped together to form what appear to be sentences (Figure 12-16⟨c⟩). These sentences are called **program statements**. Because of these characteristics, high-level languages can be *read* by programmers and are thus easier to learn and use than machine or assembly languages. Another important advantage over low-level languages is that high-level languages are usually machine independent, which means they can run on different types of computers.

As mentioned previously, all languages must be translated into machine language before they can be executed. High-level languages are translated in one of two ways: with a compiler or an interpreter.

A **compiler** converts an entire program into machine language that is usually stored on a disk for later execution. The program to be converted is called the **source program** and the machine language produced is called the **object program** or **object code**. Compilers check the program syntax, perform limited logic checking, and make sure that data that is going to be used in comparisons or calculations, such as a discount rate, is properly defined somewhere in the program. An important feature of compilers is that they produce an error listing of all program statements that do not meet the program language rules. This listing helps the programmer make the necessary changes to debug or correct the program. Figure 12-17 illustrates the process of compiling a program.

FIGURE 12-17
When a compiler is used, a source language program is compiled into a machine language object program. Usually, both the source and object programs are stored on disk. When the user wants to run the program, the object program is loaded into the main memory of the CPU and the program instructions begin executing. As instructed by the program, the CPU processes data and creates output. Errors in the source program identified during compilation are shown on an error listing that can be used to make the necessary corrections during program development.

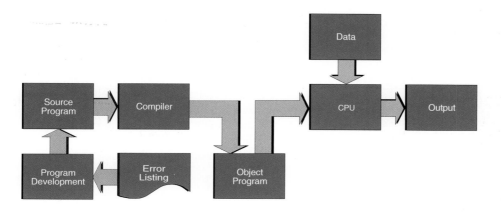

Because machine language is unique to each processor, different computers require different compilers for the same language. For example, a mainframe, minicomputer, and personal computer would each have different compilers that would translate the same source language program into the specific machine language for each computer.

While a compiler translates an entire program, an **interpreter** translates one program statement at a time and then executes the resulting machine language before translating the next program statement. When using an interpreter, each time the program is run, the source program is interpreted into machine language and executed. No object program is produced. Figure 12-18 illustrates this process.

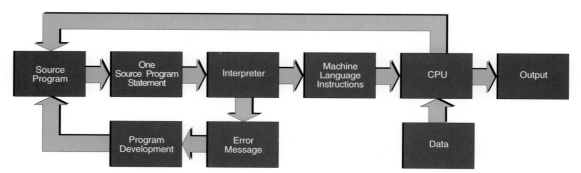

FIGURE 12-18
When an interpreter is used, one source language statement at a time is interpreted into machine language instructions that are executed immediately by the CPU. As instructed by the machine language instructions, the CPU processes data and creates output. Error messages indicating an invalid source language statement are produced as each source program statement is interpreted and are used to make the necessary corrections during program development.

Interpreters are often used with personal computers that do not have the memory or computing power required by compilers. The advantage of interpreters is that the compiling process is not necessary before program changes can be tested. The disadvantage of interpreters is that interpreted programs do not run as fast as compiled programs because the translation to machine language occurs each time the program is run. Compilers for most high-level languages are now available for the newer and more powerful personal computers.

Fourth-Generation Languages

The evolution of computer languages is sometimes described in terms of generations with machine, assembly, and high-level languages considered the first, second, and third generations, respectively. Each generation offered significant improvements in ease of use and programming flexibility over the previous generation. Although a clear definition does not yet exist, **fourth-generation languages (4GLs)**, sometimes called **very high-level languages**, continue the programming language evolution by being even easier to use than high-level languages for both the programmer and the nonprogramming user.

A term commonly used to describe fourth-generation languages is **nonprocedural**, which means that the programmer does not specify the procedures to be used to accomplish a task as is done with lower procedural language generations. Instead of telling the computer how to do the task, the programmer tells the computer *what* is to be done, usually by describing the desired output. A database query language (Figure 12-19) is an example of a nonprocedural fourth-generation language.

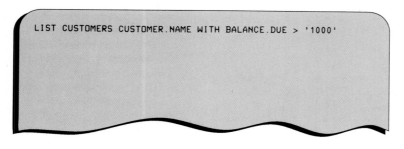

```
LIST CUSTOMERS CUSTOMER.NAME WITH BALANCE.DUE > '1000'
```

FIGURE 12-19
This database query is considered an example of a fourth-generation language because it tells the computer what the user wants, not how to perform the processing.

The advantage of fourth-generation languages is that they are *results* oriented (*what* is to be done, not *how*), and they can be used by nonprogramming personnel such as users. The disadvantage of fourth-generation languages is that they do not provide as many processing options to the programmer as other language generations and they require more computer processing power that other language generations. Most experts, however, believe that their ease of use far outweighs these disadvantages and they predict that fourth-generation languages will continue to be more widely used.

An extension of fourth-generation languages, sometimes called the fifth generation, is a natural language. A **natural language** is a type of query language that allows the user to enter a question as if he or she were speaking to another person. For example, a fourth-generation query might be stated as LIST SALESPERSON TOTAL-SALES BY REGION. A natural language version of that same query might be TELL ME THE NAME OF EACH SALESPERSON AND THE TOTAL SALES FOR EACH REGION. The natural language allows the user more flexibility in the structure of the query and can even ask the user a question if it does not understand what is meant by the initial query statement. A few natural languages are available today but they are not yet widely used.

PROGRAMMING LANGUAGES USED TODAY

Although there are hundreds of programming languages, only a few are used extensively enough to be recognized as industry standards. Most of these are high-level programming languages that can be used on a variety of computers. In this section, we discuss the popular programming languages that are commonly used, their origins, and their primary purpose.

To help you understand the differences, we show program code for each of the most popular languages. The code is from programs that solve the same problem. The problem is to compute the net price of a sale. This is done by multiplying the quantity sold times the unit price. A discount of 5% is calculated if the gross sale is over $100.00.

BASIC

BASIC, which stands for **B**eginner's **A**ll-purpose **S**ymbolic **I**nstruction **C**ode, was developed by John Kemeny and Thomas Kurtz in 1964 at Dartmouth College (Figure 12-20). They originally designed BASIC to be a simple, interactive programming language for college students to learn and use. BASIC has become one of the most popular programming languages in use on microcomputers and minicomputers today.

```
5010 REM ················P R O C E S S    A N D    D I S P L A Y········
5040 GROSS = QTY * SLSPR
5050 IF QTY > CEILING THEN NET = GROSS - (GROSS * DISC) ELSE NET = GROSS
5070 PRINT "THE NET SALES IS $";
5080 PRINT USING "$$#,###.##"; NET
5090 RETURN
```

FIGURE 12-20
An excerpt from a BASIC program.

COBOL

COBOL (**CO**mmon **B**usiness **O**riented **L**anguage) was introduced in 1960. Backed by the U.S. Department of Defense, COBOL was developed by a committee of representatives from both government and industry. Rear Admiral Grace M. Hopper was a key person on the committee and is recognized as one of the prime developers of the COBOL language. COBOL is one of the most widely used programming languages for business applications (Figure 12-21). Using an English-like format, COBOL instructions are arranged in sentences and grouped into paragraphs. The English format makes COBOL easy to write and read, but also makes it a wordy language that produces lengthy program code. COBOL is very good for processing large files and performing relatively simple business calculations. Other languages are better suited to performing complex mathematical formulas and functions.

FIGURE 12-21

An excerpt from a COBOL program. Notice the additional words in the COBOL program compared to the BASIC program in Figure 12-20. Although the extra words increase the time it takes to write a COBOL program, they also make the program easier to read and understand.

```
00100        016200 C010-PROCESS-AND-DISPLAY.
00101        016400··············································
00102        016600· FUNCTION:              CALCULATE NET SALES AMOUNT   ·
00103        016700·                         AND DISPLAY RESULTS          ·
00104        016800· ENTRY/EXIT:            B000-LOOP-CONTROL            ·
00105        016900· CALLS:                 NONE                         ·
00106        017100··············································
00107        017300    COMPUTER GROSS-SALES-WRK = QUANTITY-SOLD-WRK · SALES-PRICE-WRK.
00108        017500    IF QUANTITY-SOLD-WRK IS GREATER THAN CEILING
00109        017600       COMPUTE NET-SALES-WRK = GROSS-SALES-WRK -
00110        017700          <GROSS-SALES-WRK · DISCOUNT-RATE)
00111        017800    ELSE
00112        017900       MOVE GROSS-SALES-WRK TO NET-SALES-WRK.
00113        018100    MOVE NET-SALES-WRK TO NET-SALES-OUTPUT.
00114        018300    DISPLAY CLEAR-SCREEN.
00115        018500    WRITE PRINT-LINE FROM DETAIL-LINE
00116        018600       AFTER ADVANCING 2.
```

C

The **C** programming language was developed at Bell Laboratories in 1972 by Dennis Ritchie (Figure 12-22). It was originally designed as a programming language for writing systems software, but it is now considered a general-purpose programming language. C is a powerful programming language that requires professional programming skills to be used effectively. The use of C to develop various types of software, including commercial applications, is increasing. C programs are often used with the Unix operating system (most of the Unix operating system is written in C).

FIGURE 12-22

An excerpt from a C program.

```
float gross;
gross = qty · price;
if (qty > ceiling)
    net = gross - (gross · discount_rate);
else
    net = gross;
return(net);
```

FORTRAN

FORTRAN (FORmula **TRAN**slator) was developed by a team of IBM programmers led by John Backus. Released in 1957, FORTRAN was designed as a programming language to be used by scientists, engineers, and mathematicians (Figure 12-23). FORTRAN is considered the first high-level language that was developed and is noted for its capability to easily express and efficiently calculate mathematical equations.

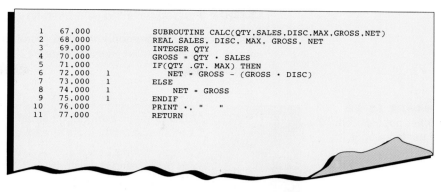

```
 1   67,000           SUBROUTINE CALC(QTY,SALES,DISC,MAX,GROSS,NET)
 2   68,000           REAL SALES, DISC, MAX, GROSS, NET
 3   69,000           INTEGER QTY
 4   70,000           GROSS = QTY • SALES
 5   71,000           IF(QTY .GT. MAX) THEN
 6   72,000    1          NET = GROSS - (GROSS • DISC)
 7   73,000    1       ELSE
 8   74,000    1          NET = GROSS
 9   75,000    1       ENDIF
10   76,000           PRINT •, "   "
11   77,000           RETURN
```

FIGURE 12-23
An excerpt from a FORTRAN program.

Pascal

The **Pascal** language was developed in 1968 by Niklaus Wirth, a computer scientist at the Institut für Informatik in Zurich, Switzerland. It was developed for teaching programming. The name Pascal is not an abbreviation or acronym, but rather the name of a mathematician, Blaise Pascal (1623–1662), who developed one of the earliest calculating machines. Pascal, available for use on both personal and large computers, was one of the first programming languages developed where the instructions in the language were designed and written so that programmers using Pascal would be encouraged to develop programs that follow structured program design (Figure 12-24).

```
BEGIN                            (• Begin procedure •)
     GROSS := SALES • QTY;
     IF QTY > CEILING
          THEN NET := GROSS - (GROSS • DISCOUNT_RATE)
          ELSE NET := GROSS;
     WRITELN('THE NET SALES IS $',NET:6:2)
END;                             (• End of procedure •)
```

FIGURE 12-24
An excerpt from a Pascal program.

Ada

The programming language **Ada** is named for Augusta Ada Byron, Countess of Lovelace, a mathematician in the 1800s, who is thought to have written the first program. The development of Ada was supported by the U. S. Department of Defense and its use is required on all U. S. government military projects. Ada was introduced in 1980 and designed to facilitate the writing and maintenance of large programs that would be used over a long period of time. The language encourages coding of readable programs that are also portable, allowing them to be transferred from computer to computer (Figure 12-25).

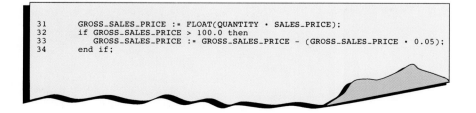

```
31     GROSS_SALES_PRICE := FLOAT(QUANTITY • SALES_PRICE);
32     if GROSS_SALES_PRICE > 100.0 then
33        GROSS_SALES_PRICE := GROSS_SALES_PRICE - (GROSS_SALES_PRICE • 0.05);
34     end if;
```

FIGURE 12-25
An excerpt from an Ada program.

Other Popular Programming Languages

In addition to the commonly used programming languages we just discussed, there are several other popular languages. Figure 12-26 lists some of these languages and their primary uses.

FIGURE 12-26
Other popular computer languages.

ALGOL	ALGOrithmetic Language. Structured programming language used for scientific and mathematical applications.
APL	A Programming Language. A powerful, easy-to-learn language that is good for processing data stored in a table (matrix) format.
FORTH	Similar to C. Creates fast and efficient program code. Originally developed to control astronomical telescopes.
LISP	LISt Processing. Popular artificial intelligence language.
LOGO	Primarily known as an educational tool to teach problem-solving skills.
MODULA-3	Similar to Pascal. Used primarily for developing systems software.
PILOT	Programmed Inquiry Learning Or Teaching. Used by educators to write computer-aided instruction programs.
PL/I	Programming Language/One. Business and scientific language that combines many of the features of FORTRAN and COBOL.
PROLOG	PROgramming in LOGic. Used for artificial intelligence.
RPG	Report Program Generator. Uses special forms to help user specify input, output, and calculation requirements of a program.

APPLICATION GENERATORS

Application generators, also called **program generators**, are programs that produce source-language programs, such as BASIC or COBOL, based on input, output, and processing specifications entered by the user. Application generators can greatly reduce the amount of time required to develop a program. They are predicated on the fact that most programs are comprised of standard processing modules, such as routines to read, write, or compare records, that can be combined together to create unique programs. These standard processing modules are stored in a library and are selected and grouped together based on user specifications. Application generators often use menu and screen generators to assist in developing an application.

A **menu generator** lets the user specify a menu (list) of processing options that can be selected. The resulting menu is automatically formatted with heading, footing, and prompt line text (Figure 12-27).

FIGURE 12-27
The left screen is part of a menu generator from ORACLE Corporation that can be used to quickly create professional looking menus on the right screen.

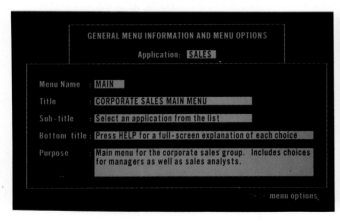

A **screen generator**, sometimes called a **screen painter**, allows the user to design an input or output screen by entering the names and descriptions of the input and output data directly on the screen. The advantage is that the user enters the data exactly as it will appear after the program is created. As each data name, such as Order No., is entered, the screen generator asks the user to specify the length and type of data that will be entered and what processing, if any, should take place before or after the data is entered. The order entry screen shown in Figure 12-28 was created in just one hour using SQL*FORMS, a screen generator product from ORACLE Corporation.

FIGURE 12-28
This order entry screen and the program to process the data were created in one hour using a screen generator from ORACLE Corporation. Using the traditional programming technique of writing individual program instructions would have taken considerably longer.

OBJECT-ORIENTED PROGRAMMING

Object-oriented programming (OOP) is a new approach to developing software that allows programmers to create **objects**, a combination of data and program instructions. Traditional programming methods keep data, such as files, independent of the programs that work with the data. Each traditional program, therefore, must define how the data will be used for that particular program. This often results in redundant programming code that must be changed every time the structure of the data is changed, such as when a new field is added to a file. With OOP, the program instructions and data are combined into objects that can be used repeatedly by programmers whenever they need them. Specific instructions, called **methods** define how the object acts when it is used by a program. The following example, illustrated in Figure 12-29, describes how OOP minimizes the number of instructions that must be defined.

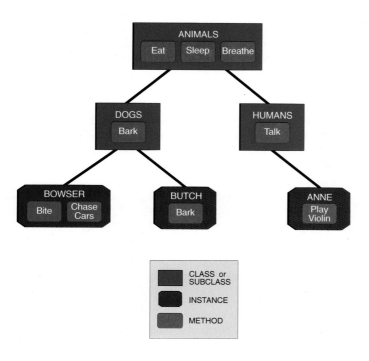

FIGURE 12-29
Object-oriented programming (OOP) allows procedures (called methods) to be combined with data to form objects. In traditional programming, procedures are defined by the program instructions that are separate from the data. In OOP, the methods define how the object will act when it is referenced and how it can be *inherited* from higher levels, called classes. For example, the method BARK can be inherited by BOWSER from the class DOGS. Objects can also have unique procedures that differ from higher levels. Thus, BUTCH can have a different BARK than BOWSER. The capability to inherit methods from higher levels makes programming more efficient because only methods unique to the specific object need to be defined. A specific occurrence of an object is called an instance.

With OOP, programmers define classes of objects. Each **class** contains the methods that are unique to that class. As shown in Figure 12-29, the class of animals could contain methods on how animals eat, sleep, and breathe. Each class can have one or more subclasses. Each subclass contains the methods of its higher level classes plus whatever methods are unique to the subclass. For example, the subclass Humans contains the method Talk. The subclass Dogs contains the method Bark. Both subclasses, Humans and Dogs, also contain the Eat, Sleep, and Breathe methods of the higher class, Animals. The OOP capability to pass methods to lower levels is called **inheritance**. A specific **instance** of an object contains all methods from its higher level classes plus any methods that are unique to the object. For example, the object Anne contains a method on how to play the violin. The object Bowser contains methods on how Bowser bites and chases cars. Although these methods may be shared by other humans and dogs, respectively, they cannot be placed at higher levels because they are not shared by all humans or dogs. When an OOP object is sent an instruction to do something, called a **message**, unlike a traditional program, the message does not have to tell the OOP object exactly what to do. *What to do* is defined by the methods that the OOP object contains or has inherited. For example, if the object Bowser was sent a message to bark, the method of barking would be defined by the bark method in the subclass Dogs. However, if the object Butch was sent the same message to bark, its actions would be defined by the bark (perhaps a growl) associated with Butch. This illustrates that higher level methods can be overridden to define actions unique to a particular object or class.

A business example of an object would include a class called Invoices. With traditional programming, each time an invoice is displayed on a screen, specific programming instructions are included in the program. With OOP, a method called Display would be part of the object Invoice. An OOP program would only have to send a message identifying the object (Invoice) and stating the desired method (Display). How to display the invoice would be defined as part of the Invoice object.

As OOP is used by an organization, the organization builds a library of OOP objects and classes that can be reused. The more extensive the library, the more powerful and efficient OOP becomes. OOP development systems, such as the Interface Builder used on NeXT computers, allow programmers to access such libraries and link objects to quickly build programs. The programming language most often associated with OOP is Smalltalk, developed by Xerox at their Palo Alto Research Center (PARC) in the 1970s. Versions of several well-known languages, including C and Pascal, also currently offer OOP features.

Closely related to OOP are object-oriented software and object-oriented operating systems. **Object-oriented software** are applications that are developed using OOP programming techniques. **Object-oriented operating systems** are operating systems specifically designed to run OOP applications. Although not widely available, several major companies, including a joint venture of IBM and Apple, are working on versions of object-oriented operating systems.

HOW TO CHOOSE A PROGRAMMING LANGUAGE

Although each programming language has its own unique characteristics, selecting a language for a programming task can be a difficult decision. Factors to be considered include the following:

1. The programming standards of the organization. Many organizations have programming standards that specify that a particular language is used for all applications.
2. The need to interface with other programs. If a program is going to work with other existing or future programs, ideally it should be programmed in the same language as the other programs.

3. The suitability of a language to the application to be programmed. As we discussed, most languages are best suited to a particular type of application. For example, FORTRAN works well with applications requiring many calculations.
4. The expertise of the available programmers. Unless another language is far superior, you should choose the language used by the existing programmers.
5. The availability of the language. Not all languages are available on all machines.
6. The need for the application to be portable. If the application will have to run on different machines, you should choose a common language so the program has to be written only once.
7. The anticipated maintenance requirements. If the user anticipates that the application will have to be modified frequently, consider a language that can be maintained easily and that supports structured programming concepts.

SUMMARY OF PROGRAMMING LANGUAGES

◆ Although procedural languages such as COBOL and BASIC will continue to be used for many years, there is a clear trend toward the creation of programs using non-procedural tools, such as fourth-generation and natural languages, that allow users to specify what they want accomplished. Your knowledge of programming languages will help you to understand how the computer converts data into information and to obtain better results if you directly participate in the programming process.

CHAPTER SUMMARY

1. A **computer program** is a detailed set of instructions that directs a computer to perform the tasks necessary to process data into information.
2. **Program development** is a series of five steps that take place when a computer program is developed. These steps include: (1) review of the program specifications, (2) program design, (3) program coding, (4) program testing, and (5) finalizing the documentation.
3. In the information system life cycle, program development occurs during the development phase.
4. **Program specifications** can include many documents such as data flow diagrams, system flowcharts, process specifications, a data dictionary, screen formats, and report layouts.
5. During **program design** a logical solution, or **logic**, for a program is developed and documented.
6. **Structured program design** is methodology that emphasizes three main program design concepts: modules, control structures, and single entry/single exit.
7. **Modules**, or **subroutines**, which perform a given task within a program, can be developed individually and then combined to form a complete program.
8. **Structure charts**, or **hierarchy charts**, are used to decompose the modules of a program.
9. The three **control structures** are: the **sequence structure** , where one process occurs immediately after another; the **selection structure**, or **if-then-else structure**, which is used for conditional program logic; and the **iteration structure** or **looping structure**.
10. The **case structure**, which is a variation of the selection structure, is used when a condition is being tested that can lead to more than two alternatives.
11. The two forms of iteration are the **do-while structure** and the **do-until structure**.
12. **Single entry/single exit** means that there is only one **entry point** and one **exit point** from each of the control structures.
13. Three commonly used program design tools are **program flowcharts**, **pseudocode**, and the **Warnier-Orr technique**.
14. Structured walk-throughs are used to review the design and logic of a program.
15. **Coding** is the process of writing the program instructions.

16. Before a program is used to process *real* data it should be thoroughly tested to make sure it is functioning correctly. A simple type of testing is **desk checking**.
17. Programs can be tested for **syntax errors** (grammar). **Logic testing** checks for incorrect results using **test data**.
18. **Debugging** refers to the process of locating and correcting program errors, or **bugs**, found during testing.
19. **Program maintenance** includes all changes to a program once it is implemented and processing real transactions.
20. A **programming language** is a set of written words and symbols that allow a programmer or user to communicate with the computer.
21. Programming languages fit into one of four categories: machine language; assembly language; high-level languages; and fourth-generation languages.
22. Before they can be executed, all programs are converted into **machine language**, the fundamental language of computers, also called **low-level language**.
23. **Assembly language** is a low-level language that is closely related to machine language. It uses **mnemonics** or **symbolic operation code**.
24. Assembly languages use **symbolic addressing** and include **macroinstructions**. Assembly language programs are converted into machine language instructions by an **assembler**.
25. **High-level languages** are easier to learn and use than low-level languages. They use sentences called **program statements**.
26. **Compilers** and **interpreters** are used to translate high-level **source programs** into machine language **object code** or **object programs**.
27. **Fourth-generation languages (4GLs)**, also called **very high-level languages**, are **nonprocedural**, which means that the user tells the computer *what* is to be done, not *how* to do it.
28. A **natural language** allows the user to enter a question as if he or she were speaking to another person.
29. Commonly used programming languages include **BASIC**, **COBOL**, **C**, **FORTRAN**, **Pascal**, and **Ada**.
30. **BASIC** is one of the most commonly used programming languages on microcomputers and minicomputers.
31. **COBOL** is the most widely used programming language for business applications.
32. **C** is an increasingly popular programming language that requires professional programming skills to be used effectively.
33. **FORTRAN** is noted for its capability to easily express and efficiently calculate mathematical equations.
34. **Pascal** contains programming statements that encourage the use of structured program design.
35. **Ada**, developed and supported by the U.S. Department of Defense, was designed to facilitate the writing and maintenance of large programs that would be used over a long period of time.
36. **Application generators**, or **program generators**, produce source-language programs based on input, output, and processing specifications entered by the user.
37. A **menu generator** lets the user specify a menu of options.
38. A **screen generator**, or **screen painter**, allows the user to design an input or output screen.
39. **Object-oriented programming (OOP)** is a new approach to developing software that allows programmers to create objects.
40. **Objects** are a combination of data and program instructions.
41. **Methods** define how the object acts when it is used by a program.
42. With OOP, each **class** contains the methods that are unique to that class.
43. **Inheritance** is the OOP capability to pass methods to lower levels of classes or objects.
44. A specific **instance** of an object contains all methods inherited from its higher level classes plus and methods that are unique to it.
45. A **message** is an instruction to do something that is sent to an OOP object.
46. **Object-oriented software** are applications that are developed using OOP programming techniques.
47. **Object-oriented operating systems** are operating systems specifically designed to run OOP applications.
48. Some of the factors that you should consider when you choose a programming language are: the programming standards of the organization; the need to interface with other programs; the suitability of a language to the application to be programmed; the expertise of the available programmers; the availability of the language; the need for the application to be portable; and the anticipated maintenance requirements.

KEY TERMS

Ada *12.17*
Application generator *12.18*
Assembler *12.13*
Assembly language *12.13*
BASIC *12.15*
Bugs *12.10*
C *12.16*
Case structure *12.5*
Class *12.20*
COBOL *12.16*
Coding *12.9*
Compiler *12.13*
Computer program *12.2*
Control structure *12.4*
Debugging *12.10*
Desk checking *12.9*
Do-until structure *12.5*
Do-while structure *12.5*
Entry point *12.6*
Exit point *12.6*
FORTRAN *12.17*
Fourth-generation language
  (4GL) *12.14*
Hierarchy chart *12.3*
High-level language *12.13*
If-then-else structure *12.4*

Inheritance *12.20*
Instance *12.20*
Interpreter *12.14*
Iteration structure *12.5*
Logic *12.3*
Logic testing *12.9*
Looping structure *12.5*
Low-level language *12.12*
Machine language *12.12*
Macroinstruction *12.13*
Menu generator *12.18*
Message *12.20*
Methods *12.19*
Mnemonics *12.13*
Module *12.3*
Natural language *12.15*
Nonprocedural *12.14*
Object *12.19*
Object code *12.13*
Object-oriented operating
  system *12.20*
Object-oriented programming
  (OOP) *12.19*
Object-oriented software *12.20*
Object program *12.13*

Pascal *12.17*
Program design *12.3*
Program development *12.2*
Program flowchart *12.6*
Program generator *12.18*
Program maintenance *12.11*
Programming language *12.12*
Program specifications *12.3*
Program statement *12.13*
Pseudocode *12.8*
Screen generator *12.19*
Screen painter *12.19*
Selection structure *12.4*
Sequence structure *12.4*
Single entry/single exit *12.6*
Source program *12.13*
Structure chart *12.3*
Structured program design *12.3*
Subroutine *12.3*
Symbolic addressing *12.13*
Symbolic operation code *12.13*
Syntax error *12.9*
Test data *12.10*
Very high-level language *12.14*
Warnier-Orr technique *12.8*

REVIEW QUESTIONS

1. What is a computer program?
2. List the five steps in program development and give a brief description of each step. Explain how the program development steps relate to the information system life cycle.
3. List at least four types of documents that might be included in the program specifications. Explain the procedures that should be followed if a programmer believes that some aspect of the design should be changed.
4. Draw the three control structures and the two variations that are used in structured program design.
5. Explain the structured programming concept of single entry/single exit. Why is it important?
6. Briefly describe three types of program design tools that are used by programmers.
7. What is desk checking?
8. List at least five types of program documentation. When should documentation be performed?
9. Describe the four categories of programming languages.
10. Explain the advantage of fourth-generation languages.
11. List six commonly used programming languages and explain their primary uses.
12. How do application generators reduce the amount of time required to program?
13. What is object-oriented programming? Explain its advantages over traditional programming methods.
14. List seven factors that you should consider when you choose a programming language.

CONTROVERSIAL ISSUES

1. Although there is a trend toward standardized operating systems, different versions of programming languages are frequently made available. Discuss the advantages and disadvantages of using a single programming language for all applications.
2. Some people believe that programming languages as we know them today will eventually be eliminated. Instead of writing program instructions in a specific computer language, programmers will be able to use a fifth-generation natural language to instruct the computer what to do. Do you think this will happen? If so, when?

RESEARCH PROJECTS

1. Choose a major application at your school or place of work such as registration, payroll, or accounting. Find out what language was used to write the application and why it was chosen. Report to your class.
2. Review the employment advertisements in your local newspaper for computer programming positions. Prepare a report discussing which programming languages are in demand.

Career Opportunities in Information Processing

13

CHAPTER

CAREERS

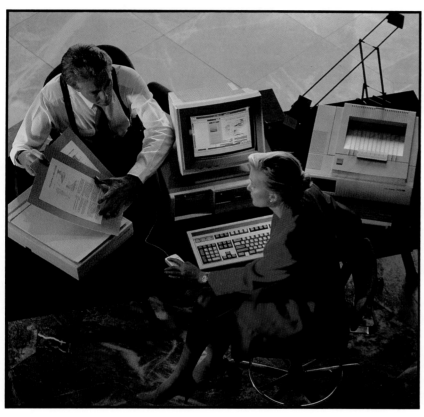

OBJECTIVES

◆ Discuss the three areas that provide the majority of computer-related jobs

◆ Describe the career positions available in an information systems department

◆ Describe information processing career opportunities in sales, service and repair, consulting, and education and training

◆ Discuss the compensation and growth trends for information processing careers

◆ Discuss the three fields in the information processing industry

◆ Discuss career development, including professional organizations, certification, and professional growth and continuing education

As society becomes more information oriented, computers are becoming an integral part of most jobs. For this reason, the knowledge you have gained from this text will apply in some way to *any* career you choose. You might, however, want to consider a career in the information processing industry itself.

The purpose of this chapter is to show you the opportunities that exist in the industry, present computer industry career trends, and discuss how to prepare for a career in information systems. Even if you don't choose a computer industry career, you will profit in whatever career you choose if you understand the jobs that computer professionals perform, because any job you choose will likely involve you with one or more of these computer professionals.

THE INFORMATION PROCESSING INDUSTRY

The information processing industry is one of the largest industries in the world with annual sales of well over $100 billion. Job opportunities in the industry come primarily from three areas: the companies that provide the computer equipment; the companies that develop computer software; and the companies that hire information processing professionals to work with these products. As in any major industry, there are also many service companies that support each of these three areas. An example would be a company that sells computer supplies such as printer paper and diskettes.

FIGURE 13-1
Personal-computer keyboards are being assembled and packaged.

The Computer Equipment Industry

The computer equipment, or hardware, industry includes all manufacturers and distributors of computers and computer-related equipment such as disk and tape drives, terminals, printers, and communications equipment (Figure 13-1).

The five largest minicomputer and mainframe manufacturers in the United States—IBM, Digital Equipment Corporation, UNISYS, Hewlett-Packard, and NCR— are huge organizations with tens of thousands of employees worldwide. Major microcomputer manufacturers include IBM, Apple, Compaq, and Tandy. The largest company, IBM, has had annual sales of over $70 billion. In addition to the major companies, the computer equipment industry is also known for the many new start-up companies that appear each year. These new companies take advantage of rapid changes in equipment technology, such as laser printers, video disks, and fiber optics, to create new products and new job opportunities. Besides the companies that make end user equipment, thousands of companies make components that most users never see. These companies manufacture chips (processor, memory), power supplies, wiring, and the hundreds of other parts that go into computer equipment.

The Computer Software Industry

The computer software industry includes all the developers and distributors of applications and system software. Thousands of companies provide a wide range of software from operating systems to complete business systems. The personal computer boom in the early 1980s provided numerous opportunities in the software industry. Thousands of individuals went into business for themselves by creating useful programs for the new microcomputers. Many of these people started by working out of their homes, developing their first software products on their own time while holding other jobs.

Today, software alone is a huge industry that includes leading companies such as MSA, ASK, Microsoft, Lotus, and Borland, with annual sales in the hundreds of millions of dollars. Most of these companies specialize in one particular type of software product such as business application software or productivity tools such as word processing or spreadsheets.

Information Processing Professionals

Information processing professionals are the people who put the equipment and software to work to produce information for the end user (Figure 13-2). This includes people such as programmers and systems analysts who are hired by companies to work in an information systems department. We discuss these and other positions available in the information processing industry in the next section.

WHAT ARE THE CAREER OPPORTUNITIES IN INFORMATION PROCESSING?

◆ The use of computers in so many aspects of life has created thousands of new jobs. Some of these occupations, such as personal computer network sales representative, didn't even exist ten years ago. We describe some of the current career opportunities, and encourage you to consider them as you prepare for your future profession.

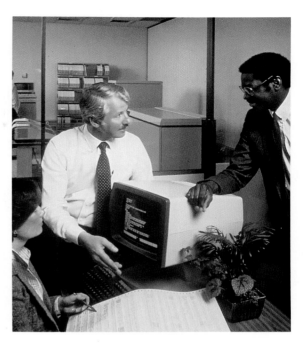

FIGURE 13-2
Computer professionals must be able to understand the end user's point of view and often meet with the user to review his or her information processing requirements.

Working in an Information Systems Department

In Chapter 1 we discussed the various jobs within an information systems department. These positions include: data entry personnel, computer operators, computer programmers, systems analysts, database administrator, manager of information systems, and vice president of information systems.

The people in these positions work together as a team to meet the information demands of their organizations. Throughout this book we have discussed the responsibilities associated with many of these positions, including the role of the systems analysts in the information system life cycle (Chapter 11) and the steps programmers perform in program development (Chapter 12). Another way to visualize the positions and their relationships is to look at an organization chart such as the one shown in Figure 13-3. In addition to management, the jobs in an information systems department can be classified into five categories:

1. Operations
2. Data administration
3. Systems analysis and design
4. Programming
5. Information center

FIGURE 13-3
The organization chart shows the many areas within an information systems department that offer employment opportunities.

Operations personnel are responsible for carrying out tasks such as operating the computer equipment that is located in the computer center. The primary responsibility of data administration is to maintain and control the organization's database. In systems analysis and design, the various information systems needed by an organization are created and maintained. Programming develops the programs needed for the information systems, and the information center provides teaching and consulting services within an organization to help users meet their departmental and individual information processing needs. As you can see, an information systems department provides career opportunities for people with a variety of skills and talents.

FIGURE 13-4
Computer retailers, such as Computerland, need salespeople who understand personal computers and have good people skills.

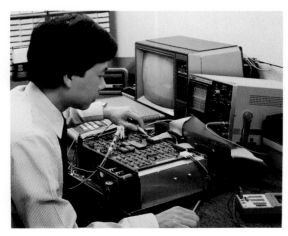

FIGURE 13-5
Computer service and repair is one of the fastest growing computer-related professions. A knowledge of electronics is essential for this occupation.

Sales

Sales representatives must have a general understanding of computers and a specific knowledge of the product they are selling. Strong interpersonal, or people, skills are important, including listening ability and strong oral and written communication skills. Sales representatives are usually paid based on the amount of product they sell, and top sales representatives are often the most highly compensated employees in a computer company.

Some sales representatives work directly for equipment and software manufacturers and others work for resellers. Most personal computer products are sold through dealers such as Computerland (Figure 13-4). Some dealers, such as Egghead Discount Software, specialize in selling the most popular software products.

Service and Repair

Being a **service and repair technician** is a challenging job for individuals who like to troubleshoot and solve problems and who have a strong background in electronics (Figure 13-5). In the early days of computers, repairs were often made at the site of the computer equipment. Today, however, malfunctioning components, such as circuit boards, are usually replaced and taken back to the service technician's office or sent to a special facility for repair. Many equipment manufacturers are now including special diagnostic software with their computer equipment that helps the service technician identify the problem. Using a modem, some computer systems can automatically telephone another computer at the service technician's office and leave a message that a malfunction has been detected.

Consulting

After building experience in one or more areas, some individuals become **consultants**, people who draw upon their experience to give advice to others. Consultants must have not only strong technical skills in their area of expertise, but must also have the people skills to effectively communicate their suggestions to their clients. Qualified consultants are in high demand for such tasks as computer system selection, system design, and communications network design and installation.

Education and Training

The increased sophistication and complexity of today's computer products has opened wide opportunities in computer education and training (Figure 13-6). Qualified instructors are needed in schools, colleges, and universities and in private industry as well. In fact, the high demand for teachers has created a shortage at the university level, where many instructors have been lured into private industry because of higher pay. This shortage probably will not be filled in the near future; the supply of Ph.D.s, usually required at the university level, is not keeping up with the demand.

FIGURE 13-6
There is a high demand in schools and industry for qualified instructors who can teach information processing subjects.

COMPENSATION AND GROWTH TRENDS FOR INFORMATION PROCESSING CAREERS

◆ Compensation is a function of experience and demand for a particular skill. Demand is influenced by geographic location, with metropolitan areas usually having higher pay than rural areas. Figure 13-7 shows the result of a salary survey of over 80,000 computer professionals across the United States and Canada.

FIGURE 13-7
Salary levels (in thousands of dollars) for various computer industry positions are based on the number of years of experience. (Source: Source EDP, 1991 Professional Compensation Data, National Statistics).

	YEARS EXP.	MEDIAN SALARY ($1,000)
PROGRAMMING:		
Commercial	<2	27
	2–3	33
	4–6	35
	>6	40
Engineering/Scientific	<2	31
	2–3	35
	4–6	38
	>6	43
Microcomputer/ Minicomputer	<2	27
	2–3	32
	4–6	34
	>6	40
Software Engineer	<2	30
	2–3	36
	4–6	41
	>6	46
Systems Software	<2	32
	2–3	38
	4–6	40
	>6	49
MANAGEMENT:		
Data Center Operations		45
Programming Development		61
Systems Development		58
Technical Services		59
MIS Director/VP		67
BUSINESS SYSTEMS:		
Consultant		45
Project Leader/Sys. Analyst		43

	YEARS EXP.	MEDIAN SALARY ($1,000)
SPECIALISTS:		
Data Base Management Analyst	<4	39
	4–6	41
	>6	49
Information Center Analyst	<4	30
	4–6	33
	>6	43
Office Automation Analyst	<4	30
	4–6	34
	>6	40
Edp Auditor	<4	35
	4–6	38
	>6	44
Technical Writer	<4	30
	4–6	32
	>6	37
Telecommunications (Planning)	<4	35
	>4	45
SALES:		
Hardware		55
Software		57
Services		56
Technical Support	<2	32
	2–3	35
	4–6	38
	>6	45
Management		68
DATA CENTER:		
Computer Operator	<2	20
	2–3	23
	4–6	25
	>6	29
Technical Data Center Analyst	<4	37
	4–6	44
	>6	46
Operations Support Technician	<4	24
	>4	30
Communications/ Network Analyst	<4	26
	>4	34

As shown in Figure 13-8, some industries pay higher than others for the same job. According to the survey, the communications, utility, and aerospace industries pay the highest salaries. These industries have many challenging applications and pay the highest rate to obtain the best qualified employees.

FIGURE 13-8
Some industries pay more for the same job position.

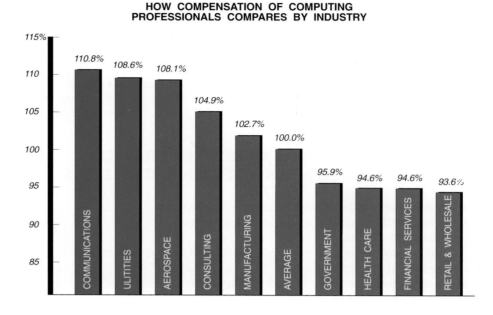

HOW COMPENSATION OF COMPUTING
PROFESSIONALS COMPARES BY INDUSTRY

According to the U.S. Bureau of Labor Statistics, the fastest growing computer career positions through 1995 will be systems analyst, applications programmer, machine operator, and computer repair technician (Figure 13-9).

FIGURE 13-9
Computer careers with the highest projected growth, as compiled by the U.S. Bureau of Labor Statistics.

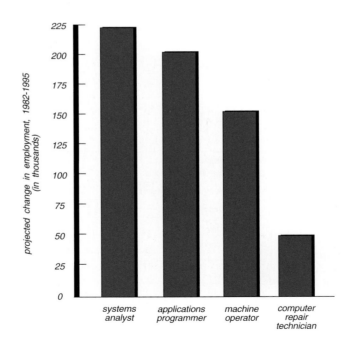

PREPARING FOR A CAREER IN INFORMATION PROCESSING

◆ To prepare for a career in the information processing industry, individuals must decide what computer field they are interested in and obtain education in the field they chose. In this section we discuss the three major computer fields and some of the opportunities for obtaining education in those fields.

What Are the Fields in the Information Processing Industry?

While this book has primarily focused on the use of computers in business, there are actually three broad fields in the information processing industry (Figure 13-10): computer information systems; computer science; and computer engineering. **Computer information systems (CIS)** refers to the use of computers to provide the information needed to operate businesses and other organizations. The field of **computer science** includes the technical aspects of computers such as hardware operation and systems software. **Computer engineering** deals with the design and manufacturing of electronic computer components and computer hardware. Each field provides unique career opportunities and has specialized requirements.

Obtaining Education for Information Processing Careers

The expanded use of computers in today's world has increased the demand for properly trained computer professionals. Educational institutions have responded to this demand by providing a variety of options for students to study information systems. Trade schools, technical schools, community colleges, colleges, and universities offer formal education and certification or degree programs in computer-related fields. If you are evaluating a program offered by one of these institutions, remember the three areas of information processing: computer information systems, computer science, and computer engineering. Frequently, schools will have separate programs for each area.

Understanding the differences among the three fields will help you to find the courses you want. For example, in a university, courses relating to computer information systems may be listed with the business courses, computer science courses may be with math, and computer engineering may be with electronic technology or electrical engineering. Because schools list and organize their computer courses in different ways, you should carefully read individual course descriptions whenever you are selecting computer education classes.

FIGURE 13-10
There are three broad fields of study in the information processing industry; each with specialized study requirements.

With the wide variety of career opportunities that exist in information processing, it is difficult to make anything other than broad general statements when it comes to discussing degree requirements for employment in the industry. As in most other industries, the more advanced degree an individual has in a chosen field, the better that individual's chances are for success. While not having a degree may limit a person's opportunities for securing a top position, it will neither prevent entry nor preclude success in information processing.

CAREER DEVELOPMENT IN THE INFORMATION PROCESSING INDUSTRY

◆ There are several ways for persons employed in the information processing industry to develop their skills and increase their recognition among their peers. These include professional organizations, certification, and professional growth and continuing education activities.

Professional Organizations

Computer-related organizations have been formed by people who have common interests and a desire to share their knowledge. Some of the organizations that have been influential in the industry include:

1. **Association for Computing Machinery (ACM).** This association is composed of persons interested in computer science and computer science education. The association has many special interest groups such as computer graphics, database, and business.
2. **Association of Information Systems Professionals (AISP).** This association was originally aimed at word processing professionals, but now includes a much broader membership, including office automation professionals.
3. **Association of Systems Management (ASM).** This group is composed of individuals interested in improving the systems analysis and design field.
4. **Data Processing Management Association (DPMA).** This is a professional association of programmers, systems analysts, and information processing managers.
5. **Institute of Electrical and Electronic Engineers (IEEE) and IEEE Computer Society (IEEE/CS).** These organizations are primarily composed of computer scientists and engineers.

Each of these organizations has chapters throughout the United States (several have chapters throughout the world), offers monthly meetings, and sponsors periodic workshops, seminars, and conventions. Some organizations have student chapters or offer reduced membership fees for students. Attending professional meetings provides an excellent opportunity for students to learn about the information processing industry and to meet and talk with professionals in the field.

In addition to these and other professional organizations, user groups exist for most makes of computers. A **user group** is a group of people with common computer equipment or software interests that meet regularly to share information. Most metropolitan areas have one or more local computer societies that meet monthly to discuss topics of common interest about personal computers. For anyone employed or simply interested in the computer industry, these groups can be an effective and rewarding way to learn and continue career development.

Certification

Many professions offer certification programs as a way of encouraging and recognizing the efforts of their members to attain a level of knowledge about their profession. The best known certification programs in the information processing industry are administered by the **Institute for the Certification of Computer Professionals (ICCP)**. The ICCP offers four certification designations: Certified Computer Programmer (CCP); Certified Data Processor (CDP); Certified Systems Professional (CSP); and Associate Computer Professional (ACP). The CCP, CDP, and CSP designations are earned by passing three examinations. The ACP designation is obtained by passing a general computer knowledge test and any one of seven programming language tests. A summary of the test requirements for all of the designations is shown in Figure 13-11. To be eligible to take the CCP, CDP, and CSP examinations, a person must have a minimum of five years of experience in the information processing industry. The ACP examination, which is designed for entry level personnel, requires no previous industry experience.

```
                    ICCP CERTIFICATION EXAMINATIONS
A.   Examination Requirements for Certified Computer Programmer
     (CCP), Certified Data Processor (CDP), and Certified Systems
     Professional (CSP)

     1.   Core Examination (required for all designations)
          a.   Human and Organization Framework
          b.   Systems Concepts
          c.   Data and Information
          d.   Systems Development
          e.   Technology
          f.   Associated Disciplines
     2.   Professional Designation Examinations
          a.   Certified Computer Programmer (CCP)
               1)   Data and File Organization
               2)   Program Design
               3)   Procedural Program Structure
               4)   Procedural Programming Considerations
               5)   Integration with Hardware and Software
          b.   Certified Data Processor (CDP)
               1)   General Management and Organization Concepts
               2)   Project Management
               3)   Information Systems Management
          c.   Certified Systems Professional (CSP)
               1)   Systems Analysis
               2)   Systems Design and Implementation
               3)   The Systems Analyst as a Professional
     3.   Specialty Examinations (one required)
          a.   Business Information Systems
          b.   Communications
          c.   Office Information Systems
          d.   Scientific Programming
          e.   Software Engineering
          f.   Systems Programming

B.   Associate Computer Professional (ACP) Examination

     1.   Core Examination (same as for CCP, CDP, and CSP)
     2.   Programming Language Examinations (one required)
          a.   FORTRAN
          b.   Pascal
          c.   BASIC
          d.   RPG
          e.   COBOL
          f.   C
          g.   ADA
```

Professional Growth and Continuing Education

Because of rapid changes in technology, staying aware of new products and services in the information processing industry can be a challenging task. One way of keeping up is by participating in professional growth and continuing education activities. This broad category includes events such as workshops, seminars, conferences, conventions, and trade shows that provide both general and specific information on equipment, software, services, and issues affecting the industry, such as computer security. Workshops and seminars usually last a day or two, while conferences, conventions, and trade shows often last a week. The largest trade show in the United States, **COMDEX**, brings together nearly 2,000 vendors to display their newest products and services to over 125,000 attendees (Figure 13-12).

FIGURE 13-11
The subject areas for each of the four certification examinations offered by the Institute for the Certification of Computer Professionals (ICCP). Three of the designations (CCP, CDP, and CSP) are designed for experienced professionals with five or more years of industry experience. The fourth designation (ACP) does not require previous industry experience.

FIGURE 13-12
COMDEX is one of the largest computer product trade shows in the world. Nearly 2,000 vendors come together to demonstrate their new equipment, software, and services to over 125,000 prospective customers.

Another way of keeping informed about what is going on in the computer industry is to regularly read one or more computer industry publications (Figure 13-13). There are hundreds of publications to choose from. Some publications, such as *Computerworld* and *InfoWorld*, are like newspapers and cover a wide range of issues. Other publications are oriented toward a particular topic area such as communications, personal computers, or a specific equipment manufacturer. Many of the more popular publications can be found in public or school libraries.

FIGURE 13-13
Computer industry publications number in the hundreds, with general- and specific-interest topics available to keep you informed.

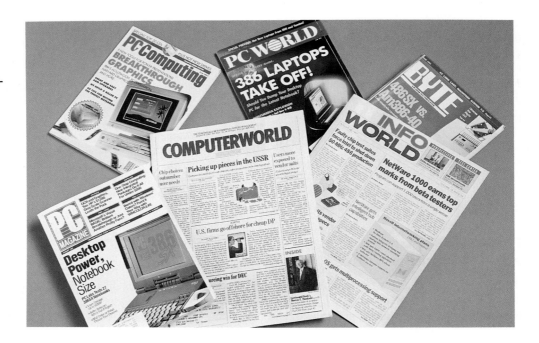

SUMMARY OF COMPUTER CAREER OPPORTUNITIES

With the increased use of computers, the prospects for computer-related career opportunities are excellent. Not only are the numbers of traditional information processing jobs, such as programmer and systems analyst, expected to increase, but the application of the computer to existing occupations will create additional job opportunities. Regardless of an individual's career choice, a basic understanding of computers should be an essential part of any employee's job skills.

CHAPTER SUMMARY

1. As society becomes more information oriented, computers are becoming an integral part of most jobs.
2. Job opportunities in the information processing industry come from three areas: computer equipment companies, computer software companies, and companies that hire information processing professionals.
3. The computer equipment industry includes all manufacturers and distributors of computers and computer-related equipment.
4. The computer software industry includes all developers and distributors of application and system software.

5. Information processing professionals are the people that put the equipment and software to work to produce information for the end user.
6. Career opportunities in information processing include: working in an information systems department, sales, service and repair, consulting, and education and training.
7. The jobs in an information systems department can be classified into five categories: (1) operations, (2) data administration, (3) systems analysis and design, (4) programming, and (5) information center.
8. **Sales representatives** are often the most highly compensated employees in a computer company.
9. Being a **service and repair technician** is a challenging job for individuals who like to solve problems and who have a strong background in electronics.
10. **Consultants**, people who draw upon their experience to give advice to others, are in high demand for such tasks as computer system selection, system design, and communications network design and installation.
11. According to the U.S. Bureau of Labor Statistics, the fastest growing computer career positions through 1995 will be systems analyst, applications programmer, machine operator, and computer repair technician.
12. The three fields in information processing are computer information systems; computer science; and computer engineering.
13. **Computer information systems (CIS)** refers to the use of computers to provide the information needed to operate businesses and other organizations.
14. **Computer science** includes the technical aspects of computers such as hardware operation and systems software.
15. **Computer engineering** deals with the design and manufacturing of electronic computer components and computer hardware.
16. Trade schools, technical schools, community colleges, colleges, and universities offer formal education and certification or degree programs in computer-related fields.
17. Computer professionals may continue to develop their skills and increase their recognition among their peers through professional organizations, certification, and professional growth and continuing education activities.
18. Professional organizations include the **Association for Computing Machinery (ACM)**, the **Association of Information Systems Professionals (AISP)**, the **Association of Systems Management (ASM)**, the **Data Processing Management Association (DPMA)**, and the **Institute of Electrical and Electronic Engineers (IEEE) and IEEE Computer Society (IEEE/CS)**.
19. A **user group** is a group of people with common computer equipment or software interests that meet regularly to share information.
20. The **Institute for Certification of Computer Professionals (ICCP)** offers four certification programs.
21. Computer professionals stay current by participating in professional growth and continuing education activities such as conferences, workshops, conventions, and trade shows.

KEY TERMS

Association for Computing Machinery (ACM) *13.8*
Association of Information Systems Professionals (AISP) *13.8*
Association of Systems Management (ASM) *13.8*
COMDEX *13.9*
Computer engineering *13.7*

Computer information systems (CIS) *13.7*
Computer science *13.7*
Consultant *13.4*
Data Processing Management Association (DPMA) *13.8*
IEEE Computer Society (IEEE/CS) *13.8*

Institute for the Certification of Computer Professionals (ICCP) *13.9*
Institute of Electrical and Electronic Engineers (IEEE) *13.8*
Sales representative *13.4*
Service and repair technician *13.4*
User group *13.8*

REVIEW QUESTIONS

1. List the three areas that provide the majority of computer related jobs.
2. Identify seven jobs within an information systems department. The jobs in an information systems department can be classified into what five categories?
3. Describe the people skills that are important for a sales representative.
4. What does a consultant do? List three areas of knowledge where consultants are in high demand.
5. What are the four fastest growing computer career positions?
6. Describe the three fields in information processing and list at least two types of jobs in each field.
7. List and describe the purpose of five computer-related professional organizations.
8. What are the four certifications administered by the Institute for the Certification of Computer Professionals (ICCP)?
9. Name two computer industry publications that are like newspapers.

CONTROVERSIAL ISSUES

1. Because the industry is changing so rapidly, computer professionals often disagree as to what should be taught in an introductory computer course. What topics do you think should be included or excluded?
2. Some people believe that computer professions such as programming should be subject to mandatory certification or licensing, like certified public accountants. Others believe that because the industry is changing so rapidly, certification programs should be encouraged but remain voluntary. Discuss the advantages and disadvantages of mandatory programs.

RESEARCH PROJECTS

1. Contact a graduate of your school who is currently working in the computer industry. Write a report on his or her current job responsibilities. Ask the graduate to comment on how his or her education prepared him or her for this current job.
2. Contact a local computer employment specialist. Ask him or her for information on entry level computer positions in your community. Report to your class.

Trends and Issues in the Information Age

CHAPTER 14

TRENDS/ISSUES

OBJECTIVES

◆ Discuss the electronic devices and applications that are part of the automated office

◆ Describe the technologies that are developing for the automated factory, including CAD, CAE, CAM, and CIM

◆ Discuss the trend toward the computer-integrated enterprise

◆ Discuss the use of personal computers in the home

◆ Describe the methods used in computer-aided instruction (CAI)

◆ Explain guidelines for purchasing personal computers

◆ Discuss social issues related to computers, such as computer crime and privacy

After reading the preceding chapters, you know what a computer is, what a computer does, how it does it, and why a computer is so powerful. You have learned about computer equipment and software and how the system development process is used to combine these elements with data, personnel, users, and procedures to create a working information system. The purpose of this chapter is to talk about current and future trends, including changes taking place in information systems in the workplace. We also discuss the use of personal computers in the home and some of the social issues related to computers such as security and computer crime, privacy, and ethics.

INFORMATION SYSTEMS IN BUSINESS

◆ The largest use of computers is in business. Millions of systems ranging from mainframes to microcomputers are installed and used for applications such as inventory control, billing, and accounting. This section discusses how these traditional applications will be affected by changes in technology and methods. It also covers the automated office, the automated factory, and the computer-integrated enterprise. Although the term automated can be applied to any process or machine that can operate without human intervention, the term is commonly used to describe computer-controlled functions.

How Will Existing Information Systems Change?

Existing business information systems will continue to undergo profound changes as new technology, software, and methods are applied to the huge installed base of traditional business system users. Important overall trends include more online, interactive systems and less batch processing. In addition, the expansion of communications networks and the increased use of relational database systems means that users will have a wider variety of data and information available for decision making, and more flexibility presenting information on reports and displays. The increased number of people using computers will make the computer-user interface even more important. Graphical user interfaces will continue to replace command- and menu-driven interfaces. These and other trends that will affect the information systems of tomorrow are shown in Figure 14-1.

FIGURE 14-1

Trends affecting information systems of tomorrow.

◄ EQUIPMENT

- Increased use of personal computers networked to other personal computers and to central minicomputers or mainframes
- Mainframes and minicomputers used as central storehouses of data with processing done on a decentralized basis by powerful personal computers
- Increased disk storage capacity using new technologies such as laser disks
- High-resolution color graphics screens that can display photo-quality pictures
- Increased use of page printers that can print high-quality graphics and text
- Reduced instruction set computers (RISC) and parallel processing greatly increasing the number of instructions that can be processed at one time
- Increased use of portable computing equipment such as notebook computers
- Handwriting recognition systems allowing users to interact with a computer using a pen-shaped stylus

SOFTWARE ►

- Fourth-generation and natural languages enabling the user to communicate with the computer in a more conversational manner
- Object orientation combining processes and methods with data
- Computer-aided software engineering (CASE) shortening the system development time frame
- Increased use of decision support and artificial intelligence systems to help users make decisions
- Widespread implementation of graphic user interfaces using icons and symbols to represent information and processes
- Integrated applications to eliminate the need for separate programs for word processing, spreadsheets, graphics, telecommunications, and other applications

◄ DATA

- Automatic input of data at the source where it is created
- Compound documents that combine text, numbers, and nontext data such as voice, image, and full-motion video

USERS ►

- Most people being computer literate, with a basic understanding of how computers work and how to use them in their jobs
- Increased responsibility for design, operation, and maintenance of information processing systems
- Users increasingly relying on computers to manage the continuing proliferation of information (the worldwide volume of printed information doubles every eight years)

◄ INFORMATION SYSTEMS PERSONNEL

- Increased interface with users
- Shift from machine and software orientation to user application orientation
- Emphasis from how to capture and process data to how to more effectively use the data available and create information
- Reduced staff levels handling increased processing work loads
- Some processing operations being outsourced to independent contractors
- Continuous need for retraining and education to keep up with new technology

The Automated Office

The **automated office**, sometimes referred to as the **electronic office**, is the term that describes the use of electronic devices such as computers, facsimile machines, and computerized telephone systems to make office work more productive. Automated office applications, such as word processing, electronic mail, voice mail, desktop publishing, facsimile, image processing, and teleconferencing, started out as separate, stand-alone applications. In recent years, however, the trend has been to integrate these applications into a network of devices and services that can share information. A brief review of each of these applications follows.

Word Processing   For many organizations, word processing was the first office application to be automated and among all organizations, word processing still ranks as the most widely used office automation technology. Today, most word processing systems are integrated with other applications. This allows the word processing applications to extract data such as names and addresses or financial data from other application files.

Electronic Mail   **Electronic mail** is the capability to use computers to transmit messages to and receive messages from other computer users. The other users may be on the same computer network or on a separate computer system reached through the use of a modem or some other communications device. Electronic mail eliminates the need to hand deliver messages or use a delivery service such as the post office or Federal Express. Electronic mail usage will grow as previously separate personal computers are attached to local area networks.

Voice Mail   **Voice mail** can be considered verbal electronic mail. Made possible by the latest computerized telephone systems, voice mail reduces the problem of telephone tag, where two people trying to reach each other wind up leaving a series of messages to please call back. With voice mail, the caller can leave a message, similar to leaving a message on an answering machine. The difference is that with a voice mail system, the caller's message is digitized (converted into binary ones and zeros) so that it can be stored on a disk like other computer data. This allows the party who was called to hear the message later (by reconverting it to an audio form) and also, if desired, add a reply or additional comments and forward the message to someone else who has access to the system. Some software applications are now incorporating voice messages as part of stored documents. For example, a budget worksheet could be created with verbal instructions on how it should be completed.

Desktop Publishing   Desktop publishing allows the user to control the process of creating high-quality newsletters, brochures, and other documents that previously would had to have been developed by professional artists. Trends in desktop publishing include more sophisticated high-resolution graphics and the increased use of color. More powerful computer systems and the availability of desktop publishing systems for different levels of user sophistication will increase their use in small as well as large organizations.

Facsimile   Facsimile, or **FAX**, machines are used to transmit a reproduced image of a document over standard phone lines (Figure 14-2). The document can contain text or graphics, can be hand-written, or be a photograph. FAX machines optically scan the document and convert the image into digitized data that can be transmitted, using a modem, over the phone. A FAX machine at the receiving end converts the digitized data back into its original image. Besides the separate FAX machines, plug-in circuit boards are also available for personal computers. Using either a separate or a built-in modem, these fax boards can directly transmit computer-prepared documents or documents that have been digitized with the use of a scanner. FAX machines are having an increasing impact on the way businesses transmit documents. Many documents that were previously sent through the mail are now sent by FAX. With the speed and convenience of a phone call, a document sent by FAX can be transmitted anywhere in the world.

Image Processing Image processing is the capability to store and retrieve a reproduced image of a document. Image processing is often used when an original document, such as an insurance claim, must be seen to verify data. Image processing and traditional applications will continue to be combined in many areas. For example, in 1988 American Express began sending cardholders copies of the individual charge slips that were related to the charges on their statement. These charge slips were recorded by an image processing system and then merged with the customer statement program.

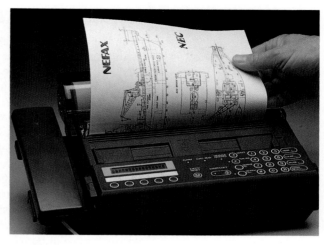

FIGURE 14-2
A facsimile (FAX) machine can send and receive copies of documents to and from any location where there is phone service and another FAX machine.

Teleconferencing **Teleconferencing** once meant three or more people sharing a phone conversation. Today, however, teleconferencing usually means **video conferencing**, the use of computers and television cameras to transmit video images and the sound of the conference participants to other participants with similar equipment at a remote location (Figure 14-3). Special software and equipment is used to digitize the video image so that it can be transmitted along with the audio over standard communications channels. Although the video image is not as clear for moving objects as is commercial television, it does contribute to the conference discussion and is adequate for nonmoving objects such as charts and graphs.

FIGURE 14-3
Video conferencing is used to transmit and receive video and audio signals over standard communications channels. This meeting is being transmitted to a video conference center at another location. The people at the other location are also being recorded and transmitted and can be seen on the TV monitor.

Summary of the Automated Office The trend toward integrated automated office capabilities will continue. Currently incompatible devices such as stand-alone FAX machines, copiers, and telephone switches will be standardized or will be provided with software that will enable them to communicate and transfer data with other devices. The higher productivity provided by automated office devices will encourage more organizations to adopt them.

The Automated Factory

As in the automated office, the goal of the **automated factory** is to increase productivity through the use of automated, and often computer-controlled, equipment. Technologies used in the automated factory include computer-aided design, computer-aided engineering, computer-aided manufacturing, and computer-integrated manufacturing.

Computer-Aided Design (CAD) Computer-aided design (CAD) uses a computer and special graphics software to aid in product design (Figure 14-4). The CAD software eliminates the laborious drafting that used to be required and allows the designer to dynamically change the size of some or all of the product and view the design from different angles. The capability to store the design electronically offers several advantages over traditional manual methods. One advantage is that the designs can be changed more easily than before. Another is that the design database can be reviewed more easily by other design engineers. This increases the likelihood that an existing part will be used in a product rather than a new part designed. For example, if a support bracket was required for a new product, the design engineer could review the design database to see if any existing products used a support bracket that would be appropriate for the new product. This not only decreases the overall design time but increases the reliability of the new product by using proven parts.

FIGURE 14-4
Computer-aided design (CAD) is an efficient way to develop plans for new products.

Computer-Aided Engineering (CAE) Computer-aided engineering (CAE) is the use of computers to test product designs. Using CAE, engineers can test the design of an airplane or a bridge before it is built (Figure 14-5). Sophisticated programs simulate the effects of wind, temperature, weight, and stress on product shapes and materials. Before the use of CAE, prototypes of products had to be built and subjected to testing that often destroyed the prototype. CAE allows engineers to create a computer prototype that can be tested under a variety of conditions. CAE allows products to be tested in some conditions, such as earthquakes, that could not previously be simulated.

FIGURE 14-5
Computer-aided engineering (CAE) allows the user to test product designs before they are built and without damaging the product.

Computer-Aided Manufacturing (CAM)

Computer-aided manufacturing (CAM) is the use of computers to control production equipment. CAM production equipment includes software-controlled drilling, lathe, and milling machines as well as robots (Figure 14-6). The use of robots has aroused much interest, partially because of preconceived ideas of robots as intelligent, humanlike machines. In practice, most industrial robots rarely look like a human and can perform only preprogrammed tasks. Robots are often used for repetitive tasks in hazardous or disagreeable environments such as welding or painting areas, or when chemicals that are hazardous to humans are used.

Computer-Integrated Manufacturing (CIM)

Computer-integrated manufacturing (CIM) is the total integration of the manufacturing process using computers (Figure 14-7). Using CIM concepts, individual production processes are linked so that the production flow is balanced and optimized and products flow at an even rate through the factory. In a CIM factory, automated design processes are linked to automated machining processes that are linked to automated assembly processes that are linked to automated testing and packaging. Under ideal CIM conditions, a product will move through the entire production process under computer control. Many companies may never fully implement CIM because it is so complex. But CIM's related concepts of minimum inventory and efficient demand-driven production are valid and will be incorporated into many manufacturers' business plans.

FIGURE 14-6
Computer-aided manufacturing (CAM) is used to control production equipment such as these welding robots on an automobile assembly line.

The Computer-Integrated Enterprise

Although in the previous sections we discuss the automated office and automated factory separately, the long-range trend is the **computer-integrated enterprise**—an organization in which all information storage and processing is performed by a network of computers and intelligent devices. In a computer-integrated enterprise, all office, factory, warehouse, and communications systems are linked using a common interface allowing authorized use in any functional area of the organization to access and use data stored anywhere in the organization. Rather than being machine or software oriented as today's systems, future systems will be document or information oriented. The user won't need to separately start a word processing, spreadsheet, or communications program. Instead, users will be able to create and distribute compound documents that contain text, graphics, numbers, and full-motion video. They will be able to record, in their own voice, comments or questions about the document before it is stored or routed to someone else in the organization. For example, a new product marketing plan could contain a text description of the product, a spreadsheet showing projected sales, and a narrated video showing the product in use. If the president of a company had questions about the plan, he or she could add questions to the plan in his or her own voice, and route the plan to the appropriate person for a response.

FIGURE 14-7
The concept of computer-integrated manufacturing (CIM) is to use computers to integrate all phases of the manufacturing process from planning and design to manufacturing and distribution.

BRINGING THE INFORMATION AGE HOME

Millions of personal computers have been purchased for home use, and the use of personal computers in the home is expected to increase. Just as the use of computers in the workplace has changed how we work, the use of computers in our homes is changing our personal lives. In the next two sections we discuss how people use personal computers in homes today, how they might use them in the future, and things you should consider when purchasing a personal computer system.

The Use of Personal Computers in the Home

People use personal computers in their homes in a variety of ways. These ways usually fall into five general categories: (1) personal services, (2) control of home systems, (3) telecommuting, (4) education, and (5) entertainment.

FIGURE 14-8
The Prodigy online information service offers the latest news, weather, sports, and financial information along with shopping, entertainment, and electronic mail.

Personal Services In many ways running a home is similar to running a small business. The productivity tools you use in the office, such as word processing, spreadsheet, and database, can also be used in the home to help you with creating documents, with financial planning and analysis, and filing and organizing data. Personal computer software is also available to assist you with home accounting applications such as balancing checkbooks, making household budgets, and preparing tax returns. In addition, using a personal computer to transmit and receive data over telephone lines allows home users to access a wealth of information and services. For example, teleshopping, electronic banking, and airline reservations are services that are becoming more popular, and information such as stock prices, weather reports, and headline news is available to home users who subscribe to online information services such as Prodigy (Figure 14-8), Genie, and CompuServe. The personal services provided by home computer use allows people to perform personal and business-related tasks quickly and conveniently in the comfort of their own homes. Without a personal computer, completing similar activities would take them considerably more time because it would frequently require them to travel to other locations to conduct this business and acquire information.

A different type of service available to users who have personal computers with communications capabilities is the access and use of electronic **bulletin board systems**, called **BBSs**, that allow users to communicate with one another and share information (Figure 14-9). While some bulletin boards provide specific services such as buying and selling used computer equipment, many bulletin boards function as electronic clubs for special-interest groups and are used to share information about hobbies as diverse as stamp collecting, music, genealogy, and astronomy. Some BBSs are strictly social; users meet new friends and conduct conversations by entering messages through their keyboards.

Control of Home Systems Another use of computers in the home is to control home systems such as security, environment, lighting, and landscape sprinkler systems. Personal computers used in this manner are usually linked to special devices such as alarms for security; thermostats for temperature control; and timing devices for lighting and sprinkler systems. For example, if the personal computer system has communications capabilities, a homeowner who is away can use a telephone or another computer to call home and change the operation of one of the control systems. Suppose a homeowner is on vacation in Texas and learns that heavy rains have been falling at home in Pennsylvania. He or she could call the computer and use the keys of a touch-tone telephone to instruct the computer to turn off the garden sprinkler system.

Most existing home control systems were installed after the home was built and often consist of separate systems to control each set of devices. This will change in the future, however. In 1990, the Electronic Industries Association released a new wiring standard called the Consumer Electronics Bus (CEBus). The CEBus sets standards for sending information throughout a home using existing electrical wiring, phone lines, TV cable, and nonwired techniques such as radio waves. In a related effort, Echelon Corporation is designing chips to be used in consumer electronics and building products. The chips will allow appliances, lighting systems, and other home products to be networked together and controlled by a single system using a consistent set of commands. Although they are not yet widely implemented, these changes will result in what many refer to as the intelligent home or smart house.

Telecommuting **Telecommuting** refers to the capability of individuals to work at home and communicate with their offices by using personal computers and communications lines. With a personal computer, an employee can access the main computer at the office. He or she can read and answer electronic mail. An employee can access databases, and can transmit completed projects. Some predictions claim that by the end of the 1990s, ten percent of the work force will be telecommuters. Most of these people will probably arrange their business schedules so they can telecommute two or three days a week. Telecommuting provides flexibility, allowing companies and employees to increase productivity and, at the same time, meet the needs of individual employees. Some of the advantages possible with telecommuting include reducing the time needed to commute to the office each week; eliminating the need to travel during poor weather conditions; providing a convenient and comfortable work environment for disabled employees or workers recovering from injuries or illnesses; and allowing employees to combine work with personal responsibilities such as child care.

Education The use of personal computers for education, called **computer-aided instruction (CAI)**, is another rapidly growing area. Whereas CAI is frequently used to describe software that is developed and used in schools, much of the same software is available for home users. CAI software can be classified into three types: drill and practice, tutorials, and simulations.

SAN DIEGO ELECTRONIC BULLETIN BOARDS

BBS	Number		BBS	Number		BBS	Number		BBS	Number
1 OMNIBUS BBS	464-6271 ¥		Digex:SDCS DIGSIG	454-8078 §		L.V. Wanderer	560-8203 §		SCH Editor's BBS	563-1598 ¥
also	280-2696		DJM BBS	588-6941 §		Mac Underground Safehouse	272-2059 ¥		Scripps Ranch	586-0703 ¥
A&B Express	447-1009 ¥Z		Dollars and Bytes	483-5477 ¥Z		Magic 102 BBS	560-1534 §		SDC BBS	754-5425 ¥
ABC	436-3525 ¥		Don's House	440-6038 ¥		Mainstreet Data	439-6624 ¥		S.D. CLIP*BOARD	279-4662 ¥
Adventure Board	224-2636 §		DOOGER'S PLACE	588-8931 §		Marzland	578-9086 §		S.D. Computer Society	549-3788 ¥
Adventure Games of America	695-3011 ∞		Dragon's Nest BBS	449-7052 ¥		MBC Broadcast	422-0239 ¥		The Seaside Connection	481-6479 ¥
Adventures In Palancia	222-1785 ¥		Dragon's Domain BBS	565-4424 ¥		MediaLine BBS	298-4027 §		Serenity	259-3704 §
Alabaster's cave	528-9218 §		The Dream Clinic	670-9522 ¥		MicroMiga	670-1095 ¥		Serenity	259-7757 Σ
Alcatraz	723-0537 ¥		Eight-Bit Tandy	571-6366 ¥		Milliway's	268-9614 ¥		Serial Port	755-3123 ¥
Amber Knights	460-9762 §		The Edge Elite	695-6949 ¥		Mister Rick's Neighborhood	695-1163 §		The Service Center	275-1448 ¥
Aquarium BBS	462-1732 §		Electro-shok Therapy	723-3065 ¥		Molakai Express	462-6319 §		Sharky's MAChine	747-8719 ¥
ARC Modem	589-0339 ¥		Elephant's Graveyard			Morning Star	575-3310 Ω		S.I.G.H. Amiga	788-0449 ¥
Artworld BBS	462-6887 ¥		(node #9):	270-3148 ¥		Mount Olympus	465-8236 §		Silver's Cave	561-7206 ¥
Ashley's BBS	565-2029 ¥		Enigma	453-1819 ¥		Mousetrap	464-2134 Ω		Skanked BBS!	480-2441 ¥
Astralite	276-7623 ¥		Especially Yours	226-3042 ¥		Multitech PC	578-9221		SKYNET II	754-1659 ¥
The Asylum	293-0158 ¥		The Evergreen Forest	426-2057 §		Mushin BBS	535-9580 §		So Cal Graphics BBS	292-0186 ¥
Atari/Amiga	691-7862 ¥		Falcon's BBS	726-8001 ¥		also	222-3097 §		Software Revenge	431-4444 §
Awesome's Place	482-3025 ¥		Family Historians	297-5746 ¥		My House	447-1422 ¥		The Software Corner	588-6238 ¥
The Ballyhoo BBS	447-1008 ¥		Far Star Prev. ST Sig atar	225-1775 ¥		Mystic Lounge	679-7691 §		The Software Market Place	669-1581 ¥
The BBS Summit	576-0077 ¥		Fax Satellite System	224-3853 ¥		Nassau Xpress	433-9777 ¥		SomeWares Bet. Heaven	436-9861 ¥
The Black Box	747-2304 ¥		The File Bank	728-4318 §		The Nesting Ground	484-7283 ¥		Sound of Money	461-2521 ¥
Bootcamp I	941-0996 §		The File Cabinet	427-5459 Ω		New-Ware	455-5226 ¥		ST-NET BBS	268-3996 Ω
Border Town BBS	466-3173 ¥		The Final Experience	670-4445 §		NEXUS Z (node #63)	486-0735 ¥		ST-SDACE	689-8157 §
The Bosn's Locker	442-9252 ¥		The Final Frontier	966-0114 §		Nassau? Ham Radio	279-3921 §		also	689-8397
Brian Smith's BBS	582-0875 ¥		Fightertown BBS	537-4217 ¥		Nola's Nemesis	461-1336 ¥		ST SIG Atari ST & Others	726-4419 §
The Bicycle Bulletin Board	720-1830 ¥		The Flare Path	561-2999 Ω		North Clairemont BBS	272-3087Ω		also	726-4419
Bullit Proof Software	284-6729 Ω		The Forgotten Realm BBS	578-4093 ¥		North San Diego Apple Club	571-9010 ¥		Star Base 23	560-2996 ¥
Bytes 'R Us	428-9773 §		Foundations Edge	287-2996 ¥		Ocean Beach BBS	224-4878 §		Starhelm Graystaff	479-3006 §
California Sands GS	541-7048 §		Foy's Trading Post	562-3646 ¥		Ocean Sports	558-2691 ¥		Suburbia?	447-5489 Ω
California Computer Connection	944-1804 §		FSMAO-2	725-6322 ¥		Oh No Not Just Another BBS	298-7475 ¥		The Surf Shack	967-6017 §
Camelot 3000	462-0542 ¥		Fuel Dump	390-7896 ¥		Orcus's Den BBS	268-4498 ¥		SW/SE Connection	479-0411 §
Casa de Cricket	823-1583 ¥		The Fun House	697-8714 ¥		Osborne-CPM User Group	299-1604 §		also	479-3006
The Chief's Mess	469-1354 §		The Funny Farm	746-6564 Ω		OtherWorlds	630-1147 §		Sys-Jam Productions	432-9057 ¥
Christ Line	268-3568 ¥		The Game Board BBS	281-0675§		Outer Limits	596-0667 ¥		Tech Pro BBS	755-7357 §
Classified Connection	566-1745 ¥		Gandall's	466-9505 ¥		PC•LawCom BBS	272-6615 ¥		TeleMac	576-1820 ¥§
The Closet BBS	480-9686 §		The General	281-4185 ¥		The General	483-1324 •		The 64 & More Store	258-0951 ¥
also	726-4419 ¥		The Ginko BBS	566-4165 ¥		P-Net (pnet03)	569-9195 ¥		Tinker Toys BBS	738-0471 ¥
CMS:Lakeside	390-2689 §		The G.T. Connection	263-0347 ¥		P-Net (pnet01)	444-7006 ¥		Trader's World	284-8729 §
CMUG	433-3162 §		The Hero Network	222-5961 ¥		Paulette's Playhouse	484-2690 ¥		The Treehouse	424-6375 ¥
Coconet Demo BBS	456-0815 ¥		High Country East	789-4391		PD-SIG	749-2741 ¥§§		Tunnels of Versarius NODE I	453-1781 √
COM2 (node #1): Remote			Hillcrest Host & BBS	291-0544 ¥		also	749-2589¥S,749-3432¥S,		The Underground Cavern	748-8157 §
BBS	471-8730 §		Hog Heaven	561-0058 ¥		also	749-6222¥§S,749-6384¥S		The Underground Press	444-4163 §
COM2 (node #2): Remote			The Family Historian	279-5746 ¥		People-Net (pnett12)	259-3704 Σ		The VOID! BBS	455-5957 ¥
BBS	471-8839 ¥		IEEE (San Diego)	452-3131 ¥		The Place BBS	479-5244 ¥		UN'x Lips Service BBS	693-0735 Ω
Commodore Connection	429-6227 ¥		I.D.I.C.	461-0982 ¥		Pro-BEAGLE	558-6151 ¥		USA BBS	443-5968 ¥
Commodore Edition	575-8364 §		Imperial Beach BBS	575-1562 ¥		Pro-Grouch	260-0492 §		USRobotics	286-0841 √
The Commodore Shop	423-7901 §		The Internal Stack II	741-2686 ¥		ProLine [avalon]	632-7161 §		USS Perpetrators	561-4681 ¥
Commodore User's Network	267-8056 §		Inve$tment Club BB$	476-0692 ¥		ProLine [mercury]	697-0261 ¥		Viking BBS	756-9567 ¥
Communication link	726-7834 §		Jim's BBS of San Diego	492-9714 ¥		ProLine [simasd]	238-2333 §		Waduki's Graphics Pad	425-5831 ¥
Communicore	484-5811 ¥		Katatania Tales	420-4120 ¥		ProLine [sol]	670-5379 §		The Warezhouse	575-7914 §
Computer Buyer's Guide	689-0500 ¥		Key Point BBS	479-8032 Ω		The Rabbit Hole	941-3505 §		The White House	432-0787 §
Computer Outlet, North County	740-0113 ¥Z		Kit's Hideout	741-0692 §		Radio-Active	268-9625 ¥		Wiłly-NET	535-0816 ¥
The Computer Room	287-6006 ¥		Knight Shadows' Grotto	792-0455 ¥		The Rasta Think Tank	282-1211 Σ		Wisdom BBS	270-3083 ¥
ComputorEdge On-Line	573-1675 ¥		Knowledge Works BBS	528-1058 ¥		The Rat's Nest	275-6129 §		The Wizard's Domain	426-5028 ¥
Cornucopia	748-8096 ¥		Lake Murray's Support BBS	460-2292 ¥		The Real Estate BBS	464-4540 ¥		Xanadu (new users)	287-2044 ¥
Cougar Country	480-3056 §Z		Lakeside Wildcat!	390-7328 Ω		R-n-S Info Foneline	268-0964 ¥		Xanadu (validated users)	287-2140 ¥
Covey's Concepts	439-5131 ¥		The Landing Strip	672-0846 Ω		Roques' Roost C-64	262-6106 §		Zeke	755-5675 ¥
Cygnus X-1 BBS	457-2665 ¥		Launching Academy	562-6337 ¥		Rom-Burner	424-7213 ¥			
The Crypt BBS	457-1836 ¥		La Verne & PC Street Again	222-9483 ¥		The RPC Library	461-6642 ¥			
Cuyamaca College	660-2010 §		The Lemonade Stand	941-6158 §		Rosie's Lair	589-4599 ¥			
Data Trax, USRobotics HST	433-8564 §		The Lemon Grove BBS	463-9037 ¥		Rudy's Place BBS	670-3040 ¥			
The Dark Alley	728-5497 ¥		Lips BBS	693-0735 ¥		Sabaline	692-1961 §			
DataWorks BBS	423-9352 Ω		Light Impressions	538-9131 §		S.D. Fantasy	476-7733 ¥			
Dave's Place	562-3248 §		L.O.L.A.	582-6969 §		San Diego PC Board (node #1)	584-4172 ¥			
Deadwood BBS	598-4088 ¥		Longshot	465-9764¥∨		San Diego PC Board (node #2)	584-1715 ¥			
dBored	748-3644 §		also	465-0327		Santee Experiment	562-8758 ¥			
The Dead Zone BBS/PDSE	755-3350 ¥		The Looney Bin	390-9470 ¥		Sawyer College of Business BBS	286-8614 ¥Z			
also	942-0848		LoticTek BBS	280-6725 ¥		Scanline	298-2023 §			
Demon's Den	284-3439 ¥					SCCG:TIBBS	278-8155 §			

Legend

§ 300/1200 baud, ¥ 300-2400 baud, § 9600 baud HSTs, Ω 14,400 baud HSTs, √ Dual Standard (14,400 HST and 9600 V.32), Σ V.32 19,200 Telebit Trailblazer, Z After hours or weekends, $ Requires a donation for access. ComputorEdge acknowledges this is not a complete list of all the BBSs in the San Diego area and reserves the right to reject or cancel, for any reason, any BBS submission for inclusion on this list.

62 October 19, 1990   COMPUTOREDGE

FIGURE 14-9

Some of the bulletin boards available in the San Diego, California area. Bulletin board systems are an excellent source for answers to questions about personal computer equipment and software.

Drill and practice software uses a flash-card approach to teaching by allowing users to practice skills in subjects such as math and language. A problem or word appears on the computer screen and the user enters the answer. The computer accepts the answer and responds by telling the student whether the answer is correct or incorrect. Sometimes the user gets second and third chances to select the correct answer before the computer software reveals the correct answer.

With **tutorial software**, the computer software uses text, graphics, and sometimes sound to teach a user concepts about subjects such as chemistry, music theory, or computer literacy. Following the instruction, tutorial software might present true/false or multiple-choice questions to help the user ensure that he or she understands the concepts. The increased use of optical disk storage provides high-quality graphics and direct access capability; it promises to greatly enhance this type of CAI.

The third type of CAI, **simulation software**, is designed to teach a user by creating a model of a real-life situation. For example, many simulation packages are available to teach business concepts. One program designed for children simulates running a lemonade stand and another program for adults simulates the stock market. In the lemonade simulation, the user makes decisions about *How many quarts of lemonade to make* and *What price to charge customers for a glass of lemonade.* The computer software accepts the user's decisions, performs computations using the software model, and then responds to the user with the amount of profit or loss for the day. Good CAI software is designed to be user friendly and motivate the user to succeed (Figure 14-10).

In addition to CAI software, some trade schools, colleges and universities are now offering students with personal computers a chance to take electronic correspondence courses from their homes. Lessons and assignments for classes are transmitted between the student and the school over communications lines.

Education in the home through CAI or electronic correspondence courses allows home users to learn at their own pace, in the convenience of their home, and at a time that fits into their personal schedule. Well-written educational software can be so entertaining that it is sometimes difficult to distinguish between it and entertainment software.

FIGURE 14-10

Computer-aided instruction (CAI) software provides a structured yet motivating way to learn. This CAI software helps the user to develop deductive reasoning, reference, and research skills while learning geography, history, economics, government, and culture.

FIGURE 14-11

Flight simulators can be both fun and educational. Some simulators offer realistic instrument consoles and flight patterns that help teach the user about flying.

Entertainment Entertainment software, or game playing, on home computers has always had a large following among the younger members of the family. However, many adults are surprised to find that entertainment software can also provide them with hours of enjoyment. Popular types of entertainment software include arcade games, board games, simulations, and interactive graphics programs. Most people are familiar with the arcade-type games (similar to video games) that are available for computers. A popular board game is computer chess. Simulations include games such as baseball and football and a variety of flight simulators that allow users to pretend they are controlling and navigating different types of aircraft (Figure 14-11).

Also available are a wide variety of interactive graphic adventure games that range from rescuing a princess from a castle's dungeon to solving a murder mystery. People can play many of these games alone or in small groups. The software usually allows players to adjust the level of play to match their abilities, that is, beginner through advanced. With entertainment software, the computer becomes a fun, skillful, and challenging game partner.

In addition to playing games, some personal computer users use their home computer as a tool for personal hobbies. Computers are used by hobbyists to design quilt and stained glass patterns, run model trains, organize stamp, doll, and photography collections, and write, transpose, play, and print musical scores.

Summary of the Use of Personal Computers in the Home As you can see, personal computers are used in homes in a variety of ways. Whether or not you now use a personal computer in your home, it is very probable that you will at some time in the near future. In fact, it is very possible that within the next decade you will have multiple computers in your home. Because computers can be used in so many different ways and also because computer technology is changing so rapidly, you should carefully choose any computer system you purchase. We discuss some general guidelines for purchasing personal computers in the next section.

Guidelines for Buying a Personal Computer

When you purchase a personal computer, you should make every effort to select a computer system that matches your individual needs as closely as possible. The six steps for purchasing a personal computer system recommend that you:

1. **Become computer literate**. This is truly the first and most important step in making a wise purchase. You might be surprised that many people buy computer equipment without understanding the capability of a personal computer or the tasks it can and cannot perform. Many times these people buy a computer like the one their neighbor or friend purchased, and expect it to meet their needs. Sometimes it does, but frequently they are disappointed. Hopefully, this will not happen to you. You already have an advantage because by reading this book, you now know a great deal about computers and have developed a foundation of knowledge on which you can base your software and equipment decisions. In short, you already are computer literate. But computer technology is changing rapidly, to stay computer literate you will need to stay current with the changes in the field. You can do this by reading periodicals or attending seminars on state-of-the-art computer technology.
2. **Define and prioritize the type of tasks you want to perform on your computer**. This step will help you to see more clearly exactly what you want to do with your computer and will help you select software and equipment that will match these needs. Define your needs in writing. Create a numbered list with the most important application at the top and the least important application at the bottom. General applications such as word processing, spreadsheets, database, and communications are easy to include on the list. You may, however, have a special application in mind such as controlling a household security system. Being computer literate will help you know if a special application is feasible. It will also help you to discuss any special needs you might have with computer professionals who can help you. Once your list is completed you can begin to evaluate the available software.
3. **Select the software packages that best meet your needs**. Publications, computer stores, and user groups are all good resources when it comes to evaluating the available software. For more on evaluating software, review the section in Chapter 2, Guidelines for Purchasing Microcomputer Applications Software.

In addition to purchasing commercial software, you can also consider selecting shareware and public domain software. **Shareware** is software that users may try out on their own systems before paying a fee. If a user decides to keep and use the software, he or she sends a registration fee to the software publisher (Figure 14-12).

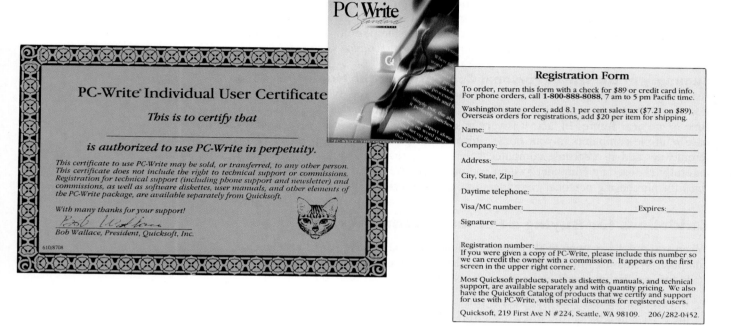

FIGURE 14-12
After trying the PC-Write software, users fill out a registration form and mail it with a fee to Quicksoft, the publisher of PC-Write. A user certificate is then sent to the user.

Public domain software is free software that is not copyrighted and can therefore be distributed among users. While the quality of shareware and public domain software varies greatly, some of the software is quite good. You can obtain this type of software from BBSs and also from public domain software libraries.

4. **Select equipment that will run the software you have selected**. The capabilities of the different types of personal computers vary greatly. For example, some personal computers can perform extensive graphics while others cannot. Selecting the software that meets your needs before selecting your equipment guides you in selecting appropriate equipment. Some software only runs on certain types of personal computers. Also, knowing the software you want to run prevents overbuying (purchasing a machine that is more powerful than you need) or underbuying (purchasing a machine that is not powerful enough). Capabilities to consider when you evaluate equipment include: processing speed of the microprocessor, memory size, system expandability, compatibility of the system with other personal computers, monochrome or color display, graphics capability, amount and type of auxiliary storage, printer type and speed, and communications capabilities. If you can't decide between two configurations, choose the system with more storage and/or processing power. Today's latest software applications require more disk space and CPU speed than applications released in prior years. This trend is expected to continue. Although you don't want to overbuy, you do want to buy a system that will meet your immediate needs and provide room for storage growth and additional applications.

5. **Select the suppliers for the software and equipment**. Your options include used equipment and software, mail order, and computer stores. Price, warranties, training, service, and repair are all details to consider when you select a supplier.

Obtaining the best overall value may not mean paying the lowest price. A store that is willing to provide you with assistance in assembling your system or furnish some training may be well worth a slightly higher price. Student purchasers should always check to see if systems and software are available through their school or if an educational discount is offered.

6. **Purchase the software and equipment**. If you have followed these guidelines you will probably feel both excited and confident with the decisions you have made. Your efforts to define your computing needs and to select software, equipment, and a supplier that will meet those needs should help you to select a personal computer system that is appropriate for you and with which you will be satisfied.

Summary of Bringing the Information Age Home

Personal computers are used in homes to aid in a variety of tasks such as personal services, control of home systems, telecommuting, education, and entertainment. When users purchase a personal computer system for the home, they should first become computer literate and evaluate their computer processing needs, then purchase software and equipment that meets those needs. The trend is clear. Personal computers will continue to bring the information age into our homes.

The changes that accompany the information age raise several issues that are related to society as a whole. We discuss some of these issues in the next section.

SOCIAL ISSUES

◆ Significant inventions such as the automobile and television have always challenged existing values and caused society to think about the right and wrong ways to use the new invention. The computer is no exception; including the social issues related to security and computer crime, privacy, and ethics.

Computer Security and Crime

Computer security and computer crime are closely related topics. **Computer security** refers to the safeguards established to prevent and detect unauthorized use and deliberate or accidental damage to computer systems and data. **Computer crime** is the use of a computer to commit an illegal act. Here we discuss three types of crimes that can be committed and the security measures that can be taken to prevent and detect them.

Software Theft Software theft, often called **software piracy**, became a major problem with the increased use of personal computers. Some people have difficulty understanding why they should pay hundreds, perhaps thousands, of dollars for what appears to be an inexpensive diskette or tape, and instead of paying for an authorized copy of the software they make an illegal copy. Estimates are that for every authorized copy of a commercial program, there is at least one illegal copy. However, it should be stated that software theft is a violation of copyright law and is a crime. Software companies take illegal copying seriously and in some cases offenders who have been caught have been vigorously prosecuted. For large users, the financial incentives for stealing software have been lowered by site licensing and multiple-copy discounts. Site licensing allows organizations to pay a single fee for multiple copies of a program used at a single location. Multiple-copy discounts reduce the fee of each additional copy of a program license.

Unauthorized Access and Use **Unauthorized access** can be defined as computer trespassing, in other words, being logged on a system without permission. Many so-called computer hackers boast of the number of systems that they have been able to access by using a modem. These hackers usually don't do any damage and merely wander around the accessed system before logging off.

Unauthorized use is the use of a computer system or computer data for unapproved and possibly illegal activities. Unauthorized use may range from an employee using the company computer for keeping his or her child's soccer league scores to someone gaining access to a bank funds system and creating an unauthorized transfer. Unauthorized use could also include the theft of computerized information such as customer lists or product plans. Courts have been taking a harsher view of both unauthorized access and use, and more frequently sentence violators to jail terms and substantial fines.

The key to preventing both unauthorized access and unauthorized use is computer security that controls and monitors an appropriate level of authorization for each user. Authorization techniques range from simple passwords to advanced biometric devices that can identify individuals by their fingerprint, voice, or eye pattern (Figure 14-13). The authorization technique should match the degree of risk associated with unauthorized access. An organization should regularly review the levels of authorization for users to determine if the levels are still appropriate.

FIGURE 14-13
Biometric security devices use biological characteristics to allow or deny access to would-be computer users. A retinal scanner reads a small area of a person's eye (left). An individual's retina pattern is as unique as a fingerprint, which can also be tested by a fingerprint recognition device (right). Other equipment exists to identify people by their voices or by their signatures.

Malicious Damage Malicious or deliberate damage to the data in a computer system is often difficult to detect because the damaged data may not be used or carefully reviewed on a regular basis. A disgruntled employee or an outsider might gain access to the system and delete or alter individual records or an entire file. One of the most potentially dangerous types of malicious damage is done by a **virus**, a computer program designed to copy itself into other software and spread through multiple computer systems. Figure 14-14 shows how a virus can spread from one system to another. Although they have existed for a some time, viruses have become a serious problem only recently.

Organizations have developed specific programs called **vaccines** to locate and remove viruses; in addition organizations are becoming more aggressive in prosecuting persons suspected of planting viruses. In what was described as the first computer virus trial, in 1988 a former programmer was convicted in Texas of planting a program in his employer's computer system that deleted 168,000 sales commission records.

A COMPUTER VIRUS: WHAT IT IS AND HOW IT SPREADS

How is a computer virus created?
A virus is a computer code that can do such things as alter programs or destroy data. Also, the virus can copy itself onto programs thereby spreading its damaging effects.

How do viruses spread?
A piece of software that has a virus attached to it is called the *host program.* Usually the virus is spread when the host program is shared. As the host program is copied for friends and business associates through swapping, electronic bulletin boards, and other usual channels, the virus is also copied. It infects the software with which it comes into contact.

Why are viruses not detected immediately?
People who copy and keep the host software are unaware that the virus exists, because the virus is designed to hide from computer users for weeks or even months.

When does a virus attack?
A virus usually attacks at the specific times or dates determined by the person who wrote the virus code. When the predetermined time or date registers on the internal clock of the computer, the virus attacks. Often the virus code will display a message to users letting them know that the virus has done its damage.

Single acts of malicious damage, especially when performed by employees with authorized access to the computer system, are very difficult to prevent. The best protection against this type of act remains adequate backup files that enable organizations to restore damaged or lost data.

FIGURE 14-14
How a virus program can be transmitted from one computer system to another.

Privacy

In the past, one way to maintain privacy was to keep information in separate locations—individual stores had their own credit files, government agencies had separate records, doctors had separate files, and so on. However, it is now technically and economically feasible to store large amounts of related data about individuals in one database. Some people believe that this increases the possibility for unauthorized use.

The concern about information privacy has led to federal and state laws regarding the storage and disclosure of personal data. Common points in these laws include: (1) information collected and stored about individuals should be limited to what is necessary to carry out the function of the business or government agency collecting the data. (2) Once collected, provisions should be made to restrict access to the data to those employees within the organization who need access to it to perform their job duties. (3) Personal information should be released outside the organization collecting the data only when the person has agreed to its disclosure. (4) When information is collected about an individual, the individual should know that data is being collected and have the opportunity to determine the accuracy of the data.

Two laws deal specifically with computers. The 1986 Electronic Communications Privacy Act (ECPA) provides the same protection that covers mail and telephone communications to the new forms of electronic communications such as voice mail. The 1988 Computer Matching and Privacy Protection Act regulates the use of government data to determine the eligibility of persons for federal benefits.

Ethics

Society is increasingly concerned about computer ethics and the difference between what is right, what is wrong, and what is criminal. Issues relate to many topics such as software copying, unauthorized access and use of computer systems, and privacy. By studying and learning the information provided in this book, you have become a computer literate member of society. As such, you will be better able to evaluate computer-related issues. The questionnaire in Figure 14-15 presents situations for you to evaluate. How do you feel about each of the questions?

FIGURE 14-15
Ethics questionnaire.

ETHICS OF INFORMATION PROCESSING

1. A computer operator runs a program at work for a friend and uses ten minutes of computer time. The program was run when the computer was idle and not being used for company business.
   Ethical _____ Unethical _____ Computer Crime _____

2. A student gives a password to another student not enrolled in a computer class for which a laboratory fee is charged. The password allows access to the school computer. The student not enrolled uses three hours of computer time in a time-sharing environment.
   Student enrolled in class:
   Ethical _____ Unethical _____ Computer Crime _____
   Student not enrolled in class:
   Ethical _____ Unethical _____ Computer Crime _____

3. A company hires a consultant to develop a payroll program. After completing the project, the consultant gives a copy of the program (without data) to a friend at another company.
   Ethical _____ Unethical _____ Computer Crime _____

4. Using a terminal, an individual breaks a security code and reviews confidential salaries of corporate executives. No use is made of the information. "I was just curious" is the individual's response when caught.
   Ethical _____ Unethical _____ Computer Crime _____

5. A bank employee electronically transfers money from a relatively inactive customer account to his own personal account and then transfers the money to a credit card account to pay current credit card charges. After money is deposited into his personal account on pay day, he electronically transfers the money back to the customer's account. No money physically changes hands, and no interest is lost to the customer's account.
   Ethical _____ Unethical _____ Computer Crime _____

6. While reviewing a list of available programs on a bulletin board, a user notices a title of a program that is the same as a popular spreadsheet package. After downloading the program onto his system, the user discovers that the program appears to be an exact copy of the spreadsheet program that is sold in computer stores for $300.00. The user keeps and uses the program.
   Ethical _____ Unethical _____ Computer Crime _____

7. A programmer is asked to write a program that she knows will generate inaccurate information for stockholders of the company. When she questions her manager about the program, she is told she must write it or lose her job. She writes the program.
   Manager: Ethical _____ Unethical _____ Computer Crime _____
   Programmer: Ethical _____ Unethical _____ Computer Crime _____

8. As a practical joke, a student enters a virus program onto the hard disk of a microcomputer in the school's computer lab. Each time another student uses that machine, the virus program is copied onto that student's diskette. The program is designed so that the first time the disk is used after the first of January a "Happy New Year" message will be displayed on the screen.
   Ethical _____ Unethical _____ Computer Crime _____

9. A photojournalist uses a computer graphics program to retouch the background of a photo that is used on the front page of the newspaper.
   Ethical _____ Unethical _____ Computer Crime _____

10. A company uses software to monitor the productivity of the clerical staff. Supervisors are notified of staff members who fall below what management considers to be the minimum productivity standards.
    Ethical _____ Unethical _____ Computer Crime _____

SUMMARY OF TRENDS AND ISSUES IN THE INFORMATION AGE

Based on current and planned developments, the impact of computers and the information age will be even greater in the future than it has been to date. However, as a society and as individuals, we have an obligation to use the computer responsibly and not abuse the power it provides. This presents constant challenges that sometimes weigh the rights of the individual against increased efficiency and productivity. The computer must be thought of as a tool whose effectiveness is determined by the skill and experience of the user. With the computer knowledge that you have acquired you will be better able to participate in decisions on how to best use computerized information systems.

CHAPTER SUMMARY

1. Existing business information systems will continue to undergo profound changes as new technology, software, and methods become available.
2. Trends will include; more online, interactive systems; less batch processing; expanded communications networks and increased use of relational database systems; and replacing command- and menu-driven interfaces with graphical-user interfaces.
3. The **automated office**, sometimes referred to as the **electronic office**, is the term that describes the use of electronic devices such as computers, facsimile machines, and computerized telephone systems to make office work more productive.
4. Word processing ranks as the most widely used office automation technology.
5. **Electronic mail** is the capability to transmit messages to and receive messages from other computer users.
6. **Voice mail** can be considered verbal electronic mail.
7. Desktop publishing involves the use of computers to produce printed documents that can combine different sizes and styles of text and graphics.
8. **Facsimile**, or **FAX**, machines are used to transmit a reproduced image of a document over standard phone lines.
9. Image processing is the capability to store and retrieve a reproduced image of a document.
10. **Teleconferencing** usually means **video conferencing**, the use of computers and television cameras to transmit video images and the sound of the conference participants to other participants with similar equipment at a remote location.
11. The goal of the **automated factory** is to increase productivity through the use of automated, and often computer-controlled, equipment.
12. **Computer-aided design (CAD)** uses a computer and special graphics software to aid in product design.
13. **Computer-aided engineering (CAE)** is the use of computers to test product designs.
14. **Computer-aided manufacturing (CAM)** is the use of computers to control production equipment.
15. **Computer-integrated manufacturing (CIM)** is the total integration of the manufacturing process using computers.
16. The long-range trend is the **computer-integrated enterprise**; an organization where all information storage and processing is performed by a network of computers and intelligent devices.
17. Personal computers are used in the home in many different ways, including: (1) personal services, (2) control of home systems, (3) telecommuting, (4) education, and (5) entertainment.
18. The personal services provided by home computer use allow people to perform personal and business-related tasks quickly and conveniently in the comfort of their own homes.
19. Electronic **bulletin board systems**, called **BBSs**, allow users to communicate with one another and share information.
20. Another use of computers in the home is to control home systems such as security, environment, lighting, and landscape sprinkler systems.

21. **Telecommuting** refers to the capability of individuals to work at home and communicate with their offices by using personal computers and communication lines.
22. The use of personal computers for education, called **computer-aided instruction (CAI)**, is a rapidly growing area.
23. **Drill and practice software** uses a flash-card approach to teaching by allowing users to practice skills in subjects such as math and language.
24. **Tutorial software** uses text, graphics, and sometimes sound to teach a user concepts about a subject and follows the instruction with questions to help the user ensure that he or she understands the concepts.
25. **Simulation software** is designed to teach a user by creating a model of a real-life situation.
26. Popular types of entertainment software include arcade games, board games, simulations, and interactive graphics programs.
27. The guidelines for purchasing a personal computer recommend that you: (1) become computer literate; (2) define and prioritize the type of tasks you want to perform on your computer; (3) select the software packages that best meet your needs; (4) select equipment that will run the software you have selected; (5) select the suppliers for the software and equipment; and (6) purchase the software and equipment.
28. **Shareware** is software that users may try out on their own systems before paying a fee.
29. **Public domain software** is not copyrighted and can therefore be distributed among users.
30. **Computer security** refers to the safeguards established to prevent and detect unauthorized use and deliberate or accidental damage to computer systems and data.
31. **Computer crime** is the use of a computer to commit an illegal act.
32. Software theft, often called **software piracy**, refers to illegal copying of software.
33. **Unauthorized access** can be defined as computer trespassing, in other words, being logged on a system without permission.
34. **Unauthorized use** is the use of a computer system or computer data for unapproved and possibly illegal activities.
35. The key to preventing both unauthorized access and unauthorized use is computer security that controls and monitors an appropriate level of authorization for each user.
36. One of the most potentially dangerous types of malicious damage is done by a **virus**, a computer program designed to copy itself into other software and spread through multiple computer systems.
37. **Vaccines** are programs that locate and remove viruses.
38. The concern about information privacy has led to federal and state laws regarding the storage and disclosure of personal data.

KEY TERMS

Automated factory *14.6*
Automated office *14.4*
Bulletin board system (BBS) *14.8*
Computer-aided design (CAD) *14.6*
Computer-aided engineering (CAE) *14.6*
Computer-aided instruction (CAI) *14.9*
Computer-aided manufacturing (CAM) *14.7*
Computer crime *14.13*

Computer-integrated enterprise *14.7*
Computer-integrated manufacturing (CIM) *14.7*
Computer security *14.13*
Drill and practice software *14.10*
Electronic mail *14.4*
Electronic office *14.4*
Facsimile (FAX) *14.4*
Public domain software *14.12*
Shareware *14.12*

Simulation software *14.10*
Software piracy *14.13*
Telecommuting *14.9*
Teleconferencing *14.5*
Tutorial software *14.10*
Unauthorized access *14.14*
Unauthorized use *14.14*
Vaccine *14.15*
Video conferencing *14.5*
Virus *14.14*
Voice mail *14.4*

REVIEW QUESTIONS

1. List at least three ways that existing information systems will change.
2. Identify and explain seven automated office applications. What is the trend with these applications?
3. What is the goal of the automated factory? Briefly explain the four technologies that are used.
4. What are some of the personal services available to home computer users?
5. What is CAI? Identify the three categories of CAI an give example of each.
6. List the six guidelines for buying a personal computer. Why is it recommended that you select your software before your equipment?
7. Explain the difference between public domain software and shareware.
8. Write a definition for computer crime. List three types of computer crime.
9. Explain why computer viruses are malicious. What is a vaccine program?
10. Discuss the four common points covered in the state and federal information privacy laws.

CONTROVERSIAL ISSUES

1. Factory and office automation has led to the reduction or elimination of many jobs. What obligation, if any, do you think companies have toward workers that are replaced by automated systems?
2. While most people agree computers can be valuable educational tools there is disagreement about how and when students should be introduced to computers. At what grade level do you think students should begin using computers? What topics should be taught using computers?

RESEARCH PROJECTS

1. Contact your school or a large company in your area and ask to see a copy of their policy on illegally copying software. Compare the policies and discuss them with your class.
2. Contact the person in charge of a computer laboratory at your school and ask him or her about computer viruses. Ask him or her if any viruses have been found in the laboratory. Also find out what procedures or software is being used to protect against viruses.

INDEX

Access arm: Contains the read/write heads and moves the heads across the surface of the disk. **6.9**

Access time: The time required to access and retrieve data stored in sectors on a diskette. **6.6**

Accounting controls: System controls to provide assurance that the dollar amounts recorded in the accounting records are correct. **11.19**

Accounting software packages, 11.11

Acoustic coupler, *See* Acoustic modem

Acoustic modem: A communications device used with a telephone handset. Also called acoustic coupler. **8.13**

Acquisition: Phase in the information system life cycle after the analysis phase. The acquisition phase has four steps: (1) summarizing the application requirements, (2) identifying potential software vendors, (3) evaluating software alternatives, and (4) making the purchase. **11.10–15**

Actuator, *See* Access arm

Ada: A programming language supported by the U.S. Department of Defense. Its use is required on all U.S. government military projects. Ada was designed to facilitate the writing and maintenance of large programs that would be used over a long period of time. **12.17**

Adding data: Updating data, such as creating a record for a new employee to include in a file or database. **7.3**

Addressing, symbolic, 12.13

Airline reservation system
  data consistency and, 3.27
  fault-tolerant systems, 9.5

ALGOrithmic Language (ALGOL), 12.18

Alphabetic characters, **3.3**
  memory storage and, 4.4
  tests for, 3.26

Alphabetic characters: Elements that comprise data; specifically, characters A–Z. **3.3**

Alphabetic field: A field that contains only alphabetic characters. **3.4**

Alphanumeric fields: Fields that contain a combination of character types, including alphabetic, numeric, and special characters. **3.4**

Alphanumeric fields, 3.4

Alphabetic menu selection, 3.18

American National Standards Institute (ANSI), 7.18–19, 12.6

American Standard Code for Information Interchange (ASCII): The most widely used coding system to represent data, primarily on personal computers and many minicomputers. **4.6**

Analog signal: A signal used on communications lines that consists of a continuous electrical wave. **8.10**

Analysis: Phase in the information system life cycle where the system is separated into its parts in order to determine how the system works. This phase consists of the preliminary investigation, detailed system analysis, and making the decision to proceed. **11.4–9**
  CASE tools and, 11.21
  data dictionary and, 11.6
  data flow diagrams and, 11.5–6
  decision on how to proceed and, 11.8
  detailed, 11.5–7
  preliminary investigation and, 11.4–5
  structured, 11.5–7
  structured English and, 11.7
  at Sutherland, 11.9

Analysis and design tools, 11.5–7

Analytical graphics: Used to selectively examine information and to interpret data through a graphic display. **2.16**

Analytical software, 5.4

Animation, 5.5

ANSI, *See* American National Standards Institute

Apple, 3.21, 9.11, 13.2

Application, computerized, 1.17

Application generators: Programs that produce source-language programs, such as BASIC or COBOL, based on input, output, and processing specifications entered by the user. Also called program generators. **12.18–19**

Application software: Programs that tell a computer how to produce information. **1.8**
  commercial, 11.10, 11.14–15
  custom, 11.14–15
  graphics and, 2.15, 5.4
  horizontal, 11.11
  integrated, 2.18–19
  loading, 1.11
  main memory and, 4.2

microcomputer, 1.9–10
  vertical, 11.11

Application software packages: Programs purchased from computer stores or software vendors. **1.8**

Appointment calendars, 2.20

A Programming Language (APL), 12.18

Architecture, of processor units, 4.13–15

Arithmetic/logic unit (ALU): Part of the CPU that performs arithmetic and logical operations. **1.5, 4.2**
  program execution and, 4.10

Arithmetic operations: Numeric calculations performed by the arithmetic/logic unit of the CPU, and include addition, subtraction, multiplication, and division. **1.5, 4.2**

Arrow keys: Keys on a keyboard that move the cursor up, down, left, or right on the screen. 2.3, **3.5**

Art
  desktop publishing and, 2.8–9
  scanners and, 3.12

Artificial intelligence: A branch of computer science applying human intelligence to computer systems. **10.11**

ASCII (American Standard Code for Information Interchange), code, 4.5, **4.6**

ASK, 13.2

Assembler: A special program that converts assembly language programs into machine language instructions. **12.13**

Assembly language: A low-level language that is similar to machine language, but uses abbreviations called mnemonics or symbolic operation code to represent the machine operation code. **12.13**

Associate Computer Professional (ACP), 13.9

Association for Computing Machinery (ACM): Professional organization composed of persons interested in computer science and computer science education. **13.8**

Association of Information Systems Professionals (AISP): Professional organization originally aimed at word processing professionals, but now includes a much broader membership, including office automation professionals. **13.8**

Association of Systems Management (ASM): Professional organization composed of individuals interested in improving the systems analysis and design field. **13.8**

Asynchronous transmission mode: Data communication method which transmits one character at a time at irregular intervals using start and stop bits. **8.10**

Attributes: Fields in a relational database. **7.15**

Automated factory: Factories that have an increase in productivity with the use of automated, and often computer-controlled, equipment. **14.6–7**

Automated office: The use of electronic devices such as computers, facsimile machines, and computerized telephone systems to make office work more productive; also known as electronic office. **14.4–5**

Auto parts sales system, 11.9

Auxiliary storage: Storage of programs and data that are not being processed. Also called secondary storage. **1.5–6, 6.2–21**
  cartridge devices, 6.14
  disk cartridges, 6.12
  diskettes, 6.3–7
  file organization and, 7.4
  file-oriented versus database system, 7.13
  hard disks, 6.7–11
  magnetic disk, 6.3–12
  magnetic tape, 6.13
  main memory and, 1.12
  mass storage devices, 6.18
  multiuser computers, 1.15–16
  optical cards, 6.19
  optical disks, 6.16–18
  reel-to-reel devices, 6.14
  removable disks, 6.10
  smart cards, 6.19
  solid-state devices, 6.18
  special-purpose devices, 6.19

Avant Garde type, 5.6

Background jobs: Assigned a lower processing priority and less CPU time. Compare with foreground jobs. **9.6**

Back support, 3.28

Backup: Procedures that provide for maintaining copies of program and data files so that in the event the files are lost or destroyed, they can be recovered. 6.12, **7.3**
  database administrator and, 7.19
  sequential files and, 7.5
  tape for, 1.16
  utility programs and, 9.14

Backus, John, 12.17

Band printers: Impact printers that use a horizontal, rotating band, and can print in the range of 300 to 2,000 lines per minute. **5.12–13**

Bandwidth: The range of frequencies that a communications channel can carry. **8.12**

Banking industry, MICR readers and, 3.15

Bar chart: Chart that displays relationships among data with blocks or bars. **2.15**

Bar code reader, *See* Laser scanners

Baseband: Coaxial cable that can carry one signal at a time at very high rates of speed. **8.3**

Base 2 number system, 4.7, 4.8

Base 16 number system, 4.7, 4.9

BASIC (Beginner's All-purpose Symbolic Instruction Code): A simple, interactive programming language. BASIC is one of the most commonly used programming languages on microcomputers and minicomputers. **12.15**

Batch control: During batch processing, balancing to a predetermined total, to ensure the accuracy and reliability of data and processing techniques. **3.25**

Batch processing: Data is collected and, at some later time, all the data that has been gathered is processed as a group, or *batch*. **3.22**, 3.23–25

Batch totaling, 11.19

Baud rate: The number of times per second that a data communications signal being transmitted changes; with each change, one or more bits can be transmitted. **8.12**

Bell Laboratories, 9.10, 12.16

Benchmark test: Test on software that measures the time it takes to process a set number of transactions. **11.13**

Bidirectional printing: Printing method of dot matrix printers, in which the print head can print while moving in either direction. **5.10**

Binary number system (base 2): Represents quantities by using only two symbols, 0 and 1, used to represent the electronic status of bits inside the processor unit, and also for addressing the memory locations. **4.5**, 4.7

  magnetic tape and, 6.14

Bit-mapped displays, *See* Dot-addressable displays

Bits: An element of a byte that can represent one of two values, on or off. There are 8 bits in a byte. **4.4**, 4.5
  buses and, 4.12
  parity, 4.7, 8.10

Bits per inch (bpi): A measure of the recording density of disk and tape. 6.5, 6.15

Bits per second (bps): A measure of the speed of data transmission; the number of bits transmitted in one second. **8.12**

Blinking: Screen feature used for emphasis in which characters or words on a screen blink. **5.18**

Blocks: Data is recorded on tape in blocks which usually consist of two or more records. **6.15**

Bold: Screen feature used for emphasis in which characters are displayed at a greater brightness level than the surrounding text. **5.6**, 5.10, 5.18

Booting: The process of loading an operating system into main memory. **9.2**

Borland, 13.2

Bottom-up design: Design approach that focuses on the data, particularly the output of the system. **11.16**

Bridge: A combination of hardware and software that is used to connect *similar* networks. **8.19–20**

Broadband: Coaxial cable that can carry multiple signals at one time. **8.3**

Bubbles, data flow diagrams and, 11.5

Buckets: The location on a disk where records in a direct file can be stored. **7.6**

Buffers: Areas of main memory used to store data that has been read or is waiting to be sent to an output device. **9.6**

Bugs: Program errors. **12.10**

Bulletin board systems (BBSs): Allow users to communicate electronically with one another and share information, using personal computers. **14.8**

Bunny suit, 4.22

Bus: Any line that transmits bits between memory and the input/output devices, and between memory and the CPU. **4.12**

Business application software industry, 13.2

Business application, typical, 1.10–13

Business systems jobs, salaries and, 13.5

Bus network: A communications network in which all the devices are connected to and share a single cable. **8.19**

Byron, Augusta Ada, 12.17

Byte: Each storage location within main memory, identified by a memory address. **4.3**

Introduction to DOS

PROJECTS

D O S

Working with Files on Disks

OBJECTIVES

You will have mastered the material in this project when you can:

- ◆ Boot your computer
- ◆ Enter the time and date, if required
- ◆ Establish the default disk drive
- ◆ Use file specifications for files stored on disk
- ◆ Distinguish between internal and external commands
- ◆ Format disks
- ◆ Clear the screen
- ◆ Copy files from one disk to another disk and to the same disk
- ◆ List a disk directory
- ◆ Rename files
- ◆ Display a file's contents and print a screen image
- ◆ Remove files

INTRODUCTION

◆ An **operating system** is a collection of programs that controls and manages the operation of the computer. These programs allow you, the computer equipment, and the application software to communicate. To use a computer to print a memo, for example, you first use the operating system to start the computer. You next enter a command that the operating system processes to start the word processing program. When you instruct the word processing program to print the memo, the operating system finds the memo file on disk, retrieves the data from the disk, and routes the output to the printer. The operating system is not part of the application software itself, but it provides essential services that the application software uses to perform its functions for you.

When you use an application program, such as a word processor, a spreadsheet, or a database manager, the application program handles the interaction with the operating system. If you are not using an application program, however, and want to list or view your disk files, for example, you must directly interact with the operating system. To use your computer effectively, you need to know when and how to interact with the operating system. In Project 1 you will learn how to use the operating system called DOS to work with your disk files.

Operating Systems for IBM PCs

Microsoft Corporation developed the operating system known as **DOS** (pronounced doss, not dose), an acronym for **Disk Operating System**. DOS has been used since 1981 in IBM PC and IBM-compatible microcomputers. **PC-DOS** is the name for versions of DOS distributed by IBM for its Personal Computer and Personal System/2 lines of microcomputers. All IBM-compatible microcomputers use versions of DOS distributed by Microsoft under the name **MS-DOS**. PC-DOS and MS-DOS are essentially the same. We use the term DOS to refer to any of the various editions of PC- or MS-DOS and cover information applicable to all versions of DOS.

DOS Versions

The numbers following the abbreviation DOS indicate the specific version and release of the product (Figure 1-1). The **version** number is the whole number and signifies a major improvement of the product. The **release** number is the decimal number and identifies minor changes or corrections to a version of the product. For example, DOS 1.1 corrected some minor problems with DOS 1.0.

DOS VERSION RELEASE	MAJOR FEATURES SUPPORTED	YEAR
5.0	Improved Memory Management, Task Switching	1991
4.0	Hard Disks Larger than 32MB, File Manager Shell, Memory Support Beyond 640KB	1988
3.3	Introduction of IBM PS/2	1987
3.2	Token-Ring Networks, 3.5" Diskette Drive	1985
3.1	Addition of Networking, 1.2MB 5.25" Diskette Drive	1984
3.0	Introduction of IBM PC/AT	1984
2.0	Introduction of IBM PC/XT	1983
1.1	Enhancements to 1.0	1982
1.0	Introduction of IBM PC	1981

FIGURE 1-1 DOS versions and releases with their major supported features

Software developers try to maintain **upward compatibility**, that is, that all the features of an earlier version and release remain supported by a later one. Downward compatibility, however, is not common. Programs or equipment that require the features of DOS 3.3, for example, will not function with DOS 3.2 or earlier versions.

Disk Configurations

You will likely use a computer with one of three common disk configurations. The first configuration has a hard disk and one diskette drive (Figure 1-2). Each drive has a **drive name**, which is a unique one-letter name preassigned to the drive. The hard disk drive name is C, and the diskette drive name is A.

The second configuration has two diskette drives and no hard disk (Figure 1-3). Drive A is the top or left drive, and drive B is the bottom or right drive.

FIGURE 1-2
Computers with a hard disk and one diskette drive

FIGURE 1-3
Computers with two diskette drives and no hard disk

The third configuration connects your computer through a local area network with other computers (Figure 1-4).

LOCAL AREA NETWORK (LAN)

FIGURE 1-4 Computers connected through a local area network (LAN)

A **local area network**, or **LAN**, is a collection of connected computers that share data. One special computer on the LAN, called the **server**, has a high-capacity hard disk that contains files that you can access from your computer. The server hard disk is usually drive F. Your computer would typically have a drive A with or without a drive C hard disk.

The DOS projects assume you have a drive A diskette drive and a drive C hard disk, unless otherwise noted. If you are using a computer with a different configuration, your instructor will instruct you on the changes you need to make for the DOS projects.

STARTING THE COMPUTER

DOS programs are stored on a hard disk or on a diskette. To begin using DOS, the operating system must be read into main memory, which is a process known as **booting**. How you begin to use the computer depends on your specific disk configuration and whether the computer has already been turned on.

On a LAN

If you are using a computer on a LAN, the laboratory attendant will have already booted your computer. You do not need to perform any start-up activities, unless your instructor gives you special instructions.

With Computer Power Off

Starting the computer by turning on the power switch is known as a **cold start**, or **cold boot**. The computer first runs some tests to diagnose its own circuitry and then loads DOS into main memory from the hard disk or your DOS diskette.

Hard Disk If you are using a computer with a hard disk, DOS is available on the hard disk. Turn on the power switch and be certain you do not insert a disk in drive A. While DOS is booting, the hard disk status light flashes on and off for a few seconds as DOS is loaded into main memory.

Two Diskette Drives and No Hard Drive If you are using a computer with two diskette drives and no hard disk, insert the DOS diskette in drive A and turn on the power switch. While DOS is booting, the status light for drive A flashes on and off, and drive A whirls for several seconds as DOS is loaded into main memory.

With Computer Power On

If the computer is already turned on, you can restart the computer without turning the power switch off and on. Restarting the computer in this way is called a **warm start**, **warm boot**, or **reset** because the computer power is already on. The warm start reloads DOS from disk but does not repeat the circuitry tests.

Hard Disk If you are using a computer with a hard disk, be certain you do not insert a disk in drive A during a warm start. Hold down the Ctrl and Alt keys, press the Delete key, and then release all three keys to begin the warm start. During the warm start the hard disk status light flashes on and off for a few seconds as DOS is loaded into main memory.

Two Diskette Drives and No Hard Drive If you are using a computer with two diskette drives and no hard disk, insert the DOS diskette in drive A before you begin a warm start. Hold down the Ctrl and Alt keys, press the Delete key, and then release all three keys to begin the warm start. During the warm start the status light for drive A flashes on and off, and drive A whirls for several seconds as DOS is loaded into main memory.

USING THE DISK OPERATING SYSTEM (DOS)

Setting the Date and Time

Many of today's computers have batteries that accurately maintain the date and time even when the computer power is off. Some computers, however, require that you enter the date and time and will display a message similar to Figure 1-5 after you boot DOS.

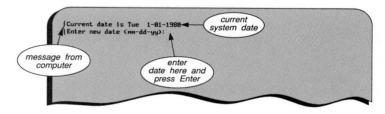

FIGURE 1-5 The request to enter the date

You would enter the month, day, and year as one-digit or two-digit numbers separated by hyphens (–), slashes (/), or, in DOS 3.3 and later versions, periods (.). If today is October 9, 1994, for example, you would type 10-9-94 and press the Enter key (Figure 1-6). Check with your instructor if you are not certain how to enter the date on your computer. If the date displayed is already correct, you do not need to enter the date. Instead, press the Enter key when the message "Enter new date: (mm-dd-yy):" appears on the screen.

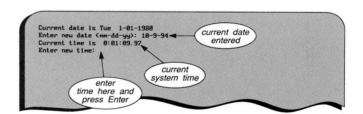

FIGURE 1-6 The request to enter the time

After you have entered the date, you enter the time in the format hh:mm:ss.xx, where hh stands for hours using the 24-hour system, mm stands for minutes, ss stands for seconds, and xx stands for hundredths of a second. If you need to enter the time, for practice, type the time as 11:50 and press the Enter key (Figure 1-7). When you do not include seconds and hundredths of seconds as in this case, DOS assumes a value of zero for them.

FIGURE 1-7 Date and time entered

The DOS Prompt

After the date and time messages and other messages tailored for your specific computer appear, DOS displays the **DOS prompt**, indicating that DOS is ready to receive your commands (Figures 1-8 through 1-10). The letter displayed before the > symbol shows which drive has been assigned as the default disk drive. The **default drive** is the drive that DOS assumes contains the disk where programs and data are located. Another term used for the default drive is **current drive** because it is the drive that is assumed to be currently used by DOS to first look at for files. If your DOS prompt is not exactly the same as one of those shown in Figures 1-8 through 1-10, your instructor will explain the difference to you.

FIGURE 1-8   DOS prompt after booting from a hard disk

FIGURE 1-9   DOS prompt after booting from a diskette

FIGURE 1-10   DOS prompt after booting from a LAN

FIGURE 1-11   Changing the default drive using a hard disk

The Default Drive

The default drive assignment will vary depending on the specific hardware you are using. A hard disk computer assigns drive C as the default drive as shown in Figure 1-8. If your computer has two diskette drives and no hard disk, drive A is the default drive, and the prompt appears as shown in Figure 1-9. Drive F is usually the default drive on a LAN as shown in Figure 1-10.

At times you will need to change the default drive assignment. Before you do, be certain that the new drive is ready. If your computer has a hard disk, it is always installed and ready, as is the server hard disk on a LAN. A diskette drive on some computers, however, must have a diskette inserted before it can be assigned as the default drive.

To change the drive assignment, you would type the letter of the new drive to be used, followed by a colon (:), and then press the Enter key. If you have a hard disk with a DOS prompt of C >, change the default to drive A by placing a diskette in drive A, typing the letter A, followed by a colon, and then pressing the Enter key. The DOS prompt will now display drive A as the default drive. Now, change the default drive back to drive C by typing C : and pressing the Enter key (Figure 1-11).

In most of our examples, we assume a hard disk on your computer with drive C as the default drive and drive A as the second drive. If you have two diskette drives and no hard disk, drive A will be your default drive and drive B your second drive. On a LAN, drive F will be your default drive and drive A your second drive. We will point out when the *procedures* for a two-diskette or LAN configuration are different than those for a hard disk configuration. In most cases, the procedures are similar for each configuration with only the drive letters differing, so we will assume you will make the appropriate changes for your configuration.

Figure 1-12, for example, shows how to change the default drive with two diskette drives from drive A to drive B and back to drive A.

Figure 1-13, on the other hand, shows how to change the default drive on a LAN from drive F to drive A and back to drive F. For practice, follow Figure 1-11, 1-12, or 1-13 to complete these appropriate two steps for your computer.

Notice that you use a **drive specifier** consisting of the colon (:) with a one-letter disk drive name. Whenever you refer to a specific disk drive, type the letter designating the drive followed by the colon, such as A:, B:, C:, or F:.

FIGURE 1-12 Changing the default drive on a two-diskette computer

Entering DOS Commands

Now that you have booted DOS, you can enter DOS commands. DOS includes a variety of commands, or instructions, to assist you in using the computer. Some commands might be called status, or informative, commands because they instruct DOS to give you information. Other commands direct DOS to perform functions for you. We show all DOS commands in capital letters for consistency. You can enter commands, drive names, and other entries to DOS, in any combination of uppercase and lowercase.

FIGURE 1-13 Changing the default drive using a LAN

ASSIGNING NAMES TO FILES

◆ A **data file** is a collection of data created by application programs and used by the programs. For instance, the data can be figures used for a spreadsheet showing sales revenues, names and addresses in a database file, or a word processing document announcing the arrival of a new employee. A **program file** contains instructions that the computer follows to perform its tasks. The program might be a DOS program or one of the application programs such as a word processing or spreadsheet program.

DOS identifies a file on a disk through the file specification for the file (Figure 1-14). A **file specification** lets DOS know exactly where to search for a file and gives its exact name. A DOS file specification has four parts: (1) the drive specifier, which you already know as A:, B:, C:, or F:; (2) a path specification (explained later in Project 2); (3) the filename; and (4) the extension.

NAME	LEGEND	DEFINITION
1. Drive specifier	d:	A drive specifier consists of the one-letter drive name and a colon. The drive name specifies the drive containing the file you are requesting. For example, A: is the drive specifier for disk drive A. If you omit the drive specifier, DOS assumes the file is located on the default drive.
2. Path specification	\path	A path is an optional reference to a subdirectory of files on the specified disk. A backslash (\) separates the drive specifier from the path. Paths are discussed in Project 2.
3. Filename	filename	A filename consists of one to eight characters.
4. Extension	ext	A filename can contain an optional extension of one to three characters. A period separates the filename and the extension.

FIGURE 1-14 The four parts to a DOS file specification

Filenames

You must assign a filename to every data and program file you place on disk so that you can later retrieve it using that filename. A **filename** consists of one to eight characters and is used by DOS to identify each file. You can use any combination of characters except: period (.), quotation mark ("), slash (/), backslash (\), brackets ([]), colon (:), broken vertical bar (|), less than (<), greater than (>), plus (+), equals (=), semicolon (;), comma (,), and space. DOS 5.0 also does not allow the question mark (?) and asterisk (*) in a filename.

In general, your filename should reflect the data stored in it. If your file contains employee records, for example, using the filename EMPLOYEE is more meaningful than using the filename FILE1, even though DOS will accept either filename.

Filename Extensions

A filename can also have an optional extension, which identifies a file more specifically or describes its purpose. An **extension** consists of one to three characters and is separated from the filename by a period. The same characters that are permitted for a filename are permitted for an extension. If you want to create a word processing document file containing a letter to Smith, for example, you could use the filename SMITH and the extension .DOC to identify the file as a document file. The entire name for the file would be SMITH.DOC. Many software packages automatically assign special extensions to the files they create.

INTERNAL AND EXTERNAL DOS COMMANDS

An **internal command** is part of DOS that is loaded into main memory when you boot. After you boot DOS, you can enter an internal command at the DOS prompt at any time. CLS, COPY, DEL, DIR, ERASE, and RENAME are examples of internal commands that you will use in Project 1.

External commands, are stored on the DOS disk as program files. They must be read from the DOS disk into main memory before they can be executed. This means that the DOS disk must be in the default drive or that you type the drive specifier so that the program can be found and loaded into main memory for execution. FORMAT and MORE are examples of external commands that you will use in Project 1.

All DOS external commands have the special extensions COM and EXE. Another special extension is BAT that is used for **DOS batch files** containing a series of DOS commands to be executed. Any DOS command with one of these three extensions (BAT, COM, and EXE) is an external command. To use external commands, simply type the filename (the extension is not required) with its required parameters and press the Enter key.

FORMAT COMMAND

You can buy disks that you can use immediately. Many disks, however, are blank and cannot be used until they have been formatted. You format a disk using the DOS **FORMAT** command. The **formatting** process establishes sectors on the disk and performs other functions that allow the disk to store data. Be careful when you select disks to use with the FORMAT command. *Formatting a disk destroys all the files previously stored on the disk.* You must be extremely careful, therefore, with the disks you format and how you type the FORMAT command. With a hard disk, take extra precaution to avoid losing files by formatting the hard disk accidentally. DOS versions 3.0 and later provide some protection against accidental formatting of a hard disk, but your own precautions are still the best insurance.

Disks vary by size and recording density, so your FORMAT command might differ from our description. If it does, your instructor will tell you what changes you need to make.

If you have a hard disk, the FORMAT program is stored on drive C, the hard disk. Be careful not to format drive C accidentally. To format a disk in drive A from a hard disk, type FORMAT A: at the C> prompt and press the Enter key (Figure 1-15).

FIGURE 1-15
Entering the FORMAT command from a hard disk

If you are using a LAN, the FORMAT program is stored on drive F, the server hard disk. To format a disk in drive A using a LAN, type FORMAT A: at the F> prompt and press the Enter key (Figure 1-16).

FIGURE 1-16
Entering the FORMAT command using a LAN

To format a disk on a two-diskette computer, place the DOS disk in drive A, making sure that drive A is the default drive. Type the command FORMAT B: and press the Enter key (Figure 1-17).

FIGURE 1-17
Entering the FORMAT command on a two-diskette computer

When you press the Enter key, DOS loads the FORMAT program into main memory and executes the program. If you are using a hard disk, a message appears on the screen instructing you to "Insert new diskette for drive A: and strike ENTER when ready" (Figure 1-18). [For DOS 5.0 Users – The message will be "Insert new diskette for drive A: and press Enter when ready...".]

FIGURE 1-18
FORMAT message for inserting a disk using a hard disk

The responses for a LAN and two-diskette computer are shown in Figures 1-19 and 1-20, respectively.

FIGURE 1-19
FORMAT message for inserting a disk using a LAN

FIGURE 1-20
FORMAT message for inserting a disk on a two-diskette computer

To complete the format process, place the disk to be formatted into the appropriate drive (drive A for a computer with a hard disk or on a LAN; drive B for a two-diskette computer) and press the Enter key. While formatting occurs, a message appears on the screen indicating that the process is underway. Figure 1-21 shows the message on a computer with a hard disk or on a LAN, and Figure 1-22 shows the message from a two-diskette computer. Messages will differ slightly depending on the version of DOS and the type of disk you are using.

FIGURE 1-21
Message appearing when formatting using a hard disk or LAN

FIGURE 1-22
Message appearing when formatting using a two-diskette computer

When the formatting process is complete, the messages shown in Figure 1-23 appear. [For DOS 5.0 Users – Your screen will show different messages.] The FORMAT program reports that the disk is formatted for a total number of bytes and that all bytes are available for storage. The next FORMAT program prompt asks you if you want to format another disk. If you do, type the letter Y and press the Enter key to continue the formatting process. If you do not, type the letter N and press the Enter key to end the FORMAT program.

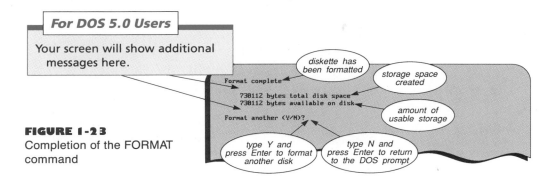

FIGURE 1-23
Completion of the FORMAT command

CLS COMMAND

◆ Frequently, as you issue several commands or perform lengthy processes, the screen becomes cluttered. To clear the screen and place the DOS prompt on the first line of the screen, you can use the **CLS** (Clear Screen) command. Type the letters CLS and press the Enter key to execute the Clear Screen command (Figure 1-24).

FIGURE 1-24
CLS (Clear Screen) command

COPY COMMAND

◆ Once you have formatted a disk, you are ready to use it to store data or program files. You can use the **COPY** command to copy a file to the same disk or a different disk. You would often use the COPY command to make *working* copies of program and data disks. Copying original files from one disk creates a second disk that you can use for everyday work to protect the original disk from damage. A similar use for the COPY command is to make a **backup copy** of a disk to guard against accidental loss of data. One frequently used technique is to make a backup copy of a file whenever you revise an existing file. In fact, some application programs create a backup file automatically, using the filename extension BAK or BAC to indicate a backup file.

Copying a File from One Disk to Another Disk

Let's practice using the COPY command by copying files from drive C to drive A. Check to see that you still have your formatted disk in drive A. If you are using a two-diskette computer, place your formatted disk in drive B, and place the Data Disk provided to instructors in drive A. In this latter case, you will copy files from drive A to drive B.

Let's begin by copying the file DOSNOTES.DOC from drive C to drive A. Your instructor will make the DOSNOTES.DOC file available to you or will give you the name of another file to copy. Type COPY C:DOSNOTES.DOC A:DOSNOTES.DOC and press the Enter key (Figure 1-25). Notice that after the word COPY you left one or more spaces, then stated the file specification of the file to be copied. In DOS terminology, this file is called the **source file**. DOS looks for a source file with a filename of DOSNOTES and an extension of DOC on drive C.

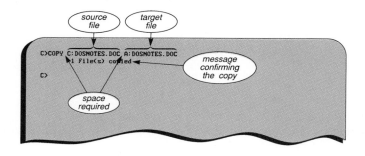

FIGURE 1-25
Copying a file to another disk

You leave one or more spaces after the source file. Then, you type the **target file**, which is the file specification of the file after it is copied. The drive specifier A: in Figure 1-25 indicates that the file is to be copied to a disk in drive A. The name of the file on drive A will be DOSNOTES.DOC. The message "1 File(s) copied" signals that the command is completed. You end up with a DOSNOTES.DOC file on both the disk in drive C and the disk in drive A.

When you copy a file from a disk in one drive to a disk in another drive, you can assign a new name to the target file. Let's copy the file DOSNOTES.DOC from drive C to the disk in drive A, giving the target file the name NOTECOPY.DUP on drive A. Type COPY C:DOSNOTES.DOC A:NOTECOPY.DUP and press the Enter key (Figure 1-26). You now have the two files with the names DOSNOTES.DOC and NOTECOPY.DUP on the disk in drive A.

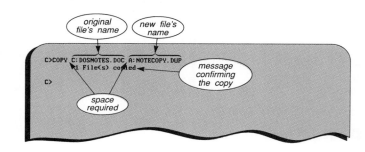

FIGURE 1-26
Coping a file to another disk
using a different name for the
target file

Copying a File to the Same Disk

You can copy a file to the same disk, but you must use a different name for the file. Let's copy the file named DOSNOTES.DOC stored on drive A onto the same disk. Give the filename DOSNOTES.BAK to the target file. Type the command COPY A:DOSNOTES.DOC A:DOSNOTES.BAK and press the Enter key (Figure 1-27).

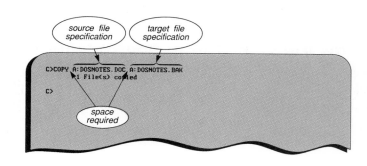

FIGURE 1-27
Copying a file to the same
disk

When the COPY command is executed, the file DOSNOTES.DOC in drive A is copied to the same disk in drive A under the name DOSNOTES.BAK. The two different extensions of DOC and BAK are used to distinguish between the files.

What would happen if you use the same file specification to designate both the source and target files? Let's try it and see. Type COPY A:DOSNOTES.DOC A:DOSNOTES.DOC and press the Enter key (Figure 1-28).

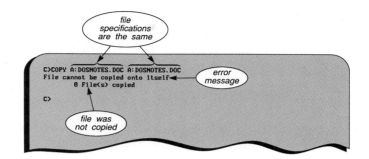

FIGURE I-28
Error in attempting to copy a
file onto itself

The messages "File cannot be copied onto itself" and "0 File(s) copied" indicate that DOS did not execute the COPY command. If you do want to make a copy of the source file, you have to reenter the COPY command using a different name for the target file.

ENTERING AND CORRECTING DOS COMMANDS

◆ Even if you are an expert typist, you will sometimes make mistakes when you enter DOS commands. Fortunately, DOS provides several keys to allow you to correct the mistakes you make.

For example, you might want to enter the command COPY C:DOSNOTES.DOC A:DOSNOTES.BAC. Instead, type COOY. Now press the Backspace key twice to delete the OY, leaving just the CO following the DOS prompt. Pressing the **Backspace** key deletes the character to the left of the cursor and moves the cursor left one position.

Next, type PU V:DOSNOTES.DOC A:DOSNOTES.BAC, but do not press the Enter key. You could press the Backspace key several times to delete all the characters you typed except the COP, which are the first three typed characters on the line. Instead, press the **Esc** key once. A backslash (\) appears at the end of the typed line, and the cursor advances to the next line (Figure 1-29). You are now back at the beginning of the line and can begin over again; this is the same result as if you had pressed the Backspace key thirty-four times.

FIGURE I-29
Using the Esc key

Let's now type COPY C:DOSNOTES.DOC A:DOSFILE.DOC and press the Enter key. You have just created a copy of the DOSNOTES.DOC file on drive C to drive A with a name for the target file of DOSFILE.DOC. Suppose you next want to recopy the same source file to drive A, but this time with a name of DOSFILE.BAK. Press the **F3** key once, and DOS automatically retypes the previous COPY command on the screen. Press the Backspace key three times, type BAK, and press the Enter key (on the next page in Figure 1-30). The F3 key retypes your previous command and is useful when you want to make minor changes at the end of your previous command.

FIGURE 1-30
Using the F3 key

DIRECTORY COMMAND (DIR)

◆ One of the functions of DOS is to store files containing programs and data on disks. To manage that file storage, DOS maintains a directory, or a list, of all the files stored on a disk. To display the directory of a disk, use the **DIR** command.

If you are using a hard disk or LAN, your disk should still be in drive A. Type DIR A: and press the Enter key. The directory of the disk in drive A displays as shown in Figure 1-31. [For DOS 5.0 Users – Your screen shows additional messages.]

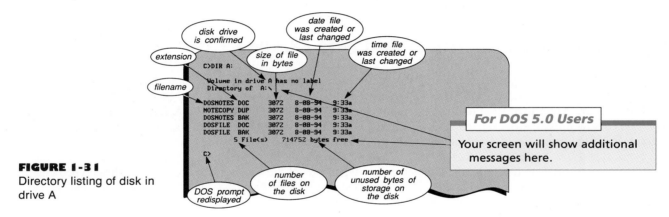

FIGURE 1-31
Directory listing of disk in
drive A

The directory itself consists of the filenames and extensions of the files on the disk, the number of bytes used to store each file on the disk, the file creation date or the date of the last change to each file, and the file creation time or the time of the last change to each file. The message at the end of the directory listing indicates the number of files on the disk (in Figure 1-31 there are five files on the disk) and the remaining space available on the disk (714752 unused bytes remain on the disk in Figure 1-31, but your number might differ if your disk has a different recording density). At the end of the directory listing, the DOS prompt reappears on the screen, indicating that DOS is ready for your next command.

RENAME COMMAND

◆ You use the **RENAME** command when you want to change the name of a file on a disk. For practice, let's change the filename NOTECOPY.DUP on drive A to NOTEFILE.DOC. Start by typing the command RENAME A:NOTECOPY.DUP NOTEFILE.DOC and pressing the Enter key (Figure 1-32). When you press the Enter key, the filename on the disk in drive A is changed from NOTECOPY.DUP to NOTEFILE.DOC. DOS does not display a message confirming a successful renaming of the file.

FIGURE 1-32
Changing the name of a file

You must be careful not to place a drive specifier on a file specification for the file's new name. Let's see what happens if you do. Type RENAME A:NOTEFILE.DOC A:NOTECOPY.DUP and press the Enter key (Figure 1-33). The message "Invalid parameter" appears because you typed the A: drive specifier for the new name for the file. DOS did not rename the file, so its name is still NOTEFILE.DOC.

FIGURE 1-33
Error when renaming a file
and using a drive specifier on
the new name for the file

If you attempt to change a file's name to a name already used by a file on the disk, DOS displays an error message and does not change the name. Let's demonstrate this. Type the command RENAME A:NOTEFILE.DOC DOSNOTES.DOC and press the Enter key (Figure 1-34). The message "Duplicate file name or File not found" indicates that DOS found a file already on the disk with a name of DOSNOTES.DOC, so DOS did not change the name of the file.

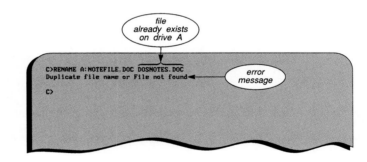

FIGURE 1-34
Error when renaming a file to
a name that already exists

DISPLAYING AND PRINTING FILES

◆ DOS allows you to display the contents of your files on the screen and to print screen images on your printer. You can use the MORE command to display files and the Print Screen key to print screen images.

MORE Command

You can use the **MORE** command to display the contents of a file on the screen. Because the MORE command is an external command, make sure you have the DOS diskette in drive A if you are using a two-diskette computer. For practice, let's display the contents of the file DOSNOTES.DOC located on drive A. Type `MORE <A:DOSNOTES.DOC` and press the Enter key (Figure 1-35); be certain that you type the less than symbol (<) immediately before A:DOSNOTES.DOC.

FIGURE 1-35

The MORE command to display a file's contents

After you press the Enter key, DOS displays the first full screen of lines from the file DOSNOTES.DOC (Figure 1-36). The message "-- More --" at the bottom of the screen indicates that more lines from the file remain to be displayed and that you should press any key to view the next screenful of lines from the file. Next, press any key to view the second screen of lines from the DOSNOTES.DOC file. DOS displays the second full screen of lines from the file, and the message "-- More --" again appears at the bottom of the screen. Once more press any key to display the next screen of lines from the file. This time you are returned to the DOS prompt, which indicates that you have viewed all the lines from the file.

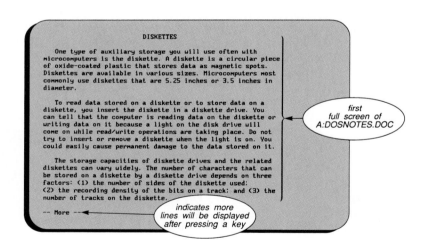

FIGURE 1-36

Display of a file using the MORE command

Print Screen

You can print the contents of the screen on the printer by using the **Print Screen** key (Shift-PrtSc on some keyboards). For practice, be sure your printer is turned on and that paper is inserted and properly aligned. Type MORE <A:DOSNOTES.DOC and press the Enter key. After the first full screen is displayed, press the Print Screen key. In response, DOS prints the contents of the screen on the printer. You can use the Print Screen key to generate a printed copy of any screen you want to study further or show to someone else.

ERASE AND DEL COMMANDS

◆ Because a disk has limited space for storing your files, you should periodically remove unneeded files from your disks to make room for new files. The **ERASE** command will erase, or remove, a file from a disk. An alternative command that functions like the ERASE command is the **DEL** (delete) command. Take care when using the ERASE or DEL command because you do not want to inadvertently remove a file you mean to keep.

Removing a File

Let's remove the file NOTEFILE.DOC from the disk in drive A. Type ERASE A:NOTEFILE.DOC and press the Enter key (Figure 1-37). You could also use the DEL command instead by typing DEL A:NOTEFILE.DOC and pressing the Enter key. DOS does not display a message confirming the file's removal. To be sure that DOS has removed the file from the disk, type DIR A: and press the Enter key (Figure 1-37). [For DOS 5.0 Users – Your screen will show additional messages.]

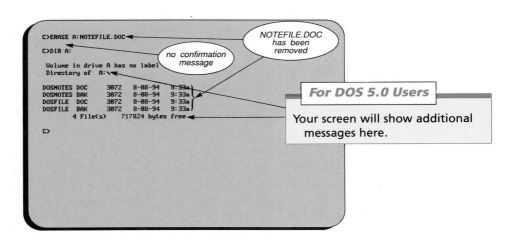

FIGURE 1-37
Removing a file from a disk

PROJECT SUMMARY

In Project 1 you learned how to boot DOS, name your files, and format disks using the FORMAT command. You also learned how to use these DOS commands to work with your files: COPY, CLS, DIR, RENAME, MORE, ERASE, and DEL. All the activities that you learned for this project are summarized in the Quick Reference following Project 2. The following is a summary of the keystroke sequence we used in Project 1.

SUMMARY OF KEYSTROKES — PROJECT 1

STEPS	KEY(S) PRESSED	RESULTS
1	Ctrl–Alt–Delete	Resets DOS.
2	10-9-94 ↵	Sets date.
3	11:50 ↵	Sets time.
4	A: ↵	Changes default drive.
5	C: ↵	Rechanges default drive.
6	FORMAT A: ↵	Formats a disk.
7	N↵	Returns to DOS after formatting.
8	CLS↵	Clears screen.
9	COPY C:DOSNOTES.DOC A:DOSNOTES.DOC ↵	Copies file.
10	COPY C:DOSNOTES.DOC A:NOTECOPY.DUP ↵	Copies file with new name.
11	COPY A:DOSNOTES.DOC A:DOSNOTES.BAK ↵	Copies file on same disk.
12	COPY A:DOSNOTES.DOC A:DOSNOTES.DOC ↵	Copies a file using erroneous same name.
13	COPY C:DOSNOTES.DOC A:DOSFILE.DOC ↵	Copies file.
14	F3 Backspace Backspace Backspace BAK ↵	Retypes command.
15	DIR A: ↵	Lists file directory.
16	RENAME A:NOTECOPY.DUP NOTEFILE.DOC	Changes file's name.
17	RENAME A:NOTEFILE.DOC A:NOTECOPY.DUP ↵	Renames with drive specifier error.
18	RENAME A:NOTEFILE.DOC DOSNOTES.DOC ↵	Renames with duplicate name error.
19	MORE <A:DOSNOTES.DOC ↵	Displays file contents.
20	Print Screen	Prints screen contents on printer. (Use Shift-PrtSc on some keyboards.)
21	ERASE A:NOTEFILE.DOC ↵	Removes file from disk.

The following list summarizes the material covered in Project 1.

1. An **operating system** is a collection of programs that controls and manages the operation of the computer.
2. The operating system known as **DOS**, an acronym for **Disk Operating System**, was developed by Microsoft Corporation. The operating system for an IBM Personal Computer is **PC-DOS**. Other compatible microcomputers use a similar operating system called **MS-DOS**.
3. The **version** number of DOS is the whole number and signifies a major improvement of the product. The **release** number is the decimal number and identifies minor changes or corrections to a version of the product.
4. **Upward compatibility** means that all the features of an earlier version and release of DOS remain supported by a later one.
5. A **drive name** is a unique one-letter name preassigned to each disk drive.
6. A **local area network**, or **LAN**, is a collection of connected computers that share data. The **server**, a special computer on a LAN, has a high-capacity hard disk that contains files that can be accessed from the other computers on the network.

7. **Booting** refers to the process of loading DOS from a disk into main memory.

8. A **cold start**, or **cold boot**, occurs when you turn on power to the computer and DOS boots from disk.

9. You can boot DOS without turning the power switch off and on by holding down the Ctrl and Alt keys and pressing the Delete key. This process is called a **warm start**, **warm boot**, or **reset**.

10. After DOS boots, you might be prompted to enter the date and time. Some computers have batteries that accurately maintain the date and time even when the computer power is off.

11. The **DOS prompt**, which typically consists of a drive name and a greater than (>) symbol, indicates that DOS is ready to receive your commands.

12. The **default drive**, or **current drive**, is the drive that DOS assumes contains the disk where programs and data are located. The default drive on a two-diskette computer is usually drive A. A computer with a hard disk generally uses drive C as its default drive. Drive F is usually the default drive on a LAN.

13. You can change the default drive by entering a valid drive specifier and pressing the Enter key. A **drive specifier** consists of the one-letter drive name, followed by a colon.

14. You can enter DOS commands in any combination of uppercase and lowercase letters.

15. A **data file** is a collection of data created by application programs and used by the programs. A **program file** contains instructions that the computer follows to perform its tasks.

16. A **file specification** lets DOS know exactly where to search for a file and gives its exact name. The file specification consists of a drive specifier, path specification, filename, and optional extension. Each **filename** is a one- to eight-character name, and each **extension** is a one- to three-character name; a period separates the filename and extension.

17. DOS has two types of commands: internal commands and external commands. **Internal commands** are a part of DOS that is loaded into main memory during booting and can be executed at any time. **External commands** are separate programs stored on the DOS disk, which must be available for the commands to execute. All DOS external commands have extensions of COM and EXE, while the BAT extension is used for **DOS batch files** containing a series of DOS commands to be executed.

18. Use the **FORMAT** command to prepare disks for storing data or program files. The **formatting** process establishes sectors on the disk and performs other functions that allow the disk to store data.

19. Use the **CLS** command to clear the screen and place the DOS prompt on the first line of the screen.

20. Use the **COPY** command to duplicate a file onto the same or another disk. Creating a working copy of a file helps protect the original file from damage. A **backup copy** of a file helps to guard against accidental loss of data.

21. A file to be copied is called the **source file**. The resulting copy is called the **target file**.

22. Use the **Backspace** key to delete the character to the left of the cursor and move the cursor one position to the left. The **Esc** key cancels the command you just typed. The **F3** key automatically retypes your previous command on the screen.

23. Enter the **DIR**, or directory, command to list the files on a disk.

24. Use the **RENAME** command to change a file's name.

25. Use the **MORE** command to display the contents of a file on the screen, one full screen at a time.

26. Press the **Print Screen** key (Shift-PrtSc on some keyboards) to print the screen's contents on the printer.

27. To remove a file from a disk, use either the **ERASE** or the **DEL** command.

STUDENT ASSIGNMENTS

STUDENT ASSIGNMENT 1: True/False

Instructions: Circle T if the statement is true and F if the statement is false.

T F   1. DOS is an example of application software.

T F   2. IBM developed DOS for use in IBM PCs.

T F   3. The DOS version number identifies minor changes or corrections to a release.

T F   4. The server hard disk on a LAN is usually drive C.

Student Assignment 1 (continued)

T F   5. During a cold start the computer first runs tests to diagnose its own circuitry.
T F   6. To begin a warm boot you hold down the Ctrl and Alt keys, press the Reset key, and then release all three keys.
T F   7. All computers require you to enter the date and time.
T F   8. The FORMAT command is an example of a DOS prompt.
T F   9. To change the default disk drive assignment to drive B, type B: and press the Enter key.
T F 10. All DOS commands must be entered in uppercase characters.
T F 11. A > is an example of a drive specifier.
T F 12. A DOS file specification can contain a filename of one to eight characters and an extension of one to three characters.
T F 13. Internal commands and external commands are the two types of DOS commands.
T F 14. The FORMAT command is an external command.
T F 15. If you are using a hard disk, you can format a diskette by entering the command FORMAT C:.
T F 16. More than one diskette can be formatted with one FORMAT command.
T F 17. To display a list of files stored on a disk, you must enter the CLS command.
T F 18. You use the Esc key to automatically retype your previous DOS command.
T F 19. The DIR command displays the remaining space available on the disk.
T F 20. When you use the RENAME command, you must enter the drive specifier as part of the file specification for the file's new name.
T F 21. The MORE command displays a file one screen at a time.
T F 22. The ERASE command can be used to remove a file from a disk.

STUDENT ASSIGNMENT 2: Multiple Choice

Instructions: Circle the correct response.

1. DOS was developed by _____.
   a. Disk Operating Systems
   b. IBM
   c. LAN
   d. Microsoft
2. The 3 in DOS 3.2 refers to the _____.
   a. default
   b. release
   c. version
   d. prompt
3. The symbol C> _____.
   a. is called the DOS prompt
   b. indicates the name of a program
   c. indicates the default disk drive
   d. both a and c
4. A file specification consists of all the following except the _____.
   a. extension
   b. drive specifier
   c. prompt
   d. filename
5. Examples of special DOS extensions are _____.
   a. BAT, COM, and EXE
   b. BAT, COM, and DOC
   c. BAT, DOC, and EXE
   d. COM, DOC, and EXE

6. The _____ command establishes sectors on a disk and performs other functions that allow the disk to store files.
   a. MORE
   b. DIR
   c. CLS
   d. FORMAT

7. Listing the files on a disk is accomplished by _____.
   a. typing MORE and pressing the Enter key
   b. typing LIST and pressing the Enter key
   c. typing DIR and pressing the Enter key
   d. typing DISPLAY and pressing the Enter key

8. To change the name of a file from FILEX.DOC to FILEA.DOC, type _____.
   a. ALTER FILEX.DOC FILEA.DOC
   b. ASSIGN FILEX.DOC FILEA.DOC
   c. CHANGE FILEX.DOC FILEA.DOC
   d. RENAME FILEX.DOC FILEA.DOC

9. To remove the file THISFILE.BAK from a disk, type _____.
   a. REMOVE THISFILE.BAK
   b. DEL THISFILE.BAK
   c. ERASE THISFILE.BAK
   d. either b or c

STUDENT ASSIGNMENT 3: Fill in the Blanks

Instructions: Fill in the blanks in the following sentences.

1. A(n) _____ is a collection of programs that controls and manages the operation of the computer.
2. Microsoft Corporation developed the operating system known as _____.
3. A(n) _____ is a unique one-letter name preassigned to a disk drive.
4. The _____ on a LAN has a high-capacity hard disk that contains files that you can access from your computer.
5. To change the default drive, you type the letter of the new drive to be used, followed by a _____.
6. In a file specification, C: is an example of a _____.
7. In a file specification, the _____ is optional and consists of one to three characters.
8. The _____ command establishes sectors on a disk and performs other functions that allow the disk to store data.
9. The _____ is the file specification of a file after it is copied.
10. The _____ key retypes your previous DOS command.
11. Use the _____ command to list the files stored on a disk.
12. Use the _____ command to change the name of a file on a disk.
13. Use the _____ command to display the contents of a file on the screen.
14. The _____ key prints the contents of the screen on the printer.

STUDENT ASSIGNMENT 4: Using DOS Commands

Instructions: Explain how to accomplish each of the following tasks using DOS.

Problem 1: Prepare a diskette using the FORMAT command and determine the amount of free space remaining on the disk.

Explanation: _____

_____

_____

_____

Student Assignment 4 (continued)

Problem 2: List the files stored on the disk in drive A and determine the name of the most recently created or changed file.
Explanation: _____

_____

_____

_____

Problem 3: Create a backup copy on the default drive of the file DOCUMENT.IT using an extension of BAK and the same filename.
Explanation: _____

_____

_____

_____

Problem 4: Change the name of the file THISFILE.DUP to THATFILE.DOC on drive B.
Explanation: _____

_____

_____

_____

Problem 5: Print the current contents of the screen on the printer.
Explanation: _____

_____

_____

_____

Problem 6: Remove the file LETTER.DOC from the disk located in drive A.
Explanation: _____

_____

_____

_____

STUDENT ASSIGNMENT 5: Understanding DOS Options

Instructions: Explain what will happen after you perform each of the following DOS commands.

Problem 1: Type FORMAT A: at the C> prompt and press the Enter key.
Explanation: _____

_____

_____

Problem 2: Type DIR B: at the A> prompt and press the Enter key.
Explanation: _____

_____

_____

Problem 3: Type RENAME A:OLDFILE.ABC NEWFILE.XYZ at the A> prompt and press the Enter key.
Explanation: _____

_____

_____

Problem 4: Type MORE <A:DOSNOTES.DOC at the C> prompt and press the Enter key.
Explanation: _____

_____

_____

STUDENT ASSIGNMENT 6: Recovering from Problems

Instructions: In each of the following situations, a problem occurred. Explain the cause of the problem and how it can be corrected.

Problem 1: You started your two-diskette computer without a disk in drive A and a message appears that you don't recognize.
Cause of problem: _____

_____

Method of correction: _____

_____

Problem 2: When DOS instructs you to "Enter new date (mm-dd-yy):", you type 6\14\94, press the Enter key, and receive an "Invalid date" message from DOS.
Cause of problem: _____

_____

Method of correction: _____

_____

Problem 3: The default drive is drive A and you type B and press the Enter key to change the default drive. DOS responds with the message "Bad command or file name".
Cause of problem: _____

_____

Method of correction: _____

_____

Problem 4: You type COPY A:DOSNOTES.DOC A:MY FILE.DOC at the A> prompt and press the Enter key. DOS responds with the message "Invalid number of parameters".
Cause of problem: _____

_____

Method of correction: _____

_____

Problem 5: You type RENAME A:OLDFILE.BAK B:NEWFILE.NEW at the A> prompt and press the Enter key. DOS responds with the message "Invalid parameter".
Cause of problem: _____

_____

Student Assignment 6 (continued)

Method of correction: _____

_____

Problem 6: You type MORE A:NOTECOPY.OLD and press the Enter key. The cursor moves down the screen a few lines, but nothing is displayed on the screen, not even the DOS prompt.
Cause of problem: _____

_____

Method of correction: _____

_____

STUDENT ASSIGNMENT 7: Creating a Working Disk Copy

Instructions: At the DOS prompt perform the following tasks to create a working disk copy of the files you created in Project 1.

1. Format a new disk.
2. The disk on which you placed files in Project 1 should now contain four files. Copy these files onto your newly formatted disk.
3. Verify that both disks contain the same files.

STUDENT ASSIGNMENT 8: Booting DOS

Instructions: Perform the following tasks on the computer you used to complete Project 1.

1. If the computer is not on a LAN:
   a. Perform a cold boot.
   b. Perform a warm boot.
2. If the computer is on a LAN:
   a. Find out from your instructor if you are allowed to perform a cold boot. If so, perform a cold boot.
   b. Find out from your instructor if you are allowed to perform a warm boot. If so, perform a warm boot.

Managing and Organizing Files on Disks

PROJECT

DOS

OBJECTIVES

You will have mastered the material in this project when you can:

◆ Create subdirectories
◆ Change the current directory
◆ Change the DOS prompt
◆ Specify a path
◆ Use wildcard characters with DOS commands
◆ Copy all files from one diskette to another
◆ List a disk directory, using /P and /W
◆ Remove subdirectories
◆ Check the status of a disk
◆ Recognize common DOS error messages

In Project 1 you learned to boot DOS, assign names to files, and format disks. You also worked with files on disk by copying, listing, renaming, displaying, and removing files. In this project you will examine the COPY and DIR commands in greater detail, especially their use when working with a large number of files. You will also learn new topics in this project that will teach you how to organize your files by application or use and how to check the status of your disks and of main memory. Finally, we present a list of the common DOS error messages you might encounter.

THE ROOT DIRECTORY AND SUBDIRECTORIES

◆ Let's first further examine the file directory displayed by the DIR command. We will again assume you are using a hard disk and one diskette drive with the drive names C and A, respectively. If you are using a different disk configuration, check with your instructor for the changes you should make in Project 2.

Insert the disk you used in Project 1 in drive A. At the DOS prompt of C>, type DIR A: and press the Enter key (Figure 2-1). [For DOS 5.0 Users – Your screen will show additional messages.] The four files on the disk in drive A displayed by the DIR command are those you placed there during Project 1.

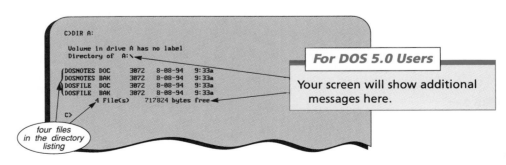

FIGURE 2-1
Directory listing of disk in drive A

Root Directory

When you need to view your files on a disk, the computer does not actually read the entire disk looking for the files. Instead, it searches the file directory, which is an index of the files on the disk. This index, created when the disk is formatted, is a special file directory called the **root directory**. As an index, the root directory contains not only the information displayed by the DIR command, but also the physical locations of the files on the disk (Figure 2-2). [For DOS 5.0 Users – Your screen will show additional messages.]

FIGURE 2-2 Directory listing of disk in drive A and the root directory and its files

The root directory on a disk is limited in size. For example, a hard disk allows for up to 512 entries, while a 360KB diskette has room for 112 entries, and 1.2MB and 1.44MB diskettes hold 224 entries. This capacity might be sufficient on a diskette, but a hard disk with many millions of bytes of storage will likely have more files than can be stored in a single directory.

If you had a few hundred file entries in the root directory, you would have difficulty managing your disk files. Imagine scanning a directory listing of several hundred files to find the names of files you created months ago. It would be better if you could somehow divide your files into smaller logical groups — for example, all school documents together, all word processing personal letters together, and all spreadsheets together. DOS also takes longer to find a file you request when you have a larger number of files. Fortunately, DOS subdirectories allow you to create these smaller groups of files.

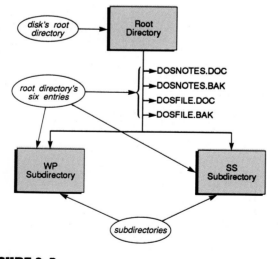

FIGURE 2-3
Root directory and the WP and SS subdirectories

Subdirectories

A **subdirectory** is a directory that you create on a disk. When you create a subdirectory, DOS places the subdirectory name in the root directory as one of its entries. You can subsequently place file entries either in the subdirectory or the root directory. Unlike the root directory, the number of files in a subdirectory is limited only by the amount of storage available on the disk. DOS users commonly refer to both the root directory and all subdirectories as directories, because a subdirectory is simply a directory within a directory by definition.

Let's assume we create two new subdirectories named WP, where we will place our word processing files, and SS, where we will place our spreadsheet files (Figure 2-3). The root directory would then contain six entries: the four files we placed there in Project 1, and the WP and SS subdirectories.

At a later time we might want to divide our WP subdirectory into two subdirectories: one for word processing program files, and the other for word processing data files. Since subdirectories themselves can have subdirectory entries, we could add a WPDOCS subdirectory to the WP subdirectory index (Figure 2-4).

MD COMMAND TO CREATE SUBDIRECTORIES

◆ You use the **MKDIR** command, usually abbreviated **MD**, to create a subdirectory. Let's create a subdirectory named DOS2 on your disk in drive A. Type MD A:\DOS2 and press the Enter key (Figure 2-5). [For DOS 5.0 Users – Your screen will show additional messages.] To see the DOS2 subdirectory entry in the root directory, next type DIR A: and press the Enter key. Notice in Figure 2-5 that the root directory now contains five files. The new fifth file is actually the DOS2 subdirectory and is identified as such by the "<DIR>" label in the directory listing.

FIGURE 2-4 Root directory and the WP, SS, and WPDOCS subdirectories

FIGURE 2-5 Root directory after creating the DOS2 subdirectory

When you use the MD command, you must follow four rules:

1. Start a subdirectory entry with the drive specifier. If the subdirectory is to be on drive A, for example, use A: to identify that drive. You can omit the drive specifier if you are creating the subdirectory on the default drive.
2. Following the drive specifier, type a backslash (\) character. In Figure 2-5 the message "Directory of A:\" indicates the root directory because the backslash alone following the drive specifier designates the root directory. When you typed MD A:\DOS2, you told DOS you wanted to create a subdirectory named DOS2 in the root directory of \ on drive A.
3. The subdirectory name, like any filename, can contain one to eight characters, followed optionally by a period and one to three characters for an extension. Subdirectory names, however, do not generally include extensions.
4. You can assign a subdirectory to an existing subdirectory.

Let's create a subdirectory named DOS2SUB and make it subordinate to the DOS2 subdirectory. Type MD A:\DOS2\DOS2SUB and press the Enter key (Figure 2-6). Just as A:\ identifies the root directory, A:\DOS2\ identifies the DOS2 subdirectory. This MD command, therefore, tells DOS to place the DOS2SUB subdirectory in the index for the DOS2 subdirectory.

FIGURE 2-6
Creating the DOS2SUB subdirectory subordinate to the DOS2 subdirectory

Next, type DIR A:\, which is an equivalent way of typing DIR A:, and press the Enter key (Figure 2-7). [For DOS 5.0 Users – Your screen will show additional messages.]

FIGURE 2-7
Directory listing of root directory after creating the DOS2 and DOS2SUB subdirectories

Notice that the directory listing for the root directory does not contain the DOS2SUB subdirectory. Something has happened, however, because the number of bytes free has changed from 716,800 to 715,776, which can be seen by comparing Figures 2-5 and 2-7. To see the entry for the DOS2SUB subdirectory, we need to view the directory listing for the DOS2 subdirectory.

To produce a directory listing for DOS2, type DIR A:\DOS2 and press the Enter key (Figure 2-8). [For DOS 5.0 Users – Your screen will show additional messages.] DOS displays the message "Directory of A:\DOS2" to tell you which directory it is listing. DOS lists the DOS2SUB subdirectory as an entry in the DOS2 index, but DOS also lists two other entries and labels them as directories: the . entry (pronounced dot), and the .. entry (pronounced dot-dot). The **dot** index entry refers to subdirectory DOS2 itself, and the **dot-dot** index entry refers to the root directory, which is the parent directory of DOS2, or the directory one level up from the DOS2 subdirectory.

FIGURE 2-8
Directory listing of DOS2 subdirectory

CD COMMAND TO CHANGE DIRECTORIES

◆ You use the **CHDIR** command, usually abbreviated **CD**, to move from one directory to another. Let's change from the root directory on drive A to the DOS2 subdirectory. Type CD A:\DOS2 and press the Enter key (Figure 2-9).

FIGURE 2-9
Changing from root directory to DOS2 subdirectory

DOS does not display a confirmation message that it changed the directory to DOS2. Now, type DIR A: and press the Enter key, and DOS lists the DOS2 directory for you (Figure 2-10). [For DOS 5.0 Users – Your screen will show additional messages.]

FIGURE 2-10
Directory listing of DOS2 subdirectory

The Current Directory

Just as there is a default, or current, disk drive, there is a current directory for each drive. The **current directory** for a drive is the directory on that drive in which you are currently working; that is, DOS looks by default for files on a drive in the current directory for that drive. When you first access a disk, the root directory is the current directory. You can, however, use the CD command to direct DOS to a subdirectory, which then becomes the current directory for that disk. Even if another drive is the default drive, your selected subdirectory remains the current directory for that drive until you change it to another directory. Drive C, for example, is our default drive, and the DOS2 subdirectory is the current directory on drive A. Whenever we access drive A, therefore, DOS looks at the DOS2 subdirectory.

So far we have used drive C as the default drive. Let's change the default drive to A; type A: and press the Enter key (Figure 2-11).

FIGURE 2-11
Changing default drive from
C to A

Notice that the DOS prompt has changed from C> to A>, which is the same prompt we would see if we were in the root directory on the A drive instead of the DOS2 subdirectory. Wouldn't it be better if DOS could somehow let us know what the current directory is for the drive?

PROMPT Command

You can use the **PROMPT** command to display the current directory on the default drive. Let's use the PROMPT command to change the DOS prompt; type PROMPT PG and press the Enter key (Figure 2-12).

FIGURE 2-12
Changing the DOS prompt

The DOS prompt has changed from A> to A:\DOS2>. We now not only know that the default drive is A, but also that the current directory on drive A is DOS2. The PROMPT command **$P parameter** tells DOS to display the current directory as part of the DOS prompt, and the **$G parameter** tells DOS to display the > symbol as part of the DOS prompt. If you have been using a LAN, you might have been seeing this form of the DOS prompt all along because most installations use this form of the PROMPT command throughout their networks when they boot their computers. You can revert back to the A> prompt by entering the PROMPT command without parameters.

Let's further practice with the PROMPT command and with changing drives and directories. We will change the default drive to C and then back to A, change the DOS prompt to A> and then back to A:\DOS2>, change to the DOS2SUB directory and produce a directory listing for it, and then change back to the DOS2 subdirectory and produce a directory listing for it. The required commands are shown in Figures 2-13 and 2-14. [For DOS 5.0 Users – Your screen will show additional messages.]

First, let's change the default drive from A to C and back again to A. Type C: and press the Enter key to change the default drive to C (Figure 2-13). The C:\> prompt indicates that you are now in the root directory on drive C. Next, type A: and press the Enter key to change the default drive back to A (Figure 2-13). The A:\DOS2> prompt tells you that you are in the DOS2 directory on drive A.

FIGURE 2-13
Changing default drives, DOS prompt, and current directories

Now, let's practice changing the DOS prompt. Type PROMPT and press the Enter key to change to the default DOS prompt of A> (Figure 2-13). Change back to the A:\DOS2> prompt by typing PROMPT PG and pressing the Enter key (Figure 2-13).

To change to the DOS2SUB directory, we could enter CD A:\DOS2\DOS2SUB, which is similar in syntax to the way we previously changed to the DOS2 directory. Because the default drive is now A, however, we do not need to enter the A:. Furthermore, because DOS2 is now the current directory on drive A, we can change to a subdirectory of DOS2 without entering the \DOS2. Consequently, type CD DOS2SUB and press the Enter key (Figure 2-13). The DOS prompt is now A:\DOS2\DOS2SUB>, which indicates that we have successfully changed to the DOS2SUB directory.

To list the files in the DOS2SUB directory, type DIR A: and press the Enter key (Figure 2-13). Once again we could have entered DIR A:\DOS2\DOS2SUB to request the directory listing, but did not need to do this because the default drive is A and the current directory on drive A is DOS2SUB. Notice that the DOS2SUB directory shows only the dot and dot-dot entries because we have not yet placed any files or subdirectories there.

To change back to the DOS2 directory, we could enter CD A:\DOS2. Instead, type CD . . and press the Enter key (Figure 2-14). The A:\DOS2> prompt indicates we successfully changed to the DOS2 directory. Recall that earlier we said that the dot-dot entry refers to the parent directory, or the directory that is one level up from the current subdirectory. In this case, DOS2 is the parent directory, so your CD command asked DOS to change from the DOS2SUB directory to the DOS2 directory.

FIGURE 2-14
Changing current directory

Finally, type DIR A: and press the Enter key to list the DOS2 directory (Figure 2-14).

SPECIFYING A PATH TO DIRECTORIES AND FILES

◆   When you use subdirectories you must learn to specify the path to a file. The **path** includes three components: (1) the drive specifier, (2) the name of the directory and the directories above it, and (3) the name of the file. The path specifies the route DOS is to take from the root directory through subdirectories leading to the file. You should specify the path whenever you want to access a file using the COPY, RENAME, ERASE, and other commands. Unless you specify the complete path, DOS might not find the file you want because it would search only the current directory of the default drive.

One way to specify the path is to include it in the command you are using. For example, let's copy the file DOSNOTES.DOC in the root directory of drive A to the DOS2 directory, using the same name for the target file. Type COPY A:\DOSNOTES.DOC A:\DOS2 and press the Enter key (Figure 2-15).

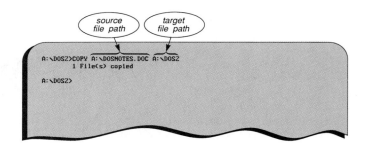

FIGURE 2-15
Specifying the path

Notice that the paths for both the source and target files have the drive specifier of A:. You also supplied the directory names of \ for the source file and \DOS2 for the target file. You entered the full name for the source file of DOSNOTES.DOC, but you did not enter the name for the target file. When you omit the filename and extension for a target file, DOS uses the filename and extension of the source file as the default. The file DOSNOTES.DOC now is in both the root and DOS2 directories.

Now you will remove the file DOSNOTES.DOC you just copied to the DOS2 directory, making sure you use the DIR command both before and after the ERASE command to verify the results of your work. Type DIR A: and press the Enter key; next, type ERASE DOSNOTES.DOC and press the Enter key; and finally, type DIR and press the Enter key (Figure 2-16). [For DOS 5.0 Users – Your screen will show additional messages.]

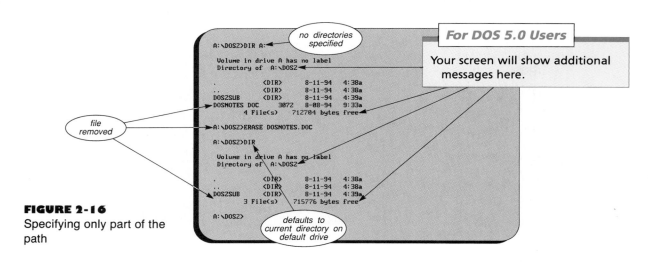

FIGURE 2-16
Specifying only part of the path

DIR A: is equivalent to DIR A:\DOS2 because DOS2 is the current directory on drive A. DIR is also equivalent to these other two forms of the DIR command because drive A is the default drive. Finally, you were able to use ERASE DOSNOTES.DOC instead of ERASE A:\DOS2\DOSNOTES.DOC because drive A is the default drive and DOS2 is the current directory on the default drive.

WILDCARD CHARACTERS

◆   You can access more than one file at a time when you use DOS commands such as COPY, RENAME, ERASE, and DEL. The wildcard characters of the asterisk (*) and the question mark (?) provide you with this multiple-file capability. You use a **wildcard character** in the file specification of a DOS command as a substitute for other characters. The asterisk represents one or more characters, whereas the question mark represents a single character.

The * Wildcard

You use the **asterisk** (*) wildcard character to represent one or more characters in a file's name. You can use the asterisk once in a filename and once in an extension. Wherever the asterisk appears, any character can occupy that position and all the remaining positions in the filename or the extension.

Let's illustrate the use of the wildcard asterisk by copying all the files from one directory to another directory. Check to be certain that your instructor has placed the DOS2 directory on your drive C hard disk. This directory contains 27 files that you will copy to the DOS2SUB subdirectory on drive A using a single COPY command. Type COPY C:\DOS2*.* A:\DOS2\DOS2SUB (Figure 2-17) and press the Enter key.

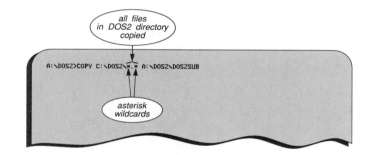

FIGURE 2-17
Copying using the * wildcard
character

DOS lists the name of each source file as it makes the copy. The message "27 File(s) copied" is your final confirmation that DOS successfully copied all the files (Figure 2-18).

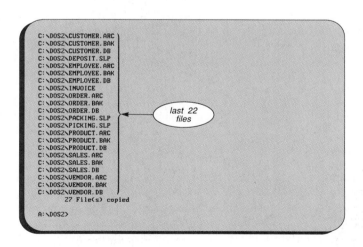

FIGURE 2-18
Copying 27 files with one
COPY command

You can use the asterisk wildcard for just the filename portion or the extension portion of the file specification. DOS just copied three files with extensions of SLP to the DOS2SUB directory on drive A. Let's copy these three files to the DOS2 directory. Type COPY A:\DOS2\DOS2SUB*.SLP and press the Enter key (Figure 2-19). The asterisk for the filename asked DOS to copy any filename with an SLP extension in the DOS2SUB directory on drive A. Notice that you did not enter any target information, so all files were copied to the current directory of DOS2 on the default drive of A.

FIGURE 2-19
Using a wildcard filename and an extension of SLP to copy multiple files

DEPOSIT.SLP, PACKING.SLP, and PICKING.SLP are the three files you just copied to the DOS2 directory. Let's remove the last two files; type ERASE P*.SLP and press the Enter key (Figure 2-20). Then type DIR and press the Enter key to verify that only the DEPOSIT.SLP file remains (Figure 2-20). [For DOS 5.0 Users – Your screen will show additional messages.]

FIGURE 2-20
Using a wildcard filename to remove multiple files

The P*.SLP used in the ERASE command asked DOS to remove any file in the current directory of DOS2 on the default drive A whose extension is SLP and whose filename starts with the letter P.

The ? Wildcard

You use the **question mark (?)** wildcard character to represent any character occupying the position in which the wildcard character appears. Whereas the asterisk wildcard can represent one or more characters, the question mark wildcard represents only a single character replacement. You can use a single question mark or several in a command to identify files.

To use the question mark wildcard, type COPY A:\DOS2\DOS2SUB\P?CKING.SLP and press the Enter key (Figure 2-21).

FIGURE 2-21
Using the ? wildcard to copy
multiple files

The two files of PACKING.SLP and PICKING.SLP met the model of the command and were copied to the DOS2 directory. Each has an extension of SLP, begins with the letter P, and has CKING in its third through seventh positions. Any character in the second position of the filename was allowed.

DIR COMMAND WITH A LARGE NUMBER OF FILES

Many directories contains many more files than can be displayed on the screen with the standard DIR command. For example, let's change to the DOS2SUB directory on drive A and produce its directory listing. Type CD DOS2SUB, press the Enter key, type DIR (Figure 2-22), and press the Enter key.

FIGURE 2-22
Changing directories and
entering the DIR command

Notice that the first few files scroll off the screen, and you can view only the last screenful of files (Figure 2-23).

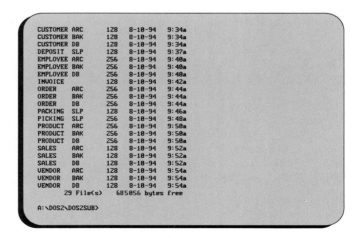

FIGURE 2-23
Last screen of DIR listing

The DIR command has two options to help in displaying large numbers of files. The first is the pause option and the second is the wide display option.

DIR Pause (/P) Option

The **DIR /P** command displays one screenful of files at a time and awaits your signal to show the next screenful. Try this option; type DIR /P (Figure 2-24) and press the Enter key.

FIGURE 2-24
Directory pause option

DOS lists the first screenful of files and pauses after displaying the message "Strike a key when ready . . ." at the the bottom of the screen (Figure 2-25). [For DOS 5.0 Users – Your screen will show a different message.]

FIGURE 2-25
First page of directory pause
option

When you are ready to view the next screenful of files, simply press any key (Figure 2-26). [For DOS 5.0 Users – Your screen will show additional messages.]

FIGURE 2-26
Last page of directory pause
option

DIR Wide Display (/W) Option

The **DIR /W** command displays the directory information in a wide format to allow more files to fit on the screen. To try this option, type DIR /W and press the Enter key (Figure 2-27). [For DOS 5.0 Users – Your screen will show additional messages.] Notice that only the file and extension names appear; the size, time, and date of the files are not listed.

For DOS 5.0 Users
Your screen will show additional messages here.

```
A:\DOS2\DOS2SUB>DIR /W

.                   ..                  AGING    RPT    BILLING  DOC    BUDGET   BAK
BUDGET   RPT    CREDIT   MEM    CUSTOMER ARC    CUSTOMER BAK    CUSTOMER DB
DEPOSIT  SLP    EMPLOYEE ARC    EMPLOYEE BAK    EMPLOYEE DB     INVOICE
ORDER    ARC    ORDER    BAK    ORDER    DB     PACKING  SLP    PICKING  SLP
PRODUCT  ARC    PRODUCT  BAK    PRODUCT  DB     SALES    ARC    SALES    BAK
SALES    DB     VENDOR   ARC    VENDOR   BAK    VENDOR   DB
          29 File(s)    685056 bytes free

A:\DOS2\DOS2SUB>
```

FIGURE 2-27
Directory wide display option

RD COMMAND TO REMOVE SUBDIRECTORIES

When you no longer need a subdirectory, you can remove, or delete, it. You use the **RMDIR** command, abbreviated **RD**, to remove a subdirectory from a disk.

Before you can remove a subdirectory, you must first remove all the files stored within it. This is a precaution that DOS takes to prevent your accidental removal of a directory containing files you need to keep. You can remove all the files by using the asterisk wildcard with the ERASE or DEL commands. You can issue this command from the subdirectory to be removed or from another directory if you give the full path. If you issue the command from another directory, make certain to use the correct subdirectory and path information or you might accidentally erase files from another part of the disk.

For practice, let's remove the DOS2SUB subdirectory. First, change to the DOS2 subdirectory and remove all files in the DOS2SUB subdirectory; type CD .. and press the Enter key. Next, type DEL A:\DOS2\DOS2SUB*.* and press the Enter key (Figure 2-28). In response to the message "Are you sure (Y/N)?", type the letter Y and press the Enter key.

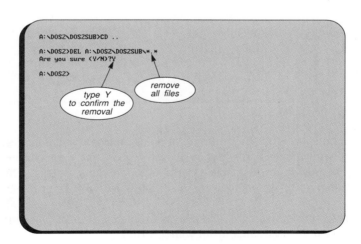

```
A:\DOS2\DOS2SUB>CD ..

A:\DOS2>DEL A:\DOS2\DOS2SUB\*.*
Are you sure (Y/N)?Y

A:\DOS2>
```

type Y to confirm the removal

remove all files

FIGURE 2-28
Removing all files from a directory

Now that you have removed all the files from the DOS2SUB subdirectory, you can also remove the subdirectory. To do this, type RD DOS2SUB and press the Enter key (Figure 2-29). No confirmation message appears, so you should use the DIR command to verify the removal of the subdirectory.

FIGURE 2-29
Removing the DOS2SUB
directory

CHKDSK Command

Another useful command is the **CHKDSK** command, which checks the condition of your disk and reports the status of main memory to you. Because the CHKDSK command is an external command, you should change the default drive to C before you enter the command. To practice with the CHKDSK command, type C:, press the Enter key, type CHKDSK A:, and press the Enter key (Figure 2-30). [For DOS 5.0 Users – Your screen will show additional messages.]

FIGURE 2-30
CHKDSK command listing

The CHKDSK command displays four lines of disk summary information. These lines indicate how many bytes can be stored on the disk, how much of this disk space is used by how many directories, how much of this disk space is used by how many files, and how much disk space is available for future storage. The CHKDSK command also reports how much main memory you have on your computer and how much is available, or free, for use by your programs.

If the CHKDSK command checks your disk and detects problems, it displays diagnostic messages instead of the status displays. If this occurs, ask for assistance from your instructor.

COMMON DOS ERROR MESSAGES

◆ When you make a mistake entering a command, DOS displays an error message that attempts to describe your specific mistake. You probably will not encounter most of the hundreds of different possible DOS error messages, but you are likely to see several of the common ones. You should refer to the DOS reference manual for a complete list of error messages and their explanations. In many cases a DOS error occurs because of a typing mistake, so your first means of correcting an error is to carefully verify the entire command you entered. The following is a list of the error messages you are likely to encounter and what each means.

ERROR MESSAGE	EXPLANATION
Bad command or file name	You used the wrong drive, path, or filename for the DOS command or application program.
Duplicate file name or File not found	You used the RENAME command and either the target filename already exists on the disk or the source filename could not be found.
Error reading drive	You do not have a diskette in the drive.
File allocation table bad	The disk might be defective and you might have to reformat it.
File cannot be copied onto itself	You used the same drive, path, and filename for both the source and target files.
File not found	You used the wrong drive, path, or filename.
Format failure	The disk you are attempting to FORMAT might be defective and unusable.
General failure	Your disk is not formatted or is not correctly inserted in the drive.
Insufficient disk space	Your disk does not have enough space to store the file.
Insufficient memory	You do not have enough usable main memory on your computer to execute the DOS command or application program.
Invalid date	You entered an invalid date.
Invalid filename or file not found	You tried to rename a file that could not be found.
Invalid number of parameters	You specified too few or too many options for the command.
Invalid parameter	You used an incorrect option for the command.
Invalid path or file name	You used an incorrect path or filename in your command.
Path not found	You entered a path that does not exist.
Program too big to fit in memory	You do not have enough usable main memory on your computer to execute the DOS command or application program.
Syntax error	Your DOS command is improperly typed.
Track 0 bad - Invalid media	You have a double-density disk in a high-density drive and entered the wrong FORMAT command.

PROJECT SUMMARY

In Project 2 you learned how to create, change, and remove subdirectories; change the current directory and specify the path; use the PROMPT and CHKDSK commands; use wildcard characters in commands; and use further options of the DIR command. All the activities that you learned for this project are summarized in the Quick Reference following Project 2.

The following is a summary of the keystroke sequence we used in Project 2.

SUMMARY OF KEYSTROKES — PROJECT 2

STEPS	KEY(S) PRESSED	RESULTS
1	DIR A: ↵	Lists file directory.
2	MD A:\DOS2 ↵	Creates subdirectory.
3	DIR A: ↵	Lists file directory.
4	MD A:\DOS2\DOS2SUB ↵	Creates subdirectory.
5	DIR A:\ ↵	Lists file directory.
6	DIR A:\DOS2 ↵	Lists file directory.
7	CD A:\DOS2 ↵	Changes directory.
8	DIR A: ↵	Lists file directory.
9	A: ↵	Changes default drive.
10	PROMPT PG ↵	Changes DOS prompt.
11	C: ↵ A: ↵	Changes default drive.
12	PROMPT ↵ PROMPT PG ↵	Changes DOS prompt.
13	CD DOS2SUB ↵	Changes directory.
14	DIR A: ↵	Lists file directory.
15	CD .. ↵	Changes directory.
16	DIR A: ↵	Lists file directory.
17	COPY A:\DOSNOTES.DOC A:\DOS2 ↵	Copies file.
18	DIR A: ↵	Lists file directory.
19	ERASE DOSNOTES.DOC ↵	Removes a file.
20	DIR ↵	Lists file directory.
21	COPY C:\DOS2*.* A:\DOS2\DOS2SUB ↵	Copies all files.
22	COPY A:\DOS2\DOS2SUB*.SLP ↵	Copies using wildcard.
23	ERASE P*.SLP ↵	Removes files.
24	DIR ↵	Lists file directory.
25	COPY A:\DOS2\DOS2SUB\P?CKING.SLP ↵	Copies using wildcard.
26	CD DOS2SUB ↵	Changes directory.
27	DIR ↵	Lists file directory.
28	DIR /P ↵	Pauses directory listing.
29	DIR /W ↵	Lists wide display directory.
30	CD .. ↵	Changes to parent directory.
31	DEL A:\DOS2\DOS2SUB*.* ↵ Y ↵	Removes all files.
32	RD DOS2SUB ↵	Removes directory.
33	C: ↵	Changes default drive.
34	CHKDSK A: ↵	Checks disk status.

The following list summarizes the material covered in Project 2.

1. The **root directory** is created by DOS during formatting and is an index of the files on the disk.
2. A **subdirectory** is a directory that you create on disk and is used to help organize your files.
3. Use the **MKDIR**, or the **MD**, command to create a subdirectory. The subdirectory entry for the MD command includes the drive specifier, a backslash, and the subdirectory name.
4. The **dot** index entry refers to its own subdirectory, and the **dot-dot** index refers to the subdirectory's parent directory.
5. Use the **CHDIR**, or **CD**, command to change from one directory to another.
6. The **current directory** for a drive is the directory on that drive in which you are currently working.
7. Use the **PROMPT** command to include the current directory as part of the DOS prompt. The prompt command **$P parameter** tells DOS to display the current directory, while the **$G parameter** tells DOS to display the > symbol.
8. The **path** to a file consists of the drive specifier, the name of the directory, and the name of the file. You use the path to specify the exact file you want to access.
9. You can use the **wildcards characters** of the **asterisk** and **question mark** in many DOS commands to replace specific characters in the file specification. Wildcards allow you to access multiple files with one command.
10. The **DIR /P** command produces a directory listing one screenful of files at a time. The **DIR /W** command displays directory information in a shorthand, wide format to allow more files to fit on the screen.
11. You remove a subdirectory by first erasing all the files in the subdirectory, then using the **RMDIR**, or **RD**, command to remove the subdirectory.
12. Use the **CHKDSK** command to verify the condition of your disk and to view a status of your disk and of main memory.

STUDENT ASSIGNMENTS

STUDENT ASSIGNMENT 1: True/False

Instructions: Circle T if the statement is true and F if the statement is false.

T F   1. The DIR A: command always produces a directory listing of the files in the root directory of drive A.
T F   2. Each disk directory keeps track of the physical locations of its files on the disk.
T F   3. The root directory has room to keep track of an unlimited number of files.
T F   4. A subdirectory can have subdirectories.
T F   5. A subdirectory name cannot have an extension.
T F   6. Only the default drive has a current directory.
T F   7. You can use only one wildcard question mark character in a command to identify files.
T F   8. The DIR /W command causes the directory listing to wait or pause after each screenful is displayed.
T F   9. Use the CHKDSK command to include the current directory as part of the DOS prompt.
T F 10. To move from one directory to another, use the MD command.
T F 11. The RD command removes a subdirectory and all its files.

STUDENT ASSIGNMENT 2: Multiple Choice

Instructions: Circle the correct response.

1. To move from one directory to another, you use the _____ command.
   a. cd
   b. md
   c. rd
   d. td
2. The _____ is the first entry in a path specification.
   a. backslash
   b. filename
   c. subdirectory
   d. drive specifier
3. Filenames are grouped on disks into _____.
   a. index lists
   b. source and target filename entries
   c. internally labeled entries
   d. directories and subdirectories
4. The _____ command uses the PG parameters.
   a. CHKDSK
   b. COPY
   c. DIR
   d. PROMPT
5. The _____ parameter tells the DIR command to display the maximum number of files on the screen.
   a. /A
   b. /G
   c. /P
   d. /W
6. The _____ command is an external command.
   a. CHKDSK
   b. COPY
   c. PROMPT
   d. RD

STUDENT ASSIGNMENT 3: Fill in the Blanks

Instructions: Fill in the blanks in the following sentences.

1. The special file directory that is created when a disk is formatted is called the _____ directory.
2. A(n) _____ is a directory that you create on a disk.
3. Use the _____ command to create a subdirectory.
4. The _____ character is used to represent the root directory.
5. Use the _____ command to move from one directory to another.
6. You can use the _____ wildcard character once in a filename and once in an extension.
7. Use the _____ parameter with the DIR command to display one screenful of files at a time.
8. Use the _____ command to delete a subdirectory.
9. You can use the _____ command to determine the amount of main memory your computer has.

STUDENT ASSIGNMENT 4: Using DOS Commands

Instructions: Explain how to accomplish each of the following tasks using DOS.

Problem 1: Copy all the files from the disk in drive B to the disk in drive A.
Explanation: _____

_____

_____

Problem 2: Verify how much free main memory you currently have on your computer.
Explanation: _____

_____

_____

Problem 3: Create a subdirectory named SUB1 on your diskette.
Explanation: _____

_____

_____

Problem 4: Erase the files in subdirectory SUB1, change to the root directory, and remove subdirectory SUB1.
Explanation: _____

_____

_____

STUDENT ASSIGNMENT 5: Understanding DOS Options

Instructions: Explain what will happen after you perform each of the following DOS commands.

Problem 1: Type COPY G*.* C: at the A> prompt and press the Enter key.
Explanation: _____

_____

_____

Problem 2: Type COPY D?S*.* A: at the C> prompt and press the Enter key.
Explanation: _____

_____

_____

Problem 3: Type PROMPT PG at the DOS prompt and press the Enter key.
Explanation: _____

_____

_____

STUDENT ASSIGNMENT 6: Recovering from Problems

Instructions: In each of the following situations, a problem occurred. Explain the cause of the problem and how it can be corrected.

Problem 1: You type COPY DOS**.* A: at the C> prompt and press the Enter key. DOS responds with the message "Invalid path or file name".

Cause of problem: _____

_____

Method of correction: _____

_____

Problem 2: You have the DOS disk in drive A, type CHKSDK A: at the A> prompt, and press the Enter key. DOS responds with the message "Bad command or file name".

Cause of problem: _____

_____

Method of correction: _____

_____

STUDENT ASSIGNMENT 7: Creating Subdirectories

Instructions: Perform the following tasks on the computer you used to complete Project 2 or on any other computer available to you.

1. Place a newly formatted disk in drive A and create these subdirectories in the root directory: SPSHEET, WORDPROC, GAMES, HOUSE, and MODEM.
2. Create two subdirectories in the SPSHEET directory: FINANCES and EXPENSES.
3. Create three subdirectories in the WORDPROC directory: WORKMEMO, PERSONAL, and WORDLIST.

STUDENT ASSIGNMENT 8: Managing Subdirectory Files

Instructions: Perform the following tasks on the computer you used to complete Project 2 or on any other computer available to you.

1. If you did not create the subdirectories in Student Assignment 7, do it now.
2. Make the HOUSE directory the current directory.
3. Copy two or more files into the HOUSE directory. You can use the files you copied onto your disk during Projects 1 and 2 or choose any other files.
4. Copy all these files from the HOUSE directory to the FINANCES directory.

STUDENT ASSIGNMENT 9: Removing Directories

Instructions: Perform the following tasks on the computer you used to complete Project 2 or on any other computer available to you.

1. If you did not create the subdirectories in Student Assignment 7, do it now.
2. Remove the GAMES directory from your disk.
3. Remove the SPSHEET directory from your disk.

STUDENT ASSIGNMENT 10: Using Wildcard Characters

Instructions: Perform the following tasks on the computer you used to complete Project 2 or on any other computer available to you.

1. If you did not create the subdirectories in Student Assignment 7, do it now.
2. Make the HOUSE directory the current directory.
3. Copy two or more files into the HOUSE directory using the ? wildcard in one or more positions of the source file-name. You can use the files you copied onto your disk during Projects 1 and 2 or choose any other files.
4. Copy two or more files into the HOUSE directory using the * wildcard in the source filename. You can use the files you copied onto your disk during Projects 1 and 2 or choose any other files.

STUDENT ASSIGNMENT 11: Subdirectories on a Hard Drive or LAN

Instructions: If you used a hard drive or LAN to complete Project 2, perform the following tasks on the computer you used to complete Project 2.

1. Determine which directories you have on drive C, if you are using a hard disk, or on drive F, if you are using a LAN.
2. Draw a diagram of this directory structure.

QUICK REFERENCE TO DOS

For each of the projects, we have provided the fundamental DOS activities in an easy-to-use quick reference format. This convenient reference tool is divided into three parts — activity, procedure, and description. All of the activities that you learn in each project are covered in the Quick Reference for that project. The numbers in parentheses that follow each activity refer to the page on which the activity is first discussed in the text.

You can use these Quick References as study aids or to quickly recall how you completed an activity. The Quick Reference is a valuable and time-saving tool, and we encourage you to use it frequently.

QUICK REFERENCE — PROJECT 1

ACTIVITY	PROCEDURE	DESCRIPTION
WARM START (DOS5)	Press Ctrl–Alt–Delete	Restart DOS if power is already on. Insert disk in drive A for two-diskette computer. Leave drive A empty for a hard disk or LAN.
SET DATE (DOS5)	Enter month Enter day Enter year Press ↵	Type one-digit or two-digit month, one-digit or two-digit day, and two-digit year, separating each with a hyphen or slash.
SET TIME (DOS5)	Enter hour Enter minute Enter second Press ↵	Type one-digit or two digit hour, one-digit or two-digit minute, and one-digit or two-digit second, separating each with a colon.
CHANGE DEFAULT DRIVE (DOS6)	Enter drive specifier Press ↵	Type single-letter drive name and a colon for the new default drive.
FORMAT DISK (DOS8)	Type format Press Spacebar Enter drive specifier	Initialize a diskette in the designated drive.
CLEAR SCREEN (DOS11)	Type cls Press ↵	Clear the screen and position DOS prompt to the top left.
COPY FILE (DOS11)	Type copy Press Spacebar Enter source file Press Spacebar Enter target file Press ↵	Duplicates the source file as the target file on the same disk or another disk.
RETYPE PREVIOUS COMMAND (DOS12)	Press F3	Automatically retype previous DOS command.
DISPLAY DIRECTORY (DOS14)	Type dir Press Spacebar Enter drive specifier Press ↵	Display file directory of the disk in the designated drive.
RENAME FILE (DOS14)	Type rename Press Spacebar Enter old file specification Press Spacebar Enter new file specification Press ↵	Change the name of the file (first filename) on the designated drive to another name (second filename).

QUICK REFERENCE — PROJECT 1 (continued)

ACTIVITY	PROCEDURE	DESCRIPTION
DISPLAY FILE (DOS15)	Type more Press `Spacebar` Type < Enter file specification Press ↵	Display the file's contents one screen at a time.
PRINT SCREEN (DOS17)	Press `Print Screen`	Print the contents of the screen on the printer.
REMOVE FILE (DOS17)	Type del or type erase Press `Spacebar` Enter file specification Press ↵	Delete the file from disk.

QUICK REFERENCE — PROJECT 2

ACTIVITY	PROCEDURE	DESCRIPTION
CREATE SUBDIRECTORY (DOS27)	Type md Press `Spacebar` Enter drive specifier Enter subdirectory name Press ↵	Create a new subdirectory.
CHANGE DIRECTORY (DOS29)	Type cd Press `Spacebar` Enter drive specifier Enter subdirectory name Press ↵	Change the current directory on a disk.
PAUSE DIRECTORY LISTING (DOS36)	Type dir Press `Spacebar` Enter path Type /p Press ↵	Display a directory listing one screenful at a time.
WIDE DIRECTORY LISTING (DOS37)	Type dir Press `Spacebar` Enter path Type /w Press ↵	Display a directory listing in a wide, condensed format.
REMOVE SUBDIRECTORY (DOS37)	Type rd Press `Spacebar` Enter drive specifier Enter subdirectory name Press ↵	Remove a subdirectory.
VERIFY DISK CONDITION (DOS38)	Type chkdsk Press `Spacebar` Enter drive specifier Press ↵	Verify and report a disk's condition.

Word Processing Using WordPerfect 5.1

PROJECTS

WORDPERFECT 5.1

WordPerfect 5.1, developed by the WordPerfect Corporation, Orem, Utah, is a comprehensive software application program designed to maximize word processing productivity. WordPerfect can be used on most microcomputers. In the following six projects, you will learn to use WordPerfect 5.1 on an IBM computer (PC, XT, AT, PS/2, and compatibles) operating under either MS-DOS or PC-DOS.

WordPerfect, as with all word processing programs, can be used to produce printed documents. These documents can be simple memos or letters, a complex business report that might include graphics, a newsletter, a legal brief, a contract, or even scholarly papers and books. WordPerfect 5.1 contains a pull-down menu interface. This means that you can use WordPerfect by selecting the actions you want to take from menus on the screen. A menu is a list of the options you can choose. The options are instructions you use to operate the software. The advantage of using menus is that you do not have to memorize commands or use command summary cards.

Before you begin Project 1, let's discuss the keys on the computer keyboard.

THE KEYBOARD

The **keyboard** is the device you use to input data into the computer to perform word processing activities. We assume you are using the enhanced keyboard (101-key) that is shown in Figure 1-1 ⟨a⟩. If you are using a standard keyboard (84-key) shown in Figure 1-1 ⟨b⟩, you will find the differences on this keyboard included in the following discussion.

As you work through the projects in this book, remember that when you press some keys, they will repeat continuously until you release the key. Thus, when you are instructed to *press* a key, you should lightly tap and quickly release the key.

FIGURE 1-1   The enhanced and standard keyboards

The Typewriter Keys

Notice the familiar **typewriter section** of the keyboard in Figure 1-1. The computer keyboard contains many other keys in addition to the keys you might be accustomed to seeing on a typewriter.

First, locate the two **Ctrl** (Control) keys on the left and right sides of the typewriter keys. Your keyboard might have only one Ctrl key on the left side of the keyboard. You can press either of the two keys and the result will be the same. This key is never used alone; it is always used with other keys to perform specific word processing functions.

Next, locate the two **Alt** (Alternate) keys on the left and right sides of the typewriter keys. Your keyboard might have only one Alt key on the left side of the keyboard. Again, you can press either of the two Alt keys and the result will be the same. Like the Ctrl key, the Alt key is never used alone; it is held down while you press other keys to perform specific word processing functions.

Now, locate the two **Shift** keys on the left and right sides of the typewriter keys. As on a typewriter you can hold down the Shift key to make lowercase letters into CAPITAL LETTERS and to type the symbols on the keyboard, such as #, $, %, &, *, and so on.

The **Caps Lock** key is located on the left side of the keyboard. When you press the Caps Lock key, any characters you type are capital letters. On most keyboards, a light indicates when the Caps Lock key has been pressed and capitalization is on. If you hold down the Shift key while Caps Lock is on, characters will be entered in lowercase. The Caps Lock key is a **toggle**, which means that you turn it off the same way you turn it on, by pressing the Caps Lock key. Remember that the Caps Lock key affects only the letter keys on the keyboard. That is, you still must use the Shift key to type symbols.

You can use the **Tab** key to indent to the next tab setting to the right, just as on a typewriter.

You can use the **Esc**, or Escape, key to quit or leave something you are doing without making a change.

The **Enter** key, sometimes called the **Return** key, is used in the same way as the Return key is used on a typewriter. To begin a new line or to add a blank line to your text, you press the Enter key just as you would on a typewriter. This key is also used to execute or activate instructions on the computer. Often you will type instructions and the letters or numbers you type will stay on the screen; the computer seems not to respond. A good rule of thumb is that *if you have typed or selected an instruction and nothing happens, press Enter ↵*. In other words, the command appears only on the screen. It will not be entered into the memory of the computer until you press the Enter key. On most keyboards the word Enter is on the key along with an arrow that looks like this ↵. Many times throughout these projects you will see this arrow instead of the word Enter. When you see this arrow, press the Enter key.

The **Backspace** key works much like the Backspace key on a typewriter. Unlike a typewriter's Backspace key, which leaves the text intact on the paper, the computer's Backspace key removes the characters when you press it.

Finally, the **Spacebar** adds blank spaces to a document as it does on a typewriter.

The Cursor Movement Keys and the Numeric Keypad

The **cursor** is a blinking underscore that indicates where the next character will be entered on the screen. Look on the right side of the keyboard and locate a set of keys with arrows pointing in different directions. If you are using an enhanced keyboard, look above these arrow keys and find another group of keys labeled Home, End, Page Up, Page Down, Insert, and Delete (Figure 1-2 ⟨a⟩). If you are using a standard keyboard the arrow keys include these labels (Figure 1-2 ⟨b⟩). Whatever keyboard you are using, the keys containing the arrows and the labels are known collectively as the **cursor movement keys**. You use the cursor movement keys to move the cursor without altering the text of the document on the screen.

FIGURE 1-2
The cursor movement keys

Next, locate the **numeric keypad**. It looks similar to a desktop calculator and is located on the far right side on the keyboard. On the standard keyboard the numeric keypad is incorporated with the arrow keys and the labels such as Home, End, and Ins. On the enhanced keyboard the numeric keypad is separate from the cursor movement keys, but it also has directional arrows and the labels. On an enhanced keyboard the keys on the numeric keypad should be used to type numbers only and *not* to move the cursor. For example, if you are entering many numbers, such as for a bookkeeping project, you could use this keypad; but if you are typing numbers only occasionally, you should use the number keys at the top of the typewriter keys.

Most enhanced keyboards automatically turn on the Num Lock (Number Lock) key when you turn on the computer. Your keyboard might display a light to indicate that the numbers have been locked to the on position. When the Num Lock key is on and you press the keys on the numeric keypad, only numbers will appear on the screen. The arrows and labels on the numeric keypad will not function. Like the Caps Lock key, Num Lock is a toggle. Thus, for example, if you want to use the numeric keypad for cursor movement, you must *unlock* the numbers by pressing the Num Lock key.

Next, locate the arrow keys. The **Left Arrow** key with the arrow pointing left ← moves the cursor one character to the left. The **Right Arrow** key with the arrow pointing right → moves the cursor one character to the right. The **Up Arrow** key with the arrow pointing up ↑ moves the cursor up one line. The **Down Arrow** key with the arrow pointing down ↓ moves the cursor down one line.

The Function Keys

The **function keys** are located either across the top or on the left side of your keyboard (Figure 1-3). In these projects we assume you are using a keyboard with the function keys across the top. Function keys are labeled F1 through F12 on the enhanced keyboard and F1 through F10 on the standard keyboard. The function keys are special keys programmed to perform specific functions. In word processing and other microcomputer application programs the function keys are used alone or used in combination with other keys to enter instructions.

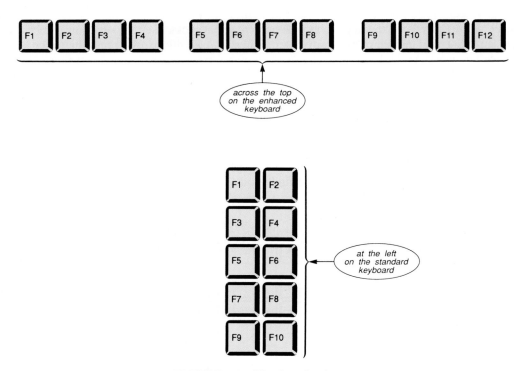

FIGURE 1-3   The function keys

ASSUMED DEFAULTS

◆ WordPerfect contains **default**, or initial, predefined settings that affect the way your screen will appear and how your documents will print. We assume you are using the default settings as they exist when WordPerfect is first installed. As you work through these projects, you might notice that some items on your screen appear differently than those illustrated in the six projects. Any differences you encounter are probably due to WordPerfect's defaults having been changed on your system. Later in this book you will learn more about defaults. For now, read the following list, which discusses the effect of the defaults on the screen display and on a printed document, and see your instructor if you have any questions:

1. **Default Drive**. WordPerfect's default is to use drive C (on a hard disk system) or drive A (on a two-disk system) for saving and retrieving documents. Your system might be set to save and retrieve documents on a different disk drive.
2. **Justification**. WordPerfect will automatically use right justification, which means that text aligns evenly at both the right and left margins. If your copy of WordPerfect has been changed to a different type of justification, your printed documents will not appear as shown in the six projects. Notice that only the *printed* copy will have justified margins. The *screen* will not display justification.
3. **Margins**. WordPerfect's default margins are each set to 1 inch. This means that the top, bottom, left, and right edges of the paper will have one inch of white space, or margins, all around. If your default margins have been changed, the Ln and Pos numbers shown in the illustrations throughout the six projects will not match yours. Also, the margins of your printed document will not match those shown in the illustrations.
4. **Menu**. WordPerfect's default is to keep the menu bar hidden, or invisible, until you request that it appear. Your system might display the menu at all times. The shortcut keys, or function key equivalents, also might not appear next to the options in the menu if your defaults have been changed.
5. **Monitor**. In these WordPerfect projects we assume you are using a monochrome, or black and white, monitor. If you are using a color monitor, the background and character colors will appear different from the illustrations in this book. The highlighted items on the menu bar will also be affected by a color monitor, as we explain in Project 1.

TYPING CONVENTIONS

◆ Each document in this book follows standard typing conventions. One blank space follows each comma, and two blank spaces follow each period. If you use conventions other than these, your documents might appear differently both on the screen and when printed on paper. Your Ln and Pos numbers might also be different from those in the illustrations.

MOUSE INSTRUCTIONS

◆ This book includes instructions for using a mouse with WordPerfect, although you do *not* need a mouse to use WordPerfect. The mouse pointer is usually displayed on the screen as a rectangle, either highlighted, in reverse video, or in a different color. When you move the mouse, the mouse pointer moves on the screen. In the six projects, mouse instructions use the words *click* and *select*. When you are instructed to click, it means to press and then release the right or left mouse button. When you are instructed to select, it means to position the mouse pointer within the option/response, then click the right or left mouse button.

THE HELP FUNCTION

◆ WordPerfect contains an on-line Help function that allows you to display on your screen information about any of WordPerfect's functions or options. You can access the Help function any time during a WordPerfect session. Check with your instructor to see if the Help files are available to you in your lab.

Creating and Editing a Document

OBJECTIVES

You will have mastered the material in this project when you can:

◆ Load WordPerfect into main memory

◆ Create, save, and print a short document

◆ Move the cursor in all directions

◆ Correct typing errors

◆ Retrieve and revise a document

◆ Display the Reveal Codes screen

◆ Exit WordPerfect and return to the DOS prompt

In Project 1 you start by turning on the computer and loading WordPerfect. Next, you type, save, and print the document shown in Figure 1-4. After you print the document, you will exit WordPerfect and return to the DOS prompt. Once you are at the DOS prompt, you reload WordPerfect, and then edit, print, and save the document you created.

As you work through this project, you may find that your screen and/or printed document appears *different* from the illustrations in this book. If this is the case, be sure you read ASSUMED DEFAULTS and TYPING CONVENTIONS in the previous section.

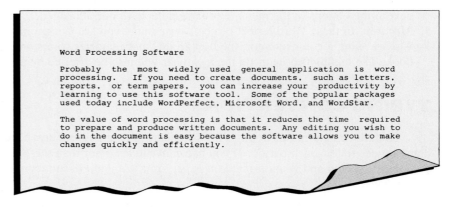

Word Processing Software

Probably the most widely used general application is word processing. If you need to create documents, such as letters, reports, or term papers, you can increase your productivity by learning to use this software tool. Some of the popular packages used today include WordPerfect, Microsoft Word, and WordStar.

The value of word processing is that it reduces the time required to prepare and produce written documents. Any editing you wish to do in the document is easy because the software allows you to make changes quickly and efficiently.

FIGURE 1-4 Document for Project 1

LOADING WORDPERFECT

◆ People normally use WordPerfect 5.1 on a hard disk system because of the amount of memory required to store this word processing software. If you are using a hard disk system or running on a networked version of WordPerfect, your instructor will show you how to access the WordPerfect program. You will be saving the work you do in this project on a disk, so be sure to put a formatted disk into drive A.

If you are running WordPerfect on a two-disk system, use the following instructions. First, load DOS so that the A> prompt displays. Remove the DOS disk and place the WordPerfect 1 disk into drive A. Place a formatted disk into drive B to save your documents. At the A> prompt, type the letters wp and press the Enter key. This tells the computer to load the WordPerfect program into the computer's main memory. When you are prompted, replace the WordPerfect 1 disk with the WordPerfect 2 disk and press the Enter key.

In this book, we assume you are using a hard disk system and that your data disk is in drive A. If your data disk is in drive B, change any reference we make to drive A to drive B.

THE WORDPERFECT SCREEN

◆ Once you have loaded WordPerfect, you see the screen in Figure 1-5, which includes the text window and the status line. If the last person to use WordPerfect exited improperly, you might see the message, "Are other copies of WordPerfect currently running (Y/N)?". If you see this message, type N and WordPerfect should continue. (If you receive a message referring to old backup files …, see your instructor for directions on how to proceed.)

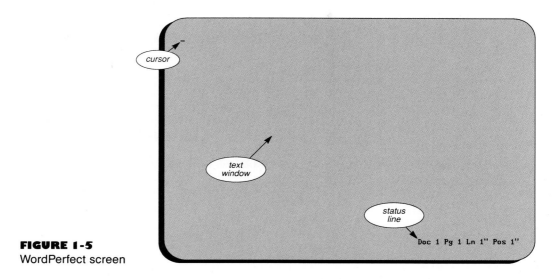

FIGURE 1-5
WordPerfect screen

The Text Window

The **text window** is the portion of the screen which displays the text you type. Notice the blinking underscore at the top left corner of the screen. This is the cursor, which points to your position on the screen. When you begin typing, text appears to the left of the cursor.

The Status Line

The **status line** is in the lower right corner of the window. This line displays information about the current document. For example, in Figure 1-5, the status line tells you that the cursor is in document 1, on page 1, on line 1" and at the 1" position. The line (Ln) and position (Pos) numbers tell you that the cursor is positioned so that text will print 1" down from the top edge of the paper and 1" in from the left edge of the paper. As you begin creating or editing a document, the status line will change to reflect the cursor's position. (Recall that we assume you are using WordPerfect's default margins. If your margins have been changed, the line and position numbers will appear differently.)

The position number on the status line will blink if you have not pressed the Num Lock key after loading WordPerfect. As you learned in the keyboard section of this book, leaving Num Lock engaged will cause numbers to be entered, when you try to use the numeric keypad to move the cursor. If the position number is blinking on your status line, press the Num Lock key.

CHANGING THE DRIVE/DIRECTORY

◆ Before you continue, you might need to change to the drive that contains your data disk so that all your documents are saved to and retrieved from your data disk. To do this, you must use the "List Files" option from the File menu.

This option appears in WordPerfect's main menu. To display this main menu, or **menu bar**, use the Alt and = keys. Hold down the Alt key and while holding it down, press = (Alt-=). The menu bar in Figure 1-6 appears. This menu bar contains all the functions that WordPerfect can perform. Any time you need to perform any action other than entering text, you will use this menu bar. (Recall that we assume your computer is set to keep this menu bar hidden. If your computer displays the menu bar at all times, pressing Alt-= will activate or deactivate the displayed menu bar.)

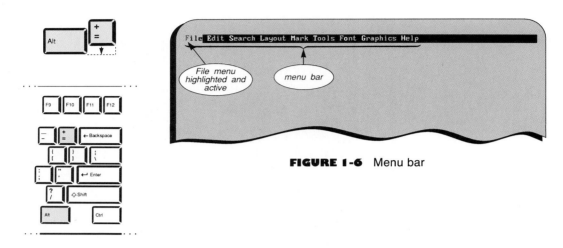

FIGURE 1-6 Menu bar

If you accidentally display the menu bar, you can press Alt-= again, the Esc key, or the F1 key to return to the text window. If you are using a mouse, click the right mouse button to cancel the menu.

To use an option, you must first highlight it. Notice that the word File appears on the screen in reverse video, or in other words, it is highlighted. This highlight indicates to you that this portion of the menu bar is active. You can now access any of the options in the File menu. You can use the arrow keys to highlight options. Press the Right Arrow key once and notice how the highlight moves from the word File to the word Edit. Since the "List Files" option is contained in the File menu, press the Left Arrow key once to activate this menu.

Once a menu name is highlighted, you must display the options it contains before you can perform any of the options. Press the Down Arrow key to pull down the menu (Figure 1-7).

FIGURE 1-7 File menu

Notice the "List Files" option on this menu. WordPerfect refers to any data or text stored on a disk as a **file**. Therefore, when you *list your files*, you are actually listing the names of the documents on your disk. Press the Down Arrow key five times until the "List Files" option is highlighted (Figure 1-8). With the "List Files" option highlighted, press the Enter key to select the option.

 Mouse Users: Click the right mouse button to display the menu bar. Select the File menu, then select "List Files".

FIGURE 1-8 Highlighting the "List Files" option

The screen in Figure 1-9 appears. Notice in the lower right corner of the screen the message, "Type = to change default Dir".

FIGURE 1-9 Listing files

You must now instruct WordPerfect which disk drive contains your data disk. Type = a:, since drive A contains your data disk (Figure 1-10).

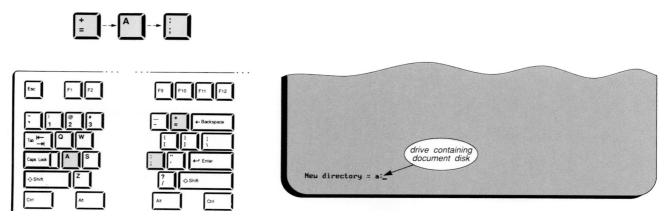

FIGURE 1-10 Changing the drive

Press the Enter key. When WordPerfect displays the message, "Dir A:*.*" (Figure 1-11), press the Esc key to return to the text window. WordPerfect will now automatically save documents to and retrieve documents from drive A. (Recall that in this book we will assume you are running WordPerfect on a hard disk and that you will save your documents to the data disk in drive A.)

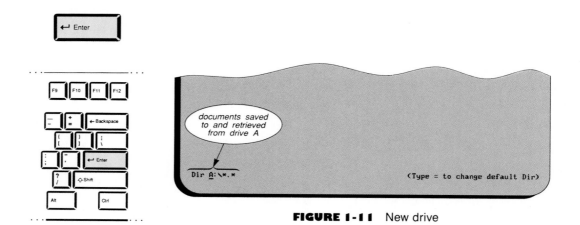

FIGURE 1-11 New drive

CREATING A DOCUMENT

◆ Before you begin typing the document in Figure 1-4, let's discuss one of WordPerfect's important features — wordwrap.

Wordwrap

Typing a document with WordPerfect is similar to using a typewriter. When you type on a typewriter, however, you must press the carriage return each time you approach the end of a line (Figure 1-12).

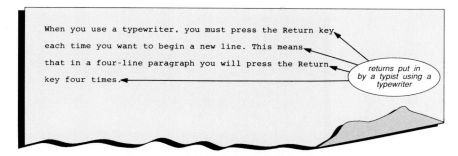

FIGURE 1-12   Typewriter carriage returns

With WordPerfect you do not need to press the Enter key each time you type to the right margin. WordPerfect allows you to type continuously and it automatically moves the cursor down one line and to the beginning of the new line when the cursor reaches the right margin (Figure 1-13). This feature is called **wordwrap**. The major advantage of wordwrap is that you are able to enter text much more quickly than if you had to press the Enter key at the end of each line.

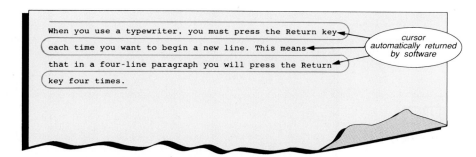

FIGURE 1-13   Document created with wordwrap

Entering Text

Now you are ready to create your document. If you make a mistake while typing, press the Backspace key. This will erase the character immediately to the left of the cursor each time you press it.

Let's correct an error with the Backspace key. Type Word Processing Softwaer. As you type, notice that the Pos indicator on the status line changes with each character you type. With the cursor immediately to the right of the error Softwaer (Figure 1-14), watch the screen as you press the Backspace key twice.

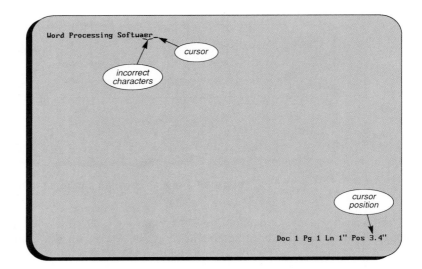

FIGURE 1-14
Correcting errors

Figure 1-15 shows the incorrect characters removed from the screen. Now, type re to correctly enter the heading.

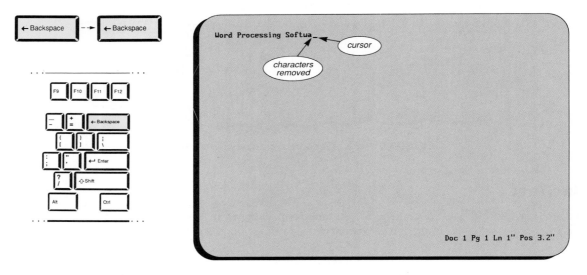

FIGURE 1-15   Correcting errors

After you correctly type the heading, press the Enter key. Notice the line number on the status line is now 1.17" (Figure 1-16).

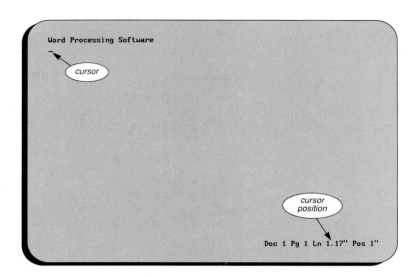

FIGURE 1-16
Entering text

Again, this is a visual reminder of where your cursor is at all times. Press the Enter key again to insert a blank line between the heading and the first line of text (Figure 1-17).

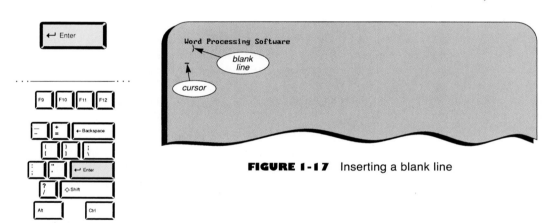

FIGURE 1-17   Inserting a blank line

Type the following text: Probably the most widely used general application is word processing, and watch the screen as you type the word processing. This word could not fit on the first line, so it was automatically moved down to the next line (Figure 1-18).

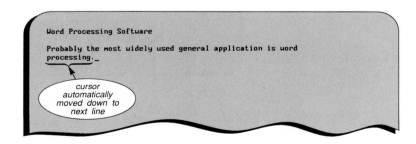

FIGURE 1-18
Wordwrap

This is wordwrap taking effect. The only time you will press the Enter key is when you want to end a line before wordwrap occurs (such as the last line of a paragraph), to insert blank lines, or to use functions.

Type the remainder of the first paragraph: If you need to create documents, such as letters, reports, or term papers, you can increase your productivity by learning to use this software tool. Some of the popular packages used today include WordPerfect, Microsoft Word, and WordStar. When you have typed the period following the word WordStar, press the Enter key twice. The first time you press the Enter key you end the paragraph and move the cursor to the next line on the screen. The second time you press the Enter key you insert a blank line between the last line of the first paragraph and the beginning of the second. Your screen should now look like Figure 1-19.

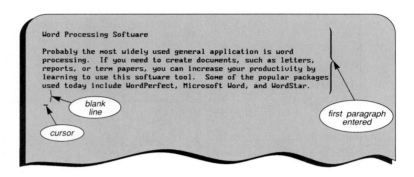

FIGURE 1-19
First paragraph entered

With your cursor positioned as shown in Figure 1-19, type the following paragraph: The value of word processing is that it reduces the time required to prepare and produce written documents. Any editing you wish to do in the document is easy because the software allows you to make changes quickly and efficiently.

When you have finished typing the second paragraph, press the Enter key to end the paragraph. Your completed document should look like Figure 1-20.

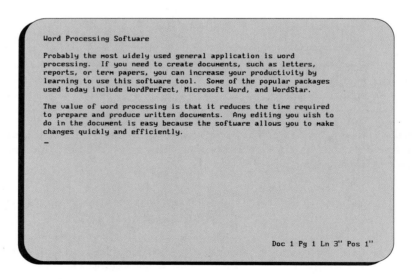

FIGURE 1-20
Completed document

CHOOSING OPTIONS WITH LETTERS

When you changed the drive so that your documents were saved on drive A, you used the arrow keys to highlight menu options. WordPerfect also provides another way of selecting options.

Display the menu bar by holding down the Alt key and, while holding it down, press = (Alt- =). Notice that each of the options in this menu contains a highlighted, or boldfaced, letter (Figure 1-21), usually the first character. Each option in this menu can be selected by typing its boldfaced letter, rather than pointing to the option with the arrow keys. If you have a color monitor, the letter used to access the option might appear in boldface or in a different color on the screen. If you have a monochrome monitor, you might or might not see these characters display boldfaced. If you are using a monochrome monitor that does not display highlighted characters, try typing the first letter of the option. If this does not access the option you want, try typing the second letter of the option, then the third, and so on.

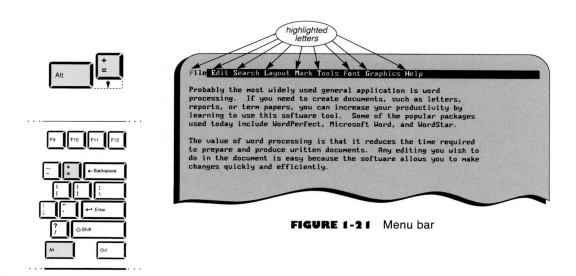

FIGURE 1-21 Menu bar

Although pointing with the arrow keys achieves the same results, you will find that this new method will be much faster. It achieves one of the major goals of word processors — to increase efficiency and decrease the number of keystrokes. For the remainder of this project and the following projects, each time we want to select an option, we will type the boldfaced character of the option. Let's try this new method to save your document to disk.

SAVING A DOCUMENT

Your document is now completed. Whenever a document is completed, it should be **saved** on a disk so that it can be retrieved for printing or revising at a later time. *If you do not save your document, it will be lost.* It's actually a good idea to save your work periodically, say every fifteen minutes or so. That way, should something unforeseen happen, such as a power outage, you will have lost only the portion of the document you entered since the last time you saved.

You can save documents on disk only by unique names. Document names can contain up to 68 characters, and can include numbers or hyphens, but not spaces or special characters. Because only the first eight characters of the document name will automatically display, it's a good idea to limit document names to eight or fewer characters. Document names should be as meaningful and as descriptive as possible so that you can recognize a document's contents by seeing its name. For instance, naming this document WPDOC would not help you to recognize its contents at a later date.

The cursor on your screen should currently be positioned at the end of the document. But the cursor might be at *any* location in the document when you select the "Save" option. The menu bar should already be displayed on your screen. If not, hold down the Alt key, and while holding it down, press = (Alt-=). Recall that you can save documents through the File menu; since File is already highlighted, press the Down Arrow key to pull down the File menu (Figure 1-22).

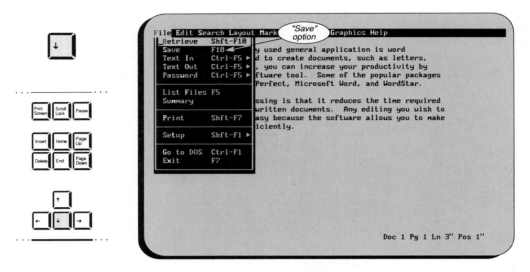

FIGURE 1-22 File menu

Again, you could point to the "Save" option with the arrow keys, but it is much faster to simply type the desired option's boldfaced letter. You can use either an uppercase or lowercase letter. WordPerfect is not case sensitive; in other words, any time you need to type letters in response to an option or message, you can use uppercase or lowercase, or a combination of the two. Because you want to save your document, type S for "Save", and the message in Figure 1-23 appears.

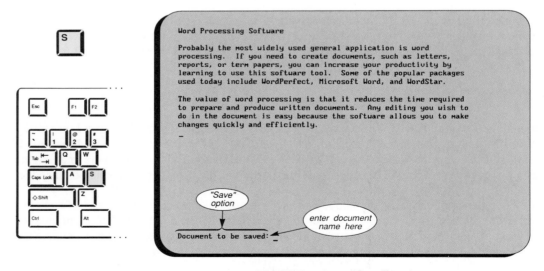

FIGURE 1-23 "Save" option

When the save message displays, you must enter the document name under which you want to save the document. Enter `proj1` as shown in Figure 1-24.

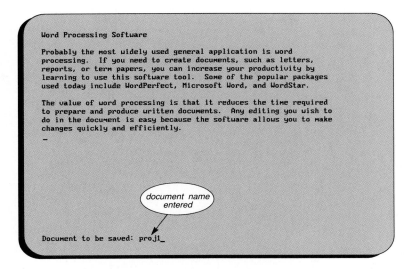

FIGURE 1-24 Entering a document name

Again, remember that you can use uppercase or lowercase letters, or a combination of the two. WordPerfect automatically converts all document names to uppercase. Now press the Enter key, and the screen in Figure 1-25 appears. This is the **document summary**, which WordPerfect automatically displays each time you save a document. At this point, you could enter specific information about the document that could be a helpful reference in the future. We will not use document summaries in this book, so press the Delete key then type Y to bypass the document summary. Your copy of WordPerfect might not display a document summary. If your screen *does not* display a document summary, do not press the Delete key.

FIGURE 1-25 Document Summary

 Mouse Users: Click the right mouse button to display the menu bar. Select the File menu, then select the "Save" option. Type `proj1` and press Enter.

The document is now saved on your data disk under the name PROJ1. WordPerfect saved the document on your data disk because this is the drive you specified in the "List Files" options at the start of this project. The name of your document now appears in the bottom border of the text window, to the left of the status line (Figure 1-26).

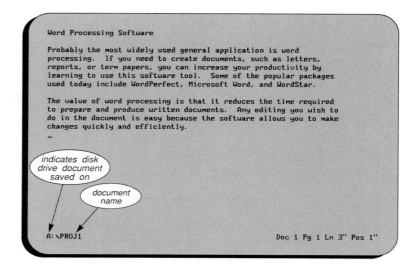

FIGURE 1-26
Saved document

PRINTING A DOCUMENT

After you type and save a document, you usually want to print it on paper. When a document is printed on paper, it is referred to as a **hard copy**. Before you continue, be sure your printer has paper inserted and properly aligned, and that the printer is turned on and ready to print.

To print the document, activate the menu bar by holding down the Alt key and while holding it down, press = (Alt- =). Press the Down Arrow key to pull down the File menu, then type P for the "Print" option. The menu in Figure 1-27 appears (your Print menu may contain additional choices). As you can see, the Print menu contains many selections, but for this project we will simply print the document.

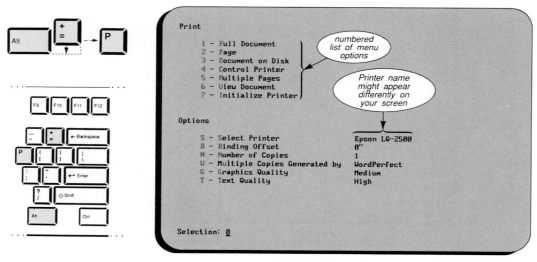

FIGURE 1-27 Print menu

Notice that this menu contains a numbered list of menu options. Because you want to print the full document, you could type the number 1 to specify menu option "1". However, the menu choices also contain boldfaced letters. As with other WordPerfect menus, you can also type the boldfaced letter (usually capitalized) to specify an option. Type F to select the "Full Document" option. The document will begin printing on the printer. The printed document, or hard copy, should look like Figure 1-4. (If the justification or margin defaults are changed on your system, your printed document will appear differently.)

 Mouse Users: Click the right mouse button to display the menu bar. Select the File menu, then select "Print". Select the "Full Document" option from the Print menu.

EXITING A DOCUMENT

As you create a document, WordPerfect creates files of its own to store your edits and options. When you have completed a WordPerfect session, you must exit the WordPerfect program. *It is extremely important that you exit the WordPerfect program properly, and that you do not simply turn off the computer when you've finished a document.* If you do not exit properly, WordPerfect is not able to erase the files it created during the session.

To exit WordPerfect and return to the DOS prompt, display the menu bar. Hold down the Alt key and while holding it down, press = (Alt-=). The File menu contains the "Exit" option, so press the Down Arrow key to display the File menu. To highlight the "Exit" option, you can press the Down Arrow key ten times. A quicker way would be to type the corresponding letter for the option. However, the "Exit" option is not an option that you can select with its first character. In this case, the second letter, x, is boldfaced. Type x, and the message in Figure 1-28 appears.

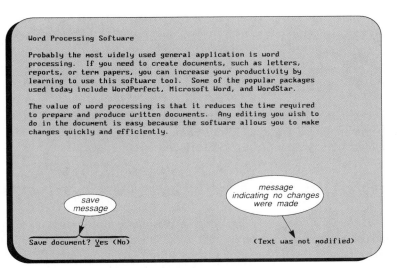

FIGURE 1-28 Exiting a document

This is a built-in safeguard to prevent you from exiting WordPerfect before saving your document. Also notice the message in the lower right corner of the screen. This message informs you that you did not make any changes to the document since the last time you saved. Because you've already saved the document since the last revision, type N for No, and the message in Figure 1-29 appears.

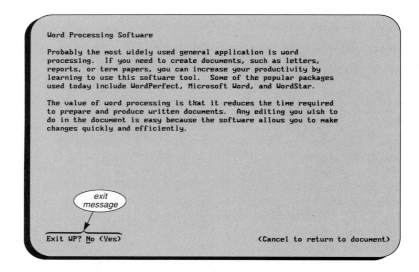

FIGURE 1-29
Exit message

Since you do, in fact, want to exit WordPerfect, type Y. You then exit WordPerfect and return to the DOS prompt. Be sure to remove your data and program disks if necessary after you return to DOS.

 Mouse Users: Click the right mouse button to display the menu bar. Select "Exit" from the File menu before you respond to the message "Save Document? Yes(No)".

You can also use the "Exit" option to clear your screen when you have finished with one document and need to begin another document. In this case, answering N to the message, "Exit WP? No (Yes)", would clear the screen and allow you to continue the WordPerfect session.

RETRIEVING AND REVISING A DOCUMENT

Suppose that after you quit the WordPerfect program and returned to DOS, you realized that you wanted to add a sentence to a paragraph in your document. To do this, you would need to load WordPerfect again, retrieve the document named PROJ1, add the sentence, and save the document in its revised form. If you are using WordPerfect on a hard disk or network, load WordPerfect as your instructor directs you. If you are using WordPerfect on a two-disk system, make sure the WordPerfect Program disk 1 is in drive A, then type wp. Replace disk 1 with disk 2 when you are prompted. Be sure to change the default drive to A, if necessary (or to drive B on a two-disk system).

Retrieving a Document

To bring your document back onto the screen so that you can edit it, you need to retrieve it. Before you retrieve a document, be sure your screen is clear. If it is not, WordPerfect will retrieve the document directly into the document on your screen. To retrieve a document, display the menu bar by holding down the Alt key and while holding it down, press = (Alt- =). Next, press the Down Arrow key to display the File menu. Recall that when you saved your document earlier in the project, you also used the File menu. Any function that involves the movement of a document to or from main memory is done by using the File menu.

Figure 1-30 shows the File menu. You can see that the "Retrieve" option is highlighted. This option will retrieve your document into the computer's main memory so that the document can appear on the screen.

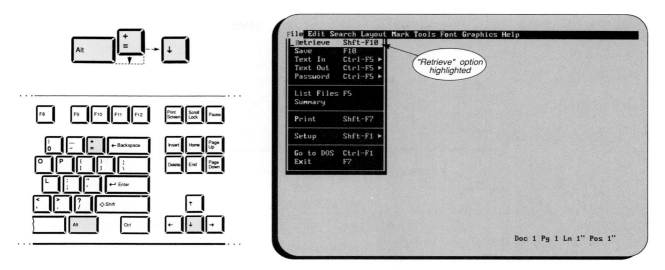

FIGURE 1-30 Retrieving a document

Press the Enter key to select the "Retrieve" option, and the message in Figure 1-31 appears.

FIGURE 1-31 "Retrieve" option

The retrieve message prompts you to enter the name of the document you want to retrieve. Again, using upper-case, lowercase, or a combination of both, type `proj1` (Figure 1-32).

Document to be retrieved: proj1_

document to be retrieved

FIGURE 1-32   Entering a document name

Press the Enter key, and the document appears on the screen, ready for you to edit or revise it (Figure 1-33). The cursor is positioned on the first character of the document. Notice that the document's filename appears in the lower left side of the text window, next to the status line.

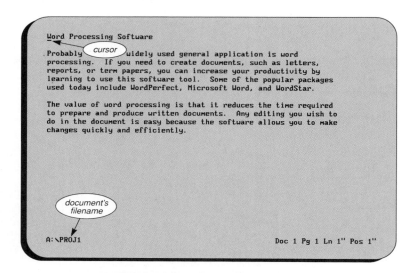

```
Word Processing Software

.Probably        uidely used general application is word
processing.  If you need to create documents, such as letters,
reports, or term papers, you can increase your productivity by
learning to use this software tool.  Some of the popular packages
used today include WordPerfect, Microsoft Word, and WordStar.

The value of word processing is that it reduces the time required
to prepare and produce written documents.  Any editing you wish to
do in the document is easy because the software allows you to make
changes quickly and efficiently.



A:\PROJ1                                      Doc 1 Pg 1 Ln 1" Pos 1"
```

cursor

document's filename

FIGURE 1-33   Retrieved document

Mouse Users: Click the right mouse button to display the menu bar. Select the "Retrieve" option from the File menu before you enter the document's filename.

Moving the Cursor

Before you begin revising your document, you need to know how to move the cursor through the text of the document. Table 1-1 lists the various keystrokes used to move the cursor through a document. You will use some of these methods in this project; you will use other methods in later projects. Be sure to practice the various methods so that you become adept at moving the cursor.

TABLE 1-1 Moving the Cursor Through the Document

ACTIVITY	KEYS
Left one character or space	←
Right one character or space	→
Down one line	↓
Up one line	↑
Left one word	Ctrl-←
Right one word	Ctrl-→
Left side of screen	Home ←
Right side of screen	Home →
Left end of line	Home Home ←
Right end of line	Home Home →
Top of screen	Home ↑
Bottom of screen	Home ↓
Top of document	Home Home ↑
Bottom of document	Home Home ↓
First line of previous page	Page Up
First line of next page	Page Down
Top of document *before any codes*	Home Home Home ↑

Let's try moving the cursor. Recall that pressing the Right Arrow key one time moves the cursor one character or space to the right. With the cursor resting on the first character of the document — the W in Word — watch the screen as you press the Right Arrow key three times. Notice that the cursor moves a character at a time to the right, and that the Pos number on the status line changes to reflect the current cursor position (Figure 1-34).

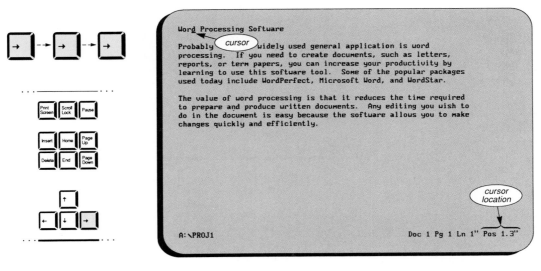

FIGURE 1-34 Using the Right Arrow key

Similarly, pressing the Left Arrow key moves the cursor one character or space to the left. Watch the screen as you press the Left Arrow key three times. The cursor is now back at its original location, the very first character of the document (Figure 1-35).

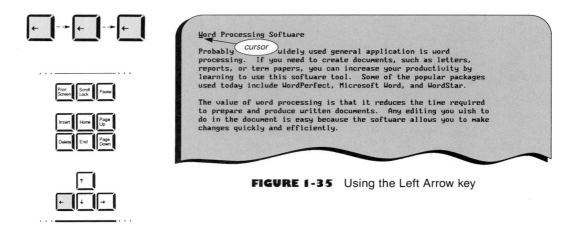

FIGURE 1-35 Using the Left Arrow key

Pressing the Down Arrow key moves the cursor directly down one line. Watch the screen as you press the Down Arrow key five times. The cursor moves directly down five lines, to the l in learning. The status line now shows that the cursor is on Ln 1.83", Pos 1" (Figure 1-36).

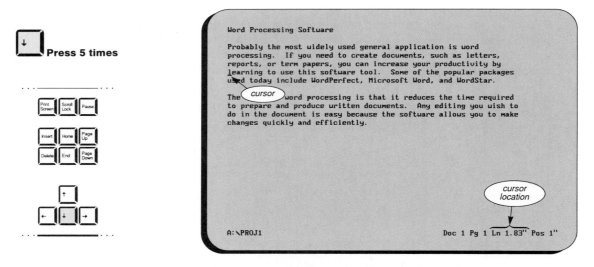

FIGURE 1-36 Using the Down Arrow key

The Up Arrow key moves the cursor directly up one line. Press the Up Arrow key five times while you watch the screen. The cursor moves up five lines, and is now in its original position at the beginning of the document.

Revising a Document

Now that you have retrieved the document, you are going to add a sentence at the end of the second paragraph. To do this, you will first position the cursor at the end of the second paragraph, which is also the end of the document. To move the cursor to the end of the document, press the Home key twice, then press the Down Arrow key. Notice that the cursor moves to the line at the end of the document, and not to the very bottom of the screen. This is because *the cursor can not be moved into areas that contain no text*. Because the text ends on the line above, the cursor moves to the last available line on the screen that contains text.

Now, let's position the cursor to insert the new sentence. Press the Left Arrow key once so the cursor rests on the space immediately following the last sentence of the document, Ln 2.83", Pos 4.2" (Figure 1-37).

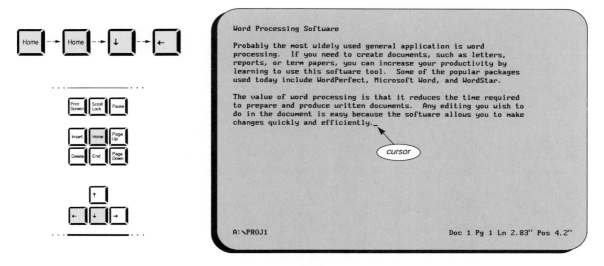

FIGURE 1-37   Positioning the cursor

Press the Spacebar twice to add two blank spaces between the period and the first character of the new sentence you are adding. Now, enter the sentence: In addition, the tedious task of typing a final draft is eliminated. As you type, notice how the sentence is inserted to the *left* of the cursor. This is because WordPerfect is automatically set to **Insert mode**, which means that text is inserted to the left of the cursor. Existing text, including the character upon which the cursor is resting, will remain intact and will adjust to accommodate the new text you type. Your document should now look like the one in Figure 1-38.

FIGURE 1-38
Adding text

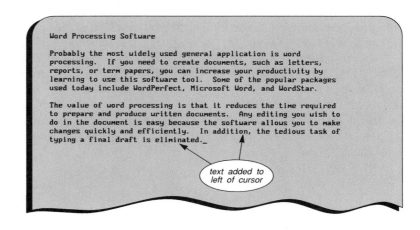

THE REVEAL CODES SCREEN

WordPerfect's text window is designed to be free of unnecessary symbols and characters, so you will be able to have a fairly accurate idea of what your document will look like once it is printed. While you are working on a document, however, WordPerfect records each keystroke you make. Some of these keystrokes are not visible to you on WordPerfect's standard screen display. Sometimes it is helpful, and even necessary, to be able to view the keystrokes that are usually invisible. You can do this by displaying the Reveal Codes screen. Let's try this now.

First, move the cursor to the beginning of the document by pressing the Home key twice, then pressing the Up Arrow key once. Display the menu bar by holding down the Alt key and while holding it down, pressing = (Alt-=). The "Reveal Codes" option is contained in the Edit menu, so type E to display the Edit menu. Select "Reveal Codes" by typing R, or by positioning the highlight directly on the "Reveal Codes" option and pressing Enter. The Reveal Codes screen is immediately displayed. (Figure 1-39).

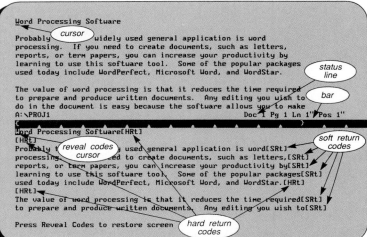

FIGURE 1-39 Reveal Codes screen

Mouse Users: Click the right mouse button to display the menu bar. Select Edit, then select "Reveal Codes".

The screen is divided by a bar into upper and lower portions. The upper portion of the screen is the screen display you are accustomed to seeing. It is clean and free of codes, and the cursor is the usual blinking underscore. The lower portion, however, contains the codes WordPerfect needs in order to generate a document in the manner you specify while you create a document. All codes appear in boldface on the Reveal Codes screen so that they are easier to identify. The cursor in the lower portion of the screen appears as a solid rectangle.

Notice the [HRt] code at the end of the first line. This is a hard return code. WordPerfect inserts this code each time you press the Enter key. The [SRt] codes indicate a soft return. WordPerfect inserts soft return codes at the end of each line where wordwrap occurs.

You are able to scroll through the Reveal Codes screen and to perform any editing tasks you ordinarily would while in the normal screen display. Watch the screen as you press the Down Arrow key until the cursor reaches the end of the document (Figure 1-40).

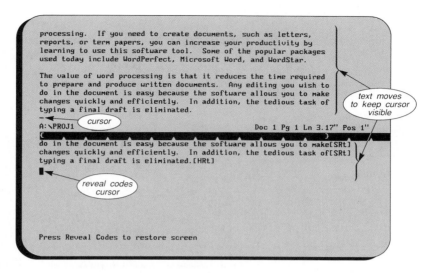

FIGURE 1-40   Scrolling in the Reveal Codes screen

Notice how the top portion of the document moves off the screen. WordPerfect does this so that the portion of the document containing the cursor is visible at all times. Notice, too, that the text in the lower portion of the screen also scrolled so that its cursor is also visible. In this project, only the [HRt] and [SRt] codes are embedded in the document. In later projects, you will learn about many other codes. For now, let's exit the Reveal Codes screen by holding down the Alt key and while holding it down, pressing = (Alt-=). Next, type E to access the Edit menu. In the Edit menu, you can either type R for "Reveal Codes" or use the Down Arrow key to highlight the "Reveal Codes" option and then press Enter. The screen is returned to its normal display (Figure 1-41).

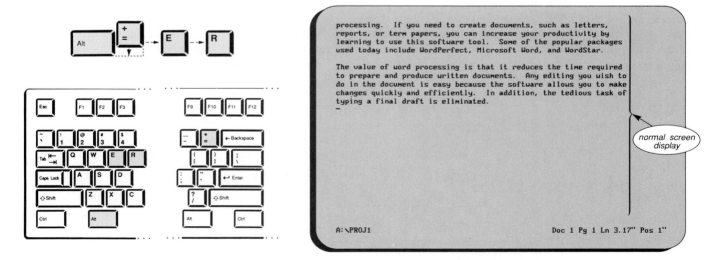

FIGURE 1-41   Exiting the Reveal Codes screen

 Mouse Users: Click the right mouse button to display the menu bar. Select Edit, then select "Reveal Codes".

SAVING A REVISED DOCUMENT

Now that you have revised the document, you should save your document again. As before, activate the menu bar by holding down the Alt key and while holding it down, pressing = (Alt- =). When the menu bar displays, press the Down Arrow key to pull down the File menu. Now, type S for "Save", and the message in Figure 1-42 appears. The "A:\" preceding the document name indicates the disk drive containing the document.

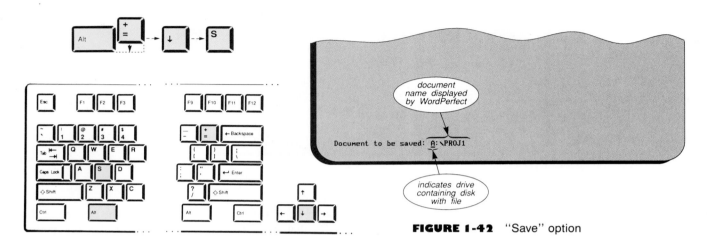

FIGURE 1-42   "Save" option

Notice that PROJ1 appears as the document name. How has this happened? The first time you saved the document, you needed to type the name under which it was to be saved. Since your document had already been saved under the name PROJ1, WordPerfect automatically displays that name each subsequent time you save the document. Press the Enter key to confirm that you want to save the document under the filename PROJ1.

When WordPerfect attempts to save this revised document under the name PROJ1, the message shown in Figure 1-43 appears. This is another of WordPerfect's safeguards. *Two different documents cannot be saved under the same document name.* Because the document on the screen differs from the document already saved on disk (recall you added a sentence), a WordPerfect prompt asks you if you want to replace the old version with the current version. Because you do want to replace the old version with the revised verion, type Y. The new version of the document, including the sentence you added, is now saved on the disk under the name PROJ1.

FIGURE 1-43   Replace message

Mouse Users: Click the right mouse button to display the menu bar. Select File, then select "Save" before you respond to the message, "Document to be saved:"

PRINTING A REVISED DOCUMENT

◆ Now that the revised document is saved, let's print a new copy. As before, activate the menu bar by holding down the Alt key and while holding it down, pressing = (Alt-=). Press the Down Arrow key to display the File menu, then type P to select the "Print" option. When the Print menu displays, type 1 or F to specify "Full Document". Your revised, printed document should look like Figure 1-44.

FIGURE 1-44 Completed document

Mouse Users: Click the right mouse button to display the menu bar. Select the "Print" option from the File menu. Select "Full Document" from the Print menu.

EXITING WORDPERFECT

◆ Recall that you should always exit WordPerfect properly when you want to end a WordPerfect session. Activate the menu bar, then pull down the File menu. Type X for "Exit". When the message, "Save Document? Yes(No)" appears, type N since you already saved the document. At the message, "Exit WP? No(Yes)", type Y. You exit Word-Perfect and return to the DOS prompt. At the DOS prompt, be sure you remove your data or program disks if necessary.

Mouse Users: Click the right mouse button to display the menu bar. Select File, then select "Exit" before you respond to the message, "Save Document? Yes(No)".

PROJECT SUMMARY

In Project 1 you learned how to load WordPerfect into the computer's main memory, and then how to create, save, and print a document. You also retrieved and revised the document you created, then you saved the revised document onto a disk. Finally, you displayed the Reveal Codes screen, scrolled through the text, and identified the codes contained in the document.

All the activities that you learned for this project are summarized in the Quick Reference following Project 6. The following is a summary of the keystroke sequence we used in Project 1.

SUMMARY OF KEYSTROKES — PROJECT 1

STEPS	KEY(S) PRESSED	RESULTS
1	wp ↵ [At C> prompt or as directed by instructor]	Loads WordPerfect.
2	Alt-=	Displays menu bar.
3	→	Activates Edit menu.
4	←	Activates File menu.
5	↓	Pulls down File menu.
6	↓[Press 5 times] ↵	Selects "List Files" option.
7	= a: ↵ Esc	Changes drive to A:.
8	Word Processing Softwaer	Enters document title.
9	Backspace Backspace	Removes incorrect characters to left of cursor.
10	re ↵	Enters correct characters and moves cursor down one line.
11	↵	Inserts blank line.
12	Probably the most widely used general application is word processing. If you need to create documents, such as letters, reports, or term papers, you can increase your productivity by learning to use this software tool. Some of the popular packages used today include Microsoft Word, WordPerfect, and WordStar. ↵ ↵	Enters text of first paragraph followed by a blank line.
13	The value of word processing is that it reduces the time required to prepare and produce written documents. Any editing you wish to do in the document is easy because the software allows you to make changes quickly and efficiently. ↵	Enters text of second paragraph.
14	Alt-=	Displays menu bar.
15	↓	Pulls down File menu.
16	S	Selects "Save" option.
17	proj1 ↵	Saves document under name PROJ1.
18	Delete	Bypasses document summary.
19	Alt-=	Displays menu bar.
20	↓	Pulls down File menu.
21	P	Displays Print menu.
22	1	Prints full document.
23	Alt-=	Displays menu bar.
24	↓	Pulls down File menu.
25	X Y Y	Exits WordPerfect and returns to DOS.

SUMMARY OF KEYSTROKES — PROJECT 1 (continued)

STEPS	KEY(S) PRESSED	RESULTS
26	wp ↵ [At C> prompt or as directed by instructor]	Loads WordPerfect.
27	Alt-= ↓	Displays File menu.
28	↵	Selects "Retrieve" option.
29	proj1 ↵	Retrieves named document.
30	→ → →	Moves cursor three characters to the right.
31	← ← ←	Moves cursor three characters to the left.
32	↓[Press 5 times]	Moves cursor down five lines.
33	↑[Press 5 times]	Moves cursor up five lines.
34	Home Home ↓	Moves cursor to end of document.
35	←	Positions cursor to enter sentence.
36	Spacebar Spacebar	Enters two blank spaces.
37	In addition, the tedious task of typing a final draft is eliminated.	Enters new sentence into document.
38	Home Home ↑	Positions cursor at top of document.
39	Alt-= → ↓ R	Displays Reveal Codes screen.
40	↓[Press 13 times]	Moves cursor through text of document.
41	Alt-= → ↓R	Exits Reveal Codes screen.
42	Alt-= ↓S ↵	Saves document under same name.
43	Alt-= ↓P 1	Prints document.
44	Alt-= ↓X Y Y	Exits WordPerfect and returns to DOS.

The following list summarizes the material covered in Project 1.

1. The **keyboard** is the device you use to input text and data into the computer to perform word processing activities.
2. The keyboard's **typewriter section** contains other keys in addition to the keys you are accustomed to seeing on a typewriter.
3. The **Ctrl** (Control) and **Alt** (Alternate) keys are used in combination with other keys to perform specific word processing functions. These keys are *never* used alone.
4. The **Shift** keys are used to type capital letters and symbols.
5. The **Caps Lock** key is also used to enter capital letters. However, even with the Caps Lock key turned on, you must still press a Shift key to type symbols.
6. The Caps Lock key is a **toggle**, which means that you turn it off the same way you turn it on.
7. The **Tab** key is used for indenting to the next tab setting to the right.
8. The **Enter** key, sometimes referred to as the Return key, is used to begin a new line, to add a blank line to the text, or to enter information or options into the computer.
9. The **Backspace** key moves the cursor back one space on the screen each time it is pressed and removes the character to the left of the cursor.
10. The **Spacebar** adds blank spaces to a document and moves the cursor to the right.
11. The **cursor**, which points to your position in the text window, is represented by a blinking underscore.
12. The **cursor movement keys**, located to the right of the typewriter section of the keyboard, are used to move the cursor.

13. The **numeric keypad** can be used to enter numbers into a document.
14. The **Left Arrow** key moves the cursor one character or space to the left.
15. The **Right Arrow** key moves the cursor one character or space to the right.
16. The **Up Arrow** key moves the cursor directly up one line.
17. The **Down Arrow** key moves the cursor directly down one line.
18. The **function keys**, labeled F1 through F12 (or through F10, on the standard keyboard), are used to perform specific functions. They can be used alone or in combination with other keys, depending upon the task that is being performed.
19. **Default**, or initial, predefined settings, affect the way your screen will appear and the way your document will print.
20. The WordPerfect screen is divided into two parts: the text window and the status line.
21. The **text window** is the portion of the screen which displays the text you type.
22. The menu contains options that you can use to achieve specific word processing functions.
23. The **status line** gives information about the cursor's location, such as document, page, and line and position number.
24. Use the Alt and = keys to activate the main menu, or **menu bar**. If you accidentally display the menu, you can cancel it by pressing Alt-=, F1, or the Esc key.
25. WordPerfect refers to any data or text stored on a disk as a **file**.
26. You can use the arrow keys to highlight options in the menu.
27. **Wordwrap** allows you to type continuously without pressing the Enter key each time the cursor reaches the right margin.
28. Options can be selected by typing their boldfaced letter, usually the first character. If the first character doesn't access the option, try the option's second letter.
29. Whenever a document is completed, it should be **saved** to a disk so that it can be retrieved for editing or printing at a later time. To avoid losing portions of text, documents should be saved every fifteen minutes or so.
30. A **document summary** appears each time a document is saved. This sheet allows you to enter information about the document for future reference.
31. When a document is printed on paper, it is referred to as a **hard copy**.
32. The File menu contains both the "Save" and "Retrieve" options. Any function that involves the movement of a document to or from main memory is done through the File menu.
33. WordPerfect is automatically set to **Insert mode**, which leaves existing text intact and inserts new text to the left of the cursor.
34. The Reveal Codes screen allows you to view the usually invisible codes that WordPerfect embeds into a document.
35. The "Retrieve" option is used to retrieve files from disk for editing or printing.
36. The "Exit" option exits WordPerfect and returns to the DOS prompt.

STUDENT ASSIGNMENTS

STUDENT ASSIGNMENT 1: True/False

Instructions: Circle T if the statement is true and F if the statement is false.

T F 1. Options in the menu bar can be accessed only by using the arrow keys; there is no other way to access them.
T F 2. The cursor is represented on the screen by a flashing diamond.
T F 3. WordPerfect's menu bar contains nine separate menus that can be pulled down.
T F 4. The status line displays information about the cursor's location.
T F 5. WordPerfect automatically converts document names to lowercase characters.
T F 6. The "Save" option is accessed through the File menu.
T F 7. Once a document is printed on paper, it is referred to as a hard copy.

T F   8. To retrieve a document through the main menu, you must first pull down the File menu.
T F   9. To move the cursor around in a document, you can use the arrow keys.
T F   10. Pressing the Up Arrow key once will move the cursor to the top of the document.

STUDENT ASSIGNMENT 2: Multiple Choice

Instructions: Circle the correct response.

1. If the menu is accidentally activated, press the _____ key(s) to cancel it and return to the text window.
   a. Alt- =
   b. Esc
   c. F1
   d. all of the above
2. The Right Arrow key moves the cursor _____.
   a. one character to the right
   b. one word to the right
   c. to the far right margin
   d. down one line
3. The Enter key is used to _____.
   a. end a paragraph
   b. select options
   c. insert a blank line
   d. all of the above
4. Once a document has been printed on paper, it is referred to as a _____.
   a. reveal codes copy
   b. data copy
   c. hard copy
   d. none of the above
5. The "Retrieve" option is accessed through the _____ menu.
   a. Exit
   b. File
   c. Edit
   d. none of the above
6. After the Print menu is pulled down, typing _____ will cause a document to begin printing on the printer.
   a. 1
   b. Alt- =
   c. F
   d. both a and c
7. The "Print" option is contained in the _____ menu.
   a. Edit
   b. File
   c. Save
   d. none of the above
8. When a document is saved to disk, a _____ appears, which enables you to enter helpful information about a document for later reference.
   a. document summary
   b. summary sheet
   c. directory
   d. none of the above
9. The "Reveal Codes" option is contained in the _____ menu.
   a. Codes
   b. File
   c. Edit
   d. none of the above

STUDENT ASSIGNMENT 3: Matching

Instructions: Put the appropriate number next to the word(s) in the second column.

1. Right or Left Arrow key   _____   Contains "Save" option
2. Up Arrow key   _____   Indicates where the Enter key was pressed
3. File menu   _____   Moves highlight between options
4. Alt-= keys   _____   Removes incorrect character to left of cursor
5. Enter key   _____   Moves cursor directly down one line
6. Backspace key   _____   Activates menu bar
7. "Exit" option   _____   Accessed through File menu
8. Down Arrow key   _____   Enters blank lines in document
9. "Retrieve" option   _____   Exits to DOS prompt
10. [HRt]   _____   Moves the cursor up one line

STUDENT ASSIGNMENT 4: Fill in the Blanks

Instructions: Fill in the blanks in the following sentences.

1. To begin the WordPerfect program, type _____ at the DOS prompt.
2. The WordPerfect screen displays the _____ in the lower right corner of the window.
3. Once a document is saved, WordPerfect displays the _____ to the left of the status line.
4. To activate the menu bar, press the _____ key(s).
5. WordPerfect automatically converts document names to _____ case characters.
6. To change the drive, select the _____ option.
7. Bringing a saved document onto the screen so that it can be viewed or edited is called _____ a document.
8. To enter a blank line into a document, press the _____ key.
9. Options can be selected with arrow keys or by typing their _____.
10. The page and position indicators are displayed on the _____ line.

STUDENT ASSIGNMENT 5: Fill in the Blanks

Instructions: Fill in the blanks in the following sentences.

1. Pressing the Right Arrow key once moves the cursor one _____ to the right.
2. The "List Files" option is contained in the _____ menu.
3. The _____ menu contains the "Save" option.
4. Once the Print menu appears, select _____ to begin printing the entire (full) document on the printer.
5. The cursor appears as a _____ on the WordPerfect screen.
6. To quickly move the cursor to the top of a document, press _____.
7. The _____ points to the position on the screen.
8. To return to the DOS prompt, select the _____ option.
9. To quickly move the cursor to the end of a document, press _____.
10. Being able to type continuously without pressing the Enter key each time the right margin is reached is the feature known as _____.

STUDENT ASSIGNMENT 6: The WordPerfect Screen

Instructions: Use the following names to label the parts of the WordPerfect screen shown here.

Text window
Cursor
Hard return code
Soft return code
Status line
Document number
Page number
Position number
Line number
Document name
Reveal Codes cursor

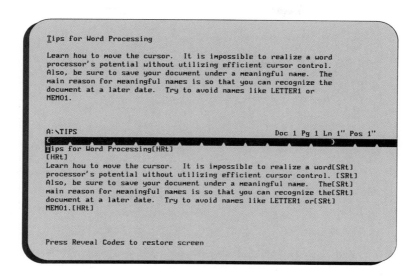

STUDENT ASSIGNMENT 7: Correcting Errors

Instructions: This document illustrates the first part of a memo that is being prepared using WordPerfect. A typing error has just occurred. The word *for* should actually read *from*. Explain the steps to correct this error.

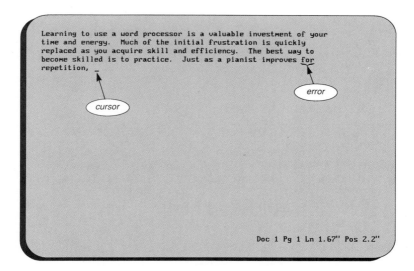

Steps: _____

_____

_____

STUDENT ASSIGNMENT 8: Correcting Errors

Instructions: This screen shows a letter that has been prepared using WordPerfect. A blank line needs to be inserted between the last sentence of the letter and the closing. Explain the steps to add a blank line above the word Sincerely.

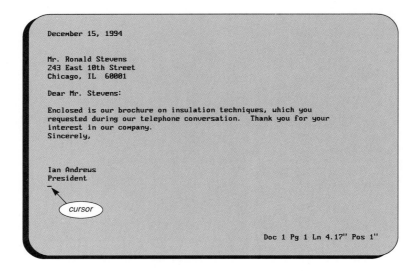

Steps: _____

_____

_____

STUDENT ASSIGNMENT 9: Creating a Document

Instructions: Perform the following tasks.

1. Type the document shown here.

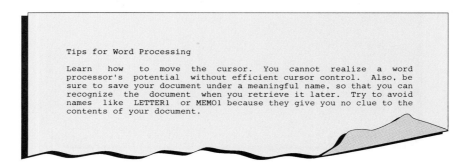

2. After you have typed the document, save it onto your disk under the name TIPS.
3. Print the document on the printer.
4. Exit WordPerfect and return to DOS.

STUDENT ASSIGNMENT 10: Retrieving and Revising a Document

Instructions: Perform the following tasks.

1. Retrieve the document TIPS created in Student Assignment 9.
2. Add the following sentence to the end of the first paragraph: These document names may make perfect sense to you when you first create the document, but will probably be meaningless after some time passes.
3. Save the document on your disk, again using the name TIPS. (You will *replace* the old version of TIPS with the new, edited version.)
4. Print the revised document. Your document should now appear as follows.

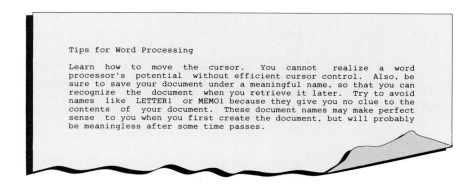

```
Tips for Word Processing

Learn  how  to  move  the  cursor.   You  cannot   realize   a   word
processor's  potential  without efficient cursor control.  Also, be
sure to save your document under a meaningful name, so that you can
recognize  the  document  when you retrieve it later.  Try to avoid
names  like  LETTER1  or MEMO1 because they give you no clue to the
contents  of  your document.  These document names may make perfect
sense  to  you when you first create the document, but will probably
be meaningless after some time passes.
```

5. Exit WordPerfect and return to DOS.

STUDENT ASSIGNMENT 11: Retrieving and Revising a Document

Instructions: Perform the following tasks.

1. Load the document TIPS, which you revised in Student Assignment 10.
2. Insert a blank line at the end of the document, then type the following as a new paragraph: When working on a document, save it frequently. Nothing is more frustrating than losing large portions of text.
3. Save the document, again under the name TIPS, then print a copy of the revised document. The document should now appear as follows.

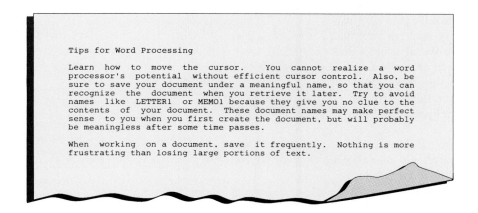

```
Tips for Word Processing

Learn  how  to  move  the  cursor.   You  cannot  realize  a  word
processor's  potential  without efficient cursor control.  Also, be
sure to save your document under a meaningful name, so that you can
recognize  the  document  when you retrieve it later.  Try to avoid
names  like  LETTER1  or MEMO1 because they give you no clue to the
contents  of  your document.  These document names may make perfect
sense  to  you when you first create the document, but will probably
be meaningless after some time passes.

When  working  on a document, save  it frequently.  Nothing is more
frustrating than losing large portions of text.
```

PROJECT 2

Formatting Text

OBJECTIVES

You will have mastered the material in this project when you can:

◆ List the files on disk

◆ Delete and restore portions of text

◆ Change WordPerfect to Typeover mode

◆ Underline, center, and boldface text

◆ Save a document under a new name

◆ Use shortcut keys to access menu options

◆ Double-space text

◆ Remove special text formats

◆ Use the Spell program

If you are using WordPerfect on a hard disk system or running on a networked version of WordPerfect, load WordPerfect as your instructor directs. Be sure to put a formatted disk into drive A so that you can save your documents.

If you are using WordPerfect on a two-disk system, at the A prompt put your data disk in drive B and the WordPerfect 1 disk in drive A. Type wp and press the Enter key. When WordPerfect prompts you, replace the WordPerfect 1 disk with the WordPerfect 2 disk, and press the Enter key.

Be sure you change the default drive/directory to drive A before beginning Project 2 so that your work will be saved on your disk in drive A. If you are using a two-disk system, change the drive to B.

In Project 2 you will use the document PROJ1 which you created in Project 1. After retrieving this document, you will learn how to edit text, how to delete and restore portions of text, and how to use Word-Perfect's Typeover mode. You will enter text with special formats, and then use the Reveal Codes screen to remove special formats from text. Finally, you will double-space the text of the document, and then use WordPerfect's Spell program to check the document for typographical and spelling errors. When this project is complete, your document will look like Figure 2-1.

<u>Word Processing Software Packages</u>

Probably the most popular and widely used general application is word processing. If you need to create documents, such as letters, reports, or term papers, you can <u>greatly</u> increase your productivity by learning to use this software tool. Some of the popular packages used today include WordPerfect, Microsoft Word, and WordStar.

The value of word processing is that it **substantially** reduces the time required to prepare and produce printed documents. Any editing you wish to do in the document is easy because the software allows you to make changes quickly and efficiently. In addition, the tedious task of typing a final draft is eliminated.

Most word processors provide you with several methods to accomplish specific goals. The method used depends on the situation. For example, you can move the cursor through the text by using several different keystrokes. Also, you can usually delete text by a character, a word, a sentence, a paragraph, or even a page at a time. Some word processing packages offer alternate methods of executing commands.

In addition most word processors provide ways for you to enhance the appearance of the text with text formatting features. These formatting features allow you to quickly and easily center, underline, boldface, or double space text in your document, usually in just a couple of keystrokes. This ease of use and efficiency have made word processing a must in most academic and business settings. By taking the time to learn a word processing package, you will increase the chances of your success.

FIGURE 2-1 Document for Project 2

RETRIEVING DOCUMENTS WITH THE LIST FILES OPTION

◆ To begin, you must first retrieve the document you created in Project 1. In Project 1, you used the "Retrieve" option by typing the name of the document you wanted to retrieve. But what if you don't recall the name you assigned to the document? Or what if you believe you entered the name correctly, but the document didn't appear on the screen? The "List Files" option allows you to view a list of the files on your disk.

Let's use "List Files" to retrieve the document PROJ1. As before, press Alt-= to activate the menu bar, then press the Down Arrow key to pull down the File menu. Next, type F for "List Files". The message in Figure 2-2 appears.

FIGURE 2-2
Listing files

Pressing the Enter key in response to this message will cause WordPerfect to list the files on the A drive, which is the drive containing your disk. Press Enter, and a list of the files on your disk appears on the screen, as shown in Figure 2-3. The list on your screen might appear somewhat different than the list in Figure 2-3.

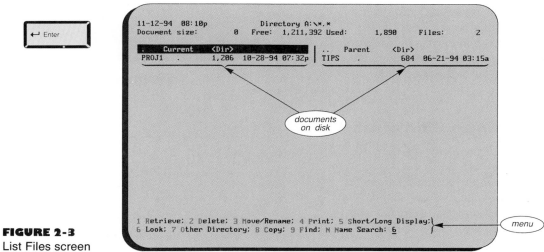

FIGURE 2-3
List Files screen

To retrieve a document, you must first highlight its name by using the arrow keys. Press the Down Arrow key until the document name PROJ1 is highlighted. Notice the menu at the bottom of the screen. "Retrieve" is number 1 on the menu, so type 1 or R, and the document PROJ1 appears on the screen, ready for editing (Figure 2-4).

The cursor is positioned on the first character of the document, Ln 1", Pos 1".

Mouse Users: Click the right mouse button to display the menu bar. Select the File menu, then select "Retrieve". Type proj1 and click the right mouse button.

CURSOR MOVEMENT

Now that the document PROJ1 is on the screen, let's make some changes to it. Recall that in Project 1 you used some keystrokes from Table 1-1 to move the cursor. Let's practice more of these cursor movements while you make changes to your document.

As you enter these changes, be sure to type them *exactly as they appear*. We ask you to make intentional spelling errors. Later in this project, you will correct these errors. The cursor should be resting on the first character of the document PROJ1.

Beginning or End of Line

You can use the Home and Left Arrow keys and the End key to move the cursor to the beginning or end of a line. Press the End key, and the cursor moves to the end of the line containing the cursor, Ln 1", Pos 3.4" (Figure 2-5).

FIGURE 2-4 Document retrieved

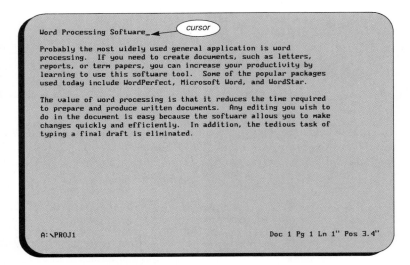

FIGURE 2-5 Pressing the End key

Now let's add a word to the heading. Press the Spacebar once to insert a blank space, then type `Pakcages` (Figure 2-6). Be sure you misspell the word as shown.

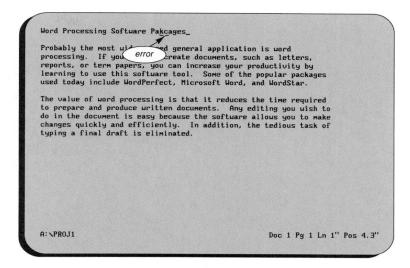

FIGURE 2-6 Adding text

Next let's move the cursor to the beginning of the line. Press the Home key, then press the Left Arrow key, and the cursor moves back to the first character of the line (Figure 2-7).

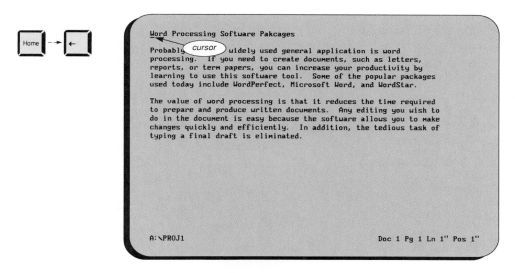

FIGURE 2-7 Moving to the beginning of a line

A Word at a Time to the Right

You can move the cursor a word at a time to the right or the left. To see how you can do this, let's move the cursor a word at a time to the right, from the word Word to the word Pakcages in the heading. The cursor should be on the first character of the document. Hold down the Ctrl key, and while holding it down, press the Right Arrow key three times. The cursor moves to the first character of the word Pakcages (Figure 2-8).

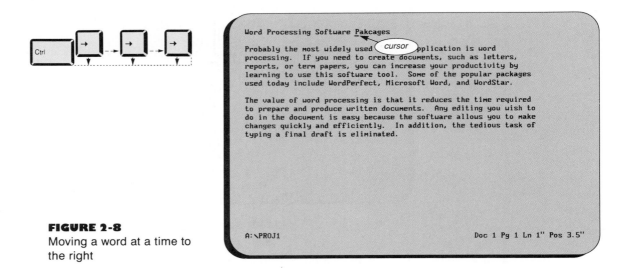

FIGURE 2-8
Moving a word at a time to the right

A Word at a Time to the Left

Just as you can move the cursor a word at a time to the right, you can also move a word at a time to the left. Let's use this cursor movement to make some more changes to your document. Press the Down Arrow key twice to move the cursor into the first sentence. The cursor is positioned at Ln 1.33", Pos 3.5", on the letter u in used. Now hold down the Ctrl key, and while holding it down, press the Left Arrow key once so that the cursor is positioned on the first character of the word widely (Figure 2-9).

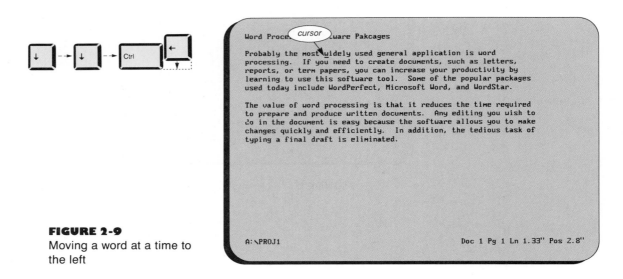

FIGURE 2-9
Moving a word at a time to the left

Again making certain you enter them *exactly as shown*, type the words `most poplar and`, then press the Spacebar once to insert a blank space (Figure 2-10). Notice that these words were inserted to the left of the cursor.

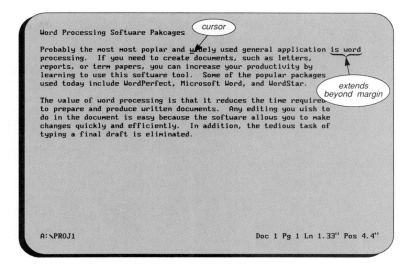

FIGURE 2-10
Adding text

Rewriting the Screen

Notice in Figure 2-10 that the sentence containing the words you added extended beyond the right margin on the screen. Sometimes WordPerfect will do this during editing if you are adding or deleting larger portions of text. When this happens, you need to rewrite the screen. Rewriting the screen causes the text to align correctly on the screen.

To rewrite the screen, you simply move the cursor through the text that needs to be aligned. In this case, pressing the Down Arrow key will move the cursor through the text. Watch the screen as you press the Down Arrow key. The text that extended beyond the right margin is automatically moved down to the next line, and the following text adjusts to accommodate it (Figure 2-11).

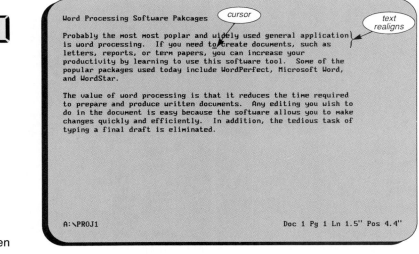

FIGURE 2-11
Rewriting the screen

Now, press the Down Arrow key until the cursor is positioned in the second line in the second paragraph. Hold down the Ctrl key and, while holding it down, press the Right Arrow key until the cursor is positioned on the first character of the word you. Type `or revising`, then press the Spacebar once to insert a blank space (Figure 2-12).

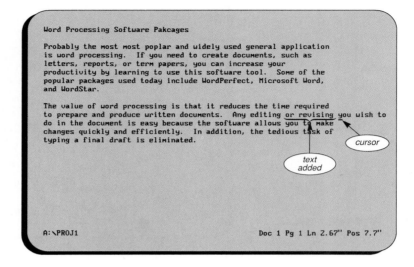

FIGURE 2-12
Adding text

The cursor remains on the letter y in you, and the text is inserted to the left. Again, rewrite the screen by pressing the Down Arrow key once.

Top or Bottom of Screen

You can use the Home key with the Up or Down Arrow key to move the cursor to the top or bottom of a screen. Let's use the Home and Down Arrow keys to move to the bottom of the screen so that you can add some text to your document. Press the Home key, then press the Down Arrow key, and the cursor moves to the first position on the last line on the screen, Ln 3.33", Pos 1" (Figure 2-13).

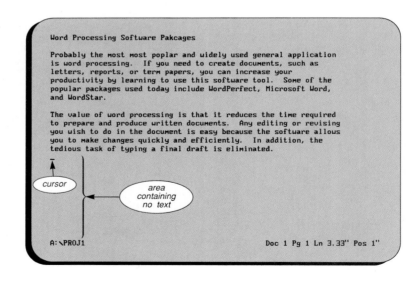

FIGURE 2-13
Moving to the bottom of the screen

Notice that the cursor moves to the last line of the document and not the last line visible on the screen. Recall that this is because *the cursor cannot be moved into areas that contain no text*. Therefore, the cursor stops at the last available line on the screen. In longer documents that contain several pages of text, you will find that using the Home key with the Up and Down Arrow keys is very helpful. These keys help you move the cursor through a screenful (24 lines, on most monitors) of text at a time.

With the cursor positioned at the end of the document, Ln 3.33", Pos 1", press the Enter key to insert a blank line and then type the following paragraph, typographical errors included: Most word processors provide you with several methods to accomplish specific goals. The method used depends on the situation. For example, you can move the cursor through the text by using several different keystrokes. Also, you can usually delete text by a charachter, a word, a sentence, a paragraph, or even a page at a time. Some word processing packages offer alteernate methods of executing commands.

Press the Enter key twice, once to end the paragraph, and once to insert a blank line (Figure 2-14). Now type the following paragraph; notice that it, too, contains some spelling errors. In addition most word processors provid ways for you to enhance the appearance of the text with text formatting features. These formatting features allow you to quickly and easily center, underline, boldface, or double space text in your document, usually in just a couple of keystrokes. This ease of use and efficiency have made word processing a must in most academic and business settings. By taking the time to learn a word processing package, you will increase the chances of your success. Press the Enter key. Your screen should now look like the one in Figure 2-15, errors and all.

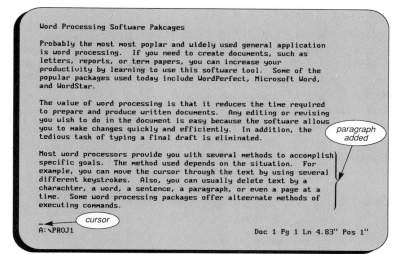

FIGURE 2-14 Adding a paragraph

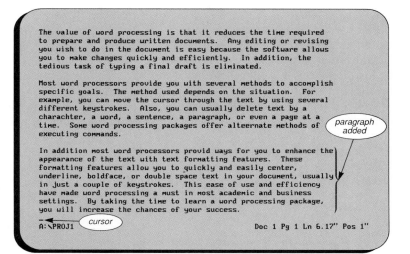

FIGURE 2-15 Adding a paragraph

Did you notice as you entered the new text that the top portion of the document moved off the screen? This is because the document is too long to fit into the lines available in the text window. WordPerfect moves the top portion of the document off the screen so that the portion containing the cursor will remain visible on the screen at all times. This is called **scrolling**. The beginning of the document still exists, as shown in Figure 2-16.

Press the Home key, then press the Up Arrow key. The cursor returns to the first character on the first line on the screen.

SAVING A DOCUMENT UNDER A NEW NAME

◆ Now that you have made some major additions to your document, you should save it so that your changes won't

FIGURE 2-16 Document position on screen

be lost. Let's call this edited document PROJ2; with this new name you won't confuse the new version of the document with PROJ1.

Notice that the document name on the screen is still PROJ1. This is because you have not yet saved your changes to the disk. Saving a document under a new name is similar to saving a document for the first time, because you must enter the document name.

To save the document, press Alt- = to activate the menu bar, then press the Down Arrow key to pull down the File menu. Now type S for "Save", and the screen in Figure 2-17 appears. (If the Document Summary appears, press Delete, then type Y.) WordPerfect automatically enters the name PROJ1.

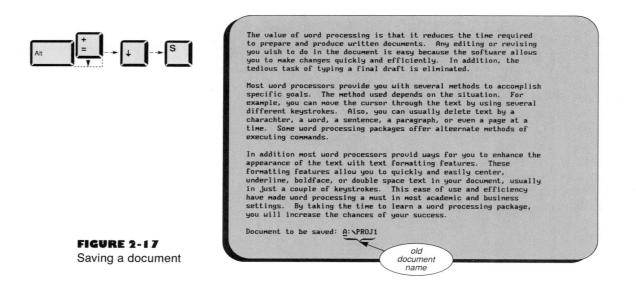

FIGURE 2-17
Saving a document

Since you want to preserve the old version of this document under the name PROJ1, type the new name proj2 (Figure 2-18), then press the Enter key. Your document is now saved on your disk under the name PROJ2.

FIGURE 2-18
Saving under a new name

If you had not given this document a new name and had saved it again under the name PROJ1, the original version of PROJ1 would have been replaced on the disk with the document you just completed.

DEFAULTS

A **default** is an automatic or predefined setting. For example, virtually every function WordPerfect performs has a default setting, which is contained in the WordPerfect program itself. WordPerfect will use the default settings *unless you instruct it otherwise*.

You have been using or changing defaults throughout this book. For example, when you changed the drive so that your work was saved onto drive A, you *changed* the default setting. You *used* a default setting when you added text to your document, allowing WordPerfect to use Insert mode.

DELETING TEXT

As with cursor movement, WordPerfect allows you to delete text several different ways. Each method can be useful depending upon the situation.

Typeover

You already know that WordPerfect's default is Insert mode, which means that text is inserted to the left of the cursor while existing text remains intact. You are now going to change the default so that WordPerfect is not in Insert mode but in what is called Typeover mode.

Sometimes it's helpful to be able to type right over text, such as when a word or sentence needs to be completely replaced by a new word or sentence. Rather than deleting the old text and inserting the new, you can use **Typeover mode**; that is, you can type the new text directly over the old text. The Insert key activates Typeover mode. Let's use the Insert key to change the word written to the word printed.

First, you must position the cursor on the first character of the word to be edited, which is the w in written. Press the Down Arrow key twice, then hold down the Ctrl key, and while holding it down, press the Right Arrow key until the cursor is on the w in written, Ln 2.67", Pos 3.3".

Now that the cursor is positioned, you need to turn on Typeover. Press Insert, and notice the word "Typeover" appears on the status line to indicate that you have pressed the Insert key (Figure 2-19). When Word-Perfect is in Typeover mode, the character on which the cursor is resting will be replaced by whatever characters you enter. Watch the screen and type the word `printed`. Notice how each character is replaced by the new characters you type (Figure 2-20).

Now press Insert again, and "Typeover" disappears from the status line. The Insert key is what is known as a toggle, which means that you press it to turn it on, and press it again to turn it off. Be sure to press the Insert key when you have finished using Typeover. If you don't, you could accidentally type over and, thereby, delete portions of your document.

A Character at a Time

You can use the Delete key to delete single characters. Thus far, you have deleted single characters by pressing the Backspace key. The Backspace key leaves the character under the cursor intact and literally *backs over* characters to the left of the cursor. Think of it as deleting *backward* through the text. The Delete key also deletes a character at a time, with a major difference: it deletes the character on which the cursor is resting, and appears to *pull in* characters from the right. Think of the Delete key as deleting *forward* through the text.

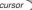

The value of word processing is that it reduces the time required to prepare and produce written documents. Any editing or revising you wish to do in the document is easy because the software allows you to make changes quickly and efficiently. In addition, the tedious task of typing a final draft is eliminated.

Most word processors provide you with several methods to accomplish specific goals. The method used depends on the situation. For example, you can move the cursor through the text by using several different keystrokes. Also, you can usually delete text by a character, a word, a sentence, a paragraph, or even a page at a time. Some word processing packages offer alternate methods of executing commands.

In addition most word processors provid ways for you to enhance the appearance of the text with text formatting features. These formatting features allow you to quickly and easily center, underline, boldface, or double space text in your document, usually in just a couple of keystrokes. This ease of use and efficiency have made word processing a must in most academic and business settings. By taking the time to learn a word processing package, you will increase the chances of your success.

Typeover   Doc 1 Pg 1 Ln 2.67" Pos 3.3"

indicates WordPerfect is in Typeover mode

FIGURE 2-19 Using Typeover

new characters replace old   *cursor*

The value of word processing is that it reduces the time required to prepare and produce printed documents. Any editing or revising you wish to do in the document is easy because the software allows you to make changes quickly and efficiently. In addition, the tedious task of typing a final draft is eliminated.

Most word processors provide you with several methods to accomplish specific goals. The method used depends on the situation. For example, you can move the cursor through the text by using several different keystrokes. Also, you can usually delete text by a charachter, a word, a sentence, a paragraph, or even a page at a time. Some word processing packages offer alteernate methods of executing commands.

In addition most word processors provid ways for you to enhance the appearance of the text with text formatting features. These formatting features allow you to quickly and easily center, underline, boldface, or double space text in your document, usually in just a couple of keystrokes. This ease of use and efficiency have made word processing a must in most academic and business settings. By taking the time to learn a word processing package, you will increase the chances of your success.

Typeover   Doc 1 Pg 1 Ln 2.67" Pos 4"

FIGURE 2-20 Using Typeover

Let's try using the Delete key. Press the Left Arrow key until the cursor is on the n in printed, Ln 2.67", Pos 3.6". Watch the screen and press Delete four times. The character under the cursor is deleted each time you press Delete, and the following characters are pulled in from the right (Figure 2-21). Now type the characters n t e d so that the word printed is again intact in your document.

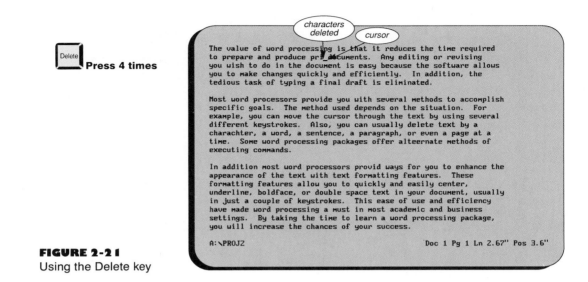

FIGURE 2-21
Using the Delete key

A Word at a Time

You can use the Ctrl and Backspace keys to delete text a word at a time to the right. Let's try this method to delete a word from your document. The cursor should still be positioned on the blank space following the word printed. Press the Down Arrow key three times, then press the Home key followed by the Left Arrow key so that the cursor is positioned on the first character of the word tedious as shown in Figure 2-22.

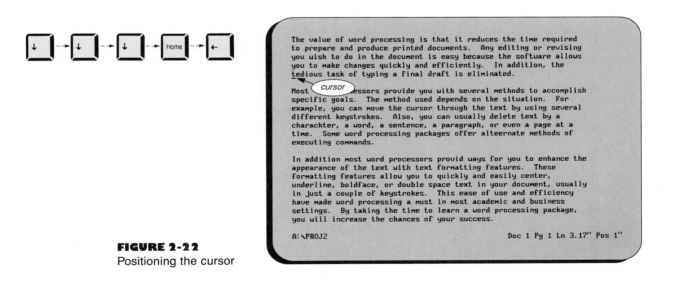

FIGURE 2-22
Positioning the cursor

Now hold down the Ctrl key and while holding it down, press the Backspace key (Ctrl-Backspace). The entire word disappears from the screen, and the text that follows adjusts to compensate for the deleted word (Figure 2-23).

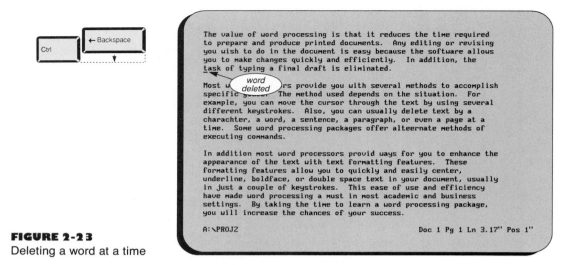

FIGURE 2-23
Deleting a word at a time

Notice that WordPerfect also deleted the space following the word tedious. This is so the spacing between words will remain consistent, and you do not need to go back and delete blank spaces that follow deleted words.

WordPerfect provides several other methods to delete text; these methods are summarized in Table 2-1.

TABLE 2-1 Deleting Text

TO DELETE	PRESS
Character directly under the cursor	Delete
Character to the left of the cursor	Backspace
Word containing the cursor	Ctrl–Backspace
From the cursor to the beginning of the word	Home Backspace
From the cursor to the end of the word	Home Delete
From the cursor to the end of the line containing the cursor	Ctrl–End
From the cursor to the end of the page	Ctrl–Page Down

BLOCKING TEXT

Sometimes you need to perform an action on a specific portion of text. For instance, rather than deleting a sentence a character at a time, you could instruct WordPerfect to delete the entire sentence at once. To do this, you must first define the area of text upon which an action will be performed. WordPerfect calls this **blocking** text, and provides several ways to do it.

Blocking isolates a portion of text so that specific actions can be performed on it without affecting the surrounding text. When you block text, you are in effect telling WordPerfect, "I am taking this portion of text and I'm going to do something special with it." The *something special* is whatever action follows, be it boldfacing, underlining, centering, or deleting.

Blocking Sentences

Entire sentences can be blocked and then deleted at one time using the Block function. To use the Block function, you must first position the cursor on the first or last character to be included in the block.

Try using the Block function to delete a sentence from your document. Hold down the Ctrl key and while holding it down, press the Left Arrow key (Ctrl-Left Arrow) until the cursor is positioned on the first character to be deleted, the I in In, Ln 3", Pos 5.6". Once the cursor is positioned, you need to turn on the Block function. Press Alt- = to display the menu bar. The Edit menu contains the Block function, so type E to display this menu (Figure 2-24).

FIGURE 2-24
Edit menu

Type B to select the "Block" option, and a flashing "Block on" message appears as shown in Figure 2-25.

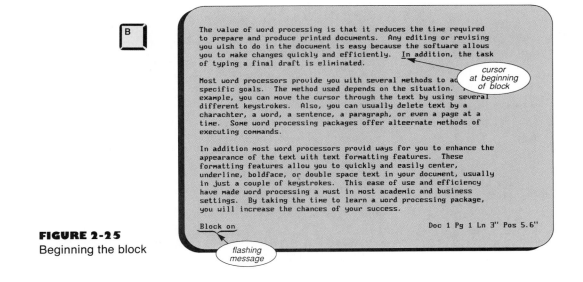

FIGURE 2-25
Beginning the block

This message indicates to you that the block will include whatever text through which the cursor moves. Any cursor movement can be used while blocking text. For example, you can extend the block a word, a line, a screen, a page at a time, and so forth.

In this case, however, you want to block the sentence. Watch the screen as you press the Down Arrow key. The text becomes highlighted as the cursor moves through it. This indicates to you that the highlighted text is included in the block, and any action specified will be performed only on the highlighted text.

Now that the sentence is blocked, you're ready to delete it. Press the Delete key and the message in Figure 2-26 appears.

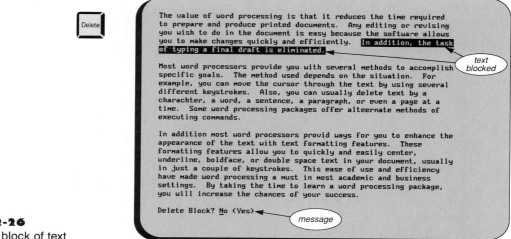

FIGURE 2-26
Deleting a block of text

This is another of WordPerfect's safeguards to prevent you from accidentally deleting portions of text that you don't want to delete. Because you do, in fact, want to delete this block, type Y, and the sentence disappears from the screen (Figure 2-27).

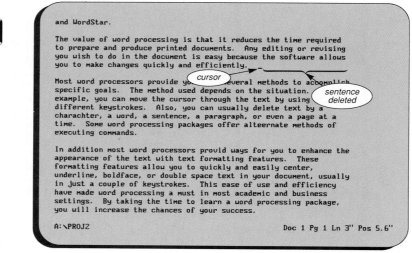

FIGURE 2-27
Block deleted from document

Notice that the flashing "Block on" message disappears when you press the Delete key. This is because once text is blocked, the function or action that follows automatically turns off the Block function. That is, once the text is blocked, pressing the Delete key deletes the text and turns off the Block function.

Mouse Users: Press the right mouse button to display the menu bar. Select the Edit menu, then select the "Block" option and click the left mouse button. Position the mouse pointer on the first character to be blocked, then press and hold down the left mouse button. Drag the mouse until the sentence is highlighted, then release the left mouse button before pressing the Delete key.

Restoring Deleted Text

You have deleted a sentence from your document, but suppose now that you changed your mind and think it should have remained in the paragraph. The F1 (Cancel) key allows you to restore deleted text.

Figure 2-27 shows the document after the sentence was deleted. The cursor is resting at the end of the second paragraph, Ln 3", Pos 5.6". Press the F1 key, and the deleted text appears in reverse video at the point of the cursor (Figure 2-28).

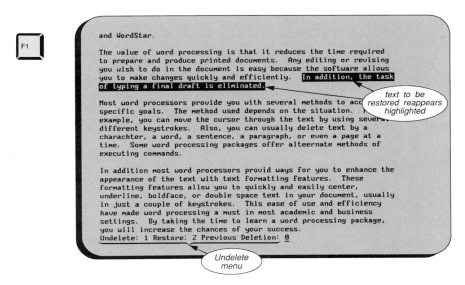

FIGURE 2-28 Restoring deleted text

The message at the bottom of the screen tells you that you can restore the highlighted text or view the previous deletion. WordPerfect stores the last two deletions in what is called a buffer, or a specially reserved portion of memory.

Because this is the text you want to restore, type 1, and WordPerfect inserts the deleted text back into your document (Figure 2-29).

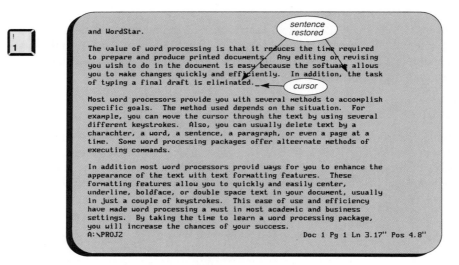

FIGURE 2-29   Text restored

Text is restored according to WordPerfect's normal Insert mode, that is, text is inserted to the left of the cursor, and existing text, including the character on which the cursor is resting, remains intact. Therefore, be certain that before you attempt to restore text, you have positioned the cursor exactly where you want the text restored.

Mouse Users: Click the right mouse button to display the menu bar. Select the Edit menu, then select "Undelete".

SHORTCUT KEYS

So far in this book, you have used WordPerfect's pull-down menus to accomplish each task. But WordPerfect also provides another method of accessing menu options. You can use the function keys to perform all the options contained in the pull-down menus. Sometimes WordPerfect users refer to these keys as the **shortcut keys**. As this name implies, you are usually able to select an option much more quickly when you use the shortcut keys than when you use the pull-down menu.

The Template

Figure 2-30 shows the WordPerfect templates. The **template** is a plastic or cardboard overlay that is placed above or around the function keys on the keyboard. The advantage of using a template is that you do not need to memorize all the functions; you need only refer to the template.

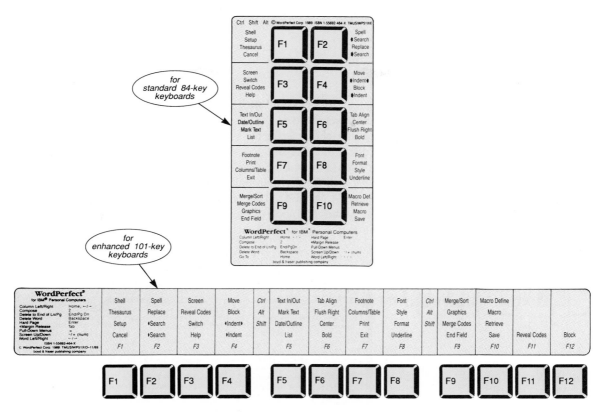

FIGURE 2-30 WordPerfect templates

The template is color coded, starting at the bottom with black. **Black** means you press the function key alone. **Green** means to hold down the Shift key and while holding it down, press the function key. **Blue** means to hold down the Alt key and while holding it down, press the function key. **Red** means you hold down the Ctrl key and while holding it down, press the function key. Each function key, therefore, has four separate values. You specify which particular function you want to perform when you press the Alt, Shift, or Ctrl key.

The Pull-Down Menu Display

Press Alt- = to display the menu bar, then press the Down Arrow key to display the File menu (Figure 2-31). Notice the combinations of keystrokes that appear after each option. These are the shortcut keys for each of the options on the menu. For example, F5 is the shortcut for the "List Files" option. This means that if you press the function key labeled F5, you would achieve the same results as if you pulled down the File menu, then selected "List Files".

All of WordPerfect's menus include the shortcut keys for each option. You can use the menu display or the template as a reference for the shortcut keys. For now, press F1 (Cancel) twice to cancel the menu bar.

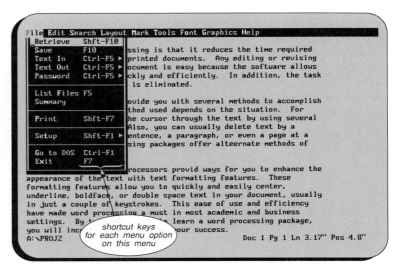

FIGURE 2-31 Shortcut keys

For the remainder of the projects, you will learn each new option by first using the pull-down menus. Thereafter, you will use the shortcut keys to select options. A list of the shortcut keys we teach in a project appears at the end of that project.

Blocking with the Shortcut Keys

Earlier in this project, you used the pull-down menu to block and then delete a sentence. Now let's try the shortcut keys to block and then delete specific words from a sentence.

First, so that the cursor is positioned on the first character of the word to be included in the block, the o in or, press the Up Arrow key three times, then hold down the Ctrl key and while holding it down, press the Right Arrow key three times (Ctrl-Right Arrow). The cursor should be at Ln 2.67", Pos 6.5". Look at the template, and notice that the word Block appears in blue next to the F4 key. Rather than pulling down the menu to begin blocking, hold down the Alt key and while holding it down, press F4 (Alt-F4). The "Block on" message immediately begins flashing, indicating that the block function is active. Extend the block to include the word revising by holding down the Ctrl key and while holding it down, pressing the Right Arrow key twice (Figure 2-32).

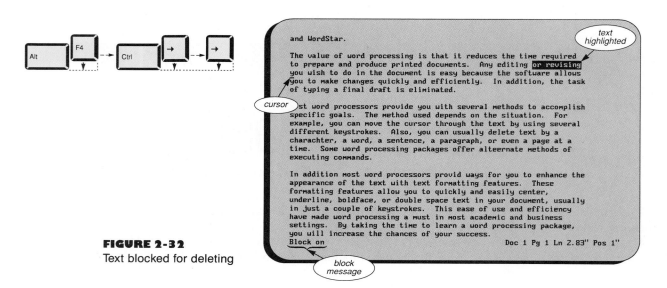

FIGURE 2-32
Text blocked for deleting

After the words or revising are blocked, proceed as you did before. Press the Delete key and answer Y to the "Delete Block? No (Yes)" message. The words disappear from the document (Figure 2-33). (You might have to press the Down Arrow key to rewrite the screen.)

FIGURE 2-33
Deleting a block

SPECIAL TEXT FORMATS

Sometimes you might want to add special touches to a document to enhance its clarity, organization, and appearance. Boldfacing, underlining, centering, double-spacing, and combinations of these are examples of special text formats.

Boldfaced Text

When you want to emphasize a word in a sentence, you can make it stand out by using the **boldface** format. This causes the word to be printed in a darker, bolder type.

To demonstrate this, let's insert a boldfaced word into your document. Press the Up Arrow key until the cursor is on the first line of the paragraph. Now hold down the Ctrl key, and while holding it down, press the Left Arrow key until the cursor is on the r in the word reduces, Ln 2.5'', Pos 5''.

Now that the cursor is positioned, let's specify boldface format. Press Alt-= to display the menu bar. The boldface format is contained in the Font menu, which cannot be accessed by typing its first letter. Type its second letter, O, and the menu displays (Figure 2-34).

FIGURE 2-34 Font menu

Because you are changing the appearance of the normal text, type A for "Appearance", and the submenu on the next page in Figure 2-35 appears.

FIGURE 2-35
Appearance submenu

A submenu is a menu within a menu. Boldfacing is specified by typing its first letter, so type B.

Notice that the Pos number on the status line is now in boldface. This is a visual reminder to you that boldfacing is turned on, and any text you enter will be boldfaced. Type the word substantially, and notice how the characters appear on your screen (Figure 2-36). You might have to press the Down Arrow key to rewrite the screen.

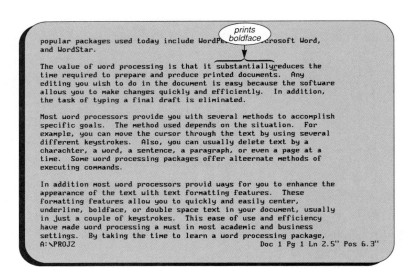

FIGURE 2-36
Adding a boldfaced word

If you have a color monitor, the word will appear either darker and bolder or possibly in a different color, depending on your monitor. On a monochrome monitor, the word will appear darker and bolder than other characters. This different appearance indicates to you that this word will print in boldface type when you print this document.

Boldfacing is a toggle, and recall that this means you must turn it off when you are finished using it. You turned on boldfacing through the Font menu, then you typed the word you wanted to boldface. Now you must turn off boldfacing. Until you do, any text that you enter at this point will be boldfaced.

Because boldfacing is a toggle, you turn it off in exactly the same way that you turned it on. Press Alt-= to display the menu bar. Type O to display the Font menu, then type A to display the "Appearance" option. Now type B for "Boldface". This turns boldfacing off, and any text you enter next will be normal print. Notice that the Pos number on the status line is no longer in boldface. Now press the Spacebar to insert a blank space to follow the boldfaced word you inserted.

Mouse Users: Click the right mouse button to display the menu bar. Select the Font menu, select "Appearance", then select "Boldface".

Underlined Text

Another special text format is underlining. The **underlining** format works much like the boldfacing format. Let's add the underlined word tedious to the last sentence of the second paragraph. Press the Down Arrow key four times, then press the Home key followed by the Left Arrow key (Home-Left Arrow). Now hold down the Ctrl key and press the Right Arrow key once so that the cursor is on the t in the word task.

Now that the cursor is positioned for the word you will add, press Alt-= to display the menu bar. As you did for boldfacing, type O for the Font menu, then A for the "Appearance" option. Underlining is specified by its first letter, so type U and notice the Pos number on the status line is now in reverse video. This reverse video display indicates to you that underlining is turned on and any text you enter next will be underlined. Now enter the word tedious (Figure 2-37).

FIGURE 2-37
Adding an underlined word

```
popular packages used today include WordPerfect, Microsoft Word,
and WordStar.

The value of word processing is that it substantially reduces the
time required to prepare and produce printed documents.  Any
editing you wish to do in the document is easy because the software
allows you to make changes quickly and efficiently.  In addition,
the tedious task of typing a final draft is eliminated.

Most word processors provide you with several methods to accomplish
specific goals.  The method used depends on the situation.  For
exa                an move the cursor through the text by using several
di   will print   okes.  Also, you can usually delete text by a
cha  underlined   ord, a sentence, a paragraph, or even a page at a
time.  Some word processing packages offer alternate methods of
executing commands.

In addition most word processors provid ways for you to enhance the
appearance of the text with text formatting features.  These                indicates
formatting features allow you to quickly and easily center,                 underlining
underline, boldface, or double space text in your document, usua            is on
in just a couple of keystrokes.  This ease of use and efficiency
have made word processing a must in most academic and business
settings.  By taking the time to learn a word processing package,
A:\PROJ2                                        Doc 1 Pg 1 Ln 3.17" Pos 2.1"
```

Notice that the monitor displays underlined text in reverse video. Regardless of how the text appears on the screen, *it will print underlined when the document is printed.*

You turn off underlining in the same way you turned it on. Press Alt-= to display the menu bar, type O for Font, then A for "Appearance". Once the Appearance submenu appears, type U for "Underline", and underlining is turned off. Any text you were to type now would appear in normal type. Notice that the Pos number on the status line no longer appears in reverse video. Press the Spacebar once to insert a blank space to follow the word tedious. If you had pressed the Spacebar before turning off underlining, the space following the underlined word tedious would also be underlined when the document was printed.

Mouse Users: Click the right mouse button to display the menu bar. Select the Font menu, select "Appearance", then select "Underline".

Centered Text

Many documents contain centered headings or titles. WordPerfect's **centering** format allows you to center text easily and quickly.

When you learned to boldface and underline text, you used these formats on text that had not yet been entered into the document. Sometimes, though, you'll want to format text that has already been typed in a document. To illustrate this, let's center our document's heading Word Processing Software Pakcages. To center the heading, you must position the cursor on the first character of the line to be centered. Move the cursor to the top of the document by pressing the Home key twice, then pressing the Up Arrow key (Home, Home, Up Arrow). The cursor should be resting on the first character of the document, the W in Word.

With the cursor positioned on the first character of the line to be centered, display the menu bar by pressing Alt-=. The "Layout" option contains the centering function, so type L to pull down this menu. The centering function is contained in the Align submenu, so type A and the submenu in Figure 2-38 appears (notice the shortcut key combination is Shift-F6).

FIGURE 2-38
Centering a line

You want to center the line, so type C, and the heading becomes centered on the line (Figure 2-39). If the heading does not immediately center, press the Down Arrow key once to rewrite the screen.

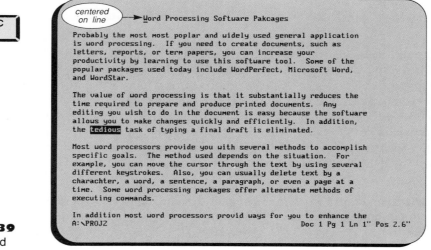

FIGURE 2-39
Line centered

Unlike the boldface and underline formats, centering is not a toggle; you do not need to turn it off when you have finished using it. Once you position the cursor and then issue the centering command, WordPerfect will center only the line containing the cursor.

If you wanted to center a heading prior to typing it, you would do it the same way you have learned to insert boldfaced and underlined text. You would first select centering from the menu, and then type the line to be centered. Once you press the Enter key, centering would end and the cursor would return to the left margin.

 Mouse Users: Click the right mouse button to display the menu bar. Select the Layout menu, select "Align", then select "Center".

Combining Text Formats

You can also combine text formats to enhance the appearance of your documents. For instance, suppose you wanted a word both underlined and boldfaced. To demonstrate, let's add boldfacing and underlining to the already centered document heading, but this time let's use the shortcut keys.

First you need to block the text to be formatted. Position the cursor on the first character of the heading, the W in Word. Now hold down the Alt key and while holding it down, press F4 to begin blocking (Alt-F4). Press the End key to extend the block to include the entire heading.

Look at the template, and notice that the word Bold appears in black next to the F6 key. Recall that black means to use the function key alone. Press F6, and the heading is now in boldface format (Figure 2-40).

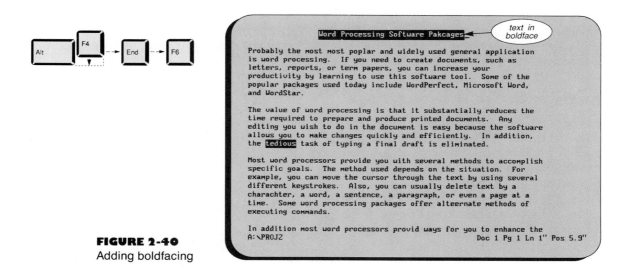

FIGURE 2-40
Adding boldfacing

Did you notice that you do not need to turn off boldfacing this time? Remember that when you block text, you do not need to turn off boldfacing or underlining. This is because you have used the Block function to specify the beginning and the end of the text to be formatted. When text is blocked, the beginning and end of the text are clearly defined. WordPerfect will add the format only to the text included in the block.

Now let's add underlining to the heading. Block the text again by positioning the cursor on the first character of the heading. Next, turn on the Block function by holding down the Alt key and while holding it down, pressing F4 (Alt-F4). Press the End key to extend the block to the end of the line.

Now that the heading is again blocked, you need to specify the underlining format. Notice that the Underline command appears in black on the F8 key. Press F8, and the heading is underlined (Figure 2-41). Again, because the text was already blocked, WordPerfect added the format only to the blocked text; you did not need to turn off underlining.

Notice that once you have added multiple text formats, the formatted words on your screen may appear in a different color within the reverse video bar (on color monitors). WordPerfect displays text with multiple formats this way so that you are aware the text contains more than one format. Although the figures in these projects will display any text with multiple formats in reverse video, be sure you understand that your monitor may enhance the characters differently if you use more than one format. Once you have combined formats, you will see how your monitor displays the characters, and recognize that it might differ from its appearance here.

This method of combining formats works for any type of format you choose, both on existing text and on text that has not yet been entered.

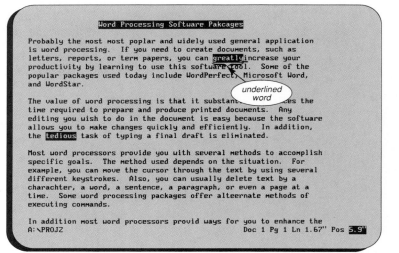

FIGURE 2-41   Adding underlining

Underlining with the Shortcut Keys

Underlining and boldfacing are both toggles. Recall that this means you must turn them off when you have finished using them, unless the text has been blocked. When you are specifying boldfacing or underlining for text that has not yet been entered, you first turn on the format, then enter the text, and finally turn off the format.

You already accomplished this when you used the menu to turn the underline and boldface formats on and off. This time, let's use the shortcut keys to add an underlined word to your document. Press the Down Arrow key four times, then hold down the Ctrl key and while holding it down, press the Left Arrow key once to move the cursor to the i in the word increase, Ln 1.67", Pos 5.2". Turn on underlining by pressing F8. Notice that the Pos number on the status line appears in reverse video. Type the word greatly, and notice that it is entered with underlining (Figure 2-42).

FIGURE 2-42   Underlining with shortcut keys

Now that the word is entered, you need to turn off underlining. Press F8 again, and underlining is turned off. The Pos number returns to its normal display, and any text you enter now will be in normal text. Press the Spacebar to add a blank space.

If you wanted to add a boldfaced word, you would do it in precisely the same manner. Position the cursor, press F6 to specify boldfacing, enter the text, then press F6 to turn off boldfacing.

Removing Special Text Formats

Recall in Project 1 that you used the Reveal Codes screen to view the embedded codes in your document. The Reveal Codes screen is also used to remove codes that control text formatting, such as underlining, boldfacing, and centering.

Suppose that you decided the underlined word tedious looked better before it was underlined. WordPerfect allows you to remove special text formats without retyping text. Let's remove the underlining from the word tedious in the second paragraph.

Press the Home key twice, then press the Up Arrow key (Home, Home, Up Arrow) to move the cursor to the top of the document. Now let's display the Reveal Codes screen with the shortcut keys. Notice on the template that the Reveal Codes command appears in blue next to the F3 key. Recall that blue means to use the function key with the Alt key. Hold down the Alt key and while holding it down, press F3 (Alt-F3). The Reveal Codes screen immediately appears (Figure 2-43).

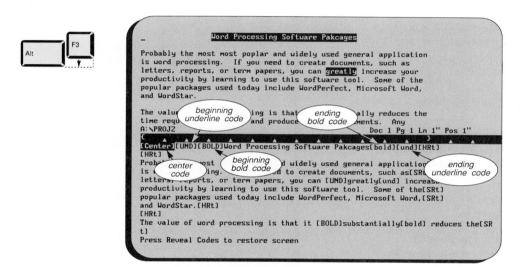

FIGURE 2-43 Reveal Codes screen

In Project 1, the only codes embedded in the document were the hard and soft return codes. In this document, however, you used centering, boldfacing, and underlining. Notice the [Center] code at the beginning of the document. WordPerfect inserted this code so that the heading will print on the center of the line when you print the document.

Now look at the [UND] and [und] codes. The uppercase code signifies the beginning of the format, and the lowercase code indicates the end of the format. Most codes that involve toggles appear in pairs. Notice, too, the [BOLD] and [bold] codes. Again, the uppercase code marks the beginning, and the lowercase code marks the end of the formatting.

To remove special text formats from the document, you simply delete one of the codes. It is not necessary to delete both the codes; deleting the first or second code in the pair will automatically remove both codes from the document. Let's try this. Press the Home key, then the Down Arrow key (Home, Down Arrow), then press the Down Arrow key three times. Now, press the Right Arrow key until the cursor is positioned directly on the [UND] code that precedes the word tedious, Ln 3.17", Pos 1.4" (Figure 2-44). Watch the upper portion of the screen as you press the Delete key. The word is immediately restored to normal text, and both codes disappear from the Reveal Codes portion of the screen (Figure 2-45).

You can use this method whenever you want to remove formatting from text. Remember, though, delete only *one* of the codes; you do not have to delete the pair.

Now that the underlining is removed, restore the screen to normal display by holding down the Alt key and while holding it down, pressing F3 (Alt-F3). The screen returns to normal display.

Double-Spacing

Often, documents or portions of documents need to be double-spaced. You are going to double-space your entire document. To accomplish this, you are going to insert a single code at the top of your document that will control the spacing of the entire document.

First, you need to position the cursor at the very top of the document *in front of any codes*. Recall from Table 1-1 that you must press the Home key *three* times to position the cursor here. Press the Home key three times, then press the Up Arrow key (Home, Home, Home, Up Arrow). The cursor moves to the top of the document in front of any codes.

FIGURE 2-44 Removing codes

FIGURE 2-45 Code deleted

Once the cursor is positioned, you need to insert the code specifying double-spacing. Display the menu bar by pressing Alt- = . The "Line Spacing" option is contained in the Layout menu, so type L to display this menu. The Line Format menu is accessed by its first letter, so type L. Notice that the shortcut key combination is Shift-F8. The menu in Figure 2-46 appears.

FIGURE 2-46
Line Format menu

Notice that menu choice "6" in the Line Format menu contains the instructions for line spacing, which is currently set to 1, or single-spacing. This is the default setting. Because you want to change the spacing, select "6", and the cursor is positioned to change the line spacing.

Because you want double-spacing, select "2" then press Enter (Figure 2-47).

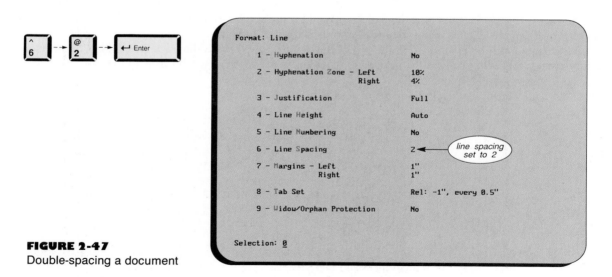

FIGURE 2-47
Double-spacing a document

When you have finished specifying settings in a menu, you must exit it. The Exit command appears in black on the template next to the F7 key. Press F7; the line spacing is set, and you exit back to the text window. The entire document is now double-spaced (Figure 2-48).

FIGURE 2-48
Double-spaced document

 Mouse Users: Click the right mouse button to display the menu bar. Select the Layout menu, then select "Line". Select menu choice "6" from Line Format menu, then type 2 and press Enter.

Page Breaks

When a document reaches a certain length, WordPerfect will automatically begin a new page. The point where the new page will begin is called a **page break**, and it appears on the screen as a single dotted line. You can let pages break where WordPerfect suggests, or you can enter your own page breaks.

The cursor should still be positioned at the top of the document, so press the Page Down key. The cursor moves to the first character that will print on the next page. Now press the Up Arrow key once and notice the dotted line that appears in the last paragraph (Figure 2-49).

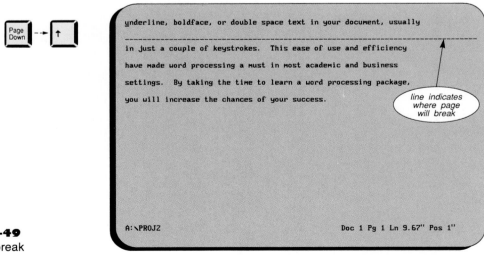

FIGURE 2-49
Soft page break

This is how WordPerfect indicates a page break. Once text fills the space alloted for a printed page, WordPerfect inserts a page break to let you know where one printed page ends and the next page begins. Page breaks that are inserted by WordPerfect are called **soft page breaks**.

Since the soft page break occurs in the middle of the last paragraph, let's enter a page break so that the entire last paragraph will print on the second page. Press the Up Arrow key three times so that the cursor is on the I in the word In. You are positioning the cursor here because this is the first character of the text you want to move down to the next page. Hold down the Ctrl key and while holding it down, press the Enter key (Ctrl-Enter). Notice that a *double* dotted line appears on the screen (Figure 2-50).

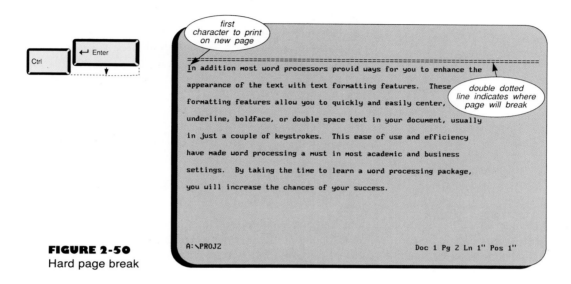

FIGURE 2-50
Hard page break

This designates a **hard page break**—one that you entered—rather than one that WordPerfect entered automatically. The original page break inserted by WordPerfect—the soft page break—disappears from the screen.

If you need to remove hard page breaks, you would position the cursor on the first character following the page break, then press the Backspace key. The double dotted line would be deleted just like any other character would be deleted.

CHECKING A DOCUMENT FOR SPELLING

WordPerfect provides a tool to help you produce error-free documents. The **Spell program** is a tool that not only assists you in finding errors, but also helps you correct them by providing you with a list of alternate word choices.

The Spell program compares each word in your document with the words contained in its dictionary. Each time the Spell program finds a word that doesn't match a word in its dictionary, the Spell program stops checking the document and displays a menu to help you correct the errors. You can check an entire document, or just a portion of one. You can also look up a selected word to see if you used the correct spelling. Let's use the Spell program to see if all of the words in our document PROJ2 are spelled correctly.

Press the Home key twice, then the Up Arrow key (Home, Home, Up Arrow) to move the cursor to the beginning of the document. If you are using WordPerfect on a hard disk or network, check with your instructor whether you need to change the speller path. If you are running WordPerfect on a two-disk system, replace your disk in drive B with the Spell disk before beginning the Spell program.

The Spell program is contained in the Tools menu, so press Alt-= to display the menu bar, then type T to display the Tools menu. "Spell" is already highlighted (notice the shortcut keys are Ctrl-F2), so press Enter. The Spell program begins by displaying the menu in Figure 2-51.

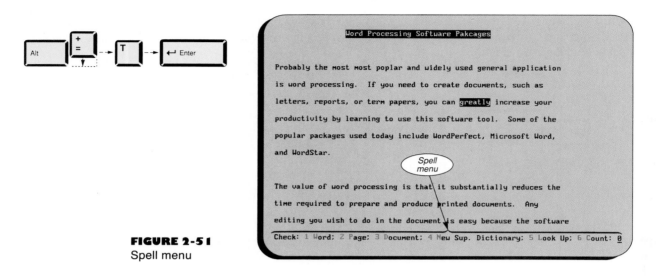

FIGURE 2-51
Spell menu

Since you want to check the entire document, select "3" from the menu, and the Spell program will begin displaying the words it considers to be errors. (Your document might contain typing errors other than the ones shown in this project. If it does, correct each additional error using the following methods.)

Mouse Users: Click the right mouse button to display the menu bar. Select the Tools menu, then select "Spell". Select menu choice "3" from the Spell menu.

Figure 2-52 shows how the Spell screen appears while your document is being checked.

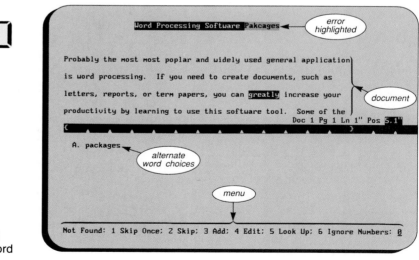

FIGURE 2-52
Correcting a word

Notice that the word Pakcages is high-lighted. This means that the Spell program cannot match this word to any word contained in its dictionary. The menu at the bottom of the screen lists the choices the Spell program provides. You have several options. You could skip (ignore) the highlighted word once or altogether, add it to the Spell dictionary, edit the word, look up a word, or change the default so that numbers are not ignored.

In this case, you need to replace the word Pakcages with the correctly spelled word Packages. Notice the word choices on the lower portion of the screen. These are alternate spellings the Spell program offers you. If the word or spelling you desire is not in this list, you could type in the correct spelling at this point by choosing "Edit" from the Spell menu. The correct word Packages is choice "A" in the list, so type A (you can use uppercase or lowercase characters). The incorrect word is replaced with the correctly spelled word Packages, and the Spell program highlights the next word it considers an error (Figure 2-53).

WordPerfect automatically replaces words to match the case of the highlighted word. Because the highlighted word was capitalized, WordPerfect inserted the correct word with capitalization also.

Notice that this next word highlighted by the Spell program is not actually misspelled. The Spell program designated this an error because it is a double word. To correct this error type 3 for "Delete 2nd;" as it is listed on the menu. The second occurrence of the repeated word is deleted and the Spell program highlights the next word for which it doesn't have a match. The next word highlighted is Microsoft (Figure 2-54).

This error is not due to incorrect spelling, either. The Spell program's dictionary simply

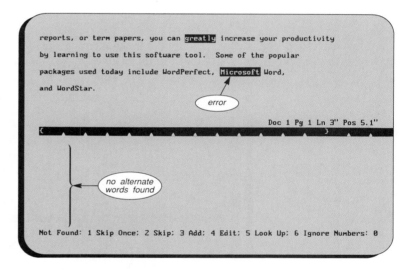

FIGURE 2-53 Double word error

FIGURE 2-54 Skipping an error

doesn't contain this word. In this instance the word is correct as is, so type 2 from the menu to skip all occurrences of this word and move on. Once you have instructed the Spell program to skip a word, it will ignore it through the entire document. The program considers subsequent occurrences of the word to be correct, and, therefore, will not highlight it again.

The next word highlighted is charachter, which is, indeed, misspelled (Figure 2-55).

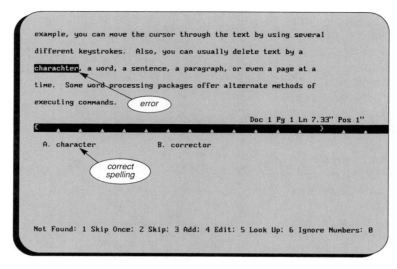

FIGURE 2-55 Misspelled word error

The correct spelling is choice "A" in the list of alternate spellings provided. Type A to confirm that this is the desired spelling. The spelling is changed in the document, and the Spell program highlights the next error (Figure 2-56).

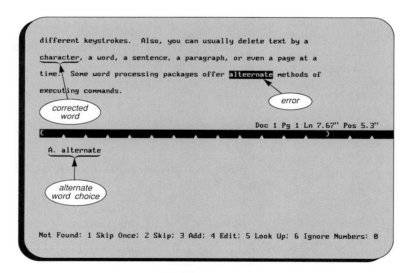

FIGURE 2-56 Misspelled word

The next error is the word alteernate, which you will correct using the same method as you did for the previously misspelled word. Type A to specify menu choice "A", and the word is replaced in the document. The Spell program now highlights the next error (Figure 2-57).

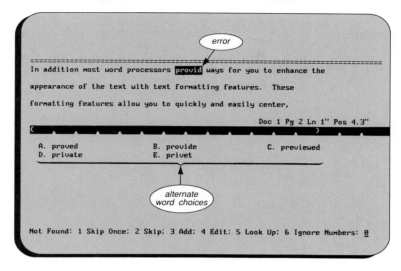

FIGURE 2-57 Misspelled word

The error here is provid, which you will correct using the same method as you did for the previously misspelled word. Type B to select menu choice "B", and the word is replaced in the document.

The Spell program has completely scanned your document, and displays the message in Figure 2-58.

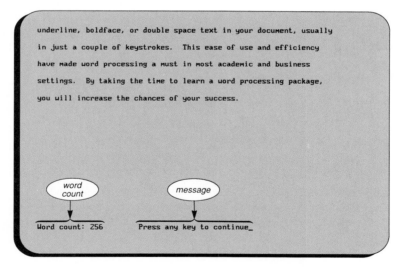

FIGURE 2-58 Exiting the Spell program

This message is a word count and tells you how many words were checked and to press any key. Press a key, and the screen returns to its normal display with the cursor at the bottom of the document. Press the Home key twice, followed by the Up Arrow key (Home, Home, Up Arrow) to move the cursor to the top of the document (Figure 2-59).

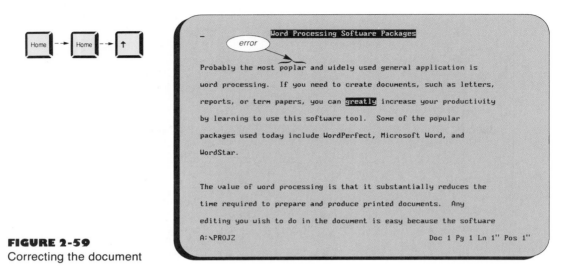

FIGURE 2-59
Correcting the document

Your document has now been run through the Spell program and contains no misspelled words. But does it? Look at the first paragraph of Figure 2-59. The word poplar should actually read popular. The Spell program did not recognize this as an error because it is, in fact, a correct spelling of a word contained in its dictionary. This is precisely why Spell programs in *any* word processing package should never be completely relied upon to check a document. Visually proofreading a document is essential if you want to find and correct *all* errors.

Let's correct this error. The cursor should be on the first character of the document. Press the Down Arrow key twice to move the cursor into the sentence containing the word poplar. Now, hold down the Ctrl key and while holding it down, press the Right Arrow key (Ctrl-Right Arrow) three times until the cursor is resting on the p in poplar. Next, press the Right Arrow key until the cursor is positioned on the l in poplar. Type the letter u (Figure 2-60).

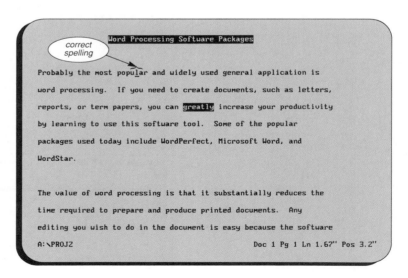

FIGURE 2-60
Corrected error

Now that your document is correct, you should save it again in its corrected form. Let's use the shortcut keys to save the document. If you are using WordPerfect on a two-disk system *be sure to remove the Spell disk from the B drive and replace it with your disk before attempting to save.*

Notice the word Save appears in black next to the F10 key on the template. Press F10, and the message in Figure 2-61 appears. (If the Document Summary appears, press Delete, then type Y to remove it.)

Notice that "PROJ2" appears as the document name. Recall that WordPerfect automatically assigns that name, since the document was most recently saved under that name. Press Enter to confirm that you want to save this document under the name PROJ2. Type Y to answer the "Replace A:\PROJ2? No (Yes)" prompt, since you do want to replace the old version with this new, corrected version.

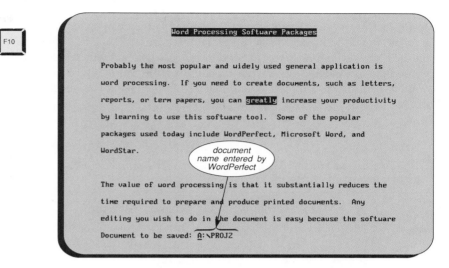

FIGURE 2-61 Saving a document

PRINTING MULTIPLE-PAGE DOCUMENTS

◆ You can print a multiple-page document in exactly the same way that you print a single-page document. Word-Perfect will automatically print all the pages of a document, although this setting can be changed if you needed to print only a portion of a document.

Let's use the shortcut keys to print your document. Be sure the printer is turned on and ready to print. Notice the word Print appears in green next to the F7 key on the template. Hold down the Shift key and while holding it down, press F7 (Shift-F7). The Print menu appears. As you did in Project 1, type 1 to select "Full Document", and your document prints on the printer with the second page breaking where you specified. Your final document should look like Figure 2-1.

EXITING WORDPERFECT

◆ Before you remove your disks and end the WordPerfect session, recall that you must exit WordPerfect correctly. Let's use the shortcut keys this time. Press F7, and the message in Figure 2-62 appears. Because you already saved your document, type N. Type Y at the "Exit WP? No (Yes)" prompt. At the DOS prompt, be sure to remove your data disk or WordPerfect program disks if necessary.

FIGURE 2-62
Exiting WordPerfect

PROJECT SUMMARY

In Project 2 you gained more practice at moving the cursor, and learned how to block and delete portions of text. You learned how to insert and remove special text formats, such as boldfaced, underlined, and centered text. You also learned how to double-space text and to insert a page break. You used some of WordPerfect's shortcut keys to access menu options. Finally, you used the Spell program to find and correct errors in your document. All the activities that you learned for this project are summarized in the Quick Reference following Project 6. The following is a summary of the keystroke sequence we used in Project 2.

SUMMARY OF KEYSTROKES — PROJECT 2

STEPS	KEY(S) PRESSED	RESULTS
1	wp ← [At C> prompt or as directed by instructor]	Loads WordPerfect.
2	[Alt-=] ↓ F←	Lists filenames on disk.
3	1	Retrieves highlighted PROJ1.
4	[End]	Moves cursor to end of line.
5	[Spacebar] Pakcages	Enters text with spelling error.
6	[Home] ←	Moves cursor to beginning of line.
7	[Ctrl-→] [Ctrl-→] [Ctrl-→]	Positions cursor.
8	↓↓ [Ctrl-←] most poplar and	Positions cursor and enters text.
9	↓	Rewrites screen.
10	↓ [Press 7 times] [Ctrl-→] [Ctrl-→] [Ctrl-→] or revising [Spacebar] ↓	Positions cursor, enters text, and rewrites screen.
11	[Home] ↓	Moves cursor to last line on screen.
12	←	Inserts blank line.
13	Most word processors provide you with several methods to accomplish specific goals. The method used depends on the situation. For example, you can move the cursor through the text by using several different keystrokes. Also, you can usually delete text by a charachter, a word, a sentence, a paragraph, or even a page at a time. Some word processing packages offer alteernate methods of executing commands. ← ←	Enters text as new paragraph and inserts a blank line.
14	In addition most word processors provid ways for you to enhance the appearance of the text with text formatting features. These formatting features allow you to quickly and easily center, underline, boldface, or double space text in your document, usually in just a couple of keystrokes. This ease of use and efficiency have made word processing a must in most academic and business settings. By taking the time to learn a word processing package, you will increase the chances of your success. ←	Enters text as new paragraph.
15	[Home] ↑	Moves cursor to top of screen.
16	[Alt-=] ↓ S PROJ2 ←	Saves document under name PROJ2.

SUMMARY OF KEYSTROKES — PROJECT 2 (continued)

STEPS	KEY(S) PRESSED	RESULTS
17	↓↓ [Ctrl–→] [Press 4 times]	Positions cursor for Typeover.
18	[Insert]	Turns on Typeover.
19	printed	Enters characters.
20	[Insert]	Turns off Typeover.
21	← [Press 4 times]	Positions cursor.
22	[Delete] [Press 4 times]	Deletes characters.
23	nted	Enters characters.
24	↓↓↓ [Home] ← [Ctrl–Backspace]	Positions cursor and deletes word.
25	[Ctrl–←] [Ctrl–←] [Ctrl–←]	Positions cursor.
26	[Alt–=] E B↓ [Delete] Y	Blocks and deletes sentence.
27	[F1] 1	Inserts previously deleted sentence back into document.
28	[Alt–=] ↓	Displays File menu.
29	[F1] [F1]	Cancels menu bar.
30	↑ [Ctrl–←] [Ctrl–←] [Ctrl–←]	Positions cursor.
31	[Alt–=] O A B substantially	Enters boldfaced word.
32	[Alt–=] O A B	Turns off boldfacing.
33	[Spacebar]	Inserts blank space.
34	↓ [Press 4 times] [Home] ← [Ctrl–→]	Positions cursor to insert underlined text.
35	[Alt–=] O A U	Begins underlining.
36	tedious	Enters underlined text.
37	[Alt–=] O A U	Turns off underlining.
38	[Spacebar]	Inserts blank space.
39	[Home] [Home] ↑	Moves cursor to top of document.
40	[Alt–=] L A C	Centers text of heading.
41	[Home] ← →	Positions cursor.
42	[Alt–F4] [End]	Blocks text of heading.
43	[F6]	Adds boldfacing to centered heading.
44	[Home] ← →	Positions cursor.
45	[Alt–F4] [End]	Blocks text of heading.
46	[F8]	Adds underlining to heading.
47	↓ [Press 4 times] [Ctrl–→]	Positions cursor.
48	[F8] greatly [F8]	Adds underlined word.
49	[Home] [Home] ↑	Moves cursor to top of document.
50	[Alt–F3]	Displays Reveal Codes screen.
51	[Home] ↓ [Press 4 times] → → →	Positions cursor on underline code.
52	[Delete]	Deletes underline code.
53	[Alt–F3]	Restores normal screen display.
54	[Home] [Home] [Home] ↑	Moves cursor to top of document prior to codes.
55	[Alt–=] L L 6 2 ↵	Sets line spacing to 2.
56	[F7]	Exits Line Format menu.

(continued)

SUMMARY OF KEYSTROKES — PROJECT 2 (continued)

STEPS	KEY(S) PRESSED	RESULTS
57	[Page Down]	Moves cursor to next page.
58	↑	Moves cursor so that page break is visible on screen.
59	↑↑↑	Positions cursor for page break.
60	[Ctrl-Enter]	Inserts page break.
61	[Home] [Home] ↑	Moves cursor to top of document.
62	[Alt-=] T↵ 3	Starts Spell program.
63	A	Inserts correctly spelled word into document.
64	3	Deletes repeated word.
65	2	Ignores error.
66	A	Inserts correctly spelled word into document.
67	B	Inserts correctly spelled word into document.
68	[Spacebar] [Or any key]	Exits Spell program.
69	[Home] [Home] ↑	Moves cursor to top of document.
70	↓↓ [Ctrl-→] [Ctrl-→] [Ctrl-→]	Positions cursor on word containing typing error.
71	→ → → u	Positions cursor and corrects typing error.
72	[F10] ↵ Y	Saves document.
73	[Shift-F7] 1	Prints document.
74	[F7] N Y	Exits WordPerfect and returns to DOS.

The following list summarizes the material covered in Project 2.

1. You can use the "List Files" option to display a list of the document names on your disk. You can then retrieve these documents by highlighting the desired name, then typing 1 from the menu.
2. When you are adding or deleting larger portions of text, it's sometimes necessary to rewrite the screen. Do this by moving the cursor through the text that needs to be aligned. The Down Arrow key is usually used for this purpose.
3. **Scrolling** allows you to move the cursor upward or downward through a document. The portion of the document containing the cursor remains visible on the screen at all times.
4. When you save a document under a new name, you must type the new document name at the Save prompt.
5. A **default** is a standard or predefined setting WordPerfect automatically uses unless instructed otherwise.
6. Pressing Insert puts WordPerfect in Typeover mode. **Typeover mode** allows you to enter characters directly over existing characters. When WordPerfect is in Typeover mode, "Typeover" appears on the status line.
7. The **Delete** key deletes text a character at a time, beginning with the character directly under the cursor and pulling in characters from the right.
8. Pressing Ctrl-Backspace deletes text a word at a time.
9. When a portion of text is highlighted, you would say it is **blocked**. This allows you to isolate a portion of text in order to perform an action upon it.
10. The "Block" option is contained in the Edit menu. The shortcut keys for blocking are Alt-F4.
11. Blocked portions of text can be deleted by pressing the Delete key.
12. The F1 (Cancel) key allows you to insert deleted text back into a document.
13. All of the options contained in the pull-down menus can be accessed through the **shortcut keys**, or function keys. As this name implies, shortcut keys can usually accomplish a task much more quickly than the pull-down menus.
14. The **template** is a plastic or cardboard overlay that is placed above or around the function keys.
15. The template is color coded as follows: **black** means to use the function key alone; **green** means to use the Shift key with the function key; **blue** means to use the Alt key with the function key; and **red** means to use the Ctrl key with the function key. Each function key, therefore, has four separate values.

16. **Boldface** and **underline** formats are contained in the Font Appearance menu. The shortcut key for boldfacing is F6, and the shortcut key for underlining is F8.
17. The **centering** format is contained in the Layout Align menu.
18. The shortcut keys used to display the Reveal Codes screen are Alt-F3.
19. Special text formats are removed from text by deleting the appropriate code in the Reveal Codes screen.
20. The Line Format menu contains the "Line Spacing" option, which allows you to change the spacing of a document.
21. The point where the new page will begin is called a **page break**.
22. **Soft page breaks**, or those inserted by WordPerfect, appear on the screen as dotted lines.
23. You can let WordPerfect break pages, or you may insert your own **hard page breaks** by pressing Ctrl-Enter at the point of the desired break. Hard page breaks appear on the screen as double dotted lines.
24. The **Spell program** locates and helps correct typing and spelling errors in a document by finding errors and then displaying a list of alternate word choices.
25. The Spell program is contained in the Tools menu. The shortcut keys are Ctrl-F2.
26. Documents should be visually proofread even after using the Spell program.
27. The shortcut keys for printing a document are Shift-F7, then 1.
28. The shortcut key for exiting a document is F7.

STUDENT ASSIGNMENTS

STUDENT ASSIGNMENT 1: True/False

Instructions: Circle T if the statement is true and F if the statement is false.

T F 1. To delete a word at a time, you would press Home-Backspace.
T F 2. To move the cursor a word at a time to the right, you would press Ctrl-Right Arrow.
T F 3. Pressing Home-Page Up moves the cursor to the first line on the screen.
T F 4. Ctrl-End moves the cursor to the very last line of the document.
T F 5. Boldfaced text is specified through the Font menu.
T F 6. The Spell program is contained in the Tools menu.
T F 7. Text can be underlined by pressing F6.
T F 8. The Spell program will find all errors in a document; it is not necessary to visually proofread a document if you run it through the Spell program.
T F 9. When printing a multiple-page document, you must tell WordPerfect how many pages the document has before you begin printing.
T F 10. To insert a soft page break, press Ctrl-Enter.

STUDENT ASSIGNMENT 2: Multiple Choice

Instructions: Circle the correct response.

1. If you hold down the Ctrl key, and while holding it down press Enter, you cause _____.
   a. text to be underlined
   b. a hard page break
   c. the cursor to move to the top of the screen
   d. none of the above
2. To display a list of document names on your disk, use the _____ option.
   a. "List Files"
   b. "Tools"
   c. "Edit"
   d. none of the above

Student Assignment 2 (continued)

3. WordPerfect is changed to Typeover mode by pressing _____.
   a. F6
   b. Ctrl-Enter
   c. Insert
   d. F8

4. Hard page breaks appear on the screen as _____.
   a. asterisks
   b. single dotted lines
   c. double dotted lines
   d. a caret (^) in the left margin

5. The shortcut keys for underline format are _____.
   a. Insert
   b. Shift-F7
   c. F6
   d. none of the above

6. The shortcut keys for boldface text are _____.
   a. Shift-F8
   b. F6
   c. F8
   d. none of the above

7. The Appearance menu is used to specify _____.
   a. boldfacing
   b. underlining
   c. both a and c
   d. none of the above

8. The shortcut keys for blocking are _____.
   a. F3
   b. F4
   c. Alt-F4
   d. Alt-F3

STUDENT ASSIGNMENT 3: Matching

Instructions: Put the appropriate number next to the words in the second column.

1.	Underline text format	_____	Alt-F3
2.	Typeover	_____	Ctrl-Backspace
3.	Block	_____	F1
4.	Restore deleted text	_____	F6
5.	Move cursor a word to the right	_____	F8
6.	Move cursor a word to the left	_____	Alt-F4
7.	Boldface text format	_____	Ctrl-→
8.	Reveal codes	_____	Ctrl-←
9.	Exit	_____	F7
10.	Delete word	_____	Insert
11.	List files	_____	F5

STUDENT ASSIGNMENT 4: WordPerfect Commands

Instructions: Next to each function, write its shortcut key(s).

1. Block   _____
2. Boldface   _____
3. List Files   _____
4. Reveal codes   _____
5. Print   _____
6. Underline   _____
7. Exit   _____
8. Save   _____
9. Cancel   _____
10. Spell program _____

STUDENT ASSIGNMENT 5: Understanding Text Formats

Instructions: The figure shows the beginning of a document. Suppose that after typing it, you realized that the heading should have been centered and underlined. Explain the steps to underline this existing text without deleting the text.

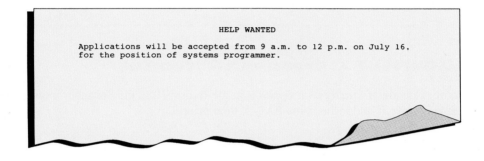

```
                          HELP WANTED

         Applications will be accepted from 9 a.m. to 12 p.m. on July 16,
         for the position of systems programmer.
```

Steps: _____

_____

_____

_____

STUDENT ASSIGNMENT 6: Removing Text Formats

Instructions: The figure shows part of a document. Suppose that after typing it, you decided that the word extremely should not be underlined. Assuming the cursor is resting on the first character of the word extremely, explain the steps to remove the underlining from this word and restore it to normal text.

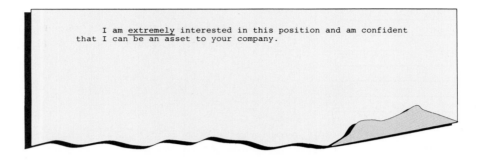

```
          I am extremely interested in this position and am confident
     that I can be an asset to your company.
```

Steps: _____

_____

_____

_____

STUDENT ASSIGNMENT 7: Creating a Document

Instructions: Create this document *exactly as it appears* in the figure. (Use the Spacebar to align the TO:, FROM:, DATE:, and RE: headings.) Save it under the name SA2-7, then print it.

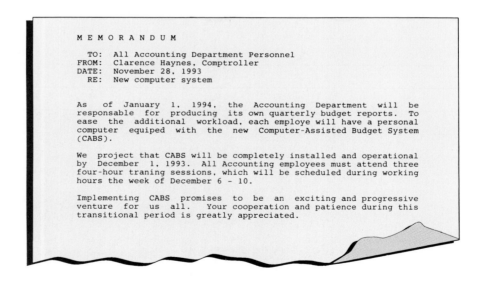

```
M E M O R A N D U M

   TO:   All Accounting Department Personnel
 FROM:   Clarence Haynes, Comptroller
 DATE:   November 28, 1993
   RE:   New computer system


As   of January 1, 1994, the Accounting Department  will  be
responsable  for  producing  its own quarterly budget reports.  To
ease  the  additional  workload, each employe will have a personal
computer  equiped  with  the  new  Computer-Assisted Budget System
(CABS).

We   project that CABS will be completely installed and operational
by  December  1, 1993.  All Accounting employees must attend three
four-hour  traning  sessions, which will be scheduled during working
hours the week of December 6 - 10.

Implementing  CABS promises  to  be  an  exciting and progressive
venture  for  us  all.   Your cooperation and patience during this
transitional period is greatly appreciated.
```

STUDENT ASSIGNMENT 8: Adding Text Formats

Instructions: Retrieve the document SA2-7 that you created in Student Assignment 7. Make the following corrections:

1. The letters CABS should appear in boldface type.
2. The titles TO:, FROM:, DATE:, and RE: in the memo heading should be boldfaced.
3. The heading should be centered and underlined.
4. The words installed and operational in the second paragraph should be underlined as shown in the figure.
5. Save the new document under the name SA2-8, then print the document. It should appear as shown in the figure.

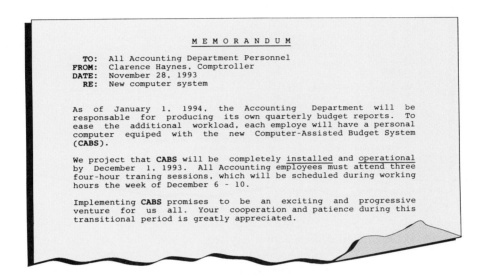

STUDENT ASSIGNMENT 9: Understanding Reveal Codes

Instructions: Retrieve the document SA2-8 that you used in Student Assignment 8. With the cursor at the top of the document, display the Reveal Codes screen. Print the Reveal Codes screen (press Print Screen twice, or check with your instructor). After the document prints, label the following codes shown in the figure:

1. beginning boldface
2. ending boldface
3. center
4. beginning underline
5. ending underline
6. hard return
7. soft return

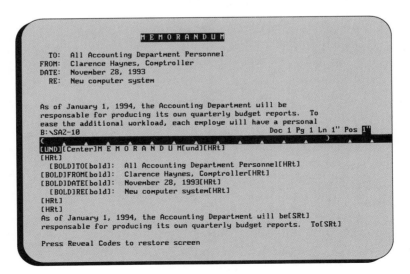

STUDENT ASSIGNMENT 10: Using the Spell Program

Instructions: Retrieve the document SA2-8 that you created in Student Assignment 8. Run the Spell program to correct the typing errors. Print the document, then save it under the name SA2-10. The document should appear as shown in the figure.

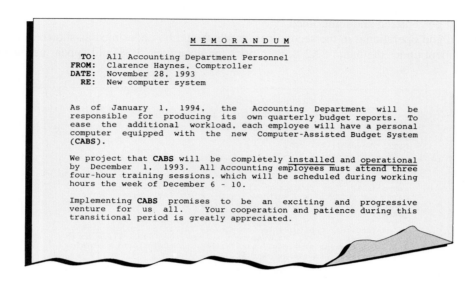

1. If you are using WordPerfect on a hard disk or network system, be sure your instructor checks to see if you need to change the spell path.
2. If you are using WordPerfect on a two-disk system, be sure to remove your disk from drive B and replace it with the Spell disk before beginning the Spell program. After the Spell program has finished, remove the Spell disk from drive B and replace it with your disk before attempting to save the document.

Moving, Searching, and Replacing Text

OBJECTIVES

You will have mastered the material in this project when you can:

◆ Move text to new locations within a document

◆ Type indented text

◆ Create a hanging indent

◆ Use the Search function

◆ Use the Replace function

◆ Quit WordPerfect and save a document at the same time

CREATING A DOCUMENT

◆ Before you begin creating the sample resume in Figure 3-1, let's discuss the new instructions for using shortcut keys. In the previous projects the options were placed in parentheses, following instructions on proper keystroke technique. By now you should be familiar with how to hold down the Ctrl, Shift, and Alt keys, and while holding them down, pressing the required key. Therefore, from this point on in the projects, instructions for using options will appear a bit differently. For instance, now when you see Shift-F7 it will mean that you should hold down the Shift key and, while holding it down, press the F7 key.

In Project 3 you will create the document shown in Figure 3-1, learn how to indent text, and create hanging indents. Once you have created the document, you will learn to use the Search function to search the text, and the Replace function to replace text within the document. You will also move text from one location to another within the document. Once the document is complete, you will save and print it using WordPerfect's shortcut keys.

Before you begin, load WordPerfect as you have done previously in Projects 1 and 2.

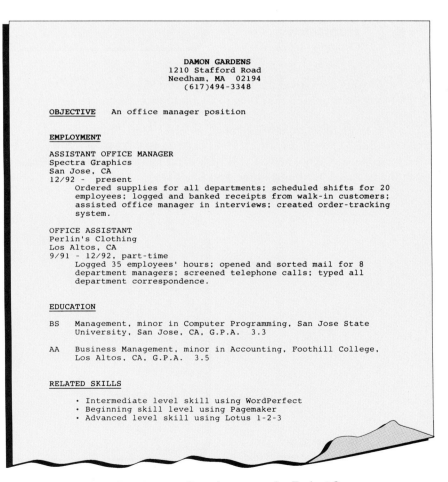

FIGURE 3-1 Sample resume for Project 3

You currently have a blank screen, ready for a new document. The heading in the sample resume (Figure 3-1) is boldfaced and centered. Recall from Project 2 that you used the menu to center a line. This time, let's try the shortcut keys.

Notice on the template that the word Center appears in green next to the F6 key. Press Shift-F6 to specify centering, and the cursor moves to the center of the line (Figure 3-2). The heading is also boldfaced, so press the F6 key to begin boldfacing.

FIGURE 3-2
Centering a line

Now that you have issued the formatting instructions, you are ready to enter the first line of the text, the name. Type the name Damon Gardens, then press F6 to turn off boldfacing. Press the Enter key to move the cursor to the next line.

The next three lines are also centered, so press Shift-F6 before entering each of the following lines: 1210 Stafford Road ↵ Needham, MA 02194 ↵ (617)494-3348 ↵. After you have entered the phone number and pressed the Enter key, your screen will look like Figure 3-3. Press the Enter key twice to insert two blank lines between the centered heading and the first line of text.

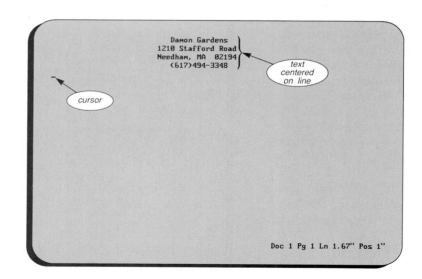

FIGURE 3-3
Entering centered text

The Caps Lock Key

Notice that the heading OBJECTIVE appears in all capital letters. You could hold down the Shift key and type each letter, but a much faster way would be to use the **Caps Lock** key. Pressing the Caps Lock key allows you to enter all uppercase letters without holding down the Shift key. Let's try using the Caps Lock key to enter the heading OBJECTIVE.

Because this heading is also boldfaced and underlined, press F6 then F8 to combine these text formats. Press the Caps Lock key once. Notice the Pos indicator on the status line is now in uppercase (POS) to remind you that you have pressed Caps Lock (Figure 3-4).

FIGURE 3-4
The Caps Lock key

Any characters you enter now will be in uppercase until you press the Caps Lock key again. Type OBJECTIVE, then press F6 and F8 again to turn off boldfacing and underlining. Press the Caps Lock key to turn off capitalization.

Press the Spacebar three times to insert three blank spaces, then type An office manager position. Press the Enter key three times, once to end the line and twice to insert two blank lines to precede the next section.

The next capitalized heading also is boldfaced and underlined. Press F6 and F8, then use the Caps Lock key to type EMPLOYMENT. Press F6 and F8 again to end boldfacing and underlining. Press the Enter key twice, then type ASSISTANT OFFICE MANAGER ↵. Press the Caps Lock key to end capitalization. Now type Spectra Graphics ↵ San Jose, CA ↵ 12/92 - present ↵. Your screen should look like the one shown in Figure 3-5.

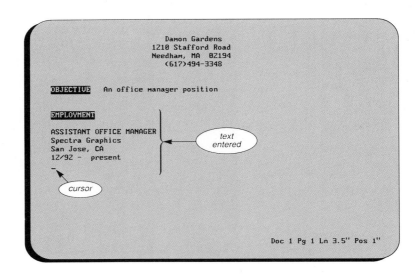

FIGURE 3-5
Entering text

INDENTED TEXT

◆ Sometimes documents contain **indented text**, or text that is set in from the margins. WordPerfect provides three different ways to indent text: at the left margin only, at both the right and left margins, or in a hanging indent.

The cursor should be positioned at the end of the document, Ln 3.5", Pos 1". The text that follows needs to be indented at the left margin. This means that text will line up at the point of the indent, rather than back at the true left margin. When you indent text, you are actually creating a temporary left margin that WordPerfect uses until you instruct it to stop.

Entering Indented Text

With the cursor positioned at the left margin (Figure 3-5), you are now ready to use the option to begin indenting. Press Alt- = to display the menu bar. The "Indent" option is contained in the Align portion of the Layout menu, so type L to display the Layout menu, then type A for "Align". Notice the two "Indent" options (Figure 3-6).

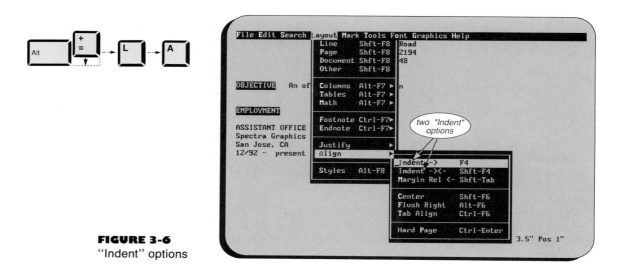

FIGURE 3-6
"Indent" options

The first option, with the single arrow pointing to the right, is used to indent the left margin only. The second option, with arrows pointing left and right, is used to indent both the right and left margins. You want to use the first option, so type I for "Indent".

The cursor moves in one tab stop (or five spaces) each time you select "Indent" from the menu. In this case you selected "Indent" once; all text will line up (or wrap) at the cursor position in Figure 3-7, which is five spaces in from the true left margin.

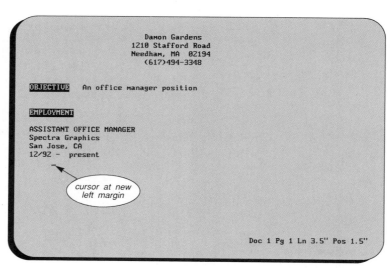

FIGURE 3-7
Indenting text

Type the following information for this section: Ordered supplies for all departments; scheduled shifts for 20 employees; logged and banked receipts from walk-in customers; assisted office manager in interviews; created order-tracking system..

After you type the word system, press the Enter key twice, once to end the line and once to insert a blank line (Figure 3-8). Notice that the cursor moved back to the true left margin when you pressed the Enter key. As with centering, indenting ends when you press the Enter key.

Mouse Users: Click the right mouse button to display the menu bar. Select the Layout menu, then select "Align", then select "Indent" with the right-pointing arrow.

Indenting Existing Text

Just as WordPerfect allows you to underline, boldface, and center existing text,
it also allows you to indent existing text. In the ASSISTANT OFFICE MANAGER section of the resume, we set the indented margin, then typed the text. In the next section, we will do the opposite: type the text, then indent it.

Type the text of this section: OFFICE ASSISTANT ↵ Perlin's Clothing ↵ Los Altos, CA ↵ 9/91 - 12/92, part-time ↵ Logged 35 employees' hours; opened and sorted mail for 8 department managers; screened telephone calls; typed all department correspondence. After you have entered the text as shown, press the Enter key three times.

As it does for most formatting options, WordPerfect indents text by inserting a code into the document. This code will affect all the text that follows it, until WordPerfect encounters the option necessary to end the format. In this case, the hard return code at the end of the text you entered will end indenting. Now you need to insert the code that begins indenting.

First position the cursor at the beginning point of the indent, the L in Logged, Ln 5", Pos 1". The shortcut key for indenting is F4, so press F4 and the paragraph becomes indented at the left margin (Figure 3-9). Press the Down Arrow key until the cursor is again positioned at the point for the new heading, at the bottom of the document, Ln 5.83", Pos 1".

FIGURE 3-8 Ending indented text

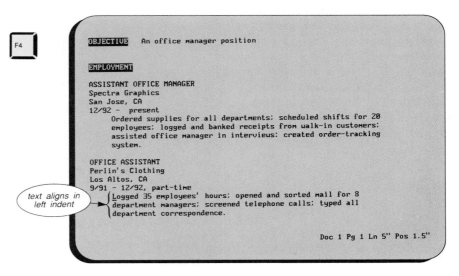

FIGURE 3-9 Indenting existing text

Hanging Indents with the Margin Release Key

A **hanging indent** indents text at the specified left margin *except for the first line*. This type of indent is especially useful for numbered text, or for a block of text like the next section of your document that shows Damon's education.

First type the boldfaced, underlined and capitalized heading by pressing F6, F8, and Caps Lock, then typing EDUCATION. Turn off boldfacing and underlining by pressing F6 and F8 again, then press Caps Lock to turn off capitalization. Press the Enter key twice to position the cursor at the beginning of the hanging indent (Figure 3-10).

To create a hanging indent, you must first instruct WordPerfect where you want the text to be indented. Press F4 and the cursor moves in one tab stop, just as it did for the previous EMPLOYMENT entries. Because the first line of a hanging indent extends back to the left margin, you must now instruct WordPerfect to move the cursor back.

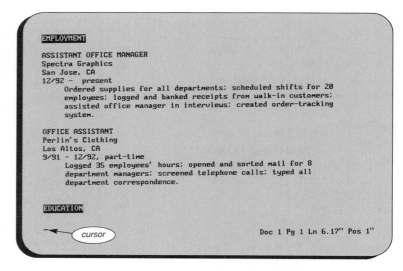

FIGURE 3-10   Entering a hanging indent

Notice that the Tab key has arrows pointing both forward and backward. If you use the Shift key with the Tab key, the cursor will move *backward* one tab stop. Press Shift-Tab, and the cursor moves back one tab stop, or to the far left margin. This keystroke is known as the **margin release** feature. You first set the temporary left margin when you pressed F4. You then released it for the *first line only* by pressing the margin release key; thus, you created a hanging indent.

Now that the cursor is positioned, type BS, then press the Tab key. The text BS remains at the true left margin; the text you enter after you press Tab will wrap at the new, temporary left margin that you set when you pressed the F4 key. Now type Management, minor in Computer Programming, San Jose State University, San Jose, CA, G.P.A. 3.3. Notice how the text of the second line automatically indents at the left margin you specified when you pressed F4 (Figure 3-11).

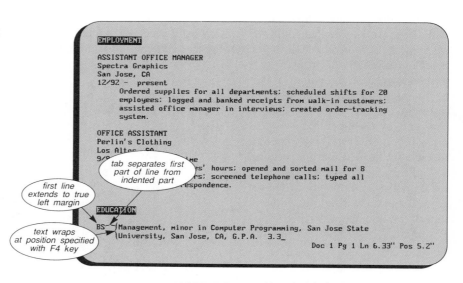

FIGURE 3-11   Hanging indent

Press the Enter key twice so that the cursor moves to the beginning of the next hanging indent (Figure 3-12).

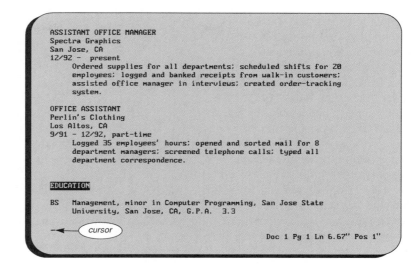

FIGURE 3-12
Adding a hanging indent

Hanging Indents with the F4 Key

In the previous entry, you used the margin release key to create the hanging indent. However, there is a quicker way of creating a hanging indent that is suitable for these entries. Because these entries have a tab in the first line of text, you can simply type the first part of the text, then use the F4 key to indent the remaining text. Let's try this quicker method for the next section of the resume.

Type AA, which is the portion of the text that will remain at the true left margin. Now press the F4 key. This instructs WordPerfect to begin indenting. Now type Business Management, minor in Accounting, Foothill College, Los Altos, CA, G.P.A. 3.5. As you type, notice how the text aligns itself in a hanging indent (Figure 3-13).

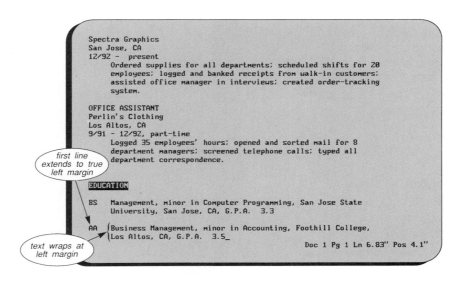

FIGURE 3-13
Hanging indent

Press the Enter key three times, once to end the paragraph and twice to insert two blank lines. This method of creating a hanging indent can be used for any type of text that has spaces or tabs separating the first portion of the text from the indented portion of the text.

Now let's input the next section of the resume. Press F6 and F8 to begin boldfacing and underlining, then type RELATED SKILLS. Turn off boldfacing and underlining by pressing F6 and F8 again, then press the Enter key twice.

The entries in this section are also indented, but only at the left margin. As you did for the EMPLOYMENT section, use F4 to indent each of the following asterisked items: * Intermediate level skill using Word-Perfect ↵ * Beginning skill level using Pagemaker ↵ * Advanced level skill using Lotus 1-2-3 ↵. Figure 3-14 shows how your screen should look after typing these entries.

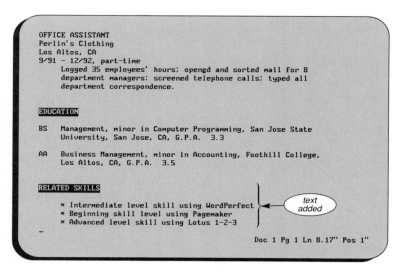

FIGURE 3-14   Adding indented text

Case Conversion

Suppose you decided that the name Damon Gardens would look better in all uppercase letters. Rather than using the Caps Lock key and retyping the text, you can use WordPerfect's Case Conversion function.

First you must block the text to be converted. Press Home, Home, Up Arrow to position the cursor at the top of the document. Press the Right Arrow key once so that the cursor is positioned on the D in Damon. Now block the text by pressing Alt-F4, then the End key.

Now that the text is blocked, you need to tell WordPerfect what action to perform. Press Alt-= to display the menu bar, then type E for Edit (Figure 3-15).

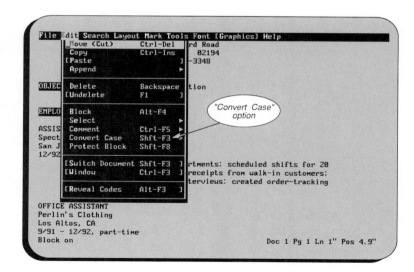

FIGURE 3-15
"Convert Case" option

Notice the "Convert Case" option on the Edit menu. Type V to select "Convert Case", and the submenu in Figure 3-16 appears.

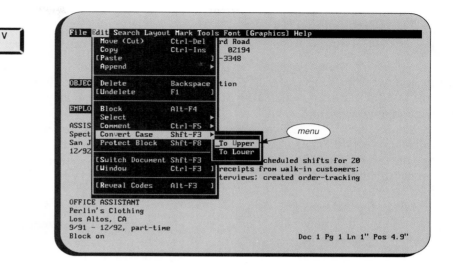

FIGURE 3-16
Convert Case menu

Because you want to convert the blocked text to uppercase, type U, and the blocked text is converted to all upper-case characters (Figure 3-17).

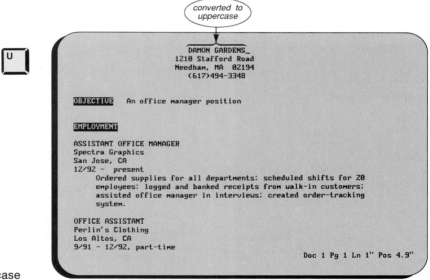

FIGURE 3-17
Case converted to uppercase

Mouse Users: Block the text to be converted, then press the right mouse button to display the menu bar. Select the Edit menu, then select "Convert Case". Position the pointer in the "To Upper" option, then click the left mouse button.

SAVING A DOCUMENT

Now that the document is complete, let's save it to disk. Press the F10 key. When the save prompt appears, type the name PROJ3, then press the Enter key. Your document is now saved on disk under the filename PROJ3.

PRINTING A DOCUMENT

◆ Now that you have saved the document, let's print a copy of it. Press Shift-F7, then type 1 to select "Full Document". Your printed document should look like the one in Figure 3-1.

MOVING TEXT

◆ Suppose that when you see a printed copy of the resume, you decide that you want the EDUCATION section to precede the EMPLOYMENT section. The Move function allows you to move text so that a document can be rearranged without retyping.

When you use the Move function, you must first specify what text you want to move. Once you have done this, you move the text by positioning the cursor at the new location for the text, and then inserting the text. You are virtually *cutting* the text from one location and then *pasting* it in its new location. Because of this, the Move function is sometimes called cutting and pasting.

To illustrate how the Move function works, let's move the entire EDUCATION section so that it precedes the EMPLOYMENT section of the resume.

WordPerfect's Move function allows you to move sentences, paragraphs, or pages. Therefore, before you learn to move the text, you must first understand how WordPerfect defines a paragraph. WordPerfect considers all text followed by a hard return code ([HRt]) to be a paragraph, even if that text consists of a single word. Figure 3-18 shows several different examples of paragraphs as defined by WordPerfect.

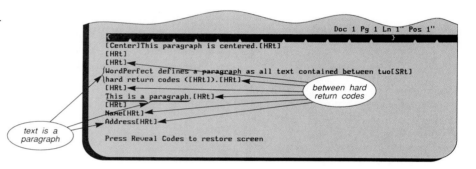

FIGURE 3-18   WordPerfect paragraphs

Moving A Paragraph

To move a paragraph, you must first position the cursor within the paragraph to be moved, in this case anywhere within the word EDUCATION (Figure 3-19).

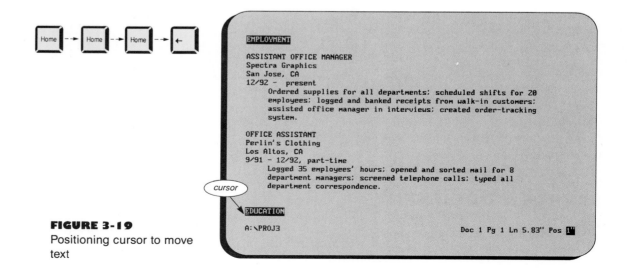

FIGURE 3-19
Positioning cursor to move text

Ordinarily, the cursor does not need to be on any particular character, only within the paragraph to be moved. In this case, however, you are moving text that has been formatted for underlining and boldfacing. Therefore, it is necessary to position the cursor at the left margin of the line containing the text, *before any codes*. This way, you ensure that the codes will be moved along with the text. Press Home, Home, Home, Left Arrow to position the cursor, then press Alt-= to display the menu bar.

The "Move" option is contained in the Edit menu, so type E to display this menu. Once the Edit menu displays, you must select the text to be moved. Type E for "Select", and the menu in Figure 3-20 appears.

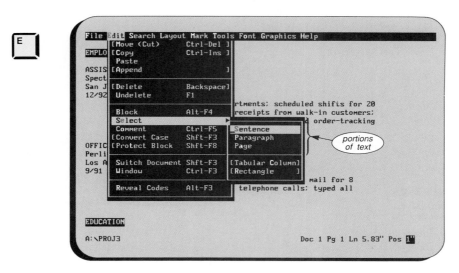

FIGURE 3-20 Defining text to be moved

You want to move a paragraph, so type P for "Paragraph", and the text of the paragraph becomes highlighted to show you that this is the text that will be moved (Figure 3-21).

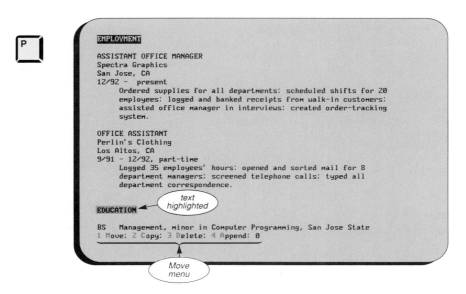

FIGURE 3-21 Move menu

You might have difficulty seeing the highlight because the word is already highlighted to signify formatting. A new menu also displays, asking if you want to move, copy, delete, or append this text. Because you want to move this text, type 1, and the text disappears from the screen (Figure 3-22). Don't panic. WordPerfect removes the text from the screen, but retains it in memory until you instruct WordPerfect where to place it in the document.

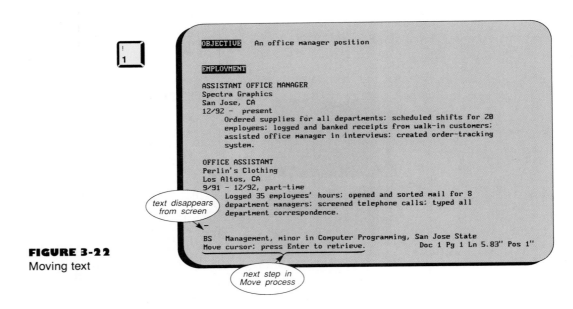

FIGURE 3-22
Moving text

The next step in the move process is to position the cursor at the new location for the text, the E in EMPLOY-MENT. Again, because this text contains formatting, press Home, Home, Home, Left Arrow to position the cursor before any codes on the line (Figure 3-23).

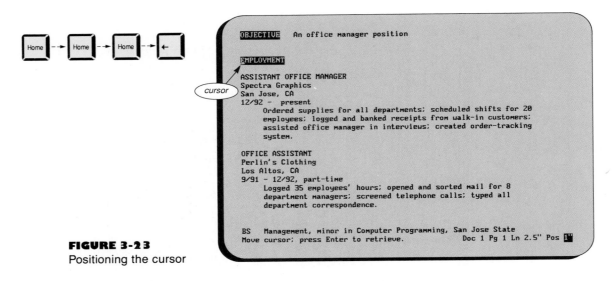

FIGURE 3-23
Positioning the cursor

When you move text, WordPerfect follows the rules for normal Insert mode. This means that the character under the cursor and all text to the right of it will be moved downward and the text will be inserted to the *left of the cursor*.

With the cursor positioned on the E in EMPLOYMENT, press the Enter key. Notice how the text under and followed by the cursor remains intact and moves down to accommodate the newly inserted text. The moved text is inserted where the cursor is positioned.

Mouse Users: Position the cursor in the paragraph to be moved, then press the right mouse button to display the menu bar. Select the Edit menu, then select "Move". Select menu choice "1", then click the left mouse button on the next menu choice "1". Move the cursor to the new location for text, then press Enter.

Moving a Block of Text

We could continue in this manner, moving each paragraph of the EDUCATION section individually. A much faster way would be to block all the paragraphs in the section, and then move them all at once. To do this, you must first position the cursor on the first character to be moved, the blank line above the text BS Management....

Once the cursor is positioned, press Alt-F4 to begin blocking, then press the Down Arrow key until all text to be moved is blocked, including the blank line following the EDUCA-TION section (Figure 3-24).

Now you're ready to move the blocked text. This time, let's try the shortcut keys. Press Ctrl-F4, and the menu in Figure 3-25 appears.

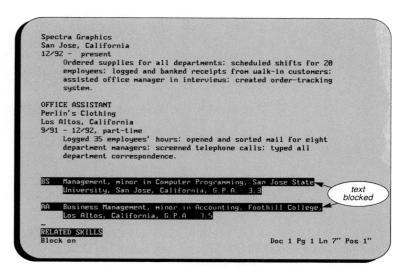

FIGURE 3-24 Blocking text to move

FIGURE 3-25
Moving blocked text

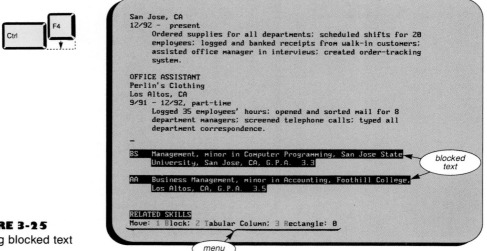

Notice that this menu is slightly different from the one that appeared when you moved a paragraph. This difference is not due to the use of the shortcut keys. Rather, this menu appears *because the portion of text to be moved has already been defined.* There is no need to specify a sentence, paragraph, or page because the text is already blocked. The menu in Figure 3-25 will appear each time you select the "Move" option and the text is already blocked.

You want to move this block, so type 1 to select "Block", and the menu in Figure 3-26 appears.

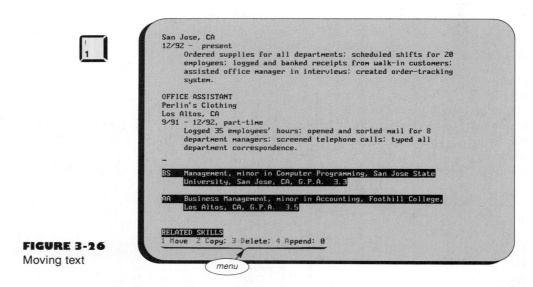

FIGURE 3-26
Moving text

From this point on, the Move function works exactly as it did previously. Type 1 for "Move", then position the cursor at the new location for the text, the line under EDUCATION. Press Enter and the text is inserted where the cursor is positioned (Figure 3-27).

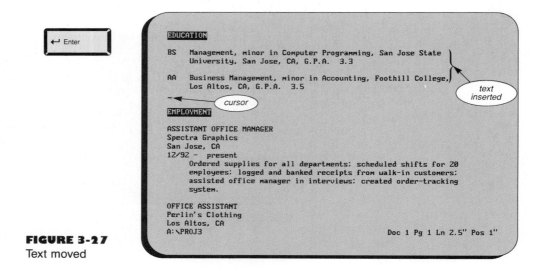

FIGURE 3-27
Text moved

When you cannot define the area of text to be moved through the Move menu, you should block the text before you invoke the Move menu. That is, if you are not moving a sentence, paragraph, or page, block the text first and then select the "Move" option.

 Mouse Users: Block the text to be moved, then proceed as you have been previously directed for moving a paragraph of text.

Moving a Word

Now let's move a single word. In the RELATED SKILLS section, notice that the first and third entries refer to level skill and the second entry refers to skill level. To remain consistent, let's move the word skill in the second entry so that it follows level as it does in the other entries. Block the word skill by positioning the cursor on the first character of the word. Next, press Alt-F4 and use the Right Arrow key to extend the block to include the space following the last character. Press Ctrl-F4 to display the Move menu. Type 1 for "Block", then type 1 for "Move". Move the cursor to the new location for the word skill, which is the u in using (Figure 3-28).

Now press the Enter key, and the word skill is inserted where the cursor is positioned.

In this project, you have moved a word, a paragraph, and a selected block of text, but WordPerfect can also move entire pages, sentences, or even a single character. Remember that whenever you want to move text, you must first define the text to be moved, position the cursor at the new location for the text, and then press the Enter key to insert the text.

FIGURE 3-28   Moving a word

SEARCHING TEXT

Suppose you used the number 8 in your document, and you decide instead you want to spell out the word eight. Rather than visually searching through the text for all the occurrences of the number 8, you can instruct WordPerfect to search the text for you.

You can search text from the point of the cursor either forward or backward, so since we want to search the entire document, press Home, Home, Up Arrow to position the cursor at the top of the document. Now press Alt-= to display the menu bar. The "Search" option is contained in the Search menu, so type S to display the Search menu (Figure 3-29).

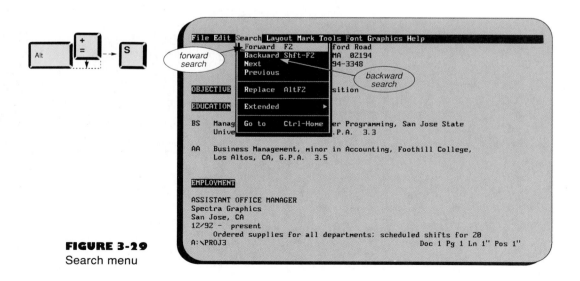

FIGURE 3-29
Search menu

The Search menu lists both forward and backward search options. You want to search forward, so select "F", and the prompt in Figure 3-30 appears.

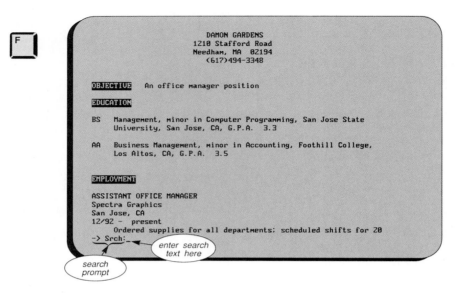

FIGURE 3-30 Search prompt

At this prompt you need to enter the text for which you want to search. Type 8 (Figure 3-31), then press F2 (the shortcut key for Search) to begin the search. Be certain you press F2 and *not the Enter key*. Pressing the Enter key will cause WordPerfect to search for the number 8 *followed by a hard return code*.

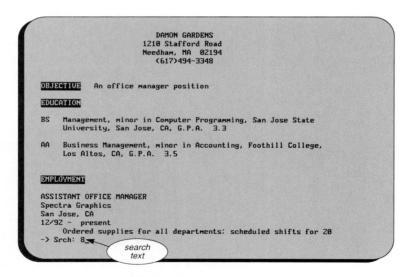

FIGURE 3-31 Entering search text

The cursor jumps to the first occurrence of 8, the text you specified when you selected the "Search" option (Figure 3-32).

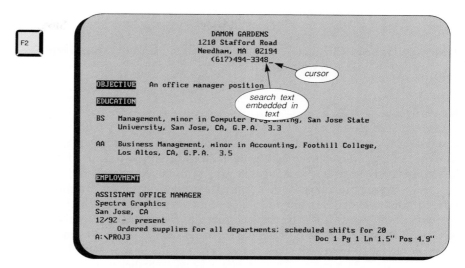

FIGURE 3-32 First occurrence of search text

Even though the text 8 is embedded in other text, WordPerfect recognizes this as an occurrence of the search text. Since you want this number to remain intact, select the "Search" option again by pressing Alt- = , then typing S. This time, you need only type N to select "Next" from the menu. WordPerfect retains the text you previously entered at the search prompt. WordPerfect retains this text until you specify other text for the search. The cursor stops at the next occurrence (Figure 3-33).

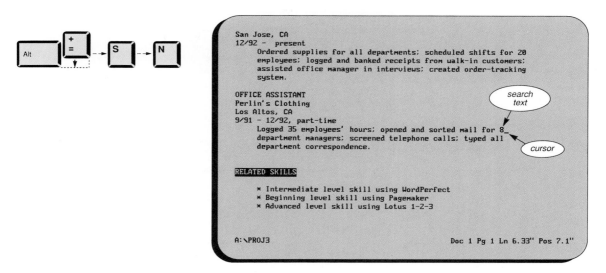

FIGURE 3-33 Next occurrence of search text

Since this is, in fact, the text you want to modify, press the Backspace key, then type the word `eight`.

In this example you searched the document for a single number, but WordPerfect can also search for whole words or phrases. To do this, you would follow the steps you followed to search for the number 8, except that you would type the whole word or phrase you are seeking.

Mouse Users: Click the right mouse button to display the menu bar. Select the Search menu, then select "Forward". Type 8, then click the right mouse button.

REPLACING TEXT

◆ WordPerfect is capable not only of searching text, but also of replacing text. The Replace function will replace each occurrence of a word or phrase with another word or phrase you specify. This feature is particularly useful for replacing a consistently misspelled or misused word with the correct word.

Let's use the Replace function to replace the state abbreviation for California with the entire state name. One major difference between the Search and Replace functions is that the Search function allows you to search a document either *forward or backward*. The Replace function is capable of searching a document from the point of the cursor *forward only*. Because of this, position the cursor at the top of the document by pressing Home, Home, Up Arrow. Display the menu bar by pressing Alt- = . Display the Search menu by typing S, then type R for "Replace". The prompt in Figure 3-34 appears. This prompt asks you whether you want to confirm each replacement. Type Y so that WordPerfect will pause and allow you to confirm each time the text is replaced.

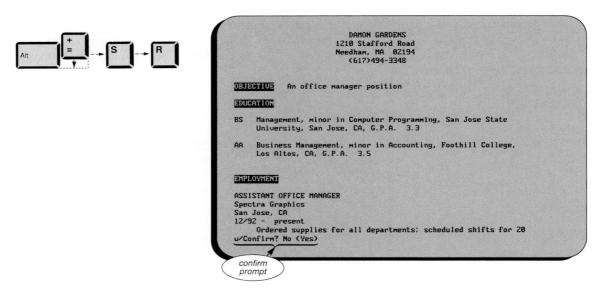

FIGURE 3-34 Confirm prompt

Once you answer the confirm prompt, you must enter the search text. Type CA. This tells WordPerfect to search for the text CA. Next you need to tell WordPerfect what the new (replacement) text will be. Press F2 (Figure 3-35) then type the replacement text California, and press F2 again to begin replacing.

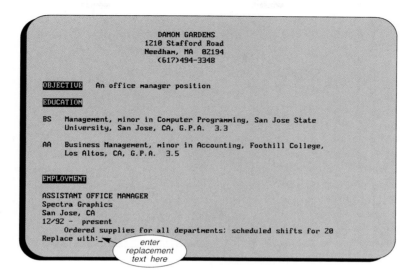

FIGURE 3-35 Entering replacement text

When WordPerfect encounters the first occurrence of CA, the cursor stops and the confirm message in Figure 3-36 appears. Because you requested that each replacement be confirmed, you must type a Y each time you want WordPerfect to replace text.

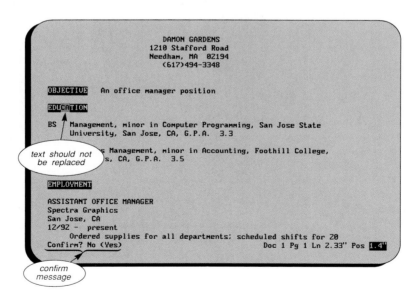

FIGURE 3-36 Replacing text

In this case, the search text is embedded in the word EDUCATION. Type N, and WordPerfect leaves the text intact and stops at the next occurrence (Figure 3-37).

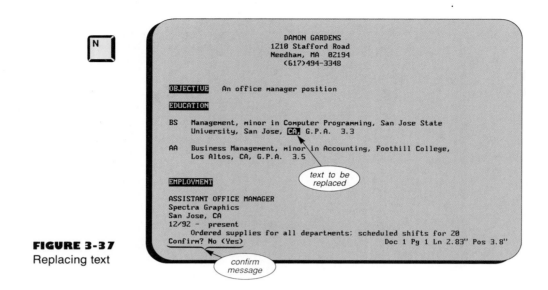

FIGURE 3-37
Replacing text

You do, in fact, want to replace this text, so type Y. The text CA is replaced with California, and the search continues until WordPerfect encounters the next CA in the document (Figure 3-38).

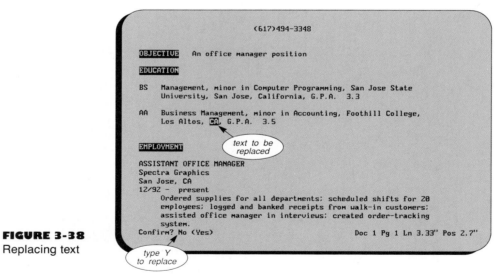

FIGURE 3-38
Replacing text

WordPerfect has encountered the next CA. Here, again, you want to replace this text with the new text, so type Y. CA is replaced with California, and WordPerfect continues searching. Type a Y each time WordPerfect stops and displays the confirm message. WordPerfect continues to search and replace until there are no more occurrences of CA in the document. In all, you should make four replacements. When WordPerfect reaches the end of the document, the Replace function ends and the cursor remains positioned at the last point where text was replaced.

Mouse Users: Press the right mouse button to display the menu bar. Select the Search menu, then select "Replace". Position the pointer in "Yes" and click the left mouse button to confirm each replacement. Enter the search text `CA`, then press the right mouse button. Enter the replacement text `California` and press the right mouse button. Click the left mouse button on "Yes" each time you want to replace text.

PRINTING A DOCUMENT

Now that the document is complete, let's print it. Make sure the printer is turned on and is ready to print. Press Shift-F7, then type 1, and the document begins printing. Your final, printed document should look like the one in Figure 3-39.

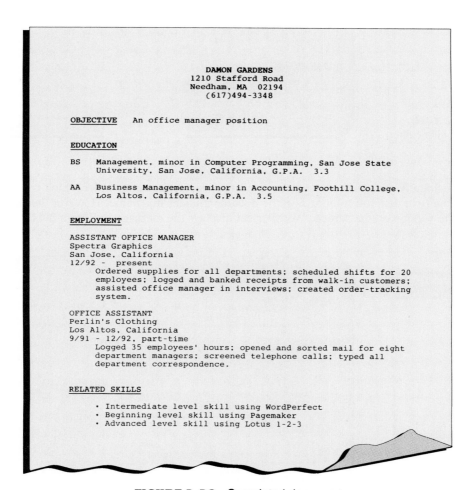

DAMON GARDENS
1210 Stafford Road
Needham, MA 02194
(617)494-3348

OBJECTIVE   An office manager position

EDUCATION

BS   Management, minor in Computer Programming, San Jose State
      University, San Jose, California, G.P.A. 3.3

AA   Business Management, minor in Accounting, Foothill College,
      Los Altos, California, G.P.A. 3.5

EMPLOYMENT

ASSISTANT OFFICE MANAGER
Spectra Graphics
San Jose, California
12/92 - present
      Ordered supplies for all departments; scheduled shifts for 20
      employees; logged and banked receipts from walk-in customers;
      assisted office manager in interviews; created order-tracking
      system.

OFFICE ASSISTANT
Perlin's Clothing
Los Altos, California
9/91 - 12/92, part-time
      Logged 35 employees' hours; opened and sorted mail for eight
      department managers; screened telephone calls; typed all
      department correspondence.

RELATED SKILLS

      • Intermediate level skill using WordPerfect
      • Beginning level skill using Pagemaker
      • Advanced level skill using Lotus 1-2-3

FIGURE 3-39 Completed document

EXITING AND SAVING AT THE SAME TIME

WordPerfect contains a built-in safeguard to prevent you from accidentally exiting without saving your work. This safeguard also allows you to save a document and exit WordPerfect at the same time.

To illustrate, let's use the "Exit" option by pressing F7. Remember that you made changes to your document since the last time you saved it. Since you want to save the document complete with the changes you made, type Y to save the document. WordPerfect displays the message in Figure 3-40.

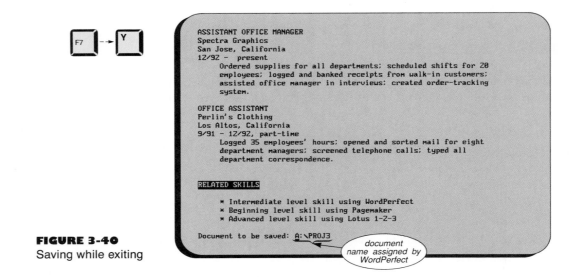

FIGURE 3-40
Saving while exiting

WordPerfect automatically assigns the document its current name, the name under which is was most recently saved. Press Enter to confirm that you want to save the document under this name. However, because the document on disk differs from the version on the screen, WordPerfect displays the message in Figure 3-41.

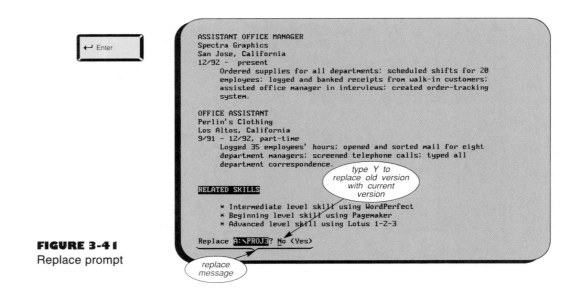

FIGURE 3-41
Replace prompt

To WordPerfect, these are two separate documents because they are not identical. *Two documents cannot be saved under the same name.* Therefore, type Y to instruct WordPerfect to replace the old version on disk with the new version. The document, including the changes you entered since the last time you saved, is saved on disk under the name PROJ3. Type Y at the "Exit WP? No (Yes)" prompt and you return to the DOS prompt.

PROJECT SUMMARY

In Project 3 you learned how to create a document with indented text and a hanging indent, and how to convert case. You learned how to move text from one location to another within a document, and how to use the Search function. You also used the Replace function to search for specified text and replace it with new text. You saved and printed the document, and then used the Exit function to save the document and exit WordPerfect at the same time. All the activities that you learned for this project are summarized in the Quick Reference following Project 6. The following is a summary of the keystroke sequence used in Project 3.

SUMMARY OF KEYSTROKES — PROJECT 3

STEPS	KEY(S) PRESSED	RESULTS
1	wp ↵ [At C> prompt or as directed by instructor]	Loads WordPerfect.
2	[Shift-F6] [F6]	Begins boldfaced, centered text.
3	Damon Gardens	Enters text.
4	[F6] ↵	Ends boldfacing and moves cursor down one line.
5	[Shift-F6] 1210 Stafford Road↵ [Shift-F6] Needham, MA 02194↵ [Shift-F6] (617) 494-3348↵↵↵	Enters text and inserts two blank lines.
6	[Caps Lock]	Turns capitalization on.
7	[F6] [F8]	Begins boldfacing and underlining.
8	OBJECTIVE	Enters heading.
9	[F6] [F8]	Ends boldfacing and underlining.
10	[Caps Lock]	Turns capitalization off.
11	[Spacebar] [Spacebar] [Spacebar]	Inserts three blank spaces.
12	An office manager position ↵↵↵	Enters text followed by two blank lines.
13	[F6] [F8]	Begins boldfacing and underlining.
14	EMPLOYMENT [F6] [F8] ↵↵	Enters text followed by blank line; turns off boldfacing and underlining.
15	ASSISTANT OFFICE MANAGER ↵	Enters text.
16	Spectra Graphics ↵ San Jose, CA ↵ 12/92 - present ↵	Enters text.
17	[Alt-=] L A I	Specifies indented text.
18	Ordered supplies for all departments; scheduled shifts for 20 employees; logged and banked receipts from walk-in customers; assisted office manager in interviews; created order-tracking system. ↵	Enters indented text and inserts a blank line.
19	OFFICE ASSISTANT↵Perlin's Clothing↵Los Altos, CA↵9/91 - 12/92, part-time ↵Logged 35 employees' hours; opened and sorted mail for 8 department managers; screened telephone calls; typed all department correspondence. ↵↵↵	Enters text and inserts two blank lines.
20	↑[Press 5 times]	Positions cursor to indent text.

(continued)

SUMMARY OF KEYSTROKES — PROJECT 3 (continued)

STEPS	KEY(S) PRESSED	RESULTS
21	F4	Indents text.
22	↓ [Press 5 times]	Positions cursor for new heading.
23	F6 F8	Begins boldfacing and underlining.
24	EDUCATION	Enters text.
25	F6 F8	Ends boldfacing and underlining.
26	↵ ↵	Inserts blank line.
27	F4 Shift-Tab BS Tab	Enters hanging indent and moves cursor to start of indented text.
28	Management, minor in Computer Programming, San Jose State University, San Jose, CA, G.P.A. 3.3↵	Enters indented text followed by blank line.
29	AA F4	Enters text and moves to start of indented text.
30	Business Management, minor in Accounting, Foothill College, Los Altos, CA, G.P.A. 3.5 ↵ ↵ ↵	Enters indented text and positions cursor for next heading.
31	F6 F8	Begins boldfacing and underlining.
32	RELATED SKILLS	Enters text.
33	F6 F8	Ends boldfacing and underlining.
34	↵ ↵	Ends line and inserts blank line.
35	F4	Begins indented text.
36	* Intermediate level skill using WordPerfect ↵ F4 * Beginning skill level using Pagemaker ↵ F4 * Advanced level skill using Lotus 1-2-3 ↵	Enters indented text.
37	F10	Invokes "Save" option.
38	proj3↵	Saves document under name PROJ3.
39	Shift-F7 1	Prints document.
40	↑ [Press 14 times]	Positions cursor on first character of EDUCATION.
41	Home Home Home →	Positions cursor at left margin prior to codes.
42	Alt-= E E P	Selects portion of text to be moved.
43	1	Removes paragraph from screen.
44	↑ [Press 20 times] Home Home Home →	Positions cursor at new location for text.
45	↵	Inserts text at new location.
46	Home Home ↓ ↑ ↑	Positions cursor on line containing word to be moved.
47	Ctrl-→ Ctrl-→ Ctrl-→ Alt-F4 → [Press 6 times]	Positions cursor and blocks word to be moved.
48	Ctrl-F4 1 1	Removes word from screen.
49	Ctrl-→	Positions cursor to insert word.
50	↵	Inserts word at new location.
51	Home Home ↑	Moves cursor to top of document.
52	Alt-= S F	Invokes "Search" option.

SUMMARY OF KEYSTROKES — PROJECT 3 (continued)

STEPS	KEY(S) PRESSED	RESULTS
53	8 F2	Enters search text and begins search.
54	Alt-= S N	Continues search.
55	Backspace	Deletes text.
56	eight	Enters text.
57	Home Home ↑	Moves cursor to top of document.
58	Alt-= S R	Invokes "Replace" option.
59	Y	Sets confirm to Yes.
60	CA F2 California F2	Enters replacement text and begins replacing.
61	Y [Press 4 times]	Confirms replacements.
62	Shift-F7 1	Prints document.
63	F7 Y ↵ Y	Saves document and exits WordPerfect.

The following list summarizes the material covered in Project 3.

1. The shortcut keys for centering are Shift-F6.
2. The **Caps Lock** key allows you to enter all uppercase letters without holding down the Shift key.
3. WordPerfect provides three different ways to **indent text**, or to set text in from the margins.
4. To indent text at the left margin only, press F4. To indent text at both the left and right margins, press Shift-F4.
5. A **hanging indent** indents text at the left margin, *except for the first line*.
6. The **margin release** feature moves the cursor back one tab stop. Press Shift-Tab to release the margin.
7. WordPerfect contains a **Case Conversion** function, which allows you to change the case of blocked text.
8. The **Move** menu enables you to move text to a different location within a document.
9. If text cannot be defined through the Move menu, block it before invoking the Move menu.
10. The Search function searches a document for specified text. Text can be searched either forward or backward through a document.
11. The Replace function searches a document for specified text, then replaces it with new text. The Replace function can be used only from the point of the cursor forward through a document.
12. You may save a document and exit WordPerfect at the same time by using the "Exit" option prior to saving changes.

STUDENT ASSIGNMENTS

STUDENT ASSIGNMENT 1: True/False

Instructions: Circle T if the statement is true and F if the statement is false.

T F 1. To indent text at the left margin, you must first block the text to be indented.
T F 2. The "Case Conversion" option is contained in the Layout menu.
T F 3. A hanging indent indents text at the left margin except for the first line.
T F 4. The F4 key indents text at both the left and right margins.
T F 5. To move text, you must always block it first.

Student Assignment 1 (continued)

T F 6. You can search a document either forward or backward.
T F 7. The Replace function must be executed each time WordPerfect stops at the word being searched for.
T F 8. WordPerfect can move only sentences or paragraphs, not words.
T F 9. The Caps Lock function is contained in the Align portion of the Layout menu.

STUDENT ASSIGNMENT 2: Multiple Choice

Instructions: Circle the correct response.

1. The Move function _____.
   a. can move text whether text consists of characters, words, sentences, or paragraphs
   b. moves text to a new location within a document
   c. can be used before or after blocking text
   d. all of the above
2. To use the Search function, _____.
   a. press F2, then type the text to be searched
   b. select Search from the menu bar, specify forward or backward search, then type the text to be searched
   c. press Alt-F2, then type the text to be searched
   d. both a and b
3. The Replace function _____.
   a. will begin from the point of the cursor
   b. can only search forward through the text
   c. will find specified text and replace it with new text
   d. all of the above
4. The "Replace" option is contained in the _____ menu.
   a. Layout
   b. Align
   c. Search
   d. Edit
5. The Move menu defines text in the following segments: _____
   a. character, paragraph, page
   b. sentence, paragraph, page
   c. word, sentence, paragraph
   d. none of the above
6. To print a document with the shortcut keys, press _____.
   a. F7, 1
   b. Shift-F7, 4
   c. Alt-F7, 1
   d. none of the above
7. To save a document with the shortcut keys, press _____.
   a. F10
   b. Shift-F10
   c. Shift-F7
   d. none of the above
8. The "Indent" option is contained in the _____ menu.
   a. Indent
   b. Search
   c. Layout
   d. none of the above

9. Press _____ to release the left margin.
   a. Alt-Tab
   b. Shift-Tab
   c. Tab, F4, F4
   d. none of the above

STUDENT ASSIGNMENT 3: Matching

Instructions: Put the number of the appropriate menu next to the words in the second column.

1. Edit   _____   "Search" option
2. Layout _____   "Replace" option
3. Search _____   Print document
4. File   _____   Exit document
           _____   Case conversion
           _____   Left-margin indent
           _____   "Move" option

STUDENT ASSIGNMENT 4: Moving Text

Instructions: Perform the following task.

In the paragraph shown in the following figure you want to move the second sentence so that it becomes the first sentence. Explain the steps to accomplish this.

> Through both lecture and hands-on exercises, the student will gain experience with some of the many features of WordPerfect 5.1. This course will provide the beginning student with a thorough introduction to word processing functions.

Steps: _____

_____

_____

STUDENT ASSIGNMENT 5: Converting Case

Instructions: Perform the following task.

In the document shown in the figure, the heading needs to be changed to all uppercase characters. Assuming the cursor is resting on the first character of the word MEMORANDUM, explain the steps to accomplish this.

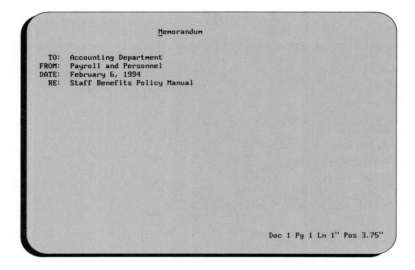

```
                              Memorandum


      TO:  Accounting Department
    FROM:  Payroll and Personnel
    DATE:  February 6, 1994
      RE:  Staff Benefits Policy Manual
```

```
                                            Doc 1 Pg 1 Ln 1" Pos 3.75"
```

Steps: _____

_____

_____

STUDENT ASSIGNMENT 6: Creating a Document

Instructions: Create the letter of recommendation in the figure, making sure you use centering, boldfacing, and underlining where shown. When you have finished the letter, print and save it under the name SA3-6.

LETTER OF RECOMMENDATION

I am writing to recommend that you hire **Damon Gardens** as an office manager. I was Damon's faculty advisor at San Jose State University during her junior and senior years, and she was a student in my MGNT 363 class.

Damon's unassuming, respectful manner stands out from the many students I have known. In the classroom I found her to be quiet and introspective, but I never underestimated her abilities. The calibre of her work was consistently high. In the MGNT 363 class case study Damon was chosen by her classmates to be their team leader. In that capacity she worked well and was respected by her team members. Damon is very conscientious and demands the best from herself.

I highly recommend Damon. She has not only strong management skills, but also the caring and sensitivity necessary to be an outstanding office manager.

Barbara P. Newman
San Jose State University
Department of Management

STUDENT ASSIGNMENT 7: Modifying a Document with the Move Function

Instructions: Perform the following tasks.

1. Retrieve the document SA3-6 that you created in Student Assignment 6.
2. Move the last sentence in the second paragraph that begins Damon is very ... and ends with the best from herself. so that it becomes the last sentence in the first paragraph.
3. Move the text Department of Management so that it precedes the university name.
4. When you have finished revising the document, print it. Then save it under the name SA3-7.

LETTER OF RECOMMENDATION

I am writing to recommend that you hire **Damon Gardens** as an office manager. I was Damon's faculty advisor at San Jose State University during her junior and senior years, and she was a student in my MGNT 363 class. Damon is very conscientious and demands the best from herself.

Damon's unassuming, respectful manner stands out from the many students I have known. In the classroom I found her to be quiet and introspective, but I never underestimated her abilities. The calibre of her work was consistently high. In the MGNT 363 class case study Damon was chosen by her classmates to be their team leader. In that capacity she worked well and was respected by her team members.

I highly recommend Damon. She has not only strong management skills, but also the caring and sensitivity necessary to be an outstanding office manager.

Barbara P. Newman
Department of Management
San Jose State University

STUDENT ASSIGNMENT 8: Using the Replace Function

Instructions: Perform the following tasks.

1. Retrieve the document SA3-7 that you revised in Student Assignment 7.
2. Use the Replace function to replace all occurrences of MGNT with Management.
3. After you have modified the document, print it and save it under the name SA3-8.

LETTER OF RECOMMENDATION

I am writing to recommend that you hire **Damon Gardens** as an office manager. I was Damon's faculty advisor at San Jose State University during her junior and senior years, and she was a student in my Management 363 class. Damon is very conscientious and demands the best from herself.

Damon's unassuming, respectful manner stands out from the many students I have known. In the classroom I found her to be quiet and introspective, but I never underestimated her abilities. The calibre of her work was consistently high. In the Management 363 class case study Damon was chosen by her classmates to be their team leader. In that capacity she worked well and was respected by her team members.

I highly recommend Damon. She has not only strong management skills, but also the caring and sensitivity necessary to be an outstanding office manager.

Barbara P. Newman
Department of Management
San Jose State University

Formatting a Document

OBJECTIVES

You will have mastered the material in this project when you can:

◆ Add page numbering to a document

◆ Change margins

◆ Use WordPerfect's default tabs

◆ Remove justification from text

◆ Set and delete custom tabs

◆ Enter and edit headers and footers

◆ Enter footnotes

◆ Use the Print View function

DOCUMENT FORMATTING

◆ In the previous projects you used WordPerfect's default settings for page formatting. All the documents you have created so far have had the same sized margins and have not had numbered pages. The document in Figure 4-1 does not use the default settings for page formatting. It contains headers and footers, page numbers, and top/bottom and left/right margins that are larger than the default margins. Since most of these settings are controlled by the Page Format and Line Format menus, you will need to use these menus to make your document appear like Figure 4-1.

In Project 4 you will create the document in Figure 4-1. You will learn how to create headers, footers, and footnotes, how to number pages, create tabbed tables, and remove justification from text. You will also learn to change margin settings, both top/bottom and right/left.

Before you begin creating the document, load WordPerfect as you have done in previous projects.

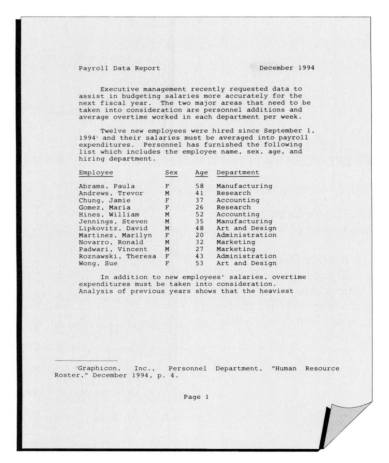

FIGURE 4-1 Document for Project 4 – Page 1

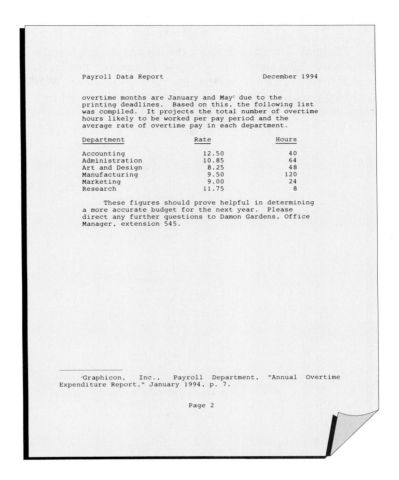

```
Payroll Data Report                      December 1994

overtime months are January and May² due to the
printing deadlines.  Based on this, the following list
was compiled.  It projects the total number of overtime
hours likely to be worked per pay period and the
average rate of overtime pay in each department.

Department                 Rate              Hours

Accounting                 12.50                40
Administration             10.85                64
Art and Design              8.25                48
Manufacturing               9.50               120
Marketing                   9.00                24
Research                   11.75                 8

     These figures should prove helpful in determining
a more accurate budget for the next year.  Please
direct any further questions to Damon Gardens, Office
Manager, extension 545.

     _____
     ²Graphicon,    Inc.,    Payroll   Department,   "Annual   Overtime
     Expenditure Report." January 1994. p. 7.

                          Page 2
```

FIGURE 4-1
Document for Project 4 –
Page 2

Press Alt-= to display the menu bar, then type L to display the Layout menu. Virtually everything that affects the printed appearance of a document is controlled by this menu. First, let's use the Page Format menu to set page numbering and to increase the top and bottom margins. Type P and the Page Format menu in Figure 4-2 appears.

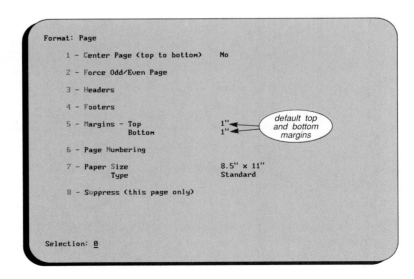

```
Format: Page

    1 - Center Page (top to bottom)    No

    2 - Force Odd/Even Page

    3 - Headers

    4 - Footers

    5 - Margins - Top                  1"        default top
                  Bottom               1"        and bottom
                                                 margins

    6 - Page Numbering

    7 - Paper Size                     8.5" x 11"
              Type                     Standard

    8 - Suppress (this page only)



Selection: 0
```

FIGURE 4-2
Page Format menu

Mouse Users: Click the right mouse button to display the menu bar. Select the Layout menu, and then select the "Page" option.

PAGE FORMAT MENU

◆ Notice in Figure 4-2 that the default settings for the top and bottom margins are 1 inch. Let's change these settings so that your document will have margins as shown in Figure 4-1, that is, two inches on each side.

A normal page of printer paper is 8 1/2 inches wide by 11 inches long. WordPerfect's default margins are automatically set so that a printed page has 1 inch top and bottom margins and 1 inch left and right margins. The result of how these default settings look on a printed page is shown in Figure 4-3.

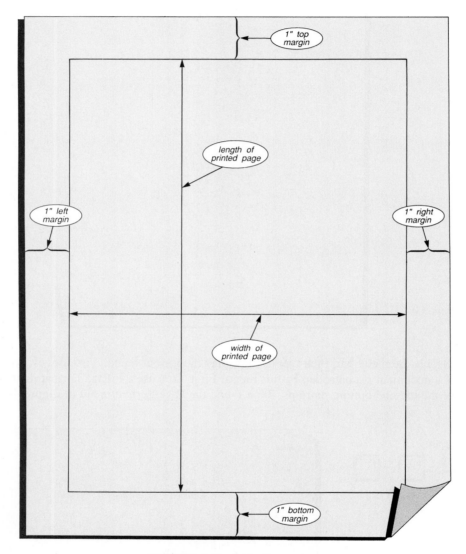

FIGURE 4-3 Default margins

Top and Bottom Margins

The top and bottom margins are controlled by menu choice "5", so type 5 and the cursor moves into the top margin setting. Type 2, then press the Enter key. The top margin is now set to 2 inches. Notice that the cursor has moved to the default setting for the bottom margin. You also need to change the bottom margin to 2 inches. Type 2 then press the Enter key (Figure 4-4), and the bottom margin is set to 2 inches.

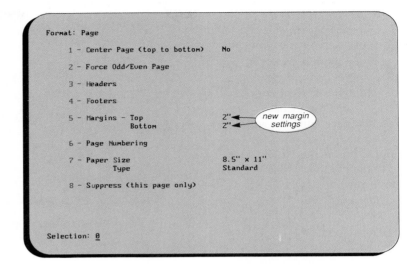

FIGURE 4-4
Changing top and bottom margins

 Mouse Users: Select menu choice "5", type 2, then press Enter. Type 2 again, then press Enter. Click the right mouse button to return to the text window.

Adding Page Numbering

When a document contains more than one page, you usually want to number the pages. WordPerfect has a feature that will automatically number pages for you. WordPerfect's default for page numbering is "No page numbering", which means that WordPerfect will not number pages unless you change this default. Since you want page numbers to print on the payroll report, we will change the page number default. Menu choice number "6" on the Page Format menu controls page numbering, so type 6 and the screen in Figure 4-5 appears.

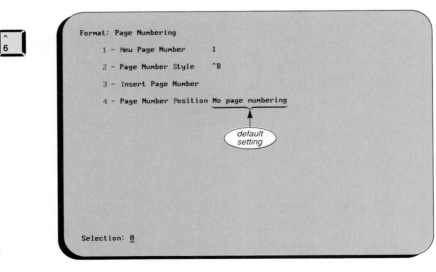

FIGURE 4-5
Page Number menu

You want to place the page numbers on the page, so type 4 and the screen in Figure 4-6 appears.

This screen shows you the different placements for page numbering. For example, selecting the number "1" would cause WordPerfect to print page numbers in the top left corner of the page. Selecting "7" would print page numbers in the lower right corner of each page. Let's use menu choice "6" so that page numbers will print centered at the bottom of each page. Type 6, then press the F7 key as instructed in the message at the bottom of the menu. Pressing F7 saves these changes and returns you to the text window. Notice that the status line now displays "Ln 2'" as the cursor position. This is because you have changed the top margin to 2 inches.

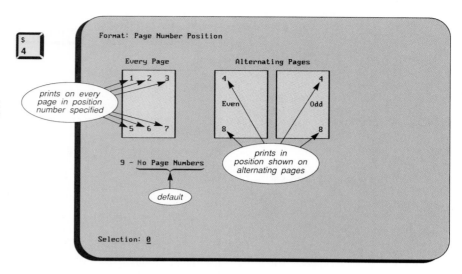

FIGURE 4-6 Specifying page number placement

Mouse Users: Click the right mouse button to display the menu bar. Select the Layout menu, then select "Page". Select menu choice "6", then select menu choice "4". Position the pointer on placement choice "6" and click the left mouse button. Click the right mouse button to exit and return to the text window.

LINE FORMAT MENU

The remaining formatting instructions you need to issue are contained in the Line Format menu. This menu is also contained in the Layout menu. Press Alt-= to display the menu bar, then type L to display the Layout menu. Now type L to display the Line Format menu (Figure 4-7).

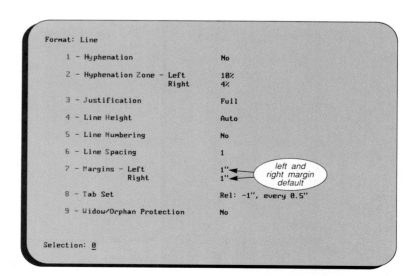

FIGURE 4-7
Line Format menu

Like the Page Format menu, the Line Format menu also controls the printed appearance of a document, but affects individual lines. Think of the Page Format menu as controlling page layout or physical shape, and the Line Format menu as controlling line placement (spacing, tabs, line height, and so on) You will also use this menu later in the project to set and delete tabs.

Left and Right Margins

So that your document appears like Figure 4-1, you need to change the left and right margins to 1.5 inches each. Menu choice "7" contains the left and right margin settings, so type 7. With the cursor positioned in the left margin setting, type 1.5, then press the Enter key. The left margin is set to 1.5 inches, and the cursor moves to the right margin setting. Now type 1.5 and press Enter again to change the right margin setting. Your final margin settings should match those shown in Figure 4-8.

```
Format: Line

     1 - Hyphenation                      No

     2 - Hyphenation Zone - Left          10%
                            Right         4%

     3 - Justification                    Full

     4 - Line Height                      Auto

     5 - Line Numbering                   No

     6 - Line Spacing                     1

     7 - Margins - Left                   1.5"      new margin
                   Right                  1.5"       settings

     8 - Tab Set                          Rel: -1", every 0.5"

     9 - Widow/Orphan Protection          No


Selection: 0
```

FIGURE 4-8
Changing the left and right margins

Mouse Users: Click the right mouse button to display the menu bar. Select the Layout menu, then select the "Line" option. Select menu choice "7", then type 1.5 and press Enter. Type 1.5 and press Enter again.

Justification

You have probably noticed that all the documents you have created so far have an even right margin. That is, the right margins are aligned so that the last letter of each line ends in the same column. Text formatted like this is said to be **justified**. When text is justified, the white (or blank) space that is usually placed at the end of each line is divided among the words in the line, and each line ends with a character. Justification sometimes results in some lines having larger spaces between some of the words.

In Figure 4-1, however, the right margins are not justified. Text is aligned only on the left, which creates what is called a **ragged right margin**. WordPerfect's default is to justify text, but you can also specify four different types of justification: left, right, full, and center. Left justification aligns the left margin and leaves the right margin ragged. Right justification causes text to justify on the right and leaves a ragged left margin. Full justification (the default) causes text to align along both the left and right margins. Center justification centers each line of text between the margins.

Now let's instruct WordPerfect to use left justification for your document. The Line Format menu should still be displayed. Menu choice "3" contains the setting for justification, so type 3 and a menu appears at the bottom of the screen (Figure 4-9).

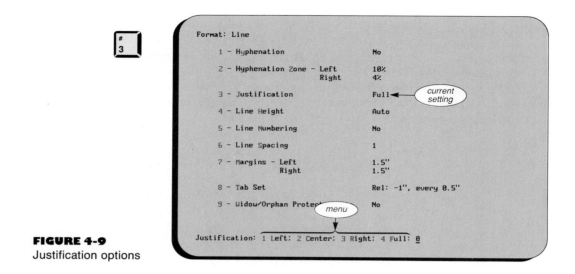

FIGURE 4-9
Justification options

Type 1 to select "Left", and notice that the Line Format menu now shows left justification (Figure 4-10).

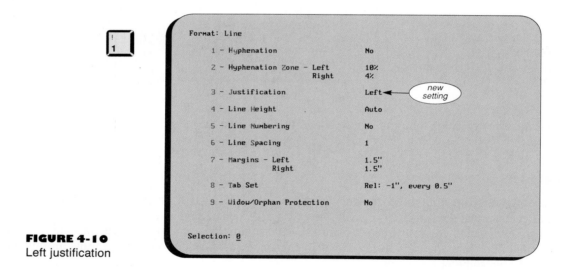

FIGURE 4-10
Left justification

We will not change the remainder of the settings on this menu at this time, so press the F7 key to exit the Line Format menu and return to the text window.

 Mouse Users: Select menu choice "3", then select the "Left" option. Click the right mouse button to return to the text window.

ENTERING TEXT

◆ You have added page numbering, changed the margins and specified left justification; you are now ready to enter text. First, recall that WordPerfect automatically inserts codes into a document. Each formatting instruction you issued is now contained — in code — in the document. Press Alt-F3 to view the Reveal Codes screen (Figure 4-11).

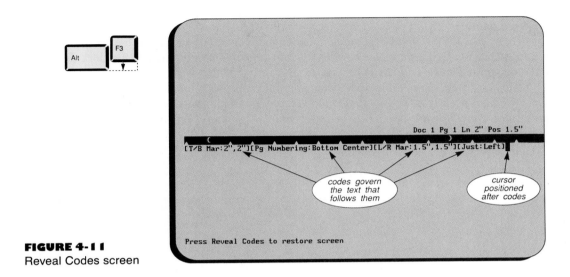

FIGURE 4-11
Reveal Codes screen

These codes govern the text that *follows* them, so be sure the cursor is positioned *after* the codes as shown in Figure 4-11. Press Alt-F3 again to exit the Reveal Codes screen. Any text you now enter will be governed by the codes preceding them. In the case of this document, this means the text will be printed with 2 inch top and bottom margins, 1 1/2 inch left and right margins; will be left-justified; and will have a page number centered at the bottom of each page.

Default Tabs

In the payroll report in Figure 4-1, the first line of the paragraph is indented five spaces at the left margin, which is the commonly accepted number of spaces for a typical paragraph indent. Because this is the tab setting most often used, WordPerfect's **default tabs** are set to every one-half inch, or five spaces. Later in this project, you will learn to change the default tabs so that you can align text at specific tab settings. For now, we will use the default tabs. Press the Tab key and the cursor moves to the first default tab, which is indented five spaces (Figure 4-12).

FIGURE 4-12 Default tabs

Now, type the text of the first paragraph: Executive management recently requested data to assist in budgeting salaries more accurately for the next fiscal year. The two major areas that need to be taken into consideration are personnel additions and average overtime worked in each department per week. Press the Enter key twice — once to end the paragraph and once to insert a blank line.

FOOTNOTES

Notice in Figure 4-1 that the document contains two footnotes. WordPerfect provides a way to insert footnotes in a document. While the footnotes contained in this document do not include underlining or boldfacing, keep in mind that you can use these formats at any time.

You can insert footnotes as they occur in a document or after you type the document. Let's insert a footnote as you type the text. Press the Tab key to indent the paragraph five spaces, then type the text of the paragraph up to the point where the footnote appears: Twelve new employees were hired since September 1, 1994 (Figure 4-13).

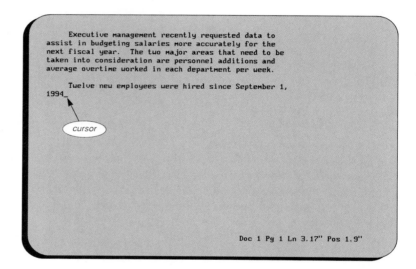

FIGURE 4-13
Cursor at footnote location

You are now ready to insert a footnote. Press Alt-= to display the menu bar, then type L to display the Layout menu (Figure 4-14).

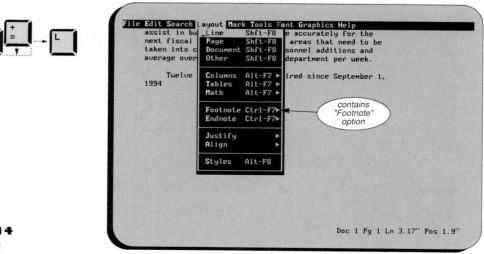

FIGURE 4-14
Layout menu

Now type F for "Footnote". Because you are creating a footnote, type C for "Create" and the screen in Figure 4-15 appears. This screen is used to enter footnote text.

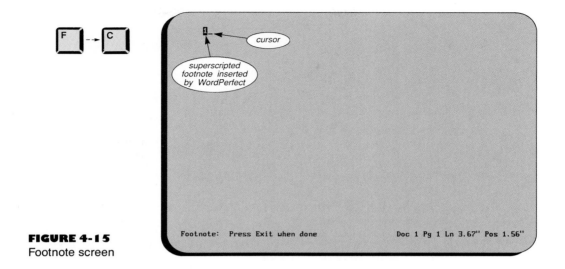

FIGURE 4-15
Footnote screen

Notice that WordPerfect has already inserted a footnote number. The number is highlighted to show you that the number will print superscripted (above the text line) as is the normal format for footnote numbers. WordPerfect will start with the number 1 and sequentially number each footnote you insert. If you add or delete footnotes, WordPerfect automatically renumbers the footnotes for you. At this point, you need only enter the text of the footnote. Type Graphicon, Inc., Personnel Department, "Human Resource Roster," December 1994, p. 4., then press the Enter key (Figure 4-16).

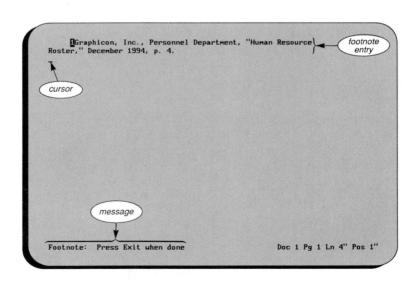

FIGURE 4-16
Entering a footnote

The message at the bottom of the screen is reminding you to press Exit when you have finished. The footnote entry is complete, so press F7 and you return to the text window. A footnote number now appears in the place you entered the footnote text (Figure 4-17).

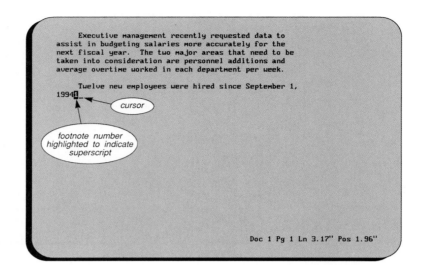

Executive management recently requested data to
assist in budgeting salaries more accurately for the
next fiscal year. The two major areas that need to be
taken into consideration are personnel additions and
average overtime worked in each department per week.

Twelve new employees were hired since September 1,
1994

cursor

footnote number
highlighted to indicate
superscript

Doc 1 Pg 1 Ln 3.17" Pos 1.96"

FIGURE 4-17
Footnote entered into document

Press the Spacebar so that a blank space follows the footnote number, then finish entering the text of the paragraph: and their salaries must be averaged into payroll expenditures. Personnel has furnished the following list which includes the employee name, sex, age, and hiring department. Press the Enter key twice, once to end the paragraph and once to insert a blank line.

Mouse Users: Click the right mouse button to display the menu bar. Select the Layout menu, select "Footnote", then select "Create". Enter the text of footnote, press the Enter key, and then press F7 to return to the text window.

CUSTOM TABS

We have previously used WordPerfect's default tabs to indent the first line of each paragraph one-half inch, or five spaces, at the left margin. Look at Figure 4-1. Notice how the columns in the table of employee information are different widths and contain different text alignments. Because of these different widths and alignments, it is unlikely that the text of the columns will line up if you use WordPerfect's default tabs. When you need to specify the alignment and width of tabs in a document, you must create custom tab stops.

Entering Tabbed Text

Like other formatting instructions, tabs are set by inserting codes into the document. This means that all text following the codes will use the tabs set. Documents can contain as many tab codes as you want. However, keep in mind that *the text is governed by the last tab code preceding it*. You can set tabs before or after typing the text to be tabbed. Let's type in the text before we set the tabs.

First, enter the underlined headings. Press F8 to begin underlining, then type Employee. Press the Tab key, then type Sex, followed by the Tab key again. Type Age, and press the Tab key. Then type Department and press F8. You have now entered the underlined headings, so press Enter twice — once to end the line and once to insert a blank line between the headings and the first line of text.

Look at Figure 4-1 and finish entering the text for this table, making sure you press the Tab key to move between columns. After you type the word Design in the last entry, press Enter to end the paragraph (Figure 4-18).

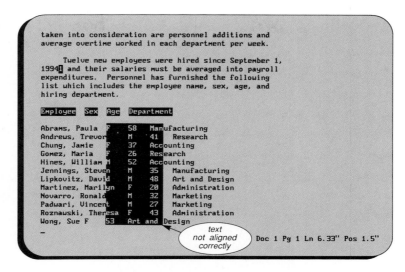

FIGURE 4-18   Entering tabbed table

Notice that the entries are not lined up correctly. This is because we have not yet set custom tabs for this paragraph, so WordPerfect is using the default tabs.

Types of Tabs

WordPerfect allows you to set five different types of tabs: left, center, right, decimal, and a dot leader, as illustrated in Figure 4-19.

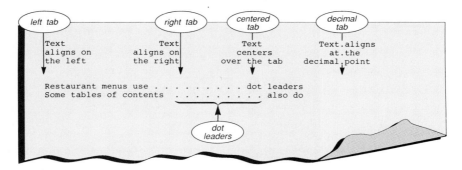

FIGURE 4-19   Tab alignments

The default setting for tabs is left-aligned. WordPerfect also allows you to set **relative** or **absolute** tabs. Relative tabs are relative to the current margin. That is, they move if you change the margin. For instance, if you set a relative tab at 1 inch, that tab will always be set one inch in from the margin, even if you change the margin setting. An absolute tab does not move; no matter where the margin is set an absolute tab set at the 1-inch position will remain at the 1-inch position. Think of relative tabs as *floating* and absolute tabs as *fixed*. WordPerfect's default tab type is relative, and that is what we will use for our tabs.

Clearing Default Tabs

You are now ready to set tabs for the table. Since the cursor is resting at the end of the table, press the Up Arrow key until the cursor precedes the text of the table (Figure 4-20).

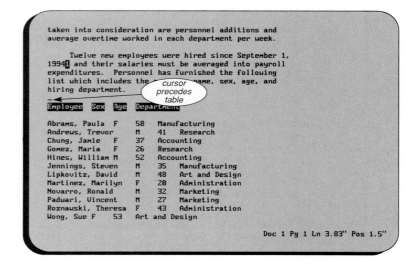

FIGURE 4-20
Positioning the cursor

You are moving the cursor here because as with all codes in WordPerfect, the tab code you will insert must *precede* the text you just typed.

Tabs are contained in the Line Format menu. This time, use the shortcut keys to display this menu. Press Shift-F8, then type 1 for Line Format, and the Line Format menu appears. Tabs are menu choice "8", so type 8 and the screen in Figure 4-21 appears.

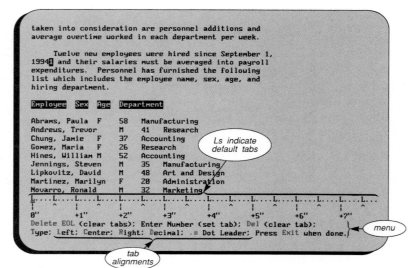

FIGURE 4-21
Tab ruler

This screen shows the **tab ruler**, which helps you position tabs on the screen. WordPerfect uses inches as its unit of measurement; the ruler indicates each tenth of one inch. This ruler is visible while you set tabs; it will disappear once you set the tabs and return to the text window. The Ls indicate the default tabs, which are set every five spaces, or one-half inch. Before you set the new tabs, you must first clear the ruler of the default tabs. Press Ctrl-End and the default tabs from the point of the cursor to the defined right margin disappear (Figure 4-22).

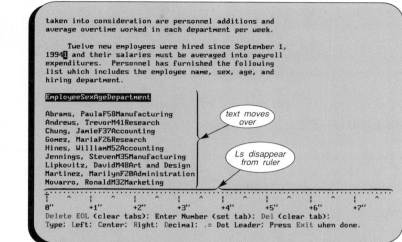

FIGURE 4-22
Clearing default tabs

Setting Tabs

Now that the default tabs are cleared, you're ready to set the tabs for the table. The first tab in the table is a left tab at the 2-inch position. You can either type the number for the setting, or you can use the arrow keys to position the cursor on the ruler. Let's try using the arrow keys. Press the Right Arrow key until the cursor is resting at the 2-inch position. Press the Tab key, and an L appears on the ruler, indicating that a left tab is set at the 2-inch position (Figure 4-23).

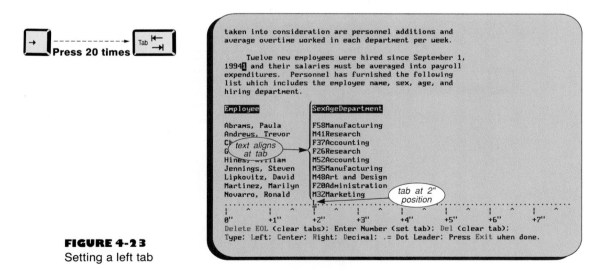

FIGURE 4-23
Setting a left tab

Notice how the text in the first tabbed column immediately aligns at the 2-inch position in response to the tab you just set.

The next tab you need to set is a left tab at the 2.7-inch position. This time, try typing the position number instead of using the arrow keys. Type 2.7, then press Enter. Again, the text aligns in response to the tab.

The last column needs a tab at the 3.2-inch position, so type 3.2, then press Enter (Figure 4-24). You have now set all the tabs for this table. Press F7 twice to exit the tab ruler and return to the text window.

Mouse Users: Click the right mouse button to display the menu bar. Select the Layout menu, then select "Line". Select menu choice "8", then select the "Delete EOL" option. Type 2 and press Enter. Type 2.7 and press Enter. Then, type 3.2 and press Enter. Click the right mouse button twice to return to the text window.

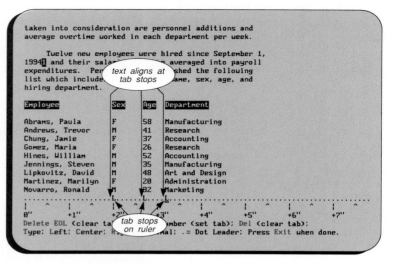

FIGURE 4-24   Tabs set on ruler

Changing Tab Settings

Suppose you decided that the Fs and Ms in the Sex column would look better if it they were centered rather than left-aligned. WordPerfect allows you to easily change tab settings.

Press Shift-F8 and type 1. Then type 8 to display the tab ruler. The tab ruler appears with the current tabs displayed. Move the cursor to the tab stop you want to change, in this case the left tab at the 2-inch position. With the cursor directly on the tab setting, type C for "Centered". The tab immediately changes to a centered tab and the text of the table centers under the tab stop (Figure 4-25). Press F7 twice to exit the tab ruler and return to the text window.

FIGURE 4-25
Changing tab alignment

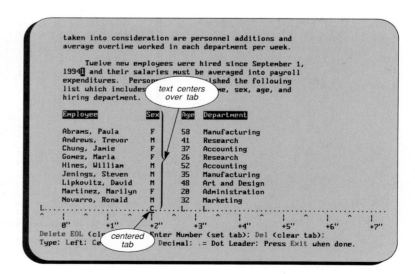

Setting Multiple Tabs

Look at Figure 4-1 and notice that the last paragraph on page 1 uses a default tab to indent the text five spaces. Because the tab codes you inserted prior to the table are still controlling the text, you must insert new tab codes for the next paragraph.

Move the cursor to the end of the document following the tabbed table. Now press the Enter key to insert a blank line. Press Shift-F8 to display the Format menu, then type 1 to display the Line Format menu. Type 8 to display the tab ruler. Press Ctrl-End to delete the existing tabs. The ruler is clear and ready to receive new tab settings.

WordPerfect allows you to quickly set multiple tabs. However, the tabs set in this fashion *must be evenly spaced*. Recall that the default tabs started at position 0 inch and were set every one-half inch, or five spaces. To reset these tabs, type 0,.5. This tells WordPerfect where to begin the tabs, and then how to space them. The numbers you just entered tell WordPerfect to start at the 0 inch position, which is the left margin, and to set tabs every .5″. Press Enter, and the default tabs reappear on the ruler (Figure 4-26).

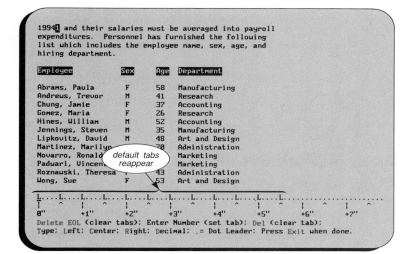

FIGURE 4-26
Resetting default tabs

Press F7 twice to return to the text window, then press the Tab key to insert a tab before the text of the next paragraph. Now type the text of the first paragraph on page 2: In addition to new employees' salaries, overtime expenditures must also be taken into consideration. Analysis of previous years shows that the heaviest overtime months are January and May. The cursor is now at the position for the next footnote (Figure 4-27).

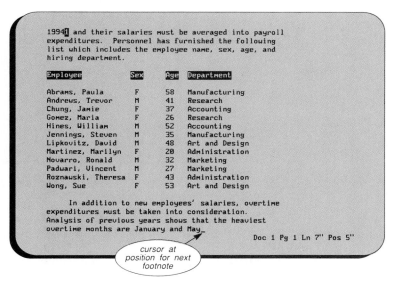

FIGURE 4-27 Entering text

This time, let's use the shortcut keys to insert the footnote. Press Ctrl-F7, and a menu appears at the bottom of the screen (Figure 4-28).

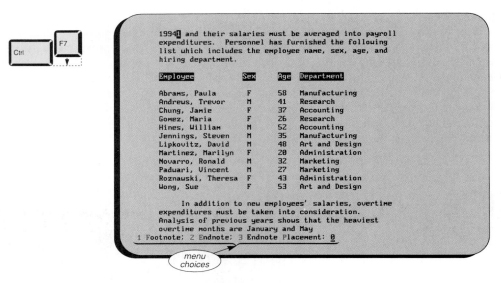

FIGURE 4-28 Footnote menu

Type 1 to select "Footnote", then type 1 again for "Create". The screen in Figure 4-29 appears.

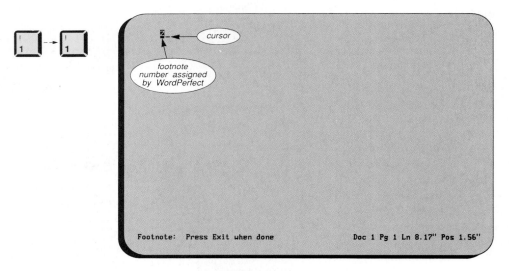

FIGURE 4-29 Adding a footnote

This is the same screen that appeared when you created a footnote using the pull-down menu. This time, though, WordPerfect inserted the footnote number 2. As you did before, enter the footnote: Graphicon, Inc., Payroll Department, "Annual Overtime Expenditure Report," January 1994, p. 7. When you have finished entering the footnote, press the Enter key; then press F7 to return to the text window. Next, press the Spacebar, then finish entering the text of the paragraph: due to the printing deadlines. Based on this, the following list was compiled. It projects the total number of overtime hours likely to be worked per pay period and the average rate of overtime pay in each department. When you have finished typing the text,

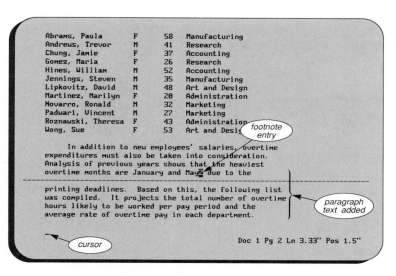

FIGURE 4-30 Entered text

press Enter twice, once to end the line and once to insert a blank line (Figure 4-30). The cursor is now positioned where the next table is to begin.

Setting Tabs Before Typing Text

Recall that you can set tabs before or after you type the text. For the first table in the payroll report, you typed the text before setting the tabs. For this table, let's set the tabs before you type the text.

With the cursor positioned as shown in Figure 4-30, press Shift-F8 to display the Format menu. Now type 1 then 8. Again, the tab ruler appears, this time with the default tabs displayed. Press Ctrl-End to delete all the default tabs.

The first tab is a decimal tab set at the 3-inch position. Type 3 and press Enter. A left tab appears on the ruler. Recall, however, that this needs to be a decimal tab, so the decimal point in each number will align. Type D and the tab ruler now displays a D at the 3-inch position, indicating that this is a decimal tab (Figure 4-31).

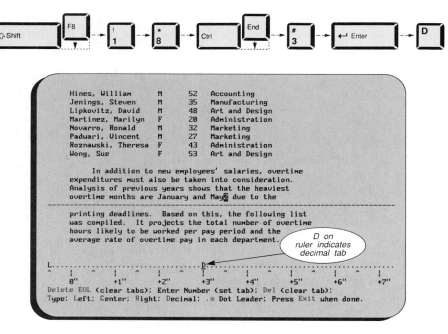

FIGURE 4-31

Setting a decimal tab

The next tab is a right tab at the 5-inch position. Type 5 and press Enter, and a left tab is set at the 5-inch position. Type R and the tab changes to a right tab (Figure 4-32). The tabs for this paragraph are now set, so press F7 twice to return to the text window.

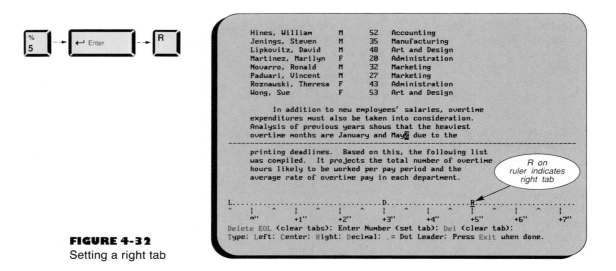

FIGURE 4-32
Setting a right tab

You're now ready to enter the text of the table. Begin by typing the underlined headings for each of the three columns, as shown in Figure 4-1. As you type, notice how the text aligns at the tabs as you enter it. After you have typed the last heading, Hours, turn off underlining and press Enter twice, once to end the line and once to insert a blank line. Refer to Figure 4-1 and continue typing the entries under the headings. Remember to use the Tab key to move between columns. When the table is complete, press the Enter key twice, once to end the line and once to insert a blank line (Figure 4-33).

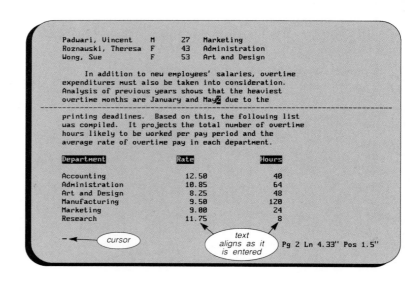

FIGURE 4-33
Entering tabbed text

The last paragraph in the document contains default tabs. Press Shift-F8, then type 1, then 8 to display the tab ruler. Press Ctrl-End to delete all the current tabs, then type 0,.5 and press Enter to reset the default tabs. Press F7 twice to return to the text window. Press the Tab key, then type the text of the last paragraph: These figures should prove helpful in determining a more accurate budget for next year. Please direct any further questions to Damon Gardens, Office Manager, extension 545. Press the Enter key to end the paragraph (Figure 4-34).

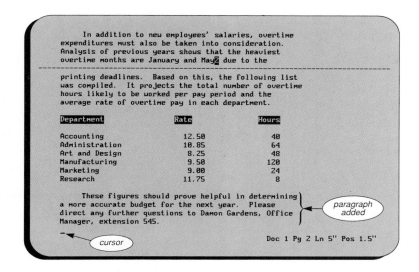

FIGURE 4-34
Adding a paragraph

Now that you have entered all of the text for the document, you are ready to insert headers and footers.

HEADERS AND FOOTERS

◆ Headers and footers are text that appear at the top and bottom margin area of each printed page, and usually repeat the report, document, or chapter name. A **header** appears at the top of the page, and a **footer** appears at the bottom of a page. You could manually locate each page break and then enter the text for a header or footer. However, WordPerfect provides a way of automatically printing headers and footers in a document.

Notice in Figure 4-1 that the payroll report contains both a header and a footer. You will use the Page Format menu to insert these into the document. You can format headers and footers as you would any regular text; that is, headers and footers can contain boldfacing, underlining, centering, tabs, and so on. You can also enter them either before or after you type the document.

Headers

Headers and footers *must be specified on the page on which they will first appear.* Thus, press Home, Home, Up Arrow to move the cursor to the top of the document. Do *not* press Home, Home, *Home*, Up Arrow to position the cursor before any codes. If you do, the cursor will move to the top of the document before the formatting codes you entered to control margins, justification, and so forth. If you enter the header or footer codes here, the header and footer text would not adhere to the formatting codes you inserted. Therefore, the margins in the document and the margins in the header and footer would be different.

Headers and footers are defined in the Page Format menu, so press Shift-F8, then type 2 to display the Page Format menu. Menu choice "3" contains the header setting, so type 3, and the screen in Figure 4-35 appears.

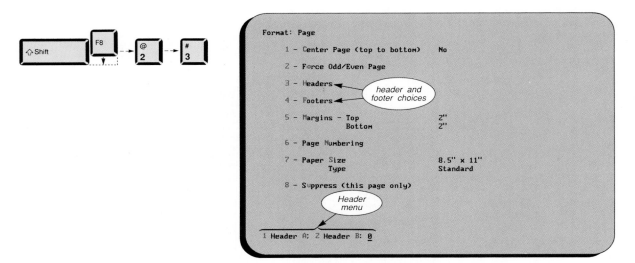

FIGURE 4-35   Defining a header

WordPerfect allows you to specify up to two headers and two footers per document (A and B). Type 1 to select "Header A" (the first header), and the menu in Figure 4-36 appears.

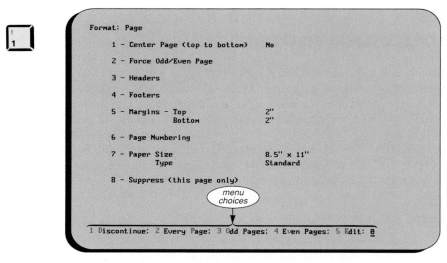

FIGURE 4-36   Specifying headers

This menu allows you to specify on which pages the header will print, to discontinue a header, or to edit an existing header. Since you want to print a header on every page, type 2, and the screen in Figure 4-37 appears.

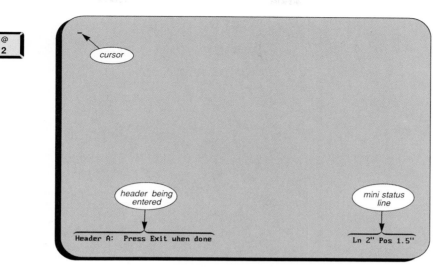

FIGURE 4-37 Header screen

The screen is almost blank, except for the mini status line, which shows you where the header will be positioned on the page. Now you must enter the text of the header. Type Payroll Data Report to Management, then press Alt-F6. This instructs WordPerfect to align the next text flush-right. Next, type December 1994 and press Enter (Figure 4-38).

FIGURE 4-38 Entering header text

The header text is now entered, so press F7 to exit the screen and return to the Page Format menu. Notice that menu choice "3" now contains a "HA Every page" setting (Figure 4-39).

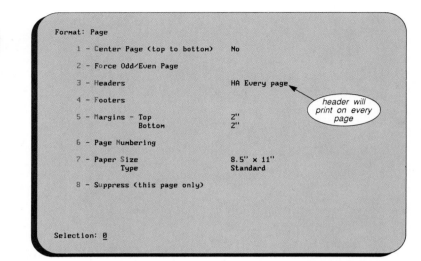

```
Format: Page

    1 - Center Page (top to bottom)      No

    2 - Force Odd/Even Page

    3 - Headers                          HA Every page

    4 - Footers

    5 - Margins - Top                    2"
                 Bottom                  2"

    6 - Page Numbering

    7 - Paper Size                       8.5" x 11"
             Type                        Standard

    8 - Suppress (this page only)



Selection: 0
```

header will print on every page

FIGURE 4-39
Header specified in menu

Mouse Users: Click the right mouse button to display the menu bar. Select the Layout menu, then select "Page". Select menu choice "3". Select the "Header A" option, then select the "Every Page" option. Enter the text of the header, press the Enter key, and then press F7 to return to the text window.

Footers

Now you are ready to enter the footer in Figure 4-1. Like headers, footers must be entered on the first page on which they will print. They *do not* need to be entered at the bottom of the page, since WordPerfect will automatically place them there. Footer text is entered in precisely the same way header text is entered.

The Page Format menu should still be displayed, so type 4 to specify "Footers", then type 1 for "Footer A". You want the footer on every page, so type 2, and the footer screen appears. Since the text for this footer is centered, press Shift-F6. Type Page, then press the Spacebar to insert a blank space. Now press Ctrl-B, and the characters "^B" appear on the screen (Figure 4-40).

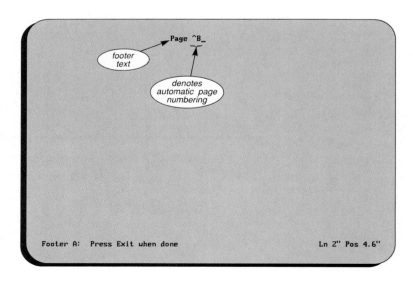

Page ^B_

footer text

denotes automatic page numbering

Footer A: Press Exit when done   Ln 2" Pos 4.6"

FIGURE 4-40
Entering footer text

These characters indicate that WordPerfect will automatically print page numbers within a header or footer. WordPerfect will begin page numbering at 1 and will sequentially number each page of the document.

Now that you have entered the header and footer, press F7 twice to return to the text window. Notice that the headers and footers *do not appear* on the screen, but they *will print* at the top or bottom of each new page when you print the document.

Mouse Users: Click the right mouse button to display the menu bar. Select the Layout menu, then select "Page". Select menu choice "4". Select the "Footer A" option, then select the "Every Page" option. Enter the text of the footer, press the Enter key, and press F7 twice to return to the text window.

Removing Page Numbering

Because you are now numbering the pages within the footer, *you must remove the page numbering you requested in the Page Format menu*. If you don't, WordPerfect will print two sets of page numbers: those specified in the footer *and* those requested through Page Format.

The cursor should be positioned at the beginning of the document, so press Alt-F3 to display the Reveal Codes screen. Position the cursor directly on the "[Pg Numbering: Bottom Center]" code (Figure 4-41), then press Delete to remove the page numbering code. Now the pages will be numbered in the footer instead of the bottom center of the page. Press Alt-F3 again to exit the Reveal Codes screen.

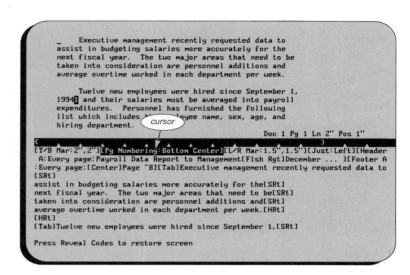

FIGURE 4-41 Page numbering code

Editing Header Text

Suppose you decided that the header for this report is too long. WordPerfect allows you to edit header or footer text as you would any other text.

To edit header or footer text you can position the cursor at any point within the portion of the document controlled by the header code. That is, as long as the header you are going to edit is the header currently in effect, the cursor does not need to be directly on the header code. In the Reveal Codes screen you saw that the cursor was on the header code. Move the cursor past the header code so that it is in the portion of the document that the code controls (Figure 4-42).

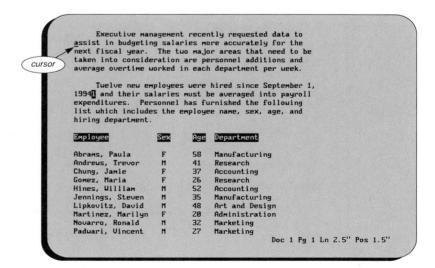

FIGURE 4-42 Positioning the cursor

Now press Shift-F8, then type 2, then 3 for the Header menu. Type 1 for "Header A", and notice on the menu that appears that "Edit" is listed as choice number "5". Type 5 and the header text appears on the screen (Figure 4-43).

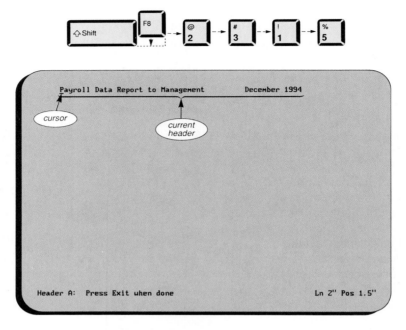

FIGURE 4-43   Editing header text

At this point, you can edit this text as you would ordinarily. Position the cursor on the first character of the word to, then press Alt-F4 to begin blocking. Extend the block to include the word Management (Figure 4-44).

FIGURE 4-44   Blocking text

Now press Delete, then answer Y to the "Delete Block? No(Yes)" prompt. The unwanted words are deleted, but the paragraph itself remains a header (Figure 4-45). Press F7 twice to exit the menu and return to the document.

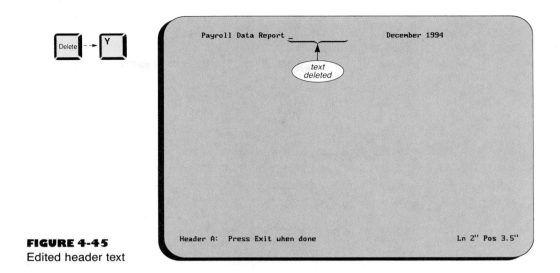

FIGURE 4-45
Edited header text

Mouse Users: Click the right mouse button to display the menu bar. Select the Layout menu, then select "Page". Select menu choice "3", then select the "Header A" option. Select "Edit", then edit the header text. Press F7 twice to return to the text window.

VIEWING DOCUMENTS

WordPerfect can show you on the screen how your document will appear when it is printed. The Print View function displays your document with all the text and page formatting visible. Page elements not normally seen on the screen, such as page numbering, headers and footers, margin changes, footnotes, and so on, will appear when you view a document. *Check with your instructor before attempting to use this function.* You must have a video monitor with graphics capabilities to use the Print View function. If you do not have a video monitor with graphics capabilities, Print View will not execute properly.

WordPerfect will display the document a page at a time beginning with the page containing the cursor. Since you want to view your document from the beginning, be sure the cursor is positioned on the first page of the document before using the Print View function. Now press Alt-= to display the menu bar. The Print menu contains the "View Document" option, so type F, then type P to display this menu (Figure 4-46).

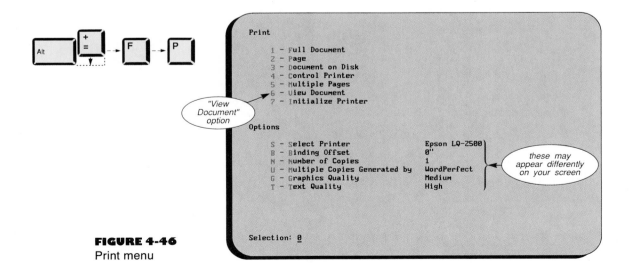

FIGURE 4-46
Print menu

Now type 6 to select the "View Document" option. The first page of your document should appear on the screen as shown in Figure 4-47. (If only part of the page appears, type 3 for "Full Page".)

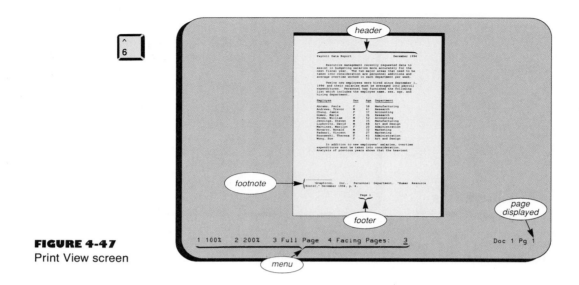

FIGURE 4-47
Print View screen

Notice that, unlike the normal screen display, the characters are not totally legible. The Print View screen is designed to show you what your document will look like when it's printed. The header and footer are visible on the screen in the placement specified, and the pages are numbered sequentially within the footer. Press Page Down, and the second page of the document appears (Figure 4-48).

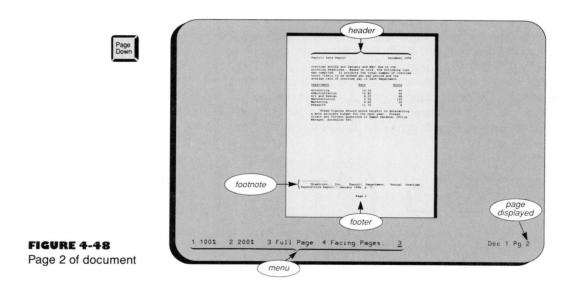

FIGURE 4-48
Page 2 of document

The menu also contains an option telling you that you can enlarge the document. Type 1 to enlarge the document so that a smaller portion displays with the text clearly legible. Type 2 to enlarge the document even further. Since our document is fine in its current form, press F7 to exit the View Document screen and return to the text *window*.

Mouse Users: Click the right mouse button to display the menu bar. Select the File menu, select "Print", then select menu choice "6". After viewing the document, click the right mouse button to exit.

SAVING, PRINTING, AND EXITING

◆ Your payroll report document is complete. Let's save it to disk before you print it. Press F10, then type PROJ4. Press Enter, and the document is saved on disk under the filename PROJ4.

Now that you have viewed and saved the report, let's print it. Be sure the printer is turned on and ready to print. Press Shift-F7, then type 1 and the document begins printing. Your final document should look like Figure 4-1.

After printing, you need to clear the screen and exit WordPerfect. At the DOS prompt, be sure to remove your student disk and WordPerfect program disks, if necessary.

PROJECT SUMMARY

In Project 4 you learned how to change margin settings and add page numbering. You learned how to set tabs, both before and after text was typed, how to change and reset tab settings, and how to quickly set evenly spaced tabs. You also learned how to left-justify text, and how to insert and edit headers and footers as well as footnotes. Once the document was complete, you learned to use the View Document function to view the document in its printed form. All the activities that you learned for this project are summarized in the Quick Reference following Project 6. The following is a summary of the keystroke sequence we used in Project 4.

SUMMARY OF KEYSTROKES — PROJECT 4

STEPS	KEY(S) PRESSED	RESULTS
1	wp ↵ [At C> prompt or as directed by instructor]	Loads WordPerfect.
2	Alt-= L P	Displays Page Format menu.
3	5 2 ↵ 2 ↵	Changes top and bottom margins to 2 inches each.
4	6 4 6 F7	Specifies page number at bottom center of page.
5	Alt-= L L	Displays Line Format menu.
6	7 1.5 ↵ 1.5 ↵	Changes left margin and right margins to 1.5 inches each.
7	3 1 F7	Specifies left justification and returns cursor to text window.
8	Alt-F3 Alt-F3	Displays then exits Reveal Codes screen.
9	Tab	Moves cursor in one tab stop.
10	Executive management recently requested data to assist in budgeting salaries more accurately for the next fiscal year. The two major areas that need to be taken into consideration are personnel additions and average overtime worked in each department per week. ↵ ↵	Enters text of first paragraph and inserts blank line.
11	Tab	Moves cursor in one tab stop.
12	Twelve new employees were hired since September 1, 1994	Enters text up to point of footnote entry.
13	Alt-= L F C	Displays footnote screen.
14	Graphicon, Inc., Personnel Department, "Human Resource Roster," December 1994, p. 4. ↵ F7	Enters footnote text and returns cursor to text window.

(continued)

SUMMARY OF KEYSTROKES — PROJECT 4 (continued)

STEPS	KEY(S) PRESSED	RESULTS
15	[Spacebar] and their salaries must be averaged into payroll expenditures. Personnel has furnished the following list which includes the employee name, sex, age, and hiring department. ↵ ↵	Inserts blank space and enters remaining text of paragraph.
16	[F8] Employee [Tab] Sex [Tab] Age [Tab] Department [F8]	Begins underlining, enters underlined headings, and ends underlining.
17	↵ ↵	Inserts blank line.
18	Abrams, Paula [Tab] F [Tab] 58 [Tab] Manufacturing ↵ Andrews, Trevor [Tab] M [Tab] 41 [Tab] Research ↵ Chung, Jamie [Tab] F [Tab] 37 [Tab] Accounting ↵ Gomez, Maria [Tab] F [Tab] 26 [Tab] Research ↵ Hines, William [Tab] M [Tab] 52 [Tab] Accounting ↵ Jennings, Steven [Tab] M [Tab] 35 [Tab] Manufacturing ↵ Lipkovitz, David [Tab] M [Tab] 48 [Tab] Art and Design ↵ Martinez, Marilyn [Tab] F [Tab] 20 [Tab] Administration ↵ Novarro, Ronald [Tab] M [Tab] 32 [Tab] Marketing ↵ Padwari, Vincent [Tab] M [Tab] 27 [Tab] Marketing ↵ Roznawski, Theresa [Tab] F [Tab] 43 [Tab] Administration ↵ Wong, Sue [Tab] F [Tab] 53 [Tab] Art and Design ↵	Enters text of table.
19	↑ [Press 15 times]	Moves cursor to precede table.
20	[Shift-F8] 1 8	Displays tab ruler.
21	[Ctrl-End]	Deletes all default tabs.
22	→ [Press 20 times] [Tab]	Sets tab at 2-inch position.
23	2.7 ↵	Sets tab at 2.7-inch position.
24	3.2 ↵	Sets tab at 3.2-inch position.
25	[F7] [F7]	Exits tab ruler and returns cursor to text window.
26	[Shift-F8] 1 8 → [Press 20 times] C [F7] [F7]	Changes left tab at 2-inch position to a centered tab.
27	[Home] [Home] ↓	Moves cursor to bottom of document.
28	[Shift-F8] 1 8 [Ctrl-End] 0,.5 ↵ [F7] [F7]	Resets default tabs and returns cursor to text window.
29	↵ [Tab]	Adds blank line and moves cursor in one tab stop.
30	In addition to new employees' salaries, overtime expenditures must also be taken into consideration. Analysis of previous years shows that the heaviest overtime months are January and May	Enters text of paragraph up to point of footnote entry.
31	[Ctrl-F7] 1 1	Displays footnote screen.

SUMMARY OF KEYSTROKES — PROJECT 4 (continued)

STEPS	KEY(S) PRESSED	RESULTS
32	Graphicon, Inc., Payroll Department, "Annual Overtime Expenditure Report," January 1994, p. 7. ↵ `F7`	Enters footnote text and returns cursor to text window.
33	`Spacebar` due to the printing deadlines. Based on this, the following list was compiled. It projects the total number of overtime hours likely to be worked per pay period and the average rate of overtime pay in each department. ↵ ↵	Enters remaining text of paragraph.
34	`Shift-F8` 1 8 `Ctrl-End`	Displays tab ruler and deletes default tabs.
35	3 ↵ D	Sets decimal tab at 3-inch position on tab ruler.
36	5 ↵ R	Sets right tab at 5-inch position on tab ruler.
37	`F8` Department `Tab` Rate `Tab` Hours `F8`	Enters underlined headings of table.
38	↵ ↵	Ends headings line and inserts blank line.
39	Accounting `Tab` 12.50 `Tab` 40 ↵ Administration `Tab` 10.85 `Tab` 64 ↵ Art and Design `Tab` 8.25 `Tab` 48 ↵ Manufacturing `Tab` 9.50 `Tab` 120 ↵ Marketing `Tab` 9.00 `Tab` 24 ↵ Research `Tab` 11.25 `Tab` 8 ↵ ↵	Enters text of table followed by a blank line.
40	`Shift-F8` 1 8 `Ctrl-End` 0,.5 ↵ `F7` `F7`	Resets default tabs.
41	`Tab`	Moves cursor in one tab stop.
42	These figures should prove helpful in determining a more accurate budget for the next year. Please direct any further questions to Damon Gardens, Office Manager, extension 545. ↵	Enters text and ends paragraph.
43	`Home` `Home` ↑	Moves cursor to top of document.
44	`Shift-F8` 2 3	Displays Header menu.
45	1	Specifies "Header A".
46	2	Specifies header to print on every page of document.
47	Payroll Data Report to Management `Alt-F6` December 1994 ↵ `F7`	Enters header text and returns cursor to Page Format menu.
48	4 1 2	Specifies "Footer A" on every page.
49	`Shift-F6`	Centers text of footer.
50	Page `Spacebar` `Ctrl-B` ↵ `F7` `F7`	Enters footer text with automatic page numbering and returns cursor to text window.
51	`Alt-F3` ← [Press until cursor is positioned on page numbering code] `Delete` `Alt-F3`	Displays Reveal Codes screen, deletes page numbering code, and exits Reveal Codes screen.
52	↓	Positions cursor past header code.

(continued)

SUMMARY OF KEYSTROKES — PROJECT 4 (continued)

STEPS	KEY(S) PRESSED	RESULTS
53	[Shift-F8] 2 3 1 5	Displays header text.
54	[Ctrl-→] [Ctrl-→] [Ctrl-→]	Positions cursor at beginning of header text to be edited.
55	[Alt-F4] [Ctrl-→] [Ctrl-→] [Delete] Y	Blocks and deletes text of running head.
56	[F7] [F7]	Returns cursor to text window.
57	[Alt-=] F P 6	Executes View Document function.
58	[Page Down]	Displays second page of document.
59	[F7]	Exits View Document screen.
60	[F10] PROJ4 ↵	Saves document under filename PROJ4.
61	[Shift-F7] 1	Prints document at printer.
62	[F7] N Y	Exits WordPerfect and returns to DOS.

The following list summarizes the material covered in Project 4.

1. Most document formatting functions are contained in the Line Format and Page Format menus.
2. WordPerfect's default top and bottom margins are set at one inch each. These margins are set through the Page Format menu.
3. WordPerfect's default left and right margins are set at 1 inch each. These margins are set through the Line Format menu.
4. WordPerfect's default for page numbering is "No page numbering", which means that page numbers will not print unless you specify that they do. This setting is contained in the Page Format menu.
5. WordPerfect's default is to use justified text. **Justified** text prints with an even right margin, and each line of justified text ends with a character. Justification is set through the Line Format menu.
6. When text is left-justified, it aligns only at the left margin, which results in a **ragged right margin**.
7. WordPerfect allows four types of justification: left, right, full (default), and center.
8. Text is governed by the codes that precede it.
9. WordPerfect's **default** tabs are set every one-half inch, or every five spaces.
10. Footnotes are contained in the Layout menu. WordPerfect will automatically assign a superscripted footnote number to each footnote you enter. Ctrl-F7 are the shortcut keys for the Footnote menu.
11. WordPerfect allows you to set five different types of tabs: left, right, center, decimal, and a dot leader. The default for tabs is left-aligned.
12. WordPerfect allows you to set **relative** or **absolute** tabs. Relative tabs move to reflect margin changes. Absolute tabs remain fixed regardless of margin changes.
13. The shortcut keys for the Format menu are Shift-F8.
14. Tabs are set through the Line Format menu. A **tab ruler**, marked in tenths of inches, appears to help you to position tabs.
15. Pressing Ctrl-End at the tab ruler clears all tab stops.
16. A **header** or **footer** is text that appears at the top or bottom margin area of each printed page and usually repeats the report, document, or chapter name.
17. Headers and footers are contained in the Page Format menu, and may contain normal text formats, like centering, underlining, boldfacing, tabs, and so on.
18. If page numbering is used in a header or footer, you must remove the page numbering code in the Reveal Codes screen. If you don't, WordPerfect will print two sets of page numbers.
19. The View Document function shows you on the screen how your document will appear when it is printed. View Document displays your document a page at a time with all text and page formatting visible.

STUDENT ASSIGNMENTS

STUDENT ASSIGNMENT 1: True/False

Instructions: Circle T if the statement is true and F if the statement is false.

T F   1. WordPerfect's default top margin is set to one inch.
T F   2. WordPerfect's default left margin is set to one inch.
T F   3. Text that appears in the area above the defined top margin of each printed page is called a header.
T F   4. WordPerfect allows three different types of justification.
T F   5. If text is formatted for full justification, text will line up on both the right and left margins.
T F   6. Tab codes govern the text that precedes them.
T F   7. There is no way to quickly set multiple tabs in WordPerfect, even if they are evenly spaced.
T F   8. Centered tabs cause text to center over the tab setting.
T F   9. The View Document function displays your document on the screen, a page at a time, in its printed form.
T F 10. Headers and footers must be entered on every page on which they will print.

STUDENT ASSIGNMENT 2: Multiple Choice

Instructions: Circle the correct response.

1. The Page Format menu allows you to change _____.
   a. top and bottom margins
   b. left and right margins
   c. justification
   d. all of the above
2. The Line Format menu allows you to change _____.
   a. page numbering
   b. top and bottom margins
   c. left and right margins
   d. all of the above
3. WordPerfect's default bottom margin is set to _____.
   a. one-half inch
   b. one inch
   c. one and one-half inches
   d. none of the above
4. WordPerfect's default right margin is set to _____.
   a. one-half inch
   b. one inch
   c. one and one-quarter inches
   d. one and one-half inches
5. WordPerfect's default tabs are set every _____.
   a. five spaces
   b. ten spaces
   c. one-half inch
   d. both a and c
6. WordPerfect's shortcut keys for displaying the Format menu are _____.
   a. Alt-F8
   b. Shift-F8
   c. Ctrl-F7
   d. none of the above

Student Assignment 2 (continued)

7. Text that appears in the top margin area of each printed page of a document is called the _____.
   a. chapter title
   b. document name
   c. footer
   d. header
8. To quickly delete all tab stops from the cursor to the defined right margin on the tab ruler, press _____.
   a. Ctrl-End
   b. Tab-Delete
   c. Alt-End
   d. none of the above
9. The Format menu contains _____.
   a. "Page Format"
   b. "Line Format"
   c. "Page numbering"
   d. all of the above
10. Footnotes are contained in the _____ menu.
   a. Line Format
   b. Page Format
   c. Print
   d. none of the above

STUDENT ASSIGNMENT 3: Matching

Instructions: Put the appropriate number next to the words in the second column.

1. Displays header options   _____   Shift-F8, 2
2. Displays justification options _____   Shift-F8, 1, 3
3. Displays tab ruler   _____   Shift-F8, 2, 3
4. Displays Page Format menu   _____   Shift-F8, 1, 8
5. View Document function   _____   Shift-F8, 2, 4
6. Displays Footnote menu   _____   Ctrl-End
7. Displays Line Format menu   _____   Shift-F8, 1
8. Deletes all tabs   _____   Shift-F7, 6
9. Displays footer options   _____   Ctrl-F7

STUDENT ASSIGNMENT 4: Identifying Default Settings

Instructions: Identify the defaults for the following settings.

Setting	Default
Top margin	_____
Bottom margin	_____
Left margin	_____
Right margin	_____
Tab stops	_____
Tab alignment	_____
Page numbering	_____
Justification	_____

STUDENT ASSIGNMENT 5: Formatting a Document

Instructions: The following document was created with top and bottom margins of 2.5 inches each, and left and right margins of 1 1/2 inches each. The first line of the first paragraph was moved in five spaces and the text of the paragraph has a ragged right margin. Explain the steps to create the document using these formats.

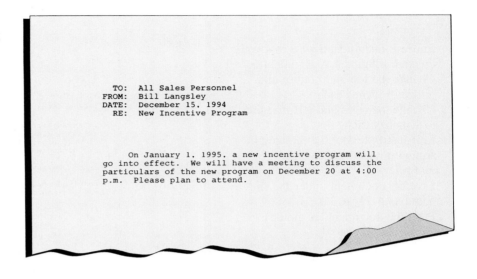

```
    TO:   All Sales Personnel
    FROM: Bill Langsley
    DATE: December 15, 1994
    RE:   New Incentive Program



        On January 1, 1995, a new incentive program will
    go into effect.  We will have a meeting to discuss the
    particulars of the new program on December 20 at 4:00
    p.m.  Please plan to attend.
```

Steps: _____

_____

_____

STUDENT ASSIGNMENT 6: Creating a Document

Instructions: Perform the following tasks.

1. Set the left margin to 1.5 inches and the right margin to 2 inches.
2. Set the top and bottom margins to 2 inches each.
3. Type the document, making sure you set a left tab at 1 inch and a right tab at 4.2 inches.
4. Save the document under the filename SA4-6.
5. Print the document. It should appear as shown.

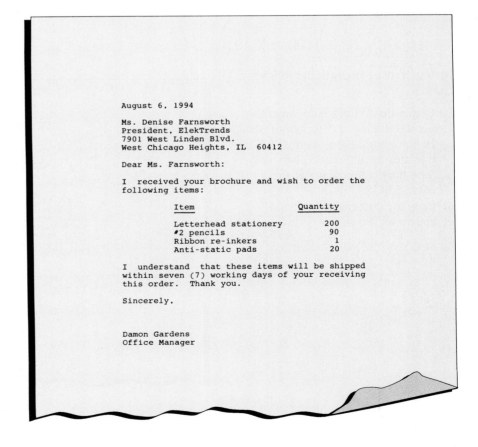

```
August 6, 1994

Ms. Denise Farnsworth
President, ElekTrends
7901 West Linden Blvd.
West Chicago Heights, IL  60412

Dear Ms. Farnsworth:

I received your brochure and wish to order the
following items:

        Item                  Quantity

        Letterhead stationery    200
        #2 pencils                90
        Ribbon re-inkers           1
        Anti-static pads          20

I understand  that these items will be shipped
within seven (7) working days of your receiving
this order.  Thank you.

Sincerely,


Damon Gardens
Office Manager
```

STUDENT ASSIGNMENT 7: Modifying a Document's Format

Instructions: Perform the following tasks.

1. Retrieve document SA4-6 that you created in Student Assignment 6.
2. Change the top and bottom margins to 3 inches each.
3. Change the right and left margins to 2 inches each.
4. Left-justify text of the paragraph so that it has a ragged right margin.
5. Save the document under the filename SA4-7.
6. Print the document. It should appear as shown.

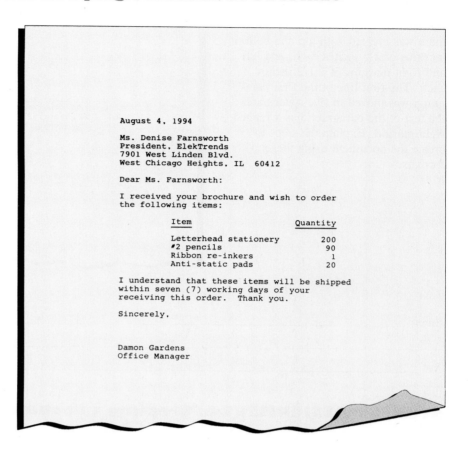

```
August 4, 1994

Ms. Denise Farnsworth
President, ElekTrends
7901 West Linden Blvd.
West Chicago Heights, IL  60412

Dear Ms. Farnsworth:

I received your brochure and wish to order
the following items:

       Item                     Quantity

       Letterhead stationery      200
       #2 pencils                  90
       Ribbon re-inkers             1
       Anti-static pads            20

I understand that these items will be shipped
within seven (7) working days of your
receiving this order.  Thank you.

Sincerely,



Damon Gardens
Office Manager
```

STUDENT ASSIGNMENT 8: Setting Tabs

Instructions: Perform the following tasks.

1. Create the following document.
2. Set a left tab at 1.5 inches for the first column, and a decimal tab at 6 inches for the second column.
3. Save the document under the name SA4-8.
4. Print the document. It should appear as shown.

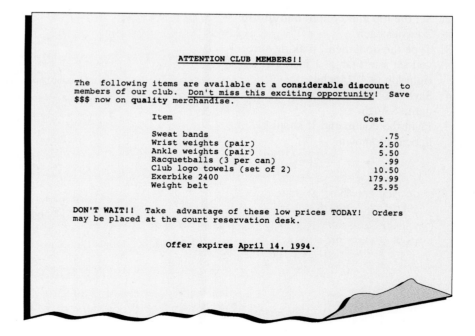

```
              ATTENTION CLUB MEMBERS!!

The  following items are available at a considerable discount  to
members of our club.  Don't miss this exciting opportunity!  Save
$$$ now on quality merchandise.

       Item                             Cost

       Sweat bands                       .75
       Wrist weights (pair)             2.50
       Ankle weights (pair)             5.50
       Racquetballs (3 per can)          .99
       Club logo towels (set of 2)     10.50
       Exerbike 2400                  179.99
       Weight belt                     25.95


DON'T WAIT!!  Take  advantage of these low prices TODAY!  Orders
may be placed at the court reservation desk.


          Offer expires April 14, 1994.
```

STUDENT ASSIGNMENT 9: Creating a Document

Instructions: Perform the following tasks.

1. Create the following document, using a top and bottom margin of 2 inches each and left and right margins of 1.5 inches each. Use hanging indents for the numbered items.

1

PROPOSAL

Part I

The following suggestions were made on how we could increase membership for the next fiscal year:

1. Review existing marketing strategies and advertising media.

2. Change the age requirement for membership. Recent surveys indicate that the 12-17 age group has become increasingly aware of physical fitness and appearance. We might want to modify our policy and offer membership to this age group.

3. Refurbish the existing racquetball/handball courts. Two years have elapsed since they were last refinished, and ordinary wear and tear have taken their toll on court appearance.

4. Provide locks for the lockers. Although we have not experienced theft, most members feel more secure if their belongings are securely locked in a locker, and most do not bring a lock with them to the club.

5. Schedule additional aerobic classes in the evening and on weekends. Aerobic instructors indicate that attendance in the morning and afternoon

Marketing Strategies   1994

2

classes are usually light, whereas the evening and weekend classes are overflowing. Attendees would feel more comfortable with a smaller class size.

6. Enlarge the existing saunas and steamrooms to approximately twice their current size. Sauna attendants have reported increased use and interest, and larger areas are needed to accommodate the growing number of users.

Marketing Strategies   1994

---

2. Create a footer as shown.
3. Change the justification to left.
4. Add page numbering in the top right corner of each page.
5. Print the document. It should appear as shown.

STUDENT ASSIGNMENT 10: Adding Footnotes

Instructions: Perform the following tasks.

1. Retrieve the document SA4-9 that you created in Student Assignment 9.
2. Add the footnote shown in the following figure.
3. Add the tabbed table with these tab settings: 1 inch centered tab, 3.3 inches decimal tab, and a 4.7 inches decimal tab.
4. Insert hard page breaks so pages break as shown in the figure.
5. Save the document under the filename SA4-10.
6. Print the document. It should appear as shown.

```
                                                              1

                          PROPOSAL

        Part I

        The following suggestions were made on how we could
        increase membership for the next fiscal year:

        1.   Review existing marketing strategies and
             advertising media.

        2.   Change the age requirement for membership.  Recent
             surveys indicate that the 12-17 age group has
             become increasingly aware of physical fitness and
             appearance.¹  We might want to modify our policy
             and offer membership to this age group.

        3.   Refurbish the existing racquetball/handball
             courts.  Two years have elapsed since they were
             last refinished, and ordinary wear and tear have
             taken their toll on court appearance.




        _____
             ¹Lake View Central High, Physical Education Department, "Self-
        Image and Self-Esteem." August 1994, p. 20.

        Marketing Strategies                        1994
```

2

4. Provide locks for the lockers. Although we have
    not experienced theft, most members feel more
    secure if their belongings are securely locked in
    a locker, and most do not bring a lock with them
    to the club.

5. Schedule additional aerobic classes in the evening
    and on weekends. Aerobic instructors indicate
    that attendance in the morning and afternoon
    classes are usually light, whereas the evening and
    weekend classes are overflowing. Attendees would
    feel more comfortable with a smaller class size.

6. Enlarge the existing saunas and steamrooms to
    approximately twice their current size. Sauna
    attendants have reported increased use and
    interest, and larger areas are needed to
    accommodate the growing number of users.

Marketing Strategies

3

Part II

The following table lists the existing yearly
membership fees as well as the suggested increased
membership fees for the next fiscal year.

Type of Membership	Current	New
Individual	210.00	265.00
Joint (2 max.)	385.00	400.00
Family < 4 members	525.00	575.00
Family > 4 members	600.00	625.00
Corporate < 25 members	2475.00	2750.00
Corporate > 25 members	4285.00	4800.00

WORDPERFECT 5.1

PROJECT 5

Merging Documents

OBJECTIVES

You will have mastered the material in this project when you can:

◆ Use the Date Text function

◆ Create a primary file

◆ Create a secondary file

◆ Edit secondary files

◆ Merge to the printer

◆ Merge to a document

◆ Print specific pages of a document

In Project 5 you will learn how to merge two documents to create a form letter. You will learn how to create both the primary and secondary files necessary in order to merge, how to edit specific copies of a form letter, and how to print specific pages of a document.

Before you begin, load WordPerfect as you have done in the previous projects.

MERGING

◆ When you merge things you combine, or blend, them together. In word processing when you perform a merge you combine, or blend, two or more documents together. Mass mailings are usually merged in some fashion so that you receive a personalized version of a form letter. You might have received a letter of this type in the mail: Yes, you, JIM Q. SMITH, may have already won $2,000,000!! This same letter is sent to millions of people with their individual names used in the text of the letter as the lucky recipient. You might also have received letters directed to Dear Customer or Current Occupant. The widespread use of computers in business has made these types of generic salutations less effective.

WordPerfect has a Merge function that allows you to individualize form letters so that each recipient's copy is personalized. Merging combines two documents, a primary file and a secondary file, into one merged document. The **primary file** contains the basic text for the letter that will remain constant. It *does not change* from letter to letter. Primary files are sometimes referred to as *template files*.

The **secondary file** contains the variable information that *will change* from letter to letter. The names, addresses, and other variable information are contained in the secondary file. Secondary files are sometimes referred to as *address files* or *data files*. The main and secondary files are created separately and are saved under separate filenames. When WordPerfect executes the Merge function, the information in the secondary file *blends* with the text of the primary file, which results in customized versions of the form letter. The merge takes place within the computer's memory and does *not* affect the text of the primary or secondary files. Both files remain intact in their original form both during and after the merge.

Suppose that you want to send the letter in Figure 5-1 to several computer supply vendors asking for product and price information. You could create a basic letter, then use Typeover to change the names and other variable information for each vendor. Or you could create one basic letter — the primary file — and a secondary file containing all the information that needs to be altered for each letter. After creating these files, you could use WordPerfect's Merge function to do the work for you and save you a great deal of time.

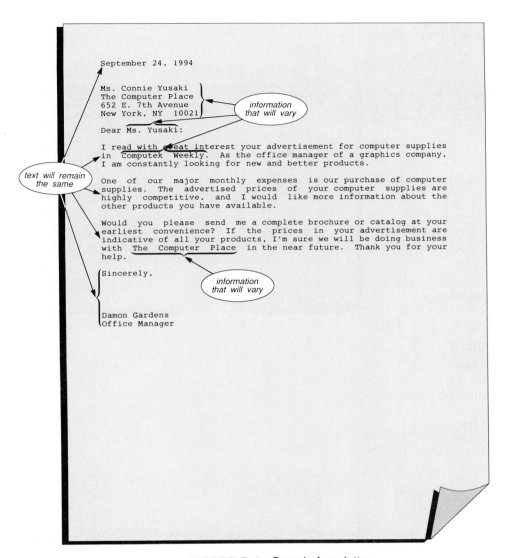

FIGURE 5-1 Sample form letter

CREATING A PRIMARY FILE

◆ Creating a primary file is like creating any other WordPerfect document, but with one difference. The difference is that you must enter special names where the variable information will appear.

The Date Function

As Figure 5-1 shows, before you begin entering the text of the primary file, you should insert the date. WordPerfect provides a quick method of inserting the current date into a document.

Position the cursor at the top of the document. Press Alt- = to display the menu bar, then type T for Tools. The menu in Figure 5-2 appears.

FIGURE 5-2
Tools menu

Notice the "Date Text" option. This option will insert the current date into a document. Type T, and the current date is inserted into the document at the point of the cursor (Figure 5-3). The date inserted into your document will be the date you are creating this document, and *not* the date shown in Figure 5-3. Your computer system also may have been programmed to use a date other than the current date. Once the date is inserted, press the Enter key three times to move the cursor down two lines.

 Mouse Users:
Select the Tools menu, then select "Date Text".

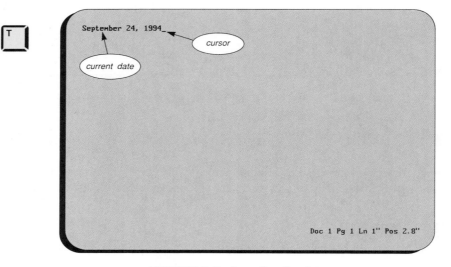

FIGURE 5-3   Inserting the date

Field Names

Now you're ready to insert the special names into the document. A **field** is a single fact about a person or object. For example, address is a field, as is name. Each time you reach a place in the primary file where the variable information — or field — will print, you will insert a **field name**. The field name acts as a placeholder for the data contained in the secondary file. When you enter field names into a WordPerfect document, WordPerfect searches the secondary

The cursor is at the point where the recipient's name should appear (Figure 5-4).

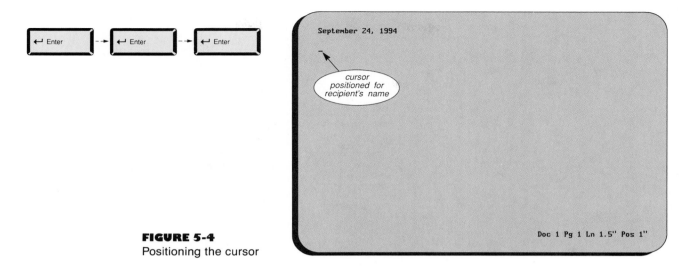

FIGURE 5-4
Positioning the cursor

Because the name will vary from letter to letter, you must insert a field name here. Field names are inserted through the Merge Codes menu contained in the Tools menu. Press Alt-= to display the menu bar, then type T for Tools. Notice the "Merge Codes" option (and the shortcut keys, Shift-F9). This option will list the various codes WordPerfect requires during a merge operation. Type R and the Merge Codes menu in Figure 5-5 appears.

FIGURE 5-5
Merge Codes menu

This menu lists many codes that WordPerfect uses to merge documents to your specifications. For this document, however, you will use only the first two codes in the menu, the {FIELD} and the {END RECORD} codes.

 Mouse Users: Select the Tools menu, then select "Merge Codes".

Entering Field Names

You are now ready to insert the first field name into your document. The cursor is already positioned on the "Field" option, so press Enter. The message in Figure 5-6 appears, asking for a field name.

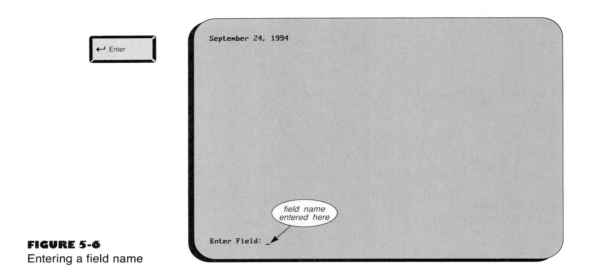

FIGURE 5-6
Entering a field name

Field names may be numbers or words; however, because numbers are easier to keep track of, let's use numbers. Type the number 1, since this is the first field of the document, then press Enter to insert the field name into the document (Figure 5-7).

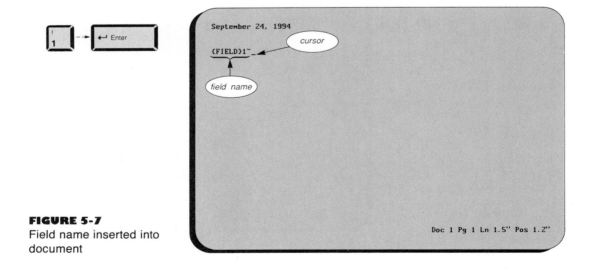

FIGURE 5-7
Field name inserted into document

This is how WordPerfect displays a field name in a document. The code alerts WordPerfect that the information that follows is a field name and not text. Press Enter to move the cursor to the next line.

The contents of this line — the company name to which you're writing — will also vary from letter to letter. Let's insert another field name. Press Alt-= to display the menu bar, type T for Tools, then R for the Merge Codes menu. Again, the cursor should be positioned on the "Field" option, so press Enter. Since this is the second field of the document, let's call this second field 2. Press Enter, then press Enter again to move the cursor to the next line.

The address will also change for each recipient, so let's enter the field name 3, but this time, let's use the short-cut keys. Press Shift-F9, and the menu in Figure 5-8 appears.

FIGURE 5-8
Merge Codes menu

This is a horizontal listing of the same menu choices contained in the pull-down menu. Type 1 for Field, then type 3 for the field name.

When you enter a field name into a document and if that field might not have an entry in the secondary file, you must enter a question mark as the last character of the field name. For example, one of the vendors this letter is being sent to does not have a street address. Whenever such a situation occurs, you must end the field name with a question mark to ensure that the printed copy of the letter will not contain blank lines. Thus, type a question mark (?), then press Enter. Field 3 is inserted into the document, so press Enter to move the cursor to the next line (Figure 5-9).

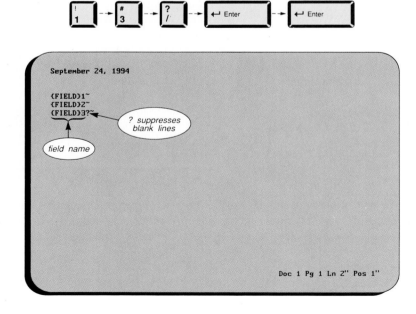

FIGURE 5-9
Inserting a field name to accommodate missing field entries

We will use the shortcut keys for the remainder of the field names. The city, state, and ZIP code will also vary, so you need to insert a field name on this line, too. Press Shift-F9, type 1, then 4 for the field name, followed by the Enter key. Press the Enter key twice to move the cursor down two lines (Figure 5-10).

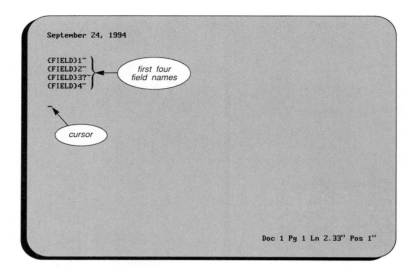

FIGURE 5-10
Entering the salutation

Type Dear, then press the Spacebar. Notice that you must press the Spacebar to include a blank space after the word Dear. You still need to use appropriate spaces and punctuation around field names exactly as if you were entering normal text. The cursor is now at the place where the recipient's name should appear, so you must insert a field name here. Press Shift-F9, type 1 for "Field", then 5 for field name, followed by the Enter key. Now type a colon (:). Press Enter twice to move the cursor down two lines (Figure 5-11).

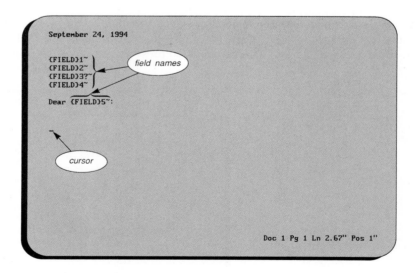

FIGURE 5-11
First five fields entered

Enter the text of the first sentence up to the place where the magazine field name needs to be inserted. Enter the following text exactly as you would in any other WordPerfect document: I read with great interest your advertisement for computer supplies in . Press the Spacebar.

Special Text Formats within Field Names

You can use special text formats, such as underlining and boldfacing, within field names. Text from the secondary file (the variable information) will print according to the codes contained in the primary file. For example, if you wanted each company name to print in bold, you would insert a bold code immediately before inserting the field name.

The next piece of variable information in our letter is the name of a magazine. To be properly punctuated, it needs to be underlined. Press F8 to begin underlining, then insert the field name by pressing Shift-F9, then typing 1 for "Field", then 6 for field number six, followed by the Enter key (Figure 5-12).

September 24, 1994

{FIELD}1~
{FIELD}2~
{FIELD}3?~
{FIELD}4~

Dear {FIELD}5~:

I read with great interest your advertisement for computer supplies
in {FIELD}6~

will print underlined

Doc 1 Pg 1 Ln 2.83" Pos 1.5"

FIGURE 5-12
Entering special text formats

Now you need to turn off underlining so that only the information for field 6 will print underlined. Press F8 to turn off underlining. When you print this letter, each printed copy will have the magazine name underlined because you surrounded the field name with underline codes. Type a period (.) to end the sentence, then press the Spacebar twice.

Entering Primary File Text

You are now ready to continue entering the text of the primary file, as shown in Figure 5-1 exactly as you would for any WordPerfect document, but stop when you reach the word with in the last line of the third paragraph: As the office manager of a graphics company, I am constantly looking for new and better products. ↵ ↵ One of our major monthly expenses is our purchase of computer supplies. The advertised prices of your computer supplies are highly competitive, and I would like more information about the other products you have available. ↵ ↵ Would you please send me a complete brochure or catalog at your earliest convenience? If the prices in your advertisement are indicative of all your products, I'm sure we will be doing business with . Press the Spacebar to insert a blank space to precede the next field name.

You have now reached the last piece of variable information in the letter, the name of the company. Recall that you already entered the company name earlier in the primary file. WordPerfect allows you to reuse field names within a document. WordPerfect will look through the secondary file until it finds the correct field entry for company. Field names need not be used in numeric order, and you can use a field name as many times as you need to throughout a document.

Press Shift-F9, then type 1 for "Field". When you inserted the company name earlier, you gave it the field name 2, so type 2 followed by the Enter key to insert the company field name (Figure 5-13).

```
September 24, 1994

{FIELD}1~
{FIELD}2~
{FIELD}3?~
{FIELD}4~

Dear {FIELD}5~:

I read with great interest your advertisement for computer supplies
in {FIELD}6~.  As the office manager of a graphics company, I am
constantly looking for new and better products.

One of our major monthly expenses is our purchase of computer
supplies.  The advertised prices of your computer supplies are
highly competitive, and I would like more information about the
other products you have available.

Would you please send me a complete brochure or catalog at your
earliest convenience?  If the prices in your advertisement are
indicative of all your products, I'm sure we will be doing business
with {FIELD}2~_

                                              Doc 1 Pg 1 Ln 4.67" Pos 1.7"
```
will print field entry for field 2

FIGURE 5-13
Inserting a duplicate field name

Now that you have entered the last field name, press the Spacebar, then type the remainder of the document: in the near future. Thank you for your help. ↵ ↵ Sincerely, ↵ ↵ ↵ ↵ ↵ Damon Gardens ↵ Office Manager ↵. The document is complete and should look like Figure 5-14.

```
Dear {FIELD}5~:

I read with great interest your advertisement for computer supplies
in {FIELD}6~.  As the office manager of a graphics company, I am
constantly looking for new and better products.

One of our major monthly expenses is our purchase of computer
supplies.  The advertised prices of your computer supplies are
highly competitive, and I would like more information about the
other products you have available.

Would you please send me a complete brochure or catalog at your
earliest convenience?  If the prices in your advertisement are
indicative of all your products, I'm sure we will be doing business
with {FIELD}2~ in the near future.  Thank you for your help.

Sincerely,




Damon Gardens
Office Manager
_
                                              Doc 1 Pg 1 Ln 6.17" Pos 1"
```

FIGURE 5-14
The completed primary file

Save the document by pressing F10, then name the document by typing P5LTR. Press Enter, and the document is saved on disk under the filename P5LTR. Now that the document is saved, you have completed the primary file. Next, you need to create the secondary file. First, exit the document but not WordPerfect, as you have done before by pressing F7.

CREATING A SECONDARY FILE

◆ The secondary file supplies the variable information for each of the field names in the primary file. During the merge, WordPerfect substitutes the information in the secondary file for the field names contained in the primary file. Secondary files contain two types of information: field entries and records.

Field Entries

A **field entry** is the information that will print for a particular field. For example, in your document, if the field is company name, the field entries are R & L Computer Supplies, Computerama, and Datatek. Each time WordPerfect encounters a field code in the primary file, it will check the field entry in the secondary file. The first step to creating a secondary file is to insert the field entries for each field. Figure 5-15 shows the field information for each of the vendors who will receive the letter.

Let's type the field entries for the first vendor. Be sure your screen is clear and ready for a new document. Type the first field entry Mr. Robert Shulman. Now that the entry is complete, you need to insert the code that instructs WordPerfect that this is the end of that field entry. Press F9, and WordPerfect inserts the {END FIELD} code shown in Figure 5-16. This code informs WordPerfect that the entry for this particular field is complete.

F9

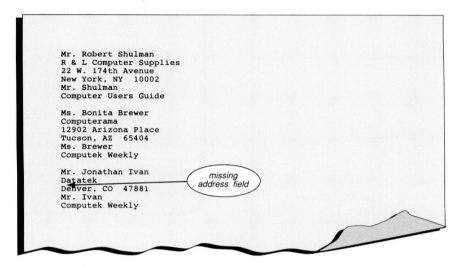

```
Mr. Robert Shulman
R & L Computer Supplies
22 W. 174th Avenue
New York, NY  10002
Mr. Shulman
Computer Users Guide

Ms. Bonita Brewer
Computerama
12902 Arizona Place
Tucson, AZ  65404
Ms. Brewer
Computek Weekly

Mr. Jonathan Ivan
Datatek          ── missing address field
Denver, CO  47881
Mr. Ivan
Computek Weekly
```

FIGURE 5-15   Field information for vendors receiving a letter

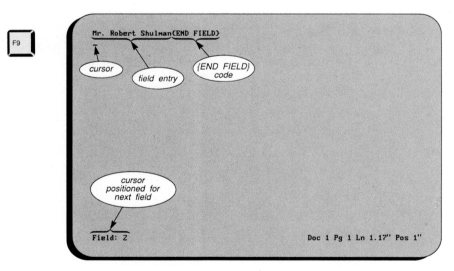

```
Mr. Robert Shulman{END FIELD}
```

cursor — field entry — {END FIELD} code

cursor positioned for next field

Field: 2   Doc 1 Pg 1 Ln 1.17" Pos 1"

FIGURE 5-16   First field entry

The status line informs you that the cursor is now positioned for field 2. WordPerfect also moves the cursor down to the next line.

Now you're ready to insert the field entry for field 2, the company name. Type R & L Computer Supplies. Press F9, and WordPerfect inserts the code and moves the cursor down one line (Figure 5-17).

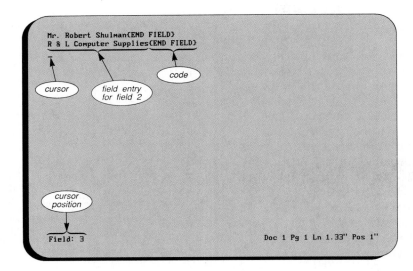

FIGURE 5-17
Entering second field entry

Insert the field entry for address (field 3) by typing 22 W. 174th Avenue, then press F9 to end the field entry. For field 4, type New York, NY 10002, then press F9 to end the field. For field 5, type Mr. Shulman then press F9. For field 6, type Computer Users Guide, and the field entries for the first letter are complete (Figure 5-18).

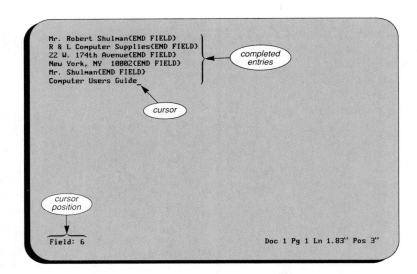

FIGURE 5-18
Completed field entries for
first letter

Now you need to instruct WordPerfect that the next group of information should result in a separate copy of the letter.

Mouse Users: Enter the information for the first field entry. Select the Tools menu, then select "Merge Codes". Select "More", then select the {END FIELD} code from the Merge Codes menu. Repeat these steps each time you finish entering the data for each field.

Entering Records

A **record** is a group of related fields. For example, a record from a telephone book would be a person's name, address, city, and telephone number. A record for our letter would be each vendor's name, company, address, city, state, ZIP code, and magazine name. These groups of facts — or groups of fields — about each vendor will become records in the secondary file.

Because the first record is now complete, you would not insert an {END FIELD} code at this point. Rather, you would insert an {END RECORD} code. Press Shift-F9 to display the Merge Codes menu, then type 2 to insert the {END RECORD} code. WordPerfect inserts the code and a hard page break (Figure 5-19).

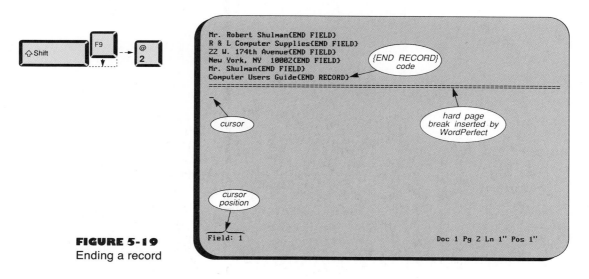

FIGURE 5-19
Ending a record

WordPerfect inserts a hard page break to ensure that each copy of the letter will automatically begin printing on a new page. Now you're ready to begin entering the field entries for the next record.

Type Ms. Bonita Brewer, then press F9. Type Computerama, then press F9. Type 12902 Arizona Place, then press F9. Type Tucson, AZ 65404, then press F9. Type Ms. Brewer, then press F9. Type Computek Weekly, press Shift-F9, then type 2 to end the record.

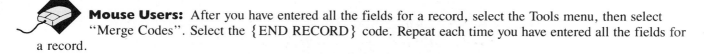

Mouse Users: After you have entered all the fields for a record, select the Tools menu, then select "Merge Codes". Select the {END RECORD} code. Repeat each time you have entered all the fields for a record.

Entering a Record with a Missing Field

Notice in Figure 5-15 that the next record contains no information for the address field. WordPerfect provides a way to fill empty fields so that your merged document will print with the address in the correct place. Recall that when you entered the field name in the primary file, you typed a question mark (?) at the end of the field name. This was to ensure that any record with this field missing would print properly. Now you need to insert a corresponding code into the secondary file.

Begin typing the field entries. Type `Mr. Jonathan Ivan`, then press F9. Type `Datatek`, then press F9. The cursor is now positioned at the point where the address should print. Press F9, and WordPerfect inserts an {END FIELD} code (Figure 5-20).

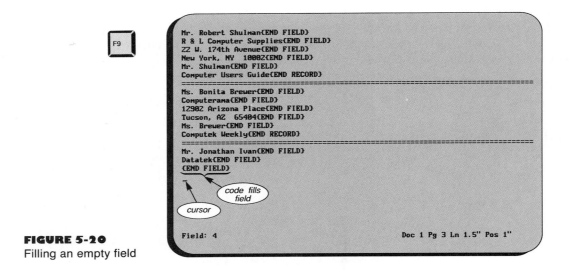

FIGURE 5-20
Filling an empty field

When the letter prints, no address line will appear. The code acts as a placeholder. WordPerfect will automatically move the next line up in the printed document so that a blank line won't print in the address.

Finish entering the information for this record. Type `Denver, CO 47881`, then press F9. Type `Mr. Ivan`, then press F9. Type `Computek Weekly`, press Shift-F9, then type 2 to end the record (Figure 5-21).

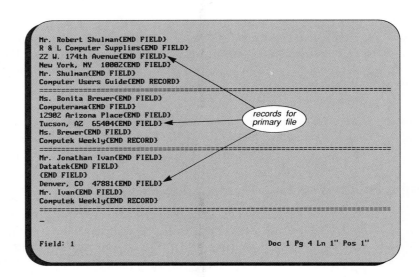

FIGURE 5-21
Completed records

Saving the Secondary File

You have entered the names and addresses of all the people to whom the letter is being sent, so your secondary file is now complete and ready to be saved. Press F10, then name the file by typing P5ADDR. When you access the "Merge" option, WordPerfect will look from the document P5LTR into P5ADDR for the variable information it needs to complete each individual letter. Press Enter, and the secondary file is saved on disk under the filename P5ADDR.

MERGING DOCUMENTS

◆ Now that you have created and saved both the primary file and the secondary file, you're ready to merge them. To begin the merge process, you must first have a clear screen. Press F7 and exit the document but not WordPerfect.

WordPerfect allows you to merge two different ways. You can merge directly to the printer or you can merge to a document, which you can then view on the screen.

Merging to the Printer

To merge directly to the printer, you must insert codes into the primary file. These merge codes instruct WordPerfect to send the merged copies directly to the printer rather than to a separate file. Let's merge to the printer so that you generate hard copies of each letter.

First, retrieve the primary file. Press Shift-F10, then type P5LTR and press Enter. Once the primary file appears on the screen, move the cursor to the bottom of the document. Now you're ready to insert the merge codes.

Press Shift-F9 to display the Merge Codes menu. Notice menu choice "6" for "More". Type 6, and the menu in Figure 5-22 appears.

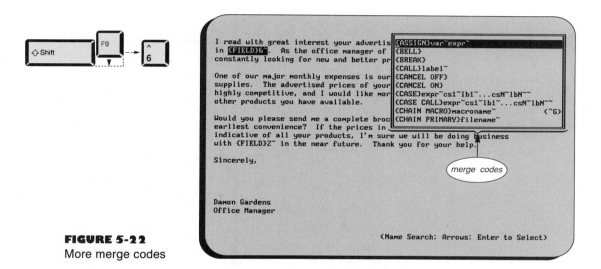

FIGURE 5-22
More merge codes

This is a list of the other codes that WordPerfect provides for merging. You may access these codes by pressing the Down Arrow key to scroll through them or by typing the first letter of the code. Because it's much quicker than scrolling, let's type the first character of the code we need, the {PRINT} code. Type P and the cursor moves to the first merge code beginning with the letter P (Figure 5-23).

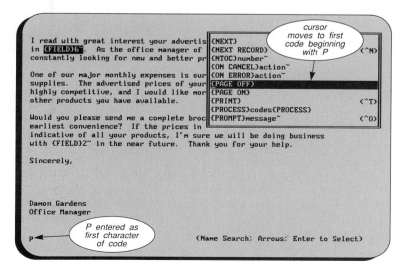

FIGURE 5-23 Selecting codes

You need to insert the code {PRINT}, so press the Down Arrow key twice until the cursor is positioned directly on the {PRINT} code as shown in Figure 5-24, then press Enter.

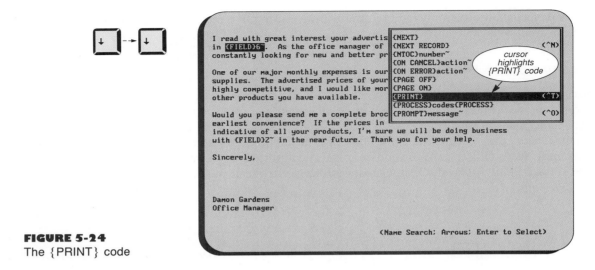

FIGURE 5-24
The {PRINT} code

You next need to insert a code so that WordPerfect will begin printing the next letter on a separate page. To do this, use the {PAGE OFF} code. Again, press Shift-F9, then type 6, then P. Position the cursor on the {PAGE OFF} code as shown in Figure 5-25, then press Enter. This code tells WordPerfect to print each copy of the letter on a separate page.

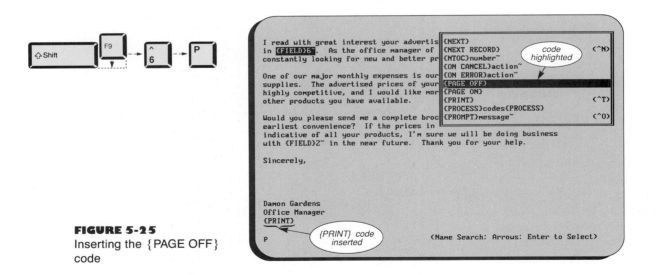

FIGURE 5-25
Inserting the {PAGE OFF}
code

Mouse Users: Position the cursor at the end of the primary file. Select the Tools menu, then select "Merge Codes", then select "More". Select the {PRINT} code. To insert the {PAGE OFF} code, select the Tools menu, select "Merge Codes", then select "More". Select the {PAGE OFF} code.

Both codes necessary to merge directly to the printer are now inserted into the primary file (Figure 5-26), so save and exit the document.

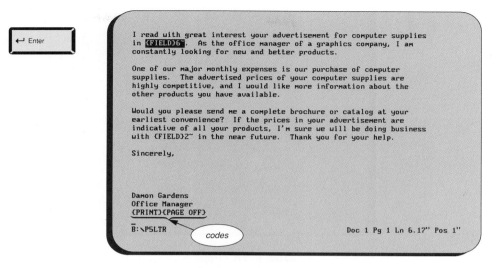

FIGURE 5-26 Codes in primary file

Your screen should be clear and ready to begin the merge. Be sure your printer is on and ready to print. Press Alt-= to display the menu bar, then type T for Tools. Notice the "Merge" option in Figure 5-27.

FIGURE 5-27 "Merge" option

Type M for "Merge", and the prompt in Figure 5-28 appears, requesting the name of the primary file.

FIGURE 5-28 Entering the primary file name

Type P5LTR, then press the Enter key. Now WordPerfect needs the name of the secondary file. Type P5ADDR (Figure 5-29), then press the Enter key.

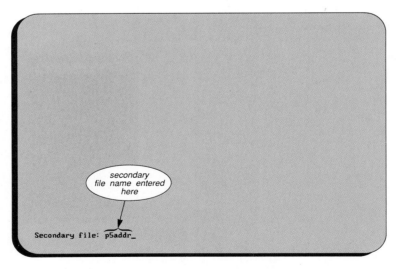

FIGURE 5-29 Entering the secondary file name

The customized letters to the various computer vendors begin printing on the printer. Neither the primary nor the secondary file displays during the merge. The message "*Merging*" appears on the status line while each copy is merged and printed. While the merge is being performed, you are unable to access any options or perform any editing. When WordPerfect has read all the records in the secondary file, the merge message disappears, and you can again edit or access options. The final letters should look like those in Figure 5-30.

```
September 24, 1994

Mr. Robert Shulman
R & L Computer Supplies
22 W. 174th Avenue
New York, NY  10002

Dear Mr. Shulman:

I read with great interest your advertisement for computer supplies
in Computer Users Guide. As the office manager of a graphics
company, I am constantly looking for new and better products.

One of our major monthly expenses is our purchase of computer
supplies. The advertised prices of your computer supplies are
highly competitive, and I would like more information about the
other products you have available.

Would you please send me a complete brochure or catalog at your
earliest convenience? If the prices in your advertisement are
indicative of all your products, I'm sure we will be doing business
with R & L Computer Supplies in the near future. Thank you for
your help.

Sincerely,


Damon Gardens
Office Manager
```

```
September 24, 1994

Ms. Bonita Brewer
Computerama
12902 Arizona Place
Tucson, AZ  65404

Dear Ms. Brewer:

I read with great interest your advertisement for computer supplies
in Computek Weekly. As the office manager of a graphics company,
I am constantly looking for new and better products.

One of our major monthly expenses is our purchase of computer
supplies. The advertised prices of your computer supplies are
highly competitive, and I would like more information about the
other products you have available.

Would you please send me a complete brochure or catalog at your
earliest convenience? If the prices in your advertisement are
indicative of all your products, I'm sure we will be doing business
with Computerama in the near future. Thank you for your help.

Sincerely,


Damon Gardens
Office Manager
```

```
September 24, 1994

Mr. Jonathan Ivan
Datatek
Denver, CO  47881

Dear Mr. Ivan:

I read with great interest your advertisement for computer supplies
in Computek Weekly. As the office manager of a graphics company,
I am constantly looking for new and better products.

One of our major monthly expenses is our purchase of computer
supplies. The advertised prices of your computer supplies are
highly competitive, and I would like more information about the
other products you have available.

Would you please send me a complete brochure or catalog at your
earliest convenience? If the prices in your advertisement are
indicative of all your products, I'm sure we will be doing business
with Datatek in the near future. Thank you for your help.

Sincerely,


Damon Gardens
Office Manager
```

FIGURE 5-30 Copies of form letter

If your letters printed with data incorrectly placed, check your secondary file to be sure that you used {END RECORD} and {END FIELD} codes in the correct places, and that you have a sufficient number of field entries for each record.

 Mouse Users: Select the Tools menu, then select "Merge". Enter the primary and secondary file names when you are prompted.

Changing the Secondary File

The merge is now complete, and the copies of the individual letters are printed. Suppose now that you decide to send this letter to two more vendors. You could accomplish this in two different ways: you could create a new secondary file, and then enter its name at the "Merge" option; or, you could add the names to the P5ADDR secondary file, and then print only the new copies of the letter. Let's use this latter method.

Retrieve the secondary file by pressing Shift-F10, then type P5ADDR. Press Enter, and when the secondary file appears, move the cursor to the bottom of the document. With the cursor positioned at the end of the document, enter the records shown in Figure 5-31, making certain you end each field entry with an {END FIELD} code and each record with an {END RECORD} code.

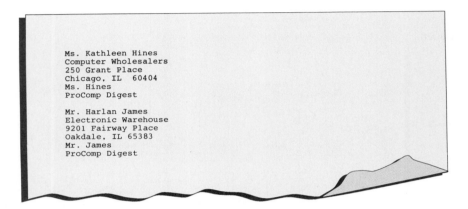

FIGURE 5-31 Additional records for secondary file

Figure 5-32 shows how your screen should look after the new records are entered.

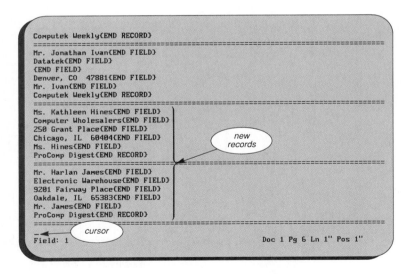

FIGURE 5-32 Edited secondary file

Now that the secondary file is complete, save it under the same name, then exit it again.

Deleting Merge Codes

Before you merge to a document, you must remove the codes you inserted that instructed WordPerfect to merge directly to the printer. If you don't remove these codes, WordPerfect will merge directly to the printer and will not display the document on your screen. Press Shift-F10, type P5LTR, then press Enter, and the primary file appears on the screen. Move the cursor to the end of the document and delete the {PRINT} and {PAGE OFF} codes. Save the document under the same filename, and exit the document.

Merging to a Document

Merging to a document is particularly helpful if certain copies of the letter need an additional sentence or minor revision, or if you want to see the document on the screen before it is printed. It is also useful because the merged copies on the screen can then be saved on disk, which would then serve as a record of who received a particular letter.

Let's merge to a document, this time with the shortcut keys. Be sure your screen is clear and ready for the merge. Press Ctrl-F9, and the menu in Figure 5-33 appears.

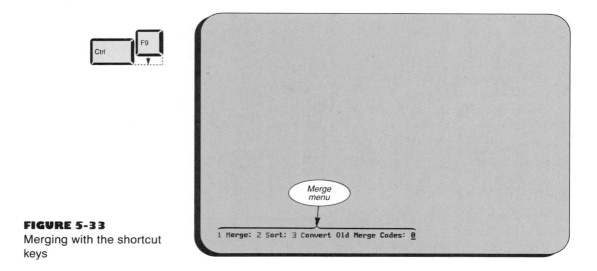

Merge
menu

1 Merge: 2 Sort: 3 Convert Old Merge Codes: 0

FIGURE 5-33
Merging with the shortcut keys

Since you want to merge, type 1, and the prompt in Figure 5-34 appears.

primary file
name entered
here

Primary file:

(List Files)

FIGURE 5-34
Entering the primary file name

From this point on, executing the merge is accomplished exactly as before. Enter the name of the primary file, P5LTR, and press Enter. Enter the name of the secondary file, P5ADDR, and press Enter. WordPerfect begins performing the merge, and displays the message "*Merging*" on the status line.

When the merge is complete, the new document containing the merged copies of the letter appears on the screen, with each copy separated by a page break. Recall that WordPerfect inserted these page breaks after you entered each {END RECORD} code so that each copy will print as a separate page.

Editing Merged Documents

Let's suppose that Electronic Warehouse has been a supplier for Graphicon for the last two years. The second to the last line of your form letter is, therefore, not appropriate, and you need to change it. Let's change this sentence so that the end of it reads … we will turn to Electronic Warehouse for our computer supply needs in the near future.

Move the cursor to the beginning of the letter to Electronic Warehouse, then position the cursor on the word be in the next to the last line of the last paragraph. Type turn to. Now press Alt-F4 to begin blocking, then press Ctrl-Right Arrow four times so that the words be doing business with are blocked. Press the Delete key and answer Y to the "Delete Block?" prompt. Now move the cursor to the i in the word in. Type for our computer supply needs, then press the Spacebar (Figure 5-35).

This vendor's copy of the letter has now been corrected. Let's print the new copies of the letter.

Printing Specific Pages

If you sent this document to the printer now, all the letters would print. Since you already printed the first three letters, you need only print the two vendors' copies you added to the secondary file, that is, to Computer Wholesalers and Electronic Warehouse. To do this, you must first position the cursor on the page you want to print, so move the cursor so that it is positioned on or beyond the first character of the fourth page of the document. The cursor can be positioned anywhere within the page to be printed, not specifically on the first character.

Press Shift-F7 to display the Print menu (Figure 5-36). Notice menu choice "2". Select this choice to print the page containing the cursor. Type 2, and page 4 begins to print.

FIGURE 5-35 Edited document

FIGURE 5-36 Print menu

When page 4 has finished printing, move the cursor to page 5. Press Shift-F7, then type 2 and page 5 will print on the printer. The two new copies should look like those in Figure 5-37.

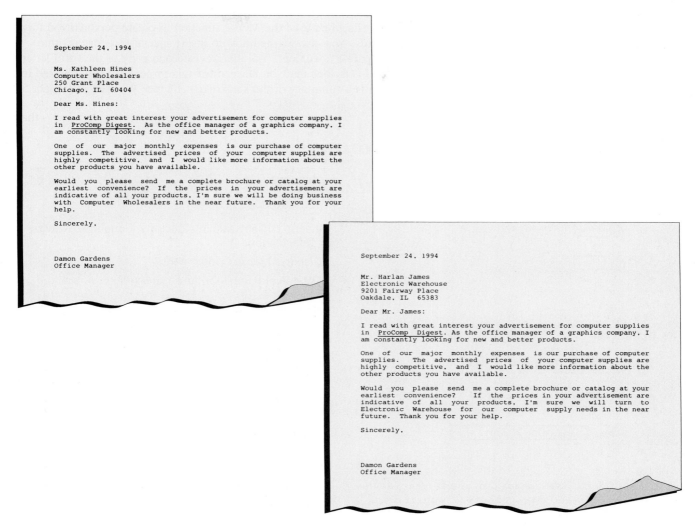

September 24, 1994

Ms. Kathleen Hines
Computer Wholesalers
250 Grant Place
Chicago, IL 60404

Dear Ms. Hines:

I read with great interest your advertisement for computer supplies in ProComp Digest. As the office manager of a graphics company, I am constantly looking for new and better products.

One of our major monthly expenses is our purchase of computer supplies. The advertised prices of your computer supplies are highly competitive, and I would like more information about the other products you have available.

Would you please send me a complete brochure or catalog at your earliest convenience? If the prices in your advertisement are indicative of all your products, I'm sure we will be doing business with Computer Wholesalers in the near future. Thank you for your help.

Sincerely,

Damon Gardens
Office Manager

September 24, 1994

Mr. Harlan James
Electronic Warehouse
9201 Fairway Place
Oakdale, IL 65383

Dear Mr. James:

I read with great interest your advertisement for computer supplies in ProComp Digest. As the office manager of a graphics company, I am constantly looking for new and better products.

One of our major monthly expenses is our purchase of computer supplies. The advertised prices of your computer supplies are highly competitive, and I would like more information about the other products you have available.

Would you please send me a complete brochure or catalog at your earliest convenience? If the prices in your advertisement are indicative of all your products, I'm sure we will turn to Electronic Warehouse for our computer supply needs in the near future. Thank you for your help.

Sincerely,

Damon Gardens
Office Manager

FIGURE 5-37   New copies of document

Mouse Users: Select the File menu, then select "Print". Select option "2" from the Print menu. Repeat for page 5.

Saving Merged Documents

Now that you've finished printing the letters, you should save the document on your screen under its own filename. This serves as an excellent record of the vendors who received a particular letter. Press F10, then type P5NEW, and press Enter to save this document. Exit WordPerfect as you have done in previous projects by pressing F7.

PROJECT SUMMARY

In Project 5 you created a primary file and a secondary file, then used the Merge function to create personalized form letters. You learned about fields, field names, and records. You also learned how to insert special text formats into fields, and how to merge both to the printer and to a separate document. You then revised one copy of the form letter, and printed only specific pages of the document. All the activities that you learned for this project are summarized in the Quick Reference following Project 6. The following is a summary of the keystroke sequence we used in Project 5.

SUMMARY OF KEYSTROKES — PROJECT 5

STEPS	KEY(S) PRESSED	RESULTS
1	wp ← [At C> prompt or as directed by instructor]	Loads WordPerfect.
2	[Alt-=] T T ← ← ←	Inserts current date into document and inserts two blank lines.
3	[Alt-=] T R	Displays Merge Codes menu.
4	← 1 ← ←	Enters field name for field 1 and moves cursor to next line.
5	[Alt-=] T R	Displays Merge Codes menu.
6	← 2 ←	Enters field name for field 2 and moves cursor to next line.
7	[Shift-F9] 1 3 ? ←	Enters field name for field 3 and moves cursor to next line.
8	[Shift-F9] 1 4 ← ←	Enters field name for field 4 and positions cursor at beginning of salutation.
9	Dear [Spacebar] [Shift-F9] 1 5 ← :	Enters salutation and field name for field 5.
10	← ←	Positions cursor at beginning point of text for letter.
11	I read with great interest your adver-tisement for computer supplies in [Spacebar]	Enters text up to point of magazine field name.
12	[F8]	Begins underlining.
13	[Shift-F9] 1 6 [F8] . [Spacebar] [Spacebar]	Enters field name for field 6, ends underlining, and enters period at end of text.
14	As the office manager of a graphics com-pany, I am constantly looking for new and better products. ← ← One of our major monthly expenses is our purchase of computer supplies. The advertised prices of your computer supplies are highly competitive, and I would like more information about the other prod-ucts you have available. ← ← Would you please send me a complete brochure or catalog at your earliest convenience? If the prices in your advertisement are indicative of all your products, I'm sure we will be doing business with [Spacebar]	Enters text up to point of company field name.

SUMMARY OF KEYSTROKES — PROJECT 5 (continued)

STEPS	KEY(S) PRESSED	RESULTS
15	[Shift–F9] 1 2 ↵ [Spacebar]	Enters company field name followed by blank space.
16	in the near future. Thank you for your help. ↵↵ Sincerely, ↵[Press 5 times] Damon Gardens ↵Office Manager↵	Enters remainder of text for letter.
17	[F10] P5LTR↵	Saves document under the filename P5LTR.
18	[F7] N N	Exits document.
19	Mr. Robert Shulman [F9] R & L Computer Supplies [F9] 22 W. 174th Avenue [F9] New York, NY 10002 [F9] Mr. Shulman [F9] Computer Users Guide [Shift–F9] 2	Enters first record.
20	Ms. Bonita Brewer [F9] Computerama [F9] 12902 Arizona Place [F9] Tucson, AZ 65404 [F9] Ms. Brewer [F9] Computek Weekly [Shift–F9] 2	Enters second record.
21	Mr. Jonathan Ivan [F9] Datatek [F9] [F9] Denver, CO 47881 [F9] Mr. Ivan [F9] Computek Weekly [Shift–F9] 2	Enters third record.
22	[F10] P5ADDR↵ [F7] N N	Saves document under the filename P5ADDR, then exits document.
23	[Shift–F10] P5LTR↵	Retrieves primary file.
24	[Home] [Home] ↓	Moves cursor to end of document.
25	[Shift–F9] 6	Displays Merge Codes menu.
26	P	Moves cursor to codes beginning with letter P.
27	↓↓↵	Inserts {PRINT} code in primary file.
28	[Shift–F9] 6 P↵	Inserts {PAGE OFF} code in primary file.
29	[F7] Y↵Y N	Saves and exits primary file.
30	[Alt–=] T M	Displays "Merge" option.
31	P5LTR↵P5ADDR↵	Enters names of primary and secondary files and merges documents to printer.
32	[Shift–F10] P5ADDR↵	Retrieves secondary file.
33	[Home] [Home] ↓	Moves cursor to bottom of document.
34	Ms. Kathleen Hines [F9] Computer Whole-salers [F9] 250 Grant Place [F9] Chicago, IL 60404 [F9] Ms. Hines [F9] ProComp Digest [Shift–F9] 2 Mr. Harlan James [F9] Electronic Warehouse [F9] 9201 Fairway Place [F9] Oakdale, IL 65383 [F9] Mr. James [F9] ProComp Digest [Shift–F9] 2	Enters new records.
35	[F7] Y↵Y N	Saves and exits secondary file.
36	[Shift–F10] P5LTR↵	Retrieves primary file.
37	[Home] [Home] ↓ [Backspace] [Backspace]	Moves cursor to end of document and removes {PRINT} and {PAGE OFF} codes.

(continued)

SUMMARY OF KEYSTROKES — PROJECT 5 (continued)

STEPS	KEY(S) PRESSED	RESULTS
38	F7 Y ← Y N	Saves and exits primary file.
39	Ctrl-F9 1 P5LTR ← P5ADDR ←	Executes merge to document on screen.
40	Page Up Page Down	Positions cursor within page of document to be printed.
41	Home ↓ ↑ ↑ End Ctrl-← Ctrl-←	Positions cursor for editing.
42	turn to Spacebar	Enters text.
43	Alt-F4 Ctrl-→ [Press 4 times]	Blocks text to delete.
44	Delete Y	Deletes blocked text.
45	Ctrl-→ Ctrl-→ for our computer supply needs Spacebar	Positions cursor and enters text.
46	Page Up	Positions cursor on page to be printed.
47	Shift-F7 2	Prints page.
48	Page Down	Positions cursor on next page of document
49	Shift-F7 2	Prints page.
50	F10 P5NEW ←	Saves document under filename P5NEW.
51	F7 N Y	Exits WordPerfect and returns to DOS.

The following list summarizes the material covered in Project 5.

1. The Merge function allows you to create personalized form letters. Many mass mailings are done through the use of a merge. WordPerfect's Merge function combines a primary file with a secondary file.
2. The **primary file** contains the basic information that will remain the same for each letter. Primary files are sometimes referred to as *template files*.
3. The **secondary file** contains the variable information that will change from letter to letter. Secondary files are sometimes referred to as *address files* or *data files*.
4. WordPerfect's Date Text function allows you to enter the current date into a document.
5. A **field** is a piece of information or fact about a person or object. For example, address, name, and phone number are all individual fields.
6. The primary file must contain **field names** where the variable information will appear. Field names act as placeholders for the information from the secondary file.
7. To use a special text format within a merged document, precede and follow the field name with the format code.
8. A **field entry** is the information that will print for a particular field.
9. A **record** is a group of related fields.
10. Each record in the secondary file must end with an {END RECORD} code.
11. The "Merge" option is accessed through the Tools menu. You may merge to a document or directly to the printer.
12. When you merge to a document, WordPerfect creates an entirely separate document on the screen containing the copies of the merged documents. This document can then be saved to disk.
13. You can print specific pages of a document through the Print menu.

STUDENT ASSIGNMENTS

STUDENT ASSIGNMENT 1: True/False

Instructions: Circle T if the statement is true and F if the statement is false.

T F   1. To use WordPerfect's Merge function you must have a primary and a secondary file.
T F   2. There is no way to edit copies of a merged letter; all letters must print exactly the same text.
T F   3. When printing individual pages of a document with the Shift-F7, 2 option, the cursor does not need to be positioned within the page to be printed.
T F   4. A field is a group of related facts about a person.
T F   5. Records must end with an {END RECORD} code.
T F   6. To merge to the printer, press Ctrl-F9, then type P.
T F   7. Secondary files are sometimes referred to as address files.
T F   8. When a field might not contain an entry in the secondary file, its name must be followed by an exclamation point in the primary file.
T F   9. You can use the same field name more than once in a primary file.
T F 10. The "Merge" option is contained in the Tools menu.

STUDENT ASSIGNMENT 2: Multiple Choice

Instructions: Circle the correct response.

1. Primary files are sometimes referred to as _____.
   a. address files
   b. template files
   c. data files
   d. none of the above
2. To insert an {END RECORD} code, press _____.
   a. F9
   b. Shift-F9, 1
   c. Shift-F9, 2
   d. none of the above
3. To insert an {END FIELD} code, press _____.
   a. F9
   b. Shift-F9, 1
   c. Shift-F9, 2
   d. none of the above
4. To fill an empty field in the secondary file, use the _____ code.
   a. {END FIELD}
   b. {END RECORD}
   c. {EMPTY FIELD}
   d. none of the above
5. To print specific pages of a document, use the _____ menu.
   a. Tools
   b. Print
   c. Merge
   d. none of the above

Student Assignment 2 (continued)

6. When you insert an {END RECORD} code, WordPerfect automatically inserts a _____.
   a. hard return
   b. field number
   c. hard page break
   d. none of the above
7. The "Date Text" option is contained in the _____ menu.
   a. Tools
   b. Merge Codes
   c. Print
   d. none of the above
8. A single fact about a person or object is called a _____.
   a. field
   b. file
   c. record
   d. none of the above

STUDENT ASSIGNMENT 3: Matching

Instructions: Put the appropriate number next to the words in the second column.

1. Shift-F7, 2   _____Displays Merge menu
2. Ctrl-F9   _____Merges to printer
3. Shift-F9, 1   _____Prints specific pages
4. Shift-F9, 2   _____Contains information that remains the same
5. Primary file   _____Inserts {END RECORD}
6. {PRINT} {PAGE OFF}   _____Inserts {END FIELD}
7. F9   _____Inserts field name into primary file
8. Secondary file   _____Contains information that will vary

STUDENT ASSIGNMENT 4: Fill in the Blanks

Instructions: Fill in the blanks in the following sentences.

1. The _____ file contains the information that will vary from letter to letter.
2. The _____ file contains the information that will remain the same in each letter.
3. The "Merge" option is accessed through the _____ menu.
4. _____ (is) are the shortcut key(s) for the Merge Codes menu.
5. _____ (is) are the shortcut key(s) for the "Merge" option.
6. _____ (is) are the shortcut key(s) for the {END FIELD} code.
7. A group of related fields is referred to as a _____.
8. The _____ and _____ must be inserted into the primary file in order to merge directly to the printer.

STUDENT ASSIGNMENT 5: Understanding the Date Function

Instructions: You want to insert the current date into a document. Explain the keystrokes to accomplish this.

Steps: _____

_____

_____

STUDENT ASSIGNMENT 6: Understanding Field Names

Instructions: You are creating a primary file in which one field might not have a field entry in the secondary file. Explain the steps to correctly insert a field name into the primary file.

Steps: _____

_____

_____

STUDENT ASSIGNMENT 7: Creating Merged Documents

Instructions: Create a primary and secondary file for the letter and addresses shown in the figures. Use the field names shown. Save the primary file as SA5-7LTR and the secondary file as SA5-7ADR.

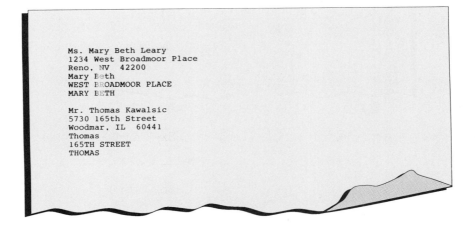

```
May 2, 1994

{FIELD}1˜
{FIELD}2˜
{FIELD}3˜

Dear {FIELD}4˜:

Thank you for your recent order from our spring catalog.  You'll be
happy to know that in addition to Greenway Gardens' values, we also
offer  huge  sweepstakes  prizes  to our valued customers.  When we
received  your  order,  we automatically entered your name into our
Garden Mania Sweepstakes.

We  are  happy to inform you that your name was randomly chosen for
entry  in  the  second  round  drawing.  Imagine  your  neighbors'
surprise  if our prize  delivery limousine drove down {FIELD}5˜ and
stopped at your house.  Imagine  your  delight  if we presented the
$1,000,000.00 check to YOU, {FIELD}6˜!

To  ensure  your  eligibility  for the second round drawing, simply
return  the  order  form  in  the  enclosed  catalog.  You need not
purchase  any  items from the catalog but be sure to take a look at
the incredible values inside.

Sincerely,




Rose Fields
President
```

```
Ms. Mary Beth Leary
1234 West Broadmoor Place
Reno, NV  42200
Mary Beth
WEST BROADMOOR PLACE
MARY BETH

Mr. Thomas Kawalsic
5730 165th Street
Woodmar, IL  60441
Thomas
165TH STREET
THOMAS
```

STUDENT ASSIGNMENT 8: Merging Documents

Instructions: Retrieve the file SA5-7LTR that you created in Student Assignment 7. Add the codes necessary to execute the "Merge" option directly to the printer. The printed copies should appear as shown in the figures.

```
May 2, 1994

Ms. Mary Beth Leary
1234 West Broadmoor Place
Reno, NV  42200

Dear Mary Beth:

Thank you for your recent order from our spring catalog.  You'll be
happy to know that in addition to Greenway Gardens' values, we also
offer  huge  sweepstakes  prizes  to our valued customers.  When we
received  your order, we automatically entered your name into our
Garden Mania Sweepstakes.

We  are  happy to inform you that your name was randomly chosen for
entry  in  the  second  round  drawing.   Imagine  your neighbors'
surprise  if our prize delivery limousine drove down WEST BROADMOOR
PLACE  and  stopped  at  your  house. Imagine  your  delight if we
presented the $1,000,000.00 check to YOU, MARY BETH!

To  ensure  your  eligibility  for the second round drawing, simply
return  the  order  form  in  the  enclosed  catalog.  You need not
purchase  any  items from the catalog but be sure to take a look at
the incredible values inside.

Sincerely,




Rose Fields
President
```

```
May 2, 1994

Mr. Thomas Kawalsic
5730 165th Street
Woodmar, IL  60441

Dear Thomas:

Thank you for your recent order from our spring catalog.  You'll be
happy to know that in addition to Greenway Gardens' values, we also
offer  huge  sweepstakes  prizes  to our valued customers.  When we
received  your order, we automatically entered your name into our
Garden Mania Sweepstakes.

We  are  happy to inform you that your name was randomly chosen for
entry  in  the  second  round  drawing.  Imagine  your  neighbors'
surprise  if our prize delivery  limousine drove down 165TH STREET
and stopped at your house. Imagine your delight if we presented the
$1,000,000.00 check to YOU, THOMAS!

To  ensure  your  eligibility  for the second  round drawing, simply
return  the  order  form  in  the  enclosed catalog.  You  need not
purchase  any items from the  catalog but be sure to take a look at
the incredible values inside.

Sincerely,




Rose Fields
President
```

STUDENT ASSIGNMENT 9: Editing the Secondary File

Instructions:　Perform the following tasks.

1. Retrieve the document SA5-7ADR that you created in Student Assignment 7.
2. Add the records shown in the figure to the secondary file.
3. Merge the document with SA5-7LTR, this time to a separate document. (Be sure to remove the codes in the primary file.)
4. Print only the new copies of the letter. They should appear as shown in the figures.
5. Save the document as SA5-9.

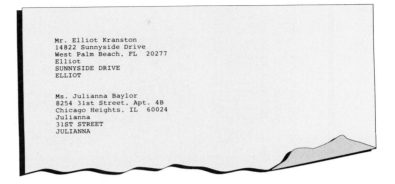

```
Mr. Elliot Kranston
14822 Sunnyside Drive
West Palm Beach, FL  20277
Elliot
SUNNYSIDE DRIVE
ELLIOT


Ms. Julianna Baylor
8254 31st Street, Apt. 4B
Chicago Heights, IL  60024
Julianna
31ST STREET
JULIANNA
```

```
May 2, 1994


Mr. Elliot Kranston
14822 Sunnyside Drive
West Palm Beach, FL  20277

Dear Elliot:

Thank you for your recent order from our spring catalog.  You'll be
happy to know that in addition to Greenway Gardens' values, we also
offer huge sweepstakes prizes  to  our valued customers.    When we
received your order,  we automatically  entered your name  into our
Garden Mania Sweepstakes.

We are happy to inform  you that your name was randomly  chosen for
entry  in  the  second  round  drawing.   Imagine  your  neighbors'
surprise if our prize delivery limousine drove down SUNNYSIDE DRIVE
and stopped at your house. Imagine your delight if we presented the
$1,000,000.00 check to YOU, ELLIOT!

To  ensure  your eligibility  for the second round drawing,  simply
return  the  order  form  in  the  enclosed catalog.   You need not
purchase  any  items from the catalog but be sure to take a look at
the incredible values inside.

Sincerely,



Rose Field
President
```

```
May 2, 1994


Ms. Julianna Baylor
8254 31st Street, Apt. 4B
Chicago Heights, IL  60024

Dear Julianna:

Thank you for your recent order from our spring catalog.  You'll be
happy to know that in addition to Greenway Gardens' values, we also
offer  huge  sweepstakes  prizes to our valued customers.    When we
received your order,  we automatically  entered  your  name into our
Garden Mania Sweepstakes.

We are  happy to inform you that  your name was randomly chosen for
entry  in  the  second  round  drawing.   Imagine  your  neighbors'
surprise if our prize delivery limousine drove down 31ST STREET and
stopped at your house. Imagine  your  delight  if  we presented the
$1,000,000.00 check to YOU, JULIANNA!

To  ensure  your  eligibility for the second round drawing,  simply
return  the  order  form  in  the  enclosed  catalog.  You need not
purchase  any items from the  catalog but be sure to take a look at
the incredible values inside.

Sincerely,



Rose Fields
President
```

STUDENT ASSIGNMENT 10: Merging Documents

Instructions: Create a merged document for the letter shown in the figure. The letter should be sent to the names and addresses listed. Notice that one recipient has a missing field in the address, and that the field for department is used twice in the body of the letter.

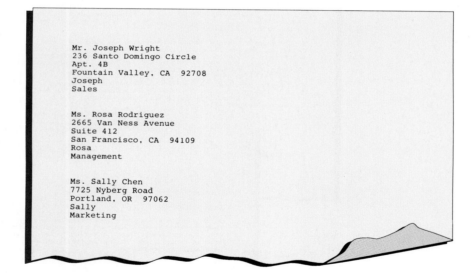

```
September 25, 1994

_____
_____
_____
_____

Dear _____ :

The new bonus plan for the _____ Department will become
effective _____.

If you have any questions, contact Suzanne Sheehy. All
_____ people are affected by this new plan.

Sincerely,


Rita Moeller
```

```
Mr. Joseph Wright
236 Santo Domingo Circle
Apt. 4B
Fountain Valley, CA  92708
Joseph
Sales


Ms. Rosa Rodriguez
2665 Van Ness Avenue
Suite 412
San Francisco, CA  94109
Rosa
Management


Ms. Sally Chen
7725 Nyberg Road
Portland, OR  97062
Sally
Marketing
```

The merged copies should appear as shown in the letters in the figures.

September 25, 1994

Mr. Joseph Wright
236 Santo Domingo Circle
Apt. 4B
Fountain Valley, CA 92708

Dear Joseph:

The new bonus plan for the Sales Department will become effective
January 31, 1995.

If you have any questions, contact Suzanne Sheehy. All Sales
people are affected by this new plan.

Sincerely,

Rita Moeller

September 25, 1994

Ms. Rosa Rodriguez
2665 Van Ness Avenue
Suite 412
San Francisco, CA 94109

Dear Rosa:

The new bonus plan for the Management Department will become
effective December 31, 1994.

If you have any questions, contact Suzanne Sheehy. All Management
people are affected by this new plan.

Sincerely,

Rita Moeller

September 25, 1994

Ms. Sally Chen
7725 Nyberg Road
Portland, OR 97062

Dear Sally:

The new bonus plan for the Marketing Department will become
effective January 15, 1995.

If you have any questions, contact Suzanne Sheehy. All Marketing
people are affected by this new plan.

Sincerely,

Rita Moeller

Macros*, Windows, Sorting, and the Thesaurus

OBJECTIVES

You will have mastered the material in this project when you can:

◆ Create a macro

◆ Insert a macro into a document

◆ Use the Window function

◆ Copy text between windows

◆ Use the Sort function

◆ Use the Thesaurus

By this point in the projects, you are already well-versed in the most basic functions of WordPerfect. In Project 6 you will use some of WordPerfect's more advanced features, such as macros, windows, sorting, and the Thesaurus, to create the documents shown in Figures 6-1 ⟨a⟩ and ⟨b⟩.

MACROS*

◆ A **macro** allows you to store on disk frequently used keystrokes. You can then use these stored keystrokes whenever you want by pressing a few keys. Notice that both Figures 6-1 ⟨a⟩ and ⟨b⟩ have a bold-faced, centered, underlined heading followed by TO:, FROM:, and RE: lines. Also, the name R & L Computer Supplies appears four times. Rather than retyping the memo heading and the vendor name, you can type them each once and then store the text in macros. When you want to use the heading or the name R&L Computer Supplies, you can simply use the macros and save yourself time and effort.

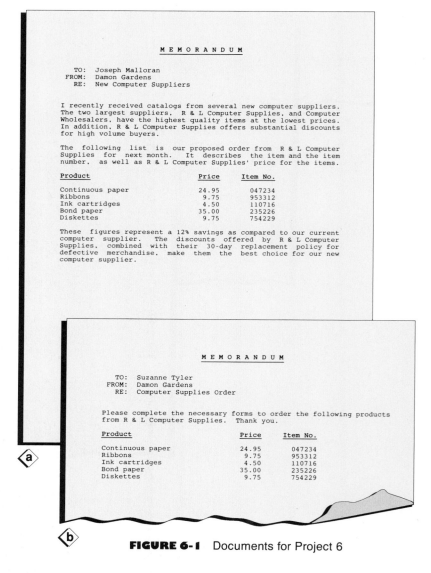

⟨a⟩
⟨b⟩

FIGURE 6-1 Documents for Project 6

✱ *Instructor's Note:* Check to be sure the Keyboard/Macro field matches the student default drive. This allows your students to save and execute macros. For more information, see the Instructor's materials or Instructor's data disk that accompany this book.

When you create a macro, you are in fact saving keystrokes on disk under a name you assign. The macro is saved as an entirely separate file with a .WPM extension and can include any amount of text you want. When you work on a document, you can enter the macro name, and the keystrokes stored in the .WPM file are inserted into the document just as if you had typed them from the keyboard.

Macro Names

Because macros are saved on disk, you must assign each macro a name. This macro name is the filename under which the keystrokes are stored on disk. You can name a macro two ways: with a single character preceded with the Alt key, such as Alt-m, or with a multiple-character name, such as memo. You can also invoke (insert) macros two ways, depending upon how you named them. Think of the macro name as the *keys* you press to retrieve the stored text, the macro. The macro itself is the stored *text* that can be retrieved into a document.

First, let's create a macro for the memo heading shown in Figures 6-1 ◁a▷ and ◁b▷. We'll use a multiple-character name for the macro, and then invoke the macro in the second part of this project, wherein we'll create the memo shown in Figure 6-1 ◁b▷.

Before you enter the text to be contained in the macro you are creating, you must first inform WordPerfect that the text you are entering should be stored in a macro. Press Alt-= to display the menu bar, then type T to display the Tools menu. Notice the "Macro" option (Figure 6-2). Type A, and the submenu in Figure 6-3 appears.

FIGURE 6-2
Tools menu

FIGURE 6-3
Macro menu

Because you need to define the macro, type D and the prompt in Figure 6-4 appears. This prompt is where you will enter the name under which the macro is stored. Macro names should be as descriptive as possible. They must have eight or fewer characters and must be unique; that is, you cannot have two separate macros stored under the same name, just like you cannot save two documents under the same filename.

Type memo for the macro name, then press the Enter key and the prompt in Figure 6-5 appears. This prompt allows you to enter a brief description of the macro so that you can identify its contents. This description will appear in the List Files screen whenever you use the Look function. Type memo heading to describe the macro's contents, then press Enter.

The "Macro Def" prompt begins blinking in the left corner of the status line (Figure 6-6). This message indicates to you that whatever text you now enter will become part of the stored text, the macro.

Creating a Macro

Now that you have named the macro, you need to enter the text that will be stored under the macro name. Enter the boldfaced, underlined, centered heading M E M O R A N D U M, making certain you turn off underlining and boldfacing when you have finished typing the heading. Press the Enter key three times to insert two blank lines. Set a right-aligned tab at .6 inches and a left tab at .8 inches for the heading of the memo. You can set tabs in a macro. The keystrokes that set the tabs become part of the macro and will be stored on disk along with the text. (If you need to, refer to Project 4 for instructions on setting tabs.) Set the tabs before you type the following: Tab TO: Tab ← Tab FROM: Tab ← Tab RE: Tab ← ← ←.

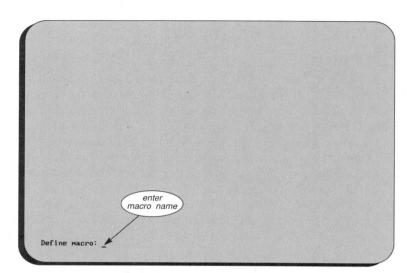

FIGURE 6-4 Naming a macro

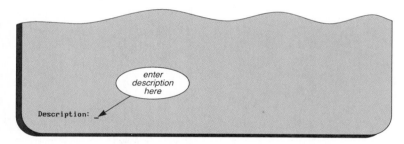

FIGURE 6-5 Entering a description

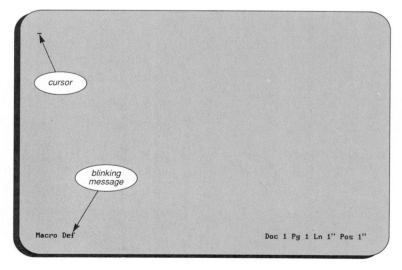

FIGURE 6-6 Entering macro text

Now that all the text you want to store has been typed, you must instruct WordPerfect that this is the end of the macro text. Press Alt-=, then type T for Tools, then A to display the Macro menu. When the Macro menu appears, type D, and the "Macro Def" message stops blinking, which means that text you enter will no longer be stored in the macro named memo.

Mouse Users: Select the "Macro" option from the Tools menu, then select "Define". Type the macro name memo and press Enter. Type the macro description memo heading and press Enter. Follow the previous directions for entering the macro text, then select "Macro Define" from the Tools menu to turn off the macro.

Entering Document Text

Let's next enter the text of Figure 6-1⟨a⟩. First, position the cursor after the tab following the word TO: in the memo heading. Fill in all of the information in the heading as shown in Figure 6-1⟨a⟩. When you have finished, your screen should look like Figure 6-7.

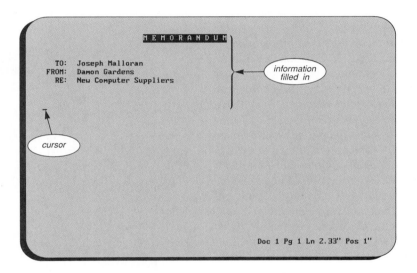

FIGURE 6-7
Completed memo heading

Continue entering the text of the memo: I recently received catalogs from several new computer suppliers. The two largest suppliers,. Press the Spacebar, and stop typing when you reach the first occurrence of the text R & L Computer Supplies (Figure 6-8).

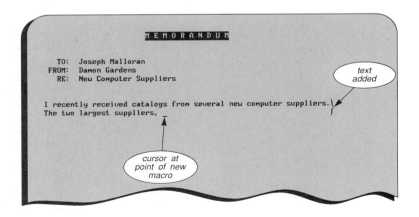

FIGURE 6-8
Entering text

Naming Macros with the Alt Key

Since the entire purpose of a macro is to save keystrokes, it's best to keep their names short. WordPerfect allows you to give a macro a one-character name preceded by the Alt key. For example, you could use the name Alt-s for a macro for the word Sincerely. Let's create a macro named Alt-r for the vendor R & L Computer Supplies.

The cursor should be at the first occurrence of the text that you want to store in the macro (Figure 6-8). This time, let's use the shortcut keys to define the macro. Press Ctrl-F10, and the "Define Macro:" prompt appears. Press Alt-r to name the macro, and the "Description:" prompt appears. Type R & L as the description, then press the Enter key. The blinking "Macro Def" message appears. Type R & L Computer Supplies. Now that the macro is complete, press Ctrl-F10 to end the macro. The text R & L Computer Supplies appeared on your screen as you typed the macro, and the macro text is also now stored on disk in a macro named Alt-r.

Invoking a Macro

As we have said before, once you create a macro, you can insert it anywhere within a document. The text stored in the macro will be inserted where the cursor is positioned, so be sure the cursor is positioned properly before you invoke a macro. Each time you want to insert the text for R & L Computer Supplies into the document, you will press Alt-r. Let's try this.

Be sure the cursor is still positioned directly after the R & L Computer Supplies text. Type a comma , , press the Spacebar, then type the following text of the document: and Computer Wholesalers, have the highest quality items at the lowest prices. In addition,. Press the Spacebar, and the cursor is positioned at the next occurrence of R & L Computer Supplies (Figure 6-9). With the cursor positioned where the macro text is to be inserted, press Alt-r, and the text R & L Computer Supplies is inserted into the document (Figure 6-10). In just two keystrokes — Alt and r — 23 keystrokes were inserted into the document.

Whenever you need to enter the same text at several places in a document you should create a macro. Macros can save a great deal of typing time, and because they are *stored* correctly spelled on disk, they can also help to reduce typing errors.

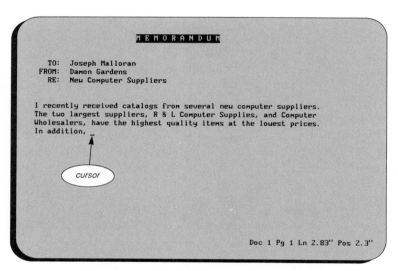

FIGURE 6-9   Cursor positioned for macro

FIGURE 6-10
Invoking a macro

Let's continue using the macro entry to complete the document. Press the Spacebar then type: offers substantial discounts for high volume buyers. ↵ ↵ The following list is our proposed order from. Press the Spacebar, and the cursor is at the next occurrence of R & L Computer Supplies (Figure 6-11). Again, invoke the macro by pressing Alt-r.

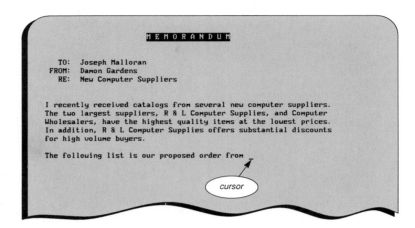

FIGURE 6-11
Inserting a macro

Press the Spacebar then type: for next month. It describes the item and the item number, as well as. Press the Spacebar, then press Alt-r. After the macro text has been inserted, type an apostrophe ', and press the Spacebar. Finish typing this paragraph: price for the items. ↵ ↵.

If you look at Figure 6-1⟨a⟩ again, you'll see that the cursor is now at the point of the document that contains a tabbed table. This table contains right tabs at 3.7 inches and 5 inches, so be sure you set tabs before you begin typing the table. The headings are both boldfaced and underlined, so press F6 and F8 to turn on these formats, making certain you turn them off after you enter the headings. Enter the following text for this table: Product Tab Price Tab Item No. ↵ ↵ Continuous paper Tab 24.95 Tab 047234 ↵ Ribbons Tab 9.75 Tab 953312 ↵ Ink cartridges Tab 4.50 Tab 110716 ↵ Bond paper Tab 35.00 Tab 235226 ↵ Diskettes Tab 9.75 Tab 754229 ↵ ↵.

Once you have entered the table, type: These figures represent a 12% savings as compared to our current computer supplier. The discounts offered by. Press the Spacebar, then press Alt-r to insert the macro. Type a comma ,, press the Spacebar to insert a blank space, then type: combined with their 30-day replacement policy for defective merchandise, make them the best choice for our new computer supplier. ↵.

Now that the document is complete, let's save it. Press F10, then type PROJ6A. Press Enter, and the document is saved on disk under the filename PROJ6A. There is no need to separately save the macro file. When you create a macro, it is automatically saved on the disk in the default drive; therefore, you do not need to save it again. Print the document by pressing Shift-F7, then typing 1. Your completed document should look like the one shown in Figure 6-1⟨a⟩. Exit the document but not WordPerfect as you have done before.

WINDOWS

Now we're ready to create the second document, which is also a memo (Figure 6-1⟨b⟩). Notice that the table contained in this document is identical to the table in PROJ6A. Rather than retyping the table and the memo heading, you can retrieve PROJ6A and copy the text into the current document with the Window function.

A **window** is the displayed portion of a document. The screen you are accustomed to seeing is actually a window. Your entire document may not always be visible in the window at one time. But the portion of the document that isn't visible still exists, even though it doesn't appear in the window. WordPerfect allows you to split the screen into two separate windows. Once these windows are opened, each window can contain a separate document.

Windows are especially useful when you need to check formatting or wording or when you need to move or copy text from one document to another. We will use the Window function to copy the table from PROJ6A to the new document you are creating. Your screen should be clear before you begin.

Switching Between Documents

Before you split the screen into two windows, you should learn about the two documents WordPerfect provides. Notice that "Doc 1" displays as the first item on the status line. WordPerfect also provides a second document (Doc 2) so that you can work on two documents at the same time, almost as if you had two computers.

Let's look at document 2. Press Shift-F3, and document 2 displays on the screen (Figure 6-12).

FIGURE 6-12
Switching to document 2

If you were now to create or retrieve a document in document 2, whatever editing, saving, or printing you did would not affect the other document, document 1. Press Shift-F3 again to switch back to document 1.

This feature is useful when you need to work on two separate documents at one time. When you split your screen into windows, however, *both* document 1 and document 2 are visible on the screen at the same time. There is no need to switch back and forth between separate documents to check formatting, wording, and so forth, because you can view both documents without switching.

 Mouse Users: Select the Edit menu, then select "Switch Document".

Opening a Window

Let's begin by opening a window. Press Alt-= to display the menu bar, then type E to display the Edit menu. Notice the "Window" option (Figure 6-13).

FIGURE 6-13
Edit menu

Type W and the prompt in Figure 6-14 appears. This prompt informs you that there are 24 lines in the current window.

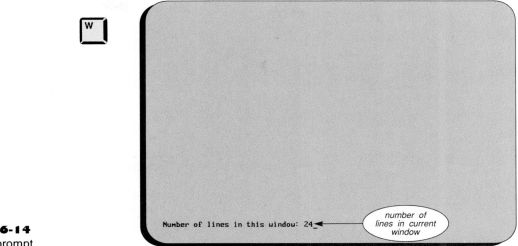

FIGURE 6-14
Window prompt

To divide the screen into two equal parts, type 12 and press Enter. Figure 6-15 shows the screen after the window has been split at line 12.

FIGURE 6-15
Screen split into two windows

The screen is divided into two portions by a bar similar to the one contained in the Reveal Codes screen. Notice that the triangular tab markers are pointing upward. This indicates to you that the cursor is currently positioned in the upper window. When you move the cursor to the lower portion, the arrows will point downward. Each window has its own status line. Notice that the status line in the upper window refers to Doc 1, and the lower window refers to Doc 2.

 Mouse Users: Select the "Window" option from the Edit menu. Type 12 and press Enter.

Moving Between Windows

The cursor can be active in only one window at a time. Right now, it is in the upper window, or Doc 1, since that was its position when the window was split. Press Shift-F3, and the cursor moves to the lower window, Doc 2 (Figure 6-16). Each time you need to move the cursor from one window to another, use Shift-F3.

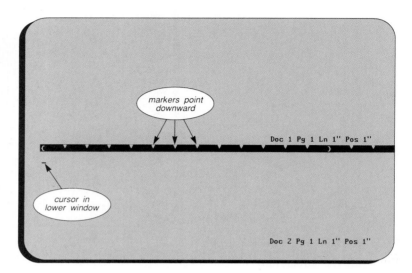

FIGURE 6-16
Moving the cursor between windows

 Mouse Users: Select the Edit menu, then select "Switch Document".

Press Shift-F3 again to move the cursor to the upper window, which should be clear and ready for a new document. Let's start the new document by invoking the macro called memo that you created earlier in this project. Because this macro name is not a single character preceded by the Alt key, you need to invoke it a bit differently. Press Alt-= to display the menu bar, then type T for Tools, then type A, and the Macro menu appears. This time, you will use the "Execute" option. Type X and the prompt in Figure 6-17 appears.

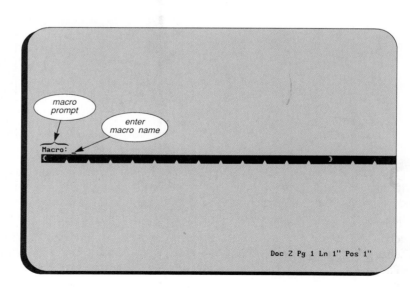

FIGURE 6-17
Invoking a macro

At the prompt, enter the macro name `memo`, then press the Enter key. The macro text is inserted into the document in the upper window (Figure 6-18).

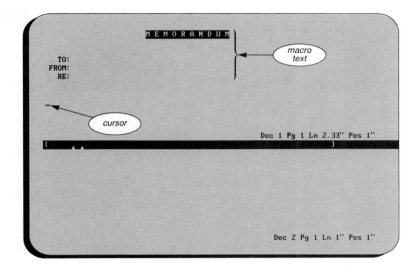

FIGURE 6-18
Macro inserted

Fill in the TO:, FROM:, and RE: lines as shown in Figure 6-1⟨b⟩, then position the cursor after the blank lines following the heading. When you have finished, your screen should look like Figure 6-19.

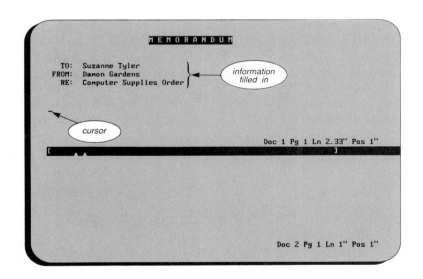

FIGURE 6-19
Completed memo heading

 Mouse Users: Select the "Macro" option from the Tools menu, then select the "Execute" option.

Now type: `Please complete the necessary forms to order the following products from.` Press the Spacebar, then press Alt-r to insert the macro text for R & L Computer Supplies. Type a period `.`, then press the Spacebar twice to insert two blank spaces. Now type: `Thank you.` Press the Enter key twice.

The next text is the tabbed paragraph you entered in PROJ6A. Rather than retyping it, you can copy it from the document in the lower window to the document you are currently creating. First you must retrieve the document PROJ6A into the lower window so that you can copy portions of it to the new document in the upper window. Press Shift-F3 to move the cursor to the lower window.

Retrieving Documents into Windows

Retrieving a document into a window is just like retrieving any WordPerfect document. With the cursor positioned in the lower window, press Shift-F10, then type PROJ6A. Press Enter and the document PROJ6A appears in the lower window (Figure 6-20). Once a document is retrieved into a window, you can perform any editing, revising, or functions in the usual way.

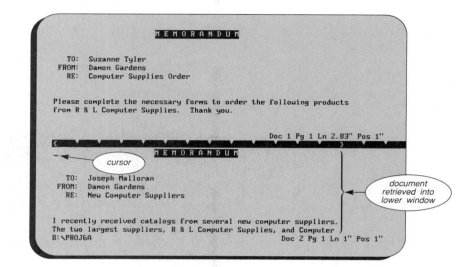

FIGURE 6-20
Retrieving a document into a window

Copying Text Between Windows

Recall that in Project 3 you learned how to move text from one location to another. In this case, however, the text does not actually need to be *moved* from one location to another. The text needs to remain in PROJ6A so that the document is intact. Rather, the text needs to be *copied* from one document to another. WordPerfect provides a way of doing this.

Move the cursor to the beginning of the line containing the tabbed headings. Check the Reveal Codes screen to be certain you are also including the [Tab Set:] code in the block. If you don't include the codes, the columns will use the default tabs and will not align correctly. Then press Alt-F4 to begin blocking; extend the block to include the entire table (Figure 6-21).

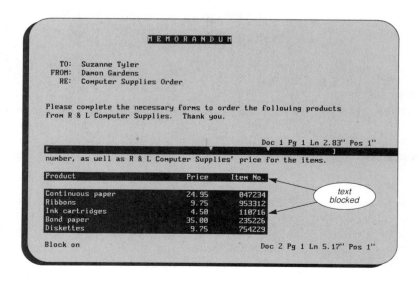

FIGURE 6-21
Text to be copied

Now press Ctrl-F4 to display the Move menu. Type 1 for "Block", and the menu in Figure 6-22 appears.

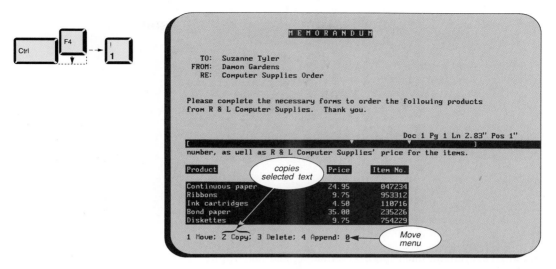

FIGURE 6-22 Copying text

Rather than using menu choice "1" to move the text, as you did in previous projects, type 2 for "Copy". The message "Move cursor; press Enter to retrieve." appears on the status line, just as it does during a move; however, the text remains intact in the document in the lower window (Figure 6-23).

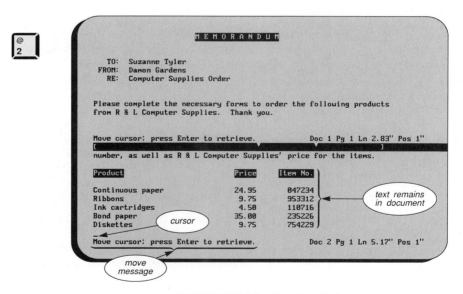

FIGURE 6-23 Copying text

From this point, copying the text is exactly like moving text. You need to move the cursor to the new location for the text, so press Shift-F3 to move the cursor to the upper window. With the cursor at the point for the table, press Enter. The table inserted into the new document is shown on the next page in Figure 6-24.

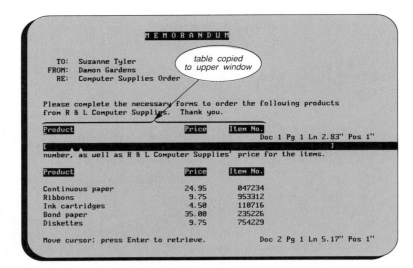

FIGURE 6-24
Text copied to upper window

Notice that the tabs remain intact, as do boldfacing and underlining. Everything — formatting, tabs, and so on — is copied from one window to the other. If the table does not align at the tabs as it does in the lower window, check the Reveal Codes screen to be sure that you copied the tab codes into the upper window.

 Mouse Users: Block the text to be copied. Select the "Copy" option from the Edit menu. Position the cursor at the point for the table, then press Enter to copy.

Exiting Documents in Windows

Now that you copied all the text you needed, you have no further use of the document in the lower window. Once you have finished with a document in a window, you should exit it. Press Shift-F3 to position the cursor in the lower window, then press F7 to exit. At the "Save Document? Yes(No)" prompt, type N since you did not alter the document. An "Exit doc 2? No(Yes)" message appears (Figure 6-25). Type Y, and WordPerfect exits the document and returns the cursor to the upper window.

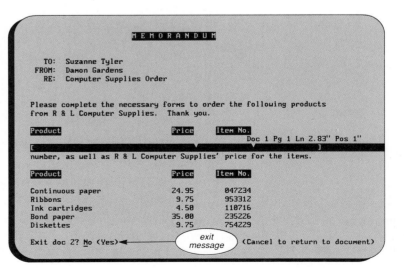

FIGURE 6-25
Exiting a document in a window

Closing Windows

Now that you have copied the text you need and exited the document in the lower window, you have no need to keep the screen split into two windows. When you no longer want to use a window, you must close it and return your screen to its normal, single-window display. The cursor should be positioned on the window you want to keep open, so be sure the cursor is positioned in the upper window. This time, let's use the shortcut keys to close the window. Press Ctrl-F3, and the menu in Figure 6-26 appears.

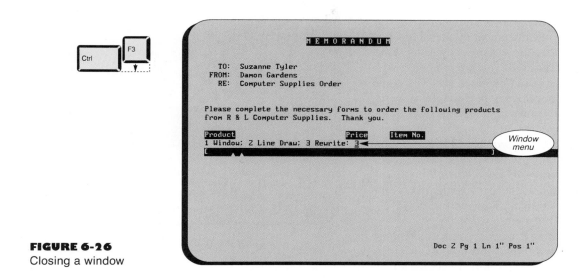

FIGURE 6-26
Closing a window

Now type 1 for "Window", and the message showing you the number of lines in the current window appears. This is the same message that appeared when you used the pull-down menu to open the window. Because you want to return the screen to its normal, 24-line display, type 24, then press Enter, and the screen returns to its normal, single-window display (Figure 6-27).

FIGURE 6-27
Single-window display

 Mouse Users: Select the "Window" option from the Edit menu. Type 24 and press Enter.

SORTING

WordPerfect contains a Sort function which enables you to sort a list of items alphabetically or numerically, in ascending or descending order. Sorting is extremely helpful, for example, if you want to arrange a list of names alphabetically or a list of addresses by state.

Items to be sorted *must be separated by tabs*. Before you sort, be certain that only one tab separates each column of the table. You should always save your document before you sort, so save your document by pressing F10, then typing PROJ6B, and pressing Enter. Once the document is saved, you are ready to sort.

Suppose it would be much easier to place the order in your document if the items were in alphabetical order. Let's use the Sort function to sort the items in the memo. Because you are going to sort *part* of a document, you should first block the items to be sorted. If you don't, WordPerfect will sort *all* the lines in the entire document, not just the list of items. Block the list of items in the tabbed table as shown in Figure 6-28.

Recall that in Project 5 you learned about fields and records when you used the Merge function. WordPerfect's Sort function also

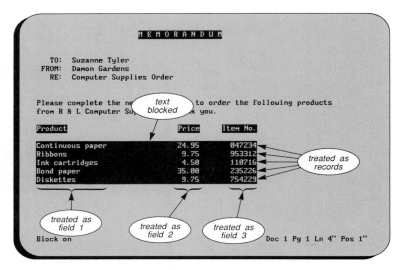

FIGURE 6-28 Blocking text to be sorted

uses the concepts of fields and records. It treats each horizontal line of the list as a record and each vertical column as a field (Figure 6-28). When sorting begins, each record will sort on the field you specify.

Once the list is blocked as shown in Figure 6-28, press Alt-= to display the menu bar, then type T for Tools, then S for the "Sort" option. The screen in Figure 6-29 appears, which shows the default settings for the "Sort" option.

FIGURE 6-29
Sort screen

Mouse Users: Select the "Sort" option from the Tools menu.

Keys, Fields, and Records

The manner in which WordPerfect sorts is determined by a key. A **key** is the item against which all other items are compared. For example, in the blocked list, if you wanted to sort by price, the key would become field 2. For now, however, let's use the default key setting, which means that items will sort on the first field, or field 1, the product name.

Type

The Type setting determines whether items are sorted alphanumerically (a combination of characters and numbers) or numerically (numbers only). If you use alphanumeric sorting, WordPerfect treats all text, including numbers, as characters rather than numeric values. The default is to sort alphanumerically, indicated by the "a" under "Typ" in Figure 6-29, and that is the setting we'll use.

Order

Notice on the Sort menu that menu choice "6" allows you to specify the "Order" in which items are sorted, either ascending (lowest to highest) or descending (highest to lowest). We will use the default, which is ascending order.

Performing a Sort

The Sort function is extremely powerful and allows you to perform quite intricate sorting. In this memo, however, you will perform a simple line sort using the defaults shown. Reading Figure 6-29 you can tell that the key is set to field 1; this means that all items will sort alphanumerically by the first field (product name) in ascending order.

Notice menu choice "1" on the Sort menu. The action is set to perform a sort, so you need only type 1 for the sort to begin. Type 1, and sorting begins. A "Records Transferred" message appears on your screen as the items are sorted. After the sort is complete, the items appear listed in the order you specified (Figure 6-30).

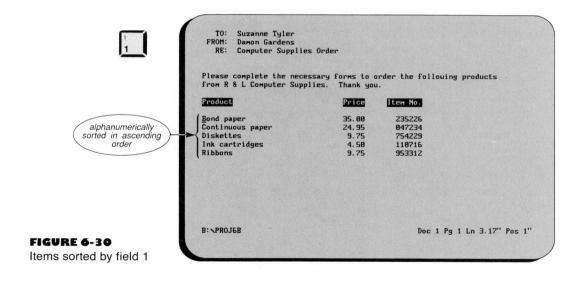

FIGURE 6-30
Items sorted by field 1

 Mouse Users: Select the "Perform Action" option from the Sort menu.

Changing the Key

Suppose now that you decided that the order would be easier to place if the items were sorted by item number rather than product name. Let's change the key so that the items will sort by item number. This time, let's use the shortcut keys to access the Sort menu.

Block the list as you did before, then press Ctrl-F9 to display the Sort menu. Because you want to change the key, type 3 and the cursor moves into the first key field. Even though you are sorting a list of numbers, you do not need to change the type to numeric. Because all the item numbers to be sorted have the same number of digits, WordPerfect is able to treat them as text and they will sort correctly. Press the Right Arrow key to move the cursor into the Field setting. Because you want the items to sort by field 3, the item number field, type 3 (Figure 6-31).

FIGURE 6-31
Changing the key

You have now instructed WordPerfect to sort the list by item number, so press F7 to exit the key field. Type 1 to perform the sort, and the items sort by item number (Figure 6-32).

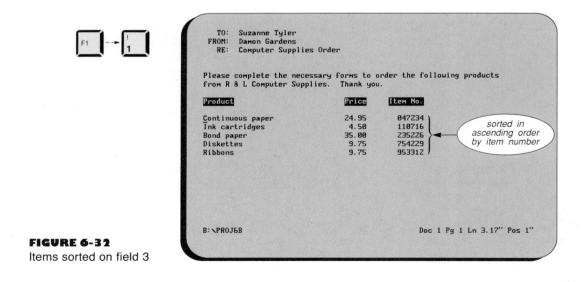

FIGURE 6-32
Items sorted on field 3

Mouse Users: Block the text, then select the "Sort" option from the Tools menu. Select the "Keys" option, then press the Right Arrow key. Type 3 and press the right mouse button. Select the "Perform Action" option to begin the sort.

THE THESAURUS

A **thesaurus** is a collection of words and their synonyms, verbs, and antonyms. WordPerfect's Thesaurus allows you to look up words to help you find just the right words for your documents. It is a helpful and powerful tool that will make your writing more effective. The Thesaurus is extremely useful if you can't think of a particular word, or to help you avoid redundancy and add variety to your writing. The Thesaurus enables you to look up words in two different ways. You can invoke the Thesaurus with the cursor positioned in the word you want to look up, or you can type the word you want to check directly in the Thesaurus screen.

Invoking the Thesaurus

Let's use the Thesaurus to look up a word in PROJ6B. First, position the cursor on the word products as shown in Figure 6-33. You do not need to block the entire word; the cursor can be positioned on any character of the word you want to check. The Thesaurus will display synonyms for the word *in which* the cursor is positioned. If you are using WordPerfect on a two-disk system, replace your data disk with the Thesaurus disk at this time.

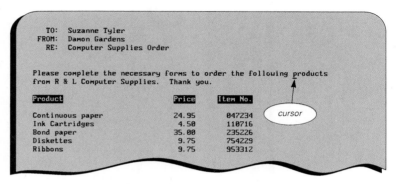

FIGURE 6-33 Positioning the cursor

To start the Thesaurus, press Alt-= to display the menu bar, then type T for Tools. Now type H to start the Thesaurus. Notice that the shortcut keys are Alt-F1. Figure 6-34 shows how your screen appears after invoking the Thesaurus. The portion of the document containing the word being checked remains displayed in the top of the screen. The bottom portion of the screen displays the Thesaurus window, which contains a list of alternate word choices for the word in the document, and the Thesaurus menu. The choices are categorized by nouns, verbs, adjectives, and antonyms (opposites).

FIGURE 6-34
Thesaurus screen

 Mouse Users: Select the "Thesaurus" option from the Tools menu.

Looking Up Alternate Words

Suppose that none of the words listed are suitable. Let's look up more choices. Notice the bullets (dots) that appear to the left of some of the words in the Thesaurus window. These bullets indicate that the words to the right may be further broken down into more choices. These words are called **headwords**. Each word listed has a letter to the left of it. When you want to break down one of the headwords shown, type the letter that appears to its left. Because it is close in meaning to the word we are checking, let's look up the word merchandise which is letter F. Type F and a list of alternate words for merchandise appears (Figure 6-35).

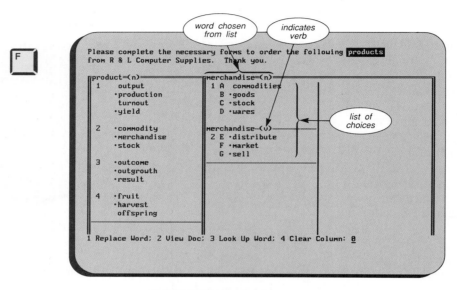

FIGURE 6-35 Looking up synonyms

Let's look up the word wares. Type D and the list of words for wares appears (Figure 6-36).

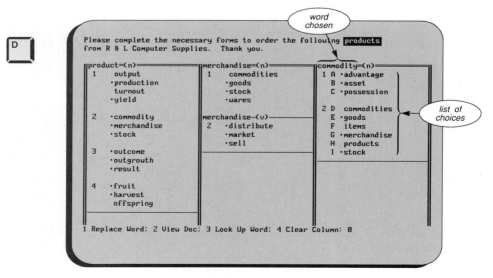

FIGURE 6-36 Looking up additional words

Replacing Words

Suppose we look down the list and we decide that the word items seems appropriate; let's use it to replace the word products. Notice menu choice "1" on the menu. Because you want to replace a word, type 1 and the prompt in Figure 6-37 appears.

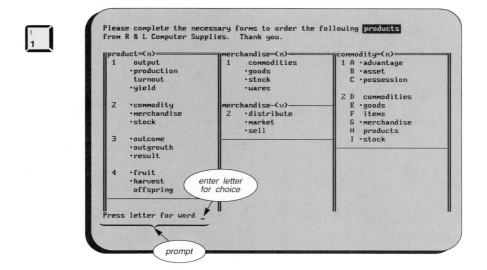

FIGURE 6-37
Replacing a word

Now you must choose the letter of the word to replace the word products in your document. Type F and the word items replaces the word products in the document (Figure 6-38), and you return to the text window. Once you type a letter to replace the word, WordPerfect automatically exits the Thesaurus.

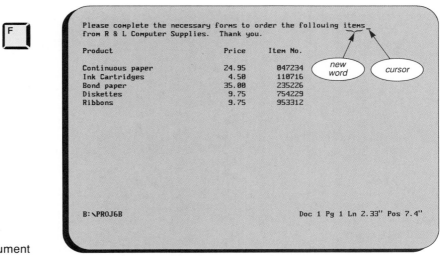

FIGURE 6-38
Word replaced in document

Words replaced from the Thesaurus menu will conform to the capitalization and formatting of the original word in the document. For instance, if the original word had been underlined, the word from the Thesaurus would be inserted as being underlined also.

 Mouse Users: Select the "Replace Word" option from the Thesaurus menu, then type F to replace the word.

Entering Words from the Keyboard

You can also directly type words for the Thesaurus to look up. Let's try this, and this time let's use the shortcut keys to start the Thesaurus. Press Alt-F1, and the Thesaurus menu appears. Notice that menu choice "3" allows you to look up a word. Type 3 and the prompt in Figure 6-39 appears.

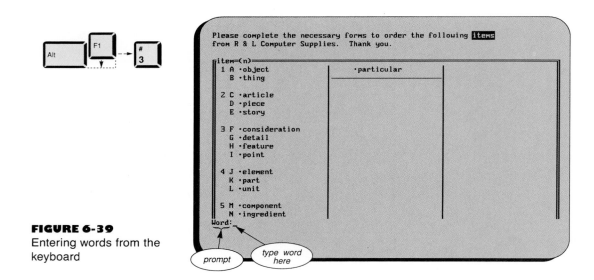

FIGURE 6-39
Entering words from the keyboard

Type productive and press Enter, and a list of alternate choices for the word productive appears on the Thesaurus screen (Figure 6-40). Press the F1 key to exit the Thesaurus without making any further changes to the document.

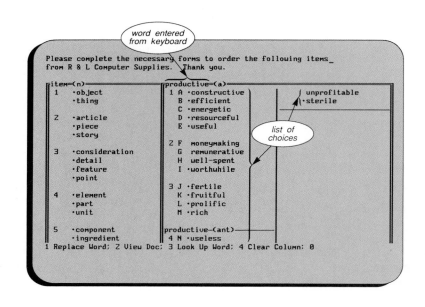

FIGURE 6-40
List of word choices

You can use this method of looking up words at any time while you are in the Thesaurus window. If you are ever in the Thesaurus and decide not to make any changes, press the F1 or the F7 key to exit the Thesaurus and return to the document. If you are using WordPerfect on a two-disk system, you should now replace the Thesaurus disk with your data disk; you should always remove the Thesaurus disk when you've finished using the Thesaurus.

SAVING AND PRINTING A DOCUMENT

◆ Now that the document is complete, save it under the filename PROJ6B, and then print it. Your final document should look like Figure 6-41. Exit WordPerfect as you have done before by pressing F7.

```
                        M E M O R A N D U M

        TO:  Suzanne Tyler
      FROM:  Damon Gardens
        RE:  Computer Supplies Order


      Please complete the necessary forms to order the following items
      from R & L Computer Supplies.  Thank you.

      Product                         Price      Item No.

      Continuous paper                24.95      047234
      Ink cartridges                   4.50      110716
      Bond paper                      35.00      235226
      Diskettes                        9.75      754229
      Ribbons                          9.75      953312
```

FIGURE 6-41 Completed document

If you receive a "Exit doc 2? No(Yes)" message, answer Y. WordPerfect will display this message if you did not exit the document in the lower window (PROJ6A) before closing the window. Be sure to remove your disks, if necessary.

PROJECT SUMMARY

In Project 6 you learned how to create and insert macros into a document. You also learned how to split the text screen into windows, and how to copy text from one document to another using windows. Finally, you sorted a list of items, and then used two ways in WordPerfect's Thesaurus to look up and replace a word in a document. All the activities that you learned for this project are summarized in the Quick Reference following Project 6. The following is a summary of the keystroke sequence we used in Project 6.

SUMMARY OF KEYSTROKES — PROJECT 6

STEPS	KEY(S) PRESSED	RESULTS
1	wp ← [At C> prompt or as directed by instructor]	Loads WordPerfect.
2	[Alt-=] T A D	Displays Macro Define menu.
3	memo ←	Enters macro name.
4	memo heading ←	Enters macro description.
5	[Shift-F6] [F6] [F8] MEMORANDUM [F6] [F8] ← ← ←	Enters centered, boldfaced, underlined heading into macro.
6	[Shift-F8] 1 8 [Ctrl-End] 0.6← R 0.8← [F7] [F7]	Sets tabs in macro.
7	[Tab] TO: [Tab] ← [Tab] FROM: [Tab] ← [Tab] RE: [Tab] ← ← ←	Enters macro text.
8	[Alt-=] T A D	Ends macro definition.
9	I recently received catalogs from several new computer suppliers. The two largest suppliers, [Spacebar]	Enters text up to point of next macro text.
10	[Ctrl-F10] [Alt-r] R & L←R & L Computer Supplies [Ctrl-F10]	Defines new macro.
11	, and Computer Wholesalers, have the highest quality items at the lowest prices. In addition, [Spacebar]	Enters text.
12	[Alt-r]	Enters macro text into document.
13	[Spacebar] offers substantial discounts for high volume buyers. ← ← The following list is our proposed order from [Spacebar]	Enters text.
14	[Alt-r]	Enters macro text into document.
15	[Spacebar] for next month. It describes the item and the item number, as well as [Spacebar]	Enters text.
16	[Alt-r]	Enters macro text into document.
17	' price for the item. ← ←	Enters text.
18	[Shift-F8] 1 8 [Ctrl-End] 3.7←R 5←R [F7] [F7]	Sets tabs for table.
19	[F6] [F8] Product [Tab] Price [Tab] Item No. [F6] [F8] ← ←	Enters boldfaced, underlined headings into table.

SUMMARY OF KEYSTROKES — PROJECT 6 (continued)

STEPS	KEY(S) PRESSED	RESULTS
20	Continuous paper `Tab` 24.95 `Tab` 047234← Ribbons `Tab` 9.75 `Tab` 953312←Ink cartridges `Tab` 4.50 `Tab` 110716←Bond paper `Tab` 35.00 `Tab` 235226←Diskettes `Tab` 9.75 `Tab` 754229← ←	Enters text for table.
21	These figures represent a 12% savings as compared to our current computer supplier. The discounts offered by `Spacebar`	Enters text.
22	`Alt-r`	Enters macro text into document.
23	, combined with their 30-day replacement policy for defective merchandise, make them the best choice for our new computer supplier. ←	Enters text.
24	`F10` PROJ6A ←	Saves document under filename PROJ6A.
25	`Shift-F7` 1	Prints document.
26	`F7` N N	Exits document.
27	`Shift-F3` `Shift-F3`	Moves cursor to Doc 2, then back to Doc 1.
28	`Alt-=` E W	Displays Window prompt.
29	12←	Splits window at line 12.
30	`Shift-F3`	Moves cursor to lower window.
31	`Shift-F3`	Moves cursor to upper window.
32	`Alt-=` T A X memo ←	Inserts macro into document.
33	↑ [Press 5 times] → [Press 5 times] Suzanne Tyler↓Damon Gardens↓Computer Supplies Order↓↓↓	Enters text into memo heading and positions cursor for new text.
34	Please complete the necessary forms to order the following products from `Spacebar`	Enters text.
35	`Alt-r`	Inserts macro into document.
36	. Thank you. ← ←	Enters text.
37	`Shift-F3`	Moves cursor to lower window.
38	`Shift-F10` PROJ6A ←	Retrieves document into lower window.
39	`Home-↓` `Home-↓` `Home` `Home` `Home-←` `Alt-F4` ↓ [Press 7 times]	Positions cursor and blocks text to be copied.
40	`Ctrl-F4` 1 2	Displays "Copy" option.
41	`Shift-F3`	Moves cursor to upper window.
42	←	Copies text.
43	`Shift-F3` `F7` N Y	Moves cursor to window 2 and exits document without saving changes.
44	`Ctrl-F3` 1 24←	Closes window and returns screen to normal display.
45	`F10` PROJ6B ←	Saves document under filename PROJ6B.

(continued)

SUMMARY OF KEYSTROKES — PROJECT 6 (continued)

STEPS	KEY(S) PRESSED	RESULTS
46	↓↓ `Alt-F4` ↓ [Press 5 times]	Positions cursor and blocks text to be sorted.
47	`Alt-=` T S	Displays Sort screen.
48	1	Sorts blocked list.
49	`Alt-F4` ↓ [Press 5 times]	Blocks text to be sorted.
50	`Ctrl-F9`	Displays Sort screen.
51	3 → 3 `F7` 1	Sorts list on field 3.
52	↑ [Press 10 times] `End` `Ctrl-←`	Positions cursor in word to be looked up.
53	`Alt-=` T H	Invokes Thesaurus.
54	F	Displays word choices for stock.
55	D	Displays word choices for wares.
56	1 F	Replaces selected word in document with items from Thesaurus.
57	`Alt-F1`	Invokes Thesaurus.
58	3 productive ←	Displays word choices for typed word.
59	`F1`	Exits Thesaurus without making changes to document.
60	`F10` PROJ6B ←	Saves document under filename PROJ6B.
61	`Shift-F7` 1	Prints document.
62	`F7` N Y	Exits WordPerfect and returns to DOS.

The following list summarizes the material covered in Project 6.

1. A **macro** allows you to store on disk frequently used text under a short name.
2. Macros can contain as many characters as you want. Macro entries are the stored *text* that can be retrieved into a document.
3. Macros can be named two ways: with a single character preceded by the Alt key, or with a multiple-character name. Macro names may contain up to eight characters, and must be unique. Think of macro names as the *keys* that are pressed to retrieve stored text into a document.
4. Macros are invoked (inserted) two ways, depending upon how they're named.
5. WordPerfect automatically assigns the extension .WPM to all macro files.
6. A **window** is the displayed portion of a document. WordPerfect allows you to split the screen into two windows. Each window can contain a separate document, but the cursor can be active in only one window at a time.
7. WordPerfect provides you with two separate documents — Doc 1 and Doc 2 — so that you can work on two documents at one time.
8. Pressing Shift-F3 moves the cursor between windows.
9. The Move menu allows you to copy text without deleting it.
10. The Sort function allows you to sort alphanumerically or numerically, in ascending or descending order.
11. The field on which items are sorted is determined by a key. A **key** is the item against which all other items in the field are compared.
12. A **thesaurus** is a collection of words and their nouns, verbs, adjectives, and antonyms. WordPerfect's Thesaurus, accessed through the Tools menu or by pressing Alt-F1, allows you to look up and replace selected words in a document.
13. A **headword** in the Thesaurus is designated by a bullet (dot). Only headwords may be further broken down in the Thesaurus screen.
14. You can exit the Thesaurus without replacing any words by pressing F1 or F7.

STUDENT ASSIGNMENTS

STUDENT ASSIGNMENT 1: True/False

Instructions: Circle T if the statement is true and F if the statement is false.

T F   1. WordPerfect's Window function allows you to split the screen into three separate windows.
T F   2. A macro stores frequently used keystrokes on disk under a short name.
T F   3. Macro names must be preceded by the Alt key.
T F   4. The "Window" option is contained in the Tools menu.
T F   5. Alt-pr is a valid macro name.
T F   6. To move the cursor between windows, press Shift-F3.
T F   7. The Thesaurus can be accessed by pressing Alt- = , then typing T, then T again.
T F   8. The cursor can be active in only one window at a time.
T F   9. Macros are inserted into a document by typing the macro name, then pressing Shift-F3.

STUDENT ASSIGNMENT 2: Multiple Choice

Instructions: Circle the correct response.

1. Macro text cannot exceed _____ characters.
    a. 4
    b. 8
    c. 12
    d. none of the above
2. The shortcut key(s) for defining a macro is (are) _____.
    a. F1
    b. Alt-F10
    c. Ctrl-F10
    d. none of the above
3. Macro names can contain up to _____ characters.
    a. 2
    b. 8
    c. 12
    d. as many as desired; there is no limit
4. Pressing Alt-F1 causes WordPerfect to _____.
    a. exit without saving a document
    b. close the window containing the cursor
    c. start the Thesaurus
    d. none of the above
5. To exit from the Thesaurus without replacing any words, press _____.
    a. Alt-F10
    b. Ctrl-F10
    c. F1
    d. none of the above
6. The "Sort" option is contained in the _____ menu.
    a. Edit
    b. Tools
    c. Macro
    d. none of the above

Student Assignment 2 (continued)

7. The displayed portion of a document is called a _____.
   a. Thesaurus
   b. macro
   c. window
   d. key
8. The "Copy" option is contained in the _____ menu.
   a. Move
   b. Thesaurus
   c. Tools
   d. none of the above
9. The default type for Sort is _____.
   a. ascending
   b. descending
   c. alphanumeric
   d. numeric

STUDENT ASSIGNMENT 3: Matching

Instructions: Put the appropriate number next to the words in the second column.

1. Alt-= , T, A, X _____ Copies blocked text
2. Ctrl-F4, 1, 2 _____ Opens or closes window
3. Shift-F3 _____ Starts Thesaurus
4. Alt-= , T, A, D _____ Moves cursor between windows
5. Alt-= , E, W _____ Defines macro
6. Alt-F1 _____ Invokes macro
7. Alt-= , T, S _____ Displays Sort menu

STUDENT ASSIGNMENT 4: Fill in the Blanks

Instructions: Fill in the blanks in the following sentences.

1. The manner in which a field is sorted is determined by the _____.
2. The shortcut keys for the Window function are _____.
3. The _____ is the key combination under which macro text is stored.
4. Pressing _____ moves the cursor between windows.
5. WordPerfect automatically assigns macro files the extension _____.
6. A _____ allows you to store frequently used text under a short name.
7. The _____ is a collection of words and their nouns, verbs, adjectives, and antonyms.
8. Pressing _____ moves the cursor between Doc 1 and Doc 2.

STUDENT ASSIGNMENT 5: Using Windows

Instructions: This screen shows a retrieved document. The screen needs to be split into two windows so that another document can be retrieved into window 2. Explain the steps to accomplish this.

```
July 11, 1994

Ms. Sarah Goetz
982 Tulip Tree Lane
West Harbor, MI  48712

Dear Ms. Goetz:

Thank you for your recent inquiry about our establishment, Biff's
Gym.  I have enclosed a brochure outlining the various fitness
programs we have available.  We at Biff's Gym recommend that you
schedule an appointment with one of our trained fitness
consultants, who will use his or her expertise to recommend the type of
training program that is best for your needs.

Our hours are listed on the brochure, and we look forward to
hearing from you very soon.  Thank you for your interest in Biff's
Gym.

Sincerely,

                                        Doc 1 Pg 1 Ln 1" Pos 1"
```

Steps:_____

_____

_____

STUDENT ASSIGNMENT 6: Understanding Macros

Instructions: The document shown in the figure needs a macro named bg inserted at the point shown. Explain the steps to accomplish this.

```
July 16, 1994

Mr. Roland Irvin
3455 Cypress Point, Apt. 2A
Harborpoint, MI  48724

Dear Mr. Irvin:

Thank you for your recent inquiry about our establishment, _

                                        Doc 1 Pg 1 Ln 2.5" Pos 6.9"
```

Steps:_____

_____

_____

STUDENT ASSIGNMENT 7: Using the Thesaurus

Instructions: Type this sentence.

I think I'll take the long way home.

Use the Thesaurus to change the word think to suppose. When you have replaced the word think, use the Thesaurus to change the word way to route. Your sentence should finally read:

I suppose I'll take the long route home.

STUDENT ASSIGNMENT 8: Understanding the Sort Function

Instructions: Perform the following tasks.

1. Create and then print the document shown in the figure, making certain you use only one tab stop to separate each column.

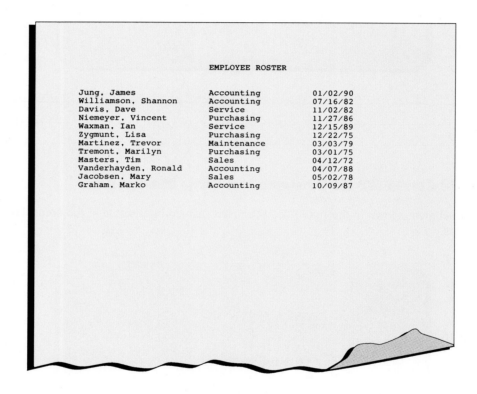

EMPLOYEE ROSTER

Jung, James	Accounting	01/02/90
Williamson, Shannon	Accounting	07/16/82
Davis, Dave	Service	11/02/82
Niemeyer, Vincent	Purchasing	11/27/86
Waxman, Ian	Service	12/15/89
Zygmunt, Lisa	Purchasing	12/22/75
Martinez, Trevor	Maintenance	03/03/79
Tremont, Marilyn	Purchasing	03/01/75
Masters, Tim	Sales	04/12/72
Vanderhayden, Ronald	Accounting	04/07/88
Jacobsen, Mary	Sales	05/02/78
Graham, Marko	Accounting	10/09/87

2. Sort the list of items alphabetically by Department name. Print the document; it should now appear as shown in the figure.

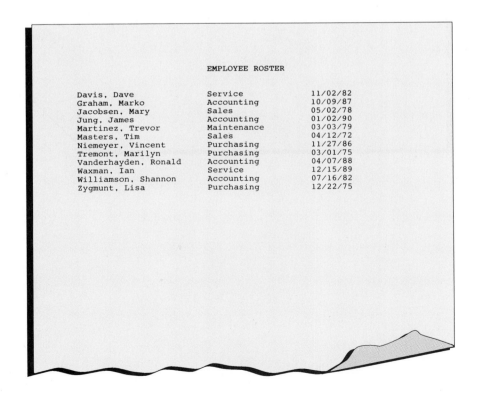

```
                         EMPLOYEE ROSTER


      Jung, James            Accounting           01/02/90
      Vanderhayden, Ronald   Accounting           04/07/88
      Graham, Marko          Accounting           10/09/87
      Williamson, Shannon    Accounting           07/16/82
      Martinez, Trevor       Maintenance          03/03/79
      Niemeyer, Vincent      Purchasing           11/27/86
      Tremont, Marilyn       Purchasing           03/01/75
      Zygmunt, Lisa          Purchasing           12/22/75
      Jacobsen, Mary         Sales                05/02/78
      Masters, Tim           Sales                04/12/72
      Waxman, Ian            Service              12/15/89
      Davis, Dave            Service              11/02/82
```

3. Sort the list alphabetically by employee last name. Print the document and save it under the filename SA6-8. The document should appear as shown in the figure.

```
                         EMPLOYEE ROSTER


      Davis, Dave            Service              11/02/82
      Graham, Marko          Accounting           10/09/87
      Jacobsen, Mary         Sales                05/02/78
      Jung, James            Accounting           01/02/90
      Martinez, Trevor       Maintenance          03/03/79
      Masters, Tim           Sales                04/12/72
      Niemeyer, Vincent      Purchasing           11/27/86
      Tremont, Marilyn       Purchasing           03/01/75
      Vanderhayden, Ronald   Accounting           04/07/88
      Waxman, Ian            Service              12/15/89
      Williamson, Shannon    Accounting           07/16/82
      Zygmunt, Lisa          Purchasing           12/22/75
```

STUDENT ASSIGNMENT 9: Creating Macros

Instructions: Create the document shown in the figure. The name Biff's Gym and Physical Fitness Emporium appears three times in this document. Create a macro named Alt-b, and insert it at the appropriate points in the document. When you have finished with the document, save it under the filename SA6-9, then print it.

```
July 11, 1994

Ms. Sarah Goetz
982 Tulip Tree Lane
West Harbor, MI  48712

Dear Ms. Goetz:

Thank you for your recent inquiry about our establishment, Biff's
Gym and Physical Fitness Emporium.  I have  enclosed a brochure
outlining  the various  fitness programs we have available.  We at
Biff's  Gym and Physical  Fitness  Emporium  recommend  that  you
schedule   an   appointment  with  one  of  our  trained  fitness
consultants,  who will  use his  or her expertise to recommend the
type of training program that is best for your needs.

Our  hours are  listed on  the brochure,  and  we  look forward to
hearing from you very soon.  Thank you for your interest in Biff's
Gym and Physical Fitness Emporium.

Sincerely,



Bruce "Biff" Lambert
President
Biff's Gym and Physical Fitness Emporium
```

For each of the projects, we have provided the fundamental WordPerfect activities in an easy-to-use quick reference format. This convenient reference tool is divided into four parts—activity, procedure, shortcut keys, and description. All of the activities that you learn in each project are covered in the Quick Reference for that project. The numbers in parentheses that follow each activity refer to the page on which the activity is first discussed in the text. In addition, we have included the shortcut keys for each activity.

You can use these Quick References as study aids or to quickly recall how you complete an activity. The Quick Reference is a valuable and time-saving tool, and we encourage you to use it frequently.

QUICK REFERENCE — PROJECT 1

ACTIVITY	PROCEDURE	SHORTCUT KEYS	DESCRIPTION
START (LOAD) (WP6)	Type wp Press ↵		Load the WordPerfect program into main memory.
CHANGE DRIVE/DIRECTORY (WP7)	Press [Alt-=] Type F Type F Press [=] Type a: Press ↵	[F5]	Change drive to A (or B).
DELETE (WP11)	Press [Backspace]		Remove incorrect characters or spaces to the left of the cursor. Character or space directly under the cursor remains intact.
SAVE (WP15)	Press [Alt-=] Type F Type S Enter filename Press ↵	[F10]	Enter filename at save prompt.
PRINT (WP18)	Press [Alt-=] Type F Type P Type 1	[Shift-F7] 1	Print entire (full) document on the printer.
EXIT (WP19)	Press [Alt-=] Type F Type X	[F7]	Type Y at the "Exit WP? No(Yes)" prompt to exit the WordPerfect program and return to DOS.
RETRIEVE (WP20)	Press [Alt-=] Type F Type R Enter filename Press ↵	[Shift-F10]	Enter filename at the "Document to be retrieved:" prompt.
REVEAL CODES (WP26)	Press [Alt-=] Type E Type R	[Alt-F3]	Repeat process to restore screen to its normal display.

QUICK REFERENCE — PROJECT 2

ACTIVITY	PROCEDURE	SHORTCUT KEYS	DESCRIPTION
LIST FILES (WP39)	Press `Alt-=` Type F Type F	`F5`	List files on disk. Retrieve file by highlighting, then typing 1.
REWRITE SCREEN (WP43)	Press ↓		Adjust text on screen to compensate for added or deleted text.
DELETE (WP47)	Press `Delete`		Delete character directly under the cursor a character at a time to the right.
TYPEOVER (WP47)	Press `Insert`		Character under the cursor is replaced by new character typed. Press Insert again to toggle off.
BLOCK (WP50)	Press `Alt-=` Type E Type B	`Alt-F4`	Move the cursor through the text to extend the block.
RESTORE (UNDELETE) (WP53)	Press `F1` Type 1		Restore deleted text at the cursor position. The surrounding text will adjust to accommodate restored text.
BOLDFACE (WP57)	Press `Alt-=` Type O Type A Type B	`F6`	Type text to be boldfaced. Repeat process to toggle off boldfacing.
UNDERLINE (WP59)	Press `Alt-=` Type O Type A Type U	`F8`	Type text to be underlined. Repeat process to toggle off underlining.
CENTER (WP60)	Press `Alt-=` Type L Type A Type C	`Shift-F6`	Type text to be centered.
DOUBLE-SPACE (WP64)	Press `Alt-=` Type L Type L Type 6 Type 2 Press `F7`	`Shift-F8` 1	Display Line Format menu, then set line spacing to 2. Press F7 to exit the menu and return to text window.
HARD PAGE BREAK (WP66)	Press `Ctrl-↵`		Position the cursor on the first character to print on the next page. Press Ctrl-Enter to insert a page break. Soft page break will automatically reposition.
SPELL PROGRAM (WP67)	Press `Alt-=` Type T Type S Type E Type 3	`Ctrl-F2` 3	Correct document by using the Spell menu.

QUICK REFERENCE — PROJECT 3

ACTIVITY	PROCEDURE	SHORTCUT KEYS	DESCRIPTION
CAPS LOCK (WP85)	Press `Caps Lock`		Press to toggle capitalization on or off.
INDENT LEFT MARGIN (WP86)	Press `Alt-=` Type L Type A Type I	`F4`	Type indented paragraph. Press Enter to return the cursor to the true left margin.
HANGING INDENT (WP88)	Press `F4` Press `Shift-Tab`		Press F4 to set temporary left margin. Press Shift-Tab to move the cursor back one tab stop. Enter text, then press Tab to align the remaining text with the temporary left margin. Type the hanging indent, then press Enter to return the cursor to the true left margin.
CASE CONVERSION (WP90)	Block text Press `Alt-=` Type E Type V Type U or L	`Shift-F3`	Select from the menu to convert blocked text to all uppercase or all lowercase characters.
MOVE (WP92)	Position cursor Press `Alt-=` Type L Type E Type P Type 1 Position cursor Press ↵	`Ctrl-F4`	Position the cursor within the portion of text to be moved. Select from the menu to determine the portion of text to be moved. Position the cursor at new location and press Enter.
SEARCH (WP97)	Press `Alt-=` Type S Type F	`F2` [or `Shift-F2` for reverse search]	Enter search text at search prompt, then press F2 to begin the search.
REPLACE (WP100)	Press `Alt-=` Type S Type R	`Alt-F2`	Enter replacement text at the replace prompt, and type Y at the confirm prompt. Press F2 to begin replacing. Type a Y each time you want to replace text.

QUICK REFERENCE — PROJECT 4

ACTIVITY	PROCEDURE	SHORTCUT KEYS	DESCRIPTION
TOP/BOTTOM MARGINS (WP114)	Press Alt-= Type L Type P Type 5	Shift-F8 2	Access the Page Format menu. Move the cursor into the Top/Bottom margin setting. Type margin setting and press the Enter key. Press F7 to exit the menu and return to text window.
PAGE NUMBERING (WP115)	Press Alt-= Type L Type P Type 6 Type 4	Shift-F8 2 6 4	Access the Page Numbering menu. Select placement for page numbering, then press F7 to exit the menu and return to text window.
LEFT/RIGHT MARGINS (WP117)	Press Alt-= Type L Type L Type 7	Shift-F8 1 7	Access the Line Format menu and move the cursor into the Left/Right margin settings. Type margin settings and press the Enter key. Press F7 to exit the menu and return to text window.
JUSTIFICATION (WP117)	Press Alt-= Type L Type L Type 3	Shift-F8 1 3	Access the Justification menu. Select the type of justification, then press F7 to exit the menu and return to text window.
FOOTNOTES (WP120)	Press Alt-= Type L Type F Type C	Ctrl-F7 1	Display the footnote entry screen. Enter footnote text, then press F7 to return to text window.
TABS (WP122)	Press Alt-= Type L Type L Type 8	Shift-F8 1 8	Display the tab ruler. Press Ctrl-End to clear all existing tabs. Enter the tab stop setting, or use the arrow keys to position tab stop settings on the tab ruler.
HEADERS/FOOTERS (WP131)	Press Alt-= Type L Type P Type 3 [header] or 4 [footer]	Shift-F8 2 3 [or 4]	Enter the text of header or footer, then press F7 to return to text window.
PAGE NUMBERING IN HEADER OR FOOTER (WP134)	Press Ctrl-B		Insert a ^B code at the point of the cursor to indicate automatic page numbering.
VIEW DOCUMENT (WP137)	Press Alt-= Type F Type P Type 6	Shift-F7 6	Document displays on the screen a page at a time. Use the menu to enlarge, scroll, or exit.

QUICK REFERENCE — PROJECT 5

ACTIVITY	PROCEDURE	SHORTCUT KEYS	DESCRIPTION
DATE TEXT (WP151)	Press Alt-= Type T Type T	Shift-F5 1	Position the cursor for the date before issuing instructions. Current date will be inserted at the point of the cursor.
ENTER FIELD NAMES (WP154)	Press Alt-= Type T Type R Press ↵ Enter field name Press ↵	Shift-F9 1	Insert field name or number into primary file.
INSERT FIELD NAME WITH MISSING ENTRY (WP159)	Press Alt-= Type T Type R Press ↵ Enter field name Press ? [question mark] Press ↵		Type field name, then press ? (question mark) before pressing the Enter key to end the field name.
END OF FIELD CODE (WP159)	Type field entry Press F9		Type each field entry, then press F9, making certain you use no blank lines between fields or records.
END OF RECORD (WP161)	Type last field entry Press Shift-F9 Type 2		After entering last field entry for the record, press Shift-F9, 2 to insert {END OF RECORD} code.
RECORD WITH A MISSING FIELD (WP161)	Press F9		Press F9 at the point of the missing field. Continue typing the following field entries using F9 at the end of each field.
MERGE TO PRINTER (WP163)	Position cursor Press Shift-F9 Type 6 Insert codes Exit document Press Ctrl-F9 Type 1		Position the cursor at the end of the primary file. Insert {PRINT} and {PAGE OFF} codes from the Merge Codes menu. Exit the document and make sure the screen is clear. Use the "Merge" option, and merged copies begin printing on the printer.
MERGE TO A DOCUMENT (WP169)	Press Alt-= Type T Type M Enter primary file name Press ↵ Enter secondary file name Press ↵	Ctrl-F9 1	Make sure the screen is clear before you begin the merge. Enter primary and secondary file names where prompted. Merged copies display on the screen.
PRINT SPECIFIC PAGES (WP170)	Position cursor Press Shift-F7 Type 2		Position the cursor anywhere within the page to be printed. Select "2" from the Print menu.

QUICK REFERENCE — PROJECT 6

ACTIVITY	PROCEDURE	SHORTCUT KEYS	DESCRIPTION
CREATE (DEFINE) A MACRO (WP183)	Press Alt-= Type T Type A Type D Enter macro name Press ↵ Enter description Press ↵ Enter macro text Press Alt-= Type T Type A Type D	Ctrl-F10	Enter the macro name, press Enter, enter the description, then press Enter. Type the text of the macro, then use the menu to end defining the macro.
INSERT (INVOKE) MACRO (WP186)	Press Alt-= Type T Type A Type X Enter macro name Press ↵	Alt-F10	Insert macro text at the point of the cursor.
WINDOWS (WP187)	Press Alt-= Type E Type W Enter number Press ↵	Ctrl-F3 1	At the "Number of lines in this window:" prompt, enter the number of lines for the current window. Type 12 to divide the screen into two equal parts (on most monitors).
SWITCH BETWEEN DOCUMENTS/ WINDOWS (WP188)	Press Shift-F3		Move the cursor between Doc 1 and Doc 2 or the upper and lower windows.
COPY TEXT (WP192)	Block text Press Ctrl-F4 Type 1 Type 2 Move cursor Press ↵		Block the text to be copied. Select Block, then select "Copy" from the Move menu. Position the cursor where you want the text to copy, then press Enter to insert the text.
SORT (WP196)	Block text Press Alt-= Type T Type S	Ctrl-F9 1	Block the list of text to be sorted. At the Sort screen, adjust keys, order, and so on, then type 1 to begin the sort.
THESAURUS (WP199)	Press Alt-= Type T Type H	Alt-F1	Position the cursor within word to be looked up before invoking the Thesaurus. Select letters to the left of word choices in the Thesaurus screen to display more word choices. Use the menu to replace, look up, or exit.

INDEX

Spreadsheets Using Lotus 1-2-3 Release 2.2

LOTUS 1-2-3 Release 2.2

LOTUS 1-2-3 Release 2.2

Building a Worksheet

OBJECTIVES

You will have mastered the material in this project when you can:

◆ Start 1-2-3

◆ Describe the worksheet

◆ Move the cell pointer around the worksheet

◆ Enter labels, numbers, and formulas into a worksheet

◆ Save a worksheet

◆ Print the screen image of the worksheet

◆ Correct errors in a worksheet

◆ Use the UNDO command

◆ Answer your questions regarding 1-2-3 using the online help facility

◆ Quit 1-2-3

In Project 1 we will develop the worksheet illustrated in Figure 1-1. It contains a company's first quarter sales report. To build this worksheet, we will enter the revenues and costs for January, February, and March. 1-2-3 calculates the profit for each month by subtracting the cost from the revenue.

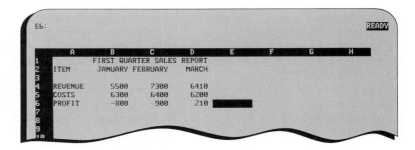

FIGURE 1-1 The worksheet we will build in Project 1.

STARTING 1-2-3

◆ Boot the computer following the procedures presented earlier in the *Introduction to DOS*. Next, follow the steps listed below if your computer has no fixed disk. If your computer has a fixed disk, follow the steps at the bottom of the next page. Several seconds will elapse while the 1-2-3 program is loaded from the disk into main memory. The status light on the disk drive turns on during this loading process. After 1-2-3 is loaded into main memory, it is automatically executed. The first screen displayed by 1-2-3 contains the copyright message shown in Figure 1-2. After a few seconds the copyright message disappears, leaving the worksheet illustrated in Figure 1-3.

Computer with No Fixed Disk Drive

To start 1-2-3 from a computer with no fixed disk drive, do the following:

1. Replace the DOS disk in drive A with the 1-2-3 system disk. If you have two disk drives, place your data disk in drive B.
2. At the A> prompt, type 123 and press the Enter key.
3. If you have only one disk drive, replace the system disk in drive A with your data disk after the program is loaded.

L2

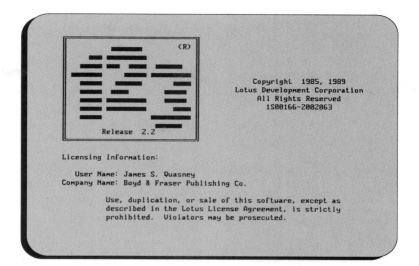

FIGURE 1-2
The copyright screen displays when you load 1-2-3.

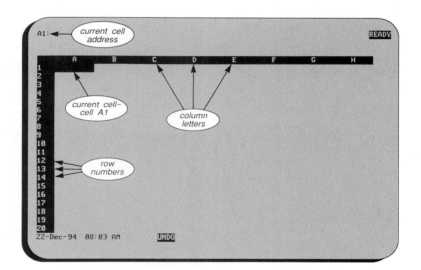

FIGURE 1-3
The worksheet

Computer with a Fixed Disk Drive

To start 1-2-3 from a fixed disk drive, do the following:

1. Use the DOS command CD to change to the subdirectory containing the 1-2-3 program.
2. Place your data disk in drive A.
3. At the DOS prompt, type 123 and press the Enter key.

THE WORKSHEET

◆ The worksheet is organized into a rectangular grid containing columns (vertical) and rows (horizontal). In the border at the top, each **column** is identified by a column letter. In the border on the left side, each **row** is identified by a row number. As shown in Figure 1-3, eight columns (A to H) and twenty rows (1 to 20) of the worksheet appear on the screen.

Cell, Cell Pointer, and Window

Within the borders is the worksheet. It has three parts: cell, cell pointer, and window. A **cell** is the intersection of a column and a row. It is referred to by its **cell address**, the coordinates of the intersection of a column and a row. When you specify a cell address, you must name the column first, followed by the row. For example, cell address D3 refers to the cell located at the intersection of column D and row 3.

One cell on the worksheet is designated the current cell. The **current cell** is the one in which you can enter data. The current cell in Figure 1-3 is A1. It is identified in two ways. First, a reverse video rectangle called the **cell pointer** displays over the current cell. Second, the **current cell address** displays on the first of three lines at the top of the screen. It is important to understand the layout of the worksheet and how to identify all cells, including the current cell.

1-2-3 has 256 columns and 8,192 rows for a total of 2,097,152 cells. Only a small portion of the rectangular worksheet displays on the screen at any one time. For this reason, the area between the borders on the screen is called a **window**. Think of your screen as a window through which you can see parts of the worksheet as illustrated in Figure 1-4.

FIGURE 1-4
The screen on your monitor is a window through which you can view a small part of the worksheet.

The Control Panel and the Status Line

The three lines above the window at the top of the screen display important information about the worksheet. The three lines—mode line, input line, and menu line—are collectively called the **control panel**. Below the window, at the bottom of the screen, is the status line. These four lines are illustrated in Figure 1-5.

Mode Line   The first line in the control panel at the top of the screen is the **mode line**. It identifies the current cell address and displays the mode of operation. If data is already in the current cell, the mode line also shows the type of entry and its contents.

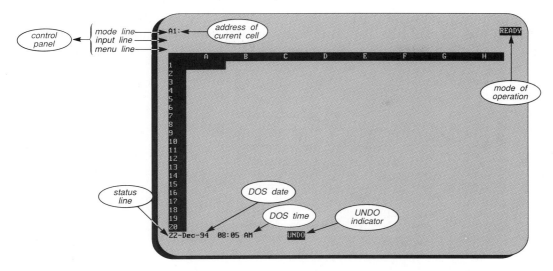

FIGURE 1-5   The control panel at the top of the screen and the status line at the bottom of the screen

The mode of operation displays on the right side of the mode line at the top of the screen. Mode indicators, like EDIT, ERROR, LABEL, MENU, POINT, READY, VALUE, and WAIT tell you the current mode of operation of 1-2-3. For now you should know that when READY displays (Figure 1-5), 1-2-3 is ready to accept your next command or data entry. When WAIT displays in place of READY, 1-2-3 is busy performing some operation that is not instantaneous, like saving a worksheet to disk.

Input Line   Just below the mode line is the input line. The **input line** displays one of three things: the characters you type as you enter data or edit cell contents; a menu of commands; or input prompts asking for additional command specifications.

Menu Line   The **menu line**, the third line in the control panel, displays information about the menu item highlighted on the input line when 1-2-3 is in MENU mode.

Status Line   The line at the very bottom of the screen is the **status line**. It displays three items: the date, the time of day as maintained by DOS, and the status indicators of 1-2-3. Status indicators, like UNDO, CALC, CAPS, CIRC, END, NUM, OVR, and SCROLL, tell you which keys are engaged and alert you to special worksheet conditions. Notice where the indicator UNDO appears at the bottom of Figure 1-5. When this indicator is on, you can use the UNDO command to restore the worksheet data and settings to what they were the last time 1-2-3 was in READY mode. We'll discuss this command in more detail later in this project.

MOVING THE CELL POINTER ONE CELL AT A TIME

◆ Before you can build a worksheet, you must learn how to move the cell pointer to the cells in which you want to make entries. Several methods let you easily move to any cell in the worksheet. The most popular method is to use the four arrow keys located between the typewriter keys and the numeric keypad. The arrow keys on a computer keyboard are illustrated on the next page in Figure 1-6.

Older keyboards do not include a separate set of arrow keys. With these older keyboards, the arrow keys are part of the numeric keypad. If you are using a keyboard without the separate arrow keys, then you must make sure that the Num Lock key is disengaged. You know that the Num Lock key is disengaged when the NUM indicator does not appear on the status line at the bottom of the screen.

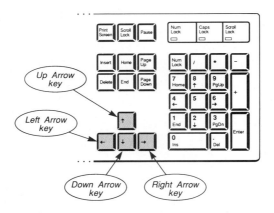

FIGURE 1-6   The arrow keys on the keyboard

We will use the separate set of arrow keys next to the typewriter keys. The arrow keys work as follows:

1. Down Arrow key (↓) moves the cell pointer directly down one cell.
2. Left Arrow key (←) moves the cell pointer one cell to the left.
3. Right Arrow key (→) moves the cell pointer one cell to the right.
4. Up Arrow key (↑) moves the cell pointer directly up one cell.

In the sample worksheet in Figure 1-1, the title FIRST QUARTER SALES REPORT begins in cell B1. Therefore, move the cell pointer from cell A1, where it is when 1-2-3 starts, to cell B1 so you can enter the title. Do this by pressing the Right Arrow key one time, as shown in Figure 1-7. Notice that the current cell address on the mode line in the upper left corner of the screen changes from A1 to B1. Remember, the current cell address on the mode line always identifies the current cell—the one in which the cell pointer is located.

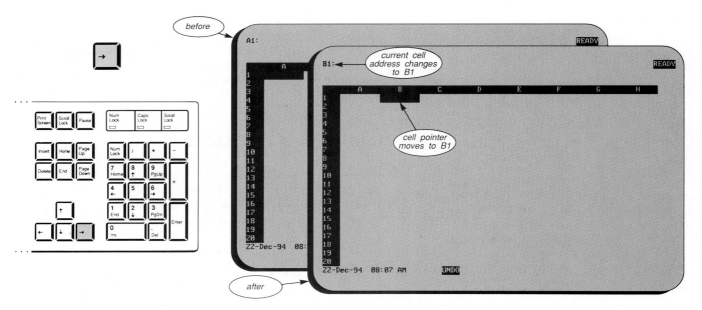

FIGURE 1-7   Press the Right Arrow key to move the cell pointer from A1 to B1.

ENTERING LABELS

◆   With the cell pointer on the proper cell (B1), you can enter the title of the worksheet. In the title FIRST QUARTER SALES REPORT, all the letters are capitals. Although it is possible to enter capital letters by holding down one of the Shift keys on the keyboard each time you type a letter, a more practical method is to press the Caps Lock key one time (Figure 1-8).

FIGURE 1-8   Press the Caps Lock key to type all capital letters.

The word CAPS on the status line at the bottom of the screen in Figure 1-8 tells you that the Caps Lock key is engaged. Therefore, all subsequent letters you type will be accepted by 1-2-3 as capital letters. Both uppercase and lowercase letters are valid in a worksheet, however, and the letters appear in the same case as you enter them. The Caps Lock key affects only the keys representing letters. Digit and special-character keys continue to transmit the lower character on the key when you press them, unless you hold down a Shift key while pressing the key. To enter a lowercase letter when the Caps Lock key is engaged, hold down the Shift key while typing the letter.

Labels That Begin with a Letter

Entering the title is simple. Just type the required letters on the computer keyboard. Type the words FIRST QUARTER SALES REPORT on the keyboard to get the display shown in Figure 1-9.

FIGURE 1-9

Typing a label on the input line with the cell pointer at B1

Figure 1-9 shows two important features. First, as soon as you enter the first character of the report title, the mode on the mode line changes from READY to LABEL. 1-2-3 determines that the entry is a **label** and not a number because the first character typed is a letter.

Second, as you type the report title, it displays on the input line followed immediately by the edit cursor. The **edit cursor** is a small, blinking underline symbol. It indicates where the next character you type will be placed on the input line.

Although the data appears at the top of the screen on the input line, it still is not in cell B1. To assign the title to cell B1, press the Enter key as shown in Figure 1-10. This causes the report title displayed on the input line to be placed in the worksheet beginning at cell B1, the cell identified by the cell pointer.

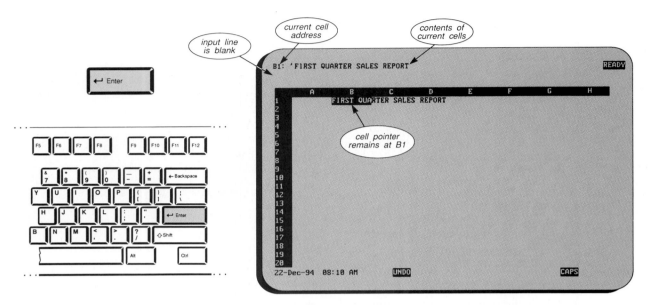

FIGURE 1-10 Pressing the Enter key assigns the label on the input line to cell B1. The cell pointer remains at B1.

If you type the wrong letter and notice the error while it is on the input line at the top of the screen, use the Backspace key (above the Enter key on the keyboard) to erase all the characters back to and including the ones that are wrong. If you see an error in a cell, move the cell pointer to the cell in question and retype the entry.

When you enter a label, a series of events occurs. First, the label is positioned left-justified in the cell where it begins. Therefore, the F in the word FIRST begins in the leftmost position of cell B1.

Second, when a label has more characters than the width of the column, the characters are placed in adjacent columns to the right as long as these columns are blank. In Figure 1-10, the width of cell B1 is nine characters. The words you entered have 26 characters. Therefore, the extra letters display in cell C1 (nine characters) and cell D1 (eight characters), since both cell C1 and cell D1 were blank when you made the 26-character entry in cell B1.

If cell C1 had data in it, only the first nine characters of the 26-character entry in cell B1 would show on the worksheet. The remaining 17 characters would be hidden, but the entire label that belongs to the cell displays in the upper left corner of the screen on the mode line whenever the cell pointer is moved to cell B1.

Third, when you enter data into a cell by pressing the Enter key, the cell pointer remains on the cell (B1) in which you make the entry.

Fourth, a label, in this case FIRST QUARTER SALES REPORT, appears in two places on the screen: in the cell and on the mode line, next to the cell address. Notice that 1-2-3 adds an apostrophe (') before the label on the mode line (Figure 1-10). This apostrophe identifies the data as a left-justified label.

With the title in cell B1, the next step is to enter the column titles in row 2 of the worksheet. Move the cell pointer from cell B1 to cell A2 by using the arrow keys (Figure 1-11). Press the Down Arrow key and then the Left Arrow key. Pressing the Down Arrow key once causes the cell pointer to move to cell B2. Then pressing the Left Arrow key once causes the cell pointer to move to cell A2. Remember that pressing an arrow key one time moves the cell pointer one cell in the direction of the arrow. The current cell address changes on the mode line from B1 to A2.

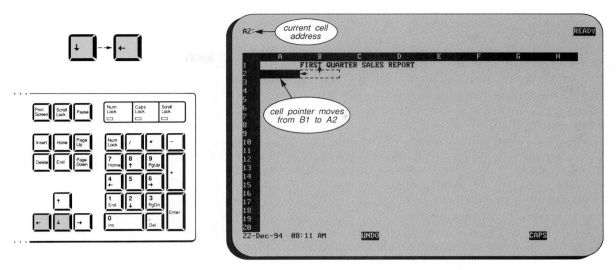

FIGURE 1-11 Moving the cell pointer from B1 to A2 using the arrow keys

With the cell pointer on A2, enter the label ITEM as shown on the input line in Figure 1-12. Since the entry starts with a letter, 1-2-3 positions the label left-justified in the current cell. To enter the label in cell A2 you could press the Enter key as you did for the report title in cell B1. But another way is to press any one of the four arrow keys, as shown on the next page in Figure 1-13. In this case, press the Right Arrow key. This is the better alternative because not only is the data entered into the current cell, but the cell pointer also moves one cell to the right. The cell pointer is at cell B2, the location of the next entry.

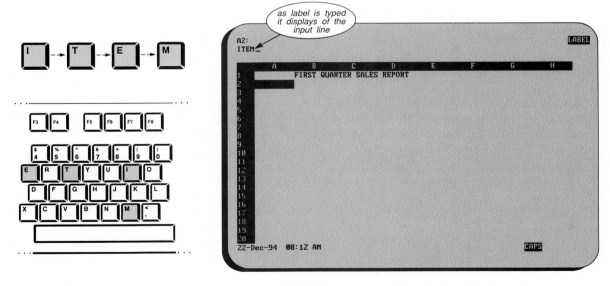

FIGURE 1-12 Typing a label on the input line

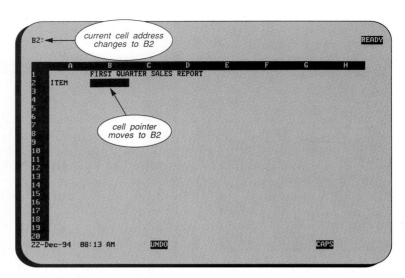

FIGURE 1-13 Pressing the Right Arrow key rather than the Enter key assigns the label on the input line to cell A2 and moves the cell pointer one cell to the right to B2.

Labels Preceded by a Special Character

The worksheet in Figure 1-1 requires that the column headings JANUARY, FEBRUARY, and MARCH be positioned right-justified in the cell, rather than left-justified. There are three different ways to position labels in a cell: left-justified, right-justified, or centered. Remember that the first character of the entry instructs 1-2-3 how to place the label in the cell.

If a label begins with a letter or apostrophe ('), 1-2-3 positions the label left-justified in the current cell. If a label begins with a quotation mark ("), it is positioned right-justified. Finally, if a label begins with a circumflex (^), it is centered within the cell. When the first character is an apostrophe, quotation mark, or circumflex, 1-2-3 does not consider the special character to be part of the label and it will not appear in the cell. However, the special character will precede the label on the mode line when the cell pointer is on the cell in question. Table 1-1 summarizes the positioning of labels in a cell.

TABLE 1-1 Positioning Labels within a Cell

FIRST CHARACTER OF DATA	DATA ENTERED	POSITION IN CELL	REMARK
1. Letter	ITEM	ITEM	Left-justified in cell.
2. Apostrophe (')	'9946	9946	Left-justified in cell. The label 9946 is a name, like the address on a house, and not a number.
3. Quotation Mark (")	"MARCH	MARCH	Right-justified in cell. This always results in one blank character at the end of the label in the cell.
4. Circumflex (^)	^MARCH	MARCH	Centered in the cell.

   With the cell pointer located at cell B2, enter the column heading "JANUARY as shown in Figure 1-14, and then press the Right Arrow key. The word JANUARY appears, right-justified, in cell B2 and the cell pointer moves to cell C2 in preparation for the next entry (Figure 1-15).

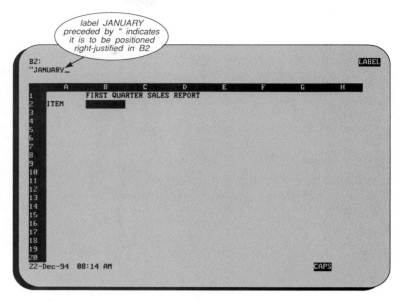

FIGURE 1-14   Begin a label with a quotation mark (") to make it right-justified.

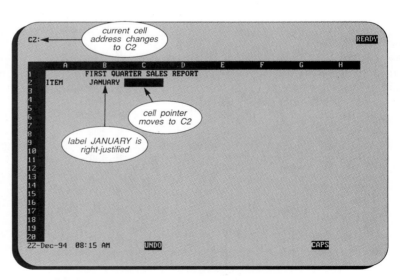

FIGURE 1-15   Pressing the Right Arrow key assigns the label on the input line to cell B2 and moves the cell pointer one cell to the right to C2.

Next, enter the month name "FEBRUARY in cell C2 and the month name "MARCH in cell D2. Enter both labels right-justified. That is, precede each month name with the quotation mark ("). Press the Right Arrow key after typing each label. With these latest entries, the worksheet appears as illustrated in Figure 1-16.

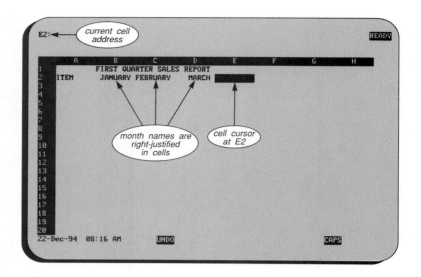

FIGURE 1-16
The three month names are entered right-justified.

The cell pointer is now located at cell E2. According to Figure 1-1 no data is to be entered into cell E2. The next entry is the label REVENUE in cell A4. Move the cell pointer from cell E2 to cell A4. Press the Down Arrow key twice and the Left Arrow key four times, as shown in Figure 1-17.

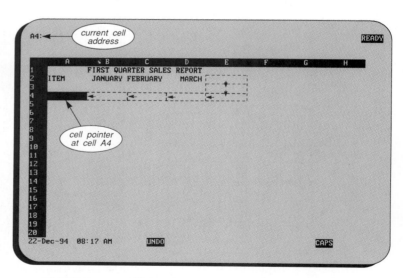

FIGURE 1-17 Using the arrow keys to move the cell pointer from E2 to A4

With the cell pointer at A4, type the label REVENUE and press the Right Arrow key. The cell pointer moves to cell B4 as shown in Figure 1-18.

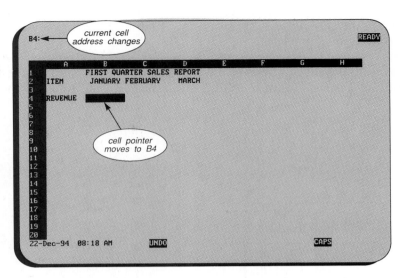

FIGURE 1-18 Pressing the Right Arrow key assigns the label on the input line to cell A4 and moves the cell pointer to B4.

ENTERING NUMBERS

◆ **Numbers** are entered into cells to represent amounts. Numbers are also called **values**. 1-2-3 assumes that an entry for a cell is a number or a formula if the first character you type is one of the following:

$$0\ 1\ 2\ 3\ 4\ 5\ 6\ 7\ 8\ 9\ (\ @\ +\ -\ .\ \#\ \$$$

Whole Numbers

With the cell pointer located at cell B4, enter the revenue amount for January. As shown in Figure 1-1, this amount is 5500. Type the amount 5500 on the keyboard without any special character preceding the number (Figure 1-19). Remember, the CAPS indicator affects only the keys that represent letters on the keyboard. Therefore, never hold down a Shift key to enter a number.

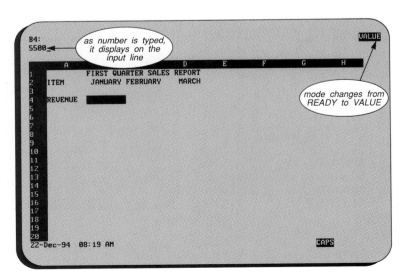

FIGURE 1-19 Entering a number on the input line

As soon as you enter the first digit, 5, the mode of operation on the mode line changes from READY to VALUE. As you type the value 5500, it displays in the upper left corner of the screen on the input line followed immediately by the edit cursor.

Press the Right Arrow key to enter the number 5500 in cell B4 and move the cell pointer one cell to the right. The number 5500 displays right-justified in cell B4 as shown in Figure 1-20. Numbers always display right-justified in a cell. As with right-justified labels, a blank is added to the right side of a number when it is assigned to a cell.

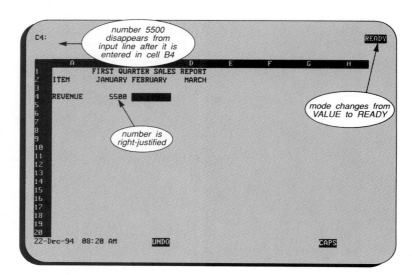

FIGURE 1-20 Pressing the Right Arrow key assigns the number on the input line to cell B4 and moves the cell pointer to C4.

After you enter the data in cell B4, the cell pointer moves to cell C4. At this point, enter the revenue values for February (7300) and March (6410) in cells C4 and D4 in the same manner as you entered the number 5500 into cell B4. After you make the last two revenue entries, the cell pointer is located in cell E4 as shown in Figure 1-21.

FIGURE 1-21
The revenues for the three months are entered into cells B4, C4, and D4.

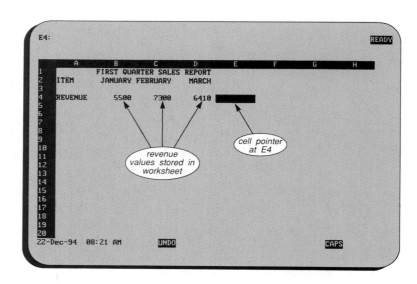

Decimal Numbers

Although the numeric entries in this project are all whole numbers, you can enter numbers with a decimal point, a dollar sign, and a percent sign. The dollar sign and percent sign will not appear in the cell, however. Other special characters, like the comma, are not allowed in a numeric entry. Table 1-2 gives several examples of numeric entries.

TABLE 1-2 Valid Numeric Entries

NUMERIC DATA ENTERED	CELL CONTENTS	REMARK
1.23	1.23	Decimal numbers are allowed.
32.20	32.2	Insignificant zero dropped.
320.	320	Decimal point at the far right is dropped.
$67.54	67.54	Dollar sign dropped.
47%	.47	Percent converted to a decimal number.

MOVING THE CELL POINTER MORE THAN ONE CELL AT A TIME

◆ After you enter the revenue values for the three months, the cell pointer resides in cell E4. Since there are no more revenue values to enter, move the cell pointer to cell A5 so that you can enter the next line of data. While you can use the arrow keys on the right side of the keyboard to move the cell pointer from E4 to A5, there is another method that is faster and involves fewer keystrokes. This second method uses the GOTO command.

The GOTO Command

The **GOTO command** moves the cell pointer directly to the cell you want. GOTO is one of many commands that you enter through the use of the function keys. As shown in Figure 1-22, each function key, except for F6, is assigned two commands — one when you press only the function key, and the other when you hold down the Alt key (or the Shift key) and then press the function key.

FIGURE 1-22 The commands associated with the function keys on the keyboard

The function keys may be located at the far left side or at the top of the keyboard. In either case, the function keys work the same. For these projects, we assume that the function keys are located at the top of the keyboard. Issue the GOTO command by pressing function key F5. 1-2-3 responds by displaying the message "Enter address to go to: E4" in the upper left corner of the screen and changing the mode from READY to POINT. This is illustrated in the top screen of Figure 1-23. When the mode is POINT, 1-2-3 is requesting a cell address.

Next, enter the cell address A5 as shown in the middle screen of Figure 1-23. Remember to enter the column letter first, followed by the row number. Now press the Enter key. The cell pointer immediately moves to cell A5 as shown in the bottom screen of Figure 1-23. Notice that not only does the cell pointer move, but also the current cell address on the mode line in the upper left corner changes from E4 to A5.

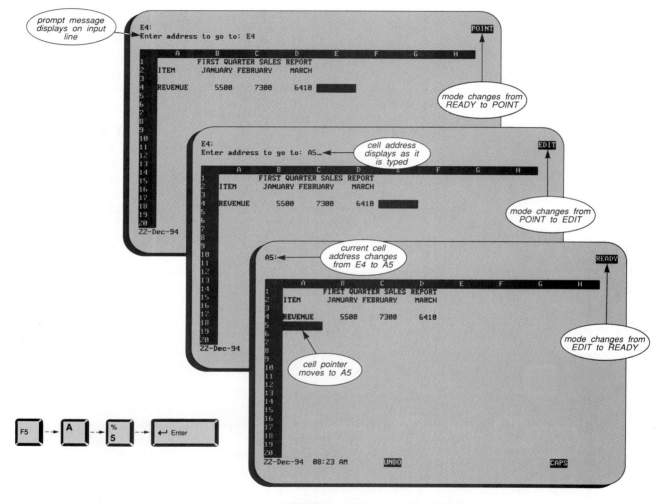

FIGURE 1-23   Using the GOTO command to move the cell pointer

With the cell pointer at cell A5, enter the label COSTS followed by the costs for January, February, and March in the same manner as for the revenues on the previous row. After entering the costs, enter the label PROFIT in cell A6. Figure 1-24 illustrates these entries.

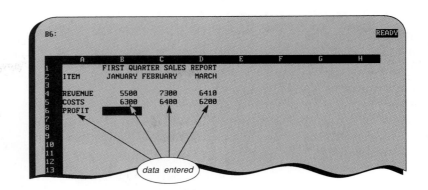

FIGURE 1-24
Costs for the three months
are entered into cells B5, C5,
and D5 and the label PROFIT
is entered into cell A6.

Summary of Ways to Move the Cell Pointer

Table 1-3 summarizes the various ways you can move the cell pointer around the worksheet. As we proceed through the projects in this book, this table will be a helpful reference. Practice using each of the keys described in Table 1-3.

TABLE 1-3   Moving the Cell Pointer Around the Worksheet

KEY(S)	RESULT
↓	Moves the cell pointer directly down one cell.
←	Moves the cell pointer one cell to the left.
→	Moves the cell pointer one cell to the right.
↑	Moves the cell pointer directly up one cell.
(Home)	Moves the cell pointer to cell A1 no matter where the cell pointer is located on the worksheet.
(End)	Moves to the border columns and rows of the worksheet in conjunction with the arrow keys.
(F5)	Moves the cell pointer to the designated cell address.
(Page Down)	Moves the worksheet under the cell pointer 20 rows down.
(Page Up)	Moves the worksheet under the cell pointer 20 rows up.
(Tab)	Moves the worksheet under the cell pointer one screenful of columns to the left.
(Shift) and (Tab)	Moves the worksheet under the cell pointer one screenful of columns to the right.
(Scroll Lock)	Causes the worksheet to move under the cell pointer when the cell pointer movement keys are used.

ENTERING FORMULAS

◆ The profit for each month is calculated by subtracting the costs for the month from the revenue for the month. Thus, the profit for January is obtained by subtracting 6300 from 5500. The result, –800, belongs in cell B6. The negative sign preceding the number indicates that the company lost money and made no profit in January.

One of the reasons why 1-2-3 is such a valuable tool is because you can assign a formula to a cell and it will be calculated automatically. In this example, the formula subtracts the value in cell B5 from the value in cell B4 and assigns the result to cell B6.

Assigning Formulas to Cells

In Figure 1-25, the cell pointer is located at cell B6. Type the formula +B4-B5 with no intervening spaces on the input line. This formula instructs 1-2-3 to subtract the value in cell B5 from the value in cell B4 and place the result in the cell to which the formula is assigned.

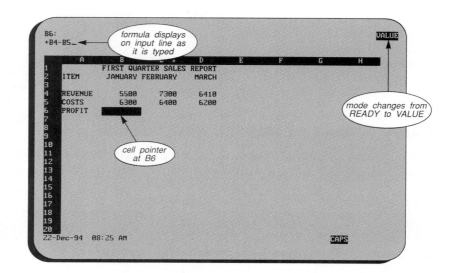

FIGURE 1-25
Entering a formula on the input line

The plus sign (+) preceding B4 is an important part of the formula. It alerts 1-2-3 that you are entering a formula and not a label. The minus sign (–) following B4 is the arithmetic operator, which directs 1-2-3 to perform the subtraction operation. Other valid arithmetic operators include addition (+), multiplication (∗), division (/), and exponentiation (^).

Pressing the Right Arrow key assigns the formula + B4–B5 to cell B6. Instead of displaying the formula in cell B6, however, 1-2-3 completes the arithmetic indicated by the formula and stores the result, –800, in cell B6. This is shown in Figure 1-26. Notice that the negative number displays in cell B6 with the minus sign on the left side of the number. Positive numbers display without any sign.

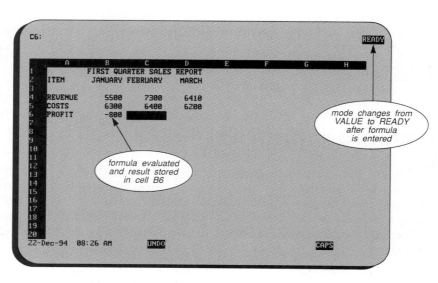

FIGURE 1-26   Pressing the Right Arrow key assigns the formula to cell B6 and moves the cell pointer to C6.

Formulas may be entered in uppercase or lowercase. That is, +b4–b5 is the same as +B4–B5. Like a number, a valid formula begins with one of the following characters: 0 1 2 3 4 5 6 7 8 9 (@ + – . # $. Otherwise, the formula is accepted as a label. Therefore, an alternative to the formula +B4–B5 is (B4–B5). The entry B4–B5 is a label and not a formula, because it begins with the letter B.

To be sure that you understand the relationship of a formula, the associated cell, and the contents of the cell, move the cell pointer back to cell B6. This procedure is shown in Figure 1-27. In the upper left corner of the screen, the mode line shows the assignment of the formula +B4–B5 to cell B6. However, in the cell itself, 1-2-3 displays the result of the formula (–800).

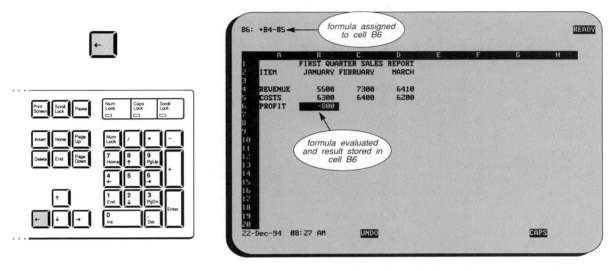

FIGURE 1-27 When the cell pointer is moved to a cell assigned a formula, the formula displays on the mode line.

Next, move the cell pointer to C6 and type the formula +C4–C5. As shown in Figure 1-28, the formula for determining the profit for February displays at the top of the screen on the input line.

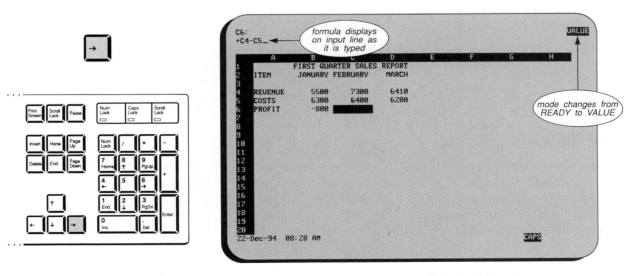

FIGURE 1-28 Entering the profit formula for February on the input line

Press the Right Arrow key. The value in cell C5 (February costs) is subtracted from the value in cell C4 (February revenue) and the result of the computation displays in cell C6 (February profit). The cell pointer also moves to cell D6, as shown in Figure 1-29. As you can see, the process for entering a formula into a cell is much the same as for entering labels and numbers.

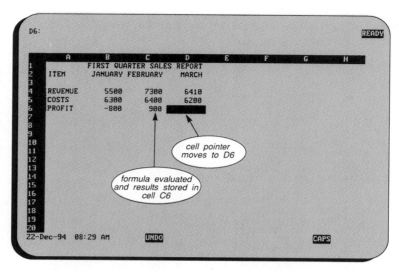

FIGURE 1-29 Pressing the Right Arrow key assigns the formula on the input line to cell C6 and the cell pointer moves to D6.

The same technique can be used to assign the formula +D4–D5 to cell D6. After pressing the Right Arrow key to conclude the entry in D6, the worksheet is complete, as illustrated in Figure 1-30.

FIGURE 1-30
Worksheet for Project 1 is complete.

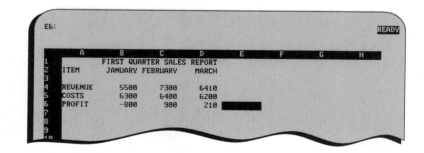

Order of Operations

The formulas in this project involve only one arithmetic operator, subtraction. But when more than one operator is involved in a formula, the same order of operations is used as in algebra. Moving from left to right in a formula, the **order of operations** is as follows: first all exponentiations ($\wedge$), then all multiplications ($*$) and divisions ($/$), and finally all additions ($+$) and subtractions ($-$). You can use parentheses to override the order of operations. Table 1-4 illustrates several examples of valid formulas.

TABLE 1-4 Valid Formula Entries

FORMULA	REMARK
+ E3 or (E3)	Assigns the value in cell E3 to the current cell.
7*F5 or + F5*7 or (7*F5)	Assigns 7 times the contents of cell F5 to the current cell.
–G44*G45	Assigns the negative value of the product of the values contained in cells G44 and G45 to the current cell.
2*(J12–F2)	Assigns the product of 2 and the difference between the values contained in cells J12 and F2 to the current cell. It is invalid to write this formula as 2(J12–F2). The multiplication sign (*) between the 2 and the left parenthesis is required.
+ A1/A1–A3*A4 + A5 ^ A6	From left to right: exponentiation (^) first, followed by multiplication (*) or division (/), and finally addition (+) or subtraction (–).

SAVING A WORKSHEET

◆ You use 1-2-3 either to enter data into the worksheet, as we did in the last section, or to execute a command. In this section we discuss the first of a series of commands that allows you to instruct 1-2-3 to save, load, modify, and print worksheets.

When a worksheet is created, it is stored in main memory. If the computer is turned off or if you quit 1-2-3, the worksheet is lost. Hence, it is mandatory to save to disk any worksheet that will be used later.

MENU Mode

To save a worksheet, place 1-2-3 in **MENU mode**. Do this by pressing the **Slash key** (/) as illustrated in Figure 1-31. First, notice in Figure 1-31 that the mode at the top right side of the screen is MENU. This means that 1-2-3 is now in MENU mode. Next, notice the menus on the input line and menu line in the control panel. A **menu** is a list from which you can choose. The Main menu appears on the input line when you first press the Slash key. A second-level menu appears immediately below on the menu line.

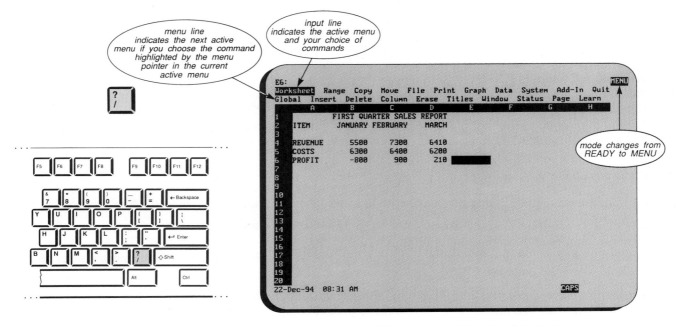

FIGURE 1-31 To save a worksheet to disk, first press the Slash key (/) to switch 1-2-3 to MENU mode.

The second-level menu lists the secondary commands that are available if you select the command highlighted by the menu pointer in the Main menu. The **menu pointer** is a reverse video rectangle that can be moved from command to command in the active menu on the input line, using the Right Arrow and Left Arrow keys. Although there are two menus on the screen, only the one on the input line is active. If you press the Right Arrow key four times, the menu pointer rests on the File command. This procedure is shown in Figure 1-32. Now compare Figure 1-31 to Figure 1-32. Notice that the second level of commands on the menu line has changed in Figure 1-32 to show the list of secondary commands that are available if you select the File command.

For a list of all the 1-2-3 commands, see the command structure charts in the Appendix following Project 6.

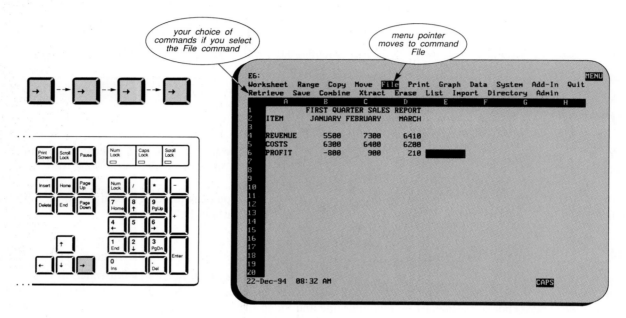

FIGURE 1-32   As you move the menu pointer to each command on the input line, the menu line indicates what the command can do.

Backing Out of MENU Mode

If you decide that you do not want to issue a command, press the **Esc key** until the mode of operation changes to READY. The Esc key, located on the top left side of the keyboard next to the digit 1 key, instructs 1-2-3 to exit MENU mode and return to READY mode.

Press the Esc key and the control panel changes from the one in Figure 1-32 to the one in Figure 1-30. Press the Slash key once and the Right Arrow key four times and the Main menu in Figure 1-32 reappears in the control panel. The Esc key allows you to *back out* of any command or entry on the input line. If you become confused while making any kind of entry (command or data), use the Esc key to reset the current entry. When in doubt, press the Esc key.

The File Save Command

To save a file, select the File command from the Main menu. There are two ways to select the File command.

1. Press the F key for File. Each command in the Main menu begins with a different letter. Therefore, the first letter uniquely identifies each command.
2. Use the Right Arrow key to move the menu pointer to the word File (Figure 1-32). With the menu pointer on the word File, press the Enter key.

Use the first method and press the F key as shown in Figure 1-33. This causes the File menu to replace the Main menu on the input line. The menu pointer is now active in the File menu.

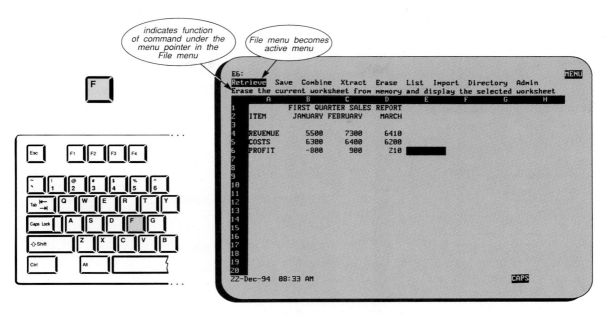

FIGURE 1-33 Typing the letter F moves the File menu
from the menu line to the input line.

Pressing the S key for Save causes the message "Enter name of file to save: A:\" followed by the blinking edit cursor to appear on the input line at the top of the screen. The mode also changes from MENU to EDIT. This procedure is shown in Figure 1-34.

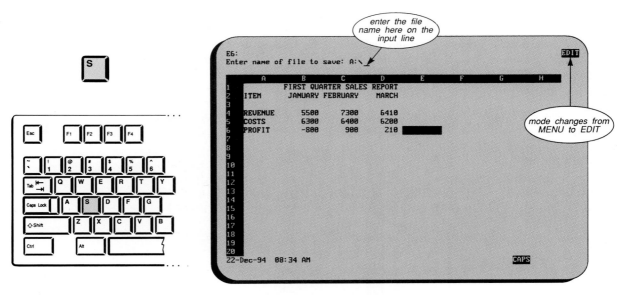

FIGURE 1-34 Typing the letter S for Save causes 1-2-3
to display the prompt message on the input line.

The next step is to select a file name. Any file name will do, provided it is eight or fewer characters in length and includes only the characters A–Z (uppercase or lowercase), 0–9, and the special characters described earlier in the *Introduction to DOS*. 1-2-3 automatically adds the file extension .WK1 to the file name. The file extension .WK1 stands for worksheet.

In this example, let's choose the file name PROJS-1. Type the file name PROJS-1 as shown in Figure 1-35. Next, press the Enter key. The file is stored on the A drive with the file name PROJS-1.WK1. Remember, 1-2-3 does not distinguish between uppercase and lowercase letters. Therefore, you can type PROJS-1 or projs-1 or ProJS-1. All three file names are the same.

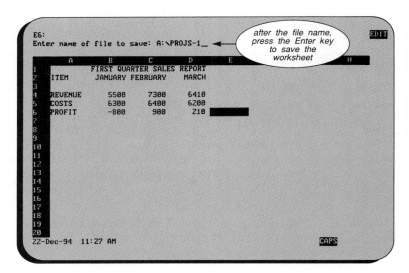

FIGURE 1-35 After you enter the file name on the input line, press the Enter key to complete the /FS command.

While 1-2-3 writes the worksheet on the disk, the mode changes from EDIT to WAIT. The status light on the A drive also lights up to show it is in use. As soon as the writing is complete, the status light goes off and 1-2-3 returns to the READY mode. This is shown in Figure 1-36.

FIGURE 1-36
When the computer is finished saving the worksheet to disk, 1-2-3 returns to READY mode.

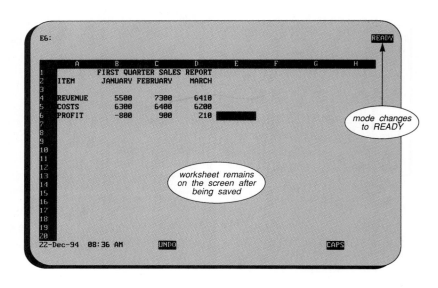

Saving Worksheets to a Different Disk Drive

If you want to save the worksheet to a different drive, enter the command /**F**ile **S**ave (/FS). Next, press the Esc key twice to delete the "A:*.wk1" from the prompt message "Enter name of file to save: A:*.wk1". Enter the drive of your choice followed by the file name. For example, to save the worksheet on the disk in drive B, enter B:PROJS-1 in response to the prompt "Enter name of file to save:". Do not attempt to save a worksheet to the B drive if it is unavailable.

To change the default drive permanently from A to B, enter the command /**W**orksheet **G**lobal **D**efault **D**irectory (/WGDD). That is, press the Slash key, then type the letters WGDD. Press the Esc key to delete the current default drive and type B: for drive B. Press the Enter key. Next, enter the commands Update and Quit (UQ). The Update command permanently changes the default drive in the 1-2-3 program. The Quit command quits the Default menu. The examples in the remainder of this book use the B drive as the default drive.

PRINTING A SCREEN IMAGE OF THE WORKSHEET

◆ The **screen image** of the worksheet is exactly what you see on the screen, including the window borders and control panel. A printed version of the worksheet is called a **hard copy**.

Anytime you use the printer, you must be sure that it is ready. To make the printer ready, turn it off and use the platen knob to align the perforated edge of the paper with the top of the print head mechanism. Then turn the printer on. With the printer in READY mode, press the Print Screen key (Shift-PrtSc on older keyboards). The screen image of the worksheet immediately prints on the printer. When the printer stops, eject the paper from the printer and carefully tear off the printed version of the worksheet (Figure 1-37).

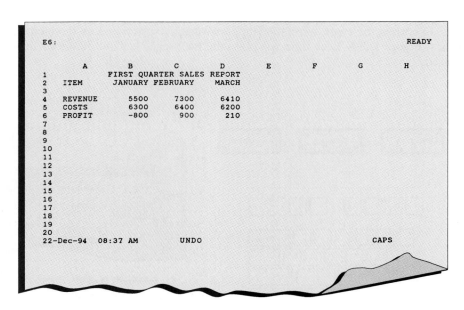

FIGURE 1-37 Press the Print Screen key to obtain a hard copy of the worksheet.

CORRECTING ERRORS

◆   There are several methods for correcting errors in a worksheet. The one you choose will depend on the severity of the error, and whether you notice it while typing the data on the input line or after the data is in the cell.

The error-correcting examples that follow are not part of the worksheet we are building in Project 1. However, you should carefully step through them since they are essential to building and maintaining worksheets.

Correcting Errors While the Data Is on the Input Line

Move the cell pointer to cell A5 and type the label COTTS, rather than COSTS, on the input line. This error is shown in Figure 1-38.

FIGURE 1-38
Incorrect data spotted on the input line

To correct the error, move the edit cursor back to position 3 on the input line by pressing the Backspace key three times (Figure 1-39). Each time you press the Backspace key, the character immediately to the left of the edit cursor is erased.

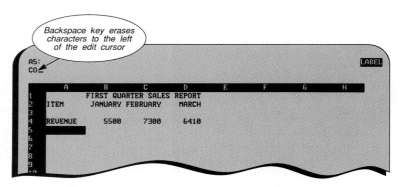

FIGURE 1-39   Press the Backspace key three times to erase the characters up to and including the first T in COTTS.

Then, as in Figure 1-40, type the correct letters STS. Now the entry is correct. Press the Right Arrow key to enter the label COSTS into cell A5.

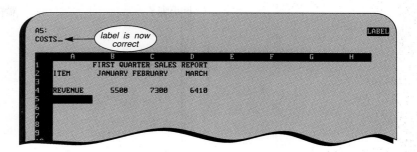

FIGURE 1-40
Enter the correct characters and press the Enter key or one of the arrow keys.

In summary, if you notice an error while the label, number, or formula is on the input line, you can do one of two things. You can use the Backspace key to erase the portion in error and then type the correct characters. Or, if the error is too severe, you can press the Esc key to erase the entire entry on the input line and reenter the data item from the beginning.

Editing Data in a Cell

If you spot an error in the worksheet, move the cell pointer to the cell with the error. You then have two ways to correct the error. If the entry is short, simply type it and press the Enter key. The new entry will replace the old entry. Remember, the cell pointer must be on the cell with the error before you begin typing the correct entry.

If the entry in the cell is long and the errors are minor, using the EDIT mode may be a better choice, rather than retyping. Move the cell pointer to cell A4 and enter the label GROSS PAY incorrectly as GRSS PSY. Figure 1-41 shows the label GRSS PSY in cell A4. You will have to insert the letter O between the letters R and S in GRSS and change the letter S in PSY to the letter A.

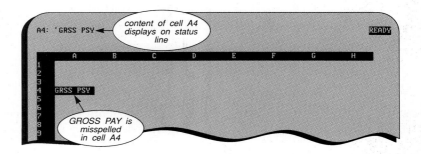

FIGURE 1-41
Error spotted in cell

The six steps in Figure 1-42 illustrate how to use the EDIT mode to correct the entry in cell A4. As shown on the next page in Step 1, first press function key F2 to switch 1-2-3 to EDIT mode. The contents of cell A4 immediately display on the input line, followed by the edit cursor. The contents of the cell can now be corrected. Table 1-5 on page L30 lists the edit keys available in EDIT mode and their functions.

FIGURE 1-42 (Step 1 of 6) Press function key F2 to switch 1-2-3 to EDIT mode.

With 1-2-3 in EDIT mode, the next step in changing GRSS PSY to GROSS PAY is to move the edit cursor on the input line to the leftmost S in GRSS PSY. Press the Left Arrow key six times as shown in Step 2 of Figure 1-42.

FIGURE 1-42 (Step 2 of 6) Press the Left Arrow key six times to move the edit cursor on the input line to the first S in GRSS PSY.

Next, type the letter O. Typing the letter O *pushes* the leftmost letter S and all the letters to the right of it to the right. The O is inserted as shown in Step 3 of Figure 1-42.

FIGURE 1-42 (Step 3 of 6) With the edit cursor on the first letter S in GRSS PSY, type the letter O.

The next step calls for moving the edit cursor to the S in PSY and changing it to the letter A. Use the Right Arrow key as shown in Step 4 of Figure 1-42. After moving the edit cursor, press the Insert key to switch from inserting characters to overtyping characters.

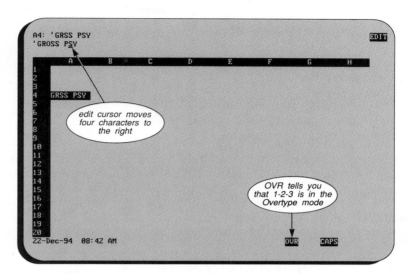

FIGURE 1-42 (Step 4 of 6) Press the Right Arrow key four times to move the edit cursor to the letter S in PSY. Press the Insert key to switch to overtype.

Type the letter A. The correct label GROSS PAY now resides on the input line (Step 5 of Figure 1-42).

FIGURE 1-42 (Step 5 of 6) With the edit cursor on the letter S in PSY, type the letter A.

Press the Enter key to replace GRSS PSY in cell A4 with GROSS PAY. This is illustrated in Step 6 of Figure 1-42.

**FIGURE 1-42
(Step 6 of 6)**
Press the Enter key to assign
the edited value to cell A4.

Pay careful attention to the six steps in Figure 1-42. It is easy to make keyboard and grammatical errors. Understanding how to use the EDIT mode will make it easier to correct mistakes. Table 1-5 summarizes the keys for editing cell entries.

TABLE 1-5 Keys for Editing Cell Entries

KEY	FUNCTION
F2	Switches 1-2-3 to EDIT mode.
↵	Completes entry. Up Arrow key or Down Arrow key also completes an entry. Either key also moves the cell pointer in the corresponding direction.
Backspace	Erases the character immediately to the left of the edit cursor.
Delete	Deletes the character on which the edit cursor is located.
Insert	Switches between inserting characters and overtyping characters. In EDIT mode, characters are inserted when the status indicator OVR does not display at the bottom of the screen. Characters are overtyped when the status indicator OVR displays at the bottom of the screen.
→	Moves the edit cursor one character to the right on the input line.
←	Moves the edit cursor one character to the left on the input line.
End	Moves the edit cursor to the end of the entry on the input line.
Home	Moves the edit cursor to the first character in the entry on the input line.

Undoing the Last Entry — The UNDO Command

As long as the UNDO indicator displays at the bottom of the screen (Figure 1-36), you can enter the UNDO command to erase the most recent cell entry. You enter the UNDO command by holding down the Alt key and pressing the function key F4 (Alt-F4).

To try the UNDO command, enter the value 7345.48 in cell B4. Before entering any other value into the worksheet, press Alt-F4. 1-2-3 erases the value 7345.48 from cell B4. To restore the value 7345.48 in B4, press Alt-F4 again. The second UNDO command *undoes* the first UNDO command.

UNDO is a time-saving command. It can be used to undo much more complicated worksheet activities than a single cell entry. For example, most commands issued from the Main menu can be undone if you enter the UNDO command before making any other entry after 1-2-3 returns from MENU mode to READY mode. The general rule is that the UNDO command can restore the worksheet data and settings to what they were the last time 1-2-3 was in READY mode.

Erasing the Contents of Any Cell in the Worksheet

It is not unusual to enter data into the wrong cell. In such a case, to correct the error, you might want to erase the contents of the cell. Let's erase the label GROSS PAY in cell A4. Make sure the cell pointer is on cell A4. Enter the command **/R**ange **E**rase (/RE). That is, press the Slash key to display the Main menu, then press the R key for Range and the E key for Erase. When the message "Enter range to erase: A4..A4" appears on the input line at the top of the screen, press the Enter key. 1-2-3 immediately erases the entry GROSS PAY in cell A4.

Erasing the Entire Worksheet

Sometimes, everything goes wrong. If the worksheet is such a mess that you don't know where to begin to correct it, you might want to erase it entirely and start over. To do this, enter the command /**W**orksheet **E**rase **Y**es (/WEY). That is, first press the Slash key to display the Main menu. Next, type the letters W for Worksheet, E for Erase, and Y for Yes.

The /**W**orksheet **E**rase **Y**es (/WEY) command does not erase the worksheet PROJS-1 from disk. This command only affects the worksheet in main memory. Remember that the /**W**orksheet **E**rase **Y**es (/WEY) command can also be a method for clearing the worksheet on the screen of its contents after you have saved it. This is especially useful when you no longer want the current worksheet displayed because you want to begin a new one.

ONLINE HELP FACILITY

◆   At any time while you are using 1-2-3, you can press function key F1 to gain access to the online help facility. When you press F1, 1-2-3 temporarily suspends the current activity and displays valuable information about the current mode or command. If you have a one-disk or two-disk system and no fixed disk drive, make sure the 1-2-3 system disk is in drive A before pressing the F1 key.

With 1-2-3 in READY mode, press the F1 key. The 1-2-3 Help Index screen shown in Figure 1-43 displays. Directions are given at the bottom of the help screen for accessing information on any 1-2-3 program subject. With the Help Index on the screen, use the arrow keys to select any one of the many 1-2-3 topics. To exit the help facility and return to the worksheet, press the Esc key.

If you press the F1 key while in any mode other than READY, 1-2-3 displays the appropriate help screen, rather than the 1-2-3 Help Index screen shown in Figure 1-43.

The best way to familiarize yourself with the online help facility is to use it. When you have a question about how a command works in 1-2-3, press F1. You may want to consider printing a hard copy of the information displayed on the screen. To print a hard copy, ready the printer and press the Print Screen key.

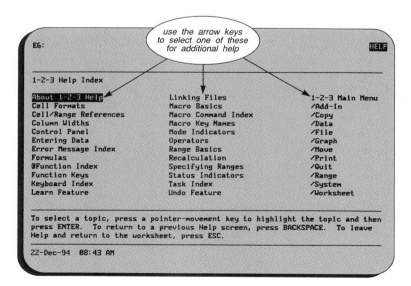

FIGURE 1-43   Press function key F1 to use the online help facility of 1-2-3.

QUITTING 1-2-3

◆ To exit 1-2-3 and return control to DOS, do the following:

1. Save the current worksheet if you made any changes to it since the last save.
2. If you loaded 1-2-3 from drive A, place the DOS disk in drive A.
3. Enter the **Quit** command (/Q). First, press the Slash key to display the Main menu. Next, type the letter Q for Quit.
4. When the message shown at the top of the screen in Figure 1-44 displays, type the letter Y to confirm your exit from 1-2-3.

If you made changes to the worksheet since the last time you saved it to disk, 1-2-3 displays the message "WORKSHEET CHANGES NOT SAVED! End 1-2-3 anyway?" Type Y to quit 1-2-3 without saving the latest changes to the worksheet to disk. Type N to return to READY mode.

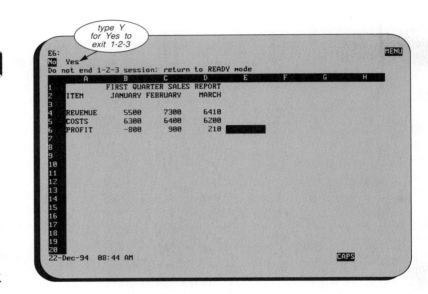

FIGURE 1-44
To quit 1-2-3 and return control to DOS, enter the command /Q and type the letter Y.

PROJECT SUMMARY

In Project 1 you learned how to move the cell pointer around the worksheet, enter data into the worksheet, save a worksheet, and print a hard copy using the Print Screen key. All the activities that you learned for this project are summarized in the Quick Reference following the Appendix. The following is a summary of the keystroke sequence we used in Project 1.

SUMMARY OF KEYSTROKES — PROJECT 1

STEPS	KEY(S) PRESSED	RESULTS
1	(Caps Lock)	Sets Caps Lock on.
2	→	Moves the cell pointer to B1.
3	FIRST QUARTER SALES REPORT ↵	Enters report heading.
4	↓ ←	Moves the cell pointer to A2.
5	ITEM →	Enters column heading.
6	"JANUARY →	Enters column heading.
7	"FEBRUARY →	Enters column heading.
8	"MARCH →	Enters column heading.
9	↓↓ ← ← ← ←	Moves the cell pointer to A4.
10	REVENUE →	Enters row identifier.
11	5500 →	Enters January revenue.
12	7300 →	Enters February revenue.
13	6410 →	Enters March revenue.
14	(F5) A5 ↵	Moves the cell pointer to A5.
15	COSTS →	Enters row identifier.
16	6300 →	Enters January costs.
17	6400 →	Enters February costs.
18	6200 →	Enters March costs.
19	(F5) A6 ↵	Moves the cell pointer to A6.
20	PROFIT →	Enters row identifier.
21	+B4-B5 →	Enters January profit formula.
22	+C4-C5 →	Enters February profit formula.
23	+D4-D5 →	Enters March profit formula.
24	/FS PROJS-1 ↵	Saves the worksheet as PROJS-1.
25	(Print Screen)	Prints the screen image of the worksheet.

The following list summarizes the material covered in Project 1.

1. The worksheet is organized in two dimensions—columns (vertical) and rows (horizontal).
2. In the border at the top of the screen, each **column** is identified by a column letter. In the border on the left side, each **row** is identified by a row number.
3. A **cell** is the intersection of a row and a column. A cell is referred to by its **cell address**, the coordinates of the intersection of a column and row.
4. The **current cell** is the cell in which data (labels, numbers, and formulas) can be entered. The current cell is identified in two ways. A reverse video rectangle called the **cell pointer** is displayed over the current cell, and the current cell address displays on the mode line at the top of the screen.
5. The area between the borders on the screen is called a **window**.
6. The three lines immediately above the window—mode line, input line, and menu line—are collectively called the **control panel**.
7. The **mode line** is the first line in the control panel. It indicates the current cell address and displays the mode of operation. If a value is already in the cell, the mode line also shows the type of entry and its contents.
8. The second line in the control panel is the **input line**. Depending on the mode of operation, it shows the characters you type as you enter data or edit cell contents; a menu of commands; or input prompts asking for additional command specifications.

9. The third line in the control panel is the **menu line**. It displays information about the menu item highlighted on the input line when 1-2-3 is in MENU mode.
10. The line at the bottom of the screen is the **status line**. It displays three items: the date and time of day as maintained by DOS and status indicators.
11. To move the cell pointer one cell at a time use the arrow keys found on the right side of the typewriter keys.
12. No matter where the cell pointer is on the worksheet, if you press the Home key, the cell pointer always moves to cell A1.
13. Three types of entries may be made in a cell: labels, numbers, and formulas.
14. A cell entry is a **label** if the first character is any character other than one that identifies it as a number or formula.
15. A cell entry is a **number** or a **formula** if the first character typed is one of the following: 0 1 2 3 4 5 6 7 8 9 (@ + – . # $.
16. A number or formula is also called a **value**.
17. You may use the **GOTO command** (function key F5) to move the cell pointer to any cell in the worksheet.
18. If a label begins with a letter or an apostrophe ('), it is positioned in the cell left-justified. If a label begins with a quotation mark ("), it is positioned right-justified. If a label begins with a circumflex (^), it is centered in the cell.
19. One of the most powerful features of 1-2-3 is the capability to assign a formula to a cell and calculate it automatically. The result of the calculation is displayed in the cell.
20. 1-2-3 uses the same order of operations as in algebra. Moving from left to right in a formula, the **order of operations** is as follows: all exponentiations (^) are completed first, then all multiplications (∗) and divisions (/), and finally all additions (+) and subtractions (–). Parentheses may be used to override the order of operations.
21. A **menu** is a list from which you can choose. To put 1-2-3 in **MENU mode**, press the **Slash key (/)**. To leave MENU mode, press the Esc key as many times as necessary.
22. The **edit cursor** shows where the next character will be placed on the input line. The **menu pointer** moves from command to command in the active menu.
23. If you get confused while making any kind of entry (command or data), press the **Esc key** to reset the current entry. When in doubt, press the Esc key.
24. To save a worksheet, enter the command **/File Save (/FS)** and the file name you intend to name the worksheet.
25. 1-2-3 automatically appends the file extension .WK1 (worksheet) to the file name.
26. The **screen image** is exactly what you see on the screen.
27. To print the screen image of the worksheet, make sure the printer is ready. Next, press the Print Screen key. After the worksheet has printed, eject the paper from the printer and carefully tear off the printed worksheet. A printed version of the worksheet is called a **hard copy**.
28. To edit the contents of a cell, press function key F2.
29. If the most recent entry into a cell is in error, use the UNDO command to erase it. You enter the UNDO command by holding down the Alt key and pressing the function key F4 (Alt-F4).
30. To erase the contents of a cell, move the cell pointer to the cell in question, enter the command **/Range Erase (/RE)**, and press the Enter key.
31. To erase the entire worksheet, enter the command **/Worksheet Erase Yes (/WEY)**.
32. At any time while you are using 1-2-3, you may press function key F1 to gain access to the online help facility.
33. To exit 1-2-3 and return control to DOS, enter the command **/Quit (/Q)**. Press the Y key to confirm your exit. Before entering the Quit command, be sure that the DOS program COMMAND.COM is available to the system.

STUDENT ASSIGNMENTS

STUDENT ASSIGNMENT 1: True/False

Instructions: Circle T if the statement is true and F if the statement is false.

T F   1. With 1-2-3, each column is identified by a letter of the alphabet and each row by a number.
T F   2. One method of moving the worksheet cell pointer is by using the arrow keys.

T F 3. A cell entry that consists of just words or letters of the alphabet is called a formula.

T F 4. The current cell address on the mode line identifies the cell that the cell pointer is on in the worksheet.

T F 5. A cell is identified by specifying its cell address, the coordinates of the intersection of a column and a row.

T F 6. When 1-2-3 first begins execution, the column width is six characters.

T F 7. Numeric data entered into a worksheet is stored left-justified in a cell.

T F 8. The GOTO command moves the cell pointer directly to a designated cell.

T F 9. When text data is entered that contains more characters than the width of the column, an error message displays.

T F 10. The cell pointer is at C6. The formula +C4–C5 causes the value in cell C5 to be subtracted from the value in cell C4. The answer is displayed in cell C6.

T F 11. If a cell entry begins with a circumflex (^), the data is left-justified in the cell.

T F 12. To move the cell pointer from cell C1 to cell A2, press the Down Arrow key one time and the Left Arrow key one time.

T F 13. When you enter a formula in a cell, the formula is evaluated and the result is displayed in the same cell on the worksheet.

T F 14. The UNDO command erases the entire worksheet.

T F 15. Typing GOTO C1 causes the worksheet cell pointer to be positioned in cell C1.

STUDENT ASSIGNMENT 2: Multiple Choice

Instructions: Circle the correct response.

1. If the first character typed on the input line is the digit 5, the mode on the mode line changes from READY to _____ .
   a. VALUE
   b. LABEL
   c. MENU
   d. EDIT

2. In the border on the left side of the worksheet, each row is identified by a _____ .
   a. number
   b. letter
   c. pointer
   d. none of the above

3. To enter the UNDO command, hold down the Alt key and press _____ .
   a. function key F4
   b. function key F5
   c. function key F6
   d. function key F7

4. A cell is identified by a cell _____ .
   a. pointer
   b. address
   c. entry
   d. none of the above

5. Which one of the following best describes the function of the Backspace key?
   a. deletes the value in the current cell
   b. deletes the character on the input line under which the edit cursor is located
   c. deletes the character to the right of the edit cursor on the input line
   d. deletes the character to the left of the edit cursor on the input line

6. The command /Quit (/Q) is used to _____ .
   a. load a new worksheet
   b. save a worksheet on disk
   c. suspend work on the current worksheet and return control to the operating system
   d. make corrections in the current entry

Student Assignment 2 (continued)

7. Which one of the following should you press to *back out* of any command or entry on the input line?
   a. Esc key
   b. Alt key
   c. Ctrl key
   d. Delete key
8. Which one of the following should you press to put 1-2-3 in HELP mode?
   a. function key F1
   b. function key F2
   c. function key F3
   d. function key F5

STUDENT ASSIGNMENT 3: Understanding the Worksheet

Instructions: Answer the following questions.

1. In the following figure, a series of arrows points to the major components of a worksheet. Identify the various parts of the worksheet in the space provided in the figure.

2. Explain the following entries that may be contained on the status line at the bottom of the screen.

   a. NUM _____
   _____

   b. 15:20 _____
   _____

   c. UNDO _____
   _____

   d. OVR _____
   _____

STUDENT ASSIGNMENT 4: Understanding 1-2-3 Commands

Instructions: Answer the following questions.

1. Indicate the value that will be assigned to cell C1 by the entry on the input line in the following figure. Assume that cell I23 contains the value 5 and cell I24 contains the value 6.

    Value: _____

2. Which keystroke causes 1-2-3 to display the mode shown in the following figure?

    Keystroke: _____

3. Indicate the sequence of keystrokes for saving a worksheet that causes the display shown on the input line in the following figure. Assume that the first letter of each command is entered to issue the commands that cause the display.

    Keystroke sequence: _____

Student Assignment 4 (continued)

4. Use the following figure to answer the questions. Where is the cell pointer located in the worksheet? Which keystroke causes the display on the input line?

Cell pointer location: _____

Keystroke: _____

STUDENT ASSIGNMENT 5: Correcting Formulas in a Worksheet

Instructions: The worksheet illustrated in the following figure contains an error in the PROFIT row for January. Analyze the entries displayed on the worksheet. Explain the cause of the error and the method of correction in the space provided below.

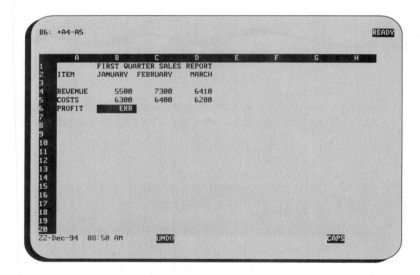

Cause of error: _____

_____

Method of correction: _____

_____

STUDENT ASSIGNMENT 6: Correcting Worksheet Entries

Instructions: The worksheet illustrated in the following figure contains errors in the PROFIT row for February (cell C6) and March (cell D6). Analyze the entries displayed on the worksheet. Explain the cause of the errors for the two months and the methods of correction in the space provided below.

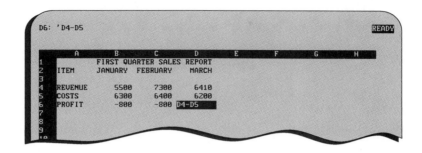

Cause of error in C6: _____

_____

Method of correction for C6: _____

_____

Cause of error in D6: _____

_____

Method of correction for D6: _____

_____

STUDENT ASSIGNMENT 7: Entering Formulas

Instructions: For each of the worksheets in this assignment, write the formula that accomplishes the specified task and manually compute the value assigned to the specified cell.

1. Use the following figure. Assign to cell A4 the sum of cell A2 and cell A3.

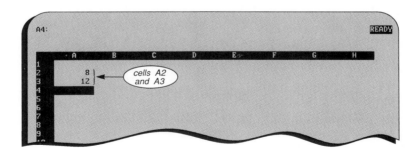

Formula: _____

Result assigned to cell A4: _____

Student Assignment 7 (continued)

2. Use the following figure. Assign to cell B5 the product of cells B2, B3, and B4, minus cell A5.

Formula: _____

Result assigned to cell B5: _____

3. Use the following figure. Assign to cell C3 five times the quotient of cell D2 divided by cell C2.

Formula: _____

Result assigned to cell C3: _____

4. Use the following figure. Assign to cell D5 the sum of cells D2 through D4 minus the product of cells C3 and C4.

Formula: _____

Result assigned to cell D5: _____

STUDENT ASSIGNMENT 8: Building an Inventory Listing Worksheet

Instructions: Perform the following tasks using a personal computer.

1. Boot the computer.
2. Load 1-2-3 into main memory.
3. Build the worksheet illustrated in the following figure. The TOTAL line in row 9 contains the totals for Part A, Part B, and Part C for each of the plants (Chicago, San Jose, and Boston). For example, the total in cell B9 is the sum of the values in cells B5, B6, and B7.
4. Save the worksheet. Use the file name STUS1-8.
5. Print the screen image of the worksheet.

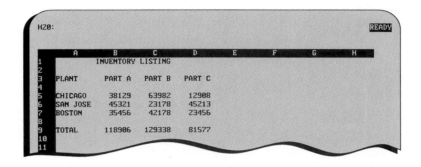

STUDENT ASSIGNMENT 9: Building a Yearly Business Expenses Comparison Worksheet

Instructions: Load 1-2-3 and perform the following tasks.

1. Build the worksheet illustrated in the following figure. Calculate the total expenses for THIS YEAR in column C and LAST YEAR in column E by adding the values in the cells representing the expenses.
2. Calculate the DIFFERENCE in column G by subtracting LAST YEAR expenses from THIS YEAR expenses.
3. Save the worksheet. Use the file name STUS1-9.
4. Print the screen image of the worksheet.

```
A1:                                                              READY

        A        B        C        D        E        F        G        H
1                            BUSINESS EXPENSES
2
3                      THIS YEAR         LAST YEAR        DIFFERENCE
4
5  ADVERTISING        12500             11280            1220
6  CAR EXPENSES        2200              2350            -150
7  ENTERTAINMENT       1435              1240             195
8  INSURANCE           3540              3280             260
9  OFFICE CLEANING      900               960             -60
10 OFFICE RENT        11375             10325            1050
11 OFFICE SUPPLIES     2100              1975             125
12 POSTAGE             1325              1550            -225
13 PRINTING            4890              4375             515
14 TELEPHONE           2350              1945             405
15 TRAVEL             13090             12150             940
16 UTILITIES           1875              1650             225
17
18 TOTAL              57580             53080            4500
19
20
22-Dec-94  08:57 AM          UNDO
```

STUDENT ASSIGNMENT 10: Building a Semiannual Income and Expense Worksheet

Instructions: Load 1-2-3 and perform the following tasks.

1. Build the worksheet illustrated in the following figure. Calculate the total income in row 10 by adding the income for gas and oil, labor, and parts. Calculate the total expenses in row 17 by adding salaries, rent, and cost of goods. Calculate the net profit in row 19 by subtracting the total expenses from the total income.
2. Save the worksheet. Use the file name STUS1-10.
3. Print the screen image of the worksheet.

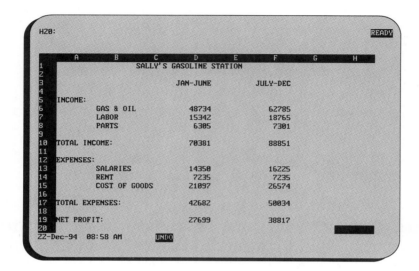

STUDENT ASSIGNMENT 11: Changing Data in the Semiannual Income and Expense Worksheet

Instructions: If you did not do Student Assignment 10, do it before you begin this assignment. With the worksheet in Student Assignment 10 stored on the disk, load 1-2-3 and perform the following tasks.

1. Retrieve the worksheet STUS1-10 you built in Student Assignment 10 from disk. Use the command /**F**ile **R**etrieve (/FR). When the list of worksheet names displays on the menu line, use the arrow keys to move the menu pointer to the worksheet name STUS1-10. Press the Enter key. The worksheet illustrated in Student Assignment 10 will display on the screen.
2. Make the changes to the worksheet described at the top of the next page in the table. Use the EDIT mode of 1-2-3. Recall that to use EDIT mode to change an entry in a cell, move the cell pointer to the cell and then press function key F2.

**List of Corrections to the Semiannual Income
and Expense Worksheet**

CELL	CURRENT CELL CONTENTS	CHANGE THE CELL CONTENTS TO
C1	SALLY'S GASOLINE STATION	SAL'S GAS STATION
D6	48734	48535
F6	62785	61523
D8	6305	63005
F8	7301	47523
D13	14350	22357
F13	16225	19876

As you edit the values in the cells containing numeric data, keep an eye on the total income (row 10), total expenses (row 17), and net profit (row 19) cells. The values in these cells are based on formulas that reference the cells you are editing. You will see that each time a new value is entered into a cell referenced by a formula, 1-2-3 automatically recalculates a new value for the formula. It then stores the new value in the cell assigned the formula. This automatic recalculation of formulas is one of the more powerful aspects of 1-2-3. After you have successfully made the changes listed in the table, the net profit for Jan–June in cell D19 should equal 76367 and the net profit for July–Dec should equal 77085.

3. Save the worksheet. Use the file name STUS1-11.
4. Print the screen image of the worksheet on the printer.

STUDENT ASSIGNMENT 12: Using the Online Help Facility

Instructions: Load 1-2-3 and perform the following tasks.

1. With 1-2-3 in READY mode, press function key F1. Print the screen image.
2. Select the topic "About 1-2-3 Help". Press the Enter key. Read and print the image of the screen.
3. Select the following help screens: Status Indicators; Control Panel; Mode Indicators; and Entering Data. Read and print the image of each help screen.
4. Press the Esc key to quit the online help facility.

Formatting and Printing a Worksheet

LOTUS 1-2-3 Release 2.2

OBJECTIVES

You will have mastered the material in this project when you can:

◆ Retrieve a worksheet from disk

◆ Increase the width of the columns in a worksheet

◆ Define a range of cells

◆ Format a worksheet

◆ Enter repeating characters into a cell using the Backslash key

◆ Copy one range of cells to another range of cells

◆ Add the contents of a range using the SUM function

◆ Determine a percentage

◆ Print a partial or complete worksheet without window borders

◆ Print the cell-formulas version of a worksheet

◆ Display the formulas assigned to cells, rather than their numeric results

The Sales Report worksheet we created in Project 1 contains the revenue, costs, and profit for each of the three months of the first quarter, but it is not presented in the most readable manner. For example, as you can see in Figure 2-1, the columns are too close together and the numbers are displayed as whole numbers, even though they are dollar figures.

In this project we will use the formatting capabilities of 1-2-3 to make the worksheet more presentable and easier to read. We will also add summary totals for the quarter, using formulas. As shown in Figure 2-2, the total revenue in cell B12 is the sum of the revenue values for January, February, and March. The total cost in cell B13 is the sum of the cost values for January, February, and March; and the total profit in cell B14 is the sum of the profit values for January, February, and March. The percent profit in cell B15 is determined by dividing the total profit by the total revenue. After the worksheet is complete, we will print it without the window borders.

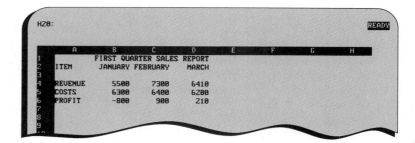

FIGURE 2-1 The worksheet we completed in Project 1.

RETRIEVING A WORKSHEET FROM DISK

◆ Recall that at the end of Project 1, the Save command was used to store the worksheet in Figure 2-1 on disk under the name PROJS-1.WK1. Since Project 2 involves making modifications to this stored worksheet, you can eliminate retyping the whole worksheet and save a lot of time by retrieving it from disk and placing it into main memory.

L44

```
E20:                                                              READY
            A          B           C           D          E
 1              FIRST QUARTER SALES REPORT
 2  ITEM          JANUARY    FEBRUARY      MARCH
 3
 4  REVENUE       5500.00     7300.00     6410.00
 5  COSTS         6300.00     6400.00     6200.00
 6  PROFIT        -800.00      900.00      210.00
 7
 8  ─────────────────────────────────────────────
 9
10  QUARTER RESULTS
11
12  TOTAL REVENUE  $19,210.00
13  TOTAL COSTS    $18,900.00
14  TOTAL PROFIT     $310.00
15  % PROFIT           1.6%
16
```

FIGURE 2-2
The worksheet we will
complete in Project 2.

After booting the computer and loading the 1-2-3 program, retrieve the worksheet PROJS-1 from the data disk. To retrieve the worksheet, enter the command **/F**ile **R**etrieve (/FR). First, press the Slash key (/) as illustrated in Figure 2-3. This causes 1-2-3 to display the Main menu on the input line at the top of the screen.

menu line indicates selections if you type letter W for Worksheet

menu pointer in Main menu

```
A1:                                                              MENU
Worksheet  Range  Copy  Move  File  Print  Graph  Data  System  Add-In  Quit
Global  Insert  Delete  Column  Erase  Titles  Window  Status  Page  Learn
         A        B        C        D        E        F        G        H
 1
 2
 3
 4
 5
 6
 7
 8
```

mode changes from READY to MENU

FIGURE 2-3 Step 1 of retrieving a worksheet from disk—
press the Slash key (/).

Next, use the Right Arrow key to move the menu pointer to the word File. The result of this activity is shown in Figure 2-4. With the menu pointer on the word File, the File menu displays on the menu line, immediately below the Main menu. To select the File menu, press the Enter key or type the letter F.

FIGURE 2-4   Step 2 of retrieving a worksheet from disk—use the arrow keys to move the menu pointer to the word File in the Main menu.

Let's press the Enter key. The menu pointer is now active in the File menu as illustrated in Figure 2-5. The Retrieve command is the first command in the list. The message on the menu line indicates the function of this command. With the menu pointer on the Retrieve command, type the letter R for Retrieve.

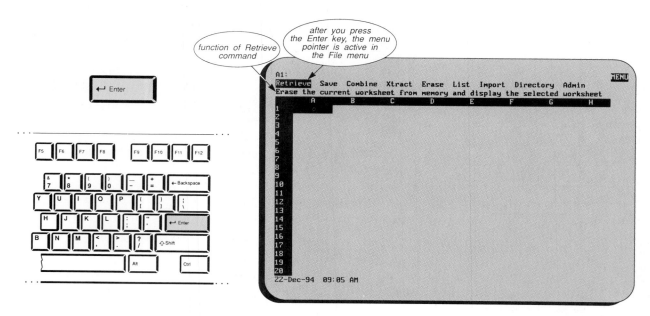

FIGURE 2-5   Step 3 of retrieving a worksheet from disk—press the Enter key to select the File command.

As illustrated in Figure 2-6, 1-2-3 displays on the menu line an alphabetized list of the file names on the default drive that have the extension .WK1. This helps you remember the names of the worksheets stored on the data disk. The list includes all the worksheets you were told to save in Project 1, including PROJS-1.WK1.

FIGURE 2-6 Step 4 of retrieving a worksheet from disk—type the letter R for Retrieve, select the worksheet name, and press the Enter key.

One way to select the worksheet you want to retrieve is to type PROJS-1 on the input line and press the Enter key. Better yet, because the menu pointer is on the file name PROJS-1.WK1 in the list in Figure 2-6, press the Enter key. This method saves keying time. While 1-2-3 is accessing the worksheet, the mode indicator in the upper right corner of the screen changes to WAIT and the status light flashes on the default drive. After the worksheet is retrieved, the screen appears as shown in Figure 2-1. According to Figure 2-2, all the new labels are in capitals. Therefore, before you modify the worksheet, press the Caps Lock key.

The tasks we want to complete in this project are to widen the columns, format the dollar amounts, and add the quarter results. The tasks may be accomplished in any sequence. Let's complete them in the following sequence:

1. Widen the columns from 9 characters to 13 characters to allow the quarter results titles and other numeric data to fit in the columns.
2. Change the numeric representations for the three months to dollars and cents—two digits to the right of the decimal place.
3. Determine the quarter results.
4. Change the percent profit to a number in percent.
5. Change the numeric representations of the quarter results to dollars and cents with a leading dollar sign.

CHANGING THE WIDTH OF THE COLUMNS

◆ When 1-2-3 first executes and the blank worksheet appears on the screen, all the columns have a default width of nine characters. You can change this default width to make the worksheet easier to read or to ensure that entries will display properly in the cells.

There are three ways to change the width of the columns in a worksheet. First, make a global change, which uniformly increases or decreases the width of all the columns in the worksheet. **Global** means the entire worksheet. Second, change the width of a series of adjacent columns. Third, make a change in the width of one column at a time. Let's use the first method and change the width of all the columns

Changing the Width of All the Columns

To change the width of all the columns, enter the command /Worksheet Global Column-Width (/WGC). When you press the Slash key, the Main menu displays at the top of the screen with the first command, Worksheet, highlighted as shown earlier in Figure 2-3. The Worksheet menu displays immediately below the Main menu. Notice that the first command in the Worksheet menu is Global. This command makes the changes to the entire worksheet. Type the letter W for Worksheet to move the menu pointer to the Worksheet menu, as shown in Figure 2-7.

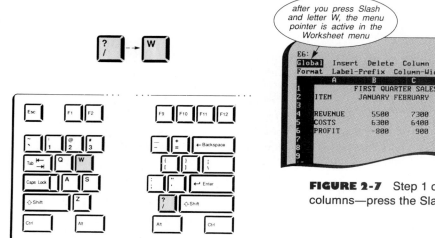

FIGURE 2-7 Step 1 of increasing the width of the columns—press the Slash key (/) and type the letter W.

Type the letter G for Global. This causes the Global menu to display on the input line and the global settings sheet to display in place of the worksheet. Press F6 if you want to view the worksheet, rather than the global settings sheet, when the Global menu is active. Press F6 again and the global settings sheet displays in place of the worksheet.

With the Global menu active, use the Right Arrow key to move the menu pointer to Column-Width. Now the menu line explains the purpose of the Column-Width command. This procedure is illustrated in Figure 2-8.

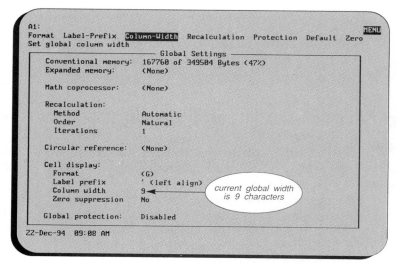

FIGURE 2-8 Step 2 of increasing the width of the columns—type the letter G and use the Right Arrow key to move the menu pointer to Column-Width in the Global menu.

Before you type the letter C for Column-Width, if you decided that you did not want to increase the width of the columns, how many times would you have to press the Esc key to *back out* of the MENU mode in Figure 2-8 and return to READY mode? If your answer is three, you're right—once for the Global command, once for the Worksheet command, and once for the Slash key (/).

Now type the letter C for Column-Width. The prompt message "Enter global column width (1..240): 9" displays on the input line at the top of the screen. This message is illustrated on the screen in Figure 2-9. The numbers 1–240 define the range of valid entries. The number 9 following the colon indicates the current global (default) column width.

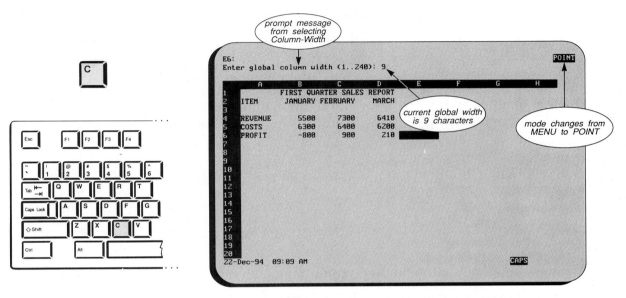

FIGURE 2-9 Step 3 of increasing the width of the columns—type the letter C for Column-Width.

Type the number 13 as shown in Figure 2-10, then press the Enter key. An alternative to typing the number 13 is to use the Right and Left Arrow keys to increase or decrease the number on the input line.

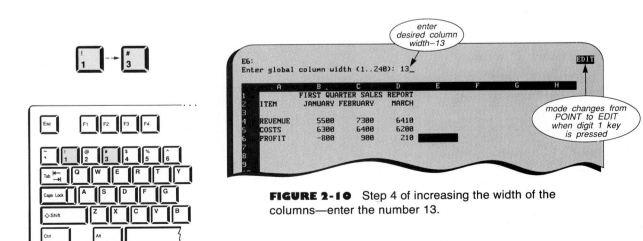

FIGURE 2-10 Step 4 of increasing the width of the columns—enter the number 13.

Figure 2-11 illustrates the worksheet with the new column width of 13 characters. Compare Figure 2-11 to Figure 2-1. Because the columns in Figure 2-11 are wider, the worksheet is easier to read. But because the columns are wider, fewer appear on the screen.

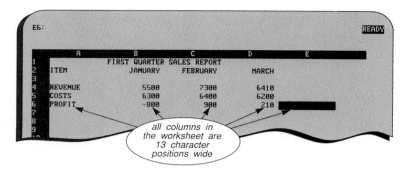

FIGURE 2-11 Step 5 of increasing the width of the columns—press the Enter key.

Changing the Width of a Series of Adjacent Columns

In Figures 2-7 through 2-11, the /Worksheet Global Column-Width (/WGC) command was used to uniformly change the width of all the columns. Since we were interested in changing only the width of columns A through E to 13 characters, we could have also used the command /Worksheet Column Column-Range Set-Width (/WCCS). This command works the same as the /Worksheet Global Column-Width (/WGC) command, except that you must enter the range of columns that will be affected by the change.

Changing the Width of One Column at a Time

You can change the width of one column at a time in the worksheet. Let's change the width of column A to 20 characters, while leaving the width of the other columns at 13 characters. To change the width of column A to 20 characters, do the following:

1. Press the Home key to move the cell pointer into column A.
2. Type the command /Worksheet Column Set-Width (/WCS). The Slash key (/) switches 1-2-3 to MENU mode. The letter W selects the Worksheet command. The letter C selects the command Column and the letter S selects the command Set-Width.
3. In response to the prompt message "Enter column width (1..240): 13" on the input line, type the number 20 and press the Enter key.

Now column A is 20 characters wide while the other columns in the worksheet are 13 characters wide. Let's change column A back to the default width of 13 characters. With the cell pointer in column A, enter the command /Worksheet Column Reset-Width (/WCR). This command changes column A back to the default width—13 characters. The UNDO command may also be used to reset the width of column A to the default width. You must be sure, however, that no other entry has been made into the worksheet, since the width was changed from 13 characters to 20 characters.

Use the GOTO command to move the cell pointer back to cell E6, where it was before the width of column A was set to 20 and then reset to 13.

DEFINING A RANGE

◆ Our next step is to format the monthly dollar amounts. The Format command requires you to specify the cells you want to format. For this reason, you need to understand the term *range* before using the Format command.

A **range** in 1-2-3 means one or more cells on which an operation can take place. A range may be a single cell, a series of adjacent cells in a row or column, or a rectangular group of adjacent cells. Hence, a range may consist of one cell or many cells. However, a range cannot be made up of cells that only run diagonally or are separated. Figure 2-12 illustrates several valid and invalid ranges of cells.

FIGURE 2-12
Valid and invalid ranges

When you are prompted by 1-2-3 to specify a range, you simply type the cell address for the first cell in the range, followed by a period (.), followed by the cell address for the last cell in the range. If a range defines a rectangular group of cells, any pair of diagonally opposite corner cells may be used to identify it. For example, the upper left cell and the lower right cell of the rectangular group of cells identify the range. Table 2-1 summarizes the ranges described in Figure 2-12.

TABLE 2-1   A Summary of the Ranges Specified in Figure 2-12

RANGE	COMMENT
A4..A4	The range is made up of one cell, A4.
C3..G3	The range is made up of five adjacent cells in row 3. The five cells are C3, D3, E3, F3, and G3.
B10..B17	The range is made up of eight adjacent cells in column B. The eight cells are B10, B11, B12, B13, B14, B15, B16, and B17.
E10..H19	The range is made up of a rectangular group of cells. The upper left cell (E10) and the lower right cell (H19) define the rectangle. The ranges H19..E10, H10..E19, and E19..H10 define the same range as E10..H19.

Now that you know how to define a range, we can move on to the next step in Project 2: formatting the numeric values in the worksheet.

FORMATTING NUMERIC VALUES

◆ The Format command is used to control the manner in which numeric values appear in the worksheet. As shown in Figure 2-2, we want to change the numeric values in the range B4 through D6 to display as dollars and cents with two digits to the right of the decimal point.

Invoking the Format Command

There are two ways to invoke the Format command. First, you can use the series of commands /**W**orksheet **G**lobal **F**ormat (/WGF) to format all the cells in the worksheet the same way. Second, you can use the commands /**R**ange **F**ormat (/RF) to format just a particular range of cells. Since this project involves formatting a range rather than all the cells in the worksheet, type /RF to activate the menu pointer in the Format menu as shown in Figure 2-13. The Format menu on the input line lists the different ways to format a range. As indicated on the third line of the control panel, the first format type in the menu, Fixed, formats cells to a fixed number of decimal places. This is the format you want to use to display the monthly amounts to two decimal places. Type the letter F for Fixed.

FIGURE 2-13 Step 1 of formatting a range of cells—press the Slash key (/) and type the letters R for Range and F for Format.

As shown in Figure 2-14, 1-2-3 displays the message "Enter number of decimal places (0..15): 2" on the input line at the top of the screen. Since most spreadsheet applications require two decimal positions, 1-2-3 displays "2" as the entry to save you time. Press the Enter key to enter two decimal positions.

FIGURE 2-14 Step 2 of formatting a range of cells—type the letter F for Fixed and 1-2-3 displays a prompt message on the input line.

Next, 1-2-3 changes to POINT mode and displays the message "Enter range to format: E6..E6" (Figure 2-15). The range E6..E6 displays at the end of the input line because the cell pointer is at cell E6. Enter the range by typing B4.D6, or use the arrow keys to select the range. (Don't be concerned that 1-2-3 displays two periods between the cell address when you press the Period key once. It is the program's way of displaying a range.) Using the arrow keys to select a range is called **pointing**. Let's use the pointing method to select a range because it requires less effort.

FIGURE 2-15 Step 3 of formatting a range of cells— press the Enter key to select two decimal places and 1-2-3 displays the prompt message on the input line, requesting the range to format.

Selecting a Range by Pointing

To select a range by pointing, first press the Backspace key (or Esc key) to change the default entry on the input line in Figure 2-15 from E6..E6 to E6. Next, use the arrow keys to move the cell pointer to B4, the upper left corner cell of the range you want. This procedure is shown in Figure 2-16.

FIGURE 2-16 Step 4 of formatting a range of cells— press the Backspace key to unlock the first end point on the input line and use the arrow keys to select end point B4.

With the cell pointer at B4, press the Period key to *lock in*, or *anchor*, the first end point, B4. The B4 on the input line changes to B4..B4. Now use the arrow keys to move the cell pointer to cell D6, the lower right corner of the desired range. Press the Down Arrow key twice and the Right Arrow key twice. As the cell pointer moves, a reverse video rectangle forms over the range covered. The range on the input line changes from B4..B4 to B4..D6 (Figure 2-17).

FIGURE 2-17 Step 5 of formatting a range of cells—press the Period key (.) to anchor the first end point and use the arrow keys to move the cell pointer to the opposite end point.

Press the Enter key. 1-2-3 immediately displays the monthly values in cells B4, C4, D4, B5, C5, D5, B6, C6, and D6 with two decimal places (dollars and cents). Everything else in the worksheet remains the same (Figure 2-18).

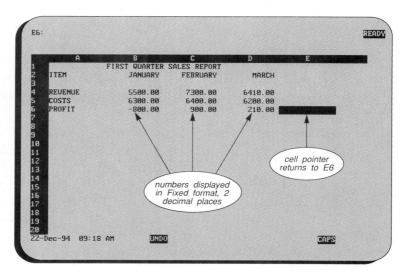

FIGURE 2-18 Step 6 of formatting a range of cells—press the Enter key and the numbers in the range B4..D6 display in Fixed format.

Don't forget that the UNDO command is available when 1-2-3 returns to READY mode after the worksheet is formatted. Thus, if you want to reset the worksheet to what it was before you formatted it, issue the UNDO command (Alt-F4).

We could have used three other ways to describe to 1-2-3 the rectangular group of cells B4..D6. Two other ways are B6..D4 and D4..B6. Can you identify the third way?

Summary of Format Commands

You can format numbers in cells in a variety of ways using the /**W**orksheet **G**lobal **F**ormat (/WGF) or /**R**ange **F**ormat (/RF) command. Table 2-2 summarizes the various format options. You will find Table 2-2 helpful when you begin formatting your own worksheets. Also, remember that 1-2-3 rounds a number to the rightmost position if any digits are lost because of the format or number of decimal positions chosen.

TABLE 2-2 Format Types for Numeric Values in the Format Menu

MENU ITEM	DESCRIPTION
Fixed	Displays numbers to a specified number of decimal places. Negative values are displayed with a leading minus sign. Examples: 38; 0.912; –45.67.
Sci	Displays numbers in a form called *scientific notation*. The letter E stands for *times 10 to the power.* Examples: 3.7E+01; –2.357E–30.
Currency	Displays numbers preceded by a dollar sign next to the leftmost digit, with a specified number of decimal places (0–15), and uses commas to group the integer portion of the number by thousands. Negative numbers display in parentheses. Examples: $1,234.56; $0.98; $23,934,876.15; ($48.34).
,	The , (comma) is the same as the Currency format, except the dollar sign does not display. Examples: 2,123.00; 5,456,023.34; (22,000).
General	This is the default format in which a number is stored when it is entered into a cell. Trailing zeros are suppressed and leading integer zeros display. Negative numbers display with a leading minus sign. Examples: 23.981; 0.563; 23401; –500.45.
+/–	Displays a single horizontal bar graph composed of plus (+) or minus (–) signs that indicate the sign of the number and the magnitude of the number. One plus or minus sign displays for each unit value. Only the integer portion of the number is used. Examples: +++++ for 6; ––– for –3.8.
Percent	Displays numbers in percent form. Examples: 34% for 0.34; .11% for 0.0011; –13.245% for –0.13245.
Date	Formats cells that contain a date or time.
Text	Displays formulas rather than their values. Numbers appear in General format. Examples: +B4–B5; 2*(F5 – G3).
Hidden	Prevents the display of the cell contents on the screen and when printed. To see what's in a hidden cell, move the pointer to that cell. The contents will display on the mode line.
Reset	Resets cells back to Global format.

Determining the Format Assigned to a Cell

You can determine the format assigned to a cell by the Range Format command by moving the cell pointer to that cell. The format displays on the mode line in the upper left corner of the screen, next to the cell address. In Figure 2-19, the cell pointer is at cell D6. Format F2 displays on the mode line in parentheses next to the cell address. F2 is an abbreviation for the format "Fixed, 2 decimal places." Recall that we assigned this format to cell D4 in Figures 2-13 through 2-18.

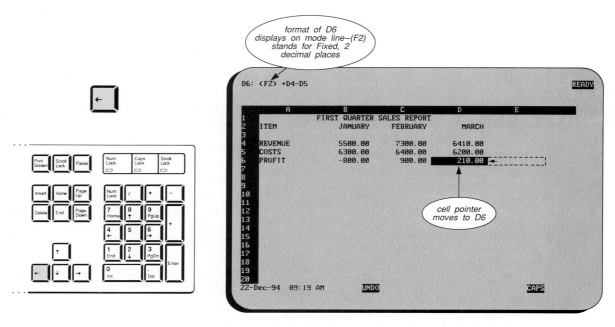

FIGURE 2-19 The format assigned to a cell displays on the mode line when the cell pointer is on the cell.

REPEATING CHARACTERS IN A CELL

In Figure 2-2, row 8 contains a dashed line. We will add the dashed line to the worksheet using repeating characters—characters that are repeated throughout a cell.

To enter the dashed line, move the cell pointer to cell A8 using the GOTO command. Recall that function key F5 invokes the GOTO command. Next, enter the cell address A8 and press the Enter key. The cell pointer immediately moves to cell A8 as shown in Figure 2-20.

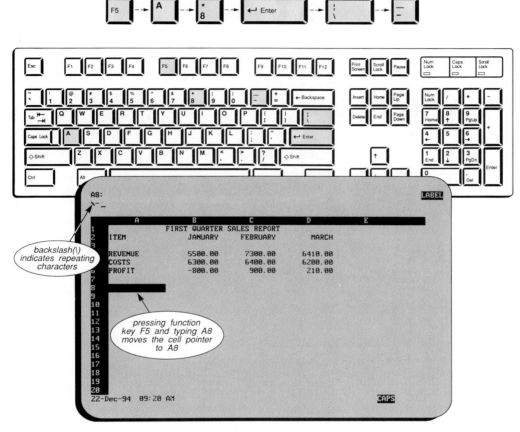

FIGURE 2-20 Moving the cell pointer to A8 and entering a repeating dash on the input line.

With the cell pointer at A8, press the Backslash key (\). The **Backslash key** signals 1-2-3 that the character or sequence of characters that follows it on the input line is to be repeated throughout the cell. Repeating the minus sign (–) creates the dashed line shown in Figure 2-2. Therefore, immediately after the Backslash key, press the Minus Sign key once as illustrated at the top of the screen in Figure 2-20.

To enter the repeating dash, press the Enter key. The dash repeats throughout cell A8 as shown in Figure 2-21. The Backslash key is not included as part of the cell entry. Like the quotation mark ("), circumflex (^), and apostrophe ('), the backslash (\) is used as the first character to tell 1-2-3 what to do with the characters that follow on the input line.

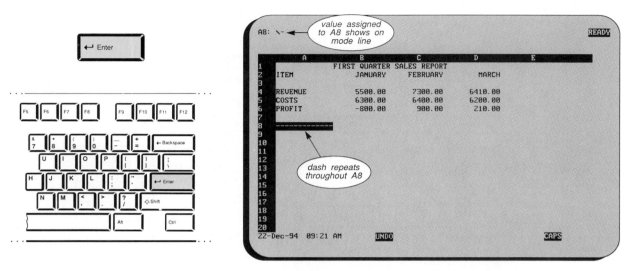

FIGURE 2-21 Press the Enter key to assign the repeating dash to cell A8.

We still need to extend the dashed line through cells B8, C8, and D8. We can move the cell pointer to each individual cell and make the same entry we made in cell A8, or we can use the Copy command. Let's use the Copy command.

REPLICATION—THE COPY COMMAND

◆ The /Copy command (/C) is used to copy, or replicate, the contents of one group of cells to another group of cells. This command is one of the most useful because it can save you both time and keystrokes when you build a worksheet. We will use the Copy command to copy the dashes in cell A8 to cells B8 through D8. Press the Slash key (/) to place 1-2-3 in MENU mode. In the Main menu list, the Copy command is the third one. Type the letter C to invoke the Copy command.

Source Range

When you select the Copy command, the prompt message "Enter range to copy FROM: A8..A8" displays on the input line as shown in Figure 2-22. The **source range** is the range we want to copy. Since A8 is the cell to copy to B8 through D8, press the Enter key.

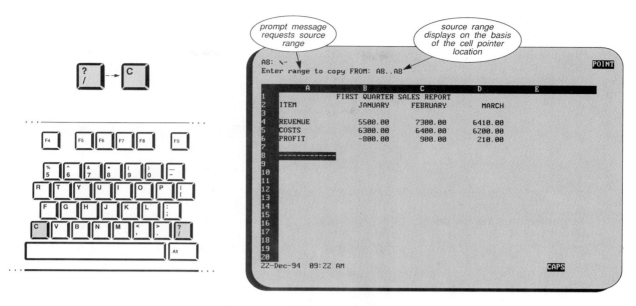

FIGURE 2-22 Step 1 of copying a range of cells—press the Slash key (/) and type the letter C for Copy.

Destination Range

After you press the Enter key, the prompt message "Enter range to copy TO: A8" displays on the input line as shown in Figure 2-23. The **destination range** is the range to which we want to copy the source range.

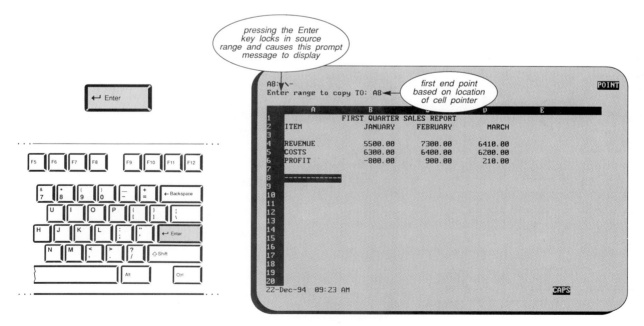

FIGURE 2-23 Step 2 of copying a range of cells—anchor the end points of the source range of cells to copy by pressing the Enter key.

Move the cell pointer to B8, the left end point of the range to copy to (Figure 2-24). Notice that following the prompt message on the input line, the cell address is now B8, the location of the cell pointer.

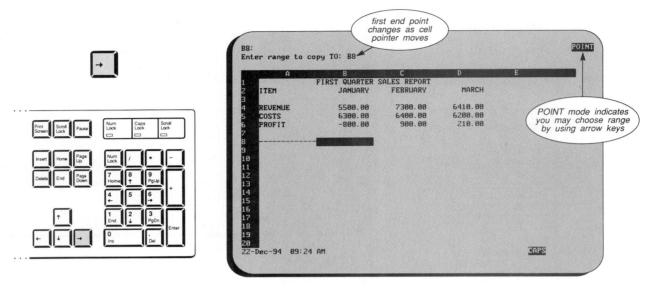

FIGURE 2-24 Step 3 of copying a range of cells—move the cell pointer to one of the end points of the destination range.

Press the Period key to anchor end point B8, and move the cell pointer to D8 as shown in Figure 2-25. Finally, press the Enter key to copy cell A8 to cells B8 through D8.

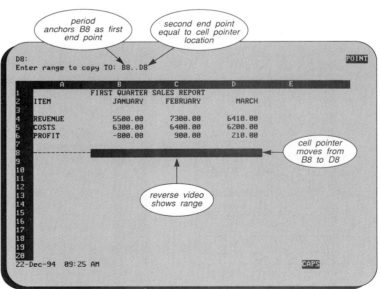

FIGURE 2-25 Step 4 of copying a range of cells—press the Period key, and move the cell pointer to the opposite end point of the destination range.

As illustrated in Figure 2-26, the dashed line is complete and the cell pointer is back at cell A8, where it was before you invoked the Copy command.

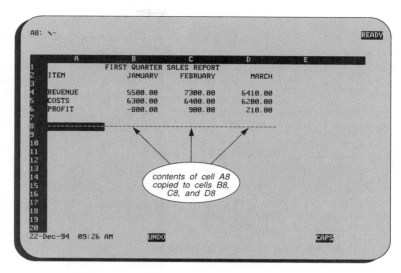

FIGURE 2-26 Step 5 of copying a range of cells—press the Enter key to anchor the end points of the destination range and complete the copy.

With the dashed line complete, move the cell pointer to A10 and begin entering the labels that identify the quarter results. First enter the label QUARTER RESULTS and press the Down Arrow key twice as shown in Figure 2-27.

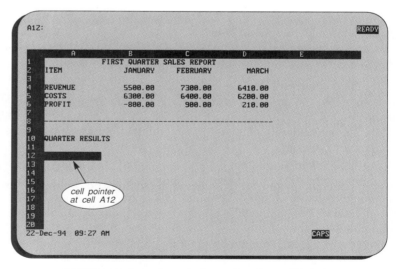

FIGURE 2-27 Step 1 of entering the total labels

Enter the remaining labels that identify the quarter results in cells A12 through A15 by using the Down Arrow key to enter each one. After you complete the label entries, the cell pointer ends up at cell A16 as illustrated in Figure 2-28. Use the GOTO command to move the cell pointer to cell B12, the location of the next entry.

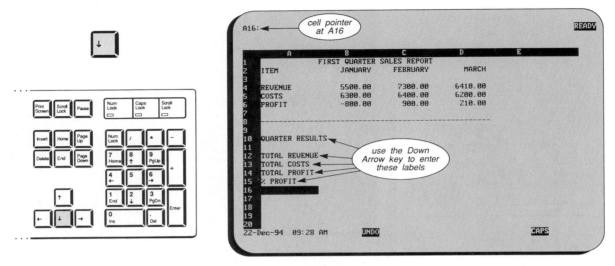

FIGURE 2-28 Step 2 of entering the total labels

SAVING AN INTERMEDIATE COPY OF THE WORKSHEET

◆ It's good practice to save intermediate copies of your worksheet. That way, if the computer loses power or you make a serious mistake, you can always retrieve the latest copy on disk. We recommend that you save an intermediate copy of the worksheet every 50 to 75 keystrokes. It makes sense to use the Save command often, because it saves keying time later if the unexpected happens.

Before we continue with Project 2, let's save the current worksheet as PROJS-2. Recall that to save the worksheet displayed on the screen you must do the following:

1. Enter the command /**F**ile **S**ave (/FS).
2. In response to the prompt message on the input line, type the new file name, PROJS-2. As soon as you type the letter P in PROJS-2, the old file name, PROJS-1, disappears from the input line. File name PROJS-1 is on the input line because we retrieved it to begin this project, and 1-2-3 assumes we want to save the revised worksheet under the same name.
3. Press the Enter key.

After 1-2-3 completes the save, the worksheet remains on the screen. You can immediately continue with the next entry.

USING BUILT-IN FUNCTIONS

◆ 1-2-3 has many **built-in functions** that automatically handle calculations. These built-in functions save you a lot of time and effort because they eliminate the need to enter complex formulas. The first built-in function we will discuss is the SUM function, since it is one of the most widely used. For the remainder of the projects in this book, the term *function* will mean built-in function.

The SUM Function

In the worksheet for Project 2, the total revenue is calculated by adding the values in cells B4, C4, and D4. Whereas the calculation can be written in cell B12 as +B4+C4+D4, an easier and more general method to produce the same result is to use the SUM function. The **SUM function** adds the values in the specified range.

With the cell pointer at B12, enter @SUM(B4.D4) as illustrated on the input line at the top of the screen in Figure 2-29. Notice that the SUM function begins with the **at symbol** (@). Beginning an entry with the @ symbol indicates to 1-2-3 that the entry is a function.

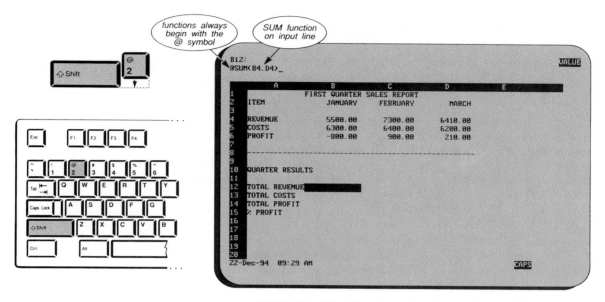

FIGURE 2-29 Entering a function on the input line

After the @ symbol, type the function name SUM (or sum) followed by a left parenthesis. Next, enter B4.D4, the range to be added. The range can be specified either by typing the beginning and ending cells or by using the pointing feature we described earlier. In this case, type the two end points of the range separated by a period (.). Finally, type the right parenthesis.

Press the Enter key as shown on the next page in Figure 2-30. As a result, 1-2-3 evaluates the sum of the entries in cells B4, C4, and D4 and displays the result in cell B12. Functions belong to the broader category called *formulas*. Therefore, 1-2-3 handles functions the same way it handles formulas—it evaluates the function and places a number in the cell. For example, in Figure 2-30, you can see on the mode line that the formula @SUM(B4..D4) is assigned to cell B12. However, the value 19210 displays in cell B12 of the worksheet. The value 19210 is the sum of the numbers in cells B4, C4, and D4.

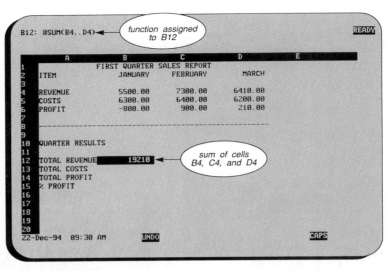

FIGURE 2-30 Press the Enter key to assign the function to B12. When a function is assigned to a cell, it is evaluated and the value displays in the cell.

Copying Functions

According to Figure 2-2, the two cells B13 and B14 require the identical function and similar ranges that we assigned to cell B12 in Figure 2-30. That is, cell B13 should contain the total costs for the quarter, or the sum of cells B5, C5, and D5. Cell B14 should contain the total profit for the quarter, or the sum of cells B6, C6, and D6. Table 2-3 illustrates the similarity between the entry in cell B12 and the entries required in cells B13 and B14.

TABLE 2-3 Three Function Entries for Cells B12, B13, and B14

CELL	FUNCTION ENTRIES
B12	@SUM(B4..D4)
B13	@SUM(B5..D5)
B14	@SUM(B6..D6)

There are two methods for entering the functions in cells B13 and B14. The first method involves moving the cell pointer to B13, entering the function @SUM(B5..D5), then moving the cell pointer to B14 and entering the function @SUM(B6..D6).

The second method, the one we recommend you use, involves the Copy command. That is, copy cell B12 to cells B13 and B14. In Table 2-3, however, the ranges do not agree exactly. Each cell below B12 has a range that is one row below the previous one. Fortunately, when the Copy command copies cell addresses, it adjusts them for the new position. This cell-address adjustment used by the Copy command is called relative addressing. In other words, after cell B12 is copied to cells B13 and B14, the contents of B13 and B14 are identical to the entries shown in Table 2-3.

Let's complete the copy from cell B12 to cells B13 and B14. With the cell pointer at B12 as shown in Figure 2-30, enter the command /Copy (/C). The prompt message "Enter range to copy FROM: B12..B12" displays on the input line as shown in Figure 2-31. Since B12 is the cell that we want to copy to cells B13 and B14, press Enter.

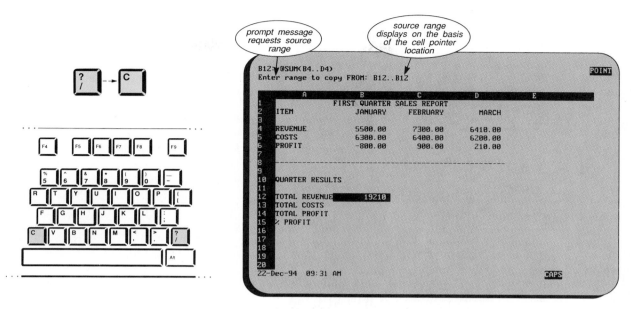

FIGURE 2-31 Step 1 of copying a function—press the Slash key (/) and type the letter C for Copy.

When you press the Enter key, the prompt message "Enter range to copy TO: B12" displays on the input line. This message is shown in Figure 2-32. Use the Down Arrow key to move the cell pointer to B13, the topmost end point of the destination range.

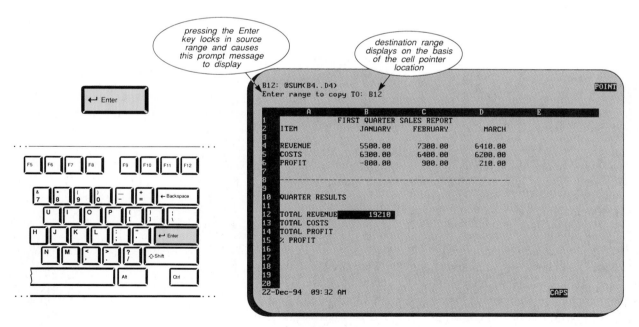

FIGURE 2-32 Step 2 of copying a function—anchor the end points of the source range of cells to copy by pressing the Enter key.

As shown in Figure 2-33, the cell address following the prompt message on the input line has changed from B12 to B13.

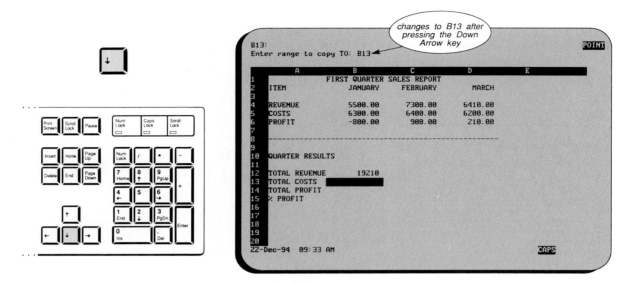

FIGURE 2-33 Step 3 of copying a function—move the cell pointer to one of the end points of the destination range.

Press the Period key to anchor the topmost end point, B13. Next, move the cell pointer to B14 as shown in Figure 2-34.

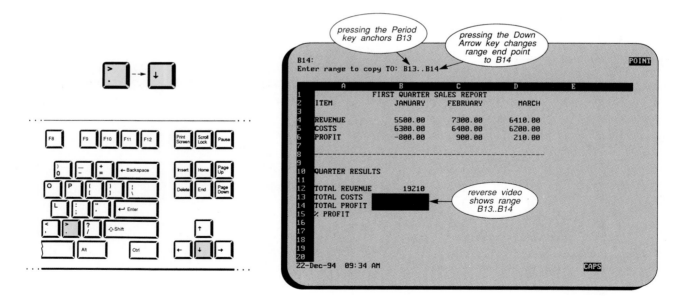

FIGURE 2-34 Step 4 of copying a function—move the cell pointer to the opposite end point of the destination range.

Finally, press the Enter key to copy the function in cell B12 to cells B13 and B14. As illustrated in Figure 2-35, cell B13 contains the total costs for the quarter and cell B14 contains the total profit for the quarter. The cell pointer remains at cell B12, where it was before invoking the Copy command.

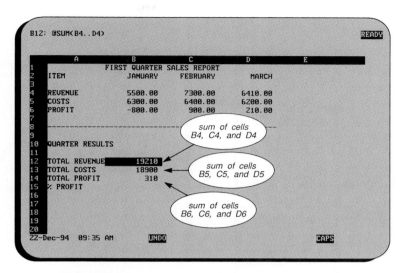

FIGURE 2-35 Step 5 of copying a function—press the Enter key to anchor the end points of the destination range and complete the copy.

Here again, you can undo the Copy command by entering the UNDO command (Alt-F4) after 1-2-3 completes the copy and returns to READY Mode.

DETERMINING A PERCENT VALUE

◆ According to Figure 2-2, the percent profit appears in cell B15. The percent profit is determined by assigning a formula that divides the total profit (cell B14) by the total revenue (cell B12). Recall that the Slash key (/) represents the operation of division, provided it is not the first key typed in READY mode and the entry is not a label.

Move the cell pointer to cell B15 and enter the formula +B14/B12 as shown on the input line in the top screen of Figure 2-36. Next, press the Enter key. 1-2-3 determines the quotient of +B14/B12 and stores the result, 0.0161374284, in cell B15. This is shown in the bottom screen of Figure 2-36.

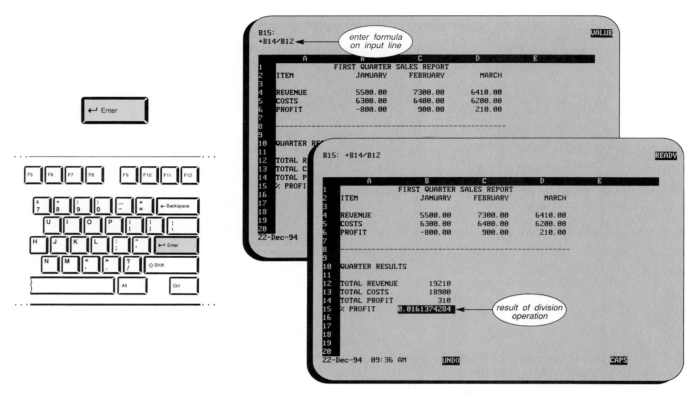

FIGURE 2-36 Entering a percentage

FORMATTING TO PERCENT AND CURRENCY

◆ Although the quarter totals displayed on the worksheet in Figure 2-36 are correct, they are not in an easy-to-read format. The dollar values are displayed as whole numbers and the percentage value is displayed as a decimal number carried out to ten places. In Figure 2-2, the dollar figures in the quarter results are displayed as dollars and cents with a leading dollar sign. Furthermore, the quotient in cell B15 is displayed as a percent with one decimal place. Let's complete the formatting for this project.

The Percentage Format

Since the cell pointer is at B15, first format the decimal value to a percentage value. With the pointer on cell B15, enter the command /**R**ange **F**ormat (/RF) as illustrated in Figure 2-37. With the menu pointer active in the Format menu, type the letter P to select the Percent format. Remember, you can also select the command Percent by moving the menu pointer to highlight the word Percent and pressing the Enter key.

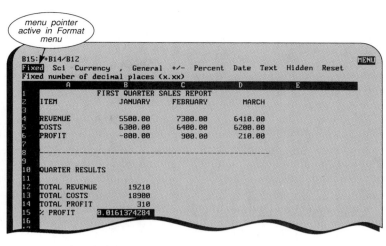

FIGURE 2-37 Step 1 of formatting Percent—press the Slash key (/), type the letter R for Range, and the letter F for Format.

When you type the letter P, 1-2-3 displays the prompt message "Enter number of decimal places (0..15): 2" on the input line. Type the number 1 for one decimal position. This procedure is shown in Figure 2-38.

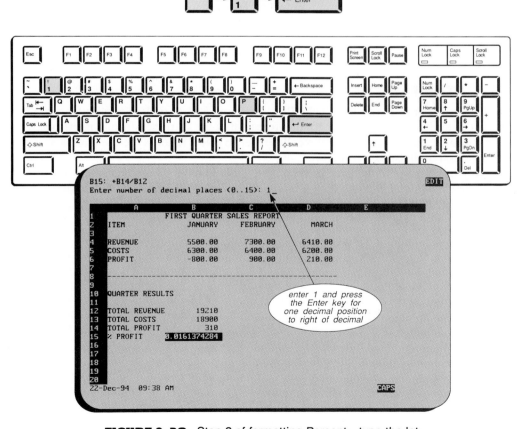

FIGURE 2-38 Step 2 of formatting Percent—type the letter P for Percent and the number 1 for decimal positions desired.

Next, press the Enter key. 1-2-3 displays the prompt message "Enter range to format: B15..B15" on the input line. Again press the Enter key, since we want to assign this format only to cell B15. The decimal number 0.0161374284, assigned to cell B15 by the formula +B14/B12, now displays as 1.6%. This result is shown in Figure 2-39.

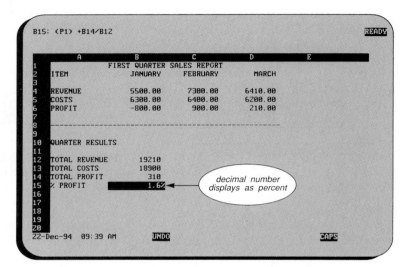

FIGURE 2-39 Step 3 of formatting Percent—press the Enter key, because the range of cells to be affected is only the cell where the cell pointer is located.

The Currency Format

The next step is to format the quarter results in cells B12, B13, and B14 to dollars and cents with a leading dollar sign. Scanning the list of available formats in Table 2-2 reveals that the Currency format is the one that displays monetary amounts with a leading dollar sign. Move the cell pointer to cell B12 and type the command **/R**ange **F**ormat **C**urrency (/RFC). This activity is shown in Figure 2-40.

Press the Enter key in response to the prompt message "Enter number of decimal places (0..15): 2" because the desired number of decimal positions is 2. As shown on the input line in Figure 2-41, 1-2-3 wants to know the range to assign the Currency format. Use the pointing method to enter the range.

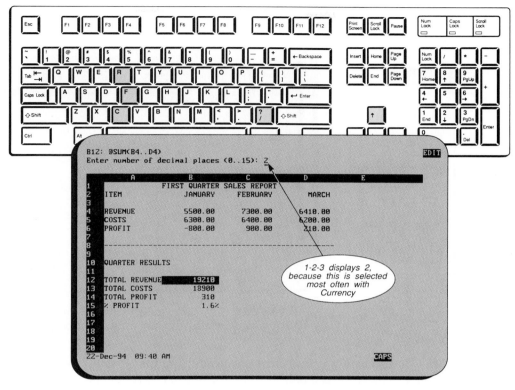

FIGURE 2-40 Step 1 of formatting Currency—move the cell pointer to one of the end points of the range of cells to be affected, press the Slash key (/), and type R for Range, F for Format, and C for Currency.

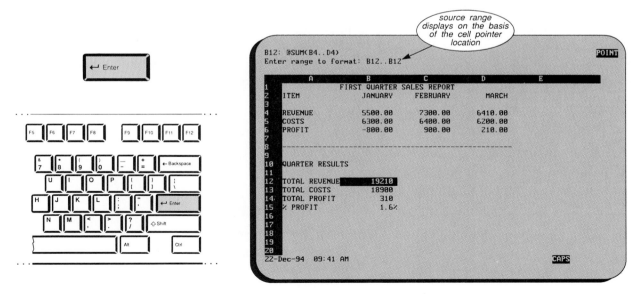

FIGURE 2-41 Step 2 of formatting Currency—press the Enter key. This sets decimal places to 2 and displays the prompt message on the input line.

The first cell address, B12, on the input line is correct. Therefore, move the cell pointer down to B14. As the cell pointer moves, 1-2-3 displays the range in reverse video. Also, the second cell address on the input line changes to agree with the location of the cell pointer. With the cell pointer on B14, the range we want to assign the Currency format is now correct (Figure 2-42).

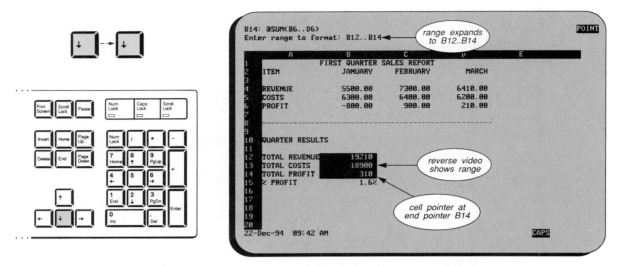

FIGURE 2-42 Step 3 of formatting Currency—use the arrow keys to select the range of cells to be affected.

Next, press the Enter key to assign the Currency format to the designated range in Figure 2-42, cells B12 through B14. Finally, press the Home key to move the cell pointer from cell B12 to cell A1 to prepare for the final step, printing the worksheet. Recall from Project 1 that regardless of where the cell pointer is in the worksheet, it immediately moves to cell A1 when you press the Home key. The complete worksheet is shown in Figure 2-43.

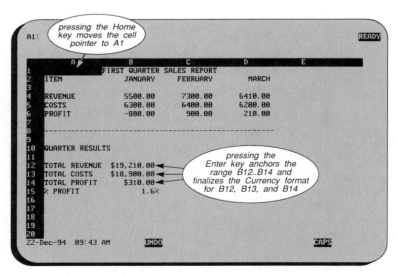

FIGURE 2-43 Step 4 of formatting Currency—press the Enter key to lock in the range B12..B14. The worksheet is complete. Press the Home key to move the cell pointer to A1.

◆ We already saved an intermediate version of the worksheet as PROJS-2. To save the worksheet again, do the following:

1. Enter the command **/F**ile **S**ave (/FS).
2. Since we saved this worksheet earlier in the session, 1-2-3 assumes we want to save it under the same file name. Therefore, it displays the name PROJS-2.WK1 on the input line at the top of the screen as shown in the first screen in Figure 2-44. This saves keying time. Press the Enter key.
3. The menu at the top of the lower screen in Figure 2-44 gives three choices—Cancel, Replace, or Backup. Type the letter R for Replace. 1-2-3 replaces the worksheet we saved earlier on disk with the worksheet on the screen.

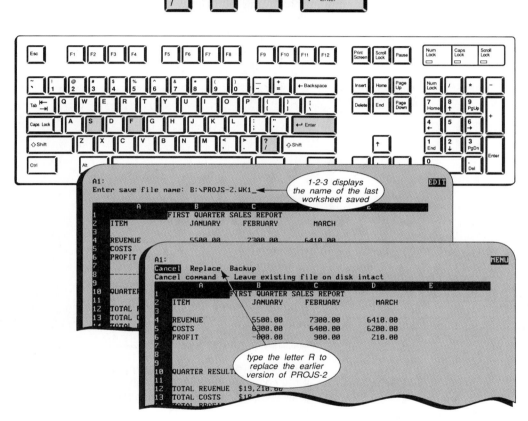

FIGURE 2-44 When a worksheet is saved a second time under the same file name, type the letter R to replace the previous version on disk.

If we type the letter C for Cancel, rather than R for Replace, the Save command is terminated, and 1-2-3 returns to READY mode. If we type the letter B for Backup, the worksheet on disk with the same name is saved under the file name PROJS-2.BAK, and the worksheet on the screen is saved under the name PROJS-2.WK1. A worksheet stored with the extension .BAK is referred to as a backup. Saving a backup copy of the worksheet is another form of protection against losing all your work.

PRINTING THE WORKSHEET

◆ In Project 1 you printed the worksheet by pressing the Print Screen key. The printed report included the window borders as well as the control panel and indicator line. However, window borders clutter the report and make it more difficult to read. In this section, we will discuss how to print the worksheet without the window borders, how to print sections of the worksheet, and how to print the actual entries assigned to the cells in a worksheet.

The Print Printer Command

To print the worksheet without window borders, type the command /**Print Printer** (/PP). This activates the menu pointer in the Print menu at the top of the screen as shown in Figure 2-45. Below the Print menu, 1-2-3 displays the print settings sheet. Press F6 if you want to view the worksheet, rather than the print settings sheet, while the Print menu is active. Press F6 again to view the print settings sheet.

Since this is the first time this report is being printed using the Print command, you must enter the range to print. Type the letter R to select Range from the Print menu. The entire worksheet is in the range A1..D15. With the cell pointer at cell A1, press the Period key to anchor A1.

FIGURE 2-45 Step 1 of printing a worksheet using the Print command—press the Slash key (/) and type the letter P twice, once for Print and once for Printer.

Next, use the arrow keys to move the cell pointer to D15. As the cell pointer moves, the reverse video enlarges to encompass the entire range (Figure 2-46). Press the Enter key to anchor end point D15. The Print menu reappears as shown in Figure 2-47.

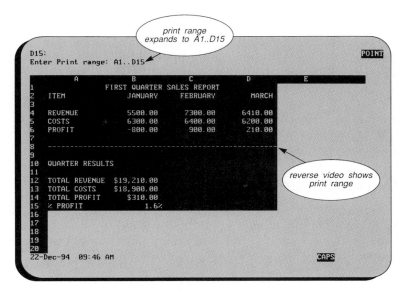

FIGURE 2-46 Step 2 of printing a worksheet using the Print command—type the letter R for Range, use the arrow keys to select the range, and press the Enter key.

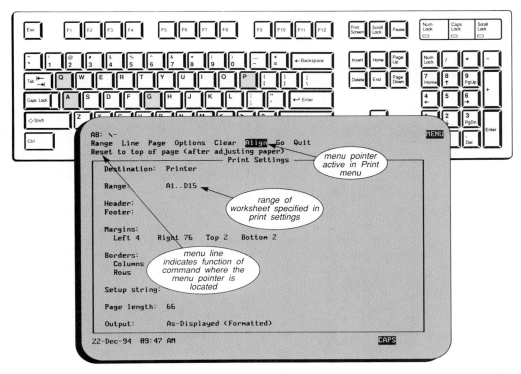

FIGURE 2-47 Step 3 of printing a worksheet using the Print command—type A for Align, G for Go, P for Page, and Q for Quit.

With the printer turned off, use the platen knob on the printer to align the perforated edge of the paper with the top of the print-head mechanism. Turn the printer on.

Type the letter A for Align. 1-2-3 has its own line counter. Invoking the Align command ensures that the program's line counter is the same as the printer's line counter; that is, that both counters are equal to zero after you turn the printer on and enter the Align command. If the two counters do not agree, the printed version of the worksheet may end up with a few inches of white space in the middle.

Next, type the letter G for Go. The printer immediately begins to print the worksheet. When the printer stops printing, type the letter P. Typing the letter P invokes the Page command, which causes the paper in the printer to move to the top of the next page. Carefully tear the paper just below the report at the perforated edge. The printed results are shown in Figure 2-48⟨a⟩.

Quitting the Print Command

The Print command is one of the few commands that does not immediately return 1-2-3 to READY mode when the command is finished executing. To return to READY mode after the Print command is complete, type the letter Q for Quit. This Quit command clears the menu from the control panel and returns 1-2-3 to READY mode with the worksheet displayed on the screen.

Printing a Section of the Worksheet

You may not always want to print the entire worksheet. Portions of the worksheet can be printed by entering the selected range in response to the Range command. Let's assume that you want to print only the quarter results as shown in Figure 2-48⟨b⟩. From Figure 2-43, you can see that the quarter results are in the range A10..B15.

To print the quarter results, enter the command /Print Printer (/PP) as shown in Figure 2-45. Next, type the letter R for Range. The screen in Figure 2-46 displays because 1-2-3 always remembers the last range entered for the Print command.

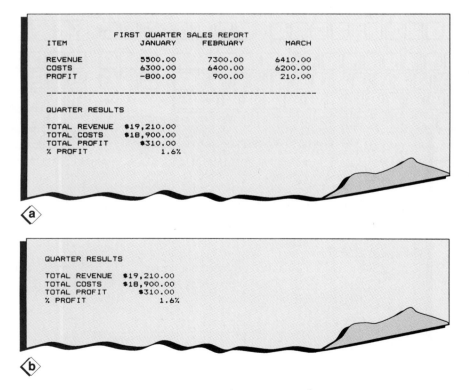

FIGURE 2-48 Complete ⟨a⟩ and partial ⟨b⟩ printed versions of the worksheet.

To change the range, press the Backspace key to free the end points A1 and D15 on the input line. Use the arrow keys to move the cell pointer to A10. Press the Period key (.) to anchor the upper left end point of the range containing the quarter results. Move the cell pointer to B15. At this point, the screen appears as shown in Figure 2-49. Press the Enter key to anchor the lower right end point.

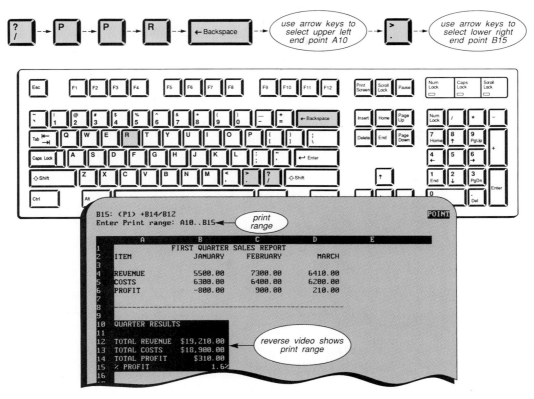

FIGURE 2-49 Printing a portion of the worksheet

Next, make sure the paper is aligned and the printer is ready. As described in Figure 2-47, type the letter A for Align and the letter G for Go to print the partial report. The partial report shown in Figure 2-48⟨b⟩ prints on the printer. When the report is complete, type the letter P to eject the paper from the printer. Finally, type the letter Q for Quit to complete the Print command. The Print menu disappears from the control panel, and 1-2-3 returns to READY mode with the worksheet displayed on the screen. At this point, if you enter the UNDO command (Alt-F4), 1-2-3 will reset the print settings to the ones shown in Figure 2-47.

Printing the Cell-Formulas Version of the Worksheet

Thus far, we have printed the worksheet exactly as it is on the screen. This is called the **as-displayed** version of the worksheet. Another variation that we print is called the cell-formulas version. The **cell-formulas** version prints what was assigned to the cells, rather than what's in the cells. It is useful for debugging a worksheet because the formulas and functions print out, rather than the numeric results.

Figure 2-50 illustrates the printed cell-formulas version of this worksheet. Each filled cell in the selected range is printed on a separate line. The cell address is printed in the left column, followed by any special formatting that was assigned to the cell, and the actual contents. The information displayed in the report is identical to the display on the mode line for the current cell.

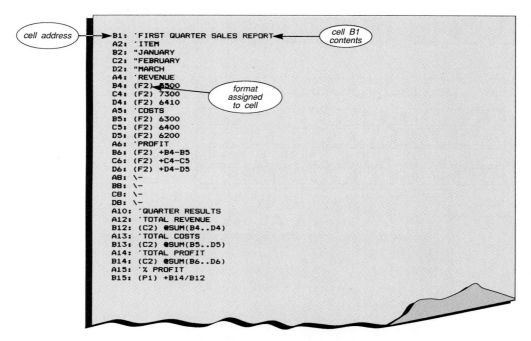

FIGURE 2-50   Cell-formulas version of the worksheet

To print the cell-formulas version of the worksheet, type the command **/Print Printer R**ange (/PPR). Enter the range A1..D15 and press the Enter key. With the menu pointer still active in the Print menu, enter the command **Options Other Cell-formulas Quit Align Go P**age (OOCQAGP). 1-2-3 prints the cell-formulas version of Project 2 as shown in Figure 2-50.

Once the Print command option has been set to print the cell-formulas version, 1-2-3 will continue to print this variation each time you use the **/Print Printer** (/PP) command until you change the print option back to as-displayed. Therefore, after printing the cell-formulas version, but before quitting the Print command, enter the command **Options Other A**s-displayed **Quit Quit** (OOAQQ). The last Quit in the chain of commands causes 1-2-3 to return to READY mode. The next time the Print command is used, 1-2-3 will print the as-displayed version. Another way to switch back to the as-displayed version is to use the UNDO command after the cell-formulas version is printed and after 1-2-3 has returned to READY mode.

Printing a Worksheet to a File

You can instruct 1-2-3 to transmit the printed version of a worksheet to a file. This can be useful if your printer is not functioning or if you prefer to print the worksheet at a later time. Use the command /**Print File** (/PF), rather than /**Print Printer** (/PP). When you enter the command /PF, 1-2-3 requests a file name. After you enter the file name, the Print menu in Figure 2-47 displays with the file name as the destination, rather than printer. From this point on, you can select commands from the Print menu as if you were printing the worksheet directly to the printer.

Later, after quitting 1-2-3, you can use the DOS command Type to display the worksheet on the screen or the DOS command Print to print the worksheet on the printer. The file extension .PRN, which stands for printer file, automatically appends to the file name you select.

Summary of Commands in the Print Menu

Table 2-4 summarizes the commands available in the Print menu.

TABLE 2-4 A Summary of Commands in the Print Menu

COMMAND	FUNCTION
Range	Allows you to specify what part of the worksheet is printed.
Line	Moves the paper in the printer one line.
Page	Advances the paper in the printer to the top of the next page on the basis of the program's page-length setting.
Options	Sets header, footer, margins, page length, borders, and special printer commands.
Clear	Sets Print command settings to their default and clears the current print-range setting.
Align	Resets the line counter for the printer.
Go	Starts printing the worksheet on the printer.
Quit	Returns 1-2-3 to READY mode.

DEBUGGING THE FORMULAS IN A WORKSHEET USING THE TEXT FORMAT

◆ **Debugging** is the process of finding and correcting errors in a worksheet. When formulas are assigned to the cells in a worksheet, the cell-formulas version is a handy tool for debugging it. Recall that the cell-formulas version shows the formulas associated with a worksheet (Figure 2-50). An alternative to printing the cell-formulas version of the worksheet is to format the worksheet to the Text type. This format allows you to see the formulas in the cells on the screen, instead of their numeric result. When the worksheet is formatted to the Text type, it is called the **text version**.

To view the text version of the worksheet, do the following:

1. Save the worksheet to disk so that you don't lose the formats currently assigned to the cells in the worksheet.
2. Enter the command /**Range Format Text** (/RFT) and enter the range A1..D15.

As shown in Figure 2-51, the formulas display in the cells instead of their numeric results. One problem with this procedure is that if a formula is longer than the width of the cell, a portion of it is hidden.

When you are finished viewing or printing the worksheet formatted to the Text type, retrieve from disk the original version of the worksheet—the one that contains the properly formatted cells.

Instead of saving the worksheet before changing the format to text, you can use the UNDO command (Alt-F4) after viewing the formulas in the cells and before making any new entries.

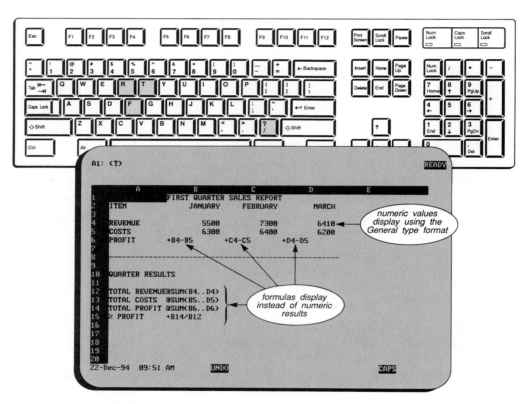

FIGURE 2-51 Display of the formulas in the cells instead of the numeric results. Use the command /Range Format Text (/RFT) and enter the range A1..D15.

PROJECT SUMMARY

In Project 2 you formatted the numeric values you entered in Project 1, added summaries, and formatted the summaries. Although this sequence of performing operations works well in many applications, it is not mandatory. For example, it may be more economical in terms of time and effort to enter portions of the data and then format it immediately, or it might be advisable to format the cells before entering the data into the worksheet. You will learn which sequence to choose as you gain experience with 1-2-3.

In Project 2 you learned how to load a worksheet, increase the size of columns, specify a range, copy cells, format a worksheet, and print a worksheet without window borders. All the activities that you learned for this project are summarized in the Quick Reference following the Appendix. The following is a summary of the keystroke sequence we used in Project 2.

SUMMARY OF KEYSTROKES — PROJECT 2

STEPS	KEY(S) PRESSED	RESULTS
1	/FR←	Retrieves PROJS-1 from disk.
2	[Caps Lock]	Sets Caps Lock on.
3	/WGC13←	Sets column width to 13.
4	/RFF← [Backspace] ←←←↑↑.↓↓ →→←	Sets monthly revenue, costs, and profit to a fixed format with two decimal places.
5	[F5] A8←	Moves the cell pointer to A8.
6	\-←	Repeats dashes in cell A8.
7	/C←→.→→←	Copies dashes in cell A8 to cells B8, C8, and D8.
8	↓↓QUARTER RESULTS↓↓	Enters title.
9	TOTAL REVENUE↓	Enters title.
10	TOTAL COSTS↓	Enters title.
11	TOTAL PROFIT↓	Enters title.
12	% PROFIT↓	Enters title.
13	[F5] B12←	Moves the cell pointer to B12.
14	/FSPROJS-2←	Saves worksheet as PROJS-2.
15	@SUM(B4.D4)←	Enters SUM function for total revenue.
16	/C←↓.↓←	Copies SUM function from cell B12 to B13 and B14.
17	↓↓↓+B14/B12←	Enters % profit formula.
18	/RFP1←←	Formats decimal number in cell B15 to percent.
19	↑↑↑/RFC←↓↓←	Formats the total revenue, costs, and profit to the Currency type.
20	[Home]	Moves the cell pointer to A1.
21	/FS←R	Saves worksheet as PROJS-2.
22	/PPRA1.D15←AGPQ	Prints the as-displayed version of the worksheet.
23	/PPRA10.B15←AGPQ	Prints a portion of the worksheet.
24	/PPRA1.D15←OOCQAGP	Prints the cell-formulas version of the worksheet.
25	OOAQQ	Changes the print option to as-displayed.
26	/RFTA1.D15←	Formats the worksheet to the Text type.

The following list summarizes the material covered in Project 2.

1. To retrieve a worksheet from disk, enter the command **/F**ile **R**etrieve (/FR). Use the Left and Right Arrow keys to move the menu pointer in the alphabetized list on the menu line to the worksheet name you want to retrieve and then press the Enter key.

2. **Global** means the entire worksheet. To change the width of all the columns in the worksheet, type the command **/W**orksheet **G**lobal **C**olumn-Width (/WGC). Enter the desired column width (1–240) on the input line and press the Enter key.

3. To change the width of a range of columns, enter the command **/W**orksheet **C**olumn **C**olumn-Range **S**et-Width (/WCCS). Enter the range of columns and the desired column width. Press the Enter key to complete the command.

4. To change the width of a specific column in the worksheet, move the cell pointer to the column in question and type the command **/W**orksheet **C**olumn **S**et-Width (/WCS). Enter the new width and press the Enter key.

5. A **range** is one or more cells upon which you want to complete an operation. A range may be a single cell, a series of adjacent cells in a column or row, or a rectangular group of adjacent cells. A range cannot be made up of cells that only run diagonally or are separated.

6. To enter a range, type the cell address at one end point of the range, followed by a period (.) to anchor the first end point, followed by the cell address at the opposite end point of the range. If it is necessary to change the first end point after it is *anchored*, press the Backspace key.

7. If a range defines a rectangular group of cells, the two end points must be diagonally opposite corner cells of the rectangle.

8. To format a range, type the command **/Range Format** (/RF). Select the type of format you want to use from the menu. Enter the number of decimal places if required. Enter the range to be affected and press the Enter key.

9. To format the entire worksheet, type the command **/Worksheet Global Format** (/WGF). Follow the same steps described for formatting a range.

10. You can also enter a range by **pointing**. Pointing involves using the arrow keys to move the cell pointer to select the end points.

11. When you use pointing to select the range, use the Backspace key to *unlock* the end points of the range on the input line.

12. 1-2-3 displays the range with the end points separated by two periods (..), even though you enter only a single period (.) to anchor the first end point.

13. There are several ways to format numeric values using the **/Worksheet Global Format** (/WGF) or **/Range Format** (/RF) command.

14. Move the cell pointer to a cell to determine the format assigned to it. The format displays in parentheses next to the cell address on the mode line at the top of the screen.

15. To repeat a series of characters throughout a cell, begin the entry by typing the **Backslash key** (\).

16. To copy a range to another range, type the command **/Copy** (/C). Enter the **source range** and then the **destination range**.

17. It is good practice to save a worksheet to disk after every 50 to 75 keystrokes.

18. A **built-in function** automatically handles calculations.

19. The **SUM function** adds the contents of the range specified in parentheses.

20. All built-in functions begin with the **@@ symbol**.

21. When you copy a function, the Copy command adjusts the range for the new position.

22. If the Slash key (/) is the first key pressed, 1-2-3 switches to MENU mode. If the Slash key follows any character in a nonlabel entry on the input line, it represents division.

23. When you save a worksheet the second time using the same file name, 1-2-3 requires that you type the letter R for Replace.

24. To print the **as-displayed** version of the worksheet without borders, type the command **/Print Printer** (/PP). If the range has not yet been established from a previous printout of the worksheet, you must enter the range to print. With the printer off, use the platen knob to align the perforated edge of the paper with the top of the print-head mechanism. Turn the printer on. Type the letter A for Align and the letter G for Go. After the worksheet is printed, type the letter P for Page. Carefully remove the printed version of the worksheet from the printer. Finally, type the letter Q for Quit.

25. To print a section of the worksheet, enter the command **/Print Printer Range** (/PPR). Use the Backspace key to *unlock* the range. Enter the desired range and continue with the steps just outlined.

26. To print the **cell-formulas** version of the worksheet, type the command **/Print Printer Options Other Cell-formulas Quit Align Go Page** (/PPOOCQAGP). It is important to change the print option back to as-displayed, so that future printouts will print the as-displayed version rather than the cell-formulas version. One way to change the printout back to as-displayed is to use the UNDO command after the cell-formulas version prints and 1-2-3 returns to READY mode.

27. To print the worksheet to a file, use the command **/Print File** (/PF). Later, after you have quit 1-2-3, you may use the DOS command Type to display the worksheet on the screen or the DOS command Print to print the worksheet on the printer.

28. To display formulas assigned to cells rather than their numeric result, assign the Text type format to the cells in the worksheet. When the worksheet is formatted to the Text type, it is called the **text version**.

STUDENT ASSIGNMENTS

STUDENT ASSIGNMENT 1: True/False

Instructions: Circle T if the statement is true or F if the statement is false.

T F   1. If you want to completely *back out* of the command /FR, press the Esc key once.

T F   2. The command /**W**orksheet **G**lobal **C**olumn-Width (/WGC) is used to set the width of all the columns in the worksheet.

T F   3. With the /**F**ile **R**etrieve (/FR) command, you are not required to type the name of the worksheet on the input line you want loaded into main memory.

T F   4. A range is made up of a minimum of two or more cells.

T F   5. When using the command /**R**ange **F**ormat (/RF), entire rows can be formatted; however, entire columns cannot be formatted.

T F   6. For a rectangular group of cells, you can enter the cell addresses of any two opposite corners to define the range.

T F   7. A range can be referenced by an entry such as B4..D6.

T F   8. With the format Currency, negative numbers display in parentheses.

T F   9. If you decide to use the point method when 1-2-3 requests a range, press the Backspace key to *unlock* the first end point, if necessary.

T F 10. If the Backslash key (\) is the first character typed on the input line, the characters that follow will repeat throughout the cell when you press the Enter key or one of the arrow keys.

T F 11. If the function @SUM(B4..D4) is assigned to cell A20, then A20 will be equal to the sum of the contents of cells B4 and D4.

T F 12. The command /**C**opy (/C) is used to copy the contents of a range of cells to another range of cells.

T F 13. The type of format assigned to a cell displays on the mode line at the top of the screen when the cell pointer is on the cell.

T F 14. When in POINT mode, anchor the first cell end point by moving the cell pointer to it and pressing the Period key.

T F 15. The Align command in the Print menu is used to align the decimal points in the selected range.

T F 16. If you save a worksheet a second time, you can use the same file name originally assigned to the worksheet.

T F 17. If the function @SUM(B4..B8) assigns a value of 10 to cell B9, and B9 is copied to C9, then C9 may or may not be equal to 10.

T F 18. It is possible to copy a single cell to a range of cells.

STUDENT ASSIGNMENT 2: Multiple Choice

Instructions: Circle the correct response.

1. Which one of the following is a valid entry for a range of cells?
   a. A1.A1
   b. B2,D2
   c. B2:D2
   d. both b and c

2. The format Comma (,) with two decimal places causes 5000 to display as _____.
   a. $5,000.00
   b. 5000.00
   c. 5,000.00
   d. $5000.00

3. Which one of the following instructs 1-2-3 to center characters in the current cell?
   a. circumflex (^)
   b. quotation mark (")
   c. apostrophe (')
   d. backslash (\)

4. Which of the following is the correct command for retrieving the worksheet PROJS-1.WK1 stored on the disk in the default drive?
   a. /FRPROJS-1 ↵
   b. /WRPROJS-1 ↵
   c. /CPROJS-1 ↵
   d. none of the above

Student Assignment 2 (continued)

5. When the command /Worksheet Global (/WG) is used, it means that _____ .
   a. only a single cell will be affected   c. only a single row will be affected
   b. only a single column will be affected   d. the entire worksheet will be affected
6. A listing on the printer of the worksheet as it displays on the screen is called the _____ version of the worksheet.
   a. cell-formulas   c. formatted
   b. as-displayed   d. content
7. Which one of the following causes the data in cells B4, C4, and D4 to be added together?
   a. @SUM(B4.D4)   c. @SUM(B4:D4)
   b. @ADD(B4.D4)   d. @SUM(B4 C4 D4)
8. Which one of the following correctly identifies the range of the rectangular group of cells with corner cells at B12, B20, E12, and E20?
   a. B12.E20   c. E20.B12
   b. B20.E12   d. all of the above

STUDENT ASSIGNMENT 3: Understanding Ranges

Instructions: List all the possible ranges for each of the designated areas in the following figure. For example, one range that identifies the first group of cells is A1..B3. There are three other ways to identify this first group of cells.

Cell group 1:   _A1..B3_   _____   _____   _____

Cell group 2:   _____

Cell group 3:   _____   _____

Cell group 4:   _____   _____

Cell group 5:   _____   _____   _____   _____

STUDENT ASSIGNMENT 4: Understanding Formats

Instructions: Using Table 2-2, fill in the *Results In* column of the following table. Assume that the column width of each cell is 10 characters. Use the character b to indicate positions containing the blank character. As examples, the first two problems in the table below are complete.

Determining the Value of a Number Based on a Given Format

PROBLEM	CELL CONTENTS	FORMAT TO	DECIMAL PLACES	RESULTS IN
1	25	Fixed	1	bbbbb25.0b
2	1.26	Currency	2	bbbb$1.26b
3	14.816	,(comma)	2	_____
4	−5281.42	Fixed	0	_____
5	123	Percent	2	_____
6	7	+/−	Not reqd.	_____
7	−3841.92	, (comma)	3	_____
8	72148.92	General	Not reqd.	_____
9	32	Percent	2	_____
10	.148	Fixed	2	_____
11	109234	Currency	0	_____
12	4.86	Scientific	1	_____
13	−1276	Currency	2	_____
14	51214.76	Scientific	0	_____
15	−5010.50	Currency	2	_____

STUDENT ASSIGNMENT 5: Correcting the Range in a Worksheet

Instructions: The worksheet illustrated in the following figure contains errors in cells B12 through B15. Analyze the entries displayed in the worksheet. Explain the cause of the errors and the method of correction in the space provided below.

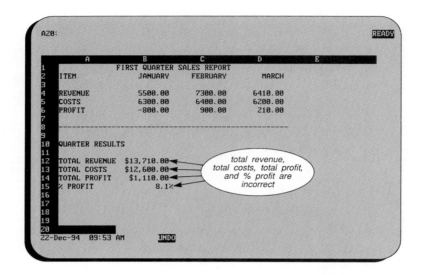

Cause of error: _____

_____

Method of correction for cell B12: _____

_____

Method of correction for cells B13, B14, and B15: _____

_____

_____

STUDENT ASSIGNMENT 6: Correcting Functions in a Worksheet

Instructions: The worksheet illustrated in the following figure contains invalid function entries in cells B12, B13, and B14. The invalid entries in these cells cause the diagnostic message ERR to display in cell B15. Analyze the entries displayed in the worksheet. Explain the cause of the errors and the method of correction in the space provided below.

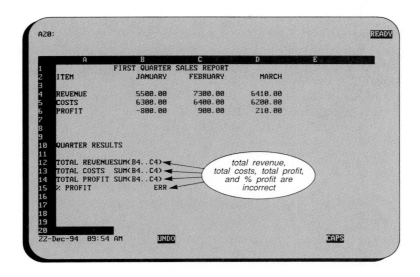

Cause of error: _____

_____

Method of correction for cell B12: _____

_____

Method of correction for cells B13, B14, and B15: _____

_____

_____

STUDENT ASSIGNMENT 7: Modifying an Inventory Worksheet

Instructions: Load 1-2-3 and perform the following tasks.

1. Load the worksheet that you created in Project 1, Student Assignment 8 (STUS1-8). This original worksheet is illustrated in the following figure ⟨a⟩.
2. Perform these modifications:
   a. Use the Comma (,) format with zero decimal places for the numbers in rows 5, 6, 7, and 9.
   b. Include the inventory total in the worksheet, as illustrated in the modified worksheet ⟨b⟩. The inventory total consists of a total for each plant (B15..B17). For example, the total for Chicago is the sum of cells B5 through D5. Separate the inventory total from the other values by a double line in row 11 (use the equal sign).
   c. Use the Comma (,) format with zero decimal places for the inventory totals.
3. Save the modified worksheet. Use the file name STUS2-7.
4. Print the entire worksheet on the printer using the **/Print Printer** (/PP) command.
5. Print only the inventory totals in the range A13..B19.
6. Print the worksheet after formatting all the cells to the Text type.

⟨a⟩ **Original worksheet**

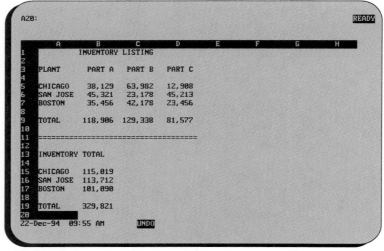

⟨b⟩ **Modified worksheet**

STUDENT ASSIGNMENT 8: Building an Office Payroll Comparison Worksheet

Instructions: Load 1-2-3 and perform the following tasks.

1. Build the worksheet illustrated in the following figure. Change the width of all the columns to 14 characters. The totals displayed in row 10 of the worksheet are the sum of the salaried personnel in column B and the hourly personnel in column C. The office totals by city (B15..B18) are the sum of the salaried personnel and the hourly personnel for each office. The total in B20 is the sum of the office totals.
2. Save the worksheet. Use the file name STUS2-8.
3. Print the as-displayed and cell-formulas versions of this worksheet.
4. Print the portion of the worksheet in the range A1..C10.

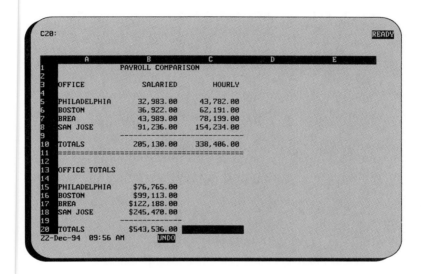

STUDENT ASSIGNMENT 9: Building an Annual Expense Worksheet

Instructions: Load 1-2-3 and perform the following tasks.

1. Build the worksheet illustrated in the following figure. Change the width of all the columns to 15 character positions. The variances in column D of the worksheet are obtained by subtracting the actual expenses from the budgeted expenses. In the summary portion of the worksheet, the percentage of budget used (C17) is obtained by dividing the total actual amount (C15) by the total budgeted amount (C14).
2. Save the worksheet. Use the file name STUS2-9.
3. Print the as-displayed and cell-formulas versions of this worksheet.
4. Print the portion of the worksheet in the range A3..B8.
5. Print the worksheet after formatting all the cells to the Text type.

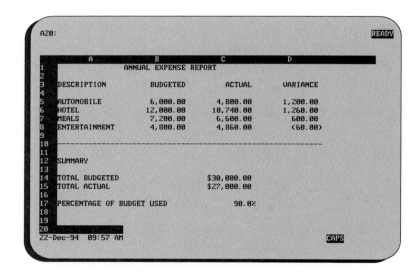

STUDENT ASSIGNMENT 10: Changing Data in the Annual Expense Worksheet

Instructions: Load 1-2-3 and perform the following tasks.

1. Retrieve the worksheet STUS2-9 from disk. The worksheet is illustrated in the figure in Student Assignment 9.
2. Decrement each of the four values in the ACTUAL column by $360.00 until the percentage of budget used in C17 is as close as possible to 80%. All four values in column C must be decremented the same number of times. You should end up with a percentage of budget used in C17 equal to 80.4%.
3. After successfully modifying the worksheet, print it on the printer.
4. Save the modified worksheet. Use the file name STUS2-10.

STUDENT ASSIGNMENT 11: Building a Monthly Sales Analysis Worksheet

Instructions: Load 1-2-3 and perform the following tasks.

1. Build the worksheet illustrated in the following figure. Change the width of all the columns to 12 characters. Then change the width of column A to 14 positions. Center all the column headings using the circumflex (^). The net sales in column D of the worksheet is determined by subtracting the sales returns in column C from the sales amount in column B. The above/below quota amount in column F is obtained by subtracting the sales quota in column E from the net sales in column D. In the summary section of the worksheet, the totals for each group are obtained by adding the values for each salesperson. The percent of quota sold in cell C20 is obtained by dividing the total net sales amount in C17 by the total sales quota amount in C18.
2. Save the worksheet. Use the file name STUS2-11.
3. Print the as-displayed and cell-formulas versions of this worksheet.
4. Print the portion of the worksheet in the range A1..F9.
5. Print the worksheet after formatting all the cells to the Text type.

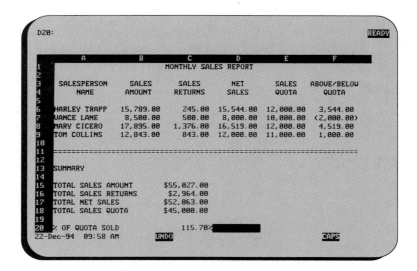

STUDENT ASSIGNMENT 12: Changing Data in the Monthly Sales Analysis Worksheet

Instructions: Load 1-2-3 and perform the following tasks.

1. Retrieve the worksheet STUS2-11 from disk. The worksheet is illustrated in the figure in Student Assignment 11.
2. Increment each of the four values in the sales quota column by $1,000.00 until the percent of quota sold in cell C20 is below, yet as close as possible to 100%. All four values in column E must be incremented the same number of times. The percent of quota sold in C20 should be equal to 98.23%.
3. Decrement each of the four values in the sales returns column by $100.00 until the percent of quota sold in cell C20 is below, yet as close as possible to 100%. All four values in column C must be decremented the same number of times. Your worksheet is correct when the percent of quota sold in C20 is equal to 99.74%.
4. After successfully modifying the worksheet, print it on the printer.
5. Save the modified worksheet. Use the file name STUS2-12.

Enhancing Your Worksheet

OBJECTIVES

You will have mastered the material in this project when you can:

◆ Display today's date and time in a worksheet using the NOW function

◆ Move a group of rows or columns to another area of the worksheet

◆ Insert and delete rows and columns

◆ Freeze the horizontal and vertical titles

◆ Enter percentage values using the percent sign (%)

◆ Copy absolute cell addresses

◆ Employ the pointing method to enter a range to be summed

◆ Print a worksheet in condensed mode

◆ Print selected nonadjacent columns

◆ Answer what-if questions

◆ Switch between manual and automatic recalculation of a worksheet

◆ Change the default settings

◆ Temporarily exit 1-2-3 and return control to DOS

◆ Produce presentation-quality printouts using the add-in program Allways

In the first two projects you learned to build, save, retrieve, format, copy, and print worksheets. In this project we continue to emphasize these topics and discuss some new ones. We especially want to examine the Copy command in greater detail. The capability to copy one range to another range is one of the most powerful features of 1-2-3.

The new topics in this project teach you to insert and delete rows and columns in a worksheet, move the contents of a range to another range, and use the add-in program Allways to produce presentation-quality printouts. In general, they make the job of creating, saving, and printing a worksheet easier.

Finally, this project illustrates using 1-2-3 to answer what-if questions, like *What if the marketing expenses decrease 3%—how would the decrease affect net income for the first quarter of the year?* This capability of quickly analyzing the effect of changing values in a worksheet is important in making business decisions. To illustrate answering what-if questions, we will prepare the quarterly budget report shown in Figure 3-1.

```
              A              B            C            D            E
 1  Quarterly Report - January through March              12/22/94
 2  Prepared by SAS                                        10:01 AM
 3
 4
 5  ITEM              JANUARY     FEBRUARY       MARCH  QUARTER TOTAL
 6  ============================================================================
 7
 8  REVENUE
 9    Sales Revenue  232,897.95   432,989.76   765,998.61   1,431,886.32
10    Other Revenue    1,232.93     3,265.81     2,145.99       6,644.73
11
12    Total Revenue  234,130.88   436,255.57   768,144.60   1,438,531.05
13
14  EXPENSES
15    Manufacturing   88,969.73   165,777.12   291,894.95     546,641.80
16    Research        25,754.40    47,988.11    84,495.91     158,238.42
17    Marketing       37,460.94    69,800.89   122,903.14     230,164.97
18    Administrative  39,802.25    74,163.45   130,584.58     244,550.28
19    Fulfillment     18,730.47    34,900.45    61,451.57     115,082.48
20
21    Total Expenses 210,717.79   392,630.01   691,330.14   1,294,677.95
22
23  NET INCOME        23,413.09    43,625.56    76,814.46     143,853.10
24
25  Budget % Values
26
27    Manufacturing       38%
28    Research            11%
29    Marketing           16%
30    Administrative      17%
31    Fulfillment          8%
```

FIGURE 3-1 A printout of the worksheet we will build in Project 3.

The worksheet in Figure 3-1 contains a company's budgeted revenue and expenses for the quarterly period of January through March. In addition, this worksheet includes the quarter total for all revenues and budgeted expenses. The total revenues for each month and the quarter total in row 12 are determined by adding the corresponding sales revenue and other revenue.

Each of the budgeted expenses—manufacturing, research, marketing, administrative, and fulfillment—is determined by taking a percentage of the total revenue. The budget percent values located in rows 27 through 31 are as follows:

1. The manufacturing expense is 38% of the total revenue.
2. The research expense is 11% of the total revenue.
3. The marketing expense is 16% of the total revenue.
4. The administrative expense is 17% of the total revenue.
5. The fulfillment expense is 8% of the total revenue.

The total expenses for each month in row 21 of Figure 3-1 are determined by adding all the corresponding budgeted expenses together. The net income for each month in row 23 is determined by subtracting the corresponding total expenses from the total revenue. Finally, the quarter totals in the far right column are determined by summing the monthly values in each row.

Begin this project by booting the computer and loading 1-2-3. A few seconds after the copyright message displays, an empty worksheet appears on the screen. All the columns in the empty worksheet are nine characters wide. This default width is not enough to hold some of the larger numbers in the worksheet we plan to build. Therefore, let's change the width of the columns.

VARYING THE WIDTH OF THE COLUMNS

◆ In the worksheet shown in Figure 3-1, column A is 17 characters wide, columns B through D are 13 characters wide, and column E is 16 characters wide. You select a column width setting on the basis of the longest column entry and the general appearance of the worksheet. Change the widths of the columns in the following manner:

1. Enter the command /Worksheet Global Column-Width (/WGC) to change the width of all the columns to 13 characters. Change the number on the input line from 9 to 13 by pressing the Right Arrow key four times followed by the Enter key as shown in Figure 3-2. We can also enter the number 13 in response to the prompt message on the input line and press the Enter key. The Global command is used to change the width of all the cells in the worksheet to 13 characters because that is the desired width of most of the columns for this project.

FIGURE 3-2 Using the command /WGC and the Right Arrow key to increase the width of all the columns in the worksheet to 13 characters

2. With the cell pointer at A1, enter the command /Worksheet Column Set-Width (/WCS) to change the width of column A to 17 characters. Again, press the Right Arrow key four times to change the number 13 to 17 on the input line. To complete the command, press the Enter key as shown in Figure 3-3. Notice on the top line of the control panel in Figure 3-3, next to the cell address, 1-2-3 displays the width of column A in brackets—[W17]. Anytime the cell pointer is in a column that has a width different from the global width, 1-2-3 displays it next to the cell address in the upper left corner of the screen.

FIGURE 3-3

Using the command /WCS and the Right Arrow key to increase the width of column A to 17 characters

3. Move the cell pointer to E1 and enter the command /Worksheet Column Set-Width (/WCS) to change the width of column E to 16 characters. This is shown in Figure 3-4.

FIGURE 3-4

Using the command /WCS and the Right Arrow key to increase the width of column E to 16 characters

As we mentioned in Project 2, columns B, C, and D could have been set to 13 characters by using the command /Worksheet Column Column-Range Set-Width (/WCCS), rather than changing the width globally as shown in Figure 3-2. This command works the same as the /Worksheet Global Column-Width (/WGC), except that you must enter the range of columns involved in the change.

With the columns set to their designated widths, we can move on to the next step, formatting the worksheet globally.

FORMATTING THE WORKSHEET GLOBALLY

In Project 2 we formatted the numbers after we entered the data. In some cases, especially when developing a large worksheet, you should consider issuing a global format before entering any data. This formats the numbers as you enter them, which makes them easier to read. The way to do this is to choose the format that is common to most of the cells. In choosing the format, don't count the empty cells or the ones with labels, because a numeric format does not affect them.

You can see from Figure 3-1 that, except for the budget percent values and the date and time, all the numbers appear as decimal numbers with two places of accuracy. These numbers also use the comma to group the integer portion by thousands. If you refer to Table 2-2 in Project 2, you will see that the required format corresponds to the Comma (,) type. Therefore, use this format for all the cells in the worksheet.

To invoke the global format command, enter the command /**W**orksheet **G**lobal **F**ormat (/WGF). This is shown in Figure 3-5.

FIGURE 3-5 Step 1 of using the /WGF command to format all the cells in the worksheet to the Comma (,) type—press the Slash key (/) and type the letters W for Worksheet, G for Global, and F for Format.

With the menu pointer active in the Format menu, press the Comma key (,). The prompt message "Enter number of decimal places (0..15): 2" displays on the input line (Figure 3-6). Since we are working with dollars and cents, we want two decimal places to display, so press the Enter key.

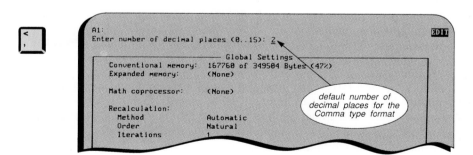

FIGURE 3-6 Step 2 of using the /WGF command to format all the cells in the worksheet to the Comma (,) type—press the Comma key (,).

The empty worksheet shown in Figure 3-7 displays. You can see that the columns are wider than nine characters. However, there is no indication of the Comma format assigned to all the cells. The format will appear as you enter data because 1-2-3 will automatically use the Comma format for any number entered into a cell.

FIGURE 3-7
Step 3 of using the /WGF command to format all the cells in the worksheet to the Comma (,) type—press the Enter key.

DISPLAYING THE DATE AND TIME

◆ With the column widths and the global format set, the next step is to enter the data into the worksheet. Enter the titles in cells A1 and A2 as you learned in Project 1. Cells E1 and E2 require today's date and time. Both values can be displayed by assigning each cell the NOW function.

The NOW Function

The **NOW function** uses the current DOS date and time that displays at the bottom of the screen to determine the number of days since December 31, 1899. It displays the value in the assigned cell as a decimal number. For this project assume that the DOS date is December 22, 1994 and the time is approximately 10:08 A.M..

To complete the time and date entries in the worksheet, move the cell pointer to E1 and enter the NOW function on the input line as illustrated in Figure 3-8.

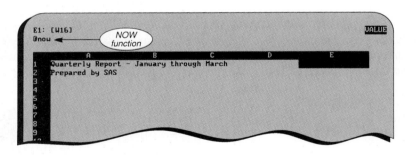

FIGURE 3-8
Entering the NOW function on the input line with the cell pointer at E1

Next, press the Down Arrow key and enter the same function in E2. Use the Up Arrow key to enter the function in E2. This places the cell pointer in E1 as shown in Figure 3-9. The value 34,690.42 in cells E1 and E2 represents the number of days since December 31, 1899. The integer portion of the number (34,690) represents the number of complete days, and the decimal portion (.42) represents the first 10 hours of December 22, 1994. Notice that the two entries are displayed in the Comma (,) format, the one assigned earlier to the entire worksheet. The next step is to format the date and time so they display in a more meaningful way.

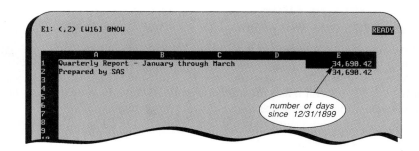

FIGURE 3-9
The NOW function assigned
to cells E1 and E2

Formatting the Date

In Figure 3-9, the cell pointer is at E1. To format the date, enter the command /**R**ange **F**ormat **D**ate (/RFD) as shown in Figure 3-10. With the menu pointer active in the Date menu, type the number 4 to select the fourth date format Long Intn'l (MM/DD/YY).

FIGURE 3-10
Formatting the date in
cell E1

1-2-3 responds by displaying the prompt message "Enter range to format: E1..E1" on the input line. E1 is the only cell we want to format, so press the Enter key. The date immediately changes in cell E1 to 12/22/94 as shown in Figure 3-11. Don't be concerned with trying to get the date in E1 to agree with 12/22/94. As long as the date in E1 represents the same day as the date on the status line at the bottom line of the screen, you have entered the NOW function correctly.

FIGURE 3-11
Date and time is displayed in
cells E1 and E2—10:10 AM
on December 22, 1994.

Formatting the Time

Move the cell pointer to E2. To format the time, enter the same command as for the date—/**R**ange **F**ormat **D**ate (/RFD). This is shown in Figure 3-10. With the menu pointer active in the Date menu, type the letter T for Time. The Time menu replaces the Date menu at the top of the screen. Select the second Time format (HH:MM AM/PM) by pressing the 2 key. Next, press the Enter key and the time in E2 displays as 10:10 AM (Figure 3-11). Here again, don't be concerned with trying to get the time in E2 to agree with 10:10 A.M.. The time in E2 should approximately agree with the time on the status line.

Updating the Time—Recalculation

The time displayed at the bottom of the screen updates every minute. However, the time displayed in a cell, as in E2, only updates when you enter a value into a cell in the worksheet. Any entry causes 1-2-3 to recalculate all the formulas and functions in the worksheet automatically.

If you are not entering values into the worksheet and want to instruct 1-2-3 to recalculate all formulas and functions, press function key F9. Pressing F9 updates the time as illustrated in Figure 3-12.

FIGURE 3-12
Press function key F9 to manually update the time in cell E2.

Date and Time Formats

Table 3-1 summarizes the date and time formats available in 1-2-3. Use this table to select formats when you want to display the date and time in a worksheet.

TABLE 3-1 Date and Time Formats
(Assume the DOS date is December 22, 1994 and the time is 3:12 PM)

FORMAT NUMBER	FORMAT TYPE	FORMAT CODE ON STATUS LINE	DATE OR TIME DISPLAYED
1	DD-MMM-YY	D1	22-Dec-94
2	DD-MMM	D2	22-Dec
3	MMM-YY	D3	Dec-94
4	Long Intn'l (MM/DD/YY)	D4	12/22/94
5	Short Intn'l (MM/DD)	D5	12/22
1	HH:MM:SS AM/PM	D6	3:12:00 PM
2	HH:MM AM/PM	D7	3:12 PM
3	Long Intn'l	D8	15:12:00
4	Short Intn'l	D9	15:12

ENTERING THE QUARTERLY BUDGET LABELS

◆   With the date and time formatted, we can enter the column headings, group titles, and row titles. Move the cell pointer to A5. Since the column headings consist of capital letters, press the Caps Lock key before entering them. Left-justify the first column heading and right-justify the rest. Recall that to left-justify a label, begin it with an apostrophe (') or a letter. For example, in A5 enter ITEM. To right-justify a label, begin the label with a quotation mark ("). For example, in B5, enter "JANUARY. The worksheet with the column headings is shown in Figure 3-13.

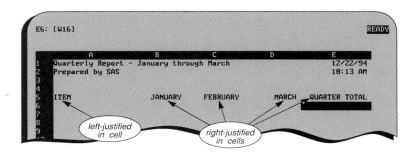

FIGURE 3-13
Column headings entered
into row 5

After completing the column headings, move the cell pointer to A6. Use the Backslash key (\) to repeat the equal sign (=) throughout cell A6. Next, use the command /Copy (/C) to copy the contents of cell A6 to cells B6 through E6. The result is a double-dashed line in row 6 as illustrated in Figure 3-14.

FIGURE 3-14
Column headings underlined

Once the column headings are complete, begin entering the group titles and row titles that are shown on the left side of Figure 3-1. All the labels are left-justified. The group subtitles are indented by two spaces to make the worksheet easier to read. Since most of the remaining labels are in lowercase letters, press the Caps Lock key to toggle off capital letters after entering the group title REVENUE in cell A8.

Do not enter the two subtitles Marketing and Administrative under the group title EXPENSES. We will add these subtitles shortly.

Figure 3-15 shows the group titles and row identifiers up to row 24. Notice in Figure 3-15 that with the cell pointer at A24, the window has moved down four rows, displaying rows 5 through 24 rather than rows 1 through 20. Once the cell pointer moves past row 20, the window begins to move down. The same applies when the cell pointer moves beyond the rightmost column on the screen.

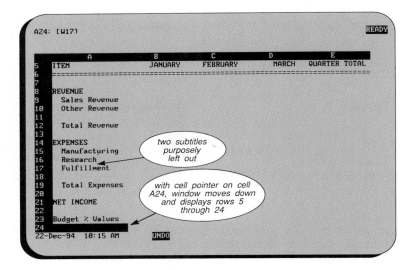

FIGURE 3-15
Group titles and subtitles entered

INSERTING AND DELETING ROWS AND COLUMNS

◆ It is not unusual to forget to include rows or columns of data when building a worksheet, or to include too many rows or columns. 1-2-3 is forgiving. It has commands to insert or delete as many rows or columns as required. Furthermore, you can do this at any time, even after a worksheet is well under way.

The Insert Command

The command /**W**orksheet **I**nsert (/WI) is used to insert empty rows or columns anywhere in the worksheet. To make room for the new rows, 1-2-3 simply opens up the worksheet by *pushing down* the rows below the insertion point. If you are inserting columns, those to the right of the insertion point are *pushed* to the right. More importantly, if the *pushed* rows or columns include any formulas, 1-2-3 adjusts the cell references to the new locations.

Remember that the two subtitles Marketing and Administrative were purposely left out from the group title EXPENSES (Figure 3-15). Let's insert, that is, open up two blank rows in the worksheet so that we can add the two subtitles. According to Figure 3-1, the two subtitles belong immediately before Fulfillment in cell A17. Therefore, move the cell pointer to A17. To complete a row insert, always position the cell pointer on the first row you want *pushed* down. This is shown in Figure 3-16. For a row insert, the column location of the cell pointer is not important.

FIGURE 3-16
Step 1 of using the /WI command to insert rows—move the cell pointer to A17, the first row you want *pushed* down.

Enter the command /Worksheet Insert (/WI) as shown in Figure 3-17.

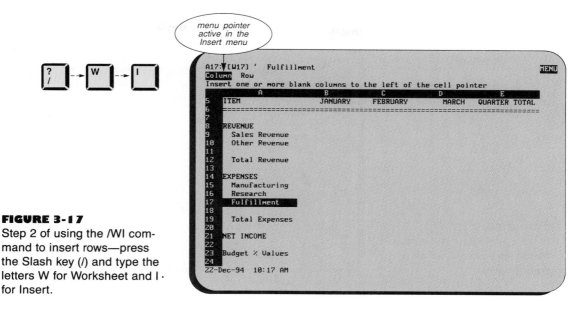

FIGURE 3-17
Step 2 of using the /WI command to insert rows—press the Slash key (/) and type the letters W for Worksheet and I· for Insert.

With the menu pointer active in the Insert menu, type the letter R for Row. 1-2-3 immediately responds on the input line at the top of the screen with the prompt message, "Enter row insert range: A17..A17". We want to add two new rows, A17 and A18. Therefore, use the Down Arrow key to increase the range on the input line from A17..A17 to A17..A18. This is illustrated in Figure 3-18.

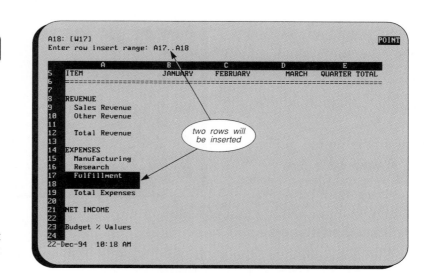

FIGURE 3-18
Step 3 of using the /WI command to insert rows—type the letter R for Row and use the Down Arrow key to select the number of rows you want to insert.

Press the Enter key and the worksheet *pushes down* all the rows beginning with row 17—the first row in the range A17..A18. This leaves rows 17 and 18 empty as shown in Figure 3-19.

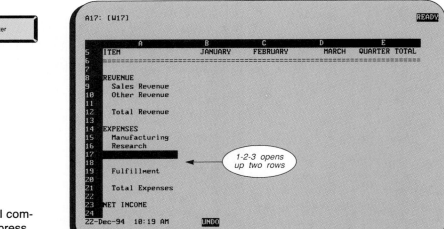

FIGURE 3-19
Step 4 of using the /WI command to insert rows—press the Enter key.

Enter the subtitle Marketing in cell A17 and the subtitle Administrative in cell A18 (Figure 3-20).

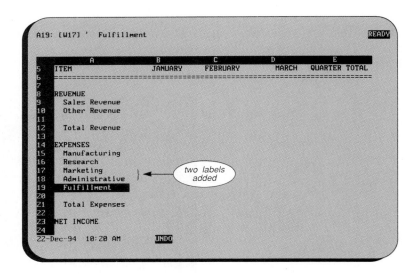

FIGURE 3-20
The two subtitles are inserted into the worksheet.

The Delete Command

You can delete unwanted rows or columns from a worksheet by using the command /**W**orksheet **D**elete (/WD). Let's delete rows 17 and 18 in Figure 3-20. After deleting these two rows, reinsert them using the command /**W**orksheet **I**nsert (/WI).

With the cell pointer at cell A17, enter the command /Worksheet Delete (/WD). Next, type the letter R to instruct 1-2-3 to delete rows rather than columns. To delete columns you would type the letter C. When 1-2-3 requests the range to delete, press the Down Arrow key to change the range from A17..A17 to A17..A18. Press the Enter key. 1-2-3 immediately *closes up* the worksheet—rows 17 and 18 disappear. The worksheet appears as it did earlier in Figure 3-16. If you had decided to close up rows 17 and 18 immediately after inserting them, you could have used the UNDO command (Alt-F4), rather than the /WD command.

Be careful when you use the /Worksheet Delete command. You do not want to delete rows or columns that are part of a range used in a formula or function elsewhere in the worksheet without carefully weighing the consequences. If any formula references a cell in a deleted row or column, 1-2-3 displays the diagnostic message "ERR" in the cell assigned the formula. ERR means that it was impossible for 1-2-3 to complete the computation.

Before moving on, reinsert the two rows above row 17 and enter the row titles Marketing and Administrative. Follow the keystroke sequence we just described and shown in Figures 3-17 through 3-20.

COPYING CELLS WITH EQUAL SOURCE AND DESTINATION RANGES

◆ The next step is to enter the subtitles in cells A27 through A31 (Figure 3-1). These subtitles are the same as the ones you entered earlier in cells A15 through A19. Therefore, you can use the Copy command to copy the contents of cells A15 through A19 to A27 through A31.

As shown in Figure 3-20, the cell pointer is at cell A19, one of the end points of the source range. Enter the command /Copy (/C). On the input line, the first end point of the source cell range (A19) is already anchored. Use the Up Arrow key to select the range A19..A15. Press the Enter key. Next, select the destination range by moving the cell pointer to A27 as shown in Figure 3-21.

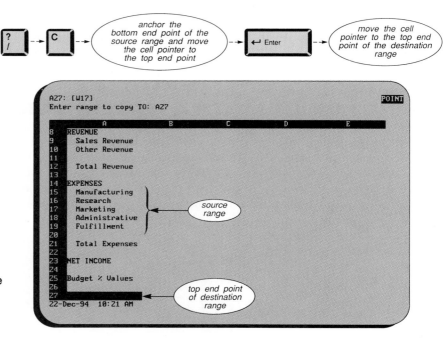

FIGURE 3-21

Step 1 of using the /C command to copy—press the Slash key (/), type the letter C for Copy, select the source range, press the Enter key, and move the cell pointer to A27.

Press the Enter key to conclude the Copy command (Figure 3-22). As shown in the figure, the source range (A15..A19) and the destination range (A27..A31) are identical.

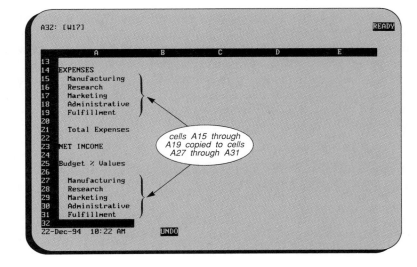

FIGURE 3-22
Step 2 of using the /C command to copy—press the Enter key. The source range (A15..A19) is copied to the destination range (A27..A31).

Two important points to consider about copying the range A15..A19 are:

1. The source range was selected by entering A19..A15. Remember that the range A19..A15 is the same as A15..A19.
2. When both the source and destination ranges are the same size, it is not necessary to anchor the second end point of the destination range. 1-2-3 only needs to know the upper left end point, in this case A27. 1-2-3 copies the five cells in the source range beginning at cell A27. It always copies below the upper left end point of the destination range.

ENTERING NUMBERS WITH A PERCENT SIGN

◆ The five budget percent values begin in cell B27 and extend through cell B31. Use the arrow keys to move the cell pointer from its present location to B27. Rather than entering the percent value as a decimal number (.38), as we did in Project 2, enter it as a whole number followed immediately by a percent sign (%). 1-2-3 accepts the number (38%) as a percent and displays it in the cell using the global format assigned earlier to the worksheet. After you enter the five budget percent values, the worksheet appears as shown in Figure 3-23.

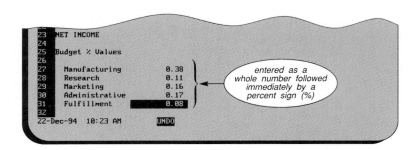

FIGURE 3-23
The five budget percent values in cells B27 through B31

To format the five budget percent values to the Percent format, enter the command **/R**ange **F**ormat **P**ercent (/RFP). When 1-2-3 displays the prompt message "Enter number of decimal places (0..15): 2" on the input line, type the digit zero and press the Enter key. The prompt message "Enter range to format: B31..B31" displays on the input line. Enter the range B31..B27. The first end point (B31) is anchored. Use the Up Arrow key to move the cell pointer to B27. The range on the input line now reads B31..B27. Press the Enter key. The five budget percent values display in percent form as shown in Figure 3-24.

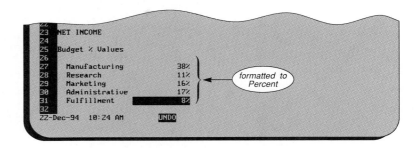

FIGURE 3-24
The five budget percent values in cells B27 through B31 formatted to the Percent type

FREEZING THE TITLES

◆ The worksheet for this project extends beyond the size of the window. When you move the cell pointer down or to the right, the column and row titles disappear off the screen. This makes it difficult to remember where to enter the data. To alleviate this problem, 1-2-3 allows you to **freeze the titles** so that they remain on the screen no matter where you move the cell pointer. The title and column headings in rows 1 through 6 are called the horizontal titles and the row titles in column A are called the vertical titles.

The Titles Command

To freeze the titles in this worksheet, press the Home key so that most of the titles are visible on the screen. Next, use the GOTO command to move the cell pointer to B7. The horizontal titles are just above cell B7 and the vertical titles are just to the left of cell B7. Enter the command **/W**orksheet **T**itles (/WT) as shown in Figure 3-25.

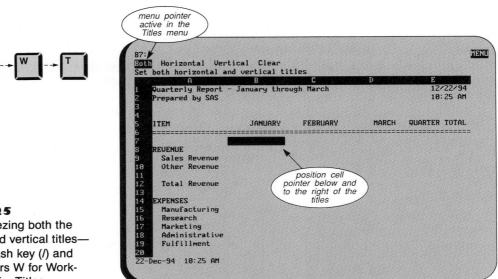

FIGURE 3-25
Step 1 of freezing both the horizontal and vertical titles—press the Slash key (/) and type the letters W for Worksheet and T for Titles.

With the menu pointer active in the Titles menu, type the letter B for Both. This keeps the titles visible regardless of where you move the cell pointer, as shown in Figure 3-26.

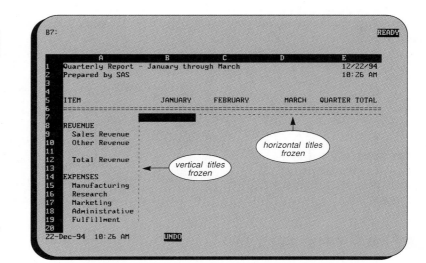

FIGURE 3-26
Step 2 of freezing both the horizontal and vertical titles—type the letter B to freeze both.

Unfreezing the Titles

Once you specify a title area, you cannot move the cell pointer into this area of the worksheet using the cursor movement keys. If you want to make a change to the titles after freezing them, you must **unfreeze** them. To unfreeze the titles, enter the command /Worksheet Titles Clear (/WTC). Once the titles are unfrozen, you can move the cell pointer anywhere on the worksheet, including the title area, to make your desired changes. To refreeze the titles, move the cell pointer to the cell (B7) just below the horizontal titles and just to the right of the vertical titles and enter the command /Worksheet Titles Both (/WTB).

MOVING THE CONTENTS OF CELLS

◆ The command /**M**ove (/M) moves the contents of a cell or range of cells to a different location in the worksheet. To illustrate the use of this command, let's make a mistake by entering the sales revenue (232897.95, 432989.76, and 765998.61) that belongs in cells B9 through E9 into cells B7 through E7—two rows above its location according to Figure 3-1. This type of error is common, especially when you're not careful about cell-pointer placement.

The sales revenues for January, February, and March are 232,897.95, 432,989.76, and 765,998.61. The quarter total in column E is the sum of the sales revenue for the three months. Enter the three numbers in cells B7, C7, and D7. Use the Right Arrow key after typing each number on the input line. With the cell pointer at E7, enter the function @SUM(B7..D7). 1-2-3 evaluates the function and stores the number 1,431,886.32 in E7 (232,897.95 + 432,989.76 + 765,998.61).

The values in cells C7, D7, and E7 are shown in Figure 3-27. Notice that with the cell pointer at F7, the row identifiers in column A display along with columns C, D, E, and F. However, column B does not display because the titles in column A are frozen.

FIGURE 3-27 The sales revenue data entered into the wrong row

As we indicated earlier, the data entered in row 7 belongs in row 9. Let's correct the mistake and move the data from row 7 to row 9. With the cell pointer at F7, enter the command /Move (/M). 1-2-3 displays the message "Enter range to move FROM: F7..F7" on the input line. Press the Backspace key to *unlock* the first end point. Move the cell pointer to E7 and press the Period key. Next, move the cell pointer to B7. The range to be moved is shown in Figure 3-28. Press the Enter key to lock in the range to be moved.

FIGURE 3-28 Step 1 of using the /M command to move data from one range to another—press the Slash key (/), type the letter M, and select the range of cells to move.

Next, 1-2-3 displays the message "Enter range to move TO: F7" on the input line. Move the cell pointer to E9. Press the Period key to anchor the first end point. Move the cell pointer to B9 as shown in Figure 3-29.

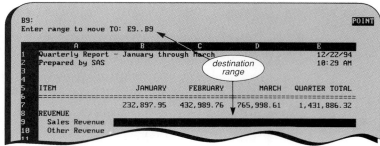

FIGURE 3-29 Step 2 of using the /M command to move data from one range to another—press the Enter key to lock in the range to move. Next, select the destination range.

To complete the command, press the Enter key and move the cell pointer to B10. Figure 3-30 illustrates the result of moving the contents of cells B7 through E7 to B9 through E9.

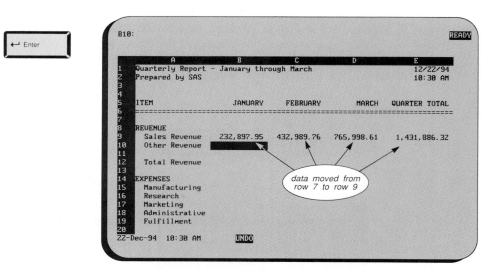

FIGURE 3-30 Step 3 of using the /M command to move data from one range to another—press the Enter key.

Some points to consider about the Move command are:

1. The Move and Copy commands are not the same. Where the Copy command copies one range to another, the Move command moves the contents of one range to another. Use the Move command to rearrange your worksheet. Use the Copy command to duplicate a range.
2. When you move a range containing a formula or function that references cell addresses, the referenced cell addresses are not changed relative to the new position, unless they refer to cells within the moved range. This was the case with the function in cell E7. Recall that we assigned the function @SUM(B7..D7) to cell E7. Following the Move command, the function assigned to cell E9 reads @SUM(B9..D9).
3. You can undo a Move command by entering the UNDO command, provided you do so prior to entering any other value or command.

DISPLAYING FORMULAS AND FUNCTIONS IN THE CELLS

◆ Enter the other revenue data in row 10 for January, February, and March (Figure 3-31). Leave the quarter total in column E alone for now. The monthly total revenue in row 12 is equal to the sum of the corresponding monthly revenues in rows 9 and 10. Therefore, assign cell B12 the function @SUM(B9..B10) as shown in Figure 3-31.

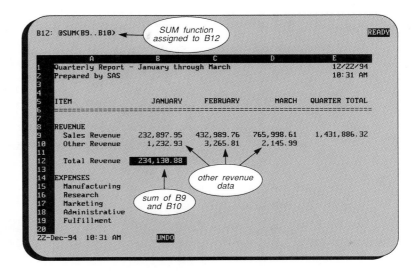

FIGURE 3-31

Other revenue and formula for January total revenue entered into worksheet

Use the /Copy (/C) command to copy the SUM function in cell B12 to cells C12 and D12. Remember, the Copy command adjusts the cell references in the function so that it adds the contents of the cells above the cell to which the SUM function is copied. Once the Copy command has been entered, 1-2-3 requests the source cell range and the destination cell range. In this case the source cell range is B12 and the destination cell range is C12..D12 (Figure 3-32).

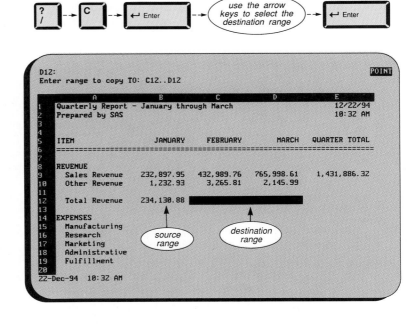

FIGURE 3-32

Using the /C command to copy cell B12 to cells C12 and D12—press the Slash key (/), type the letter C, press the Enter key to select the source range, use the arrow keys to select the destination range, and press the Enter key.

After you enter each range, press the Enter key. The result of the copy is shown in cells C12 and D12 in Figure 3-33. When entering or copying formulas, you might find it useful to view them in the cells, instead of their numeric result. Therefore, to illustrate what is actually copied, let's change the format from Comma (,) to Text for the range B9..E19 in the worksheet. Remember from Project 2 that the Text format instructs 1-2-3 to display the formula assigned to a cell, rather than the numeric result.

Enter the command /**R**ange Format Text (/RFT). 1-2-3 responds with the prompt message "Enter range to format: B12..B12" on the input line. Enter the range B9..E19 as shown in Figure 3-33 and press the Enter key.

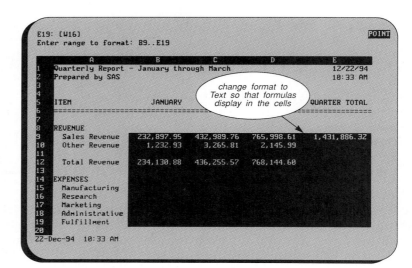

FIGURE 3-33

Step 1 of using the /RFT command to format cells B9..E19 to the Text type— press the Slash key (/), type the letters R for Range, F for Format, and T for Text, and select the range B9..E19.

The functions in the worksheet (cells E9, B12, C12, and D12) now display in their respective cells and the numeric entries display using the General type format. This is shown in Figure 3-34. Later, we will reassign the Comma (,) format to the range B9..E19.

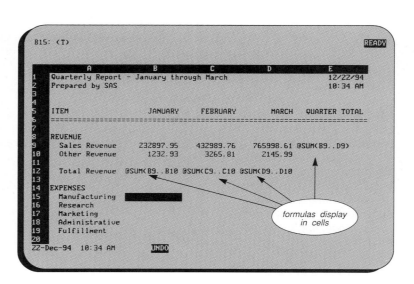

FIGURE 3-34

Step 2 of using the /RFT command to format cells B9..E19 to the Text type— press the Enter key.

ABSOLUTE VERSUS RELATIVE ADDRESSING

◆ The next step is to determine the five monthly budgeted expenses in the rectangular group of cells B15 through D19. Each of these budgeted expenses is equal to the corresponding budgeted percent (cells B27 through B31) times the monthly total revenue (cells B12 through D12). The formulas for each of the cells in this range are similar. They differ in that the total revenue varies by the month (column) and the budgeted percent value varies by the type of expense (row).

Relative Addressing

We would like to be able to enter the formula +B27*B12 once in cell B15 (January budgeted manufacturing expense) and then copy this formula to the remaining cells in the rectangular group B15 through D19. However, we know that when a formula with relative addresses, like B27 and B12, is copied across a row or down a column, 1-2-3 automatically adjusts the cell references in the formula as it copies to reflect its new location.

Specifying cells in a formula using **relative addressing** has worked well in the previous examples of copying formulas, but it won't work here because the five budgeted percent values are all located in one column and the monthly total revenues are all located in one row. For example, if we copy +B27*B12 in cell B15 to cell C15, then cell C15 equals +C27*C12. This adjustment by the Copy command is because B27 and B12 are relative addresses. The C12 is okay, because it represents the total revenue for February, but cell C27 is blank. What we need here is for 1-2-3 to maintain cell B27 as it copies across the first row.

Absolute and Mixed Cell Addressing

1-2-3 has the capability to keep a cell, a column, or a row constant when it copies a formula or function by using a technique called **absolute addressing**. To specify an absolute address in a formula, add a dollar sign ($) to the beginning of the column name, row name, or both. For example, $B$27 is an absolute address and B27 is a relative address. Both reference the same cell. The difference shows when they are copied. A formula using $B$27 instructs 1-2-3 to use the same cell (B27) as it copies the formula to a new location. A formula using B27 instructs 1-2-3 to adjust the cell reference as it copies. Table 3-2 gives some additional examples of absolute addressing. A cell address with one dollar sign before either the column or the row is called a **mixed cell address**—one is relative, the other is absolute.

When you enter or edit a formula, you can use the function key F4 to cycle the cell address the edit cursor is on, or immediately to the right of, from relative to absolute to mixed.

TABLE 3-2 Absolute Addressing

CELL ADDRESS	MEANING
$A$22	Both column and row references remain the same when this cell address is copied.
A$22	The column reference changes when you copy this cell address to another column. The row reference does not change—it is absolute.
$A22	The row reference changes when you copy this cell address to another row. The column reference does not change—it is absolute.
A22	Both column and row references are relative. When copied to another row and column, both the row and column in the cell address are adjusted to reflect the new location.

Copying Formulas with Mixed Cell Addresses

With the cell pointer at B15, enter the formula $B27*B$12 as shown in Figure 3-35. Because B15 was in the range formatted to Text earlier, the formula displays in the cell, rather than the value. It is not necessary to enter the formula $B27*B$12 with a leading plus sign because, in this case, the $ indicates that the entry is a formula or a number. The cell reference $B27 (budgeted manufacturing % value) means that the row reference (27) changes when you copy it to a new row, but the column reference (B) remains constant through all columns in the destination range. The cell reference B$12 (January expenses) in the formula means that the column reference (B) changes when you copy it to a new column, but the row reference (12) remains constant through all rows in the destination range. Let's copy the formula $B27*B$12 in cell B15 to the rectangular group of cells B15 through D19.

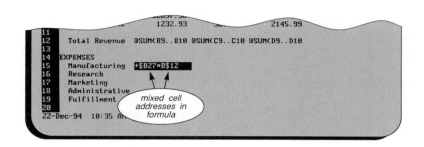

FIGURE 3-35

Formula with mixed cell addresses entered into cell B15

The cell pointer is located at B15 as shown in Figure 3-35. Enter the command /Copy (/C). When the prompt message "Enter range to copy FROM: B15..B15" displays on the input line, press the Enter key. When the message "Enter range to copy TO: B15" displays on the input line, use the arrow keys to select the range B15..D19. This is shown in Figure 3-36. Notice that cell B15 is copied on top of itself, because B15 is one of the end points of the destination range.

FIGURE 3-36

Step 1 of using the /C command to copy cell B15 to the range B15..D19—press the Slash key (/), type the letter C for Copy, press the Enter key, and select the destination range.

Press the Enter key. The Copy command copies the formula in cell B15 to the rectangular group of cells B15 through D19 as shown in Figure 3-37. Take a few minutes to study the formulas in Figure 3-37. You should begin to see the significance of mixed cell addressing. For example, every aspect of the five formulas in cells B15 through B19 is identical, except for the row in the first cell reference (budgeted % value). You can see in columns C and D, that the column in the second cell reference (monthly total revenue) changes based on the column in which the formula is located.

FIGURE 3-37

Step 2 of using the /C command to copy cell B15 to the range B15..D19—press the Enter key.

Switching from Text Format to the Global Comma Format

Let's change cells B9 through E19 from the Text format back to the Comma format, the one selected earlier as the global format. Recall that we switched the format of these cells from the global format (Comma) to Text so that we could view the formulas in the cells. To reset the format, move the cell pointer to the lower left end point (B19) of the range B19..E9. Enter the command /Range Format Reset (/RFR). When 1-2-3 requests the range, use the arrow keys to select the rectangular group of cells B19..E9. Press the Enter key. The format of the range B19..E9 is reset to the global format (Comma). The results of the formulas, rather than the formulas themselves, display in the cells (Figure 3-38).

```
B19: (,2) +$B31*B$12                                                    READY

         A              B            C             D           E
1   Quarterly Report - January through March                  12/22/94
2   Prepared by SAS                                            10:38 AM
3
4
5   ITEM              JANUARY      FEBRUARY       MARCH    QUARTER TOTAL
6   ==================================================================
7
8   REVENUE
9     Sales Revenue   232,897.95   432,989.76   765,998.61   1,431,886.32
10    Other Revenue     1,232.93     3,265.81     2,145.99
11
12    Total Revenue   234,130.88   436,255.57   768,144.60
13
14  EXPENSES
15    Manufacturing    88,969.73   165,777.12   291,894.95
16    Research         25,754.40    47,988.11    84,495.91
17    Marketing        37,460.94    69,800.89   122,903.14
18    Administrative   39,802.25    74,163.45   130,584.58
19    Fulfillment      18,730.47    34,900.45    61,451.57
20
22-Dec-94  10:38 AM        UNDO
```

FIGURE 3-38

Range B9..E19 reformatted to the Comma (,) type

POINTING TO A RANGE OF CELLS TO SUM

The total expenses for January (cell B21) are determined by adding the five monthly budgeted expenses in cells B15 through B19. The total expenses for February (C21) and March (D21) are found in the same way.

To sum the five monthly budgeted expenses for January, move the cell pointer to B21 and begin entering the SUM function. For this entry, let's apply the pointing method to enter the range to sum. Enter @sum(on the input line. Remember that function names can be entered in lowercase. After typing the open parenthesis, use the Up Arrow key to move the cell pointer to B15, the topmost end point of the range to sum. As the cell pointer moves upward, 1-2-3 changes the cell address following the open parenthesis on the input line. Move the cell pointer until it reaches B15 (Figure 3-39).

Press the Period key (.) to lock in the first end point of the range to sum. Next, use the Down Arrow key to move the cell pointer to B19 (Figure 3-40). To complete the entry, press the Close Parenthesis key and the Enter key.

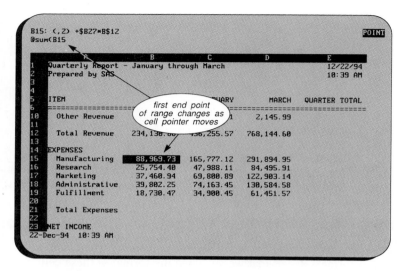

FIGURE 3-39 Step 1 of entering the SUM function using the pointing method—after the open parenthesis, use the arrow keys to select the first end point of the range.

FIGURE 3-40
Step 2 of entering the SUM function using the pointing method—press the Period key (.), use the arrow keys to select the second end point of the range, press the Close Parenthesis key, and press the Enter key.

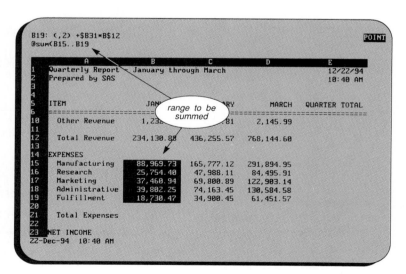

As shown in cell B21 of Figure 3-41, 1-2-3 displays the sum (210,717.79) of the five January budgeted expenses stored in cells B15 through B19.

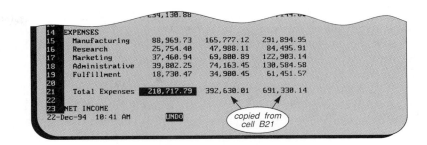

FIGURE 3-41
SUM function in cell B21
copied to cells C21 and D21

Pointing versus Entering a Range of Cells

The pointing method used to enter the range for the SUM function in cell B21 saves keying time. Anytime you need to enter a range, you may use the arrow keys to point to it. Alternatively, you may type the cell addresses. Once you begin typing a cell address, 1-2-3 is no longer in POINT mode.

Copying the Total Expenses and Net Income for Each Month

The next step in this project is to determine the total expenses in row 21 for February and March. To accomplish this task, copy the function in cell B21 to cells C21 and D21. Enter the command /Copy (/C). After entering the source range (B21), press the Enter key. Next, select the destination range (C21..D21) and press the Enter key. Figure 3-41 shows the result of copying cell B21 to cells C21 and D21.

You can now determine the net income for each month in row 23 by subtracting the total expenses for each month in row 21 from the total revenue for each month in row 12. Move the cell pointer to B23 and enter the formula +B12-B21. Copy this formula to cells C23 and D23. The result of entering the formula in cell B23 and copying it to C23 and D23 is shown in Figure 3-42.

FIGURE 3-42
Formula in cell B23 copied to
cells C23 and D23

Summing Empty Cells and Labels

To complete the worksheet, determine the quarter totals in column E. Use the GOTO command to move the cell pointer to the quarter total in cell E9. Since cell E9 is not on the screen (Figure 3-42), the GOTO command causes the window to move so that cell E9 is positioned in the upper left corner, just below and to the right of the titles.

Recall that the quarter total for the sales revenue in cell E9 was determined earlier (Figure 3-30). The functions required for all the row entries (E10, E12, E15 through E19, E21, and E23) are identical to the function in cell E9. Therefore, let's copy the function in cell E9 to these cells.

Unfortunately, the cells in the destination range are not contiguous, that is, connected. For example, in the range E10 through E23, the function is not needed in E11, E13, E14, E20, and E22. We have three choices here: (1) use the Copy command several times and copy the function in E9 to E10, E12, E15 through E19, E21, and E23; (2) enter the function manually in each required cell; or (3) copy the function to the range E10 through E23. If we select the third method, we have to use the command **/R**ange **E**rase (/RE) to erase the function from E11, E13, E14, E20, and E22, the cells in which the function is not required. Let's use the third method.

With the cell pointer at E9, enter the command **/C**opy (/C). When 1-2-3 displays the prompt message "Enter range to copy FROM: E9..E9", press the Enter key. For the destination range, leave E9 anchored as the first end point and use the Down Arrow key to move the cell pointer to E23. This is shown in Figure 3-43.

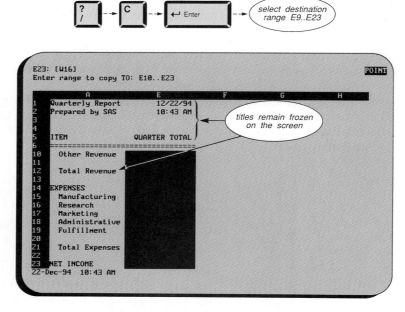

FIGURE 3-43 Step 1 of using the /C command to copy cell E9 to the range E9..E23—press the Slash key (/), type the letter C for Copy, press the Enter key, and select the destination range.

Press the Enter key and the function in cell E9 is copied to the cells in the range E9..E23 (Figure 3-44).

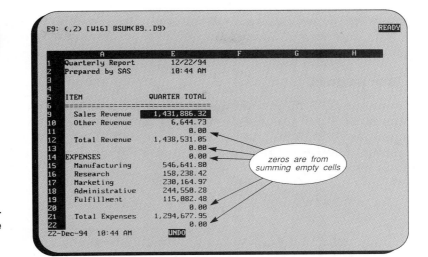

FIGURE 3-44

Step 2 of using the /C command to copy cell E9 to the range E9..E23—press the Enter key.

Notice the zeros in cells E11, E13, E14, E20, and E22. The formula in cell E11 reads @SUM(B11..D11). 1-2-3 considers empty cells and cells with labels to be equal to zero when they are referenced in a formula or function. Since cells B11, C11, and D11 are empty, the SUM function assigned to E11 produces the zero display. You need to erase the functions in the cells displaying zero. Recall from Project 1 that the command /**R**ange **E**rase (/RE) erases the contents of a cell. Use this command to erase the zeros in cells E11, E13, E14, E20, and E22.

After the zeros in column E are erased, use the command /**W**orksheet **T**itles **C**lear (/WTC) to unfreeze the titles. Finally, press the Home key to move the cell pointer to A1. The worksheet is complete as shown in Figure 3-45.

FIGURE 3-45

The completed worksheet

SAVING AND PRINTING THE WORKSHEET

◆ Save the worksheet on disk for later use. Use the command **/F**ile **S**ave (/FS) and the file name PROJS-3. As we discussed in Project 2, when you create a large worksheet such as this one, it is prudent to save the worksheet periodically—every 50 to 75 keystrokes. Then, if there should be an inadvertent loss of power to the computer or other unforeseen mishap, you will not lose the whole worksheet.

Printing the Worksheet

After you save the worksheet as PROJS-3, obtain a hard copy by printing the worksheet on the printer. Recall from Project 2, that to print the worksheet you use the command **/P**rint **P**rinter (/PP). This command activates the menu pointer in the Print menu and displays the printsheet settings (Figure 3-46). Type the letter R for Range. The cell pointer is at one end point of the range to print, A1. Use the arrow keys to move the cell pointer to E31. Press the Enter key to anchor the second end point.

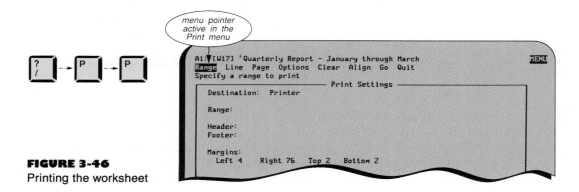

FIGURE 3-46
Printing the worksheet

Next, check the printer to be sure it is ready. Type the letter A for Align and the letter G for Go. The worksheet prints on the printer as shown in Figure 3-47. Finally, type the letter P for Page to move the paper through the printer so that you can tear the paper at the perforated edge below the printed version of the worksheet.

```
Quarterly Report - January through March                    12/22/94
Prepared by SAS                                             10:47 AM


ITEM                JANUARY      FEBRUARY        MARCH   QUARTER TOTAL
=====================================================================

REVENUE
  Sales Revenue   232,897.95    432,989.76   765,998.61   1,431,886.32
  Other Revenue     1,232.93      3,265.81     2,145.99       6,644.73

  Total Revenue   234,130.88    436,255.57   768,144.60   1,438,531.05

EXPENSES
  Manufacturing    88,969.73    165,777.12   291,894.95     546,641.80
  Research         25,754.40     47,988.11    84,495.91     158,238.42
  Marketing        37,460.94     69,800.89   122,903.14     230,164.97
  Administrative   39,802.25     74,163.45   130,584.58     244,550.28
  Fulfillment      18,730.47     34,900.45    61,451.57     115,082.48

  Total Expenses  210,717.79    392,630.01   691,330.14   1,294,677.95

NET INCOME         23,413.09     43,625.56    76,814.46     143,853.10

Budget % Values

  Manufacturing        38%
  Research             11%
  Marketing            16%
  Administrative       17%
  Fulfillment           8%
```

FIGURE 3-47   The printed version of the worksheet in Project 3

Printing the Worksheet in Condensed Mode

If you have a graphics printer, you can print more than 80 characters per line by printing the worksheet in condensed mode. This mode can be helpful if the worksheet is wider than the screen. The **condensed mode** allows nearly twice as many characters to fit across the page. To print a worksheet in the condensed mode, do the following:

1. Enter the command /**P**rint **P**rinter **O**ptions **S**etup (/PPOS). Enter the code \015 and press the Enter key.
2. With the Printer Options menu at the top of the screen, enter the command **M**argins **R**ight. Type in a right margin of 132. Press the Enter key and type the letter Q to quit the Printer Options menu.
3. Select the range to print and follow the usual steps for printing the worksheet. The condensed printed version of the worksheet prints on the printer as shown in Figure 3-48.

```
Quarterly Report - January through March              12/22/94
Prepared by SAS                                       10:48 AM


ITEM              JANUARY    FEBRUARY      MARCH   QUARTER TOTAL
==============================================================


REVENUE
  Sales Revenue  232,897.95  432,989.76  765,998.61  1,431,886.32
  Other Revenue    1,232.93    3,265.81    2,145.99      6,544.73

  Total Revenue  234,130.88  436,255.57  768,144.60  1,438,531.05

EXPENSES
  Manufacturing   88,969.73  165,777.12  291,894.95    546,641.80
  Research        25,754.40   47,988.11   84,495.91    158,238.42
  Marketing       37,460.94   69,800.89  122,903.14    230,164.97
  Administrative  39,802.25   74,163.45  130,584.58    244,550.28
  Fulfillment     18,730.47   34,900.45   61,451.57    115,082.48

  Total Expenses 210,717.79  392,630.01  691,330.14  1,294,677.95

NET INCOME        23,413.09   43,625.56   76,814.46    143,853.10

Budget % Values

  Manufacturing     38%
  Research          11%
  Marketing         16%
  Administrative    17%
  Fulfillment        8%
```

FIGURE 3-48 A printout of the worksheet in the condensed mode

If the printer does not print in condensed mode, check the printer manual to be sure the current dip switch settings on the printer allow for it. You may have to change these settings. If you continue to experience problems, check the printer manual to be sure that code \015 instructs the printer to print in condensed mode. This code works for most printers.

To change 1-2-3 back to the normal print mode, do the following:

1. Enter the command /**P**rint **P**rinter **O**ptions **S**etup (/PPOS). Enter the code \018 and press the Enter key.
2. With the Printer Options menu at the top of the screen, enter the command **M**argins **R**ight. Type in a right margin of 76. Press the Enter key and type the letter Q to quit the Printer Options menu.
3. With the menu pointer in the Print menu, follow the steps we outlined earlier for printing the worksheet in the normal mode.

Using Borders to Print Nonadjacent Columns

Up to this point, we have printed only columns that are side by side in the worksheet. Consider Figure 3-49. This partial printout is called a summary report, since only the row titles in column A and the corresponding totals in column E are printed.

We can print such a report through the use of the Borders command in the Printer Options menu. The Borders command prints specified columns to the left of the selected range or it prints specified rows above the selected range.

To print the summary report in Figure 3-49, do the following:

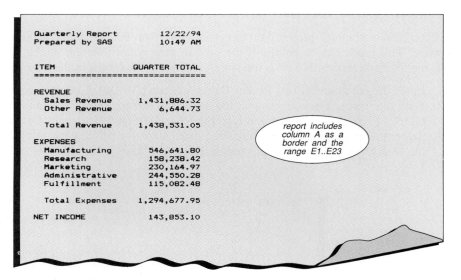

```
Quarterly Report        12/22/94
Prepared by SAS         10:49 AM


ITEM                  QUARTER TOTAL
=====================================

REVENUE
  Sales Revenue        1,431,886.32
  Other Revenue            6,644.73

  Total Revenue       1,438,531.05

EXPENSES
  Manufacturing         546,641.80
  Research              158,238.42
  Marketing             230,164.97
  Administrative        244,550.28
  Fulfillment           115,082.48

  Total Expenses      1,294,677.95

NET INCOME              143,853.10
```

report includes column A as a border and the range E1..E23

FIGURE 3-49 A summary report made up of nonadjacent columns

1. Move the cell pointer to column A and enter the command /**Print Printer Options Borders** (/PPOB). Type C for Column and press the Enter key to select column A as the border. Type Q to quit the Printer Options menu.
2. With the Print menu at the top of the screen, select E1..E23 as the range to print.
3. Press A for Align and G for Go.

In Figure 3-49, column A prints as the border and column E prints because it was selected as the range to print. To clear column A as the border, select the Clear command in the Print menu. When the Clear menu displays at the top of the screen, type B for Borders.

Other Printer Options

There are other printer options that can enhance your worksheet. Table 3-3 summarizes the commands found in the **Printer Options** menu.

TABLE 3-3 A Summary of Commands in the Printer Options Menu

COMMAND	DEFAULT SETTING	FUNCTION
Header	none	Prints a line of text at the top of every page of the worksheet.
Footer	none	Prints a line of text at the bottom of every page of the worksheet.
Margins	Left 4 Right 76 Top 2 Bottom 2	Sets the margins.
Borders	none	Prints specified columns or rows on every page.
Setup	none	Sends commands to the printer, for example, to print the worksheet in condensed mode.
Pg-Length	66	Sets printed lines per page.
Other		Selects the As-Displayed or Cell-Formulas version to print.
Quit		Returns to the Print menu.

Many of the options you set with the /**Print Printer Options** (/PPO) command are saved with the worksheet and stay in effect when you retrieve it. Remember, if you change any of the printer options and you want the changes to stay with the worksheet, be sure to save the worksheet after you finish printing it. That way you won't have to change the options the next time you retrieve the worksheet.

If you use the command /**Worksheet Erase** (/WE) to clear the worksheet on the screen or restart 1-2-3, the printer options revert back to the default settings shown in Table 3.3.

WHAT-IF QUESTIONS

A powerful feature of 1-2-3 is the capability to answer **what-if questions**. Quick responses to these questions are invaluable when making business decisions. Using 1-2-3 to answer what-if questions is called performing **what-if analyses** or **sensitivity analyses**.

A what-if question for the worksheet in Project 3 might be, *What if the manufacturing budgeted percentage is decreased from 38% to 35%—how would this affect the total expenses and net income?* To answer questions like this, you need only change a single value in the worksheet. The recalculation feature of 1-2-3 answers the question immediately by displaying new values in any cells with formulas or functions that reference the changed cell.

Let's change the manufacturing budgeted percentage from 38% to 35% (Figure 3-50). Before the change, as shown in the top screen of Figure 3-50, the manufacturing budgeted percentage is 38%. After the change is made, the manufacturing budgeted percentage is 35%. When we make the change, all the formulas are immediately recalculated. This process generally requires less than one second, depending on how many calculations must be performed. As soon as the 35% replaces the 38% in cell B27, the new expenses and new net income values can be examined (bottom screen of Figure 3-50).

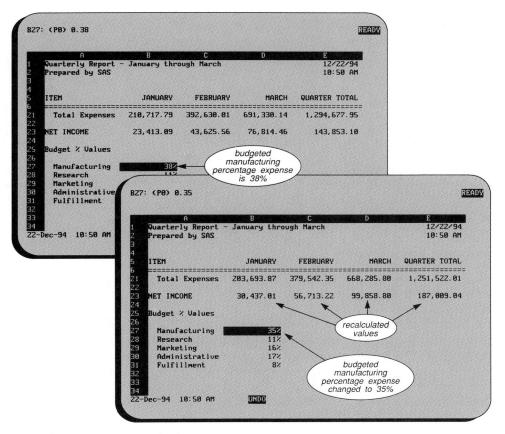

FIGURE 3-50 Using 1-2-3 to answer what-if questions by changing one value in the worksheet

By changing the value in B27 from 38% to 35%, the total January expenses decrease from 210,717.79 to 203,693.87, and the January net income increases from 23,413.09 to 30,437.01. The February and March figures change the same way. The quarter total expenses decrease from 1,294,677.95 to 1,251,522.01, and the quarter net income increases from 143,853.11 to 187,009.04. Thus, if the budgeted manufacturing expenses are reduced, it is clear that net income increases.

After the change, as shown in the bottom screen of Figure 3-51, you can change more than one percentage. Let's change all the percentages. The new calculations display immediately.

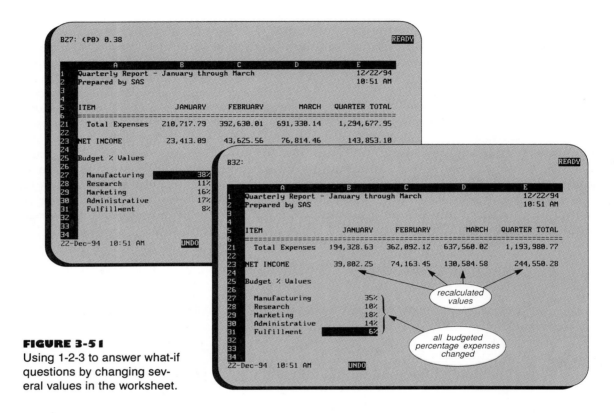

FIGURE 3-51
Using 1-2-3 to answer what-if questions by changing several values in the worksheet.

In Figure 3-51, we ask the question, *What if we change all the budgeted percent values to the following: Manufacturing (35%); Research (10%); Marketing (18%); Administrative (14%); Fulfillment (6%)—how would these changes affect the total expenses and the net income?* By merely changing the five values on the worksheet, all formulas are automatically recalculated to provide the answer to this question.

Manual versus Automatic Recalculation

Each time you enter a value in the worksheet, 1-2-3 automatically recalculates all formulas and functions in those cells that changed since the worksheet was last recalculated, and in the cells that depend on those cells. This feature is called **automatic recalculation**.

An alternative to automatic recalculation is manual recalculation. With **manual recalculation**, 1-2-3 only recalculates after you instruct it to. To change recalculation from automatic to manual, enter the command /Worksheet Global Recalculate (/WGR). With the menu pointer active in the Recalculate menu, type the letter M for Manual. Then recalculation of formulas takes place *only* after you press function key F9. To change back to automatic recalculation, use the same command but type the letter A for Automatic rather than M for Manual.

When you save a worksheet, the current recalculation mode is saved along with it. For an explanation of the other types of recalculation available with 1-2-3, enter the command /WGR and press function key F1. When you are finished with the online help facility, press the Esc key to return to your worksheet.

CHANGING THE WORKSHEET DEFAULT SETTINGS

◆ 1-2-3 comes with default settings. We have already discussed some of the more obvious ones—column width is nine characters, format is General, and recalculation of formulas is Automatic. Some of the default settings, like the format, can be changed for a range or for the entire worksheet. When you make a change to the entire worksheet using the command /Worksheet Global (/WG), the change is saved with the worksheet when you issue the /File Save (/FS) command.

There is another group of default settings that affect all worksheets created or retrieved during the current session, until you quit 1-2-3. To view or change these settings, type the command /Worksheet Global Default (/WGD). This command displays the Global Default menu and default settings sheet as shown in Figure 3-52. Then use the arrow keys or first letters of the commands in the Global Default menu to select features to change. Remember, when you are in MENU mode, you can display the worksheets, rather than the settings sheet, by pressing F6.

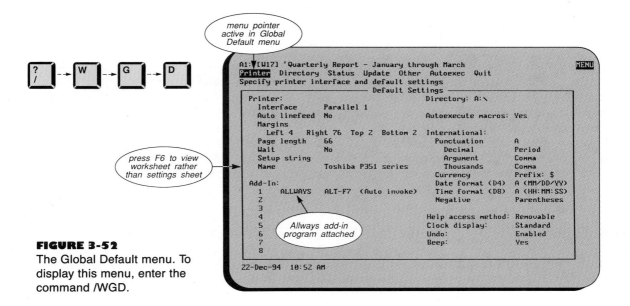

FIGURE 3-52
The Global Default menu. To display this menu, enter the command /WGD.

Once you select the desired settings, you have the choice of saving the changes for the current session or saving them permanently. To save the changes for the current session, type the letter Q to quit the Global Default menu. To save the changes permanently, type the letters U for Update and then Q for Quit. If you typed the letter U for Update, the new settings become the defaults for the current and future 1-2-3 sessions. Table 3-4 describes the features you can change by typing the command /WGD.

TABLE 3-4 A Summary of Commands in the Global Defaults Menu

COMMAND	FUNCTION
Printer	Specifies printer interface and default settings.
Directory	Changes the default directory.
Status	Displays default settings.
Update	Permanently changes default settings in configuration file.
Other	Changes international, help, add-in programs, and clock settings.
Autoexec	Instructs 1-2-3 whether to run autoexecute macros named \0 (zero).
QUIT	Quits Global Default menu.

INTERACTING WITH DOS

◆ Up to this point, we have used the File command to save and retrieve worksheets from disk. This command can also be used to carry out several other file management functions normally done at the DOS level. Table 3-5 summarizes the major file management commands available in 1-2-3.

TABLE 3-5 File Management Commands

COMMAND	FUNCTION	DUPLICATE DOS COMMAND
/FE	Erases a file from disk.	ERASE or DEL
/FL	Displays the names of the files of a particular type.	DIR
/FD	Changes the current directory to a new one.	CHDIR or CD

Other DOS commands and programs can be executed by placing 1-2-3 and your worksheet in a wait state. A **wait state** means that 1-2-3 has given up control to another program, like DOS, but still resides in main memory. To leave 1-2-3 temporarily, enter the command /System (/S). (If you do not have a fixed disk, place the DOS disk in the A drive before entering the /S command.)

You can use the System command to leave 1-2-3 to format a disk. Once the disk is formatted, you can return to 1-2-3 and the worksheet by typing the command Exit in response to the DOS prompt. One word of advice—save your worksheet before using the System command, especially if you plan to execute an external DOS command.

PRINTING THE WORKSHEET USING ALLWAYS

◆ Allways is a spreadsheet publishing add-in program that comes with Release 2.2 of 1-2-3. **Add-in** means the program is started while 1-2-3 is running. Allways allows you to produce presentation-quality printouts as shown in Figure 3-53.

To use Allways, you must be running 1-2-3 on a hard-disk or network system with at least 512K main memory. In addition, Allways must be attached, that is, available to 1-2-3 as an add-in program. To check if it is attached and ready to use, enter the command /Worksheet Global Default (/WGD). If Allways is attached, "ALLWAYS" displays in the add-in program list as shown in the lower left corner of the default settings sheet in Figure 3-52. The Alt-F7 that you see to the right of "ALLWAYS" in Figure 3-52 means that you can start this program while 1-2-3 is on the screen by pressing Alt-F7.

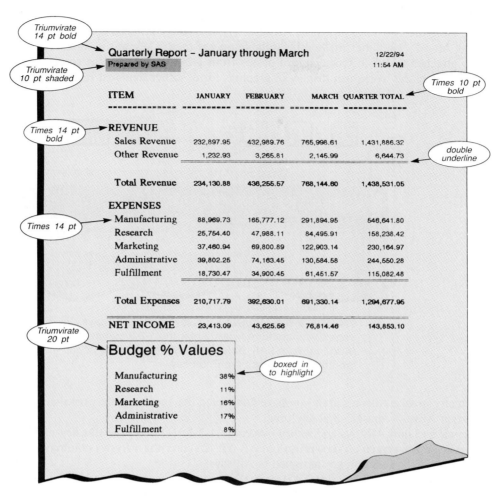

FIGURE 3-53   The worksheet in Project 3 printed using the spreadsheet publishing add-in program Allways

As shown in Figure 3-53, Allways allows you to improve the appearance of a report significantly. With Allways you can:

- Change the font (typeface and size)
- Boldface and underline text and numbers
- Adjust the height of rows and width of columns
- Shade cells
- Draw horizontal and vertical lines
- Outline a cell or range of cells
- Display the worksheet at 60% to 140% of its normal size
- Include a 1-2-3 graph in the same report as the worksheet (Project 5)
- Print in color if you have a color printer attached to your system

Another nice feature of Allways is that if you have a graphics monitor, you get a *What you see is what you get* (**Wysiwyg**) display on the screen that is nearly identical to what will print.

Starting and Quitting Allways

With 1-2-3 running, there are two ways to invoke Allways: (1) enter the command **/A**dd-In **I**nvoke (/AI) and select Allways; or (2) press Alt-F7. The latter method is available only if the F7 key was assigned the Allways program when it was initially attached to 1-2-3. Once control passes from 1-2-3 to Allways, the screen in Figure 3-54 appears. Notice that the characters in the worksheet display in graphics form, rather than text form, as they do in 1-2-3.

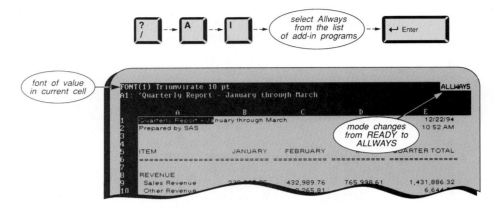

FIGURE 3-54 Project 3 displayed under Allways. To transfer control to Allways, enter the 1-2-3 command /Add-In Invoke (/AI). Select Allways from the list of add-in programs, and press the Enter key.

You would normally invoke Allways after you have completed the entries in the worksheet; but you can switch back and forth between Allways and 1-2-3 at any time.

There are three ways to quit Allways and return control to 1-2-3: (1) press the Esc key until 1-2-3 and the original worksheet reappear on the screen as shown in Figure 3-45; (2) enter the Allways command **/Q**uit (/Q); or (3) hold down the Alt key and press the function key assigned to Allways.

With the worksheet for Project 3 (Figure 3-45) on the screen, practice switching back and forth between 1-2-3 and Allways. As you move from 1-2-3 to Allways and back again to 1-2-3, the display on the screen switches between the one shown in Figure 3-45 (text display) and the one shown in Figure 3-54 (graphics display). Once you get a feel for how easy it is to transfer control between the two programs, switch to Allways to continue with this project.

The Allways Online Help Facility

To view Allways help screens, press the F1 key just as you do in 1-2-3. Allways displays a help screen that describes the activity you are currently performing in the program. For example, if you want information on the command **/L**ayout **O**ptions, enter /LO and press the F1 key.

The Allways Control Panel

The control panel in Allways is similar to the one in 1-2-3. The first line displays the format of the current cell: the font, color of data, boldface, underline, lines, or shading. The mode of operation also displays on the first line. The ALLWAYS mode means that you are in Allways (Figure 3-54). This mode is the same as READY mode in 1-2-3.

The second line of the control panel shows the address and contents of the current cell. As with 1-2-3, when you press the Slash key (/), the Main menu appears on the second line. If you press the Slash key in the middle of any command sequence, the Main menu will reappear. The third line in the control panel displays information about the menu item highlighted when Allways is in MENU mode.

The line at the bottom of the Allways screen displays the date, time, and status indicators, as does the line at the bottom of the 1-2-3 screen.

Type Styles and Cell Formats

When you initially enter Allways, all values in the cells are assigned the same font — Triumvirate 10 point (Figure 3-54). The **font** is a typeface (Triumvirate) of a particular size (10 point). A **point** is equal to 1/72 of an inch. Thus, 10 point is equal to about 1/7 of an inch. Figures 3-55 and 3-56 illustrate a variety of typefaces and point sizes.

Allways makes available two typefaces and four different point sizes for a total of eight different fonts. These eight *active* fonts can be changed as described in the 1-2-3 reference manual. The most important font is Font 1 — Triumvirate 10 point — because it is the one that is assigned to all the values in the worksheet when you first enter Allways.

This is Triumvirate
This is Times
This is Courier

FIGURE 3-55   Different typefaces

This is Times 10 point
This is Times 12 point
This is Times 14 point
This is Times 17 point
This is Times 20 point
This is Times 24 point

FIGURE 3-56   The Times typeface shown in different point sizes

Additional publishing terms with which you should be familiar are shading, bold, double underline, outlining a range of cells, and grid. **Shading** is the darkening of a range of cells and is useful for creating contrast (line 2 of Figure 3-53).

If a range of cells is **bold** or **boldface**, then the characters are darkened to make them stand out (line 1 of Figure 3-53). A **double underline** results in a double bar at the base of a range of cells. This is shown in Figure 3-53 below the row entitled Other Revenue.

You can request Allways to outline a range of cells. When we say a range **outlined**, we mean that a box has been drawn around it. The box highlights the range of cells as shown at the bottom of Figure 3-53.

Grid lines are dotted lines that surround each cell. The dotted lines run along the rows and columns of the worksheet. You can instruct Allways to display and print your worksheet with a grid by using the command /Layout **O**ptions Grid (/LOG). You can also toggle the grid on and off by pressing Alt-G. With Project 3 on the screen, press Alt-G to create a grid on the worksheet. After the grid appears, press Alt-G again. The grid disappears. Since a grid is not called for in this project, make sure the grid is off before continuing.

Saving and Synchronizing Format Changes

To preserve the format changes made with Allways, return control to 1-2-3 and save the worksheet to disk. A separate Allways file with the same file name as the worksheet, but with an extension of .ALL, is saved along with the worksheet. The next time you load the worksheet and invoke Allways, the format changes will be the same as they were when you saved it earlier.

Allways automatically synchronizes the formats assigned to cells that are changed with 1-2-3. That is, after formatting with Allways, you can return to 1-2-3 and make any changes you want to the worksheet, such as moving cells, inserting columns or rows, or deleting columns or rows. Allways will automatically adjust the cell formats to agree with the most recent worksheet modifications.

Allways Main Menu

When you press the Slash key (/) in ALLWAYS mode, the Main menu displays. Table 3-6 summarizes the functions of these commands.

TABLE 3-6 A Summary of Commands in the Allways Main Menu

COMMAND	FUNCTION
Worksheet	Sets column widths, row heights, and page breaks.
Format	Changes font, boldface, underline, color, lines, or shading of a range of cells.
Graph	Inserts or deletes a graph from the current worksheet.
Layout	Changes page size, margins, headers, footers, prints borders, and grid lines.
Print	Prints worksheet on printer or file and configures printer.
Display	Enlarges or reduces worksheet display, displays worksheet in text or graphics, turns graphs on or off, and sets colors.
Special	Copy, move, or import formats. Justifies labels in a range.
Quit	Returns control to 1-2-3.

For the remainder of this project we will use Allways to format and print the worksheet so that it looks like Figure 3-53. Just as in 1-2-3, Allways allows you to make the format changes to the worksheet in any order you want. We will make the format changes in the following order:

1. Change A1 to Triumvirate 14-point font.
2. Change A5 and A8..31 to Times 14-point font.
3. Change A25 to Triumvirate 20-point font.
4. Shade A2.
5. Bold cells A1, A5..E5, A8, A12..E12, A14, A21..E21, and A23..E23.
6. Double underline B10..E10, B19..E19, and A22..E22.
7. Outline in the range A25..B31.
8. Change the width of column A from 17 to 18 characters.
9. Print the worksheet.
10. Preserve the format changes by returning to 1-2-3 and saving the worksheet.

Changing The Font

With the Allways program in control of the computer and the cell pointer at A1, change the font of the worksheet title. Enter the command /Format Font (/FF). The Slash key (/) instructs Allways to display the Main menu shown in the top screen of Figure 3-57. When you press the first F for Format, Allways displays the Format menu as shown in the middle screen of Figure 3-57. Typing the second letter F for Font, instructs Allways to display the Font menu. With the Font menu on the screen, highlight Triumvirate 14 point by pressing the Down Arrow key twice. This procedure is shown in the bottom screen of Figure 3-57.

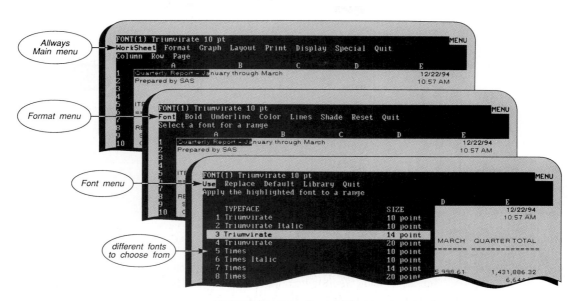

FIGURE 3-57 Step 1 of changing the font—press the Slash key (/), type the letter F for Format, type the letter F for Font, and use the Down Arrow key to select Triumvirate 14 point.

To assign the highlighted Triumvirate 14-point font to the worksheet title in A1, press the Enter key. Allways responds by prompting you to enter the range of cells to which the new font will be assigned. This procedure is shown in the top screen of Figure 3-58. Since we want to assign the font only to A1, press the Enter key. The contents of cell A1 display using the Triumvirate 14-point font as shown in the bottom screen of Figure 3-58.

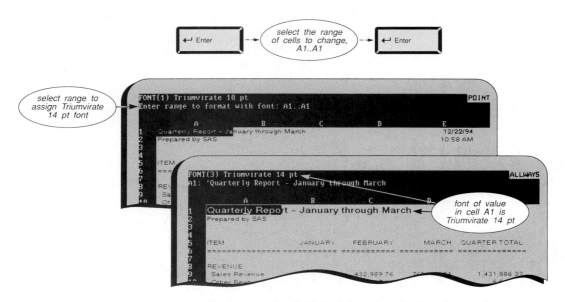

FIGURE 3-58 Step 2 of changing the font—press the Enter key to select Triumvirate 14 point and then press the Enter key again to select the range A1..A1.

Our next step is to change the font in cell A5 to Times 14 point. Move the cell pointer to A5 and enter the command **/Format Font** (/FF). Use the arrow keys to select Times 14 point from the Font menu (bottom screen of Figure 3-57) and press the Enter key. When Allways displays the prompt message "Enter range to format with font: A5..A5", press the Enter key. The characters in cell A5 display in Times 14-point font as shown in Figure 3-59.

FIGURE 3-59 Triumvirate 10 point in cell A5 changed to Times 14 point. Use the command **/Format Font** (/FF).

Move the cell pointer to cell A8 to change the font in the range A8..A31 to Times 14 point. Enter the command **/Format Font** (/FF). The Font menu in the bottom screen of Figure 3-57 displays. Select Times 14 point and press the Enter key. When the prompt message "Enter range to format with font: A8..A8" displays on the second line, use the Down Arrow key to expand the range to A8..A31. Press the Enter key. Allways assigns Times 14-point font to the range A8..A31 as shown in Figure 3-60.

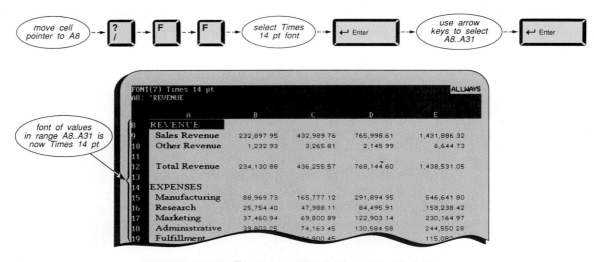

FIGURE 3-60 Triumvirate 10 point in range A8..A31 changed to Times 14 point

In Figure 3-53, the title Budget % Values shown in cell A25 is printed using Triumvirate 20-point font. There-fore, use the GOTO command to move the cell pointer from A8 to A25. Here again, enter the command /**F**ormat **F**ont (/FF). When the Font menu shown in the bottom screen of Figure 3-57 displays, select Triumvirate 20-point font. Press the Enter key. Respond to the prompt message asking for the range by pressing the Enter key, as we want to assign the new font only to cell A25. The screen shown in Figure 3-61 displays.

FIGURE 3-61   Times 14 point in cell A25 changed to Triumvirate 20 point

Shading Cells

In the top left corner of the formatted report in Figure 3-53, the label "Prepared by SAS" is shaded. This label is located in cell A2. To move the cell pointer from A25 to A2, press Home and then press the Down Arrow key. Next, enter the command /**F**ormat **S**hade (/FS). As shown in the top screen of Figure 3-62, the Shade menu has four options: Light, Dark, Solid, and Clear. Type the letter L for Light. Allways displays the prompt message "Enter range to shade: A2..A2". Since we want to shade only A2, press the Enter key. Allways shades A2 as shown in the bottom screen of Figure 3-62.

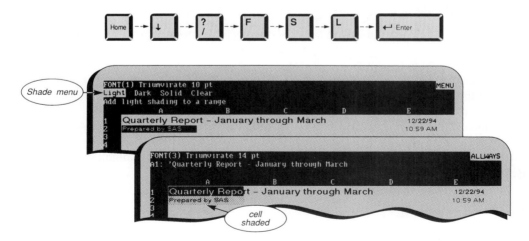

FIGURE 3-62   Shading a cell. Top screen shows Shade menu. Bottom screen shows cell A2 lightly shaded.

An alternative to using the command /Format Shade (/FS) to shade an individual cell is to position the cell pointer on the cell and press Alt-S. Each time you press this combination of keys, the shade changes from clear to light to dark to solid and back to clear. To use the Alt and S keys to shade a range of cells, first press the Period key (.) to anchor the cell pointer and use the arrow keys to highlight the range. With the range highlighted, enter Alt-S. To complete the command, press one of the arrow keys to move the highlight off the selected range.

Boldfacing Cells

The worksheet in Figure 3-53 calls for boldfacing a number of cells. Let's start by boldfacing the worksheet title in A1. Use the Up Arrow key to move the cell pointer to A1. Enter the command /Format Bold Set (/FBS). Allways displays the prompt message "Enter range to bold: A1..A1". Press the Enter key. The worksheet title in cell A1 changes to bold as shown in Figure 3-63.

FIGURE 3-63
Boldfacing the title of the worksheet in A1 by using the command /Format Bold Set (/FBS)

You can also bold an individual cell by positioning the cell pointer on the cell and pressing Alt-B. If you press this combination of keys again, Allways clears the boldface from the cell. Hence, Alt-B turns bold on or off in the current cell. Alt-B can also be used to bold a range of cells. Before you press the combination of keys, press the Period key to select the range. Once the range is highlighted, press Alt-B. To complete the command, press one of the arrow keys to move the highlight off the selected range.

Use Alt-B and the following steps to complete the boldfacing in this project.

1. Move the cell pointer to A5. Press the Period key. Use the Right Arrow key to highlight the range A5..E5. Press Alt-B.
2. Move the cell pointer to A8. Press Alt-B.
3. Move the cell pointer to A12. Press the Period key. Use the Right Arrow key to highlight the range A12..E12. Press Alt-B. Press the Down Arrow key one time.
4. Move the cell pointer to A14. Press Alt-B.
5. Move the cell pointer to A21. Press the Period key. Use the Right Arrow key to highlight the range A21..E21. Press Alt-B. Press the Down Arrow key one time.
6. Move the cell pointer to A23. Press the Period key. Use the Right Arrow key to highlight the range A23..E23. Press Alt-B. Press the Down Arrow key one time.

After completing step 6, the range A9..E23 displays as shown in Figure 3-64.

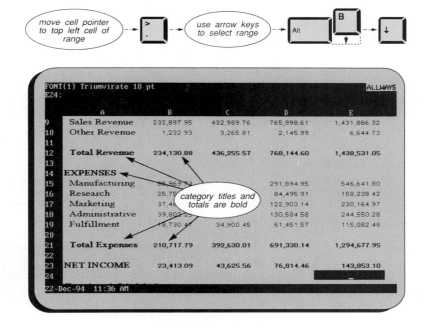

FIGURE 3-64
Boldfacing a range of cells.
Use the Period key (.) to
select the range, and then
press Alt-B.

Underlining Cells

As shown in Figure 3-53, the rows designated Other Revenue (cells B10..E10) and Fulfillment (cells B19..E19), and the empty cells A22..E22, are double underlined. Let's double underline the range B10..E10 first.

Use the GOTO command to move the cell pointer to B10. Enter the command /**F**ormat **U**nderline (/FU). As shown in the top screen of Figure 3-65, the Underline menu has three options: Single, Double, and Clear. Type the letter D for Double. Allways displays the prompt message "Enter range to double underline: B10..B10". Use the Right Arrow key to highlight the range B10..E10. Press the Enter key. The range B10..E10 is double underlined as shown in the bottom screen of Figure 3-65.

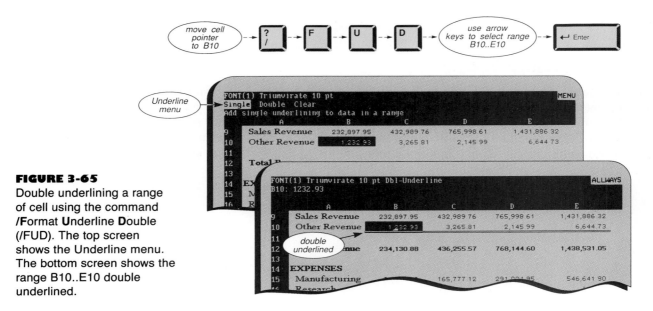

FIGURE 3-65
Double underlining a range
of cell using the command
/**F**ormat **U**nderline **D**ouble
(/FUD). The top screen
shows the Underline menu.
The bottom screen shows the
range B10..E10 double
underlined.

You can also use the Alt-U to underline an individual cell or range of cells. Each time you press Alt-U, the underlining changes from single to double to clear (no underline). To use Alt-U to underline a range of cells, first press the Period key to anchor the cell pointer; then use the arrow keys to highlight the range you want to underline. With the range highlighted, press Alt-U. To complete the command, press any one of the arrow keys to move the highlight off the selected range.

Use Alt-U to complete the required double underlining as described in Figure 3-53. Issue the GOTO command to move the cell pointer to B19. Press the Period key to activate range selection. Use the Right Arrow key to highlight the range B19..E19. Press Alt-U twice. Press the Down Arrow key to move the highlight off the range B19..E19.

Next, issue the GOTO command to move the cell pointer to A22. Press the Period key. Use the Right Arrow key to highlight the range A22..E22. Press Alt-U twice. Press the Down Arrow key. The worksheet displays as shown in Figure 3-66.

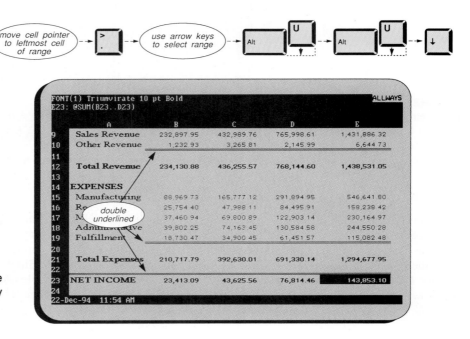

FIGURE 3-66
Double underlining a range of cells. Use the Period key (.) to select the range and then press Alt-U twice.

Outlining a Range of Cells

To outline the title Budget % Values at the bottom of the worksheet (Figure 3-53), use the GOTO command to move the cell pointer to A25. Enter the command /Format Lines Outline (/FLO). When Allways displays the prompt message "Enter range to outline: A25..A25", use the arrow keys to select the range A25..B31 as shown in the top screen of Figure 3-67. Press the Enter key. A box outlines the range A25..B31 as shown in the bottom screen of Figure 3-67. You can also outline a range of cells by first selecting the range using the Period key and then pressing Alt-L.

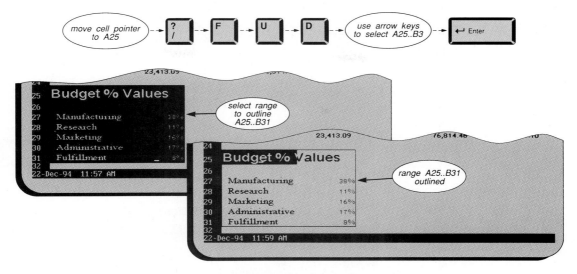

FIGURE 3-67 Outlining a range of cells using the command /Format Lines Outline (/FLO). The top screen shows the range selected. The bottom screen shows the range A25..B31 outlined.

In addition to outlining a range of cells, the /Format Lines (/FL) command can be used to draw vertical lines along the right or left edge of a range of cells or to draw horizontal lines along the top or bottom of a range of cells. You can also use /FL to draw a grid over a range of cells. For more information on drawing lines, enter /Format Lines (/FL), and press F1 to use the Allways online help facility.

Summary of Shortcut Keys for Invoking Commands

Shortcut keys allow you to execute a command sequence by holding down the Alt key and pressing a typewriter key. Table 3-7 summarizes the shortcut keys that invoke Allways commands. Use this table to speed the entry of your commands.

TABLE 3-7 Shortcut Keys for Invoking Allways Commands

KEYS	DESCRIPTION
Alt-B	Boldface (Set/Clear)
Alt-G	Grid lines (On/Off)
Alt-L	Lines (Outline/All/None)
Alt-S	Shade (Light/Dark/Solid/None)
Alt-U	Underline (Single/Double/None)
Alt-1	Set font 1
Alt-2	Set font 2
Alt-3	Set font 3
Alt-4	Set font 4
Alt-5	Set font 5
Alt-6	Set font 6
Alt-7	Set font 7
Alt-8	Set font 8

PROJECT 3 ENHANCING YOUR WORKSHEET

Changing the Widths of Columns and Heights of Rows Using Allways

When you use Allways to increase the point size in a range of cells, some characters may be truncated (chopped off) in those cells. You can overcome this problem by instructing Allways to increase the column width of the range of cells. Changing the column width in Allways does not affect the column width in 1-2-3.

Sometimes a value just fits into the cell, such as Total Expenses in cell A21 (Figure 3-68). In such cases, chances are that when the worksheet is sent to the printer, the last character will be partially or completely truncated. Therefore, we need to increase the width of column A from 17 characters to 18 characters.

FIGURE 3-68
Increasing the width of column A. Use the command **/W**orksheet **C**olumn **S**et-Width (/WCS). Use the Right or Left Arrow key to increase or decrease the column width.

To change the width of column A, move the cell pointer to A21. (Actually, the cell pointer can be in any cell in column A.) Enter the command /Worksheet Column Set-Width (/WCS). The screen shown in Figure 3-68 appears. Notice the prompt message at the top of the screen and the vertical dotted line along the right edge of column A. Press the Right Arrow key to increase the width by 1, and the vertical line on the screen moves to the right to show the new column width. With the column width at 18.00, press the Enter key. Column A is now 18 characters wide. Press the Home key to move the cursor to A1. The completed worksheet is shown in Figure 3-69.

FIGURE 3-69
Format modifications to Project 3 completed

Consider one last point about the column width—as the prompt message indicates in Figure 3-68, Allways allows you to enter a column width to the nearest hundredths (two decimal places). You can type in the width you desire or you can increase or decrease the width by 1/10 of a character by holding down the Ctrl key and pressing the Right or Left Arrow key. Pressing the Right or Left Arrow key by itself increases or decreases the column width by 1 character.

Allways automatically adjusts the height of a row on the basis of the greatest point size assigned to the cells in the row. You can manually adjust the height of a row by moving the cell pointer into the row and entering the /**W**orksheet **R**ow **S**et-Height (/WRS) command. You can also adjust the height of several adjacent rows by using the Period key to select the rows prior to issuing the /WRS command.

Printing the Worksheet

To print the worksheet using Allways, enter the command /**P**rint (/P). This command activates the menu pointer in the Print menu (Figure 3-70). Type the letters R for Range and S for Set. Use the arrow keys to move the cell pointer to E31. Press the Enter key to anchor the second end point. The Print menu shown in Figure 3-70 reappears.

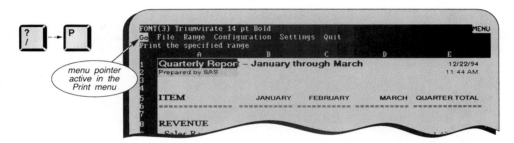

FIGURE 3-70 Printing the worksheet using Allways

Check to be sure the printer is ready. Type the letter G for Go. The worksheet prints on the printer as shown earlier in Figure 3-53. Move the paper through the printer so that you can tear the paper at the perforated edge below the printed version of the worksheet.

If the worksheet fails to print when you type the letter G for Go and you get an "Out of Memory" message on the status line at the bottom of the screen, return control to 1-2-3 and save the worksheet. After the worksheet is saved, return control to Allways and issue the print command again. If the worksheet still fails to print, use the command /**W**orksheet **G**lobal **D**efault **O**ther **U**ndo **D**isable (/WGDOUD) to turn off the UNDO command and free up main memory. After disabling the UNDO command, issue the print command again.

One additional point about the Print command—once you establish a print range, Allways displays a dotted outline that defines the range whenever you switch from 1-2-3 to Allways.

Saving the Worksheet with Allways Format Changes

To preserve the format changes we have made to Project 3 using Allways, we need to save the worksheet to disk. To do this, return control to 1-2-3, and enter the command /**F**ile **S**ave **R**eplace (/FSR). 1-2-3 saves the worksheet as PROJS-3.WK1 and the corresponding Allways format changes as PROJS-3.ALL.

The Display Command

The /**D**isplay (/D) command in Allways allows you to control how the worksheet displays on the screen. Table 3-8 summarizes the functions of the commands in the Display menu.

TABLE 3-8 A Summary of Commands in the Allways Display Menu

COMMAND	FUNCTION
Colors	Sets color for background, foreground, and cell pointer.
Graphs	Turns the display of integrated graphs on or off. (Press F10 to issue this command.)
Mode	Switches display between text and graphics.
Quit	Quits Display menu and returns to ALLWAYS mode.
Zoom	Reduces or enlarges the display of the worksheet. (Use Alt-F4 to enlarge the worksheet. Press Alt-F4 repeatedly to enlarge the worksheet up to 140% of its normal size. Use F4 to reduce the size of the worksheet down to 60% of its normal size.)

The two screens in Figure 3-71 show the Project 3 worksheet reduced to 60% and enlarged to 140%.

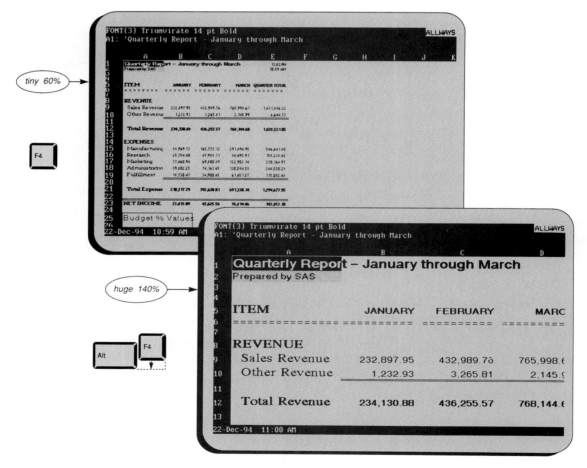

FIGURE 3-71 Minimizing and maximizing the display of the worksheet. Use the command /**D**isplay **Z**oom (/DZ) or use Alt-F4 to enlarge the display and F4 to reduce it.

PROJECT SUMMARY

In this project you learned a variety of ways to enhance a worksheet and simplify the steps of building, formatting, and printing large worksheets. You were introduced to the capabilities of 1-2-3 to answer what-if questions. Finally, you learned how to change the default settings, interact with DOS through 1-2-3, and produce presentation-quality printouts through Allways. All the activities that you learned for this project are summarized in the Quick Reference following the Appendix. The following is a summary of the keystroke sequence we used in Project 3.

SUMMARY OF KEYSTROKES — PROJECT 3

STEPS	KEY(S) PRESSED	RESULTS
1	/WGC → → → → ↵	Sets width of all columns to 13.
2	/WCS17↵	Sets width of column A to 17.
3	→ → → → /WCS16↵	Sets width of column E to 16.
4	/WGF,↵	Sets format of all columns to Comma (,).
5	← ← ← ←Quarterly Report - January through March↓	Enters report title in A1.
6	Prepared by SAS↵	Enters author of worksheet in B1.
7	F5 E1↵@now↓	Enters @NOW function in E1.
8	@now↑	Enters @NOW function in E2.
9	/RFD4↵	Formats date in E1.
10	↓/RFDT2↵	Formats time in E2.
11	F5 A5↵ Caps Lock	Moves cell pointer to A5 and engages Caps Lock.
12	ITEM→ "JANUARY →	Enters column titles in A5 and B5.
13	"FEBRUARY→ "MARCH→	Enters column titles in C5 and D5.
14	"QUARTER TOTAL↵	Enters column title in E5.
15	F5 A6↵\ = ↵	Underlines title in column A.
16	/C↵→.→ → → ↵	Underlines titles in columns B through E.
17	↓↓REVENUE↓ Caps Lock	Enters group title in A8 and disengages Caps Lock.
18	' Sales Revenue↓' Other Revenue↓↓	Enters group subtitles in A9 and A10.
19	' Total Revenue↓↓	Enters group subtitle in A12.
20	EXPENSES↓' Manufacturing↓	Enters group title in A14 and group subtitle in A15.
21	' Research↓' Fulfillment↓↓	Enters group subtitles in A16 and A17.
22	' Total Expenses↓↓NET INCOME↓↓	Enters group subtitle in A19 and group title in A21.
23	Budget % Values↓	Enters group title in A23.
24	F5 A17↵	Moves cell pointer to A17.
25	/WIR↓ ↵	Inserts two rows.
26	' Marketing↓' Administrative↓	Enters group subtitles in A18 and A19.
27	/CA15.A19↵A27↵	Copies group subtitles in A15..A19 to A27..A31.
28	F5 B27↵	Moves cell pointer to B27.
29	38%↓11%↓16%↓17%↓8%↵	Enters budget % values in B27..B31.

(continued)

SUMMARY OF KEYSTROKES — PROJECT 3 (continued)

STEPS	KEY(S) PRESSED	RESULTS
30	/RFP0 ← ↑↑↑↑ ←	Sets format of B27..B31 to Percent.
31	(Home) (F5) B7 ←	Moves cell pointer to B7.
32	/WTB	Freezes row and column titles.
33	232897.95 → 432989.76 → 765998.61 →	Enters sales revenue in B7..D7.
34	@SUM(B7.D7) →	Sums sales revenue (B7..D7) in E7.
35	/M (Backspace) ←.← ← ← ←↓↓←.← ← ← ←	Moves sales revenue from B7..E7 to B9..E9.
36	↓↓↓ ← ← ← ←	Moves cell pointer to B10.
37	1232.93 → 3265.81 → 2145.99↓↓← ←	Enters other revenue in B10..D10 and moves cell pointer to B12.
38	@SUM(B9.D10) ←	Sums revenue (B9..D10) in B12.
39	/C ← → . → ←	Copies B12 to C12..D12.
40	/RFTB9.E19 ←	Sets format of B9..E19 to Text.
41	↓↓↓$B27*B$12 ←	Moves cell pointer to B15 and enters formula.
42	/C ←.↓↓↓↓ → → ←	Copies B15 to B15..D19.
43	(F5) B19 ←/RF,←B19.E9 ←	Sets format of B19..E9 to Comma (,).
44	↓↓@SUM(↑↑↑↑↑↑.↓↓↓↓) ←	Assigns the sum of B15..B19 to B21.
45	/C ← → . → ←	Copies B21 to C21..D21.
46	↓↓+B12-B21 ←	Assigns formula +B12-B21 to B23.
47	/C ← → . → ←	Copies B23 to C23..D23.
48	(F5) E9 ←	Moves cell pointer to E9.
49	/C ←E9.E23 ←	Copies E9 to E9..E23.
50	↓↓/RE ←	Erases E11.
51	↓↓/RE↓ ←	Erases E13..E14.
52	↓↓↓↓↓↓↓/RE ←	Erases E20.
53	↓↓/RE ←	Erases E22.
54	/WTC (Home)	Clears titles and moves cell pointer to A1.
55	/FSPROJS-3 ←	Saves worksheet as PROJS-3.
56	/PPRA1.E31 ←	Sets A1..E31 as the print range.
57	AGPQ	Prints the worksheet.

SUMMARY OF KEYSTROKES — PROJECT 3   Using Allways

STEPS	KEY(S) PRESSED	RESULTS
1	/A|ALLWAYS ←	Invokes ALLWAYS.
2	/FF↓↓←←	Assigns Triumvirate 14-point font to A1.
3	[F5] A5←/FF↓↓↓↓↓↓←←	Assigns Times 14-point font to A5.
4	↓↓↓/FF↓↓↓↓↓↓←A8.A31←	Assigns Times 14-point font to A8..A31.
5	[F5] A25←/FF↑↑↑←←	Assigns Triumvirate 14-point font to A25.
6	[Home]↓/FSL←	Shades A2.
7	↑/FBS←	Boldfaces A1.
8	[F5] A5←.→→→→ [Alt-B] ↓	Boldfaces A5..E5.
9	[F5] A8← [Alt-B]	Boldfaces A8.
10	[F5] A12←.→→→→ [Alt-B] ↓	Boldfaces A12..E12.
11	[F5] A14← [Alt-B]	Boldfaces A14.
12	[F5] A21←.→→→→ [Alt-B] ↓	Boldfaces A21..E21.
13	[F5] A23←.→→→→ [Alt-B] ↓	Boldfaces A23..E23.
14	[F5] B10←/FUD→→→←	Draws double underline in B10..E10.
15	[F5] B19←.→→→ [Alt-U] [Alt-U] ↓	Draws double underline in B19..E19.
16	[F5] A22←.→→→→ [Alt-U] [Alt-U] ↓	Draws double underline in A22..E22.
17	[F5] A25←/FLO→↓↓↓↓↓↓←	Boxes in A25..B31.
18	[F5] A21←/WCS→← [Home]	Sets width of column A to 17.
19	/PRSA1.E31←G	Prints the worksheet (A1.E31).
20	/Q	Quits ALLWAYS.
21	/FSR	Saves worksheet as PROJS-3.

The following list summarizes the material covered in Project 3.

1. After setting the column width for the entire worksheet, use the command /**W**orksheet **C**olumn **S**et-Width (/WCS) to set the width of individual columns requiring a different width.

2. Use the command /**W**orksheet **G**lobal **F**ormat (/WGF) to format all the cells in the worksheet to the same type.

3. To display the date and time as a decimal number, use the **NOW function**. The whole number portion is the number of complete days since December 31, 1899. The decimal portion represents today's time.

4. Use the command /**R**ange **F**ormat **D**ate (/RFD) to format today's date and time. Use Table 3-1 for a summary of the date and time formats.

5. The time stored in a cell is updated only after you make an entry into the worksheet or after you press function key F9.

6. To insert rows or columns into a worksheet, move the cell pointer to the point of insertion and enter the command /**W**orksheet **I**nsert (/WI). Type the letter R to insert rows or the letter C to insert columns. Use the arrow keys to select how many rows or columns you want to insert.

7. To delete rows or columns from a worksheet, move the cell pointer to one of the end points of the range you want to delete. Enter the command /**W**orksheet **D**elete (/WD). Type the letter R to delete rows or the letter C to delete columns. Use the arrow keys to select how many rows or columns you want to delete.

8. Enter a percentage value in percent form by appending a percent sign (%) to the right of the number.

9. To **freeze the titles** so that they remain on the screen as you move the cell pointer around the worksheet, use the command /**W**orksheet **T**itles (/WT). You then have the choice of freezing vertical (row) titles, horizontal (column) titles, or both. Use the same command to **unfreeze** the titles.

10. To move a range to another range, use the command /**M**ove (/M).
11. With the Copy command, a cell address with no dollar sign ($) is a **relative address**. A cell address with a dollar sign appended to the front of both the column name and row number is an **absolute address**. A cell address with a dollar sign added to the front of the column name or to the front of the row number is a **mixed cell address**.
12. When you enter a formula or function, you may use the arrow keys to point to the range.
13. It is valid to copy a cell to itself. This is necessary when you copy the end point of the destination range.
14. An empty cell or a cell with a label has a numeric value of zero.
15. Use the command /**P**rint **P**rinter **O**ption (/PPO) to change the printer default settings.
16. **Condensed mode** allows nearly twice as many characters to fit across the page. Use the command /**P**rint **P**rinter **O**ptions **S**etup (/PPOS) to print a worksheet in the condensed mode.
17. The capability to answer **what-if questions** is a powerful and important feature of 1-2-3. Using 1-2-3 to answer what-if questions is called performing **what-if-analyses** or **sensitivity analyses**.
18. Once a worksheet is complete, you can enter new values into cells. Formulas and functions that reference the modified cells are immediately recalculated, thus giving new results. This feature is called **automatic recalculation**.
19. Use the command /**W**orksheet **G**lobal **R**ecalculation (/WGR) to change from automatic to **manual recalculation**.
20. To change the default settings for the worksheet, use the command /**W**orksheet **G**lobal **D**efault (/WGD).
21. Default settings changed with the command /WGD remain in force for the entire session, until you quit 1-2-3.
22. To permanently change the default settings, type the letter U for Update before quitting the Global Default menu.
23. The File command may be used to list the names of the files on disk, delete files, and change the current directory.
24. The System command allows you to temporarily place 1-2-3 in a **wait state** and return control to DOS. Once control returns to DOS, you may execute DOS commands. To return to 1-2-3, enter the command Exit.
25. Allways is a spreadsheet publishing add-in program that comes with Release 2.2 of 1-2-3. **Add-in** means the program is started while 1-2-3 is running.
26. There are two ways to invoke Allways: (1) enter the command /**A**dd-**I**n **I**nvoke (/AI) and select Allways; or (2) hold down the Alt key and press F7. The latter method is available only if the F7 key was assigned the Allways program when it was initially attached to 1-2-3.
27. **Wysiwyg** stands for *What you see is what you get*.
28. The **font** is a typeface of a particular size. A **point** is equal to 1/72 of one inch.
29. To preserve the format changes made with Allways, return control to 1-2-3 and save the worksheet to disk.
30. To change the font of a cell or range of cells, enter the command /**F**ormat **F**ont (/FF).
31. Shade a cell or range of cells by entering the command /**F**ormat **S**hade (/FS). The Shade menu has four options: Light, Dark, Solid, and Clear.
32. Bold a cell or range of cells by entering the command /**F**ormat **B**old **S**et (/FBS).
33. To underline a cell or range of cells, enter the command /**F**ormat **U**nderline (/FU). The Underline menu has three options: Single, Double, and Clear.
34. To outline a range of cells, enter the command /**F**ormat **L**ines **O**utline (/FLO).
35. **Shortcut keys** allow you to execute an Allways command sequence by holding down the Alt key and pressing a typewriter key. Some of the more important shortcut keys are: Alt-B for bold; Alt-S for shade; Alt-U for underline; and Alt-L for lines.
36. To use the shortcut keys on a range of cells, use the Period key to select the range and then press the shortcut key. To conclude the command, use one of the arrow keys to move the highlight off the range.
37. To change the column width in Allways, enter the command /**W**orksheet **C**olumn **S**et-Width (/WCS).
38. To change the height of rows, enter the /**W**orksheet **R**ow **S**et-Height (/WRS) command.
39. To print the worksheet using Allways, enter the command /**P**rint (/P). Select the range and then press G for Go.
40. The /**D**isplay (/D) command in Allways allows you to control how the worksheet displays on the screen.

STUDENT ASSIGNMENTS

STUDENT ASSIGNMENT 1: True/False

Instructions: Circle T if the statement is true and F if the statement is false.

T F   1. When you insert rows in a worksheet, 1-2-3 *pushes down* the current row and rows below the point of insertion to open up the worksheet.

T F   2. The /Worksheet Global Format (/WGF) command does not require that you enter a range in the worksheet to be affected.

T F   3. Use the NOW function to display the system date and time.

T F   4. To reset the format in a range to the global format, use the command /Range Format Reset (/RFR).

T F   5. Labels, such as a name, are not affected by a global numeric format.

T F   6. Use the command /Worksheet Titles Clear (/WTC) to unfreeze the titles.

T F   7. When using the /Worksheet Titles (/WT) command, the title and column headings that run across the worksheet are called horizontal titles.

T F   8. The range B10..B15 is the same as B15..B10.

T F   9. A percentage value, like 5.3%, can not be entered exactly as 5.3% on the input line.

T F   10. When you start Allways, the default font is designated font 1 in the Font menu.

T F   11. If a cell within the range summed by the SUM function contains a label, 1-2-3 displays an error message.

T F   12. You can use the arrow keys to select the range for the SUM function.

T F   13. D23 is an absolute address and $D$23 is a relative address.

T F   14. When numbers are displayed using the Text format, they display right-justified in the cells.

T F   15. Use the /Move (/M) command to move the contents of a cell or range of cells to a different location in the worksheet.

T F   16. The /Display (/D) command allows you to reduce the display of the worksheet to a maximum of 40% of its normal display.

T F   17. The format changes made with Allways are preserved as part of the .WK1 file when the worksheet is saved.

T F   18. To double underline a cell in Allways, move the cell pointer to the cell you want to double underline, and press Alt-U twice.

T F   19. ALLWAYS mode in Allways is similar to MENU mode in 1-2-3.

T F   20. Press Alt-B to boldface the current cell.

STUDENT ASSIGNMENT 2: Multiple Choice

Instructions: Circle the correct response.

1. Which one of the following commands is used to delete rows or columns from a worksheet?
   a. /Worksheet Unprotect (/WU)
   b. /Worksheet Erase (/WE)
   c. /Worksheet Label (/WL)
   d. /Worksheet Delete (/WD)

2. Which one of the following is an absolute address?
   a. $B$45 b. !G!45 c. G45 d. #G#45

3. Which one of the following functions is used to display the time?
   a. TODAY b. TIME c. NOW d. CLOCK

4. The command /Print Printer Options (/PPO) may be used to change _____ .
   a. the margins
   b. the page length
   c. from normal mode to condensed mode
   d. all of the above

5. The /File (/F) command can be used to _____ .
   a. format disks
   b. change the current directory
   c. erase worksheets from disk
   d. both b and c

Student Assignment 2 (continued)

6. If cell B14 is assigned the label TEN, then the function @SUM(B10.B14) in cell C25 considers B14 to be equal to _____ .
   a. 10   c. an undefined value
   b. 0   d. 3
7. The command /Move (/M) results in the same change to the worksheet as _____ .
   a. /Worksheet Erase (/WE)   c. /Worksheet Insert (/WI)
   b. /Copy (/C)   d. none of the above
8. The command /Worksheet Global Default (/WGD) can be used to _____ .
   a. display default settings   c. return control to DOS
   b. select a format for the worksheet   d. delete files
9. Which one of the following keys is used with Allways to select a range of cells before a shortcut key command is entered?
   a. Slash (/)   d. Circumflex (˜)
   b. Comma (,)   e. Number sign (#)
   c. Period (.)
10. Which of the following are the initial commands in the command sequence to instruct Allways to outline a range of cells?
   a. /Format Underline (/FU)
   b. /Format Font (/FF)
   c. /Format Display (/FD)
   d. /Format Lines (/FL)
   e. /Format Shade (/FS)

STUDENT ASSIGNMENT 3: Understanding Absolute, Mixed, and Relative Addressing

Instructions: Fill in the correct answers.

1. Write cell D15 as a relative address, absolute address, mixed address with the row varying, and mixed address with the column varying.

   Relative address: _____   Mixed, row varying: _____

   Absolute address: _____   Mixed, column varying: _____

2. In the following figure, write the formula for cell B8 that multiplies cell B1 times the sum of cells B4, B5, and B6. Write the formula so that when it is copied to cells C8 and D8, cell B1 remains absolute. Verify your formula by checking it with the values found in cells B8, C8, and D8 below.

Formula for cell B8: _____

3. In the figure at the bottom of page L144, write the formula for cell E4 that multiplies cell A4 times the sum of cells B4, C4, and D4. Write the formula so that when it is copied to cells E5 and E6, cell A4 remains absolute. Verify your formula by checking it with the values found in cells E4, E5, and E6.

   Formula for cell E4: _____

4. In the figure at the bottom of page L144, write the formula for cell B10 that multiplies cell B1 times the sum of cells B4, B5, and B6. Write the formula so that when it is copied to cells C10 and D10, 1-2-3 adjusts all the cell addresses according to the new location. Verify your formula by checking it with the values found in cells B10, C10, and D10.

   Formula for cell B10: _____

5. In the figure at the bottom of page L144, write the formula for cell F4 that multiplies cell A4 times the sum of cells B4, C4, and D4. Write the formula so that when it is copied to cells F5 and F6, 1-2-3 adjusts all the cell addresses according to the new location. Verify your formula by checking it with the values found in cells F4, F5, and F6.

   Formula for cell F4: _____

STUDENT ASSIGNMENT 4: Writing 1-2-3 Commands

Instructions: Write the 1-2-3 command to accomplish the task in each of the following problems. Write the command up to the point where you enter the range or type the letter Q to quit the command.

1. Move the range of cells A12..C15 to F14..H17. Assume the cell pointer is at A12.

   Command: _____

2. Return control to DOS temporarily.

   Command: _____

3. Insert three rows between rows 5 and 6. Assume the cell pointer is at A6.

   Command: _____

4. Freeze the vertical and horizontal titles. Assume that the cell pointer is immediately below and to the right of the titles.

   Command: _____

5. Delete columns A, B, and C. Assume the cell pointer is at A1.

   Command: _____

6. Switch control to the add-in program Allways.

   Command: _____

7. Change 1-2-3 from automatic to manual recalculation.

   Command: _____

8. Change to print in condensed mode with a right margin of 132.

   Command: _____

9. Change the left print margin to 1 and the right print margin to 79 for the current worksheet only.

   Command: _____

10. Set columns A and B as borders. Assume the cell pointer is at B1.

    Command: _____

Student Assignment 4 (continued)

11. Reset the format in the range A1..B10 to the global format. Assume the cell pointer is at A1.

    Command: _____

12. List the Allways command sequence for assigning bold to the range A10..E25 using the shortcut key.

    Command: _____

13. List the shortcut key commands to minimize and maximize the display of a worksheet using Allways.

    Command: Minimize _____   Maximize _____

STUDENT ASSIGNMENT 5: Correcting the Range in a Worksheet

Instructions: The worksheet illustrated in the following figure contains errors in cells C21 through E21. Analyze the entries displayed on the worksheet, especially the formula assigned to B21 and displayed at the top of the screen. Cell B21 was copied to C21..D21. Explain the cause of the errors and the method of correction in the space provided below.

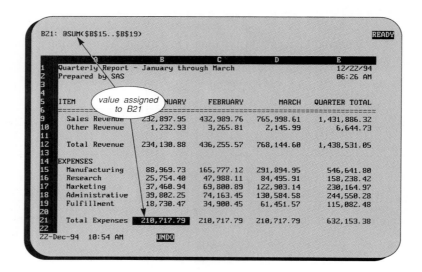

Cause of errors: _____

_____

Method of correction for cell B21: _____

_____

Method of correction for cells C21 through E21: _____

_____

_____

STUDENT ASSIGNMENT 6: Correcting Errors in a Worksheet

Instructions: The worksheet illustrated in the figure at the top of the next page contains errors in the range B15..E23. This worksheet contains the same formulas as the worksheet in Project 3. Analyze the entries displayed on the worksheet. Explain the cause of the errors and the method of correction in the space provided below. (Hint: Check the cells that are referenced in the range B15..E23.)

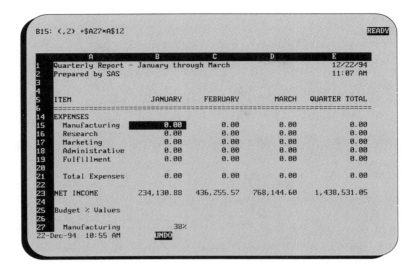

B15: (,2) +$A27*A$12   READY

	A	B	C	D	E
1	Quarterly Report - January through March				12/22/94
2	Prepared by SAS				11:07 AM
5	ITEM	JANUARY	FEBRUARY	MARCH	QUARTER TOTAL
14	EXPENSES				
15	Manufacturing	0.00	0.00	0.00	0.00
16	Research	0.00	0.00	0.00	0.00
17	Marketing	0.00	0.00	0.00	0.00
18	Administrative	0.00	0.00	0.00	0.00
19	Fulfillment	0.00	0.00	0.00	0.00
21	Total Expenses	0.00	0.00	0.00	0.00
23	NET INCOME	234,130.88	436,255.57	768,144.60	1,438,531.05
25	Budget % Values				
27	Manufacturing	38%			

22-Dec-94 10:55 AM   UNDO

Cause of errors: _____

_____

Method of correction: _____

_____

STUDENT ASSIGNMENT 7: Building a Projected Price Increase Worksheet

Instructions: Load 1-2-3 and perform the following tasks.

1. Build the worksheet illustrated in the following figure. Increase the width of columns B through E to 13 characters. Enter the title, column headings, model numbers in column A, and corresponding current prices in column B. The entries in the columns labeled 12.5% INCREASE, 16.25% INCREASE, and 21.5% INCREASE are determined from formulas. Multiply one plus the percent specified in the column heading by the current price. For example, assign C9 the formula 1.125*B8. To determine the total current price in cell B19, enter a formula that adds the products of the on-hand column and the corresponding current price. Copy this total formula in cell B19 to cells C19 through E19 to determine the totals in the remaining columns.

A20:   READY

	A	B	C	D	E	F
1			LOWLAND'S STEREO			22-Dec
2						11:07 AM
3		PROJECTED CD PRICE INCREASES FOR NEXT QUARTER				
5	MODEL	CURRENT	12.5%	16.25	21.5%	
6	NUMBER	PRICE	INCREASE	INCREASE	INCREASE	ON HAND
9	CD-101	275.00	309.38	319.69	334.13	18
10	CD-201	320.00	360.00	372.00	388.80	27
11	CD-325	375.00	421.88	435.94	455.63	32
12	CD-500	520.00	585.00	604.50	631.80	15
13	CD-750	625.00	703.13	726.56	759.38	23
14	CD-800	700.00	787.50	813.75	850.50	36
15	CD-825	725.00	815.63	842.81	880.88	21
16	CD-900	775.00	871.88	900.94	941.63	34
17	CD-990	825.00	928.13	959.06	1002.38	23
19	TOTAL	$133,515.00	$150,204.38	$155,211.19	$162,220.73	

22-Dec-94 10:56 AM   UNDO

Student Assignment 7 (continued)

2. Save the worksheet as STUS3-7.
3. Print the worksheet in the condensed mode. Reset 1-2-3 back to the normal print mode.
4. Print the cell-formulas version of the worksheet.
5. Print only the first 18 rows of the model number and current price columns.
6. Print the worksheet after formatting all the cells to the Text type.

STUDENT ASSIGNMENT 8: Building a Payroll Analysis Worksheet

Instructions: Load 1-2-3 and perform the following tasks.

1. Build the worksheet illustrated in the following figure. Change the global width to 13 characters. Change the width of column A to 19 characters. Enter the title, column headings, row titles, employee names in column A, and corresponding current hourly pay rate in column B. Use the NOW function to display the current date and time in cells E18 and E19. It is not necessary that the date and time in your worksheet agree with the date and time in the figure. Finally, enter the proposed percent increase in cell B15 and hours per week in cell B16.

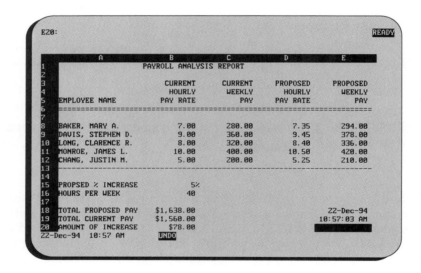

Enter the following formulas once and copy them to complete the remainder of the worksheet:
   a. Cell C8—current weekly pay = hours per week × current hourly pay rate
   b. Cell D8—proposed hourly pay rate = current hourly pay rate × (1 + proposed percent increase in B15)
   c. Cell E8—proposed weekly pay = hours per week × proposed hourly pay rate
   Format the numbers in rows 8 through 12 to the Fixed type with two decimal places. Format the totals in rows 18 through 20 to the Currency type with two decimal places.
2. Save the worksheet as STUS3-8.
3. Print the worksheet in condensed mode. Reset 1-2-3 back to the normal print mode.
4. Print only the range A1..C13.

5. Answer the following what-if questions. Print the worksheet for each question.
   a. What is the total proposed pay if the proposed percent increase is changed to 10%?
   b. What is the total proposed pay if the proposed percent increase is changed to 7.5%?
6. Use Allways to print the worksheet as shown in the figure below. Incorporate the following format changes:
   a. Change the font in B1 to Times 14 point.
   b. Change the font over the range A15..B20 to Times 10 point.
   c. Bold A1, A3..E5, and A15..B20.
   d. Shade dark E8..E12.
   e. Outline A15..B16.
   f. Double underline A20..B20.

PAYROLL ANALYSIS REPORT

EMPLOYEE NAME	CURRENT HOURLY PAY RATE	CURRENT WEEKLY PAY	PROPOSED HOURLY PAY RATE	PROPOSED WEEKLY PAY
BAKER, MARY A.	7.00	280.00	7.35	294.00
DAVIS, STEPHEN D.	9.00	360.00	9.45	378.00
LONG, CLARENCE R.	8.00	320.00	8.40	336.00
MONROE, JAMES L.	10.00	400.00	10.50	420.00
CHANG, JUSTIN M.	5.00	200.00	5.25	210.00

| PROPOSED % INCREASE | 5% |
| HOURS PER WEEK | 40 |

TOTAL PROPOSED PAY	$1,638.00		22-Dec-94
TOTAL CURRENT PAY	$1,560.00		02:06:01 PM
AMOUNT OF INCREASE	$78.00		

7. Save the worksheet with the Allways format characteristics as STUS3-8A.

STUDENT ASSIGNMENT 9: Building a Book Income Worksheet

Instructions: Load 1-2-3 and perform the following tasks.

1. Build the worksheet illustrated in the following figure. Set column A to a width of 18 characters and columns B through E to a width of 13 characters. The calculations for each author are determined as follows:
    a. The royalty in column C is the net sales of the book multiplied by the author's royalty percentage in cell B30 or B31.
    b. The manufacturing costs in column D are the net sales of the book multiplied by the manufacturing budgeted percent in cell B35.
    c. The net income in column E for each book is determined by subtracting the royalty and manufacturing costs from the net sales.
    d. The report totals in rows 25 and 26 are the sum of the individual book titles for each author.

```
                          BOOK INCOME REPORT
        ---------------------------------------------------------------
        AUTHOR:            JONES

        BOOK TITLE         NET SALES      ROYALTY   MANU. COSTS   NET INCOME

        Texas Belle        147,962.00    21,454.49    40,393.63    86,113.88
        You're OK          734,145.87   106,451.15   200,421.82   427,272.90
        Thanks For Nothing 915,923.56   132,808.92   250,047.13   533,067.51

        ---------------------------------------------------------------
        AUTHOR:            SMYTHE

        BOOK TITLE         NET SALES      ROYALTY   MANU. COSTS   NET INCOME

        The Dull Day       349,923.56    43,040.60    95,529.13   211,353.83
        Simple Times       765,123.34    94,110.17   208,878.67   462,134.50
        Computer Brain   1,097,324.57   134,970.92   299,569.61   662,784.04

        ---------------------------------------------------------------
        REPORT TOTALS

        AUTHOR             NET SALES      ROYALTY   MANU. COSTS   NET INCOME

        Jones            1,798,031.43   260,714.56   490,862.58 1,046,454.29
        Smythe           2,212,371.47   272,121.69   603,977.41 1,336,272.37

        ===============================================================
        Royalty:
        Jones                 14.5%
        Smythe                12.3%


        Manufacturing Cost                                         Dec-94
        All Books             27.3%                               02:55 PM
```

2. Save the worksheet. Use the file name STUS3-9.
3. Print the worksheet.
4. Print only the range A3..E9.
5. Print the worksheet after formatting all the cells to the Text type.

STUDENT ASSIGNMENT 10: Changing Manufacturing Costs and Royalty Rates in the Book Income Worksheet

Instructions: Load 1-2-3 and perform the following tasks.

1. Retrieve the worksheet STUS3-9 from disk. The worksheet is illustrated in the figure in Student Assignment 9.
2. Answer the following what-if questions. Print the worksheet for each question. Each question is independent of the others.
   a. If the manufacturing percentage cost in cell B35 is reduced from 27.3% to 25.7%, what is the net income from all of Jones's books?
   b. If Smythe's royalty percentage in cell B31 is changed from 12.3% to 15.8%, what would be the royalty amount for the book *Simple Times*?
   c. If Jones's royalty percentage in cell B30 is reduced from 14% to 13.5%, Smythe's royalty percentage is increased from 12.3% to 14.3%, and the manufacturing percentage costs are reduced from 27.3% to 24%, what would be the net incomes for Jones and Smythe?

STUDENT ASSIGNMENT 11: Building a Salary Budget Worksheet

Instructions: Load 1-2-3 and perform the following tasks.

1. Build the worksheet illustrated in the following figure. Change the width of all the columns in the worksheet to 15 characters. Then change the width of column A to 20 characters. Enter the title, column headings, row titles, date, time, and current salary for full- and part-time employees. Determine the projected salaries in column C by using the salary increase in cell B27 and the current salaries in column B. Determine the salaries by department by multiplying the total salaries in row 12 by the corresponding sales allocation percent value in the range B21..B24. Use the SUM function to determine the annual totals in column D.

```
                A              B              C              D
 1   SALARY BUDGET - CURRENT AND PROJECTED SALARIES         12/22/94
 2   PREPARED BY ACCOUNTING                                 10:59 AM
 3
 4
 5                          CURRENT        PROJECTED
 6   SALARY TYPE           JAN - JUNE      JULY - DEC     ANNUAL TOTAL
 7   ====================================================================
 8
 9   FULL TIME            1,250,500.00    1,313,025.00    2,563,525.00
10   PART TIME              750,500.00      788,025.00    1,538,525.00
11
12   TOTAL SALARIES       2,001,000.00    2,101,050.00    4,102,050.00
13
14   SALARIES BY DEPARTMENT
15       Accounting         200,100.00      210,105.00      410,205.00
16       Production         600,300.00      630,315.00    1,230,615.00
17       Sales              500,250.00      525,262.50    1,025,512.50
18       Distribution       700,350.00      735,367.50    1,435,717.50
19
20   SALES ALLOCATION % VALUES
21       Accounting                            10%
22       Production                            30%
23       Sales                                 25%
24       Distribution                          35%
25
26
27   SALARY INCREASE %                          5%
28
```

2. Save the worksheet using the file name STUS3-11.
3. Print the worksheet.
4. Print the portion of the worksheet in the range A14..D18.

Student Assignment 11 (continued)

5. Use Allways to print the worksheet as shown in the following figure. Incorporate these format changes:
    a. Bold A1, A5..D7, and A9..A27.
    b. Double underline B10..D10, A18..D18, A27..B27.
    c. Outline A20..B24.
    d. Shade dark D9..D10.
6. Minimize the display to 60%. Maximize the display to 140%.
7. Save the worksheet with the Allways format characteristics as STU3-11A.

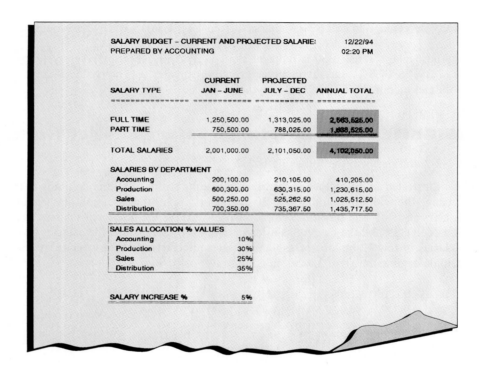

STUDENT ASSIGNMENT 12: Changing Sales Allocation Percent Values and Salary Increase Percent in the Salary Budget Worksheet

Instructions: Load 1-2-3 and perform the following tasks.

1. Retrieve the worksheet STUS3-11 from disk. The worksheet is shown in the first figure in Student Assignment 11.
2. Answer the following what-if questions. Print the worksheet for each question. Each question is independent of the other.
    a. If the four sales allocation percent values in the range B21..B24 are each decreased by 1% and the salary increase in cell B27 is changed from 5% to 4%, what are the annual totals in the Salary Budget worksheet?
    b. If the salary increase percent is cut in half, what would be the total projected salaries?

LOTUS 1-2-3 Release 2.2

Building a Worksheet with Functions and Macros

PROJECT 4

OBJECTIVES

You will have mastered the material in this project when you can:

◆ Assign a name to a range and refer to the range in a formula using the assigned name

◆ Apply the elementary statistical functions AVG, COUNT, MAX, MIN, STD, and VAR

◆ Determine the monthly payment of a loan using the financial function PMT

◆ Enter a series of numbers into a range using the Data Fill command

◆ Employ the IF function to enter one value or another in a cell on the basis of a condition

◆ Determine the present value of an annuity using the financial function PV

◆ Determine the future value of an investment using the financial function FV

◆ Build a data table to perform what-if analyses

◆ Store keystrokes as a macro and execute the macro

◆ Use the learn feature of 1-2-3 to enter macros into the worksheet

◆ Write program-like macros to automate your worksheet

◆ Divide the screen into multiple windows

◆ Protect and unprotect cells

In this project we will develop two worksheets, Project 4A and Project 4B. The worksheet for Project 4A, shown in Figure 4-1, is a grading report that displays a row of information for each student enrolled in DP 101. The student information includes a student identification number, three test scores, a test score total, and total percent correct. At the bottom of the worksheet is summary information for each test and all three tests grouped together. The summary includes the number of students that took the test, the highest and lowest test scores, the average test score, standard deviation, and variance. The standard deviation is a statistic used to measure the dispersion of test scores. The variance is used to make additional statistical inferences about the test scores.

```
DP 101                Grading Report              22-Dec-94

                 Test 1      Test 2      Test 3     Total    Percent
Student            139         142         150        431    Correct
==========================================================================
1035               121         127         142        390     90.5
1074               114         113         132        359     83.3
1265                79          97         101        277     64.3
1345                85         106          95        286     66.4
1392               127         124         120        371     86.1
3167               101         120         109        330     76.6
3382               110         104         120        334     77.5
3597                92         104         100        296     68.7
4126               105         100          96        301     69.8
5619               125         135         143        403     93.5
7561               112         130         123        365     84.7
--------------------------------------------------------------------------
Count               11          11          11         11
Lowest Grade        79          97          95        277
Highest Grade      127         135         143        403
Average Grade    106.5       114.5       116.5      337.5
Std Deviation     15.2        12.6        16.8       41.4
Variance         230.2       159.0       282.8     1711.2
```

FIGURE 4-1 The grading report we will build in Project 4A.

Project 4B has three parts. The first part is shown in Figure 4-2. This worksheet determines the monthly payment and an amortization table for a car loan. An amortization table shows the beginning and ending balances and the amount of payment that applies to the principal and interest for each period. This type of worksheet can be very useful if you are planning to take out a loan and want to see the effects of increasing the down payment, changing the interest rate, or changing the length of time it takes to pay off the loan.

FIGURE 4-2
The monthly payment and amortization table we will build for the Crown Loan Company in Part 1 of Project 4B.

The second part of this worksheet is shown in Figure 4-3. Here we use a data table to analyze the effect of different interest rates on the monthly payment and total amount paid for the car loan. A data table is an area of the worksheet set up to contain answers to what-if questions. By using a data table you can automate your what-if questions and organize the answers returned by 1-2-3 into a table. For example, the data table in Figure 4-3 displays the monthly payments and total cost of the loan for interest rates varing between 8.5% and 15% in increments of 0.5%.

FIGURE 4-3
The data table we will build for the Crown Loan Company in Part 2 of Project 4B.

The third part of Project 4B involves writing the four macros shown in Figure 4-4. A macro is a series of keystrokes or instructions that are stored in a cell or a range of cells associated with that particular worksheet. They are executed by pressing only two keys: the Alt key and the single letter macro name. Macros save you time and effort. For example, they allow you to store a complex sequence of commands in a cell. Later you can execute the macro (stored commands) as often as you want by simply typing its name.

```
            A             B          C             D                    E
 22                 Crown Loan Company Worksheet Macros
 23
 24   Macro                     Macro Name    Function
 25   ===========               ==========    ==================================
 26   /FS~R                      \S           Saves worksheet
 27
 28   /PPAGPQ                    \P           Prints worksheet
 29
 30   /PPOOCQAGOOAQPQ            \C           Prints cell-formulas version
 31
 32
 33   {HOME}                     \D           Accept loan information
 34   {GOTO}B3~/RE~                           --Clear cell B3
 35   {DOWN}{DOWN}/RE~                         --Clear cell B5
 36   {DOWN}{DOWN}/RE~                         --Clear cell B7
 37   {GOTO}E3~/RE~                            --Clear cell E3
 38   {DOWN}{DOWN}/RE~                         --Clear cell E5
 39   {HOME}                                  --Move to cell A1
 40   /XLPurchase Item:~B3~                    --Accept item
 41   /XNPurchase Price:~B5~                   --Accept price
 42   /XNDown Payment:~B7~                     --Accept down payment
 43   /XNInterest Rate in %:~E3~               --Accept interest rate
 44   /XNTime in Years:~E5~                    --Accept time in years
 45   {HOME}                                  --Move to cell A1
 46   /XQ                                     --End of macro
 47
```

FIGURE 4-4   The four macros we will build for the Crown Loan Company in Part 3 of Project 4B.

When executed, the macro in cell A26 of Figure 4-4 saves the worksheet. The one in cell A28 prints the worksheet on the basis of the previously defined range. The macro in cell A30 prints the cell-formulas version of the worksheet on the basis of the previously defined range. The multicell macro in the range A33..A46 is a type of computer program. When it executes, it automatically clears the cells containing the loan information in Figure 4-2, requests new loan data on the input line, and displays the new loan information.

PROJECT 4A — ANALYZING STUDENT TEST SCORES

◆   Begin Project 4A with an empty worksheet and the cell pointer at A1, the home position. The first step is to change the widths of the columns in the worksheet. Set the width of column A to 13 characters, so that the row identifier "Std Deviation" fits in cell A22 (Figure 4-1). Change the width of the rest of the columns in the worksheet from 9 to 11 characters so that all the student information fits across the screen. To change the columns to the desired widths, do the following:

1. Enter the command /**W**orksheet **G**lobal **C**olumn-Width (/WGC). Change the default width on the input line from 9 to 11 and press the Enter key.
2. With the cell pointer at A1, enter the command /**W**orksheet **C**olumn **S**et-Width (/WCS). Change the number 11 on the input line to 13 and press the Enter key.

If you reverse steps 1 and 2, the results will still be the same. That is, you can change the width of column A first and then change the width of the rest of the columns. The command /WGC affects only those columns that were not previously changed by the /WCS command.

The next step is to add the titles and student data to the worksheet. Enter the course number, worksheet title, date, column headings, maximum possible points for each test, student number, test scores, and summary identifiers as specified in Figure 4-1. Follow the first 20 steps in the Summary of Keystrokes—Project 4A at the end of this project. The first 20 rows display as shown in Figure 4-5.

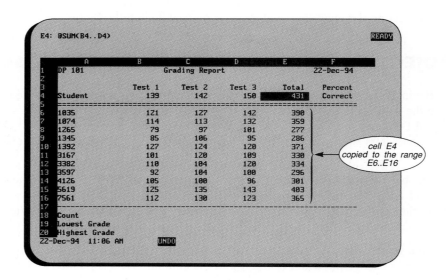

FIGURE 4-5

Labels and student data are entered into the grading report.

With the student data in the worksheet, the totals and summaries can be determined. Let's start with the maximum number of points for all three tests in cell E4. Use the GOTO command to move the cell pointer from cell A1 to cell E4 and enter the function @SUM(B4..D4). The range B4..D4 contains the maximum possible points for each test.

The SUM function in cell E4 is the same one required in the range E6..E16 to determine the total number of points received by each student. Hence, use the Copy command to copy cell E4 to the range E6..E16. With the cell pointer at E4, enter the command /Copy (/C), press the Enter key to lock in the source range, and use the Down Arrow key and Period key to select the destination range E6..E16. Press the Enter key. The total number of points received by each student displays in the range E6..E16 (Figure 4-6).

FIGURE 4-6

Student test totals are entered into column E of the grading report.

Once the total number of points received by each student is part of the worksheet, the total percent correct in column F can be determined. Move the cell pointer to F6 and enter the formula +E6/$E$4*100. The numerator in this formula, cell E6, is equal to the total number of points for the first student. The denominator, cell E4, is equal to the maximum number of points for the three tests. Multiplying the quotient +E6/$E$4 by 100 converts the ratio to a percent value. This procedure is used to display a percent value rather than formatting it in the Percent type because the column heading already indicates that the values in column E are in percent. Recall that the Percent type adds a percent sign (%) to the right side of the number.

Copy cell F6 to the range F7..F16. Notice that the dollar sign ($) character in the denominator of the formula in cell E6 makes cell E4 an absolute cell address. Therefore, when the formula in cell F6 is copied, the relative address E6 in the numerator changes based on the new location and the absolute address $E$4 in the denominator stays the same.

Format the percent correct in column F to the Fixed type with one decimal place. Enter the command /**R**ange **F**ormat **F**ixed (/RFF). Select one decimal position and press the Enter key. Enter the range F6..F16 and press the Enter key. The worksheet with each student's percent correct formatted to the Fixed type with one decimal place is illustrated in Figure 4-7.

FIGURE 4-7
Total percent correct for each student is formatted to the Fixed type with one decimal position.

The next step is to determine the summaries in rows 18 through 23. To make the job of entering these summaries easier, we need to discuss range names.

Assigning a Name to a Range of Cells

One of the problems with using a range is remembering the end points that define it. The problem becomes more difficult as worksheets grow in size and the same range is referred to repeatedly. This is the situation in the summary rows at the bottom of the grading report. For example, each summary item for Test 1 in cells B18 through B23 reference the same range, B6..B16. To make it easier to refer to the range, 1-2-3 allows you to assign a name to it. You may then use the name to reference the range, rather than the cell addresses of the end points. A range name can consist of up to 15 characters. Let's assign the name TEST1 to the range B6..B16.

Move the cell pointer to B6, one of the end points of the range B6..B16. Enter the command **/R**ange **N**ame (/RN). With the menu pointer active in the Range Name menu (Figure 4-8), type the letter C for Create.

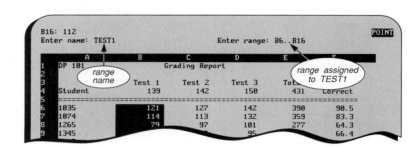

FIGURE 4-8
The display after entering the command **/R**ange **N**ame (/RN)

1-2-3 responds with the prompt message "Enter name:" on the input line (Figure 4-9). Enter the name TEST1 and press the Enter key. The prompt message "Enter range: B6..B6" immediately displays on the input line. Use the arrow keys to select the range B6..B16 as shown in Figure 4-9. Press the Enter key. The range name TEST1 can now be used in place of B6..B16.

FIGURE 4-9
Range name TEST1 assigned to the range B6..B16

As shown in the Range Name menu in Figure 4-8, there are several Range Name commands. These commands are summarized in Table 4-1. When 1-2-3 is in POINT mode, you can display a list of all the range names associated with the current worksheet by pressing function key F3.

TABLE 4-1 A Summary of Commands in the Range Name Menu

COMMAND	FUNCTION
Create	Assigns a name to a range. The name can be no longer than 15 characters.
Delete	Deletes the specified range name.
Labels	Assigns the label in the current cell as a name to the cell above, below, to the right, or to the left of the current cell.
Reset	Deletes range names associated with the worksheet.
Table	Places an alphabetized list of range names in the worksheet beginning at the upper left corner cell of the specified range.

Statistical Functions — AVG, COUNT, MIN, MAX, STD, and VAR

1-2-3 has several statistical functions that return values that are handy for evaluating a group of numbers, like the test scores in the grading report. The statistical functions are summarized in Table 4-2.

TABLE 4-2   Statistical Functions

FUNCTION	FUNCTION VALUE
AVG(R)	Returns the average of the numbers in range R by summing the nonempty cells and dividing by the number of nonempty cells. Labels are treated as zeros.
COUNT(R)	Returns the number of cells that are not empty in range R.
MAX(R)	Returns the largest number in range R.
MIN(R)	Returns the smallest number in range R.
STD(R)	Returns the standard deviation of the numbers in range R.
SUM(R)	Returns the sum of the numbers in range R.
VAR(R)	Returns the variance of the numbers in range R.

In the grading report, cell B18 displays the number of students that received a grade for Test 1. This value can be obtained by using the COUNT function. With the cell pointer at B18, enter the function @COUNT(TEST1). 1-2-3 immediately displays the value 11—the number of students that received a grade for Test 1. This is shown in Figure 4-10. Remember, the range name TEST1 is equal to the range B6..B16.

FIGURE 4-10
COUNT, MIN, and MAX functions entered into the grading report for Test 1

In cells B19 and B20, the grading report contains the lowest score and the highest score received on Test 1. Student 1265 received the lowest score—79. Student 1392 received the highest score—127. To display the lowest score obtained on Test 1, enter the function @MIN(TEST1) in cell B19. To display the highest score, enter the function @MAX(TEST1) in cell B20. The results of entering these functions are shown in cells B19 and B20 in Figure 4-10.

The next step is to determine the average of the scores received on Test 1. Enter the function @AVG(TEST1) in cell B21. As illustrated in Figure 4-11, the average score for Test 1 in cell B21 is 106.454545. 1-2-3 arrives at this value by summing the scores for Test 1 and dividing by the number of nonempty cells in the range B6..B16.

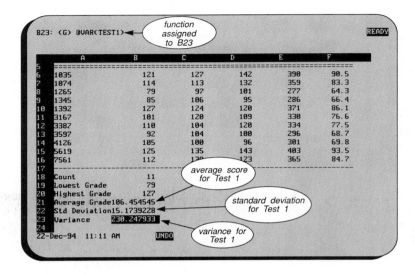

FIGURE 4-11
AVG, STD, and VAR functions entered into the grading report for Test 1

The last two summary lines require the use of the functions STD and VAR. As indicated in Table 4-2, the STD function returns the standard deviation and the VAR function returns the variance. To complete the summary lines for Test 1, enter the functions @STD(TEST1) in cell B22 and @VAR(TEST1) in cell B23. The results are shown in Figure 4-11.

The same six functions that are used to summarize the results for Test 1 are required for Test 2, Test 3, and the sum of the test scores for each student in column E. With the cell pointer at B23, enter the command /Copy (/C). Copy the source range B23..B18 to the destination range C23..E18.

As the functions in column B are copied to the new locations in columns C, D, and E, 1-2-3 adjusts the range TEST1 (B6..B16) to C6..C16 for Test 2, D6..D16 for Test 3, and E6..E16 for the sum of the test scores in column E.

To complete the worksheet, format the last three rows in the worksheet to the Fixed type with one decimal place. With the cell pointer at B23, enter the command /Range Format Fixed (/RFF). In response to the prompt message "Enter number of decimal places (0..15): 2" on the input line, type the number 1 and press the Enter key. Next, 1-2-3 displays the prompt message "Enter range to format: B23..B23". Use the arrow keys to select the range B23..E21 and press the Enter key. The complete grading report is shown in Figure 4-1.

Saving and Printing the Worksheet

To save the grading report worksheet to disk, enter the command /File Save (/FS). In response to the prompt message on the input line, enter the file name PROJS-4A, and press the Enter key.

Perform these steps to obtain a printed version of the worksheet.

1. Make sure the printer is ready.
2. Press the Home key to move the cell pointer to A1.
3. Enter the command /Print Printer Range (/PPR) and select the range A1..F23.
4. Type the letters A for Align and G for Go.
5. After the worksheet prints on the printer, type the letter P for Page. Recall that the Page command moves the paper through the printer to the top of the next page.
6. Type the letter Q to quit the /PP command and carefully remove the grading report from the printer.

Erasing the Worksheet from Main Memory

After saving and printing the grading report, erase it from main memory so that you can begin Project 4B. Recall from Project 1, that to erase the current worksheet, enter the command **/Worksheet Erase** (/WE). Finally, type the letter Y for Yes. 1-2-3 responds by clearing all the cells in the worksheet and changing all the settings to their default values.

PROJECT 4B — DETERMINING THE MONTHLY PAYMENT FOR A CAR LOAN

◆ The car loan payment worksheet is shown in Figures 4-2, 4-3, and 4-4. It is by far the most complex worksheet undertaken thus far. For this reason, we will use the divide and conquer strategy to build it. This strategy involves completing a section of the worksheet and testing it before moving on to the next section. Let's divide the worksheet into five sections:

1. Determine the monthly payment on a five-year loan for a 1993 Chevy Van with a sticker price of $18,500.00, down payment of $4,000.00, at an interest rate of 11.5%—range A1..E7 in Figure 4-2.
2. Display the amortization schedule—range A8..E20 in Figure 4-2.
3. Generate the data table—range F1..H20 in Figure 4-3.
4. Create the simple macros—range A22..E30 in Figure 4-4.
5. Create the multicell macro—range A33..E46 in Figure 4-4.

The first step in determining the car loan payment is to change the column widths. Set the width of column A to 12 characters and set the global width of the columns in the worksheet to 15 characters. Change the widths of the columns as follows:

1. With the cell pointer at A1, enter the command **/Worksheet Column Set-Width** (/WCS) to change the width of column A to 12 characters.
2. Enter the command **/Worksheet Global Column-Width** (/WGC). Change the default value 9 on the input line to 15 and press the Enter key.

With the column widths set, enter the worksheet title, the date, the six cell titles, and the five data items in the range A1..E7 (Figure 4-12). Assign cell E1 the NOW function.

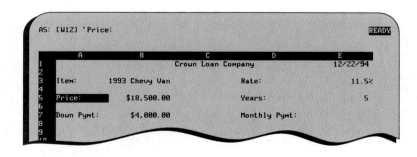

FIGURE 4-12

Labels and data entered into the Crown Loan Company worksheet

Use the command **/Range Format** (/RF) to change the format of the cells assigned numeric data in the range A1..E7 as follows:

1. Cell E1 to the Long Intn'l (MM/DD/YY) type.
2. Cells B5, B7, and E7 to the Currency type with two decimal positions.
3. Cell E3 to the Percent type with one decimal position.

The formatted worksheet with the cell pointer at A5 is shown in Figure 4-12.

Assigning a Label Name to an Adjacent Cell

In Project 4A we used the command /Range Name Create (/RNC) to assign the name TEST1 to the range B6..B16. Later, when we built the summary lines, we used the name TEST1 several times in functions to reference the range B6..B16, because the name TEST1 is easier to remember than the range B6..B16. Another advantage of using range names is that they make it easier to remember what the range represents in the worksheet. This is especially helpful when you are working with complex formulas or functions.

The function for determining the monthly payment in cell E7 uses the purchase price (B5), down payment (B7), rate (E3), and years (E5). Let's name each of these cells. In this case, we'll use a second technique for assigning names to the individual cells. Rather than typing in a new name for each cell, use the adjacent cell title—the label located immediately to the left of each cell you want to name. For example, use the label Price: in cell A5 to name cell B5.

With the cell pointer at A5, enter the command /Range Name Label (/RNL). By entering the command Label, you instruct 1-2-3 to use a label in the worksheet as the name, rather than to create a new name. With the menu pointer active in the Range Name Label menu (Figure 4-13), type the letter R for Right. This command allows you to assign any adjacent cell to the label name. Typing the letter R tells 1-2-3 to assign the cell to the right of the label name.

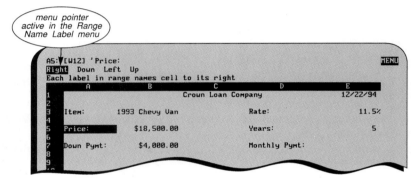

FIGURE 4-13
Display after entering the command /Range Name Label (/RNL)

Next, 1-2-3 requests that the range containing the labels that you want to assign to the cells to the right. Use the Down Arrow key to select the range A5..A7. Press the Enter key. You can now use the name Price: to refer to cell B5 and Down Pymt: to refer to cell B7.

Name cells E3, E5, and E7 in a similar fashion. Move the cell pointer to D3. Enter the command /Range Name Label (/RNL). Type the letter R for Right, select the range D3..D7, and press the Enter key. You can now use Rate: to refer to cell E3, Years: to refer to cell E5, and Monthly Pymt: to refer to cell E7.

Three points to remember about the /RNL command are: first, if a label in a cell is subsequently changed, the old label remains the name of the range; second, numbers cannot be used as range names; and third, 1-2-3 uses only the first 15 characters of the label as the name.

Determining the Loan Payment — PMT

1-2-3 has several financial functions that save you from writing out long, complicated formulas. One of the most important of these is the PMT function. This function determines the payment of a loan on the basis of the amount of the loan (principal), the interest rate (interest), and the length of time required to pay back the loan (term). If the term is in months, the PMT function returns the monthly payment. The general form of the PMT function is:

@PMT(principal,interest,term)

To display the monthly payment of the car loan in cell E7, move the cell pointer to E7 and enter the function:

```
@PMT($Price:-$Down Pymt:,$Rate:/12,$Years:*12)
```

The first argument ($Price:–$Down Pymt:) is the principal. The second argument ($Rate:/12) is the interest rate charged by the Crown Loan Company compounded monthly. The third argument ($Years:*12) is the number of months required to pay back the loan. As illustrated in cell E7 of Figure 4-14, it will cost $318.89 per month for 5 years to purchase the 1993 Chevy Van with a sticker price of $18,500.00, down payment of $4,000.00, at an annual interest rate of 11.5%.

Notice that we preceded all the names in the function arguments with a dollar sign ($). We do this because the function will be copied to another part of the worksheet later, and we want the cell references to remain the same.

Remember, 1-2-3 automatically recalculates the formula in E7 when a new entry is made into a cell referenced in the formula assigned to E7. If you change the purchase price, the amount of the down payment, the interest rate, the number of years, or any combination of these, 1-2-3 immediately adjusts the monthly payment displayed in cell E7.

The Data Fill Feature

The next step is to add the amortization table in cells A8..E16 (Figure 4-2). Enter the double underline in row 8, the column headings in rows 9 and 10, and the single underline in row 11 as shown in Figure 4-15.

In the range A12..A16, the series of numbers 1 though 5 represent the years. You can enter these numbers one at a time or you can use the Data Fill command. The **Data Fill command** allows you to quickly enter a series of numbers into a range using a specified increment or decrement. In this case, the series of numbers in the range A12..A16 that begins with 1, increments by 1, and ends with 5.

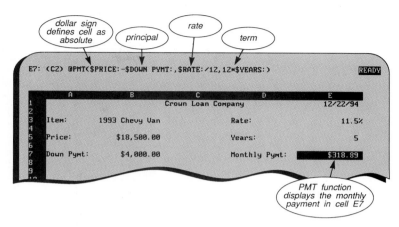

FIGURE 4-14 The PMT function entered into cell E7

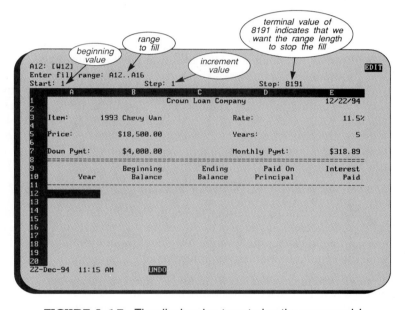

FIGURE 4-15 The display due to entering the command / Data Fill (/DF)

With the cell pointer at A12, enter the command /**D**ata **F**ill (/DF). In response to the prompt message "Enter Fill range: A12" on the input line, press the Period key to anchor the first end point, A12. Use the Down Arrow key to move the cell pointer to the second end point (A16) and press the Enter key. Next, 1-2-3 requests the start, increment, and stop values. In response to the prompt messages on the input line, enter a start value of 1, an increment value of 1, and a stop value of 8191. The length of the range (five cells) will terminate the Data Fill command before it reaches the stop value 8191. The entries are shown at the top of the screen in Figure 4-15.

Press the Enter key and the range A12..A16 is filled with the series of numbers 1 through 5 (Figure 4-16).

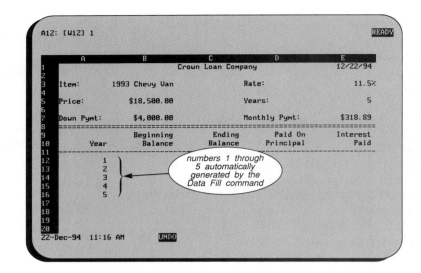

FIGURE 4-16
The display after using the
Data Fill command

Move the cell pointer to B12 and enter the beginning balance for year 1. This value is equal to the amount of the loan, which is +Price:-Down Pymt: or +B5-B7.

Before you enter any more values in the amortization table, format cells B12 through E20 to the Comma (,) type with two decimal positions. The Comma (,) type with two decimal positions displays the numbers in the form of dollars and cents. Although labels will be part of the range (B12..E20), recall that a numeric format is used only if a numeric value is stored in the cell. Enter the command /**R**ange **F**ormat **,** (/RF,). Press the Enter key to select two decimal positions. Enter the range B12..E20 and press the Enter key.

Determining the Yearly Ending Balance — PV

Another important financial function is the PV function. This function returns the present value of an annuity. An annuity is a series of fixed payments made at the end of each of a fixed number of terms at a fixed interest rate. This function can be used to determine how much the borrower of the car loan still owes at the end of each year (C12..C16).

The general form of the PV function is:

@PV(payment,interest,term)

Use this function to determine the ending balance after the first year (C12) by using a term equal to the number of months the borrower must still make payments. For example, if the loan is for five years (60 months, therefore 60 payments), as it is in Figure 4-16, then the borrower still owes 48 payments after the first year. After the second year, the number of payments remaining is 36, and so on.

The entry for cell C12 that determines the ending balance is:

@PV($Monthly Pymt:,$Rate:/12,12*($Years:-A12))

The first argument, $Monthly Pymt:, refers to cell E7, the monthly payment. The second argument, $Rate:/12, refers to the interest rate in cell E3. The third argument, 12*($Years:-A12), indicates the number of monthly payments that still must be made—48 after the first year. Notice that each name in the three arguments of the PV function for cell C12 is preceded by a dollar sign ($). This tells 1-2-3 to treat these cell references as absolute. That is, when 1-2-3 copies the PV function in cell C12 to cells C13 through C16, the cell references in the arguments will not be adjusted.

Making Decisions — The IF Function

If you assign the PV function just described to cell C12 and copy it to cells C13 through C16, the ending balances for each year of a five-year loan will display properly as illustrated in Figure 4-2. If the loan is for a period of time less than five years, the ending balances displayed for the years beyond the time the loan is due are invalid. For example, if a loan is taken out for three years, the ending balance for years four and five in the amortization table should be zero. However, the PV function will display negative values even though the loan has already been paid off.

What is needed is a way to assign the PV function to the range C12..C16 as long as the corresponding year in the range A12..A16 is less than or equal to the number of years in cell E5, which contains the number of years of the loan. If the corresponding year in column A is greater than the number of years in cell E5, cells C12 through C16 must be assigned the value zero. 1-2-3 has a function that can handle this type of decision making. It is called the IF function.

The IF function is useful when the value you want assigned to a cell is dependent on a condition. A **condition** is made up of two expressions and a relation. Each **expression** may be a cell, a number, a label, a function, or a formula.

The general form of the IF function is:

@IF(condition,true,false)

The argument **true** is the value you want to assign to the cell when the condition is true. The argument **false** is the value you want to assign to the cell when the condition is false. For example, assume @IF(A1 = A2,C3 + D4,C3–D4) is assigned to cell B12. If the value assigned to A1 is equal to the value assigned to A2, then the sum of the values in C3 and D4 is assigned to B12. If the value assigned to A1 does not equal the value assigned to A2, then B12 is assigned the difference between the values in C3 and D4.

Valid relations and examples of their use in IF functions are shown in Table 4-3.

TABLE 4-3 Valid Relational Operators and Their Use in Conditions

RELATIONAL OPERATOR	MEANING	EXAMPLE
=	Equal to	@IF(A5 = B7,A22–A3,G5 ∧ E3)
<	Less than	@IF(E12/D5 < 6,A15,B13–5)
>	Greater than	@IF(@SUM(A1..A5) > 100,1,0)
< =	Less than or equal to	@IF(A12 < = $YEARS,A4 * D5,1)
> =	Greater than or equal to	@IF(@NOW > = 30000,H15,J12)
< >	Not equal to	@IF(5 < > F6,"Valid","Invalid")

The logical operators NOT, AND, and OR also may be used to write a **compound condition**—two or more conditions in the same IF function. A summary of the logical operators is given in Table 4-4. Multiple logical operators in the same compound condition are evaluated from left to right.

TABLE 4-4 Valid Logical Operators and Their Use in Conditions

LOGICAL OPERATOR	MEANING	EXAMPLE
#NOT#	The compound condition is true if, and only if, the simple condition is false.	@IF(#NOT#($A$2 = A6),2,4)
#AND#	The compound condition is true if, and only if, both simple conditions are true.	@IF($J6 = R$4#AND#G5–S2 > D2, D4 * D6,T3/D2)
#OR#	The compound condition is true if, and only if, either simple condition is true or both simple conditions are true.	@IF(A1 > $PRINCIPAL#OR#B7 = E4, "Contact","OK")

By using the IF function, you can assign the PV function or zero as the ending balance to cells C12 through C16. In cell C12 enter the IF function:

@IF(A12<=$Years:,@PV($Monthly Pymt:,$Rate:/12,12*($Years:-A12)),0)

   condition   *true task*   *false task*

If the condition A12< = $Years: is true, then 1-2-3 assigns C12 the PV function. If the condition is false, then 1-2-3 assigns C12 the value zero.

Use the command /Copy (/C) to copy cell C12 to the range C13..C16. The results of this copy are shown in Figure 4-17.

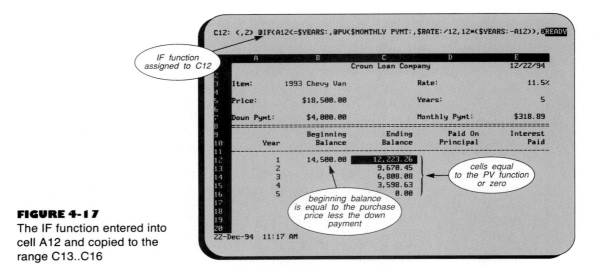

FIGURE 4-17
The IF function entered into cell A12 and copied to the range C13..C16

Let's go back now and complete the entries in the beginning balance column, cells B13 through B16. The beginning balance in B13 is equal to the ending balance in cell C12. Therefore, enter +C12 in cell B13 and copy this cell to B14 through B16. The beginning balance for each year in cells B12 through B16 displays as shown in Figure 4-18.

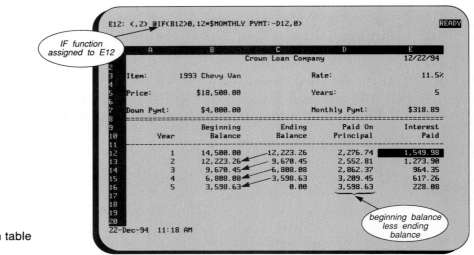

FIGURE 4-18
The amortization table filled in

The total amount paid on the principal each year in column D is determined by subtracting the ending balance from the beginning balance. Enter the formula +B12-C12 in cell D12. Copy cell D12 to cells D13 through D16 (Figure 4-18).

The total amount of interest paid each year by the borrower to the lender in column E is equal to 12 times the monthly payment in cell E7 less the amount paid on the principal. Here again, use the IF function because the loan may be for less than five years. Interest is paid in any year in which the beginning balance is greater than zero. Therefore, in cell E12, enter the IF function @IF(B12>0,12*$Monthly Pymt:-D12,0). Copy cell E12 to cells E13 through E16. The interest paid each year for a loan of $14,500.00 at 11.5% for 5 years is shown in column E of the worksheet in Figure 4-18.

To complete the amortization table, add the single underline in row 17 and the labels that identify the totals in cells C18 through C20. In cell D18, enter the function @SUM(D12..D16). This agrees with the original amount of the loan, $14,500.00. In cell E18, enter the function @SUM(E12..E16). Cell E18 displays the total interest paid for the loan, $4,633.57. In cell E19, enter the name +Down Pymt:. Cell E19 displays $4,000.00, the amount in cell B7. Finally, in cell E20, enter the formula +D18+E18+E19. Cell E20 displays the total cost of the 1993 Chevy Van (Figure 4-19).

FIGURE 4-19
Part 1 of Project 4B
complete

With the amortization table complete, try various combinations of loan data to evaluate the what-if capabilities of 1-2-3. If you change the purchase price (B5), down payment (B7), interest rate (E3), term (E5) or any combination of these values, 1-2-3 will immediately change the monthly payment and the numbers in the amortization table.

Saving the Worksheet

Before continuing with Project 4B, save the worksheet as PROJS-4B. Enter the command /File Save (/FS). Enter the file name PROJS-4B and press the Enter key. The worksheet is saved on the default drive.

Using a Data Table to Answer What-If Questions

The next step is to build the data table at the right side of the amortization table (Figure 4-3). A **data table** has one purpose—it organizes the answers to what-if questions into a table. We have already seen that if a value is changed in a cell referenced elsewhere in a formula, 1-2-3 immediately recalculates and stores the new value in the cell assigned the formula. You may want to compare the results of the formula for several different values, but it would be unwieldy to write down or remember all the answers to the what-if questions. This is where a data table comes in handy.

Data tables are built in an unused area of the worksheet. You may vary one or two values and display the results of the specified formulas in table form. Figure 4-20 illustrates the makeup of a data table.

In Project 4B, the data table shows the impact of changing interest rates on the monthly payment and the total cost of the loan. The interest rates range from 8.5% to 15% in increments of 0.5%. Therefore, in this data table we are varying one value, the interest rate (E3). We are interested in its impact on two formulas: the monthly payment (E7) and the total cost (E20).

To construct the data table, enter the headings in the range F1..H5 as described in Figure 4-3. Next, move the cell pointer to F7 and use the command **/D**ata **F**ill (/DF) to enter the varying interest rates. Select the range F7..F20. Use a start value of 8.5%, an increment value of 0.5%, and a stop value of 8191. After you press the Enter key, the range F7..F20 contains the varying interest rates. Format the interest rates to the Percent type with one decimal position (Figure 4-21).

In cell G6 enter +E7, the cell with the monthly payment formula. In cell H6 enter +E20, the cell with the total cost of the loan formula. Format the range G6..H20 to the Comma (,) type with two decimal positions. Move the cell pointer to F6. The range F1..H20 of the worksheet is shown in Figure 4-21.

This cell must be empty	Formula-1	Formula-2	. . .	Formula-k
Value-1				
Value-2	1-2-3 places results of formulas here on the basis of the values in the left-hand column.			
Value-3				
Value-4				
Value-n				

(a) Data table with one value varying

Assign formula to this cell	Value-2a	Value-2b	. . .	Value-2k
Value-1a				
Value-1b	1-2-3 places results of the formula in the upper left corner cell here on the basis of the two corresponding values.			
Value-1c				
Value-1d				
Value-1n				

(b) Data table with two values varying

FIGURE 4-20 General forms of a data table with one value varying (a) and two values varying (b).

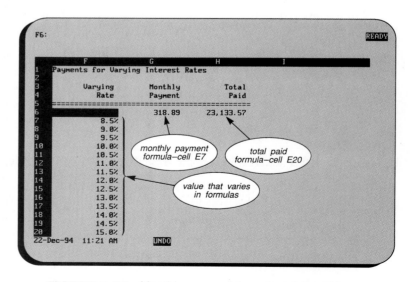

FIGURE 4-21 Monthly payment formula, total paid formula, and varying interest rates entered into the worksheet in preparation for applying a data table in the range F6..H20.

To define the data table, enter the command /**D**ata **T**able **1** (/DT1). 1-2-3 responds by displaying the prompt message "Enter Table range: F6" on the input line. Press the Period key to anchor F6 as one of the end points. Use the arrow keys to move the cell pointer to H20 and press the Enter key. (The data table itself does not include the headings above F6.) 1-2-3 responds with the prompt message "Enter Input cell 1: F6" on the input line. The **input cell** is defined as the cell in the worksheet that contains the value you want to vary. For this data table, vary the interest rate in cell E3 (also called Rate:). Therefore, enter the name `Rate:` in response to the prompt message on the input line and press the Enter key.

The data table, in the range F6..H20, immediately fills with monthly payments and total loan costs for the corresponding varying interest rates, as shown in Figure 4-22.

FIGURE 4-22
Data table in the range F6..H20 is filled with answers to what-if questions regarding varying interest rates.

Look over the table. Notice how it allows you to compare the monthly payments and total loan costs for different interest rates. For example, at 10%, the monthly payment on the loan of $14,500.00 for 5 years is $308.08. At 10.5%, the monthly payment is $311.66 for the same loan. The two numbers at the top of the table, in cells G6 and H6, are the same as the monthly payment and total cost displayed in cells E7 and E20.

Some important points to remember about data tables are:

1. You can have only one active data table in a worksheet. If you want to move or establish a new data table, use the command /**D**ata **T**able **R**eset (/DTR) to deactivate the current data table.
2. For a data table with one varying value, the cell in the upper left corner of the table (F6) must be empty. With two values varying, assign the formula you want to analyze to the upper left corner cell of the table (Figure 4-20(b)).
3. If you change any value in a cell referenced by the formula that is part of the data table but does not vary in the data table, you must press function key F8 to instruct 1-2-3 to recalculate the data table values.

MACROS

◆ A **macro** is a series of keystrokes entered into a cell or a range of cells. The macro is assigned a name using the command /**R**ange **N**ame **C**reate (/RNC). Later, when you enter the macro name, the keystrokes stored in the cell or range of cells execute one after another, as if you entered each keystroke manually at the keyboard. A macro can be as simple as the series of keystrokes required to save a worksheet or as complex as a sophisticated computer program.

Whether simple or complex, macros save time and help remove the drudgery associated with building and using a worksheet. You should consider using a macro when you find yourself repeatedly typing the same keystrokes; when the series of keystrokes required is difficult to remember; or if you want to automate the use of the worksheet.

Designing a Simple Macro

In Project 2 we suggested that you save your worksheet every 50 to 75 keystrokes. If you follow this suggestion, you will be frequently entering the series of keystrokes shown in Table 4-5. This is an excellent example of how a macro can save you time and effort.

TABLE 4-5   Series of Keystrokes for Saving a Worksheet Under the Same File Name

KEYSTROKE	PURPOSE
/	Switches 1-2-3 to MENU mode.
F	Selects File command.
S	Selects Save command.
←	Saves worksheet under the same file name.
R	Replaces the worksheet on disk.

One of the keystrokes in Table 4-5 is the Enter key(←). In a macro, we use the **tilde character** (˜) to represent the Enter key. Therefore, /FS˜R represents the series of keystrokes in Table 4-5.

After determining the makeup of the macro, the next step is to move the cell pointer to a cell in an unused area of the worksheet. According to Figure 4-4, the macros for this project are to be placed below the amortization table. Hence, use the GOTO command and move the cell pointer to A22.

Documenting Macros

We recommend that all macros be documented, even the simple ones. **Documenting** a macro means writing a comment off to the side of the cell or range containing the macro. The comment explains the purpose of the macro, and if it is complex, how it works. To document this macro, as well as the other macros in this worksheet, first enter the macro title and column headings in cells A22 through E25 (Figure 4-23).

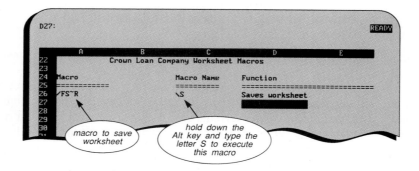

FIGURE 4-23   The macro \S is entered into cell A26 and documented in cells C26 and D26.

Entering and Naming a Macro

Move the cell pointer to A26 and enter the macro '/FS˜R. It is important that you begin the macro with an apostrophe or one of the other characters that defines the entry as a label (^, "). If you don't begin the macro with an apostrophe, 1-2-3 immediately switches to MENU mode because the Slash key (/) is the first character entered.

With the macro in cell A26, enter the command /**R**ange **N**ame **C**reate (/RNC) and assign the macro name \S to cell A26. A macro name can consist of up to 15 characters. It is to your advantage, however, to use a name made up of only two characters in which the first character is the backslash (\) and the second character is a letter. In this way you can invoke the macro by holding down the Alt key and pressing the second letter in the macro name. Complete the documentation in cells C26 and D26. Figure 4-23 illustrates the \S macro in cell A26 and the corresponding documentation.

The macro name \0 (zero) has special meaning to 1-2-3. If you name a macro \0, then 1-2-3 automatically executes the macro whenever you first load the worksheet from disk into main memory.

Invoking a Macro

After entering the macro '/FS˜R in cell A26 and naming it \S, execute it by pressing Alt-S. 1-2-3 automatically executes the series of keystrokes in cell A26 and saves the worksheet. The \S macro is part of the worksheet that is saved. Hence, the macro will be available the next time you load the worksheet into main memory.

An alternative method of executing macros is to press Alt-F3. Alt-F3 displays a menu of range names at the top of the screen. Select the macro name, in this case, \S, from the menu, and press the Enter key. 1-2-3 immediately executes the \S macro. This second method of invoking a macro *must be used* to execute macros whose names are longer than two characters or begin with a character other than the backslash (\).

Adding More Macros to the Worksheet

When 1-2-3 executes a macro, it starts at the specified cell. After executing the keystrokes in this cell, it inspects the adjacent cells. First it checks the cell below, then the cell to the right. If they are empty, the macro terminates. If they are not empty, 1-2-3 considers the nonempty cell to be part of the macro and executes its contents. Hence, 1-2-3 is finished executing a macro when the cells below and to the right are empty. It is for this reason that when you add additional macros to a worksheet, make sure that there is at least one empty cell between each macro.

With this rule in mind, enter the macro /PPAGPQ in cell A28 and /PPOOCQAGOOAQPQ in cell A30. Also enter the corresponding documentation in cells C28 through D30 (Figure 4-24). Use the command /**R**ange **N**ame **C**reate (/RNC) and assign the names \P to cell A28 and \C to cell A30.

FIGURE 4-24

The macros \P and \C are entered into cells A28 and A30 and documented in the range C28..D30.

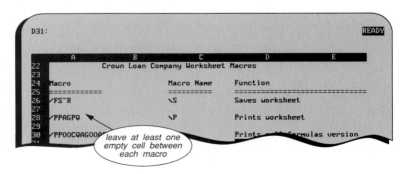

The \P macro in cell A28 prints the worksheet on the basis of the previous printer range setting. It also ejects the paper in the printer and quits the Print command. Build a print macro like this one when you expect to print the worksheet often. To prepare to execute the \P macro, use the /**P**rint **P**rinter **R**ange (/PPR) command to set the range to A1..E20. Invoke the \S macro again to save the print range permanently.

Now, imagine you are the loan officer for the Crown Loan Company. A customer comes in and requests information on the 1993 Chevy Van we discussed earlier. With the monthly payment and the amortization table on the screen, you can print a copy of the loan information and give it to the customer. First, make sure the printer is ready. Next, hold down the Alt key and press the letter P. The monthly payment and amortization table shown in Figure 4-19 prints on the printer.

The \C macro in cell A30 prints the cell-formulas version of the worksheet according to the previously defined printer range. After printing the as-displayed version of the range A1..E20, hold down the Alt key and type the letter C. This invokes the \C macro. Notice that after the printer is done printing the cell-formulas version, the macro resets the print setting to the as-displayed version.

Creating Macros Using the Learn Feature of 1-2-3

1-2-3 has a macro learn feature that automatically records your keystrokes and allows you to test the command sequence at the same time. You enter the keystrokes, such as /PPAGPQ, and 1-2-3 saves the command sequence in a specified cell as a macro. To illustrate the learn feature, let's erase the macro /PPAGPQ in cell A28 by using the command /**R**ange **E**rase (/RE). With cell A28 blank, do the following:

1. Enter the command/**W**orksheet **L**earn **R**ange (/WLR). Specify the range A28..A28.
2. Turn on the learn feature by pressing Alt-F5. The LEARN status indicator displays at the bottom of the screen to inform you that the learn feature is active.
3. Enter the command /PPAGPQ. 1-2-3 carries out the command sequence and prints the range A1..E20 on the printer. (Recall that the range A1..E20 was established earlier.) More importantly, 1-2-3 records the command sequence.
4. Turn off the learn feature by pressing Alt-F5.
5. Press F9 to recalculate the worksheet.

After step 5, the command sequence entered in step 3 is assigned to cell A28. If you hadn't already assigned the name \P to A28, then after step 5 you would name the macro by using the /**R**ange **N**ame **C**reate (/RNC) command.

Guarding Against Macro Catastrophes

Take care when you apply macros to a worksheet. If you enter the wrong letter, forget the tilde (˜) when it's required, place macros in adjacent cells, or transpose characters in a macro, serious damage in the form of lost data can occur. For this reason we recommend you save the worksheet before executing a macro for the first time.

You should also use **STEP mode** of 1-2-3 to test the macro. STEP mode allows you to watch 1-2-3 execute the macro keystroke by keystroke just as if you entered the keystrokes one at a time at the keyboard. Let's execute the \S macro again using STEP mode. To place 1-2-3 in STEP mode, hold down the Alt key and press function key F2. The indicator "STEP" appears on the status line at the bottom of the screen. Next, invoke the \S macro by holding down the Alt key and pressing the S key. With STEP mode active, 1-2-3 displays two items at the bottom of the screen on the left side of the status line: the cell address of the macro being executed and the contents of that cell. Also, the keystroke that corresponds to the command being executed within the macro is highlighted. Now press any key on the keyboard to execute the next keystroke in the macro.

If you encounter an error while in STEP mode, terminate the macro by holding down the Ctrl key and pressing the Break key. Next, press the Esc or Enter key and the macro terminates execution. Edit the macro and execute it once again using STEP mode. Continue in this fashion until the macro is doing exactly what you intend it to do. To quit STEP mode, press Alt-F2. This process of finding and correcting errors in a macro is called debugging.

Macro Commands and Macro Words

The final step in Project 4B is to enter the macro that extends from cell A33 through A46. Before entering this macro, we need to discuss macro commands and macro words. **Macro commands** are used to write programs that can guide you or another user of the worksheet through complex tasks such as accepting data into various cells. Some of the macro commands are listed in Table 4-6. Notice that each macro command is enclosed in curly braces { }. For a complete list of the macro commands, press function key F1 and go to the Help Index of the online help facility. Select the title Macro Command Index from the Help Index. Select subroutine. Press the Enter key to scroll through the macros. Press the Esc key to return to the worksheet.

TABLE 4-6 Frequently Used Macro Commands

COMMAND	EXAMPLE	EXPLANATION
{BRANCH location}	{BRANCH TALL}	Transfers macro control to the macro command with the label TALL.
{GETLABEL prompt,location}	{GETLABEL "Purchase Item: ",B3}	Displays the prompt message "Purchase Item:" followed by a space on the input line, accepts a label, and assigns it to B3.
{GETNUMBER prompt,location}	{GETNUMBER "Purchase Price: ",B5}	Displays the prompt message "Purchase Price:" followed by a space on the input line, accepts a number, and assigns it to B5.
{IF condition}	{IF B10< = 40}{BRANCH SHORT}	If cell B10 has a value less than or equal to 40, then macro control transfers to the macro command with the label SHORT, else macro control passes to the cell below.
{QUIT}	{QUIT}	Ends the execution of a macro.
{RETURN}	{RETURN}	Returns control to the command following the corresponding subroutine call.
{subroutine}	{BONUS}	Executes the macro beginning at BONUS. Saves the location of the macro command following {BONUS} for the corresponding {RETURN}.

Macro words are used to handle special circumstances in a macro, like moving the cell pointer from one cell to another. Except for the tilde (˜), which represents the Enter key, all macro words are enclosed in curly braces { }. The frequently used words are listed in Table 4-7. For a complete list of the macro words, load 1-2-3, press function key F1, and select Macro Key Names from the Help Index. After reading or printing the screens, press the Esc key to return to the worksheet.

TABLE 4-7 Frequently Used Macro Words That Represent Special Keys on the Keyboard

CATEGORY	MACRO WORD
Cell pointer	{UP} {DOWN} {RIGHT} {LEFT} {PGUP} {PGDN} {HOME} {END} {BACKSPACE}
Function keys	{EDIT} {NAME} {ABS} {GOTO} {WINDOW} {QUERY} {TABLE} {CALC} {GRAPH}
Special keys	{ESC} {DEL} {INS} {MENU}
Enter key	˜
Interaction	{?}

The cell pointer movement macro words in Table 4-7 move the pointer, as if you pressed the key named within the curly braces. The function key macro words operate the same as pressing one of the function keys. The macro word {?} makes the macro pause and wait for keyboard input from the user. For example, the macro /FR{?} ˜ may be used to retrieve a worksheet from disk. The macro word {?} following /FR tells the macro to pause and wait for the user to select a file name. When you press the Enter key after entering the file name, the macro resumes execution and accepts the name entered on the input line.

Interactive Macros

The macro defined in cells A33 through A46 in Figure 4-4 automates the entry of the loan data in cells B3, B5, B7, E3, and E5. The instructions in cells A34 through A39 clear the cells that contain the loan data. The instructions in cells A40 through A44 prompt the user to enter the loan data. Each {GETLABEL} and {GETNUMBER} command displays a prompt message and halts the execution of the macro until the user responds by entering a value on the input line. {QUIT} in cell A46 terminates the macro.

Enter the macro and documentation in the range A33..D46 as shown in Figure 4-4. Use the command /**R**ange **N**ame **C**reate (/RNC) and assign cell A33 the macro name \D. It is not necessary to assign the range A33..A46 to the macro name \D, since a macro executes downward until it comes across an empty cell. Invoke the \D macro and reenter the loan data for the 1993 Chevy Van shown in Figure 4-19. In a step-by-step fashion, Table 4-8 explains how the \D macro works. Use Table 4-8 to step through the macro activity when you execute it.

TABLE 4-8 Step-by-Step Explanation of the \D Macro in the Range A33..A46

STEP	CELL	ENTRY	FUNCTION
1	A33	{HOME}	Moves the cell pointer to A1.
2	A34	{GOTO}B3˜/RE˜	Moves the cell pointer to B3 and erases the contents.
3	A35	{DOWN}{DOWN}/RE˜	Moves the cell pointer to B5 and erases the contents.
4	A36	{DOWN}{DOWN}/RE˜	Moves the cell pointer to B7 and erases the contents.
5	A37	{GOTO}E3˜/RE˜	Moves the cell pointer to E3 and erases the contents.
6	A38	{DOWN}{DOWN}/RE˜	Moves the cell pointer to E5 and erases the contents.
7	A39	{HOME}	Moves the cell pointer to A1.
8	A40	{GETLABEL "Purchase Item: ",B3} ˜	Accepts the purchase item (1993 Chevy Van) and assigns it to cell B3.
9	A41	{GETNUMBER "Purchase Price: ",B5} ˜	Accepts the purchase price (18500) and assigns it to cell B5.
10	A42	{GETNUMBER "Down Payment : ",B7} ˜	Accepts the down payment (4000) and assigns it to cell B7.
11	A43	{GETNUMBER "Interest Rate in %: ",E3} ˜	Accepts the interest rate (11.5) and assigns it to cell E3.
12	A44	{GETNUMBER "Time in Years: ",E5} ˜	Accepts the time (5) and assigns it to cell E5.
13	A45	{HOME}	Moves the cell pointer to A1.
14	A46	{QUIT}	Quits the macro.

WINDOWS

◆ When you have a large worksheet like the one in Project 4B, it is helpful to view two parts of the worksheet at one time. 1-2-3 lets you divide the screen into two horizontal windows or two vertical windows. For example, by dividing the screen into two horizontal windows, you can view the \D macro in cells A33..A46 and the cells (A1..E7) that are affected by this macro at the same time.

To show two windows, press the Home key and use the arrow keys to move the cell pointer to A8. Enter the command /**W**orksheet **W**indow **H**orizontal (/WWH). The rows above row 8 display in the top window and rows 8 through 19 display in the lower window.

Immediately after a window split, the cell pointer is active in the window above or to the right of the split. You can move the cell pointer from window to window by pressing function key F6. Press function key F6 and use the Page Down and Down Arrow keys to move the cell pointer to A44. As shown in Figure 4-25, the top window shows the cells that are modified by the \D macro in the lower window.

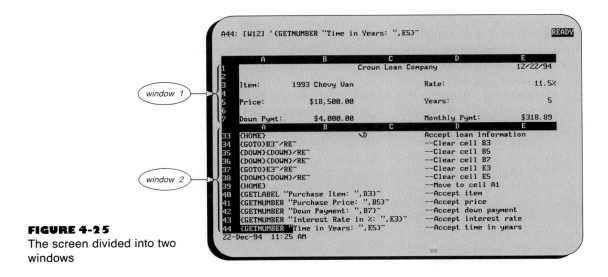

FIGURE 4-25
The screen divided into two windows

Press function key F6 to move the cell pointer to the top window. Execute the \D macro a second time. Step through the macro in the lower window and watch the cells change in the top window.

It is important to understand that the entire worksheet is available through any window. If you make a change to a cell in one window, the change will show up in any other window. Table 4-9 summarizes the window commands available when you enter the command /**W**orksheet **W**indow (/WW).

TABLE 4-9   A Summary of Commands in the Worksheet Window Menu

COMMAND	FUNCTION
Horizontal	Splits the screen from side to side.
Vertical	Splits the screen from top to bottom.
Sync	Causes windows that are aligned horizontally or vertically to scroll together.
Unsync	Causes each window to scroll independently.
Clear	Returns the screen to a single window.

Synchronizing Windows

If you look closely at the two windows in Figure 4-25, you'll notice that they are synchronized, that is, the same column letters are aligned in both windows. The windows scroll together. You can unsynchronize the windows so that they scroll independent of one another. To unsynchronize the windows, enter the command /Worksheet Window Unsync (/WWU). To synchronize the windows after unsynchronizing them, enter the command /Worksheet Window Sync (/WWS).

Clearing the Windows

To return to the normal worksheet display with one window, enter the command /Worksheet Window Clear (/WWC). This command switches the screen from two windows back to one window.

CELL PROTECTION

◆ Cells are either protected or unprotected. When you create a new worksheet, all cells are unprotected. **Unprotected cells** are cells whose values may be changed at any time, but **protected cells** cannot be changed. If a cell is protected and the user attempts to change its value, the computer beeps and 1-2-3 displays the error message "Protected cell" on the status line at the bottom of the screen.

Once the worksheet has been fully tested and displays the correct results, you should protect the cells that you don't want changed by mistake. You should protect cells that contain information that will not change or is unlikely to change, cells that contain macros, and cells whose values are determined by formulas. In the case of Project 4B, we want to protect all the cells in the worksheet except for B3, B5, B7, E3, E5, and the data table in the range F6..H20.

The first step in protecting cells is to protect all the cells in the worksheet. Once all the cells are protected, you can be selective and *unprotect* those that you want to change. To protect all the cells in the worksheet, enter the command /Worksheet Global Protection Enable (/WGPE). Next, move the cell pointer to B3. Enter the command /Range Unprotect (/RU). Press the Enter key when 1-2-3 requests the range to unprotect. Do the same for cells B5, B7, E3, and E5. Finally, move the cell pointer to F6 and unprotect the range F6..H20, which contains the data table information.

You can check whether a cell is unprotected by moving the cell pointer to the cell in question. The letter U displays on the mode line at the top of the screen if the cell is unprotected. The letters PR display if the cell is protected. If you mistakenly unprotect the wrong cell, you may protect it by using the command /Range Protect (/RP). This command is meaningless unless global protection has been enabled (turned on).

If for some reason you need to modify the cells that are in a protected area, such as the macros, disable (turn off) global protection by using the command /Worksheet Global Protection Disable (/WGPD). Once you are finished modifying the cells, enable (turn on) global protection. The worksheet will be protected exactly as it was before you disabled (turned off) global protection.

Saving and Printing the Worksheet

To save the Crown Loan Company worksheet to disk with the cells protected, invoke the \S macro by holding down the Alt key and pressing the S key. To obtain a printed version of the worksheet,

1. Enter the command /Print Printer Range (/PPR) and select the range A1..H46.
2. Type the letter Q to quit the Print menu.
3. Invoke the \P macro by holding down the Alt key and typing the letter P.

1-2-3 prints the three parts of the worksheet on multiple pages. After the printer stops, carefully remove the Crown Loan Company worksheet from the printer. The complete worksheet is shown in Figures 4-2, 4-3, and 4-4.

OBTAINING A SUMMARY OF ALL THE 1-2-3 FUNCTIONS

◆ 1-2-3 has over 100 useful functions. We have discussed those most widely used. You may find the others to be useful in certain situations. For a complete listing and description of the functions available, load 1-2-3 and press function key F1. Select the title @Function Index. Press the Up Arrow key once when the @Function Index displays. Select @Function by Categories at the bottom of the screen. Print the screen for each category of functions by pressing the Print Screen key. After you are finished, press the Esc key to return to the worksheet.

PROJECT SUMMARY

In Project 4 we developed two worksheets. Project 4A introduced you to statistical functions and range names. Project 4B taught you how to use the IF, PMT, and PV functions, the data fill feature, data tables, and macros. You also learned how to protect cells in the worksheet and how to use multiple windows to see different parts of the worksheet at the same time. All the activities that you learned for this project are summarized in the Quick Reference following the Appendix. The following is a summary of the keystroke sequence we used in Projects 4A and 4B.

SUMMARY OF KEYSTROKES — PROJECT 4A

STEPS	KEY(S) PRESSED	RESULTS
1	/WGC → → ←	Sets width of all columns to 11.
2	/WCS → → ←	Sets width of column A to 13.
3	DP 101 → → Grading Report → → →	Enters report title in row 1.
4	@NOW ←/RFD1 ←	Enters NOW function in F1 and formats F1 to Date 1.
5	F5 B3 ← "Test 1 → "Test 2 → "Test 3 → "Total → "Percent ←	Enters column titles in row 3.
6	F5 A4 ← Student → 139 → 142 → 150 → → "Correct ←	Enters column titles and total test points in row 4.
7	F5 A5 ← \ = ←/C ← . → → → → → → ←	Underlines column titles.
8	↓ ' 1035 → 121 → 127 → 142 ←	Enters student 1035 ID and test scores.
9	F5 A7 ← '1074 → 114 → 113 → 132 ←	Enters student 1074 ID and test scores.
10	F5 A8 ← '1265 → 79 → 97 → 101 ←	Enters student 1265 ID and test scores.
11	F5 A9 ← '1345 → 85 → 106 → 95 ←	Enters student 1345 ID and test scores.
12	F5 A10 ← '1392 → 127 → 124 → 120 ←	Enters student 1392 ID and test scores.
13	F5 A11 ← '3167 → 101 → 120 → 109 ←	Enters student 3167 ID and test scores.
14	F5 A12 ← '3382 → 110 → 104 → 120 ←	Enters student 3382 ID and test scores.
15	F5 A13 ← '3597 → 92 → 104 → 100 ←	Enters student 3597 ID and test scores.
16	F5 A14 ← '4126 → 105 → 100 → 96 ←	Enters student 4126 ID and test scores.
17	F5 A15 ← '5619 → 125 → 135 → 143 ←	Enters student 5619 ID and test scores.
18	F5 A16 ← '7561 → 112 → 130 → 123 ←	Enters student 7561 ID and test scores.

(continued)

SUMMARY OF KEYSTROKES — PROJECT 4A (continued)

STEPS	KEY(S) PRESSED	RESULTS
19	F5 A17←\-←/C←.→→→→→←	Underlines students' test scores in A6..F16.
20	↓Count↓Lowest Grade↓Highest Grade↓Average Score↓Std Deviation↓Variance← Home	Enters row titles in column A below students' scores and moves cell pointer to A1.
21	F5 E4←@SUM(B4.D4)←	Sums total test scores (B4..D4) in E4.
22	/C←E6.E16←	Copies E4 to E6..E16.
23	F5 F6←+E6/$E$4*100←	Assigns formula +E6/$E$4*100 to F6.
24	/C←F6.F16←	Copies F6 to F6..F16.
25	/RFF1←F6.F16←	Sets format of F6..F16 to Fixed.
26	F5 B6←/RNCTEST1←B6.B16←	Assigns the range name TEST1 to B6..B16.
27	F5 B18←@COUNT(TEST1)↓@MIN(TEST1)↓@MAX(TEST1)↓	Assigns @COUNT(TEST1), @MIN(TEST1), and @MAX(TEST1) to B18, B19, and B20.
28	@AVG(TEST1)↓@STD(TEST1)↓@VAR(TEST1)←	Assigns @AVG(TEST1), @STD(TEST1), and @VAR(TEST1) to B21, B22, and B23.
29	/CB18.B23←C18.E23←	Copies B18..B23 to C18..E23.
30	/RFF1←↑↑→→→→←	Sets format of B21..E23 to Fixed.
31	/FSPROJS-4A←	Saves worksheet as PROJS-4A.
32	Home /PPRA1.F23←	Sets A1..F23 as the print range.
33	AGPQ	Prints the worksheet.
34	/WEY	Erases the worksheet.

SUMMARY OF KEYSTROKES — PROJECT 4B

STEPS	KEY(S) PRESSED	RESULTS
1	/WCS12←	Sets width of column A to 12.
2	/WGC15←	Sets global width to 15.
3	→→Crown Loan Company→→	Enters report title in C1.
4	@NOW←/RFD4←	Enters NOW function in E1 and formats E1 to Date 4.
5	F5 A3←Item:↓↓Price:↓↓Down Pymt:←	Enters row titles in A3, A5, and A7.
6	F5 D3←Rate:↓↓Years:↓↓Monthly Pymt:←	Enters row titles in D3, D5, and D7.
7	F5 B3←'1993 Chevy Van↓↓18500↓↓4000←/RFC←.↑↑←	Enters loan data in B3, B5, and B7. Sets format of B5 and B7 to Comma (,).
8	F5 E3←11.5%←/RFP1←←↓↓5↓↓/RFC←←	Enters loan data in E3, E5, and E7. Sets format of E3 to Percent. Sets format of E7 to Comma (,).
9	F5 A5←/RNLR.↓↓←	Assigns label names in A5..A7 to B5..B7.
10	F5 D3←/RNLR.↓↓↓↓←	Assigns label names in D3..A7 to E3..E7.
11	F5 E7←@PMT($Price:-$Down Pymt:,$Rate:/12,$Years:*12)←	Assigns PMT function to E7.
12	F5 A8←\=←/C←.→→→→←	Underlines loan information in A1..E7.
13	F5 B9←"Beginning→"Ending→"Paid On→"Interest↓	Enters column titles in row 9.

SUMMARY OF KEYSTROKES — PROJECT 4B (continued)

STEPS	KEY(S) PRESSED	RESULTS
14	"Paid← "Principal← "Balance← "Balance← "Year↓	Enters column titles in row 10.
15	\-←/C←.→→→→←	Underlines column titles in A9..E10.
16	↓/DF.↓↓↓↓←1←←←	Generates numbers 1 through 5 in A12..A16.
17	→+Price:-Down Pymt:←	Assigns beginning balance to B12.
18	/RF,←B12.E20←	Sets format of B12..E20 to Comma (,).
19	→@IF(A12<=$YEARS:,@PV($Monthly Pymt:, $Rate:/12,12*($Years:-A12)),0)←	Assigns ending balance to C12.
20	/C←.↓↓↓↓←	Copies C12 to C12..C16.
21	↓←+C12←/C←.↓↓↓←	Assigns C12 to B13 and copies B13 to B13..B16.
22	[F5] D12←+B12-C12←/C←.↓↓↓↓←	Assigns +B12-C12 to D12 and copies D12 to D12..D16.
23	→@IF(B12>0,12*$Monthly Pymt:-D12,0) ←/C←.↓↓↓↓←	Assigns interest paid to E12 and copies E12 to E12..E16.
24	[F5] A17←\-←/C←.→→→→←	Underlines amortization table tin A9..E17.
25	[F5] C18←"Subtotal↓"Down Pymt↓ "Total Cost←	Enters row titles to C18..C20.
26	[F5] D18←@SUM(D12.D16)→	Assigns sum of D12..D16 to D18.
27	@SUM(E12.E16)↓	Assigns sum of E12..E16 to E18.
28	+Down Pymt:↓	Assigns down payment to E19.
29	+D18+E18+E19←	Assigns total cost of car to E20.
30	/FSPROJS-4B←	Saves worksheet as PROJS-4B.
31	[F5] F1←Payments for Varying Interest Rates↓↓	Enters data table title in F1.
32	"Varying→"Monthly→"Total↓	Enters data table column titles in F3..H3.
33	"Paid←"Payment←"Rate↓	Enters data table column titles in F4..H4.
34	\=→\==→\=↓	Underlines data table column titles in F3..H4.
35	[F5] F7←/DFF7.F20←8.5%←0.5%←←	Generates numbers .085 to .15 in increments of .05 in the range F7..F20.
36	/RFP1←F7.F20←	Sets format of F7..F20 to Percent.
37	↑→+E7→+E20←	Assigns monthly payment in E7 to G6 and total amount paid in E20 to H6.
38	/RF,←G6.H20←	Sets format of G6..H20 to Comma (,).
39	/DT1H6.F20←Rate:←	Defines G6..H20 as data table 1 with the rate in E3 (Rate:) varying.
40	[F5] A22←→Crown Loan Company Worksheet Macros←	Enters title of area in worksheet where macros will be defined.
41	[F5] A24←Macro→→Macro Name→Function↓	Enters macro column titles in A24..D24.
42	\=→\=←←==========←←\=↓	Underlines macro column titles in A24..D24.
43	'/FS~R→→'\S→Saves worksheet under same name←	Enters save worksheet macro, name of macro, and documentation in A26, C26, and D26.
44	←←/RNC\s←←	Names macro in A26 \S.
45	[Alt-S]	Executes \S macro to save worksheet.

(continued)

SUMMARY OF KEYSTROKES — PROJECT 4B (continued)

STEPS	KEY(S) PRESSED	RESULTS
46	↓↓'/PPAGPQ → → '\P→Prints worksheet↵	Enters print worksheet macro, name of macro, and documentation in A28, C28, and D28.
47	← ← ←/RNC\P↵ ↵	Names macro in A28 \P.
48	↓↓'/PPOOCQAGOOAQPQ → → '\C→Prints cell-formulas version↵	Enters print cell-formulas macro, name of macro, and documentation in A30, C30, and D30.
49	← ← ←/RNC\c↵ ↵	Names macro in A30 \C.
50	/PPRA1.E20↵Q	Sets A1..E20 as the print range.
51	Alt-P	Executes \P macro to print worksheet.
52	Alt-C	Executes \C macro to print cell-formulas version of worksheet.
53	↓↓↓{HOME} → → '\D→Accept loan information↵	Enters step 1 of macro, name of macro, and documentation in A33, C33, and D33.
54	← ← ←/RNC\D↵ ↵	Names macro beginning in A33 \D.
55	↓{GOTO}B3~/RE~ → → → '--Clear cell B3↵	Enters step 2 of macro and documentation in A34 and D34.
56	F5 A35↵{DOWN}{DOWN}/RE~ → → → '--Clear cell B5↵	Enters step 3 of macro and documentation in A35 and D35.
57	F5 A36↵/CA35↵A36↵ → → → '--Clear cell B7↵	Enters step 4 of macro and documentation of A36 and D36.
58	F5 A37↵{GOTO}E3~/RE~ → → → '--Clear cell E3↵	Enters step 5 of macro and documentation of A37 and D37.
59	F5 A38↵{DOWN}{DOWN}/RE~ → → → '--Clear cell E5↵	Enters step 6 of macro and documentation of A38 and D38.
60	F5 A39↵{HOME} → → → '--Move to cell A1↵	Enters step 7 of macro and documentation of A39 and D39.
61	F5 A40↵{GETLABEL "Purchase Item: ",B3}~ → → → '--Accept purchase item↵	Enters step 8 of macro and documentation of A40 and D40.
62	F5 A41↵{GETNUMBER "Purchase Price: ",B5}~ → → → '--Accept purchase price↵	Enters step 9 of macro and documentation of A41 and D41.
63	F5 A42↵{GETNUMBER "Down Payment: ",B7}~ → → → '--Accept down payment↵	Enters step 10 of macro and documentation of A42 and D42.
64	F5 A43↵{GETNUMBER "Interest Rate in %: ",E3}~ → → → '--Accept interest rate↵	Enters step 11 of macro and documentation of A43 and D43.
65	F5 A44↵{GETNUMBER "Time in Years: ",E5}~ → → → '--Accept time in years↵	Enters step 12 of macro and documentation of A44 and D44.
66	F5 A45↵{HOME} → → → '--Move to cell A1↵	Enters step 13 of macro and documentation of A45 and D45.
67	F5 A46↵{QUIT} → → → '--End of macro↵	Enters step 14 of macro and documentation of A46 and D46.
68	Alt-D 1993 Chevy Van↵18500↵4000↵ 11.5%↵5↵	Executes \D macro and enters requested loan information.
69	/WGPE	Enables cell protection.
70	→ ↓↓/RU↵	Unprotects B3.
71	↓↓/RU↵	Unprotects B5.
72	↓↓/RU↵	Unprotects B7.

SUMMARY OF KEYSTROKES — PROJECT 4B (continued)

STEPS	KEY(S) PRESSED	RESULTS
73	[F5] E3 ↵ /RU ↵	Unprotects E3.
74	↓↓/RU ↵	Unprotects E5.
75	[F5] F6 ↵ /RUF6.H20 ↵ [Home]	Unprotects data table in F6..H20.
76	[Alt–S]	Executes \S macro to save worksheet.
77	/PPRA1.H46 ↵ Q	Sets A1..H46 as the print range.
78	[Alt–P]	Executes \P macro to print worksheet.

The following list summarizes the material covered in Project 4.

1. If you intend to reference a range repeatedly, assign a name to it. To name a range, use the command **/R**ange Name Create (/RNC).
2. The Range Name command allows you to create range names, delete range names, assign labels as range names, clear all range names, and insert the list of range names in the worksheet. Refer to Table 4-1.
3. Several statistical functions in 1-2-3 are AVG, COUNT, MAX, MIN, STD, and VAR. Refer to Table 4-2.
4. The command **/R**ange Name Label (/RNL) allows you to assign a label in a cell as the name of the cell immediately above, below, to the right, or to the left.
5. The PMT function determines the payment of a loan on the basis of the amount of the loan (principal), the interest rate (interest), and the length of time required to pay back the loan (term). The general form of the PMT function is @PMT(principal,interest,term).
6. The command **/D**ata **F**ill (/DF) allows you to quickly enter a series of numbers into a range using a specified increment or decrement.
7. The PV function can be used to return the amount the borrower still owes at the end of a period at any time during the life of a loan. The general form of the PV function is @PV(payment,interest,term).
8. The general form of the IF function is @IF(condition,true,false). When the IF function is assigned to a cell, the value displayed will depend on the condition. If the condition is **true**, the cell is assigned the true value. If the condition is **false**, the cell is assigned the false value.
9. A **condition** is made up of two expressions and a relation. Each **expression** may be a number, label (in quotation marks), function, or formula. Refer to Table 4-3 for a list of the valid relations.
10. The true and false values in an IF function may be a number, label (in quotation marks), function, or formula.
11. A **compound condition** is one that includes a logical operator like #AND#, #OR#, and #NOT#. Refer to Table 4-4 for examples. Multiple logical operators in the same compound condition are evaluated from left to right.
12. A **data table** is used to automate asking what-if questions and organize the values returned by 1-2-3.
13. A data table may have one value or two varying values. The **input cell** is defined as the cell in the worksheet that contains the value to vary.
14. A **macro** is a series of keystrokes entered into a cell or range of cells. The macro is assigned a name using the command **/R**ange Name Create (/RNC).
15. A macro name can consist of 15 characters. Execute a macro by pressing Alt-F3. Select the desired macro from the list displayed.
16. If the macro name is two characters long with the first character the backslash (\) and the second character a letter, then you can execute the macro by holding down the Alt key and pressing the key that corresponds to the second letter in the macro name. If you name a macro \0 (zero), then 1-2-3 automatically executes the macro whenever the worksheet is first loaded from disk into main memory.
17. If you have more than one macro associated with a worksheet, each macro should be separated by an empty cell.
18. The **tilde character** (˜) is used to represent the Enter key in a macro.
19. All macros should be documented. **Documenting** a macro means writing a comment off to the side of the cell or range containing the macro.
20. Use the learn feature of 1-2-3 to enter and test macros at the same time.

21. A poorly designed macro can damage a worksheet. Before you execute a new macro, save the worksheet. To test a macro, place 1-2-3 in **STEP mode**, hold down the Alt key, and press function key F2. When you are finished testing the macro, hold down the Alt key and press function key F2 to toggle STEP mode off.

22. If you encounter an error in a macro while in STEP mode, hold down the Ctrl key and press the Break key to stop the macro followed by the Esc or Enter key.

23. **Macro commands** are used to write programs. Refer to Table 4-6.

24. **Macro words** represent special keys, like the pointer movement and function keys. Refer to Table 4-7.

25. 1-2-3 allows you to divide the screen into two windows for viewing different parts of the worksheet at the same time. Use the command **/Worksheet Window (/WW)**. Refer to Table 4-9.

26. **Unprotected cells** are cells whose values may be changed at any time, but **protected cells** cannot be changed.

27. To protect cells in a worksheet that you do not want the user to change, enter the command **/Worksheet Global Protection Enable (/WGPE)**. Once all the cells in the worksheet are protected, use the command **/Range Unprotect (/RU)** to unprotect the cells you want the user to be able to change. If you unprotect the wrong cell, use the command **/Range Protect (/RP)** to protect it.

28. To correct the values in protected cells, enter the command **/Worksheet Global Protection Disable (/WGPD)**. After the cells are corrected, enable (turn on) global protection. 1-2-3 remembers the cells you unprotected earlier.

STUDENT ASSIGNMENTS

STUDENT ASSIGNMENT 1: True/False

Instructions: Circle T if the statement is true and F if the statement is false.

T F   1. If there are seven cells in range R and five of the cells each have a value of 5 and two of the cells are empty, then the function @AVG(R) returns a value of 5.

T F   2. A data table allows you to automate what-if questions.

T F   3. You may assign a single cell a name using the **/Range Name Create (/RNC)** command.

T F   4. The @MIN(R) function returns the smallest number in the range R.

T F   5. To fill a range from top to bottom with the sequence of numbers 1, 2, 3, 4, and 5, use the **/Data Fill (/DF)** command with a start value of 5, a step value of 1, and a stop value of 1.

T F   6. The command **/Worksheet Erase (/WE)** may be used to erase the contents of the cells in the worksheet.

T F   7. The PMT function may be used to determine the monthly payment on a loan.

T F   8. The command **/Range Name Label (/RNL)** is used to name a cell that contains a label.

T F   9. The learn feature of 1-2-3 is used to enter macros.

T F 10. You may vary one, two, or three values in a data table.

T F 11. 1-2-3 recalculates the values in a data table when you press function key F8.

T F 12. To invoke a macro, hold down one of the Shift keys and type the letter that names the macro.

T F 13. The logical operator #OR# requires both conditions to be true for the compound condition to be true.

T F 14. The IF function is used to assign one value or another to a cell on the basis of a condition that may be true or false.

T F 15. The macro commands allow you to write programs.

T F 16. The **/Worksheet Window (/WW)** command allows you to divide the screen into two windows.

T F 17. To protect cells in the worksheet, global protection must be disabled (turned off).

T F 18. Each macro should be separated by at least one empty cell.

T F 19. STEP mode is used to enter a macro into a cell.

T F 20. To name a macro, use the **/Range Name Create (/RNC)** command.

STUDENT ASSIGNMENT 2: Multiple Choice

Instructions: Circle the correct response.

1. Which one of the following functions is used to assign one value or another value to a cell on the basis of a condition?
   a. IF   b. FALSE   c. CHOOSE   d. TRUE
2. Which one of the following functions returns the payment on a loan?
   a. PMT   b. TERM   c. PV   d. RATE
3. Which one of the following functions returns the average of the numbers in a range?
   a. MAX   b. COUNT   c. AVG   d. MIN
4. Which one of the following allows you to assign a name to one or more adjacent cells?
   a. **/R**ange Name Label (/RNL)   c. **/R**ange Name Create (/RNC)
   b. **/W**orksheet Name Create (/WNC)   d. **/R**ange Name Table (/RNT)
5. Which one of the following relations is used to represent not equal to?
   a. $<>$ b. $>$ c. $<$ d. none of these
6. Which one of the following is used to instruct 1-2-3 to terminate the Data Fill command?
   a. the last cell in the selected range terminates the command
   b. the STOP parameter terminates the command
   c. either a or b can terminate the command
   d. none of the above
7. Which one of the following characters represents the Enter key in a macro?
   a. backslash ($\backslash$)   b. curly braces ({ })   c. circumflex (^)   d. tilde (~)
8. Which one of the following turns the learn feature of 1-2-3 on and off?
   a. Alt-F9   b. Alt-F5   c. Alt-F7   d. Alt-F2

STUDENT ASSIGNMENT 3: Understanding Functions

Instructions: Enter the correct answers.

1. Write a function that will determine the monthly payment on a loan of $75,000, over a period of 20 years, at an interest rate of 8.4% compounded monthly.

   Function: _____

2. Write a function that will display the largest value in the range F1..F13.

   Function: _____

3. Write a function that will find the average of the nonempty cells in the range C18..F18.

   Function: _____

4. Write a function that will count the nonempty cells in the range C12..C43.

   Function: _____

5. When there are multiple logical operators in a compound condition, 1-2-3 determines the truth value of each simple condition. It then evaluates the logical operators left to right. Determine the truth value of the compound conditions below, given the following cell values: E1 = 500   F1 = 500   G1 = 2   H1 = 50   I1 = 40
   a. E1<400#OR#G1 = 1   Truth value: _____
   b. F1<300#AND#I1<50#OR#G1 = 2   Truth value: _____
   c. #NOT#(F1>600)#OR#G1 = 0#AND#I1 = 40   Truth value: _____
   d. E1 + F1 = 800#AND#H1*4/10 = 30   Truth value: _____

Student Assignment 3 (continued)

6. The cell pointer is at F15. Write a function that assigns the value zero or 1 to cell F15. Assign zero to cell F15 if the value in cell B3 is greater than the value in cell C12, else assign 1 to cell F15.

   Function: _____

7. The cell pointer is at F15. Write a function that assigns the value Credit OK or Credit Not OK to cell F15. Assign the label Credit OK if the value in cell A1 is not equal to the value in cell B1 or the value of cell C12 is less than 500. If both conditions are false, assign the label Credit Not OK.

   Function: _____

STUDENT ASSIGNMENT 4: Understanding Macros

Instructions: Enter the correct answers.

1. Describe the function of each of the following macros.
   a. /FS˜R/QY

      Function of macro: _____

   b. /RE˜

      Function of macro: _____

   c. /RFC2˜{?}˜

      Function of macro: _____

   d. /C˜{?}˜

      Function of macro: _____

   e. /PPOML2˜MR78˜Q

      Function of macro: _____

   f. /PPR{?}˜AGPQ

      Function of macro: _____

   g. {DOWN}{DOWN}/RE˜

      Function of macro: _____

   h. /DF{?}˜1˜2˜˜

      Function of macro: _____

2. Describe the function of each of the following macro commands and macro words.

a. tilde (~)   Function: _____   g. {UP}   Function: _____

b. curly braces ({ })   Function: _____   h. {QUIT}   Function: _____

c. {GETNUMBER}   Function: _____   i. {IF}   Function: _____

d. {?}   Function: _____   j. Alt-F2   Function: _____

e. {HOME}   Function: _____   k. Alt-F3   Function: _____

f. {GOTO}   Function: _____   l. Alt-F5   Function: _____

STUDENT ASSIGNMENT 5: Using the Data Fill Command

Instructions: Enter the worksheet illustrated in the following figure. The worksheet is a multiplication table. Change the global width of the columns to 6 characters. Use the Data Fill command twice, once to enter the numbers 1 to 18 in column A, and once to enter the numbers 2 to 22 by 2 in row 1. Enter the formula $A3*B$1 in cell B3. Copy the formula to the range B3..L20. Save the worksheet as STUS4-5. Print the as-displayed version of the worksheet. Format all the cells in the worksheet to the Text type and print the worksheet.

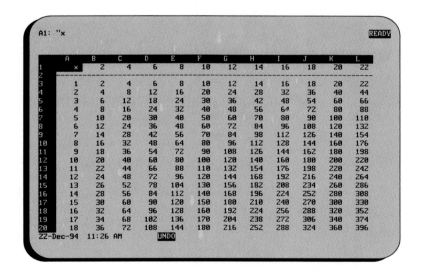

STUDENT ASSIGNMENT 6: Using the Data Table Command

Instructions: Create the worksheets as described in Parts 1 and 2.

Part 1: The worksheet illustrated in the following figure contains a data table with one value (time) varying. At the top of the worksheet, the PMT function is used to determine the monthly mortgage payment for a loan of $100,000.00 at 9.5% annual interest for 30 years. The data table indicates the monthly payment for the same loan for different terms (10 years, 15 years, 20 years).

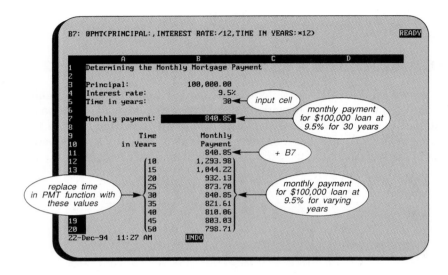

Do the following to create the worksheet in the figure:

a. Increase the global column width to 17.

b. Format the entire worksheet to the Comma (,) type with two decimal places.

c. Enter the labels and numeric values in the range A1 through B5 and in cell A7. Format cell B4 to the Percent type with one decimal position. Format cell B5 to the Fixed type with zero decimal positions.

d. Use the Range Name Label command to assign the labels in cells A3 through A7 to B3 through B7.

e. Assign the PMT function shown on the input line in the previous figure to cell B7.

f. Enter the labels in the range A9..B10.

g. Use the Data Fill command to enter the multiples of five shown in the range A12..A20. Format A12..A20 to the Fixed type with zero decimal positions.

h. Assign cell B11 the formula +B7.

i. Use the command /Data Table 1 (/DT1) to create a data table in the range A11..B20. Use B5 (time in years) as the input cell.

j. After the data table displays, save the worksheet using the file name STUS4-6A.

k. Print the worksheet.

l. Select and enter several other sets of numbers into cells B3, B4, and B5. When necessary, use function key F8 to reset the data table.

Part 2: The worksheet illustrated in the following figure contains a data table with two values varying. It also uses the FV function in cell B7 to determine the future value of a fund. The FV function tells you how much money you will have in a fund if you pay a fixed payment and earn a fixed interest rate over a period of time.

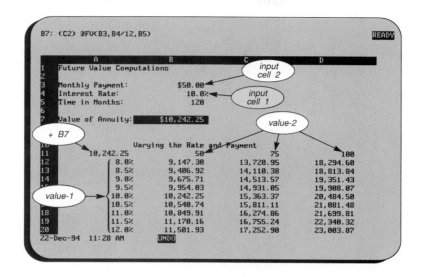

The data table describes the future values for varying interest rates and varying monthly payments. For example, if you invest $75.00 per month instead of $50.00 per month and if the interest rate is 11.5%, then you will have $16,755.24 rather than $10,242.25 at the end of 10 years.

Do the following to create the worksheet in the previous figure:

a. Increase the global column width to 17.
b. Enter the labels and numeric values in the range A1 through B5 and in cell A7.
c. Assign the FV function @FV(B3,B4/12,B5) to cell B7 to determine the future value of a fund in which you invest $50.00 per month at 10% interest, compounded monthly, for 10 years (120 months).
d. Use the Data Fill command to build the percent values in the range A12..A20. Assign +B7 to cell A11.
e. With the cell pointer at A11, enter the command /Data Table 2 (/DT2). Enter the data table range A11..D20.
f. Enter an input cell-1 value of B4 and an input cell-2 value of B3. Press the Enter key. The data table should fill as shown in the previous figure.
g. Format the worksheet according to the figure.
h. Save the worksheet using the file name STUS4-6B.
i. Print the worksheet.
j. Try several different investment combinations in cells B3, B4, and B5. Use function key F8 to instruct 1-2-3 to recalculate the data table if you change the value in cell B5.

STUDENT ASSIGNMENT 7: Building a Biweekly Payroll Worksheet

Instructions: Load 1-2-3 and perform the following tasks.

1. Build the worksheet illustrated in the following figure. For each employee, use these formulas to determine the gross pay in column E, federal tax in column F, state tax in column G, and net pay in column H:
   a. If Hours ≤ 80, then Gross Pay = Rate * Hours, otherwise Gross Pay = Rate * Hours + 0.5 * Rate * (Hours − 80).
   b. If (Gross Pay − Dependents * 38.46) > 0, then Federal Tax = 20% * (Gross Pay − Dependents * 38.46), otherwise Federal Tax = 0.
   c. State Tax = 3.2% * Gross Pay.
   d. Net Pay = Gross Pay − (Federal Tax + State Tax).

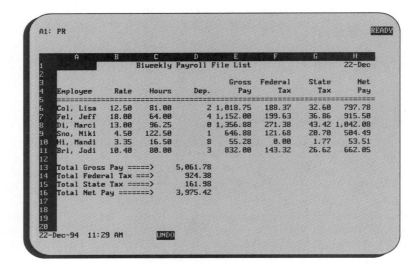

2. Use the Range Name Create command to name cells B6, C6, and D6 so that you can use the variable names described in step 1 when you enter the formulas in cells E6, F6, G6, and H6.
3. Protect all the cells in the worksheet except those in the range C6..C11. Try to enter values into the protected cells.
4. Save the worksheet as STUS4-7.
5. Print the worksheet.
6. Print the cell-formulas version of the worksheet.
7. Print the worksheet after formatting all the cells to the Text type.
8. Retrieve STUS4-7. Increase the number of hours worked for each employee by 7.5 hours. Print the as-displayed version of the worksheet with the new values.

STUDENT ASSIGNMENT 8: Building a Future Value Worksheet

Instructions: Load 1-2-3 and perform the following tasks.

1. Build the worksheet illustrated in the following figure. Set column A to a width of 16 characters and the rest of the columns to a width of 14 characters. Use the Range Name Label command to name B3, B5, E3, and E5. Use the label to the right of each cell in the figure as the label name. Determine the future value in cell E5 from the function @FV($Monthly Pymt:, $Rate:/12,12*$Time:). The FV function tells you how much money you will have in a fund if you pay a fixed payment and earn a fixed interest rate over a period of time. Enter the following data: monthly payment, 250; rate of interest, 10%; time in years, 10. Print the range A1..E19.

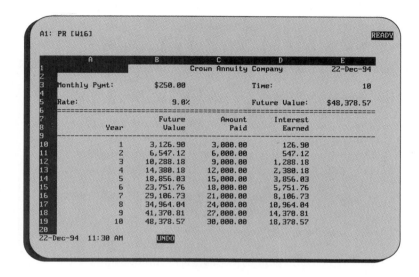

Determine the values in the table in rows 10 through 19 as follows:

a. Use the Data Fill command to create the series of numbers in the range A10..A19.
b. Assign the function @IF(A10< = $Time:,@FV($Monthly Pymt:,$Rate:/12,12*A10),0) to B10 and copy B10 to B11..B19.
c. Assign the function @IF(A10< = $Time:,12*A10*$Monthly Pymt:,0) to C10 and copy C10 to C11..C19.
d. Assign the formula +B10–C10 to D10 and copy D10 to D11..D19.
e. Format the cells in the worksheet as shown in the figure.

2. Enable cell protection. Unprotect B3, B5, and E3.
3. Save the worksheet. Use the file name STUS4-8.
4. Determine the future value for the following: monthly payment, 500; rate of interest, 11.5%; time in years, 10. For this data, the future value is equal to $111,701.61.
5. Print the worksheet with the future value for the data described in step 4.
6. Print only the range A1..E5 with the future value for the data described in step 4.

STUDENT ASSIGNMENT 9: Building a Data Table for the Future Value Worksheet

Instructions: Load 1-2-3 and perform the following tasks.

1. Load STUS4-8, the future value worksheet, which you created in Student Assignment 8. This worksheet is illustrated in the figure in Student Assignment 8. Determine the future value for the following: monthly payment, 1200; rate of interest, 10%; time in years, 7.
2. Do the following to create the data table shown in the following figure.
   a. Disable cell protection.
   b. Use the Data Fill command to enter the series of numbers 6.5% to 12.5% in increments of 0.5% in the range F8..F20.
   c. Assign +E5 (future value) to cell G7.
   d. Assign the formula +Future Value:−Time:*12*Monthly Pymt: to cell H7.
   e. Use the command /**D**ata **T**able **1** (/DT1) to establish the range F7..H20 as a data table.
   f. Enter an input cell value of B5, the interest rate.
   g. Format the data table as shown in the figure.
   h. Enable cell protection. Unprotect the range F7..H20.

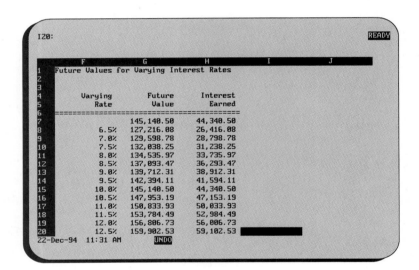

3. Save the worksheet using the file name STUS4-9.
4. Print the complete worksheet (A1..H20) with the future value for the data described in step 1.

STUDENT ASSIGNMENT 10: Building Macros for the Future Value Worksheet

Instructions: Load 1-2-3 and perform the following tasks.

1. Load STUS4-9, the future value worksheet, which was created in Student Assignments 8 and 9. This worksheet is illustrated in the figures in Student Assignments 8 and 9.
2. Enter the three macros shown in the following figure.

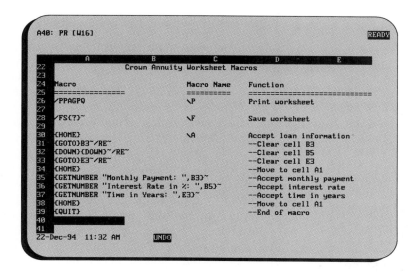

3. Change the printer range to A1..E19.
4. Use STEP mode to test each macro. For the \F macro in cell A28, use the file name STUS4-10. For the \A macro beginning in cell A30, use the following data: monthly payment, 350; rate of interest, 8%; time in years, 7. For this data, the future value equals $39,239.66.
5. Enable cell protection for the worksheet.
6. Press function key F8 to recalculate the data table.
7. Use the \F command to save the worksheet a second time.
8. Print the complete worksheet (A1..H39) with the future value for the data described in step 4.

STUDENT ASSIGNMENT 11: Building Macros for the Biweekly Payroll Worksheet

Instructions: Load 1-2-3 and perform the following tasks.

1. Load STUS4-7, the weekly payroll worksheet, which was created in Student Assignment 7. This worksheet is illustrated in the figure in Student Assignment 7.
2. Disable cell protection and add macros that will do the following:
   a. Save the worksheet under the file name entered by the user (\S).
   b. Print the range A1..H16 (\P).
   c. Erase the current hours worked and accept the new hours worked (\A).
3. Enable cell protection for the worksheet.
4. Use STEP mode to test each macro. For the save macro, use the file name STUS4-11. For the accept hours worked macro, enter the following hours worked: Col, Lisa—78.5; Fel, Jeff—84.5; Di, Marci—120; Sno, Niki—80; Hi, Mandi—80; Bri, Jodi—132.5.
5. Use the save macro to save the worksheet a second time. Use the file name STUS4-11.
6. Print the worksheet (A1..H16) for the data described in step 4.
7. Print the macros entered in step 2.

Graphing with 1-2-3 and Allways

OBJECTIVES

You will have mastered the material in this project when you can:

◆ Create a pie chart

◆ Create a line graph

◆ Create a multiple-line graph

◆ Create a scatter graph

◆ Create a simple bar graph

◆ Create a side-by-side bar graph

◆ Create a stack-bar graph

◆ Create an XY graph

◆ Assign multiple graphs to the same worksheet

◆ Dress up a graph by adding titles and legends

◆ Save a graph as a PIC file

◆ Save a worksheet with the graph settings

◆ Print a graph

◆ View the current graph and graphs saved on disk

◆ Use Allways to place a graph alongside the data in a worksheet

As we have seen in the previous four projects, a worksheet is a powerful tool for analyzing data. Sometimes, however, the message you are trying to convey gets lost in the rows and columns of numbers. This is where the graphics capability of 1-2-3 becomes useful. With only a little effort, you can have 1-2-3 create, display, and print a graph of the data in your worksheet and get your message across in a dramatic pictorial fashion. With the Graph command, you can select a pie chart, a line graph, a variety of bar graphs, an XY graph, or a scatter graph. We will study these types of graphs in this project.

We will use the year-end sales analysis worksheet shown in Figure 5-1 to illustrate all the graphs except the XY graph. The worksheet in Figure 5-1 includes the quarter sales for each of six cities in which King's Computer Outlet has a store. Total sales for each quarter and the year are displayed in row 13. The total sales for each of the six cities are displayed in column F.

Before going any further, let's build the worksheet shown in Figure 5-1. As a guide, follow the first 23 steps in the list of keystrokes given in the Project Summary section at the end of this project.

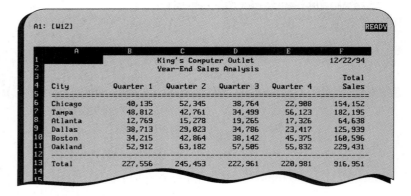

FIGURE 5-1 The year-end sales analysis report we will use to illustrate graphing with 1-2-3.

THE GRAPH COMMAND

◆ With the worksheet in Figure 5-1 in main memory, the first step in drawing a graph is to enter the command /Graph (/G). The Graph menu and the graph settings sheet display as shown in Figure 5-2.

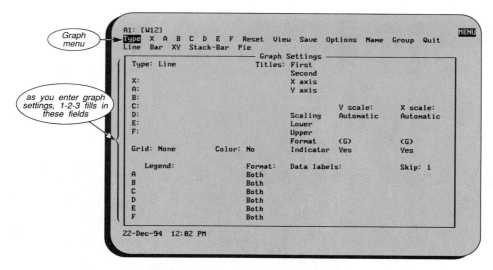

FIGURE 5-2   The Graph menu of 1-2-3—enter the command /Graph (/G).

The functions of the commands listed in the Graph menu are described in Table 5-1.

TABLE 5-1   A Summary of Commands in the Graph Menu

COMMAND	FUNCTION
Type	Allows you to select the type of graph you want to display—Line, Bar, XY, Stack-bar, Pie.
X	Defines a range of labels for the X axis for a line or bar graph. Defines a range of labels to describe each piece of a pie chart. In an XY graph the X range is assigned the X coordinates.
ABCDEF	Allows you to define up to six Y-axis data ranges. For example, in a multiple-line graph each data range is represented by a line.
Reset	Clears the current graph specifications.
View	Displays the current graph.
Save	Saves the current graph to disk. 1-2-3 automatically adds the extension .PIC to the graph file.
Options	Allows you to define titles or labels for the X and Y axes and for the top of the graph.
Name	Allows you to save a set of graph settings by name. In this way you can have several different graphs associated with the same worksheet.
Group	Allows you to define multiple graph data ranges when the ranges are located in consecutive columns or rows.
Quit	Quits the Graph command.

PIE CHARTS

◆ A **pie chart** is used to show how 100% of an amount is divided. Let's create the pie chart in Figure 5-3. This pie chart shows the percentage of total annual sales for each of the six cities where King's Computer Outlet has a store.

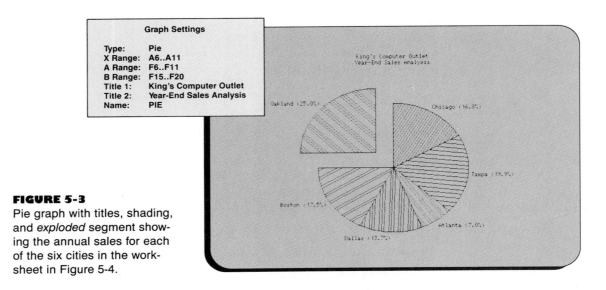

Graph Settings

Type:	Pie
X Range:	A6..A11
A Range:	F6..F11
B Range:	F15..F20
Title 1:	King's Computer Outlet
Title 2:	Year-End Sales Analysis
Name:	PIE

FIGURE 5-3

Pie graph with titles, shading, and *exploded* segment showing the annual sales for each of the six cities in the worksheet in Figure 5-4.

The total annual sales for each of the six stores are in the range F6..F11 of the worksheet in Figure 5-4.

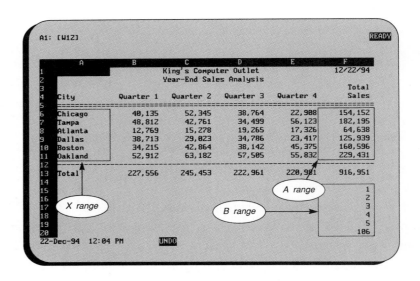

FIGURE 5-4

Ranges specified in the worksheet for the pie graph in Figure 5-3

To create any graph using 1-2-3, you need to enter the type of graph, the ranges in the worksheet to graph, graph titles, and graph options. Collectively, these are called the **graph settings** and they display on the graph settings sheet when the Graph menu is active. Remember, function key F6 toggles the display between the graph settings sheet and the worksheet when the Graph menu is active.

With the Graph menu on the screen (Figure 5-2), enter the command **T**ype **P**ie (TP). This command tells 1-2-3 to create a pie chart as the current graph. The **current graph** is the one that displays when you enter the command **/G**raph **V**iew (/GV).

Selecting the A Range

After typing the letter P for Pie, the menu pointer returns to the Graph menu, (Figure 5-2). For a pie chart, you can select only one data range to graph, and it must be assigned as the A range. As shown in Figure 5-4, assign the annual sales for each city (F6..F11) as the A range. Type the letter A. 1-2-3 responds by displaying the prompt message "Enter first data range: A1" on the input line. Enter the range F6..F11 and press the Enter key.

Selecting the X Range

The X range is used to identify each *slice*, or segment, of the pie. You must select a range that can identify the cells in the A range. Since the A range is equal to the annual sales for each of the six cities, select the names of the cities (A6..A11) to identify each segment of the pie. With the menu pointer in the Graph menu, type the letter X. 1-2-3 responds by displaying the prompt message "Enter x-axis range: A1" on the input line. Enter the range A6..A11 and press the Enter key.

After defining the A range and X range, 1-2-3 has enough information to draw a *primitive* pie chart, one that shows the characteristics assigned thus far. With the menu pointer in the Graph menu, type the letter V for View and the primitive pie chart in Figure 5-5 displays on the screen. After viewing it, press any key on the keyboard to redisplay the Graph menu and graph settings. Once a range has been assigned you may view the pie chart at any time and make changes if you feel the pie chart is not being drawn the way you want it.

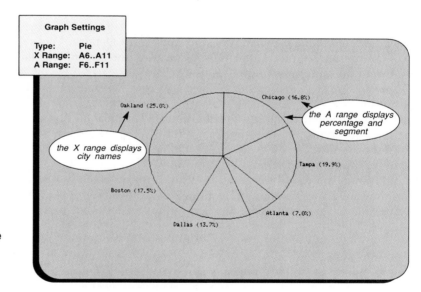

FIGURE 5-5
Primitive pie chart with no titles or shading. It shows the proportion of annual sales contributed by each city in the form of a *slice of the pie.*

It is the A range that causes the pie in Figure 5-5 to be divided into segments. Each segment is proportionate to the annual sales for each city. The A range is also responsible for the percentage value displayed within parentheses outside each segment. The city names outside each segment of the pie are the labels assigned as the X range.

In certain instances, you may want to assign the same group of cells to both the A and X ranges. When both ranges are assigned the same group of cells, the values in the A range that determine the size of each segment of the pie are also used to identify (label) each segment.

Selecting the B Range

The B range is used to enhance the pie chart and make it more presentable and easier to read. Through the use of the B range, you can create segment shading and *explode* a pie chart. An **exploded pie chart** is one in which one or more segments are offset or slightly removed from the main portion of the pie so that they stand out (Figure 5-3).

The B range is usually set up off to the side or below the worksheet. To shade and explode the pie chart in Figure 5-5 so that it looks more like Figure 5-3, you need to choose six adjacent cells for the B range, one for each pie segment. In each cell, enter a code number between 0 and 7. Each code represents a different type of shading. A code of zero instructs 1-2-3 to leave the corresponding segment of the pie chart unshaded.

Let's use the range F15..F20 to enter the code numbers. The first of the six cells, F15, will refer to the first entry in the A range, Chicago. The last of the six cells will refer to the last entry in the A range, Oakland.

To enter the shading codes, first quit the Graph menu by typing the letter Q. Use function key F5 to move the cell pointer to F15. Enter the shading codes 1 through 5 in the range F15..F19. To explode one or more segments of the pie chart, add 100 to the shading values. Explode the segment representing Oakland by entering the number 106, rather than 6, in cell F20. The six shading codes are shown in the range F15..F20 in Figure 5-4.

Select the range F15..F20 by entering the command /**Graph B** (/GB). Enter the range F15..F20 and press the Enter key. Type the letter V to view the pie chart. The pie chart (without titles) displays as shown earlier in Figure 5-3. Except for the graph titles, the pie chart is complete. After viewing the pie chart, press any key to redisplay the Graph menu and graph settings.

Adding a Title to the Pie Chart

To add graph titles above the pie chart, type the letter O for Options. This causes the Graph Options menu to display at the top of the screen. With the Graph Options menu on the screen, type the letter T for Titles. We are allowed two title lines—First Line and Second Line—up to 39 characters each. Type the letter F for First Line. Enter the title King's Computer Outlet and press the Enter key. Type the letters T for Titles and S for Second Line. Enter the second line of the title Year-End Sales Analysis and press the Enter key.

To quit the Graph Options menu, type the letter Q for Quit. 1-2-3 returns to the Graph menu. The graph settings for the pie chart are complete as shown in Figure 5-6. Type the letter V for View and 1-2-3 displays the pie chart with titles as shown earlier in Figure 5-3. To terminate the View command, press any key on the keyboard and the Graph menu redisplays on the screen.

If the title you plan to use for a graph is identical to one in the worksheet, you can press the Backslash (\) key followed by the cell address in place of the title. For example, you could have entered \C1 for the first title and \C2 for the second title, since the titles are identical to the worksheet titles in cells C1 and C2 (Figure 5-4).

Naming the Pie Chart

With the menu pointer in the Graph menu and the pie chart complete, the next step is to name the graph settings. That way you can develop a new graph from the same worksheet and still have the pie chart settings stored away to view and modify at a later time. To assign a name to the graph settings, type the letter N for Name. The Graph Name menu displays at the top of the screen as shown in Figure 5-6. Type the letter C for Create. 1-2-3 displays the prompt message "Enter graph name:" on the input line. Enter the name PIE for pie chart and press the Enter key. After assigning the name, 1-2-3 returns control to the Graph menu.

FIGURE 5-6

The Graph Name menu display after entering the command /Graph Name (/GN)

The graph settings shown in Figure 5-6 are now stored under the name PIE. Graph names, like PIE, can be up to 15 characters long and should be as descriptive as possible. Table 5-2 summarizes the commands available in the Graph Name menu.

TABLE 5-2 A Summary of Commands in the Graph Name Menu

COMMAND	FUNCTION
Use	Lists the directory of graph names associated with the current worksheet. Assigns the selected named set of graph settings as the current graph and displays the graph.
Create	Saves the current graph settings as a part of the worksheet so that another graph can be built. This command does not save the graph settings to disk.
Delete	Deletes the named set of graph settings.
Reset	Deletes all graph names and their settings.
Table	Creates a table of named graphs in the worksheet.

The Effect of What-If Analyses on the Pie Chart

Once you have assigned the pie chart settings to the worksheet, any values changed in the worksheet will show up in the pie chart the next time it is drawn. For example, quit the Graph menu and change the sales amount for Quarter 1 for Chicago in cell B6 from 40,135 to 45,550. Press the F10 key to view the pie chart. When the worksheet is displayed on the screen, it is quicker to press the F10 key to display the current graph than it is to enter the command /GV. Compare the displayed pie chart to the one in Figure 5-3. Notice that the segments representing all six cities have changed because of the change in the first quarter sales for Chicago. After viewing the pie chart, press any key on the keyboard to return to the worksheet. Before continuing with this project, change the sales amount for Chicago in cell B6 back to 40,135.

Saving the Worksheet with the Pie Chart Graph Settings

When you assign a name, like PIE, to the current set of graph settings using the /GNC command, they are not saved to disk. To save the named graph settings, you must save the worksheet itself using the File Save command. When the /FS command is used, both the current graph settings and any named graph settings are saved with the worksheet. To complete the save, first type the letter Q to quit the Graph menu. When the worksheet reappears on the screen, enter the command /File Save (/FS). When the file name PROJS-5A appears on the input line, press the Enter key. Finally, type the letter R for Replace.

Later, when you retrieve the worksheet, the pie chart settings will be available and you can display or print the pie chart at any time. If you retrieve the worksheet and decide to change any of the pie chart settings, you must save the worksheet again or the latest changes will be lost.

Printing the Pie Chart

Printing a graph is a three-step process: first, save the graph to disk using the command /Graph Save (/GS); second, quit 1-2-3; and third, load the PrintGraph program (PGRAPH) into main memory and print the graph. The PrintGraph program allows you to print graphs that have been saved with the /Graph Save (/GS) command.

Let's print the pie chart by following the three steps we just described. With 1-2-3 in READY mode, enter the command /Graph Save (/GS). In response to the prompt message on the input line, enter the file name PIE-5A and press the Enter key. The pie chart (not the worksheet) is saved to disk under the name PIE-5A with an extension of .PIC (picture). We call a graph file, like PIE-5A.PIC, a **PIC file**. With a snapshot of the graph saved, quit the Graph menu and quit 1-2-3.

Next, load the PrintGraph program into main memory. If you have a computer with a fixed disk, then at the DOS prompt enter PGRAPH and press the Enter key. If you have a computer with no fixed disk, replace the 1-2-3 system disk in the A drive with the PrintGraph disk and make sure the disk with PIE-5A.PIC is in the B drive. At the DOS prompt, enter PGRAPH and press the Enter key. After several seconds the PrintGraph menu displays on the screen (Figure 5-7).

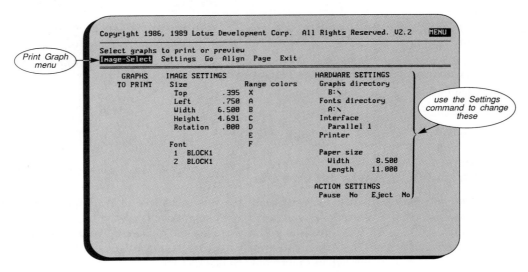

FIGURE 5-7   The PrintGraph menu

Table 5-3 describes the commands available in the PrintGraph menu.

TABLE 5-3   A Summary of Commands in the PrintGraph Menu

COMMAND	FUNCTION
Image-Select	Allows you to specify the graph to print.
Settings	Lets you set the default drive; adjust the size of the graph; select colors, fonts, and the hardware.
Go	Starts printing the graph.
Align	Resets the PrintGraph line counter.
Page	Ejects the paper in the printer to the top of the next page.
Exit	Ends the PrintGraph session.

With the PrintGraph menu on the screen, type the letter I for Image-Select. PrintGraph displays the Image-Select menu (Figure 5-8). This menu includes a list of all the PIC files on the default drive. Use the Up Arrow and Down Arrow keys to highlight the one to print. In our case, there is only one PIC file and it is highlighted. Press the Enter key to select PIE-5A. The PrintGraph menu shown in Figure 5-7 redisplays on the screen.

Check the printer to be sure it is in READY mode. Type the letters A for Align and G for Go. The pie chart prints on the printer. Type the letter P for Page to advance the paper to the top of the next page. If the graph fails to print properly, refer to the section entitled Solving PrintGraph Problems in the Lotus 1-2-3 Release 2.2 reference manual.

To the right of the list of PIC files in the Image-Select menu in Figure 5-8 are instructions explaining how to select a graph from the list. The Spacebar is used to mark or unmark the highlighted graph in the list. A graph name that is marked has a number sign (#) displayed to the left of the name. All marked graph names print when you use the Go command in the PrintGraph menu. Hence, when you print a second graph, you should unmark the previous one or it will print also.

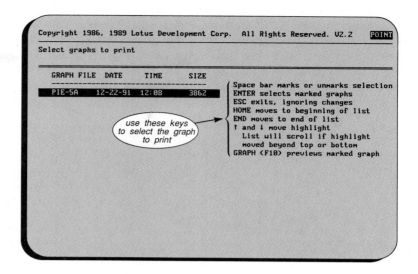

FIGURE 5-8
The Image-Select menu

The GRAPH key is the function key F10. You can press this key to display the highlighted graph on the screen. When you are finished viewing the graph, press any key to return to the Image-Select menu.

To quit PrintGraph, type the letters E for Exit and Y for Yes to confirm your exit from the PrintGraph program. At the DOS prompt, type 123 to reenter the spreadsheet program.

LINE GRAPHS

Line graphs are used to show changes in data over time. For example, a line graph can show pictorially whether sales increased or decreased during quarters of the year. The lines are drawn on X and Y axes. You can have from one to six lines in the graph. Each line represents a different data range in the worksheet. We will create two line graphs, one with a single data range and another with six data ranges.

First, we will create a line graph with a single data range that shows the trend of the total sales for the four quarters (Figure 5-9). Begin by resetting the current graph settings associated with PROJS-5A. That is, clear the pie chart—the current graph—to begin the line graph because the settings are different.

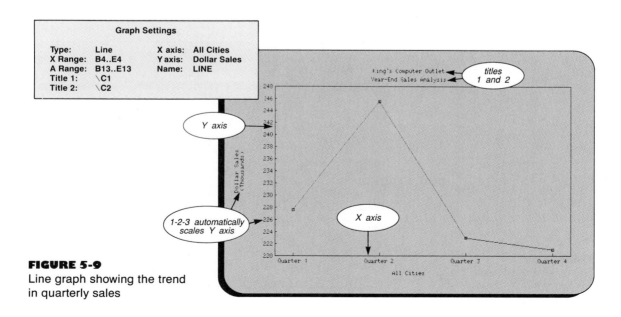

FIGURE 5-9
Line graph showing the trend in quarterly sales

With the Graph menu on the screen, type the letter R for Reset. The Graph Reset menu displays at the top of the screen as shown in Figure 5-10. The graph settings can be reset on an individual basis (X, A, B, C, D, E, F) or for the entire graph (Graph). In this case, reset all the graph settings. With the menu pointer in the Graph Reset menu, type the letter G for Graph. The pie chart settings disappear from the screen since it is no longer the current graph. Remember, however, that the pie chart settings are stored under the name PIE and can be accessed at any time using the **/G**raph **N**ame **U**se (/GNU) command (Table 5-2).

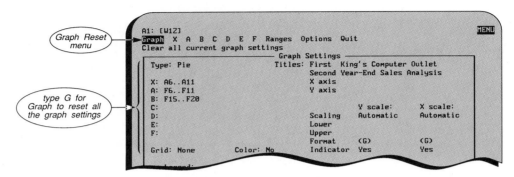

FIGURE 5-10 The Graph Reset menu—enter the command /Graph Reset (/GR).

The menu pointer returns to the Graph menu after erasing the pie chart settings. We can now proceed to build the line graph in Figure 5-9. There are four steps involved:

1. With the Graph menu on the screen, enter the command **T**ype **L**ine (TL).
2. Define the X range—the cells that contain the desired labels for the X axis.
3. Define the A range—the cells that include the values that the line graph will represent.
4. Enter the title of the line graph and titles for the X and Y axes.

Selecting the X Range

With the menu pointer in the Graph menu, type the letter X and assign the range B4..E4 as the X range. As shown in Figure 5-11, cells B4 through E4 contain the labels Quarter 1, Quarter 2, Quarter 3, and Quarter 4. These labels display along the X axis in the line graph (Figure 5-9).

FIGURE 5-11

Range settings for line graph in Figure 5-9

Selecting the A Range

The next step is to select the A range. Assign to the A range the cells that include the values to graph. This is also called the Y-axis data range. With the menu pointer in the Graph menu, type the letter A and enter the range B13..E13. The A range is shown in the worksheet in Figure 5-11.

Adding Titles to the Line Graph

You can add three different titles to the line graph: (1) line graph title (you are allowed two of these); (2) X-axis title; (3) Y-axis title. Let's add the same line graph titles used for the pie chart. To add these titles, type the letter O for Options while the Graph menu is on the screen. The Graph Options menu shown in Figure 5-12 displays. Type the letters T for Titles and F for First. Enter \C1 and press the Enter key. \C1 instructs 1-2-3 to use the label assigned to cell C1 in the worksheet as the first title. Next, type the letters T and S to enter the second title. Enter \C2 and press the Enter key. The label in cell C2 serves as the second title.

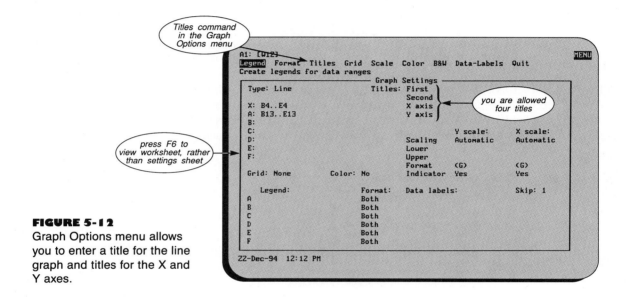

FIGURE 5-12
Graph Options menu allows you to enter a title for the line graph and titles for the X and Y axes.

Enter the X-axis title by typing the letters T and X and the label `All Cities`. Press the Enter key. Enter the Y-axis title by typing the letters T and Y and the label `Dollar Sales`. Press the Enter key. Finally, type the letter Q to quit the Graph Options menu.

Viewing the Line Graph

With the menu pointer in the Graph menu, type the letter V for View. The line graph previously shown in Figure 5-9 displays. Notice that 1-2-3 automatically scales the numeric labels along the Y axis on the basis of the numbers in the A range. The small squares that the line graph passes through represent the points whose coordinates are the corresponding values in the X and A ranges.

You can see from Figure 5-9 that the line graph is useful for showing a trend. The line graph clearly shows that sales for King's Computer Outlet increased significantly during the second quarter and then fell sharply in the third quarter. Finally, there was a slight drop in sales during the fourth quarter. Here again, if we change any numeric values in the worksheet, the line graph will show the latest values the next time we invoke the View command. After viewing the graph, press any key to redisplay the Graph menu.

Naming the Line Graph

With the line graph complete and the menu pointer active in the Graph menu, type the letters N for Name and C for Create. When 1-2-3 requests the graph name, enter the name L I NE and press the Enter key. The line graph settings are stored under the name LINE.

Saving and Printing the Line Graph

To save the named graph settings (LINE) with the worksheet to disk, type the letter Q to quit the Graph menu. Enter the command /File Save (/FS). Press the Enter key when the file name PROJS-5A appears on the input line. Type the letter R for Replace to rewrite the file to disk. Now there are two sets of graph settings associated with PROJS-5A—PIE and LINE. The line graph continues to be the current graph.

Make a hard copy of the line graph in the same manner we described for the pie chart. That is, with the menu pointer in the Graph menu, type the letter S for Save and name the graph LINE-5A. Quit the Graph menu and quit 1-2-3. At the DOS prompt, enter PGRAPH. When the PrintGraph menu displays, type the letter I for Image-Select and select the PIC file LINE-5A. Turn the printer on, type A for Align, G for Go, and P for Page. When the printing activity is complete, quit PrintGraph, load 1-2-3, and retrieve PROJS-5A.

Multiple-Line Graphs

1-2-3 allows up to six Y-axis data ranges (A–F) and the range of corresponding labels (X) to be assigned to a line graph. When more than one data range is assigned to a line graph, it is called a **multiple-line graph**. The multiple-line graph in Figure 5-13 includes six lines, each representing the four quarterly sales for one of the six cities in the worksheet. Multiple-line graphs like this one are used not only to show trends, but also to compare one range of data to another.

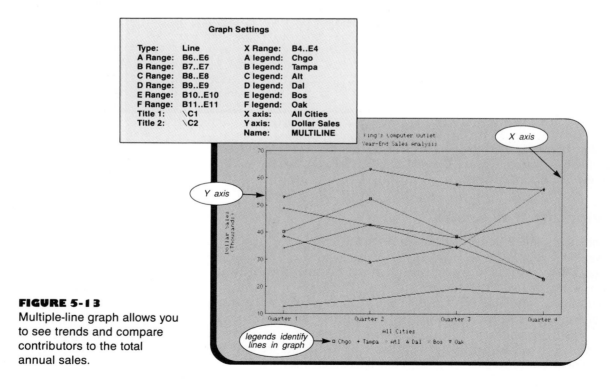

FIGURE 5-13
Multiple-line graph allows you to see trends and compare contributors to the total annual sales.

The multiple-line graph in Figure 5-13 uses the same titles, X range, and graph type as the line graph in Figure 5-9, the current graph associated with the worksheet. Therefore, rather than resetting the current graph settings, modify them.

Selecting the Data Ranges One at a Time

With the menu pointer active in the Graph menu, assign to the six data ranges A through F the quarterly sales of the six cities shown in Figure 5-14. Type the letter A for the A range. Enter the range B6..E6 and press the Enter key. Follow the same procedure for the other five ranges—assign the B range B7..E7, the C range B8..E8, the D range B9..E9, the E range B10..E10, and the F range B11..E11.

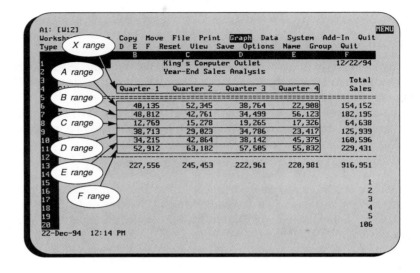

FIGURE 5-14
Multiple-line graph range settings

Selecting the Data Ranges as a Group

If the majority of the data ranges are in adjacent rows or adjacent columns, you can use the Group command in the Graph menu (Figure 5-2) to select all the data ranges at once, rather than one by one. In Figure 5-14, the data ranges A through F are in adjacent rows, and the X range is separated from the rest of the data ranges by row 5. Let's use the Group command to assign the range B5..E11 to X through F, and then let's change the X range to B4..E4.

With the Graph menu active, type the letter G for Group. 1-2-3 responds by prompting you to enter the range. Enter B5..E11 and press the Enter key. 1-2-3 then asks if the selected range should be assigned by columns or rows to the data ranges. Since Figure 5-14 shows that the data ranges are in rows, type the letter R. 1-2-3 responds by assigning X range B5..E5, A range B6..E6, B range B7..E7, C range B8..E8, D range B9..E9, E range B10..E10, and F range B11..E11. To complete the selection, change the X range. With the Graph menu still on the screen, type the letter X. Change the X range to B4..E4.

This alternative method for selecting the data ranges saves time because you can assign all the data ranges with two commands instead of seven.

Assigning Legends to the Data Ranges

Before quiting the Graph menu, enter legends that help identify each of the six lines that are drawn in the multiple-line graph. Without legends, the multiple-line graph is useless because you cannot identify the lines in the graph.

To enter the legend that identifies the A range, type the letters O for Options, L for Legend, and A for A range. From Figure 5-14 you can determine that the A range was assigned the quarterly sales for Chicago (B6..E6). Therefore, enter the label Chgo in response to the prompt message "Enter legend for A range:" on the input line. Assign the abbreviated city names as the legends for the B through F ranges as described at the top of Figure 5-13.

Viewing the Multiple-Line Graph

Next, type the letter V for View and the multiple-line graph illustrated in Figure 5-13 displays on the screen. The six lines in the graph show the trend in quarterly sales for each of the six cities. The graph also allows us to compare the sales for the six cities. To identify the line that represents a particular city, scan the legends at the bottom of the graph in Figure 5-13. Before each abbreviated city name is a special character called a symbol, like the square for Chicago. The line that passes through the square in the graph represents Chicago's four quarterly sales. After viewing the multiple-line graph, press any key to return control to the Graph menu.

Naming the Multiple-Line Graph

To assign a name to the multiple-line graph specifications, type the letters N for Name and C for Create. When 1-2-3 requests the graph name, enter the name MULTLINE and press the Enter key. The multiple-line graph settings are stored under the name MULTLINE.

There are now three graphs associated with the worksheet—PIE, LINE, and MULTLINE. However, there is only one current graph. At this point, the current graph is the multiple-line graph because it was the last one created.

Saving and Printing the Multiple-Line Graph

Type Q to quit the Graph menu. The worksheet in Figure 5-1 reappears on the screen. Save the worksheet. This ensures that the graph settings under the name MULTLINE are saved with the worksheet on disk. Enter the command /**F**ile **S**ave (/FS). When the file name PROJS-5A appears on the input line, press the Enter key. Type the letter R to replace the old version of PROJS-5A with the new one.

After saving the worksheet, enter the command /**G**raph **S**ave (/GS) to save the multiple-line graph as a PIC file using the name MLINE-5A. Quit the graph menu and quit 1-2-3. At the DOS prompt enter PGRAPH. Follow the steps for printing a graph outlined earlier.

Scatter Graphs

A **scatter graph** displays the points (symbols) in a graph without any connecting lines. Sometimes a scatter graph is better able to illustrate what a multiple-line graph is attempting to show. To create the scatter graph shown in Figure 5-15, you need only instruct 1-2-3 not to connect the symbols with lines in the multiple-line graph. Remember, the multiple-line graph is still the current graph.

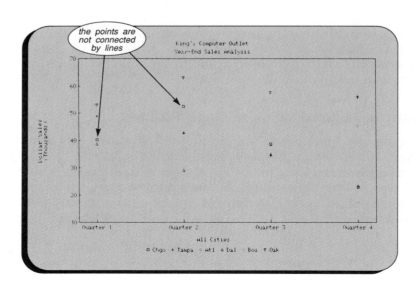

FIGURE 5-15
The scatter graph is an alternative to the multiple-line graph.

Changing the Multiple-Line Graph to a Scatter Graph With the Graph menu on the screen, type the letters O for Options, F for Format, and G for Graph. The default setting for the Format Graph command is Both. This means that both lines and symbols are displayed for the current multiple-line graph. Change this to Symbols so that only the symbols are displayed. Type the letter S for Symbols. Finally, type the letter Q twice, once to quit the Format section of the Graph Options menu and once to quit the Graph Options menu.

Viewing the Scatter Graph Type the letter V and the original multiple-line graph (Figure 5-13) displays as a scatter graph (Figure 5-15). Here again, the symbols are identified by the legends displayed below the scatter graph. Press any key to redisplay the Graph menu.

Naming, Saving, and Printing the Scatter Graph To assign a name to the scatter graph settings, type the letters N for Name and C for Create. When 1-2-3 requests the graph name, enter the name SCATTER and press the Enter key. Type the letter Q to quit the Graph menu and save the worksheet to disk using the File Save command. Now there are four graphs associated with the worksheet—PIE, LINE, MULTLINE, and SCATTER.

To print the scatter graph, first save it as a PIC file using the /Graph Save (/GS) command and the file name SCAT-5A. Next, quit 1-2-3 and use PGRAPH to print the PIC file SCAT-5A.

BAR GRAPHS

◆ The **bar graph** is the most popular business graphic. It is used to show trends and comparisons. The bar graph is similar to a line graph, except that a bar rather than a point on a line represents the Y-axis value for each X-axis value. Unlike the line graph that shows a continuous transition from one point to the next, the bar graph emphasizes the magnitude of the value it represents.

We will discuss three types of bar graphs: simple bar graphs, side-by-side bar graphs, and stack-bar graphs. The following examples change the preceding line graphs to bar graphs. The range settings, titles, and legends remain the same.

Simple Bar Graphs

A **simple bar graph** has a single bar for each value in the X range. The graph settings for a bar graph are similar to those for a line graph. Let's create the bar graph in Figure 5-16. It is a bar graph of the same data used earlier for the line graph shown in Figure 5-9. Recall that the line graph showed the trend in total sales for the four quarters.

FIGURE 5-16
A simple bar chart is useful for comparing and showing trends.

Using a Named Graph   The first step in creating the bar graph is to assign the line graph settings stored under the graph name LINE as the current graph. Therefore, with the Graph menu on the screen, type the letters N for Name and U for Use. 1-2-3 displays an alphabetized list of all the graph names associated with the worksheet PROJS-5A—LINE, MULTLINE, PIE, and SCATTER. With the menu pointer on the name LINE, press the Enter key. The line graph shown earlier in Figure 5-9 immediately displays on the screen. Press any key on the keyboard and the Graph menu reappears. The graph settings for the line graph (LINE) now represent the current graph.

Changing the Line Graph to a Bar Graph   With the Graph menu on the screen, type the letters T for Type and B for Bar. The current graph is now a bar graph, rather than a line graph. To improve the appearance of the bar graph and make it easier to read, add a horizontal grid. Type the letter O for Options. With the Graph Options menu displayed, type the letters G for Grid and H for Horizontal. Quit the Graph Options menu by typing the letter Q for Quit.

Viewing the Simple Bar Graph   Type the letter V for View. The simple bar graph shown in Figure 5-16 displays on the screen. Notice that it gives a more static view of the total sales for each quarter as compared to the line graph in Figure 5-9. The horizontal grid in the simple bar graph makes it easier to recognize the magnitude of the bars that are not adjacent to the Y axis. When you are finished viewing the graph, press any key on the keyboard. The Graph menu reappears on the screen.

Naming, Saving, and Printing the Simple Bar Graph   To name the simple bar graph, type the letters N for Name and C for Create. Enter the graph name BAR and press the Enter key. Type the letter Q to quit the Graph menu. Use the command /File Save (/FS) to save the worksheet to disk. Press the Enter key when the file name PROJS-5A appears on the input line. Next, press the letter R to replace PROJS-5A on disk with the latest version. Now there are five graphs associated with the worksheet—PIE, LINE, MULTLINE, SCATTER, and BAR.

    Save the simple bar graph as a PIC file by entering the command /Graph Save (/GS). When 1-2-3 requests a file name, enter BAR-5A and press the Enter key. Use PrintGraph to print the bar graph.

Side-by-Side Bar Graphs

Like a line graph, a bar graph can have from one to six independent bars (data ranges) for each value in the X range. When a bar graph has more than one bar per X value, we call it a **side-by-side bar graph** (Figure 5-17). This type of graph is primarily used to compare data. For example, you might want to compare the sales in each quarter for Oakland to the sales of the rest of the cities.

Using a Named Graph   To create a side-by-side bar graph, let's assign the graph name MULTLINE as the current graph. With the menu pointer in the Graph menu, type the letters N for Name and U for Use. When the list of named graphs display on the screen, select the name MULTLINE and press the Enter key. The multiple-line graph displays on the screen and is assigned to the worksheet as the current graph. Press any key to redisplay the Graph menu.

Changing the Multiple-Line Graph to a Side-by-Side Bar Graph   Change the current graph from a multiple-line graph to a side-by-side bar graph by typing the letters T for Type and B for Bar. All the other graph settings (A–F ranges, titles, and legends) remain the same. Add the horizontal grid, as we did earlier with the simple bar graph, by typing the letters O for Options, G for Grid, and H for Horizontal. Quit the Graph Options menu by typing the letter Q.

Viewing the Side-by-Side Bar Graph   Type the letter V for View. The side-by-side bar graph shown in Figure 5-17 displays on the screen. The different shading that you see for each bar (data range) is automatically done by 1-2-3. The legends below the graph indicate which shaded bar corresponds to which city. Compare Figure 5-17 to Figure 5-13. The side-by-side bar graph is much easier to interpret than the multiple-line graph. For example, it is clear that Oakland had the greatest sales during the first three quarters. For the fourth quarter, Oakland had about the same sales as Tampa. After viewing the graph, press any key to redisplay the Graph menu.

Graph Settings

Type:	Bar	A legend:	Chgo
X Range:	B4..E4	B legend:	Tampa
A Range:	B6..E6	C legend:	Atl
B Range:	B7..E7	D legend:	Dal
C Range:	B8..E8	E legend:	Bos
D Range:	B9..E9	F legend:	Oak
E Range:	B10..E10	X axis:	All Cities
F Range:	B11..E11	Y axis:	Dollar Sales
Grid:	Horiz	Name:	SIDEBAR
Title 1:	\C1		
Title 2:	\C2		

FIGURE 5-17
A side-by-side bar graph allows you to compare the sales in each city on a quarterly basis.

Naming, Saving, and Printing the Side-by-Side Bar Graph   With the Graph menu on the screen, type the letters N for Name and C for Create to name the side-by-side bar graph. Enter the graph name SIDEBAR and press the Enter key. Next, type the letter Q to quit the Graph menu.

Use the command /File Save (/FS) to save the worksheet to disk. Press the Enter key when the file name PROJS-5A appears on the input line. Finally, type the letter R for Replace. Now there are six graphs associated with the worksheet—PIE, LINE, MULTLINE, SCATTER, BAR, and SIDEBAR.

With the worksheet on the screen, enter the command /Graph Save (/GS) to save the side-by-side bar graph as a PIC file. Use the file name MBAR-5A. Quit 1-2-3 and load PrintGraph into main memory. Type the letter I for Image-Select and highlight MBAR-5A. Press the Enter key and the PrintGraph menu redisplays. Type the letters A for Align and G for Go. The side-by-side bar graph shown in Figure 5-17 prints on the printer.

Stack-Bar Graphs

One of the problems with the side-by-side bar graph in Figure 5-17 is that it does not show the combined total sales for the six cities for any quarter. An alternative graph to consider is the stack-bar graph. A **stack-bar graph** has a single bar for every value in the X range (Figure 5-18). Each bar is made up of shaded segments. Each segment or piece of the total bar represents an element (city) as a distinct contributor. Together, the stacked segments make up a single bar that shows the cumulative amount (total quarterly sales) of all elements for each value in the X range (quarter).

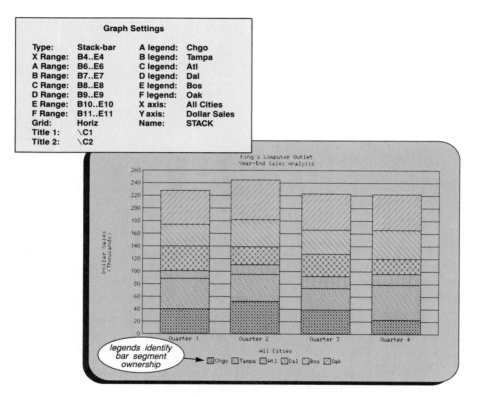

Graph Settings			
Type:	Stack-bar	A legend:	Chgo
X Range:	B4..E4	B legend:	Tampa
A Range:	B6..E6	C legend:	Atl
B Range:	B7..E7	D legend:	Dal
C Range:	B8..E8	E legend:	Bos
D Range:	B9..E9	F legend:	Oak
E Range:	B10..E10	X axis:	All Cities
F Range:	B11..E11	Y axis:	Dollar Sales
Grid:	Horiz	Name:	STACK
Title 1:	\C1		
Title 2:	\C2		

FIGURE 5-18 A stack-bar graph allows you to compare the sales in each city on a quarterly basis. It also shows the total sales for each quarter.

Changing the Side-by-Side Bar Graph to a Stack-Bar Graph   The side-by-side bar graph is still the current graph associated with the worksheet. Therefore, let's modify it to display the stack-bar graph shown in Figure 5-18. With the Graph menu on the screen, enter the command **Type Stack-bar (TS)**. This command changes the side-by-side bar graph (Figure 5-17) to a stack-bar graph (Figure 5-18). All the other side-by-side bar graph settings (A–F ranges, titles, horizontal grid, and legends) remain the same for the stack-bar graph.

Viewing the Stack-Bar Graph   Type the letter V for View. The stack-bar graph shown in Figure 5-18 displays on the screen. Compare Figure 5-18 to Figure 5-17. Notice how the stack-bar graph shows both the quarterly contributions of each city and the total sales for each quarter. The stack-bar graph is an effective way of showing trends and contributions from all segments, while still showing a total for each quarter.

Naming, Saving, and Printing the Stack-Bar Graph   With the stack-bar graph still on the screen, press any key to redisplay the Graph menu. Type the letters N for Name and C for Create to name the stack-bar graph. Enter the graph name STACK and press the Enter key. Quit the Graph menu by typing the letter Q.

Save the worksheet to disk. Enter the command **/File Save** (/FS). Press the Enter key when the file name PROJS-5A appears on the input line. Press the letter R for Replace. Now there are seven graphs associated with the worksheet—PIE, LINE, MULTLINE, SCATTER, BAR, SIDEBAR, and STACK.

Save the stack-bar graph as a PIC file by entering the command **/Graph Save** (/GS). Use the file name SBAR-5A. Finally, use PrintGraph to print the stack-bar graph.

ADDITIONAL GRAPH OPTIONS

Three graph options that we did not cover in this project are the Data-Labels, Scale, and Color/B&W commands.

Data-Labels

Data-labels are used to explicitly label a bar or a point in a graph. Select the actual values in the range that the bar or point represents. 1-2-3 then positions the labels near the corresponding points or bars in the graph (Figure 5-19).

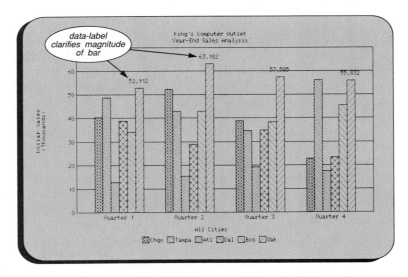

FIGURE 5-19   Data-labels are useful for clarifying and emphasizing various segments of the graph.

To illustrate the use of data-labels, make the SIDEBAR graph settings the current graph by entering the command **/Graph Name Use** (/GNU). When the alphabetized list of named graphs display on the screen (Figure 5-20), use the Down Arrow key to select SIDEBAR and press the Enter key. 1-2-3 immediately displays the side-by-side bar graph shown in Figure 5-17. Press any key on the keyboard and the Graph menu reappears on the screen.

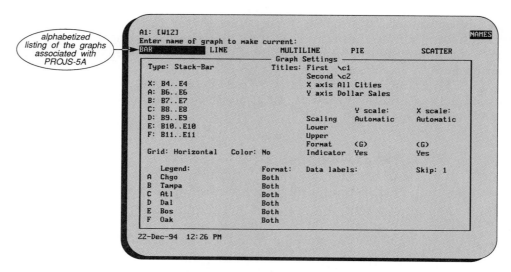

FIGURE 5-20 Directory of named graphs associated with the worksheet PROJS-5A—enter the command /Graph Name Use (/GNU).

Let's emphasize the four bars in Figure 5-17 that represent the quarterly sales for Oakland by displaying the actual quarterly sales above each corresponding bar. Enter the command **Options Data-Labels** (OD). This command causes the Data Labels menu to display.

Type the letter F to select the F range because it was assigned the range representing the four quarterly sales for Oakland. The worksheet reappears on the screen and 1-2-3 responds with the prompt message "Enter data label for F range data: A1". Type the range B11..E11 and press the Enter key. The range B11..E11 contains the four quarterly sales for Oakland. Therefore, select the same range for the F data-label that was selected earlier for the F range.

After you press the Enter key, 1-2-3 prompts you to enter the desired position of the data-labels in the graph. A response to this prompt is only possible for line and XY graphs. For simple and side-by-side bar graphs, 1-2-3 automatically positions data-labels above each bar. Hence, press the Enter key. Next, type the letter Q twice, once to quit the Data-Labels section of the Graph Options menu and once to quit the Graph Options menu. Finally, type the letter V for View. The modified side-by-side bar graph in Figure 5-19 displays on the screen. Notice how the data-labels above the four bars representing Oakland emphasize and clarify them in the graph.

Press any key to redisplay the Graph menu. Type the letter Q to quit the Graph menu. The worksheet shown earlier in Figure 5-1 reappears on the screen.

Scale Command

When you build a graph, 1-2-3 automatically adjusts the graph to include all points in each data range. The Scale command in the Graph Options menu may be used to override 1-2-3 and manually set the scale on the X or Y axis or both. This command may also be used to specify the display of labels on the X axis and to format the numbers that mark the X and Y axes.

Color/B&W Commands

If your monitor can display colors, the Color command in the Graph Options menu causes bars, lines, and symbols to display in contrasting colors. Alternatively, the B&W command causes the bar and stack-bar graphs to have cross-hatched patterns. The Color and B&W commands are mutually exclusive.

XY GRAPHS

◆ XY graphs differ from the graphs we have discussed thus far. Rather than graphing the magnitude of a value at a fixed point on the X axis, an **XY graph** plots points of the form (x,y), where x is the X-axis coordinate and y is the Y-axis coordinate. Adjacent points are connected by a line to form the graph (Figure 5-21). The XY graph is the type of graph used to plot mathematical functions.

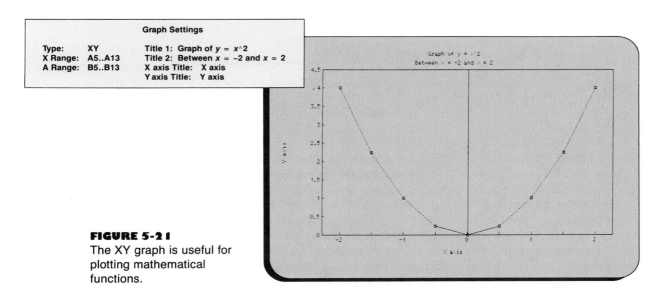

FIGURE 5-21
The XY graph is useful for plotting mathematical functions.

In an XY graph, both the X and Y axes are automatically scaled relative to the low and high values, so that all (x,y) points display and the graph fits on the screen. You can switch to manual scaling and scale either the X or Y axis yourself by using the Scale command in the Graph Options menu.

To illustrate an XY graph, we will use the worksheet in Figure 5-22. As the title indicates, this worksheet includes a table of x and y coordinates for the function $y = x^2$. The x coordinates are in the range A5..A13. They begin at –2 and end at 2 in increments of 0.5. The x coordinates are formed in the worksheet by using the Data Fill command. The y coordinates are determined by assigning the formula +A5^2 to cell B5 and then copying B5 to the range B6..B13. Enter the worksheet in Figure 5-22 by following the first six steps in the Summary of Keystrokes—PROJS-5B in the Project Summary at the end of this project.

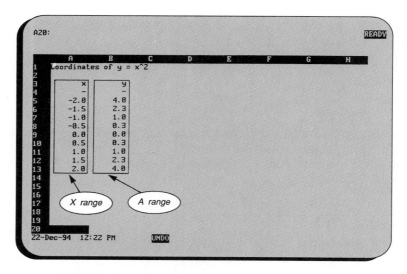

FIGURE 5-22 The worksheet we will use to plot the function $y = x^2$.

To plot the function $y = x^2$ in the form of an XY graph, enter the command /Graph **T**ype **XY** (/GTX). Next, type the letter X to define the X range. Assign the X range the x coordinates (cells A5 through A13). Type the letter A to define the A range. Assign the A range the y coordinates (cells B5 through B13).

To complete the XY graph, let's enhance it using the Graph Options menu. Enter Graph of y = x^2 on the first line of the title and enter Between x = -2 and x = 2 on the second line. Enter the X-axis label X axis and the Y-axis label Y axis. Type the letter Q to quit the Graph Options menu.

With the menu pointer in the Graph menu, type the letter V for View. The XY graph shown in Figure 5-21 displays on the screen. To return to the Graph menu after viewing the graph, press any key on the keyboard.

Quit the Graph menu and save the worksheet shown in Figure 5-22 as PROJS-5B. Print the XY graph in Figure 5-21 by saving it as a PIC file using the file name XYGRAPH.PIC. Finally, quit 1-2-3 and use PrintGraph to print the XY graph.

ADDING A GRAPH TO THE WORKSHEET USING ALLWAYS

In the previous sections we printed the graph independent of the worksheet by using PrintGraph. In this section we will demonstrate how to use the add-in program Allways to place a graph alongside the data in a worksheet, and how to print the graph and data in the same report. Allways allows you to add up to 20 graphs in a worksheet and you can place them wherever you like. Once a graph is part of the worksheet, you can enhance its appearance by resizing it, shading its background, changing the graph title to a larger font, or drawing a box around the graph. To illustrate how to add a graph to the worksheet, we will place the graph of $y = x^2$ next to the table of coordinates in the worksheet as shown in Figure 5-23.

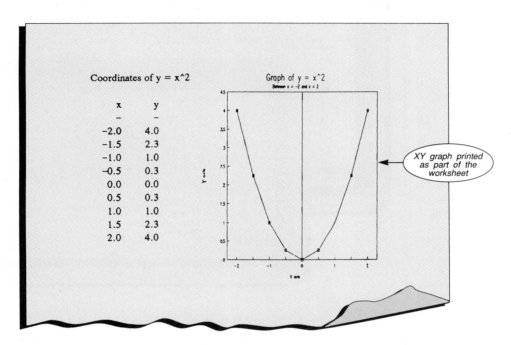

FIGURE 5-23 The XY graph is included in the worksheet through the use of the Allways command **/G**raph **A**dd (/GA).

Starting Allways

With the worksheet in Figure 5-22 on the screen and the XY graph saved under the name XYGRAPH.PIC, enter the command /Add-In Invoke (/AI). Select the add-in program Allways and press the Enter key. The worksheet with the table of coordinates shown earlier in Figure 5-21 displays on the screen in graphics form, rather than in text form.

Adding the Graph to the Worksheet

Enter the Allways command /Graph (/G). The Graph menu displays as shown in the top screen of Figure 5-24. Type the letter A for Add. Allways displays a list of the PIC files on the default drive. Select XYGRAPH and press the Enter key. Allways prompts you to enter the range of cells where you want the graph to appear in the worksheet. Enter the range D1..H13 and press the Enter key. Allways responds by crosshatching the range to indicate where the graph will display (bottom screen of Figure 5-24).

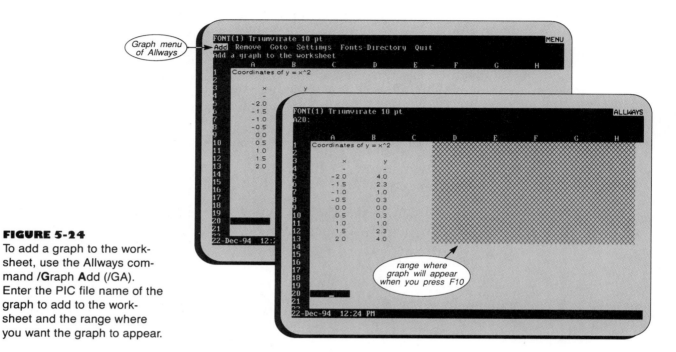

FIGURE 5-24

To add a graph to the worksheet, use the Allways command /Graph Add (/GA). Enter the PIC file name of the graph to add to the worksheet and the range where you want the graph to appear.

Press the F10 key to display the graph (Figure 5-25), rather than the crosshatched design. The F10 key serves as a toggle key. Press it once and the graph appears in the specified range. Press it again and the crosshatched design appears in place of the graph. The advantage of displaying the crosshatched design in the range is that Allways redisplays the worksheet faster when you are enhancing it because Allways does not have to continually redraw the graph.

FIGURE 5-25

Press the F10 key to display the XYGRAPH.PIC graph in the specified range of the worksheet.

Compare the graph in Figure 5-25 to the one in Figure 5-21. Notice that Allways automatically sizes the graph in Figure 5-25 so that it fits in the specified range.

Before printing the worksheet, let's change the table of coordinates font to Times 14 point and resize the graph.

Changing the Font

Press the Home key to move the cell pointer to A1. Enter the Allways command **/F**ormat **F**ont (/FF). Select Times 14 point from the menu of fonts. Press the Enter key. Next, select the entire table of coordinates (A1..B13) and press the Enter key. The table of coordinates display in Times 14-point font as shown in Figure 5-26.

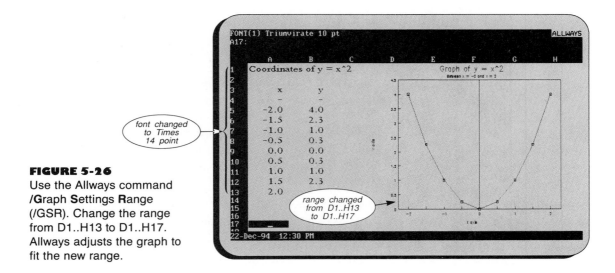

font changed to Times 14 point

range changed from D1..H13 to D1..H17

FIGURE 5-26
Use the Allways command **/G**raph **S**ettings **R**ange (/GSR). Change the range from D1..H13 to D1..H17. Allways adjusts the graph to fit the new range.

Resizing the Graph

Once the graph displays in the worksheet, you can resize it by increasing or decreasing the graph range. Enter the command **/G**raph **S**ettings (/GS). Allways prompts you to enter the name of the graph you want to adjust. Select XYGRAPH from the list. Next, type the letter R for Range. Allways highlights the old range (D1..H13) and prompts you to enter the new range. Enter the range D1..H17 and press the Enter key. Finally, type the letter Q to return to ALLWAYS mode. Allways immediately adjusts the graph to fit the new range as shown in Figure 5-26. Compare Figure 5-26 to Figure 5-25 and notice the difference in the graph sizes.

Printing the Worksheet with the Graph

To print the worksheet (table of coordinates and graph), enter the Allways command **/P**rint **R**ange **S**et (/PRS). Select the range A1..H17 and press the Enter key. Check to be sure the printer is ready. Type the letter G for Go. The worksheet containing both the table of coordinates and the graph prints on the printer as shown earlier in Figure 5-23.

If an "Out of Memory" message appears on the status line at the bottom of the screen, return control to 1-2-3 and save the worksheet. After the worksheet is saved, return control to Allways and issue the print command again. If the worksheet still fails to print, return control to 1-2-3 and enter the command **/W**orksheet **G**lobal **D**efault **O**ther **U**ndo **D**isable (/WGDOUD) to disable the UNDO command. After disabling the UNDO command, return control to Allways and issue the print command again.

Saving the Worksheet

To preserve the graph in the worksheet, use 1-2-3 to save it to disk. Use the Allways command **/Q**uit (/Q). Enter the 1-2-3 command **/F**ile **S**ave **R**eplace (/FSR). 1-2-3 saves the worksheet as PROJS-5B.WK1 and the corresponding Allways format changes as PROJS-5B.ALL.

The next time the worksheet is loaded into main memory and displayed using Allways, the graph will appear as part of the worksheet.

The Graph Commands

To add or modify a graph in a worksheet, enter the Allways command /Graph (/G). The Graph menu shown in the top screen of Figure 5-24 displays. Table 5-4 summarizes the function of each of the commands in the Graph menu.

TABLE 5-4 A Summary of Commands in the Allways Graph Menu

COMMAND	FUNCTION
Add	Adds a graph to the worksheet.
Remove	Erases a graph from the worksheet.
Goto	Moves the cell pointer to the specified graph.
Settings	Specifies fonts, scaling, colors, margins, and graph replacement.
Fonts-Directory	Defines the directory where the graph fonts are located.
Quit	Quits the Graph command.

The command /Graph Settings (/GS) displays the Graph Settings menu. This menu is primarily used to enhance the appearance of the graph in the worksheet. Table 5-5 summarizes the commands available in the Graph Settings menu.

TABLE 5-5 A Summary of Commands in the Allways Graph Settings Menu

COMMAND	FUNCTION
PIC-File	Replaces a graph in the worksheet with another graph.
Fonts	Sets fonts for text in graphs.
Scale	Sets the scaling factor for fonts.
Colors	Sets colors for the graph data ranges.
Range	Resizes the graph or moves it to another area of the worksheet.
Margins	Sets margins for the graph.
Default	Restores the default graph settings.
Quit	Returns control to ALLWAYS mode.

PROJECT SUMMARY

In this project we created several graphs. All the activities that you learned for the projects are summarized in the Quick Reference following the Appendix. The following is a summary of the keystroke sequence we used in Project 5.

SUMMARY OF KEYSTROKES — PROJS-5A
(Figure 5-1 and Associated Graphs)

STEPS	KEY(S) PRESSED	RESULTS
1	/WGC12↵ (Build worksheet)	Sets width of all columns to 12.
2	→ →King's Computer Outlet↓	Enters line 1 of report title in row 1.
3	Year-End Sales Analysis→ → →↑	Enters line 2 of report title in row 2.
4	@NOW↵	Enters @NOW function in F1.
5	/RFD1↵	Formats F1 to Date 1.
6	↓↓"Total↵	Enters line 1 of column headings in F3.
7	F5 A4↵City→ "Quarter 1→ "Quarter 2→	Enters first part of line 2 of column headings in row 4.
8	"Quarter 3→ "Quarter 4→ "Sales↵	Enters second part of line 2 of column headings in row 4.
9	F5 A5↵\ = ↵/C↵.→ → → → → ↵	Underlines column titles.
10	↓Chicago→40135→52345→38764→22908↵	Enters Chicago sales in row 6.
11	F5 A7↵Tampa→48812→42761→34499→56123↵	Enters Tampa sales in row 7.
12	F5 A8↵Atlanta→12769→15278→19265→17326↵	Enters Atlanta sales in row 8.
13	F5 A9↵Dallas→38713→29023→34786→23417↵	Enters Dallas sales in row 9.
14	F5 A10↵Boston→34215→42864→38142→45375↵	Enters Boston sales in row 10.
15	F5 A11↵Oakland→52912→63182→57505→55832↵	Enters Oakland sales in row 11.
16	F5 A12↵\-↵/C↵.→ → → → → ↵	Underlines sales.
17	F5 F6↵@SUM(B6.E6)↵	Sums B6..E6 in F6.
18	/C↵.↓↓↓↓↓↵	Copies F6 to F6..F11.
19	F5 A13↵Total→	Enters row title in A13.
20	@SUM(B6.B11)↵	Sums B6..B11 in B13.
21	/C↵.→ → → →↵	Copies B13 to B13..F13.
22	/RF,0↵B6.F13↵ HOME	Sets format of B6..F13 to Comma (,) and moves cursor to A1.
23	/FSPROJS-5A↵	Saves worksheet as PROJS-5A.
24	/GTP (Build pie chart)	Selects pie chart.
25	AF6.F11↵	Defines A range as F6..F11.
26	XA6.A11↵Q	Defines X range as A6..A11 and quits Graph command.
27	F5 F15↵1↓2↓3↓4↓5↓106↵	Enters values in F15..F20 to crosshatch and explode pie chart.
28	/GBF15.F20↵	Defines B range as F15..F20.
29	OTFKing's Computer Outlet↵	Enters first title line to pie chart.
30	TSYear-End Sales Analysis↵Q	Enters second title line to pie chart.
31	V	Views pie chart.
32	↵NCPIE↵Q	Assigns pie chart characteristics to the graph name PIE and quits Graph command.
33	/FS↵R	Saves worksheet with PIE as PROJS-5A.

(continued)

SUMMARY OF KEYSTROKES — PROJS-5A (continued)
(Figure 5-1 and Associated Graphs)

STEPS	KEY(S) PRESSED		RESULTS
34	/GS		Initiates saving a snapshot image of the pie graph.
35	PIE-5A ↵		Enters PIC file name PIE-5A.PIC.
36	RG	(Build line graph)	Resets current graph settings.
37	TL		Selects line graph.
38	XB4.E4 ↵		Defines X range as B4..E4.
39	AB13.E13 ↵		Defines A range as B13..E13.
40	OTF\C1↵TS\C2↵		Enters first and second title lines to line graph.
41	TXAll Cities ↵TYDollar Sales ↵Q		Enters x-axis and y-axis titles to line graph.
42	V		Views line graph.
43	↵NCLINE↵Q		Assigns line graph characteristics to the graph name LINE and quits Graph command.
44	/FS↵R		Saves worksheet with PIE and LINE as PROJS-5A.
45	/GSLINE-5A ↵		Saves a snapshot image of the line graph as LINE-5A.PIC.
46	AB6.E6 ↵	(Build multiple-line graph)	Changes A range to B6..E6.
47	BB7.E7 ↵		Defines B range as B7..E7.
48	CB8.E8 ↵		Defines C range as B8..E8.
49	DB9.E9 ↵		Defines D range as B9..E9.
50	EB10.E10 ↵		Defines E range as B10..E10.
51	FB11.E11 ↵		Defines F range as B11..E11.
52	OLAChgo↵LBTampa↵LCAtl↵		Defines A, B, and C legends.
53	LDDal↵LEBos↵LFOak↵Q		Defines D, E, and F legends.
54	V		Views multiple-line graphs.
55	↵NCMULTLINE↵Q		Assigns multiple-line graph characteristics to the graph name MULTLINE and quits Graph command.
56	/FS↵R		Saves worksheet with PIE, LINE, and MULTLINE as PROJS-5A.
57	/GSMLINE-5A ↵		Saves a snapshot image of the multiple-line graph as MLINE5A.PIC.
58	OFGSQQ	(Build scatter graph)	Changes multiple-line graph to scatter graph.
59	V		Views scatter graph.

SUMMARY OF KEYSTROKES — PROJS-5A (continued)
(Figure 5-1 and Associated Graphs)

STEPS	KEY(S) PRESSED		RESULTS
60	←NCSCATTER←Q		Assigns scatter graph characteristics to the graph name SCATTER and quits Graph command.
61	/FS←R		Saves worksheet with PIE, LINE, MULTLINE, and SCATTER as PROJS-5A.
62	/GSSCAT-5A←		Saves a snapshot image of the multiple-line graph as SCAT5A.PIC.
63	NU→←	(Build simple bar graph)	Selects LINE graph characteristics.
64	←TB		Selects bar graph.
65	OGHQ		Selects horizontal grid.
66	V		Views scatter graph.
67	←NCBAR←Q		Assigns bar graph characteristics to the graph name BAR and quits Graph command.
68	/FS←R		Saves worksheet with PIE, LINE, MULTLINE, SCATTER, and BAR as PROJS-5A.
69	/GSBAR-5A←		Saves a snapshot image of the multiple-line graph as BAR5A.PIC.
70	NUMULTLINE←	(Build side-by-side bar graph)	Selects MULTLINE graph characteristics.
71	←TB		Selects bar graph.
72	OGHQ		Selects horizontal grid.
73	V		Views side-by-side bar graph.
74	←NCSIDEBAR←Q		Assigns side-by-side bar graph characteristics to the graph name SIDEBAR and quits Graph command.
75	/FS←R		Saves worksheet with PIE, LINE, MULTLINE, SCATTER, BAR, and SIDEBAR as PROJS-5A.
76	/GSMBAR-5A←		Saves a snapshot image of the side-by-side bar graph as MBAR5A.PIC.
77	TS	(Build stack-bar graph)	Selects stack-bar graph.
78	V		Views stack-bar graph.
79	←NCSTACK←Q		Assigns stack-bar graph characteristics to the graph name STACK and quits Graph command.
80	/FS←R		Saves worksheet with PIE, LINE, MULTLINE, SCATTER, BAR, SIDEBAR, and STACK as PROJS-5A.
81	/GSSBAR-5A←		Saves a snapshot image of the stack-bar graph as SBAR-5A.PIC.

SUMMARY OF KEYSTROKES — PROJS-5B
(Figures 5-21 through 5-26)

STEPS	KEY(S) PRESSED	RESULTS
1	/WEY	Erases current worksheet.
2	Coordinates of y = x^2↓↓	Enters table title in A1.
3	"x → "y↓"-←"-↓	Enters column titles in A3..B4.
4	/DFA5.A13←-2←0.5←←	Generates numbers –2 through 2 in A5..A13.
5	→ +A5^2←/C←B6.B13←	Enters +A5^2 in B5 and copies B5 to B6..B13.
6	/RFF1←A5.B13←	Formats A5..B13 to Fixed.
7	/GTX (Start XY graph)	Selects XY chart.
8	XA5.A13←	Defines X range as A5..A13.
9	AB5.B13←	Defines A range as B5..B13.
10	OTFGraph of y = x^2←	Enters first title line to XY graph.
11	TSBetween x = -2 and x = 2←	Enters second title line to XY graph.
12	TXX axis←	Enters x-axis title to XY graph.
13	TYY axis←Q	Enters y-axis to XY graph.
14	V	Views XY graph.
15	←Q/FSPROJS-5B←	Quits Graph command and saves worksheet with XY graph characteristics as PROJS-5B.
16	/GSXYGRAPH←Q	Saves a snapshot image of the XY graph as XYGRAPH.PIC.
17	/AIALLWAYS←	Invokes ALLWAYS.
18	/GAXYGRAPH←D1.H13←Q F10	Adds XY graph to worksheet in range D1..H13. Quits Graph command and displays XY graph rather than crosshatched design.
19	/FF↓↓↓↓↓↓←A1.B13←	Enters Times 14-point font to A1..B13.
20	/GS←RD1.H17←Q	Resizes the XY graph using the range D1..H17.
21	/PRSA1.H17←G	Prints the worksheet with the XY graph.
22	/Q	Returns control to 1-2-3.
23	/FSR	Saves the worksheet with the Allways settings as PROJS-5B.
24	/Q	Returns control to DOS.

The following list summarizes the material covered in Project 5.

1. 1-2-3 allows you to create, display, and print a graph of the data in your worksheet and get your message across in a dramatic pictorial fashion.
2. The first step in drawing a graph is to enter the command /**Graph** (/G). This command activates the menu pointer in the Graph menu.
3. A **pie chart** is used to show how 100% of an amount is divided.
4. With a pie chart, you are allowed only three ranges. The A range specifies the data that is used to segment the pie. The X range is assigned the range of labels that identify the segments. The B range is used to shade and explode segments of the pie chart.
5. The type of graph, the ranges in the worksheet to graph, graph titles, and graph options are called the **graph settings**. They display on the graph settings sheet when the Graph menu is active.
6. The **current graph** is the one that displays when you enter the command /**Graph View** (/GV).
7. An **exploded pie chart** is one in which one or more segments are offset or slightly removed from the main portion of the pie so that they stand out.

8. Through the Graph Options menu, you can assign two title lines of 39 characters each to identify the graph. Except on the pie chart, you may also add titles up to 39 characters each for the X axis and Y axis. Titles may be entered by keying in the title or by keying in a cell address preceded by a backslash (\).

9. When numbers are changed in a worksheet, the current graph will reflect the changes the next time it is displayed.

10. The command **/Graph Name Create** (/GNC) can be used to store the current graph settings under a name. This allows you to have more than one set of graph settings associated with a worksheet. To assign a named set of graph settings as the current graph, use the command **/Graph Name Use** (/GNU).

11. To save any named graph settings to disk, you must save the worksheet. Use the **/File Save** (/FS) command.

12. The command **/Graph Reset** (/GR) allows you to reset all the current graph settings or any individual ones.

13. Printing a graph is a three-step process: first, save the graph to disk as a PIC file; second, quit 1-2-3; and third, use the PrintGraph program (PGRAPH) to print the graph. A **PIC file** is a snapshot of the graph saved.

14. **Line graphs** are used to show trends. You can have from one to six lines drawn in the graph. Each line represents a different data range (A through F) in the worksheet.

15. In a line graph, assign the labels for the X axis to the X range and assign the data ranges to the A through F ranges.

16. When more than one line is assigned to a line graph, it is called a **multiple-line graph**. Multiple-line graphs are used to show trends and comparisons.

17. The Group command in the Graph menu allows you to assign multiple data ranges when the ranges are located in consecutive rows or columns.

18. To identify the lines in a multiple-line graph, use the Legends command in the Graph Options menu.

19. A **scatter graph** displays the points in a graph without any connecting lines.

20 To create a scatter graph, follow the steps for a multiple-line graph. Next, through the Graph Options menu, use the Format Graph Symbols command to draw the symbols and delete the connecting lines.

21. A **bar graph** is used to show trends and comparisons.

22. A **simple bar graph** has a single bar (A range) for each value in the X range.

23. To add a horizontal grid to a graph, display the Graph Options menu and type the letters G for Grid and H for Horizontal.

24. A **side-by-side bar graph** is used to compare multiple data ranges. A side-by-side bar graph may have up to six bars per X-range value.

25. A **stack-bar** graph shows one bar per X-range value. However, the bar shows both the sum of the parts and the individual contributors.

26. Data-labels are used to explicitly label a bar or point in a graph. You may label any of the six data ranges A through F.

27. 1-2-3 automatically scales the Y axis for bar and line graphs and the X and Y axes for XY graphs. If you prefer to set the scales manually, use the Scale command in the Graph Options menu.

28. The Color and B&W commands in the Graph Options menu are used to display graphs in color or in black and white.

29. **XY graphs** are used to plot mathematical functions. In an XY graph the X range is assigned the X-axis values and the A range is assigned the Y-axis values.

30. The add-in program Allways allows you to place a graph alongside the data in a worksheet and to print the graph and data in the same report.

31. Allways allows you to add up to 20 graphs to a worksheet.

32. To add a graph to the worksheet, first use the 1-2-3 command **/Graph Save** (/GS) to save the graph as a PIC file. Next, use the Allways command **/Graph Add** (/GA) to add the graph to the worksheet.

33. Once the graph is part of the worksheet, use the F10 key to toggle between displaying the graph and the cross-hatched design in the range.

34. To resize the graph in the worksheet, use the command **/Graph Settings Range** (/GSR).

STUDENT ASSIGNMENTS

STUDENT ASSIGNMENT 1: True/False

Instructions: Circle T if the statement is true and F if the statement is false.

T F 1. The PrintGraph program is used to print WK1 files.
T F 2. A PIC file contains a worksheet.
T F 3. The Save command in the Graph Options menu saves a snapshot of the current graph.
T F 4. A line graph is used to show a trend.
T F 5. A line graph can have at most from one to four lines.
T F 6. To store the graph settings assigned to a worksheet under a name, save the worksheet using the Save command in the Graph menu.
T F 7. A pie chart can have from one to six data ranges.
T F 8. The X range is used to shade the segments of a pie chart.
T F 9. Data-labels are used to clarify a bar or a point in a graph.
T F 10. Legends are used to identify the bars and lines in a graph.
T F 11. If the title for a graph is the same as a label in a cell of the corresponding worksheet, enter the cell address preceded by a backslash (\) for the title.
T F 12. Multiple-line graphs are used to show trends and comparisons.
T F 13. The XY command in the Graph Type menu is used to display a bar graph.
T F 14. 1-2-3 automatically scales the axes in a graph unless you use the Scale command in the Graph Options menu.
T F 15. A stack-bar graph differs from a side-by-side bar graph in that it shows the combined total of the contributors.
T F 16. Side-by-side bar graphs are used to compare data ranges for the same period.
T F 17. A scatter graph shows a random sample of points in the graph.
T F 18. Once a graph is part of a worksheet, it can be moved to another range, resized, or deleted from the worksheet.
T F 19. The Reset command in the Graph Options menu allows you to reset individual graph specifications, like the ranges A through F.
T F 20. A graph must be saved as a PIC file before it can be added to the worksheet using the add-in program Allways.

STUDENT ASSIGNMENT 2: Multiple Choice

Instructions: Circle the correct response.

1. A side-by-side bar graph can have up to _____ bars per value in the X range.
   a. 3   b. 5   c. 6   d. 8
2. A line graph is used to show _____ .
   a. how 100% of an amount is divided   c. how two or more data ranges compare
   b. trends   d. none of these
3. Which of the following ranges are meaningless for a pie chart?
   a. X   b. A   c. B   d. C through F
4. Which of the following types of graphs can you draw with 1-2-3?
   a. line   b. bar   c. pie   d. XY   e. all of these
5. Which one of the following commands in the Graph menu displays the current graph?
   a. View   b. Type   c. Save   d. both a and b
6. In a stack-bar graph each bar shows _____ .
   a. the total amount for a label in the X range   c. none of these
   b. the contribution of each participant   d. both a and b

7. To explode a segment of a pie chart, add _____ to the corresponding cell in the _____ range.
   a. 100, C   b. 10, B   c. 1000, A   d. none of these
8. Data-labels are used to _____ .
   a. assign a title to the graph
   b. define which bar or line belongs to which data range
   c. clarify points and bars in a graph
   d. scale the X and Y axes

STUDENT ASSIGNMENT 3: Understanding Graph Commands

Instructions: Describe the function of each of the following 1-2-3 commands.

a. /G _____
b. /GRG _____
c. /GNU _____
d. /GO _____
e. /GTB _____
f. /GTP _____
g. /GOTF _____
h. /GRXQ _____
i. /GS _____
j. /GV _____
k. /GQ _____
l. /GND _____
m. /GTS _____
n. /GNC _____
o. /GOL _____
p. /GG _____

STUDENT ASSIGNMENT 4: Understanding the Graph Options

Instructions: Describe the purpose of the following titled sections in the Graph Options menu.

a. DATA-LABELS

Purpose: _____

b. TITLES

Purpose: _____

c. LEGEND

Purpose: _____

d. SCALE

Purpose: _____

e. FORMAT

Purpose: _____

f. GRID

Purpose: _____

g. COLOR

Purpose: _____

h. B&W

Purpose: _____

i. QUIT

Purpose: _____

STUDENT ASSIGNMENT 5: Drawing a Pie Chart

Instructions: Load 1-2-3. Retrieve the worksheet PROJS-2 built in Project 2 (Figure 2-2).

Draw a pie chart that shows the revenue contribution for each month to the total quarterly revenue in the first quarter sales report. The pie chart should resemble the one shown in the following figure. Use these graph settings:

Type = Pie
X range = B2..D2
A range = B4..D4
B range = E4..E6
   (explode the March revenue)
Title 1 = \B1
Title 2 = TOTAL REVENUE

   Save the worksheet with the
graph settings as STUS5-5. Save
the graph as STUSP5-5.PIC. Use
PrintGraph to print the pie chart.

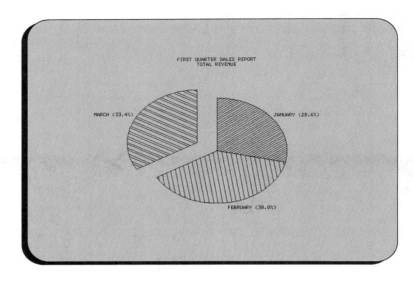

STUDENT ASSIGNMENT 6:   Drawing a Multiple-Line Graph and a Side-by-Side Bar Graph

Instructions: Load 1-2-3. Retrieve the worksheet PROJS-2 built in Project 2 (Figure 2-2). Draw a multiple-line graph and a side-by-side bar graph that show the trends in the revenue, costs, and profit of the first quarter sales report. Use Allways to add graphs to the worksheet and enhance the worksheet's appearance.

Part 1: Draw the multiple-line graph. This graph should resemble the one shown in the following figure. Use these graph settings, and name the multiple-line graph MULTLINE. Save the multiple-line graph as STUSM5-6.PIC. Save the worksheet as STUS5-6. Use PrintGraph to print the multiple-line graph.

Type = Line
X range = B2..D2
A range = B4..D4
B range = B5..D5
C range = B6..D6
Title 1 = \B1
Y-axis title = Dollars
A legend = \A4
B legend = \A5
C legend = \A6

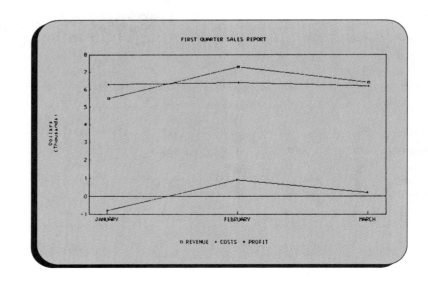

Part 2: Draw a side-by-side bar graph to show the same trends for the first quarter. This graph should resemble the one shown in the following figure. Use the same graph settings given above for the multiple-line graph, and name the graph SIDEBAR. For the side-by-side bar graph, change the Type to Bar. Save the side-by-side bar graph as STUSS5-6.PIC. Save the worksheet as STUS5-6. Use Print-Graph to print the side-by-side bar graph.

Part 3: Add the multiple-line graph and side-by-side graph to the worksheet STUS5-6 as shown in the figure below and to the right. Use Allways to modify the worksheet in the following ways:

1. Increase the width of column A to 15 characters.
2. Change the report title in cell B1 and the totals title in cell A10 to Times 14-point font.
3. Add the multiple-line graph in the range A17..C34.
4. Add the side-by-side graph in the range D17..F34.
5. Print the range A1..F34.

   Return control to 1-2-3 and save the worksheet as STUS5-6.

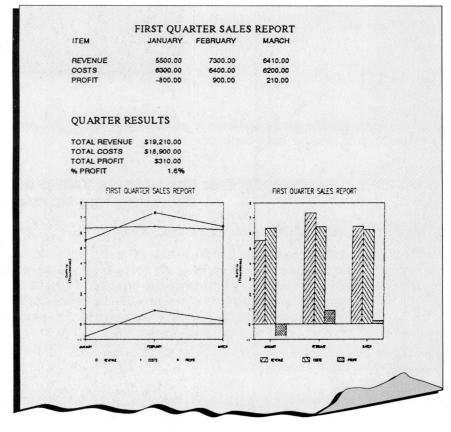

STUDENT ASSIGNMENT 7: Drawing a Stack-Bar Graph

Instructions: Load 1-2-3. Retrieve the worksheet STUS3-10 built in Student Assignment 10 of Project 3.

Draw a stack-bar graph that shows the individual contributions of each expense category and the total estimated expenses for each of the three months. The stack-bar graph should resemble the one shown in the following figure. Use these graph settings:

Type = Stack-bar
X range = B6..C6
A range = B15..C15
B range = B16..C16
C range = B17..C17
D range = B18..C18
Title 1 = Current and Projected Salaries

Y-axis title = Dollars
A legend = Accounting
B legend = Production
C legend = Sales
D legend = Distribution
Grid = Horizontal

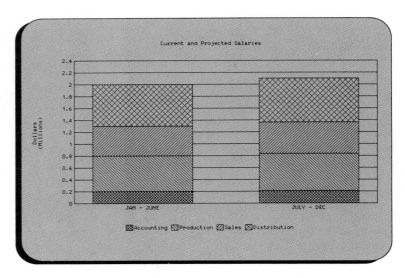

Save the worksheet with the stack-bar graph settings as STUS5-7. Save the stack-bar graph as STUSS5-7.PIC. Use PrintGraph to print the stack-bar graph.

STUDENT ASSIGNMENT 8: Building a Table of Coordinates and Drawing the Corresponding XY Graph

Instructions: Load 1-2-3. Complete Parts 1 and 2 below.

Part 1: Build the table of coordinates for the function $y = 2x^3 + 6x^2 - 18x + 6$ shown on the next page in the top screen of the figure and draw the corresponding XY graph shown on the next page in the bottom screen of the figure.

For the worksheet, use the Data Fill command to build the column of X coordinates in the range A6..A20. Start with –5, increment by 0.5, and stop at 8191. Assign to B6 the formula 2*A6^3 + 6*A6^2–18*A6 + 6. Copy B6 to the range B7..B20. Format the range A6..B20 to the Fixed type with 1 decimal position. For the XY graph in the figure, use these graph settings:

Type = XY
X range = A6..A20
A range = B6..B20
Title 1 = Graph of y = 2x^3 + 6x^2 – 18x + 6
X-axis title = X axis
Y-axis title = Y axis

Save the worksheet with XY graph settings as STUS5-8. Save the graph as STUSX5-8.PIC. Use PrintGraph to print the XY graph.

Part 2: Add the XY graph in the bottom screen of the previous figure to the worksheet STUS5-8 as shown in the figure below. Use Allways to modify the worksheet in the following ways:

1. Change the report title in A1 to Times 14-point font.
2. Add the XY graph in the range D3..H20.
3. Print the range A1..H20.

Return control to 1-2-3 and save the worksheet as STUS5-8.

Sorting and Querying a Worksheet Database

LOTUS 1-2-3 Release 2.2

OBJECTIVES

You will have mastered the material in this project when you can:

◆ Define the terms database, DBMS, field, field name, and record

◆ Differentiate between records in ascending and descending sequence

◆ Sort a database on the basis of a primary key

◆ Sort a database on the basis of both primary and secondary keys

◆ Establish criteria for selecting records in a database

◆ Find records in a database that match specified criteria

◆ Extract records from a database that match specified criteria

◆ Apply the database functions to generate information about the database

◆ Utilize the lookup functions to select values from a list or a table

◆ Search for strings in the worksheet

◆ Replace strings in the worksheet

In this project we will discuss some of the database capabilities of 1-2-3. A **database** is an organized collection of data. For example, a telephone book, a grade book, and a list of company employees are databases. In these cases, the data related to a person is called a **record**, and the data items that make up a record are called **fields**. In a telephone book database, the fields are name, address, and telephone number.

A worksheet's row and column structure can easily be used to organize and store a database (Figure 6-1). Each row of a worksheet can be used to store a record and each column can store a field. Additionally, a row of column headings at the top of the worksheet can be used as **field names** to identify each field.

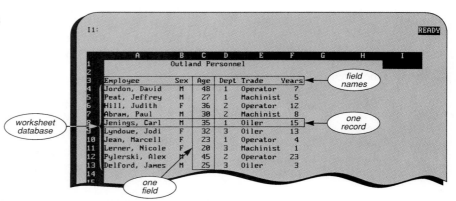

FIGURE 6-1 The worksheet database we will use to illustrate the database capabilities of 1-2-3.

A **database management system (DBMS)** is a software package that is used to create a database and store, access, sort, and make additions, deletions, and changes to that database. Although somewhat limited by the number of records that can be stored, 1-2-3 is capable of carrying out many of the DBMS functions. We have already used 1-2-3 as a database management system when we built, formatted, and enhanced our worksheets in the earlier projects.

In this project we will focus on the two functions of a DBMS that we have not yet discussed—sorting and accessing records. We also discuss the special database and table lookup functions and the Search command available with 1-2-3. For the remainder of this project, the term *database* will mean *worksheet database*.

The database for this project is illustrated in Figure 6-1. It consists of 10 personnel records. Each record represents an employee for the Outland Company. The names, columns, types, and sizes of the fields are described in Table 6-1. Since the database is visible on the screen, it is important that it be readable. Therefore, most of the field sizes (column widths) in Table 6-1 are determined from the column headings (field names) and not the maximum length of the data as is the case with most database management systems. For example, column E represents the Trade field, which has a width of nine characters because the longest trade designation is machinist (nine characters). Column F, which represents the years of seniority, is five characters wide because the field name Years is five letters long. The column headings in the row immediately above the first record (row 3) play an important role in the database commands issued to 1-2-3.

TABLE 6-1 Field Descriptions for the Outland Personnel Database

FIELD NAME	COLUMN	TYPE OF DATA	SIZE
Employee	A	Label	16
Sex	B	Label	5
Age	C	Numeric	5
Dept	D	Label	6
Trade	E	Label	9
Years	F	Numeric	5

Build the database shown in Figure 6-1 by following the steps listed in the Summary of Keystrokes—PROJS-6 in the Project Summary at the end of this project.

SORTING A DATABASE

◆ The information derived from a database is easier to work with and more meaningful if the records are arranged in sequence on the basis of one or more fields. Arranging the records in sequence is called **sorting**. Figure 6-2 illustrates the difference between unsorted data and the same data in ascending and descending sequence. Data that is in sequence from lowest to highest in value is in **ascending sequence**. Data that is in sequence from highest to lowest in value is in **descending sequence**.

DATA IN NO PARTICULAR SEQUENCE	DATA IN ASCENDING SEQUENCE	DATA IN DESCENDING SEQUENCE
7	1	9
5	3	7
9	5	5
1	7	3
3	9	1

FIGURE 6-2 Data in various sequences

The Sort Menu

To sort a database, enter the command **/D**ata **S**ort (/DS). The Sort menu displays in the control panel at the top of the screen, and the sort settings sheet displays in place of rows 1 through 10 in the worksheet (Figure 6-3). The commands available in the Sort menu are described in Table 6-2.

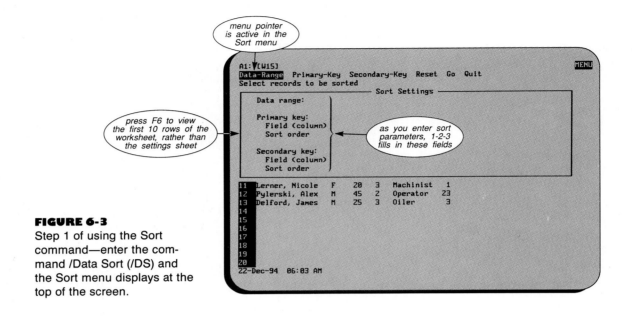

FIGURE 6-3

Step 1 of using the Sort command—enter the command /Data Sort (/DS) and the Sort menu displays at the top of the screen.

TABLE 6-2 A Summary of Commands in the Sort Menu

COMMAND	FUNCTION
Data-Range	Prompts you to specify the range of the database to sort.
Primary-Key	Prompts you to enter the field (column) you want to sort the records on and the sequence.
Secondary-Key	Prompts you to enter a second field (column) you want to sort on within the primary-key field, and the sequence for the secondary-key field. Used to *break ties* on the primary-key field.
Reset	Clears all sort settings.
Go	Causes the database to be sorted on the basis of the sort settings.
Quit	Quits the Data command and returns control to READY mode.

To illustrate the use of the Data Sort command, we will first sort the database in Figure 6-1 into ascending sequence on the basis of the employee name field (column A). Next, we will sort the same database on years of seniority (column F) within the sex code (column B). That is, the sex code will be the primary-key field and years of seniority will be the secondary-key field.

Sorting the Records by Employee Name

With the menu pointer active in the Sort menu (Figure 6-3), do the following:

1. Enter the data range.
2. Enter the primary-key field.
3. Enter the Go command.

To enter the data range, type the letter D for Data-Range. The **data range** defines the fields and records to be sorted in the database. The data range almost always encompasses *all* the fields in *all* the records below the column headings, although it can be made up of fewer records or fewer fields. Be aware, however, that if you do not select all the fields (columns) in the database, the unselected fields will not remain with the records they belong to and the data will get mixed up.

When you type the letter D for Data-Range, 1-2-3 responds by displaying the prompt message "Enter data range: A1" on the input line. Use the arrow keys and Period key to select the range A4..F13 as shown in Figure 6-4. Press the Enter key and the Sort menu shown at the top of the screen in Figure 6-3 reappears on the screen.

The next step is to enter the primary-key field. With the Sort menu on the screen and the cell pointer at A4, type the letter P for Primary-Key. 1-2-3 responds by displaying the prompt message "Primary sort key: A4" on the input line. Since column A is the employee name field and the cell pointer is in column A, press the Enter key. As shown in Figure 6-5, 1-2-3 responds with a second prompt message requesting the desired sequence of the sort. Type the letter A for ascending sequence and press the Enter key.

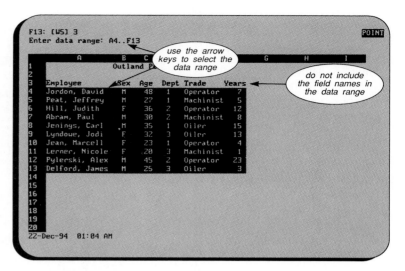

FIGURE 6-4 Step 2 of using the Sort command—enter the data range. The data range usually encompasses all the fields in all the records of the database.

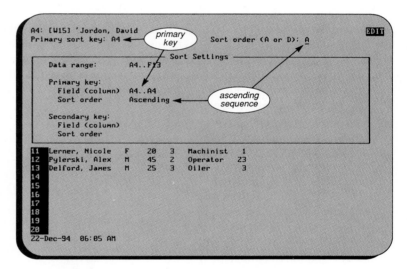

FIGURE 6-5 Step 3 of using the Sort command—enter the primary key and desired sequence for sorting the database by employee name.

To complete the sort, type the letter G for Go. 1-2-3 sorts the records and displays them in ascending sequence according to employee name. Following the completion of the Go command, control returns to READY mode as shown in Figure 6-6. Whereas the records in Figure 6-1 are in no particular sequence, the same records in Figure 6-6 are now in ascending sequence by employee name.

To complete this portion of the project, save and print a hard copy of the sorted database. Save the database using the file name PROJS-6A. Print the database following the same procedures used in the previous projects.

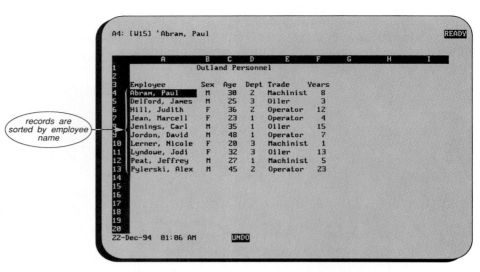

FIGURE 6-6   The database sorted by employee name in ascending sequence after typing the letter G for Go

Sorting the Records by Years of Seniority within Sex Code

In this example, we will use two sort keys. Our goal is to order the records so that the secondary-key field, years of seniority (column F), is ordered in descending sequence within the primary-key field, sex code (column B). We will sort the primary-key field into ascending sequence. Therefore, the female with the most years of seniority will be at the top of the list, and the male with the least seniority will be at the bottom of the list. This nested sorting always assumes that the primary-key field contains duplicate values.

To start this portion of the project, load the original database PROJS-6 (Figure 6-1) into main memory and enter the command **/Data Sort** (/DS). With the menu pointer active in the Sort menu (Figure 6-3), type the letter D for Data-Range. Next, select all the records in the database (A4..F13) as shown in Figure 6-4. Press the Enter key and the Sort menu shown earlier in Figure 6-3 reappears on the screen.

After the data range is set, enter the primary-key field. To accomplish this, type the letter P for Primary-Key. Move the cell pointer to column B (sex code) and press the Enter key. Type the letter A for ascending sequence. The primary-key field selections are shown on the input line in Figure 6-7. Press the Enter key to finalize the primary-key selections.

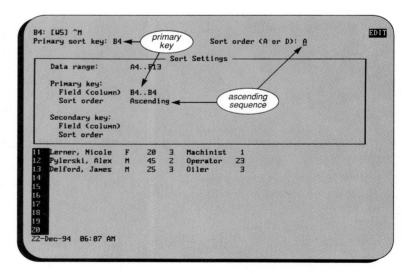

FIGURE 6-7   Entering the primary key and desired sequence for sorting the database by years of seniority within sex code

Type the letter S for Secondary-Key. 1-2-3 responds by displaying a prompt message on the input line requesting the secondary key. Move the cell pointer to column F, the one that contains the years of seniority, and press the Enter key. In response to the second prompt message on the input line, leave the D for descending sequence. The secondary-key field selections are shown in Figure 6-8. Press the Enter key to return control to the Sort menu.

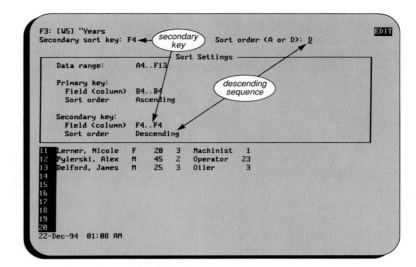

FIGURE 6-8

Entering the secondary key and desired sequence for sorting the database by years of seniority within sex code

To complete the sort, type the letter G for Go. 1-2-3 sorts the records and places them in ascending sequence according to the sex-code field in column B. Within the sex code, the records are in descending sequence according to the years of seniority in column F. This is shown in Figure 6-9. Following the completion of the Go command, 1-2-3 displays the sorted records and returns to READY mode.

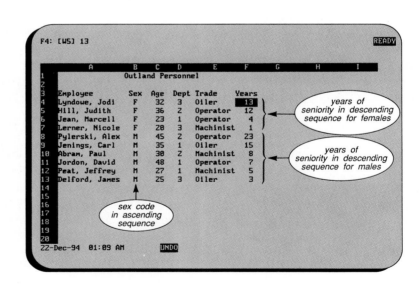

FIGURE 6-9

The database sorted by years of seniority within sex code

Save and print a hard copy of the sorted database. Use the file name PROJS-6B.

QUERYING A DATABASE

◆ One of the most powerful aspects of a DBMS is its capability to select records from a database that match specified criteria. This activity is called **querying a database**. Records that match the criteria can be highlighted, copied to another part of the worksheet, or deleted.

The Query Menu

To query a database, enter the command **/Data Query** (/DQ). The Query menu displays in the control panel at the top of the screen, and the query settings sheet displays in place of rows 1 through 6 in the worksheet (Figure 6-10). The function of each of the Query commands is described in Table 6-3.

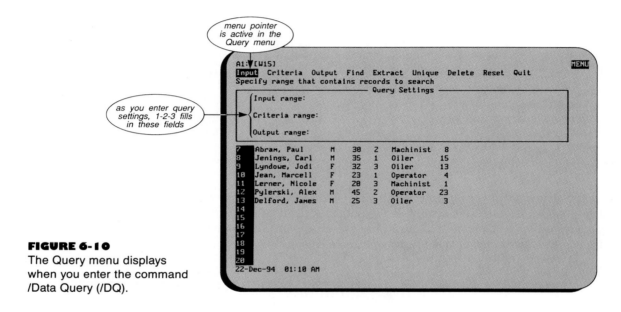

FIGURE 6-10
The Query menu displays when you enter the command /Data Query (/DQ).

TABLE 6-3 A Summary of Commands in the Query Menu

COMMAND	FUNCTION
Input	Prompts you to enter the range of the database to be queried. Usually the entire database is selected.
Criteria	Prompts you to enter the range of cells that includes the conditions for record selection. The conditions are entered into the worksheet off to the side or below the database.
Output	Prompts you to enter a range of cells to which records can be copied. The Output range is defined in the worksheet off to the side or below the database.
Find	Moves the cell pointer to the first record in the database that passes the test. The cell pointer moves one record at a time as you press the Up Arrow or Down Arrow key. When you invoke the Find command, the cell pointer extends to include the entire record. Pressing the Esc key or Enter key cancels the search.
Extract	Copies all selected records from the database to the Output range. The records that pass the test are selected from the database. Records that fail the test are not copied to the Output range.
Unique	Same as the Extract command, except that it copies only the first of any duplicate records.
Delete	Deletes all records from the database that pass the test.
Reset	Resets the Input, Output, and Criteria settings.
Quit	Quits the Data command and returns control to READY mode.

The Find Command

The Find command is used to search for records in the database that meet certain criteria. The command highlights the first record in the database that passes the test and continues to highlight records that pass the test as you press the Up and Down Arrow keys. If no more records pass the test in the direction you are searching, the computer beeps at you and the last record meeting the criteria remains highlighted.

With the database PROJS-6 (Figure 6-1) in main memory, let's search for records representing males who work in department 2 (Sex = M AND Dept = 2). To complete the search, do the following:

1. Choose an unused area off to the side of the database and set up the criteria.
2. Type the command /Data Query (/DQ) and enter the Input range.
3. Enter the Criteria range.
4. Type the letter F for Find.

The first step in setting up the Criteria range is to select an unused area of the worksheet. Let's begin the Criteria range at cell H3. Copy cell B3 (Sex) to cell H3 and cell D3 (Dept) to cell I3. You can bypass the Copy command and enter the field names through the keyboard, but the field names in the Criteria range must agree exactly with the field names in the database, or the search won't work properly. To ensure that they are the same, it's best to use the Copy command.

Under each field name in the Criteria range, enter the value for which you want to search. In our example, we want to search for males who work in department 2. Therefore, enter the letter M in cell H4. (1-2-3 considers lower-case m and uppercase M to be the same in a Criteria range.) In cell I4, enter the label 2 (^2 or "2 or '2). These entries for the Criteria range are shown in Figure 6-11. The Criteria range must contain at least two rows—the field names in the first row and the criteria in the second row.

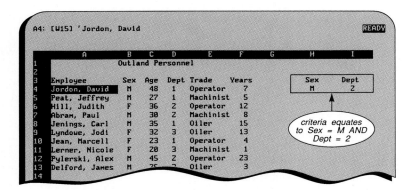

FIGURE 6-11 Step 1 of using the Find command—enter the criteria in unused cells off to the side of the database before issuing the Data Query command.

After building the Criteria range, enter the command **/D**ata **Q**uery (/DQ). The Query menu displays as shown in Figure 6-10. Type the letter I for Input and use the arrow keys to select the entire database (A3..F13). This is shown in Figure 6-12. The field names in row 3 must be included in the Input range. Press the Enter key.

FIGURE 6-12

Step 2 of using the Find command—enter the command /Data Query Input (/DQI). Enter the Input range, which should encompass all the fields in all the records of the database, including the field names at the top.

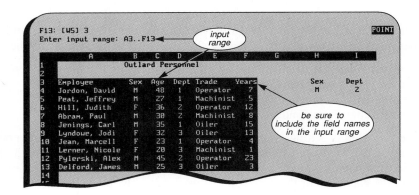

Earlier, the Criteria range (H3..I4) was set up. Now it must be selected. Therefore, type the letter C for Criteria. Select the range H3..I4 as illustrated in Figure 6-13 and press the Enter key.

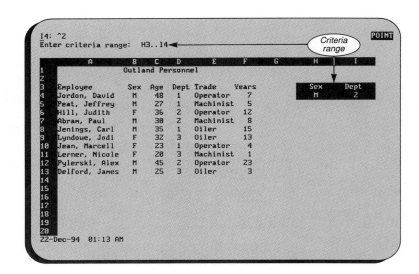

FIGURE 6-13

Step 3 of using the Find command—select the Criteria range.

Next, type the letter F for Find. As shown in the top screen of Figure 6-14, the first record that passes the test (Sex = M AND Dept = 2) is highlighted. Press the Down Arrow key and the next record that passes the test is highlighted. This is shown in the bottom screen of Figure 6-14. If you press the Down Arrow key again, the computer will beep at you because there are no more records that pass the test below the highlighted one. If you press the Up Arrow key, the previous record that passed the test is highlighted again.

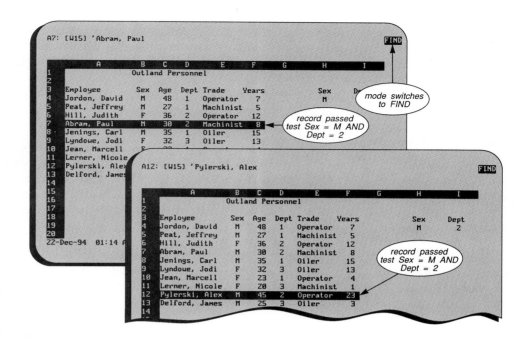

FIGURE 6-14
Step 4 of using the Find command—use the Up and Down Arrow keys to highlight the next record that passes the criteria.

After typing the letter F to invoke the Find command, you can move the elongated cursor to the very first record by pressing the Home key. You can move it to the last record by pressing the End key. These two keys allow you to start the search at the top or the bottom of the database. To terminate the Find command, press the Enter key or the Esc key to return to the Data Query menu.

While the Find command is still active, you can edit the record that is highlighted. Use the Right Arrow and Left Arrow keys to move from one field to another. Because the entire record is highlighted, the cell pointer does not move to the different fields when you use the arrow keys. However, you can determine the field location of the cell pointer because the cell address displays at the top of the screen on the status line. The blinking underline cursor that is active in the current cell also indicates the location of the cell pointer. When the cell address of the field you want to change displays in the upper left corner of the control panel, you can retype the contents or use the F2 key to edit them. If you decide the original values were correct before pressing the Enter key to complete the change, you can press the Esc key to discard the change.

To complete this portion of this project, save and print the database and criteria. Use the file name PROJS-6C.

More About the Criteria Range

The way you set up the Criteria range determines which records pass the test when you use the Find command. The following paragraphs describe several different examples of valid field names and logical expressions within a Criteria range.

No Conditions   If the Criteria range contains no values below the field names, all the records pass the test. For example, if you use the Criteria range at the right, then all the records in the Input range pass the test and the Find command highlights every record in the Input range, one at a time.

Sex	Trade

Conditions with Labels   The values below the field names in the Criteria range can be labels, numbers, or formulas. For example, if you want to select all the records in the database that represent employees who are operators, use the criteria at the right. In this example Operator is a label. If you use the Find command, this Criteria range causes 1-2-3 to use the condition Trade = Operator to evaluate each record. If the condition is true, the record passes the test and it is highlighted. If Trade does not equal Operator, the record fails the test and it is bypassed.

Trade
Operator

More than one type of trade can be listed in the Criteria range. For example, if you want to select records that represent employees who are operators or employees who are oilers (Trade = Operator OR Trade = Oiler), you can set up a Criteria range with the entries at the right. In this example, the Criteria range is three rows long.

Trade
Operator
Oiler

The global characters question mark (?) and asterisk (*) can be used within labels. The asterisk (*) means *any characters at this position and all remaining positions*. The question mark (?) means *any character at this position*. These **global characters** are also called **wild-card characters**. For example, the Criteria range at the right causes all records whose trade begins with the letter O to be selected. In our database, records with the trade of oiler or operator pass the test. The remaining records fail the test.

Trade
O*

The Criteria range at the right causes all records to be selected that represent employees whose trade is five characters long, begins with the letter O, and ends with the letters er. With regard to the placement of wild-card characters in a label, the question mark (?) can be used in any character position. The asterisk (*) can be used only at the end of a label.

Trade
O??er

Labels can also be preceded by the tilde (˜) to exclude a match. To select the records representing employees that work in any department other than department 3, you may use the criteria at the right. The department numbers in our database are labels, not numbers. The tilde (˜) can only precede labels. Table 6-4 summarizes the special symbols that may be used with labels in a Criteria range.

Dept
˜3

TABLE 6-4 A Summary of Special Symbols That Can Be Used with Labels in a Criteria Range

SYMBOL	MEANING	EXAMPLE
*	Any characters at this position and all remaining positions	Tr*
?	Any character at this position	M??T
˜	Not	˜F

Conditions with Numbers   If you want to select records that represent employees who are 30 years old, enter the criteria in the entry at the right. In this example, 1-2-3 uses the expression Age = 30 to determine if each record passes the test when the Find command is used. It is invalid to begin a number with any of the special characters we described earlier for labels, like *, ?, and ˜.

Age
30

Conditions with Formulas   Formula criteria are entered into the Criteria range beginning with a plus sign (+). The plus sign is followed by the address of the cell of the first record immediately below the specified field name in the Input range. The cell address is followed by a relational operator and the value to which to compare the field name. (Table 4-3 in Project 4 contains a list of the valid relational operators.) If you want to select all records that represent employees who are older than 25, use the criteria at the right.

Age
+C4>25

The cell address C4 is the first cell in the database below the field name Age (Figure 6-15). Since C4 is a relative cell address, 1-2-3 adjusts the row as it goes through the database, passing and failing records. Hence, when you invoke the Find command, cell address C4 is used only to evaluate the first record. Thereafter, the 4 in C4 is adjusted to 5, 6, and so on, as each record in the database is evaluated.

In the previous example, the formula $+C4>25$ was shown in the cell below the field name Age. Actually, when a condition containing a formula is assigned to the cell, 0 or 1 displays. The number displayed in the cell assigned the formula $+C4>25$ depends on the value in cell C4. If it is greater than 25, then 1 (true) displays. If C4 contains a value less than or equal to 25, then 0 (false) displays. You can use the command **/R**ange Format **T**ext (/RFT) to display the formula in the Criteria range, rather than the numeric value 0 or 1.

Compound conditions may be formed by using the logical operators #AND#, #OR#, and #NOT#. (Table 4-4 in Project 4 provides an explanation of their meaning.) In the following example, all records are selected that meet the criteria Age < 37 AND Years ≥ 10.

Age
$+C4<37\#AND\#+F4>=10$

The compound condition may include numeric fields that are not directly under the field name. In this case, C4 refers to the Age field and F4 refers to the Years field.

Mixing Conditions with Formulas and Labels If the criteria require both a label and a formula, use multiple field names. For example, if you wanted to find all records in the employee database that represent operators with more than 10 years of seniority (Trade = Operator AND Years > 10), use the criteria at the right.

Trade	Years
Operator	$+F4>10$

To select records that meet the criteria Trade = Operator OR Years > 10, use the entry at the right. Because the expressions Operator and $+F4>10$ are in different rows, 1-2-3 selects records that represent employees who are operators or have more than 10 years of seniority.

Trade	Years
Operator	
	$+F4>10$

The Delete Command

You can use the Delete command in the Data Query menu to delete all records that pass the test described in the Criteria range. As each record is deleted, all those below it move up toward the top of the database. Since the Delete command physically removes records from the database, it is strongly recommended that before executing this command, you save the database to disk.

The Extract Command

The Extract command copies data from the records that pass the test to the designated fields in the Output range. The Output range is a group of cells off to the side or below the database. The first row of the Output range includes duplicates of the field names in the Input range that you want to extract. This command is very powerful because it allows you to build a database that is a subset of the original one. The subset database can be printed, saved as a new database, or queried like any other database.

Again, load the employee database PROJS-6 (Figure 6-1) into main memory. Assume that your manager wants you to generate a list of all those employees who meet the criteria:

Age ≥ 27 AND NOT(Dept = 3) AND Years < 10

In the list, include the employee name, department, and sex code of all the records that pass the test.

To complete the extract, do the following:

1. Choose an area off to the side of the database and set up the criteria.
2. Choose an area below the database and set up an area to receive the extracted results.
3. Invoke the command **/D**ata **Q**uery (/DQ) and enter the Input range.
4. Enter the Criteria range.
5. Enter the Output range.
6. Type the letter E for Extract.

The criteria for this query involve three fields—Age, Dept, and Years. Use the cells in the range G3 through I4 for the Criteria range. Copy the three field names Age, Dept, and Years from the database in row 3 to cells G3, H3, and I3. The first condition in the previously stated criteria is Age ≥ 27. Therefore, in cell G4, enter the formula +C4>=27. This is shown in Figure 6-15. (Cells G4 through I4 have been formatted to the Text type so that the formulas display, rather than the numeric values 0 or 1.) The second condition is NOT(Dept = 3). Therefore, in cell H4, enter ~3. The condition for the third field is Years < 10. In cell I4, enter +F4<10.

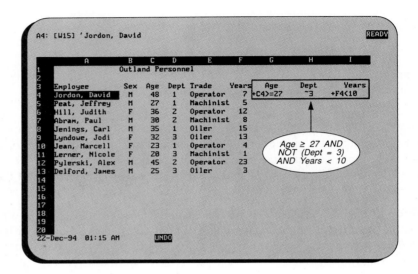

FIGURE 6-15
Step 1 of using the Extract command—enter the criteria in unused cells off to the side of the database.

The next step is to set up the Output range. This involves copying the names of the fields at the top of the database (row 3) to an area below the database. Since we want to extract the employee name, department, and sex code, copy the three field names to row 16 as illustrated in Figure 6-16.

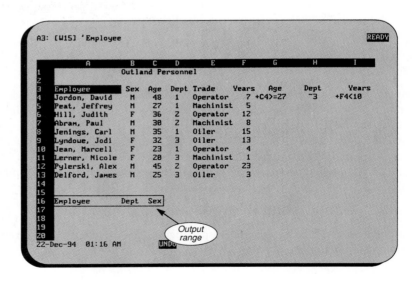

FIGURE 6-16
Step 2 of using the Extract command—copy the field names for the Output range below the database.

Enter the command /**D**ata **Q**uery (/DQ). The Query menu shown at the top of the screen in Figure 6-10 displays. Type the letter I for Input. Use the arrow keys to select the entire database, including the field names in row 3 (A3..F13). The Input range is shown in Figure 6-17. Press the Enter key.

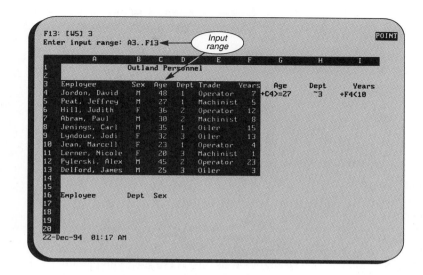

FIGURE 6-17

Step 3 of using the Extract command—enter the command /Data Query (/DQ) and enter the Input range. The Input range usually encompasses all the fields in all the records of the database, including the field names.

With the menu pointer in the Query menu, type the letter C for Criteria. Select the Criteria range G3..I4 as shown in Figure 6-18. Press the Enter key.

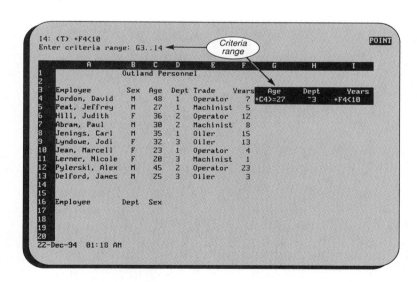

FIGURE 6-18

Step 4 of using the Extract command—enter the Criteria range.

Now type the letter O for Output. Select the range A16..C16 (Figure 6-19). Press the Enter key.

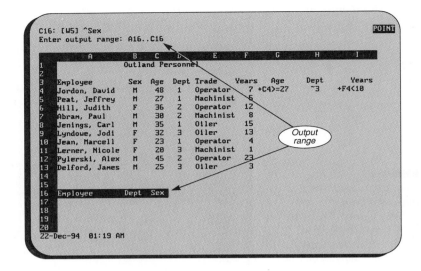

FIGURE 6-19
Step 5 of using the Extract command—enter the Output range.

After the Input, Criteria, and Output ranges are set, type the letter E for Extract. This causes 1-2-3 to select the records that meet the criteria specified in the range A3..I4. For each record selected, it copies the employee name, department, and sex code to the next available row beneath the field names in the Output range. Type the letter Q to quit the Data Query command. The results of the extract display below the database as shown in Figure 6-20. Save and print the database, criteria, and records extracted. To save the database, use the file name PROJS-6D.

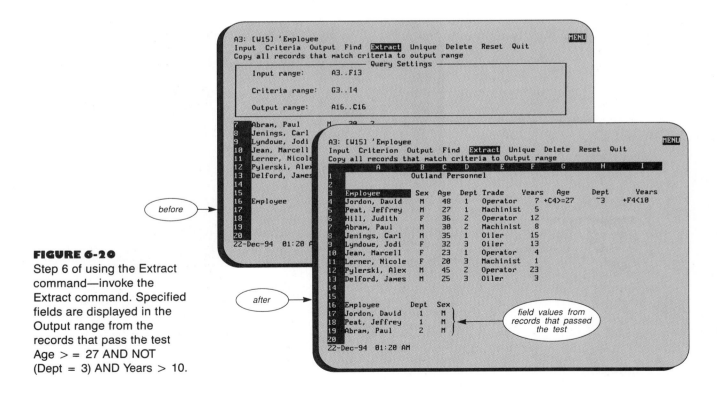

FIGURE 6-20
Step 6 of using the Extract command—invoke the Extract command. Specified fields are displayed in the Output range from the records that pass the test Age > = 27 AND NOT (Dept = 3) AND Years > 10.

In the previous example, the Output range was defined to be the row containing the field names (A16..C16). When the Output range is defined in this fashion, any number of records can be extracted from the database. The alternative is to define a rectangular Output range. In this case, if more records are extracted than rows in the Output range, 1-2-3 displays the diagnostic message "Too many records for Output range".

THE DATABASE FUNCTIONS

1-2-3 has seven functions for evaluating numeric data in the database. The functions, which are similar to the statistical functions discussed in Project 4, are described in Table 6-5.

TABLE 6-5 Database Statistical Functions

FUNCTION	FUNCTION VALUE
DAVG(I,O,C)	Returns the average of the numbers in the Offset column (O) of the Input range (I) that meet the criteria (C).
DCOUNT(I,O,C)	Returns the number of nonempty cells in the Offset column (O) of the Input range (I) that meet the criteria (C).
DMAX(I,O,C)	Returns the largest number in the Offset column (O) of the Input range (I) that meet the criteria (C).
DMIN(I,O,C)	Returns the smallest number in the Offset column (O) of the Input range (I) that meet the criteria (C).
DSTD(I,O,C)	Returns the standard deviation of the numbers in the Offset column (O) of the Input range (I) that meet the criteria (C).
DSUM(I,O,C)	Returns the sum of the numbers in the Offset column (O) of the Input range (I) that meet the criteria (C).
DVAR(I,O,C)	Returns the variance of the numbers in the Offset column (O) of the Input range (I) that meet the criteria (C).

The purpose of these functions is to return a statistic, like the average, on the values in the column of the records that meet the specified criteria. For example, with the database in Figure 6-1 in main memory, let's compute the average age of the male employees and the average age of the female employees.

The first step is to set up the criteria for each average. For the average age of females, use the criteria shown in cells H3 and H4 in Figure 6-21. Likewise, for the average age of males, use the criteria shown in cells I3 and I4. Next, enter the labels that identify the averages. This is shown in cells A16 and A17 in Figure 6-21.

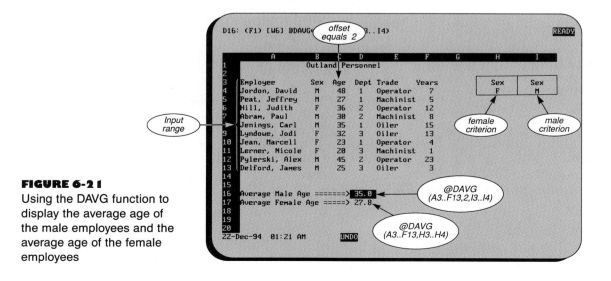

FIGURE 6-21

Using the DAVG function to display the average age of the male employees and the average age of the female employees

You can now assign the DAVG function to cells D16 and D17. This function has three arguments—Input range, offset, and Criteria range. Since the arguments in the function define the ranges, this function does not require that the ranges be defined through the Data Query command.

Set the Input range to the entire database (A3..F13). The offset argument defines the field in the database to be used in the computation. The offset of the leftmost field (Employee) is 0. The offset of the Sex field is 1. The offset of the Age field is 2, and so on. Hence, use the value 2 for the offset argument in the DAVG function. The third argument is the range of cells that make up the criteria—H3..H4 for females and I3..I4 for the males.

With the cell pointer at D16, enter the function @DAVG(A3..F13,2,I3..I4). This causes the average age of the male employees to display in cell D16. Press the Down Arrow key and enter @DAVG(A3..F13,2,H3..H4). This function causes the average age of the female employees to display in cell D17. Format cells D16 and D17 to the Fixed type with one decimal position. The effect of entering these two functions and formatting the results is shown in Figure 6-21. To complete this portion of the project, save and print the database, criteria, and averages. Save the database using the file name PROJS-6E.

THE LOOKUP FUNCTIONS

◆ Three functions that we have not yet discussed are the CHOOSE, VLOOKUP, and HLOOKUP functions. These three functions are called **lookup functions** because they allow you to look up values in a list or a table that is part of the worksheet.

The CHOOSE Function

The CHOOSE function selects a value from a list on the basis of an index. The general form of the CHOOSE function is @CHOOSE$(x, y_0, y_1, y_2, ..., y_n)$, where the value of x determines the value in the list (y_0, y_1, y_2, ..., y_n) to store in the cell. If x equals 0, the first value (y_0) is stored in the cell. If x equals 1, the second value (y_1) is stored in the cell, and so on. The list can contain values, quoted strings, cell addresses, formulas, range names, or a combination of these.

Consider the partial worksheet in Figure 6-22. The table in the range E1..E7 contains costs. B1 is assigned the index that determines the value in the list that the function returns. The CHOOSE function is assigned to cell B3. It is entered as follows: @CHOOSE(B1,0,E2,E3,E4,E5+.02,E6*.95,E7,.46). Since B1 is equal to 3, the CHOOSE function returns the fourth value in the list—the value of cell E4.

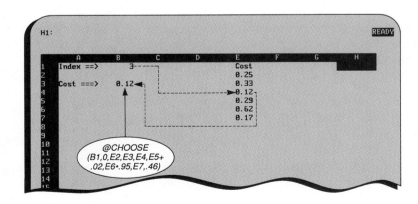

FIGURE 6-22
Using the CHOOSE function to select a value from the list of arguments following the index

If you change the value of B1 to some other number between 0 and 7, the function will store a different value in B3. If the value in B1 exceeds the number of items in the list, the diagnostic message "ERR" is assigned to B3. An index value of zero in cell B1 causes the CHOOSE function to assign zero to B3. If cell B1 is assigned a value of 7, the function returns the value .46 from the list and stores it in cell B3.

The VLOOKUP and HLOOKUP Functions

The VLOOKUP and HLOOKUP functions are useful for looking up values in tables, like tax tables, discount tables, and part tables. The general form of the VLOOKUP function is @VLOOKUP(x,range,offset). The first argument, x, is called the search argument. It is compared to values in the leftmost column of the multiple-column table defined by the second argument, range. The leftmost column of the range is called the range column. Offset defines the column from which a value is returned when a hit is made in the range column. A hit occurs when a value is found in the range column that is closest to but not greater than the search argument x.

The offset in the VLOOKUP function can be zero or positive. The offset value of the range column is zero. A positive offset causes a value to be selected from a column to the right of the range column.

While the VLOOKUP function looks up values in a table arranged vertically, the HLOOKUP function looks up values in a table arranged horizontally. Vertical tables are used more often than horizontal tables.

Consider the top screen of Figure 6-23. Column B contains a list of student test scores. A grade scale table is in the range F5..G9. Look up the corresponding letter grade in the grade scale table for each student test score and assign it to the appropriate cell in column D. For example, a test score of 78 returns the letter grade C; a test score of 99 returns the letter grade A. To look up the letter grades for the student test scores, enter the function @VLOOKUP(B5,$F$5..$G$9,1) in cell D5, the location of the letter grade for student number 1035.

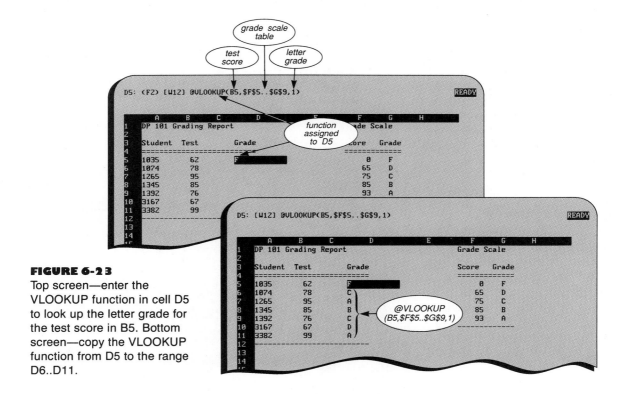

FIGURE 6-23

Top screen—enter the VLOOKUP function in cell D5 to look up the letter grade for the test score in B5. Bottom screen—copy the VLOOKUP function from D5 to the range D6..D11.

The first argument in the VLOOKUP function is cell B5, the test score for student number 1035. The second argument, $F$5..$G$9, defines the grade scale table. The third argument, 1, is the offset. It instructs 1-2-3 to assign the corresponding value in the grade scale table that is located one column to the right of the range column—column F.

Copy the VLOOKUP function in cell D5 to the range D6..D11. As the copy takes place, the first argument in the VLOOKUP function, B5, is adjusted to B6, B7, B8, and so on. The result of copying the VLOOKUP function is shown in the bottom screen of Figure 6-23. In this case, the VLOOKUP function in cells D5 through D11 returns the letter grades that correspond to the student test scores.

THE SEARCH AND REPLACE COMMANDS

◆ The /**R**ange Search (/RS) command is used to locate a string in labels and formulas within a specified range of the worksheet. A **string** consists of a series of characters that make up a cell entry. Use the Find command to locate a string. Use the Replace command to locate and replace one string with another.

The Find Command

To illustrate the use of the Find command, let's locate the string Oiler in the Outland Personnel worksheet shown in Figure 6-1. To find the string Oiler, do the following:

1. Enter the command /**R**ange Search (/RS).
2. Select the range A4..F13 to search.
3. Type the word `Oiler` as shown in the top screen of Figure 6-24. 1-2-3 does not differentiate between uppercase and lowercase letters. Hence, Oiler and oiler are the same.
4. Type the letter L for Labels. As shown in the bottom screen of Figure 6-24, you have three selections: Formulas, Labels, and Both. The Labels command tells 1-2-3 to search only those cells containing labels in the worksheet. Formulas means 1-2-3 will search cells containing only formulas. The command Both instructs 1-2-3 to search cells that contain either labels or formulas.
5. Type the letter F for Find as shown in the top screen of Figure 6-25.

   1-2-3 begins the search at the upper left cell of the specified range. It continues the search down and to the right. When 1-2-3 finds the word Oiler, it highlights the cell as shown in the bottom screen of Figure 6-25. Type the letter N to locate the next occurrence of Oiler. Type the letter Q to Quit the search and return 1-2-3 to READY mode.

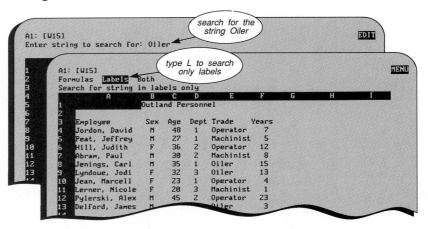

FIGURE 6-24 Initiating a search

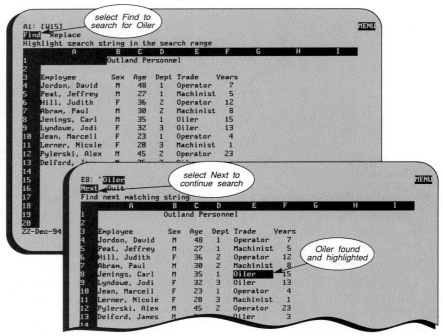

FIGURE 6-25 Completing the search

The Replace Command

The Replace command is similar to the Find command, except that the search string is replaced by a new string. To illustrate how the Replace command works, let's replace all occurrences of the word Oiler with Boiler. To initiate this command, follow the first four steps described for the Find command in the previous section (Figure 6-24).

With the top screen of Figure 6-25 displayed, type the letter R for Replace, instead of F for Find. 1-2-3 responds by displaying the prompt message "Enter replacement string:". Type the word `Boiler` as shown in the top screen of Figure 6-26 and press the Enter key. When 1-2-3 displays the menu shown in the middle screen of Figure 6-26, type the letter R for Replace. The first occurrence of Oiler is replaced with Boiler and 1-2-3 continues to search the worksheet. When it finds the next occurrence of Oiler, it redisplays the menu shown in the middle screen of Figure 6-26. This next occurrence is not changed until you select one of the commands. The bottom screen of Figure 6-26 shows all occurrences of Oiler changed to Boiler.

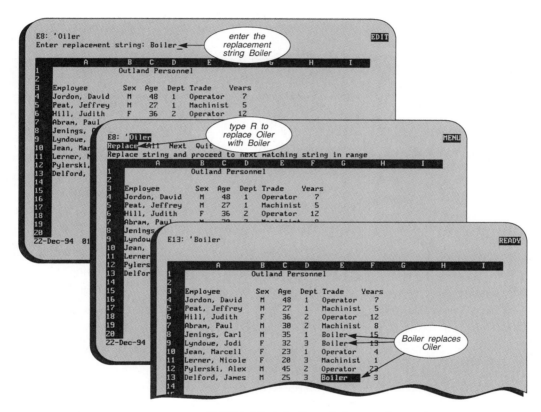

FIGURE 6-26 Completing a string replacement

Table 6-6 describes the functions of the Replace commands available in the middle screen of Figure 6-26.

TABLE 6-6 A Summary of the Commands in the Range Search Replace Menu

COMMAND	FUNCTION
Replace	Replaces the highlighted string and highlights the next cell containing the search string.
All	Replaces all remaining occurrences of the search string.
Next	Finds the next occurrence of the search string without changing the cell that is highlighted.
Quit	Stops the search and returns 1-2-3 to READY mode.

PROJECT SUMMARY

In this project you learned how to sort and query a worksheet database. The database was sorted in two different ways, first by employee name and then by years of seniority within sex code. Querying a database involves searching for records that meet a specified criteria. The selected records can be highlighted, extracted, or deleted.

Powerful database functions can be used to generate information about the database. In this project you were introduced to the lookup functions. These functions are used to return a value from a list or table. Finally, we discussed the Search and Replace. All the activities that you learned for this project are summarized in the Quick Reference following the Appendix. The following is a summary of the keystroke sequence we used in Project 6.

SUMMARY OF KEYSTROKES — PROJS-6 (Figure 6-1)

STEPS	KEY(S) PRESSED	RESULTS
1	/WCS16↵	Sets width of column A to 16.
2	→/WCS5↵	Sets width of column B to 5.
3	→/WCS5↵	Sets width of column C to 5.
4	→/WCS6↵	Sets width of column D to 6.
5	→→/WCS5↵	Sets width of column E to 5.
6	[F5] B1↵Outland Personnel↓	Enters report title in B1.
7	↓←Employee→	Enters column A title in A3.
8	^Sex→	Enters column B title in B3.
9	"Age→	Enters column C title in C3.
10	^Dept→	Enters column D title in D3.
11	Trade→	Enters column E title in E3.
12	"Years↵	Enters column F title in F3.
13	[F5] A4↵Jordon, David→^M→48→^1→Operator→7↵	Enters Jordon's record in row 4.
14	[F5] A5↵Peat, Jeffrey→^M→27→^1→Machinist→5↵	Enters Peat's record in row 5.
15	[F5] A6↵Hill, Judith→^F→36→^2→Operator→12↵	Enters Hill's record in row 6.
16	[F5] A7↵Abram, Paul→^M→30→^2→Machinist→8↵	Enters Abram's record in row 7.
17	[F5] A8↵Jenings, Carl→^M→35→^1→Oiler→15↵	Enters Jenings's record in row 8.
18	[F5] A9↵Lyndowe, Jodi→^F→32→^3→Oiler→13↵	Enters Lyndowe's record in row 9.
19	[F5] A10↵Jean, Marcell→^F→23→^1→Operator→4↵	Enters Jean's record in row 10.
20	[F5] A11↵Lerner, Nicole→^F→20→^3→Machinist→1↵	Enters Lerner's record in row 11.
21	[F5] A12↵Pylerski, Alex→^M→45→^2→Operator→23↵	Enters Pylerski's record in row 12.
22	[F5] A13↵Delford, James→^M→25→^3→Oiler→3↵	Enters Delford's record in row 13.
23	[Home]	Moves the cell pointer to A1.
24	/FSPROJS-6↵	Saves the database worksheet as PROJS-6.

SUMMARY OF KEYSTROKES —
Sorting PROJS-6 by Employee Name (Figure 6-6)

STEPS	KEY(S) PRESSED	RESULTS
1	/FRPROJS-6↵	Retrieves the database worksheet PROJS-6.
2	/DS	Enters the Sort command.
3	DA4.F13↵	Selects A4..F13 as the data range.
4	PA4↵A↵	Selects column A as the primary key for ascending sort.
5	G	Sorts records in range A4..F13.
6	/PPRA1.F13↵AGPQ	Prints the database worksheet.
7	/FSPROJS-6A↵	Saves the database worksheet as PROJS-6A.

SUMMARY OF KEYSTROKES —
Sorting PROJS-6 by Years of Seniority within Sex Code (Figure 6-9)

STEPS	KEY(S) PRESSED	RESULTS
1	/FRPROJS-6↵	Retrieves the database worksheet PROJS-6.
2	/DS	Enters the Sort command.
3	DA4.F13↵	Selects A4..F13 as the data range.
4	PB4↵A↵	Selects column B as the primary key for ascending sort.
5	SF4↵↵	Selects column F as the secondary key for ascending sort.
6	G	Sorts records in range A4..F13.
7	/PPRA1.F13↵AGPQ	Prints the database worksheet.
8	/FSPROJS-6B↵	Saves the database worksheet as PROJS-6B.

SUMMARY OF KEYSTROKES —
Finding Records That Meet the Criteria Sex = M AND Dept = 2 (Figure 6-14)

STEPS	KEY(S) PRESSED	RESULTS
1	/FRPROJS-6↵	Retrieves the database worksheet PROJS-6.
2	[F5] B3↵/C↵H3↵	Copies B3 to H3.
3	[F5] D3↵/C↵I3↵	Copies D3 to I3.
4	[F5] H4↵^M→^2↵	Enters label M in H4 and label 2 in I3.
5	/DQ	Enters the Query command.
6	IA3.F13↵	Selects A3..F13 as the input range.
7	CH3.I4↵	Selects H3..I4 as the criteria range.
8	F↓↓	Finds records that meet criteria.
9	[Esc]	Quits the Find command.
10	/PPRA1.I13↵OMR77↵QAGPQ	Prints the database worksheet.
11	/FSPROJS-6C↵	Saves the database worksheet as PROJS-6C.

SUMMARY OF KEYSTROKES —
Extracting Records That Meet the Criteria Age > = 27
AND NOT (Dept = 3) AND Years < 10 (Figure 6-20)

STEPS	KEY(S) PRESSED	RESULTS
1	/FRPROJS-6↵	Retrieves the database worksheet PROJS-6.
2	[F5] C3↵/C↵G3↵	Copies C3 to G3.
3	→/C↵H3↵	Copies D3 to H3.
4	→ →/C↵I3↵	Copies F3 to I3.
5	→ ↓+C4>=27→ ˆ˜3→ +F4<10↵	Enters criteria in G4..I4.
6	/RFT↵ ← ← ↵	Formats G4..I4 to Text.
7	[F5] A3↵/C↵A16↵	Copies A3 to A16.
8	[F5] D3↵/C↵B16↵	Copies D3 to B16.
9	[F5] B3↵/C↵C16↵	Copies B3 to C16.
10	/DQ	Enters the Query command.
11	IA3.F13↵	Selects A3..F3 as the input range.
12	CG3.I4↵	Selects G3..I4 as the criteria range.
13	OA16.C16↵	Selects A16..C16 as the output range.
14	EQ	Extracts records from the input range and places them in the output range. Quits the Extract command.
15	/PPRA1.I20↵OMR77↵QAGPQ	Prints the database worksheet.
16	/FSPROJS-6D ↵	Saves the database worksheet as PROJS-6D.

SUMMARY OF KEYSTROKES —
Using the Database Function DAVG (Figure 6-21)

STEPS	KEY(S) PRESSED	RESULTS
1	/FRPROJS-6↵	Retrieves the database worksheet PROJS-6.
2	[F5] B3↵/C↵H3.I3↵	Copies B3 to H3..I3.
3	[F5] H4↵ˆF→ ˆM↵	Enters the labels F and M in H4 and I4.
4	[F5] A16↵Average Male Age =======>↓	Enters row title in A16.
5	Average Female Age =====>↵	Enters row title in A17.
6	[F5] D16↵@DAVG(A3.F13,2,I3.I4)↓	Enters DAVG function for males in D16.
7	@DAVG(A3.F13,2,H3.H4)↑	Enters DAVG function for females in D17.
8	/RFF1↵↓↵	Formats D16..D17 to Fixed.
9	/PPRA1.I17↵AGPQ	Prints the database worksheet.
10	/FSPROJS-6E ↵	Saves the database worksheet as PROJS-6E.

The following list summarizes the material covered in Project 6.

1. A **database** is an organized collection of data.
2. The data related to a person, place, or thing is called a **record**.
3. The data items that make up a record are called **fields**.
4. Each row in a worksheet can be used to store a record.
5. Each column in a worksheet can be used to store a field.

6. The row immediately above the first record contains the **field names**.
7. A **database management system (DBMS)** is a software package that is used to create a database and store, access, sort, and make additions, deletions, and changes to that database.
8. **Sorting** rearranges the records in a database in a particular sequence on the basis of one or more fields.
9. Data that is in sequence from lowest to highest is in **ascending sequence**.
10. Data that is in sequence from highest to lowest is in **descending sequence**.
11. To sort a database, enter the command **/Data Sort (/DS)**. Enter the data range and the sort keys. To complete the sort, enter the Go command.
12. The **data range** defines the fields and records to be sorted in the database. The data range for a sort is usually all the records in the database. Never include the field names in the data range.
13. A sort key, like the primary key, is assigned a column and a sort sequence.
14. Selecting records in a database on the basis of a specified criteria is called **querying a database**. Records that match the criteria can be highlighted, copied to another part of the worksheet, or deleted.
15. To query a database, enter the command **/Data Query (/DQ)**.
16. Before you enter the Data Query command, the criteria should be present in the worksheet. If you use an Output range, the field names for the Output range should also be present in the worksheet.
17. The Find command highlights records that pass the criteria.
18. To apply the Find command to a database, use the Data Query command to define the Input range and Criteria range. Finally, type the letter F for Find.
19. The criteria used to pass records include the field names and the values to which the field names are compared. Field names can be compared to labels, numbers, and formulas.
20. **Global**, or **wild-card**, **characters** are allowed in labels in the criteria. The two valid wild-card characters are the asterisk (*), which means *any characters in this position and all remaining positions*, and the question mark (?), which means *any character at this position*. The question mark (?) can be used anywhere in the label. The asterisk (*) can be used only at the end of a label.
21. A label preceded by a tilde (˜) in the criteria range negates the condition.
22. The criteria can include the logical operators AND, OR, and NOT.
23. The Delete command in the Data Query menu is used to delete selected records from the database.
24. The Extract command is used to copy selected records from the database to the Output range.
25. 1-2-3 includes database statistical functions to generate information about the database.
26. The **lookup functions**, CHOOSE, VLOOKUP, and HLOOKUP allow you to look up values in a list or table that is part of the worksheet.
27. A **string** consists of a series of characters that make up a cell entry.
28. To search for a string or replace a string with another in the worksheet, use the command **/Range /Search (/RS)**.

STUDENT ASSIGNMENTS

STUDENT ASSIGNMENT 1: True/False

Instructions: Circle T if the statement is true and F if the statement is false.

T F 1. The Reset command in the Sort menu resets the database back to its original sequence.
T F 2. The series of numbers 1, 3, 4, 5, 6 is in ascending sequence.
T F 3. A database management system is a worksheet.
T F 4. A database is an organized collection of data.
T F 5. The Extract command copies selected records to the Output range.
T F 6. To query a database, you must first select unused cells off to the side or below the database and set up the criteria.
T F 7. A sort key is identified by any cell in the column containing the field by which you want to sort.
T F 8. In a sort operation, the secondary-key field has a higher priority than the primary-key field.
T F 9. The tilde (˜) is used to OR a condition in the Criteria range.
T F 10. The wild-card character asterisk (*) may be used only at the front of a label that is part of the criteria.

Student Assignment I (continued)

T F   11. A Criteria range consisting of field names and empty cells below the field names will cause all the records in the database to be selected.

T F   12. The Criteria range must contain at least two rows and two columns.

T F   13. The DAVG function returns the average number of records in the database.

T F   14. The Offset column is relative to the leftmost field in the Input range.

T F   15. The database functions require that you define the Input range and Criteria range by invoking the Data Query command.

T F   16. It is required that the field names in the Output range be the same as the field names in the Input range.

T F   17. The /Range Search (/RS) command causes 1-2-3 to search for a string from right to left in the worksheet, one row at a time.

T F   18. The VLOOKUP and HLOOKUP functions are the same, except that VLOOKUP verifies the search of the table and HLOOKUP does not.

T F   19. An Offset column value of zero causes the VLOOKUP function to return the value in the range column that is closest to but not greater than the search argument.

T F   20. The Offset column in the VLOOKUP function cannot be negative.

STUDENT ASSIGNMENT 2: Multiple Choice

Instructions: Circle the correct response.

1. Which one of the following series of numbers is in ascending sequence?
   a. 1, 2, 3, 4, 5   c. 1, 3, 5, 3, 1
   b. 5, 4, 3, 2, 1   d. none of these

2. Which one of the following commands in the Query menu is used to highlight records?
   a. Extract   c. Unique
   b. Find   d. Criteria

3. To properly execute the Find command, the _____ and _____ range must be set.
   a. Input, Output   c. Input, Criteria
   b. Data-Range, Output   d. Data-Range, Criteria

4. Which one of the following characters represent *any character in this position*?
   a. tilde (˜)   c. question mark (?)
   b. number sign (#)   d. asterisk (*)

5. To copy all records that satisfy the criteria to the Output range, use the _____ command.
   a. Find   c. Extract
   b. Delete   d. Output

6. Which one of the following database functions returns the number of nonempty cells in the Offset column (O) of the records in the Input range (I) that meet the Criteria range (C)?
   a. DMAX(I,O,C)   c. DCOUNT(I,O,C)
   b. DAVG(I,O,C)   d. DVAR(I,O,C)

7. If a database has four fields, the rightmost column has an Offset value of _____ .
   a. 5   c. 3
   b. 4   d. 0

8. Which one of the following functions is used to search a columnar table?
   a. VLOOKUP   c. SEARCH
   b. CHOOSE   d. HLOOKUP

STUDENT ASSIGNMENT 3: Understanding Sorting

Instructions: Enter the database in the following figure and save it as STUS6-3. Sort the seven records on the basis of the problems that follow. Begin each problem by loading STUS6-3. Print the original worksheet and each sorted worksheet. Save each sorted worksheet as STUS6-3x where x is equal to the problem number.

1. Sort the database into descending sequence by cost.
2. Sort the database by district within division. Both sort keys are to be in ascending sequence.
3. Sort the database by department within district within division. All three sort keys are to be in descending sequence. (Hint: First sort on division. Next, sort *only* the first division by department within district. Continue sorting each division separately.)
4. Sort the database into descending sequence by division.
5. Sort the database by department within district within division. All three sort keys are to be in ascending sequence. (Hint: See the hint in problem 3.)

DIVISION	DISTRICT	DEPARTMENT	COST
2	1	2	1.21
1	2	2	2.22
2	1	3	1.57
1	2	1	3.56
1	1	1	1.11
2	1	1	1.45
1	2	3	2.10

STUDENT ASSIGNMENT 4: Understanding Criteria

Instructions: Write the criteria required to select records from the database in Figure 6-1 according to the following problems. To help you better understand what is required for this assignment, we have answered the first problem.

1. Select records that represent male employees who are less than 25 years old.

Criteria:

Sex	Age
M	+C4<25

2. Select records that represent employees whose trade is machinist or oiler.

Criteria:

3. Select records that represent employees whose last names begin with P or who work in department 2.

Criteria:

Student Assignment 4 (continued)

4. Select records that represent female employees who are at least 30 years old and have at least 10 years of seniority.

Criteria:

5. Select records that represent male employees or employees who are at least 30 years old.

Criteria:

6. Select records that represent male machinist employees who are at least 28 years old and whose last names begin with P.

Criteria:

STUDENT ASSIGNMENT 5: Understanding Database and Lookup Functions

Instructions: Load 1-2-3 and perform the following tasks.

1. Consider Figure 6-21 on page L243. Write a database function and the criteria that will assign to the current cell the number of years of seniority for the female employee with the maximum years of seniority. Use a Criteria range of I3..I4.
2. Consider Figure 6-21. Write a database function and the criteria that will assign to the current cell the average years of seniority of the male employees. Use a Criteria range of I3..I4.
3. Consider Figure 6-21. Write a database function and the criteria that will assign to the current cell the sum of the ages of the female employees. Use a Criteria range of I3..I4.
4. Consider Figure 6-21. Write a database function and the criteria that will assign to the current cell the average years of seniority for both the male and female employees. Use a Criteria range of I3..I4.
5. Consider Figure 6-22 on page L244. Use the CHOOSE function to assign cell B3 twelve times the cost in column E. Select the cost in column E on the basis of the index value in cell B1.
6. Consider the VLOOKUP function in the top screen of Figure 6-23 on page L245. Complete the following problems independently and write down the results displayed in column D:
   a. Decrease all test scores in column B by 10 points.
   b. Increase all test scores in column B by 10 points.
   c. Reset the test scores in column B to their original values and change the offset argument in the VLOOKUP function to zero.

STUDENT ASSIGNMENT 6: Building and Sorting a Database of Prospective Programmers

Instructions: Load 1-2-3 and perform the following tasks.

1. Build the database illustrated in the following figure. Use the field sizes listed in the table.
2. Save and print the database. Use the file name STUS6-6.
3. Sort the records in the database into decending sequence by name. Print the sorted version.
4. Sort the records in the database by years within sex. Select descending sequence for the sex code and ascending sequence for the years. Print the sorted version.

Field Descriptions for the Prospective Programmer Database

FIELD NAME	COLUMN	TYPE OF DATA	SIZE
Name	A	Label	16
Sex	B	Label	5
Age	C	Numeric	5
Years	D	Numeric	7
BASIC	E	Label	7
COBOL	F	Label	7
C	G	Label	5
RPG	H	Label	5
123	I	Label	5
DBASE	J	Label	7

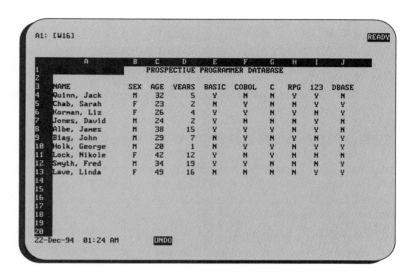

STUDENT ASSIGNMENT 7: Finding Records in the Prospective Programmer Database

Instructions: Load 1-2-3 and perform the following tasks.

1. Load the database created in Student Assignment 6 (STUS6-6). This worksheet is illustrated in the figure in Student Assignment 6.
2. For the Criteria range, copy row 3 (A3..J3) to row 15 (A15..J15).
3. In columns E through J of the database, the letter Y indicates that a prospective programmer knows the language or software package identified by the field name. The letter N indicates no experience with the language or software package. Find records that meet the following criteria. Treat each set of criteria in problems a through e separately.
   a. Find all records that represent prospective programmers who are male and can program in COBOL.
   b. Find all records that represent prospective programmers who can program in BASIC and RPG and use 1-2-3.
   c. Find all records that represent prospective male programmers who are at least 29 years old and can use dBASE.
   d. Find all records that represent prospective programmers who know 1-2-3 and dBASE.
   e. Find all records that represent prospective programmers who know at least one programming language and can use 1-2-3 or dBASE. (Hint: Your Criteria range should have 9 rows; including the field names.)
   f. All prospective programmers who did not know dBASE were sent to a seminar on the software package. Use the Find command to locate the records of these programmers and change the entries from the letter N to the letter Y under the field name dBASE. Save and print the database and the accompanying Criteria range. Use the file name STUS6-7.

STUDENT ASSIGNMENT 8: Extracting Records from the Prospective Programmer Database

Instructions: Load 1-2-3 and perform the following tasks.

1. Load the database created in Student Assignment 6 (STUS6-6). This worksheet is illustrated in the figure in Student Assignment 6.
2. For the Criteria range, copy row 3 (A3..J3) to row 15 (A15..J15). For the Output range, copy the field names NAME, SEX, and AGE (A3..C3) to K3..M3. Change the widths of column K to 16, column L to 5, and column M to 5. Extract the three fields from the records that meet the criteria in problems a through e. Treat each extraction in problems a through e separately. Print the worksheet after each extraction.
    a. Extract from records that represent prospective programmers who are male.
    b. Extract from records that represent prospective programmers who can program in BASIC and RPG.
    c. Extract from records that represent prospective male programmers who are at least 30 years old and can use 1-2-3.
    d. Extract from records that represent prospective programmers who know RPG and dBASE.
    e. Extract from records that represent prospective programmers who do not know how to use any programming language.
3. Save the database with the Criteria range specified in 2e. Use the file name STUS6-8.

STUDENT ASSIGNMENT 9: Property Tax Rate Table Lookup

Instructions: Load 1-2-3 and perform the numbered tasks to build the worksheet shown in the following figure. This worksheet uses the VLOOKUP function in cell C5 to look up the tax rate in the tax table in columns F and G. The VLOOKUP function employs cell C3 as the search argument. From the tax rate, the tax amount due in cell C7 can be determined.

1. Change the widths of column A to 11, column C to 13, and column F to 10. Leave the widths of the remaining columns at 9 characters.
2. Enter the title, column headings, and row identifiers.
3. Format cells C3 and C7 and range F4..F9 to the Comma (,) type with two decimal positions. Enter 57900 in cell C3. Format cell C5 and range G4..G9 to the Percent type with one decimal position.
4. Enter the table values in the range F4..G9.
5. Assign the function @VLOOKUP(C3,F4..G9,1) to cell C5.

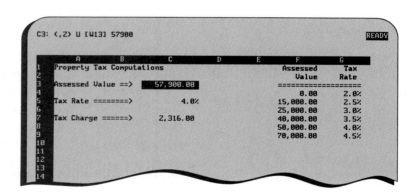

6. Assign the formula +C3*C5 to cell C7. This cell displays the tax amount due.
7. Test the worksheet to ensure that the VLOOKUP function is working properly.
8. Use the command /**W**orksheet **G**lobal **P**rotection **E**nable (/WGPE) to enable (turn on) cell protection. Unprotect cell C3.
9. Save the worksheet. Use the file name STUS6-9.
10. Determine the tax rate and tax charge for the following assessed valuations: $9,850.00; $40,000.00; $62,550.00; $42,500.00; and $452,750.00. Remember that commas are not allowed in a numeric entry. Print the worksheet for each assessed valuation.

APPENDIX

Command Structure Charts for Release 2.2

This appendix includes structure charts for each of the commands in the Main menu of Release 2.2. The purple commands indicate features added in Release 2.2.

The Worksheet Command

The Range Command

The Copy and Move Commands

The File Command

The Print Command

The Graph Command

The Data Command

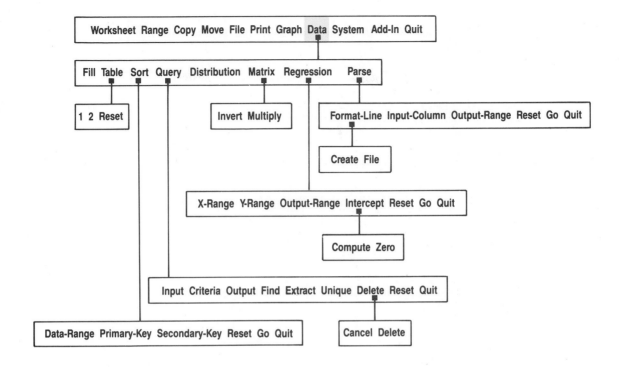

Worksheet Range Copy Move File Print Graph **Data** System Add-In Quit

Fill Table Sort Query Distribution Matrix Regression Parse

1 2 Reset

Invert Multiply

Format-Line Input-Column Output-Range Reset Go Quit

Create File

X-Range Y-Range Output-Range Intercept Reset Go Quit

Compute Zero

Input Criteria Output Find Extract Unique Delete Reset Quit

Data-Range Primary-Key Secondary-Key Reset Go Quit

Cancel Delete

The System Command

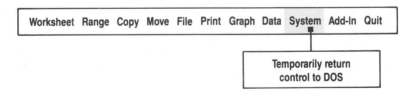

Worksheet Range Copy Move File Print Graph Data **System** Add-In Quit

Temporarily return
control to DOS

The Add-In Command

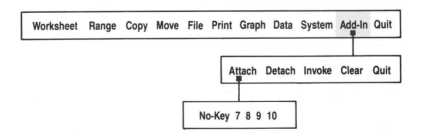

Worksheet Range Copy Move File Print Graph Data System **Add-In** Quit

Attach Detach Invoke Clear Quit

No-Key 7 8 9 10

The Quit Command

The PrintGraph Command

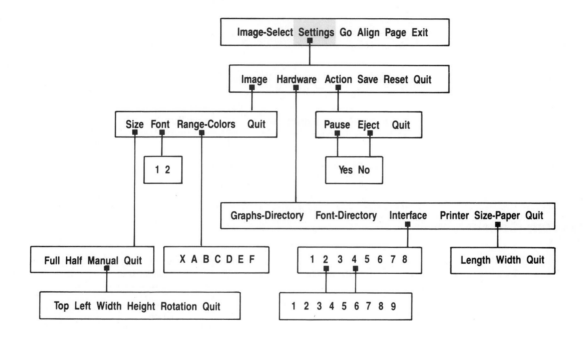

For each of the projects, we have provided the fundamental Lotus 1-2-3 activities in an easy-to-use quick reference format. This convenient reference tool is divided into three parts—activity, procedure, and description. All of the activities that you learn in each project are covered in the Quick Reference for that project. The numbers in parentheses that follow each activity refer to the page number on which the activity is first discussed in the text.

You can use these Quick References as study aids or to quickly recall how you complete an activity. The Quick Reference is a valuable and time-saving tool, and we encourage you to use it frequently.

QUICK REFERENCE — PROJECT 1

ACTIVITY	PROCEDURE	DESCRIPTION
START 1-2-3 (L2)	Type 123 Press ↵	Loads the 1-2-3 program into main memory.
MOVE CELL POINTER ONE CELL AT A TIME (L5)	↓ ↑ → ←	Press arrow keys to move cell pointer.
MOVE CELL POINTER MORE THAN ONE CELL AT A TIME (L15)	Press F5 Enter destination cell Press ↵	Use the GOTO command (F5) to move cell pointer to any cell in the worksheet including a cell which does not appear on the screen.
SAVE (L21)	Press / Type F Type S Enter file name Press ↵	Enters file name at the Save prompt. If the file name exists, type R to replace it.
PRINT SCREEN IMAGE (L25)	Press Print Screen	Prints exactly what you see on the screen.
CORRECT ERRORS ON INPUT LINE (L26)	Press Backspace	Erases character to left of cursor.
EDIT CELL CONTENTS (L27)	Press F2	Before pressing F2, move cell pointer to cell with error. Press ← or → to move cursor to character to correct. Toggle on overtype and type correct character.
UNDO (L30)	Press Alt-F4	Restores worksheet data and settings to what they were the last time 1-2-3 was in READY mode.
ERASE CELL CONTENTS (L31)	Press / Type R Type E Press ↵	Erases the contents of a cell.
ERASE WORKSHEET (L31)	Press / Type W Type E Type Y	Erases the worksheet in main memory. This command does not erase the worksheet from disk.
HELP (L31)	Press F1	Temporarily suspends the current activity and displays help. Press Esc key at any time to return to READY mode.
QUIT 1-2-3 (L32)	Press / Type Q Type Y	Quits 1-2-3 and returns control to DOS.

QUICK REFERENCE — PROJECT 2

ACTIVITY	PROCEDURE	DESCRIPTION
LOAD (L45)	Press / Type F Type R Select file name Press ↵	Use arrow keys to select file name.
CHANGE WIDTH OF ALL COLUMNS (L48)	Press / Type W Type G Type C Enter width Press ↵	Type the global width or use Left and Right Arrow keys to enter the global width.
CHANGE WIDTH OF ADJACENT COLUMNS (L50)	Press / Type W Type C Type C Type S Select columns Press ↵ Enter width Press ↵	Use Left and Right Arrow keys to select the columns. Type the width or use Left and Right Arrow keys to enter the width.
CHANGE WIDTH OF ONE COLUMN (L50)	Press / Type W Type C Type S Enter width Press ↵	Type the width or use Left and Right Arrow keys to enter the width.
FORMAT NUMERIC VALUES OVER A RANGE (L52)	Press / Type R Type F Select format Select decimal places Select range Press ↵	Select decimal places only if requested.
REPEAT CHARACTERS (L57)	Press \ Enter character(s) Press ↵	Character(s) will repeat throughout cell.
COPY (L58)	Press / Type C Enter source range Press ↵ Enter destination range Press ↵	Cell references in formulas are adjusted as copy takes place.
PRINT (L74)	Press / Type P Type P Select print range Press ↵ Type A Type G Type P Type Q	1-2-3 remembers the last print range entered.

QUICK REFERENCE — PROJECT 3

ACTIVITY	PROCEDURE	DESCRIPTION
FORMAT NUMERIC VALUES GLOBALLY (L95)	Press / Type W Type G Type F Select format Select decimal places Press ↵	Select decimal places only if requested.
INSERT ROWS OR COLUMNS (L100)	Press / Type W Type I Type R or C Select range Press ↵	If inserting rows, all rows including the one cell pointer is on, are pushed down. If inserting columns, all columns including the one cell pointer is on, are pushed to the right.
DELETE ROWS OR COLUMNS (L102)	Press / Type W Type D Type R or C Select range Press ↵	Make sure rows or columns to be deleted do not include data referenced elsewhere in formulas.
FREEZE TITLES (L105)	Press / Type W Type T Type B or H or V	Type B for both row and column titles. Type H for only column titles. Type V for only row titles.
MOVE (L106)	Type M Enter source range Press ↵ Enter destination range Press ↵	When moving a range containing a formula or function that references cell addresses, the referenced cell addresses are not changed relative to the new position, unless they refer to cells within the moved range.
INVOKE ALLWAYS (L126)	Press / Type A Type I Select ALLWAYS Press ↵	If a function key has been assigned to ALLWAYS, hold down the Alt key and press the assigned function key.
CHANGE FONT IN ALLWAYS (L128)	Press / Type F Type F Select font Press ↵ Select range Press ↵	Use arrow keys to select the desired font.
SHADE CELLS IN ALLWAYS (L131)	Press / Type F Type S Select shade Select range Press ↵	The shade can be light, dark, solid, or clear. The shortcut key is Alt-S.

(continued)

QUICK REFERENCE — PROJECT 3 (continued)

ACTIVITY	PROCEDURE	DESCRIPTION
BOLDFACING CELLS IN ALLWAYS (L132)	Press / Type F Type B Type S Select range Press ↵	The shortcut key is Alt-B.
UNDERLINING CELLS IN ALLWAYS (L133)	Press / Type F Type U Select underline Select range Press ↵	The shortcut key is Alt-U.
OUTLINING CELLS IN ALLWAYS (L134)	Press / Type F Type L Type O Select range Press ↵	The shortcut key is Alt-L.
CHANGE WIDTHS OF COLUMNS AND HEIGHTS OF ROWS IN ALLWAYS (L136)	Press / Type W Select column or row Type S Enter width or height Press ↵	Type the width or height or use arrow keys to enter the width or height.
PRINT IN ALLWAYS (L137)	Press / Type P Type R Type S Select range Press ↵ Press G	1-2-3 remembers the last print range entered.
ZOOM IN ALLWAYS (L138)	Press / Type D Type Z Select size	The size can be tiny, small, normal, large, or huge. The shortcut key to reduce the size is F4. The shortcut key to increase the size is Alt-F4.

QUICK REFERENCE — PROJECT 4

ACTIVITY	PROCEDURE	DESCRIPTION
NAME A RANGE (L157)	Press / Type R Type N Type C Enter name Press ↵ Enter range Press ↵	A range name can consist of up to 15 characters.
LABEL NAMES (L162)	Press / Type R Type N Type L Select adjacent cell Enter range Press ↵	An adjacent cell is to the right, down, to the left, or up.
DATA FILL (L163)	Press / Type D Type F Enter range Enter start Enter step Enter stop Press ↵	Range or stop value terminates data fill.
DATA TABLE 1 (L169)	Press / Type D Type T Type 1 Enter range Press ↵ Enter input cell Press ↵	Press F8 to recalculate a data table.
DATA TABLE 2 (L169)	Press / Type D Type T Type 2 Enter range Press ↵ Enter input cell-1 Press ↵ Enter input cell-2 Press ↵	Assigns formula to evaluate to upper left corner cell of range. Press F8 to recalculate a data table.
NAME MACRO (L171)	Press / Type R Type N Type C Enter name Press ↵ Enter range Press ↵	A range name can consist of up to 15 characters.

QUICK REFERENCE — PROJECT 4 (continued)

ACTIVITY	PROCEDURE	DESCRIPTION
INVOKE A MACRO (L171)	Alt-(macro name)	An alternative method for executing a macro is to press Alt-F3 and select the macro from the menu of range names.
SPLIT WINDOWS (L175)	Move cell pointer to split location Press / Type W Type W Type H or V	Type H for horizontal split. Type V for vertical split. Type /WWC to switch from two windows back to one window. Press F6 to deactivate current window and activate the other one.
CELL PROTECTION (L176)	Press / Type W Type G Type P Type E	This command sequence protects all cells. Use the /Range Unprotect (/RU) command to unprotect cells into which data is to be entered.

QUICK REFERENCE — PROJECT 5

ACTIVITY	PROCEDURE	DESCRIPTION
BUILD GRAPH (L193)	Press / Type G Type T Select graph type Enter ranges	Selects between line, bar, XY, stack-bar, and pie.
VIEW GRAPH (L194)	Press / Type G Type V	The shortcut key to view current graph is F10.
GRAPH OPTIONS (L196)	Press / Type G Type O Select option	Use the Options menu to select legends, formats, titles, grid, scale, color, B&W, and data-labels.
NAME GRAPH (L196)	Press / Type G Type N Type C Enter graph name Press ↵	A graph name can consist of up to 15 characters.
SAVE GRAPH SETTINGS (L197)	Press / Type F Type S Enter file name Press ↵	Graph settings are saved with the worksheet. Enter file name at the Save prompt.
SAVE PIC FILE (L197)	Press / Type G Type S Enter file name Press ↵	A PIC file is a snapshot of the current graph.
PRINT PIC FILE (L198)	Quit 1-2-3 Load PGRAPH Type I Highlight graph name Press ↵ Type A Type G Type P	When a graph name is highlighted, use the Spacebar to mark and unmark for printing. A number sign (#) to the left of a graph name indicates it is marked for printing.
ADD GRAPH TO WORKSHEET USING ALLWAYS (L213)	Press / Type G Type A Select graph name Press ↵ Enter range Press ↵	Press F10 to display graph in worksheet rather than crosshatched design.
RESIZING GRAPH USING ALLWAYS (L215)	Press / Type G Type S Select graph name Press ↵ Type R Enter range Press ↵ Type Q	Up to 20 graphs can be added to the worksheet.

QUICK REFERENCE — PROJECT 6

ACTIVITY	PROCEDURE	DESCRIPTION
SORT RECORDS (L230)	Press / Type D Type S Type D Select data range Press ↵ Type P Select sort key Press ↵ Select sort sequence Press ↵ Type G	If a secondary key is involved in the sort, enter it immediately after the primary sort key is entered.
FIND RECORDS (L235)	Press / Type D Type Q Type I Select input range Press ↵ Type C Select criteria range Press ↵ Type F	The criteria is entered into worksheet before initiating the query. After typing F, use arrow keys to find the next record that meets the criteria. Press ↵ or Esc to return to Data Query menu.
EXTRACT RECORDS (L239)	Press / Type D Type Q Type I Select input range Press ↵ Type C Select criteria range Press ↵ Type O Select output range Press ↵ Type E	The criteria is entered into worksheet before initiating the query. The column headings for the output range are entered before initiating the query.
SEARCH (L246)	Press / Type R Type S Select range Press ↵ Enter search string Press ↵ Select search type Type F Type N	Search type may be F for Formulas, L for Labels, or B for Both. Typing Q during the search activity returns 1-2-3 to READY mode.
REPLACE (L247)	Press / Type R Type S Select range Press ↵ Enter search string Press ↵ Select search type Type R Enter replace string Press ↵ Type R	Search type may be F for Formulas, L for Labels, or B for Both. To replace all occurrences, type A rather than R after entering the replace string. Typing Q during the replace returns 1-2-3 to READY mode.

◆ INDEX

Database Management Using dBASE IV Version 1.1

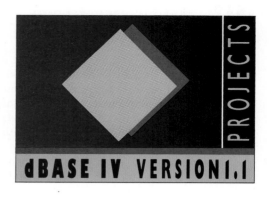

dBASE IV VERSION 1.1

Creating, storing, sorting, and retrieving data are important tasks. In their personal lives, most people keep data in a variety of records such as the names, addresses, and telephone numbers of friends and business associates, records of investments, and records of expenses for income tax purposes. These records must be arranged so that the data can be accessed easily when required. In business, information must also be stored and accessed quickly and easily. Personnel and inventory records must be kept; payroll information and other types of data must be accumulated and periodically updated. Like personal records, business records must be organized so that the information they contain can be retrieved easily and rapidly.

The term **database** describes a collection of data organized in a manner that allows access, retrieval, and use of that data. A database is a structure that can hold data concerning many different types of objects (technically called **entities**) as well as relationships between these objects. For example, a company's database might hold data on such objects as sales reps and customers. In addition, the database would include the relationship between sales reps and customers; that is, we could use the data in the database to determine the sales rep who represents any particular customer and to determine all the customers who are represented by any given sales rep.

Figure 1 gives a sample of such a database. It consists of two tables: SLSREP and CUSTOMER. The columns in the SLSREP table include the sales rep number, name, address, total commission, and commission rate. For example, the name of sales rep 3 is Mary Jones. She lives at 123 Main St. in Grant, Michigan. Her total commission is $2,150.00 and her commission rate is 5 percent.

SLSREP_NUMBER	SLSREP_NAME	SLSREP_ADDRESS	TOTAL_COMMISSION	COMMISSION_RATE
3	Mary Jones	123 Main,Grant,MI	2150.00	.05
6	William Smith	102 Raymond,Ada,MI	4912.50	.07

sales rep 3 → 3

CUSTOMER_NUMBER	NAME	ADDRESS	CURRENT_BALANCE	CREDIT_LIMIT	SLSREP_NUMBER
124	Sally Adams	481 Oak,Lansing,MI	418.75	500	3
256	Ann Samuels	215 Pete,Grant,MI	10.75	800	6
315	Tom Daniels	914 Cherry,Kent,MI	320.75	300	6
412	Susan Lin	16 Elm,Lansing,MI	908.75	1000	3
567	Joe Baker	808 Ridge,Harper,MI	201.20	300	6
587	Judy Roberts	512 Pine,Ada,MI	57.75	500	6
622	Dan Martin	419 Chip,Grant,MI	575.50	500	3

customers of sales rep 3

FIGURE 1   Sample database of sales reps and customers

The first five columns in the customer table include the customer number, name, address, current balance, and credit limit. The name of customer 622 is Dan Martin. He lives at 419 Chip St. in Grant, Michigan. His current balance is $575.50, which happens to exceed his $500 credit limit.

The last column in the customer table serves a special purpose. It *relates* customers and sales reps. Using this column, we can see that Dan Martin's sales rep is sales rep 3 (Mary Jones). Likewise, we can see that, in addition to Dan Martin, Mary Jones represents customers 124 (Sally Adams) and 412 (Susan Lin). We do this by first looking up Mary's number in the SLSREP table and then looking for all the rows in the CUSTOMER table that contain this number in the SLSREP_NUMBER column.

In a sense, the tables shown in Figure 1 form a database even if they are simply kept on paper. But for easy and rapid access, they should be kept on a computer. All we would need is a tool that would help users access such a database. A database management system is such a tool. A **database management system**, or **DBMS**, is a software product that can be used easily to create a database; to add, delete, and change data in the database; to sort the data in the database; and to retrieve data from the database in a variety of ways.

The most widely used DBMS available for personal computers is the dBASE family from Ashton-Tate. The newest and most dynamic entry in the family is dBASE IV. dBASE IV is a powerful DBMS. Its commands let users easily create and manage databases they need for either personal or business needs. dBASE IV is one of a general category of database management systems called **relational**. In simplest terms, this means that the data in the database can be visualized exactly as you saw in Figure 1, that is, as a collection of tables, each consisting of a series of rows and columns. From this point on, we will refer to dBASE IV as dBASE.

dBASE IV VERSION1.1

PROJECT 1

Creating a Database

OBJECTIVES

You will have mastered the material in this project when you can:

◆ Plan a database

◆ Load and use dBASE

◆ Use menus and options within the Control Center

◆ Create a database file

◆ Add records to a database file

◆ Correct errors in a database file

◆ Delete records from a database file

◆ Produce a report showing all records in a database file

◆ Back up a database file

In Project 1 you will learn how to create a database using dBASE. To illustrate the process, we will work through a sample problem that relates to creating and accessing a company's employee records.

The employee record form (Figure 1-1) is the basis of the database. Each record contains an employee number, the employee name, the date hired, a department name, the employee's pay rate, and an entry indicating whether the employee is a member of the union. The records taken as a whole comprise a **file**. Each form that contains information about a single employee is called a **record**, and the individual units of information within each record are called **fields**. Thus, in this example, Date Hired is a field, all the information about Anthony P. Rapoza is a record, and Anthony Rapoza's record along with the records of all the other employees in this company make up the file.

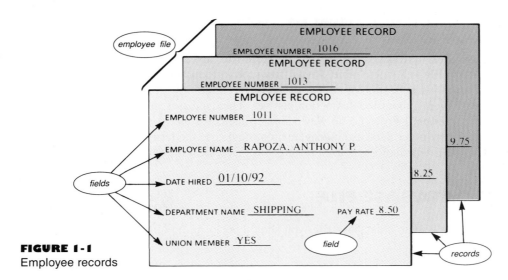

FIGURE 1-1
Employee records

For another perspective, consider the sample table shown in Figure 1-2. Notice that it presents the same data as Figure 1-1, but in a more concise format. The rows in this table are the records. The columns are the fields. The whole table is a file.

EMPLOYEE NUMBER	EMPLOYEE NAME	DATE HIRED	DEPARTMENT NAME	PAY RATE	UNION MEMBER
1011	Rapoza, Anthony P.	01/10/92	Shipping	8.50	T
1013	McCormack, Nigel L.	01/15/92	Shipping	8.25	T
1016	Ackerman, David R.	02/04/92	Accounting	9.75	F
1017	Doi, Chan J.	02/05/92	Production	6.00	F
1020	Castle, Mark C.	03/04/92	Shipping	7.50	T
1022	Dunning, Lisa A.	03/12/92	Marketing	9.10	F
1025	Chaney, Joseph R.	03/23/92	Accounting	8.00	F
1026	Bender, Helen O.	04/12/92	Production	6.75	T
1029	Anderson, Mariane L.	04/18/92	Shipping	9.00	T
1030	Edwards, Kenneth J.	04/23/92	Production	8.60	T
1037	Baxter, Charles W.	05/05/92	Accounting	11.00	F
1041	Evans, John T.	05/19/92	Marketing	6.00	F
1056	Andrews, Robert M.	06/03/92	Marketing	9.00	F
1057	Dugan, Mary L.	06/10/92	Production	8.75	T
1066	Castleworth, Mary T.	07/05/92	Production	8.75	T

records

fields

FIGURE 1-2 Employee table

Similar terminology is used in dBASE. Rather than the term file, however, dBASE uses the term database file. Thus, in dBASE, a **database file** is a single table. Recall from the introduction that a relational database is not necessarily a single table, but usually a collection of tables. In dBASE terminology, this means that a database is a collection of database *files*. Don't worry about the distinction just yet. The databases in our first four projects consist of a single database file (table). Not until Project 5 do we encounter databases that contain more than one database file.

You should know that many other database management systems use the terms **table** (for file), **row** (for record), and **column** (for field). dBASE terminology is used throughout this text, however.

PLANNING A DATABASE FILE

Before you use dBASE to create a database file, you should perform the following four steps:

1. Select a name for the database file.
2. Define the structure of the database file; that is, determine the fields that will be a part of the file.
3. Name the fields.
4. Determine the type and width of each field.

Naming a Database File

When using dBASE, you must assign a name to each database file. The rules for forming a name are:

1. The name can be up to eight characters in length.

2. The first character must be a letter of the alphabet.
3. The remaining characters can be letters, numbers, or the underscore (_).
4. Blank spaces are not allowed within a file name.

   You should select names that are as meaningful as possible so it's easier to identify the database file later. In the sample problem, let's use the name EMPLOYEE.

Defining the Structure of a Database File

To define the structure of the database file, you must determine the fields that will make up the file. The fields you want to include in the database stored on disk must be based on the type of information that the user needs to extract from the database. For example, let's suppose that we know we will require access to each of the fields on the employee form, that is, the employee number field, the employee name field, the date hired field, the department name field, the pay rate field, and the field that indicates whether the employee is a member of the union. We will include these six fields in the structure of EMPLOYEE. (dBASE allows records to have up to 128 fields and to be up to 4,000 characters long. We certainly have no problems with either of these limits.)

Naming the Fields

You must assign a unique name to each field in the database. The rules for forming field names are:

1. A field name can contain up to ten characters.
2. The first character must be a letter of the alphabet.
3. The remaining characters can be letters, numbers, or the underscore (_).
4. Blank spaces are not allowed within the field name.

   Figure 1-3 illustrates the field names that are used in the sample database file.

FIELD DESCRIPTION	FIELD NAME
EMPLOYEE NUMBER	NUMBER
EMPLOYEE NAME	NAME
DATE HIRED	DATE
DEPARTMENT NAME	DEPARTMENT
PAY RATE	PAY_RATE
UNION MEMBER	UNION

FIGURE 1-3
Fields in employee file

   You should select meaningful field names that are closely related to the contents of the field. For example, the field name for the Pay Rate field is PAY_RATE. (The underscore is often used to join words together to improve readability because blanks are not allowed within field names.)

Defining Field Types

Next, you must determine the type of each field in the database. There are several field types in dBASE. The most common are:

1. **Character fields** — These fields store any printable character that can be entered from the keyboard. This includes letters of the alphabet, numbers, special characters, and blanks.
2. **Date fields** — These fields store dates in the form MM/DD/YY (month/day/year), unless otherwise specified.
3. **Numeric fields** — These fields store either integer numbers or decimal numbers. Integer numbers do not contain a decimal point, whereas decimal numbers do. Numeric fields may contain a plus (+) or minus (–) sign. Accuracy is to 15 digits. A field must be defined as numeric if it is to be used in a calculation.

4. **Logical fields** — These fields store a single value representing a true or false condition. The entry must be T (True), F (False), Y (Yes), or N (No). Lowercase letters can also be used.
5. **Memo fields** — These fields store large blocks of text such as words or sentences and are useful for comments. For example, we might want to store a comment about each employee's work habits as part of the employee's record. We do not use such fields in our example.

Figure 1-4 illustrates the field type for the various fields used in the sample problem. Notice that the employee number field is specified as a character field because a field that is not involved in calculations, even if it contains all numbers, should be defined as a character field. The employee name field is defined as a character field, the date hired field as a date field, the department name field as a character field, the pay rate field as a numeric field, and the union member field as a logical field. The chart also indicates which fields are to be indexed. Although we won't discuss the concept of indexing quite yet, we do need to specify which fields are to be indexed to dBASE at this point. (In this project, we always tell you which fields should be indexed.)

FIELD DESCRIPTION	FIELD NAME	FIELD TYPE	WIDTH	DECIMAL POSITIONS	INDEX
EMPLOYEE NUMBER	NUMBER	CHARACTER	4		Y
EMPLOYEE NAME	NAME	CHARACTER	20	*decimal positions only necessary for numeric fields*	N
DATE HIRED	DATE	DATE	8		N
DEPARTMENT NAME	DEPARTMENT	CHARACTER	10		N
PAY RATE	PAY_RATE	NUMERIC	5	2	N
UNION MEMBER	UNION	LOGICAL	1		N

FIGURE 1-4 Field characteristics for employee file

Indicating Width and Decimal Position

dBASE knows that date fields have width 8 and logical fields have width 1. For other types of fields, you must specify the width. In addition, for numeric fields, you must specify the decimal position. The width of the field indicates the maximum number of characters the field can hold. The decimal position specifies the location of the decimal point. For example, a decimal position of 2 indicates that there are two positions to the right of the decimal point. The entries in Figure 1-4 describe the database that we are creating in the sample problem.

We define the PAY_RATE field as having a width of five characters. This means that the maximum value that can be stored in the PAY_RATE field is 99.99. In a numeric field, the decimal point is counted when specifying the field width because it occupies a screen position.

USING dBASE

Loading dBASE

Before you use dBASE, you must load it into main memory. Since the process depends on how your particular installation is set up, you should check with your instructor concerning the specific details of this process. The steps shown in Figure 1-5 give one possible approach. They will only be accurate if you are storing your files on a diskette in drive A and dBASE is stored in a directory called dbase on drive C. You can type the commands in uppercase or lowercase, and their functions are as follows.

1. The first command creates the required path to the directory containing dBASE. It assumes that dBASE is located in a directory called dbase on drive C. (If dBASE has been installed in the usual manner, the required path command will execute automatically when you boot your computer, so you can skip this step. Check with your instructor to see if this is the case.)

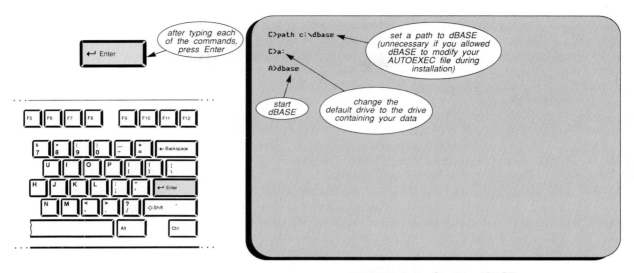

FIGURE 1-5 Starting dBASE

2. The second command makes the drive where you will place your data files the default drive. It assumes that your data files will be placed on a diskette in drive A. If this is not the case, you need to change this command accordingly.
3. The third command loads and starts dBASE.

   After you have completed these steps, dBASE is loaded into main memory and the dBASE license agreement is displayed on the screen. To proceed, press Enter again. If you don't press Enter, dBASE takes you on to the next screen after a short pause. Pressing Enter at this point simply speeds up the process.

The Control Center

Let's begin by looking at some of the important screens you will use in dBASE as well as some of the keys you will use to accomplish various tasks. To begin, start dBASE in the manner we just described. Your screen should look like Figure 1-6. This is called the **Control Center**. It is the screen from which you begin most of your work. Let's look at the various portions of the Control Center.

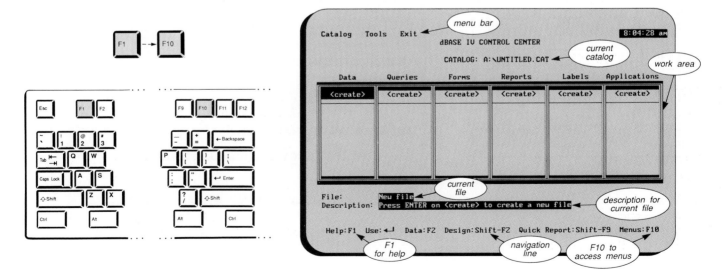

FIGURE 1-6 Control Center

The area at the top of the screen where you see the words Catalog, Tools, and Exit is called the menu bar. Each of the three terms (Catalog, Tools, and Exit) represents a menu. A **menu** is simply a list of actions from which you can choose. As you work with dBASE, the words listed at the top of the screen may change, but the list itself always plays the same role. It is a collection of menus that you access to select the action you want to take next.

Farther down the screen is a line that begins with CATALOG:. A **catalog** is simply a collection of related files. It is like a file folder that helps you organize your paperwork. You have a chance to create and use catalogs throughout this text. The various files you create will be grouped into these catalogs. The CATALOG line on the screen indicates which catalog is currently in use. Presently it indicates that a special catalog, called UNTITLED, is in use. We show you how to switch from one catalog to another and what happens when you do.

The big box on the screen is called the **work area** and it is also referred to as the **panel**. It contains a list of files of various types that are in the current catalog. At any given point, either one of these files or the word <create> will be highlighted. The highlighted file appears after the word File and a description of it appears after the word Description. If the word <create> is highlighted, the file name and description will appear as shown in Figure 1-6. Each column in the Control Center relates to a given task and is also referred to as a task panel.

Finally, the line at the bottom of the screen is called the **navigation line**. It tells you how certain special keys function. The navigation line in Figure 1-6, for example, shows that you can press function key 1 (the key labeled F1 on your keyboard) to obtain help or press F10 to use the menus.

All of this detail may seem confusing, but once you master a few simple techniques, you will be able to work your way through the various steps without much difficulty. We now turn our attention to the way we work with dBASE.

Pressing Esc

The key labeled Esc is called the Escape key. Sometimes you might find that you unintentionally chose the wrong option. In other cases, you might not want to proceed with some action you have started, but you're not sure how to get out. In such situations, simply press Esc. Sometimes this immediately returns you to the Control Center. Other times, you may first be asked to indicate whether you really want to escape from the task on which you are working. In still others, you may need to press Esc more than once to return to the Control Center.

To illustrate the use of the Esc key, press F10. Your screen should look like Figure 1-7. The Catalog menu is currently on your screen, and if you wanted to, you could make a choice from this menu. Let's suppose that you decide not to make a choice after all. Simply press Esc and the menu is removed from your screen. You are then returned to the same screen you were on before you pressed F10. The Esc key is handy to use when you find that you don't want to proceed in a particular task.

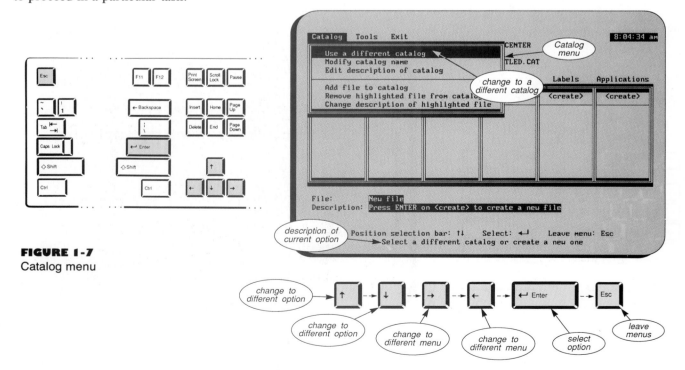

FIGURE 1-7
Catalog menu

Using Menus

Next, we examine the way you use menus in dBASE. Press F10 again, producing the screen shown in Figure 1-7. You are now in the Menu mode, where you indicate the option you want by selecting it from a menu. (Don't worry about the meaning of the specific choices for now.)

The menu currently visible on the screen is the Catalog menu. The possible choices — "Use a different catalog", "Modify catalog name", and so on — are listed in the box. Notice that the first choice, "Use a different catalog", is currently highlighted. When you press the Down Arrow key several times, the highlight moves down through some of the other choices. Whenever an option is highlighted, a brief description of the option appears at the bottom of the screen, under the navigation line. Depending on what actions you took before you pressed F10, some of these options may not be currently available to you. The highlight automatically skips over such options. Press the Right Arrow key once. Your screen should now look like Figure 1-8. You now see a different menu, the Tools menu.

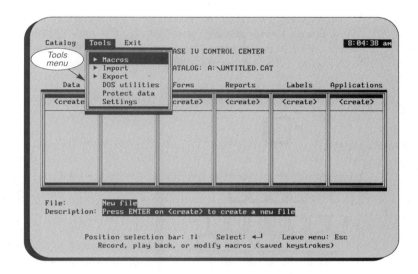

FIGURE 1-8
Tools menu

Press the Right Arrow key again and you will see the Exit menu (Figure 1-9). Press the Left Arrow key twice and you are returned to the Catalog menu.

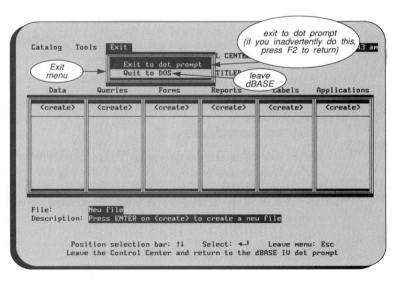

FIGURE 1-9 Exit menu

To recap, you bring the menus to the screen by pressing F10. You move from one menu to another by using the Left and Right Arrow keys. Within a menu, you move from one option to another by using the Up and Down Arrow keys.

The final step in the process is to actually make the selection. First, make sure the option you want is highlighted by using the appropriate arrow keys. Then, simply press Enter.

Another way to select an option from a menu is to hold the Alt key down and type the first letter of the menu. The options will then be displayed. Release the Alt key and type the first letter of the option you want. Use the approach with which you are most comfortable. (Be aware that the keystroke summary at the end of each project reflects the use of the F10 and arrow keys.)

The Dot Prompt

Besides using the Control Center, you can also use the **dot prompt** in dBASE. The only reason we mention it here is so that if you inadvertently switch to this mode, you will recognize it and be able to return to the Control Center. For example, when you want to exit dBASE, you should select the "Quit to DOS" option from the Exit menu (Figure 1-9). If you select "Exit to dot prompt" by mistake, you will find yourself in the **dot prompt mode** and your screen should look like Figure 1-10. Notice the single dot near the lower left corner of the screen. This is the dot prompt.

FIGURE 1-10 Dot prompt screen

Fortunately, if you ever find yourself at the dot prompt, you can easily return to the Control Center by pressing F2. The Control Center appears once again on your screen.

"Press any key to continue..."

When you use dBASE, you often see the message "Press any key to continue...". This message means exactly what it says: Press any key whatsoever and you will continue what you are doing. It typically appears when you are displaying a report on the screen. dBASE displays one screenful of the report and then this message. You can look at the portion of the report that is on the screen for as long as you want. When you are ready to move on, simply press any key, and the next portion of the report appears.

Selecting a Catalog

Before you access data in a particular database, you should first select the appropriate catalog, that is, the catalog for that database. Select the "Use a different catalog" option from the Catalog menu, and your screen should look like Figure 1-11. The box on the right-hand side of the screen lists the available catalogs. Like many other lists you will encounter, this list contains an item called <create>. This option is used to create a new catalog, which is precisely what you need to do at this point. Make sure <create> is highlighted and press Enter.

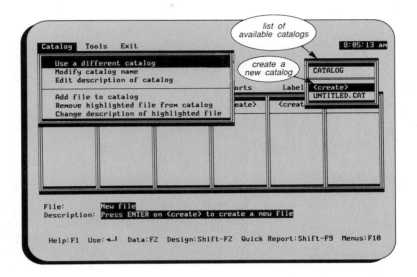

FIGURE 1-11
Changing catalogs

dBASE then asks you to name the catalog. Type EMPCAT (for EMPloyee CATalog) and press Enter. (You can use either uppercase or lowercase letters when you type EMPCAT.) Your screen should now look like Figure 1-12. Notice that the catalog you created, EMPCAT, is now the active catalog.

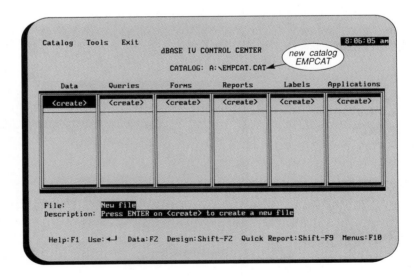

FIGURE 1-12
Control Center

"Abandon Operation"

Make sure you are at the Control Center with no menus visible and press Esc. You then see a screen similar to Figure 1-13. The question in the box asks, "Are you sure you want to abandon operation?". You will see such a box frequently. Since the No choice is already highlighted, you would not abandon what you are doing if you were to press Enter. You would simply be returned to the Control Center screen. To choose Yes instead, use the Left Arrow key to move the highlight to it and then press Enter. If you choose Yes, you do abandon whatever you are working on. In this particular situation, if you select Yes, you abandon the Control Center and are taken to the dot prompt. (Remember that you can return to the Control Center by pressing F2.) Select "No" to return to the Control Center.

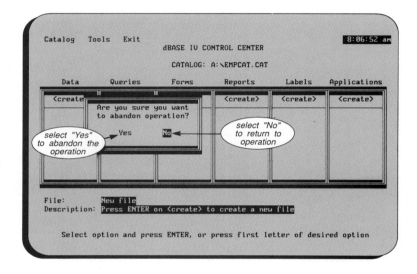

FIGURE 1-13
"Abandon operation" question

Getting Help

dBASE has an extensive help facility. You can get help on a variety of topics while you are at the computer. Simply press F1. When you do, you will see a screen similar to Figure 1-14. You may only need to read the information on that screen, but, as you see on the bottom line of this screen, you can also press F4 to move to the next screen of help information or F3 to move back to the previous screen.

FIGURE 1-14
Help screen

You can select "Contents" to see a table of contents of help information or "Related Topics" to get information on other topics that are related to the topic at which you are currently looking. You can also select "Print" to get a printed copy of the information. To select any of these, move the highlight to the option you want and press Enter. When you have finished looking, press Esc.

When you request help, the information you get is information concerning the task on which you are working. However, you can use the table of contents to obtain help on any topic. Practice using the various options within the help facility. Use the table of contents. Select related topics. The better you become in obtaining help, the better off you'll be later when you need it. Remember that you can always get out of "Help" by pressing Esc.

Leaving dBASE

To leave dBASE, you should be at the Control Center. Press F10 to change to Menu mode and move to the Exit menu. The first choice, "Exit to dot prompt", would take you to the dot prompt you saw earlier, but this is not what you want. You want the second choice, "Quit to DOS". Press the Down Arrow key to highlight this choice and then press Enter.

Practice

At this point, it's a good idea for you to practice using dBASE. Do this by moving through the various options we looked at. While you do, pay close attention to the effect on the last two lines on the screen. Try getting help. Try leaving dBASE and starting it again. Try pressing Esc to move to the dot prompt and then pressing F2 to get back to the Control Center. You should do this until you are very comfortable with these techniques.

CREATING THE DATABASE

Beginning the Process

Make sure the highlight is on <create> in the Data column and press Enter. You are now taken to the screen used to design a database (Figure 1-15). On this screen, you will enter the information on all the fields in the database file. The status line shows that:

1. You are creating a database file.
2. The default drive is A: (yours might be different).
3. You are creating a new file. If you were working on a file that already existed, its name would appear in the spot currently occupied by <NEW>.
4. You are currently working on the first field.
5. So far there is only this one field.

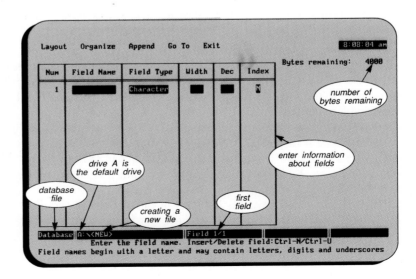

FIGURE 1-15
Database Design screen

Defining the Structure

Next, you define the structure of the database by specifying for each field: the field name, the field type, the field width, decimal places (if appropriate), and whether to index the field. The screen in Figure 1-15 is designed to help you enter this information.

In the upper right-hand portion of the screen, the number of remaining bytes is displayed. (A byte is a single position of main memory. It is the amount of main memory required to store a single character. Thus you can think of the terms byte and character as being synonymous.) In dBASE, a record can contain a maximum of 4,000 bytes, or characters, so initially the number of remaining bytes is 4,000. As we add fields, this number decreases, continually reflecting the number of bytes we still have available.

In this box are screen headings for field name, type, width, dec, and index. Beneath the headings are reverse video blocks that are used to indicate where the field name is entered, where the field type is selected, where the width of the field is specified, where the number of decimal positions (for numeric fields) are entered, and where we indicate whether an index is to be created for the field. The cursor is in the first position of the area where the field name is to be entered. The number 1 to the left of the cursor merely indicates that this is the area in which you will define the first field.

The entry on the bottom line of the screen provides information to help you make the appropriate entry in the field name portion of the display. This message changes as the cursor moves from one portion of the screen to the next.

Now let's define the fields for the employee records database that we described earlier in the project (Figure 1-4). Begin by typing the name of the first field you want to define. In the example, the first field is the employee number field. Recall from Figure 1-4 that the field name is NUMBER. Therefore, enter NUMBER as the first field name (Figure 1-16).

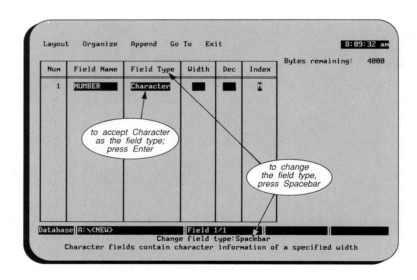

FIGURE 1-16
Selecting field type

If the entry in the field name portion of the screen has fewer than ten characters, you must press Enter to move the cursor to the next area on the screen. Since the word NUMBER has only six characters, press Enter. After you do this, the cursor moves to the Field Type column on the screen. Under the Field Type column is the word Character within the reverse video block (Figure 1-16).

Next, you will specify the type of field being defined. You accomplished this by simply pressing the Spacebar until the desired field type is displayed. Do this a few times. After you have pressed it once, the entry in the Field Type column changes to the word Numeric; a second time changes it to Float (a type we won't use); the next time, it changes to Date; and so on. Keep pressing the Spacebar until it is back to the word Character, at which point, the whole sequence would start all over again.

Because the employee number field is not used in calculations, it should be defined as a character field. To specify that NUMBER is a character field, make sure the word Character is displayed on the screen and press Enter. The cursor then advances to the Width column.

Now you must type the width of the field. The example allows the employee number field to have a maximum of four digits. Therefore, type the number 4 and press Enter, producing the display shown in Figure 1-17. Because there can be no decimal entries for a character field, the cursor moves automatically to the Index column. As Figure 1-4 indicated, the index entry for this field should be Y, whereas for all the other fields it should be N. Type the letter Y (in either uppercase or lowercase) at this point.

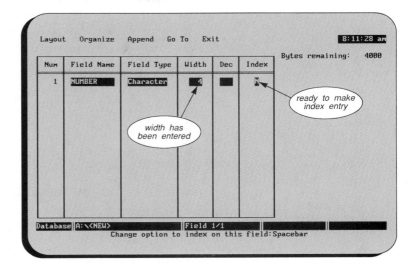

FIGURE 1-17
Database Design screen

Since the entries for the NUMBER field are now complete, the cursor and the reverse video display move to the next line. The entries for the NAME field are illustrated in Figure 1-18. Make these entries in the same way that you did for the NUMBER field.

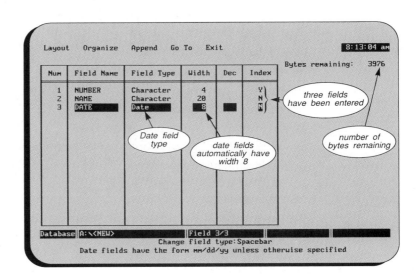

FIGURE 1-18
Database Design screen

In Figure 1-18, the name and type of the DATE field have also been entered. Type the name of this field (DATE) and then press Enter. Notice that the number of bytes remaining is 3976 because so far we have used up 24 bytes (NUMBER occupies 4 bytes and NAME occupies 20). Since we have not completed the entries for the DATE field, the number of bytes remaining does not yet reflect the bytes necessary to store the date.

When you press Enter after typing DATE, the cursor moves to the Field Type column. Because DATE is to be treated as a Date field, press the Spacebar repeatedly until the word Date appears in the Field Type column (remember this was already done in the figure) and then press Enter. dBASE automatically specifies the width as 8. (The slashes in a date count as positions in the field.)

Make the remaining entries as shown in Figure 1-19. Because the name DEPARTMENT occupies all positions in the field name portion of the display, when you type the last character (the ending T in DEPARTMENT), a beep sounds and the cursor automatically advances to the next column.

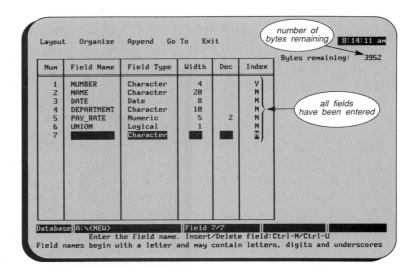

FIGURE 1-19
Database Design screen

If you make a mistake in any of these entries, use the keys shown in Figure 1-20 to go back and correct it. (Shift-Tab means hold down the Shift key and press the Tab key. Ctrl-N means hold down the Ctrl key and type the letter N.)

KEY	PURPOSE
↑	Moves the highlight up one row
↓	Moves the highlight down one row
→	Moves the cursor one position to the right
←	Moves the cursor one position to the left
Tab	Moves the cursor one column to the right
Shift–Tab	Moves the cursor one column to the left
Backspace	Moves the cursor one position to the left and erases the character that was in that position
↵	Completes the current entry and moves the cursor to the next column. If you are in the last column in a row, moves to the first column in the next row
Ctrl–N	Inserts a blank row at the current cursor position
Ctrl–U	Deletes the row at the current cursor position

FIGURE 1-20 Special keys used when designing a database

Completing the Process

When you have made all the entries, you will have defined all the fields in the database. To indicate to dBASE that you are done, press F10 to change to Menu mode, use the Right Arrow key to move to the Exit menu (Figure 1-21), and select the "Save changes and exit" option.

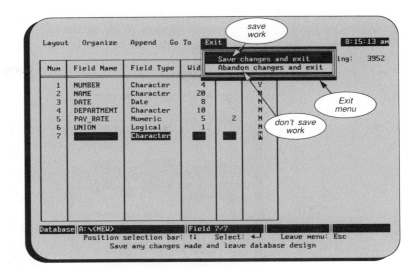

FIGURE 1-21
Leaving database design

dBASE then asks you to name this database file. Names for files can be up to eight characters long and can contain letters, numbers, and underscores (_). Type EMPLOYEE as the name for this file and press Enter. You are returned to the Control Center and the file you just created, EMPLOYEE, is active and displayed at the bottom of the screen.

In general, file names can contain a three-character extension (the characters following the period in the name of the file). dBASE adds its own extensions to file names. All you do is indicate the regular part of the name and dBASE does the rest automatically. On some screens you will see these extensions, but you don't need to do anything with them.

The final step is to enter a description of this EMPLOYEE file. This is not required, but it will help you differentiate between files later. Select the "Change description of highlighted file" option from the Catalog menu (Figure 1-22). (Since you have just worked on the EMPLOYEE file, it is already highlighted. If it weren't, you would have to move the highlight to it using the arrow keys before selecting this option.)

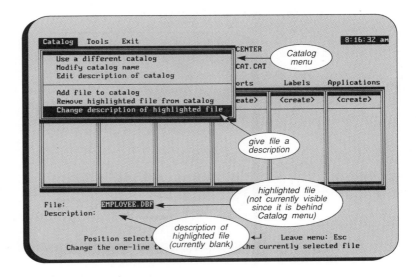

FIGURE 1-22
Control Center

Enter the words Employee database file, and then press Enter. Your screen should now look like Figure 1-23. Notice that the description you just entered appears on the screen. Also notice in the Data column that the word EMPLOYEE appears *above* the line. This indicates that the file is currently active. If it were not active, EMPLOYEE would be below the line.

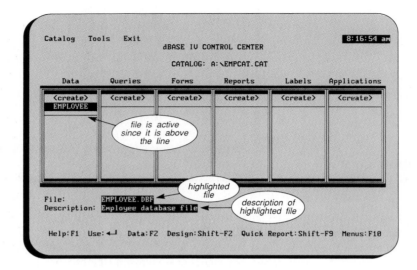

FIGURE 1-23
Control Center

ENTERING DATA USING THE EDIT SCREEN

Adding Data

To add records to the active database file (the one above the line), press F2. (Notice that F2 is one of the keys described on the screen.) This takes you to the Edit screen (Figure 1-24). You use this screen to add new records or to change existing records.

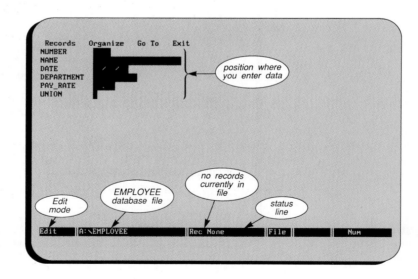

FIGURE 1-24
Edit Screen

You enter your data in the upper portion of the screen. This area consists of the field names from your database file, followed by reverse video blocks that represent the maximum number of characters that you can enter in each field. Notice that the DATE field contains two slashes. When you enter the date, type a two-digit month, a two-digit day, and a two-digit year; for example, 05 09 92. dBASE will position the date correctly around the slashes. The PAY_RATE field contains a decimal point in the screen display because you defined it as a field with a width of 5 and two positions to the right of the decimal place.

When you are entering a value for UNION, it's a good idea to restrict yourself to just entering T (for true) or F (for false) even though dBASE allows you to enter Y (for yes) or N (for no). It is easy to get confused if you use T or F some of the time and Y or N other times. Furthermore, when dBASE displays this data, it displays T or F. If you enter Y, it is displayed as a T. If you enter N, it is displayed as an F. Thus it makes sense to use only T or F.

Enter the data, up to the union code, as shown in Figure 1-25. Notice that you enter the name Rapoza, Anthony P. as Rappozi, Athony P. This will give you a chance later to experiment with making corrections. Enter the data one field at a time. The cursor automatically moves to the next line if the data you entered fills up the entire width of the field. If not, you must press Enter after you have entered the data for a field. When you enter the pay rate, type the value including the decimal point (for example, 8.50). dBASE properly positions the value around the decimal point in the area reserved for the pay rate.

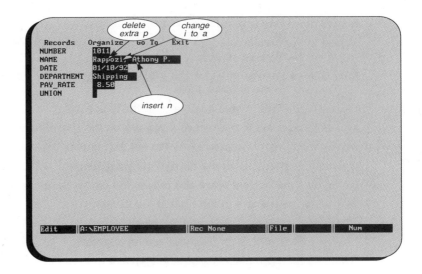

FIGURE 1-25
Edit screen

Correcting Errors During Data Entry

If you make a typing mistake when you are entering data, you can correct the error (provided you have not yet pressed Enter) by merely pressing the Backspace key as many times as necessary to delete the unwanted characters and then retyping the data.

dBASE also provides very powerful editing capabilities for correcting errors made after you have pressed Enter. For example, let's suppose that, after you have entered the data for the PAY_RATE in the first record, you discover that you erroneously entered the name Rapoza, Anthony P. as Rappozi, Athony P. (Figure 1-25). Three errors are apparent. First there is an extra p in the last name. Second, the last character in the last name should be an a instead of an i. Third, an n should be inserted after the first character in the first name.

When you correct data, you can use the Up and Down Arrow keys and the Right and Left Arrow keys to move the cursor to the location where you must make a correction. You could simply retype the data in its entirety, this time making sure you do it correctly. Often a quicker alternative is to use the Delete and Insert keys to delete and insert data. Figure 1-26 illustrates the keys that are used for moving the cursor and inserting and deleting data. Let's correct the name by using these keys.

KEY	PURPOSE
↑	Moves the cursor up one row
↓	Moves the cursor down one row
→	Moves the cursor one position to the right
←	Moves the cursor one position to the left
Tab	Moves to the next field
Shift–Tab	Moves to the previous field
Page Down	Moves to the next record if you are on the Edit screen
	Moves down one screenful if you are on the Browse screen
Page Up	Moves to the previous record if you are on the Edit screen. Moves up one screenful if you are on the Browse screen
Home	Moves to beginning of field if you are on the Edit screen. Moves to first field in the record if you are on the Browse screen
End	Moves to the end of field if you are on the Edit screen
	Moves to last field in the record if you are on the Browse screen
Backspace	Moves the cursor one position to the left and erases the character that was in that position
Delete	Deletes the character at the current cursor position
↵	Completes the current entry and moves the cursor to the next field
Ctrl–Y	Deletes all characters to the right of the cursor
F2	Changes between the Edit and Browse screens
Esc	Leaves the current record without saving changes
Insert	Switches between Insert mode and Replace mode. If in Insert mode, "Ins" will be displayed on the status line

FIGURE 1-26 Special keys used when entering data

To delete the extra p in the last name, use the Up Arrow and Right Arrow keys to move the cursor so that it is under the second of the extra p's in Rappozi. When the cursor is in position, press the Delete key, producing the display shown in Figure 1-27. When you press the Delete key, the extra p will be deleted. The field now reads: Rapozi, Athony P. The cursor is positioned under the letter o.

FIGURE 1-27
Edit screen

To change the last character in the name Rapozi from an i to an a, position the cursor under the i by pressing the Right Arrow key twice. Then, with the cursor positioned under the incorrect character, type the correct letter (a). The results are shown in Figure 1-28. When you type the letter a, it replaces the letter i and the cursor moves one position to the right. The entry now reads Rapoza, Athony P.

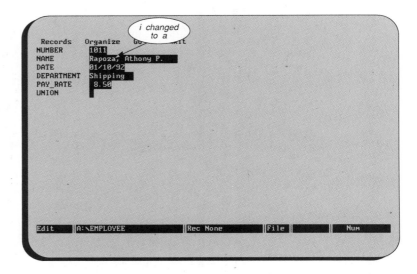

FIGURE 1-28
Edit screen

The next step is to insert an n before the t in the name Athony by pressing the Right Arrow key three times to place it under the letter t, pressing the Insert key to enter the Insert mode, and then typing the letter n. The result is shown in Figure 1-29.

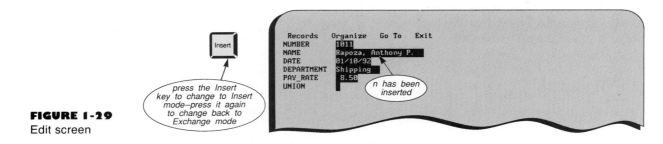

FIGURE 1-29
Edit screen

When you press the Insert key, the abbreviation "Ins" appears in the lower portion of the screen, indicating that Insert mode is in effect. When using Insert mode, each character you type is inserted at the location of the cursor. The character above the cursor and all characters to the right of the cursor are moved one position to the right. When you typed the letter n, it was inserted at the location of the cursor and the characters thony P. were all shifted one position to the right. After you complete the insertion, press the Insert key again to exit from the Insert mode. The abbreviation "Ins" no longer appears on the screen.

When you have corrected the name, you can resume normal data entry.

Resuming Normal Data Entry

When you enter the union code, dBASE allows you to type either a T or F (True or False) or a Y or N (Yes or No). As we mentioned earlier, it is a good idea to restrict yourself to only T or F. Thus, enter T for those employees with a Y in the UNION column and an F for those employees with an N. Complete the entry for this first record by entering a T for the union code. A new screen automatically appears that contains the field names and blank reverse video blocks so that you may enter the data for record 2.

Make the entries for record 2 and record 3 as illustrated in Figures 1-30 and 1-31. Notice that you are to make some mistakes in the data for record 2. We will use these to illustrate the process of correcting errors after records have already been added to the database file.

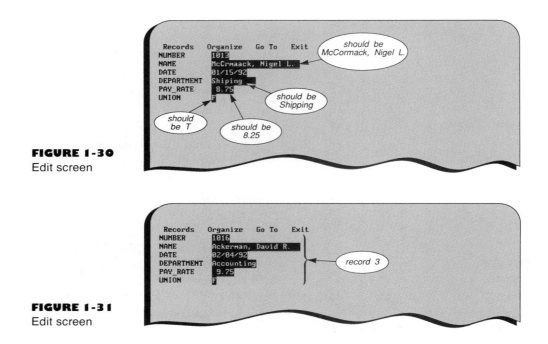

FIGURE 1-30
Edit screen

FIGURE 1-31
Edit screen

When you have entered these records, terminate the data entry process by pressing F10 and selecting the "Exit" option from the Exit menu (Figure 1-32). At this point, you are returned to the Control Center. The data you have entered is automatically saved so that there is no need for a special *save* step as you often encounter in using word processors or spreadsheet programs.

FIGURE 1-32
Edit screen

Using F2 to Transfer Between Screens

If you have some records in your database file, the F2 key possesses an interesting property. If you are at the Edit screen and press F2, you move to a different screen, the Browse screen. (We'll look at the Browse screen later.) Press F2 again and you move back to the Edit screen. If you keep pressing F2, you flip back and forth between these two screens. The only thing you really need to know about this property of F2 is that if you press F2 from the Control Center or any other screen and you end up at the wrong screen, simply press F2 a second time.

Activating a Database File

As long as you continue working on the EMPLOYEE database file, it remains active. If you leave dBASE, however, EMPLOYEE is no longer active. Thus, if you don't have time to add all the records in a single sitting, you must be able to reactivate the EMPLOYEE database file the next time you start dBASE.

Leave dBASE by selecting the "Quit to DOS" option from the Exit menu. Then restart dBASE. We now want to reactivate the EMPLOYEE database file. Highlight EMPLOYEE in the Data column and then press Enter. Your screen should look like Figure 1-33. To activate the file, make sure "Use file" is highlighted and press Enter. (If you wanted to change something about the structure of the file, such as adding an additional field, you would select the "Modify structure/order" option.)

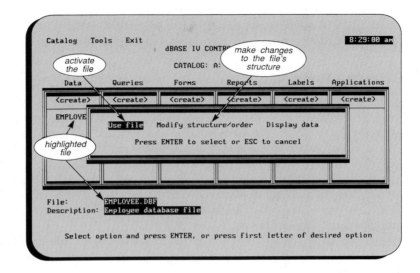

FIGURE 1-33
Control Center

Adding Records

You should now add the remaining records shown in Figure 1-2. To do this, use F2 to get to the Edit screen. The last time you did this, the form on the screen was blank and you could begin adding your records. Since no records were in the file, dBASE assumed you wanted to add new records. This time, however, you already have some records in your file. In this case, dBASE assumes you want to change some of these records. The first record is currently displayed on the screen. By making new entries in any of the fields, you will be changing this record. This is, in fact, one way to correct existing data.

What we want to do, however, is to add records. If you select the "Add new records" option from the Records menu (Figure 1-34), you will see a blank form and you can now enter additional records.

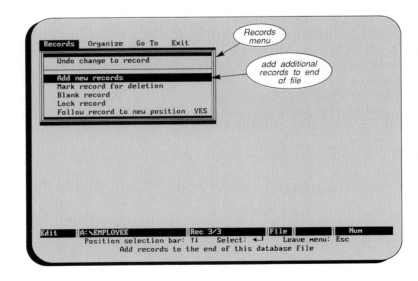

FIGURE 1-34
Edit screen

You should now add the rest of the records shown in Figure 1-2. If you make any mistakes in entering a particular record and discover them while you are still working on the record, you can correct them using the same techniques you used to correct Anthony Rapoza's name. If you don't discover them in time, don't worry about it. In the next section, we will see how to make changes to existing records.

You do not need to add all the records in one sitting. Just remember that if you leave dBASE, you will have to reactivate the EMPLOYEE file, press F2, and then select "Add additional records" to resume adding your data.

When you are adding records, if you inadvertently press Enter while the highlight is in the first position of the first field of the form, dBASE assumes you have finished entering your data and returns you to the Control Center. If this should happen, simply add the remaining records in the same fashion we described in the previous paragraph.

Changing Existing Records

To make a change to an existing record, get to the Edit screen as you did before. Now bring the record you want to change to the screen by using either the Page Up key (which moves you to the previous record) or the Page Down key (which moves you to the next record). Since the number of the record currently on the screen is always displayed on the status line and since your database file is very small, this is not a problem. (This would be very cumbersome if your file were large. Fortunately, there are other ways to do this. For now, however, simply follow this procedure.) When you have the desired record on the screen, repeatedly press Enter until the cursor is on the field you want to change. Correct the data in the field. One way to correct the data is to completely retype the contents of the field with the correct data. Another way is to use combinations of the arrow keys, the Insert key, and the Delete key as you did earlier. Use whichever seems simplest to you.

When you have corrected the data in the field, press Enter. If you need to make other changes to this record, make them in the same way. If you need to correct other records, use Page Up or Page Down to move to them and make the corrections. When you are done, press F10 to move to the Menu mode and select the "Exit" option from the Exit menu.

At this point, feel free to experiment with making changes. Don't make the corrections to record 2, however, since we will make those changes in a different way. Be sure to correct any mistakes you made in your data entry. If you didn't make any mistakes, try changing the department of Mark Castle to Marketing and the pay rate of John Evans to 7.00. After you have done both of these, undo them. That is, change the department for Mark Castle back to Shipping and the pay rate for John Evans back to 6.00.

ENTERING DATA USING THE BROWSE SCREEN

The Browse Screen

Remember that pressing F2 while you were on the Edit screen took you to another screen, called the Browse screen. We will now look at the Browse screen. We can use this screen to view existing data, make changes to existing data, and add new data just as we can with the Edit screen. Press F2 at this time to change to the Browse screen. (If you are currently at the Control Center, you may need to press F2 twice: once to get to the Edit screen and a second time to move to the Browse screen.)

Your screen may now look like Figure 1-35. (You may have more records showing than the screen in the figure.) We are currently positioned at record 15, the last record in the file. Press Page Up.

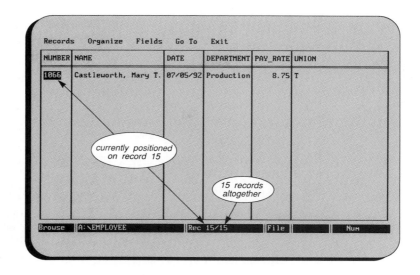

FIGURE 1-35
Browse screen

Unlike the Edit screen where Page Up moves you back a single record, Page Up on the Browse screen moves up a screenful at a time. In this case, Page Up moves back to the beginning of the file (Figure 1-36).

```
     Records   Organize   Fields    Go To    Exit

    NUMBER NAME                     DATE     DEPARTMENT PAY_RATE UNION

     1011  Rapoza, Anthony P.     01/10/92 Shipping       8.50 T
     1013  McCrmaack, Nigel L.    01/15/92 Shiping        8.75 F      need to fix
     1016  Ackerman, David R.     02/04/92 Accounting     9.75 F      record 2
     1017  Doi, Chan J.           02/05/92 Production     6.00 T
     1020  Castle, Mark C.        03/04/92 Shipping       7.50 T
     1022  Dunning, Lisa A.       03/12/92 Marketing      9.10 F
     1025  Chaney, Joseph R.      03/23/92 Accounting     8.00 F
     1026  Bender, Helen O.       04/12/92 Production     6.75 T
     1029  Anders   currently     04/18/92 Shipping       9.00 T
     1030  Eduar   positioned on  04/23/92 Production     8.60 T
     1037  Baxte      record 1    05/05/92 Accounting    11.00 F
     1041  Evans, Jo...           05/19/92 Marketing      6.00 F
     1056  Andreus, Robert M.     06/03/92 Marketing      9.00 F
     1057  Dugan, Mary L.         06/10/92 Production     8.75 T
     1066  Castleworth, Mary T.   07/05/92 Produ          25 T
                                              15 records
                                              altogether
    Browse  A:\EMPLOYEE              Rec 1/15        File          Num
```

FIGURE 1-36
Browse screen

Changing Existing Records

Not only can you use the Browse screen to view several records at a time, you can also use it to change existing records. We will use it to correct the mistakes in record 2. To correct a particular record, we must be positioned on the record. In dBASE terms, the record must be the **current active record**, often simply called the **current record**. If we were on the Edit screen, this would be the record that is currently displayed. In the Browse screen, it would be the record on which the highlight appears.

To move the highlight to another record, that is, to change the current record, we use the Up and Down Arrow keys. The Up Arrow key moves the highlight to the previous record and the Down Arrow key moves it to the next record. Press the Down Arrow key to move the highlight to record 2.

To make a change to a field, move the highlight to the field. To move the highlight one field to the right, press the Tab key. To move it to the left, press Shift-Tab (hold down the Shift key while you press the Tab key). At this point, press the Tab key once, moving the highlight to the NAME field (Figure 1-37). Correct the name by changing it to McCormack, Nigel L. You can correct it either by typing the correct name over the incorrect one, or by using the Insert and Delete keys as you did when you corrected the Anthony Rapoza name. Complete the correction by pressing Enter.

FIGURE 1-37
Browse screen

Correct the rest of the record by changing the department to Shipping, the pay rate to 8.25, and the union to T. Since your last entry was in the final field of record 2, the highlight advances to record 3 (Figure 1-38). You should now complete any corrections you need to make to any other records in this database file.

FIGURE 1-38
Browse screen

Printing the Contents of Your Database File

Let's pause now to print a copy of the data in our database file. Fortunately, there is a very simple way to do this. It's called *Quick Report*, and all we need to do to use it is to press Shift-F9 (hold the Shift key down while you press F9). This is available from the Control Center. In fact, if you look back to Figure 1-23, which shows the Control Center, you'll see "Quick Report: Shift-F9" on the screen. We don't have to be at the Control Center to use it, however. We can use it from the Edit or Browse screen just as well.

Try Quick Report now. Press Shift-F9, and the box shown in Figure 1-39 appears. If you have a printer attached to your computer and want a printed copy of the report, select "Begin printing". If you don't have a printer or just don't want to print the report at this time, but you would like to see what the report looks like, select "View report on screen". If you view the report on the screen, you will see one screenful at a time.

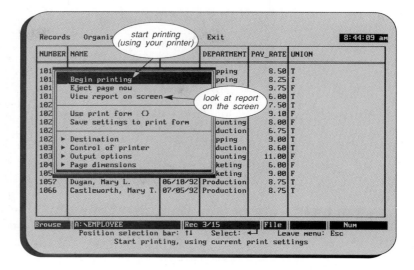

FIGURE 1-39
Print menu

After each screenful is displayed, a message appears indicating that you can press Esc if you don't want to see any more or press the Spacebar to see the next screenful. If you decide you don't want to print the report on your printer and you don't want to view it on the screen, press Esc and you are returned to the Browse screen.

After you request that the report be printed or displayed on the screen, dBASE creates a special file that it uses for its own purposes. Don't worry about this, but be aware that you will see messages displayed on the screen indicating that this special file is being created. Ignore these messages and wait for the report to appear.

Adding Records on the Browse Screen

You can add data using the Browse screen just as you can with the Edit screen, but instead of entering the data into a form, you enter it into a table. To add records, you could select the "Add new records" option from the Records menu, just as you did at the Edit screen, but another method is possible. Press Page Down to move to the last record, and then press the Down Arrow key to move to a position on the screen where there are no records. You are asked if you want to add new records (Figure 1-40).

FIGURE 1-40
Browse screen

You should type Y so that you can enter the data shown in Figure 1-41. When you are done, finish the process by selecting the "Exit" option from the Exit menu.

FIGURE 1-41
Browse screen

DELETING RECORDS

◆ Let's suppose that Ashley Francis (the employee you just added) doesn't belong in the database after all. In addition, perhaps in typing your data you added other employees that shouldn't be there. To fix our database, we need to delete these records.

The process for deleting records is very similar to that for changing them. Go to the Edit screen and use Page Up or Page Down to bring the record to be deleted to the screen. (You could also go to the Browse screen and use the Up or Down Arrow keys to move to the record you want to delete.) In either case, rather than changing the contents of some field, just press Ctrl-U to delete the record currently on the screen. Use this technique to delete the record for employee 2211 (Ashley Francis). If you mistakenly added any employees other than the ones shown in Figure 1-2, delete them as well.

When you delete records from a database file, the records are not actually removed from the file at that time. Instead, dBASE merely marks them as being deleted. You need to take special action to physically remove these records from the file. Until you take such action, the records are actually still in the file. dBASE does, however, indicate which records have been so marked. When records are being edited and the currently highlighted record happens to be one that has been marked for deletion, the letters "Del" will appear near the right-hand end of the status line. Move to the record for Ashley Francis (unless you are already there) and notice the "Del" on the screen. If you move to another record, you will not see these letters.

Once you have marked any records that you want deleted, you should take the required action to remove them from the database file. Select the "Erase marked records" option from the Organize menu (Figure 1-42).

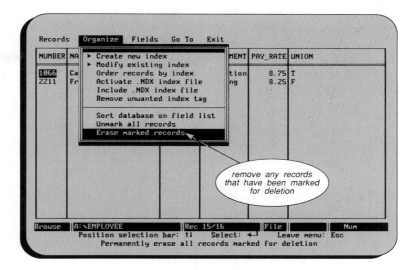

FIGURE 1-42
Database Design screen

When you answer Yes to the question displayed on the screen (Figure 1-43), the records will be permanently removed from the database file. When you have finished, select the "Exit" option from the Exit menu.

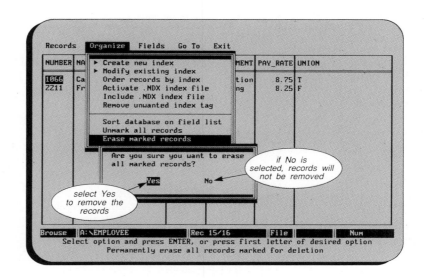

FIGURE 1-43
Database Design screen

If you inadvertently delete the wrong record, you can *un*delete it by pressing Ctrl-U a second time, provided you have not yet selected "Erase marked records." Once the records have been permanently removed, however, undeleting the record will no longer be possible.

BACKING UP YOUR DATABASE FILES

To be safe, it is a good idea to periodically make a copy of your database files. This copy is called a **backup copy**, and the database file itself is called the **live copy**. If you discover a problem with a database file, you can copy the backup version over the live one. This returns the database file to the state it was in when you made the backup.

You can make backup copies while you are in dBASE, but a simpler method is to use the DOS COPY command after you have exited dBASE.

To copy the database file EMPLOYEE.DBF located on drive A and create a backup copy named EMPBACK.DBF also located on drive A, for example, you can use the first command shown in Figure 1-44. (In this example we chose EMPBACK.DBF; you can choose any name you want. Just make sure the name is easy for you to recognize.) A separate related file, EMPLOYEE.MDX, should also be backed up. The second command in Figure 1-44 makes a copy of this file called EMPBACK.MDX.

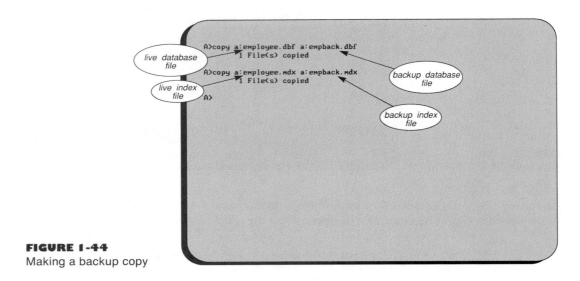

FIGURE 1-44
Making a backup copy

If you discover a problem, you can restore EMPLOYEE.DBF and EMPLOYEE.MDX to the states they were in when the backups were made by typing the commands shown in Figure 1-45.

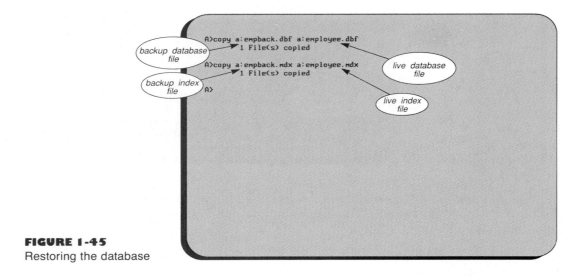

FIGURE 1-45
Restoring the database

If you want to place the backup copy on a separate diskette, place the other diskette in drive B and change the letters that precede EMPBACK.DBF and EMPBACK.MDX to the letter B.

PROJECT SUMMARY

In Project 1 you learned how to access dBASE and how to create a database file. You also learned how to add records to a database file and how to correct any errors you might have made. You learned one way to display the contents of a database file. Finally, you saw how to make a copy of the database file for backup purposes. All the activities that you learned for this project are summarized in the Quick Reference following Project 6. The following is a summary of the keystroke sequence we used in Project 1.

SUMMARY OF KEYSTROKES — PROJECT 1

STEPS	KEY(S) PRESSED	RESULTS
1	DBASE ←[At DOS prompt]	Starts dBASE.
2	F10 Esc	Illustrates use of Esc.
3	F10 → → ← ← Esc	Illustrates using menus.
4	Esc ← ←	Moves to dot prompt.
5	F2	Moves to Control Center.
6	F10 ← ←EMPCAT←	Creates catalog.
7	F1	Gets help.
8	Esc	Returns to Control Center from help.
9	F10 → → ↓←	Quits dBASE.
10	DBASE ←[At DOS prompt]	Starts dBASE.
11	←	Creates database file.
12	NUMBER← ←4←Y←NAME← ←20← ←DATE← SPACE SPACE SPACE ← ←DEPARTMENT←10← ←PAY_RATE ← SPACE ←5←2← ←UNION← SPACE [Press 4 times]← F10 → [Press 4 times]←EMPLOYEE←	Creates database.
13	F10 ↓[Press 5 times]←Employee database file←	Enters description.
14	F2	Moves to Edit screen.
15	1011Rappozi, Anthony P. ←011092Shipping←8.50	Partially enters record.
16	↑[Press 4 times]→ → → Delete → →a→ → → Insert n Insert ←[Press 4 times]T	Enters record correctly.
17	1013McCrmaack, Nigel L. ←011592Shiping←8.75F	Enters record incorrectly.
18	1016Ackerman, David R. ←020492Accounting9.75F	Enters record.
19	F10 → → → ←	Exits to Control Center.
20	F10 → → ↓←	Leaves dBASE.
21	DBASE ←[At DOS prompt]	Starts dBASE.
22	↓←←	Activates EMPLOYEE file.
23	F2 [Press once or twice to move to Edit screen]	Moves to Edit screen.
24	F10 ←	Enters new records.
25	1017Doi, Chang J. ←020592Production6.00F	Enters record.
26	1020Castle, Mark C. ←030492Shipping←7.50T	Enters record.

(continued)

SUMMARY OF KEYSTROKES — PROJECT 1 (continued)

STEPS	KEY(S) PRESSED	RESULTS
27	1022Dunning, Lisa A. ↵031292Marketing↵9.10F	Enters record.
28	1025Chaney, Joseph R. ↵032392Accounting8.00F	Enters record.
29	1026Bender, Helen O. ↵041292Production6.75T	Enters record.
30	1029Anderson, Mariane L.041892Shipping↵9.00T	Enters record.
31	1030Edwards, Kenneth J. ↵042392Production8.60T	Enters record.
32	1037Baxter, Charles W. ↵050592Accounting11.00F	Enters record.
33	1041Evans, John T. ↵051992Marketing↵6.00F	Enters record.
34	1056Andrews, Robert M. ↵060392Marketing↵9.00F	Enters record.
35	1057Dugan, Mary L. ↵061092Production8.75T	Enters record.
36	1066Castleworth, Mary T.070592Production8.75T	Enters record.
37	F10 → → → ↵	Returns to Control Center.
38	F2 [Press once or twice to move to Browse screen] Page Up	Moves to Browse screen (record 1).
39	↓ Tab	Moves to name field on record 2.
40	McCorma↵ Tab Shipping↵8.25T	Corrects data.
41	Shift-F9 ↵	Prints report.
42	Page Down	Moves to last record.
43	↓Y	Enters new records.
44	2211Francis, Ashley↵070892Shipping↵8.25F	Enters record.
45	F10 → [Press 4 times] ↵	Returns to Control Center.
46	F2 [Press once or twice to move to Edit screen]	Moves to Edit screen.
47	Page Up or Page Down [Use if necessary to move to Ashley Francis]	Moves to record for Ashley Francis.
48	Ctrl-U	Deletes record.
49	F10 → ↓[Press 8 times]↵ ← ↵	Removes marked records.
50	F10 → → → ↵	Returns to Control Center.
51	F10 → → ↓ ↵	Leaves dBASE.
52	copy a:employee.dbf a:empback.dbf ↵	Backs up EMPLOYEE database file.
53	copy a:employee.mdx a:empback.mdx ↵	Backs up related file.

The following list summarizes the material covered in Project 1.

1. A **database** is a structure that can hold data concerning many different types of objects (technically called **entities**) as well as relationships between these objects.
2. A **database management system**, or **DBMS**, is a software product used easily to maintain a database.
3. A **relational** DBMS is one in which a database is a collection of tables, each consisting of a series of rows and columns.
4. An individual unit of information, such as an employee number or name, is called a **field**. A group of related fields is called a **record**. A collection of records is called a **file**. Sometimes **table**, **row**, and **column** are used in place of file, record, and field, respectively.
5. In dBASE, each individual file (table) is called a **database file**. Thus, in dBASE, a database can actually be a collection of database files. (Throughout the first four projects, each database consists of just a single database file.)

6. **Character fields** are fields that may be used to store any printable character. **Date fields** are fields that can only be used to store dates. **Numeric fields** are fields that can only be used to store numbers. Arithmetic operations can only be applied to numeric fields. **Logical fields** consist of a single value representing a true or false condition. They can hold only T (True), F (False), Y (Yes), or N (No). **Memo fields** are fields that may be used to store large blocks of text such as words or sentences.

7. The **Control Center** is the place from which you begin your work. It contains a list of files of various types in a box called the **work area**, also referred to as the **panel**, as well as a collection of menus. (A **menu** is a list of actions from which you can choose.) Each column in the Control Center relates to a given task and is also referred to as the task panel. The line at the bottom of the screen is called the **navigation line**. It indicates how special keys function.

8. A **catalog** is a collection of related files. The files in the active catalog are the ones that are displayed at the Control Center.

9. To use menus, press F10 to change to Menu mode. Use the Left and Right Arrow keys to move from one menu to another. Use the Up and Down Arrow keys to move from one selection within a menu to another. When you have the choice you want highlighted, press Enter.

10. The **dot prompt mode** is a mode of operating with dBASE in which a single dot, called the **dot prompt**, appears on the screen. To change from the Control Center to the dot prompt mode, select the "Exit to dot prompt" option from the Exit menu. To change from the dot prompt mode to the Control Center, press F2.

11. To leave dBASE, select the "Quit to DOS" option from the Exit menu.

12. To get help, use the F1 key.

13. To change to a different catalog, use the "Use a different catalog" option from the Catalog menu, and then select the desired catalog. If the catalog does not yet exist, select <create>, and then enter the name of the catalog.

14. To create a database file, select <create> in the Data column, and then describe each of the fields that make up the database file. When you are done, select the "Exit" option from the Exit menu and indicate the name of the database file you have created. Select the "Change description of highlighted file" option from the Catalog menu to enter a description for the database file.

15. To add or change records, press F2 at the Control Center. You will then change to the Edit screen. You can then change back and forth between the Edit screen and the Browse screen by pressing F2. If there are no records in the file, you will automatically be adding records. If there are records in the file, you will be editing existing records. To add new ones, select the "Add new records" option from the Records menu.

16. The record on which you are currently positioned is called the **current active record**, or the **current record**. If you were on the Edit screen, this would be the record that is currently displayed. In the Browse screen, it would be the record on which the highlight appears.

17. To move between records when you are entering or editing data, use the Page Up and Page Down keys if you are on the Edit screen. If you are on the Browse screen, use the Up or Down Arrow key.

18. To print a report of all the data in your database file, press Shift-F9 (for Quick Report).

19. A **backup copy** of a database file is a copy that is made and stored as a safety measure. If problems occur in the database file that is actively used, called the **live copy**, copying the backup version over the live version returns the database file to the state it was in when the backup was made.

20. You can make a backup copy of a database file by using the DOS COPY command after you have exited dBASE. In the event of a problem, you can copy the backup copy over the live version by using a similar COPY command.

STUDENT ASSIGNMENTS

STUDENT ASSIGNMENT 1: True/False

Instructions: Circle T if the statement is true and F if the statement is false.

T F 1. A record is composed of one or more files.

T F 2. The four steps to be performed prior to using dBASE IV commands to create a database are: Define the structure of the database; Name the fields in the database; Determine the type and width of each field in the database; Determine a record name for the records in the database.

Student Assignment 1 (continued)

T F   3. Each field in a dBASE IV database must be given a unique name.

T F   4. You can use blank spaces within a dBASE IV field name.

T F   5. The width of a dBASE IV date field is eight characters.

T F   6. The line on the screen that indicates such things as the default drive and the currently active database file is called the information line.

T F   7. To create a dBASE IV database, highlight <create> in the Data column of the Control Center and press Enter.

T F   8. In all cases, after you have entered a field name when you are creating a database, you must press the Enter key to move the cursor to the next entry to be made.

T F   9. When creating a dBASE IV database, if you enter the width of a Character field and press Enter, the cursor will automatically move to the Decimal positions field.

T F 10. Suppose you are creating a dBASE IV database and the cursor is in the Type column. If you press the Spacebar until Logical appears and then press Enter, the cursor will automatically advance to the width column.

T F 11. To indicate to dBASE IV that all fields have been defined, select the "Save changes and exit" option from the Exit menu.

T F 12. When you are entering data for a record in a dBASE IV database, the field names are displayed on the screen and are followed by reverse video blocks representing the maximum number of characters that can be entered in each field.

T F 13. To get help on the currently highlighted option, press F1.

T F 14. When you press the Insert key, the letters "Ins" appear on the screen, indicating that the Insert mode is in effect. Similarly, when you press the Delete key, the letters "Del" appear on the screen, indicating that the Delete mode is in effect.

T F 15. To add records to an existing database file, select the "Add new records" option from the Records menu.

T F 16. To activate a previously created database, highlight the database in at the Control Center and select the "Database file" option from the Activate menu.

STUDENT ASSIGNMENT 2: Multiple Choice

Instructions: Circle the correct response.

1. A database management system _____.
   a. requires too much main memory to be used on personal computers
   b. will normally be used only by computer programmers and cannot be used by people who want to make inquiries into a database to obtain information
   c. is not a very powerful piece of software and, therefore, is not used for very many applications
   d. is an application software package that can be used to create a database and store, access, sort, and make additions, deletions, and changes to that database
2. A record in dBASE IV is composed of a _____.
   a. series of databases
   b. series of files
   c. series of records
   d. series of fields
3. To create a dBASE IV database file, _____.
   a. move the highlight to <create> in the Data column and press Enter
   b. use the "Create" option from the Database File menu
   c. use the "Database file" option from the Create menu
   d. move the highlight to Database File in the Create column

4. To get help on the currently highlighted option, _____.
   a. type help
   b. press the Esc key and then type help
   c. press F1
   d. press F2
5. How do you print a quick report of data in a database file?
   a. select the "Quick report" option from the Report menu
   b. press Shift-F9
   c. press F2
   d. select the "Report" option from the Retrieve menu and then select "Quick report"
6. To activate a database file, _____.
   a. highlight the file at the Control Center and select the "Activate" option from the Tools menu
   b. highlight the file at the Control Center, press Enter, and then select "Use file"
   c. select the "Database file" option from the Tools menu and then type the name of the database file you want to activate
   d. type the name of the database file after you type DBASE at the DOS prompt

STUDENT ASSIGNMENT 3: Understanding dBASE Options

Instructions: Explain what happens after you perform each of the following actions.

Problem 1: You press Enter while the license agreement is on the screen.

Explanation: _____

_____

_____

Problem 2: You highlight a database file at the Control Center and press Enter.

Explanation: _____

_____

_____

Problem 3: You are on the Browse screen and press F2.

Explanation: _____

_____

_____

Problem 4: You are on the Browse screen and press Esc.

Explanation: _____

_____

_____

STUDENT ASSIGNMENT 4: Using dBASE

Instructions: Explain how to accomplish each of the following tasks using dBASE.

Problem 1: Move from the dBASE license screen to the Control Center.

Explanation: _____

_____

_____

Problem 2: Specify a field as a character field.

Explanation: _____

_____

_____

Problem 3: Move to the next record while adding data.

Explanation: _____

_____

_____

Problem 4: Insert a letter in the middle of a name.

Explanation: _____

_____

_____

Problem 5: Print the contents of a database file.

Explanation: _____

_____

_____

Problem 6: Change data in an already existing database file.

Explanation: _____

_____

_____

STUDENT ASSIGNMENT 5: Recovering from Problems

Instructions: In each of the following cases, a problem occurred. Explain the cause of the problem and how you can correct it.

Problem 1: Your screen contains a display you don't recognize. You know it is definitely not the option you meant to select.

Cause of Problem:_____

_____

Method of Correction: _____

_____

Problem 2: You tried to print a list on your printer. The list appeared on the screen, but *not* on the printer. Your printer is on.

Cause of Problem: _____

_____

Method of Correction: _____

_____

Problem 3: The Control Center has disappeared and the dot prompt is on the screen.

Cause of Problem: _____

_____

Method of Correction: _____

_____

STUDENT ASSIGNMENT 6: Listing Records

Instructions: List all the records in the EMPLOYEE database file. Explain the steps to accomplish this.

Steps: _____

_____

_____

STUDENT ASSIGNMENT 7: Adding a Record

If you complete Assignment 7, you should also complete Assignments 8 through 10. If not, your EMPLOYEE database file will not have the correct data in it for the remaining projects.

Instructions: Add the following record to the EMPLOYEE database file. Then list all the records in the file. Explain the steps to accomplish this.

EMPLOYEE NUMBER	EMPLOYEE NAME	DATE HIRED	DEPARTMENT NAME	PAY RATE	UNION MEMBER
1089	Vander Molen, Ann P.	08/10/92	Shipping	10.25	T

Steps: _____

_____

_____

STUDENT ASSIGNMENT 8: Changing a Record

Instructions: Use the Edit screen to change the department for Ann Vander Molen (the record you added in Assignment 7) to Marketing. Then list all the records in the file. Explain the steps to accomplish this.

Steps: _____

_____

_____

STUDENT ASSIGNMENT 9: Changing a Record

Instructions: Use the Browse screen to change the pay rate for Ann Vander Molen (the record you added in Assignment 7) to 10.75. Then list all the records in the file. Explain the steps to accomplish this.

Steps: _____

_____

_____

STUDENT ASSIGNMENT 10: Deleting a Record

Instructions: Delete Ann Vander Molen (the record you added in Assignment 7). Permanently remove this record from the database file. Then list all the records in the file. Explain the steps to accomplish this.

Steps: _____

_____

_____

MINICASES

CREATING AND DISPLAYING A DATABASE

Each project ends with four minicases. In each project, Minicase 1 involves a database of customers, Minicase 2 involves a database of parts, Minicase 3 deals with a database containing data about movies, and Minicase 4 deals with a database containing information about the inventory of a bookstore.

The minicases are cumulative. That is, the assignment for Minicase 1 in Project 2 builds on the assignment for Minicase 1 from Project 1. Thus, be sure you work through the minicase completely before proceeding to the the next project. If not, you may encounter difficulty later on.

MINICASE 1: Customers

Instructions: Create a database file to store information about the customers of an organization. Use the data and field characteristics in the following tables.

CNUM	CNAME	CADDR	BAL	SNAME	STDATE	DSC
124	Adams, Sally	481 Oak,Lansing,MI	419	Gomez, Maria	02/14/90	T
256	Samuel, Anna	215 Pete,Grant,IN	11	Smith, Wilhelm	03/12/90	T
311	Tranh, Tuan	48 College,Ira,IL	200	Brown, Doyle	05/12/90	F
315	Stevens, Ken	914 Cherry,Kent,MI	321	Smith, Wilhelm	07/11/90	T
405	Tao, Chan	519 Watson,Ira,IL	202	Brown, Doyle	11/15/90	F
412	Adams, Sally	16 Elm,Lansing,MI	909	Gomez, Maria	02/03/91	F
522	Lee, Kuan	108 Pine,Ada,MI	50	Brown, Doyle	06/04/91	T
567	Baker, Gina	808 Ridge,Clair,MI	201	Smith, Wilhelm	08/12/91	T
587	Roberts, Ian	512 Pine,Ada,MI	58	Smith, Wilhelm	11/15/91	F
622	Martin, Ida	419 Chip,Grant,IN	576	Gomez, Maria	04/12/92	F

FIELD NAME	FIELD TYPE	FIELD WIDTH	DECIMAL POSITIONS	INDEX	FIELD DESCRIPTION
CNUM	Numeric	3		Y	Customer number
CNAME	Character	12		N	Customer name
CADDR	Character	18		N	Customer address
BAL	Numeric	4		N	Customer balance
SNAME	Character	14		N	Name of customer's sales rep
STDATE	Date	8		N	Customer start date
DSC	Logical	1		N	Discount? (T or F)

Perform the following tasks using dBASE:

1. Create a catalog called CUSTCAT and make sure the catalog is active.
2. Create the database file and enter the given data. Use the name CUSTOMER for the database file.
3. After you have created the database file and entered the data, use Quick Report (Shift-F9) to produce a report of all data in the database file.
4. Leave the database file that you created on your disk for use with assignments in later projects.

MINICASE 2: Parts

Instructions: Create a database file to store information about the parts sold by an organization. Use the data and field characteristics in the following tables.

PNUMB	PDESC	UOH	ITEMCLSS	WHSE	PRICE	LSDATE	DISC
AX12	HAIR DRYER	52	HAIR CARE	3	27.99	02/12/92	T
AZ52	SKATES	20	SPORTING GOODS	2	49.99	01/15/92	F
BA74	DARTBOARD	40	SPORTING GOODS	1	34.99	11/02/91	T
BH22	CURL. IRON	95	HAIR CARE	3	10.95	01/19/92	T
BT04	CONV. OVEN	11	APPLIANCES	2	149.99	08/25/91	F
BZ66	BLENDER	12	APPLIANCES	3	99.99	03/01/92	T
CA14	FOOTBALL	2	SPORTING GOODS	3	19.99	01/05/92	F
CB03	POOL TABLE	2	SPORTING GOODS	1	299.99	02/06/92	F
CX11	COFF. MAKER	32	APPLIANCES	3	34.95	03/05/92	T
CZ81	WEIGHTS	11	SPORTING GOODS	2	108.99	01/29/92	T

FIELD NAME	FIELD TYPE	FIELD WIDTH	DECIMAL POSITIONS	INDEX	FIELD DESCRIPTION
PNUMB	Character	4		Y	Part number
PDESC	Character	11		N	Part description
UOH	Numeric	4		N	Units on hand
ITEMCLSS	Character	15		N	Item class
WHSE	Numeric	2		N	Warehouse number
PRICE	Numeric	7	2	N	Price
LSDATE	Date	8		N	Last sold date
DISC	Logical	1		N	Discount? (T or F)

Perform the following tasks using dBASE:

1. Create a catalog called PARTCAT and make sure the catalog is active.
2. Create the database file and enter the given data. Use the name PART for the database file.
3. After you have created the database file and entered the data, use Quick Report (Shift-F9) to produce a report of all data in the database file.
4. Leave the database file that you created on your disk for use with assignments in later projects.

MINICASE 3: Movies

Instructions: You own several video tapes of movies and want to keep information about your tapes on your computer. You assign each movie a number. You then record this number as well as other pertinent information about the movie. In this minicase, you will create a database file for you video tapes. Use the data and field characteristics in the following tables.

MNUM	MTITLE	YEAR	MTYPE	LNG	DNAME	BW
001	Annie Hall	1977	COMEDY	93	Allen, Woody	F
002	Dr. Strangelove	1964	COMEDY	93	Kubrick, Stanley	T
003	A Clockwork Orange	1971	SCI FI	136	Kubrick, Stanley	F
004	North by Northwest	1959	SUSPEN	136	Hitchcock, Alfred	F
005	Rope	1948	SUSPEN	80	Hitchcock, Alfred	F
006	Psycho	1960	HORROR	109	Hitchcock, Alfred	T
007	Interiors	1978	DRAMA	95	Allen, Woody	F
008	The Birds	1963	HORROR	119	Hitchcock, Alfred	F
011	Manhattan	1979	COMEDY	96	Allen, Woody	T
012	Vertigo	1958	SUSPEN	128	Hitchcock, Alfred	F
014	2001 A Space Ody.	1968	SCI FI	141	Kubrick, Stanley	F
021	Stagecoach	1939	WESTER	99	Ford, John	T
022	Rear Window	1954	SUSPEN	112	Hitchcock, Alfred	F
023	Mogambo	1953	WESTER	116	Ford, John	F
024	Grapes of Wrath	1940	DRAMA	128	Ford, John	T

FIELD NAME	FIELD TYPE	FIELD WIDTH	DECIMAL POSITIONS	INDEX	FIELD DESCRIPTION
MNUM	Character	3		Y	Movie number
MTITLE	Character	18		N	Movie title
YEAR	Numeric	4		N	Year movie was made
MTYPE	Character	6		N	Movie type
LNG	Numeric	4		N	Length of movie (minutes)
DNAME	Character	18		N	Name of director
BW	Logical	1		N	Black and white? (T or F)

Perform the following tasks using dBASE:

1. Create a catalog called MOVCAT and make sure the catalog is active.
2. Create the database file and enter the given data. Use the name MOVIE for the database file.
3. After you have created the database file and entered the data, use Quick Report (Shift-F9) to produce a report of all data in the database file.
4. Leave the database file that you created on your disk for use with assignments in later projects.

MINICASE 4: Books

Instructions: Create a database file to store information about the books sold at a bookstore. Use the data and field characteristics in the following tables.

CODE	TITLE	AUTHOR	PUBLISHER	TYP	PRICE	PB	OH
0189	Kane and Abel	Jeffrey Archer	Pocket Books	FIC	4.95	T	2
1351	Cujo	Stephen King	Signet	HOR	5.95	T	1
138X	Death on the Nile	Ag. Christie	Bantam Books	MYS	3.50	T	3
2226	Ghost from Grand	Ar. C. Clarke	Bantam Books	SFI	17.95	F	3
2295	Four Past Midnight	Stephen King	Viking	HOR	22.95	F	0
2766	The Prodigal Dghtr	Jeffrey Archer	Pocket Books	FIC	4.95	T	2
3743	First Among Equals	Jeffrey Archer	Pocket Books	FIC	3.50	T	0
3906	Vortex	Clive Cussler	Bantam Books	SUS	4.95	T	1
6128	Evil Under the Sun	Ag. Christie	Pocket Books	MYS	3.95	T	3
6171	Dragon	Clive Cussler	Simon and Shu.	SUS	21.95	F	4
6328	Vixen 07	Clive Cussler	Bantam Books	SUS	4.95	T	2
7405	Night Probe	Clive Cussler	Bantam Books	SUS	4.95	T	0
7443	Carrie	Stephen King	Signet	HOR	5.95	T	1
9373	Lady Boss	Jackie Collins	Simon and Shu.	FIC	21.95	F	2

FIELD NAME	FIELD TYPE	FIELD WIDTH	DECIMAL POSITIONS	INDEX	FIELD DESCRIPTION
CODE	Character	4		Y	Book code
TITLE	Character	18		N	Book title
AUTHOR	Character	14		N	Book author
PUBLISHER	Character	14		N	Book publisher
TYP	Character	3		N	Book type
PRICE	Numeric	5	2	N	Price
PB	Logical	1		N	Paperback? (T or F)
OH	Numeric	2		N	Units on hand

Perform the following tasks using dBASE:

1. Create a catalog called BOOKCAT and make sure the catalog is active.
2. Create the database file and enter the given data. Use the name BOOK for the database file.
3. After you have created the database file and entered the data, use Quick Report (Shift-F9) to produce a report of all data in the database file.
4. Leave the database file that you created on your disk for use with assignments in later projects.

dBASE IV VERSION 1.1

Displaying Records in a Database

OBJECTIVES

You will have mastered the material in this project when you can:

◆ Activate a previously created database file

◆ Display all records and all fields

◆ Display only selected fields

◆ Display only records meeting a given condition

◆ Use both simple and compound conditions

◆ Count the number of records satisfying a given condition

◆ Calculate sums and averages

A major benefit of a database management system is that once the database has been created, you can rapidly access and easily display its records and fields. For example, after accessing the employee database file illustrated in Project 1, you can use dBASE options to display a single employee record or specific collections of records such as the records of employees who work in the accounting department or of those who are members of the union.

In this project, you will learn the dBASE options that you can use to display various records and fields in a database. In addition, you will learn the options you can use to count various types of records and to calculate totals and averages.

To be ready to work through the material in this project, you need to start dBASE in the same manner you did in Project 1.

ACTIVATING THE DATABASE

◆ A database file must be active to be accessed. The name of the file that is active appears above the line in the Data column. Thus, in Figure 2-1, the EMPLOYEE file is active and ready to be used. Assuming that you have just started dBASE, your EMPLOYEE file will not be active. Therefore, you need to move the highlight to EMPLOYEE, press Enter, and then select "Use file" from the options presented.

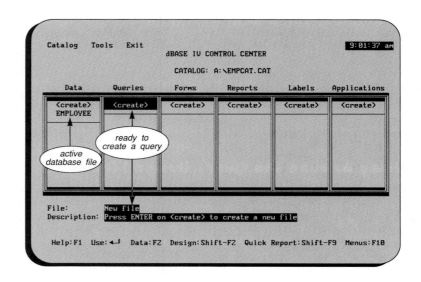

FIGURE 2-1
Control Center

INTRODUCTION TO QUERIES

You can access data in a file by using what are called **queries**. (Generally, to query means to ask for information; specifically, we are asking dBASE for information.) When we create queries, we specify the conditions that the data we want must satisfy. For example, we might specify that the pay rate of certain employees must be $6.00. We can also specify the fields that we want included. We might choose, for example, to include only the name, department, and pay rate.

To begin creating a query, you first make sure your database file is active and then select < create > in the Queries column of the Control Center (Figure 2-1). You then see the Query Design screen (Figure 2-2). This is the screen we use to design our queries.

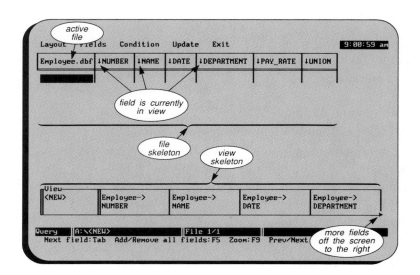

FIGURE 2-2
Query Design screen

The Query Design Screen

Let's take a look at the important parts of the Query Design screen (Figure 2-2). Near the top is a **file skeleton**. It lists the name of the database file together with all the fields in the file. We use this skeleton to define the conditions for our queries, that is, the requirements that must be satisfied in order for a record to be displayed. Near the bottom of the screen is the **view skeleton**. It specifies the fields that will be included, that is, the fields that will be displayed when we see the results of the query.

In the file skeleton, notice the down arrows in front of the fields. A down arrow in front of a field indicates that it is included in the view skeleton. Initially, all fields are included in the view skeleton, so all fields in the file skeleton will have these down arrows. This need not always be the case, however.

On the screen in Figure 2-2, the view skeleton has a right-pointing arrow at the far right-hand end. This arrow indicates that there are additional fields off the right-hand edge of the screen. Similarly, a left-pointing arrow at the left-hand edge of the screen indicates additional fields in that direction.

Moving Around the Query Design Screen

Two types of movements within the Query Design screen are important to learn. The first is moving within a skeleton. Pressing the Tab key takes you one field to the right. Pressing Shift-Tab (holding the Shift key down while you press the Tab key) moves you one field to the left. In either case, if you move to a field that is not currently displayed on the screen, the fields are shifted so that the field to which you are moving is visible.

The second type of movement is from one skeleton to another. You can move to the next skeleton on the screen by pressing F4. You can move back to the prior skeleton by pressing F3. Take some time now to practice moving around this screen.

Applying a Query

When we have finished designing a query, we would like to see the results. We say we would like our query to be **applied**. All we need to do is to press F2. This takes us to the Browse screen where the results of our query will be displayed. (Remember that F2 takes us to either the Browse or the Edit screen. If it takes us to the Edit screen, all we need to do is press F2 a second time to view the Browse screen.) At the Browse screen, only the records that satisfy our conditions are displayed and only the fields that we selected are included.

Printing the Results

Having applied our query, we can see the results on the screen. If we would like the results printed, we press Shift-F9. The results are then printed using Quick Report (as you did in Project 1).

Leaving the Browse Screen

To leave the Browse screen, use the Exit menu. Choosing the "Exit" option from this menu returns us directly to the Control Center. We could use the other option, "Transfer to Query Design", to return to the Query Design screen, if, for example, we want to make some changes to our query and then reuse it.

Abandoning a Query

For now, we won't need to save any of our queries. If you don't want to save a query, choose "Abandon changes and exit" from the Exit menu of the Query Design screen. If you have applied the query and are currently on the Browse or Edit screen, you can simply select "Exit" from the Exit menu to return directly to the Control Center without saving the query. In either case, as a safety measure, a dBASE prompt asks if you are sure that you don't want to save the query. By answering that you do not, you will return to the Control Center without your work being saved.

QUERY EXAMPLES

Displaying All Records

To display all records, we simply do not enter any conditions to restrict the records to be displayed. We merely press F2 to apply our query (Figure 2-3), and the results include all records.

FIGURE 2-3
Browse screen

After you have viewed the records, select the "Transfer to Query Design" option from the Exit menu to return directly to the Query Design screen (Figure 2-4). If you want to take a break now, choose "Exit" and you return directly to the Control Center. When you are ready to return to this material, activate your database file and select <create> from the Queries column.

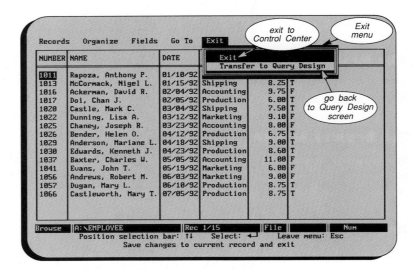

FIGURE 2-4
Browse screen

Displaying Selected Fields

For many situations, you may be interested in displaying only particular fields; for example, each employee's name, department, and pay rate. Fortunately, you do not have to display all the fields in a record.

The view skeleton (the list of fields near the bottom of the screen) indicates which fields are part of the view, that is, which fields we will see when we apply the query. Initially, the view skeleton contains all fields. There are several ways to change the skeleton so that it contains precisely the fields we want. The simplest way relies on the following characteristics of the F5 key:

1. If the highlight is under a field name in the file skeleton and that field is currently in the view skeleton, pressing F5 removes the field. If the field is not in the view skeleton, pressing F5 adds the highlighted field to the end of the list of fields currently in the view skeleton.
2. If the highlight is under the name of the database file in the file skeleton and if there are fields currently in the view skeleton, pressing F5 removes all fields. (You might need to press F5 twice.) If no fields are currently in the view skeleton, pressing F5 adds all fields.

We can always use these properties of the F5 key to construct the precise view skeleton we want. First, we move the highlight under the database file name in the file skeleton and then use F5 to remove all fields. Next, we add the fields in the order we want. To add any field, move the highlight under it in the file skeleton and press F5. If you make a mistake, just start over. Move the highlight back under the database file name, use F5 to delete all fields, and then reselect the fields.

Let's construct a query to display the NAME, DEPARTMENT, and PAY_RATE fields for all employees. First, remove all fields by placing the highlight under Employee.dbf and pressing F5. Your screen should now look like Figure 2-5. Notice that the view skeleton is gone. Next, move the highlight to the NAME field and press F5. At this point, your screen should look like Figure 2-6. Notice that only one field is currently in the view skeleton. Now, move the highlight to the DEPARTMENT field and press F5. Then move the highlight to the PAY_RATE field and press F5. At this point, your screen should look like Figure 2-7.

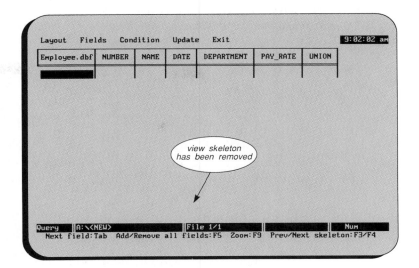

FIGURE 2-5
Query Design screen

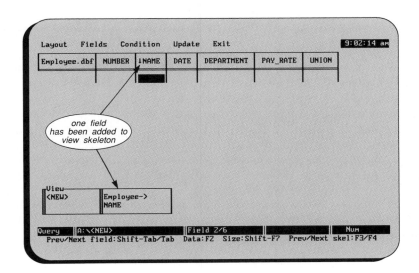

FIGURE 2-6
Query Design screen

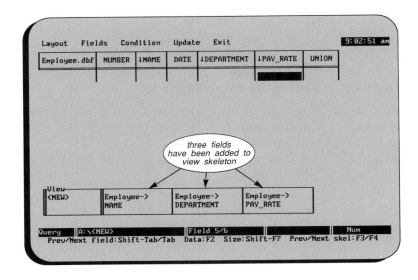

FIGURE 2-7
Query Design screen

Since the view skeleton is exactly what you want, you are done. Press F2 to see the results (Figure 2-8). (Remember that F2 displays data that meet the query you designed.) Notice that the view skeleton contains precisely the fields you specified.

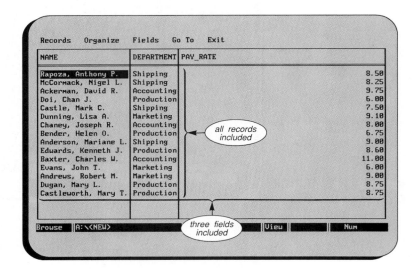

FIGURE 2-8
Browse screen

If your view skeleton has more fields than will fit on the screen and you want to see what is in it, you can press F4 to move to the view skeleton and then repeatedly press the Tab key to move through all the fields. When you are done, you can press F3 to move back to the file skeleton.

The remaining queries in this project assume that all the fields are in the view skeleton unless specifically indicated. If you return directly to the Query Design screen, your view skeleton will still contain only the fields that were in the last query. Move the highlight under Employee.dbf and press F5 twice to remove the view skeleton. Then press F5 one more time. The view skeleton once again is complete. If you start the next query from scratch, that is, you begin by selecting <create> in the Queries column of the Control Center, your view skeleton will automatically be complete.

The last column on the Browse screen often looks a little odd because dBASE always sizes the last column so that it occupies whatever space is left on the screen. Fortunately, if you print these results (using Shift-F9), you won't see this strange spacing.

Conditions

One nice feature of dBASE is its capability to display records and fields based on certain conditions. A **condition** is an expression that evaluates to either true or false. Suppose, for example, that you only wanted information about employee 1030. You don't want to see a report of all employees and have to scan through it looking for this one employee. You only want to display the employee for whom the condition NUMBER is equal to 1030 is true.

Using Character Fields in Conditions

To find the employee whose number is 1030, you need to type the number 1030 in the NUMBER column. If the field is a character field, you must enclose the entry in quotation marks ("). Since the NUMBER field is of character type, you must make the entry as shown in Figure 2-9.

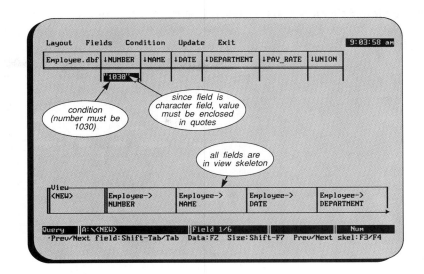

FIGURE 2-9
Query Design screen

Remember that you press the Tab key to move a column to the right and you press Shift-Tab (hold the Shift key down and press the Tab key) to move a column to the left. Make sure the highlight is in the NUMBER column, then type "1030" (including the quotes), and press Enter.

To see the results of the query, press F2 to move to the Browse screen. Your screen should look like Figure 2-10. Only the employee whose number is 1030 appears. To return to the Query Design screen, select "Transfer to Query Design" from the Exit menu.

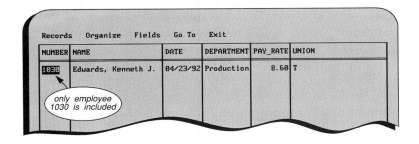

FIGURE 2-10
Browse screen

Clearing Out Prior Conditions

If you go back to the Control Center after you have seen the results of your query and then later begin a new query, you start fresh. No conditions are in place. If, however, you go directly to the Query Design screen from the Browse screen, the conditions you entered previously are still there. You must make sure you clear out the previous entries before entering the conditions for your next query. If you don't, you will not get the results you are expecting. To clear out an entry, move the highlight to it and press Ctrl-Y (hold down the Control key and type the letter Y).

Sometimes, in the previous query, you might have entered a condition in a column that was not then visible on the screen. In such a case, you might not even realize that there is a previous entry that needs to be cleared. The safest practice is to simply tab through all the columns looking for previous entries before you start the next query. If you find any entries along the way, delete them with Ctrl-Y.

If you have returned to the Query Design screen directly from the Browse screen, "1030" will still be in the NUMBER column. Clear it out by placing the highlight in the column and then pressing Ctrl-Y. Then you are ready to move on to the next query.

Using Numeric Fields in Conditions

The only difference between using a numeric field and using a character field in a condition is that you don't enclose numeric values in quotes. To find all employees whose pay rate is $6.00, for example, type 6.00 (no dollar sign) in the PAY_RATE column (Figure 2-11). Press F2 to see the results (Figure 2-12).

FIGURE 2-11
Query Design screen

FIGURE 2-12
Browse screen

Using Operators

In the last query, you really were using = (equals). That is, you were asking for all employees for whom the pay rate *equals* 6.00. *Equals* is called an operator. You could have used several other operators besides equals (Figure 2-13). (The last two operators listed in the figure are special-purpose operators, which we will look at in later examples.) *If you don't enter an operator, dBASE assumes that you mean equals.* That is why, in the preceding query, you didn't have to enter = 6.00.

OPERATOR	MEANING
=	Equals
>	Greater than
> =	Greater than or equal to
<	Less than
< =	Less than or equal to
< >	Not equal to (can also use #)
Like	Matches the given pattern
Sounds like	Sounds like the given entry

FIGURE 2-13
Operators available for conditions

Next, try to produce a list of all employees whose pay rate is greater than $9.00. This time, you need to select greater than rather than equals. The correct symbol is > and you *must* enter it. You cannot leave it out as you can with equals. Thus, type >9.00 in the PAY_RATE column. This time, let's include only the NAME, DEPARTMENT, and PAY_RATE fields. Change your view skeleton accordingly, and press F2 to see the results (Figure 2-14).

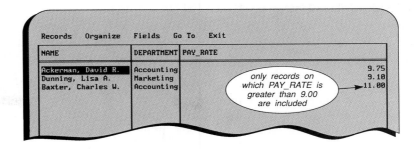

FIGURE 2-14
Browse screen

Special Conditions for Character Fields

Three special conditions are available for character fields: exact match, pattern matching, and sounds like.

Exact Match To find an exact match, simply type the desired character string (collection of characters) in the desired column. You must enclose the character string in quotation marks. This is exactly what you did when you found employee number 1030. (When you enter a value containing letters, you must be very careful about using uppercase or lowercase letters. Later on, for example, you will search for records in which DEPARTMENT is Accounting. If you enter ACCOUNTING, you will not find any records because dBASE considers ACCOUNTING to be different from Accounting.)

Pattern Matching To find entries that match a given pattern, use the word LIKE, followed by the desired pattern. In specifying the pattern, you can use two special symbols, called *wild cards*. (These, incidentally, are the same wild cards you can use in DOS.) The first of these is the asterisk (*), which represents any collection of characters. The other is the question mark (?), which represents a single character. You must enclose the pattern in quotes.

To find all the employees named Mary, we need to find all the employees whose name contains Mary somewhere within it. We can use the condition LIKE "*Mary*" as shown in Figure 2-15. The characters LIKE "*Mary*" indicate that we are looking for names that have any collection of characters, followed by Mary, followed by any other collection of characters.

FIGURE 2-15
Query Design screen

The results are shown in Figure 2-16.

FIGURE 2-16
Browse screen

The other symbol, ?, represents only a single character rather than a collection of characters. Thus "?Mary?" would be true only for those names that consist of a single character, followed by Mary, followed by another single character. Although in this case it would not be appropriate because the names we want have more than a single character before and after Mary, the question mark can come in handy in a few situations. Normally, however, you will use the asterisk.

Sounds Like   You can even find records if you just know what a character string is supposed to sound like. Let's suppose you do not know how to spell an employee's name, but you know that the name sounds like DOY. To find such employees, type the words SOUNDS LIKE DOY, in the appropriate column (Figure 2-17).

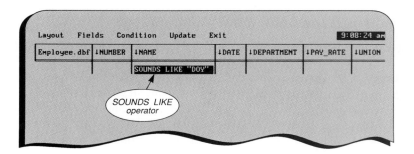

FIGURE 2-17
Query Design screen

The results of this query are shown in Figure 2-18. Notice that dBASE picked out the employee whose name is Doi, which probably does sound like DOY.

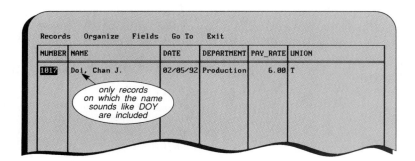

FIGURE 2-18
Browse screen

You can see in this case that it didn't matter that we entered DOY in uppercase letters. We were interested in only the sound of the name. Certainly the sound would be the same whether we entered DOY or Doy.

Using Logical Fields in Conditions

We use logical fields (fields whose type is Logical) in conditions just about like any other type of field. The only difference is that the values we place in the column can be only the letter T (for true) or the letter F (for false). In addition, these letters must be enclosed between periods. To find all employees for whom the UNION field contains the value T, for example, type .T. as shown in Figure 2-19.

FIGURE 2-19
Query Design screen

The results of this query are shown in Figure 2-20.

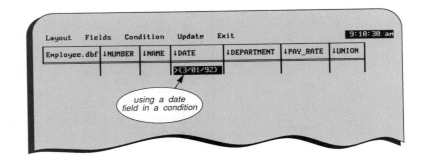

FIGURE 2-20
Browse screen

Date Conditions

You can use dates in conditions by enclosing them in curly braces ({ }). To find all employees whose date of hire is after 3/01/92, for example, make the entry as shown in Figure 2-21. Notice that the entry contains a greater than sign (>), followed by the date, and that the date is enclosed in braces.

FIGURE 2-21
Query Design screen

The result of this query is shown in Figure 2-22.

FIGURE 2-22
Browse screen

Compound Conditions

The conditions you have used so far are called **simple conditions**. They consist of a single value and an operator placed in a single field. Simple conditions can be combined using AND or OR to form **compound conditions**. Some database packages actually have you use the words AND and OR, but dBASE queries do it a little differently.

Using AND   To connect two or more simple conditions with AND, enter the conditions on the same line. To find all employees whose department is Accounting *and* whose pay rate is more than $9.00, for example, type both conditions on the same line as shown in Figure 2-23. The results are shown in Figure 2-24.

 If both conditions involve the same column, separate the conditions with a comma. To find all customers whose pay rate is greater than $7.00 *and* less than $9.00, for example, type the conditions as shown in Figure 2-25. The results are shown in Figure 2-26.

FIGURE 2-23 Query Design screen

FIGURE 2-24 Browse screen

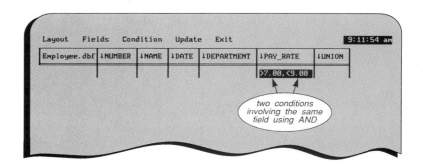

FIGURE 2-25
Query Design screen

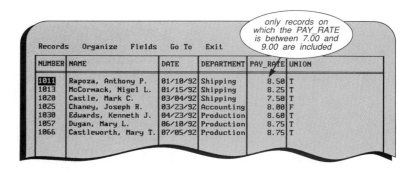

FIGURE 2-26
Browse screen

Using OR   To connect two or more simple conditions with OR, enter the conditions on separate lines. For example, to find all employees whose department is Accounting or who are in the union, type "Accounting" in the DEPART-MENT column as shown in Figure 2-27.

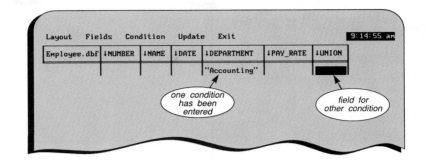

FIGURE 2-27
Query Design screen

Next, move to the UNION column and press the Down Arrow key. A second line is added automatically. Type the next condition .T. on this new line (Figure 2-28).

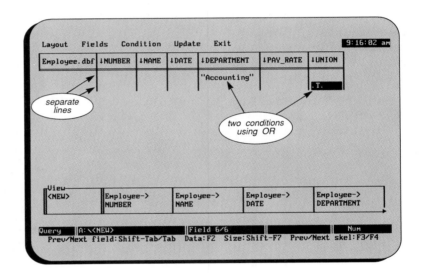

FIGURE 2-28
Query Design screen

The results of this query are shown in Figure 2-29.

FIGURE 2-29
Browse Screen

When you clear out the entries in this query in preparation for another, make sure you clear out both lines. **When you clear out the entry in the second line and press the Up Arrow key to move back to the first line, the entire second line disappears.**

SUMMARY CALCULATIONS

Summary Operators

dBASE has several built-in computations we can use. These are called the **summary operators**, and they are listed in Figure 2-30.

SUMMARY OPERATOR	MEANING
AVG	Average
COUNT	Count
MAX	Maximum (largest value)
MIN	Minimum (smallest value)
SUM	Total

FIGURE 2-30
Summary operators

To use one of these operators, simply type it in the desired column. To count the number of employees in the Accounting department, for example, type "Accounting" in the DEPARTMENT column since the records we are counting must satisfy this condition (Figure 2-31).

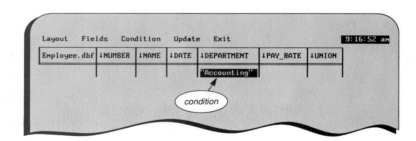

FIGURE 2-31
Query Design screen

Next, type the word COUNT in some column. In this example, it doesn't matter whether we count employee numbers, names, or anything else. Let's put it in the NUMBER column (Figure 2-32).

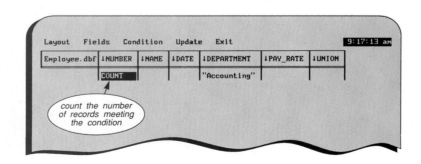

FIGURE 2-32
Query Design screen

To see the results, press F2. Your screen should then look like Figure 2-33. The count is displayed in the NUMBER column as you requested. All the other columns remain blank.

As another example, let's calculate both the count of the number of employees in the Accounting department as well as the total of their pay rates. Make sure the DEPARTMENT column contains Accounting, and type the word SUM in the PAY_RATE column. Make sure the NUMBER column contains the word COUNT (Figure 2-34). The results are shown in Figure 2-35.

Grouping

Suppose that you want to break down the average pay rates by department. That is, you would like to see the average pay rate for all employees in Accounting, the average pay rate for all employees in Marketing, and so on. This process is known as **grouping**, and we say that we *group* employees by department. Enter the summary operators you want as you did before. In this case, enter the words GROUP BY in the DERPARTMENT column and enter AVG in the PAY_RATE column (Figure 2-36).

FIGURE 2-33 Browse screen

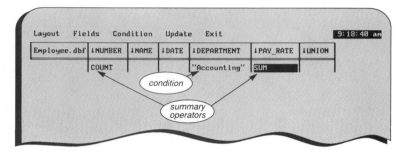

FIGURE 2-34 Query Design screen

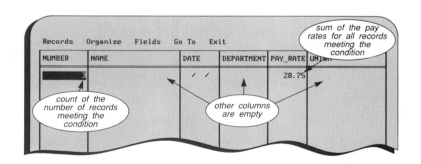

FIGURE 2-35
Browse screen

FIGURE 2-36
Query Design screen

When you apply this query, you will see one line for each department. There will be a line on which the department is Accounting, one on which it is Marketing, and so on. Each of these lines will also include the average pay rate for all employees in that department (Figure 2-37).

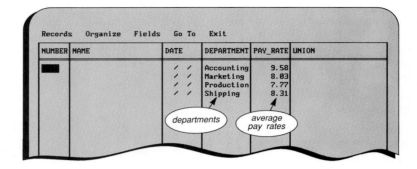

FIGURE 2-37
Browse screen

You may decide that you would rather not have any columns displayed other than DEPARTMENT and PAY_RATE. To delete the other columns, return to the Query Design screen and modify the view skeleton so that it contains only DEPARTMENT and PAY_RATE (Figure 2-38).

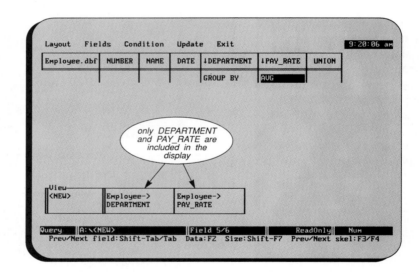

FIGURE 2-38
Query Design screen

When you press F2 to apply the query again, you only see these two columns (Figure 2-39).

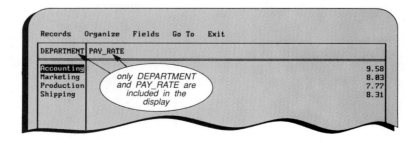

FIGURE 2-39
Browse screen

P R O J E C T   S U M M A R Y

In Project 2 you learned how to use queries to display only the records in which you were interested. You learned how to include only certain fields in the display. You also learned how to calculate counts, sums, and averages. All the activities that you learned for this project are summarized in the Quick Reference following Project 6. The following is a summary of the keystroke sequence we used in Project 2.

SUMMARY OF KEYSTROKES — PROJECT 2

STEPS	KEY(S) PRESSED	RESULTS
1	DBASE ← [At DOS prompt]	Starts dBASE.
2	↓ [To highlight EMPLOYEE] ← ←	Activates EMPLOYEE database file.
3	→ ←	Moves to Query Design screen.
4	(F2) (F10) → [Press 4 times] ↓ ←	Applies query and returns.
5	(F5) (Tab) (Tab) (F5) (Tab) (Tab) (F5) (Tab) (F5)	Changes view skeleton.
6	(F2) (F10) → [Press 4 times] ↓ ←	Applies query and returns.
7	(Shift-Tab) [Press 5 times] (F5) (F5) (F5)	Reconstructs view skeleton.
8	(Tab) "1030" ←	Creates query.
9	(F2) (F10) → [Press 4 times] ↓ ←	Applies query and returns.
10	(Ctrl-Y)	Clears out previous query.
11	(Tab) [Press 4 times] 6.00 ←	Creates query.
12	(F2) (F10) → [Press 4 times] ↓ ←	Applies query and returns.
13	>9.00 ←	Creates query.
14	(Shift-Tab) [Press 5 times] (F5) (Tab) (Tab) (F5) (Tab) (Tab) (F5) (Tab) (F5)	Changes view skeleton.
15	(F2) (F10) → [Press 4 times] ↓ ←	Applies query and returns.
16	(Ctrl-Y)	Clears out previous query.
17	(Shift-Tab) [Press 5 times] (F5) (F5) (F5)	Reconstructs view skeleton.
18	(Tab) (Tab) LIKE "*Mary*" ←	Creates query.
19	(F2) (F10) → [Press 4 times] ↓ ←	Applies query and returns.
20	SOUNDS LIKE "DOY" ←	Creates query.
21	(F2) (F10) → [Press 4 times] ↓ ←	Applies query and returns.
22	(Ctrl-Y)	Clears out previous query.
23	(Tab) [Press 4 times] .T. ←	Creates query.

SUMMARY OF KEYSTROKES — PROJECT 2 (continued)

STEPS	KEY(S) PRESSED	RESULTS
24	[F2] [F10] → [Press 4 times] ↓ ↵	Applies query and returns.
25	[Ctrl-Y]	Clears out previous query.
26	[Shift-Tab] [Shift-Tab] [Shift-Tab] >{3/01/92} ↵	Creates query.
27	[F2] [F10] → [Press 4 times] ↓ ↵	Applies query and returns.
28	[Ctrl-Y]	Clears out previous query.
29	[Tab] "Accounting" ↵ [Tab] >9.00 ↵	Creates query.
30	[F2] [F10] → [Press 4 times] ↓ ↵	Applies query and returns.
31	[Shift-Tab] [Ctrl-Y] [Tab] >7.00,<9.00 ↵	Creates query.
32	[F2] [F10] → [Press 4 times] ↓ ↵	Applies query and returns.
33	[Ctrl-Y]	Clears out previous entry.
34	[Shift-Tab] "Accounting" ↵ [Tab] [Tab] ↓ .T. ↵	Creates query.
35	[F2] [F10] → [Press 4 times] ↓ ↵	Applies query and returns.
36	[Ctrl-Y] ↑ [Shift-Tab] [Shift-Tab] [Ctrl-Y]	Clears out previous query.
37	"Accounting" ↵ [Shift-Tab] [Shift-Tab] [Shift-Tab] COUNT ↵	Creates query (we could have left "Accounting" from previous query).
38	[F2] [F10] → [Press 4 times] ↓ ↵	Applies query and returns.
39	[Tab] [Press 4 times] SUM ↵	Creates query.
40	[F2] [F10] → [Press 4 times] ↓ ↵	Applies query and returns.
41	[Ctrl-Y] [Shift-Tab] [Ctrl-Y] [Shift-Tab] [Shift-Tab] [Shift-Tab] [Ctrl-Y]	Clears out previous query.
42	[Tab] [Tab] [Tab] GROUP BY ↵ [Tab] AVG ↵	Creates query.
43	[F2] [F10] → [Press 4 times] ↓ ↵	Applies query and returns.

The following list summarizes the material covered in Project 2.

1. To activate a database file, move the highlight to it, press Enter, and then select "Use file".
2. To access data in a database, create a **query** by selecting <create> in the Queries column and then indicating the conditions that the records you want must satisfy. Optionally, you can select to include only certain fields.
3. The Query Design screen contains a **file skeleton** that you use to indicate conditions and a **view skeleton** that you use to indicate the list of fields that will appear in the results of the query. To move within a skeleton, press Tab to move to the right and Shift-Tab to move to the left. To move to the next skeleton, press F4. To move to the previous skeleton, press F3.
4. To see the results of a query, press F2. In technical terms, you are **applying** the query.
5. To print the results of a query, press Shift-F9 (for Quick Report).
6. To change the view skeleton, place the highlight under the file name in the file skeleton and press F5 until the view skeleton disappears. Then, for each field you want in the view skeleton, move the highlight under the field name in the file skeleton and press F5.
7. A **condition** is an expression that evaluates to either true or false.

8. A **simple condition** consists of a single value and an operator in a single field. To enter a simple condition, type the condition and the operator in the appropriate column in the file skeleton.
9. To enter a **compound condition** using AND, type the individual conditions on the same line. If they are in the same column, separate them with a comma.
10. To enter a compound condition using OR, type the individual conditions on separate lines.
11. To perform a summary calculation, place the appropriate **summary operator** in the appropriate column.
12. To group data when performing summary calculations, place the words GROUP BY in the column that is to be used for **grouping**.

STUDENT ASSIGNMENTS

STUDENT ASSIGNMENT 1: True/False

Instructions: Circle T if the statement is true and F if the statement is false.

T F   1. At the Control Center, dBASE IV will automatically display a list of database files in the currently selected catalog.
T F   2. To activate a database file, you first choose the "Database file" option from the Tools menu and then type the full name of the database file.
T F   3. To begin constructing a query, select <create> in the Queries column of the Control Center.
T F   4. The portion of the Query Design screen that specifies which fields are included in the query is called the view skeleton.
T F   5. A right arrow at the end of the file skeleton indicates that there are additional fields off to the right.
T F   6. To move from one skeleton on the Query Design screen to the next, press F4.
T F   7. When you first begin constructing a query, the view skeleton will not contain any fields.
T F   8. You can clear out a condition in a field in the file skeleton by moving the cursor to it and pressing Ctrl-Y.
T F   9. To connect two or more conditions with AND on the Query Design screen, enter them on the same line of the view skeleton.
T F 10. A condition consisting of a single field, a comparison operator, and a value is called a simple condition.
T F 11. When you are entering a condition into a field, dBASE IV automatically shows you the type and width of the field.
T F 12. It is impossible to build a search condition in dBASE IV to select only those employees whose names begin with the letter D.
T F 13. When building a search condition, if you are entering a string of characters, you must enclose them in quotes.
T F 14. Logical fields cannot be used in simple conditions.
T F 15. To print the results of a query, press Shift-F9.
T F 16. To count all records in a database file that satisfy a condition, type the word COUNT in some column, press F2, and then enter the condition.

STUDENT ASSIGNMENT 2: Multiple Choice

Instructions: Circle the correct response.

1. To activate a database file, highlight the file at the Control Center, press Enter, and select _____.
   a. "Use file"
   b. "Activate file"
   c. "Start file"
   d. "Database file"

Student Assignment 2 (continued)

2. The portion of the Query Design screen in which you enter conditions is called the _____.
   a. condition area
   b. status area
   c. file skeleton
   d. view skeleton
3. To move from one field in a skeleton to the next field, press _____.
   a. Tab
   b. Shift-Tab
   c. Enter
   d. F4
4. To _____ a query, press F2.
   a. complete
   b. create
   c. apply
   d. use
5. To add a field to the view skeleton that is not already present, move the cursor to the field in the file skeleton and press _____.
   a. F2
   b. F3
   c. F4
   d. F5
6. A(n) _____ at the end of the file skeleton indicates that there are additional fields off to the right.
   a. left arrow
   b. right arrow
   c. asterisk
   d. down arrow

STUDENT ASSIGNMENT 3: Understanding dBASE Options

Instructions: Explain what happens after you perform each of the following actions.

Problem 1: You are on the Query Design screen and press F2.

Explanation: _____

_____

_____

Problem 2: You are on the Browse screen and select "Transfer to Query Design" from the Exit menu.

Explanation: _____

_____

_____

Problem 3: You are in a column on the Query Design screen and press Ctrl-Y.

Explanation: _____

_____

_____

Problem 4: You type two conditions on the same line of the Query Design screen.

Explanation: _____

_____

_____

STUDENT ASSIGNMENT 4: Using dBASE

Instructions: Explain how to accomplish each of the following tasks using dBASE.

Problem 1: Create a query.

Explanation: _____

_____

_____

Problem 2: Move from the file skeleton to the view skeleton on the Query Design screen.

Explanation: _____

_____

_____

Problem 3: Move from one field to the previous field in the file skeleton of the Query Design screen.

Explanation: _____

_____

_____

Problem 4: Display the NUMBER and NAME fields for all records.

Explanation: _____

_____

_____

Problem 5: Display the records for those employees whose last name begins with Mc.

Explanation: _____

_____

_____

Problem 6: Count the number of employees whose pay rate is more than $8.00.

Explanation: _____

_____

_____

STUDENT ASSIGNMENT 5: Recovering from Problems

Instructions: In each of the following cases, a problem occurred. Explain the cause of the problem and how it can be corrected.

Problem 1: You attempted to create a query containing a compound condition involving OR. When you looked at your display, you realized that the condition you created must have involved AND.

Cause of Problem:_____

_____

Method of Correction: _____

_____

Problem 2: You attempted to calculate the sum of the wage rates for all employees in the Shipping department. dBASE indicated the result was zero. You know this is not the case.

Cause of Problem:_____

_____

Method of Correction: _____

_____

Problem 3: You pressed F2 from the Query Design screen. When you looked at the results, you realized you should have had more records displayed than the ones that actually appeared.

Cause of Problem:_____

_____

Method of Correction: _____

_____

STUDENT ASSIGNMENT 6: Using the Query Design Screen

Instructions: Activate the EMPLOYEE database file, move to the Query Design screen, and apply the query. Then, print the results, return to the Query Design screen, and return to the Control Center. Explain the steps to accomplish this.

Steps: _____

_____

_____

STUDENT ASSIGNMENT 7: Selecting Fields

Instructions: Display the NAME, PAY_RATE, DATE, and UNION fields for all records in the EMPLOYEE database file. Explain the steps to accomplish this.

Steps: _____

_____

_____

STUDENT ASSIGNMENT 8: Using Simple Conditions

Instructions: Display all employees whose pay rate is more than $9.50. Explain the steps to accomplish this.

Steps: _____

_____

_____

STUDENT ASSIGNMENT 9: Using Compound Conditions

Instructions: Display all employees who are in the union and whose pay rate is more than $8.50. Explain the steps to accomplish this.

Steps: _____

_____

_____

STUDENT ASSIGNMENT 10: Using Calculations

Instructions: Count the number of employees in the Marketing department. Sum their pay rates. Find their average pay rate. Explain the steps to accomplish this.

Steps: _____

_____

_____

MINICASES

DISPLAYING RECORDS IN A DATABASE

MINICASE 1: Customers

Instructions: Use the database you created in Minicase 1 of Project 1 for this assignment. List the step(s) necessary to perform each task and then execute it on the computer. You should obtain a printed copy of the results of each query by pressing Shift-F9 (Quick Report).

1. Activate the CUSTCAT catalog and the CUSTOMER database file.

Steps: _____

_____

_____

2. Display all the records in the database file.

Steps: _____

_____

_____

Minicase I (continued)

3. Display the customer number, name, address, balance, and start date fields for all customers.

Steps: _____

_____

_____

4. Display the name field, then the address field, the balance field, the customer number field, and the start date field for all customers.

Steps: _____

_____

_____

5. Display the record for customer 311.

Steps: _____

_____

_____

6. Display the record for the customer whose balance is $909.

Steps: _____

_____

_____

7. Display the records for all customers who are represented by Maria Gomez. (Hint: Be sure to enter the last name first, followed by a comma, and then the first name, since this is the way the data is stored in the database file.) Include the customer number, name, and balance fields.

Steps: _____

_____

_____

8. Display the record for any customer whose name is Sally Adams.

Steps: _____

_____

_____

9. Display the records for all customers who are entitled to a discount.

Steps: _____

_____

_____

10. Display the records for all customers who are represented by Doyle Brown and whose balance is over $100.

Steps: _____

_____

_____

11. Display the records for all customers who are represented by Doyle Brown or whose balance is over $100.

Steps: _____

_____

_____

12. Count the number of records in the database file.

Steps: _____

_____

_____

13. Sum the balances of all customers.

Steps: _____

_____

_____

14. Sum the balances of all customers represented by Maria Gomez.

Steps: _____

_____

_____

15. Average the balance for all customers.

Steps: _____

_____

_____

16. Average the balance for all customers who are entitled to a discount.

Steps: _____

_____

_____

17. Calculate the average balance for customers of each sales rep.

Steps: _____

_____

_____

MINICASE 2: Parts

Instructions: Use the database you created in Minicase 2 of Project 1 for this assignment. List the step(s) necessary to perform each task and then execute it on the computer. You should obtain a printed copy of the results of each query by pressing Shift-F9 (Quick Report).

1. Activate the PARTCAT catalog and the PART database file.

Steps: _____

_____

_____

Minicase 2 (continued)

2. Display all the records in the database file.

Steps: _____

_____

_____

3. Display the part number, part description, item class, and price fields for all parts.

Steps: _____

_____

_____

4. Display the item class field, then the part number field, the part description field, and the price field for all parts.

Steps: _____

_____

_____

5. Display the record for part CA14.

Steps: _____

_____

_____

6. Display the record which contains the part whose price is $10.95.

Steps: _____

_____

_____

7. Display the records for all parts in the SPORTING GOODS item class. Include the part number, part description, price, and last sold date fields.

Steps: _____

_____

_____

8. Display the records for all parts located in warehouse 3.

Steps: _____

_____

_____

9. Display the records for all parts that are eligible for a discount.

Steps: _____

_____

_____

10. Display the records for all parts that are in the SPORTING GOODS item class and have a price that is greater than $100.00.

Steps: _____

_____

_____

11. Display the records for all parts that are in the SPORTING GOODS item class or have a price that is greater than $100.00.

Steps: _____

_____

_____

12. Count the number of records in the database file.

Steps: _____

_____

_____

13. Sum the number of units on hand for all parts.

Steps: _____

_____

_____

14. Sum the number of units on hand for all parts whose item class is HAIR CARE.

Steps: _____

_____

_____

15. Average the price for all parts.

Steps: _____

_____

_____

16. Average the price for all parts whose item class is SPORTING GOODS.

Steps: _____

_____

_____

17. Average the price for parts in each item class.

Steps: _____

_____

_____

MINICASE 3: Movies

Instructions: Use the database you created in Minicase 3 of Project 1 for this assignment. List the step(s) necessary to perform each task and then execute it on the computer. You should obtain a printed copy of the results of each query by pressing Shift-F9 (Quick Report).

1. Activate the MOVCAT catalog and the MOVIE database file.

Steps: _____

_____

_____

2. Display all the records in the database file.

Steps: _____

_____

_____

3. Display the movie number, title, movie type, and director name for all movies.

Steps: _____

_____

_____

4. Display the movie title field, then the director name field, the movie number field, and movie type field for all movies.

Steps: _____

_____

_____

5. Display the record for movie 11.

Steps: _____

_____

_____

6. Display the record for any movies made in 1978.

Steps: _____

_____

_____

7. Display the records for all movies for which the type is COMEDY. Include the movie number, title, year made, and length.

Steps: _____

_____

_____

8. Display the records for all movies directed by Woody Allen. (Hint: Be sure to enter the last name first, followed by a comma, and then the first name, since this is the way the data is stored in the database file.)

Steps: _____

_____

_____

9. Display the records for all movies that are in black and white.

Steps: _____

_____

_____

10. Display the records of all movies of type SUSPEN which are more than 100 minutes in length.

Steps: _____

_____

_____

11. Display the records of all movies which are of type SUSPEN or which are more than 100 minutes in length.

Steps: _____

_____

_____

12. Count the number of records in the database file.

Steps: _____

_____

_____

13. Sum the length of all the movies.

Steps: _____

_____

_____

14. Sum the length of all movies whose type is SUSPEN.

Steps: _____

_____

_____

15. Average the length of all the movies.

Steps: _____

_____

_____

16. Average the length of all movies directed by Woody Allen.

Steps: _____

_____

_____

17. Average the length of the movies directed by each director.

Steps: _____

_____

_____

MINICASE 4: Books

Instructions: Use the database you created in Minicase 4 of Project 1 for this assignment. List the step(s) necessary to perform each task and then execute it on the computer. You should obtain a printed copy of the results of each query by pressing Shift-F9 (Quick Report).

1. Activate the BOOKCAT catalog and the BOOK database file.

Steps: _____

_____

_____

2. Display all the records in the database file.

Steps: _____

_____

_____

3. Display the code, title, author, and price fields for all books.

Steps: _____

_____

_____

4. Display the title field, then the author field, the code field, and price field for all books.

Steps: _____

_____

_____

5. Display the record for the book whose code is 6171.

Steps: _____

_____

_____

6. Display the records for all books whose price is $4.95.

Steps: _____

_____

_____

7. Display the records for all books published by Viking. Include the code, title, author, and units on hand fields.

Steps: _____

_____

_____

8. Display the records for all books written by Jeffrey Archer.

Steps: _____

_____

_____

9. Display the records for all paperback books.

Steps: _____

_____

_____

10. Display the records of all books published by Bantam Books whose type is SUS.

Steps: _____

_____

_____

11. Display the records of all books that are published by Bantam Books or whose type is SUS.

Steps: _____

_____

_____

12. Count the number of records in the database file.

Steps: _____

_____

_____

13. Sum the price of all books.

Steps: _____

_____

_____

14. Sum the price of all paperback books.

Steps: _____

_____

_____

15. Average the price of all books.

Steps: _____

_____

_____

16. Average the price of all books published by Pocket Books.

Steps: _____

_____

_____

17. Average the price of the books published by each publisher.

Steps: _____

_____

_____

Sorting and Report Preparation

OBJECTIVES

You will have mastered the material in this project when you can:

◆ Sort the records in a database file

◆ Display the sorted records

◆ Describe the sequence in which records are sorted

◆ Sort on multiple fields

◆ Create a report file using dBASE

◆ Print a report using a report file you have created

◆ Implement subtotals in a report

The records in a database file are initially arranged in the order in which you enter them. Some applications, however, may require that the records in a database be rearranged in some other sequence. For example, you may want to list employees alphabetically by name. Sorting is the method we use. **Sorting** simply means rearranging the records in the database file so they are in some desired order. Sorting is an important capability in any database management system.

In Project 1, the employee records were entered in the database in a date hired sequence (Figure 3-1). But the records could be arranged in several ways to display the data in a useful form. For example, the records could be arranged in alphabetical order by last name, in ascending or descending sequence by pay rate, or in alphabetical order within the various departments.

NUMBER	NAME	DATE	DEPARTMENT	PAY_RATE	UNION
1011	Rapoza, Anthony P.	01/10/92	Shipping	8.50	.T.
1013	McCormack, Nigel L.	01/15/92	Shipping	8.25	.T.
1016	Ackerman, David R.	02/04/92	Accounting	9.75	.F.
1017	Doi, Chang J.	02/05/92	Production	6.00	.T.
1020	Castle, Mark C.	03/04/92	Shipping	7.50	.T.
1022	Dunning, Lisa A.	03/12/92	Marketing	9.10	.F.
1025	Chaney, Joseph R.	03/23/92	Accounting	8.00	.F.
1026	Bender, Helen O.	04/12/92	Production	6.75	.T.
1029	Anderson, Mariane L.	04/18/92	Shipping	9.00	.T.
1030	Edwards, Kenneth J.	04/23/92	Production	8.60	.T.
1037	Baxter, Charles W.	05/05/92	Accounting	11.00	.F.
1041	Evans, John T.	05/19/92	Marketing	6.00	.F.
1056	Andrews, Robert M.	06/03/92	Marketing	9.00	.F.
1057	Dugan, Mary L.	06/10/92	Production	8.75	.T.
1066	Castleworth, Mary T.	07/05/92	Production	8.75	.T.

records are in sequence by date hired field

FIGURE 3-1 Records sorted by date

If you need to list employees in alphabetical order by last name, you must sort the records in the database file using the employee name field as the basis of the sorting operation (Figure 3-2). A field used as a basis of a sorting operation is called a **key field**. Figure 3-3 displays records that have been sorted by pay rate, using the PAY_RATE field as the key field.

records are in alphabetical order by last name

NUMBER	NAME	DATE	DEPARTMENT	PAY_RATE	UNION
1016	Ackerman, David R.	02/04/92	Accounting	9.75	.F.
1029	Anderson, Mariane L.	04/18/92	Shipping	9.00	.T.
1056	Andrews, Robert M.	06/03/92	Marketing	9.00	.F.
1037	Baxter, Charles W.	05/05/92	Accounting	11.00	.F.
1026	Bender, Helen O.	04/12/92	Production	6.75	.T.
1020	Castle, Mark C.	03/04/92	Shipping	7.50	.T.
1066	Castleworth, Mary T.	07/05/92	Production	8.75	.T.
1025	Chaney, Joseph R.	03/23/92	Accounting	8.00	.F.
1017	Doi, Chang J.	02/05/92	Production	6.00	.T.
1057	Dugan, Mary L.	06/10/92	Production	8.75	.T.
1022	Dunning, Lisa A.	03/12/92	Marketing	9.10	.F.
1030	Edwards, Kenneth J.	04/23/92	Production	8.60	.T.
1041	Evans, John T.	05/19/92	Marketing	6.00	.F.
1013	McCormack, Nigel L.	01/15/92	Shipping	8.25	.T.
1011	Rapoza, Anthony P.	01/10/92	Shipping	8.50	.T.

FIGURE 3-2   Records sorted by name

records are sorted by pay rate

NUMBER	NAME	DATE	DEPARTMENT	PAY_RATE	UNION
1041	Evans, John T.	05/19/92	Marketing	6.00	.F.
1017	Doi, Chang J.	02/05/92	Production	6.00	.T.
1026	Bender, Helen O.	04/12/92	Production	6.75	.T.
1020	Castle, Mark C.	03/04/92	Shipping	7.50	.T.
1025	Chaney, Joseph R.	03/23/92	Accounting	8.00	.F.
1013	McCormack, Nigel L.	01/15/92	Shipping	8.25	.T.
1011	Rapoza, Anthony P.	01/10/92	Shipping	8.50	.T.
1030	Edwards, Kenneth J.	04/23/92	Production	8.60	.T.
1066	Castleworth, Mary T.	07/05/92	Production	8.75	.T.
1057	Dugan, Mary L.	06/10/92	Production	8.75	.T.
1029	Anderson, Mariane L.	04/18/92	Shipping	9.00	.T.
1056	Andrews, Robert M.	06/03/92	Marketing	9.00	.F.
1022	Dunning, Lisa A.	03/12/92	Marketing	9.10	.F.
1016	Ackerman, David R.	02/04/92	Accounting	9.75	.F.
1037	Baxter, Charles W.	05/05/92	Accounting	11.00	.F.

FIGURE 3-3   Records sorted by pay rate

The capability to sort on more than one field is important in sorting. For example, using the employee database file, assume you need to prepare a list of employees in alphabetical order by last name within each department. Output from such a sorting operation is illustrated in Figure 3-4. Notice how the names are in alphabetical order within each department; that is, the names are arranged alphabetically within Accounting, alphabetically within Marketing, alphabetically within Production, and alphabetically within Shipping.

dBASE provides an option that can be used to perform sorting operations. In addition, dBASE provides an option for preparing business-type reports with report and column headings, space control, and totaling for numeric fields. We will see how to use these options to create a variety of professional looking reports.

records are sorted by name within each department

NUMBER	NAME	DATE	DEPARTMENT	PAY_RATE	UNION
1016	Ackerman, David R.	02/04/92	Accounting	9.75	.F.
1037	Baxter, Charles W.	05/05/92	Accounting	11.00	.F.
1025	Chaney, Joseph R.	03/23/92	Accounting	8.00	.F.
1056	Andrews, Robert M.	06/03/92	Marketing	9.00	.F.
1022	Dunning, Lisa A.	03/12/92	Marketing	9.10	.F.
1041	Evans, John T.	05/19/92	Marketing	6.00	.F.
1026	Bender, Helen O.	04/12/92	Production	6.75	.T.
1066	Castleworth, Mary T.	07/05/92	Production	8.75	.T.
1017	Doi, Chang J.	02/05/92	Production	6.00	.T.
1057	Dugan, Mary L.	06/10/92	Production	8.75	.T.
1030	Edwards, Kenneth J.	04/23/92	Production	8.60	.T.
1029	Anderson, Mariane L.	04/18/92	Shipping	9.00	.T.
1020	Castle, Mark C.	03/04/92	Shipping	7.50	.T.
1013	McCormack, Nigel L.	01/15/92	Shipping	8.25	.T.
1011	Rapoza, Anthony P.	01/10/92	Shipping	8.50	.T.

FIGURE 3-4 Records sorted on two fields

SORTING

As illustrated in Figure 3-5, three steps occur when the records in the file EMPLOYEE are sorted. The records in the EMPLOYEE file are read into main memory ①, sorted in main memory ②, and then stored on the disk ③. In the example, the new sorted file is stored on disk using the file name SORTFLE1. After the sorting operation is completed, two separate files are actually stored on disk: the original file (EMPLOYEE) and the sorted file (SORTFLE1).

FIGURE 3-5
Sorting records

The Sort Option

We illustrate the Sort option by sorting the EMPLOYEE database file, the file you used in Projects 1 and 2. This file is currently in sequence by date hired because that's the way we entered the data. If we wanted to sort the records alphabetically by last name, we would have to use the NAME field as the key field. Since NAME is a character field, we can use it as the key field. Character, numeric, and date fields can be sorted, but logical and memo fields cannot.

Creating a Sorted File

To sort records in this file, highlight the EMPLOYEE file at the Control Center and press Enter as you have done before. This time, however, choose "Modify structure/order" rather than "Use file". You are then taken to the Database Design screen (Figure 3-6).

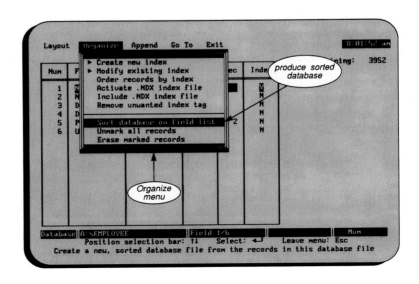

FIGURE 3-6
Database Design screen

The Organize menu should be displayed on your screen. If it is not, press F10 and use the Right or Left Arrow key to bring it to the screen. Select "Sort database on field list". Your screen should then look like Figure 3-7.

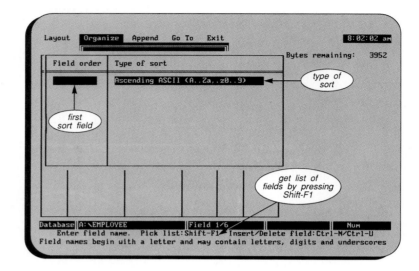

FIGURE 3-7
Database Design screen

dBASE is now prompting you to indicate the key field. You could just type the name of the field you want, but it is usually easier to press Shift-F1. As you can see on your screen, this produces a *pick list*, which is simply a list of items from which you can choose. In this case, pressing Shift-F1 produces a list of available fields in the EMPLOYEE database file (Figure 3-8). Move the highlight to the field you want (NAME) and press Enter. Next, indicate the type of sort you want. When you indicate the type of sort, you are really specifying the *sort sequence*.

FIGURE 3-8
Database Design screen

Sort Sequence

When you are sorting fields defined as numeric fields, the data in the fields are sorted based on their algebraic values. For example, if three records contain the values + 10, –25, and + 90 in a temperature field, and the records are sorted in ascending sequence, the values would be arranged as follows: –25, + 10, + 90.

The sequence in which character data is typically sorted is based on the **American Standard Code for Information Interchange**, called the **ASCII code**. A portion of a chart illustrating the ASCII code is illustrated in Figure 3-9.

ASCII VALUE	CHARACTER	ASCII VALUE	CHARACTER	ASCII VALUE	CHARACTER	ASCII VALUE	CHARACTER	ASCII VALUE	CHARACTER
032	Space	051	3	070	F	089	Y	108	l
033	!	052	4	071	G	090	Z	109	m
034	" (lowest value)	053	5	072	H	091	[	110	n
035	#	054	6	073	I	092	\	111	o
036	$	055	7	074	J	093	]	112	p
037	%	056	8	075	K	094	^	113	q
038	&	057	9	076	L	095	—	114	r
039	'	058	:	077	M	096	`	115	s
040	(	059	;	078	N	097	a	116	t
041	)	060	<	079	O	098	b	117	u
042	*	061	=	080	P	099	c	118	v
043	+	062	>	081	Q	100	d	119	w
044	,	063	?	082	R	101	e	120	x
045	-	064	@	083	S	102	f	121	y
046	.	065	A	084	T	103	g	122	z (highest value)
047	/	066	B	085	U	104	h		
048	0	067	C	086	V	105	i		
049	1	068	D	087	W	106	j		
050	2	069	E	088	X	107	k		

FIGURE 3-9   ASCII codes

In this chart you can see that numbers are lower in the sorting sequence than uppercase letters, and uppercase letters are lower in the sorting sequence than lowercase letters. For example, if in an auto supply store, a part number field contained part numbers A33, 333, and a33, and these part numbers were sorted in ascending sequence, the fields would be sorted as follows: 333, A33, a33. The number 333 would be first because it does not begin with a letter. A33 is next because it begins with capital A. Then a33 is last because it begins with a lowercase a.

dBASE attempts to indicate this on the screen by placing (A..Za..z0..9) in parentheses after the words Ascending ASCII. This is technically incorrect, however. The sequence dBASE has placed on the screen would indicate letters come *before* numbers, which is not the case.

Other possible sort types are available in dBASE. To change from one to another, press the Spacebar (just as you did to change from one field type to another when you first designed your database). The types you cycle through in this process are Descending ASCII (z..aZ..A9..0), Ascending Dictionary (Aa..Zz0..9), and Descending Dictionary (zZ..aA9..0). Usually you will select "Ascending ASCII", but it's nice to know the others are available. In this text, unless you are specifically told otherwise, select "Ascending ASCII". Since this sequence is already on the screen, all you need to do is press Enter.

Finishing the Process

You could now enter a second sort field if you wanted; but, in this example, we have no second sort field, so simply press Enter. A prompt appears asking for a name for the sorted file (Figure 3-10). Any legitimate file name is allowed, except that you cannot sort a file onto itself. Thus, EMPLOYEE is not a possibility as the file name. In this example, use the file name SORTFLE1.

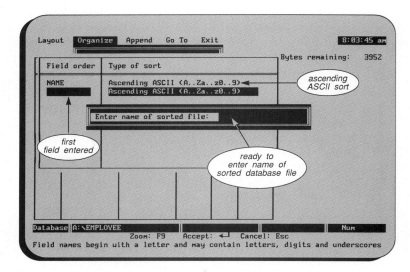

FIGURE 3-10
Database Design screen

After you have typed the file name, press Enter to actually sort the data. During the sort operation, dBASE provides messages on the screen indicating the percentage of the file that has been sorted. When the message indicates that the file has been 100% sorted, the sort is complete. The number of records sorted is also displayed. Enter `Employees sorted by name` as the description of the sorted file. A new sorted file, named SORTFLE1, has now been created and placed in your catalog. Return to the Control Center by selecting the "Save changes and exit" option from the Exit menu.

Displaying a Sorted File

Although you have created this new sorted file, EMPLOYEE is still considered to be the active database file. Thus any option you select, for example, Browse, will operate on the records in EMPLOYEE. To use the sorted version, you must first activate it. Highlight the sorted file at the Control Center, press Enter, and select "Use file". Your screen should then look like Figure 3-11.

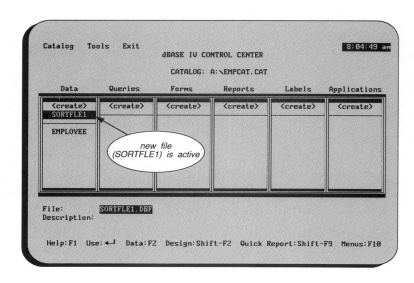

FIGURE 3-11
Control Center

To see the effect of the sort, press F2 to get to the Browse screen (Figure 3-12). (If F2 takes you to the Edit screen, press F2 a second time and you will be at the Browse screen.) Notice that the records are indeed sorted by NAME. After you have finished looking at this display, select the "Exit" option from the Exit menu to return to the Control Center.

Sorting on Multiple Fields

Records can be sorted on the basis of more than one field. Figure 3-4, for example, illustrated the concept of sorting records in alphabetical order by name within each department. Let's try to sort on more than one field. First, highlight EMPLOYEE at the Control Center, press Enter, and then select "Modify structure/order" as you did before. This time, select both key fields in the same way you selected NAME in the previous example. Remember, though, you must select the more significant field first. In this example, records are sorted by name *within* department. Therefore, the more significant field is the DEPARTMENT field, so you must select it first. In both cases, you can select "Ascending ASCII" as the sort type. The remainder of the process is identical to the process you used in creating SORTFLE1, except that this time you use the name SORTFLE2 for the sorted file (Figure 3-13). Enter `Employees by name within department` as the description of the sorted file.

When the sort has been completed, activate SORTFLE2 and press F2 to transfer to the Browse screen (Figure 3-14). Notice that the records are sorted by department and that within each department, the records are sorted by name. After you have finished looking at this display, select the "Exit" option from the Exit menu to return to the Control Center.

Sorting is valuable when it is important for data to appear in some particular order. Although a special order may be desirable even when we view data using the Browse screen, it is often crucial in reports. The process of creating reports makes good use of the sorted files we created in this section.

FIGURE 3-12 Browse screen

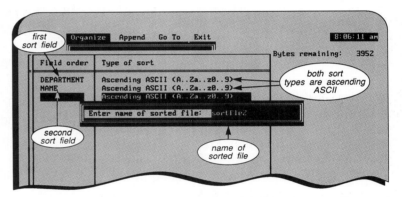

FIGURE 3-13 Database Design screen

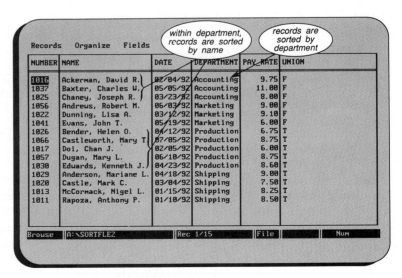

FIGURE 3-14 Browse screen

REPORTS

◆ In previous examples, you have looked at data using the Browse screen. You have also printed the data using Quick Report (Shift-F9). The format of the displayed output was very restrictive. However, dBASE allows you to produce reports containing such items as a page number, date, page and column headings, and totals. You can thus format reports with a professional appearance.

Introduction to Reports

The report in Figure 3-15 lists the name, department, pay rate, and weekly pay amount for all employees. (The weekly pay amount is the pay rate times 40.) The top area of the report is called the **page header**. A page header appears at the top of each page in the report. The body of the report consists of **detail** lines. One detail line is printed for each record. The bottom area, the one containing the total of the weekly pay amounts, is called the **report summary**. It appears once at the end of the report. Even if this report were 50 pages long, there would still be only one report summary and it would appear at the very end.

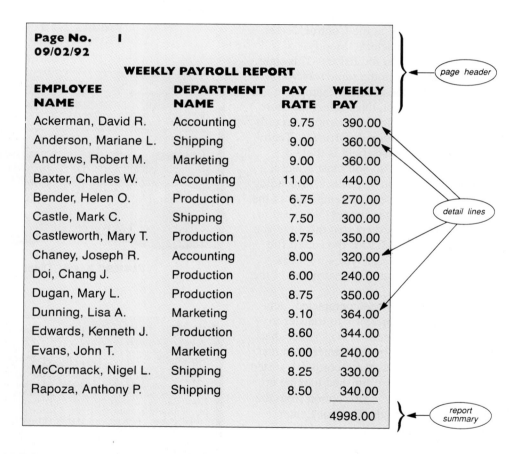

Page No. 1			
09/02/92			
WEEKLY PAYROLL REPORT			
EMPLOYEE NAME	**DEPARTMENT NAME**	**PAY RATE**	**WEEKLY PAY**
Ackerman, David R.	Accounting	9.75	390.00
Anderson, Mariane L.	Shipping	9.00	360.00
Andrews, Robert M.	Marketing	9.00	360.00
Baxter, Charles W.	Accounting	11.00	440.00
Bender, Helen O.	Production	6.75	270.00
Castle, Mark C.	Shipping	7.50	300.00
Castleworth, Mary T.	Production	8.75	350.00
Chaney, Joseph R.	Accounting	8.00	320.00
Doi, Chang J.	Production	6.00	240.00
Dugan, Mary L.	Production	8.75	350.00
Dunning, Lisa A.	Marketing	9.10	364.00
Edwards, Kenneth J.	Production	8.60	344.00
Evans, John T.	Marketing	6.00	240.00
McCormack, Nigel L.	Shipping	8.25	330.00
Rapoza, Anthony P.	Shipping	8.50	340.00
			4998.00

FIGURE 3-15
Weekly Payroll Report

Figure 3-15 is quite typical of simple reports. The page header contains the date the report was produced, the title of the report, the page number, and headings for the various columns in the report. The detail lines contain values in various fields. The report summary contains a statistic, in this case the sum of all the weekly pay amounts.

Sometimes you want to group records in a report; that is, you want to create separate collections of records sharing some common characteristic. In the report in Figure 3-16, for example, the records have been grouped by department. There are four separate groups: one each for Accounting, Marketing, Production, and Shipping.

When you group, you might include in your report two other types of objects: a group intro and a group summary. A **group intro** (or, formally, a group introduction) *introduces* the records in a particular group. In Figure 3-16 the group intro indicates the department. A **group summary** provides certain *summary* information about the records in the group. In Figure 3-16, the group summary gives the total of the weekly pay amounts for all records in the group.

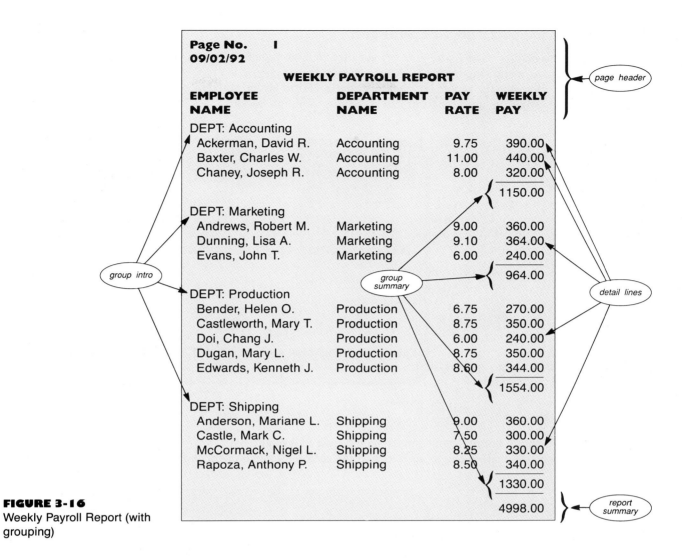

FIGURE 3-16
Weekly Payroll Report (with grouping)

Beginning the Report-Creation Process

Let's use dBASE to create your first report. Before you begin, make sure the database file you are going to use for the report is active. We will use SORTFLE1, so highlight it, press Enter, and then select "Use file". Then select <create> in the Reports column. The Report Design screen now appears (Figure 3-17).

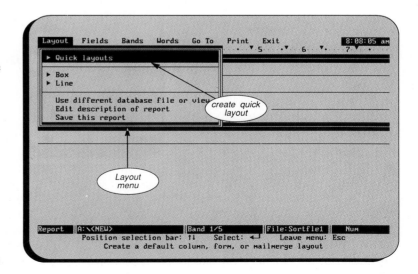

FIGURE 3-17
Report Design screen

Using Quick Layouts to Get Started

A useful shortcut to getting started with a report is called "Quick layouts". To use this shortcut, select "Quick layouts" from the Layout menu (Figure 3-17). A prompt asks you to choose the type of report you want (Figure 3-18). "Column layout" organizes the report in columns of data. "Form layout" produces a report that looks more like a form. "Mailmerge layout" is used for form letters. Select "Column layout".

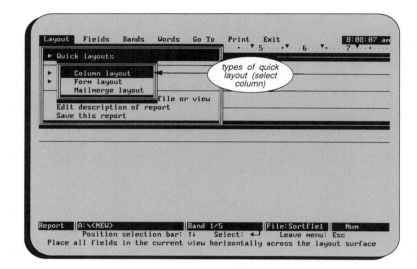

FIGURE 3-18
Report Design screen

Report Bands

After you select "Column layout", your screen should look like Figure 3-19. We will look at the specific entries on this screen in the next section. For now, let's look at the screen's general characteristics.

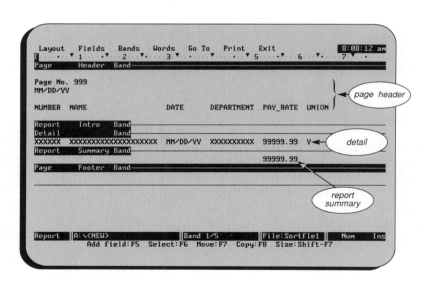

FIGURE 3-19
Report Design screen

Each of the different portions of the report is described in what is often termed a **band**. Notice that there is a page header band, a detail band, and a report summary band, all of which correspond to sections of the report you want to create. There are also two other bands: a report intro band and a page footer band. A **report intro** appears once at the beginning of a report, regardless of how many pages the report contains. A page footer appears at the bottom of each page. Reports seldom require either a report intro or a page footer, although it's nice to have them available in case you run into a report that requires them.

To specify the layout of a report, you need to describe each of the bands you intend to include in the report. This means you need to indicate the precise positions of each item that will appear in the band.

At any given moment during the process, only one band is active. The active band is the band on which the cursor is currently positioned. To move from one band to another, use the Up and Down Arrow keys. Press the Down Arrow key a few times. Notice that you move down through the bands and that the band in which you are currently positioned is highlighted, indicating it is active. Also notice that the number following the word Band on the status line contains the number of the active band.

The Quick Layout

Let's look at the specifics of the layout that dBASE has created for you (Figure 3-19). The block of lines that follows the words Page Header Band is the page header, and it prints at the top of each page. There is currently no report intro band. The detail band contains all the fields from the database file. Finally, a report summary band prints once at the end of the report.

To get an idea of what this would look like on a report, press F10 and select the Print menu (Figure 3-20). Using this menu, you could print the report on your printer by selecting "Begin printing". However, as an alternative, let's see how the report would look on the screen by selecting "View report on screen".

FIGURE 3-20
Report Design screen

After a brief period, the report appears (Figure 3-21). As you can see, it look's just like the quick reports you produced earlier by pressing Shift-F9.

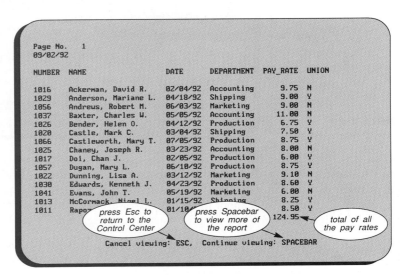

FIGURE 3-21
Viewing report

Whenever you view a report on the screen, dBASE shows you the first screenful and then displays the message shown at the bottom of the screen in Figure 3-21. As the message indicates, press Esc if you do not want to see any more of the report and press the Spacebar to see more. (In this case, there is no more to the report, so it doesn't matter which key you press.) In either case, when you have finished, you are returned to the Report Design screen.

The "View report on screen" option is a helpful feature that you should use often. As you are designing a report, you frequently move objects around on the screen. You add new fields, move existing fields, and delete existing fields. You change the text (letters) on the screen. It is helpful to see periodically exactly what the report will look like given the current entries on the screen. The "View report on screen" option gives you the opportunity to verify that you have done your work correctly.

The Report Design Screen

In the page header band of the Report Design screen, you see things such as Page No., NUMBER, NAME, DATE, and so on. These are printed on the page header exactly as they are shown here in precisely the same position. Thus, Page No. prints on the second line of the page starting in the first column; NUMBER prints on the fifth line on the page starting in the first column; NAME follows NUMBER with two blank spaces in between; and so on.

Notice also the 999 and MM/DD/YY. It certainly doesn't make sense to print Page No. 999 at the top of each page and then MM/DD/YY on the next line. Similarly, you don't want each detail line to start with XXXXXX and then be followed by XXXXXXXXXXXXXXXXXXXX. Fortunately, this is not what these symbols mean. They indicate the position at which the data in some particular field will be printed and what it will look like. The 999 indicates the place where the page number will appear on the report. The MM/DD/YY indicates the position in which the date will appear. The other 9s and the Xs indicate positions where various fields from our file as well as additional calculated fields will appear. The 9s indicate that the field to be printed is numeric, and the Xs indicate that the field is a character field. In addition, if a numeric field contains a decimal point, the decimal point appears at the correct position within the group of 9s.

You might want to know how you can tell whether the XXXXXX indicates that the data in some field will be inserted in the report at this spot or that the report will actually contain six Xs. Also, if XXXXXX is the data from some field, which field? Fortunately, dBASE provides an easy way to tell. Move the cursor down to the group of Xs at the beginning of the detail band (Figure 3-22). As soon as you move into the group of Xs, the whole group becomes highlighted, not just the position where the cursor is located. Notice also that a description of the NUMBER field appears on the last line of the screen. This indicates that the contents of the NUMBER field will be displayed at this position. Also notice that the line number and column number of the current cursor position in the band are both displayed on the status line. (Line numbers and column numbers both start with 0, rather than 1, as you might expect.)

FIGURE 3-22
Report Design screen

One aspect to moving the cursor may surprise you at first. Press the Right Arrow key. Notice that you don't move to the second position in the field, as you might expect. Instead, you move to the position immediately past the end of the field. This always happens. You cannot move the cursor around within any of the fields. Press the Left Arrow key to move back into the first field. You will be positioned at the beginning of the field.

Correcting Mistakes

Before you start working on your report, let's look at a few tips for correcting any mistakes you might make as you create the report. The more you work with the Report Design screen, the easier it will be to correct mistakes. But, until you become comfortable with the various correction methods, follow these few simple tips:

1. Use Ctrl-Y to delete the cursor line, the line on which the cursor is located.
2. Use Ctrl-N to insert a blank line before the cursor line.
3. Use the "Add line" option from the Words menu to insert a blank line after the cursor line.

If you have an extra line you don't want, delete it with Ctrl-Y. If you need an additional line, insert one. If you have made mistakes on a particular line that you don't know how to fix, use Ctrl-Y to delete it and then Ctrl-N to insert a new line. This combination erases the contents of the line. Now reconstruct the line the way it should be. If you need to insert a field on the line, move the cursor to the position for the field, select the "Add field" option from the Fields menu, select the desired field, press Enter, and then press Ctrl-End. (We'll cover this in more detail later in this project.) If you need to insert characters, move the cursor to the position where you want to insert these characters and simply type them.

Occasionally, you might decide that it would be simpler to start over rather than making a number of individual corrections. To do this, select "Abandon changes and exit" from the Exit menu. A dBASE prompt then asks you if you are sure you want to abandon the operation. Answer yes and you are returned to the Control Center without any of your work being saved. You can now start the process from scratch.

There is one potential problem with this approach. If you need to remove the last line in the band, you may find that moving the cursor to it and pressing Ctrl-Y simply erases its contents. The line remains in the band. If this happens, move the contents of the previous line to the last line and then remove the previous line. These steps are:

1. Move the cursor to the beginning of the previous line, press F6, move the cursor to the last nonblank character on the previous line, and press Enter. You have now selected the line.
2. Press F7, move the cursor to the beginning of the last line, and press Enter. You have now moved the contents of the previous line to the last line.
3. Move the cursor back to the previous line and press Ctrl-Y. This will delete the previous line.

Selecting Fields and Text

dBASE allows you to easily move, delete, or resize fields on the screen. You can also move and delete text. By text, we mean characters. On the current screen, the entries Page No., NUMBER, NAME, DATE, DEPARTMENT, PAY_RATE, and UNION are all text. In any case, before you take any of these actions, you must *select* the portion of the screen with which you want to work.

We can illustrate the process of making a selection by specifying the NUMBER field in the detail band. First, move the cursor into this field. Next, press F6 as indicated on the screen. Your screen should now look like Figure 3-23. As the message on the screen indicates, you complete the selection process by pressing Enter. Since you want to select only this single field, press Enter. If you wanted to select a larger portion of the screen, you would first use the arrow keys to move the cursor to the other end of the portion you want to select before pressing Enter. In either case, once you have pressed Enter, the selection is made.

FIGURE 3-23
Report Design screen

Removing Fields from a Report

To remove a field from a report, select it as we have done previously, and then press the Delete key. Delete the NUMBER field from the detail band in this way. Your screen should then look like Figure 3-24. Notice that the field is now removed. Similarly, remove the DATE field and the UNION field from the detail band.

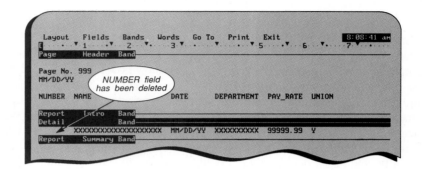

FIGURE 3-24
Report Design screen

As we remove fields from the detail band, the page header will no longer be accurate. Don't worry about this. We will fix it shortly.

Moving Fields on a Report

You now need to move the NAME field to the beginning of the band. First, select the field by moving the cursor to it, pressing F6, and then pressing Enter. Next, press F7. (Notice the message near the bottom of your screen indicating that F7 is used to move a field.) Figure 3-25 shows how the screen looks after you have pressed F7. The message "Position selection with cursor keys, complete with ENTER" means that you should move the cursor to the position where you want the field to begin, and then press Enter. Move the cursor to the beginning of the detail band and press Enter.

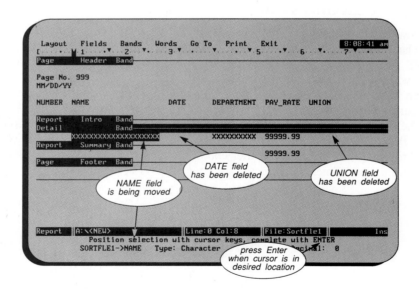

FIGURE 3-25
Report Design screen

As you move the cursor, you will see a faint strip the exact size of the field move along with it. This helps you make sure you get the position you want. In this case, getting the right position is not a problem because you want the very first position in the band. In other cases, though, this feature can come in very handy.

In many cases, the field would now be moved. Here, however, we need to take one additional step. If the new position results in a portion of the field covering an existing field, a prompt asks you: "Delete covered text and fields? (Y/N)". dBASE is warning you that the movement you are requesting would cause the deletion of an existing field, in this case, the deletion of the old NAME field. This is perfectly acceptable because we don't need the old NAME field. Therefore, type the letter Y and the field will now be moved.

Move the DEPARTMENT field in the same manner so that only one space separates it from NAME.

Resizing Fields on a Report

Although we want to include the PAY_RATE field in the report, we don't need it to occupy as many positions as it currently does. Let's change it so that it occupies only five positions rather than eight (the decimal point counts as a position). The entry on the screen should read 99.99 rather than 99999.99. You need to change the size of this entry. On your screen, you can see the word Size, followed by Shift-F7, on the next-to-the-last line. As you might guess, this is how you change the size.

Select the PAY_RATE field in the detail band by moving the cursor to it, pressing F6, and then pressing Enter. Next, press Shift-F7. The message "Size field with cursor keys, complete with ENTER" appears on your screen. Move the cursor to the left until only five positions are included and then press Enter. You have now resized the field (Figure 3-26).

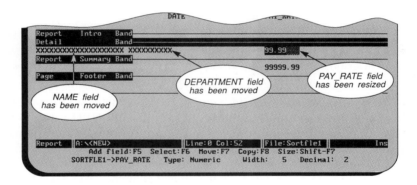

FIGURE 3-26
Report Design screen

You must also move the pay rate to the position shown in Figure 3-27.

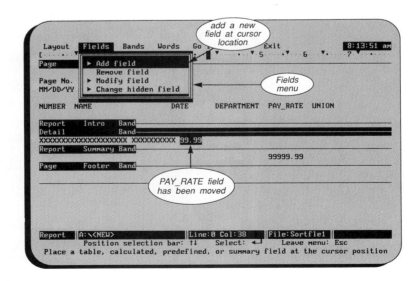

FIGURE 3-27
Report Design screen

Adding Fields

Sometimes, you need to add additional fields; for example, to add the weekly pay rate to the detail band. To add a field, move the cursor to the location where you want to place the field, then move your cursor so that it follows the PAY_RATE field with a single space in between. Next, select the "Add field" option from the Fields menu. Your screen should look like Figure 3-28.

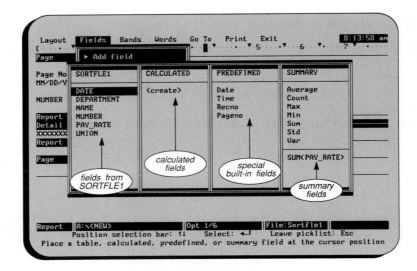

FIGURE 3-28
Report Design screen

The box on the screen shows the fields you can select to add to your report. The first column, SORTFLE1, contains fields from your database file. The third column, PREDEFINED, contains special dBASE fields. The fourth column, SUMMARY, allows you to add fields that give statistics such as sums and averages. These columns do not contain what you need, so you must create an additional field that is calculated from existing fields (weekly pay is equal to PAY_RATE multiplied by 40).

To create this field, select <create> in the second column, CALCULATED. Your screen should now look like Figure 3-29, except that the WEEKLY_PAY and PAY_RATE * 40 entries will not yet appear on your screen. You now need to make these two entries.

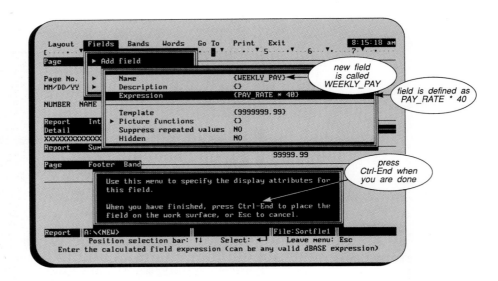

FIGURE 3-29
Report Design screen

To enter WEEKLY_PAY, be sure the highlight is on the line labeled Name. Press Enter, type WEEKLY_PAY, and press Enter again. By doing this, you have assigned a name, specifically, WEEKLY_PAY, to this new field. You could, if you wanted to, enter a description of this field by making an entry in the row labeled Description, but since a description is not necessary, we won't bother making one.

You also must enter an expression that indicates how the contents of the field are to be calculated. Move the highlight to the line labeled Expression, press Enter, type PAY_RATE * 40, and press Enter again. This indicates that the value of WEEKLY_PAY for a record is to be obtained by taking the value of PAY_RATE on the record and multiplying it by 40. In these expressions, you can also use the plus sign (+) for addition, the minus sign (–) for subtraction, and a slash (/) for division.

You can use the bottom portion of the box containing Template, Picture functions, and so on to create some special effects in your output. Your reports, however, will look fine without them, and we will not use them here. You have now completed the description of this new field. To finish the process, press Ctrl-End as indicated on the screen.

Your screen should now look like Figure 3-30. The new field has been placed where you designated. You still need to resize the field so that it is two positions smaller than its current size. Do this now.

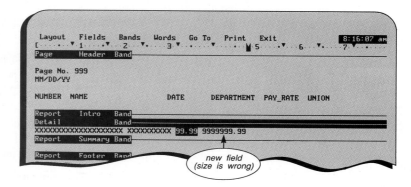

FIGURE 3-30
Report Design screen

Changing the Report Summary

Let's correct the report summary band. First, delete the sum of the pay rates since we don't want it on the report. Move the highlight into the field (the group of 9s in the report band). Your screen should now look like Figure 3-31. Make sure the field you just added (WEEKLY_PAY) is sized and positioned as shown in the figure. Your highlight should now be on the field that is the sum of pay rates. As you can see on the screen, the *operation* is SUM and the field that is *summarized* is PAY_RATE. Select this field by pressing F6 and Enter. Next, delete it by pressing the Delete key.

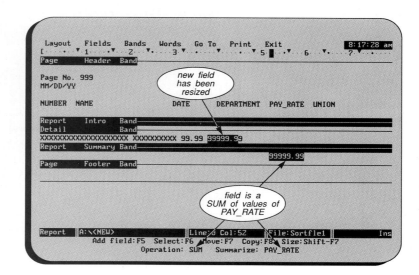

FIGURE 3-31
Report Design screen

Next, add the sum of the weekly pay amounts. Move your cursor so that it is directly below the first 9 in the group of 9s representing WEEKLY_PAY (the last group of 9s in the detail band). Select the "Add field" option from the Fields menu (Figure 3-32). Since you want to calculate a sum, select "Sum" from the SUMMARY column.

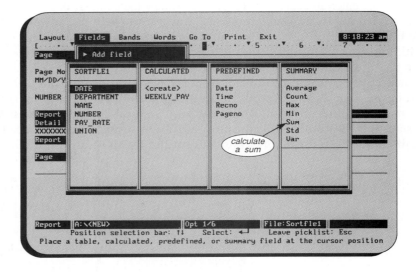

FIGURE 3-32
Report Design screen

Your screen should now look like Figure 3-33. (The word SUM should already appear on the Operation line, but there should not yet be any entry on the line labeled "Field to summarize on".) Make sure the highlight is on the line labeled "Field to summarize on" and press Enter. You then see a list of fields, including the new field you just created, WEEKLY_PAY. Select it and your screen should match the one in the figure.

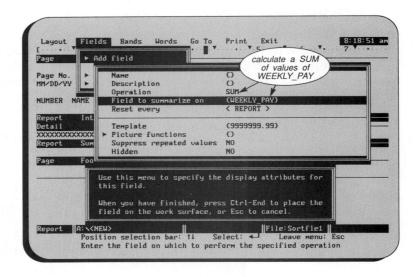

FIGURE 3-33
Report Design screen

You do not need to make any other changes on this screen, so press Ctrl-End. Your screen should then look like Figure 3-34. The new field has been added, but it is the wrong size. Resize it so that it matches the size shown in Figure 3-35.

Next, let's make this field look more like a total by adding a line of hyphens right above the position where we have the sum of the weekly pay amounts. Place the cursor at the beginning of the line and press Ctrl-N to insert a new line above the cursor line. Then you can type eight hyphens in this new line in the positions shown in the report summary band of Figure 3-36.

Changing the Page Header

Let's correct the page header so that it looks like the one in Figure 3-36. The simplest way to do this is to move the cursor to the beginning of the line following the MM/DD/YY, press Ctrl-Y twice to delete two lines, and then press Ctrl-N four times to insert four new lines. This erases everything underneath the page number and date and gives you the right number of lines.

To make any of the entries shown in the page header band in the figure, move the cursor to the location you want and type the letters you want. If you should make a mistake, place the cursor on the incorrect letter and press the Delete key.

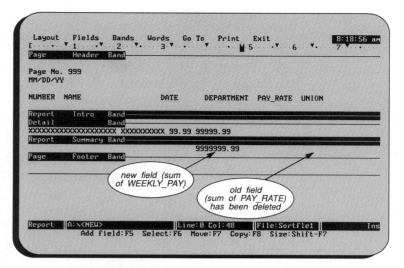

FIGURE 3-34 Report Design screen

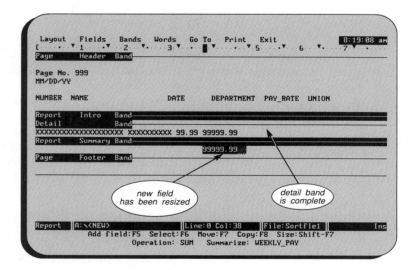

FIGURE 3-35
Report Design screen

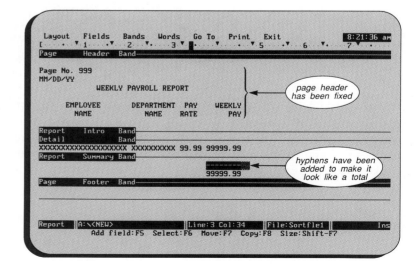

FIGURE 3-36
Report Design screen

Changing the Left Margin

When your page header band is correct, you are almost done. The only remaining change is to the left margin. If you don't adjust the left margin, the report will begin at the left-hand edge of the paper. Let's allow five spaces as a left margin; that is, the report will begin in position 6. To change the left margin, select the "Page dimensions" option from the Print menu (Figure 3-37). The entry you want to change is labeled "Offset from left". Move the highlight to it, press Enter, type the number 5, and press Enter again. Then you can leave the menu by pressing Esc twice.

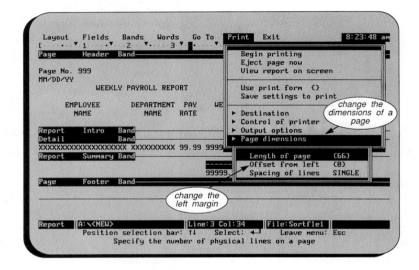

FIGURE 3-37
Report Design screen

Saving the Report

Before you save the report, it's a good idea to view it on the screen. If you discover anything you don't like about the report layout when you view it, you can change it at this time. Assuming the report is the way you want it, the report description is now complete. To finish, choose the "Save changes and exit" option from the Exit menu (Figure 3-38). A dBASE prompt then asks you what you want to name this report file. Type REPORT1 and press Enter.

FIGURE 3-38
Report Design screen

By changing the left margin, you made changes to what dBASE terms the *print form*. Since you did, a dBASE prompt asks you if you want to save them. Answer yes. dBASE then prompts you to save them with the same name you gave your report. There is no good reason to give them a different name, so simply press Enter. This last step may seem a little complicated, but don't worry. All the answers you need to give are highlighted. Thus, you can simply keep pressing Enter until you return to the Control Center.

When you return to the Control Center, you will see the report you created listed in the Reports column (Figure 3-39). Now is a good time to add a description to this report. You will appreciate the description when you have several reports listed in the column. Make sure REPORT1 is highlighted and then select the "Change description of highlighted file" option from the Catalog menu. You are then asked for a description. Enter something that is descriptive of the report such as Weekly Payroll Report.

Printing a Report

As you have seen, you can print the report from the Report Design screen. Usually, however, you only go to the Report Design screen when you want to change the design of a report. Most of the time, you print the report from the Control Center. Highlight the report, press Enter, and then select "Print report" (Figure 3-40).

You then see the same Print menu that you encountered on the Report Design screen (Figure 3-41). All the options function in exactly the same way. Thus you could see the report on the screen by selecting "View report on screen". You could also change the length of a page or the line spacing using the "Page dimensions" option. If you want to print the report on your printer, select the "Begin printing" option.

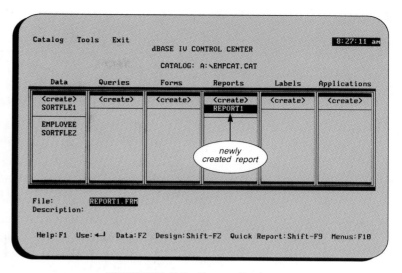

FIGURE 3-39 Report Design screen

FIGURE 3-40 Control Center

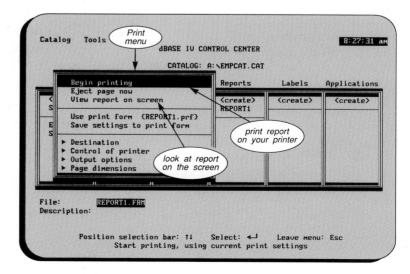

FIGURE 3-41 Control Center

Either print your report or view your report on the screen. It should look like Figure 3-42.

| Page No.   1 |
| 09/02/92 |

WEEKLY PAYROLL REPORT

EMPLOYEE NAME	DEPARTMENT NAME	PAY RATE	WEEKLY PAY
Ackerman, David R.	Accounting	9.75	390.00
Anderson, Mariane L.	Shipping	9.00	360.00
Andrews, Robert M.	Marketing	9.00	360.00
Baxter, Charles W.	Accounting	11.00	440.00
Bender, Helen O.	Production	6.75	270.00
Castle, Mark C.	Shipping	7.50	300.00
Castleworth, Mary T.	Production	8.75	350.00
Chaney, Joseph R.	Accounting	8.00	320.00
Doi, Chang J.	Production	6.00	240.00
Dugan, Mary L.	Production	8.75	350.00
Dunning, Lisa A.	Marketing	9.10	364.00
Edwards, Kenneth J.	Production	8.60	344.00
Evans, John T.	Marketing	6.00	240.00
McCormack, Nigel L.	Shipping	8.25	330.00
Rapoza, Anthony P.	Shipping	8.50	340.00
			4998.00

FIGURE 3-42
Weekly Payroll Report

GROUPING

◆ Earlier in the project, you saw two reports (Figures 3-15 and 3-16). You have just produced the first one. We now turn our attention to the second report (also shown in Figure 3-43). This report involves **grouping**, that is, creating separate collections of records that share some common characteristic. The records in this report have been grouped by department. There are four separate groups: one for Accounting, one for Marketing, one for Production, and one for Shipping.

This report includes two new types of objects: a group intro and a group summary. In the sample report, the group intro indicates the department and the group summary gives the total of the weekly pay amounts for all records in the group.

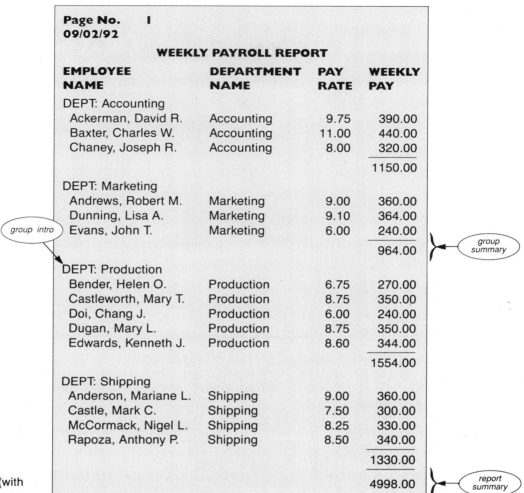

FIGURE 3-43
Weekly Payroll Report (with grouping)

Modifying a Report Design

We could design this report from scratch just as we did the last one. There is no need to go to all that trouble, however, since we already have a report that is close to the one we want, namely REPORT1. Rather than create a new report, let's make things easier by modifying this existing one.

Make sure your SORTFLE1 database file is active, move the highlight to REPORT1, and press Enter. Next, select "Modify layout" from the options presented. You are then returned to the Report Design screen. The current design appears on the screen (Figure 3-44). You can now make changes to this design in exactly the same manner you did when you first created it.

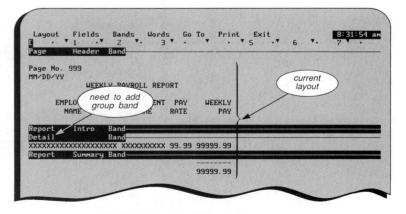

FIGURE 3-44 Report Design screen

Adding a Group Band

To group records in a report, we use a new type of band, called a **group band**. To add the necessary group band to the report, place your cursor on the report intro band because as we will see, the group band follows the report intro band. Next, select the "Add a group band" option from the Bands menu (Figure 3-45).

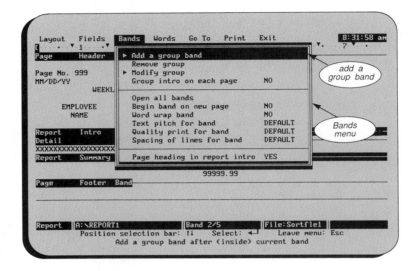

FIGURE 3-45
Report Design screen

At this point, you are asked to enter the value on which grouping takes place (Figure 3-46). You can enter a field value, an expression value, or a record count. You will virtually always use a field value. Make sure the highlight is on "Field value" and press Enter.

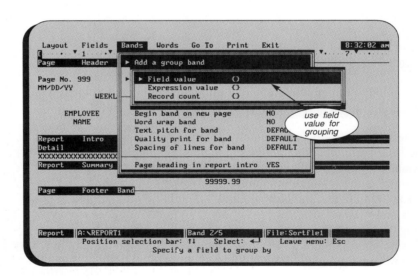

FIGURE 3-46
Report Design screen

A list of all the fields in the view then appears. Select DEPARTMENT because this is the field on which the grouping is to take place. Your screen should now look like Figure 3-47.

Notice that two new bands have appeared, one labeled "Group 1 Intro Band" and the other labeled "Group 1 Summary Band." The collection of all employees in the same department is a group. Whatever we specify in the Group 1 intro band is displayed immediately *before* each group (it *intro*duces the group). Whatever we specify in the Group 1 summary band will be displayed immediately *after* each group, in other words it provides a *summary* for the group. Thus we now need to describe these two bands. Before we do, we will look briefly at another topic, opened and closed bands.

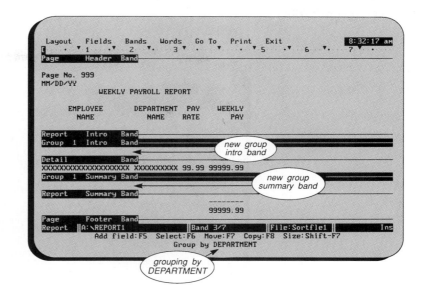

FIGURE 3-47
Report Design screen

Opened and Closed Bands

Look at the report intro band and the Group 1 intro band in Figure 3-47. Do you notice a difference? A blank line follows the Group 1 intro band, but none follows the report intro band. Any band that does not have at least one line following it is *closed* and the contents of the band, whatever they may be, will not be printed on the report. The other bands are *open* and their contents will print. Currently, the Group 1 intro band consists of just a single blank line. This will still appear on the report, however. The group of employees in any given department is preceded by a single blank line.

To close a band that is currently open or to open a band that is currently closed, move the cursor to the line that gives the name of the band and press Enter. Try closing the Group 1 intro band. Watch the blank line disappear. Open it again by pressing Enter and the line reappears.

Fixing the Group Bands

Let's fix the group intro band. Move the cursor to the beginning of the first line of the band and type DEPT:. Move the cursor one position past the colon (:) and select the "Add field" option from the Fields menu (Figure 3-48).

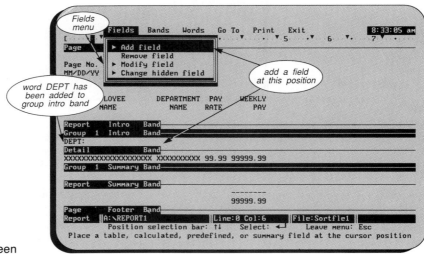

FIGURE 3-48
Report Design screen

You are then presented with a list of fields as you have seen before. Select DEPARTMENT. Your screen then looks like Figure 3-49. You don't need to make any changes in this box, so press Ctrl-End.

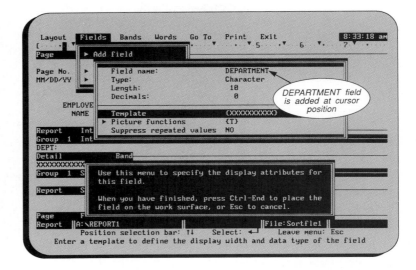

FIGURE 3-49
Report Design screen

Now let's fix the group summary band. Move the cursor to the blank line in the band and add two additional lines by pressing Ctrl-N twice. Add eight hyphens in the position shown in Figure 3-50. Next, move the cursor down one line and immediately under the first of the hyphens. Bring the Fields menu to the screen (in the figure this has already been done).

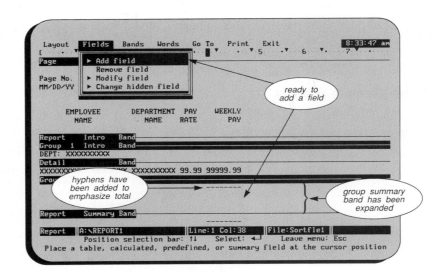

FIGURE 3-50
Report Design screen

Select the "Add field" option and then select "Sum". In the box that appears, select WEEKLY_PAY as the field to summarize on, just as you did in the report summary band. Finish the process by changing the size of the field so that it matches the size shown in Figure 3-51.

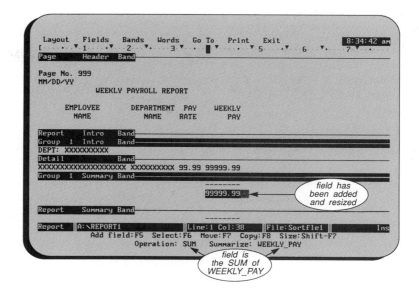

FIGURE 3-51
Report Design screen

Saving the Report

To save the new report, you could select "Save changes and exit" from the Exit menu as you did before, but don't. Since you were working on an existing report, dBASE would not ask you for a name for this report. Instead, it saves the report under the original name, REPORT1, which means you would lose the old report. If this is not a problem for you, then save the report.

Let's suppose, however, that you still would like to have the original REPORT1. You should save your work under a different name such as REPORT2. Select the "Save this report" option from the Layout menu. Your screen should then look like Figure 3-52. The name of the original report is displayed in the "Save as" box. Using the arrow keys or the Backspace key, change the name from REPORT1 to REPORT2 and then press Enter. This report is then saved as REPORT2. You have completed the second report, but you were not returned to the Control Center because you did not choose "Exit". To return to the Control Center, select the "Abandon changes and exit" option from the Exit menu. (In this case, "Abandon changes" would mean abandon your changes to REPORT1, which is exactly what you want.)

Once you are back to the Control Center, add a description for this file as you have done before. You might enter something such Weekly Payroll Report by Department.

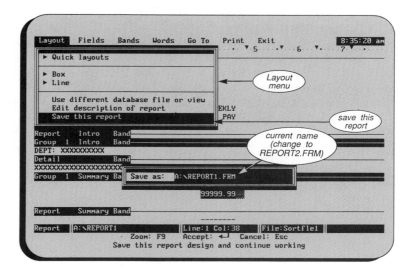

FIGURE 3-52
Report Design screen

Printing the Report

If you produce the report as you did before, you will see something unusual. (Figure 3-53 shows only the first part of the report, but the report continues on in this fashion.) There is a group for Accounting, followed by a group for Shipping, one for Marketing, and then *another one* for Accounting. What's wrong? The problem is that the records are not sorted correctly. All the records for a given department must be together for the report to work correctly. This is not the case in SORTFLE1.

Page No. I 09/02/92			
WEEKLY PAYROLL REPORT			
EMPLOYEE NAME	**DEPARTMENT NAME**	**PAY RATE**	**WEEKLY PAY**
DEPT: Accounting			
Ackerman, David R.	Accounting	9.75	390.00
			390.00
DEPT: Shipping			
Anderson, Mariane L.	Shipping	9.00	360.00
			360.00
DEPT: Marketing			
Andrews, Robert M.	Marketing	9.00	360.00
			360.00
DEPT: Accounting			
Baxter, Charles W.	Accounting	11.00	440.00
			440.00
DEPT: Production			
Bender, Helen O.	Production	6.75	270.00
			270.00

FIGURE 3-53 Weekly Payroll Report (with incorrect grouping)

Fortunately, another file that you created, SORTFLE2, contains the records sorted by NAME within DEPART-MENT, which is precisely the correct order. Activate this file in the usual manner and produce the report again.

Since you are attempting to use a database file that is different from the one you used when you created the report, a dBASE prompt asks you if you want to use the current view (the current database file) or the original database file (SORTFLE1) for the report (Figure 3-54). Select "Current view" and you will see a report that looks like the one you were trying to produce.

What if you were not so fortunate? What if SORTFLE2 did not already exist? You would need to create it now in exactly the fashion we described earlier in this project.

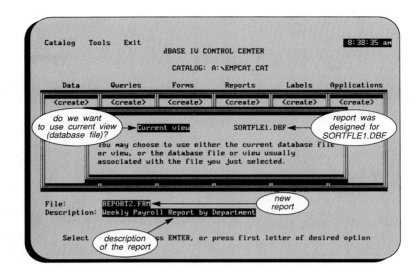

FIGURE 3-54
Control Center

REMOVING FILES

◆ Sometimes you might want to remove a file from your catalog and delete it from your disk. If you never remove files, your disk and your catalogs can become cluttered quickly. Thus, if you have files that you don't think you will need again, you should remove them. In your case, SORTFLE1 and SORTFLE2 are good candidates for removal as once you make any further changes in EMPLOYEE, the data in these two files is out of date. If you need them again later, you should recreate them using the new data in EMPLOYEE.

To delete a file, first move the highlight to it. To be deleted, a file, must *not* be active. If it is, press Enter and then select "Close file". Now choose the "Remove highlighted file from catalog" option from the Catalog menu. As a safety feature, a dBASE prompt asks you if you are sure you want to remove it from the catalog. Answer yes. The file is no longer in the catalog, but it is still on your disk. You are next asked if you also want to remove it from the disk. Unless you have some special need for the file, you should usually remove it from the disk as well, so answer yes.

PROJECT SUMMARY

In Project 3 you learned how to sort a database file producing a file containing the same records but in the order you desire. You also learned how to design a report and use the dBASE report facility to create a report file, a file that contained the report layout to dBASE. You used this report file to produced a report with the desired layout. Finally, you saw how to use subtotals in reports. All the activities that you learned for this project are summarized in the Quick Reference following Project 6.

The following is a summary of the keystroke sequence we used in Project 3.

SUMMARY OF KEYSTROKES — PROJECT 3

STEPS	KEY(S) PRESSED	RESULTS
1	DBASE ←[At DOS prompt]	Starts dBASE.
2	↓[To highlight EMPLOYEE] ← → ←	Moves to Database Design screen with EMPLOYEE active.
3	↓[Press 6 times] ← Shift-F1 ↓↓ ←[Press 4 times]SORTFLE1 ←Employees sorted by name ← F10 → → → ←←	Creates first sort file.
4	↓[To highlight SORTFLE1] ← ← F2	Moves to Browse screen with SORTFLE1 active.
5	F10 →[Press 4 times] ←	Returns to Control Center.
6	↓[To highlight EMPLOYEE] ← → ←	Moves to Database Design screen with EMPLOYEE active.
7	↓[Press 6 times] ← Shift-F1 ↓ ← ← ← Shift-F1 ↓↓ ← [Press 4 times]SORTFLE2 ←Employees by name within department ← F10 → → → ←←	Creates second sort file.
8	↓↓ ← ← F2 F10 →[Press 4 times] ←	Activates SORTFLE2 and browses.
9	↓↓ ← ←	Activates SORTFLE1.
10	→ → → ← ← ←	Starts report creation.
11	F10 →[Press 5 times]↓↓ ← Esc [Any key]	Views report.
12	↓[Press 9 times] F6 ← Delete	Deletes NUMBER field.
13	→[Press 11 times] F6 ← Delete	Deletes DATE field.
14	→[Press 16 times] F6 ← Delete	Deletes UNION field.
15	←[Press 19 times] F6 ← F7 ←[Press 8 times]←Y	Moves NAME field.
16	→[Press 21 times] F6 ← F7 ←[Press 19 times]←	Moves DEPT field.
17	→[Press 22 times] F6 ← Shift-F7 ← ← ← ←	Resizes PAY_RATE field.
18	F6 ← F7 ←[Press 20 times]←	Moves PAY_RATE field.
19	→ → F10 ←[Press 4 times]← → ← ←WEEKLY_PAY←↓↓ ←PAY-RATE * 40← Ctrl-End	Enters WEEKLY_PAY field.
20	← F6 ← Shift-F7 ← ← ←	Resizes WEEKLY_PAY field (Detail band is done).
21	↓↓ ←[Press 14 times] F6 ← Delete	Deletes sum of PAY_RATE.
22	←[Press 14 times] F10 ← → → → ↓[Press 4 times]← ↓↓↓ ← → ← Ctrl-End	Enters sum of WEEKLY_PAY.
23	← F6 ← Shift-F7 ← ← ←	Resizes sum of WEEKLY_PAY.
24	←[Press 38 times]	Moves to beginning of line.
25	Ctrl-N	Enters blank line.
26	→[Press 38 times]-[Press Hyphen key 8 times]	Underlines weekly pay (Report summary band is done).

SUMMARY OF KEYSTROKES — PROJECT 3 (continued)

STEPS	KEY(S) PRESSED	RESULTS
27	↑[Press 7 times] ← [Press 45 times] `Ctrl-Y` `Ctrl-Y` `Ctrl-N` [Press 4 times]	Places correct number of blank lines in page header.
28	[Place each of the following at the indicated position] WEEKLY PAYROLL REPORT [Line:3 Col:13] EMPLOYEE [Line:5 Col:8] DEPARTMENT [Line:5 Col:21] PAY [Line:5 Col:32] WEEKY [Line:5 Col:40] NAME [Line:6 Col:10] NAME [Line:6 Col:24] RATE [Line:6 Col:32] PAY [Line:6 Col:43]	Completes page header band.
29	`F10` →[Press 4 times to get to Print menu]↓ [Press 6 times]←↓←5← `Esc` `Esc`	Changes margin.
30	`F10` → ←REPORT1 ← ← ←	Creates first report.
31	`F10` ↓[Press 5 times]←Weekly Payroll Report ←	Enters report description.
32	← ← ←	Prints report.
33	← → ←	Moves to Report Design screen.
34	↓[Press 9 times] `F10` → → ← ← ↓ ←	Enters group band.
35	↓DEPT: → `F10` ← ←↓← `Ctrl-End`	Finishes Group intro.
36	↓[Press 4 times] `Ctrl-N` `Ctrl-N` [Move cursor to Line:0 Col:38 of group summary]–[Press Hyphen key 8 times]	Enters underlines.
37	[Move cursor to Line:1 Col:38 of group summary] `F10` ← → → → ↓[Press 4 times]←↓↓↓← → ← `Ctrl-End`	Enters sum of weekly pay.
38	← `F6` ← `Shift-F7` ← ← ←	Finishes report.
39	`F10` ← ↓[Press 5 times] ← ←[Press 5 times]2←	Saves as REPORT2.
40	`F10` →[Press 6 times]↓ ←	Returns to Control Center.
41	↓ `F10` ↓[Press 5 times]←Weekly Payroll Report by Department←	Enters report description.
42	← ← ←↓↓[To highlight SORTFLE2]← ←	Activates SORTFLE2.
43	→ → →↓↓[To highlight REPORT2]←[Press 4 times]	Prints report using current view (SORTFLE2).
44	← ← ← ← ←	Closes SORTFLE2.
45	↓↓[To highlight SORTFLE1] `F10` ↓[Press 4 times]← ← ← ← ←	Removes SORTFLE1 from catalog and disk.
46	↓↓[To highlight SORTFLE2] `F10` ← ← ← ← ←	Removes SORTFLE2 from catalog and disk.

The following list summarizes the material covered in Project 3.

1. A **key field** is a field that is used as a basis of a **sorting** operation.
2. To sort the records in a database file, producing a new database file, use the "Sort database on field list" option from the Organize menu.
3. To sort on multiple keys, select the keys in order of importance.
4. To display the records in a sorted file, the sorted file must be activated.
5. The **American Standard Code for Information Interchange**, usually called the **ASCII code**, is a code used for storing data.

6. Numeric fields are sorted on the basis of their algebraic values. Character data is usually sorted on the basis of the ASCII code.
7. To create a report, highlight <create> in the Reports column of the Control Center and press Enter.
8. The various portions of a report (**page header**, **report intro**, **group intro**, **detail**, **group summary**, and **report summary**) are specified by making entries in appropriate **bands** in the Report Design screen.
9. The page dimensions of a report can be changed by using the "Page dimensions" option from the Print menu.
10. To terminate the report-creation process, choose either "Save" (to save your work) or "Abandon" (to exit without saving your work) from the Exit menu.
11. To print a report from the Control Center, highlight the report, press Enter, and then choose "Print report".
12. To change the layout of an existing report, highlight the report at the Control Center, press Enter, and then select "Modify layout".
13. To specify **grouping** on a report, add a **group band**.

STUDENT ASSIGNMENTS

STUDENT ASSIGNMENT 1: True/False

Instructions: Circle T if the statement is true and F if the statement is false.

T F 1. You can accomplish the rearranging of records in a database file into some sequence other than the order in which the records were entered by sorting the records in the database file.
T F 2. When you use dBASE IV, you can sort records using only one key field.
T F 3. To get a list of fields available as sort keys, press F1.
T F 4. The file that contains the sorted records is automatically active at the end of the sort operation.
T F 5. When the "Sort" option is executed, the file which is to be sorted must be the active file.
T F 6. If you sort with multiple key fields, it doesn't matter in which order you specify the fields.
T F 7. To begin creating a report, select <create> in the Reports column of the Control Center.
T F 8. When you are creating a report design, you can have dBASE IV create an initial design for you by selecting the "Quick layouts" option from the Layout menu.
T F 9. When you move the cursor into a field in a report design, the name of the field will be displayed near the bottom of the screen.
T F 10. To delete a field from the Report Design screen, move the cursor to it, press F6, press Enter, and then press the Delete key.
T F 11. Unless you change it, the left margin will be zero in any report created by the dBASE IV report feature.
T F 12. To delete a line in a report band, press Ctrl-X.
T F 13. To open a band, select the "Open band" option from the Bands menu and then select the band you want to open from the list that is presented.
T F 14. To modify an existing report, highlight the report at the Control Center and then select "Modify layout".
T F 15. Group bands are used to specify subtotals when you are using the dBASE IV report facility.
T F 16. The maximum number of lines possible for a page heading using the report facility of dBASE IV is four.

STUDENT ASSIGNMENT 2: Multiple Choice

Instructions: Circle the correct response.

1. A field used as a basis of a sorting operation is called a _____.
   a. sort field
   b. sequence field
   c. key field
   d. basis field

2. When sorting in dBASE IV, the file containing the data to be sorted _____.
   a. must be specified when you choose the "Sort" option
   b. must be the active file
   c. must be both the active file and specified when you choose the "Sort" option
   d. must not be the active file
3. If you want dBASE to create an initial report layout for you, select the _____ of the Layout menu.
   a. "Initial layout"
   b. "Quick layouts"
   c. "Create layout"
   d. "Start"
4. To delete a line in the Report Design screen, press _____.
   a. Esc
   b. Ctrl-N
   c. Ctrl-Y
   d. Delete
5. To move a field on a report, select it, and then press _____.
   a. F6
   b. F7
   c. Shift-F7
   d. Delete
6. To include subtotals on a report, use a _____ band.
   a. group intro
   b. subtotal
   c. report summary
   d. group summary

STUDENT ASSIGNMENT 3: Understanding dBASE Options

Instructions: Explain what happens after you perform each of the following actions.

Problem 1: You select two fields for the "Sort database on field list" option from the Organize menu.

Explanation: _____

_____

_____

Problem 2: You highlight <create> in the Reports column of the Control Center and press Enter.

Explanation: _____

_____

_____

Problem 3: You select "Quick layouts" from the Layout menu on the Report Design screen.

Explanation: _____

_____

_____

Problem 4: You are on a line in the Page Header Band of the Report Design screen and press Ctrl-Y.

Explanation: _____

_____

_____

STUDENT ASSIGNMENT 4: Using dBASE

Instructions: Explain how to accomplish each of the following tasks using dBASE.

Problem 1: Sort a database file on two fields.

Explanation: _____

_____

_____

Problem 2: After sorting a database file, display all the records in the sorted file.

Explanation: _____

_____

_____

Problem 3: Begin creating a report. (Describe the steps that must occur up to the point where you first see the Report Design screen.)

Explanation: _____

_____

_____

Problem 4: Specify a two-line heading for a column.

Explanation: _____

_____

_____

Problem 5: Cause totals not to be calculated for some numeric field in a report.

Explanation: _____

_____

_____

Problem 6: Include subtotals in a report.

Explanation: _____

_____

_____

STUDENT ASSIGNMENT 5: Recovering from Problems

Instructions: In each of the following cases, a problem occurred. Explain the cause of the problem and how it can be corrected.

Problem 1: You were on the Report Design screen. Once you completed the design for your report, you left the Report Design screen. Later, when you attempted to use the report you created, you found that it did not exist.

Cause of Problem:_____

_____

Method of Correction: _____

_____

Problem 2: You were creating a sorted file. When you specified a name for the file, dBASE rejected it.

Cause of Problem:_____

_____

Method of Correction: _____

_____

Problem 3: You specified a report using the Report Design screen. The report involved a database called STUDENT that contained student data. In the report, you indicated that records were to be grouped by MAJOR, which is one of the fields in each student's record. After printing the report, you notice that it starts with a group of two students in Geology, then one student in History, followed by two students in Music and then another student in Geology.

Cause of Problem:_____

_____

Method of Correction: _____

_____

STUDENT ASSIGNMENT 6: Sorting on One Key

Instructions: Sort the EMPLOYEE database file on pay rate. Display the results. Explain the steps to accomplish this.

Steps: _____

_____

_____

STUDENT ASSIGNMENT 7: Sorting on Multiple Keys

Instructions: Sort the EMPLOYEE database file on pay rate within department. Explain the steps to accomplish this.

Steps: _____

_____

_____

STUDENT ASSIGNMENT 8: Creating a Report

Instructions: Create and print a report called EMPREPT for the EMPLOYEE database file. Include the NUMBER, NAME, DATE, and PAY_RATE fields. The report should include a total of all the pay rates. The data on the report should be sorted by pay rate. Explain the steps to accomplish this.

Steps: _____

_____

_____

STUDENT ASSIGNMENT 9: Modifying a Report

Instructions: Modify EMPREPT so the DEPARTMENT field is included. It should appear between the NAME and DATE fields. Once you have done this, print the new version of the report. Explain the steps to accomplish this.

Steps: _____

_____

_____

STUDENT ASSIGNMENT 10: Grouping in a Report

Instructions: Modify EMPREPT so a subtotal is taken whenever there is a change in DEPARTMENT. Once you have done this, print the new version of the report. Explain the steps to accomplish this.

Steps: _____

_____

_____

MINICASES

SORTING RECORDS AND REPORT PREPARATION

MINICASE 1: Customers

Instructions: Use the CUSTOMER database file that you created in Minicase 1 of Project 1 in the following problems. These problems require sorting the database and preparing reports from the database.

Problem 1: Sorting Records

a. Sort the records in the CUSTOMER database file in ascending order by customer name. Use SORTFLE1 as the name for the sorted file. Explain the steps to accomplish this.

Steps: _____

_____

_____

b. After the records have been sorted, print the contents of the sorted file using Quick Report (Shift-F9).

Problem 2: Sorting Records on Multiple Fields

a. Sort the records in the CUSTOMER database file in ascending order by customer name within sales rep name. Use SORTFLE2 as the name for the sorted file. Explain the steps to accomplish this.

Steps: _____

_____

_____

b. After the records have been sorted, print the contents of the sorted file using Quick Report (Shift-F9).

Problem 3: Creating a Report

a. Create a report for the CUSTOMER database file. Call the report CUSTRPT1. The report is to contain a page number, date, and report and column headings. Include the customer number, customer name, customer address, sales rep name, and balance fields on the report. The report should contain a final total of the balance field.
b. Print a copy of your report. Use the data contained in SORTFLE1 to prepare the report.
c. Modify the report format so that a subtotal is taken when there is a change in sales rep name. Call the new report CUSTRPT2. Include a group intro giving the sales rep name and a group summary giving the subtotal.
d. Print a copy of the modified report. Use the data contained in the file named SORTFLE2 to prepare the report.

MINICASE 2: Parts

Instructions: Use the PART database file that you created in Minicase 2 of Project 1 in the following problems. These problems require sorting the database and preparing reports from the database.

Problem 1: Sorting Records

a. Sort the records in the PART database file in ascending order by part description. Use SORTFLE1 as the name for the sorted file. Explain the steps to accomplish this.

Steps: _____

_____

_____

b. After the records have been sorted, print the contents of the sorted file using Quick Report (Shift-F9).

Problem 2: Sorting Records on Multiple Fields

a. Sort the records in the PART database file in ascending order by description within item class. Use SORTFLE2 as the name for the sorted file. Explain the steps to accomplish this.

Steps: _____

_____

_____

b. After the records have been sorted, print the contents of the sorted file using Quick Report (Shift-F9).

Problem 3: Creating a Report

a. Create a report for the PART database file. Call the report PARTRPT1. The report is to contain a page number, date, and report and column headings. Include the part number, description, units on hand, item class, and price fields on the report. The report should contain a final total of the units on hand field.
b. Print a copy of your report. Use the data contained in SORTFLE1 to prepare the report.
c. Modify the report format so that a subtotal is taken when there is a change in item class. Call the new report CUSTRPT2. Include a group intro giving the item class and a group summary giving the subtotal.
d. Print a copy of the modified report. Use the data contained in the file named SORTFLE2 to prepare the report.

MINICASE 3: Movies

Instructions: Use the MOVIE database file that you created in Minicase 3 of Project 1 in the following problems. These problems require sorting the database and preparing reports from the database.

Problem 1: Sorting Records

a. Sort the records in the MOVIES database file in ascending order by movie title. Use SORTFLE1 as the name for the sorted file. Explain the steps to accomplish this.

Steps: _____

_____

_____

Minicase 3 (continued)

b. After the records have been sorted, print the contents of the sorted file using Quick Report (Shift-F9).

Problem 2: Sorting Records on Multiple Fields

a. Sort the records in the MOVIE database file in ascending order by movie title within movie type. Use SORTFLE2 as the name for the sorted file. Explain the steps to accomplish this.

Steps: _____

_____

_____

b. After the records have been sorted, print the contents of the sorted file using Quick Report (Shift-F9).

Problem 3: Creating a Report

a. Create a report for the MOVIES database file. Call the report MOVRPT1. The report is to contain a page number, date, and report and column headings. Include the movie number, title, type, director name, and length fields on the report. The report should contain a final total of the length field.
b. Print a copy of your report. Use the data contained in SORTFLE1 to prepare the report.
c. Modify the report format so that a subtotal is taken when there is a change in movie type. Call the new report CUSTRPT2. Include a group intro giving the movie type and a group summary giving the subtotal.
d. Print a copy of the modified report. Use the data contained in the file named SORTFLE2 to prepare the report.

MINICASE 4: Books

Instructions: Use the BOOK database file that you created in Minicase 4 of Project 1 in the following problems. These problems require sorting the database and preparing reports from the database.

Problem 1: Sorting Records

a. Sort the records in the BOOKS database file in ascending order by title. Use SORTFLE1 as the name for the sorted file. Explain the steps to accomplish this.

Steps: _____

_____

_____

b. After the records have been sorted, print the contents of the sorted file using Quick Report (Shift-F9).

Problem 2: Sorting Records on Multiple Fields

a. Sort the records in the BOOKS database file in ascending order by title within author. Use SORTFLE2 as the name for the sorted file. Explain the steps to accomplish this.

Steps: _____

_____

_____

b. After the records have been sorted, print the contents of the sorted file using Quick Report (Shift-F9).

Problem 3: Creating a Report

a. Create a report for the BOOKS database file. Call the report BOOKRPT1. The report is to contain a page number, date, and report and column headings. Include the book code, title, author, publisher, price, and paperback fields on the report. The report should contain a final total of the price field.
b. Print a copy of your report. Use the data contained in SORTFLE1 to prepare the report.
c. Modify the report format so that a subtotal is taken when there is a change in author. Call the new report CUSTRPT2. Include a group intro giving the author and a group summary giving the subtotal.
d. Print a copy of the modified report. Use the data contained in the file named SORTFLE2 to prepare the report.

dBASE IV VERSION 1.1

More on Adding, Changing, and Deleting

OBJECTIVES

You will have mastered the material in this project when you can:

◆ Add records to a previously created database file using the Edit screen

◆ Change records in a database file using the Edit screen

◆ Position the record pointer

◆ Change records in a database file using an update query

◆ Change records in a database file using the Browse screen

◆ Mark records for deletion using the Edit screen

◆ Mark records for deletion using the Browse screen

◆ Mark records for deletion using an update query

◆ Unmark records using an update query

◆ Physically remove marked records from a database file

The previous projects have illustrated many of the functions that can be performed when using dBASE. You have created a database file, displayed various records in the file, sorted the file, and prepared reports using the data in the file.

For the database file to be useful, however, the information in it must be kept up to date. This means that you must be able to perform three basic functions: add records to the file, change records in the file, and delete records from the file. The dBASE options that you can use to perform these functions are explained in this project.

Some of these options should be somewhat familiar to you since you used them when you initially created your database files in Project 1. In that project, you learned to add records so that you could enter the data for your database file. You also saw briefly how to change and delete records in case you made a mistake when you were entering data. In this project, we expand on the ideas presented in Project 1.

ADDING RECORDS

◆ To illustrate the commands necessary to add records to a file, let's use the EMPLOYEE database file we created in Project 1, shown again on the next page in Figure 4-1. We want to add two employees to the EMPLOYEE file, and we can use the Edit screen to add these records.

RECORD#	NUMBER	NAME	DATE	DEPARTMENT	PAY_RATE	UNION
1	1011	Rapoza, Anthony P.	01/10/92	Shipping	8.50	.T.
2	1013	McCormack, Nigel L.	01/15/92	Shipping	8.25	.T.
3	1016	Ackerman, David R.	02/04/92	Accounting	9.75	.F.
4	1017	Doi, Chang J.	02/05/92	Production	6.00	.T.
5	1020	Castle, Mark C.	03/04/92	Shipping	7.50	.T.
6	1022	Dunning, Lisa A.	03/12/92	Marketing	9.10	.F.
7	1025	Chaney, Joseph R.	03/23/92	Accounting	8.00	.F.
8	1026	Bender, Helen O.	04/12/92	Production	6.75	.T.
9	1029	Anderson, Mariane L.	04/18/92	Shipping	9.00	.T.
10	1030	Edwards, Kenneth J.	04/23/92	Production	8.60	.T.
11	1037	Baxter, Charles W.	05/05/92	Accounting	11.00	.F.
12	1041	Evans, John T.	05/19/92	Marketing	6.00	.F.
13	1056	Andrews, Robert M.	06/03/92	Marketing	9.00	.F.
14	1057	Dugan, Mary L.	06/10/92	Production	8.75	.T.
15	1066	Castleworth, Mary T.	07/05/92	Production	8.75	.T.

FIGURE 4-1 Employee data

After you have loaded dBASE, activate the EMPLOYEE file as you have done before. Next, move to the Edit screen by pressing F2. (If pressing F2 takes you to the Browse screen instead, press F2 a second time.) Your screen should now look like Figure 4-2. Notice that this is the same display you saw when you first created the file. You are currently positioned at the beginning of the file.

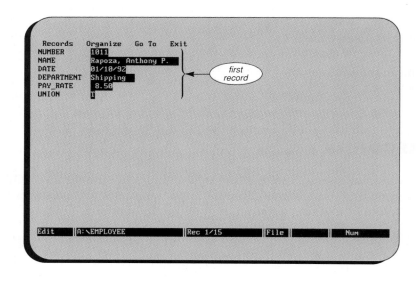

FIGURE 4-2
Edit screen

To add records, press F10 to change to Menu mode and select the "Add new records" option from the Records menu (Figure 4-3). At this point, your form is cleared out and you are ready to enter additional records.

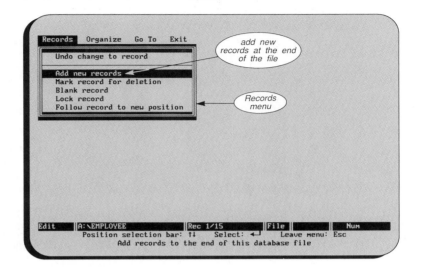

FIGURE 4-3
Edit screen

Enter the first additional record as shown in Figure 4-4.

FIGURE 4-4
Edit screen

After you have entered this first record, another screen appears and you can enter the information for the second record (Figure 4-5). After you have entered the data for this record, a screen for a third record appears. Because you have no more records to add to the file, select the "Exit" option from the Exit menu. The new additions have been added to the end of the EMPLOYEE file, and you are returned to the Control Center.

FIGURE 4-5
Edit screen

Figure 4-6 shows the EMPLOYEE file after the two records have been added. Notice that records 16 and 17 have been added to the file.

RECORD#	NUMBER	NAME	DATE	DEPARTMENT	PAY_RATE	UNION
1	1011	Rapoza, Anthony P.	01/10/92	Shipping	8.50	.T.
2	1013	McCormack, Nigel L.	01/15/92	Shipping	8.25	.T.
3	1016	Ackerman, David R.	02/04/92	Accounting	9.75	.F.
4	1017	Doi, Chang J.	02/05/92	Production	6.00	.T.
5	1020	Castle, Mark C.	03/04/92	Shipping	7.50	.T.
6	1022	Dunning, Lisa A.	03/12/92	Marketing	9.10	.F.
7	1025	Chaney, Joseph R.	03/23/92	Accounting	8.00	.F.
8	1026	Bender, Helen O.	04/12/92	Production	6.75	.T.
9	1029	Anderson, Mariane L.	04/18/92	Shipping	9.00	.T.
10	1030	Edwards, Kenneth J.	04/23/92	Production	8.60	.T.
11	1037	Baxter, Charles W.	05/05/92	Accounting	11.00	.F.
12	1041	Evans, John T.	05/19/92	Marketing	6.00	.F.
13	1056	Andrews, Robert M.	06/03/92	Marketing	9.00	.F.
14	1057	Dugan, Mary L.	06/10/92	Production	8.75	.T.
15	1066	Castleworth, Mary T.	07/05/92	Production	8.75	.T.
16	1070	Fisher, Ella C.	07/15/92	Accounting	8.00	.F.
17	1075	Caine, William J.	08/16/92	Marketing	9.25	.F.

new records have been added

FIGURE 4-6 Updated employee data

CHANGING RECORDS

In most database files, you need to make periodical changes to the data in one or more records. Three options within dBASE that you can use to make such changes are Edit, Browse, and update queries.

Using Edit

To illustrate the Edit option, assume that employee 1016 received a pay increase from $9.75 to $10.00 per hour. This pay rate change should be made to the PAY_RATE field for this employee. You should press F2 to move to the Edit screen from the Control Center. The active record appears on the screen in a form that should now be very familiar to you (Figure 4-7). (If you just completed making the additions in the previous section, you should be positioned at the last record as shown in the figure. If you took a break and have just begun from scratch, you are positioned at the first record instead.)

FIGURE 4-7
Edit screen

If the record you wanted to update happened to be the one displayed on the screen, you could simply begin the update process. In this case, it is not. Thus, you must first bring the desired record to the screen. In a small file like this one, you can repeatedly press Page Up (to move to the previous record) or Page Down (to move to the next record) until you have found the record you want. When the desired record is on the screen (Figure 4-8), you can proceed with the update.

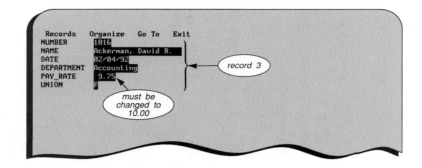

FIGURE 4-8
Edit screen

Initially, the cursor is in the first position of the first field. Press the Down Arrow key four times to position the cursor in the PAY_RATE field, and enter the new pay rate 10.00. Since this is the only change, finish the process by selecting the "Exit" option from the Exit menu. (If there were other changes, you would make them before taking this action.)

The change is saved and you are returned to the Control Center. A display of the EMPLOYEE file illustrating the pay rate change appears in Figure 4-9.

RECORD#	NUMBER	NAME	DATE	DEPARTMENT	PAY_RATE	UNION	
1	1011	Rapoza, Anthony P.	01/10/92	Shipping	8.50	.T.	
2	1013	McCormack, Nigel L.	01/15/92	Shipping	8.25	.T.	pay rate has been changed
3	1016	Ackerman, David R.	02/04/92	Accounting	10.00	.F.	
4	1017	Doi, Chang J.	02/05/92	Production	6.00	.T.	
5	1020	Castle, Mark C.	03/04/92	Shipping	7.50	.T.	
6	1022	Dunning, Lisa A.	03/12/92	Marketing	9.10	.F.	
7	1025	Chaney, Joseph R.	03/23/92	Accounting	8.00	.F.	
8	1026	Bender, Helen O.	04/12/92	Production	6.75	.T.	
9	1029	Anderson, Mariane L.	04/18/92	Shipping	9.00	.T.	
10	1030	Edwards, Kenneth J.	04/23/92	Production	8.60	.T.	
11	1037	Baxter, Charles W.	05/05/92	Accounting	11.00	.F.	
12	1041	Evans, John T.	05/19/92	Marketing	6.00	.F.	
13	1056	Andrews, Robert M.	06/03/92	Marketing	9.00	.F.	
14	1057	Dugan, Mary L.	06/10/92	Production	8.75	.T.	
15	1066	Castleworth, Mary T.	07/05/92	Production	8.75	.T.	
16	1070	Fisher, Ella C.	07/15/92	Accounting	8.00	.F.	
17	1075	Caine, William J.	08/16/92	Marketing	9.25	.F.	

FIGURE 4-9 Updated employee data

Positioning the Record Pointer

Remember, you can change the record pointer by pressing Page Up (to move back to the previous record) and Page Down (to move to the next one). Unless you only need to move a record or two, this method can be very cumbersome. It is quicker to use the Go To menu (Figure 4-10). The menu's first option, "Top record", moves you directly to the first record in the database file. The next option, "Last record", moves you to the last record. If you select the third option, "Record number", a dBASE prompt asks you for the number of the record to which you want to move. When you enter the number you want, you are taken directly to that record.

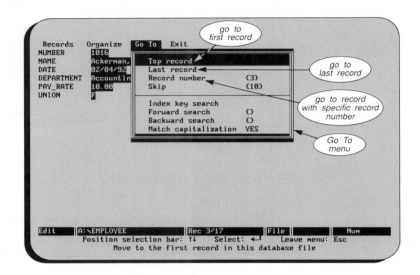

FIGURE 4-10
Edit screen

If you are not on the Edit screen already, use F2 to move there. Select the "Record number" option from the Go To menu, type the number 10, and press Enter. As you will see, record 10 becomes the current record. Now select "Top record", and record 1 becomes the current record (Figure 4-11).

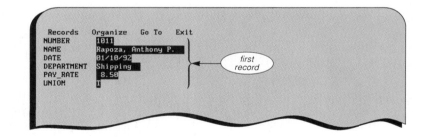

FIGURE 4-11
Edit screen

What if you don't know the number of the record you want? What if you only know something about the record? For example, suppose you want to make a change to the data for employee 1016, but you don't know where this employee is located in the file. This is where the "Forward search" and "Backward search" options on the Go To menu can be very helpful. To use these options, make sure your cursor is in the NUMBER field and select "Forward search" from the Go To menu. You are then asked to enter a *search string*, that is, the particular value for which you are looking (Figure 4-12).

FIGURE 4-12
Edit screen

Enter 1016 and press Enter. dBASE then locates this employee for you (Figure 4-13).

FIGURE 4-13
Edit screen

You may be wondering how dBASE knew that you wanted to search for a record on which the value of NUMBER was 1016. Why didn't dBASE search the NAME, PAY_RATE, or any other field? The answer is that dBASE uses the field in which the cursor is currently positioned as the field to search. This is why you were instructed to make sure the cursor was in the NUMBER field before beginning your search.

When you select "Forward Search", you are asking dBASE to search starting with the current record and move forward until it finds the record you want. If there is no such record, you receive an appropriate message. What if, however, the record you want is earlier in the file than the current record? In this case you would use the "Backward search" option. If you don't know the direction to move, you can play it safe with the "Top record" option, moving to the first record and then beginning a forward search.

Using Update Queries

Another option that you can use to change data is a special kind of query, called an **update query**. We illustrate this option by changing the pay rate of employee 1016 to $10.25.

To use a query for update, begin creating a query as you have done before. First, select < create > in the Queries column of the Control Center. You should then see the Query Design screen (Figure 4-14).

FIGURE 4-14
Query Design screen

Now, select "Specify update operation" from the Update menu of the Query Design screen (Figure 4-15).

FIGURE 4-15
Query Design screen

You then see a list of possible update operations (Figure 4-16). To change data in existing records, select "Replace values in Employee.dbf".

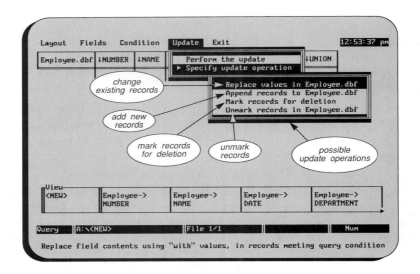

FIGURE 4-16
Query Design screen

Next, you are asked if you want to proceed or cancel the request (Figure 4-17). As the message in the box points out, if you proceed with the update query, the view skeleton will be deleted. This is not a problem because it is the file skeleton that you use to specify the update. You should select "Proceed".

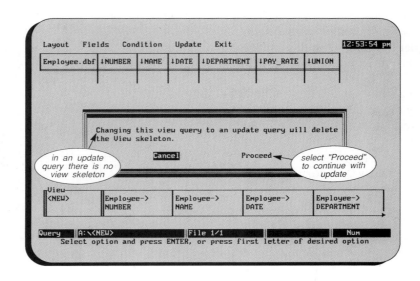

FIGURE 4-17
Query Design screen

Your screen then looks like Figure 4-18. The word "Target" above Employee.dbf indicates that this database file is the *target* of the update. The word "Replace" that appears underneath Employee.dbf indicates that the update operation is *replacing* existing data.

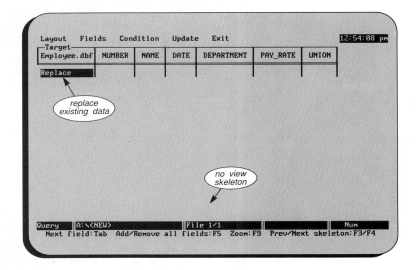

FIGURE 4-18
Query Design screen

At this point, you are going to enter a condition and a replacement expression. You want to change the pay rate of employee 1016. The condition is that the employee number be 1016, so enter "1016" in the NUMBER column (Figure 4-19). Be sure to enclose it in quotes. (Remember that NUMBER is a character field.) Unlike the searches on the Go To menu, when we use the Query Design screen, values for character fields must be enclosed in quotes.

FIGURE 4-19
Query Design screen

A replacement expression indicates what the new values should be. It is preceded by the word WITH. To replace the current pay rate with 10.25, enter WITH 10.25 in the PAY_RATE column (Figure 4-20).

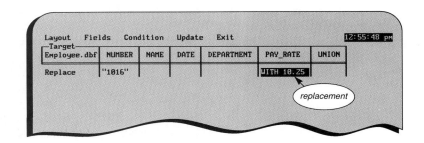

FIGURE 4-20
Query Design screen

Next, select the "Perform the update" option from the Update menu (Figure 4-21).

FIGURE 4-21
Query Design screen

Your update is made, and you should see the screen shown in Figure 4-22. Notice that the screen shows how many records were replaced, in this case, only one. As indicated on the screen, you can press F2 to see the results of the update. If you do not need to see the results, simply press any other key.

FIGURE 4-22
Query Design screen

Update queries furnish a very rapid approach to updating. By entering a condition that can identify several records rather than just one such as Marketing in the DEPARTMENT column, many records can be changed at the same time, namely, all the records on which the department is Marketing.

The change can also involve a computation. To give every employee in the Marketing department a 5% raise, for example, you would enter the expression WITH PAY_RATE * 1.05 in the PAY_RATE column. (The asterisk represents multiplication.) This expression indicates that the value of the pay rate is to be replaced by the previous value multiplied by 1.05. You can also use the plus sign (+) for addition, the minus sign (–) for subtraction, and the slash (/) for division in these expressions.

When you have finished, select "Abandon changes and exit" from the Exit menu to return to the Control Center.

Using Browse

The Browse screen furnishes yet another method of making changes to records in a database. The Browse screen displays several records on the screen at one time and as many fields as will fit horizontally on the screen. Press F2 to move to the Browse screen. (As always, if you are at the Edit screen, press F2 a second time.)

The Browse screen displays records, beginning with the current active record and moving toward the end of the file. To begin with the first record, make sure the first record is the current active record. If not, press Page Up until it is. Your screen should now look like Figure 4-23. The current active record (in this case, record 1) is highlighted. You can move the highlight to any other record by pressing the Down Arrow or Up Arrow key.

You can move the cursor a field to the right by pressing the Tab key and a field to the left by pressing Shift-Tab. Now move the cursor to the PAY_RATE field (Figure 4-25).

To change a field in a record, you must highlight the record to be changed. For example, to change the pay rate of Helen Bender from $6.75 to $7.00, move the highlight to record 8 by pressing the Down Arrow key seven times (Figure 4-24).

FIGURE 4-23 Browse screen

FIGURE 4-24
Browse screen

FIGURE 4-25
Browse screen

Next, enter 7.00, the new pay rate (Figure 4-26).

FIGURE 4-26
Browse screen

If changing the pay rate for Helen Bender is the only change you are making, select the "Exit" option from the Exit menu. The change is then saved, and you are returned to the Control Center. If you needed to make changes to several records, you would probably want to make all the changes before exiting.

Records can also be added to a file using the Browse option by moving the reverse video block highlighting each record past the last data record. The message "Add new record? (Y/N)" appears on the screen. If you type a Y, spaces are displayed at the bottom of the screen so that you can enter a new record. If you type an N, the highlight remains on the bottom row. The most common method of adding records, however, is to use the Edit screen, as you saw earlier.

DELETING RECORDS

◆ Deleting records from a file is sometimes necessary. For example, if an employee no longer works for the company, the employee's record should be removed (deleted) from the EMPLOYEE file. This can be accomplished by using Edit, Browse, or update queries.

When you delete records from a database file using any of these options, the records are not actually removed from the file at that time. Instead, dBASE merely marks them as being deleted. You must use the "Erase marked records" option from the Organize menu on the Database Design screen to physically remove these records from the file. Until you do, the records are still in the file. dBASE, however, indicates which records have been marked. When records are being edited and the current active record happens to be one that has been marked for deletion, the letters "Del" appear near the right-hand end of the status line.

dBASE provides another option, called "Unmark", that allows you to remove this deletion mark, that is, to undelete these records. This option comes in handy if you ever delete the wrong records. Once you use the "Erase marked records" option, however, such records are physically removed and can no longer be brought back. You should always be very careful, both when you choose to initially mark records and also when you decide to erase the marked records.

Deleting Records with Edit

You normally use the Edit screen to change data in one or more records in a database file, as well as to add new records. You can also use it to mark records for deletion. To mark a record, simply bring the record to the screen using any of the methods we discussed earlier. When the record is on the screen, hold the Ctrl key down and type the letter U. The record is then marked for deletion and the letters "Del" appear near the lower right-hand corner of the screen.

You can use the same process to unmark a record. If a marked record is on the screen, hold the Ctrl key down and type the letter U to unmark it. The record once more becomes an active record in the file, and the letters "Del" disappear from the screen.

Deleting Records with Browse

You can mark records for deletion using the Browse screen by positioning the highlight on the record to be marked, holding down the Ctrl key, and typing the letter U. The record is then marked for deletion. As with the Edit screen, if the record was already marked, taking this action unmarks it.

Deleting Records Using Update Queries

Let's illustrate how to delete records by using an update query to delete the employee record for Andrews, Robert M. To use a query for marking records for deletion, first select the "Specify update operation" option from the Update menu of the Query Design screen and then select "Mark records for deletion" (Figure 4-27).

FIGURE 4-27
Query Design screen

Your screen now looks like Figure 4-28. Notice that the operation is "Mark", which stands for mark records for deletion.

FIGURE 4-28
Query Design screen

Next, move the highlight to the NAME column, enter "Andrews, Robert M." in quotes as the condition (Figure 4-29) and press Enter. No records have yet been marked. To mark the record, select "Perform the update" from the Update menu.

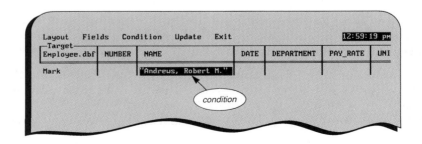

FIGURE 4-29
Query Design screen

A prompt will ask you if it is OK to mark this record for deletion (Figure 4-30). Type the letter Y and press Enter. The record for Robert M. Andrews is marked for deletion.

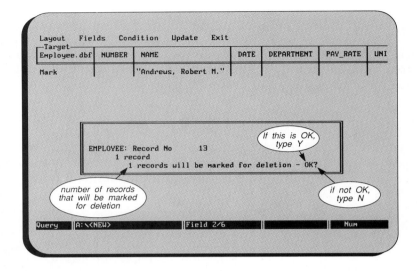

FIGURE 4-30
Query Design screen

Normally, if you have only a single record to delete, you can use either the Edit or Browse screen. If you need to delete all the records that satisfy a certain condition (such as all the employees in a given department), update queries are ideal.

Unmarking Records

The only difference between marking and unmarking records is that unmarking removes the deletion mark rather than adding the deletion mark. To unmark records, select "Specify update operation" and then "Unmark records". You can now enter any condition you want, and then select "Perform the update". Use this option to unmark the record for Robert M. Andrews (Figure 4-31) because we want him to remain in the database file.

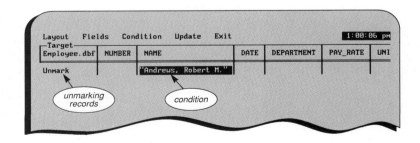

FIGURE 4-31
Query Design screen

Erasing Marked Records

When you want to permanently remove marked records from a database file, move to the Database Design screen. Do this by highlighting the file name at the Control Center, pressing Enter, and then selecting "Modify structure/order". Next, select the "Erase marked records" option from the Organize menu. A dBASE prompt then asks you if you are sure you want to erase these records. Select "Yes" and the records are removed. At this point, select the "Exit" option from the Exit menu to return to the Control Center. The marked records are no longer in the file and cannot be recalled.

PROJECT SUMMARY

In Project 4 you learned how to change the data in a database file and how to add records using the Edit screen. You saw how to change data using the Edit screen, the Browse screen, and update queries. Using these same facilities, you also learned how to mark records for deletion, and how to unmark records. Finally, you physically removed marked records using the "Erase marked records" option. All the activities that you learned for this project are summarized in the Quick Reference following Project 6. The following is a summary of the keystroke sequence we used in Project 4.

SUMMARY OF KEYSTROKES — PROJECT 4

STEPS	KEY(S) PRESSED	RESULTS
1	DBASE ← [At DOS prompt]	Starts dBASE.
2	↓ [To highlight EMPLOYEE] ← ←	Activates EMPLOYEE database file.
3	F2 [Once or twice as required to move to Edit screen] F10 ←	Prepares to enter new records.
4	1070Fisher, Ella C. ←071592Accounting8.00F	Enters record.
5	1075Caine, William J. ←081692Marketing←9.25F	Enters record.
6	F10 → → → ←	Returns to Control Center.
7	F2 Page Up or Page Down [Use to make record 3 the current active record.] ↓ [Press 4 times]10.00 F10 → → → ←	Changes record with Edit.
8	F2 F10 → → ↓ ↓ ← ← 10 ←	Moves to record 10.
9	F10 ↑ ↑ ←	Moves to record 1.
10	F10 ↓ [Press 4 times] ← 1016 ←	Moves to record for employee 1016.
11	F10 → ←	Moves to Control Center.
12	→ ←	Moves to Query Design screen.
13	F10 → → → ← ← → ←	Begins update query.
14	Tab "1016" ← Tab [Press 4 times]WITH 10.25 ←	Enters update query.
15	F10 ↑ ← ←	Applies update query.
16	F10 → ↓ ← ← ←	Returns to Control Center.
17	F2 F2	Moves to Browse screen.
18	↓ [Press 7 times] Tab [Press 4 times]7.00 F10 → [Press 4 times] ←	Changes record with Browse.
19	[Make sure <create> in the Queries column is highlighted] ←	Moves to Query Design screen.
20	F10 → → → ← ↓ ↓ ← → ←	Begins update query to mark records for deletion.
21	Tab Tab "Andrews, Robert M." ← F10 ↑ ←Y← ←	Marks record for deletion.
22	F10 ↓ ← ↓ ← F10 ↑ ← ←	Unmarks (recalls) record.
23	F10 → ↓ ← ← ←	Returns to Control Center.

The following list summarizes the material covered in Project 4.

1. To add records, use the Edit screen. Select the "Add new records" option from the Records menu.
2. To change records while viewing one record at a time, use the Edit screen.

3. To position the record pointer to a record containing a certain value, use the "Forward search" or "Backward search" option from the Go To menu.
4. To make the same change to all records satisfying a certain condition, use an **update query**.
5. To change records while viewing several records at a time, use the Browse screen.
6. Deleting records does not remove them from a database file. Rather, such records are marked for deletion. To physically remove such records from the file, use the "Erase marked records" option of the Organize menu on the Database Design screen.
7. To mark records for deletion, use either the Edit or the Browse screen. In either case, move to the record that is to be deleted, hold the Ctrl key down, and type the letter U. (The letters "Del" on the status line indicate that the current active record has been deleted.)
8. To unmark records that have been marked for deletion, use either the Edit or the Browse screen. In either case, move to the deleted record, hold the Ctrl key down, and type the letter U. (The letters "Del" disappear from the screen.)
9. To mark all records that satisfy a certain condition, use an update query.
10. To unmark all records that satisfy a certain condition, use an update query.

STUDENT ASSIGNMENTS

STUDENT ASSIGNMENT 1: True/False

Instructions: Circle T if the statement is true and F if the statement is false.

T F 1. Whenever you choose the "Add new records" option, a screen will appear prompting you to enter record 1. This is the first new record which you will add to the active file.
T F 2. Once you have created an update query, you can execute the query by selecting the "Perform the update" option from the Update menu.
T F 3. When you use the Browse screen, the current active record is highlighted on the screen.
T F 4. To mark a record for deletion when you are using the Browse screen, make sure the record to be marked for deletion is highlighted. Then, hold down the Ctrl key and type the letter U.
T F 5. To create an update query to change values in the CUSTOMER database file, select the "Specify update operation" option from the Update menu and then select "Replace values in Customer.dbf".
T F 6. To change records while you are viewing a single record at a time, use the Edit screen.
T F 7. To move to the first record in a database file, select the "First record" option of the Go To menu.
T F 8. A replacement expression in an update query must begin with the word WITH.
T F 9. When you create an update query to delete records, you will not use a replacement expression.
T F 10. To make the same change to all records that satisfy some condition, use an update query.
T F 11. To delete a record using the Edit screen, bring the record to the screen and type the word delete.
T F 12. When you bring a record that has been marked for deletion to the screen using the Edit screen, the letters "Del" appear in the status line.
T F 13. One way to undelete all records that have been marked for deletion but have not been physically removed from the database file is to use an update query.
T F 14. To permanently remove records that have been marked for deletion, use the "Remove" option.
T F 15. It is possible to undelete records using the Edit screen.
T F 16. In an update query, the view skeleton contains all fields.

STUDENT ASSIGNMENT 2: Multiple Choice

Instructions: Circle the correct response.

1. Which of the following functions is not performed to keep records in a database file up to date?
   a. delete records from the file
   b. move records from one location on the disk to another location
   c. add records to the file
   d. change records in the file
2. To change records while viewing several records at a time, use _____.
   a. the Edit screen
   b. an update query
   c. the Browse screen
   d. the Replace screen
3. In an update query, a replacement expression must be preceded by the word _____.
   a. WITH
   b. EQUALS
   c. CHANGE
   d. TO
4. To make the same change to all records that satisfy some condition, use _____.
   a. the Edit screen
   b. an update query
   c. the Browse screen
   d. the Replace screen
5. To delete a record using the Edit screen, _____.
   a. bring the record to the screen, hold the Ctrl key down and type the letter U
   b. bring the record to the screen and type the word delete
   c. bring the record to the screen and press Delete
   d. bring the record to the screen, hold the Ctrl key down and press Delete
6. The quickest way to delete all the records that satisfy a certain condition is to use _____.
   a. the Edit screen
   b. an update query
   c. the Browse screen
   d. the Delete screen

STUDENT ASSIGNMENT 3: Understanding dBASE Options

Instructions: Explain what will happen after you perform each of the following actions.

Problem 1: You are on the Edit screen and select the "Top record" option from the Go To menu.

Explanation: _____

_____

_____

Problem 2: You select the "Specify update operation" option from the Update menu on the Query Design screen.

Explanation: _____

_____

_____

Student Assignment 3 (continued)

Problem 3: You are on the Browse screen and press Ctrl-U.

Explanation: _____

_____

_____

Problem 4: You select the "Erase marked records" option from the Organize menu.

Explanation: _____

_____

_____

STUDENT ASSIGNMENT 4: Using dBASE

Instructions: Explain how to accomplish each of the following tasks using dBASE.
Problem 1: Add records at the end of the active database file.

Explanation: _____

_____

_____

Problem 2: Use the Edit screen to make a change to the fourth field on the fifth record of a database file you have just activated.

Explanation: _____

_____

_____

Problem 3: Use the Browse screen to make a change to the fourth field on the fifth record of a database file you have just activated.

Explanation: _____

_____

_____

Problem 4: Give a 5% raise to all employees in the Marketing department.

Explanation: _____

_____

_____

Problem 5: Permanently remove all members of the Marketing department.

Explanation: _____

_____

_____

Problem 6: Unmark all employees in the Shipping department who have been marked for deletion.

Explanation: _____

_____

_____

STUDENT ASSIGNMENT 5: Recovering from Problems

Instructions: In each of the following cases, a problem occurred. Explain the cause of the problem and how it can be corrected.

Problem 1: You were certain you made a change using the Browse screen and yet, when you later examined the data, you found that the change was not made.

Cause of Problem:_____

_____

Method of Correction: _____

_____

Problem 2: You used an update query to delete all employees whose pay rates are under $7.50. When you later examined the data, you found that you had deleted those employees whose pay rates were greater than $7.50.

Cause of Problem:_____

_____

Method of Correction: _____

_____

Problem 3: You had deleted a number of records incorrectly. Before discovering this, however, you chose the "Erase marked records" option.

Cause of Problem:_____

_____

Method of Correction: _____

_____

STUDENT ASSIGNMENT 6: Adding Records

Instructions: Add the following records to the EMPLOYEE database file. Add the first record using the Edit screen and add the second record using the Browse screen. Then, list all the records in the file. Explain the steps to accomplish this.

EMPLOYEE NUMBER	EMPLOYEE NAME	DATE HIRED	DEPARTMENT NAME	PAY RATE	UNION MEMBER
1112	Molinski, Sara L.	09/12/92	Marketing	9.25	F
1124	Vollink, Jay Q.	09/18/92	Shipping	10.75	T

Steps: _____

_____

_____

STUDENT ASSIGNMENT 7: Finding Records

Instructions: Use the "Forward search" option to find employee 1112. Then, change her date hired to 09/15/91 and list all the records in the database file. Explain the steps to accomplish this.

Steps: _____

_____

_____

STUDENT ASSIGNMENT 8: Changing Records

Instructions: Use the Edit screen to change the pay rate of employee 1112 to $9.75. Use the Browse screen to change the pay rate of employee 1124 to $10.25. Use an update query to add fifty cents (.50) to the pay rate of all employees in the Accounting department. Once you have made these changes, list all the records in the database file. Next, use an update query to subtract fifty cents from the pay rate of all employees in the Accounting department. Explain the steps to accomplish this.

Steps: _____

_____

_____

STUDENT ASSIGNMENT 9: Deleting Records

Instructions: Use an update query to delete all employees whose number is greater than 1110. Explain the steps to accomplish this.

Steps: _____

_____

_____

STUDENT ASSIGNMENT 10: Removing Marked Records

Instructions: Permanently remove the marked records from your database file. Then, list all the records in the file. Explain the steps to accomplish this.

Steps: _____

_____

_____

MINICASES

ADDING, CHANGING, AND DELETING RECORDS

MINICASE 1: Customers

Instructions: Use the CUSTOMER database file that you created in Minicase 1 of Project 1 in the following problems. These problems require adding, changing, and deleting records in the database.

Problem 1: Adding Records to a Database File

a. Using the Edit screen, add the following records to the database file. Explain the steps to accomplish this.

CNUM	CNAME	CADDR	BAL	SNAME	STDATE	DSC
687	Koch, Hans	52 48th,Holt,IL	0	Brown, Doyle	05/12/92	F
699	Ting, K. L.	311 Bass,Harper,MI	112	Gomez, Maria	06/26/92	F
702	Evans, Terry	22 Hubbell,Ira,IL	349	Gomez, Maria	07/11/92	T
753	Owen, Lee	783 Maple,Kent,MI	1260	Smith, Wilhelm	08/03/92	F

Steps: _____

_____

_____

b. After you have added the records to the database file, obtain a printed listing of the records by pressing Shift-F9.

Problem 2: Deleting Records from a Database File

a. Using an update query, delete the record for customer 311. (Do not permanently remove it from the file. Simply mark it for deletion.) Explain the steps to accomplish this.

Steps: _____

_____

_____

b. The record for customer 311 should remain in the file. Explain the steps to make the record a part of the original file and no longer marked for deletion.

Steps: _____

_____

_____

Problem 3: Changing the Records in a Database File

a. Using an update query, change the sales rep name for customer 702 to Brown, Doyle. Explain the steps to accomplish this.

Steps: _____

_____

_____

b. Using the Edit screen, change the balance for customer 702 to 249. Explain the steps to accomplish this.

Steps: _____

_____

_____

c. Obtain a printed listing of the records in the file after you have made the preceding changes.

Problem 4: The Browse Screen

a. Delete the records for customers 687, 699, 702, and 753. Then, permanently remove these records from the database file.

b. Complete Problems 1, 2, and 3 of this minicase using the Browse screen to add, delete, and change records.

MINICASE 2: Parts

Instructions: Use the PART database file that you created in Minicase 2 of Project 1 in the following problems. These problems require adding, changing, and deleting records in the database.

Problem 1. Adding Records to a Database File

a. Using the Edit screen, add the following records to the database file. Explain the steps to accomplish this.

PNUMB	PDESC	UOH	ITEMCLSS	WHSE	PRICE	LSDATE	DISC
DG11	BWLNG BALL	12	SPORTING GOODS	2	59.99	02/12/92	F
EF86	WASHER	5	APPLIANCES	1	419.95	01/19/92	T
KA29	FREEZER	7	APPLIANCES	2	319.99	03/02/92	F
KZ50	CLIPPER KIT	45	HAIR PRODUCTS	3	24.95	11/19/91	T

Steps: _____

_____

_____

b. After you have added the records to the database file, obtain a printed listing of the records by pressing Shift-F9.

Problem 2: Deleting Records from a Database File

a. Using an update query, delete the record for part BA74. (Do not permanently remove it from the file. Simply mark it for deletion.) Explain the steps to accomplish this.

Steps: _____

_____

_____

b. The record for part BA74 should remain in the file. Explain the steps to make the record a part of the original file and no longer marked for deletion.

Steps: _____

_____

_____

Problem 3: Changing the Records in a Database File

a. Using an update query, change the item class for part KZ50 to HAIR CARE. Explain the steps to accomplish this.

Steps: _____

_____

_____

b. Using the Edit screen, change the price for part EF86 to 399.95. Explain the steps to accomplish this.

Steps: _____

_____

_____

c. Obtain a printed listing of the records in the file after you have made the preceding changes.

Problem 4: The Browse Screen

a. Delete the records for parts DG11, EF86, KA29, and KZ50. Then, permanently remove these records from the database file.

b. Complete Problems 1, 2, and 3 of this minicase using the Browse screen to add, delete, and change records.

MINICASE 3: Movies

Instructions: Use the MOVIE database file that you created in Minicase 3 of Project 1 in the following problems. These problems require adding, changing, and deleting records in the database.

Problem 1. Adding Records to a Database File

a. Using the Edit screen, add the following records to the database file. Explain the steps to accomplish this.

MNUM	MTITLE	YEAR	MTYPE	LNG	DNAME	BW
035	Purple Rose of Cr.	1984	COMEDY	82	Allen, Woody	F
038	Love and Death	1975	COMEDY	85	Allen, Woody	F
042	The Lady Vanishes	1938	SUSPEN	97	Hitchcock, Alfred	T
046	Trouble With Harry	1955	COMEDY	99	Hitchcock, Alfred	F

Steps: _____

_____

_____

b. After you have added the records to the database file, obtain a printed listing of the records by pressing Shift-F9.

Problem 2: Deleting Records from a Database File

a. Using an update query, delete the record for movie 4. (Do not permanently remove it from the file. Simply mark it for deletion.) Explain the steps to accomplish this.

Steps: _____

_____

_____

b. The record for movie 4 should remain in the file. Explain the steps to make the record a part of the original file and no longer marked for deletion.

Steps: _____

_____

_____

Problem 3: Changing the Records in a Database File

a. Using an update query, change the Year field for movie 046 to 1957. Explain the steps to accomplish this.

Steps: _____

_____

_____

Minicase 3 (continued)

b. Using the Edit screen, change the LNG field for movie 024 to 111. Explain the steps to accomplish this.

Steps: _____

_____

_____

c. Obtain a printed listing of the records in the file after you have made the preceding changes.

Problem 4: The Browse Screen

a. Delete the records for movies 35, 38, 42, and 46. Then, permanently remove these records from the database file.
b. Complete Problems 1, 2, and 3 of this minicase using the Browse screen to add, delete, and change records.

MINICASE 4: Books

Instructions: Use the BOOK database file that you created in Minicase 4 of Project 1 in the following problems. These problems require adding, changing, and deleting records in the database.

Problem 1: Adding Records to a Database File

a. Using the Edit screen, add the following records to the database file. Record the steps used.

CODE	TITLE	AUTHOR	PUBLISHER	TYP	PRICE	PB	OH
4656	Cyclops	Clive Cussler	Pocket Books	SUS	5.95	T	1
7317	The Dark Half	Stephen King	Signet	HOR	5.95	T	3
5450	Cradle Will Fall	M. H. Clark	Dell	SUS	6.95	T	2
5812	Longshot	Dick Francis	Putnam	MYS	19.95	F	2

Steps: _____

_____

_____

b. After you have added the records to the database file, obtain a printed listing of the records by pressing Shift-F9.

Problem 2: Deleting Records from a Database File

a. Using an update query, delete the record for book 2226. (Do not permanently remove it from the file. Simply mark it for deletion.) Explain the steps to accomplish this.

Steps: _____

_____

_____

b. The record for book 2226 should remain in the file. Explain the steps to make the record a part of the original file and no longer marked for deletion.

Steps: _____

_____

_____

Problem 3: Changing the Records in a Database File

a. Using an update query, change the publisher for book 5450 to Pocket Books. Explain the steps to accomplish this.

Steps: _____

_____

_____

b. Using the Edit screen, change the price for book 5450 to 7.45. Explain the steps to accomplish this.

Steps: _____

_____

_____

c. Obtain a printed listing of the records in the file after you have made the preceding changes.

Problem 4: The Browse Screen

a. Delete the records for books 4656, 7317, 5450, and 5812. Thus, permanently remove these records from the database file.

b. Complete Problems 1, 2, and 3 of this minicase using the Browse screen to add, delete, and change records.

PROJECT **5**

dBASE IV VERSION1.1

Additional Topics

OBJECTIVES

You will have mastered the material in this project when you can:

◆ Change the characteristics of fields in a database file

◆ Add new fields to a database file

◆ Delete existing fields from a database file

◆ Create indexes for database files

◆ Use indexes in place of sorting

◆ Use indexes for rapid retrieval

◆ Create a view relating two database files

◆ Use a view for retrieving data from two database files

In this project you will learn how to make changes to the structure of a database. You will be able to change the characteristics of existing fields, add fields, and delete fields. You will also learn about indexes and how they can be used to increase the efficiency of retrieval. Finally, you will learn about views and how they can be used to allow easy access to more than a single database file.

CHANGING THE DATABASE STRUCTURE

Why Change the Structure?

The structure of a database file might need to change for a variety of reasons. Changes in the needs of users of the database might require additional fields to be added. For example, suppose we need to store the number of hours an employee has worked. Such a field needs to be added to the EMPLOYEE file since it is not there already.

Characteristics of a given field might need to change. For example, suppose we discover that Mary Castleworth's name is stored incorrectly in the database. Rather than Castleworth, Mary T., it should be Castleworth, Marianne K. There is no problem changing the middle initial from T to K. There is a big problem changing the first name from Mary to Marianne. There is not enough room in the NAME field to hold the correct name! To accommodate this change, we must increase the width of the NAME field.

A field currently in the database file may become unnecessary. If no one ever uses the DEPARTMENT field, for example, there is no point in having it in the database file. It is occupying space and yet serving no useful purpose. Therefore, we should remove it from the database file.

Sometimes you discover that the database structure you created earlier has some inherent problems. Did it bother you, for example, that you had to type a complete department name when entering each employee? Wouldn't it be easier to simply type a code number? This would make the process of entering data simpler. It would also save space in the database because a one- or two-character code number does not take as much storage space as a ten-character department name. Finally, using a code cuts down on errors during data entry. If you only have to type the number 01 rather than the name Accounting, for example, you are less likely to make mistakes. Such mistakes can have serious consequences. If, for example, Accouning is entered incorrectly as an employee's department, that employee is omitted from any list of employees whose department is Accounting.

Thus, you might want to store the code number rather than the department name. What are you to do, however, if you are supposed to print the department name on some crucial reports? You can create a separate table of department numbers and names. Thus, rather than the single table that you have been using (Figure 5-1), you will have two (shown on the next page in Figure 5-2).

EMPLOYEE NUMBER	EMPLOYEE NAME	DATE HIRED	DEPARTMENT NAME	PAY RATE	UNION MEMBER
1011	Rapoza, Anthony P.	01/10/92	Shipping	8.50	Y
1013	McCormack, Nigel L.	01/15/92	Shipping	8.25	Y
1016	Ackerman, David R.	02/04/92	Accounting	10.25	N
1017	Doi, Chang J.	02/05/92	Production	6.00	Y
1020	Castle, Mark C.	03/04/92	Shipping	7.50	Y
1022	Dunning, Lisa A.	03/12/92	Marketing	9.10	N
1025	Chaney, Joseph R.	03/23/92	Accounting	8.00	N
1026	Bender, Helen O.	04/12/92	Production	7.00	Y
1029	Anderson, Mariane L.	04/18/92	Shipping	9.00	Y
1030	Edwards, Kenneth J.	04/23/92	Production	8.60	Y
1037	Baxter, Charles W.	05/05/92	Accounting	11.00	N
1041	Evans, John T.	05/19/92	Marketing	6.00	N
1056	Andrews, Robert M.	06/03/92	Marketing	9.00	N
1057	Dugan, Mary L.	06/10/92	Production	8.75	Y
1066	Castleworth, Mary T.	07/05/92	Production	8.75	Y
1070	Fisher, Ella C.	07/15/92	Accounting	8.00	N
1075	Caine, William J.	08/16/92	Marketing	9.25	N

FIGURE 5-1 Employee data in a single file

EMPLOYEE NUMBER	EMPLOYEE NAME	DATE HIRED	PAY RATE	UNION MEMBER	DEPT NUMB
1011	Rapoza, Anthony P.	01/10/92	8.50	Y	04
1013	McCormack, Nigel L.	01/15/92	8.25	Y	04
1016	Ackerman, David R.	02/04/92	10.25	N	01
1017	Doi, Chang J.	02/05/92	6.00	Y	03
1020	Castle, Mark C.	03/04/92	7.50	Y	04
1022	Dunning, Lisa A.	03/12/92	9.10	N	02
1025	Chaney, Joseph R.	03/23/92	8.00	N	01
1026	Bender, Helen O.	04/12/92	7.00	Y	03
1029	Anderson, Mariane L.	04/18/92	9.00	Y	04
1030	Edwards, Kenneth J.	04/23/92	8.60	Y	03
1037	Baxter, Charles W.	05/05/92	11.00	N	01
1041	Evans, John T.	05/19/92	6.00	N	02
1056	Andrews, Robert M.	06/03/92	9.00	N	02
1057	Dugan, Mary L.	06/10/92	8.75	Y	03
1066	Castleworth, Mary T.	07/05/92	8.75	Y	03
1070	Fisher, Ella C.	07/15/92	8.00	N	01
1075	Caine, William J.	08/16/92	9.25	N	02

department number

department name

DEPT NUMB	DEPARTMENT NAME
01	Accounting
02	Marketing
03	Production
04	Shipping

FIGURE 5-2
Employee data stored in two files

Notice that the first table in Figure 5-2 has no DEPARTMENT column, but instead has a column for code numbers (DEPT_NUMB). The second table also has a DEPT_NUMB column as well as a column that contains the department name. Using these two tables still allows you to list the name of the department for each employee. To find the department name for Anthony Rapoza, for example, you would first find that he works in department 04 by looking in the DEPT_NUMB column in his row. Then, you would look for the row in the second table that contained 04 in the DEPT_NUMB column. Finally, you would look in the next column on that same row and see that department 04 is Shipping. Thus, Anthony Rapoza works in Shipping.

Suppose you also need to maintain some other information for each department, for example, the department's office location, phone number, and annual budget. With the approach that you have been using so far (Figure 5-1), you would need to add more columns to the employee table: a column for location, a column for phone number, and a column for annual budget. The location, phone number, and annual budget of the Shipping department would appear on the first, second, fifth, and ninth rows in the employee table because each of those rows contains Shipping department employees. Doesn't this seem cumbersome? With the new approach (Figure 5-2), the new information is added, not to the employee table, but to the department table. In this case, the location, phone number, and annual budget of the Shipping department appear only on the fourth row because that is the only row on which Shipping occurs. We will not add the additional columns; we will just have the department number and department name columns as shown in Figure 5-2.

You now have a database that consists of more than one table, or, in dBASE jargon, more than one database file. You need a way of relating the two tables, that is, of using information from both. This is done by using what is called a view. But before you can learn about views, you must change the structure of the database from the one shown in Figure 5-1 to the one shown in Figure 5-2. You must also look at an important concept called an index.

To change the structure,

1. Create and fill in the department database file (called DEPT).
2. Change the length of the NAME field in the EMPLOYEE database file to 24.
3. Add the DEPT_NUMB field to the EMPLOYEE file.
4. Fill in the DEPT_NUMB field with the appropriate values.
5. Delete the DEPARTMENT field from the EMPLOYEE database file.

Creating Additional Files

Before making changes to the EMPLOYEE file, create the file of departments that we mentioned in the previous section. Make sure the highlight is on <create> in the Data column of the Control Center and press Enter. Describe the two fields shown in Figure 5-3 and then press Enter. When dBASE displays the "Save as:" prompt, enter DEPT and press Enter.

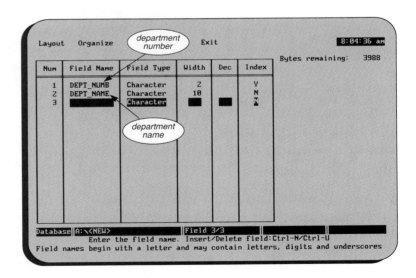

FIGURE 5-3
Database Design screen

Press F2 to get to the Edit screen and add the data that is shown in Figure 5-4 to this file. The first record has 01 for a department number and Accounting for a department name; the second record has 02 for a number and Marketing for a name; and so on. Make sure to enter the zeros in the department number field. When you have added these four records, select the "Exit" option from the Exit menu.

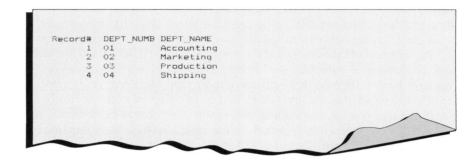

FIGURE 5-4
Data for DEPT database file

Selecting the Database File to Be Changed

Before changing the structure of a database file, you must select it. Move the highlight to the EMPLOYEE file and press Enter. Rather than choosing the "Use file" option as you have done before (Figure 5-5), select "Modify structure/order".

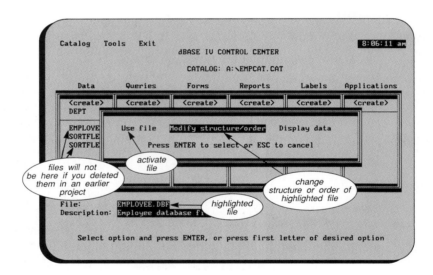

FIGURE 5-5
Control Center

You then see the Database Design screen. The Organize menu should be displayed. Press Esc to remove it. Your screen should look like Figure 5-6. Notice that your current structure is displayed.

FIGURE 5-6
Database Design screen

Changing the Characteristics of Fields

To change the characteristics of any field, repeatedly press Enter until the data to be changed is highlighted. In your case, move the highlight to the Width column in the second row, type 24 (the new width for the NAME field), and press Enter.

Adding New Fields

Keep pressing the Down Arrow until you have arrived at the bottom of the current list of fields. A new line is created for you. Enter DEPT_NUMB as the name of the new field, choose Character for the type, type the number 2 as the width, and type the letter Y under "Index" as shown in Figure 5-7. Another new line has been created for you. Since there are no other fields to add, press Enter. Select the "Exit" option from the Exit menu to return to the Control Center.

FIGURE 5-7
Database Design screen

Press Enter when a prompt asks you if you want to save your changes, and the changes are made. The line at the bottom of your screen reads, "Database records will be APPENDED from backup fields of the same name only!!" This simply means that, if you changed the name of any field, dBASE would not be able to keep the current data.

When the process is complete, use F2 to move to the Browse screen and then press Page Up to move to the top of the file. Your screen should then look like Figure 5-8. Notice that no entries have yet been filled in for that new field, DEPT_NUMB, on the right. Notice also that the NAME field is wider than it was before.

FIGURE 5-8
Browse screen

Making Entries for New Fields

To fill in the DEPT_NUMB entries, you could use either Edit or Browse and simply proceed through each and every record. Whenever you encounter a record on which the value for DEPARTMENT is Accounting, set DEPT_NUMB to 01; if the value is Marketing, set DEPT_NUMB to 02; and so on. Does this approach seem cumbersome to you? Even with only seventeen records, it probably seems like a lot of busy work. What if there were several thousand records? It would take a long time to make these changes, with many chances to make errors. Fortunately, there is an easier way. You can use update queries, as you did in Project 4.

To make these changes with update queries, move to the Query Design screen by selecting < create > in the Queries column. Then, select "Specify update operation" from the Update menu. Select "Replace values in Employee.dbf" from the list presented to you (Figure 5-9).

FIGURE 5-9
Query Design screen

Since the condition for the query is that the department must be Accounting, enter "Accounting" (include the quotes) in the DEPARTMENT column (Figure 5-10).

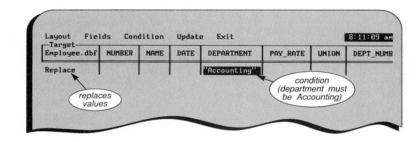

FIGURE 5-10
Query Design screen

Enter the replacement value of 01 by entering WITH "01" (include the quotes) in the DEPT_NUMB column (Figure 5-11).

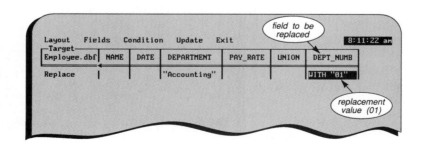

FIGURE 5-11
Query Design screen

The update query is now complete, so select "Perform the update" from the Update menu. At this point, the update takes place and you see the screen shown in Figure 5-12. Notice that four records have been replaced. Press any key to remove the message.

FIGURE 5-12
Query Design screen

In exactly the same way, change the value for DEPT_NUMB to 02 for all records in which DEPARTMENT is Marketing, 03 for all records in which DEPARTMENT is Production, and 04 for all records in which DEPART-MENT is Shipping. The changes are then complete, and all the records contain an appropriate value in the DEPT_NUMB field. When you have finished all the updates, use the Exit menu to return to the Control Center. You do not need to save your query.

Making Other Corrections

To make additional corrections, use F2 to move to the Edit screen, and then move to record 15 as shown in Figure 5-13.

FIGURE 5-13
Edit screen

Change the name from Castleworth, Mary T. to Castleworth, Marianne K. (Figure 5-14). If you have correctly changed the length of the NAME field, you should have enough room to make this change. Select the "Exit" option from the Exit menu when you are done.

FIGURE 5-14
Edit screen

Use F2 to move to the Browse screen, and press Page Up to move to the beginning of the file. Your display should now look like Figure 5-15. Notice that the DEPT_NUMB column contains the correct values and that the name Marianne Castleworth is now correct. Select the "Exit" option from the Exit menu to return to the Control Center.

Deleting Fields

The DEPARTMENT field is no longer required, so let's delete it. Highlight EMPLOYEE, press Enter, and then choose "Modify structure/order" as you did before. Press Esc to remove the Organize menu from the screen. Your display should now look like Figure 5-16.

Press the Down Arrow enough times to move the highlight to the fourth row (DEPARTMENT). Press Ctrl-U. (Does this seem familiar? It is exactly the same way you delete records when you use either the Edit screen or the Browse screen.) The field then disappears (Figure 5-17). Since deleting this record is the only change you need to make, return to the Control Center by selecting the "Save changes and exit" option from the Exit menu.

Now, use F2 to move to the Browse screen and press Page Up to go to the beginning of the file. You should see the display shown in Figure 5-18. Notice that there is no DEPARTMENT column. Return to the Control Center by selecting the "Exit" option from the Exit menu.

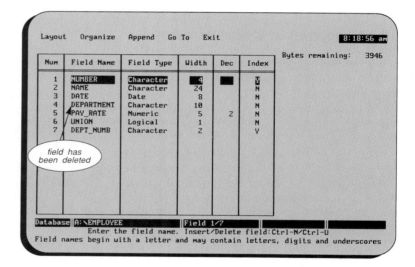

FIGURE 5-15 Browse screen

FIGURE 5-16 Database Design screen

FIGURE 5-17 Database Design screen

FIGURE 5-18
Browse screen

INDEXES

What Is an Index?

You are already familiar with the concept of an index. The index in the back of a book contains important words or phrases together with a list of pages on which the given words or phrases can be found. An **index** for a database file is similar. Figure 5-19, for example, shows the EMPLOYEE database file along with an index built on NAME. Technically, the expression on which the index is built, in this case NAME, is called the **index key**. When we use this index, the items of interest are employee names rather than key words or phrases. Each employee name occurs in the index along with the number of the record on which the employee name is found. If you were to use this index to find Helen Bender, for example, you would find her name in the index, look at the corresponding record number (8), and then go immediately to record 8 in the EMPLOYEE file, thus finding her much more rapidly than if you had to look at each employee one at a time. This is precisely what dBASE does when using an index. Thus, indexes make the process of retrieving an employee much more efficient.

EMPLOYEE NAME	REC NUM
Ackerman, David R.	3
Anderson, Mariane L.	9
Andrews, Robert M.	13
Baxter, Charles W.	11
Bender, Helen O.	8
Castle, Mark C.	5
Castleworth, Marianne K.	15
Chaney, Joseph R.	7
Doi, Chang J.	4
Dugan, Mary L.	14
Dunning, Lisa A.	6
Edwards, Kenneth J.	10
Evans, John T.	12
McCormack, Nigel L.	2
Rapoza, Anthony P.	1

FIGURE 5-19 Use of an index

REC NUM	EMPLOYEE NUMBER	EMPLOYEE NAME	DATE HIRED	PAY RATE	UNION MEMBER	NUMB
1	1011	Rapoza, Anthony P.	01/10/92	8.50	Y	04
2	1013	McCormack, Nigel L.	01/15/92	8.25	Y	04
3	1016	Ackerman, David R.	02/04/92	10.25	N	01
4	1017	Doi, Chang J.	02/05/92	6.00	Y	03
5	1020	Castle, Mark C.	03/04/92	7.50	Y	04
6	1022	Dunning, Lisa A.	03/12/92	9.10	N	02
7	1025	Chaney, Joseph R.	03/23/92	8.00	N	01
8	1026	Bender, Helen O.	04/12/92	7.00	Y	03
9	1029	Anderson, Mariane L.	04/18/92	9.00	Y	04
10	1030	Edwards, Kenneth J.	04/23/92	8.60	Y	03
11	1037	Baxter, Charles W.	05/05/92	11.00	N	01
12	1041	Evans, John T.	05/19/92	6.00	N	02
13	1056	Andrews, Robert M.	06/03/92	9.00	N	02
14	1057	Dugan, Mary L.	06/10/92	8.75	Y	03
15	1066	Castleworth, Marianne K.	07/05/92	8.75	Y	03
16	1070	Fisher, Ella C.	07/15/92	8.00	N	01
17	1075	Caine, William J.	08/16/92	9.25	N	02

Another benefit of indexes is that they provide an extremely efficient alternative to sorting. Look at the record numbers in the index and suppose dBASE uses the index to list all employees. That is, dBASE simply follows down the record number column, listing the corresponding employees as it goes. In this example, dBASE would first list the employee on record 3 (David Ackerman), then the employee on record 9 (Mariane Anderson), then the employee on record 13 (Robert Andrews), and so on. dBASE lists the employees in alphabetical order without sorting the file.

Creating Indexes

To create an index, move to the Database Design screen. At the screen, highlight the EMPLOYEE database file at the Control Center, press Enter, and then select "Modify structure/order". Your screen should now look like Figure 5-20. The Organize menu is currently on the screen. Select the first choice, "Create new index", to create a new index.

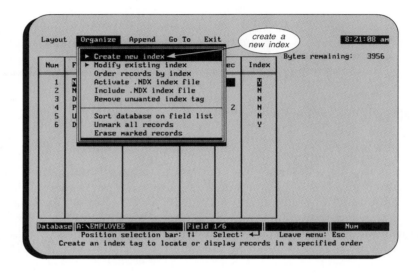

FIGURE 5-20
Database Design screen

Some indexes already exist. Any field for which you entered the letter Y in the Index column already has an index. Thus, you would not need to go through the process for these fields.

When you select "Create new index", you see the screen shown in Figure 5-21. Use this screen to specify details about your index.

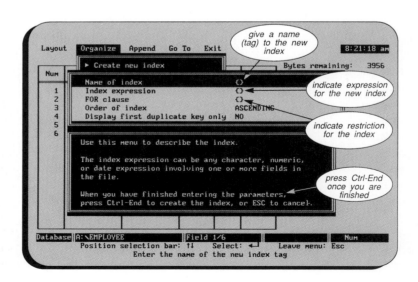

FIGURE 5-21
Database Design screen

Single-Field Indexes

Most indexes only involve a single field. We will illustrate the process of creating a single-field index by creating one for the field called NAME; that is, NAME is the index key. To specify an index, we must give it a name, also called a **tag**. We must also specify the index key, that is, the expression on which the index is created. You can do these in either order. Let's specify the expression first.

Move the cursor to the line labeled "Index expression" and press Enter. You could type in the expression, which, in this case, would be NAME. As an alternative, you can press Shift-F1 (remember our pick list) to get a list of possibilities (Figure 5-22) and then select NAME from the list. In either case, you finish the process by pressing Enter a second time. Now move back to the line labeled "Name of index" and indicate a name for the index. Enter NAME as the name of the index by pressing Enter, typing NAME, and pressing Enter again. (If your index expression is a single field, it's a good idea to also use this field name as a name for the index as we have done here.)

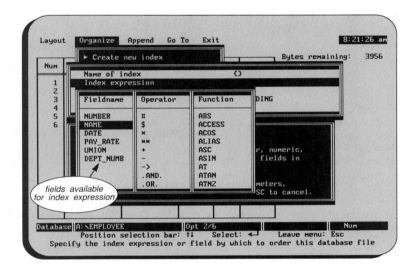

FIGURE 5-22
Database Design screen

At this point, you have entered all the required information, so press Ctrl-End. You now see the screen shown in Figure 5-23. Notice that the entry in the index column for the NAME field has been changed to Y since this field now has an index.

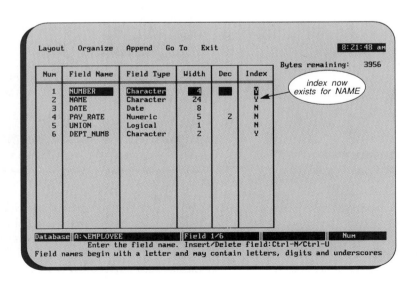

FIGURE 5-23
Database Design screen

Using Indexes for Sorting

Indexes can also be used as an alternative to sorting. For example, dBASE could use the index on the NAME field to make the records in the database file *appear* to be ordered by name. Since each database file can potentially have several different indexes, we need a way to specify to dBASE the one that we want it to use. Select the "Order records by index" option from the Organize menu (Figure 5-24).

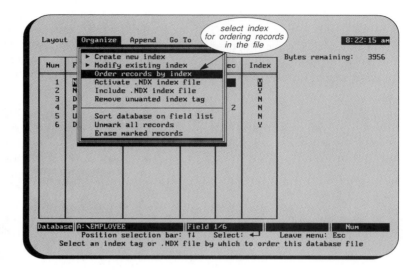

FIGURE 5-24
Database Design screen

You then see a list of the names of the available indexes (Figure 5-25). To the left of this box is a box that contains the index expression for whichever index is currently highlighted. Ignore the other box for now. Select the index called NAME by moving the highlight to it and pressing Enter. This index is now used to order the records.

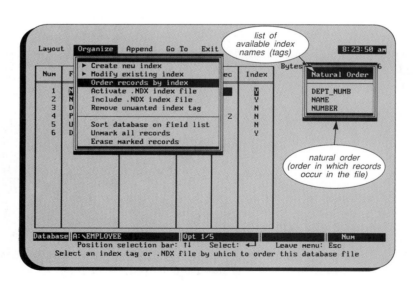

FIGURE 5-25
Database Design screen

To see the ordering, use F2 to move to the Browse screen and press Page Up, if necessary, to move to the beginning of the file. Your display should look like Figure 5-26. Notice that the records do indeed appear to be sorted by name.

FIGURE 5-26
Browse screen

Multiple-Field Indexes

An index can also be built on a combination of fields. The process is almost identical to that used to build an index on a single field. To build an index on the combination of DEPT_NUMB and NAME, for example, the only difference from the preceding example is that the index key is defined to be DEPT_NUMB + NAME. You could type just this expression. Alternatively, you could press Shift-F1 for a list of available options, choose DEPT_NUMB, type the plus sign (+), press Shift-F1 for another list, and choose NAME. For the name of the index, let's use DPNMNAME.

To create such an index, return to the Database Design screen and select "Create new index" from the Organize menu. Make the entries as we indicated in the previous paragraph and as shown in Figure 5-27. Press Ctrl-End to finish the process.

FIGURE 5-27
Database Design screen

To use this index, select the "Order records by index" option from the Organize menu (Figure 5-28). Notice that DPNMNAME is included in the list of index names. Move the highlight to it, as shown in the figure, and the box to the left will show the index expression (DEPT_NUMB + NAME) for this index. Finish selecting it by pressing Enter.

FIGURE 5-28
Database Design screen

Again use F2 to move to the Browse screen and press Page Up, if necessary, to move to the beginning of the file. Your display should now look like Figure 5-29. Notice that this time the records appear to be sorted by name within department.

FIGURE 5-29
Browse screen

Unfortunately, to build an index on a combination of fields, *both fields must be of character type*. This means that you could not use the same technique to build an index on the combination of DEPT_NUMB and PAY_RATE, for example. There are ways around this problem, but they are beyond the scope of this text. Fortunately, the situations in which you would need to do this are not very common. If you ever find yourself in such a situation, look up the word index in a dBASE reference manual.

Using Indexes for Retrieval

Indexes can also be used to find records rapidly. To illustrate this, let's use the index on the NUMBER field. This index already exists, so we don't need to create it. All we need to do is select it, so move to the Edit screen and again select the "Order records by index" option from the Organize menu. This time select NUMBER from the list of index names presented to you.

Let's suppose that you want to find employee 1037. Choose "Index key search" from the Go To menu (Figure 5-30).

FIGURE 5-30
Edit screen

You are then asked to enter a search string for NUMBER. Enter 1037, as shown in Figure 5-31, and then press Enter.

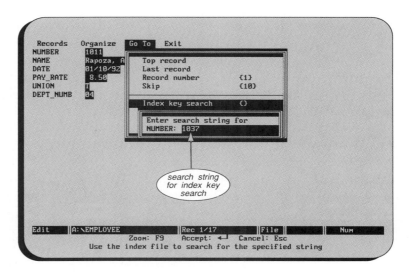

FIGURE 5-31
Edit screen

If there were no such employee, dBASE would display a message indicating this. If, as is the case here, there is such an employee, this employee's record becomes the current active record (Figure 5-32).

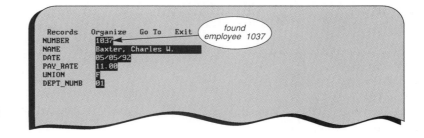

FIGURE 5-32
Edit screen

At this point, you might question what value this option has. You may recall that you used the "Forward search" option to accomplish the same task back in Project 2. Why is this "Index key search" option necessary since you could accomplish the same task without it?

The answer is that the "Index key search" option, which only works if you are using an index, is *much* more efficient than the "Forward search" option. The "Index key search" option uses the index to go directly to the desired record. The "Forward search" option steps through every record looking for one that matches the condition.

In the case of a file with only a handful of records, this doesn't make much difference. Imagine a file with 50,000 records, however, in which the record you want happens to be record 40,176. Think how much time it would take dBASE to look at the first 40,175 records before it found the one you want. In such a case, the difference between "Index key search" and "Forward search" is dramatic.

Removing Unwanted Indexes

Occasionally, you might find that you created an index, but now you never use it. If this is the case, you should probably get rid of the index. It occupies space on your disk. In addition, dBASE must keep this index up to date; that is, when you change the data in your database file, dBASE must make appropriate changes to the index. If you are not going to use the index, there is no point in wasting the space or in having dBASE do the extra work.

Removing an index is a simple matter. You do it in the same way you choose an index to order records. The only difference is that you choose the "Remove unwanted index tag" option from the Organize menu rather than "Order records by index". In both cases, you are presented with a list of possible indexes. In this case, choose the index you want to remove and press Enter. The process is then complete, and the index is removed.

VIEWS

What Is a View?

To access data from more than one database file in dBASE, you use a **view**. In general terms, a view is a pseudo-table, or pseudo-database file, that can combine two or more existing database files. Saying it is a pseudo-database file means that the view appears to the user to be a database file, but it doesn't really exist in the same way that a database file does. Instead, dBASE assembles the data for you at the time you use the view.

To see how views work, consider the EMPLOYEE and DEPT database files in Figure 5-33.

EMPLOYEE NUMBER	EMPLOYEE NAME	DATE HIRED	PAY RATE	UNION MEMBER	DEPT NUMB
1011	Rapoza, Anthony P.	01/10/92	8.50	Y	04
1013	McCormack, Nigel L.	01/15/92	8.25	Y	04
1016	Ackerman, David R.	02/04/92	10.25	N	01
1017	Doi, Chang J.	02/05/92	6.00	Y	03
1020	Castle, Mark C.	03/04/92	7.50	Y	04
1022	Dunning, Lisa A.	03/12/92	9.10	N	02
1025	Chaney, Joseph R.	03/23/92	8.00	N	01
1026	Bender, Helen O.	04/12/92	7.00	Y	03
1029	Anderson, Mariane L.	04/18/92	9.00	Y	04
1030	Edwards, Kenneth J.	04/23/92	8.60	Y	03
1037	Baxter, Charles W.	05/05/92	11.00	N	01
1041	Evans, John T.	05/19/92	6.00	N	02
1056	Andrews, Robert M.	06/03/92	9.00	N	02
1057	Dugan, Mary L.	06/10/92	8.75	Y	03
1066	Castleworth, Marianne K.	07/05/92	8.75	Y	03
1070	Fisher, Ella C.	07/15/92	8.00	N	01
1075	Caine, William J.	08/16/92	9.25	N	02

DEPT NUMB	DEPARTMENT NAME
01	Accounting
02	Marketing
03	Production
04	Shipping

current active record

matching department numbers

FIGURE 5-33 Relating database files

A special kind of relationship, called a **one-to-many relationship**, exists between these two files. In other words, *one* department is associated with many employees, but each employee is associated with one department. Department 01, for example, is associated with employees 1016, 1025, 1037, and 1070. Employee 1016, on the other hand, is associated with *only* department 01. DEPT is called the *one* database file, and that EMPLOYEE is called the *many* database file in this relationship.

When two database files are related in this way, they can become part of a view. In such a case, you work with the many database file and dBASE automatically keeps track of which record in the one file is associated with the current active record in this many file. For example, if record 1 (employee 1011) is the current active record, dBASE knows that the related record in the DEPT file is record 4 (department 04) since the department numbers match (the arrow in Figure 5-33). dBASE allows you to use not only fields in the EMPLOYEE file, but also any fields in the DEPT file. Thus, if you list the department name for employee 1011, you get Shipping since it is the name on the related record in the DEPT file. If you make record 3 the current active record (Figure 5-34), the corresponding record in the DEPT file is record 1 (department 01). The department name for this employee is therefore Accounting.

EMPLOYEE NUMBER	EMPLOYEE NAME	DATE HIRED	PAY RATE	UNION MEMBER	DEPT NUMB
1011	Rapoza, Anthony P.	01/10/92	8.50	Y	04
1013	McCormack, Nigel L.	01/15/92	8.25	Y	04
1016	Ackerman, David R.	02/04/92	10.25	N	01
1017	Doi, Chang J.	02/05/92	6.00	Y	03
1020	Castle, Mark C.	03/04/92	7.50	Y	04
1022	Dunning, Lisa A.	03/12/92	9.10	N	02
1025	Chaney, Joseph R.	03/23/92	8.00	N	01
1026	Bender, Helen O.	04/12/92	7.00	Y	03
1029	Anderson, Mariane L.	04/18/92	9.00	Y	04
1030	Edwards, Kenneth J.	04/23/92	8.60	Y	03
1037	Baxter, Charles W.	05/05/92	11.00	N	01
1041	Evans, John T.	05/19/92	6.00	N	02
1056	Andrews, Robert M.	06/03/92	9.00	N	02
1057	Dugan, Mary L.	06/10/92	8.75	Y	03
1066	Castleworth, Marianne K.	07/05/92	8.75	Y	03
1070	Fisher, Ella C.	07/15/92	8.00	N	01
1075	Caine, William J.	08/16/92	9.25	N	02

DEPT NUMB	DEPARTMENT NAME
01	Accounting
02	Marketing
03	Production
04	Shipping

current active record

matching department numbers

FIGURE 5-34 Relating database files

When you access such a view, you don't have to be aware of these details. dBASE handles them for you automatically. You simply indicate that you want to include the department name on a display or report, and dBASE ensures that the correct one is included.

Beginning the View-Creation Process

In dBASE, we use the same Query Design screen you saw earlier to create views. In simplest terms a view *is a saved query*; that is, dBASE considers any query you save to be a view. If you saved any of the queries you created in Project 2, you created a view. Those views are very simple views, containing data from only one database file, but they are views nonetheless.

Now, activate your EMPLOYEE database file, one of the two that will be in this view, in the usual manner. Then, select <create> from the Queries column. Your screen should look like Figure 5-35, just like the initial screen you saw when you designed your queries in Project 2.

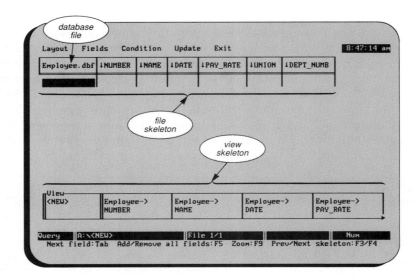

FIGURE 5-35
Query Design screen

Using Indexes

As you have seen, the use of indexes can greatly improve efficiency. dBASE uses indexes in queries and views, but only if you indicate that indexes are to be included. You do this by using the "Include indexes" option from the Fields menu (Figure 5-36). If the word following "Include indexes" is YES, dBASE uses any indexes. Since it is not, move the highlight to this option and press Enter to change the NO to YES. You won't see the change because the menu disappears. If you want to see that your change was made, you could bring the menu back to the screen by pressing F10. After you have looked at it, remove the menu from the screen by pressing Esc.

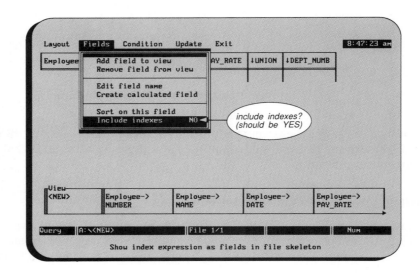

FIGURE 5-36
Query Design screen

Your screen should look like Figure 5-37. The number signs (#) that precede NUMBER and NAME indicate that there are indexes for those fields that dBASE can use. Notice that a number sign is not in front of DATE because we did not create an index for DATE.

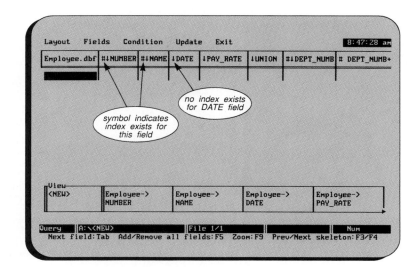

FIGURE 5-37
Query Design screen

Adding Database Files

So far only the EMPLOYEE file is included in your query. You also need to include the DEPT file. Select "Add file to query" from the Layout menu (Figure 5-38) and you are presented with a list of possible files. Select DEPT.

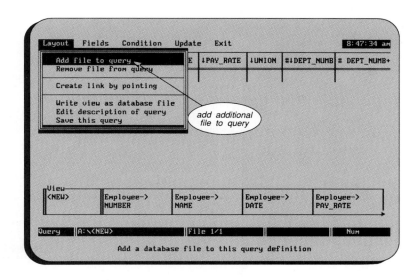

FIGURE 5-38
Query Design screen

Your screen should then look like Figure 5-39. There are now two file skeletons, one for EMPLOYEE and one for DEPT. Try repeatedly pressing F4. Notice how you move from one skeleton to the next. Each time you press F4 you move to the next skeleton on the screen. If you're on the last skeleton, the view skeleton, you'll move back to the first one, the skeleton for EMPLOYEE. Now, try repeatedly pressing F3. You'll see that the same thing happens, except that you move in the opposite direction. These keys let you easily transfer from one skeleton to another.

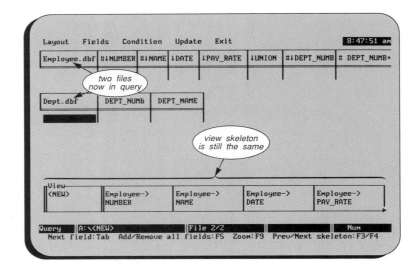

FIGURE 5-39
Query Design screen

Using F4, move to the file skeleton for DEPT and include indexes just as you did for EMPLOYEE (select the "Include indexes" option from the Fields menu). Your screen should look like Figure 5-40. Notice the number sign (#) in front of the DEPT_NUMB field indicating that an index exists for this field.

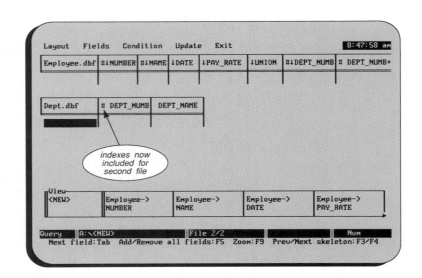

FIGURE 5-40
Query Design screen

Linking the Database Files

Having two database files included in the view is not the only thing we need to do. We also need to indicate how these database files are to be linked, that is, how records in EMPLOYEE are to be matched with records in DEPT. We know that this is to be done by matching values in the two DEPT_NUMB fields. We need to indicate this to dBASE, however.

Move to the file skeleton for EMPLOYEE and then move to the DEPT_NUMB field within this skeleton by repeatedly pressing the Tab key. Then, select the "Create link by pointing" option from the Layout menu (Figure 5-41).

FIGURE 5-41
Query Design screen

dBASE inserts "LINK1" in the column in which your cursor is positioned (Figure 5-42). A message instructs you to move the cursor to the other field in the linking process and then to press Enter. Press F4 to move to the skeleton for DEPT, use the Tab key to move to the DEPT_NUMB field (unless you're there already), and press Enter.

FIGURE 5-42
Query Design screen

At this point, your screen should look like Figure 5-43. Notice that both DEPT_NUMB columns now include "LINK1". This is the way dBASE indicates that these are the fields it will use to link the two files.

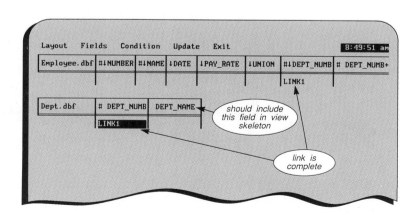

FIGURE 5-43
Query Design screen

Changing the View Skeleton

You now have included both files, and you have linked them. The view skeleton has not changed, however; it still includes only fields from EMPLOYEE. You do not need to include the DEPT_NUMB field in DEPT because this field should exactly match the DEPT_NUMB field in EMPLOYEE, which is already included in the view skeleton. (The DEPT_NUMB field in EMPLOYEE is currently off the right-hand edge of the screen.) You should include DEPT_NAME, however. Move the cursor to it and press F5. (Remember that you use F5 to add fields to the view skeleton.) DEPT_NAME is then added to the view skeleton.

Finishing the View-Creation Process

When you have made all the required entries for your view on the Query Design screen, select the "Save changes and exit" option from the Exit menu. When you are asked for a name, enter EMPDEPT. You have now saved your query as EMPDEPT. Thus, you have created a view and called it EMPDEPT. Remember that a view is the same as a saved query. It is displayed in the Queries column of the Control Center.

Using Views

Since you just created the view, it is automatically active. It appears above the line in the Queries column. If it is not, you can activate it in the same way you activate a database file. Move the highlight to it, press Enter, and then select "Use view".

To see the data in this view, make sure the view is active and press F2 to move to the Browse screen. Your screen should look like Figure 5-44. Notice that all the fields from the EMPLOYEE database file as well as the DEPT_NAME field from the DEPT file are included. Notice also "ReadOnly" on the status line. This simply indicates that you can use this view to read data, that is, look at it, but not to update data. To update data, you must update either the EMPLOYEE or DEPT database files rather than the view.

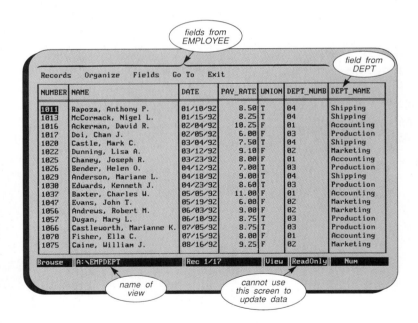

FIGURE 5-44
Browse screen

Suppose you don't want to see all the data shown in Figure 5-44. You only want to see the employee number, name, and department name, and only those employees who were hired after March 1, 1992. To see employees meeting that description, select the "Transfer to Query Design" option from the Exit menu. You are then taken back to the Query Design screen, and the query you created for your view is displayed. You can now make appropriate changes to it and then press F2 to see the results of your new query.

Suppose also that you want to change the view skeleton to Figure 5-45. The simplest way is to move the cursor under Employee.dbf. Press F3 or F4, and then move the cursor under Employee.dbf by using Tab or Shift-Tab.

When the cursor is under Employee.dbf, press F5 as many times as it takes to remove all the fields in EMPLOYEE from the view skeleton. In this example, you only need to press it once. In other situations, you may need to press it twice. Fortunately, it's very easy to tell how many times you should press it. Just look at the view skeleton, and press F5 until the fields disappear.

Next, move the cursor under Dept.dbf and press F5 until all the fields from Dept.dbf are removed from the view skeleton. In this case, you need to press F5 twice. The first time you press F5, *all* fields from DEPT are included in the skeleton because they're not already there; the second time, they are removed. Now move the cursor under the NUMBER field and press F5. This field is then included in the view skeleton. Do the same for both NAME and DEPT_NAME to complete your view skeleton.

Next, enter your condition. Move the cursor to the DATE column and type the condition as shown in Figure 5-46.

Then press F2 to see the results. Your screen should look like Figure 5-47. Notice that the results are exactly the ones we wanted.

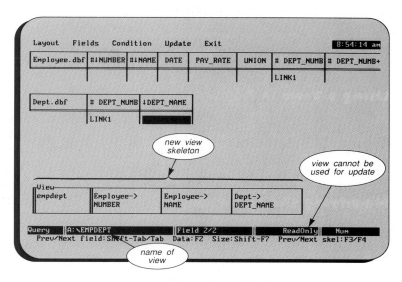

FIGURE 5-45 Query Design screen

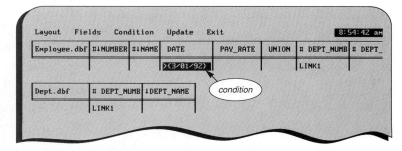

FIGURE 5-46 Query Design screen

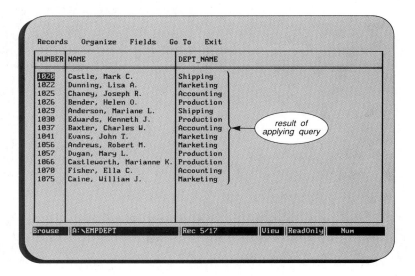

FIGURE 5-47
Browse screen

Return to the Control Center by selecting the "Exit" option from the Exit menu. Since you changed the definition of a query, dBASE asks you if you want to save it. *Be sure you answer no.* Saving it would replace the old definition. Our view would then consist of only the rows and columns shown in Figure 5-47, which is not what we want. Fortunately, the "No" choice is highlighted, so all you need to do is press Enter.

Using a View in Reports

Creating a report using a view involves the same procedures you followed in Project 3 when you created a report for a database file. When you use Quick layout, for example, all the fields in the view are included in the report. Whenever you add a new field, all the fields in the view will be available. When you produce the report, you should make sure the EMPDEPT view is active.

Modifying the Structure of a View

Occasionally, you might need to change the structure of a view. Highlight the view at the Control Center and press Enter. Your screen would then look like Figure 5-48. To merely use the view, you can select "Use view". If you want to change the structure, however, select "Modify query". You are then taken to the Query Design screen where the query for your view is already on the screen. You can now make any necessary changes to the query. When you are done, save your work. The structure of your view is then changed. You shouldn't need to make any changes unless you made some mistake earlier.

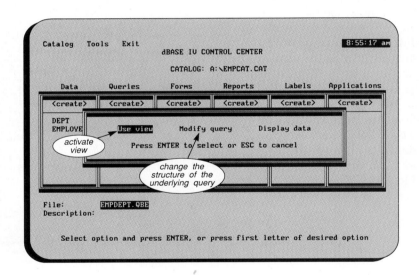

FIGURE 5-48
Control Center

Sorting a View on a Single Field

You can specify that the data in a view be sorted in some particular order right from the Query Design screen. You don't need to go to the Database Design screen as you did for a database file.

To specify sort order in a view, highlight the view, press Enter, and then select "Modify query" to move to the Query Design screen. Next, move the cursor to the field on which you want to sort the data. If, for example, you wanted to sort the query on NAME, you would move the cursor to the NAME field in the skeleton for EMPLOYEE.

To sort on the field in which the cursor is located, select the "Sort on this field" option from the Fields menu (Figure 5-49). You then see the same list of possible sort types you saw when you sorted a database file (Figure 5-50). Select the "Ascending ASCII" option.

Your screen should look like Figure 5-51. The entry "Asc1" in the NAME field indicates two things. First, the abbreviation Asc is the dBASE code for Ascending ASCII. Second, the number 1 indicates that this is the first sort field. This number only becomes meaningful if we have more than one sort field.

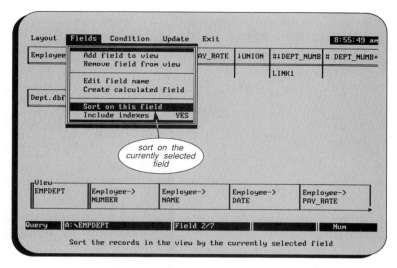

FIGURE 5-49 Query Design screen

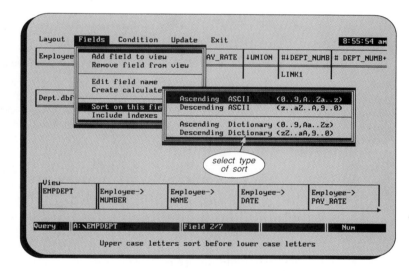

FIGURE 5-50
Query Design screen

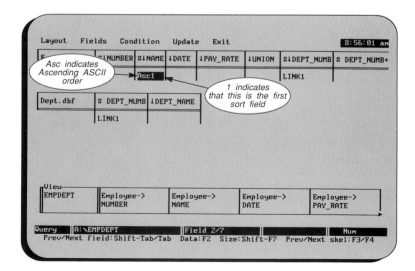

FIGURE 5-51
Query Design screen

Press F2 to see the results of this query. As you can see (Figure 5-52), the data does appear to be sorted by NAME. Since the NAME field is indexed and you requested that indexes be included, dBASE uses this index to display the data in sorted order. Without it, dBASE would have had to physically sort the data, which is a much slower process.

FIGURE 5-52
Browse screen

Now, let's sort the view on multiple fields. If you want to move on to this step now, select the "Transfer to Query Design" option from the Exit menu. If you don't want to do it at this time, select the "Exit" option from the Exit menu to return directly to the Control Center. (We don't want to save this change to the query, so be sure to answer no when the prompt asks you if you want to save the new query design.)

Sorting a View on Multiple Fields

You can also sort on more than one field. We can illustrate this by sorting the data by NAME within DEPT_NUMB. First, return to the Query Design screen. If you are on the Browse screen, you could select the "Transfer to Query Design" option from the Exit menu. If you are at the Control Center, highlight EMPDEPT in the Queries column, press Enter, and select "Modify query".

If you have returned from the Browse screen, you still have "Asc1" in the NAME column. You must delete it before you move on. Move the cursor to the NAME column and repeatedly press the Spacebar to erase the previous entry. As a shortcut, you could press Ctrl-Y. If you came directly from the Control Center, you will not have such an entry to remove. You are now ready to specify the sort keys you want.

Select the sort keys in order of importance. Since DEPT_NUMB is the more important of the two, select it first. You could use either the DEPT_NUMB column in the EMPLOYEE file or the DEPT_NUMB column in the DEPT file. The other sort key, NAME, is in the EMPLOYEE file. We will use the DEPT_NUMB column in the same file.

You select the DEPT_NUMB field in the EMPLOYEE file as a sort key in exactly the same way you selected NAME in the previous example. Move the cursor to it, select the "Sort on this field" option from the Fields menu, and then select "Ascending ASCII".

Your screen should then look like Figure 5-53. Notice that two entries are in the DEPT_NUMB column separated by commas. The first, "LINK1", is the entry used to link the tables. The second, "Asc2", indicates that the sort type is Ascending ASCII.

You may be wondering why the second entry reads "Asc2" rather than "Asc1". This is just the way dBASE works. dBASE automatically assigns the next higher number within each work session.

You are now ready to select the second sort field, NAME. You do this in the same way you selected DEPT_NUMB. Your screen should then look like Figure 5-54. Notice that the entry in the NAME column is "Asc3". Again dBASE has assigned the next higher number. There is something important about this number, however. In the present query, two entries are like this. There is "Asc2" in the DEPT_NUMB column and "Asc3" in the NAME column. Whichever column has the *smaller* number will be treated as the more important sort key. It doesn't matter specifically what the numbers are, just which one is smaller. This is why it's important to select the more important key first.

To see the results, press F2. Your screen should look like Figure 5-55. Notice that the overall sort order is by DEPT_NUMB and that the employees within any given department are sorted by name.

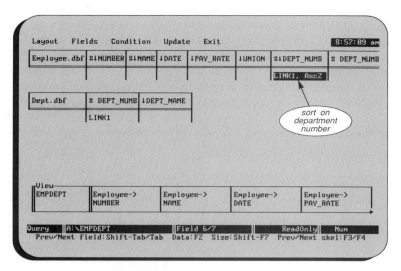

FIGURE 5-53 Query Design screen

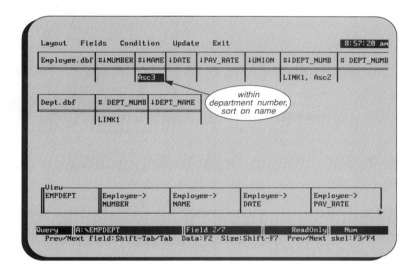

FIGURE 5-54
Query Design screen

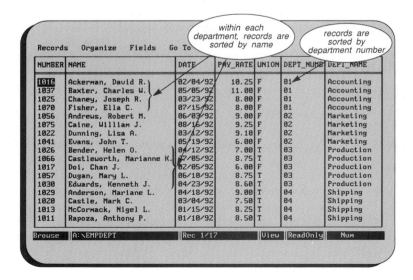

FIGURE 5-55
Browse screen

Even though indexes existed for both DEPT_NUMB and NAME, dBASE cannot use them to make the sort efficient. (The reason is beyond the scope of this book.) But an alternative method allows dBASE to use an index. To see this method, return to the Query Design screen and remove the Asc entries in both the NAME and DEPT_NUMB columns. Be sure to leave the entry "LINK1" in the DEPT_NUMB column. Next, use the Tab key to move the cursor past the DEPT_NUMB column. You will see an extra column as shown in Figure 5-56. This column is the additional index you created when you built an index on the combination of DEPT_NUMB and NAME. Remember that this index causes data to appear to be sorted by name within department number, which is exactly what you want. Thus, select this as the sort field, just as you selected sort fields earlier, and the entry "Asc4" will appear in this column. If you now press F2, you will see the same results that you did before. In this case, however dBASE can produce them much more efficiently.

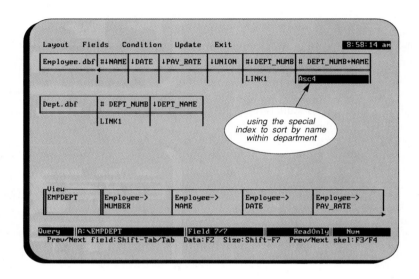

FIGURE 5-56
Query Design screen

Because your database is small, you probably will not notice the added efficiency. In a very large database, however, the difference in efficiency can be dramatic.

Now that we have finished, selecte the "Exit" option from the Exit menu. Since we don't want to save the changes to the query, answer no when the prompt asks you if you want to save the new query design.

Sorting Queries

Although the preceding discussion explains how to sort views, remember that views are nothing more than stored queries. Thus, in the preceding discussion, we were also learning how to sort queries. The same techniques apply to sorting a query whether or not the query will ultimately be saved.

Special Considerations

When using views, you must remember the following special considerations:

1. When you have activated a view, the name of the view rather than the name of a database file, is displayed in the status bar.
2. To update any of the data, update the appropriate database file. For example,
   a. To add a new employee, activate the EMPLOYEE database file and use the Edit screen to add the employee.
   b. To change the name of an employee, activate the EMPLOYEE database file and use the "Edit" option.
   c. To add a new department, activate the DEPT database file and then use the Edit screen.
3. Data never exists in the form in which it is represented in a view. Rather, dBASE draws data from the underlying database files and assembles it in the form required for the view *at the time you access the view*. The helpful thing about this arrangement is that, whenever changes are made to any of the database files that are included in the view, you automatically see the results of these changes the next time you use the view. You don't need to recreate the view in order to access the current data.

PROJECT SUMMARY

In Project 5 you learned how to change the structure of a database file. You saw how to add new fields, change the characteristics of existing fields, and delete fields. You learned how to create indexes, which can be used in place of sorting and how to increase the efficiency of retrieval. You created a view encompassing data from two database files. And you observed that data can be retrieved from a view in the same way as it can from an individual database file. All the activities that you learned for this project are summarized in the Quick Reference following Project 6. The following is a summary of the keystroke sequence we used in Project 5.

SUMMARY OF KEYSTROKES — PROJECT 5

STEPS	KEY(S) PRESSED	RESULTS
1	DBASE ← [At DOS prompt]	Starts dBASE.
2	←DEPT_NUMB← ←2←YDEPT_NAME← ←10← ← ←DEPT←N	Creates DEPT file.
3	F2 01Accounting02Marketing← 03Production04Shipping← F10 → → → ←	Enters records to DEPT.
4	↓ ← → ← Esc	Moves to Database Design screen with EMPLOYEE active.
5	↓ ← ←24← ←	Changes length of NAME field.
6	↓[Press 4 times]DEPT_NAME← ←2←Y← ←	Enters DEPT_NUMB field.
7	F2 Page Up	Browses Employee database.
8	F10 →[Press 4 times]←	Returns to the Control Center.
9	→ ←	Moves to Query Design screen.
10	F10 → → → ← ← → ←	Begins update query.
11	Tab [Press 4 times]"Accounting"← Tab Tab Tab WITH "01"←	Completes update query.
12	F10 ↑← ←	Makes first change.
13	WITH "02"← Shift-Tab Shift-Tab Shift-Tab Ctrl-Y "Marketing"← F10 ←←	Makes second change.
14	"Production"← Tab Tab Tab WITH "03"← F10 ←←	Makes third change.
15	WITH "04"← Shift-Tab Shift-Tab Shift-Tab Ctrl-Y "Shipping← F10 ←←	Makes final changes.
16	F10 →↓←←←	Returns to Control Center.
17	F2 Page Down [Press 14 times]↓Castleworth, Marianne K. F10 → → → ←	Changes name.
18	F2 F2 Page Up	Browses Employee database.
19	F10 →[Press 4 times]←	Returns to the Control Center.
20	← ← → ← Esc	Moves to Database Design screen.
21	↓↓↓ Ctrl-U	Removes field.
22	F10 → → → ← ←	Saves changes.
23	F2 Page Up	Browses Employee database.
24	F10 →[Press 4 times]←	Returns to the Control Center.
25	← → ← ←	Creates index.
26	↓ ←NAME← ↑↑ ←NAME← Ctrl-End	Completes first index.

(continued)

SUMMARY OF KEYSTROKES — PROJECT 5 (continued)

STEPS	KEY(S) PRESSED	RESULTS
27	F10 ↓↓←↓↓←	Selects index to use.
28	F2 F2 F10 →[Press 4 times]↓↓←	Views database in name order and returns to database design.
29	←DPNMNAME←←DEPT_NUMB+NAME← Ctrl-End	Completes second index.
30	F10 ↓↓←↓↓←	Selects index to use.
31	F2	Views database in name order within department.
32	F2 F10 →↓↓←↓[Press 4 times]←	Moves to Edit screen and selects NUMBER index.
33	F10 →↓[Press 4 times]←1037←	Seeks employee 1037.
34	F10 →←	Returns to Control Center.
35	→←	Moves to Query Design screen.
36	F10 →↓↓↓←	Includes indexes.
37	F10 ←←←	Enters DEPT to query.
38	F10 →←	Includes indexes for DEPT.
39	F3 Tab [Press 6 times]	Moves to link field in EMPLOYEE.
40	F10 ←↓↓←	Starts link.
41	F4 Tab ←	Finishes link.
42	Tab F5	Includes DEPT_NAME in view skeleton.
43	F10 →[Press 4 times]←EMPDEPT←	Saves as EMPDEPT.
44	F2 F2	Moves to Browse screen.
45	F10 →[Press 4 times]↓←	Moves to Query Design screen.
46	F3 Shift-Tab [Use to move highlight under Employee.dbf] F5 F4 Shift-Tab [Use to move highlight under Dept.dbf] F5 F5	Erases view skeleton.
47	F3 Tab F5 Tab F5 F4 Tab Tab F5	Creates new view skeleton.
48	F3 Tab >{03/01/92}←	Enters condition.
49	F2 F10 →[Press 4 times]←←	Applies query and returns to Control Center.
50	[Make sure EMPDEPT is highlighted] ←→←	Modifies the view.
51	F3 Tab [Use to move to NAME] F10 →↓↓←←	Modifies query to sort on NAME.
52	F2 F10 →[Press 4 times]↓←	Applies query and returns to Query Design screen.
53	Ctrl-Y Tab [Press 4 times] F10 ↓↓←← Shift-Tab [Press 4 times] F10 ←←	Modifies query to sort on NAME within DEPT_NUMB.
54	F2 F10 →[Press 4 times]↓←	Applies query and returns to Query Design screen.
55	Ctrl-Y Tab [Press 4 times]→[Press 5 times] Delete [Press 6 times] Tab F10 ↓←←	Modifies query to use special index.
56	F2 F10 →[Press 4 times]←←	Applies query and returns to Control Center without saving new query design.

The following list summarizes the material covered in Project 5.

1. To change the structure of a database file, highlight the database file at the Control Center, press Enter, and select "Modify structure/order".
2. To change the characteristics of a field, move the highlight to the data to be changed and enter the new value.
3. To add a field, move the highlight to the beginning of the first row past all the existing fields, and then type in the name and characteristics of the new field.
4. To make mass changes to the new field, use an update query.
5. To delete a field, move the highlight to the field to be deleted on the Database Design screen, hold the Ctrl key down and type the letter U.
6. An **index key** is the field or combination of fields on which an **index** is built. The name of an index is called a **tag**.
7. To build an index, use the "Create new index" option from the Organize menu on the Database Design screen. Specify a name and expression for the index.
8. To build an index on multiple fields, the fields should be character fields. Enter the names of the fields separated by plus signs.
9. To make an individual index active, select it using the "Order records by index" option from the Organize menu on the Database Design screen. Records in the database file then appear to be sorted in order of the index key.
10. An index may be used to allow rapid retrieval of individual records on the basis of the index key.
11. In general terms, a **view** is a pseudo-table (or pseudo-database file). Although the same is true in dBASE, a view is specifically a saved query.
12. A **one-to-many relationship** between two database files occurs when one record in one of the files is related to many records in the second but each record in the second is related to only one record in the first. The first database file is called the *one* database file and the second is called the *many* database file.
13. To create a view, first create a query that describes exactly the database files, records, and fields you want in the view, and then save the query.
14. To activate a view, highlight it at the Control Center, press Enter, and then select "Use view".
15. Once activated, a view may be used in displays and reports just as though it were a database file.
16. To update any of the data in a view, update the appropriate database file.

STUDENT ASSIGNMENTS

STUDENT ASSIGNMENT 1: True/False

Instructions: Circle T if the statement is true and F if the statement is false.

T F 1. You can use "Modify structure/order" to change the order of records in a database file.
T F 2. It is possible to delete a field from a database file.
T F 3. You want to change the value of a field called SLSRNUMB to 01 for all records on which SLSRNAME is ANN JONES. The simplest way to do this is to use an update query.
T F 4. Indexes provide an efficient alternative to sorting.
T F 5. Indexes allow you to rapidly find database files.
T F 6. The database file on which an index is to be created must be the active file.
T F 7. To create an index on the combination of the ORDNUMB and PARTNUMB fields (both are character fields), define the index expression to be ORDNUMB + PARTNUMB.
T F 8. The "Forward search" option will make use of an index that happens to be active.
T F 9. A database file can only have one index at any given point in time.
T F 10. You are selecting the field or fields on which an index is to be built and you don't remember the names of the fields. You can obtain a list of the available fields by pressing F1 for help.
T F 11. A query is a saved view.
T F 12. In order to relate database files in a view, select the "Create link by pointing" option from the Layout menu.

Student Assignment I (continued)

T F   13. When you create a view, if you don't take some special action, all the fields from all the database files you have selected will be included in the view.

T F   14. You should use the underlying database files and not the view itself when you want to retrieve data from the view.

T F   15. To activate a view, highlight the view at the Control Center, press Enter, and select "Use view".

T F   16. Before you choose the "Create link by pointing" option, the cursor must be positioned in one of the two fields that will link the databases.

STUDENT ASSIGNMENT 2: Multiple Choice

Instructions: Circle the correct response.

1. To change the structure of a database file _____.
   a. you must name the database file when you choose "Modify structure/order"
   b. the database file must be active
   c. there can be no records in the database file
   d. all of the above
2. Which of the following represent benefits to indexes?
   a. they provide an efficient alternative to sorting
   b. they allow you to rapidly find records
   c. they allow you to rapidly find database files
   d. both a and b
3. You are selecting the field or fields on which an index is to be built and you don't remember the names of the fields. You can obtain a list of the available fields by _____.
   a. looking at the screen since such a list is automatically displayed
   b. pressing Shift-F1
   c. pressing F1
   d. typing the word List
4. To begin creating a view, _____.
   a. select <create> in the View column
   b. select <create> in the Queries column
   c. select the "View" option from the Create menu
   d. highlight the name of the view, press Enter, and select "Create"
5. Which option do you use to relate database files in a view?
   a. "Relate database files"
   b. "Link database files"
   c. "Create link by pointing"
   d. "Create relationship"
6. You should use the underlying database files and not the view itself when you want to _____.
   a. retrieve data from the view
   b. update the data in the view
   c. activate the view
   d. delete the view

STUDENT ASSIGNMENT 3: Understanding dBASE Options

Instructions: Explain what happens after you perform each of the following actions.

Problem 1: You highlight a database file at the Control Center, press Enter, and then select "Modify structure/order". Once you arrive at the next screen, you press Enter.

Explanation: _____

_____

_____

Problem 2: You select the "Perform the update" option from the Update menu on the Query Design screen.

Explanation: _____

_____

_____

Problem 3: You select the "Create new index" option from the Organize menu on the Database Design screen. You next select "Index expression" and then press Shift-F1.

Explanation: _____

_____

_____

Problem 4: You select the "Create link by pointing" option from the Layout menu on the Query Design screen.

Explanation: _____

_____

_____

STUDENT ASSIGNMENT 4: Using dBASE

Instructions: Explain how to accomplish each of the following tasks using dBASE.

Problem 1: Increase the length of a field in an existing database file.

Explanation: _____

_____

_____

Problem 2: Add a new field to an existing database file between the second and third fields.

Explanation: _____

_____

_____

Problem 3: Delete the fifth field from an existing database file.

Explanation: _____

_____

_____

Student Assignment 4 (continued)

Problem 4: Create an index on a combination of character fields.

Explanation: _____

_____

_____

Problem 5: Use an index to rapidly find a record.

Explanation: _____

_____

_____

Problem 6. Relate the database files in a view.

Explanation: _____

_____

_____

STUDENT ASSIGNMENT 5: Recovering from Problems

Instructions: In each of the following cases, a problem occurred. Explain the cause of the problem and how it can be corrected.

Problem 1: You attempted to find a record using the "Index key search" option from the Go To menu and were unable to find a record you know is there.

Cause of Problem:_____

_____

Method of Correction: _____

_____

Problem 2: When you display the data in a view, none of the data from the *many* database file matches anything from the *one* database file. You know this is not correct.

Cause of Problem:_____

_____

Method of Correction: _____

_____

Problem 3: You were changing the structure of a database file intending to delete the fifth field. You looked up at your display and found you deleted the fourth field instead.

Cause of Problem:_____

_____

Method of Correction: _____

_____

STUDENT ASSIGNMENT 6: Changing the Structure

Instructions: Change the structure of the DEPT database file. Increase the width of the DEPT_NAME field to accommodate Shipping and Receiving as the name for department 04 and then change the name of this department. Add a third field called NUMB_EMP (number of employees). This field is to be numeric with a width of 3 and no decimal places. Fill in this field appropriately. (The entry for NUMB_EMP for department 01 should be the number of employees in department 01; the entry for department 02 should be the number in department 02; and so on.) Explain the steps to accomplish this.

Steps: _____

_____

_____

STUDENT ASSIGNMENT 7: Using Indexes

Instructions: Create an index called DPNMNUMB on the DEPT_NUMB and NUMBER fields in the EMPLOYEE database file. Activate the EMPLOYEE database file and order records by this new index. List all the records. In what order do they appear? Move to the Edit screen, use the "Index key search" option and enter the value 02. On which record are you now positioned? Press Page Down. What is true of the record now on the screen? What will happen as you continue to press Page Down? Explain the steps to accomplish this.

Steps: _____

_____

_____

STUDENT ASSIGNMENT 8: Creating Views

Instructions: Create a view called EMPDEPT2. Include the NUMBER, NAME, and PAY_RATE fields from the EMPLOYEE database file as well as the DEPT_NAME and NUMB_EMP fields from the DEPT database file in this view. Explain the steps to accomplish this.

Steps: _____

_____

_____

STUDENT ASSIGNMENT 9: Using Views

Instructions: Activate the EMPDEPT2 view. List all the data in the view. Then, list all the fields but only the records on which the pay rate is more than $9.00. Explain the steps to accomplish this.

Steps: _____

_____

_____

STUDENT ASSIGNMENT 10: Changing the Structure

Instructions: Change the structure of the DEPT database file. First, change the name of department 04 back to Shipping. Next, change the width of the DEPT_NAME field back to 10 (its original value) and then delete the NUMB_EMP field. Remove the new index. Finally, erase the EMPDEPT2 view from your disk. (Move to the dot prompt, enter ERASE EMPDEPT2.VUE, and press Enter.) Explain the steps to accomplish this.

Steps: _____

_____

_____

M I N I C A S E S

Instructions: Modify the structure of the CUSTOMER database file that you created in Minicase 1 of Project 1. Change the structure from:

CUSTOMER

CNUM	CNAME	CADDR	BAL	SNAME	STDATE	DSC
124	Adams, Sally	481 Oak,Lansing,MI	419	Gomez, Maria	02/14/90	T
256	Samuel, Anna	215 Pete,Grant,IN	11	Smith, Wilhelm	03/12/90	T
311	Tranh, Tuan	48 College,Ira,IL	200	Brown, Doyle	05/12/90	F
315	Stevens, Ken	914 Cherry,Kent,MI	321	Smith, Wilhelm	07/11/90	T
405	Tao, Chan	519 Watson,Ira,IL	202	Brown, Doyle	11/15/90	F
412	Adams, Sally	16 Elm,Lansing,MI	909	Gomez, Maria	02/03/91	F

to:

CUSTOMER

CNUM	CNAME	CADDR	BAL	SNUM	STDATE	DSC
124	Adams, Sally	481 Oak,Lansing,MI	419	01	02/14/90	T
256	Samuel, Anna	215 Pete,Grant,IN	11	02	03/12/90	T
311	Tranh, Tuan	48 College,Ira,IL	200	03	05/12/90	F
315	Stevens, Ken	914 Cherry,Kent,MI	321	02	07/11/90	T
405	Tao, Chan	519 Watson,Ira,IL	202	03	11/15/90	F
412	Adams, Sally	16 Elm,Lansing,MI	909	01	02/03/91	F

SLSREP

SNUM	SNAME
01	Gomez, Maria
02	Smith, Wilhelm
03	Brown, Doyle

1. Make the following changes.
   a. Expand the length of the CNAME field to accommodate Stevens, Kenneth as the name for customer 315.
   b. Add a second database file containing two fields, SNUM and SNAME and use it to relate sales rep numbers and names.
   c. Remove the SNAME field from the original database file. Add in its place a new field, SNUM.
   d. Then, fill in the correct values in the new field.
2. Perform the following tasks. Whenever you are asked to list something, press Shift-F9 to obtain a printed copy.
   a. Create the new database file using the name SLSREP. The SNUM field is a CHARACTER field with width 2. The SNAME field is a CHARACTER field with width 14. The entry in the Index column for the SNUM field should be Y. The entry for the other field should be N.
   b. Add the indicated sales rep numbers and names.
   c. Change the length of the CNAME field in the CUSTOMER database file to accommodate Stevens, Kenneth. Then, make the change.
   d. Add the SNUM field to the CUSTOMER database file following the BAL field. The index entry should be Y.
   e. Fill in the SNUM field in the CUSTOMER database file with appropriate data (01 on records where SNAME is Gomez, Maria, 02 on records where SNAME is Smith, Wilhelm, and so on).
   f. Delete the SNAME field from the CUSTOMER database file.
   g. Create an index on the CNAME field in the CUSTOMER database file. Use it to list the records in CNAME order.
   h. Create an index on the combination of SNUM and CNAME fields in the CUSTOMER database file. Use it to list the records ordered by CNAME within SNUM.
   i. Create an index on the CNUM field in the CUSTOMER database file. Use this index and the "Index key search" option to locate the record containing customer 315. Display the record. Explain the steps to locate the record.

   Steps: _____
   _____

   _____

   j. Create a view called CUSTVIEW. Include both the CUSTOMER and SLSREP database files in this view. Use the SNUM field in both files to relate the two. Include all fields from the CUSTOMER database file except SNUM in this view. Include the SNAME field from the SLSREP database file.
   k. Using this view, display the customer number, name, balance, and sales rep name for all customers.
   l. Using this view, display the customer number, name, balance, and sales rep name for all customers whose credit limit is at least $500.
   m. What do you think about the change that was made? Is it a good idea? What are the advantages? What are the disadvantages?

   _____

   _____

MINICASE 2: Parts

Instructions: Modify the structure of the PART database file that you created in Minicase 2 of Project 1. Change the structure from:

PART

PNUMB	PDESC	UOH	ITEMCLASS	WHSE	PRICE	LSDATE	DISC
AX12	HAIR DRYER	52	HAIR CARE	3	27.99	02/12/92	T
AZ52	SKATES	20	SPORTING GOODS	2	49.99	01/15/92	F
BA74	DARTBOARD	40	SPORTING GOODS	1	34.99	11/02/91	T
BH22	CURL. IRON	95	HAIR CARE	3	10.95	01/19/92	T
BT04	CONV. OVEN	11	APPLIANCES	2	149.99	08/25/91	F
.							
.							
.							

to:

PART

PNUMB	PDESC	UOH	ICDE	WHSE	PRICE	LSDATE	DISC
AX12	HAIR DRYER	52	HC	3	27.99	02/12/92	T
AZ52	SKATES	20	SG	2	49.99	01/15/92	F
BA74	DARTBOARD	40	SG	1	34.99	11/02/91	T
BH22	CURLING IRON	95	HC	3	10.95	01/19/92	T
BT04	CONVECTION OVEN	11	AP	2	149.99	08/25/91	F
.							
.							
.							

CLASS

ICDE	ITEMCLSS
AP	APPLIANCES
HC	HAIR CARE
SG	SPORTING GOODS

1. Make the following changes.
   a. Expand the length of the PDESC field to accommodate CONVECTION OVEN as the description for part BT04.
   b. Add a second database file containing two fields, ICDE and ITEMCLSS, and use it to relate item class codes and item class descriptions.
   c. Remove the ITEMCLSS field from the original database file. Add a new field, ICDE, in its place.
   d. Then, fill in the correct values in the new field.
2. Perform the following tasks. Whenever you are asked to list something, press Shift-F9 to obtain a printed copy.
   a. Create the new database file using the name CLASS. The ICDE field is a CHARACTER field with width 2. The ITEMCLSS field is a CHARACTER field with width 15. The entry in the Index column for the ICDE field should be Y. The entry for the other field should be N.

b. Add the indicated class codes and descriptions.

c. Change the length of the PDESC field in the PART database file to accommodate CONVECTION OVEN. Then, make the change. In addition, change the description of part BH22 to CURLING IRON, and the description of part CX11 to COFFEE MAKER.

d. Add the ICDE field to the PART database file following the UOH field. The index entry should be Y.

e. Fill in the ICDE field in the PART database file with appropriate data (AP on records where ITEMCLSS is APPLIANCES, HC on records where PDESC is HAIR CARE, and so on).

f. Delete the ITEMCLSS field from the PART database file.

g. Create an index on the PDESC field in the PART database file. Use it to list the records in PDESC order.

h. Create an index on the combination of ICDE and PDESC fields in the PART database database file. Use it to list the records ordered by PDESC within ICDE.

i. Create an index on the PNUMB field in the PART database file. Use this index and the "Index key search" option to locate the record containing part BT04. Display the record. Explain the steps to locate the record.

Steps: _____

_____

_____

j. Create a view called PARTVIEW. Include both the PART and CLASS database files in this view. Use the ICDE field in both files to relate the two. Include all fields from the PART database file except ICDE in the view. Include the ITEMCLSS field from the CLASS database file.

k. Using this view, display the part number, description, item class, price, and last sale date for all parts.

l. Using this view, display the part number, description, item class, price, and last sale date for all parts with at least 50 units on hand.

m. What do you think about the change that was made? Is it a good idea? What are the advantages? What are the disadvantages?

_____

_____

MINICASE 3: Movies

Instructions: Modify the structure of the MOVIE database file that you created in Minicase 3 of Project 1. Change the structure from:

MOVIE

MNUM	MTITLE	YEAR	MTYPE	LNG	DNAME	BW
001	Annie Hall	1977	COMEDY	93	Allen, Woody	F
002	Dr. Strangelove	1964	COMEDY	93	Kubrick, Stanley	T
003	Clockwork Orange	1971	SCI FI	136	Kubrick, Stanley	F
004	North by Northwest	1959	SUSPEN	136	Hitchcock, Alfred	F
005	Rope	1948	SUSPEN	80	Hitchcock, Alfred	F
.						
.						
014	2001: A Space Ody.	1968	SCI FI	141	Kubrick, Stanley	F
.						
.						
.						

Minicase 3 (continued)

to:

MOVIE

MNUM	MTITLE	YEAR	MTYPE	LNG	DNUM	BW
001	Annie Hall	1977	COMEDY	93	01	F
002	Dr. Strangelove	1964	COMEDY	93	04	T
003	Clockwork Orange	1971	SCI FI	136	04	F
004	North by Northwest	1959	SUSPEN	136	03	F
005	Rope	1948	SUSPEN	80	03	F
.						
.						
014	2001: A Space Odyssey	1968	SCI FI	141	04	F
.						
.						

DIRECTOR

DNUM	DNAME
01	Allen, Woody
02	Ford, John
03	Hitchcock, Alfred
04	Kubrick, Stanley

1. Make the following changes.
   a. Expand the length of the MTITLE field to accommodate *2001: A Space Odyssey* as the name for movie 14.
   b. Add a second database file containing two fields, DNUM and DNAME, and use it to relate director numbers and names.
   c. Remove the DNAME field from the original database file. Add a new field, DNUM, in its place.
   d. Then, fill in the correct values in the new field.
2. Perform the following tasks. Whenever you are asked to list something, press Shift-F9 to obtain a printed copy.
   a. Create the new database file using the name DIRECTOR. The DNUM field is a CHARACTER field with width 2. The DNAME field is a CHARACTER field with width 18. The entry in the Index column for the DNUM field should be Y. The entry for the other field should be N.
   b. Add the indicated director numbers and names.
   c. Change the length of the MTITLE field in the MOVIE database file to accommodate *2001: A Space Odyssey*. Then, make the change.
   d. Add the DNUM field to the MOVIE database file following the LNG field. The index entry should be Y.
   e. Fill in the DNUM field in the MOVIE database file with appropriate data (01 on records where DNAME is Allen, Woody, 02 on records where DNAME is Ford, John, and so on).
   f. Delete the DNAME field from the MOVIE database file.
   g. Create an index on the MTITLE field in the MOVIE database file. Use it to list the records in MTITLE order.
   h. Create an index on the combination of MTYPE and MTITLE fields in the MOVIE database database file. Use it to list the records ordered by MTITLE within MTYPE.

i. Create an index on the MNUM field in the MOVIE database file. Use this index and the "Index key search" option to locate the record containing movie 005. Display the record. Explain the steps to locate the record.

Steps: _____

_____

_____

j. Create a view called MOVVIEW. Include both the MOVIE and DIRECTOR database files in this view. Use the DNUM field in both files to relate the two. Include all fields from the MOVIE database file except DNUM in the view. Include the DNAME field from the DIRECTOR database file.
k. Using this view, display the movie number, title, type, length, and director number for all movies.
l. Using this view, display the movie number, title, type, length, and director number for all movies which are in black and white.
m. What do you think about the change that was made? Is it a good idea? What are the advantages? What are the disadvantages?

_____

_____

Instructions: Modify the structure of the BOOK database file that you created in Minicase 4 of Project 1. Change the structure from:

BOOK

CODE	TITLE	AUTHOR	PUBLISHER	TYP	PRICE	PB	OH
0189	Kane and Abel	Jeffrey Archer	Pocket Books	FIC	4.95	T	2
1351	Cujo	Stephen King	Signet	HOR	5.95	T	1
138X	Death on the Nile	Ag. Christie	Bantam Books	MYS	3.50	T	3
2226	Ghost from Grand	Ar. C. Clarke	Bantam Books	SFI	17.95	F	3
2295	Four Past Midnight	Stephen King	Viking	HOR	22.95	F	0
.							
.							
.							

to:

BOOK

CODE	TITLE	AUTHOR	PCDE	TYP	PRICE	PB	OH
0189	Kane and Abel	Jeffrey Archer	PB	FIC	4.95	T	2
1351	Cujo	Stephen King	SI	HOR	5.95	T	1
138X	Death on the Nile	Ag. Christie	BB	MYS	3.50	T	3
2226	Ghost from Grand Bank	Ar. C. Clarke	BB	SFI	17.95	F	3
2295	Four Past Midnight	Stephen King	VI	HOR	22.95	F	0
.							
.							
.							

Minicase 4 (continued)

PUBLISH

PCDE	PUBLISHER
BB	Bantam Books
PB	Pocket Books
SI	Signet
SS	Simon and Shu.
VI	Viking

1. Make the following changes.
   a. Expand the length of the TITLE field to accommodate *Ghost from the Grand Bank* as the title for the book whose code is 2226.
   b. Add a second database file containing two fields, PCDE and PUBLISHER, and use it to relate publisher codes with the names of the publishers.
   c. Remove the PUBLISHER field from the original database file. Add a new field, PCDE, in its place.
   d. Then, fill in the correct values in the new field.
2. Perform the following tasks. Whenever you are asked to list something, press Shift-F9 to obtain a printed copy.
   a. Create the new database file using the name PUBLISH. The PCDE field is a CHARACTER field with width 2. The PUBLISHER field is a CHARACTER field with width 14. The entry in the Index column for the PCDE field should be Y. The entry for the other field should be N.
   b. Add the indicated publisher codes and names.
   c. Change the length of the TITLE field in the BOOK database file to accommodate *Ghost from the Grand Bank*. Then, make the change. In addition, change the title of the book whose code is 2766 to *The Prodigal Daughter*.
   d. Add the PCDE field to the BOOK database file following the AUTHOR field. The index entry should be Y.
   e. Fill in the PCDE field in the BOOK database file with appropriate data (BB on records where PUBLISHER is Bantam Books, PB on records where PUBLISHER is Pocket Books, and so on).
   f. Delete the PUBLISHER field from the BOOK database file.
   g. Create an index on the TITLE field in the BOOK database file. Use it to list the records in TITLE order.
   h. Create an index on the combination of TYP and TITLE fields in the BOOK database database file. Use it to list the records ordered by TITLE within TYP.
   i. Create an index on the CODE field in the BOOK database file. Use this index and the SEEK option to locate the record containing book 2226. Display the record. Explain the steps to locate the record.

      Steps: _____

      _____

      _____

   j. Create a view called BOOKVIEW. Include both the BOOK and PUBLISH database files in this view. Use the PCDE field in both files to relate the two. Include all fields from the BOOK database file except PCDE in the view. Include the PUBLISHER field from the PUBLISH database file.
   k. Using this view, display the book code, title, author, publisher, and price for all books.
   l. Using this view, display the book code, title, author, publisher, and price for all books whose type is FIC.
   m. What do you think about the change that was made? Is it a good idea? What are the advantages? What are the disadvantages?

      _____

      _____

dBASE IV VERSION 1.1

PROJECT 6

Generating Applications

OBJECTIVES

You will have mastered the material in this project when you can:

◆ Create a custom form

◆ Create a new view from an existing view

◆ Modify a report to accommodate a change in structure

◆ Create an application using the applications generator

◆ Run an application you have created

You have come a long way in these projects. You can now create database files, add new data to your database files, change existing data, and delete records from your database files. You can query those files in a variety of ways. You can create reports that present data from your files in a professional looking manner. You know how to create indexes to speed retrieval and also to order the records in your files. You have learned to create views that relate data in more than one database file.

The only problem is that you have to go through the Control Center, remembering the correct series of steps to execute, each time you want to do use your database. What you need to do, however, is to create your own menu system, in which all you have to do is select an option from a menu. This way you could put all your updates, reports, and so on together in one single system. Such a system is called an **application system**, or simply an **application**.

Creating an application system could be a lengthy and complex process. Fortunately, there are tools, called applications generators, whose sole purpose is to enable us to create application systems quickly and easily. dBASE contains such an applications generator, and you will use it in this project to create an application system for the EMPLOYEE database. You will also learn to create custom forms for data entry as well as to modify reports when the structure of the underlying database changes. Specifically, you will modify your reports to incorporate the changes you made to the structure of the EMPLOYEE database file in Project 5.

DESIGNING APPLICATIONS

 Before you can create an application system, you need to do seven things.

1. Decide what database files are needed and what indexes should be created for those database files.
2. Create all these database files and indexes.
3. Create a custom data entry form for each database file.
4. Decide what reports you require.
5. If any report requires data from more than one database file, create a view for the report.
6. Create the reports themselves.
7. Determine what menus you need and what the choices in these menus will be.

In the application system we create in this project, the main menu will have four choices, "Updates," "Reports," "Utilities," and "Exit." Each of these menus leads to other appropriate menus. You would pick the "Updates" option to see a menu allowing the various possible types of updates to the database. Picking "Reports" allows you to select from a list of available reports. "Utilities" leads to a menu of such functions as backing up the various database files. Other Utilities menu options allow you to repair any indexes that have become damaged (a real possibility in dBASE). Finally, you would select the Exit menu to leave the system. You are given two choices: "Return to dBASE IV," which takes you back to the Control Center, or "Exit to DOS," which takes you out of dBASE and directly back to DOS.

CREATING CUSTOM FORMS

You have already used the Edit screen to add new records to a database file as well as to change existing records. When you did, you used a form on the screen to enter data. Although the form did provide you some assistance in the task, the form was not particularly attractive. The fields were simply stacked on top of each other. The names shown on the screen were the names of the fields, which are not as descriptive as we might like. In this section, we create custom forms that you can use in place of the ones normally supplied by dBASE. We create custom forms for the EMPLOYEE and DEPT database files. Just as you did with reports, if you happen to make some mistakes as you are creating the form and wish to simply start over, select "Abandon changes and exit" and answer yes to the question of whether you want to abandon your work. You can then start fresh.

Using Quick Layout

To design a form, the database file for which the form is intended should be active, so you should activate EMPLOYEE. Next, select <create> in the Forms column to begin creating your custom form. At this point, your screen should look like Figure 6-1. Although you can create a form totally from scratch, it is usually simplest to let dBASE get you started. Select "Quick layout" (remember that you have a similar choice when you create reports).

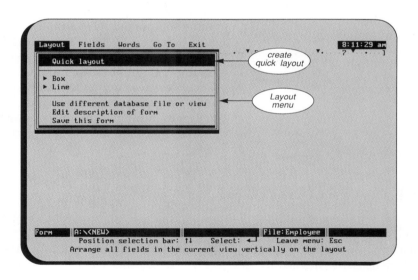

FIGURE 6-1
Forms Design screen

At this point, dBASE creates the form shown in Figure 6-2. (Does it look familiar? It is precisely the form you normally see on the Edit screen. Just as with reports, the 9s and Xs represent the fields.) We will now modify this form to produce the custom form we want.

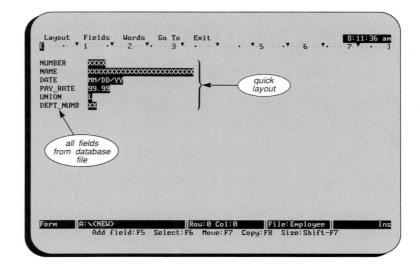

FIGURE 6-2
Forms Design screen

Adding Blank Lines

Let's begin by adding blank lines as shown in Figure 6-3. First move the cursor to the beginning of the word NUMBER and press Ctrl-N twice. Next, move the cursor to the beginning of NAME and press Ctrl-N twice. Move the cursor again to the beginning of PAY_RATE and press Ctrl-N. Repeat the process for UNION and DEPT_NUMB. Notice that the blank lines separating the fields make the form easier to read. (In this form, NAME and DATE do not have a blank line in between them. We often do this to group fields functionally. For example, we would probably not put blank lines between such fields as NAME, ADDRESS, CITY, STATE, and ZIP since they form a functional unit.)

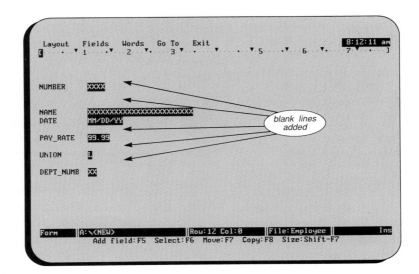

FIGURE 6-3
Forms Design screen

Moving Fields and Characters

It is now time to move the fields. When you moved a field or text in a report, you selected it by moving the cursor to the field, pressing F6, and then pressing Enter. You then pressed F7 (for "Move"), moved the cursor to the new location, and pressed Enter. You do exactly the same thing here.

Select the NUMBER field (the XXXX) and then move it to the location shown in Figure 6-4. Don't worry if you are not in precisely the same column as the one shown on the screen. The main thing is to line up the other fields with the position in which you place this one.

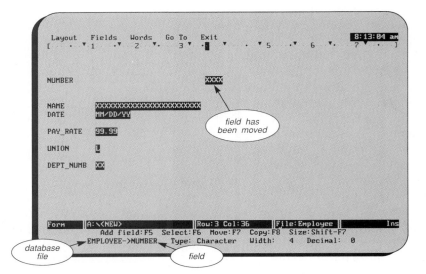

FIGURE 6-4
Forms Design screen

Next, move the remaining fields into the positions shown in Figure 6-5.

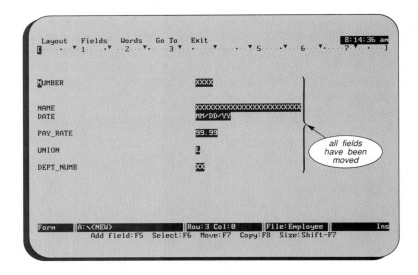

FIGURE 6-5
Forms Design screen

The words NUMBER, NAME, DATE, and so on are called prompts. They prompt the user to enter data and indicate the type of data that is to be entered. When the cursor is next to the word NAME, for example, the user knows it is time to enter a name. We certainly want prompts on our form. We would like them to be a little more descriptive, however.

At this point, go back to the prompts (NUMBER, NAME, DATE, and so on) and replace them with the ones shown in Figure 6-6. To delete a character, move the cursor to it and press the Delete key. To insert a new character, move the cursor to the desired location and type the character. Thus, to replace NUMBER by Employee Number:, move the cursor to the N in NUMBER, press the Delete key key six times, and then type Employee Number.

Next, move the characters you have typed to the positions shown in Figure 6-7. To move a series of characters, first select the series you want to move by placing the cursor at the first character, pressing F6 ("Select"), moving the cursor to the last character, and pressing Enter. Next, press F7 ("Move"), move the cursor to the new location, and press Enter. Notice a faint strip that is exactly the size of the selected portion. This strip moves right along with the cursor, helping you judge exactly where you should position the cursor to complete the move.

Finally, let's help anyone who uses this form to know that they should enter only T or F in the union field. Type (T or F) at the position shown on the screen in Figure 6-7.

Adding Boxes

We can improve the look of a form by adding boxes to set off important portions. In this form, we place a double box around the employee number and a single box around the rest. Before you do, move the cursor to the first position in the line immediately preceding the employee number. Next, choose the "Box" option from the Layout menu (Figure 6-8).

You are next asked if you want a single or double line, or if you want to use some special character. Choose "Double line". You are then instructed to move the cursor to the upper left corner of the box and press Enter. In our case, the upper left corner is at the beginning of the line above the line containing the employee number. You are already in this position, so press Enter. You are then instructed to "Stretch box with cursor keys, complete with Enter". Move the cursor to the end of the line below the line that contains the employee number and press Enter. The box is now in place (Figure 6-9).

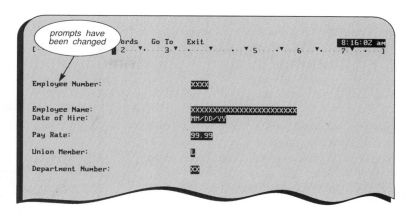

FIGURE 6-6 Forms Design screen

FIGURE 6-7 Forms Design screen

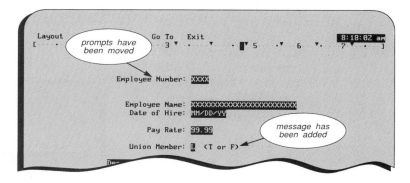

FIGURE 6-8 Forms Design screen

FIGURE 6-9 Forms Design screen

Now place a single box in the position shown in Figure 6-10. The only difference in the process is that you choose "Single line" rather than "Double line."

Saving the Form

You save your form exactly as you have saved your reports and queries. Choose "Save changes and exit" from the Exit menu and then give a name that is descriptive of the form. In your case, call it EMPLOYEE to emphasize the fact that it is a form for the EMPLOYEE database.

You may be wondering if giving a database file the same name as a form could cause a problem. After all, both files are stored on your disk and files stored on a disk must have unique names. Fortunately, this is not a problem because the files are of different types, and consequently dBASE assigns them different extensions. Thus, as far as DOS is concerned, they do have different names.

When you have returned to the Control Center, you will see your form in the Forms column (Figure 6-11).

Creating a Second Form

At this point, activate the DEPT database file and create a form for the DEPT database file as shown in Figure 6-12. Call this form DEPT.

Using the Form

When you first create a form, the form is active. Activating a different database file, activating a different form, or leaving dBASE will deactivate the form. To reactivate the form later, you should first activate the corresponding database file. You should do this now using the EMPLOYEE database file as shown in Figure 6-13. Next, move the highlight to the name of the form in the Forms column and press Enter.

You are then given two choices: "Display data" and "Modify layout" (Figure 6-14). If you wanted to change the layout of the form, you would choose "Modify layout." But let's suppose you just want to use the form; choose "Display data", and the form is again considered to be active.

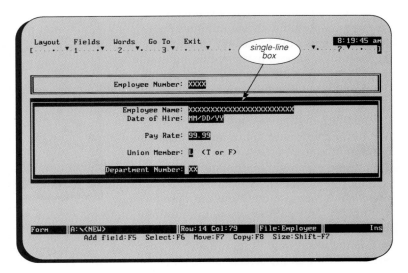

FIGURE 6-10 Forms Design screen

FIGURE 6-11 Control Center

FIGURE 6-12 Forms Design screen

When the form is active and you press F2 to move to the Edit screen, the normal dBASE form is replaced with your own custom form (Figure 6-15). Notice that the form shown on the screen is precisely the one you created. Other than the new form, there is no difference in the use of the Edit screen. You can still use it to add records and to make changes exactly as you did before. You can still press Page Down to move to the next record. You can still use the Go To menu to find records. Once you have seen the form, return to the Control Center in the usual manner.

CREATING VIEWS

A report that uses only a single database file causes no problem when we create the application. If a report requires data from more than one database file, however, we need to use a view for the report. If the data for the report must be sorted in some particular order, we must make sure the view is sorted appropriately.

We currently have two payroll reports, REPORT1 and REPORT2, that we created earlier. Both reports were created using the fields in the original EMPLOYEE database file. We changed the structure of this file in Project 5, making these reports invalid.

The main problem with the payroll reports is that they include the DEPART-MENT field which is no longer part of EMPLOYEE. Remember, we replaced DEPARTMENT by DEPT_NUMB (department number) and created a separate database file (DEPT) that contained DEPT_NUMB and DEPT_NAME. The DEPT_NAME field is the one we would like to use in place of DEPARTMENT. Thus, we need fields from *both* the EMPLOYEE database file *and* the DEPT database file. Therefore, we need to use views.

View for REPORT1

We already have a view, EMPDEPT, that contains all the fields we want, but it is not sorted in the order we would like. Therefore, we will create a new view that is just like EMPDEPT except that it is sorted correctly.

FIGURE 6-13 Control Center

FIGURE 6-14 Control Center

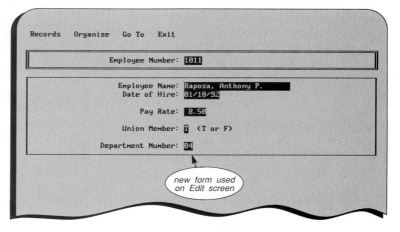

FIGURE 6-15 Edit screen

The simplest way to do this is to highlight EMPDEPT in the Queries column, press Enter, and then select "Modify query". You should then see the Query Design screen displaying the query you created for EMPDEPT (Figure 6-16). (You might be at a different position within the skeleton for EMPLOYEE, in which case your screen would be slightly different.)

Now we want to modify this query so that it is appropriate for the first of the payroll reports (the one sorted by name). Move the highlight to the NAME field and select the "Sort on this field" option from the Fields menu. (Remember that this is how we sort views.) Your screen should be similar to Figure 6-17.

If we now select "Save changes and exit" from the Exit menu, the view EMPDEPT would be changed. Rather than do this, let's create a new view. Select the "Save this query" option from the Layout menu (Figure 6-18). The name of the current view is displayed on the screen. Let's use the name REPORT1 for the new view to make it clear that we are designing this view to use with the REPORT1 report. (As with database files and forms, the fact that you are giving a view the same name as a report does not cause a problem.) To enter this name for the new view, repeatedly press the Backspace key until the name EMPDEPT.QBE is deleted. Then, enter REPORT1 and press Enter. (You don't need to include the QBE extension. dBASE does this automatically.)

View for REPORT2

Now let's create a view for the other payroll report, REPORT2. The only difference between this view and view REPORT2 is that REPORT2 is sorted by name within department number. Remember that we created a special index for sorting on this combination. We can use that index here.

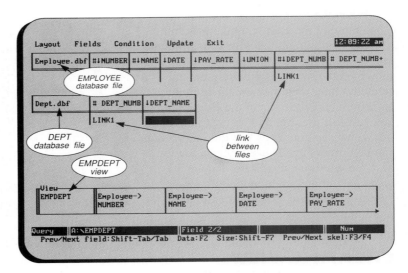

FIGURE 6-16 Query Design screen

FIGURE 6-17 Query Design screen

FIGURE 6-18 Query Design screen

First, remove the "Asc1" from the NAME column by pressing Ctrl-Y. Next, use the Tab key to move to the column for the special index on DEPT_NUMB + NAME. Select the "Sort on this field" option from the Fields menu. Your screen should then look like Figure 6-19. Save this query as REPORT2 in exactly the same manner you saved REPORT1. You are done, so you can leave the Query Design screen by selecting the "Abandon changes and exit" option from the Exit menu.

Your screen should look like Figure 6-20. Notice that the two queries you created now appear in the Queries column.

CREATING REPORTS

◆ We'll now create three reports. The first two are modified versions of REPORT1 and REPORT2 that work with the views you just created. The third is a simple list of employees and is the report we will include in our application.

Modifying REPORT1

To correct the weekly payroll report (REPORT1), we need to replace the DEPARTMENT field with the DEPT_NAME field. First, activate the REPORT1 view because we are using this view for the report. Next, highlight REPORT1 in the Reports column, press Enter, and select "Modify layout" (Figure 6-21). Then, select "Current view" from the choices dBASE presents you.

Before you see a report on the screen, you will see a message "DEPARTMENT not found in REPORT1". This message indicates that the DEPARTMENT field in the report is not present in the view. We will correct this problem in a moment, so press any key to remove the message from the screen.

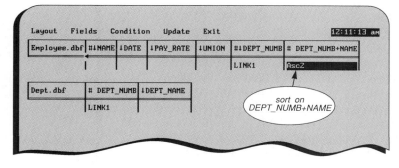

FIGURE 6-19 Query Design screen

FIGURE 6-20 Control Center

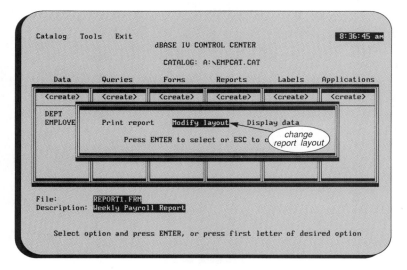

FIGURE 6-21 Control Center

To correct the problem, first move the highlight to the DEPARTMENT field (the second field in the detail band). Select the field by pressing F6 and then Enter. Then, delete the field by pressing the Delete key. The DEPARTMENT field has now been removed. Now choose the "Add field" option from the Fields menu. The list of available fields includes all fields in the view (Figure 6-22). Select the DEPT_NAME field.

You then see the same box you have seen before whenever you added fields. Since all the details in it are acceptable as they are, press Ctrl-End to complete the process. The new field has now been added. This is the only change we needed to make, so select the "Save changes and exit" option from the Exit menu. The first report is now complete.

FIGURE 6-22   Report Design screen

Modifying REPORT2

To correct the departmental version of the report (REPORT2), we also need to replace the DEPARTMENT field with the DEPT_NAME field. In addition, we need to change the group intro because it contains the DEPARTMENT field. Finally, we need to change the way the report is grouped because we used the DEPARTMENT field for grouping.

To make these changes, return to the Control Center and activate the REPORT2 view. Then, highlight REPORT2 in the Reports column, press Enter, and select "Modify layout". Again you will see a message indicating that DEPARTMENT is not found in the view. Press any key to remove the message from the screen and move on.

Replace the DEPARTMENT field in the detail band with DEPT_NAME as you did in the other report. Next, remove the DEPARTMENT field from the group intro band. Rather than simply replace it with the DEPT_NAME field, however, let's include both DEPT_NUMB and DEPT_NAME. First, add the DEPT_NUMB field in the position shown in Figure 6-23. (The DEPT_NUMB field is represented by the pair of Xs in the group intro band.)

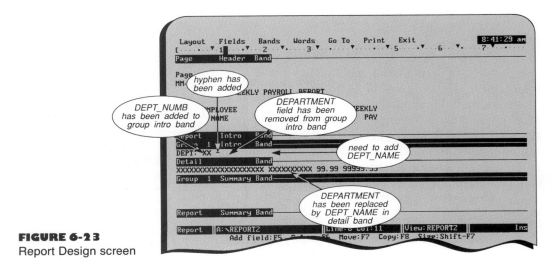

FIGURE 6-23
Report Design screen

Next, add the hyphen shown in Figure 6-23 by moving the cursor to that position and typing a hyphen. Finally, move the cursor one position to the right and add the DEPT_NAME field.

All that remains is to change the field on which grouping is to take place. Move the cursor into the line labeled "Group 1 Intro Band" and select the "Modify group" option from the Bands menu (Figure 6-24).

FIGURE 6-24
Report Design screen

Your screen should then look like Figure 6-25.

FIGURE 6-25
Report Design screen

Now, change DEPARTMENT to DEPT_NUMB because we want to group by department number. Press Enter and then select DEPT_NUMB. When you are done, save your changes. The report is now complete. This new version of the report is shown in Figure 6-26.

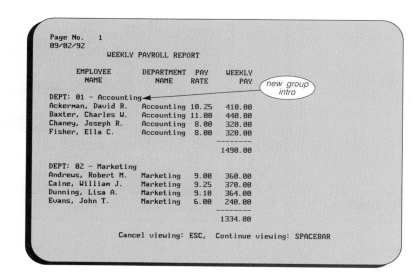

FIGURE 6-26
Viewing report on screen

Creating the Employee List

Let's now create the employee list that we will use as the report for our application. First, activate the EMPLOYEE database file, select <create> in the Reports column, select "Quick layout" (using Column layout), and then save the report as EMPLIST. This report is not particularly well laid out, but we can use it to illustrate the use of reports in applications.

APPLICATIONS

Creating Applications

The dBASE applications generator is a large and powerful tool with many options. We will use one specific option to generate what is called a *quick* application. This application will contain options to add records to our database file, edit or delete the records in the database file, remove deleted records from the database file, reindex the database file, and print a report. Unfortunately, we can only include one report in this application and that report can only consist of data from the database file. We cannot use a view to include data from other database files in this report. Of course, we can still produce such reports from the Control Center.

Before you create this application, make sure your EMPLOYEE database file is active. Then, select <create> in the Applications column. Next, a dBASE prompt will ask you if you want to create a dBASE program or an application with the applications generator. Select "Applications Generator".

Your screen should now look similar to Figure 6-27, although the entries that you see in this figure will not yet appear on your screen. This is the screen on which we enter basic information concerning our application. Make the entries as shown in the figure: enter EMPAPP as the name of the application; Employee Application System as the description; EMPLOYEE for the database/view; EMPLOYEE for the "Set INDEX to" entry; and NUMBER for order. After each entry, press Enter. When you are done, press Ctrl-End.

When you are making these entries for your own applications in the future, you can assign your own application name and description. You will not need to change the menu type or enter a menu name. You will enter the name of the database file that your application will use for both the "Database/view" and "Set INDEX to" entries. When you enter the name of your database file, you can either type the name or press Shift-F1. Pressing Shift-F1 produces a *pick list*, a list of available files. You can then choose the one you want from the list. Finally, you will enter the tag of the index you want to use to order the records. This is also the index that you will use if you select the "Seek" option when you are editing records.

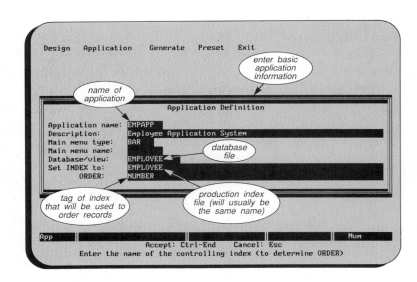

FIGURE 6-27
Application Design screen

You will next see the screen shown in Figure 6-28. This is the Application Design screen. The only option you need on this screen is the "Generate quick application" from the Application menu. Select this option now. Your screen should look like Figure 6-29.

Most of the entries you need to make in the box on the screen have already been made for you, based on the information you entered earlier. The only other entries you will need to make are the screen format file and the report format file.

Press Enter to move the cursor to "Screen format file". Enter EMPLOYEE (the name of the screen format file) and press Enter. Your cursor should now be on the "Report format file". Enter EMPLIST (the name of your employee report) and press Enter. In both cases, you could press Shift-F1 to produce a pick list, and then pick the entries you want from the list instead of typing the entry. You are now done with this screen, so press Ctrl-End.

You will next see a prompt asking you if you want to *generate* your application. We have been specifying the various details concerning our application. To actually use the application, however, you need to run a program. One of the functions of the applications generator is to generate (create) such a program—a program that matches the details you have specified.

Select "Yes". The applications generator will now create this program for you. Once this process has finished, a prompt will instruct you to press any key. Press any key, and then select the "Save changes and exit" option from the Exit menu. You will be returned to the Control Center, and your application will appear in the Applications column.

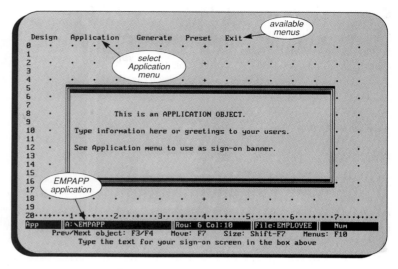

FIGURE 6-28 Application Design screen

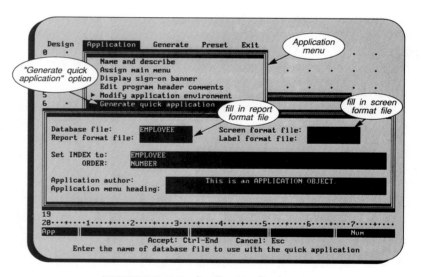

FIGURE 6-29 Application Design screen

If you ever find that you need to change anything concerning your application, highlight the application and press Enter. A prompt will then give you two choices: "Run application" and "Modify application". Select "Modify application," and you will be returned to your application with only your sign-on message visible.

Again select the "Generate quick application" option from the Application menu. Once you have made the necessary changes, press Ctrl-End. A prompt again asks you if you want to generate the application. In the process, you will see a message indicating that the program to be generated already exists. You are asked if the new application can overwrite the old one. Since this is exactly what you want, answer Y (Yes) and press Enter. At this point, the generation proceeds. When it is complete, select "Save all changes and exit" from the Exit menu, and you are returned to the Control Center.

Running Applications

To run an application you have created, select the application in the Applications column. You will then be asked if you want to run the application or modify it. Select "Run application". For security reasons a dBASE prompt then asks you if you are sure you want to run the application. Answer Yes.

You should see your application menu (Figure 6-30). If you select "Add Information", you will be able to add new records to EMPLOYEE using your form. If you select "Change Information", you can edit existing records using your form. The "Browse Information" option takes you to the Browse screen. If you exit any of these options, you will be returned directly to your Application menu.

The "Discard Marked Records" option removes any records you have previously marked. The "Reindex Database" option recreates any indexes. The "Reindex Database" option is convenient if you ever receive error messages concerning indexes. Simply select this option and the problems should disappear. For either of these options, all you do is select the option. The operation will occur, and you will be returned to your Application menu.

The only option that requires any extra steps is "Print Report". Select this option, and you will see the screen shown in Figure 6-31. This screen gives you the option of starting your report at a particular record. If you want all the records, and in all probability you always will, simply select "Return". You then see one final menu (Figure 6-32) on which you identify where you would like your report to be sent. If you would like the report printed, select "Printer". If not, select "Screen". When you are instructed to "Press any key," do just that. You will then be returned to your Application menu.

Feel free to try any other options at this time. Once you are done, you can leave your application by selecting "Exit From Empapp". You are then be returned to the Control Center.

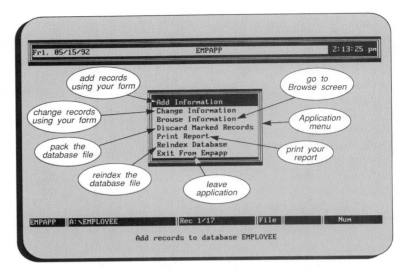

FIGURE 6-30 Running an application

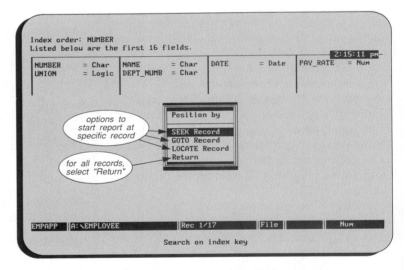

FIGURE 6-31 Application Design screen

FIGURE 6-32 Application Design screen

PROJECT SUMMARY

In Project 6 you learned how to create custom forms, modify existing views and reports, and create applications. All the activities that you learned for this project are summarized in the Quick Reference following Project 6. The following is a summary of the keystroke sequence we used in Project 6.

SUMMARY OF KEYSTROKES — PROJECT 6

STEPS	KEY(S) PRESSED	RESULTS
1	DBASE ← [At DOS prompt]	Starts dBASE.
2	↓↓ [To highlight EMPLOYEE] ← ←	Activates EMPLOYEE database file.
3	→ → ←	Begins screen design.
4	←	Uses quick layout.
5	↓ Ctrl-N Ctrl-N ↓↓↓ Ctrl-N Ctrl-N ↓ [Press 4 times] Ctrl-N ↓↓ Ctrl-N ↓↓ Ctrl-N	Inserts blank lines.
6	↑[Press 9 times] →[Press 11 times] F6 ← F7 →[Press 25 times] ← ↓↓↓ ← ← F6 ← F7 →[Press 25 times] ← ↓ ←[Press 18 times] F6 ← F7 →[Press 25 times] ← ↓↓ ←[Press 21 times] F6 ← F7 →[Press 25 times] ← ↓↓ ←[Press 25 times] F6 ← F7 →[Press 25 times] ← ↓↓ ←[Press 24 times] F6 ← F7 →[Press 25 times] ←	Moves fields.
7	↑[Press 10 times] ←[Press 36 times] Delete [Press 6 times] Employee Number: ↓↓↓ ←[Press 16 times] Delete [Press 4 times]Employee Name: ↓ ←[Press 14 times] Delete [Press 4 times]Date of Hire: ↓↓ ←[Press 13 times] Delete [Press 8 times]Pay Rate: ↓↓ ←[Press 9 times] Delete [Press 5 times]Union Member: ↓↓ ←[Press 13 times] Delete [Press 9 times]Department Number:	Changes prompts.
8	↑[Press 10 times] ←[Press 18 times] F6 →[Press 15 times] ← F7 →[Press 4 times] ← ↓↓↓ ←[Press 19 times] F6 → [Press 13 times] ← F7 →[Press 8 times] ← ↓ ←[Press 21 times] F6 →[Press 12 times] ← F7 →[Press 10 times] ← ↓↓ ←[Press 22 times] F6 →[Press 8 times] ← F7 → [Press 18 times] ← ↓↓ ←[Press 26 times] F6 →[Press 12 times] ← F7 →[Press 10 times] ← ↓↓ ←[Press 22 times] F6 →[Press 17 times] ← F7 ← Y ↑↑ →[Press 22 times](T or F)	Moves prompts.
9	↑[Press 9 times] ←[To first column] F10 ↓ ← ↓ ← ← ↓↓ → [To last column] ← ↓ ←[To first column] F10 ← ↑ ← ← ↓ [Press 9 times] →[To last colunn] ←	Enters boxes.
10	F10 →[Press 4 times] ← EMPLOYEE ←	Saves and names your form.
11	← ← ↓ ← ←	Activates DEPT.

(continued)

SUMMARY OF KEYSTROKES — PROJECT 6 (continued)

STEPS	KEY(S) PRESSED	RESULTS
12	→ → ←	Begins screen design.
13	←	Uses quick layout.
14	Ctrl-N Ctrl-N ↓[Press 4 times] Ctrl-N Ctrl-N	Enters blank lines.
15	↑ →[Press 11 times] F6 ← F7 →[Press 29 times] ←↓↓↓ ←[Press 20 times] F6 ← F7 →[Press 29 times] ←↑↑↑ ←[Press 40 times] Delete [Press 9 times] Department Number:↓↓↓ ←[Press 18 times] Delete [Press 9 times]Department Name:	Changes prompts.
16	↑↑↑ ←[Press 16 times] F6 →[Press 17 times]← F7 → [Press 4 times]←↓↓↓ ←[Press 21 times] F6 →[Press 15 times]← F7 →[Press 8 times]← ↑[Press 4 times] ←[To first column] F10 ↓←↓←←↓↓→[To last column]←↓ ←[To first column] F10 ←↑←←↓↓ →[To last column]←	Enters boxes.
17	F10 →[Press 4 times]←DEPT←	Saves and names your form.
18	← ← ↓ ← ←	Activates EMPLOYEE.
19	→ → ← ←	Uses form.
20	F10 → → → ←	Returns to Control Center.
21	←↓←→←	Moves to Query Design screen.
22	F4 [To EMPLOYEE skeleton] Tab [To NAME column] F10 →↓↓←←	Sorts.
23	F10 ←↓[Press 5 times]← Backspace [Press 11 times] REPORT1←	Creates REPORT1 view.
24	Ctrl-Y Tab [Press 5 times] F10 →←←	Sorts.
25	F10 ←← Backspace [Press 5 times]2←	Creates REPORT2 view.
26	F10 →[Press 4 times]↓←	Leaves Query Design screen.
27	↓←←[To activate the REPORT1 view]→→↓←→←←	Moves to Report Design screen.
28	↓[Press 11 times]→→ F6 ← Delete	Deletes field.
29	F10 →←↓← Ctrl-End	Enters field.
30	F10 →[Press 5 times]←	Saves changes.
31	←←↓↓←←[To activate the REPORT2 view]→→↓↓ ←→←←	Moves to Report Design screen.
32	↓[Press 13 times]→→ F6 ← Delete	Deletes field.
33	F10 →←↓← Ctrl-End	Enters field.
34	←←←↑↑→[Press 6 times] F6 ← Delete	Deletes field.
35	F10 ←↓↓← Ctrl-End	Enters field.
36	→ -[Press Hyphen key]→ F10 ←↓← Ctrl-End	Enters field.
37	↑ F10 →↓↓←←↓↓←	Modifies group band.
38	F10 →[Press 4 times]←	Saves your work.

SUMMARY OF KEYSTROKES — PROJECT 6 (continued)

STEPS	KEY(S) PRESSED	RESULTS
39	← ← ← ↓ ↓ ← ←[To activate EMPLOYEE database file] → → → ← ← ← `F10` →[Press 6 times] ← EMPLIST ←	Creates EMPLIST.
40	→ → ← → ←	Begins application creation.
41	EMPAPP ← Employee Application System ← ← ← EMPLOYEE ← EMPLOYEE ← NUMBER ← `Ctrl–End`	Enters basic application information.
42	`F10` → ↓[Press 5 times] ← ← EMPLOYEE ← EMPLIST ← `Ctrl–End`	Enters remaining application information.
43	←[Any key] → → → ←	Generates application.
44	↓ ← ← ← ←	Runs application.
45	↓[Press 4 times] ←	Selects "Print Report".
46	↓ ↓ ↓ ← ↓ ←[Any key]	Prints report.
47	↓ ↓ ←	Leaves application.

The following list summarizes the material covered in Project 6.

1. A system that allows users to take actions by selecting options from menus is called an **application system** or **application**. A tool to allow rapid development of application systems is called an applications generator.
2. To create a custom form, first activate the associated database file and then select <create> in the Forms column.
3. To place boxes on a form, use the "Box" option from the Layout menu.
4. To use a custom form, highlight the form, press Enter, and select "Display data".
5. To modify an existing view, highlight the view, press Enter, and select "Modify query".
6. To save a query under a different name, use the "Save this query" option from the Layout menu.
7. To change the layout of a report, highlight the report, press Enter, and then select "Modify layout".
8. To change the field on which records are grouped in a report, place the highlight on the group intro band and use the "Modify group" option from the Bands menu.
9. To create a new application, select <create> in the Applications column.
10. To create a quick application, select the "Generate quick application" option from the Application menu. Fill in the requested information, and press Ctrl-End.
11. To run an application, highlight the application at the Control Center, press Enter, and then select "Run application".
12. To modify an application, highlight the application at the Control Center, press Enter, and then select "Modify application".

STUDENT ASSIGNMENTS

STUDENT ASSIGNMENT 1: True/False

Instructions: Circle T if the statement is true and F if the statement is false.

T F 1. To begin creating a custom form, select <create> in the Forms column.
T F 2. To add a blank line to a form, press Ctrl-U.
T F 3. To move a field on a form, select it and then press F4.
T F 4. To add a box to a form, choose the "Box" option from the Layout menu.
T F 5. To modify the layout of an existing form, move the highlight to the form at the Control Center, press Enter, and select "Modify layout".
T F 6. To save a query under a different name, use the "Save this query" option from the Layout menu.
T F 7. If a report contains a field that is not in the active database file, you will not be able to change the layout of the report.
T F 8. To obtain a pick list, press Shift-F1.
T F 9. To create an application, select <create> from the Application menu.
T F 10. If you modify an existing application, you will see a message during generation that a program already exists.
T F 11. When you select the "Print report" option in a quick application, the first menu you encounter will ask if you want to send the report to the screen or the printer.
T F 12. To generate the program for an application, you must select the "Generate program" option from the Application menu.
T F 13. One limitation when you create a quick application is that you cannot use a custom form to edit data.
T F 14. A quick application can contain only one report.
T F 15. To run an application, select the "Run" option from the Application menu.
T F 16. To modify an existing application, highlight the application at the Control Center, press Enter, and then select "Modify application".

STUDENT ASSIGNMENT 2: Multiple Choice

Instructions: Circle the correct response.

1. How do you begin creating a custom form?
   a. select <create> in the Data column and then select "Custom form"
   b. select "Custom form" from the Create menu
   c. highlight a database file at the Control Center, press Enter, and select "Modify layout"
   d. select <create> in the Forms column
2. To move a field on a form, select it and then press _____.
   a. F6
   b. F7
   c. Shift-F7
   d. F1
3. Which option do you use to add a box to a form?
   a. the "Box" option from the Design menu
   b. the "Box" option from the Layout menu
   c. the "Add box" option from the Fields menu
   d. the "Add box" option from the Design menu

4. What happens when you attempt to modify a report that contains a field that is not in the active database file?
   a. you will immediately be returned to the Control Center
   b. you will get a message, but can still modify the report
   c. you will get a message and as soon as you press a key, you are returned to the Control Center
   d. nothing happens
5. To create an application, _____.
   a. select <create> in the Applications column and then select "Application generator"
   b. select <create> in the Applications column and then select "dBASE program"
   c. select "Create application" from the Tools menu
   d. select "Create/modify application" from the Application menu
6. Which of the following is true concerning a quick application?
   a. it can contain two reports
   b. it can use two database files
   c. it contains options to remove marked records and to reindex a database
   d. it can send reports only to the printer, not to the screen

STUDENT ASSIGNMENT 3: Understanding dBASE Options

Instructions: Explain what happens after you perform each of the following actions.

Problem 1: Select the "Box" option from the Layout menu on the Forms Design screen.

Explanation: _____

_____

_____

Problem 2: Select the "Save this query" option from the Layout menu on the Query Design screen.

Explanation: _____

_____

_____

Problem 3: Select the "Add fields" option from the Fields menu on the Report Design screen.

Explanation: _____

_____

_____

Problem 4: Select the "Generate quick application" option from the Application menu on the Application Design screen.

Explanation: _____

_____

_____

STUDENT ASSIGNMENT 4: Using dBASE

Instructions: Explain how to accomplish each of the following tasks using dBASE.

Problem 1: Create a custom form.

Explanation: _____

_____

_____

Problem 2: Add a box to a custom form.

Explanation: _____

_____

_____

Problem 3: Create a view that is identical to an existing view but that is sorted in a different order.

Explanation: _____

_____

_____

Problem 4: Add a field to a report.

Explanation: _____

_____

_____

Problem 5: Create a quick application.

Explanation: _____

_____

_____

Problem 6: Run an application you have created.

Explanation: _____

_____

_____

STUDENT ASSIGNMENT 5: Recovering from Problems

Instructions: In each of the following cases, a problem occurred. Explain the cause of the problem and how it can be corrected.

Problem 1: You try to run an application and get the message "No program file found for this application".

Cause of Problem: _____

_____

Method of Correction: _____

_____

Problem 2: You are running your application, and you have selected the option to edit your data. Instead of seeing your custom form, however, you see a message indicating the form cannot be found.

Cause of Problem:_____

_____

Method of Correction: _____

_____

Problem 3: You try to modify the layout of a report. Instead of seeing your report design, you see a message telling you that a particular field doesn't exist.

Cause of Problem:_____

_____

Method of Correction: _____

_____

STUDENT ASSIGNMENT 6: Creating Forms

Instructions: Create a custom form called EMPFORM. This form is designed for a user who is only allowed to update the NUMBER, NAME, DATE, and DEPT_NUMB fields so include only these fields in your form. Explain the steps to accomplish this.

Steps: _____

_____

_____

STUDENT ASSIGNMENT 7: Creating Views

Instructions: Create a view called EMPREPT. Include both the EMPLOYEE and DEPT database files in this view. Include in the view the NUMBER, NAME, DEPT_NAME, DATE, and PAY_RATE fields. Sort the data in the view by NUMBER within DEPT_NAME. Explain the steps to accomplish this.

Steps: _____

_____

_____

STUDENT ASSIGNMENT 8: Creating Reports

Instructions: Modify the report called EMPREPT that you created in the assignments in Project 3 so that the report will work with the EMPREPT view. Print a copy of the report. Explain the steps to accomplish this.

Steps: _____

_____

_____

STUDENT ASSIGNMENT 9: Creating Applications

Instructions: Create an application for the DEPT database file. This application should be similar to the one you created for the EMPLOYEE database file. Create a report of departments for this application. Explain the steps to accomplish this.

Steps: _____

_____

_____

_____

STUDENT ASSIGNMENT 10: Running Applications

Instructions: Run the application you created in Student Assignment 9. Try each of the updates. Print the report. Explain the steps to accomplish this.

Steps: _____

_____

_____

_____

MINICASES

GENERATING APPLICATIONS

Your instructor may want you to hand in printed documentation of your screen forms. Such documentation is stored in a file whose name is the name you assigned to your form together with an extension of FMT. Thus, if you called your form EMPLOYEE, the file name will be EMPLOYEE.FMT. Once you leave dBASE, you can print this file by entering the word TYPE followed by the name of the file, followed by >PRN. Thus, to print EMPLOYEE.FMT, the command would be TYPE CUSTFORM.FMT>PRN.

MINICASE 1: Customers

Instructions: Use the CUSTOMER database that you created in Minicase 1 of Project 1 and modified in Minicase 1 of Project 5 in this assignment. Also use the CUSTVIEW view that you created in Project 5.

1. Perform the following tasks using dBASE:
   a. Create custom update forms for the CUSTOMER and SLSREP database files. Name the forms CUSTOMER and SLSREP, respectively. They should be similar in style to the ones you have seen in the text.
   b. Create views called CUSTRPT1 and CUSTRPT2. You will use these views for the reports you created in Project 3. These views should be the modified versions of the CUSTVIEW view you created in Project 5.
   c. Create a report called CUSTRPT3 that is a list of all the records in the CUSTOMER database file.
   d. Create an application system for this database. Give it the same structure and options as the one we created in the text. Use the CUSTOMER database file in the place of the EMPLOYEE database file. Use CUSTRPT3 as the report.

MINICASE 2: Parts

Instructions: Use the PART database that you created in Minicase 2 of Project 1 and modified in Minicase 2 of Project 5 in this assignment. Also use the PARTVIEW view that you created in Project 5.

1. Perform the following tasks using dBASE:
   a. Create custom update forms for the PART and CLASS database files. Name the forms PART and CLASS, respectively. They should be similar in style to the ones you have seen in the text.
   b. Create views called PARTRPT1 and PARTRPT2. You will use these views for the reports you created in Project 3. These views should be the modified versions of the PARTVIEW view you created in Project 5.
   c. Create a report called PARTRPT3 that is a list of all the records in the PART database file.
   d. Create an application system for this database. Give it the same structure and options as the one we created in the text. Use the PART database file in the place of the EMPLOYEE database file. Use PARTRPT3 as the report.

MINICASE 3: Movies

Instructions: Use the MOVIE database that you created in Minicase 3 of Project 1 and modified in Minicase 3 of Project 5 in this assignment. Also use the MOVVIEW view that you created in Project 5.

1. Perform the following tasks using dBASE:
   a. Create custom update forms for the MOVIE and DIRECTOR database files. Name the forms MOVIE and DIRECTOR, respectively. They should be similar in style to the ones you have seen in the text.
   b. Create views called MOVRPT1 and MOVRPT2. You will use these views for the reports you created in Project 3. These views should be the modified versions of the MOVVIEW view you created in Project 5.
   c. Create a report called MOVRPT3 that is a list of all the records in the MOVIE database file.
   d. Create an application system for this database. Give it the same structure and options as the one we created in the text. Use the MOVIE database file in the place of the EMPLOYEE database file. Use MOVRPT3 as the report.

MINICASE 4: Books

Instructions: Use the BOOK database that you created in Minicase 4 of Project 1 and modified in Minicase 4 of Project 5 in this assignment. Also use the BOOKVIEW view that you created in Project 5.

1. Perform the following tasks using dBASE:
   a. Create custom update forms for the BOOK and PUBLISH database files. Name the forms BOOK and PUBLISH, respectively. They should be similar in style to the ones you have seen in the text.
   b. Create views called BOOKRPT1 and BOOKRPT2. You will use these views for the reports you created in Project 3. These views should be the modified versions of the BOOKVIEW view you created in Project 5.
   c. Create a report called BOOKRPT3 that is a list of all records in the BOOK database file.
   d. Create an application system for this database. Give it the same structure and options as the one we created in the text. Use the BOOK database file in the place of the EMPLOYEE database file. Use BOOKRPT3 as the report.

For each of the projects, we have provided the fundamental dBASE IV Version 1.1 activities in an easy-to-use quick reference format. This convenient reference tool is divided into three parts—activity, procedure, and description. All of the activities that you learn in each project are covered in the Quick Reference for that project. The numbers in parentheses that follow each activity refer to the page on which the activity is first discussed in the text.

You can use these Quick References as study aids or to quickly recall how you complete an activity. The Quick Reference is a valuable and time-saving tool, and we encourage you to use it frequently.

QUICK REFERENCE — PROJECT 1

ACTIVITY	PROCEDURE	DESCRIPTION
BOOT AND LOAD (dB6)	Turn power on	Follow the procedures to power up your system and load DOS.
LOAD dBASE (dB6)	Place your data disk in drive A Type a: Press ↵ Type path c:\dbase Press ↵	Set up a path to the directory containing dBASE. Necessary only if the correct path has not yet been set up. See your instructor to check whether this is the case.
	Type dbase Press ↵	Also, may wait a few seconds.
ESCAPE FROM AN OPERATION (dB8)	Press Esc	Next two steps are necessary only if you are prompted to abandon the operation.
	Press ← Press ↵	
SELECT AN OPTION (dB9)	Press F10 Press ← or → as required Press ↑ or ↓ as required Press ↵	Move to the menu containing the option. Move the highlight to the option.
MOVE FROM CONTROL CENTER TO DOT PROMPT (dB10)	Select "Exit to dot prompt"	From the Exit menu of the Control Center.
MOVE FROM DOT PROMPT TO CONTROL CENTER (dB10)	Press F2	Move from dot prompt to Control Center.
GET HELP (dB12)	Press F1 Press Esc	Display help information. Remove help information from the screen.
CHANGE A CATALOG (dB11)	Select "Use a different catalog" Select catalog	From the Catalog menu. Change catalog.
LEAVE dBASE (dB13)	Select "Quit to DOS"	From the Exit menu of the Control Center.
CREATE A CATALOG (dB9)	Select "Use a different catalog" Select <create> Type catalog name Press ↵	From the Catalog menu of the Control Center. Create catalog. Name catalog.

QUICK REFERENCE — PROJECT 1 (continued)

ACTIVITY	PROCEDURE	DESCRIPTION
CREATE A DATABASE FILE (dB13)	Select < create >	From the Data column. Make sure the catalog that will contain the database file is active before you begin.
	Specify the fields	Define the structure.
	Select "Save changes and exit"	From the Exit menu.
	Type database file name	
	Press ↵	Name the database file.
ACTIVATE A DATABASE FILE (dB23)	Select the database file	From the Data column. Before you take this step, check to see if the database file appears above the line in the Data column. If it does, it is already active.
	Select "Use file"	
TRANSFER BETWEEN EDIT AND BROWSE SCREENS (dB22)	Press F2	If there are no records in the database file, you will be unable to transfer to the Browse screen.
ADD RECORDS USING THE EDIT SCREEN (dB23)	Make sure database file is active	
	Press F2	If you are taken to the Browse screen, press F2 a second time.
	Select "Add new records"	From the Records menu. If there are no records in the file, you do not need to select this option.
	Type data for new records	
	Select "Exit"	From the Exit menu.
CHANGE RECORDS USING THE EDIT SCREEN (dB24)	Make sure database file is active	
	Press F2	If you are taken to the Browse screen, press F2 a second time.
	Press Page Up or Page Down as required	Move to the record to change.
	Make changes	
	Select "Exit"	From the Exit menu.
CHANGE RECORDS USING THE BROWSE SCREEN (dB25)	Make sure database file is active	
	Press F2	If you are taken to the Edit screen, press F2 a second time.
	Press ↑ or ↓ as required	Move to the record to change.
	Make changes	
	Select "Exit"	From the Exit menu.
PRINT THE CONTENTS OF THE ACTIVE DATABASE FILE (dB26)	Press Shift-F9	
	Select "Begin printing"	Print the contents of the file.
ADD RECORDS USING THE BROWSE SCREEN (dB27)	Make sure database file is active	
	Press F2	If you are taken to the Edit screen, press F2 a second time.
	Press Page Down and ↓ as required	Move past the last the record in the file.
	Type Y	Respond to the prompt "Add new records".
	Type new records	
	Select "Exit"	From the Exit menu.

(continued)

QUICK REFERENCE — PROJECT 1 (continued)

ACTIVITY	PROCEDURE	DESCRIPTION
DELETE RECORDS (dB28)	Make sure database file is active	
	Press F2	Press once or twice at the Control Center to move to the Edit screen.
	Press Page Up or Page Down as required	Move to the record to be deleted.
	Press Ctrl–U	Mark the record for deletion. If you have other records to delete, mark them in the same way.
	Select "Erase marked records"	From the Organize menu.
	Select "Exit"	From the Exit menu.
MAKE A BACKUP COPY (dB29)	Select "Quit to DOS"	From the Exit menu at the Control Center.
	Type COPY	
	Press Spacebar	
	Type name of live database file	
	Press Spacebar	
	Type name of backup database file	
	Press ↵	
	Type name of related file	
	Press Spacebar	
	Type name of backup file	
	Press ↵	Make backup copies of database file and related file.
RESTORE A DATABASE FILE (dB30)	Select "Quit to DOS"	From the Exit menu at the Control Center.
	Type COPY	
	Press Spacebar	
	Type name of backup database file	
	Press Spacebar	
	Type name of live database file	
	Press ↵	
	Type name of backup-related file	
	Press Spacebar	
	Type name of live file	
	Press ↵	Restore the database file.

QUICK REFERENCE — PROJECT 2

ACTIVITY	PROCEDURE	DESCRIPTION
MOVE TO THE QUERY DESIGN SCREEN (dB44)	Activate database file	
	Select <create>	From the Queries column.
APPLY A QUERY (dB45)	Press `F2`	
	Select "Transfer to Query Design"	From the Exit menu. Transfer back to Query Design screen.
PRINT THE RESULTS (dB45)	Press `Shift-F9`	
	Select "Begin printing"	Prints the results.
ABANDON A QUERY (dB45)	Select "Abandon changes and exit"	From the Exit menu on the Query Design screen.
	Type Y	Abandon query.
DISPLAY ALL RECORDS (dB45)	Press `F2`	Make sure you have not entered any conditions. Display all the records.
DISPLAY SELECTED FIELDS (dB46)	Press `Tab` or `Shift-Tab` as required	Move highlight under database file.
	Press `F5`	Erase View skeleton. You may need to press F5 twice.
	Press `Tab` or `Shift-Tab` as required	Move highlight under field to be included. Repeat this step and the next for each field to be included.
	Press `F5`	Include field.
USE A CONDITION (dB48)	Press `Tab` or `Shift-Tab` as required	Move to the column for the condition.
	Type condition	
	Press ↵	Enter the condition.
	Press `F2`	Display results.
CLEAR OUT PREVIOUS CONDITION (dB49)	Press `Tab` or `Shift-Tab` as required	Move to the column for the condition.
	Press `Ctrl-Y`	Erase condition.
USE NUMERIC FIELDS IN CONDITIONS (dB50)	Type number	Do not enclose the number in quotation marks.
USE OPERATORS IN CONDITIONS (dB50)	Type operator	The possible operators are =, >, >=, <, <=, <>, LIKE, SOUNDS LIKE.
	Press `Spacebar`	
	Type value	Complete the condition.
USE EXACT MATCH CONDITION (CHARACTER FIELDS) (dB51)	Type desired character string	Enclose the character string in quotation marks.
USE PATTERN MATCHING CONDITION (dB51)	Type LIKE	
	Press `Spacebar`	
	Type pattern	Using the asterisk (*) and/or question mark (?) wild cards. The pattern must be enclosed in quotes.
USE SOUNDS LIKE CONDITION (dB52)	Type SOUNDS LIKE	
	Press `Spacebar`	
	Type character string	Enclose the character string in quotation marks.
USE LOGICAL FIELDS IN CONDITIONS (dB52)	Type value	Value .T. (for true) or .F. (for false).

(continued)

QUICK REFERENCE — PROJECT 2 (continued)

ACTIVITY	PROCEDURE	DESCRIPTION
USE DATE FIELDS IN CONDITIONS (dB53)	Type date	Enclose the date in braces ({ }).
CREATE COMPOUND CONDITIONS USING AND (dB54)	Type conditions	On the same line. If they are in the same column, separate them by commas.
CREATE COMPOUND CONDITIONS USING OR (dB55)	Type first condition Press ↓ Type second condition	Create compound condition using OR.
COUNT RECORDS (dB56)	Type COUNT Enter condition	In any column. The condition is optional.
CALCULATE A SUM (dB56)	Type SUM Enter condition	In any column that is to be totaled. The condition is optional.
CALCULATE AN AVERAGE (dB56)	Type AVG Enter condition	In any column that is to be averaged. The condition is optional.
GROUP (dB57)	Type GROUP BY Enter condition	In the column used for grouping. The condition is optional.

QUICK REFERENCE — PROJECT 3

ACTIVITY	PROCEDURE	DESCRIPTION
SORT ON A SINGLE FIELD (dB77)	Select database file	From the Data column of the Control Center.
	Select "Modify structure/order"	
	Select "Sort database on field list"	From the Organize menu.
	Press `Shift-F1`	Create pick list.
	Select sort key	
	Select sort type	Use Spacebar to select type of sort.
	Press ←	Complete selection of sort type.
	Press ←	Indicate there are no additional sort keys.
	Type name of sorted file	
	Press ←	Name the sorted file.
	Type Y	If a prompt asks if it is all right to overwrite the existing file.
	Type description for sorted file	If a prompt asks for a description.
	Press ←	
	Select "Save changes and exit"	From the Exit menu.
USE A SORTED FILE (dB78)	Activate sorted file	Activate sorted file, since the sort operation does not automatically activate it.
SORT ON MULTIPLE FIELDS (dB81)	Select database file	From the Data column of the Control Center.
	Select "Modify structure/order"	
	Select "Sort database on field list"	From the Organize menu.
	Press `Shift-F1`	Create pick list.
	Select first sort key	
	Select sort type	Use Spacebar to select type of sort.
	Press ←	Complete selection of sort type.
	Press `Shift-F1`	Create pick list.
	Select second sort key	
	Select sort type	Use Spacebar to select type of sort.
	Press ←	Complete selection of sort type.
	Press ←	Indicate there are no additional sort keys.
	Type name of sorted file	
	Press ←	Name the sorted file.
	Type Y	If a prompt asks if it is all right to overwrite the existing file.
	Type description for sorted file	If a prompt asks for a description.
	Press ←	
	Select "Save changes and exit"	From the Exit menu.
BEGIN REPORT CREATION (dB83)	Activate database file	
	Select <create>	From the Reports column.
	Select "Quick layouts"	From the Layout menu.
	Select "Column layout"	Complete quick layout.
ADD A BLANK LINE (dB87)	Press ↑, ↓, ← as required	Move the cursor to the beginning of the line where you want to insert a blank line.
	Press `Ctrl-N`	Insert blank line.
DELETE A LINE (dB87)	Press ↑, ↓ as required	Move the cursor to the line.
	Press `Ctrl-Y`	Delete the line.

(continued)

QUICK REFERENCE — PROJECT 3 (continued)

ACTIVITY	PROCEDURE	DESCRIPTION
SELECT A FIELD (dB87)	Press ↑, ↓, ←, → as required Press F6 Press ↵	Move the cursor into the field. Select the field.
SELECT TEXT (dB87)	Press ↑, ↓, ←, → as required Press F6 Press ↑, ↓, ←, → as required Press ↵	Move the cursor to the beginning of the text. Move the cursor to the end of the text. Select the text.
REMOVE FIELD FROM A REPORT (dB88)	Select the field Press Delete	Delete the field.
MOVE FIELDS ON A REPORT (dB88)	Select the field Press F7 Press ↑, ↓, ←, → as required Press ↵ Type Y or N	Move the cursor to the new position for the field. If the new position covers part of an existing field, a dBASE prompt will ask if this is acceptable. Answer either yes or no.
RESIZE FIELDS ON A REPORT (dB89)	Select the field Press Shift-F7 Press ← or → as required Press ↵	Change the size of the field.
ADD A FIELD TO A REPORT (dB90)	Press ↑, ↓, ←, → as required Select "Add field" Select the field Press Ctrl-End	Move the cursor to the position for the new field. From the Fields menu. Add the field.
ADD A CALCULATED FIELD TO A REPORT (dB90)	Press ↑, ↓, ←, → as required Select "Add field" Select <create> Press ↵ Type name for new field Press ↵ Press ↓ ↓ Press ↵ Type expression Press ↵ Press Ctrl-End	Move the cursor to the position for the new field. From the Fields menu. From the CALCULATED column. Name the new field. Use the plus sign (+) for addition, the minus sign (–) for subtraction, the asterisk (*) for multiplication, and the backslash (/) for division in these expressions. Complete the expression. Add the new field.
FINISH THE REPORT CREATION (dB94)	Select "Save changes and exit" Type name for report file Press ↵	From the Exit menu. If you have previously saved this report, you will not be asked for a name. If you were required to type a name for the report file.

QUICK REFERENCE — PROJECT 3 (continued)

ACTIVITY	PROCEDURE	DESCRIPTION
PRINT A REPORT (dB95)	Activate database file	
	Select the report	From the Reports column.
	Select "Print report"	
	Select "Begin printing"	Print the report.
MODIFY A REPORT DESIGN (dB97)	Activate the database file	
	Select the report	From the Reports column.
	Select "Modify layout"	
	Make changes	
	Select "Save changes and exit"	From the Exit menu.
ADD A GROUP BAND TO A REPORT (dB98)	Press ↑, ↓, ←, → as required	Move cursor to report intro band.
	Select "Add a group band"	From the Bands menu.
	Select "Field value"	
	Select field	Select the field on which to group.
ADD A SUMMARY FIELD TO THE REPORT SUMMARY (dB99)	Press ↑, ↓, ←, → as required	Move cursor to position for field.
	Select "Add field"	From the Fields menu.
	Select operator	The appropriate summary operator (such as Sum) from the SUMMARY column.
	Select "Field to summarize on"	
	Press ↵	
	Select the field	
	Press Ctrl–End	Add summary field.
REMOVE FILES (dB103)	Press ↑, ↓, ←, → as required	Move highlight to file at Control Center. If the file is currently active, you will need to use the next two steps to close it. If not, skip these steps.
	Press ↵	
	Select "Close file"	
	Select "Remove highlighted file from catalog"	From the Catalog menu.
	Select "Yes"	Remove file from the catalog.
	Select "Yes" or "No" as required	If you want to delete it from the disk, select "Yes." If not, select "No".

QUICK REFERENCE — PROJECT 4

ACTIVITY	PROCEDURE	DESCRIPTION
ADD RECORDS USING THE EDIT SCREEN (dB113)	Press F2	If you are taken to the Browse screen, press F2 a second time.
	Select "Add new records"	From the Records menu. If there are no records in the file, do not select this option.
	Type data	The data for the new records.
	Select "Exit"	From the Exit menu.
CHANGE RECORDS USING THE EDIT SCREEN (dB116)	Press F2	If you are taken to the Browse screen, press F2 a second time.
	Press Page Up , Page Down as required	Move to the record to change.
	Make changes	
	Select "Exit"	From the Exit menu.
LOCATE A RECORD (dB118)	Make sure database file is active	
	Press F2 once or twice	Move to either Edit or Browse screen (your choice).
	Press ↑, ↓ as required	Move the cursor to the field to search. It is essential that the cursor be in the right field before you begin the search.
	Select "Forward search"	From the Go To menu.
	Type value	The value for which you want to search. Be sure to erase any previous entry before typing the new one.
	Press ↵	Locate the record.
USE UPDATE QUERY TO CHANGE RECORDS (dB119)	Make sure database file is active	
	Select <create>	From the Queries column.
	Select "Specify update operation"	From the Update menu.
	Select "Replace values"	
	Select "Proceed"	
	Enter condition	The condition that indicates the records to be changed.
	Enter replacement expression	The expression that indicates change to be made.
	Select "Perform the update"	From the Update menu.
	Press any key	
	Select "Abandon changes and exit"	From the Exit menu.
	Select "Yes"	Do not save the query.
CHANGE RECORDS USING THE BROWSE SCREEN (dB123)	Make sure database file is active	
	Press F2	If you are taken to the Edit screen, press F2 a second time.
	Press ↑, ↓ as required	Move to the record to change.
	Make changes	
	Select "Exit"	From the Exit menu.

QUICK REFERENCE — PROJECT 4 (continued)

ACTIVITY	PROCEDURE	DESCRIPTION
ADD RECORDS USING THE BROWSE SCREEN (dB124)	Make sure database file is active Press `F2`	If you are taken to the Edit screen, press F2 a second time.
	Press `Page Down` , ↓ as required	Move past the last the record in the file.
	Type Y	Respond to the prompt to "Add new records".
	Type new records	
	Select "Exit"	From the Exit menu.
USE UPDATE QUERY TO MARK RECORDS (dB124)	Make sure database file is active	
	Select <create>	From the Queries column.
	Select "Specify update operation"	From the Update menu.
	Select "Mark records for deletion"	
	Select "Proceed"	
	Enter condition	The condition to identify records to be marked.
	Select "Perform the update"	From the Update menu.
	Type Y	
	Press any key	
	Select "Abandon changes and exit"	From the Exit menu.
	Select "Yes"	
USE UPDATE QUERY TO UNMARK RECORDS (dB126)	Make sure database file is active	
	Select <create>	From the Queries column.
	Select "Specify update operation"	From the Update menu.
	Select "Unmark records"	
	Select "Proceed"	
	Enter condition	The condition to identify records to be unmarked.
	Select "Perform the update"	From the Update menu.
	Press any key	
	Select "Abandon changes and exit"	From the Exit menu.
	Select "Yes"	
PERMANENTLY REMOVE MARKED RECORDS (dB126)	Make sure database file is active	
	Select "Erase marked records"	From the Organize menu.

QUICK REFERENCE — PROJECT 5

ACTIVITY	PROCEDURE	DESCRIPTION
CHANGE FIELD CHARACTERISTICS (dB143)	Select database file	From the Data column of the Control Center.
	Select "Modify structure/order"	Do not select "Use file" as you usually do.
	Press `Esc`	Remove the Organize menu from the screen.
	Press ↓ as required	Move the highlight to the field to be changed.
	Press `Tab` as required	Move the highlight to the data to be changed. You can use either Tab or Enter.
	Type new entry	
	Select "Save changes and exit"	From the Exit menu.
	Press ↵	Confirm you are done.
ADD A NEW FIELD (dB143)	Select the database file	From the Data column of the Control Center.
	Select "Modify structure/order"	
	Press `Esc`	Remove the Organize menu from the screen.
	Press ↓ as required	Move the highlight to the position for the new field. If the new field is to be added at the end, you are ready to type the contents for the field. If not, use the following step to make room for the new field.
	Press `Ctrl-N`	Make room for the field.
	Type entries	Make the entries for the new field.
	Select "Save changes and exit"	From the Exit menu.
	Press ↵	Confirm you are done.
DELETE A FIELD (dB146)	Select the database file	From the Data column of the Control Center.
	Select "Modify structure/order"	
	Press `Esc`	Remove the Organize menu from the screen.
	Press ↓ as required	Move the highlight to the field to be deleted.
	Press `Ctrl-U`	Delete the field.
	Select "Save changes and exit"	From the Exit menu.
	Press ↵	Confirm you are done.
CREATE AN INDEX ON A SINGLE FIELD (dB148)	Select database file	From the Data column of the Control Center.
	Select "Modify structure/order"	
	Select "Create new index"	From the Organize menu.
	Press ↵	
	Type name (tag) for index	For a single-field index, the name should be the same as the name of the field.
	Press ↵	Indicate you are done.
	Press ↵	Enter an index expression.
	Press `Shift-F1`	Produce a pick list.
	Select field	The field for the index (the index key).
	Press ↵	Indicate the expression is complete.
	Press `Ctrl-End`	Indicate you are done.
	Select "Save changes and exit"	From the Exit menu.
	Press ↵	Confirm you want to save changes.
USE AN INDEX FOR SORTING (dB150)	Make sure database file is active	
	Press `F2`	Move to either the Edit or the Browse screen.
	Select "Order records by index"	From the Organize menu.
	Select index tag	The tag for the index. The records will now appear to be ordered by this index.

QUICK REFERENCE — PROJECT 5 (continued)

ACTIVITY	PROCEDURE	DESCRIPTION
CREATE AN INDEX ON MORE THAN ONE FIELD (dB151)	Select the database file	From the Data column of the Control Center.
	Select "Modify structure/order"	
	Select "Create new index"	From the Organize menu.
	Press ↵	
	Type name (tag) for index	The name should represent the combination of fields that you are using for the index.
	Press ↵	Indicate you are done.
	Press ↵	Enter an index expression.
	Press Shift–F1	Produce a pick list.
	Select field	The first field (major key) for the index.
	Type plus sign	
	Press Shift–F1	Produce a pick list.
	Select field	The second field (minor key) for the index.
	Press ↵	Indicate the expression is complete. If the key has more fields, repeat the previous four steps for each additional field.
	Press Ctrl–End	Indicate you are done.
	Select "Save changes and exit"	From the Exit menu.
	Press ↵	Confirm you want to save changes.
USE AN INDEX TO FIND A RECORD (dB152)	Make sure database file is active	
	Press F2	Move to either the Edit or the Browse screen.
	Select "Order records by index"	From the Organize menu.
	Select index tag	The tag for the index.
	Select "Index key search"	From the Go To menu.
	Type search string	If there is no matching record, dBASE will display a message. If there is such a record, it will become the current active record and will be displayed on the screen.
REMOVE UNWANTED INDEXES (dB154)	Make sure database file is active	
	Press F2	Move to either the Edit or the Browse screen.
	Select "Remove unwanted index tag"	From the Organize menu.
	Select tag	The tag for the index you want to remove.
BEGIN THE VIEW-CREATION PROCESS (dB156)	Activate a database file	
	Select < create >	From the Queries column.
	Select "Include indexes"	From the Fields menu.
	Select "Add file to query"	From the Layout menu.
	Select other database file	
	Select "Include indexes"	From the Fields menu.

(continued)

QUICK REFERENCE — PROJECT 5 (continued)

ACTIVITY	PROCEDURE	DESCRIPTION
LINK THE DATABASE FILES (dB158)	Press `F3`	Move to the skeleton for the first database file.
	Press `Tab` or `Shift-Tab` as required	Move to the linking field.
	Select "Create link by pointing"	From the Layout menu.
	Press `F4`	Move to the skeleton for the second database file.
	Press `Tab` or `Shift-Tab` as required	Move to the linking field.
	Press ↵	Complete the link.
ADD A FIELD TO THE VIEW SKELETON (dB160)	Press `F3` or `F4` as required	Move to the file skeleton containing the field.
	Press `Tab` or `Shift-Tab` as required	Move to the field.
	Press `F5`	Adds field (unless field is already present, in which case pressing F5 will remove it).
REMOVE A FIELD FROM THE VIEW SKELETON (dB160)	Press `F3` or `F4` as required.	Move to the file skeleton containing the field.
	Press `Tab` or `Shift-Tab` as required	Move to the field.
	Press `F5`	Removes field (unless field is not present, in which case pressing F5 will add it).
FINISH THE VIEW CREATION (dB160)	Select "Save changes and exit"	From the Exit menu.
	Type name	The name of the saved query (view).
	Press ↵	Complete the process.
USE A VIEW (dB160)	Select view	From the Queries column.
	Select "Use view"	Activate the view
SORT THE DATA IN A VIEW ON A SINGLE FIELD (dB162)	Press `F3`, `F4`, `Tab`, `Shift-Tab` as required	Move the highlight to the sort key.
	Select "Sort on this field"	From the Fields menu.
	Select sort type	
SORT THE DATA IN A VIEW ON MULTIPLE FIELDS (dB164)	Press `F3`, `F4`, `Tab`, `Shift-Tab` as required	Move the highlight to the major sort key.
	Select "Sort on this field"	From the Fields menu.
	Select sort type	Move the highlight to the minor sort key.
	Select "Sort on this field"	From the Fields menu.
	Select sort type	If there are more than two fields, repeat these steps for each additional sort key.

QUICK REFERENCE — PROJECT 6

ACTIVITY	PROCEDURE	DESCRIPTION
BEGIN FORM CREATION (dB182)	Make sure database file is active Select < create > Select "Quick layout"	From the Forms column. From the Layout menu.
ADD A BLANK LINE (dB183)	Press ↑, ↓, →, ← as required Press Ctrl–N	Move the cursor to the beginning of the line where you want to insert a blank line. Insert a blank line.
SELECT A FIELD (dB183)	Press ↑, ↓, ←, → as required Press F6 Press ↵	Move the cursor into the field. Select the field.
SELECT TEXT (dB183)	Press ↑, ↓, ←, → as required Press F6 Press ↑, ↓, ←, → as required Press ↵	Move the cursor to the beginning of the text. Move the cursor to the end of the text. Select the text.
MOVE A FIELD OR TEXT (dB183)	Select the field or text Press F7 Press ↑, ↓, ←, → as required Press ↵ Type Y or N	 Move the cursor to the new position for the field. If the new position covers part of an existing field, a dBASE prompt will ask if this is acceptable. Answer either yes or no.
ADD BOXES (dB185)	Select "Box" Select box type Press ↑, ↓, ←, → as required Press ↵ Press ↑, ↓, ←, → as required Press ↵	From the Layout menu. Box type "Double line" (for a double box) or "Single line" (for a single box). Move the cursor to the upper left-hand corner of the box. Move the cursor to the lower right-hand corner of the box.
FINISH FORM CREATION (dB186)	Select "Save changes and exit" Type name	From the Exit menu. The name of the form. You will not need to do this if you have previously saved your form.
USE A FORM (dB186)	Make sure database file is active Select the form Select "Display data"	 From the Forms column. Display data using your form.
MODIFY A FORM (dB189)	Make sure database file is active Select the form Select "Modify layout" Make changes Save the form	 From the Forms column. Save your changes.
BEGIN APPLICATION CREATION (dB192)	Make sure database file is active Select < create > Select "Applications Generator" Enter information Press Ctrl–End	 From the Applications column. Enter basic application information. Complete the process.

(continued)

QUICK REFERENCE — PROJECT 6 (continued)

ACTIVITY	PROCEDURE	DESCRIPTION
CREATE QUICK APPLICATION (dB193)	Select "Generate quick application"	From the Application menu.
	Type name	Enter name of format file.
	Type name	Enter name of report file.
	Press Ctrl–End	Complete the process.
RUN APPLICATION (dB194)	Select application	From the Applications column.
	Select "Run application"	
	Select "Yes"	Answer yes to the follow-up question.

INDEX